W9-BEH-202

Why You Need This New Edition

This ninth edition of *Social Gerontology: A Multidisciplinary Perspective*, continues to reflect the profound changes in the way society views aging and older adults—a more optimistic viewpoint that people can, to some extent, influence their own experience of aging.

Since the last edition, however, there has been a dramatic shift in the economic context in which we age. Growing numbers of older people must continue to, or return to, work because of lost retirement income, the high cost of health care, or unexpected rises in their housing costs. The ninth edition examines many of these systemic changes, most of which were not even thought of as possibilities when the last edition was published.

The authors have thoroughly updated the text to encompass a wide range of topics with exciting new research in many domains, including social, health, and long-term care policies and programs.

Here are just some of the new topics and research findings discussed in the ninth edition:

1. Critiques on **extending both years and quality of life** by preventing or managing chronic diseases, enhancing active aging, and maintaining productivity are highlighted.

2. New evidence-based findings on **health and long-term care**, including unpaid family caregivers and underpaid direct care workers, as well as public policies supporting them, such as consumer-directed care, integrated care systems, care transition models, and innovations in home- and community-based care are discussed.

3. Recent developments in the areas of **preventing, diagnosing, and treating depression, anxiety, and dementia** such as Alzheimer's disease are reviewed.

4. The benefits of **health promotion**, **spirituality**, and **religiosity** for achieving and maintaining active aging are demonstrated.

5. The chapters on **informal supports and family caregiving** recognize the distinctive needs of lesbian, gay, bisexual, and transsexual (LGBT) partners, grandparents as primary caregivers of grandchildren, and parents caring for adult children with long-term disabilities, along with the policy and programmatic barriers confronting them.

6. The sections on **technology,** including growing computer use by elders, and universal design that helps people "age in place," are expanded.

7. Research and interventions to **change the culture of long-term care** and to develop elder-friendly communities are described.

8. The evolution of **newer models of community-based long-term care** such as assisted living, adult family homes, and adult day care are discussed.

9. The growing research on **LGBT older adults**, attendant policy, and practice implications are incorporated in many chapters.

10. Both the resilience of, and the historical disadvantage faced by **older women and elders of color,** are emphasized.

11. Given the dramatically changing political arena, the chapters on social, health, and long-term care policies reflect contemporary debates related to federal and state budget cuts, the impact of the 2003 Medicare prescription drug law, the 2009 health care debates, and **older adults' political participation** in these discussions.

12. **Culturally competent methods** to understand and respectfully meet the needs of an increasingly diverse older population are also identified throughout.

PEARSON

NINTH EDITION

SOCIAL GERONTOLOGY

A MULTIDISCIPLINARY PERSPECTIVE

Nancy R. Hooyman
University of Washington

H. Asuman Kiyak
University of Washington

Allyn & Bacon

Boston   Columbus   Indianapolis   New York   San Francisco   Upper Saddle River
Amsterdam   Cape Town   Dubai   London   Madrid   Milan   Munich   Paris   Montreal   Toronto
Delhi   Mexico City   Sao Paulo   Sydney   Hong Kong   Seoul   Singapore   Taipei   Tokyo

Publisher: Karen Hanson
Editorial Assistants: Courtney Shea and Alyssa Levy
Associate Editor: Mayda Bosco
Executive Marketing Manager: Kelly May
Marketing Assistant: Elaine Almquist
Production Editor: Claudine Bellanton
Manufacturing Buyer: Debbie Rossi
Cover Administrator/Designer: Joel Gendron
Editorial Production and Composition Service: Elm Street Publishing Services and Integra Software Services Pvt. Ltd.

Credits appear on page 788, which constitutes an extension of the copyright page.

Library of Congress Cataloging-in-Publication Data

Hooyman, Nancy R.
    Social gerontology: a multidisciplinary perspective/Nancy R. Hooyman, H. Asuman Kiyak. — 9th ed.
        p. cm.
    Includes bibliographical references and index.
    ISBN 0-205-76313-8 (alk. paper)—ISBN 0-205-52561-X (alk. paper)
      1. Gerontology.   2. Aging.   3. Older people—United States.   I. Kiyak, H. Asuman, 1951-   II. Title.
    HQ1061.H583 2009
    305.26—dc22   2009043774

10 9 8 7 6 5   V031   17   16   15   14

Allyn & Bacon
is an imprint of

PEARSON   www.pearsonhighered.com   ISBN 13: 978-0-205-76313-9
                                                                            ISBN 10:   0-205-76313-8

*In dedication to students, faculty, and practitioners
who are committed to enhancing the well-being of older
adults and their families.*

—NRH and HAK

*With love and gratitude to Joe and Lara for their
support and patience.*

—HAK

*With hope that our young adult children, Kevin, Mani, and
Lara, will inherit a world that supports active aging.*

—NRH and HAK

CONTENTS

C h a p t e r   **4 Managing Chronic Diseases and Promoting
Well-Being in Old Age   117**

C h a p t e r **7** Love, Intimacy, and Sexuality in Old Age   276

p a r t **four**

The Social Context of Aging   **309**

C h a p t e r **8** Social Theories of Aging   **312**

Chapter **9** The Importance of Social Supports: Family,
Friends, Neighbors, and Communities   **339**

C h a p t e r **10** Opportunities and Challenges
of Informal Caregiving   393

PREFACE

Similar to the last edition, this edition of *Social Gerontology: A Multidisciplinary Perspective* reflects a profound change in the way society views aging and older adults. We are moving from the widely held perspective that aging represents inevitable decline, to the more optimistic viewpoint that people can, to some extent, influence their own experience of aging. To a large degree, our lifestyles during youth and middle age affect our health, cognitive and emotional well-being, and social lives in later years. This dramatic paradigm shift in the field of gerontology is attributable to two parallel and interactive processes. First, a growing body of research demonstrates the role of individual choices and behaviors in whether we age in a healthy, active manner, or with multiple chronic diseases and without supportive social networks. While genetic and societal factors, especially educational and economic opportunities, affect aspects of aging, many recent studies offer evidence that even older adults who have dementia, chronic systemic diseases, or are living in poverty, can be resilient and experience active aging in ways that were rarely recognized in the past.

On the other hand, we bring a social constructionist perspective to the concepts of successful aging, recognizing the growing structurally determined disparities among older adults in their access to resources and opportunities to age "successfully" or "optimally." Another trend in the past 20 years has been society's recognition of the continuing contribution of older adults to our cultural, family, and work lives, as reflected in the increasing attention given to older adults' productivity and civic engagement. This includes cross-generational alliances related to environmental issues and social justice. We are moving away from the perspective that aging means withdrawal from active participation in society, to one where older adults remain an integral part of our communities. Yet, we also recognize that some older adults prefer contemplative and solitary activities and experience high levels of well-being without remaining "productive" in a traditional sense. Additionally, many elders face societal barriers to productivity and civic engagement.

What has shifted dramatically since the last edition, however, is the economic context in which we age. The economic status of older adults has been profoundly affected by the 2008–2009 worldwide recession. Growing numbers of older people must continue to work, or return to work, because of lost retirement income, the high cost of health care, or unexpected rises in their housing costs. After decades of a pattern of early retirement, older adults are faced with declining retirement income and are now retiring later, generally for financial reasons. In other instances, older adults have been disproportionately hurt by workforce reductions and increasingly find it difficult to move into other jobs, except for jobs in the part-time poorly paid service sector. Although adults ages 65 and older benefit from Medicare, this does not cover all their acute care expenses, and even less so, their long-term care. Accordingly, the poverty rate among older adults, especially women and elders of color, is growing after decades of decline while social and health services to support elders' well-being are being cut nationwide. Adult children are moving back home because of home foreclosures or turning increasingly to their parents or grandparents for financial support. And cuts in Medicare and Medicaid translate into inadequate care for the neediest, as well as reductions in other services to the older population. The economic crisis has affected the elder care workforce and has produced challenges in recruiting students to work with older adults. Many of these economic changes were simply unimaginable a decade ago—or even when the prior edition of this text was completed.

The subtitle, *A Multidisciplinary Perspective,* reflects our focus on aging as a process with multiple facets—physiological, emotional, cognitive, cultural, economic, and interpersonal—all of which interact to influence our social functioning and well-being. It is a fascinating process because these changes occur differently in each one of us. There is considerable truth to the statement that, as we grow older, we become more unlike each other.

Aging is also a process that attracts the attention of the media, politicians, businesses and industry, and the general public, largely because of the visibility and influence of aging baby boomers. Changes in the numbers and proportion of older people in our population have numerous implications for societal structures, the families, health and social services, long-term care, retirement policies, political processes, educational and recreational services, religious institutions, volunteerism, and housing. These changes are of growing concern because of the problems of poverty, inadequate housing, and chronic disease faced by some older people, particularly women, immigrants, persons of color, the oldest-old, and those living alone. Public officials, as well as individuals in the private sector, must address the challenge of planning for a not-so-distant future when older people will comprise 20 percent of the U.S. population.

These changes have also meant that a growing number of colleges and universities now offer courses in gerontology, the study of aging. The goal of many of these courses is to prepare students to understand the process of aging and the diversity among older people, and to be able to work effectively with older adults and their families. These programs also attempt to enhance students' personal understanding of their own and others' aging. Frequently, students take such a course simply to meet a requirement, but they quickly learn how relevant the aging process is to their own lives. Thus, instructors are often faced with the need to help students see the connection between learning about aging and understanding their own behavior, the behavior of their parents, grandparents and other relatives, and eventually the behavior of their clients, consumers, or patients.

This book was first triggered by our experiences in teaching gerontology courses. In doing so, we were unable to locate a textbook that conveyed the excitement and relevance of understanding the aging process or one that adequately addressed the interaction between the biological, physiological, psychological, and social aspects of aging. We were frustrated by the lack of a text that was comprehensive, thorough, and current in its review of the rapidly growing research on older adults. As a sociologist/social worker and a psychologist, we have been committed to writing and continuously updating a text that can be useful to a wide range of disciplines, including nursing, social work, sociology, psychology, health education, architecture, and the allied health professions. We are pleased that we have created a text that both undergraduate and graduate students find helpful and even inspiring, both personally and professionally.

Aims and Focus

The primary focus of this book is on social gerontology. As the title implies, however, our goal is to present the diversities of the aging experience, the interaction between biological, psychological, social and cultural forces on aging, and the heterogeneity of the older population in a multidisciplinary manner. As you will see throughout the 17 chapters, a careful examination of the social lives of older people requires a basic understanding of the historical, cultural, biological, physiological, psychological, and social contexts of aging across the life course. It is important to understand the changes that occur within the aging individual, how these modifications influence interactions with social and physical environments, and how the older person, and often their family members are, in turn, affected by such interactions. Throughout this book, a unifying theme is the impact of these dynamic interactions between older people and their environments, including inequities based on age, gender, race, and sexual orientation, on their quality of life and physical and mental well-being.

Social gerontology encompasses a wide range of topics with exciting research in so many domains. This book does not cover all these areas but rather highlights major research findings that illuminate the complex processes of aging. Through such factual information, we intend to dispel some of the myths and negative attitudes about aging. We also hope to encourage readers to pursue this field, academically, professionally, and for the personal rewards that come from gaining insight into older people's lives. Because the field is so complex and rapidly changing, some recent research findings may appear to contradict earlier studies as well as many of your own beliefs about aging and the older population. We have attempted to be thorough in presenting a multiplicity of theoretical perspectives and empirical data to ensure that the reader has as full and accurate a picture of the field as possible. We have tried to include up-to-date content throughout, but because the field—and especially social, health, and long-term care policies and programs—changes so rapidly, some of the issues raised in this edition will inevitably be out of date by the time the text is published. We encourage you to keep up with these changes by reading journals and periodicals that report on recent research findings and policies related to aging and older adults.

Features

This book begins by reviewing major demographic, societal, and cultural changes and their implications for the development of the field of social gerontology, as well as methods used to study aging and older people. Issues affecting immigrants, as well as other countries with significant increases in their populations of elders are also discussed. We then turn to the normal biological and physiological changes that affect older people's daily functioning, as well as their risk of chronic diseases and disability, how they cope with these conditions, and their use of health and long-term care services, including new models of disease management, care transitions, and health promotion. The third section considers normal age-related psychological changes in sensory functions, learning and memory, cognitive ability, creativity, personality, and sexuality, as well as mental disorders faced by some older adults. Given our emphasis on how such physical and psychological changes affect the social aspects of aging, the fourth section examines social theories of aging, the social context of family, friends, neighbors and other multigenerational supports, current living arrangements and community-based innovations in long-term care, productivity and social/civic engagement in the later years, and the conditions under which people die. Throughout the book, the differential effects that these changes have on three rapidly growing, but historically underserved populations, women, LGBT adults, and elders of color, are identified. Two chapters focus specifically on such differences, as well as the strength and resilience of older women and persons of color. We conclude by turning to the larger context of social, health, and long-term care policies, which faced constant challenges during the 2009 health care reform debates and budget reductions at all levels of government.

To underscore the application of research findings to everyday situations, most chapters integrate discussions of policy and practice implications of the aging process, career opportunities, and some predictions regarding the experiences of future cohorts of elders. *Points to Ponder,* updated tables, figures, and boxes providing summaries or case examples, and highlights from current news stories about elders attempt to bring to life many of the concepts discussed in these chapters.

New to This Edition

The positive responses of faculty and students to the first eight editions suggest that we have been successful in achieving our goals for this book. Based on feedback from faculty members who have used the text in different colleges and universities, nationally and internationally, the ninth edition builds on and expands many of the changes made in the previous edition. The book is designed to be completed in a 16-week semester, but readers can proceed at a faster pace and select only the chapters most relevant to their focus of study. Themes that underlie each chapter are the importance of congruence between elders and their environment, the interaction between the biological, psychological, and social aspects of aging on resilience and active aging, all within a life course perspective that takes account of historical, economic, cultural, and structural contexts and inequities by race, class, gender, sexual orientation, and functional ability.

New research findings are presented on extending both years and quality of life by preventing or managing chronic diseases, enhancing active aging, and maintaining productivity (i.e., contributing to society in a wide range of ways) through both paid and unpaid activities. These concepts are also critiqued. We have added new evidence-based findings on health and long-term care, including unpaid family caregivers and underpaid direct care workers, as well as public policies supporting them, such as consumer-directed care, integrated care systems, chronic care coordination, and new options for home and community-based care. Recent developments in the areas of preventing, diagnosing, and treating depression, anxiety, and dementias such as Alzheimer's disease are reviewed. The benefits of health promotion and of spirituality for achieving and maintaining active aging also have growing research support, as demonstrated in this edition. The chapters on informal supports and family caregiving recognize the growing number of grandparents as primary caregivers of grandchildren and of parents caring for adult children with long-term disabilities, and the policy and programmatic barriers confronting them. The sections on technology, including increasing computer use by elders and universal design that help people "age in place," are expanded. At the same time, however, we recognize that some older adults face cognitive and physical declines that preclude their living autonomously. Research and interventions to change the culture of long-term care facilities and to develop elder-friendly communities are described. The evolution of newer models of community-based long-term care such as assisted living, adult family homes, and adult day health is discussed. The growing research on LGBT older adults and attendant policy and practice implications are incorporated in many chapters. Both the resilience of and the historical disadvantage faced by older women and elders of color are emphasized. Given the dramatically changing political arena, the chapters on social, health, and long-term care policies reflect contemporary debates related to federal and state budget cuts, the impact of the 2003 Medicare prescription drug law, the 2009 health care debates and older adults' political participation in these discussions. Culturally competent methods to understand and respectfully meet the needs of an increasingly diverse older population are also identified throughout.

Each chapter begins with bulleted points covered in that chapter. The glossary defines key terms introduced in that chapter, while more resources, especially Internet resources, are added at the end of each chapter.

Supplements

For Instructors

Instructor's Manual and Test Bank (ISBN: 0-205-79416-5). Designed to make your lectures more effective and to save you preparation time, the Instructor's Manual contains chapter summaries, chapter outlines, lists of key terms and people, discussion topics, classroom activities and projects, suggested films, and suggested websites. The Test Bank contains multiple choice, true-false, short answer, and essay questions.

MyTest (ISBN: 0-205-79424-6). This computerized software allows instructors to create their own personalized exams, to edit any or all of the existing test questions and to add new questions. Other special features of this program include random generation of test questions, creation of alternate versions of the same test, scrambling question sequence, and test preview before printing. For easy access, this software is available via Pearson's Instructor Resource Center at www.pearsonhighered.com.

PowerPoint Presentations (ISBN: 0-205-79321-5). The PowerPoint presentations for *Social Gerontology*, Ninth Edition will bring your class alive. You have the option in every chapter of choosing from any of the following types of slides: Lecture & Line Art, Clicker Response System, and/or Special Topics PowerPoints. The Lecture & Line Art PowerPoint slides follow the chapter outline and feature images from the textbook integrated with the text. The Clicker Response System allows you to get immediate feedback from your students regardless of class size. The Special Topics PowerPoint slides allow you to integrate rich, supplementary material into your course with minimal amount of preparation time. Additionally, all of the PowerPoints are uniquely designed to provide students with a clear visual of succinct points for each concept. They are available to adopters at www.pearsonhighered.com.

For Students

MySocKit for *Social Gerontology*, Ninth Edition. MySocKit (www.mysockit.com) is a new online resource that contains chapter summaries, practice tests, flashcards, *New York Times* articles, audio and video activities, writing and research tutorials, access to scholarly literature on aging through Research Navigator, and materials for using the "Growing Old in a New Age" telecourse (formerly published in a print telecourse guide). MySocKit is available with *Social Gerontology*, Ninth Edition, when a MySocKit access code card is value-packed with the text.

A Note on Terminology

As with most other disciplines, the field of gerontology is constantly evolving, as is recognition of problems of language that makes sweeping generalizations or has negative connotations. The commonly used terms *the elderly, the aged,* and *seniors* are frequently associated with negative images of the older population. For this reason, we have chosen the terms *older adults, older persons,* and *elders* throughout this textbook. The first two terms parallel those of *younger person/adult*. The term *elder,* used widely among Native Americans, typically conveys respect and honor. Another change in terminology is our use of the word *Latino* in place of *Hispanic* wherever appropriate. This is because a growing number of scholars in this community have suggested that *Hispanic* has been associated with colonialism and the conquest of Spanish-speaking people in the Americas. Except where dictated by publications, such as reports of the U.S. Census Bureau (where *Hispanic* is the standard term), we have chosen to refer to older adults from Spanish-speaking origins as *Latinos* and *Latinas*.

Acknowledgments

We are grateful to the many people who have contributed significantly to the successful completion of the ninth edition of *Social Gerontology*. In particular, we thank Kevin Kawamoto, Associate Professor at the University of Hawaii, and University of Washington students Brittany Barrett, Charles Pitre Hoy-Ellis, Kathleen Nelson, and Mark Williams, for their assistance with literature and Web site searches and updating references. Thanks also to Julia Bruk for her diligent search for new photos and illustrations for each chapter. The willingness of these colleagues and students to do whatever tasks necessary allowed us to concentrate on the big picture! We also thank our many colleagues around the United States who have given us valuable and candid feedback about the eighth edition that has helped us in preparing the ninth edition. They include: Maria Lena Claver, California State University, Long Beach; Angela Hauger, The College of St. Scholastica; Richard D. MacNeil, The University of Iowa; and Melanie Horn Mallers, California State University, Fullerton. It is feedback from faculty and students who value this text that motivates and sustains us through the intense efforts needed to update each edition. It means a great deal to both of us when a student or faculty member approaches us at a conference or meeting to convey how much they learned from the text. We hope this new edition excites a new generation of students about seeking careers in gerontology.

Our families and good friends have been a mainstay of support throughout the preparation of all nine editions of this book, and we take this opportunity to express our gratitude to all of them.

ABOUT THE AUTHORS

Nancy R. Hooyman Nancy R. Hooyman holds the Hooyman Professorship of Gerontology and is dean emeritus at the School of Social Work at the University of Washington. Her M.S.W and Ph.D. in sociology and social work are from the University of Michigan. She is nationally recognized for her scholarship in aging and multigenerational policy and practice, gender inequities in family caregiving, and feminist gerontology. In addition to this textbook, Dr. Hooyman is the co-author of *Living through Loss: Interventions across the Life Span; Taking Care of Aging Family Members;* and *Feminist Perspectives on Family Care: Policies for Gender Justice,* and editor of *Transforming Social Work Education: The First Decade of the Hartford Geriatric Social Work Initiative.* She has published over 120 articles and chapters and is a frequent national and international presenter on issues related to gerontology, multigenerational perspectives in aging, and older women. She is Co-Principal Investigator of the Council on Social Work Education's National Center for Gerontological Social Work Education, funded by the John A. Hartford Foundation, and an advisory board member and national research mentor for the Hartford Geriatric Social Work Faculty Scholars Program. A Fellow in the Gerontological Society of America, Dr. Hooyman is past-chair of GSA's Social Research, Policy and Practice Section. She received the Significant Lifetime Achievement in Social Work Education Award from the Council on Social Work Education in 2009.

H. Asuman Kiyak H. Asuman Kiyak is Director of the Institute on Aging, professor in the School of Dentistry, and adjunct professor in the Departments of Architecture and Psychology at the University of Washington. She obtained her M.A. and Ph.D. in psychology at Wayne State University. Professor Kiyak has been the recipient of major research grants from NIH, CDC, AOA, the State of Washington, and private foundations in the areas of health promotion and health service utilization by older adults, and in person–environment adaptation to Alzheimer's disease by patients and their caregivers. She has published over 130 articles and 35 chapters in these areas and is known nationally and internationally for her research on geriatric dental care and the application of psychological theory to health promotion. In 2000, she received the Distinguished Scientist Award from the International Association for Dental Research and has served as president of the Geriatric Oral Research and the Behavioral Sciences and Health Services Research Groups of IADR. Dr. Kiyak was principal investigator of a large clinical trial in geriatric dentistry funded by the National Institute of Dental and Craniofacial Research, and two studies of a community-based health promotion study funded by the CDC. She has collaborated with Intel to test new technologies and to sponsor conferences on this topic to help older adults remain active and independent. In 2003 she was named Distinguished Professor of Geriatrics at UCLA and received the Teaching Excellence Award from the University of Washington Educational Outreach division. Professor Kiyak is a Fellow in the Gerontological Society of America.

The Field of Social Gerontology

Toward Understanding Aging

From the perspective of youth and middle age, old age seems a remote and, to some, an undesirable period of life. Throughout history, humans have tried to prolong youth and to delay aging. The attempts to discover a substance to rejuvenate the body and mind have driven explorers to far corners of the globe and inspired alchemists and scientists to search for ways to restore youth and extend life. Indeed, the discovery of Florida by Ponce de León in 1513 was an accident, as he searched for a fountain in Bimini whose waters were rumored to bring back one's youth. Medieval Latin alchemists believed that eating gold could add years to life and spent many years trying to produce a digestible form of gold. In the seventeenth century, a popular belief was that smelling fresh earth each morning could prolong one's youth. The theme of prolonging or restoring youth is evident today in advertisements for skin creams, soaps, vitamins, and certain foods; in the popularity of cosmetic surgery and Botox treatments; in books, movies, and TV shows that feature attractive, youthful-looking older characters; and even in anti-aging medical research that is testing methods to replace depleted hormones in an attempt to rejuvenate aging skin and physical and sexual functioning. One organization, by its name, suggests that aging is a process that can be fought or prevented. The International Academy of Anti-Aging Medicine actually promotes preventive and naturopathic medicine, but its name suggests a more negative view of aging than does its goal. Given the historical and societal focus on youth, most Euro-Americans are unprepared for many of the physical and cognitive signs of aging.

All these concerns point to underlying fears and denial of aging. Many of these arise from misconceptions about what happens to our bodies, our minds, our status in society, and our social networks as we reach our 70s, 80s, and beyond. They arise, in part, from negative attitudes toward older people within mainstream Western culture. These attitudes are sometimes identified as manifestations of **ageism**, a term that

As Leo Tolstoy noted, "Old age is the most unexpected of all things that happen to a man."

was coined by Robert Butler (the first Director of the National Institute on Aging) to describe stereotypes about old age (1969). As is true for sexism and racism, ageism attributes certain traits to all members of a group solely because of a characteristic they share—in this case, their age. In fact, ageism is one prejudice that we are all likely to encounter if we live long enough, regardless of our gender, race, ethnicity, social class, functional ability or sexual orientation. A frequent result of ageism is discriminatory behavior against older persons. For example, some age-based advocates complain that older workers are encouraged to retire early because of stereotypes about older people's abilities and productivity. Instead, advocates suggest that employers should consider each worker's skills and experience—not age—when organizational restructuring requires layoffs. Although attitudes toward older adults have improved in the past

four decades, partially because of expanded education about the aging process, pockets of negative attitudes persist, along with a "new ageism" that resents elders for their perceived economic progress and tax burden (Palmore, 2004).

To distinguish the realities of aging from the social stereotypes requires an understanding of the "normal" changes that can be expected in the aging body, mental and emotional functioning, and social interactions and status. Aging can then be viewed as another phase of growth and development—a universal biological phenomenon. Accordingly, the normal processes due to age alone need to be differentiated from pathological changes or disease. As life expectancy increases, the older proportion of our population expands, and more of us can look forward to becoming older ourselves; concerns and questions about the aging process attract growing public and professional attention.

1

The Growth of Social Gerontology

The Field of Gerontology

The growing interest in understanding the process of aging has given rise to the multidisciplinary field of **gerontology,** the study of the biological, psychological, and social aspects of aging. Gerontologists include researchers and practitioners in such diverse fields as biology, medicine, nursing, dentistry, social work, physical and occupational therapy, psychology, psychiatry, sociology, economics, political science, architecture, pharmacy, and anthropology. These individuals are concerned with multiple aspects of aging, from studying and describing the cellular processes involved to seeking ways to improve the quality of life for older people and their families. **Geriatrics** focuses on how to prevent or manage the diseases that often occur as people age. As a specialty within the health professions, geriatrics is receiving more attention with the increased number of older people who have long-term health problems. But the number of health professionals trained in geriatrics is currently inadequate to meet growing needs.

Gerontologists view aging in terms of four distinct processes that are examined throughout this book:

- *Chronological aging* is the definition of aging based on a person's years lived from birth. Thus, a 75-year-old is chronologically older than a 45-year-old. Chronological age is not necessarily related to a person's biological, physical, psychological, or social age, as we will emphasize throughout this book. For example, we may remark that someone "looks younger (or older)" or "acts younger (or older)" than her or his age. This implies that the individual's *biological* or *psychological* or *social age* is incongruent with the person's *chronological age.*
- *Biological aging* refers to the physical changes that reduce the efficiency of organ systems, such as the lungs, heart, and circulatory system. This type of aging can be determined by measuring the efficiency and functional abilities of an individual's organ systems, as well as physical activity levels. Indeed, some have referred to this as *functional aging* (Hayflick, 1996).
- *Psychological aging* includes the changes that occur in sensory and perceptual processes, cognitive abilities (e.g., memory, learning, and intelligence), adaptive capacity, and personality. Thus, an individual in her 70s who is intellectually active and adapts well to new situations can be considered psychologically young.
- *Social aging* refers to an individual's changing roles and relationships with family, friends, and other informal supports, both paid and unpaid productive roles, and within organizations such as religious and political groups.

Social gerontologists study the impact of these aging processes on both older people and social structures. They also examine effects of

AN OLDER ADULT WITH DIVERGENT CHRONOLOGICAL, BIOLOGICAL, PSYCHOLOGICAL, AND SOCIAL AGES

Mr. Roberts is an 80-year-old retired university professor in biology. He has no chronic diseases and continues his longtime exercise routine: running five miles three times a week and weight lifting for core body strength four times a week. His physician tells him that his vital signs resemble that of a 40-year-old. Mr. Roberts has decided to keep his mind active by learning a new language and taking piano lessons, so he spends six hours per week in a college class on Spanish, two hours taking piano lessons, and many hours each day practicing both. His social life is rich with friends of all ages; he and his wife socialize with old and new friends at least twice a week, and he volunteers at the local food bank two mornings per week as a way to serve his community.

social attitudes toward aging on older adults and opportunities available to them. For example, as a society, we have tended to undervalue older people and to assume that most of them are forgetful, unemployable, nonproductive, uninterested in interacting with younger people, and asexual. As a result, they have been limited in their access to activities such as jobs in high-tech fields or stigmatized in long-term care facilities if they express their needs for intimacy or sexuality. The research reviewed throughout this book demonstrates that these stereotypes are not true for the vast majority of older adults who continue to participate actively in society.

With the rapid growth in the number and diversity of older persons, societal myths and stereotypes are increasingly being challenged. The public has become more aware of older citizens' strengths, contributions to society, and potential for civic engagement. Accordingly, older people's status and the way they are viewed by other segments of the population are changing. Contemporary advertising, for example, reflects the shifting status of older people from a group that is viewed as weak, ill, and poor to one perceived as politically and economically powerful and therefore a growing consumer market.

The emergence of age-based advocacy groups and increased political activity of older adults in the past 50 years have changed not only public perceptions but also policies and programs. Organized groups of older people have responded to congressional attempts to change retirement and pension policies, housing options, health and long-term care policy, Social Security reform—although they do not speak with a unified voice on all issues and their organizing may not be proactive but in reaction to changes in policies and programs. As described in Chapter 16, with scarce public resources and the economic crisis, the need for cross-generational collaboration is gradually replacing age-based advocacy.

Equally significant in this area of study are the social, economic, and health problems that continue to affect a large percentage of older people. Even though older adults today are financially better off than they were 50 years ago, slightly less than 10 percent still fall below the U.S. government's official poverty line. In the economic crisis that emerged in 2008, most older adults lost significant retirement income because of declining returns on their investments. This may result in increased rates of poverty among aging adults in future years. Poverty is an even greater problem for women, elders of color, those living alone, and the oldest of the old. Although less than five percent of the older population resides in nursing homes at any given time, the number who will require long-term care at some point in their lives is increasing. Growing percentages of older people in the community face living increased years with chronic diseases that may limit their daily activities. At the same time, health and long-term care costs have escalated. In general, older people pay a higher proportion of their income for health and long-term care than they have at any time in the past, and they often lack access to publicly supported home- and community-based services. Therefore, many gerontologists

are also concerned with developing public policy, program and practice interventions to address these problems.

Social Gerontology

The purpose of this book is to introduce you to *social gerontology*. This term was first used by Clark Tibbitts in 1954 to describe the area of gerontology that is concerned with the impact of social and sociocultural conditions on the process of aging and its social consequences. This field has grown as the extent to which aging differs across cultures, historically underserved groups, and societies has been recognized.

Social gerontologists are interested in how the older population and the diversity of aging experiences both affect and are affected by the social structure. As noted above, the fact that older people are now the fastest-growing population segment in the United States has far-reaching social implications for families and communities, health and long-term care, the workplace, retirement practices, long-term care facilities, housing design, and patterns of government and private spending. Already it has led to the growth of specialized services such as assisted living and adult day-health programs, and a leisure and travel industry aimed at the older population. Changes in the sociopolitical structure, in turn, affect civic engagement initiatives. For example, the greater availability of secondary and higher education and health promotion programs offers hope that future generations of older people will be better educated, healthier, economically more secure and socially engaged than the current cohort, presuming a growing economy in the future.

What Is Aging?

Contrary to the messages on birthday cards, aging does not start at age 40 or 65. Even though we are less conscious of age-related changes in earlier life stages, we are all aging from the moment of birth. In fact, **aging** in general refers to changes that take place in the organism throughout the life span—good, bad, and neutral. Younger stages are referred to as *development* or *maturation*, because the individual develops and matures, both socially and physically, from birth through adolescence. After age 30, additional changes occur that reflect normal declines in all organ systems. This is called **senescence.** Senescence happens gradually throughout the body, ultimately reducing the viability of different bodily systems and increasing their vulnerability to disease. This is the final stage in the development of an organism.

Our place in the social structure also changes throughout our lives. Every society is *age-graded;* that is, it assigns different roles, expectations, opportunities, status, and constraints to people of different ages. For example, there are common societal expectations about the appropriate age to attend school, begin work, have children, and retire—even though people may deviate from these expectations and some of these expectations are now changing as people live longer. To call someone a *toddler, child, young adult,* or an *old person* is to imply a full range of social characteristics. As we age, we pass through a sequence of defined stages, each with its own social norms and characteristics. In sum, age is a social construct with social meanings and implications.

The specific effects of age grading, or age stratification, vary across cultures and historical time periods. A third-world society, for instance, has very different expectations associated with stages of childhood, adolescence, and old age from mainstream American society. Even within our society, those who are old today have different experiences of aging than previous or future groups of older people; and expectations about when to go to school, shift careers, or start a family are changing dramatically. The term **cohort** is used to describe groups of people who were born at approximately the same time and therefore share many common experiences. For example, cohorts now in their late 80s experienced the Great Depression, World War II, and the Korean War, which shaped their lives. For example, members of the Depression era cohort have tended to be frugal throughout their lives. The oldest-old includes large numbers of immigrants who came to the United States in the first third of the twentieth century and many who have grown up in rural areas. Their average levels of education are lower than those of later cohorts, such as those growing up during the Vietnam War. Such factors set today's oldest-old population apart from other cohorts and must be taken into account in any studies of the aging process as well as policies and practice.

The Older Population Is Diverse

Throughout this book, we refer to the phenomenon of aging and the population of older people. As noted earlier in this chapter, these terms are based to some extent on chronological criteria, but, more importantly, on individual differences in functional age, such as the ability to perform activities of daily living. In fact, each of us may differ in the way we define old age. You may know an 80-year-old who seems youthful and a 50-year-old whom you consider old. Older people also define themselves differently. Some individuals, even in their 80s, do not want to associate with "those old people," whereas others readily join age-based organizations and are proud of the years they have

---

POINTS TO PONDER

For each age group below, list one activity or event that you think is typical for that age. These might include marriage, attending school, or learning to ride a bike. Then think of an activity or event that is not so typical.

	TYPICAL	ATYPICAL
Toddler (ages 2–4)		
Child (ages 4–12)		
Young adult (ages 18–24)		
Old person (age 65+)		

lived. There are significant differences among the "young-old" (ages 65–74), the "old-old" (ages 75–84), and the "oldest-old" (ages 85 and over) (Riley & Riley, 1986). In addition, intragenerational diversity in terms of gender, race, and sexual orientation exists even within these divisions.

Older people vary greatly in their health status, productive activities, and family and social situations. Growing numbers are employed full- or part-time; most are retired. Most are relatively healthy; some are frail, confused, or homebound. Most still live in a house or apartment; a small percentage is in nursing homes, and growing numbers are in assisted living facilities and adult family homes. Some receive comfortable incomes from pensions and investments, although these have declined in the worldwide economic downturn that started in 2008; many depend primarily on Social Security and have little discretionary income. Most men over age 65 are married, whereas women are more likely to become widowed and live alone as they age. For all these reasons, we cannot consider the social aspects of aging without also assessing the impact of individual variables such as physiological changes, health status, psychological well-being, social class, gender, sexual orientation, and race. Recognizing this, many chapters of *Social Gerontology* focus on how these multiple factors intersect and influence elders' social functioning and current concepts of active aging, resilience, and productivity.

Although the terms *elders, elderly,* and *older persons* are often used to mean those over 65 years in chronological age, this book is based on the principle that aging is a complex process that involves many different biological, psychological and social factors and is unique to each individual.

POINTS TO PONDER

Discuss with friends and family some common terms used to describe older adults, such as "elderly," "old folks," and "elders." What images of aging and older people do these terms convey?

Rather than chronological age, the more important distinction is functional ability—that is, the ability to perform activities of daily living that require cognitive and physical well-being. In addition, the authors deliberately use the term *older adults, older people, elders,* or *people as they age* throughout the book. The reasons for this choice of more neutral terminology are:

1. There is no comparable term for "the elderly" among younger populations, while "older adults" or "older people" are similar to the concept of "young people."
2. Growing numbers of older adults do not like the term "seniors" or "elderly."
3. The word "elder" connotes respect in many cultures (Kaiser, 2006; Lesnoff-Caravaglia, 2002; Levy, 2001; Palmore, 2000).

An Active Aging Framework

The concept of **active aging** is a widely accepted perspective in gerontology. It is defined by the World Health Organization as "the process of optimizing opportunities for health, participation, and security in order to enhance quality of life as people age" (WHO, 2002, p. 2). This concept focuses on ways to improve quality of life for all older people, including those who are frail, disabled, or require assistance with daily activities. Active aging is consistent with the growing emphasis on autonomy and choice in aging, regardless of physical and mental decline, and benefits both the individual and society. Such a definition shifts our thinking about old age from a time of passivity to one of continued participation in the family, community, workplace, and religious and political life. It serves as a useful framework for this textbook, since we present a growing number of studies that support the importance of active aging for physical, psychological, and social well-being in the later years.

Consistent with the life-course approach underlying this book, the active-aging perspective implies that aging is a lifelong process. As a result,

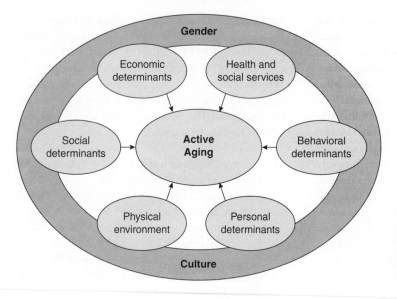

FIGURE 1.1   The Determinants of Active Aging

SOURCE: World Health Organization, *Active ageing: A policy framework* (WHO: 2002). Reprinted by permission of the World Health Organization.

it is understood that people's lifestyles, socioeconomic status, health care, and educational and social activities in their childhood, youth, and middle years determine the quality of their lives in their later years. This is also an important assumption of other models of active aging that we will introduce later in this book, including the concepts of *successful, positive, vital, resilient, robust,* and *productive aging.* Accordingly, the determinants of active aging, as shown in Figure 1.1, include individual behaviors, personal characteristics, the physical environment (e.g., neighborhood, living situation) and social environment (e.g., informal and formal support networks), economic security, and access to and use of health and social services across the life course. This model also places great importance on status variables such as ethnicity, race, gender, and sexual orientation that influence opportunities for active aging, such as access to education, employment, and health care beginning from childhood. A closely related concept is **resilience,** or individuals' ability to thrive despite adversity in their lives. We have all known older adults who have suffered multiple losses throughout their lives but have turned those losses into opportunities for forgiveness and growth, in part because of the protective effects of family, community, and cultural and religious affiliation.

As noted above, the concept of **life course** is central to this model. A life course approach captures how earlier life experiences and decisions affect opportunities in later life and for future generations within and across cultures and time. By placing families and individuals in the larger context of historical, demographic, economic, and social changes, the life course perspective differs from a life-span approach that is focused on individual development. A life course perspective recognizes that gender or racial inequities that limit opportunities earlier in the life cycle are often intensified in old age, frequently resulting in increased economic and health disparities and cumulative inequities for older women and persons of color. Gender, ethnicity, race, sexual orientation, childhood poverty, educational levels, and generational differences have all been identified as associated with health disparities and as social justice issues for elders (Alwin & Wray, 2005; O'Rand & Hamil-Luker, 2005; Whitfield & Hayward, 2003; Williams, 2005). At the same time, however, many older adults, including those from historically underserved groups, have demonstrated remarkable resilience and strengths, making the most of lifelong experiences despite adversity and setbacks throughout their lives (Cohen,

2005). The terms *active aging, resilience,* and *health disparities and health care disparities across the life course* will be used throughout this text. Another perspective central to this text is *the person in the environment,* discussed next.

A Person–Environment Perspective on Social Gerontology

Consistent with the framework of the interaction of physiological, psychological, and social changes with aging, this textbook approaches topics in social gerontology from a **person-environment perspective.** This model suggests that the environment is not a static backdrop, but changes continually as the older person takes from it what he or she needs, controls what can be

modified, and adapts to conditions that cannot be changed. Adaptation thus implies a dual process in which the individual adjusts to some characteristics of the social and physical environment (e.g., completing the numerous forms required by Medicare) and brings about changes in others (e.g., lobbying to expand Medicare benefits to cover prescription drugs).

Environmental Press

The **competence model** is one useful way to view the dynamic interactions between the person's physical and psychological characteristics and the social and physical environment (Lawton & Nahemow, 1973; Lawton, 1989; Parmelee & Lawton, 1990). *Environment* in this model, which is shown in Figure 1.2, may

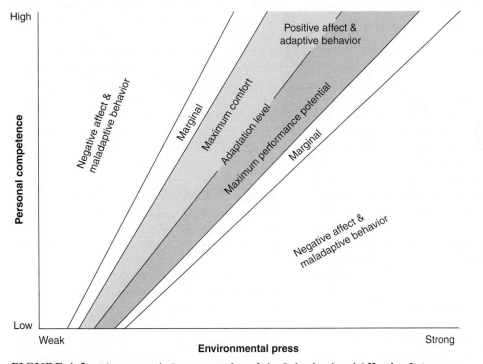

FIGURE 1.2　**Diagrammatic Representation of the Behavioral and Affective Outcomes of Person–Environment Transactions**

SOURCE: M. P. Lawton and L. Nahemow, Ecology and the aging process. In C. Eisdorfer and M. P. Lawton (Eds.), *Psychology of adult development and aging* (Washington, D.C.: American Psychological Association, 1973), p. 661. Copyright © 1973 by the American Psychological Association. Reprinted by permission of the author and publisher.

refer to the larger society, the community, the neighborhood, or the home. **Environmental press** is defined as the demands that social and physical environments make on the individual to adapt, respond, or change. The environmental-press model can be approached from a variety of disciplinary perspectives. A concept fundamental to social work, for example, is that of human behavior and the environment, and the need to develop practice and policy interventions that achieve a better fit between the person and his or her social environment. Health care providers are increasingly aware of the necessity to take account of social and physical environmental factors (e.g., family caregivers and other informal supports as well as the elder's living situation) in their assessments of health problems.

Architects and advocates for persons with disabilities are developing ways to make physical environments more accessible and congruent. Psychologists are interested in how physical and social environments may be modified to maximize the older person's ability to learn new tasks and perform familiar ones such as driving, taking tests, and self-care. Sociologists study the ways in which the macroenvironment (the larger political and economic structures and policies) affects and is affected by an individual's interactions with it. Because the concepts of this model are so basic to understanding the position of older people and to developing ways to improve the quality of their lives, such environmental interactions are referred to throughout this text.

Environmental press can range from minimal to quite high. For example, often very little environmental press is present in an institutional setting where an individual is not responsible for self-care (such as personal grooming and housekeeping) and may have few resources to stimulate the senses or challenge the mind. Other environments can create a great deal of press—for example, a multigenerational household in which an older person plays a pivotal role. An increase in the number of people sharing the living arrangement or a move to a new home intensifies the environmental demands. As the demands change, individuals must adapt in order to maintain their sense of competence.

Individuals perform at their maximum level when the environmental press slightly exceeds the level at which they adapt. In other words, the environment challenges them to test their limits but does not overwhelm them. If the level of environmental demand becomes too high, the individual experiences excessive stress or overload. When the environmental press is far below the individual's adaptation level, sensory deprivation, boredom, learned helplessness, and dependence on others may result. However, a situation of mild to moderate stress, just below the person's adaptation level, results in maximum comfort. It is important to challenge the individual in this situation as well to prevent a decline to boredom and inadequate stimulation. In either situation—too much or too little environmental press—the person or the environment must change if the individual's adaptive capacity is to be restored and quality of life enhanced.

As implied above, *individual competence* is another concept central to this model. This is defined by Lawton and Nahemow (1973) as the theoretical upper limit of an individual's abilities to function in different areas. Some of the capacities needed to adapt to environmental press include good health, effective problem-solving and learning skills, and the ability to manage the basic activities of daily living such as dressing, grooming, and cooking (Parmelee & Lawton, 1990). As suggested by the model in Figure 1.2, the higher a person's competence, the higher the levels of environmental press that can be tolerated. Thus, an older person with multiple physical disabilities and chronic illnesses has reduced physical competence, which may limit the level of physical demands with which he or she can cope.

COPING WITH P–E INCONGRUENCE

Sometimes P–E incongruence can be temporary, as in the following example of an elder who must adjust to life in a new community:

Mrs. Jackson recently moved to Minneapolis from her home in Atlanta in order to be near her only daughter, although she does not know anyone else in the new community. Her daughter has found a beautiful high-rise apartment for seniors so Mrs. Jackson can live among other retired older adults. Although the building is new and has many safety features to help elders live independently, Mrs. Jackson feels overwhelmed by all the built-in monitoring systems and appliances that seem to be controlling her life, and she does not like being on the 10th floor looking down on the street after a lifetime of living in a one-story home surrounded by her lovely flower garden in Atlanta. She has not met anyone in the building from her part of the country or with a similar work and family history to hers, so she keeps mostly to herself. Going out on her own and exploring the city is out of the question because it is too cold for her to walk outdoors or to go window-shopping, and she does not feel safe in a new city.

On the other hand, this individual may still maintain a high level of psychosocial competence, enjoy the company of others, and experience life satisfaction.

Environmental Interventions

The competence model has numerous implications for designing prevention and intervention strategies to enhance the quality of older adults' lives. Most services for older people are oriented toward minimizing environmental demands and increasing supports. These services may focus on changing the physical or the social environment, or both. Physical environmental modifications (such as ramps and handrails) and community services (such as Meals On Wheels and escort vans equipped for

wheelchairs) reestablish the older person's level of adaptation and ease the burdens of daily coping. Such arrangements are essential to the well-being of some older people who require environmental adaptations or occasional assistance from informal and paid caregivers to enhance their autonomy. For example, many older people with chronic conditions are able to remain in their own homes because of environmental modifications such as emergency systems that allow them to call for help, computers that aid them with communication, and medication reminders. Other examples of both environmental and individual interventions to enhance older people's choices are considered throughout this text.

A fine line exists, however, between minimizing excessive environmental press and creating an environment that is not stimulating or is "too easy" to navigate. Well-intentioned families, for example, may do too much for an older person, assuming responsibility for daily activities so that their older relative no longer has to exert any effort and may no longer feel he or she is a contributing family member. Likewise, nursing home staff may not challenge residents to perform such daily tasks as getting out of bed or going to the dining hall. Protective efforts such as these can remove necessary levels of environmental press, with the result that the person's social, psychological, and physical levels of functioning may decline. Understimulating conditions, then, can be as negative in their effects on older people as those in which there is excessive environmental press.

Organization of the Text

This book is divided into five parts:

- Part One is a general introduction to the field of social gerontology and the demographics of an aging society and includes a brief history of the field, the growth of the older population, a discussion of research methods and designs, and descriptions of aging in other countries and cultures as well as the lives of older immigrants to the United States.

• Part Two addresses the physiological changes that influence social aging. It begins with a review of normal age-related changes in the body's major organ systems, including modifications in the sensory system and their social/environmental effects. It also discusses the most frequent chronic diseases among older people, how these diseases can be managed, factors that influence health care behavior (e.g., when and why older people are likely to seek professional care), and health promotion programs aimed at improving their physical, psychological, and social functioning.

• In Part Three, we move to the psychological context of aging; this includes normal and disease-related changes in cognitive functioning (learning, intelligence, and memory), theories of personality development and coping styles, psychological and cognitive disorders in late life, such as depression and dementia, the use of mental health services, as well as the universal need for love, intimacy, and sexuality in the later years.

• Part Four explores the social issues of aging, beginning with a discussion of current social theories on aging; the importance of the support of family, friends, and neighbors; informal caregiving of older adults; and how the array of housing and long-term care options for older adults affects their social interactions and sense of competence. Issues related to productivity, employment, retirement, and income are next explored, followed by a review of unpaid productive roles and civic engagement in the community, educational and religious institutions, and politics. This part concludes with topics related to dying, grief and widowhood. The last two chapters of Part Four present both the challenges and strengths of elders of color and older women.

• Part Five goes beyond the individual's social context to address societal challenges—particularly social, health, and long-term care policy issues and debates.

Each part begins with an introduction to the key issues of aging that are discussed in that section. Throughout each chapter, the diversity of the older population and of the aging process itself is highlighted in terms of chronological age, gender, culture, race, ethnicity, social class, functional ability, and sexual orientation. Where appropriate, the dynamic interaction between older people and their environment is emphasized. How age-related changes are measured and the methods for improving measurement in this field are also discussed.

We encourage you to read the facts and examples in the boxed material, which illustrate some of the key concepts discussed in the chapters. At the end of each chapter, you will find a brief description of emerging trends, possible future directions relevant to the chapter's topic, and, where relevant, implications for careers in gerontology. These projections are based on population trends and biological, social, and psychological research that allow us to glean some ideas of what aging and old age will be like in the future.

Why Study Aging?

As you begin this text, you may find it useful to think about your own motivations for learning about older adults and the aging process. You may be in a required course, questioning its relevance, and approaching this text as something you must read to satisfy requirements. Or you may have personal reasons for wishing to learn about aging. You may be concerned about your own age-related changes, wondering whether reduced energy or alterations in physical features are inevitable with age. After all, because middle and old age together encompass a longer time span than any other stage of our lives, it is important that we understand and prepare for these years. Perhaps you are in a transition phase, looking forward to the freedom made possible by retirement and the "empty nest." Through increased knowledge about the aging process, you may be hoping to make decisions that can enhance your own active aging. Or perhaps you are assisting aging relatives, friends, and neighbors, wanting to know what can be done to help them maintain their autonomy, their housing options, and how you can improve your own caregiving abilities.

Learning about aging not only gives us insight into our own interpersonal relationships, self-esteem, competence, and meaningful activities as we grow older; it also helps us comprehend the aging process of our parents, grandparents, clients, patients, and friends. It is important to recognize that change and growth take place throughout the life course and that the concerns of older people are not distinct from those of the young, but represent a continuation of earlier life periods. Such understanding can improve our effectiveness in communicating with relatives, friends, or professionals. In addition, such knowledge can help challenge any assumptions or stereotypes we may hold about behavior appropriate to various ages.

Perhaps you wish to work professionally with older people but are unsure how your interests can fit in with the needs of the older population. The exciting and diverse range of career opportunities in both community and institutional settings and growing geriatric workforce needs are discussed throughout this book. If you are already working with older people, you may genuinely enjoy your work, but you may also be concerned about the social, economic, and health problems facing some older adults and thus feel a responsibility to change these negative social conditions. As a professional or future professional working with older people, you are probably eager to learn more about both policy and practice issues that can enhance their active aging, resilience, and quality of life.

Regardless of your motivations for reading this text, chances are that, like most Americans, you have some misconceptions about older people and the aging process. As products of our youth-oriented society, we all sense the pervasiveness of negative attitudes about aging, although our own personal experiences with older people may counter many stereotypes and myths. By

studying aging and older people, you will not only become more aware of the older population's competence and contributions in many areas, but also be able to differentiate the normal changes that are associated with the aging process from disease-related modifications. Such an understanding may serve to reduce some of your own fears about aging, as well as positively affect your professional and personal interactions with older people.

Our challenge as educators and authors is to present you with the facts and concepts that will give you an accurate picture of the experience of aging. We also want to convey to you the excitement and importance of learning about the field of social gerontology. We hope that by the time you have completed this text, you will have acquired information that strengthens positive attitudes toward living and working with older people and toward your own experience of aging. First, we will describe some career opportunities in this field, whether you want to specialize in work with older adults and their families or you choose a career that includes older adults as patients, service recipients, or a population that benefits from your expertise. Later, we will turn to the demographic changes that are creating the largest population of people age 65 and older in the history of the United States.

Careers in Aging

Those who work in the field of aging may be *geriatricians, gerontological workers, gerontological specialists,* or *gerontologists.* The term *geriatrics* typically refers to the work of health professionals in the branch of medical science that deals with diseases, other health problems, and health promotion and prevention specific to older adults. Geriatricians are physicans trained in geriatrics; there are also geriatric social workers, geriatric nurses, geriatric pharmacists, and people in other allied health professions who have received specialized training to work with older people and their families. In fact, the membership of the American Geriatrics Society includes a wide range of health care providers who are trained to prevent and manage the multiple health concerns of older adults. Gerontology, which is broader than geriatrics, refers to the psychological, social, and biological phenomena associated with aging, as well as policies and programs that address older adults' wide range of needs.

The classifications of gerontological workers, gerontological specialists, and gerontologists are based on their degree of training related to aging. Gerontological workers have no formal training in this field but nevertheless provide services to or for older persons. These people include social workers who work in a child welfare agency interacting with older grandparents, physicians whose patients have aged, nurse aides in a long-term care setting, or home care workers. Gerontological specialists have received training in gerontology through a certificate, continuing education, a minor in college, or a postdoctoral training, but their primary training is in another discipline. For example, physical and occupational therapists, social workers, nurses, and physicians may take additional courses, complete an internship or residency in geriatrics, or obtain a certificate as part of their professional training that allows them to specialize in working with older people. In contrast, gerontology is the primary training at the bachelor's, master's, or doctoral levels for gerontologists. A growing number of colleges and universities today offer degrees in gerontology. As described in this section, most professionals who work for or with older people today fall into the category of gerontological specialists, without a degree in the field but with some training or specialization in gerontology (Grabinski, 2007; Stepp, 2007).

No matter what your area of interest—health care, mental health, design, technology, law, business, or one of many others—there are numerous and growing opportunities to work with or on behalf of older adults and their families. A degree in social work with additional training in gerontology is necessary to become a professional advocate, such as a professional geriatric care manager (PGCM). Those who are interested in designing or adapting housing and products for older

people would do well to combine their degrees in architecture or interior or industrial design with coursework in gerontology. Similarly, experts in computer science, industrial or human factors engineering, and information technology who want to develop, test, and improve technology for older users must first understand the normal physiological, social, and psychological processes of aging and how systemic diseases and cognitive impairment can result in the need for technological aids. Information specialists, librarians, and experts in lifelong learning and continuing education can also benefit from this knowledge as they work with a growing population of older students and clients. Attorneys who practice elder law, estate planning, or file lawsuits in areas such as elder abuse, age or disability discrimination, or advocacy for older clients must understand the normal aging process and the impact of disease and dementia on their clients. Even those who decide to obtain a degree in business and work in the fields of accounting, marketing, advertising, banking, or financial planning should obtain some training in gerontology through additional coursework, certificates in aging, or continuing education courses. Such knowledge is vital for helping younger adults plan for their old age and for assisting older persons in maintaining quality of life. For those seeking to develop or influence policies affecting older adults, advocacy at the individual or population level requires extensive knowledge of age-associated needs, the aging process, and health and social policies affecting state and local programs for older citizens. A degree in public administration, law, or social work, combined with training in gerontology, can prepare individuals to work as advocates for the rights of older persons. As noted by Dr. Marie Bernard, Director of the National Institute on Aging, "You can do virtually anything . . . The doors are wide open. There are so many things you can do in this field." (American Geriatrics Society, 2009).

The growing population of older adults and their family caregivers will require more health care providers with the knowledge, values, and skills to manage their needs in community and long-term care settings. It has been estimated that by 2030, 3.5 million formal health care providers—a 35 percent increase from current levels—will be needed just to maintain the current ratio of providers to the total population. Similarly, all health care providers are predicted to spend at least 50 percent of their time working with older adults. This means that health care professionals in medicine, nursing, pharmacy, dentistry, and social work must enhance their competence in geriatric health care (IOM, 2008). Additionally, one of the fastest-growing occupational areas is direct care, including such workers as nurse aides, home health aides, and personal care aides with skills to work with older adults. Other health professionals trained in gerontology and geriatrics will be needed, especially those who focus on prevention and rehabilitation. These include physician assistants; nutritionists; recreational, physical, occupational, and speech therapists; as well as audiologists. Due to these needs, the Eldercare Workforce Alliance, a national coalition, addresses the immediate and future workforce crisis in caring for an aging America.

Growth of the Older Population

The increasing size of the older population is the single most important factor affecting current interest in the field of gerontology. In 1900, people age 65 and older accounted for approximately 4 percent of the U.S. population—less than 1 in 25. By 2008, slightly more than 100 years later, this segment of our population had grown to almost 39 million, or 12.7 percent of the U.S. population (AOA, 2008; U.S. Census Bureau, 2009b). This represents a twelve-fold increase in the older population during this period, compared with a three-fold increase in those under age 65. Population growth for the older age group declined slightly between 1990 and 2005 because of the low birthrates experienced during the Great Depression (1929–1935). With the first baby boomers turning 60 in 2006, the population over 65 will again increase significantly after 2010. Thus, demographers

predict that by 2030 the population age 65 and older may be as high as 72 million, representing a 100 percent increase over 30 years, compared with a 30 percent growth in the overall population (U.S. Census Bureau, 2009b).

Changes in Life Expectancy

Why have these changes in the older population occurred? Chiefly because people are living longer. In 1900, the average **life expectancy** at birth in the U.S. (i.e., the average length of time one could expect to live if one were born that year) was 47 years. At that time, approximately 772,000 people were between the ages of 75 and 84 in the United States, and only 123,000 age 85 and older. In 2008, there were over 5.4 million in the oldest group. The average life expectancy is now much longer: 78.1 years. About four out of five individuals can currently expect to reach age 65, at which point there is a better than 50 percent chance of living past age 80 (AOA, 2008; U.S. Census Bureau, 2009a, 2009b).

According to the Census Bureau, life expectancy at birth is expected to increase to 82.6 in 2050. Sex differences in life expectancy have declined since 1980, when females born that year could expect to live 7.4 years longer than men; in 2006, the difference was only 5.3 years. Projections by the Census Bureau assume a fairly constant 5- to 6-year difference in male-female life expectancy well into the future. Therefore, females born in 2006 are expected to reach age 80.7, compared to 75.4 for males in that birth cohort (U.S. Census Bureau, 2009a). Differences continue to be greater between African American females and males, with current life expectancies at birth of 76.9 and 70, respectively. Even in the year 2050, however, male life expectancy will be less than 80 years, compared to 84.3 years for women (NCHS, 2007; AOA, 2008). Of course, these projections do not take into account natural disasters or potential new diseases that could differentially increase mortality risks for men and women. On the other hand, death rates due to hypertension and stroke have already started to decline because

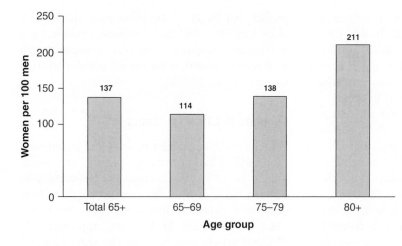

FIGURE 1.3   **Number of Women per 100 Men by Age: 2007**
SOURCE: U.S. Census Bureau, 2009.

of lifestyle changes. Since both health conditions are somewhat more likely to affect men, the decline may narrow the gender differential and increase life expectancy more for men. Nevertheless, the trend illustrated in Figure 1.3, where women outnumber men at every age after 65, will continue at least until mid-century.

Most gains in life expectancy have occurred in the younger ages. For example, during the period from 1900 to 2007, the average life expectancy at birth increased from 47 years to 78.1 years. Although less dramatic, gains in life expectancy beyond age 65 also occurred during this same period, from about 12.3 to 18.7 years (20.3 years for women, 17.4 for men) (AOA, 2008). The gains that took place in the early years of life are largely attributable to the eradication in the twentieth century of many diseases that caused high infant and childhood mortality. On the other hand, survival beyond age 65 may increase significantly in future cohorts, when heart disease and cancer become less fatal but more chronic or long-term diseases, along with obesity, predominate. Already there has been an acceleration of years gained. Between 1900 and 1960, only 2.4 years were gained beyond age 65, while the gain since 1960 has been 4.3 years (Federal Interagency Forum, 2008).

This shift results mostly from advances in medicine. A hundred years ago, adults generally died from acute diseases, particularly influenza and pneumonia. Few people survived these diseases long enough to need care for chronic or long-term conditions. Today, death from acute diseases is rare. Maternal, infant, and early childhood death rates have also declined considerably. The result is a growing number of people who survive to old age, often with one or more health problems requiring long-term care. Nevertheless, life expectancy at age 65 is lower in the U.S. than in Japan, Switzerland, and Canada. In particular, Japanese men can expect to live 1.2 years longer than American men, and Japanese women 3.2 years longer than American women at age 65 (Federal Interagency Forum, 2008).

Today more former presidents are alive than in the past.

Maximum Life Span

It is important to distinguish life expectancy from **maximum life span.** While life expectancy is a probability estimate based on environmental conditions such as disease and health care, as described previously, maximum life span is the maximum number of years a given species could expect to live if environmental hazards were eliminated. There appears to be a maximum biologically determined life span for cells that comprise the organism, so that even with the elimination of all diseases, we could not expect to live much beyond 120 years. For these reasons, more persons will expect to live longer, but the maximum number of years they can expect to live will not be increased in the foreseeable future unless, of course, some extraordinary and unanticipated biological discoveries occur. The longest documented human life was of Jeanne Calment, a Frenchwoman who died at age 122. Research on some biological factors that may increase longevity for future cohorts is discussed in Chapter 3.

Perhaps the most important goal of health planners and practitioners should be to approach a *rectangular survival curve;* that is, the "ideal curve." As seen in the survival curve in Figure 1.4 (page 18), developments in medicine, public hygiene, and health care have already increased the probability that people will survive into the later years. The ideal situation is one where all people would survive to the maximum life span, creating a rectangular curve. The survival curves of developed countries serve as a model for developing countries; that is, about 50 percent of all babies born today in developed countries will reach age 85, or more than two-thirds of the maximum life span of 120 years (CDC, 2005). Although the U.S. is approaching this ideal curve, it will not be achieved until the diseases of middle age—including cancer, heart disease, diabetes, and kidney diseases, along with obesity—can be totally prevented or at least effectively managed as chronic conditions.

The oldest-old are disproportionately represented in institutional settings such as nursing homes, assisted living, adult family homes, and

GENETIC OR BEHAVIORAL EXPLANATIONS OF LONGEVITY

Journalist Dan Buettner has traveled to world regions where it is not unusual to find vigorous, active centenarians. He labeled these "Blue Zones," places with large numbers of long-living residents who share in common healthy lifestyles, diets, engagement in their community, and a positive world view (Buettner, 2008). Yet these elders in different parts of the world—Okinawa, Sardinia, the northwestern region of Costa Rica, and Loma Linda, California—share other characteristics that cannot be replicated by others who want to emulate their lifestyles in efforts to increase their longevity. The residents of these Blue Zones share genetic qualities and cultural norms that have tied the community together for hundreds of years, and they live in more remote, less stressful environments than the majority of elders. While some aspects of their lifestyles may be adopted—such as strong connections with family and friends, participating in physical labor into advanced old age, walking and exercise, a low-calorie, plant-based diet, and a positive outlook—several societal and genetic factors cannot be replicated.

WHO ARE THE OLDEST-OLD?

- Not surprisingly, the great majority are women (71 percent).
- Their educational level is lower than for those age 65 to 74 (8.6 years vs. 12.1 in 1990).
- Most women are widowed compared to men (78.3 percent vs. 34.6 percent).
- Their mean personal income is lower than for the young-old cohorts.
- A higher proportion live below or near poverty compared to their counterparts age 65 to 69 years) (http://SSA.gov/policy/pubs, 2000).
- The current cohort of the oldest-old includes 15 percent who are foreign born. Many immigrated from European countries in the early 1900s, while others are later immigrants from China, Japan, the Philippines, Vietnam, and Latin America. The typical challenges of aging may be exacerbated for these nonnative English speakers as they try to communicate with health care providers. Misdiagnoses of physical, psychological, and cognitive disorders may occur in such cases.

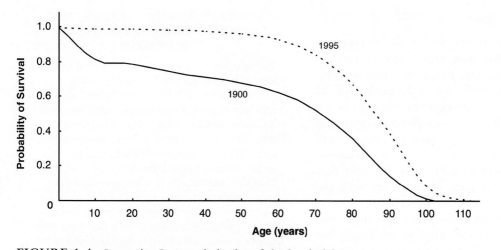

FIGURE 1.4   Increasing Rectangularization of the Survival Curve
SOURCE: J. R. Wilmoth and S. Horiuchi, Rectangularization Revisited: Variability of Age at Death within Human Populations. *Demography*, Vol. 36, No. 4 (Nov., 1999), pp. 475–495.

hospitals, because they are more likely to have multiple health problems that often result in physical frailty, and up to 50 percent may have some form of cognitive impairment. Among the 1.2 million elders in nursing homes, about 50 percent are age 85 and older. However, the incidence of relocation to a long-term care facility among historically disadvantaged populations is lower. For example, the rate for African Americans age 85 and older is only about two-thirds the overall rate for this age group. The oldest-old blacks are far more likely to be living with relatives other than a spouse or partner (40 percent). Only 27 percent of the oldest-old (regardless of their race or ethnicity) live with a spouse or partner, compared with 63 percent of people age 65 to 74 (AOA, 2008; U.S. Census Bureau, 2005). Although functional health is

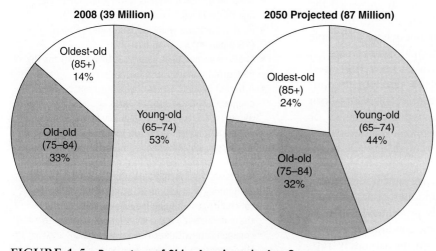

FIGURE 1.5   Percentage of Older Americans by Age Group
SOURCE: U.S. Census Bureau, 2008, U.S. Administration on Aging, 2008.

more impaired in the oldest-old, a study of Medicare expenditures during the last year of life showed that medical costs were not highest for this age group. Contrary to common misperceptions, Medicare expenditures during the last year of life for people age 85 and older were 60 to 70 percent lower than the average charges for the group who died at ages 65 to 74, regardless of gender and race. These findings reflect the shorter hospitalizations and less aggressive terminal health care received by the oldest-old (Hoover et al., 2002; Levinsky et al., 2001). These costs may be even lower for future cohorts of the oldest-old, who are likely to be healthier and more active than today's population.

The Oldest-Old

Ages 85 and Older

The population age 85 and older, also referred to as the "oldest-old," has grown more rapidly than any other age group. In 2008, of the nearly 39 million persons age 65 and over in the U.S.:

- Thirteen million, or 33 percent, were age 75 to 84.
- Another 5.4 million, or 14 percent, were age 85 and older (Federal Interagency Forum, 2008; U.S. Census Bureau, 2008a).
- The oldest-old population of Americans has increased by a factor of 23.
- The old-old (ages 75–84) have increased twelve-fold.
- The young-old (ages 65–74) grew eightfold.

It is also important to consider the distribution of selected age groups now and in the future. The young-old (ages 65–74) currently represent 53 percent of the older population; those over 85 make up 14 percent. Those over age 85 increased by more than 500 percent from 1960 to 2007. As Table 1.1 illustrates, between 1990 and 2007, the oldest-old population increased more than

TABLE 1.1 Population Increase per Age Group: United States (in millions)

YEAR	AGE		
	15–44	**65+**	**85+**
1960		16.6	0.9
1990	118	31.1	3.02
2007	126.3	37.9	5.3
Increase (%) (1990–2007)	7%	21.9%	75%

SOURCE: U.S. Census Bureau, 2007.

10 times the growth of 15- to 44-year-olds and more than three times that of the total population aged 65 and older. This does not mean that their absolute numbers are higher than the younger groups in Table 1.1 but that their rate of growth is much faster. Demographers project this age group to reach 19 million by 2050, almost four times their current number. This translates into 24 percent oldest-old by 2050 (see Figure 1.5). This is primarily attributable to the aging of baby boomers, who will start to turn 85 after 2030. The baby boom generation, defined as those born between 1946 and 1964, currently numbers 69 million. However, these projections vary, depending on assumptions about changes in chronic disease morbidity and mortality rates (AOA, 2008), as we will see in Chapter 4. The impact of such a surge in the oldest-old on the demand for health services, especially hospitals and long-term care settings, will be dramatic.

Centenarians

Projections by the U.S. Census Bureau also suggest a substantial increase in the population of centenarians, people age 100 and older. In 2006, more than 73,000 Americans had reached this milestone, almost double their numbers in 1990. Baby boomers are expected to survive to age 100 at rates never before achieved; one in 26 Americans can expect to live to be 100 by 2025, compared with only one in 500 in 2000 (AOA, 2008).

With increases in life expectancy, oldest-old adult children may live with centenarian parents, as in this photo of a 90-year-old daughter enjoying a meal with her 112-year-old mother.

As more Americans become centenarians, there is growing interest in their genetics and lifestyles that may have influenced their longevity. Data from the Georgia Centenarian Study support other findings of greater survival among women, as well as racial crossover effects in advanced old age (i.e., persons of color who live to age 85 are "hardier" than their Caucasian counterparts). In a follow-up of 137 people age 100 at entry into the study, African American women, on average, survived twice as many months as white men, who lived the shortest time beyond 100. White women had the next best survival rates and lived slightly longer than African American men (Poon et al., 2000). Overall, genetics appears to be a primary factor, especially given the predominance of healthy 80-year-old adult children of centenarians, but lifestyle factors, social support, and personality are also salient (Christensen, 2001).

The New England Centenarian Study points to genetic factors that determine how well the older person copes with disease (Perls & Silver, 1999; Perls & Terry, 2003; Perls & Wood, 1996; Terry et al., 2004). This study suggests that the oldest-old are hardy because they have a higher threshold for disease and disability and show slower rates of disease progression than their peers who develop chronic diseases and disabilities at younger ages and die earlier. Perls and colleagues illustrate this hypothesis with the case of a 103-year-old man who displayed few symptoms of Alzheimer's disease; however, at autopsy, the man's brain had a high number of neurofibrillary tangles, which are a hallmark of the disease. Contrary to the once prevalent belief that dementia is a concomitant of advanced age, as many as 30 percent of centenarians have no memory problems, 20 percent have some, and 50 percent have serious problems. In one study of 69 centenarians who were tested for dementia, none of these robust elders showed significant levels of dementia, either in their neuropsychological testing or in the neuropathological studies of their brains (Samuelsson et al., 1997; Silver et al., 1998).

Rates of dementia were slightly higher in the New England Centenarian Study, where 59 percent of women scored in the moderate–severe range, and 17 percent in the normal range. In contrast, only 33 percent of centenarian men scored in the moderate–severe dementia range and 30 percent in the normal range (Terry, Sebastiani, Andersen & Perls, 2008). Even among centenarians with some cognitive impairment at age 100, however, 90 percent had been cognitively intact until well into their 90s. Indeed, other researchers who have studied dementia in older adults have suggested that the genetic mutations most closely associated with Alzheimer's disease are not present in the oldest-old. Environmental factors that emerge much later in life appear to cause dementia in these survivors (Kaye, 1997).

The likelihood of a genetic advantage is also supported by the finding that male siblings of centenarians are 17 times more likely as the general population, and female siblings eight times more likely, to survive to age 100. As further evidence for the robustness of centenarians, all of the 79 people who were age 100 had lived independently into their early 90s, and on average, took only one medication (Perls et al., 1998; Willcox et al., 2006b).

> ### CENTENARIANS' ZEST FOR NEW EXPERIENCES
>
> The obituary of a 103-year-old woman who died of a stroke noted that she celebrated her 100th birthday by taking her first hot-air balloon ride. To her it was no big deal, just something she wanted to do. Her daughter described her as "go, go, go, all the time. She liked to have fun."
>
> SOURCE: (Brown, 2009).

Older men who survive to age 90, in particular, represent the hardiest segment of their birth cohort. Between ages 65 and 89, women score higher on tests of cognitive function. However, after age 90, men perform far better on these tests. Even at age 80, 44 percent of men were found to be robust and independent, compared with 28 percent of women. In an analysis of 523 women and 216 men age 97 and older, researchers in the New England Centenarian Study found that men in this age group had better functional health then their female counterparts. More than three times as many men (60 percent vs. 18 percent of women) scored 90 or higher on the Barthel Activities of Daily Living Index, where a score of 80–100 represents fully independent functioning. Even among the small group of centenarians (32 percent of this sample) who had "late onset" of major chronic diseases (at age 85 or later), twice as many men as women (50 percent vs. 27 percent respectively) had Barthel ADL Index scores of 90 or higher (Terry, et al., 2008).

Chronic disease onset occurs later or not at all among most centenarians. A retrospective analysis of more than 400 persons in the New England Centenarian Study found that 45 percent had none of the ten most common chronic diseases (i.e., diabetes, hypertension, heart disease, chronic obstructive pulmonary disease, osteoporosis, stroke, cancer, Parkinson's disease, thyroid conditions, dementia) until after age 80. Another 13 percent had escaped any of these diseases, and 42 percent were classified as "survivors" because they had been diagnosed with one or more of these diseases before age 80 but had functioned adequately into their 90s and 100s (Evert, Lawler, Bogan & Perls, 2003).

The Okinawa Centenarian Study supports the importance of both genetic and environmental factors in explaining extreme longevity (see box, p. 17). Since 1976, researchers have examined more than 600 centenarians in this isolated prefecture of Japan. Most of the elders possess genetic patterns that place them at lower risk of autoimmune diseases, but even those without these patterns have lower rates of coronary heart disease, cancer, and stroke mortality than other Japanese people. They also have lower blood levels of cholesterol, homocysteine, and free radicals. Researchers attribute these biochemical advantages to a low-calorie diet with a high intake of folate, vitamins B6, B12, D, calcium, omega-3 fats, and high-fiber foods. The traditional Okinawan lifestyle includes high physical activity, social integration at all ages, a deep spirituality, adaptability, and optimistic attitudes. In fact, Okinawans who move from the island and abandon their traditional diet and lifestyle experience higher mortality rates from diseases that are rare among lifelong Okinawans (Bernstein et al., 2004; Suzuki, Willcox, & Willcox, 2001; Willcox et al., 2006a, 2006b).

Further evidence for the resilience of centenarians comes from the Swedish Centenarian Study (Samuelsson et al., 1997). Among 143 respondents:

- 52 percent were able to perform their activities of daily living with little or no assistance.
- 39 percent had a disorder of the circulatory system.
- 80 percent had problems with vision and hearing.
- 27 percent had some signs of dementia and all performed worse on a test of cognitive function (memory and attention) than 70- to 80-year-olds.

Overall, centenarians appear to be healthy for a longer period of time. Nevertheless, almost 50 percent live in nursing homes, compared with 16 percent of all persons age 85 and older (AOA, 2008; Griffith, 2004). This may be because about 25 to 30 percent of centenarians no longer have living children or siblings but often rely on nieces, nephews, and longtime friends (Christensen, 2001).

Population Pyramids

The increase in longevity is partly responsible for an unusually rapid rise in the *median age* of the U.S. population—from 28 in 1970 to 36.8 years in 2009, meaning that half the population was older than 36.8 years and half younger (U.S. Census Bureau, 2009a). From a historical perspective, an 8-year increase in the median age over a 30-year period is a noteworthy demographic event. The other key factors contributing to this rise include a dramatic decline in the birthrate after the mid-1960s, high birthrates from 1890 to 1915 and just after World War II (these baby boomers are now all older than the median), and the large number of immigrants before the 1920s. The median age will rise as more Americans live into their 80s and 90s; to age 39 by 2030 (U.S. Census Bureau, 2009a).

One of the most dramatic examples of the changing age distribution of the American population is the shift in the proportion of older adults in relation to young persons, as illustrated in Figure 1.6. In 1900, when 4 percent of the population was age 65 and over, 40 percent was young persons age 0 to 17 years. By 2005, reduced birthrates in the 1970s and 1980s had resulted in a decrease of young persons to 25 percent of the population. The U.S. Census Bureau predicts that, by 2030, the proportion of young and old persons will be similar, with those age 0 to 17 forming 23.5 percent of the population and older adults about 19 percent. After 2030, the death rate will be greater than the birthrate because baby boomers will be in the oldest cohorts (U.S. Census Bureau, 2009b).

The *population pyramid* illustrates the changing proportions of young and old persons in the population. Figure 1.7 contrasts the population pyramids for the years 2000, 2025, and 2050. Each horizontal bar represents a 10-year *birth cohort* (i.e., people born within the same 10-year period). By comparing these bars, we can determine the relative proportion of each birth cohort. As you can see in the first graph, the distribution of the population in 2000 had already moved from a true pyramid to one with a bulge in the 35- to 54-year-old group; this represents the population of baby boomers. This pyramid grows more column-like over the years, as shown in the other two graphs. These changes reflect the aging of the baby boomers (note the "pig in a python" phenomenon as this group moves up the age ladder), combined with declining birthrates and reduced death rates for older cohorts.

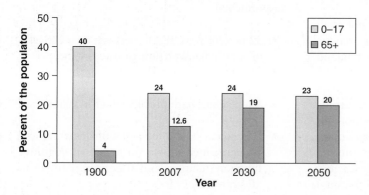

FIGURE 1.6 Actual and Projected Distribution of Children and Older Adults in the Population: 1900–2050
SOURCE: U.S. Census Bureau, 2009.

(NP-P2) Projected Resident Population of the United States as of July 1, 2000, Middle Series

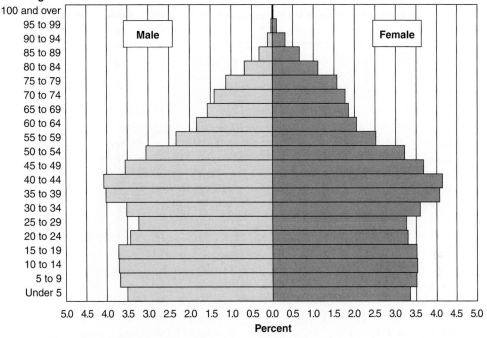

(NP-P3) Projected Resident Population of the United States as of July 1, 2025, Middle Series

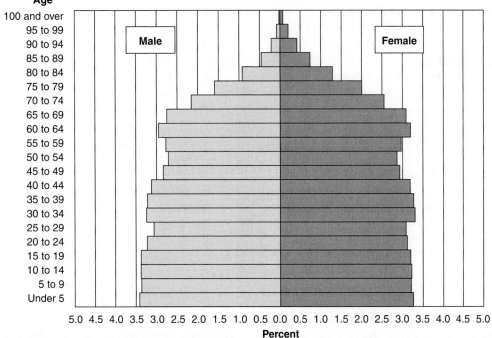

FIGURE 1.7 Projected Resident Populations of the United States for 2000, 2025, and 2050
SOURCE: National Projections Program, Population Division, U.S. Census Bureau, Washington, DC 20233.

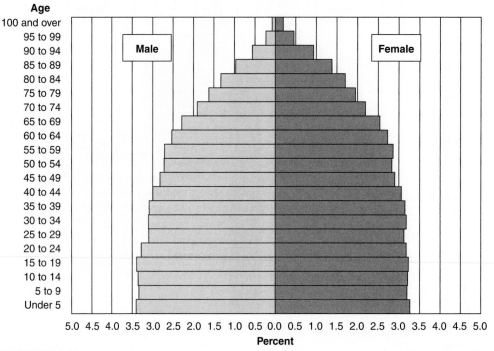

(NP-P4) Projected Resident Population of the United States as of July 1, 2050, Middle Series

FIGURE 1.7 **(Continued)**

Support Ratios

One aspect of the changing age distribution in our population that has raised public concern is the so-called "old-age support ratio." The way this ratio has generally been used is to indicate the relationship between the proportion of the population that is employed (defined as "productive" members of society) and the proportion that is not in the workforce (and is thus viewed as "dependent" or as "requiring support"). This rough estimate is obtained by comparing the percent of the population age 20 to 64 (the working years) to the proportion age 19 and under (yielding the youth dependency ratio) and over 65 (yielding the old-age support ratio). This ratio has increased steadily, showing that proportionately fewer employed persons support retired older persons today. In 1910, the ratio was less than 0.10 (i.e., 10 working people per retired older person),

compared with 0.21 in 2000 (i.e., five working people per retired person). Assuming that the lower birthrate continues, by the year 2030, a ratio of 0.36 (or fewer than three working people per retired person) is expected (U.S. Census Bureau, 2006a). These changes since 1960, along with projections through 2030, are illustrated in Figure 1.8.

Such a crude measure of support ratios is problematic, however. Many younger and older persons are actually in the labor force and not dependent, while many people of labor-force age may not be employed. Another flaw is that support ratios do not take account of the labor-force participation rates of different groups. For example, older workers, both men and women, have continued to remain employed during the economic downturn. In addition, baby boomers are setting the trend toward starting new careers in middle age and continuing to work in their

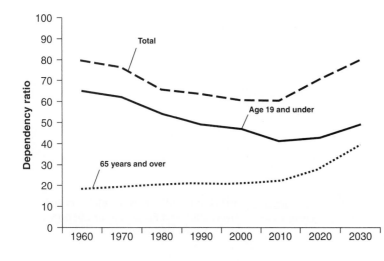

FIGURE 1.8   Number of Dependents per 100 Persons Aged 18–64 Years: Estimates and Projections 1960–2030
SOURCE: U.S. Census Bureau, International Data Base, Census 2000 Summary File 1.

later years, increasingly out of economic necessity. When these variations are taken into account, the total support ratio in the year 2050 will remain lower than recent historical levels, even though it increases as the population ages. Moreover, despite population aging, those under the age of 16 will continue to constitute the largest "dependent" group into this century. Therefore, we need to be cautious when policy makers predict "burdens" on the younger population and blame rising costs of Social Security primarily on the changing support ratio (Reynolds, 2004). What is unknown, however, is how the economic crises of 2008–2009 and the increasing numbers of unemployed adults will affect this dependency ratio in the next 10 years.

Population Trends

In addition to the proportional growth of the older population in general, other demographic trends are of interest to gerontologists. These include statistics related to the social, ethnic, racial, gender, and geographic distribution of older populations. This section reviews some of these trends, beginning with the changing demographics of populations of color in the United States.

Elders of Color*

Because of lifelong socioeconomic inequities in access to health and preventive health services, elders of color have a lower life expectancy than whites. For example, in 2006, life expectancy at birth was 81 years for white females and 77 for African American females. White males could expect to live 75.4 years, compared with 70 years for their black counterparts. Nevertheless, the greatest improvement in life expectancy—an increase of five years between 1990 and 2006—occurred for the latter group. White males' life expectancy increased three years during that same period (NCHS, 2007).

Today, 19 percent of the population over age 65 are persons of color (9 percent African American, 6 percent Latino, 3 percent Asian or Pacific Islander, and less than 1 percent American Indian or Native Alaskan (AOA, 2008); they include a smaller proportion of older people and a

*For purposes of this text, we are using the term *elders of color* or *people of color* to refer to four federally protected groups: African Americans, Latinos (including Mexican Americans/Chicanos, Puerto Ricans, Cubans, and Latin Americans), American Indians, and Asian/Pacific Islanders (API). These groups share the experience of collective discrimination and oppression by reason of their race. The terms *historically underserved* and *disadvantaged populations* are also used throughout the text to refer to these four groups.

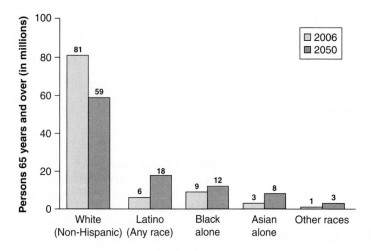

FIGURE 1.9   **Persons 65 Years and Over: 2006 and Projected for 2050 (%)**
SOURCE: Federal Interagency Forum, 2008.

larger proportion of younger adults than the white population. The difference results primarily from the higher fertility and mortality rates among the nonwhite population under age 65 than among the white population under age 65. The proportion of older persons is predicted to increase at a *higher* rate for the nonwhite population than for the white population. This is partly because of the large percentage of children in these groups, who, unlike their parents and especially their grandparents, are expected to reach old age (AOA, 2008; U.S. Census Bureau, 2006c). Figure 1.9 illustrates these differential patterns of growth. A more detailed discussion of elders of color is provided in Chapter 14.

Geographic Distribution

Data on the geographic location of older populations within the United States is important for a variety of reasons. For example, the differing needs of rural and urban older people may affect service delivery and local government policy decisions. Statistical information on older adults state-by-state is necessary in planning for the distribution of federal funds, such as through the Older Americans Act. The following are some of the most salient statistics on the geographic distribution of older adults today. The implications of these changes are considered in later chapters, including their impact on living arrangements;

social, health, and long-term care policies; and cross-cultural issues.

Although older adults live in every state and region of the United States, they are not evenly distributed:

- The Northeast continues to be the region with the oldest population; those over age 65 represent 13.8 percent of its population.
- The Western states have approximately 11 percent elders.
- In the Midwest and the South, the proportion of older adults declined between 1990 and 2000, from 13 percent to 12.8 percent, and from 12.6 percent to 12.4 percent, respectively (AOA, 2007).

POINTS TO PONDER

The majority of people age 65 and older (80.5 percent), live in metropolitan areas, with 19.5 percent in rural areas. About 37 percent of those in metropolitan areas live in cities, 63 percent in suburbs and smaller communities (AOA, 2008). Despite their low distribution in rural communities, older adults make up a greater percentage of rural populations than in the general population: 19.5 percent of all residents in rural areas and small towns versus 13 percent of the total U.S. population (AOA, 2008). What do you think accounts for this higher proportion of elders in rural communities?

More than half (54 percent) of all persons 65 and older lived in 10 states in 2007, with the highest number of older people in California (U.S. Census Bureau, 2009c):

- California (4 million older residents)
- Florida (3.1 million)
- New York (2.5 million)
- Texas (2.4 million)
- Pennsylvania (about 1.9 million)
- Ohio, Illinois, Michigan, New Jersey, and North Carolina (over 1.1 million each)

This does not necessarily mean that all these states have a higher *proportion* of older Americans than the national average, but their absolute numbers are large. Some states have a much higher proportion of residents over 65 than the national average. For example, in 2007, older people represented:

- 18.5 percent of the population in Florida
- almost 16 slightly percent in Pennsylvania and 15.5 percent in Rhode Island
- about 15 percent in West Virginia, Iowa, North Dakota, and Connecticut (AOA, 2008)

In contrast, elders comprised just 7 percent of the population of Alaska and 8.8 percent of the population of Utah, although this represents more than a 20 percent increase since 1997 (AOA, 2008; U.S. Census Bureau, 2009a).

Because of these disparate proportions of older adults in their states' populations, it is not surprising that a northeastern state, Maine, has the highest median age (40.7 years), and Utah the lowest (28 years). In some cases (such as that of Florida), migration of retired persons to the state explains the increase, whereas in others (such as West Virginia and North Dakota), migration of younger persons out of the state leaves a greater proportion of older people. More than 20 percent of some rural counties in these states are age 65 and older. Other states may simply reflect the generalized "graying of America." These regional differences are expected to continue in this century, although

there are some unexpected shifts, such as the greatest percentage increase (4.2 percent) of older adults in Nevada, followed by a 3.8 percent growth in older residents in Alaska. Residential relocation is relatively rare for older people in the United States. In a typical year, only about 4 percent of people age 65 and older move, compared with 17 percent of people under age 65 (AOA, 2008). The movement that occurs tends to be within the same region of the country and similar types of environments; that is, people over age 65 generally move within the same county (AOA, 2008; U.S. Census Bureau, 2006a). These trends and their implications for person–environment fit in the later years are described further in Chapter 11.

Educational and Economic Status

In 1960, less than 20 percent of the population age 65 and older had finished high school. By 2007, 76 percent of the new cohort age 65 and older had completed high school and 19 percent held a bachelor's degree or more. No gender differences were found in high school completion rates, but racial and generational differences are striking. Among whites, 81 percent had at least a high school diploma in 2007, compared to 58 percent of older African Americans, 42 percent Latinos, and 72 percent for Asians (AOA, 2008; Federal Interagency Forum, 2008). As a result of historical patterns of discrimination in educational opportunities, a disproportionate ratio of older persons of color today has less than a high school education. Since educational level is so closely associated with economic well-being, these racial differences have a major impact on poverty levels of persons of color across the life course and particularly in old age. Other implications of these gaps in educational attainment are discussed in Chapter 14.

Not surprisingly, baby boomers, as well as people currently age 65 to 69, are more educated than the old-old and oldest-old. More than three-fourths (77 percent of the former vs. 68 percent of those 75 years and older) have at least a high school education. For this reason, the median educational level today is 12.1 years for the young-old, 10.5 years for the old-old, and 8.6 years for the oldest-old. Because of cultural values and gender inequities in previous generations, fewer white women age 65 and older (15 percent) have college degrees than do white men (25 percent). Among African Americans, the pattern is mixed; for those age 70 and older, more black women than men completed college, while for the 65- to 69-year-olds, fewer women did so. It is noteworthy that an even greater proportion of people over age 25 today (84.5 percent) have at least a high school education; 27.5 percent have a bachelor's degree or more (He et al., 2005). This suggests that future generations of older people will be better educated—many with college degrees—than their grandparents are today. The implications of this shift for political activism, employment, and the nature of paid and unpaid productive roles are explored in later chapters.

In recent years, the proportion of older people in the labor force has increased, sometimes out of a desire to continue their careers, but more frequently out of economic necessity. Although comprising only 3.8 percent of the U.S. labor force, 20.5 percent of men and 12.6 percent of women age 65 and older reported working outside the home, a proportion that has been increasing since 2002. Among elders who work, more than 50 percent of women and more than 40 percent of men are employed in a part-time or temporary capacity, which means they lack benefits. Many older adults prefer to work part-time but are unable to find such jobs (AOA, 2008; Bureau of Labor Statistics, 2008).

Social Security is the primary source of income for many older adults, comprising 37 percent of the aggregate of all elders' sources of income, compared with 28 percent from current employment, 18 percent from private pensions, and 15 percent from assets (Federal Interagency Forum, 2008). In fact, increases in Social Security benefits along with annual cost-of-living adjustments are major factors underlying the improved economic status of the older population. In 2007, the median household income for those 65 and older was $27,798, which is 45 percent higher than the median income for this age group in 1974, after correcting for inflation (AOA, 2008; Federal Interagency Forum, 2008). In 2007, only 9.7 percent of older people subsisted on incomes below the poverty level, compared to 35 percent in the late 1950s, and slightly lower than the 11.3 percent of Americans under age 65 who are poor, although this proportion may have increased as a result of the worldwide economic downturn in 2008–2009. Another 6.4 percent of older Americans are classified as "near-poor," with income levels between poverty and 125 percent of the poverty level (AOA, 2008; Federal Interagency Forum, 2008; U.S. Census Bureau, 2007). The improved economic status of the older population as a whole masks the growing rates of poverty among older women, elders of color, the oldest-old, and those living alone. Older women are twice as likely to be poor as their male counterparts. Older African Americans and Latinos are more likely to be poor than whites, although their situation is improving (23 and 19 percent, respectively vs. 7 percent for whites) (Federal Interagency Forum, 2008). Poverty is higher among elders in central cities (12.2 percent), in rural areas and small towns) (10.8 percent), and in the South (10.8 percent each) (AOA, 2008). The current and projected economic status of the older population is discussed in detail in Chapters 12, 14, and 15.

Impact of Demographic Trends

As noted later in this book, these trends have wide-ranging implications, especially in terms of federal and state spending. The growth in numbers and proportions of older people has already placed pressures on our health, long-term care, and social service systems, as discussed in Chapters 16 and 17. Although the high cost of health care is the primary factor related to growing expenditures, the increase in life expectancy also has changed people's expectations about the quality of life in late adulthood. Those facing retirement have generally anticipated living 20 to 30 years in relatively good health, with adequate retirement incomes. When these expectations are not met because of catastrophic medical costs, widowhood, or loss of retirement income or employer-sponsored pensions, older adults may not be prepared to manage such changes in their lifestyles. For other segments of the older population, particularly women and elders of color, old age may represent a continuation of a lifetime of poverty or near-poverty. Fortunately, for most older people, the problems associated with old age—particularly chronic illness and the attendant costs—are forestalled until their 70s and 80s. Nevertheless, the rapid growth in numbers of frail elders, the majority of whom are women, may severely strain the health and income systems designed to provide resources in old age.

Longevity in Health or Disease?

Future cohorts of older people may be healthier and more autonomous well into their 80s and 90s. A strong argument was first put forth to this effect almost 30 years ago by Fries (1980, 1990), who suggested that more people will achieve the maximum life span in future years because of healthier lifestyles and better health care during their youth and middle years. Furthermore, Fries argued that future cohorts will have fewer debilitating illnesses and will, in fact, experience a phenomenon he labeled **compression of morbidity** (i.e., experiencing only a few years of major illness in very old age). The concept of compressed morbidity implies that premature death is minimized because disease and functional decline are compressed into a brief period of 3 to 5 years before death. In fact, major chronic diseases like arthritis, arteriosclerosis, and respiratory problems now appear 10 to 25 years later than for past cohorts. As a result, people generally die a "natural death" from the failure of multiple organ systems, not because of disease per se (Hazzard, 2001). There is evidence that compression of morbidity is occurring, because mortality rates among older adults are declining at about 1 percent per year and disability rates at about 2 percent per year (Fries, 2002). These

healthier older adults of the future may therefore expect to die a "natural death," or death due to the natural wearing out of all organ systems, by approximately age 100. If this process does occur, it will have significant impacts on future generations in terms of active aging and their need for health and long-term care. More home health care services will be needed, but skilled nursing facilities for the frail oldest-old will still be required.

Additional evidence from a review of large national health surveys also indicates that today's older population, especially age 65 to 74, is generally healthier than previous cohorts, in part due to reduction of lifestyle risk factors (Fries, 2002). Analyses of the Longitudinal Study on Aging and the National Health Interview Survey (NHIS) from 1982 through 1993 for respondents who were age 70 and older in each year reveal that rates of disability are declining or stabilizing. At the same time, recovery from acute disabilities (e.g., due to falls) is improving. This may be due to more aggressive rehabilitation efforts for older adults. It is also consistent with the findings from National Long-Term Care Survey from 1982 through 1999, where disability rates declined from 26 percent in 1982 to less than 20 percent in 1999 (Manton & Gu, 2001). A more recent National Institute on Aging study identified disability rates of 14 percent in 2005 (Schoeni, Freedman, & Martin, 2008). However, this trend may be reversed with growing rates of obesity and its accompanying chronic diseases and relatively low exercise rates among older adults (Fries, 2002). Additionally, the level of functional impairment has increased among elders with obesity (Alley, 2007). Not surprisingly, rates of disability vary across populations of color and ethnicity and by social class:

- 19 percent for non-Hispanic white men and women
- 27 percent for Latino men and 28 percent for Latina women
- 29 percent for African American men and 28 percent for African American women (Reville & Schoeni, 2003–2004)

This means that future generations of the oldest-old may have lower health care expenditures and less reliance on acute care services but may still need community-based services to support their autonomy.

The concept of **active versus dependent life expectancy** (Katz et al., 1983) is useful in this context. Katz and others distinguish between merely living a long life and living to a healthy old age. This is consistent with the concept of maintaining active aging. Instead of death, they define the endpoint of "active" life expectancy as the need to rely on others for most activities of daily living. As life expectancy has increased beyond age 65, only about 25 percent of these years are spent depending on others for assistance with functions such as bathing or meal preparation (Manton & Land, 2000; WHO, 2002).

- A 65-year-old woman today has almost 20 years remaining, 15.7 in active life expectancy, 4 in dependency.
- A 65-year-old man can look forward to living 16.2 more years, with 13.7 of these years representing active life expectancy (Social Security Administration, 2006).

Not surprisingly, differences in life conditions of older persons with inadequate income and those above the median income have led to the finding that active life expectancy differs by 1 to 2.5 years between the poor and non-poor. This may result in a growing bimodal distribution of older people remaining healthier and free of disease (as predicted by Fries) and another, probably larger, distribution of older adults surviving diseases that would have been fatal years ago but living with "battle scars." This latter group may be the segment of the population that is distorting projections for compressed morbidity; as we have seen in the reviews of the NHIS findings, this latter group also appears to be increasing in size and is most likely to require long-term care services in the future. As noted above, this group may become even larger as the growing trend toward obesity affects more people age 65 and older. Between 1980 and 2000, rates of obesity increased from 27 percent to 39 percent among older women and from 24 percent to 33 percent among older men (U.S. Census Bureau, 2006b). This pattern may trigger an increase in obesity-related diseases such as heart disease and diabetes. On the other hand, the adoption of healthier lifestyles by some adults, e.g., physical exercise and maintaining a lean body weight—as well as advances in preventing and treating heart disease, musculoskeletal problems, and stroke—may result in a longer active life expectancy (Freedman, Martin, & Schoeni, 2002; Schoeni et al., 2008).

How Aging and Older Adults Are Studied

You are undoubtedly aware that more researchers are studying older people and the process of aging more now than in the past. Some of the concerns that have motivated this increasing professional interest in the field have probably influenced your own decision to study gerontology. In this section, we turn to the question of how the older population is studied: What are the particular challenges of social gerontological research, and how are they addressed? Methods of conducting research in this field are described.

Development of Gerontology as a Scientific Discipline

Although the scientific study of social gerontology is relatively recent, it has its roots in biological studies of the aging processes and in the psychology of human development. Biologists have long explored the reasons for aging in living organisms. Several key publications and research studies are milestones in the history of the field.

One of the first textbooks on aging, *The History of Life and Death,* was written in the thirteenth century by Roger Bacon. With great foresight, Bacon suggested that life expectancy could be extended if health practices such as personal and public hygiene were improved. The first scientist to explain aging as a developmental process, rather than as stagnation or deterioration, was a nineteenth-century Belgian mathematician-statistician named Adolph Quetelet. His interest in age and creative achievement preceded the study of these issues by social scientists by 100 years. His training in the field of statistics also led him to consider the problems of **cross-sectional research**—that is, the collection of data on people of different ages at one time, instead of **longitudinal research**, the study of the same person over a period of months or years. These problems are examined further in the next section of this chapter. The first published reference to gerontology as a scientific concept is attributed to Elie Metchnikoff, a French researcher whose book, *The Problem of Age, Growth, and Death,* was published in 1908. In 1922, American psychologist G. Stanley Hall published one of the first books on the social-psychological aspects of aging in the United States. Titled *Senescence, the Last Half of Life,* it remains a landmark text in social gerontology because it provides the experimental framework for examining changes in cognitive processes and social and personality functions.

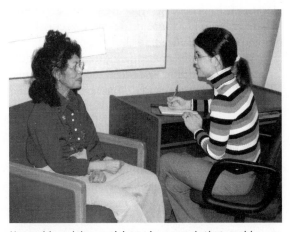

Many older adults participate in research that could benefit others.

> ### THE GERONTOLOGICAL SOCIETY OF AMERICA
>
> Today, the GSA has over 5,000 members. It is the major professional association for people in diverse disciplines focused on research in aging. The GSA's mission is "to add life to years, not just years to life." This emphasizes the goal of most gerontologists—to enhance quality of life in the later years, not just to extend it.

Formal Development of the Field

As society grew more aware of issues facing the older population, the formal study of aging emerged in the 1940s. In 1945, the Gerontological Society of America (GSA) was founded, bringing together the small group of researchers and practitioners who were interested in gerontology and geriatrics at that time. Gerontology became a division of the American Psychological Association in 1945 and, later, of the American Sociological Association.

The *Journal of Gerontology,* which the GSA began to publish in 1946, served as the first vehicle for transmitting new knowledge in this growing field. In 1988, it became two journals, *The Journals of Gerontology,* composed of *Psychological Sciences and Social Sciences* and *Biological Sciences and Medical Sciences,* which reflected the growth of gerontological research. Today, the burgeoning periodicals in diverse disciplines focused on gerontology have resulted in an exponential growth of research publications in this field. Gerontology has also become increasingly more interdisciplinary; that is, specialists in diverse areas of the basic, clinical, behavioral, and social sciences, as well as engineering and design professions, are working together on research projects aimed at improving the aging process and the lives of older people.

Major Research Centers Founded

An interest in the physiological, psychological, and social factors associated with aging grew in the late

1950s and early 1960s. In 1946, a national gerontology research center, headed by the late Nathan Shock (a leader in geriatric medicine), was established at Baltimore City Hospital by the National Institutes of Health. This federally funded research center undertook several studies of the physiological aspects of aging, using a cross-sectional approach. In 1958, Dr. Shock and his colleagues began a longitudinal study of physiological changes in healthy middle-aged and older men living in the community by testing them every two years on numerous physiological parameters. They later started to examine the cognitive, personality, and social-psychological characteristics of these men. Much later, in 1978, older women were included in their samples. Known as the **Baltimore Longitudinal Studies of Aging,** these assessments of changes associated with healthy aging are still continuing, now under the direction of the National Institute on Aging. More than 2,200 volunteers, men and women age 20 to 90, have participated and today 1,400 are continuing to participate in this study of the basic processes of aging. Relatively recently, persons of color have been recruited as research subjects; 13 percent are African Americans, mostly in the younger cohorts. The results of this ongoing research effort provide valuable information about normal age-related changes in physiological and psychological functions. As more persons of color in this longitudinal study grow older, they will provide valuable insights into the process of normal age-related changes versus disease in these populations.

Concurrently with the Baltimore Longitudinal Studies, several university-based centers were developed to study the aging process and the needs of older adults. One of the first, the Duke University Center on Aging, was founded in 1955 by one of the pioneers in gerontology, Ewald Busse. The University of Chicago, under Robert Havighurst's direction, developed the first research center devoted exclusively to the social aspects of aging. The Kansas City studies of adult development represent the first major social-psychological studies of adult development and were conducted by researchers from the Chicago center. Research

and training centers on aging have since evolved at many other universities, generally stimulated by government sponsorship of gerontological research through the National Institute on Aging (founded in 1974), the National Institute of Mental Health (which established its Center for Studies of the Mental Health of the Aging in 1976), and the Administration on Aging (founded in 1965).

Research Methods

Before examining the issues and areas of special concern to social gerontologists, we first consider the ways in which such information about the aging process is gathered. The topic of research methodologies in gerontology may seem an advanced one to introduce in a basic text, but, in fact, it is essential to understanding the meaning and validity of information presented throughout this book.

The study of aging presents particular conceptual and methodological difficulties. A major one is how research is designed and data interpreted regarding age changes. A point that complicates research in aging and produces some misleading interpretations of data is how to distinguish *age changes* from *age differences*. This differentiation is necessary if we are to understand the processes of aging and the conditions under which age differences occur. If we wish to determine what changes or effects are experienced as an individual moves from middle age to old age and to advanced old age, we must examine the same individual over a period of years, or at least months. In order to understand age changes, longitudinal research is necessary—that is, the repeated measurement of the same person over a specified period of time.

Unfortunately, the time and cost of such studies prevent many researchers from undertaking longitudinal research. Instead, much of the research in this field focuses on age differences, by comparing people of different chronological ages at the same measurement period. These studies, cross-sectional in nature, are the most common ones in gerontology.

The unique problems inherent in how gerontological research is designed and how data are interpreted are evident in the following question: Given that aging in humans is a complex process that proceeds quite differently among individuals in varied geographic, cultural, and historical settings and occurs over a time span as long as 100 to 120 years, how does one study it? Obviously, scientists cannot follow successive generations—or even a single generation of subjects—throughout their life span. Nor can they be expected to address the entire range of variables that affect aging—including lifestyle, social class, cultural beliefs, gender, race and ethnicity, public policies, and so on—in a single study.

The Age/Period/Cohort Problem

The problem in each case is that of distinguishing *age differences* (ways that one generation differs from another) from *age changes* (ways that people normally change over time). This has been referred to as the "age/period/cohort" problem. (The word *cohort,* you will recall, refers to those people born at roughly the same time. *Period,* or time of measurement effect, refers to the impact of the specific historical period involved.) The concept of cohort is an important one in gerontology because historical events differentiate one generation from another in attitudes and behaviors. People in the same cohort are likely to be more similar to each other than to people in other cohorts because of comparable social forces acting on them during a given era. For example, the Depression era cohort has very different attitudes toward saving than the baby boom cohort.

Cross-Sectional Studies

As noted earlier, the most common approach to studying aging is cross-sectional; that is, researchers compare a number of subjects of different ages on the same characteristics in order to determine age-related differences. One reason that cross-sectional studies are frequently used is that, compared to other designs, data can be readily gathered. Some examples might include a comparison of the lung capacity of men aged 30 with those who are age 40, 50, 60, 70, and 80, or a study comparing church attendance by American adults under age 65 with those over age 65. The average differences among different age groups in each study might suggest conclusions about the changes that come with age.

The danger with such cross-sectional studies is that these differences might not be due to the process of aging, but rather to particular cultural and historical conditions that shaped each group of subjects being studied. For example, a higher rate of church attendance among today's older adults than among younger adults probably reflects a change in social attitudes toward attending church, as opposed to an increased need for spiritual and religious life as one grows older.

Even in studies of biological factors, such as lung capacity, many intervening variables may threaten the validity of comparative results. In this case, they include the effects of exercise, smoking, and other lifestyle factors, genetic inheritance, and exposure to pollution (this, in turn, might be a product of work environments and social class) on relevant outcome variables.

The major limitation of cross-sectional studies occurs when differences among younger and older respondents are erroneously attributed to growing old. For example, some researchers have found that the older the respondent, the lower his or her score on intelligence tests. As a result, cognitive abilities have been misinterpreted as declining with age. In fact, such differences may be due to the lower educational levels and higher test anxiety of this cohort of older adults compared to younger adults, not to age. This is an example of *confounding,* or a joint effect of two variables on an outcome of interest. In this case, age effects are confounded by the impact of cohort differences. Because many issues in social gerontology center on distinguishing age from cohort effects, a number of research designs have emerged that attempt to do this. They include *longitudinal* and *sequential* designs.

Longitudinal Studies: Design and Limitations

Longitudinal designs permit inferences about *age changes*. They eliminate cohort effects by studying the same people over time. Each row in Table 1.2 represents a separate longitudinal study in which a given cohort (e.g., A, B, or C) is measured once every 10 years. Despite the advantages of longitudinal designs over the cross-sectional approach, they still have limitations. First, the longitudinal method does not allow a distinction between age and time of testing. Second, it cannot separate the effects of events extraneous to the study that influence people's responses in a particular measurement period.

Another problem with longitudinal studies is the potential for practice effects. This is a particular concern in studies that administer aptitude or knowledge tests, where repeated measurement with the same test improves the test-taker's performance because of familiarity or practice. For example, a psychologist who is interested in age-related changes in intelligence could expect to obtain improvements in people's scores if the same test is administered several times, with a brief interval (e.g., less than one year) between tests. In such cases, it is difficult to relate the changes to maturation unless the tests can be varied or parallel forms of the same tests can be used.

Longitudinal studies also present the problem of *attrition,* or dropout. Individuals in experimental studies and respondents in surveys that are administered repeatedly may drop out for many reasons—death, illness, loss of interest, or frustration with poor performance. To the extent that people who drop out are not different from the original sample in terms of demographic characteristics, health status, and intelligence, the researcher can still generalize from the results obtained with the remaining sample. However, more often it is the case that dropouts differ significantly from those who stay until the end. As we shall see in Chapter 5, those who drop out of longitudinal studies of intelligence are more likely

- to be in poorer health,
- to score lower on intelligence tests, and
- to be more socially isolated.

TABLE 1.2 Illustration of Alternative Research Designs in Gerontology

DESIGN	TIME OF MEASUREMENT			
	1970	1980	1990	2000
Cross-sectional		A B C		
Longitudinal	A_1	A_2		
		B_1	B_2	
		C_1	C_2	C_3
Cohort-sequential	A_1	A_2		
		B_1	B_2	
Time-sequential		B C		C D
Cross-sequential		B_1 C_1	B_2 C_2	

Cohort A was born in 1930; Cohort B was born in 1940; Cohort C was born in 1950; Cohort D was born in 1960.

AN EXAMPLE OF MISINTERPRETING LONGITUDINAL DATA

Imagine a study that attempted to determine attitudes about retirement. If a sample of 55-year-old workers had been interviewed in 1980, before mandatory retirement was changed to age 70, and again in 1990, after mandatory retirement was eliminated, it would be difficult to determine whether the changes in the workers' attitudes toward retirement occurred because of their increased age and proximity to retirement or because of the modifications in retirement laws during this period.

In contrast, older participants who remain in a longitudinal study are generally

- more educated,
- healthier, and
- more motivated.

The problem of **selective survival** affects most studies of older people (Schaie, 2005). Over time, the birth cohort loses members so that those who remain are not necessarily representative of all members of the original group. Those who survive, for example, probably were healthiest at birth and maintained their good health throughout their lives—variables that tend to be associated with higher socioeconomic status.

Sequential Designs

Some alternative research designs have emerged in response to the problems of cross-sectional and longitudinal methods. One is the category of **sequential research designs** (Schaie, 1967, 1973, 1977, 1983). They combine the strengths of cross-sectional and longitudinal research designs. These

---

EXAMPLE OF A COHORT-SEQUENTIAL DESIGN

An investigator may wish to compare changing attitudes toward federal aging policies among the cohort born in 1930 and the cohort born in 1940 and follow each one for 10 years, from 1980 to 1990 for the first cohort and from 1990 to 2000 for the second. This approach is useful for many social gerontological studies in which age and cohort must be distinguished. However, it still does not separate the effects of cohort from historical effects or time of measurement. As a result, historical events that occurred just before one cohort entered a study (in this case, the Great Depression) but later than another cohort entered may influence each cohort's attitude scores differently.

EXAMPLE OF A TIME-SEQUENTIAL DESIGN

A group of 70-year-olds and a group of 60-year-olds might be compared on their attitudes toward religious activities in 1990. The latter group could then be compared with a new group of 60-year-olds in 2000. This would give some information on how people approaching old age at two different historical periods view the role of religion in their lives.

---

include the cohort-sequential, time-sequential, and cross-sequential methods, which are illustrated in Table 1.2.

A *cohort-sequential* design is an extension of the longitudinal design, whereby two or more cohorts are followed for a period of time so that measurements are taken of different cohorts at the same ages but at different points in time.

The *time-sequential* design is useful for distinguishing between age and time of measurement or historical factors. It can be used to determine if changes obtained are due to aging or to historical factors. The researcher using this design would compare two or more cross-sectional samples at two or more measurement periods.

The third technique is the *cross-sequential* design, which combines cross-sectional and longitudinal designs (Schaie, 1983). These three sequential designs are becoming more widely used by gerontological researchers, especially in studies of intelligence. Table 1.3 summarizes potential confounding effects in each of these methods.

Despite the growth of new research methods, social gerontology is based largely on cross-sectional studies. For this reason, it is important to carefully read the description of a study and its results in order to make accurate inferences about age *changes* as opposed to age *differences* and to determine whether the differences found between groups of different ages are due to cohort effects or to the true effects of aging.

TABLE 1.3 **Potential Confounding Effects in Developmental Studies**

DESIGN	CONFOUNDING EFFECT		
	AGE × COHORT CONFOUNDED	AGE × TIME OF MEASUREMENT CONFOUNDED	COHORT × TIME OF MEASUREMENT CONFOUNDED
Cross-sectional	Yes	No	No
Longitudinal	No	Yes	No
Cohort-sequential	No	No	Yes
Time-sequential	Yes	No	No
Cross-sequential	No	Yes	No

SOURCE: Adapted from M. F. Elias, P. K. Elias, and J. W. Elias, *Basic processes in adult developmental psychology* (St. Louis: C. V. Mosby, 1977).

Problems with Representative Samples of Older Persons in Research

Accurate sampling can be difficult with older populations. If the sample is not representative, the results are of questionable validity. However, comprehensive lists of older people are not readily available. Membership lists from organizations such as AARP tend to overrepresent those who are healthy, white, and financially secure. Studies in long-term care facilities tend to overrepresent those with chronic impairments. Because whites represent 81 percent of

the population over age 65 today, it is not surprising that they are more readily available for research.

Reaching older persons of color through organizational lists can be especially difficult. More effective means of recruiting these groups include the active participation of community leaders such as ministers and respected elders in churches attended by the population of interest. The problem of ensuring diverse samples of research participants is compounded by the mistrust toward research among elders of color. Many African Americans, in particular, know about the unethical practices of the Tuskegee Syphilis Study in the early twentieth century and are reluctant to participate in research today, despite significant improvements in the ethics of human research. Researchers must be sensitive to these issues when attempting to recruit elders of color into research projects.

Such a disproportionate focus on whites and lack of data on historically underserved groups has slowed the development of gerontological theories that consider the impact of race, ethnicity, and culture on the aging process. Yet even as researchers and funding agencies emphasize the need to include more people of color in all types of research, multiple

---

EXAMPLE OF A CROSS-SEQUENTIAL DESIGN

A researcher interested in examining the effects of cohort and historical factors on attitudes toward federal aging policy might compare two groups: people who were age 40 and 50 in 1990 and the same people in 2000 when they are age 50 and 60, respectively. This would permit the assessment of cohort and historical factors concurrently, with one providing information on changes from age 40 to 50 and the other representing changes from age 50 to 60.

continuing to outlive men. The growth in the population over age 85 has been most dramatic, reflecting major achievements in disease prevention and health care since the start of the twentieth century. More recently, there has been increased attention given to learning about the aging process by studying centenarians. Those who live to be 100 and older may have a biological advantage over their peers who die at a younger age. Studies have found greater tolerance to stress and fewer chronic illnesses in centenarians. Populations of color are less likely to live beyond age 65 than their white counterparts, but population projections anticipate a much higher rate of population growth for elders of color in the next 20 years. Because of the lower life expectancy of historically disadvantaged populations, increasing attention is given to health and economic disparities from birth to old age (Zarit & Pearlin, 2005).

confounding factors must be considered. For example, Latino elders represent U.S.-born as well as immigrant populations who have come here from countries as diverse as Mexico, Cuba, and Argentina and speak different Spanish dialects. Therefore, any research that includes racial groups must distinguish among subgroups by language, place of birth, nationality, ethnicity and religion, not just the broader categories of Latino, African American, and Asian. It is not necessary to include all possible subgroups of a particular racial population in a given study. However, it behooves the researcher to state clearly who is represented in order to assure appropriate generalizability of the findings.

The growth in the numbers and proportions of older people, especially the oldest-old, requires that both public and private policies affecting employment and retirement, health and long-term care, and social services be modified to meet the needs and enhance the quality of life of those who are living longer. Fundamental issues need to be resolved about who will receive what societal resources and what roles informal (e.g., families) and formal sectors will play in sharing the responsibilities of elder care.

Summary

A primary reason for the growing interest in gerontology is the dramatic increase in the population over age 65. This growth results from a reduction in infant and child mortality and improved treatment of acute diseases of childhood and adulthood, which in turn expands the proportion of people living to age 65 and beyond. In the United States, average life expectancy from birth has increased from 47 years in 1900 to 78.1 in 2007, with women

Gerontology has grown as a field of study since early philosophers and scientists first explored the reasons for changes experienced with advancing age. Roger Bacon, in the thirteenth century, Adolph Quetelet in the early nineteenth century, Botkin in the late nineteenth century, and Ivan Pavlov and G. Stanley Hall in the early twentieth century made pioneering contributions to this field. During the early 1900s in Europe and the United States, the impact of an increasing aging population on social and health resources began to be felt.

Social gerontological research has expanded since the 1940s, paralleling the rapid growth of the older population and its needs, along with its resilience.

The growing older population and associated social concerns have stimulated great interest in gerontological research. However, existing research methodologies are limited in their ability to distinguish the processes of aging per se from cohort, time, and measurement effects. Cross-sectional research designs are most often used in this field, but these can provide information only on age differences, not on age changes. Longitudinal designs are necessary for understanding age changes, but they suffer from the possibility of subject attrition and the effects of measuring the same individual numerous times. Newer methods in social gerontology—known as cohort-sequential, time-sequential, and cross-sequential designs—test multiple cohorts or age groups over time. They also are limited by possible confounding effects but represent considerable improvement over traditional research designs.

Because research methods in gerontology have improved, there is now a better understanding of many aspects of aging. Research findings to date provide the empirical background for the theories and topics to be covered in the remaining chapters. Despite the recent explosion of knowledge in gerontology, gaps remain in what is known about older people and the aging process. The problem is particularly acute in our understanding of aging among historically underserved groups. Throughout the text, we will call attention to areas in which additional research is needed and suggest implications for gerontological practice and policy.

GLOSSARY

active aging a model of viewing aging as a positive experience of continued growth and participation in family, community, and societal activities, regardless of physical and cognitive decline

active versus dependent life expectancy a way of describing expected length of life, the term *active* denoting a manner of living that is relatively healthy and independent in contrast to being *dependent* on help from others

ageism negative attitudes, beliefs, and conceptions of the nature and characteristics of older persons that are based on age that distort their actual characteristics, and abilities.

aging changes that occur to an organism during its life span, from development to maturation to senescence

Baltimore Longitudinal Studies of Aging a federally funded longitudinal study that has examined physiological, cognitive, and personality changes in healthy middle-aged and older men since 1958, and in women since 1978

cohort a group of people of the same generation sharing a statistical trait such as age, ethnicity, or socioeconomic status (for example, all African American women between the ages of 60 and 65 in 1999)

competence model a conception or description of the way persons perform, focusing on their abilities vis-à-vis the demands of the environment

compression of morbidity given a certain length of life, a term referring to relatively long periods of healthy, active, high-quality existence and relatively short periods of illness and dependency in the last few years of life

cross-sectional research research that examines or compares characteristics of people at a given point in time and attempts to identify factors associated with contrasting characteristics of different groupings of people

environmental press features of the social, technological, natural environment that place demands on people

geriatrics clinical study and treatment of older people and the diseases that affect them

gerontology the field of study that focuses on understanding the biological, psychological, social, and political factors that influence older people's lives

life course   a broader concept than individual life-span development that takes account of cultural, historical, and societal contexts that affect people as they age

life expectancy   the average length of time persons in a given society, and subgroups defined by age, gender, race, and ethnicity are expected to live

longitudinal research   research that follows the same individual over time to measure change in specific variables

maximum life span   biologically programmed maximum number of years that each species can expect to live

person–environment (P–E) perspective   a model for understanding the behavior of people based on the idea that persons are affected by personal characteristics, such as health, attitudes, and beliefs, as they interact with and are affected by the characteristics of the cultural, social, political, and economic environment

resilience   capacity to overcome adversity, in part due to protective personal, family, community, and societal factors

selective survival   elders who remain in longitudinal studies tend to be the healthiest and from the higher socioeconomic levels of their cohort

senescence   gradual decline in all organ systems, especially after age 30

sequential research designs   research designs that combine features of cross-sectional and longitudinal research designs to overcome some of the problems encountered in using those designs

RESOURCES

Log on to MySocKit (www.mysockit.com) for information about the following:

- AOA—Administration on Aging
- Alliance for Aging Research
- American Federation for Aging Research
- Gerontological Society of America
- MedWeb: Geriatrics
- National Institute on Aging (NIA)

REFERENCES

AARP. (2000). *Global Aging Report, 5,* 4–5.

Administration on Aging (AOA). (2008). A profile of older Americans: Retrieved 2008, from http://www.aoa.gov/PROF/statistics/profile/2007/8.aspx

Alley, D. E. & Chang, V. W. (2007). The changing relationship of obesity and disability. *Journal of the American Medical Association, 17,* 2020–2027.

Alwin, D. & Wray, L. A. (2005). Life-span developmental perspective on social status and health. *Journal of Gerontology: Psychological Sciences, 60B,* 7–14.

American Geriatrics Society. (2009). *Career opportunities caring for older adults.* Retrieved 2009, from http://www.americangeriatrics.org/education/career_caring.shtml

Bernstein, A. M., Willcox, B. J., Tamaki, H., Kunishima, N., Suzuki, M., Willcox, D. C., et al. (2004). First autopsy study of Okinawan centenarians: Absence of many age-related diseases. *Journal of Gerontology: Medical Sciences, 59A,* 1195–1199.

Brown, C. (2009). She was not your average senior citizen. *Seattle Times,* April 16, 2009, p. B2.

Buettner, D. (2008). *The blue zone.* Washington DC: National Geographic Society.

Bureau of Labor Statistics. (2008). *Spotlight on statistics: Are there more older people in the workplace?* Retrieved 2008, from http://www.bls.gov/cgi-bin/spotlight/2008/older_workers/home.htm

Butler, R. (1969). Ageism: Another form of bigotry. *The Gerontologist, 9,* 243.

Centers for Disease Control and Prevention (CDC). (2005). *Trends in causes of death among older persons in the United States: 2005.* Retrieved 2006, from http://www.cdc.gov/nchs/data/ahcd/agingtrends/06olderpersons

Christensen, D. (2001). Making sense of centenarians: Genes and lifestyle help people live through a century. *Science News.*

Cohen, G. D. (2005). *The mature mind: The positive power of the aging brain.* Cambridge, MA: Perseus Books.

Evert, J., Lawler, E., Bogan, H., & Perls, T. T. (2003). Morbidity profiles of centenarians: survivors, delayers and escapers. *Journals of Gerontology: Medical Sciences, 58,* 232–237.

Federal Interagency Forum on Aging-Related Statistics (2008). *Older Americans 2008: Key indicators of well-being.* U.S. Government Printing Office.

Freedman, V. A., Martin, L. G., & Schoeni, R. F. (2002). Recent trends in disability and functioning among older adults in the United States. *Journal of the American Medical Association, 288,* 3137–3146.

Fries, J. F. (1980). Aging, natural death, and the compression of morbidity. *New England Journal of Medicine, 303,* 130–135.

Fries, J. F. (1990). The compression of morbidity: Near or far? *Milbank Quarterly, 67,* 208–232.

Fries, J. F. (2002). Reducing disability in older age. *Journal of the American Medical Association, 288,* 3164–3166.

Grabinski, C. J. (2007). *101 careers in gerontology.* New York: Springer Publishing.

Griffith, R. W. (2004). What centenarians can tell us. Retrieved April 2009, from http://www.healthandage.com/public/health-center

Hayflick, L. (1996). *How and why we age* (2nd ed.). New York: Ballantine Books.

Hazzard, W. R. (2001). Aging, health, longevity, and the promise of biomedical research. In E. J. Masoro & S. N. Austad (Eds.). *Handbook of the biology of aging* (5th ed.). San Diego: Academic Press.

He, W., Sengupta, M., Velkoff, V., & DeBarros, K. A. (2005). *65+ in the United States: 2005.* U.S. Census Bureau, Current Population Reports. Washington, DC: U.S. Government and Printing Office, 23–29.

Hoover, D., Crystal, S., Kumar, R., Sambamoorthi, U., & Cantor, J. (2002). Medical expenditures during the last year of life. *Health Services Research, 37,* 1625–1642.

Kaiser, F. (2006). *I say senior, you say senior, suddenly senior.* Retrieved October 2006, from http://www.suddenlysenior.com/boomerhatessenior.html

Katz, S., Branch, L. G., Branson, M. H., Papsidero, J. A., Beck, J. C., & Greer, D. S. (1983). Active life expectancy. *New England Journal of Medicine, 309,* 1218–1224.

Kaye, J. A. (1997). Oldest-old healthy brain function. *Archives of Neurology, 54,* 1217–1221.

Lawton, M. P. (1989). Behavior-relevant ecological factors. In K. W. Schaie & C. Scholar (Eds.). *Social structure and aging: Psychological processes.* Hillsdale, NJ: Erlbaum.

Lawton, M. P. & Nahemow, L. (1973). Ecology and the aging process. In C. Eisdorfer & M. P. Lawton (Eds.). *Psychology of adult development and aging.* Washington, DC: American Psychological Association.

Lesnoff-Caravaglia, G. (2002). Response to "Ageism in Gerontological Language" or growing old absurd. *The Gerontologist, 42,* 431.

Levy, B. R. (2001). Eradication of ageism requires addressing the enemy within. *The Gerontologist, 41,* 578–579.

Manton, K. G. & Land, K. C. (2000). Active life expectancy estimates for the U.S. elderly population. *Demography, 37,* 253–265.

Manton, K. G. & Gu, X. L. (2001). Changes in the prevalence of chronic disability in U.S. black and non-black population above age 65 from 1982 to 1999. *Proceedings of the National Academy of Sciences, 98,* 6354–6359.

National Center for Health Statistics (NCHS). (2007). *Health United States, 2007.* Hyattsville, MD: NCHS.

O'Rand, A. M. & Hamil-Luker, J. (2005). Processes of cumulative adversity: Childhood disadvantage and increased risk of heart attack across the life course. *Journal of Gerontology, 60B, Special Issue II,* S117–S124.

Parmelee, P. A. & Lawton, M. P. (1990). The design of special environments for the aged. In J. E. Birren & K. W. Schaie (Eds.). *Handbook of the psychology of aging* (3rd ed.). San Diego: Academic Press.

Perls, T. T., Alpert, L., Wagner, G. G., Vijg, J., & Kruglyak, L. (1998). Siblings of centenarians live longer. *Lancet, 351,* 1560–1565.

Perls, T. T. & Silver, M. H. (1999). *Living to 100: Lessons in living to your maximum potential at any age.* New York: Basic Books.

Perls, T. T. & Terry, D. F. (2003). Genetics of exceptional longevity. *Experimental Gerontology, 38,* 725–730.

Perls, T. T. & Wood, E. R. (1996). Acute care costs of the oldest old: They cost less, their care intensity is less, and they go to nonteaching hospitals. *Archives of Internal Medicine, 156,* 754–760.

Poon, L. W., Johnson, M. A., Davey, A., Dawson, D. V., Siegler, I. C., & Martin, P. (2000). Psychosocial predictors of survival among centenarians. In P. Martin, A. Rott, B. Hagberg, & K. Mongan (Eds.). *Centenarians.* New York: Springer Publishing.

Reville, R. T. & Schoeni, R. F. (2003–2004). The fraction of disability caused at work. *Social Security Bulletin, 65,* 31–38.

Reynolds, C. (2004). Boomers, act II. *American Demographics, 26,* 10–11.

Riley, M. W. & Riley, J. (1986). Longevity and social structure: The potential of the added years. In A. Pifer & L. Bronte (Eds.). *Our aging society: Paradox and promise.* New York: W.W. Norton.

Samuelsson, S. M., Baur, B., Hagberg, B., Samuelsson, G., Norbeck, B., Brun, A., et al. (1997). The Swedish Centenarian Study: A multidisciplinary study of five consecutive cohorts at the age of 100. *International Journal of Aging and Human Development, 45,* 223–253.

Schaie, K. W. (1967). Age changes and age differences. *The Gerontologist, 7,* 128–132.

Schaie, K. W. (1973). Methodological problems in descriptive developmental research on adulthood and aging. In J. R. Nesselroade & H. W. Reese (Eds.). *Lifespan developmental psychology: Methodological issues.* New York: Academic Press.

Schaie, K. W. (Ed.). (1983). *Longitudinal studies of adult psychological development.* New York: Guilford Press.

Schaie, K. W. (1996). *Intellectual development in adulthood.* Cambridge: Cambridge University Press.

Schaie, K. W. (2005). *Developmental influences on adult intelligence: The Seattle Longitudinal Study.* New York: Oxford University Press.

Schoeni, R. V., Freedman, V. A., & Martin, L. G. (2008). Why is late-life disability declining? *The Milbank Quarterly, 86,* 47–69.

Silver, M. H., Newell, K., Hyman, B., Growdon, J., Hedley, E. T., & Perls, T. (1998). Unraveling the mystery of cognitive changes in old age. *International Psychogeriatrics, 10,* 25–41.

Social Security Administration. (2006). Retrieved October 2006, from http://www.ssa.gov/OACT/TR06/V_demographic.html

Stepp, D. D. (2007). *Directory of educational programs in gerontology and geriatrics* (8th ed.). Washington DC: Association for Gerontology in Higher Education.

Suzuki, M., Willcox, B. J., & Willcox, D. C. (2001). Implications from and for food cultures for cardiovascular disease. *Asia Pacific Journal of Clinical Nutrition, 10,* 165–171.

Terry, D. F., Sebastiani, P., Andersen, S. L., & Perls, T. T. (2008). Disentangling the roles of disability and morbidity in survival to exceptional old age. *Archives of Internal Medicine, 168,* 277–283.

Terry, D. F., Willcox, M. A., McCormick, M. A., & Perls, T. T. (2004). Cardiovascular disease delay in centenarian offspring. *Journal of Gerontology: Medical Sciences, 59A,* 385–389.

U.S. Census Bureau. (2006a). *Median age of the total population: 2005.* Retrieved October 2006, from http://www.factfinder.census.gov

U.S. Census Bureau. (2006b) Retrieved October 2006, from www.census.gov/cgi-bin/ipc/idbagg

U.S. Census Bureau. (2006c). Population Division, Interim Statistics. *Population projections by age: 2005.* Retrieved October 2006, from http://www.census.gov/population/projections/SummaryTab C1.pdf

U.S. Census Bureau. (2007). Population Estimates Program (PEP). Retrieved November 2009, from http://www/census.gov/popest/estimates/php

U.S. Census Bureau. (2009a). Population Division, Interim Statistics. *Population projections by age, sex and race for 2008.* Retrieved March 2009, from http://factfinder.census.gov/servlet/DatasetMainPageServlet?program=PEP&Submenuid=&lang=en&ts

U.S. Census Bureau. (2009b). Statistical abstract of the United States: 2009. Retrieved 2009, from http://www.census.gov/compendia/statab/2009edition.html

U.S. Census Bureau. (2009c). *Facts for features.* Retrieved April 2009, from http://www.census.gov/Press-Release/ww/releases/archives/facts_for_features

Whitfield, K. E. & Hayward, M. (2003). The landscape of health disparities among older adults. *Public Policy and Aging Report, 13,* 1–7.

Williams, D. (2005). The health of U.S. racial and ethnic populations. *Journals of Gerontology, 60B,* 53–62.

Willcox, D. C., Willcox, B. J., Todoriki, H., Curb, J. D., & Suzuki, M. (2006a). Caloric restriction and human longevity: What can we learn from the Okinawans? *Biogerontology, 7,* 173–177.

Willcox, B. J., Willcox, D. C., He, Q., Curb, J. D., & Suzuki, M. (2006b). Siblings of Okinawan centenarians share lifelong mortality advantages. *Journal of Gerontology: Biological Sciences, 61A,* 345–354.

World Health Organization (WHO). (2002). *Active Ageing: A Policy Framework.* Geneva, Switzerland: WHO.

Zarit, S. H. & Pearlin, L. I. (2005). Special issue on health inequalities across the life course. *Journal of Gerontology: Social Sciences, 60B, Special Issue II,* S5–S7.

2

Aging in Other Countries and Across Cultures in the United States

This chapter describes the phenomenon of global aging, including

- The increasing population of older adults in both industrialized, and developing, countries
- The impact of demographic shifts on employment and retirement patterns in other countries
- How modernization has affected elders' roles in traditional societies
- The impact of modernization on filial piety
- Challenges faced by older immigrants in the United States

Global Trends

The rapid pace of economic development in most countries has resulted in shifts from rural agricultural societies to more urbanized industrial landscapes with accompanying changes in social and family structures, improved life expectancy, and more people living into advanced old age. However, in many regions of the world where young adults must migrate to cities for job opportunities, older adults are left behind without family members living nearby. These changes in intergenerational contact are compounded when adult children immigrate to other countries for better job and educational opportunities. In this chapter, we explore the impact of global aging, where increased populations of older persons combine with the cultural

43

THE IMPORTANCE OF UNDERSTANDING AGING ACROSS CULTURES

Global aging is among the most pivotal changes of our time. Stark demographic differences among nations will significantly shape almost every aspect of national and international life. Demographics affect growth rates, intergenerational distribution of income, the structure of markets, the balance of savings and consumption, and many other economic variables. Socially, the world will change as well, as families come to have three, four, sometimes even five generations alive at one time. International relations, too, will change as some countries grow and others shrink. The stakes are high.

SOURCE: George P. Shultz, Stanford Center on Longevity, March 2007. (from the preface of a report by the Standford Center on Longevity, *How Population Aging Differs Across Countries: A Briefing on Global Demographics* on page 6.)

changes and economic patterns that disrupt traditional family and social structures.

The Phenomenon of Global Aging

All world regions are experiencing an increase in the absolute and relative size of their older populations, but tremendous variation will occur in aging patterns across countries and regions (Hayutin, 2007). Global aging is occurring for two major reasons: More people are living longer and fertility rates have declined in many regions of the world. The United Nations' definition of *population aging* is the rapid growth of the population age 60 and older. This age group is expected to grow by more than 50 percent in the developed nations between 2009 and 2050 (from 264 million to 416 million). The projected increase for those age 60 and older is even higher for developing nations—475 million in 2009 to 1.6 billion in 2050, when about 80 percent of the world's older adults will be living in developing countries (United Nations 2008; 2009). This parallels the fact that all world population growth is taking place in the developing countries and is likely to continue to do so (Bloom & Canning, 2007). The growth rate for those age 80 and older is higher than for the general population

age 60 and older: 3.9 percent per year worldwide, 3.3 percent in the most developed countries, and 3.8 percent in the least developed. As a result, the population age 65 and older will increase from 5.5 percent of the total population of less-developed countries in 2005 to 14.6 percent in 2050. The comparable figures for more developed countries are 15.3 percent and 25.9 percent, respectively. The number of persons age 65 or older in the world is expected to expand from an estimated 495 million in 2009 to 974 million in 2030. This will result in a world population in which 12 percent will be 65 years of age or older by the year 2030, compared with 7 percent today (He et al., 2005; United Nations, 2007; 2009).

As seen in the projections for population growth in the United States, described in Chapter 1, the global age distribution will change from a pyramid to a cylindrical form (Figure 2.1). This is due to a reduction in fertility rates worldwide, even in the less-developed countries of Africa and South America. In fact, for the 49 least developed countries, fertility rates are projected to drop from the current 4.39 children per woman to 2.41 by 2050 (United Nations, 2009). It is estimated that 120 countries will reach total fertility rates below replacement levels (i.e., 2.1 children per woman) by 2025, compared to 22 countries in 1975 and 70 in 2000 (WHO, 2002). The situation is particularly critical in Japan, where the fertility rate in 2006 was 1.25 children per woman. Low fertility rates combined with increased life expectancy in more developed countries have created what is called a "demographic divide" and resultant conflicts over how to address labor force shortages while providing employment to younger workers, possibly by changes in these countries' retirement policies (Bloom & Canning, 2007).

Life expectancy and the current numbers and expected growth of the older population differ substantially between industrialized and developing countries. Currently, 60 percent of older adults live in developing countries, which may increase to 75 percent by 2020. For example, in 2008, the population age 65 and older for Western and Southern European countries was 18 percent. Japan has the highest proportion of elders in the

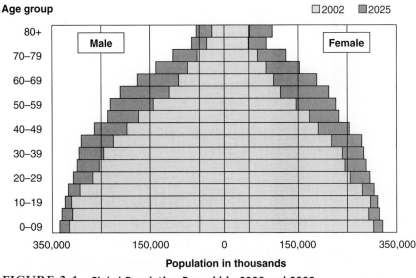

FIGURE 2.1   Global Population Pyramid in 2002 and 2025
SOURCE: World Health Organization, *Active ageing: A policy framework*. WHO, 2002. Reprinted by permission of the World Health Organization.

JAPAN'S AGING CRISIS

Japan is experiencing the most rapid rate of population aging in the world. In 1970, 7 percent of its population was 65 or older, but this increased to 22 percent in 2008. This group could make up 40 percent of Japan's population by 2050. Even more striking is the prediction that 7.2 percent will be age 80 and older in 2020, compared with 4.1 percent in the United States. By 2050, Japan is expected to have one million people age 100 and older. Baby boomers in Japan account for approximately 8.6 percent of the workforce, so their retirement will be a blow to Japan's economy at a time when the overall labor force is shrinking and fewer workers are available to pay into a pension system. Nevertheless, politicians and Japanese society in general resist immigration as a way to increase the number of young workers contributing to the economic support of retirees. Reports by the United Nations and demographers project a need for 13 million to 17 million new immigrants by 2050 in order to prevent the collapse of Japan's pension system. Yet in the past 25 years, only one million foreigners have been accepted as immigrants in this insular country.

SOURCE: AARP, 2006; Bloom and Canning, 2007; Population Reference Bureau, 2008b.

world (22 percent), followed by Italy (20 percent). Other developed countries with high proportions are Germany and Greece (19 percent) and Sweden (18 percent) (Population Reference Bureau, 2008a).

A major reason for such large proportions is increased life expectancy beyond age 65 in developed countries, as illustrated in Table 2.1 by comparisons of different world regions and some

TABLE 2.1   Life Expectancy at Birth of World Regions and Some Countries

REGION	TOTAL	MALES	FEMALES
World	68	67	70
More-developed	77	74	81
Least-developed	55	53	56
Sub-Saharan Africa	50	49	51
W. Europe	80	77	83
S. Europe	79	76	82
N. Europe	79	76	81
Japan	82	79	86
Canada	80	78	83
U.S.	78	75	81

SOURCE: Population Reference Bureau, 2008b.

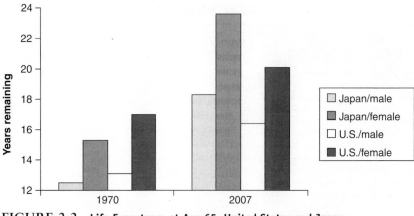

FIGURE 2.2   **Life Expectancy at Age 65: United States and Japan**
SOURCE: United Nations, 2007a.

countries and by life expectancy trends in the United States and Japan (Figure 2.2). In less than 40 years, the U.S. and especially Japan have made great strides in keeping people alive into advanced old age. In particular, Japanese men and women have gained considerable advantage since 1970—almost five years for men and an additional seven years for women beyond (NCHS, 2005). In contrast, sub-Saharan, Western, Eastern, and Middle African countries had only 3 percent of their population age 65 and older (Population Reference Bureau, 2008a). Overall, extreme societal aging will likely occur in Europe and a few Asian countries for the next few decades, while the developing world will remain comparatively young, intensifying the demographic divide. But this will shift by 2050, when developing countries will be as old as the developed countries are today, as captured changes in their median ages, discussed below (Hayutin, 2007).

The median age (the age at which half the population is younger and half is older, described in Chapter 1), of these regions also varies but is increasing in all countries:

- 29 worldwide
- 44.2 in Japan
- 40 in Western Europe
- 36.7 in the United States
- 20 in Latin America (United Nations, 2009)

Even in Africa, with fertility rates three times higher than that of developed countries and high mortality rates, the median age will increase from 19 today to 27.4 in 2050. Figure 2.3 shows this projected increase in the median age of three developed countries and for Mexico. In less than 45 years, the median age in Italy, the "oldest" country, will be 52.5, followed closely by Japan at 52.3. The United States will show a much smaller increase, from a median age of 36.7 currently to 41.5 in 2050. This is due primarily to higher birthrates in the United States compared to these other countries. Mexico's median age is also expected to increase significantly, from the current 26.3 to 38 by 2050, even though fertility rates in Mexico will remain high (United Nations, 2009).

At the same time, the less developed regions of the world expect to show a nearly fivefold increase in their oldest population, from 3.8 percent in 1975 to 17 percent in 2075. This fivefold growth rate is projected to occur in just 30 years (2000–2030) in Malaysia and Mexico, compared with slightly less than a doubling of the older population in the United States during this same period (Kinsella & Velkoff, 2001). An even greater rise in the proportion of the old-old (ages 75–84) and oldest-old (age 85 and older) is anticipated in these countries, from the current 0.5 percent to 3.5 percent in 2075. In absolute numbers, China

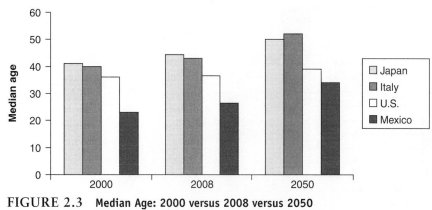

FIGURE 2.3   Median Age: 2000 versus 2008 versus 2050
SOURCE: United Nations, 2009.

currently has the largest number of people 65 and older (102 million), which is expected to reach 322 million by 2050. The Chinese population age 80 and older is also the largest in the world (13 million vs. 9.2 million in the United States), and is projected to reach 100 million by 2050. This increase in the general population of elders and among the old-old is attributable mostly to China's continued low birthrate—12 births per one thousand population compared with 21 worldwide. As a result, the median age of China is projected to rise from 33 in 2005 to 42 by 2030 (Kaneda, 2006; Population Reference Bureau, 2008a; United Nations, 2005). This will result in a top-heavy rectangular population structure, as illustrated by Figure 2.4 (page 48), which is much more dramatic than the increases described globally in Figure 2.1. Reasons for the growth of the old-old in developing countries include:

- improved sanitation
- medical care
- immunizations
- better nutrition
- declining birthrates

Unfortunately, this rapid growth in developing countries has not led to adequate public policy and strategic planning to meet care needs. While an industrialized country like France took 115 years to double its population of elders, it will take China only 27 years to do so. Such an increase requires government planning, but few developing countries have had the resources to focus on this coming crisis because of their priority on more immediate needs and younger populations (Hayutin, 2007; Kinsella & Phillips, 2005; United Nations, 2009; U.S. Census Bureau, 2006). The less-developed regions of the world are also coping with the tremendous impact of high fertility rates as they struggle to provide jobs, education, and housing for growing numbers of young people (Hayutin, 2007). Even with the continued high infant mortality rates in countries such as those in sub-Saharan Africa and the Middle East, children

GOVERNMENT EFFORTS TO INCREASE BIRTHRATES

In response to dramatic declines in birthrates, leaders of several industrialized countries have proposed tax benefits and financial incentives to encourage women to bear more children. Former Russian President Vladimir Putin proposed a cash bonus of $9,000 per baby, as well as assistance in the form of cash and child care. However, economists are not optimistic that this will reverse the trend toward low fertility and a declining number of workers to support Russia's aging population. Meanwhile, some French politicians have advocated national support for child care and foster grandparents to assist mothers working outside the home (Chivers, 2006).

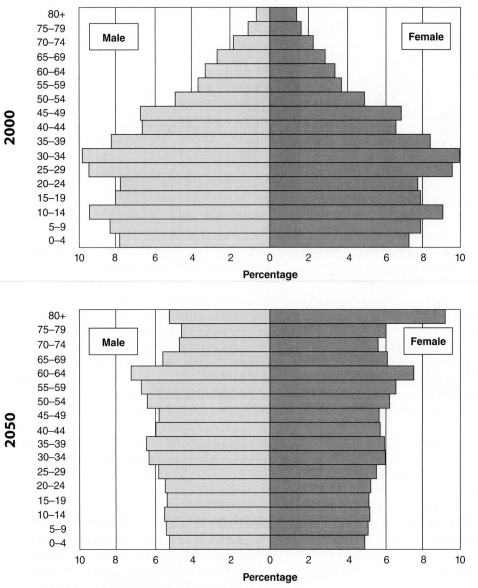

FIGURE 2.4   **Population Pyramids, China: 2000 and 2050**
SOURCE: *World Population Prospects: The 2004 Revision* (2005).

under 15 represent 43 percent of the population in less-developed regions, compared with 17 percent in more-developed regions (Population Reference Bureau, 2008).

Economic Implications for Industrialized Countries

Life expectancy in industrial nations has improved by 6 years for men and 8.5 years for women since 1953, most markedly among those at the highest socioeonomic levels, in higher-level occupations, and with the most education (United Nations, 2009). The rate has been greatest over the past 20 years, with a significant impact on the availability of workers to support retired persons. Although retirement patterns are shifting because of the global economic crisis, the dependency ratio for older retired persons will still drop from 3.5:1 (3.5 workers to support one retiree) in 1990 to about 2:1 in 2030 in the industrialized countries of Europe and in Japan. The Economic Policy Committee of the European Union projects a decline in the working-age population of its member nations (ages 15–64) by an average of 7 percent between 2005 and 2030 compared to an increase in the population of elders by 52 percent. The decline is projected to be 3.9 percent in Italy, 8.1 percent in Germany, and as high as 19.4 percent in Russia. This is even greater than the shrinkage in Japan's working-age population, projected at 15.7 percent between 2005 and 2030 (European Commission, 2005; United Nations, 2007).

A parallel concern for European countries is the "graying" of their workforce and perceptions that older adults with pensions are benefitting more than younger generations. Until recently, state pension plans and early retirement incentives to avoid layoffs in the European Union (EU) countries made it attractive for workers to retire in their 50s and early 60s. This allowed companies and governments to hire less expensive younger workers. But with the decline in the younger population and as middle-aged workers begin to retire, many companies are experiencing

problems in replacing these skilled workers with new employees who have the necessary qualifications. EU countries project a decline in their 20- to 29-year-old population by 20 percent in the next two decades, coupled with an increase in the 50 to 64 age group by 25 percent (Von Nordheim, 2003).

The proportion of older adults who continue to be employed in EU countries declines precipitously with age. For example, 80 percent of men and 68 percent of women in their late 80s are in the workforce in the United Kingdom; this declines to 10 and 5 percent, respectively, by their late 60s. By age 75, only 1 to 2 percent of Britons are employed (Heywood & Siebert, 2008). One indicator of the success of national governments and labor unions to retain older workers is the proportion of adults age 65 and older who are full- or part-time employees:

- 3.8 percent of the U.S. workforce is age 65 and older
- 2 percent of the UK workforce
- Only 0.5 percent of France's workforce (OECD, 2005)

In response, EU leaders have implemented changes in pensions and social security systems to achieve a goal of having 50 percent of their employees be age 55 to 64. One strategy is to raise the age of full retirement by an additional five years by 2010 (Commission of European Communities, 2004). These are difficult objectives because across the 25-member EU, less than 40 percent of workers fall in the 55 to 64 age range, with an average retirement age of 60. This ranges from an average retirement age of 57 in Poland to 63 in Portugal. Portugal's population of older adults is projected to grow from 17 percent today to 33 percent by 2050. This rapid growth, combined with concerns about the significant share of its gross domestic product (GDP) being spent for pension expenditures and health care, has forced the national government to change its retirement policies. Portugal's Ministry of Labor and Social Security has placed restrictions on early retirement and calculation of pension benefits in an effort to encourage workers to postpone their retirement (SSA, 2005). As another example, the legal retirement age of 65 in Germany is older than in other EU countries, but the federal government has initiated legislation for raising this to 67. This represents a major reform of Germany's state pension system and will be implemented incrementally, beginning in 2012 and taking full effect by 2029. At the same time, in response to growing numbers of retirees who depend on its pension fund and fear that Germany risks becoming a "pensioner's democracy" in which the "old plunder the young" (Oldies with muscle, 2008), the German government will decrease full state pensions from the current 54 percent to 43 percent of the individual's salary by 2030 (Wagner, 2006).

Alternatively, many developed countries are implementing incentives for and removing barriers against longer employment, such as improving the quality of working conditions for older workers (United Nations, 2009). For example, the United Kingdom has taken a proactive position to prevent age discrimination in recruiting, selecting, and retaining workers. A program initiated in 2000 by the U.K. government, "New Deal 50," offers training grants

THE CRISIS IN EUROPE'S PENSION SYSTEMS

Pension programs in European nations have already started to feel the pinch of a growing population of retirees. The average portion of gross domestic product spent on pensions is 10 percent for the European Union; 14 percent in Italy. It will most likely rise in Italy if the current law that allows retirement at age 57 persists. Some regional government workers in Italy can retire even earlier; in Sicily, for example, male government workers can retire after 25 years on the job and women after 20 years. While other European countries like France and Germany are enacting legislation to require 40 years of employment or extending the retirement age to 67, efforts by the Italian government to protect its pension system by changing retirement laws have met with fierce resistance from labor unions.

of £1500 (almost $3,000) to prepare older adults to return to the workforce and a working tax credit of £40–60 per week to supplement their earnings (Taylor, 2003). ASDA, a large U.K. retailer, has been successful in recruiting and retaining mature workers. They proudly point to the fact that 19 percent of their workforce is age 50 and older. ASDA offers workshops to promote the company to potential employees over age 50; it also allows up to 3 months unpaid leave and a "grandparent leave" of one week after the birth of a grandchild. These actions have benefited the company directly; ASDA stores with the highest proportion of older workers report only one-third the absenteeism rates of the average in other stores (Personnelzone, 2004).

An innovative solution to prevent the "brain drain" of older workers was devised by Bosch, a German electronics company. Retiring employees complete a questionnaire about the knowledge they have gained during their careers. Project managers access the information from a database if they need workers with specific abilities. The retirees are then employed for short periods on projects that require such skills (Bosch Management Support, 2004).

Although Australia is facing less of a workforce crisis than European countries, many Australian companies have recognized the importance of hiring and retaining experienced workers. For example, Westpac, a financial services company planned to expand its financial advising division. To do so, it recruited 900 experienced workers who were age 55 and older and interested in starting a second career. The company's leaders viewed older workers as an asset because they could communicate better with their older clients (Nixon, 2002). What is unknown is how these retirement projections, pension patterns, and retirement incentives will change due to the global economic crisis, which has resulted in many adults needing to work longer primarily to build up their retirement funds after their investments precipitously declined in 2008–2009.

In addition to raising the age for receiving full retirement benefits, industrialized countries are also faced with whether or not to permit more immigration of young workers. Already, more than 25 percent of all workers in Australia are immigrants. However, this is a controversial proposal for many countries where immigrants often are not easily assimilated because of languages, religions, and cultures divergent from those of the host country. As noted above, Japan is particularly resistant to opening up immigration. But resistance is also strong in many Western European countries that do not define themselves as multicultural societies and fear losing their national identity (Haub, 2007). These tensions erupted into riots in late 2005 in the suburbs of Paris, where young Muslim immigrants from North Africa protested policies and practices by

employers and the French government that discriminated against foreign workers. And in Germany, those opposed to immigration raise the rallying cry of "children instead of Indians" (Bloom & Canning, 2007). Other solutions to labor shortages favored by such countries are to encourage more women to join the labor force, persuade part-time workers to become full-time, and raise the birthrate (Haub, 2007). Resistance to immigrants meeting workforce needs is likely to intensify with the growing unemployment rates due to the worldwide recession in 2008–2009.

The Impact of Modernization on Older Adults' Roles in Traditional Societies

The social position and experiences of older persons vary across cultures. Not surprisingly, the greatest differences in the status of older adults are between traditional societies and the modernized world, with its rapidly changing values, norms, and lifestyles. Examining the different ways that other societies have addressed issues affecting their elders can shed light on the process of aging in our society. The field of "comparative sociocultural gerontology" or an "anthropology of aging" has helped researchers differentiate what aspects of aging are universal or biological and which factors are largely shaped by the sociocultural system (Sokolovsky, 1997; Infeld, 2002).

Understanding how aging in contemporary American society differs from that experienced elsewhere and which factors are socioculturally determined can also suggest strategies for improving environments in which to grow old. Within the constraints of this one chapter, we can only glance at a few other cultures. For a more complete view, we urge you to turn to the available literature on the anthropology of aging, including the *Journal of Cross-Cultural Gerontology*. While this chapter explores aging

JAPAN'S DECLINING IMMIGRANT POPULATION

When Japan has allowed immigrants, they have been very selective. Between 1990 and the early 2000s, the government issued work visas to 366,000 Brazilians and other South Americans of Japanese descent. These guest workers were the largest group of foreign blue-collar workers in Japan, employed by the industrial sector and performing jobs that native-born Japanese refused. During the economic crisis that accelerated in late 2008, Japan's unemployment levels rose to a high of 4.4 percent and its exports dropped by 45.6 percent. The government undertook an emergency program to offer South American guest workers $3,000 each for their airfare and $2,000 for each dependent to return to their home country. This offer was contingent on these immigrants agreeing not to return or apply for worker visas later. These changes, made in response to the growing economic crisis in Japan, may be shortsighted as the country's working age population declines and its population ages. Despite its rising unemployment rate, Japan continues to have a shortage of staff to care for frail elders and has not made efforts to retrain its industrial workers for these types of jobs (Tabuchi, 2009).

Older people in Asian cultures enjoy teaching traditional arts to younger generations.

in other countries and among immigrants to the United States, Chapter 14 focuses on the cultural and ethnic diversity represented by elders of color within contemporary American society.

Resources Held by Older Adults

Definitions of old age—as well as the authority exercised by older people—have traditionally rested on the material and political resources controlled by them. These resources include:

- traditional skills and knowledge
- security bestowed by property rights
- civil and political power
- information control
- contributions to the general welfare from routine services performed by older people (such as child care)

Traditional systems of **social stratification** conferred respect and authority to older adults who controlled these resources or skills (Glascock, 1997). Older people's social rank in traditional cultures was generally determined by the balance between the cost of maintaining them and the

societal contributions they were perceived to make. As age became a less important criterion for determining access to and control of traditional and political resources, older members of society lost some of their status and authority.

Modernization Theory

A number of explanations have been advanced for the declining status of the old in modern society. **Modernization theory,** a major explanation, was defined by Cowgill (1974a, 1974b, 1986) as:

> The transformation of a total society from a relatively rural way of life based on animate power, limited technology, relatively undifferentiated institutions, parochial and traditional outlook and values, toward a predominantly urban way of life, based on inanimate sources of power, highly differentiated institutions, matched by segmented individual roles, and a cosmopolitan outlook which emphasizes efficiency and progress (Cowgill, 1974a, p. 127).

As society becomes modernized, older people lose political and social power, influence, and leadership. These social changes also may lead to reduced engagement by aging persons in community life. In addition, younger and older generations tend to become separated socially, morally, and intellectually. Youth is glorified as the embodiment of progress and achievement, as well as the means by which society can attain such progress. Over time, the characteristics of modernization that contribute to the lower status of older adults are:

- health technology
- scientific technology as applied in economic production and distribution
- urbanization
- literacy and mass education

As noted in Chapter 1, *health technology* has reduced infant mortality and maternal deaths and prolonged adult life, thereby increasing the number of older persons. With more elders in the labor market, competition between generations for jobs intensified, and retirement developed as a means of forcing older people out of the labor market. However, as described above, this has resulted in a shortage of workers in many industrialized countries.

Scientific technology creates new jobs primarily for the young, with older workers more likely to remain in traditional occupations that become obsolete. The rapid development of high-tech industries today and the generational differences in the use of the Internet illustrate this phenomenon. Some older workers feel marginalized and alienated if they are not able to contribute to a technologically skilled workforce.

In the early stages of modernization, when a society is relatively rural, young people are attracted to *urban areas,* whereas older parents and grandparents remain on the family farm or in rural communities. The resulting residential segregation of the generations has a dramatic impact on family interactions. The geographical and occupational mobility of the young, in turn, leads to greater social distance between generations and to a reduced status of the old. All parts of the world are becoming increasingly urbanized, with 50 percent of the world's population now living in cities compared to 30 percent in 1950. Even in developing countries, urban populations are expected to double over the next 30 years, with the highest rates of urban growth in the poorest areas (Hayutin, 2007).

Rapid urbanization in many developing countries has disrupted the tradition of family support for their elders. Modern migration programs in India, while providing resources for young and old, have resulted in younger people obtaining more education and creating a sense of superiority over their illiterate elders. Rapid urbanization has left almost 30 percent of old people in rural areas in India without family nearby to care for them (Dandekar, 1996; Vincentnathan & Vincentnathan, 1994). Meanwhile, families who eke out a meager living in urban areas have little means to assist their elders who live with them. In

the economically more successful countries of East Asia, such as Japan and South Korea, older people have benefited from improvements in health care, income, and long-term care services, but at the cost of power, respect, and prestige that was accorded previous generations of older adults (Silverman, Hecht, & McMillin, 2000). The phenomenon of rapid urban population growth globally is expected to continue through 2030, with projections of 4 to 6 percent per year in parts of Africa, Asia, and South America (United Nations, 2005). This will accelerate the problem of isolated elders in rural areas as their children seek opportunities in urban centers.

Another example of how modernization has eroded traditional family supports is Taiwan, where young adults' support for multigenerational households has steadily declined. Accordingly, adult children in China report feeling less obligated to help their parents if this conflicts with the demands of their job (Hsu, Lew-Ting, & Wu, 2001; Zhan, 2004). In such instances, it becomes vital for national and local governments to provide services such as public housing, health care, pension plans, and policies that support family care of elders. These programs may also serve to reduce tensions between generations. Some demographers have suggested that the improved health and financial status of older populations and a trend toward individualism have resulted in more older adults choosing to live apart from their adult children. In contrast, other demographers have found that increases in the socioeconomic status of older persons or their adult children do not result in significant changes in traditional family structures and the value of family interdependence (Cameron, 2000; Kinsella & Velkoff, 2001).

Occupation and education appear to have a reversed J-shaped relationship to modernization. In the early phases of rapid social change (illustrated by nations such as China and the Philippines), the occupational and educational status of older adults shows a decline, but later improves (exemplified by New Zealand, Canada, and the United States). This suggests that, as societies move beyond an initial state of

ROLE CHANGES AND SUICIDE AMONG OLDER ADULTS

Evidence of global differences in adaptation to role loss with age is reflected in suicide rates among older women. Although the rate among women in the United States *drops* as they age, the suicide rate *increases* dramatically in Japan, tripling from 11.6 per 100,000 at age 40 to 39.3 at age 65 and older. In Taiwan, there is also a striking increase, from 10.4 to 34.6 per 100,000 in this same age range (Hu, 1995). In general, women age 75 and older in Asian countries have higher suicide rates than their counterparts in English-speaking countries. Suicide rates for men age 75 and older are higher than for any other age group in Asian countries, especially in rural China and Singapore, but less so in Japan (Pritchard & Baldwin, 2002).

THE UNDERPINNINGS OF FILIAL PIETY IN ASIAN CULTURE

In his writings, Confucius emphasized that young people should respect, not just provide care for, their elders:

Filial piety today is taken to mean providing nourishment for parents, but dogs and horses are provided with nourishment. If it is not done with reverence for parents, what is the difference between men and animals?

SOURCE: From *Analects*, Book 2, Chapter 7, quoted in Sung, 2000.

rapid modernization, status differences between generations decrease and the relative standing of older people may rise, particularly when reinforced by social policies such as Social Security, which have improved older adults' financial well-being. Societies in advanced stages of modernization may become more concerned about the older population's devalued status. Through public education, social policies, and the media, they then attempt to create more opportunities for, and positive images of, older people. This has already been occurring in the U.S., in part because of the aging of the baby boomers, who have the political clout and resources to change popular stereotypes of aging. Advertising and television programs increasingly portray older persons as vital, active, involved, and physically attractive.

Impact of Modernization on Filial Piety

Most societies have some norms of respectful treatment toward their elders, but considerable variability exists in practice. For example, **filial piety**—a sense of reverence and deference toward elders—in China and Taiwan was not universal but was affected by family resources,

the number of living children, and geographic location (Ikels, 1997). The norms of filial piety were more often practiced by wealthy families in traditional rural China. Despite the Confucian reverence for age, known as *xiao*, older people in lower-class families had fewer resources to give them status. But the tradition was maintained because of Confucian ideals that required children to obey and serve their parents.

Life for older people in China has undergone a major transformation within a relatively short time period. As government policies have been altered, the "political economy" has had an impact on elders' status. For example, women have benefited from changes such as not having to submit to arranged marriages or having their feet bound as well as from increased job opportunities. National social insurance also benefits older Chinese citizens. However, the practice of educating sons and not daughters in traditional China has resulted in older cohorts in which women are illiterate and economically dependent on their children in old age. For this reason, researchers have found older women in China today to be more disadvantaged than men in their functional health as well as their economic status (Zeng, Liu, & George, 2003). This problem is compounded by China's one-child-per-family policy that began in 1979, combined with preferences for male children. Although the policy is less rigid now, it has resulted in a disproportionate number of older adults to working-age younger adults and of males to females. In addition, the break up of communes that provided support for childless elders in the past has also placed many elders at risk. These problems are expected to continue as future cohorts of older people have fewer children, especially daughters and daughters-in-law, to care for them in times of need. These changes will also reduce multigenerational living arrangements in China (Cheng & Chan, 2006). Additionally, China's Social Security fund and pension systems have been markedly reduced by declining investments due to the volatile global economic markets.

The rising standard of living in China has benefited many young adults, who often migrate to urban areas for job opportunities. This results in a concentration of older adults in rural areas, where 65 percent of China's general population and 77 percent of its older adults reside (He, Sengupta, Zhang, & Guo, 2007). As noted above, this pattern of migration by younger workers to urban areas also occurs in other Asian countries such as the Philippines, Indonesia, and Thailand, resulting in sharp declines in three-generational coresidence (Knodel & Ofstedal, 2002; Zhang, 2004). The loss of this long-held tradition of multigenerational living, an important pillar of filial piety, may significantly affect the older adult who is left behind. A survey in a rural region of China compared elders living in three-generational households or with grandchildren in **skipped-generation households** (i.e., where grandparents were caring for grandchildren after the parents had relocated to urban areas for employment) with elders who lived alone or with a spouse. Those in traditional multigenerational households reported greater life satisfaction and less depression than their counterparts in single-generation households. Stronger emotional ties with and financial assistance from their adult children mitigated the negative effects of living alone on elders' well-being (Silverstein, Cong, & Li, 2006).

In response to these population and economic demands, China has increased its publicly funded housing and government-funded welfare programs for all older adults—not just for childless elders, as in the past. A private residential-care-facility industry and community-based services are also developing in response to the anticipated 24 percent older population by 2050 (Kaneda, 2006; Zhan et al., 2006). In Singapore, a more radical approach to caring for a growing older population has emerged. In 1997, the government opened a special court where older persons can bring legal claims against their children for not providing assistance in their old age.

Overcoming the Impact of Modernization on Intergenerational Relations

Despite these changes in older adults' status and family relations in traditional societies, strong cultural values can mitigate many of the negative effects of modernization on older people. This is vividly illustrated in modern, industrialized, and urban Japanese society. Confucian values of filial piety and ancestor worship help to maintain older persons' relatively high status and integration in family life, as well as their leadership in national politics. Traditional values of reciprocity and lifelong indebtedness to one's parents are a major reason for continued three-generational households in Japan, even though the modernization of Japanese society and a declining economy have increased financial demands on the nuclear family. Almost half of working-age Japanese women today are employed outside the home. Unprecedented numbers of older people in Japan have increased the societal costs of caring for older members and created dilemmas for younger family members who are responsible for their support. Therefore, it is not surprising that the majority of respondents to a survey by the Japanese Ministry of Health and Welfare (57.3 percent) viewed the aging population as a serious problem, and 68 percent thought that the birthrate in Japan should be encouraged to grow (National Institute of Population and Social Security Research, 2004).

Even the oldest-old have important roles in most Asian families.

Nevertheless, the majority of middle-aged persons in Japan still believe that the care of older parents is the children's responsibility. Indeed, negligence toward one's parents is a source of great public shame. Society also assumes increasing responsibility for the care of Japan's elders; all those age 70 and older receive free basic medical services, which serves as a model for other Asian countries. The Japanese government provides incentives for home care by families; they can receive subsidies to remodel their homes in order to accommodate joint households as well as a tax credit for providing elder-parent care (Kim & Maeda, 2001). The number of nursing homes and long-stay hospitals in Japan has also grown, but in Tokyo, long waiting lists for admission to nursing homes mean that many older adults have to move from familiar environments to find institutional care (Gerontological Society of America, 2009). The percentage of parents living with children has declined due to urbanization, industrialization, the growing number of employed women, and the declining number of children since 1950. Nevertheless, the proportion of older parents living in multigenerational households is still higher than in any other industrialized nation. In 1995,

56 percent of people over age 65 lived with their children and grandchildren, although this is a decline from 1980, when 70 percent of older households were multigenerational. By 2010, this is projected to drop even further, to 42 percent (National Institute of Population and Social Security Research, 2006). Meanwhile, the number of households consisting of only the older couple has increased. Urban–rural differences in family expectations are demonstrated by the fact that 25 percent of people age 75 and older in Tokyo live alone, compared with 15 percent in rural regions. All these trends suggest that traditional customs of caring for aging parents in adult children's homes are altering.

Even so, middle-aged women remain the primary caregivers to Japanese elders, as in most other countries. As older adults continue to live longer, they may increasingly require goods and services at the perceived expense of younger members (e.g., children) and may place even greater demands on middle-aged women in Japan. With the growing proportion of educated, professional women and newer cohorts influenced more by Western values than by Confucianism, many women do not want to leave their jobs to become caregivers to their parents or parents-in-law. Because of public concerns about long-term care needs of its growing population of oldest-old, the Japanese Diet passed the Public Long-Term Care Insurance Act in 1997 and intitiated the Long-Term Care Insurance System in 2000 (AARP, 2006; Maeda, 1998). This national policy guarantees comprehensive long-term care for all Japanese persons age 65 and older and for those age 40 to 64 who may require long-term care. Funding is provided by a combination of mandatory insurance premiums paid by older persons, a co-pay of all incurred expenses, and general taxes paid to federal, prefecture, and municipal governments. Recognizing the escalating costs of institutional care, policymakers established an "Active Aging Society" framework by emphasizing prevention, such as exercise programs and nutrional counseling, and a community-wide care system, which

"RETIRED HUSBAND SYNDROME"

A new medical diagnosis has been coined in Japan. Labeled "Retired Husband Syndrome" (or RHS), the condition has been observed among women whose husbands have retired by age 60 to 65 and remain at home full-time, demanding their wives' attention and care. From a generation where wives remained at home and were subservient to their husbands, many of these women develop psychosomatic symptoms related to the stress of having to serve their husbands full-time after retirement. With the projected increase in Japanese men retiring, RHS is expected to increase dramatically among women 60 and older in Japan.

SOURCE: A. Faiola, *Washington Post*, October 17, 2005.

provides prevention-oriented care management (AARP, 2006).

More community-based long-term care options are needed to fully implement Japan's long-term service system. Nevertheless, this universal long-term care program appears to partially relieve the burden on Japanese families and hospitals, where most long-term care occurs. Policy makers in other developed countries are closely watching Japan's program as a possible model for day-to-day care of their oldest-old while still preserving filial piety.

A strong belief in filial piety also plays a dominant role in family attitudes and government policies regarding care for aging parents in South Korea, where the number of people 65 and older has increased threefold in 25 years. Surveys of young Koreans reveal that more than 90 percent believe that adult children must care for their older parents, and in fact, 90 percent of older adults cite family as their primary source of support. These values are supported by the the fact that 65 percent of people age 65 and older live with their adult children, even in urbanized areas like Seoul. In particular, daughters-in-laws are expected to provide most of the primary care for their aging parents-in-law. Such filial duties are performed within

the framework of "serving" elders rather than "caring" for them; this conveys a less egalitarian relationship (Lan, 2002). The government of South Korea promotes family-based caregiving by sponsoring a "Respect for Elders Day" and a "Respect for Elders Week," as well as prizes to honor outstanding examples of filial piety. These initiatives help reduce Koreans' expectations for long-term care services from the government, although changing demographics today have placed a greater burden on families, with average family size down to 3.0 and with 46 percent of all married women in Korea working outside the home (Levande, Herrick, & Sung, 2000; Sung, 2000, 2001).

Other Asian countries where filial piety persists, despite changing work and family patterns, are Singapore, Thailand, and the Philippines, where the majority of parents age 60 and older live with their children (Kinsella & Velkoff, 2001). The importance of filial piety generally supersedes modern social and economic demands in these Asian countries.

However, immigration to a Western country may change elders' definitions of filial piety. A study of older Chinese and Korean immigrants in San Francisco examined their views on **biculturalism,** or the process of integrating two cultures into one's lifestyle. The Chinese participants in this study had lived in the U.S. an average of 24 years; the Koreans 16 years. These elders described how their perspectives of family social support had altered as they became more peripheral to the nuclear families created by their adult children. They were more likely to live alone, relying on employment, Social Security, and Supplemental Security Income (SSI) to support themselves. Their changing perceptions of filial piety were also evident in their recogniton that they were no longer authority figures to their adult children and grandchildren. While this suggests what appears to be a successful adaptation to immigration, it also highlights the loss of filial piety as Asian immigrant elders become more bicultural (Wong, Yoo, & Stewart, 2006).

A Cross-Cultural View of Elders' Roles in Contemporary Societies

As discussed in Chapter 1, every society defines people as old on some basis, whether chronological, functional, or generational, and assigns that group a particular set of rights, privileges, and duties that differ from those of its younger members. To illustrate, older persons in our society today qualify for Social Security and Medicare on the basis of their age, although the age of eligibility is increasing as life expectancy grows. As another example, in some religious groups, only the oldest members are permitted to perform the most sacred rituals. Societies generally distinguish two, sometimes three, classes of elders:

- those who are no longer fully productive economically but are physically and mentally able to attend to their daily needs
- those who are functionally dependent, require long-term care, and are regarded as social burdens and thus may be treated negatively
- those who continue to participate actively in the economy and the social system through farming or self-employment, care of grandchildren, or household maintenance, while younger adults work outside the home

Consistent with the social exchange theory discussed in Chapter 8, older people who can no longer work but who control resources essential to fulfill the needs of younger group members generally offset the societal costs incurred in maintaining them. In some social systems, political, judicial, religious, or ritual power and privileges are vested in older people as a group, and this serves to mediate social costs. For instance, in societies such as those of East Africa, politically powerful positions are automatically assigned to men who reach a certain age (Keith, 1990).

Control over knowledge, especially ritual and religious traditions, has traditionally provided elders with a critical source of power. The aged shaman is an example, revered in many societies for knowledge or wisdom. The importance of older members' protecting cultural values is illustrated in India, where traditional Hindu law prescribes a four-stage life cycle for high-caste men: student, householder, ascetic, and mendicant. In the last two stages, older religious men are expected to renounce worldly attachments to seek enlightenment in isolated retreats. This practice ensures that the pursuit of the highest form of knowledge is limited to older men of higher castes (Sokolovsky, 1997).

Knowledge as the basis of older people's power has been challenged as traditional societies become more urbanized or assimilated into the more modernized culture. Over the course of the twentieth century, American Indian elders lost their roles as mentors and counselors to younger tribal members. Their knowledge of tribal customs and stories, language, agricultural skills, and folk medicine was no longer valued as family structures changed and people migrated away from the reservation (Baldridge, 2001). Among some American Indian tribes, however, a revival of interest and pride in native identity and spirituality has occurred, thus raising the esteem of elders who possess ritual knowledge. For example, they are the only ones who know the words and steps for many traditional songs and dances. Knowledge of the group's culture, particularly its arts and handicrafts, native songs, and epics has enhanced the social status of older persons in native cultures. Similarly, the search for one's heritage or roots has led to increased contacts between younger generations seeking this information from older persons who often are a great repository of family histories. The growing desire for ethnic or tribal identity among many American Indians, which has led to a conscious restoration of old patterns, illustrates that modernization does not automatically erode the status of elders.

On the other hand, rapid societal changes created by modernization and accompanying sociodemographic shifts, poverty, and the HIV/

AIDS epidemic have placed unexpected burdens on older people in many African countries, who are disproportionately expected to contribute to supporting younger generations. Although much smaller in proportion than in other regions of the world, people age 60 and older comprise a growing share of the population, ranging from 6.8 percent in South Africa to 4.3 percent in Zimbabwe. With increasing migration of younger family members to urban centers, older adults in rural parts of Africa cannot rely on their adult children to care for them. Instead, many provide a critical role as caregivers themselves to grandchildren left behind by parents who seek employment in distant cities. This responsibility has been compounded by the growing number of AIDS orphans, especially in sub-Saharan Africa. Given that the population age 15 to 49 has been hardest hit by AIDS, older adults are often left to care for their grandchildren as well as extended family members. In most cases, they receive very little government support for their surrogate parenting. To make matters worse, most African countries provide little, if any, Social Security or pension benefits for their older citizens (Darkwa & Mazibuko, 2002; UNAIDS, 2000). The role of grandparents as primary caregivers for grandchildren or great-grandchildren, because their adult children are unable or unwilling to provide care, is now a global phenomenon (United Nations, 2008).

Singapore is another rapidly aging country; by 2050 their median age is expected to be similar to that of Japan and Italy. The state is preparing for its aging population through initiatives to encourage self-sufficiency. Government subsidies support 90 percent of older Singaporeans to live in public housing or to purchase their own homes. The Singaporean government has also invested in improvements to the country's infrastructure to allow people to age in place, by building barrier-free homes and expanding transportation options. A mandatory savings plan of risk-free bonds requires deposits throughout the working years and withdrawals only during retirement. In addition, the government controls health care costs for elders. Although the mandatory retirement age in Singapore is 62, employers can rehire workers for another 3 years (Loong, 2009). Other countries are planning for increased numbers of older retirees by encouraging more self-sufficiency and personal responsibility.

Immigrants from Traditional Cultures to the United States

In 2005, the U.S. had more foreign-born residents than any other country: approximately 38 million, representing 20 percent of all immigrants in the world. The countries that placed second and third had fewer than one-third that number: 12 million in Russia and 10 million in Germany. The growth of international migrants is also highest in the U.S.: 15 million between 1990 and 2005. The United Nations projects even higher rates of future immigration to the U.S.: 1.1 million per year between 2010 and 2050. Most of these are voluntary immigrants, not refugees, who seek better economic opportunities for their families. The great majority of immigrants are younger families. Although older adults represent less than 10 percent of the total, it is estimated that 4.5 million older immigrants will reside in the U.S. by 2010. Almost 17 percent are new to the U.S. and have lived here less

Social activities with others from their native country can help older immigrants adapt to life in the United States.

than 10 years, which has implications for how they have adapted to our society (Borjas, 2007; Population Reference Bureau, 2008b). Because of changes in the Immigration and Naturalization Act to give preferential entry for family members through the Family Reunification Act, most older immigrants arrive as "immediate relatives of U.S. citizens." They generally follow their adult children who preceded them to this country (Gorospe, 2006; Moon & Rhee, 2006). This older immigrant population is:

- less likely to be educated (almost half have not completed high school)
- less likely to be proficient in English (including 58 percent of elders from Asian countries)
- more likely to live in poverty
- less likely to have health care coverage (45 percent of all elders who have no health insurance are foreign-born)
- less likely to use health and social services
- more likely than their U.S.-born peers to receive government benefits such as Medicaid (Asian American Justice Center, 2006; He, 2001; Moon & Rhee, 2006)

HELPING ISOLATED OLDER IMMIGRANTS

The "community ambassadors" program in Fremont, California was started by city leaders. It helps older immigrants who move to the U.S. to live with their adult children and often move out when conflicts arise in cultural values and lifestyles. Those who continue to live with their children remain at home alone when the younger generation leaves for work or school, often feeling dependent and depressed because they cannot speak English to function independently. Community ambassadors are other immigrants from the same countries who help elders obtain medical and legal services, enroll them in government benefit programs, provide transportation, and otherwise fill gaps left by the elders' families.

SOURCE: National Public Radio, "Elderly Immigrants Flow into California," March 17, 2008.

Adult children who precede their parents to the new country often encourage them to immigrate because they are concerned about providing care for their aging parents from a distance, especially when other siblings are unavailable in the home country. In some cases, the assistance is mutually beneficial because the parents live with or near their adult children in order to help in family-owned businesses and as caregivers for grandchildren. However, elders' immigration for the sake of their children and grandchildren can disrupt their lives and psychological well-being at a time when their own health may be declining. Social isolation and depression often result. Depression rates as high as 26 percent have been found among immigrant elders and may be linked to financial problems, lack of health insurance coverage, multiple chronic diseases, and grief over leaving their home and friends in their native country (Gelfand, 2003; Min, Moon, & Lubben, 2005; Mui & Kang, 2006; van der Geest, Mul, & Vermeulen, 2004). As noted above, many of these older immigrants lack economic and educational resources. They are generally not proficient in English and rely on their children for financial and social support, thereby making acculturation more difficult. Language and cultural barriers compound the elders difficulties in accessing Western health care. For example, older immigrants must rely on their adult children to seek health services and manage the accompanying paperwork, shifting the balance of power and respect and making the older adult dependent on the child for this assistance. In a study of older Chinese immigrants in Boston, the most depressed were elders with the most chronic diseases and worst self-ratings of health (Wu, Tran, & Amjad, 2004).

Older refugees to Western countries face even more problems adjusting to their new country. In the past 40 years, waves of Indochinese refugees have come to the United States from countries experiencing political strife, war, and unrest. Property and other resources in their native lands that afforded them importance and power were generally stripped from them. Being

POINTS TO PONDER

Think about immigrant and refugee groups in your community. What is your impression of ways that elders in such families are involved, or not involved, in the lives of their children and grandchildren? What impact do a common language and shared cultural values appear to have on their interactions? To what extent have cultural differences created family conflicts and reduced the status of elders?

in the United States has brought them a different life than the one they might have imagined for their later years. These older refugees do not have the ability to provide material goods, land, or other financial support, which has traditionally given them status. Accordingly, traditional power has been eroded as families have started new lives in this culture and the balance of power has shifted within these families. Indeed, financial self-sufficiency is a major determinant of adjustment to life in the U.S. among older Indochinese refugees, regardless of education, gender, and English proficiency. In a study of refugee elders from Cambodia, Vietnam, Ukraine, and Jewish elders from the former Soviet Union, reports of loneliness and isolation were widespread. However, the majority of these refugees were unaware of any social or health services that could help them adapt to their new situation (Strumpf et al., 2001). Refugees from countries in the midst of civil war often experience even greater mental health problems. Traumas such as torture, massacre of family and friends, and abrupt separation from family members can have long-lasting negative effects, even after escaping to the political safety of the U.S. (Morioka-Douglas, Sacks, & Yeo, 2004).

Living Arrangements of Older Immigrants

Coresidence with adult children varies across nationality among immigrants. In an analysis of U.S. census data on almost 64,000 older immigrants, the living arrangements of Latino (mostly Cuban and Mexican), Asian (mostly from China or Southeast Asia), and non-Hispanic white (mostly from Europe) immigrants were compared (Wilmoth, 2001). Significant differences emerged across immigrant groups, with the highest rates of independent living among white, Japanese, and Cuban immigrants. Living in another family member's home was more common among other Asian groups and elders from Mexico, especially among those who were unmarried, had lower incomes and less than a college education, and those with a physical disability. As noted above, coresidence may not always benefit the older immigrant, especially if their adult children live in a suburban community far from an ethnic enclave, such as Chinese and Southeast Asian neighborhoods in urban settings. Elders who choose to live in these ethnic enclaves lose their immediate access to family but gain the benefit of socializing with their peers and finding health and social service providers who speak their native language. In some cases, immigrant elders who opt to live in ethnic enclaves in the city sacrifice the material comfort of life in the suburbs in order to be close to such reminders of "home." For these older adults, their residence takes on a meaning beyond physical safety and comfort and can serve to ameliorate their sense of displacement from their home country (Becker, 2003).

When immigrant elders need long-term care, traditional norms of filial piety generally play a dominant role in the decision by elders and their adult children about what services to use. Research with immigrant Latino families has found that they mobilize a wide network of extended family and friends to provide care in the community (Gelfand, 2003). Among families from Southeast Asia, regardless of religion (Sikh, Hindu, Muslim, or Christian), those who continue to hold filial piety beliefs are less likely to feel burdened by caring for an older parent (Gupta & Pillai, 2002). Indeed, among some immigrant groups, placing an older family member in a nursing home is viewed as a denial of one's filial obligations. These values of providing long-term care

IMMIGRANTS WORKING IN LONG-TERM CARE FACILITIES

More and more workers in the direct-services labor force are young immigrants. Their clients are often white, middle-class, and the oldest-old. Nowhere is this more evident than in long-term care facilities such as assisted living and nursing homes. In some communities, immigrants make up as many as half of the nurses, aides, and housekeeping staff of long-term care facilities. In 2005, foreign-born women had the greatest likelihood of being employed in direct-care jobs, with the highest rates among Latinas (Leutz, 2007). Communication with older clients may suffer because of poor English proficiency among staff, hearing impairments among elders, stereotypes held by each group regarding the other, and in some instances, the elders' verbal abuse of the staff. These facilities are a microcosm of the increasingly diverse American society. When strategically managed, they can also create opportunities for cross-cultural dialog and the celebration of diversity.

to frail elders at home can strengthen bonds in immigrant families. However, as noted above, if adult children are already burdened by financial problems, work demands, and interpersonal conflicts with their other family members, their parents' expectations of caregiving in the home can create psychological distress for them (Moon & Rhee, 2006).

One long-term care option that is gaining popularity among older immigrants and their families is adult day-health centers. Some are located in enclaves of older immigrants from Latin America or Southeast Asian countries or China, so they reach out to these populations by hiring staff who are native speakers of these languages and by offering culturally appropriate programming and meals. One such example, that has been replicated nationally, is the adult day-health program of the El Portal Latino Alzheimer's Project in Los Angeles (Aranda, Villa, Trejo, Ramirez, & Ranney, 2003). Others were started by leaders in these immigrant communities to serve vulnerable

elders who live alone or are left home alone during the day while their adult children work and their grandchildren attend school (Medical News Today, 2009).

Financial Dilemmas Facing Immigrant Elders

Financial self-sufficiency is an important determinant of an elder's social position in the family, whether they are immigrants or native-born Americans. As described in more detail in Chapter 12, in order to receive Social Security benefits, a worker must have been employed at least 10 years (or 40 quarters) in a job that has these benefits. For this reason, many older immigrants seek employment when they first enter the U.S. If they are legal immigrants and work at least 10 years, they can obtain Social Security benefits. As a result, an increasing proportion of older immigrants, especially men, remain employed for the mandatory 10 years, then quit working. Recognizing that less-educated immigrants are unlikely to have personal assets and to depend largely on employment income, it is not surprising that this group is more likely to work than their college-educated counterparts. In 2005:

- 20 percent of older workers were foreign-born and had less than a high school education
- 19 percent were foreign-born and had completed high school
- 11 percent were foreign-born and college graduates (Borjas, 2007)

The poverty rate for older non-citizens is approximately twice that of older U.S. citizens. As a result, they are more likely to rely on government assistance, such as Medicaid and SSI, than their citizen counterparts. For example, 21 percent of immigrants accessed government cash assistance programs in 1994, compared with 4 percent of older adults who were citizens (Nam & Jung, 2008). However, major policy changes took place in 1996 that severely limited non-citizen immigrants' access to these benefits.

Euphemistically labeled "welfare reform," this change enacted by the U.S. Congress placed significant limits on non-citizen immigrants' eligibility for and access to public assistance benefits, including SSI and food stamps. These rules, aimed at reducing the federal government's costs at the time, transferred decisions and responsibility for welfare programs to state and local governments. The immediate and long-term effects of this policy change have been to reduce income security for poor families and older immigrants who were not U.S. citizens when welfare reform was enacted. This problem differentially affects older persons, depending on the state where they reside. In states where budgetary and philosophical attitudes toward welfare programs are negative, immigrants have faced lower benefits, restrictions on eligibility, and time limits. In states such as California, which has the largest number of non-citizen immigrants, the percentage of immigrant households receiving public assistance has declined sharply, particularly given the magnitude of the recession in the state. Many who are eligible have not applied for needed assistance because they think that they are ineligible or that it may result in deportation. Others who could become eligible for Medicaid and SSI by becoming citizens do not seek this status because they do not have the necessary English proficiency to pass the naturalization tests (Angel, 2003; Caro & Morris, 2004; Carroll, 2002; Estes et al., 2006; Gorospe, 2006).

Summary

Population aging is a global phenomenon that is occurring at different rates in developed as well as developing countries, reflecting the demographic transition from high-fertility rural agrarian societies to low-fertility urban industrialized societies. The largest proportions of elders are in industrialized countries, especially in Europe and Japan, where life expectancy and the median age have increased dramatically in the past 20 years.

However, the greatest proportion of older people live in developing countries. A key challenge associated with global aging, intensified by declining birthrates, is that fewer workers are available to support the growing proportion of older people. China is already facing a crisis from its one-child-per-family policy resulting in fewer workers, daughters and daughters-in-law to provide care for its burgeoning population of elders. Many developing countries, focused on the immediate needs of younger populations, have not yet established adequate public policies to address the growth of their older populations. In contrast, many industrialized countries, especially in the European Union, are attempting to implement new retirement policies intended to increase the number of older workers while reducing the burden on their state pension programs. Not surprisingly, these attempts to raise the retirement age are being met with resistance by many workers who had expected to retire with full benefits between age 55 and 64, as in the past. Other industrialized countries are actively recruiting middle-aged adults as employees and offering incentives, such as flexible work schedules, for their existing older workers to continue on the job. On the other hand, more older adults worldwide are realizing that they need to continue to be employed well past age 65 because of the global economic crisis. Japan has implemented a comprehensive long-term care policy and system of care that is being watched closely by other countries.

A basic principle governing the status of older adults is the need to achieve a balance between their contributions to society and the costs of supporting them. The process of modernization and technological development often conflicts with traditions of filial piety. But the family continues to play an essential role in supporting its oldest members in most societies. The extent to which older citizens are engaged in society appears to vary with the nature of their power resources, such as their material possessions, knowledge, and social authority. In most of their exchanges, older people seek to maintain reciprocity and to be active, autonomous agents in the management of their own lives. That is, they prefer to give money, time, caregiving or other resources in exchange for services. This theoretical perspective, described as social exchange theory in Chapter 8, suggests that communities should seek ways to increase older people's exchange resources so that they are valued by society.

Control of resources as a basis for social interactions between members of a society is important throughout the life course. However, it becomes even more crucial in old age, because retirement generally results in a decline in one's level of control over material and social resources. As their physical strength diminishes and their social world correspondingly shrinks, many older people face the challenge of altering their environments and using their capacities in ways that will help them maintain reciprocal exchanges and protect their competence and self-determination. A 2008 review of the Madrid International Plan for Acting on Ageing, which was adopted by the United Nations in 2002, urged action in terms of national policies and practices to promote the health, employment, and human rights of older adults globally. It called for more attention to disease prevention efforts in order to reduce health and economic disparities that are intensified in old age, advocacy on behalf of elders to promote their empowerment and decision-making, positive incentives for working longer, and identifying ways for older adults to contribute to social and economic progress (United Nations 2008).

Such strategies are relevant as well to older immigrants who may still have full physical and cognitive functions but have lost material resources from their homeland that would have given them power and prestige. Older people who immigrate to the United States often do so to be with their adult children and generally help with child care or the family business. Although this may represent a reciprocal exchange, immigration in the later years can also deprive elders of their autonomy and opportunities for active aging. Some experience psychological and physical health problems; others face financial burdens, especially since welfare reform in the mid-1990s placed restrictions on non-citizen immigrants' access to Medicaid. Attempts by elders to maintain control over their environment in the face of changing personal capacities and resources are consistent with the person–environment model presented in Chapter 1. This issue will be discussed in detail in subsequent chapters on biological, psychological, and social changes with aging. The relatively limited information on cross-cultural issues in gerontology suggests a need for more anthropologists, sociologists, and economists to direct their research toward comparing how the aging process and elders are viewed in different cultures and countries and how varied economic systems are adapting to the growth of this population.

GLOSSARY

biculturalism the process of changing one's lifestyle by integrating one's native culture with that of the host country

filial piety a sense of reverence for and deference to elders that encourages care for one's aging family members

modernization theory advances in technology, applied sciences, urbanization, and literacy which, in this context, are related to a decline in the status of older people

skipped generation households often because of economic necessity, the middle generation moves out of the home and grandparents assume responsibility for the day-to-day care of grandchildren

social stratification divisions among people (e.g., by age, ethnic group) for purposes of maintaining distinctions between different strata by the significant characteristics of those strata

REFERENCES

AARP. (2006). Interview with Mr. Tatsuo Honda, Japan's National Institute of Population and Social Security Research. *AARP Global Aging Issues*, 2006. Retrieved April 2009, from http://www.aarp.org/reserach/intl/globalaging/apr_06_newsmaker.html

Angel, J. L. (2003). Devolution and the social welfare of elderly immigrants: Who will bear the burden? *Public Administration Review, 63,* 79–89.

Aranda, M., Villa, V., Trejo, L., Ramirez, R., & Ranney, M. (2003). El Portal Latino Alzheimer's Project: Model program for Latino caregivers of Alzheimer's disease-affected people. *Social Work, 48,* T1.

Asian American Justice Center and Asian Pacific American Legal Center. (2006). *A community of contrasts: Asian and Pacific Islanders in the United States.* Washington, DC.

Baldridge, D. (2001). Indian elders: Family traditions in crisis. *American Behavioral Scientist, 44,* 1515–1527.

Becker, G. (2003). Meanings of place and displacement in three groups of older immigrants. *Journal of Aging Studies, 17,* 129–149.

Bloom, D. & Canning, D. (2007). Demographic change, fiscal sustainability and macroeconomic performance. *Public Policy and Ageing Report, 17,* 18–23.

Borjas, G. J. (2007). *Social security eligibility and the labor supply of elderly immigrants.* Paper presented at 9th annual Joint Conference for the Retirement Research Consortium.

Bosch Management Support. (2004). *Handfeste unterstutzung statt allgemainer Ratschlage-eine feste verbindung auf Zeit, 2.*

Cameron, L. (2000). The residency decision of elderly Indonesians: A nested logit analysis. *Demography, 37,* 17–27.

Caro, F. G. & Morris, R. Devolution and aging policy. *Journal of Aging and Social Policy, 14,* 1.

Carroll, D. (2002). *TANF reauthorization: A California perspective.* Sacramento, CA: California Budget Project.

Cheng, S. T. & Chan, A. C. M. (2006). Filial piety and psychological well-being in well older Chinese. *Journal of Gerontology: Psychological Sciences, 61B,* P262–P269.

Chivers, C. J. (2006). Russians, busy making shrouds, are asked to make babies. *The New York Times,* May 14, p. 4.

Cowgill, D. (1974a). Aging and modernization: A revision of the theory. In J. F. Gubrium (Ed.), *Late life communities and environmental policy.* Springfield, IL: Charles C. Thomas.

Cowgill, D. (1974b). The aging of populations and societies. In F. Eisele (Ed.). *Political consequences of aging. The annals of the American Academy of Political and Social Science, 415,* 1–18.

Cowgill, D. (1986). *Aging around the world.* Belmont, CA: Wadsworth.

Dandekar, K. (1996). *The elderly in India.* Thousand Oaks, CA: Sage.

Darkwa, O. K. & Mazibuko, F. N. M. (2002). Population aging and its impact on elderly welfare in Africa. *International Journal of Aging and Human Development, 54,* 107–123.

Estes, C. L., Goldberg, S., Wellin, C., Linkins, K. W., Shostak, S., & Beard, R. L. (2006). Implications of welfare reform on the elderly: A case study of provider, advocate and consumer perspectives. *Journal of Aging and Social Policy, 18,* 41–63.

European Commission. (2005). *Green paper on demographic change.* Brussels, EU.

Gelfand, D. E. (2003). *Aging and ethnicity: Knowledge and services* (2nd ed.). New York: Springer.

Gerontological Society of America. (2009). Tokyo running short on care facilities. *Gerontology News,* March 9.

Gorospe, E. (2006). Elderly immigrants: Emerging challenge for the U.S. healthcare system. *Internet Journal of Healthcare Administration, 4.*

Gupta, R. & V. K. Pillai. (2002). Elder caregiving in South Asian families: Implications for social services. *Journal of Comparative Family Studies, 33,* 565–576.

Haub, C. (2007). Global aging and the demographic divide. *Public Policy and Aging Report, 17,* 1, 3–6.

Hayutin, A. M. (2007a). Graying of the global population. *Public Policy and Ageing Report, 17,* 12–17.

Hayutin, A. M. (2007b). *How population aging differs across countries.* Stanford Center on Longevity.

He, W. (2001). The older foreign-born population in the United States: 2000. *Current Population Reports.* U.S. Census Bureau, Washington, DC, 23–211.

He, W., Sengupta, M., Velkoff, V., & DeBarros, K. A. (2005). *65+ in the United States: 2005. Current Population Report 23–29.* Washington, DC: U.S. Census Bureau.

He, W., Sengupta, M., Zhang, K., & Guo, P. (2007). Health and healthcare of the older population in urban and rural China: 2000. *International Population Reports, P95/07–2.* Washington, DC: U.S. Census Bureau.

Heywood, J. S. & Siebert, W. S. (2008). *Understanding the market for older workers.* IEA Discussion Paper no. 23. Retrieved 2008, from http://www.iea.org.uk/files/upld-book446pdf?.pdf

Hsu, H. C., Lew-Ting, C. Y., & Wu, S. C. (2001). Age, period, and cohort effects on the attitude toward supporting parents in Taiwan. *The Gerontologist, 41,* 742–750.

Hu, Y. H. (1995). Elderly suicide risk in family context: A critique of the Asian family care model. *Journal of Cross-Cultural Gerontology, 10,* 199–217.

Ikels, C. (1997). Long-term care and the disabled elderly in urban China. In J. Sokolovsky (Ed.). *The cultural context of aging* (3rd ed.). Westport, CT: Bergin and Garvey.

Infeld, D. L. (Ed.). (2002). *Disciplinary approaches to aging: Anthropology of aging* (Vol. 4). New York: Routledge.

Kaneda, T. (2006). *China's concern over population aging and health.* Retrieved October 2006, from http://www.prb.org.

Keith, J. (1990). Age in social and cultural context: Anthropological perspectives. In R. Binstock & L. George (Eds.). *Handbook of aging and the social sciences* (3rd ed.). New York: Academic Press.

Kim, I. K. & Maeda, D. (2001). Comparative study on sociodemographic changes and long-term care needs of the elderly in Japan and South Korea. *Journal of Cross-Cultural Gerontology, 16,* 237–255.

Kinsella, K. & Velkoff, V. A. (2001). *An aging world: 2001.* U.S. Census Bureau Series. Washington, DC: U.S. Government Printing Office, 95/01–1.

Kinsella, K. & Phillips, D. (2005). The challenge of global aging. *Population Bulletin, 60.*

Knodel, J. & Ofstedal, M. B. (2002). Patterns and determinants of living arrangements. In A. I. Hermalin (Ed.). *Well-being of the elderly in Asia: A four-country comparative study.* Ann Arbor: University of Michigan Press.

Lan, P. C. (2002). Subcontracting filial piety. *Journal of Family Issues, 23,* 812–835.

Leutz, W. (2007). *Immigration and the elderly: Foreign-born workers in long-term care.* American Immigration Law Foundation.

Levande, D. I., Herrick, J. M., & Sung, K. T. (2000). Eldercare in the United States and South Korea. *Journal of Family Issues, 21,* 632–651.

Loong, L. H. (2009). Preparing for an aging population: The Singapore experience. *The Journal (AARP),* Winter, 12–17.

Maeda, D. (1998). *Recent policy of long-term care in Japan.* Paper presented at meetings of the American Public Health Association, Washington DC.

Medical News Today. (2009). New Jersey elderly immigrants increasingly using adult day health care centers. Retrieved February 2009, from http://www.medicalnewstoday.com/articles/137406.php

Min, J., Moon, A., & Lubben, J. (2005). Determinants of psychological distress over time among older Korean Americans and non-Hispanic white elders. *Journal of Mental Health and Aging, 9,* 210–222.

Moon, A. & Rhee, S. (2006). Immigrant and refugee elders. In B. Berkman & S. D'Ambruoso (Eds.). *Handbook of social work in health and aging.* New York: Oxford Press.

Morioka-Douglas, N., Sacks, T., & Yeo, G. (2004). Issues in caring for Afghan American elders: Insights from literature and a focus group. *Journal of Cross-Cultural Gerontology, 19,* 27–40.

Mui, A. C. & Kang, S. Y. (2006). Acculturation stress and depression among Asian immigrant elders. *Social Work, 51,* 243–250.

Nam, Y. & Jung, H. J. (2008). Welfare reform and older immigrants' food stamp program participation and food insecurity. *The Gerontologist, 48,* 42–50.

National Center for Health Statistics (NCHS). (2005). *Health United States, 2005, with chartbook on trends in the health of Americans.* Hyattsville, MD: NCHS.

National Institute of Population and Social Security Research. (2004). *Key learning from the 2nd public opinion survey on population issues in Japan.* Retrieved 2004, from http://www.ipss.go.jp/English/pospi_2nd/chosa.html

National Institute of Population and Social Security Research. (2006). *Housing with seniors: 1975–2010.* Retrieved October 2006, from http://www.jinjapan.org/insight/html/focus10/page08.html

Nixon, S. (2002). Looming labour crisis puts the focus on grey force. *Sydney Morning Herald,* October 2.

OECD. (2005). *Ageing and employment policies.* Paris: OECD.

Oldies with muscle. (2008). *The Economist,* 70–71.

Personnelzone Direct. (2004). *SAGA predicts thousands will delay retirement.* Retrieved February 2004, from http://www.personnelzone.com

Population Reference Bureau. (2008a). *2008 World population data sheet.* Washington DC: USAID.

Population Reference Bureau. (2008b). World population highlights. *Population Bulletin, 63.*

Pritchard, C. & Baldwin, D. S. (2002). Elderly suicide rates in Asian and English-speaking countries. *Acta Psychiatrica Scandinavica, 105,* 271–275.

Silverman, P., Hecht, L., & McMillin, J. D. (2000). Modeling life satisfaction among the aged: A comparison of Chinese and Americans. *Journal of Cross-Cultural Gerontology, 15,* 289–305.

Silverstein, M., Cong, Z., & Li, S. (2006). Intergenerational transfers and living arrangements of older people in rural China. *Journal of Gerontology: Social Sciences, 61B,* S256–S266.

Social Security Administration (SSA). (2005). *International update.* SSA Publication No. 13–11712.

Sokolovsky, J. (Ed.). (1997). *The cultural context of aging* (3rd ed.). Westport, CT: Bergin and Garvey.

Strumpf, N. E., Glicksman, A., Goldberg-Glen, R. S., Fox, R. C., & Logue, E. H. (2001). Caregiver and elder experiences of Cambodian, Vietnamese, Soviet Jewish, and Ukrainian refugees. *International Journal of Aging and Human Development, 53,* 233–252.

Sung, K. T. (2000). Respect for elders: Myths and realities in East Asia. *Journal of Aging and Identity, 5,* 197–205.

Sung, K. T. (2001). Family support for the elderly in Korea: Continuity, change, future directions and cross-cultural concerns. *Journal of Aging and Social Policy, 12,* 65–77.

Tabuchi, H. (2009). Japan is paying immigrants to go home and not come back. *The New York Times,* April 26, p. 1.

Taylor, P. (2003). Policy-making towards older workers in the U.K. In H. Buck & B. Dworschak (Eds.), *Ageing and work in Europe.* Stuttgart.

United Nations. (2005). *World Population Prospects.* (Vol. II). Department of Economic and Social Affairs: Population Division.

United Nations. (2007a). *World Population Aging 2007.* Department of Economic and Social Affairs: Population Division.

United Nations. (2007b). *World Population Prospects.* (Vol. IV). Department of Economic and Social Affairs: Population Division.

United Nations. (2007c). *Global summit on grandparents and kinship caregivers.* Retrieved October 2009, from www.un.org/News/briefings/docs/2007/070402_grandparents.doc.htm

United Nations. (2009a). *Opportunities and challenges for an aging world.* AARP United Nations Briefing Series. Retrieved April 2009, from www.aarpinternational.org/2008UNBriefingSeries

United Nations. (2009b). World population to exceed 9 billion by 2050. Retrieved April 2009, from http://www.un.org/esa/population/publications/wpp2008/pressrelease.pdf

United Nations AIDS Programme (UNAIDS). (2000). *HIV/AIDS in Africa: Fact sheet.* Retrieved 2000, from http://www.unaids.org

U.S. Census Bureau. (2006). International Data Base. Retrieved 2006, from www.census.gov/ipc/www/idbnew.html

Van der Geest, S., Mul, A., & Vermeulen, H. (2004). Linkages between migration and the care of frail older people: Observations from Greece, Ghana, and The Netherlands. *Ageing and Society, 24,* 431–450.

Vincentnathan, S. G. & Vincentnathan, L. (1994). Equality and hierarchy in untouchable intergenerational relations and conflict resolutions. *Journal of Cross-Cultural Gerontology, 9,* 1–19.

Von Nordheim, F. (2003). EU policies in support of member states' efforts to retain, reinforce and re-integrate older workers in employment. In H. Buck & B. Dworschak (Eds.). *Ageing and work in Europe.* Stuttgart.

Wagner, J. (2006). German government agrees to first-pillar reform. *Global Action on Aging.* Retrieved October 2006, from http://www.globalagin.org/pension/world/2006/firstpillar.htm

Wilmoth, J. M. (2001). *Social integration of older immigrants in 21st century America.* Syracuse University Policy Brief No. 29. Syracuse, NY: Syracuse University.

Wong, S. T., Yoo, G. J., & Stewart, A. L. (2006). The changing meaning of family support among older Chinese and Korean immigrants. *Journal of Gerontology: Social Sciences, 61B,* S4–S9.

World Health Organization (WHO). (2002). *Active Ageing: A policy framework.* Geneva, Switzerland: WHO.

Wu, B., Tran, T. V., & Amjad, Q. A. (2004). Chronic illnesses and depression among Chinese immigrant elders. *Journal of Gerontological Social Work, 43,* 79–95.

Yee, B. W. K. (1997). The social and cultural context of adaptive aging by Southeast Asian elders. In

J. Sokolovsky (Ed.). *The cultural context of aging* (3rd ed.). Westport, CT: Bergin and Garvey.

Zeng, Y., Liu, Y., & George, L. K. (2003). Gender differentials of the oldest old in China. *Research on Aging, 25,* 65–80.

Zhan, H. J. (2004). Willingness and expectations: Intergenerational differences in attitudes toward filial responsibility in China. *Marriage and Family Review, 36,* 175–200.

Zhan, H. J., Liu, G., Guan, X., & Bai, H. G. (2006). Recent developments in institutional elder care in China: Changing concepts and attitudes. *Journal of Aging Social Policy, 18,* 85–108.

Zhang, H. (2004). Living alone and the rural elderly: Strategy and agency in post-Mao rural China. In C. Ikels (Ed.). *Filial piety: Practice and discourse in contemporary East Asia.* Palo Alto, CA: Stanford University Press.

The Biological and Physiological Context of Social Aging

If we are to understand how older people differ from younger age groups, and why the field of gerontology has evolved as a separate discipline, we must first review the *normal* changes in biological and physiological structures as well as diseases that impair these systems and affect older persons' day-to-day functioning. Part Two provides this necessary background.

• Chapter 3 describes normal changes in major organ systems and how they may influence older adults' abilities to perform activities of daily living and to interact with their social and physical environments. This area of research has received considerable attention as biogerontologists have searched for explanations for the basic processes of aging. Numerous theories have emerged to explain observable changes such as wrinkles, gray hair, stooped shoulders, and slower response time; as well as changes at the cellular and organ level that can only be inferred from tests of physiologic function. These changes include alterations in the heart, lungs, kidneys, and bones, as well as in sensory systems. There are many normal changes in these organ systems that do not imply disease but may slow down the older adult. Furthermore, significant differences in the degree of change experienced have been observed among people and among organ systems within the same person. The effects of genetic factors versus health enhancement behaviors—such as vigorous exercise, nutrition, and an active socially engaged lifestyle—on the extent of physical aging are discussed.

• Chapter 3 highlights some of the exciting new discoveries in biological research that show the potential for modifying cellular processes and using human growth hormones to slow down aging and to increase the proportion of the population that reaches the maximum life span of humans. Some of the current debates surrounding ways to extend cell life and promote cell regeneration are also presented in Chapter 3.

• Age-related changes in the five major senses are also discussed in Chapter 3. Because sensory functions are so critical for our daily interactions with our social and physical environments, and because many of the normal declines observed in sensory systems are a model of changes throughout the body, it is useful to focus on each sensory system and its role in linking individuals with their environments. Recommendations are made for modifying the environment and for interacting effectively with older people who are experiencing significant declines in vision, hearing, taste, smell, touch, and kinesthetic functioning.

• Chapter 4 focuses on secondary aging—diseases of the organ systems described in Chapter 3, and how these diseases can affect active aging. Acute and chronic diseases are differentiated, and the impact of these diseases on the demand for health care, long-term care, and social services among different segments of the older population is presented. For nearly every chronic disease, inequities by gender, race, ethnicity, and social class exist that affect life expectancy, morbidity, and mortality rates. We also discuss HIV-AIDS among older persons and the implications of this disease for long-term care.

• Because automobile accidents among older people often result from psychomotor and vision changes associated with aging, we consider in Chapter 4 methods to reduce auto fatalities through new programs in driver training and through better environmental design.

• Additionally, Chapter 4 provides some striking statistics on older people's utilization of health services, barriers to their use, and recommendations for enhancing culturally competent services. Most existing medical, dental, and mental health services do not adequately address the distinctive needs of the older population, especially those with low income and less education, as well as elders of color and immigrants. As a result, older people who could benefit most from the services often are unable to access them.

• Health promotion and wellness programs have proved successful in maintaining and even improving older people's health in many areas, including exercise, preventing falls and managing osteoporosis and nutrition. Chapter 4 depicts some components of health-promoting programs and the research evidence of their benefits.

Throughout Part Two, the tremendous variations in how people age physically are emphasized. Because of lifestyle, environmental and genetic factors and barriers to adequate care, some people will show dramatic declines in all their organ systems at a relatively early age. Most older people, however, will experience slower rates of decline and at different levels across the organ systems. For example, some people may suffer from chronic heart disease, yet at the same time maintain strong bones and muscle strength. In contrast, others may require medications for painful osteoarthritis, even as their heart and lungs remain in excellent condition.

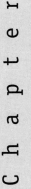

3

The Social Consequences of Physical Aging

Most people define aging in terms of its most visible features—graying or balding, hair, sagging and wrinkled skin, stooped shoulders, and a slower walk or shuffling gait. Although these are the most visible signs of old age among humans, numerous other alterations occur in our internal organs—the heart, lungs, kidneys, stomach, bladder, and central nervous system. These changes are not as easy to detect because they are not visible. In fact, x-rays and computer-assisted images of organ systems are not very useful for showing most changes that take place. It is primarily by measuring the **functional capacity** of these systems (i.e., the performance ability of the heart, lungs, kidneys, and other organs) that their relative efficiency across the life span can be determined.

As noted in Chapter 1, biological aging, or **senescence,** is defined as the normal process of changes over time in the body and its components. It is a gradual process common to all living organisms that eventually affects an individual's functioning vis-à-vis the environment but does not necessarily result in disease or death. It is not, in itself, a disease. But aging and disease are often linked in most people's minds, because declines in organ capacity and our immune system make us more vulnerable to sickness. Because certain diseases such as Alzheimer's, arthritis, and heart conditions have a higher incidence with age, we may erroneously equate age with disease. However, a more accurate conception of the aging process is a gradual accumulation of irreversible functional losses to which the average person tries to accommodate. As discussed in Chapter 1, people can still maintain an active lifestyle as they experience age-related changes in their biological and physiological systems. In order to achieve active aging, individuals may alter their physical and social environments by reducing the demands placed on their remaining functional capacity (e.g., relocating to a one-story home or apartment to avoid stairs, driving only during the day, avoiding crowds). This is consistent with the person–environment model of aging; as their physical competence declines, older people may simplify their physical environment to reestablish homeostasis or their comfort zone. It also suggests their resilience as they cope effectively with changes.

Individual differences are evident in the rate and severity of physical changes. As noted in the introduction to this chapter, not all people show the same degree of change in any given organ system, nor do all the systems decline at the same rate and at the same time. Individual aging depends largely on genetic inheritance, nutrition and diet, physical activity, and environment. Thus, while one 78-year-old feels "old" because of aches and pains due to arthritis but uses her excellent cognitive skills at work every day, another 78-year-old may retain her physical functioning but may live in a nursing home due to advanced dementia. One way of understanding these variations in biological aging is to examine the major theories that have been advanced to explain the changes in all living organisms over time.

Biological Theories of Aging

Popular culture, as reflected in books and magazines, is full of stories about "antiaging therapies," "fighting aging," and "preventing death." The problem with these optimistic projections is that no single scientific theory has yet been able to explain what causes aging and death. Without a clear understanding of this process, it is impossible to prevent, or certainly to stop this normal mechanism of all living organisms.

The process of aging is complex and multidimensional, involving significant loss and decline in some physiological functions and minimal change in others. Scientists have long attempted to find the causes for this process. Some theories posit that aging is a process that is programmed into the genetic structure of each species. Yet genetic heritability within a species accounts for only 35 percent of the variance in life span. More likely it is the rate of damage to DNA and its ability to repair itself that predicts longevity (Rattan & Clark, 2005). Other theories state that aging represents an accumulation of stimuli from the environment that produce stress on the organism. Any theory of aging must be based on the scientific method, using systematic tests of hypotheses and empirical observations. It is generally agreed that in order to be viable, biological theories on aging must meet four criteria:

1. The process must be universal; that is, all members of a species must experience the phenomenon.
2. The process must be deleterious or result in physiological decline.
3. The process must be progressive; that is, losses must be gradual over time.
4. Finally, the losses must be intrinsic; that is, they cannot be corrected by the organism.

These guidelines are useful for excluding biological phenomena that are different from aging per se. For example, they help to distinguish disease from normal aging. While diseases are often deleterious, progressive, and intrinsic, they are not universal (e.g., not all older adults will develop arthritis or Alzheimer's disease). Most biological theories of aging have one of two general orientations: (1) Aging occurs due to random genetic mutations and oxidative stress, or (2) aging is a result of programmed senescence (Bengtson, Gans, Putney, & Silverstein, 2009). Each of the following biological theories meets these criteria for viability. Even though the theories advance our understanding of aging, none of them fully explains what *causes* aging. The theories that will be discussed in this section are based on extensive research with animals and humans.

- Wear and tear
- Cellular aging
- Immunological theory
- Cross-linkage
- Free radical or oxidative stress
- Mitochondrial DNA mutation theory

One of the earliest theories of biological aging, the **wear-and-tear theory,** suggests that, like a machine, the organism simply wears out over time (Wilson, 1974). In this model, aging is a preprogrammed process; that is, each species has a biological clock that determines its maximum life span and the rate at which each organ system will deteriorate. For example, fruit flies (drosophilae) have a natural life span of a few hours, butterflies a few weeks, dogs up to 20 years, and humans about 120 years. This process is compounded by the effects of environmental stress on the organism (e.g., nutritional deficiencies). Cells continually wear out, and existing cells cannot repair damaged components within themselves. This is particularly true in tissues that are located in the striated skeletal and heart muscles and throughout the nervous system; these tissues are composed of cells that cannot undergo cell division. As we will see later, these systems are most likely to experience significant decline in their ability to function effectively with age.

The **cellular aging theory** suggests that aging occurs as cells slow their number of replications.

Hayflick and Moorehead (1961) first reported that cells grown in culture (i.e., in controlled laboratory environments) undergo a finite number of replications, approaching 50 doublings. Cells from older subjects replicate even fewer times, as do cells derived from individuals with progeria and Werner syndrome—both rare genetic anomalies in which aging is accelerated and death may occur by age 15 to 20 in the former and by 40 to 50 in the latter condition. It appears that cells are programmed to follow a biological clock and stop replicating after a given number of times. The number of divisions a normal cell undergoes depends on the specific cell type. Telomeres at the end of chromosomes shorten with each cell division and keep track of the number of divisions it undergoes. Once the telomere shortens to a critical length, the cell stops replicating. In addition, each cell has a given level of DNA that is eventually depleted. This in turn reduces the production of RNA, which is essential for producing enzymes necessary for cellular functioning. Hence, the loss of DNA and subsequent reduction of RNA eventually result in cell death. Although early research suggested that aging at the level of cells could explain aging at the organ level, there is growing evidence that cellular senescence, particularly for T-cells that are critical for immune function, sets the stage for higher-level aging processes (Chang & Harley, 1995; Dagarag, Evazyan, Rao, & Effros, 2004; Effros, 2009a; Hayflick, 2000).

The **immunological theory** of aging makes use of the findings of cellular aging theory in its observations that *replicative senescence* occurs with aging, defined as the declining ability of T cells in aging organisms to replicate. This theory posits that aging is a function of the body's immune system becoming defective over time. The immune system, which serves as an important protective function early in life, becomes less efficient and impaired in making the body resistant to pathogens that attack and interfere with normal functioning. According to this theory, failure of the immune system reduces the organism's ability to fight infections in the later years. This process may be responsible for cardiovascular disease, Alzheimer's disease, cancer, diabetes, and inflammatory diseases that are associated with aging and in many cases may have an immunological etiology (Effros, 2001; 2009a; Walford, 1969). There is evidence that inflammatory exposure early in life can persist throughout adulthood; low-grade chronic inflammation may even predict death late in life (Wikby et al., 2006).

The role of telomeres in explaining the aging process has led to several significant research findings but not a theory of aging. As noted above, **telomeres** are the series of protective DNA structures at the end of human chromosomes. These structures shorten with multiple cell divisions, and as they reach very short lengths, the cell cycle ends. Shortening of telomeres may be a biomarker for declining health status. Researchers have found that people with telomeres in the shortest quartile at age 60 and older were seven to eight times more likely to die of infection compared with elders in the longest telomere quartile. Shortened telomeres are also found to be associated with ulcerative colitis, cirrhosis of the liver, and colon cancer. A study of healthy centenarians (i.e., free of hypertension, heart disease, cancer, stroke, diabetes, and chronic obstructive pulmonary disease) identified significantly longer telomeres than in their peers who had two or more of these conditions (Cawthorn, Smith, O'Brien, Silvatchenko, & Kerber, 2003; Terry, Nolan, Andersen, Perls, & Cawthon, 2008; Effros, 2009b; Rudolph et al., 2000). Recognizing the potential role of telomere shortening on aging and age-related diseases, researchers have focused on ways to maintain the length of telomeres through the enzyme **telomerase.** Early studies introduced a gene with the catalytic component of human telomerase to various cell types. These experiments were successful in stabilizing the length of telomeres, normalizing cell function and replication, and not causing tumor growth. More recent studies tested a chemical telomerase activator on cell function. This intervention also enhanced telomerase

activity, prevented loss of telomeres, and improved antiviral function. These findings offer promise for preventing age-related disease and some forms of cancer, and also for HIV-AIDS immunity (Bodnar, Kim, Effros, & Chiu, 1996; Bodnar et al., 1998; Effros, 2009b).

The *oxidative stress model of aging,* or the **free radical theory,** as it was first proposed (Finch 1990; Hamilton et al., 2000; Harman, 1956, 1993), states that the progressive and irreversible accumulation of oxidative damage to cells explains the age-related loss of physiological function. Oxidative stress occurs when an organism cannot easily detoxify or repair the damage caused by free radicals and other reactive oxygens. These reactive oxygens are formed as a normal by-product of oxygen metabolism. Although people are exposed to oxidative damage from birth, the process accelerates in older adults and leaves them vulnerable to degenerative, age-related diseases. This may occur because of an age-related decline in the organism's antioxidant defenses and repair systems. Antioxidants serve the function of fighting off attacks on DNA by free radicals. These are highly reactive molecules that break off in cells and possess an unpaired electron. They are produced normally by the use of oxygen within the cell but are multiplied by smoking, exposure to ultraviolet radiation, and psychological stress. They interact with other cell molecules and may cause DNA mutations, cross-linking of connective tissue, changes in protein behavior, and other damage. Such reactions continue until one free radical pairs with another or meets an *antioxidant.* The antioxidants are chemical inhibitors that can safely absorb the extra electron and prevent oxygen from combining with susceptible molecules to form free radicals and damage DNA. They are created by cells in the body, but aging results in slower production of antioxidants (Finch, 1990; Thavanati, Kanala, de Dios, & Garza, 2008).

Some researchers have proposed that ingesting antioxidants such as vitamins E and C, beta carotene, and selenium can inhibit free radical damage; this can then slow the aging process by delaying the loss of immune function and reducing the incidence of many diseases associated with aging. However, more research is needed before these implications can be drawn (Aldwin & Gilmer, 2004; Beckman & Ames, 1998; Grune & Davies, 2001).

Nevertheless, it appears that free radicals are not totally destroyed. Those that survive in the organism damage the proteins needed to make cells in the body by interacting with the oxygen used to produce protein. As a result, free radicals may destroy the fragile process of building cells and the DNA strands that transmit messages of genes. Some argue that this continuous pounding by dangerous oxidants wears down the organism over time, not just by interfering with cell-building, but also by requiring antioxidants to be ever-vigilant. This damage to cell tissue by free radicals is implicated in normal aging, as well as in the development of some cancers, cardiovascular disease, Alzheimer's disease, immune system disorders, and cataracts.

Molecular biologists have explored this theory further by splicing genes to measure the cumulative effects of free radicals in cells, with the goal of developing ways to counter the effects. It may be that synthetic antioxidants can be administered to older people as the body's natural supply is depleted. Animal studies show dramatic enhancements of memory and physical activity with high doses of antioxidants. For example, two drugs containing the enzymes superoxide dismutase and catabase (known to have antioxidant properties) are found to extend the life span of worms by more than 50 percent. These drugs may also be effective in reducing the damage caused by strokes or Parkinson's disease (Melov et al., 2000). Until research with higher-level animals supports the promising results emerging from worm studies, it is difficult to predict whether humans will experience similar benefits.

The **mitochondrial DNA mutation theory** of aging offers another perspective on the biological process of aging. There is evidence that mutated forms of mitochondrial DNA (mtDNA) accumulate in the body with aging. However, it is unclear if this is a cause or a byproduct of age-related deterioration and death. The idea of mitochondrial changes playing a role in aging was first proposed by Harman (1972), who suggested that aging is caused by oxygen species that are normal byproducts of cellular function, but attack the mitochondria and thereby damage the cell. Subsequent researchers have hypothesized that aging may be due to errors made during the cell's attempt to repair or replicate damaged DNA in the mitochondria (Khrapko & Vijg, 2008; Vijg, 2007). Evidence for the impact of mutated mtDNA on aging are the accumulations observed in muscle tissue, which undergoes significant loss of mass by age 80, and in parts of the brain where lesions associated with Parkinson's disease are located. But researchers have not yet demonstrated that these DNA deficits are sufficient to cause muscle loss and Parkinson's disease. Some animal studies have increased mtDNA mutation rates and found several symptoms of aging. Others have introduced mtDNA mutations in younger mice; their life spans were not reduced but they showed signs of premature aging. Nevertheless, one cannot assume definitive causal links between mtDNA mutations and the aging process (Campisi & Vijg, 2009; Kujoth et al, 2005; Trifunovic et al, 2004).

It should not be presumed that the step from understanding to reversing the process of aging will be achieved soon. It is often erroneously assumed that scientific discoveries of the *cause* of a particular physiological process or disease can immediately lead to *preventing* or reversing that condition. Unfortunately, that step is a difficult one to make, as evidenced by the challenges in cancer research. Scientists have long observed the structural changes in cancer cells, but the reasons for these changes are far from being understood. Without a clear understanding of *why* a particular biological process takes place, it is impossible to move toward reversing or delaying that process.

Can Aging Be Reversed or Delayed?

Growth Hormones

Genetic researchers have made great strides in the past 30 years in their understanding of the aging process. Indeed, contrary to our long-held assumptions about aging, many scientists are convinced that aging is *reversible*. New research on telomeres is one example of this development. Another approach is the possibility of introducing new hormones into the body to replace the depleted hormones in genes that serve as chemical messengers. Researchers at the National Institute on Aging, Veterans Administration centers, and universities around the country are testing the effects of injecting growth hormones into aging animals and humans. So far, many startling discoveries have occurred, such as increased lean muscle mass and vertebral bone density and reduced fat levels. These changes, in turn, have led to increased activity and vigor. While these effects are short-lived, it may not be long before a human growth hormone is marketed that can safely be administered on a regular basis, like daily doses of vitamins.

Some researchers have tested the effects of the hormone dehydroepiandrosterone, or DHEA, on muscle strength, cardiovascular formation, and bone density. This hormone is secreted by the adrenal glands, and the body converts it into testosterone and estrogen. Production of DHEA increases from age 7 to 30, when it stabilizes, then begins to decline. By age 80, the body has less than 5 percent of the level of DHEA it produced in its peak. Animal studies have shown that administering DHEA to adult mice results in increased activity levels and learning speed. However, research evidence with humans is not sufficient to recommend the regular, long-term use of DHEA. One of the few long-term clinical trials with DHEA gave older men and women supplements for two years. Bone mineral density improved in only one area of several that were measured, while insulin sensitivity, muscle strength, and quality of life showed no gains. The authors recommend physical exercise instead of DHEA to improve these parameters in older adults' well-being (Dhatariya & Nair, 2003; Nair et al., 2006).

Caloric Restriction

Numerous studies using animal models (mice, fruit flies, fish) have demonstrated that reducing caloric intake by 30 to 50 percent increases the life span of experimental animals by as much as 50 percent, because it delays the onset of pathology. Dietary restriction does not, however, include limiting nutrients. Caloric restriction (CR) that is accomplished mostly through reducing fat intake is most successful in extending the life of experimental animals without causing malnutrition. Yet it is evident from these studies that the restriction of fat, protein, or carbohydrate intake alone is not sufficient; total caloric intake must also be reduced. Nor have the same benefits been identified from merely increasing the intake of antioxidants or specific vitamins. The benefits of CR are greatest when it is initiated soon after birth; however, even when mice were placed on such diets in early middle age, their average life span increased by 10 to 20 percent. This does not mean that maximum life span was increased, but that more mice on CR lived longer than their average life expectancy compared to the control group. Other benefits of CR in studies using rodents include slowing the rate of aging, lower levels of cholesterol and fat tissue, higher levels of lean muscle mass as the animal aged, and higher levels of physical performance. In fact, CR

POINTS TO PONDER

How would you feel if your aging process could be reversed? What might happen to society if more people could achieve the maximum life span of 120 years? What are some of the ethical and resource allocation issues raised by scientific efforts to reverse or slow the aging process?

ANTIAGING AS BIG BUSINESS

The promise of extending the human life span beyond the currently accepted 120 years has spawned many new biotech companies, whose primary goal is to find the ultimate "antiaging pill." Numerous biotechnology companies are conducting research on antiaging chemicals. The names of the leading companies in this field reflect their corporate mission and include Elixir, LifeGen, Longevity, and Chronogen.

SOURCE: *The New York Times,* September 21, 2003, Sect. 3, pp. 1, 10.

has even been found to extend the reproductive capacity of female mice (McShane, Wilson, & Wise, 1999; Martini et al., 2008; You, Sonntag, Leng, & Carter, 2007).

Until the results of longitudinal studies with primates are available, these conclusions are not generalizable to humans. The first such major study of CR with primates is ongoing at the Baltimore Longitudinal Studies of the Gerontology Research Center (Ingram et al., 2004; Lane et al., 2002; Messaoudi et al., 2006; Roth, Ingram, & Lane, 2001). This study has examined the effects of feeding rhesus monkeys 30 percent less than their normal caloric intake. After 6 years on this diet, the monkeys showed higher activity levels, lower body temperature, less body fat, lower fasting glucose and insulin levels, and a slower decline in DHEA levels produced by the adrenal glands than an age-matched control group of monkeys that were fed freely, with no CR. Another study of rhesus monkeys also compared a group that was fed a diet of less than 30 percent of their normal intake, enriched with vitamins and minerals, with an age-matched group that was fed 20 percent more than their average intake. These animals were followed from age 6 to 17. During that time, more of the control group monkeys died; additionally, more experienced problems with glucose regulation, progressing to diabetes in two animals. In general, muscle mass declined among the control group animals, starting at age 10. In contrast, CR animals

retained more muscle mass even beyond age 14 as they reached old age (Colman, Beasley, Allison, & Weindruch, 2008).

These results provide the first evidence in primates that CR may delay the aging process by slowing down metabolism, thereby reducing the number of free radicals created in the organism. Lower caloric intake may also maintain the production of adrenal steroids, such as DHEA, without artificially replacing them. CR also reduces the growth of tumors, delays declines in kidney function, decreases the loss of muscle mass, and slows other age-related changes ordinarily found in these animals. It also delays the onset of auto-immune disease, hypertension, Type II diabetes, cataracts, glaucoma, and cancers in these animals; and it appears to improve immune response and wound healing.

In one of the few human studies of CR, 18 middle-aged adults who had reduced their calorie intake for an average of 6 years showed improved cardiovascular function and lower blood pressure, triglycerides, low-density lipids, glucose, and insulin (Fontana et al., 2004). Similarly, a study of 36 adults who restricted their calories by 25 percent for 6 months found significant reductions in cardiovascular disease risk whether CR was combined with aerobic exercise or not (the risk declined 38 percent and 29 percent, respectively). This occurred as a result of its impact on blood pressure and lipid levels (Lefevre et al., 2009). These studies offer evidence that CR may help humans improve their active life expectancy, but further research is needed to determine the relative benefits of lifelong CR versus starting in middle age or later (Holloszy & Fontana, 2007; Masoro, 2001, 2003; Mattison et al., 2003; Miller, 2009).

Antiaging Compounds

Recent studies have found that living organisms produce specific enzymes that can be boosted to survive the damage caused by stressors such as ionizing radiation, and can delay cell death. Although this research has focused on simple organisms such as yeast, fruit flies, and worms (specifically the nematode *Caenorhabditis elegans* or *C. elegans*), the findings provide evidence that cellular enzymes can be boosted by compounds such as *resveratrol* (Howitz et al., 2003). Resveratrol is a type of polyphenol, a chemical that is found in red wine, and seems to be responsible for the preventive benefits observed in red wine against heart disease. In laboratory studies, Howitz and colleagues found that adding these enzyme boosters to yeast cells increased their life span (that is, extended their length of life) by 70 percent. A more recent study by researchers at the National Institute on Aging compared the effects of resveratrol with caloric restriction on age-related changes in mice. They observed a reduction in total cholesterol and reduced inflammation of the heart, better bone health, enhanced balance and motor coordination in both groups of mice, compared with a control group that remained on a high-calorie diet. In this study, the lifespan of mice on resveratrol did not increase significantly (Pearson, et al., 2008). These findings may eventually lead to important discoveries that can slow the aging process in humans, but it will require many more years of research to move beyond single cells and simple organisms to complex mammals.

Researchers with the Baltimore Longitudinal Studies (introduced in Chapter 1) are also searching for a medication that can alter cellular metabolism to mimic the effects of caloric restriction. One such compound is 2-deoxy-D-glucose (2DG), which is found to reduce insulin levels in the blood and slow tumor growth in rodents. This compound causes cells to produce smaller amounts of glucose by-products in the same way as caloric restriction, and in turn slow the formation of free radicals. Research with mice demonstrates significant benefits in reducing blood glucose, body temperature, and damage to nerve cells. However, the NIA researchers have also found that 2DG can have toxic effects in higher doses or when used for prolonged periods. This may limit its application to primates, but these findings may open the door to testing other compounds that can mimic caloric restriction (Lane et al., 2002).

Instead of "antiaging," biogerontologists today are focused on **prolongevity,** or the idea that

> ## PROMISING RESEARCH FOR PROMOTING HEALTHY AGING
>
> Resveratrol, found in the skin of grapes and in red wine, has been offered as a partial explanation for the "French paradox," the puzzling fact that people in France enjoy a high-fat diet yet suffer less heart disease than Americans. Researchers have concluded that resveratrol activates a protein, *sirtuin,* which restores chromosomes in genes, protecting them against the effects of aging and extending the life span, even neutralizing the risks of diabetes from an unhealthy diet. While viewed as a major landmark on the molecular genetics of aging, the findings should not encourage people to think that red wine could reverse the effects of eating badly. In fact, a person would have to drink at least one hundred bottles of red wine a day or take megadoses of resveratrol supplements to reach the levels of the substance given to mice. Scientists at this point caution against taking large doses of resveratrol nutritional supplements until more is known about its effects in humans and its actions on genes. Their goal is to develop a safe and effective form of this product (Bauer et al., 2006; Oberdoerffer et al., 2008).

the length of healthy life can be extended and some diseases associated with aging eliminated. This relates to healthy life span, or the number of years in good health and with quality of life. The concept of prolongevity does not change the fundamental processes of aging, but may provide explanations rather than simply describing the processes of aging (Fishman, Binstock, & Lambrix, 2008; Hayflick, 2004a, 2004b; Kirkland & Peterson, 2009; Miller, 2009; Olshansky, Hayflick, & Carnes, 2002; Tatar, 2009).

Research on Physiological Changes with Age

It is difficult to distinguish normal, age-related changes in many human functions from changes that are secondary to disease or other factors. Until the late 1950s, much of our knowledge about aging came from cross-sectional comparisons of healthy young persons with older adults who had multiple chronic diseases. These comparisons led to the not-surprising conclusion that the organ systems of older persons function less efficiently than those of younger persons.

Since the 1950s, a series of longitudinal studies have been undertaken with healthy younger and middle-aged persons to determine changes in various physiological parameters. The first of these studies began in 1958 at the Gerontology Research Center in Baltimore, as described in Chapter 1 (Shock, 1962). Many of the people in the original sample are still participating. Other researchers around the country are examining physiological functions longitudinally. The information that follows is derived largely from their work.

Aging in Body Composition

In this section, *normal* changes in the human body—both visible and invisible—are reviewed. These include alterations in:

- muscle mass, fat tissue, and water (body composition)
- skin
- hair

CHANGES IN BODY COMPOSITION Although individuals vary greatly in body weight and composition, the proportion of body weight contributed by water generally declines with age for both men and women: on average, from 60 percent to 54 percent in men, and from 52 percent to 46 percent in women (Blumberg, 1996). Lean body mass in muscle tissue is lost, whereas the proportion of fat increases (see Figure 3.1). This decline in muscle mass and increase in fat is known as *sarcopenia*. Because of an increase in fibrous material, muscle tissue loses its elasticity and flexibility. After age 50, the number of muscle fibers steadily decreases; muscle mass typically declines by 40 percent between ages 30 and 80 (Rincon, Muzumdar, & Barzilai, 2006). However, as illustrated by **master athletes,** older people who maintain a vigorous exercise program can prevent a significant loss of muscle tone, as described in Chapter 4. The loss of muscle mass and water and increase in fat tissue all have significant effects on older adults' ability to metabolize many medications, which can lead to adverse reactions such as disorientation, falls, and overmedication. Some drugs are processed by muscle tissue, some in fat, and some in water

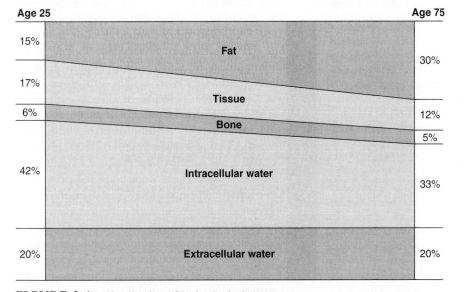

FIGURE 3.1 **Distribution of Major Body Components**

SOURCE: Reprinted with permission from the American Geriatrics Society. R. J. Goldman, Speculations on vascular changes with age. (*Journal of the American Geriatrics Society,* Vol. 18, 1970), p. 766.

throughout the human body. With the changes in body composition described here, these medications may remain in fat tissue longer than needed or may be too concentrated relative to the available water and muscle volume.

These changes in muscle mass, water, and fat are also associated with weight alterations—from increased weight for some people in the middle years, until after age 75 when there is a tendency toward lower weight and lower calorie intake. This is why we rarely see people in their 80s and 90s who are obese, but at the same time it is rare to see older adults with excellent muscle tone. The balance of sodium and potassium also changes, with the ratio of sodium increasing by 20 percent between ages 30 and 70, which has implications for restricting salt intake.

The changes in body composition that we have described have numerous implications for older people's diets; although older adults generally require fewer total calories per day than active younger people, they need to consume a higher proportion of protein, calcium, and vitamin D to offset the depletion of these nutrients and to ensure that they obtain nutrient-rich calories (Blumberg, 1996). However, many older individuals do not change their diet during the later years unless advised specifically by a physician.

LEARNING FROM MASTER ATHLETES

The National Senior Games Association, committed to promoting healthy lifestyles through sports and fitness, involves thousands of participants in the Senior Olympics, a state and national competitive athletics event. Older athletes defy expectations about inevitable physiological decline. For example, an 88-year-old shot-put thrower in the 1999 Senior Olympics claimed that his return to competitive track and field eliminated his migraine headaches. An 86-year-old who played guard for an NFL team in the 1930s broke records for his age group. Whether they have maintained their physical activity levels since youth or begun in middle or old age, older master athletes can teach gerontologists about the effects of healthy lifestyles on biological aging.

Others, especially those living alone, eat poorly balanced meals. This combination of poor nutrition and age-associated changes in body composition are found to be linked to diabetes and cardiovascular disease, because of alterations in carbohydrate metabolism and insulin resistance (Rincon et al., 2006).

CHANGES IN THE SKIN   Changes in the appearance and texture of skin and hair are often the most visible signs of aging. These also tend to have deleterious consequences on how older people view themselves and are perceived by others. The human skin is unique among that of all other mammals in that it is exposed directly to the elements, with no protective fur or feathers to shield it from the direct effects of sunlight. In fact, ultraviolet light from the sun, which damages the elastic fibers beneath the skin's surface, is primarily responsible for the wrinkled, dried, and tougher texture of older people's skin—known as *photoaging* or *extrinsic aging*. Indeed, UV radiation may be the main culprit in skin aging, suggesting the value of protecting the skin throughout the life course. Human skin cells collected from exposed parts of the body grow much more slowly than skin from areas protected from the sun (e.g., underarms). This is evident when one compares the appearance of the skin of two 75-year-olds: one a retired farmer who has worked under the sun most of his life, the other a retired office worker who has spent most of his years indoors. The farmer generally will have more wrinkles, darker pigmentation known as **melanin** (which has been produced by the body to protect it from ultraviolet rays), and drier skin with a leathery texture. He is also more likely to have so-called *age spots* or *liver spots*—harmless from a health standpoint but of concern sometimes for their appearance. As one might expect, people who spend most of their lives in sunny climates are more prone to these changes. Concern about the negative consequences of extensive exposure to the sun is more prevalent today, and people of all ages are taking more precautions, such as wearing sunscreen and UV-protective clothing (Ramirez & Schneider, 2003).

Besides these environmental factors, the human body itself is responsible for some of the changes in the skin with age. The outermost layer of skin, the epidermis, constantly replenishes itself by shedding dead cells and replacing them with new cells. As an individual gets older, the process of cell replacement is slowed, up to 50 percent between ages 30 and 70. More importantly, the connective tissue that makes up the second layer of skin, the *dermis,* thins because the number of dermal cells diminishes and makes it less elastic with age. These changes result in reduced elasticity and thickness of the outer skin layer, longer time required for the skin to spring back into shape, and increased sagging and wrinkling. Sometimes women in their 20s and 30s may experience these problems earlier than men. This is because women tend to have less oil in the sebaceous glands. However, the process of skin aging varies widely, depending on the relative amount of oil in the glands, exposure to the sun, and heredity. Despite its changing appearance, the skin can still perform its protective function throughout old age.

Wound healing is also slower in older persons. Thus, people over age 65 require more time than those under age 35 to form blisters as a means of closing a wound and then to grow new epithelial tissue to replace blistered skin. This is one of the reasons why the bedsores of bed-bound elders can take so long to heal and may prove deadly.

The sebaceous and sweat glands, located in the dermis, generally deteriorate with age. Changes also occur in the deepest, or *subcutaneous,* skin layers, which tend to lose fat and water. The alterations in subcutaneous skin are compounded by a reduction in the skin's blood circulation, which can damage the effectiveness of the skin's temperature-regulating mechanism and make older people more sensitive to hot and cold temperatures. As a result, an older person's comfort zone for ambient temperature is generally three to five degrees warmer than that for a younger person. It also takes longer for an older person to adjust after being exposed to either hot or cold extreme temperatures. This leaves the older individual much more vulnerable to **hypothermia** (low body temperature, sometimes resulting in brain damage and death) and **hyperthermia** (heat stroke), as evidenced by reports of increased accidental deaths among older adults during periods of extremely cold winter weather and prolonged heat spells. For example, the long heat wave in Europe during August, 2003 claimed over 15,000 lives in France alone, most of whom were older people who lacked adequate ventilation in their homes and apartments (In France, nothing gets in the way of vacation, 2003). A similar heat wave in Europe in July, 2006 resulted in a far lower death rate, with only 112 French elders dying. The lower death rate compared to 2003 was attributed to better preparation by the medical community and public service announcements reminding people to stay indoors and drink plenty of water.

To prevent hypothermia, it is recommended that indoor temperatures in older people's homes be set above 68°F during winter months and that humidity be minimized. Some older people who are concerned about conserving energy and money may set their thermostats below 68°F and compensate by layering their clothes to keep warm. As a preventive measure, the Department of Health and Human Services, as well as many local governments, offers funds to help low-income individuals pay for heating costs (NIH, 2006).

CHANGES IN THE HAIR   As we age, the appearance and texture of our hair changes. Hair is thickest in early adulthood and decreases by as much as 20 percent in diameter by age 70. This is why so many older people have fine, limp-looking hair. This change is compounded by the increased loss of hair with age. Although up to 60 strands of hair are lost daily during youth and early adulthood, the hair is replaced regularly through the action of estrogen and testosterone. As we age, however, more hairs are lost than replaced, especially in men. Some men experience rapid hair loss, leading to a receding hairline or even complete baldness by their mid-40s. Some older women also find that their hair thins so much that they cannot hide bald spots. Reasons for the observed variation in hair loss are not clear, but genetic factors appear to play a role.

Gray hair results from pigment loss in the hair follicles. As we age, less pigment is produced at the roots. Eventually, all the hair becomes colorless or white in appearance. The gray color of some people's hair is an intermediate stage of pigment loss. In fact, some people may never experience a total loss of pigment production but will live into an advanced old age with relatively dark hair. Others may experience graying in their 20s. In our society, the graying of hair tends to have more stigma associated with it for women than for men, and women are more likely to tint or color their hair.

Changes in Organ Systems

Although some change occurs with age in all organ systems, this chapter focuses on alterations in the:

- musculoskeletal and kinesthetic system
- respiratory system
- cardiovascular system
- urinary system
- gastrointestinal system
- endocrine system
- nervous system

Solid
bone matrix
Weakened
bone matrix

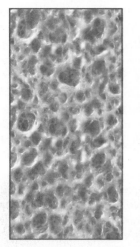 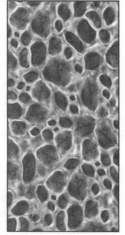

With osteoporosis, both trabecular and cortical bones become more brittle and lace-like.

CHANGES IN THE MUSCULOSKELETAL AND KINESTHETIC SYSTEM   Stature or height declines an average of three inches with age, although the total loss varies across individuals and between men and women. Indeed, the Baltimore Longitudinal Studies found that a gradual reduction in height begins around age 30, averaging one-sixteenth inch per year. We reach our maximum size and strength at about age 25, after which our cells decrease steadily in number and size. This decline occurs in both the trunk and the extremities, and may be attributable to the loss of bone mineral density. This loss is, in turn, is due to a decline in estrogen levels with menopause in women. A decline in testosterone may explain the similar, but less dramatic, loss of bone mineral in older men (Rudman et al., 1991). The spine becomes more curved, and discs in the vertebrae become compacted. This is why older people are sometimes described as literally shrinking. Such loss of height is intensified for individuals with **osteoporosis**, a disease that makes the bones less dense, more porous, and hence more prone to fractures. For older people who have no natural teeth remaining, it is not unusual to lose a considerable volume of bone in the jaw, or alveolar bone. This results in a poor fit of dentures and a painful feeling when chewing or biting with dentures. The loss of bone mass characteristic of osteoporosis is

---

INCONGRUENCE BETWEEN THE ENVIRONMENT AND OLDER ADULTS' MOTOR FUNCTIONING AND BALANCE

Mrs. Gutiérrez, age 83, lives alone and is determined to be as autonomous as possible. Her neighbors watch carefully, however, when she goes out to walk her small dog. She shuffles, moves very slowly, and often has to stop and grab hold of something to avoid falling. When her son and daughter-in-law visit, they shudder when she climbs on a stool to reach a can or bottle on the upper cabinet shelves. Her son has tried to make her home safer by moving the food to lower shelves, putting grab bars in the bathroom, and removing throw rugs. Such changes can accommodate normal age-related changes in her kinesthetic and motor functioning.

not a normal process of aging but a disease that occurs more frequently among older women, as discussed in Chapters 4 and 15.

Another normal change with aging is that shoulder width decreases as a result of bone loss, weakened muscles, and loss of elasticity in the ligaments. This results in reduced range of motion, making it difficult for some older people to reach high cupboards or turn their heads to see cars behind them. Regular exercise to strengthen shoulder muscles can slow such loss of upper-body mobility. Crush fractures of the spine cause the vertebrae to collapse, to such an extent that over time, some older people (especially women) appear to be stoop-shouldered or hunched—a condition known as **kyphosis.** Stiffness in the joints is also characteristic of old age; this occurs because cartilage between the joints wears thin, and fluid that lubricates them decreases. Strength and stamina also decline with aging. Maximum strength at age 70 has been found to be 65 to 85 percent of the maximum capacity of a 25-year-old. This drops to 50 percent by age 80, although older persons who maintain an active physical fitness program show much less decline in strength. Grip strength declines by 50 percent in men between age 30 and 75, and to a lesser degree in women (Frontera et al, 2008; Jansen et al, 2008).

The **kinesthetic system** lets an individual know his or her position in space; adjustments in body position become known through kinesthetic cues. Because of age-related changes in the central nervous system—which controls the kinesthetic mechanism—as well as muscle weakness, diminished vision, and spinal injury, older people demonstrate a decreased ability to orient their bodies in space and to detect externally induced changes in body position. Other physiological and disease-related changes, such as damage to the inner ear, may exacerbate this problem. Older persons need more external cues to orient themselves in space, because they can be incorrect by 5 to 20 degrees in estimating their position compared to younger people. If both visual and surface cues of position are lost, older people experience postural sway or inability to maintain a vertical stance. This is why healthy older adults may complain that "things are spinning."

Not surprisingly, these alterations in motor functioning and in the kinesthetic system result in greater caution among older adults, who then tend to take slower, shuffling, and more deliberate steps. Older people are more likely to seek external spatial cues and supports while walking. As a result, they are less likely to go outside in inclement weather for fear of slipping or falling. Some may complain of dizziness and vertigo. These normal, age-related changes combined with the problems of slower reaction time, muscle weakness, and reduced visual acuity make it far more likely that older people will fall and injure themselves. However, attempts to improve balance through general and aerobic exercise, lifting weights, yoga, and Tai Chi, and systematic programs to increase visual cues are effective in enhancing the postural stability of healthy older persons (Nikolaus & Bach, 2003; Wolf et al., 2003). Other advantages of exercise programs for older adults are discussed in Chapter 4.

CHANGES IN THE SENSE OF TOUCH *Somesthetic,* or touch, sensitivity also deteriorates with age. This is partially due to changes in the skin and to age-related loss in the number of nerve endings. Reduced touch sensitivity is especially prevalent in the fingertips, palms, and lower extremities. Age differences in touch sensitivity of the fingertips are much more dramatic than

POINTS TO PONDER

Look around your own home or your parents' home. What physical factors can you identify that would be a hazard for an 80-year-old woman living there? Think about lighting, stairs, floors, cabinets, and so on. What changes could make the home congruent with an older person's needs?

those in the forearm. Using two-point discrimination tests (i.e., the minimum distance at which the subject detects the two points of a caliper), researchers have found that older persons need two to four times the separation of two points that younger persons do. This has significant implications for daily tasks that require sensitivity of the fingertips, such as selecting medications from a pillbox.

Pain perception is an important aspect of touch sensitivity. Older adults are less able to discriminate among levels of painful stimuli than younger persons. One reason for this may be that nerve cells in the skin become less efficient with age. As a result, burns are often more serious in older people because they do not respond to the heated object or flame until it is too late.

The distinction between pain perception and pain behavior is a critical one. Tolerance for pain is a subjective experience, which may be related to cultural, gender, and personality factors. Increased complaints of pain may be a function of depression and psychosomatic needs in some older people. On the other hand, some individuals may attempt to minimize their pain by not reporting above-threshold levels of unpleasant stimuli. This is consistent with a frequently observed attitude among many older adults that pain, illness, and discomfort are inevitable corollaries of aging and "just something to live with." In fact, most elders probably underreport actual pain experienced. For example, an older person may not report symptoms of a heart attack unless or until it is severe. This has significant implications for health-seeking behaviors, as described in Chapter 4.

CHANGES IN THE RESPIRATORY SYSTEM Almost every organ system shows some decline in functional (or reserve) capacity with age, as illustrated by several physiological indices in Figure 3.2. It is important to keep in mind that this graph is based on *cross-sectional* data collected from healthy men in these age groups;

results from the Baltimore Longitudinal Studies of Aging show more variability when longitudinal data for each cohort are examined. On average, many organ systems show a functional decline of about 1 percent per year after age 30. Complex functions that require the integration of multiple systems experience the most rapid decline. For example, maximum breathing capacity—which requires coordination of the respiratory, nervous, and muscular systems—is greatly reduced. Accordingly, normal changes in the respiratory and cardiovascular system become most evident with age. These changes are responsible for an individual's declining ability to maintain physical activity for long periods and the increasing tendency to fatigue easily. With aging, the muscles that operate the lungs lose elasticity so that respiratory efficiency is reduced. Gradual declines in organ function are caused by increasing rates of cell loss and the inability of tissues to repair themselves with aging, resulting in impaired replication and reserve capacity of the organ. Indeed, this loss of reserve capacity with aging may be responsible for some diseases associated with aging (Hornsby, 2001). Nevertheless, exercise can sometimes slow the loss of reserve capacity.

Vital capacity, or the maximum amount of oxygen that can be brought into the lungs with a deep breath, declines as people age. The average decline for men is estimated to be 50 percent between ages 25 and 70, or a decrease from six quarts of air to three quarts. Breathing may become more difficult after exercise, such as climbing up several flights of stairs, but it does not necessarily impair the older person's daily functions. It may simply mean that the person has to move more slowly or rest on the stairway landing. However, the rate of decline in vital capacity is slower in physically active men than in healthy but sedentary men. A longitudinal study that followed well-trained endurance athletes (average age 62 at baseline) and a control group of sedentary men (average age 61 at baseline) over 8 years suggests that

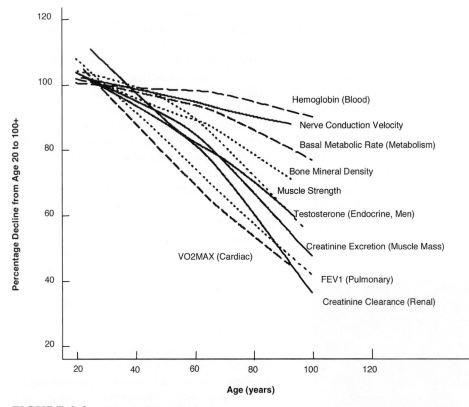

FIGURE 3.2 **Aging in Organ Systems**
SOURCE: Courtesy of Dr. Jeffrey Metter, National Institute on Aging, Baltimore Longitudinal Studies on Aging 2009.

aging per se plays only a small role in the decline of the respiratory system:

- The maximum volume of oxygen declined in master athletes by 5.5 percent
- The maximum volume of oxygen decreased in sedentary men by 12 percent (Rogers et al., 1990)

Of all the organ systems, the respiratory system suffers the most punishment from environmental pollutants and infections. This makes it difficult to distinguish normal, age-related changes from pathological or environmentally induced diseases. Cilia, which are hairlike structures in the airways, are reduced in number and less effective in removing foreign matter, which diminishes the amount of oxygen available. This decline, combined with reduced muscle strength in the chest that impairs cough efficiency, makes older adults more susceptible to chronic bronchitis, emphysema, and pneumonia. Older people can avoid serious loss of lung function by remaining active, pacing their tasks, taking part in activities that do not demand too much exertion, and avoiding strenuous physical activity on days when the air quality is poor.

CARDIOVASCULAR CHANGES AND THE EFFECTS OF EXERCISE
Structural changes in the heart and blood vessels include a reduction in bulk, a replacement of heart muscle with fat, a loss of elastic tissue, and an increase in collagen. Within the muscle fibers, an age pigment composed of fat and protein,

known as *lipofuscin,* may take up 5 to 10 percent of the fiber structure. These changes produce a loss of elasticity in the arteries, weakened vessel walls, and **varicosities,** or an abnormal swelling in veins that are under high pressure (e.g., in the legs). In addition to loss of elasticity, the arterial and vessel walls become increasingly lined with lipids (fats), creating the condition of **atherosclerosis,** which makes it more difficult for blood to be pumped through the vessels and arteries. This buildup of fats and lipids occurs to some extent with normal aging, but it is exacerbated in some individuals whose diet includes large quantities of saturated fats. Such nutritional risk factors for heart disease are reviewed in Chapter 4.

Biking can help maintain respiratory and cardiovascular function.

Blood pressure is expressed as the ratio of **systolic** to **diastolic pressure.** The former refers to the level of blood pressure (in millimeters) during the contraction phase (systole), whereas the latter refers to the stage when the chambers of the heart are filling with blood. For example, a blood pressure of 120/80 indicates that the pressure created by the heart to expel blood can raise a column of mercury 120 millimeters. During diastole, in this example, the pressure produced by blood rushing into the heart chambers can raise a column of mercury 80 millimeters. In normal aging (i.e., no signs of cardiovascular disease), systolic blood pressure increases somewhat, but the diastolic blood pressure does not (see Figure 3.3). Extreme elevation of blood pressure is not normal and is associated with unhealthy diet, obesity, and an inactive lifestyle, all of which have negative cumulative effects over the years. The harmful consequences of abnormally high or low blood pressure are examined in Chapter 4.

Heart rate varies from person to person, remaining relatively high in physically active elders. Resting heart rates also decrease with aging, although physically well-conditioned older people tend to have heart rates more similar to the average younger person.

These changes in the heart and lungs cause them to be less efficient in utilizing oxygen. This, in turn, reduces an individual's capacity to maintain physical activity for long periods. Nevertheless, physical training for older persons can significantly reduce blood pressure and increase their aerobic capacity (Vincent et al., 2002). Studies of master athletes show that physical training results in a greater volume of oxygen, more lean body weight, reduced levels of low density lipoprotein (LDL) cholesterol, also known as "bad cholesterol," and higher levels of high-density lipoprotein (HDL), or good cholesterol, than is found in sedentary older persons. However, these levels in master athletes are worse than in younger athletes, underscoring the reality that normal changes in the body's physiology and their effects on its operation cannot be eliminated completely. For

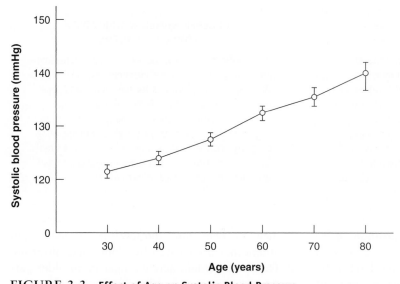

FIGURE 3.3   **Effect of Age on Systolic Blood Pressure**
SOURCE: J. D. Tobin, Physiological indices of aging. In D. Danon, N. W. Shock, and M. Marois (Eds.), *Aging: A challenge in science and society,* Vol. 1 (New York: Oxford University Press, 1981).

example, world-class sprinters are generally in their late teens or early 20s, but marathon runners are normally in their late 20s or early 30s, because strength and neuromuscular coordination peak earlier than stamina. After age 30, running speed declines by a few percent each year (Hayflick, 1996).

Nevertheless, moderate exercise—such as a brisk walk 3 to 4 times per week, yard work, or even housework—appears to slow down these age-related changes. Aerobic capacity, as measured by maximum volume of oxygen intake, is found to increase significantly among older persons after 24 weeks of low-intensity or high-intensity training (e.g., walking vs. jogging for 30 minutes). Both low- and high-intensity exercise resulted in improved aerobic capacity (Vincent et al., 2002). However, high-intensity training can also lead to more **orthopedic injuries** than low-intensity training. For this reason, walking may be the best exercise for improving aerobic capacity in many older adults. It should be noted that exercise by itself may not be

sufficient for reducing LDL cholesterol levels in the blood, which is associated with heart disease. Instead, reduced intake of animal fats, tropical oils, transfats, and refined carbohydrates appears to be essential for lowering these elements in the blood. Although there are limitations, such findings justify optimism that physical health can be considerably improved through lifestyle changes, even after age 65 and well into one's 80s. Aerobic exercise and a healthy lifestyle can significantly

---

HOW TO CALCULATE MAXIMUM ACHIEVABLE HEART RATE

The maximum heart rate achievable by sustained exercise is directly associated with age. An easy way to calculate this is: 220 minus age in years. For example:

- For a 25-year-old, 220 − 25 = 195 beats per minute
- For a 70-year-old, 220 − 70 = 150 beats per minute

AN OLDER ADULT CAN IMPROVE CARDIOVASCULAR FUNCTION

Mrs. Carson had gained weight after retiring at age 66. She was never very interested in exercise. However, a medical checkup at age 68 revealed high LDL and total cholesterol, as well as marginally high blood pressure. She began an exercise program of walking 30 minutes, five times weekly, and cut down her intake of red meat. After 6 months she had lost 10 pounds, her blood lipids were in the normal range, and her blood pressure was 120/70, ideal for a woman her age.

AN OLDER WOMAN WITH BLADDER CONTROL PROBLEMS

Mrs. RedHorse, age 75, has experienced increasing problems with urinary incontinence, especially since she began using diuretics for her high blood pressure. This has forced her to curtail many of her favorite activities, such as her daily walks with her dog, overnight visits to her daughter's home, shopping trips to the mall, and her afternoon tea breaks. She feels frustrated and is too embarrassed to talk with her physician or daughter about this problem.

increase active life expectancy by postponing and shortening the period of morbidity (e.g., days of sickness) that one can expect in the later years. The significance of some lifestyle habits for maintaining good health in old age is discussed further in Chapter 4.

CHANGES IN THE URINARY SYSTEM   Both kidney and bladder functions change with age. The kidneys play an important role in regulating the body's internal chemistry by filtering blood and urine through an extraordinary system of tubes and capillaries, known as glomeruli. As blood passes through these filters, it is cleaned, and the necessary balance of ions and minerals is restored. In the process, urea (e.g., water and waste materials) is collected and passed through the ureter and the bladder, where it is excreted in the form of urine. With age, the kidneys decrease in volume and weight, and the total number of glomeruli correspondingly decreases by 30 percent from age 30 to age 65. The kidneys also lose their capacity to absorb glucose, as well as their concentrating and diluting ability. This contributes to increased problems with dehydration and hyponatremia (i.e., a loss of salt in the blood). Of all organ systems, **renal function**—defined by the rate at which blood is filtered through the kidneys—deteriorates most dramatically with age, irrespective of disease. These changes have significant implications for an older person's tolerance for certain medications

such as penicillin, tetracycline, digoxin, and others that are cleared by glomerular filtration. The drugs remain active longer in an older person's system and may be more potent than in a younger person, indicating a need to reduce drug dosage and frequency of administration.

Compounding this problem, bladder function also deteriorates with age. The capacity of the bladder may be reduced by as much as 50 percent in some older persons. At the same time, however, the sensation of needing to empty the bladder is delayed. The latter condition may be more a function of central nervous system dysfunction than changes in the bladder. As a result, **urinary incontinence** is common in older adults. As many as 30 percent of older people living in the community and at least 50 percent of those in nursing homes suffer from difficulties with bladder control. The problem may be made worse by a stroke, dementia, or other diseases associated with the nervous system, such as Parkinson's (Pringle-Specht, 2005; Thom & Brown, 1998).

Because of changes in the kidney and the bladder, older people may be more sensitive to the effects of alcohol and caffeine. Both of these substances inhibit the production of a hormone that regulates urine production. This hormone, known as antidiuretic hormone (ADH), ordinarily signals to the kidneys when to produce urine in order to keep the body's chemistry balanced. When it is temporarily inhibited by the consumption of alcohol, coffee, or tea, the kidneys no longer receive messages and, as a result, produce urine constantly. This, in turn, dehydrates the body. It appears that ADH production is slowed with aging, so substances that inhibit its production increase the load on the kidneys and the bladder. These changes can force older people to avoid social outings—even a trip to the grocery store—out of fear that they may not have access to a bathroom. Unfortunately, because of the social stigma associated with incontinence, older adults may be reticent about mentioning such problems to their physician or family members. Relatives may be puzzled as to why their previously active elder is now isolating herself. Possible treatments for urinary incontinence, as well as ways that older people can alter their daily habits to accommodate bladder problems, are discussed more fully in Chapter 4.

CHANGES IN THE GASTROINTESTINAL SYSTEM The gastrointestinal system includes the esophagus, stomach, intestines, colon, liver, and biliary tract. Although the esophagus does not show age-related changes in appearance, some functions show alterations. These may include a decrease in the contraction of the muscles and more time for the cardiac sphincter (a valve-like structure that allows food to pass into the stomach) to open, thus taking more time for food to be transmitted to the stomach. The result of these changes may be a sensation of being full before having consumed a complete meal. This, in turn, may reduce the pleasure a person derives from eating and result in inadequate nutrient intake. The sensation also explains why older people may appear to eat such small quantities at mealtimes.

Secretion of digestive juices in the stomach apparently diminishes after age 50, especially among men. As a result, older people are more likely to experience the condition of **atrophic gastritis,** or a chronic inflammation of the stomach lining. Gastric ulcers are more likely to occur in middle age than in old age, but older people are at greater risk for colon and stomach cancer. Because of this risk, older people who

complain of gastrointestinal discomfort should be urged to seek medical attention for the problem, instead of relying on home remedies or over-the-counter medications for heartburn or digestive problems.

As with many other organs in the human body, the small and large intestines decrease in weight after age 40. There are also functional changes in the small intestine, where the number of enzymes is reduced, and simple sugars are absorbed more slowly, resulting in diminished efficiency with age. The smooth muscle content and tone in the wall of the colon also decrease. Anatomical changes in the large intestine are associated with the increased incidence of chronic constipation in older persons.

Behavioral factors are probably more critical than organic causes of constipation, however, as discussed in Chapter 4. Spasms of the lower intestinal tract are an example of the interaction of physiological with behavioral factors. Although they may occur at any age, such spasms are more common among older persons. These spasms are a form of functional disorder—that is, a condition without any organic basis, often due to psychological factors. Many gastrointestinal conditions that afflict older people are unrelated to the anatomical changes described previously. Nevertheless, they are very real problems to older people who experience them. For these reasons, many physicians routinely do a complete checkup, including a colonoscopy, of the gastrointestinal system in their patients age 50 and older, every 2 to 3 years.

The liver also grows smaller with age, by about 20 percent, although this does not appear to have much influence on its functions. However, the ability to process medications that are dependent on liver function does deteriorate. Jaundice occurs more frequently in older people and may be due to changes in the liver or the obstruction of bile in the gall bladder. In addition, high alcohol consumption may put excessive strain on the older person's liver, resulting in the often-deadly disease of cirrhosis of the liver.

CHANGES IN THE ENDOCRINE SYSTEM The endocrine system is made up of cells and tissues that produce a variety of hormones. One of the most obvious age-related changes in the endocrine system is **menopause,** resulting in a reduced production of two important hormones in women—**estrogen** and progesterone. Many other hormones besides estrogen and progesterone also decline with aging. These include testosterone, thyroid, growth hormones, and insulin. Changes in insulin levels with aging may affect the older person's ability to efficiently metabolize **glucose** in the diet, resulting in high blood sugar levels. It is unclear if the changes in hormone production are a cause or an effect of aging. Nevertheless, much of the research aimed at reversing or delaying aging has focused on replacing other hormones whose levels decline with aging. As noted earlier, some support for hormone replacement is found in animal studies; for example, by stimulating the hypothalamus in the brain (which produces growth hormones) of old female rats, researchers activated the development of eggs and increased protein synthesis in these animals. Thyroid hormones administered to old rats have been found to increase the size of the thyroid and the efficiency of their immune systems (Hayflick, 1996).

CHANGES IN THE IMMUNE SYSTEM Many complex changes occur in the immune system with aging. The concept of *immunosenescence* implies that aging results in a significant decline of the immune system, increasing the older person's susceptibility to infectious disease and risk of death. However, recent research findings contradict the prevailing wisdom that the aging process always results in deterioration or immunodeficiency (i.e., an inadequate response to infectious organisms). Studies of centenarians show highly effective immune responses when compared to some young-old persons (Effros, 2001; Solana, 2003). Nevertheless, the fact that most deaths in people age 80 and older are caused by infections implicates failure of the immune system in these cases. This may be because of the lower production and poorer response of

T-cells, B-cells, and lymphocytes with aging. Declines in these critical cells for creating antibodies to infectious organisms are aggravated by a reduction in CD3, CD4, CD8, and CD28 molecules that are critical as a secondary activator signal for T-cells.

The variation across organ systems in cellular composition is noteworthy. Although healthy adults show declines in the production of these cells in blood, T cells in the tonsils and spleen actually *increase* with age. Based on studies of old and young mice, aging appears to cause a qualitative change in immune responses. The quantity of antibody production may be high, but it is activated more slowly and less efficiently in older animals. Age-related changes in some physiological processes—such as a decline in lipid metabolism and pulmonary function, reduced acid secretion in the gut, and delines in sex hormones—may all influence immune function. As noted in the description of biological theories of aging, altered immune function is linked to many age-related illnesses, including prostate and skin cancers as well as cardiovascular disease. More research is needed with long-lived animals such as rhesus monkeys to test interventions against these diseases and pathogens that cause infections in humans (Swain & Nikolich-Zugich, 2009).

CHANGES IN THE NERVOUS SYSTEM The brain is composed of billions of **neurons,** or nerve cells, and billions of glial cells that support these. We lose some of both types of cells as we grow older. Neuronal loss begins at age 30, well before the period termed "old." It is compounded by alcohol consumption, cigarette smoking, and breathing polluted air. The frontal cortex experiences a greater loss of cells than other parts of the brain. A moderate degree of neuronal loss does not create a major decline in brain function, however. In fact, contrary to popular belief and common jokes about neuronal loss, we can function with fewer neurons than we have, so their loss is not the reason for mild forgetfulness in old age. Even in the case of Alzheimer's disease and other

dementias, severe loss of neurons may be less significant than changes in brain tissue, blood flow, and receptor organs (Thomas et al., 1996).

Other aging-related changes in the brain include a reduction in its weight by 10 percent, an accumulation of lipofuscin (i.e., an age pigment composed of fat and protein), and slower transmission of information from one neuron to another. The reduction in brain mass occurs in all species and is probably due to loss of fluids. The gradual buildup of lipofuscin, which has a yellowish color, causes the outer cortex of the brain to take on a yellow-beige color with age. As with the moderate loss of neurons, these changes do not appear to alter brain function in old age. That is, difficulties in solving problems or remembering dates and names cannot be attributed to these slight alterations in the size and appearance of the brain. Indeed, research comparing age-related changes in brain structures of healthy men and women shows that men experience greater loss of cerebrospinal fluid volume, but this does not translate to any greater or less change in memory or learning among men with normal aging (Coffey et al., 1998).

Age-related changes in neurotransmitters and in the structure of the synapse (the junction between any two neurons) are shown to impair cognitive and motor function. Electroencephalograms, or readings of the electrical activity of the brain, demonstrate a slower response in older brains than in the young. These changes may be at least partially responsible for the increase in reaction time with age. The Baltimore Longitudinal Studies of Aging found that reaction time declines by as much as 20 percent between age 20 and 60 (Hayflick, 1996). Neuronal loss and reduced blood flow may slow reaction time. Reaction time is a complex product of multiple factors, primarily the speed of conduction and motor function, both of which are slowed by the increased time needed to transmit messages at the synapses.

The reduced speed with which the nervous system can process information or send signals for action is a fairly widespread concern, even in middle age when people begin to notice lagging reflexes and reaction time. As a result, such tasks as responding to a telephone or doorbell, crossing the street, completing a paper-and-pencil test, or deciding among several alternatives generally take longer for older people than for the young. Most people adjust to these changes by creatively modifying their physical environment or personal habits, such as allowing more time to do a task and avoiding rush situations; for example:

- leaving the house one hour before an appointment instead of the usual 15 minutes
- shopping for groceries in smaller stores and when they are not crowded
- avoiding freeway driving

Such person–environment adaptations are perhaps most pronounced in the tasks associated with driving. The older driver tends to be more cautious, to slow down well in advance of a traffic signal, to stay in the slower lane, and to avoid driving during rush hour. Despite this increased caution, accident rates are high among older drivers, as discussed in the next chapter.

Changes in the central nervous system that accompany aging also affect the senses of hearing, taste, smell, and touch. Despite these alterations, intellectual and motor function does not appear to deteriorate significantly with age. The brain has tremendous reserve capacity that takes over as losses begin. It is only when neuronal loss, inadequate function of neurotransmitters, and other structural changes are severe that the older person experiences significant loss of function. The changes in the brain that appear to be associated with dementia are discussed in Chapter 6.

Changes in Sleep Patterns with Aging

Older people often complain that they can no longer sleep well, with up to 40 percent in community surveys complaining of sleep problems. These complaints have a basis in biological changes that occur with aging. Results of laboratory studies of sleep-wake patterns of adults

TIPS FOR IMPROVING SLEEP

Sleep disturbances can be alleviated by improving one's **sleep hygiene.** These include:

- increasing physical exercise during the day
- increasing exposure to natural light during the day
- reducing the intake of caffeine and other stimulants
- avoiding napping during the day
- improving the sleeping environment (e.g., a quieter bedroom with heavy curtains to block out the light, because exposure to light can change circadian rhythms) (Vitiello, 1996)

have consistently revealed normal age-related changes in electroencephalogram (EEG) patterns, sleep stages, total sleep time, and sleep efficiency, with a longer time to fall asleep (latency) and increasing episodes of waking at night (Lesage & Scharf, 2007; Ohayon et al., 2004; Vitiello, Larsen, & Moe, 2004). Sleep progresses over five stages:

- non-REM sleep; i.e., no rapid eye movements during sleep (stages 1–4)
- REM (rapid eye movement) sleep (stage 5)

Sleep stages occur in a linear pattern from stage 1 through stage 4, then REM sleep in stage 5. Stage 4 is when deep sleep takes place. Each cycle is repeated four or five times through the night. Brain wave activity differs in a characteristic pattern for each stage.

Many of these brain waves slow down with aging, and the length of time in each stage changes. In particular, comparisons of studies across the life span reveal increased time in stages 1 and 2, when sleep is lighter. Time spent in REM sleep declines and occurs earlier in the cycle. During these stages, older people—more so than the young—are easily awakened, often by environmental stimuli, such as a honking horn or a train passing by, that might not disturb a younger person (Ohayon et al., 2004).

Changes in circadian rhythms, or the individual's cycle of sleeping and waking within a 24-hour period, are characterized by a movement from a two-phase pattern of sleep (awake during the day, asleep during the night) to a multiphasic rhythm that is more common in infants—daytime napping and shorter sleep cycles at night. These changes may be associated with alterations in core body temperatures in older people, discussed earlier in this chapter.

When older persons compensate by taking more daytime naps, night sleep can be further disrupted. Most often, older people who report sleep disturbances to their primary physician are prescribed sleeping pills (sedative-hypnotic medications); this age group represents the highest users of such medications, receiving almost one-half of all sedative-hypnotic drugs prescribed. Yet medications do not necessarily improve their sleep patterns, especially if used long term (Vitiello, 2000). Many hypnotics, if used for a long time to treat sleep disorders, can instead produce a paradoxical effect by resulting in insomnia.

A true sleep disturbance is one that interferes with daytime activities. Researchers who have examined older people with sleep complaints have found that chronic diseases, depression, anxiety, limited mobility, alcohol and prescription drug use are more likely to cause disturbed sleep in this population than aging per se. These conditions are more common among nursing home residents and may explain why sleep disorders occur more often in this population (Lesage & Scharf, 2007; Ohayon, 2004). In a study of community-dwelling older adults, only 3.2 percent in one group and 1.4 in another could be classified as experiencing a significant sleep disorder, after excluding all persons who had medical or psychiatric conditions that could affect sleep (Vitiello, Moe, & Prinz, 2002). A larger study of almost 12,000 people (ages 15 and older) in Canada found that increased age was not significantly related to insomnia, but life stress, smoking, low education and income, multiple health problems, and activity limitations were all associated with insomnia at any age (Sutton, Moldofsky, and Badley, 2001). However, some true *disorders of sleep* can occur with aging. These include respiratory problems such as **sleep apnea** (defined as a 5- to 10-second cessation of breathing) and *nocturnal myoclonus,* or **periodic limb movement disorder (PLMD),** a neuromuscular disturbance affecting the legs during sleep. Generally, these conditions are treated with medications, although behavior training to modify sleeping position, weight loss, and devices to improve breathing are useful for sleep apnea.

Sleep disturbance in older persons with dementia is not uncommon and can disrupt both the elder's and caregiver's quality of life. This often leads to premature nursing home placement of elders with dementia. For these reasons, many families seek medical help for their relative's insomnia, resulting in the use of sedative-hypnotic medications that may further aggravate the elder's sleep disturbance. Medications should not be the treatment of first choice for this population. Instead, nonpharmacological therapies, along with behavioral and environmental interventions (e.g., preventing daytime napping, keeping the elder physically active during the day), should be used to treat sleep problems in dementia patients. One study tested the impact of nonpharmacological interventions with nursing home residents. This included increased exposure to outdoor light and physical activity during the day, establishing a bedtime routine, and reducing light and noise in residents' rooms at night. Even after adjusting for cognitive impairment, medical conditions, behavioral problems, and age, the researchers found that nursing home residents whose sleep hygiene had improved also showed better rest/activity rhythms compared to elders who maintained their usual sleep habits (Martin, Mailer, Harker, Josephson, & Alessi, 2007; McCurry et al., 2000; Vitiello & Borson, 2001).

In general, sleep disorders in older persons should be treated because they can increase the risk of stroke, myocardial infarction, and even death. In a large study of community-dwelling older adults, daytime sleepiness was associated with increased death rates in men and women (1.40 times the rate for men with normal sleep and 2.12 times the rate for women). Frequent or early morning awakenings, however, had no discernible effect on mortality (Newman et al., 2000). Among nursing home residents, excess daytime sleep is associated with lower survival rates (Endeshaw, Ouslander, Schnelle, & Bliwise, 2007). Poor sleep quality increases the risk of falls among older adults in residential care facilities. In one study, elders who reported sleep disturbance were 3.2 times more likely to have fallen in the past year, while those who awoke two times or more per night were 50 percent more likely to have fallen. This high risk of falls was unrelated to using walking aids or having poor vision (Hill et al., 2007).

Changes in Sensory Functions

Our ability to see, hear, touch, taste, and smell has a profound influence on our interactions with our social and physical environments and on quality of life. Given this importance and the gradual decline in our sensory abilities with aging, it is critical that we understand these changes and how they can influence our competence level as we age. A popular belief is that, as we get older, we cannot see, hear, touch, taste, or smell as well as we did when we were younger. This appears to be true. The decline in all our sensory receptors with aging is normal; in fact, it begins relatively early. We reach our optimum capacities in our 20s, maintain this peak for a few years, and gradually experience a decline, with a more rapid rate of deterioration after the ages of 45 to 55. Having said this, we should note that there is tremendous diversity among individuals in the rate and severity of sensory decline. Some older persons may have better visual acuity than most 25-year-olds; many 75-year-olds can hear better than most younger persons; and many elders have a more intense

POINTS TO PONDER

Think about the wine taster who, in old age, may still be considered the master of his trade, performing a job that requires excellent taste discrimination. Perfume developers also attain their expertise over many years. What other jobs require intrinsic sensory abilities as well as skills that take years to master?

sense of smell than their younger counterparts. Although age per se does not determine deterioration in sensory functioning, it is clear that many internal changes do occur. The older person who has better visual or hearing acuity than a 25-year-old probably had even better sensory capacities in the earlier years. When studying sensory and perceptual functions, it is important to focus on *intraindividual* changes with age, not *interindividual* differences. Unfortunately, most of the research on sensory changes with age is cross-sectional—that is, it is based on comparing older and younger persons, so that only age differences, not changes, can be obtained.

DISTINCTIONS IN TERMINOLOGY RELATED TO SENSORY FUNCTIONS

- *Sensation* is the process of taking in information through the sense organs.
- *Perception* is a higher function in which the information received through the senses is processed in the brain.
- *Sensory threshold* is the minimum intensity of a stimulus that a person requires in order to detect the stimulus. This differs for each sensory system.
- *Recognition threshold* is the intensity of a stimulus needed in order for an individual to identify or recognize it. As might be expected, a greater intensity of a stimulus is necessary to recognize than to detect it.
- *Sensory discrimination* is defined as the minimum difference necessary between two or more stimuli in order for a person to distinguish between them.

Some sensory functions, such as hearing, may show an early decline, yet others, such as taste and touch, change little until well into advanced old age. Over time, however, sensory decrements affect an older person's social functions. Because these alterations are usually gradual, people adapt and compensate by using other, still-intact sensory systems. For example, they may draw upon the following person–environment compensation strategies to maintain their level of competence by:

- standing closer to objects and persons in order to hear or see
- using nonverbal cues such as touch and different body orientations
- utilizing external devices such as bifocals or hearing aids
- reducing the level of excessive stimulation in their environment, such as moving to a quieter table in a restaurant

To the extent that people can alter their environment to conform to their changing needs, sensory decline need not be incapacitating. It becomes more difficult for individuals to use compensatory mechanisms if the environment does not allow for modification to suit individual needs, if the decline in any one system is severe, or if several sensory systems deteriorate at the same time. Such multiple problems are more likely to occur in advanced old age. This is because, with normal aging, sensory and recognition thresholds increase, and the individual needs a higher level of the stimulus and greater distinctions between multiple stimuli in order to distinguish between them.

Changes in Vision

Vision impairments increase with age. When 55- to 64-year-olds are compared with those over age 85, the prevalence of visual problems increases fourfold from 55 per 1,000 people to 225 per 1,000. As a result, older adults are more likely to be challenged by daily tasks that require good visual skills, such as reading small print or signs on moving vehicles, threading a needle, or adapting to sudden changes in light level when entering a dark room after being out in the sun. In addition, visual impairments can cause significant problems with activities of daily living, increase the risk of falls and fractures, and result in depression. Along with eye charts, a widely used assessment tool is the Functional Vision Screening Questionnaire (Aldwin & Gilmer, 2004; Desai et al., 2001; Stuen, 2006).

EFFECTS OF STRUCTURAL CHANGES IN THE EYE   Most age-related impairments in vision are attributable to changes in parts of the eye (see Figure 3.4). However, these problems are aggravated by alterations in the central nervous system that block the transmission of stimuli from the sensory organs. Changes in the visual pathways of the brain and in the visual cortex may be a possible source of some of the alterations in visual sensation and perception with age. The parts of the eye that show the greatest age-related modifications are:

- the cornea
- the pupil
- rods and cones in the retina
- the lens

The cornea is usually the first part of the eye to be affected by age-related changes. The surface of the cornea thickens with aging, and the blood vessels become more prominent. The smooth, rounded surface of the cornea becomes flatter and less smooth, and may take on an irregular shape. The older person's eye appears to lose its luster and is less translucent than it was in youth. In some cases, a fatty yellow ring, known as the *arcus senilis*, may form around the cornea. But this is not a sign of impending vision loss and has no impact on vision.

At its optimal functioning, the pupil is sensitive to light levels in the environment, widening in response to low-light levels and contracting when light levels are high. With aging, the pupil appears to become smaller and more fixed in size. The opening of the pupil is reduced in old age, commonly to about two-thirds its original maximum. That is, the older person's pupil is less able to respond to low light levels by dilating or opening to the extent needed. The eye also responds more slowly to alterations in light conditions. This problem is compounded by a slower shift from cones to rods under low-light conditions. As a result, older individuals may have considerable difficulty functioning in low-light situations

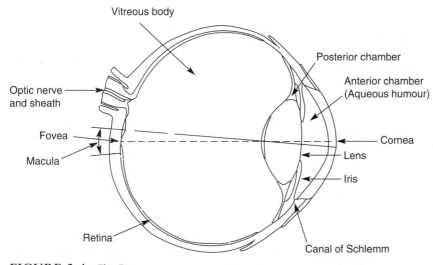

FIGURE 3.4   **The Eye**

PROBLEMS WITH RESTAURANT ENVIRONMENTS

Many older people may feel frustrated when they go to a special restaurant for an evening dinner, only to find that the tables are lit by candles. This makes it difficult to read the menu, to see the way to the table, and even to have eye contact with companions. Family and friends may be frustrated in such situations if they do not understand that the older person's complaints about the restaurant stem from these changes in vision, not from a lack of appreciation for their efforts. Some older people cope with these problems by avoiding such restaurants altogether or going there only during daylight hours.

It is important for restaurant owners to provide good lighting at each table and write their menus in large, legible print against a white background. In response to the growing number of baby boomers who are experiencing problems of visual accommodation, some restaurants have begun to stock reading glasses with different levels of magnification to lend to their customers!

or adjusting to significant changes in ambient light. In fact, older people may need three times more light than younger persons to function effectively; for example, highway signs must be 65 to 75 percent closer than for younger drivers to be readable at night. Illumination levels also affect older people's ability to read text written in small font (such as a menu with less than 12-point font in a dimly lit restaurant) and with low contrast between text and background. When 80-year-olds were compared with 30-year-olds, low levels of illumination (10-lux*) caused the former to make twice as many errors as the latter, even with high contrast between figure and ground. However, at the highest illumination levels (1,000-lux), older adults benefited from high contrast and performed as well as young adults. Unfortunately, most homes and offices do not provide such high lighting levels (Fozard & Gordon-Salant, 2001).

*Lux is a unit of measurement for illumination, referring to the amount of light received by a surface at a distance of one meter from a light source.

These changes may also reduce the older person's ability to discern images in conditions of poor light contrast (e.g., driving at twilight or under foggy or rainy conditions) and to detect details in moving objects. Even among healthy older persons who are still driving, age-related visual changes may significantly alter their abilities under marginal conditions. For these reasons, older people may choose to avoid such activities, especially driving among fast-moving traffic on freeways at night when bright headlights create glare against asphalt surfaces, and driving in rain. Although this is a safe method of coping with age-related difficulties in low-light situations, it can restrict the older person's social activities. In such instances, families and professionals may have to encourage older people to use other forms of transportation, such as buses, light rail and taxis, thereby avoiding the problem of too little environmental stimulation relative to the person's competence. More often, however, older people want to keep driving as long as possible, even when they experience such difficulties, because driving is linked with autonomy and control in their daily lives (Horowitz & Higgins, 2000).

PROBLEMS RELATED TO OXYGEN AND FLUID LEVELS
Problems in rod and cone function may be related to a reduced supply of oxygen to the retina. This may be due to a deficiency of vitamin A. However, there is little research evidence to suggest that increased intake of vitamin A in old age can improve visual functioning under low-light conditions.

Two fluid-filled chambers are in the eye: *aqueous humour* fills the anterior, or front portion of the eye, and *vitreous humour* is found in the posterior chamber, behind the lens. The aqueous humour drains through the canal of Schlemm. In the disease state known as **glaucoma,** drainage is less efficient, or excess production of the aqueous humour occurs and causes pressure on the optic nerve. Glaucoma is not a normal part of aging, but it increases in frequency with age and can be managed with a daily routine of medications if it is caught early. Unfortunately, it is an insidious disease that progresses slowly and may not be detected until it is more advanced. More severe cases may require surgery or, more recently, laser treatment. In its later stages, glaucoma may result in tunnel vision, which is a gradual narrowing of an individual's field of vision, such that peripheral vision is lost and the individual can focus only in the center, affecting elders' safe mobility. Untreated glaucoma is the second leading cause of blindness in the U.S. and the primary cause of blindness among African Americans. It is more prevalent and more difficult to treat in African Americans, with rates of 15 percent compared to 7 percent in whites age 70 and older (Braille Institute, 2004; Desai et al., 2001; Stuen, 2006).

EFFECTS OF AGING ON THE LENS   Perhaps the greatest age-related changes in the eye occur in the lens. In fact, the lens is a model system for studying aging because it contains some of the oldest cells in the body, formed during the earliest stages of the embryo's development. Furthermore, the lens is a relatively simple structure biochemically; all of its cells are of the same type and are composed of protein.

Collagen is the primary protein in the lens and thickens and hardens with age. This change

in collagen makes the lens less elastic, thereby reducing its ability to alter its shape (i.e., from rounded to elongated and flat) as it focuses from near to far. Muscles that help stretch the lens also deteriorate with age, thereby compounding the problem of changing the shape of the lens. This process, known as **accommodation,** begins to deteriorate in middle age and is manifested in increasing problems with close vision. By the time many people reach their 40s and 50s, they need to hold their reading material at arm's length and often turn to reading glasses or bifocals.

By age 60, accommodative ability is significantly deteriorated. Decrements in accommodation may cause difficulties for the older person when shifting from near to far vision; for example, looking across a room, walking up or down stairs, reading and glancing up, and writing notes while looking up at a blackboard or a lecturer. The hardening of the lens due to changes in collagen tissue does not occur uniformly. Rather, there is differential hardening, with some surfaces allowing more light to enter than others. This results in uneven refraction of light through the lens and onto the retina. When combined with the poor refraction of light through the uneven, flattened surface of the cornea, extreme sensitivity to glare often results. This problem becomes particularly acute in environments with a single source of light aimed at a shiny surface—such as a large window at the end of a long, dark corridor with highly polished floors; streetlights on a rain-slicked highway; or a bright, single, overhead incandescent light shining on a linoleum floor. These conditions may contribute to older people's greater caution and anxiety while driving or walking.

From childhood through early adulthood, the lens is a transparent system through which light can easily enter. With normal aging, the lens becomes more opaque, and less light passes through it (especially shorter wavelengths of light). These changes compound the problems of poor vision in low light that were described earlier. Some older persons experience a more severe opacification (clouding of the lens), to

---

SUGGESTIONS FOR IMPROVING PERSON–ENVIRONMENT FIT FOR PEOPLE EXPERIENCING VISION CHANGES

- Use widely contrasting colors on opposite ends of the color spectrum, such as red and yellow, green and orange.
- Clearly define edges and corners—such as stairs, walls, and doors—with color or texture.
- Avoid using blue and green together to define adjoining spaces such as stairs and stair landings, floors and ramps, and curbs and curb cuts, especially where the junction represents different levels.
- Avoid shiny floor and wall surfaces that can cause glare.
- Avoid placing a single, large window at the end of a long, dark corridor.

the point that the lens prevents light from entering. This disease condition, known as an **age-related cataract (ARC),** is the fourth leading cause of blindness in the U.S. and the primary basis for blindness worldwide (Asbell et al., 2005; Braille Institute, 2004). Symptoms of ARC include:

- cloudy or fuzzy vision
- double vision
- problems with glare from bright light
- problems with color discrimination

Researchers in the Framingham eye study examined the development of ARC in the same individuals over a number of years. In a reexamination of survivors almost 14 years later, the incidence rate was 50 percent for people who were age 55 to 59 at the beginning of the study. It jumped to 80 percent for older adults who had been age 70 to 74 at the start (Milton & Sperduto, 1991). In other words, the prevalence of ARC increases tenfold between ages 52 and 85. There is strong evidence for a relationship between the development of cataracts with age combined with the lack of antioxidants (such as vitamins A, C, and E) and oxidative damage to the lens. Both the frequency and amount of alcohol consumed are associated with the development of ARC, as are a history of gout, excess exposure to sunlight, and use of steroids (Asbell et al., 2005; Robman & Taylor, 2005; Stuen, 2006; Truscott, 2005; Zubenco, Zubenco, Maher, & Wolf, 2007).

A cataract may occur in any part of the lens—in the center, the peripheral regions, or scattered throughout. If the lens becomes totally opaque, cataract surgery may be required to extract the lens. It carries relatively little risk, even for very old persons, and can significantly enhance quality of life. Indeed, this is the most frequent outpatient surgical procedure performed on people over age 65. A lens implant in place of the extracted lens capsule is the most common treatment. Almost 50 percent of people 85 years and older in a U.S. survey reported that they had

undergone cataract surgery, compared with about 20 percent at age 70 to 74. Older women were more likely to report cataract surgery than their male counterparts (Desai et al., 2001). When the older person first obtains a replacement lens, it takes some time to adjust to performing daily activities. Patients who receive a lens implant show improvement not just in visual function, but also in objective assessments of activities of daily living and manual function within a few months.

In addition to getting harder and more opaque, the lens becomes more yellow with age, especially after age 60. The increasingly more opaque and yellowing lens acts as a filter to screen out wavelengths of light, thus reducing the individual's color sensitivity and ability to discriminate among colors that are close together in the blue-green range. Older people may have problems selecting clothing in this color range, sometimes resulting in poorly coordinated outfits. Deterioration in color discrimination may also be due to age-related changes in the visual and neural pathways.

OTHER CHANGES IN VISION *Depth and distance perception* also deteriorate with aging, because of a loss of convergence of images formed in the two eyes. This is caused by differential rates of hardening and opacification in the two lenses, uneven refraction of light onto the retina, and reduced visual acuity in aging eyes. As a result, the ability to judge distances and depths declines rapidly after age 75, particularly in low-light situations and in the absence of orienting cues, such as stairs with no color distinctions at the edges and pedestrian ramps or curb cuts with varying slopes. Narrower peripheral vision (the ability to see on either side without moving the eyes or the head) is another age-related change. Since our peripheral vision makes us aware of approaching objects, older adults can be startled when a car, bicycle or other fast-moving object seems to appear suddenly out of nowhere. This problem becomes particularly acute when driving; for example, an older person may not see cars approaching from the left or right at an intersection or in a passing situation.

Some older persons experiencing **age-related macular degeneration (AMD)** lose acuity in the center of their visual field. The macula is that point in the retina with the best visual acuity, especially for seeing fine detail. Macular degeneration is the leading cause of blindness in adults in the U.S. (Braille Institute, 2004). It occurs if the macula receives less oxygen than it needs, resulting in destruction of the existing nerve endings. The incidence of macular degeneration grows with age, even more dramatically than cataracts. Rates of AMD increase significantly with age, from 18 percent among those age 70 to 74, to 47 percent among people 85 and older (Desai et al., 2001). The condition is more common in older women and in white elders than in men and African Americans. There is evidence for both a genetic basis and environmental risk factors for AMD, such as long-term exposure to UV light, smoking, and lack of antioxidants. Researchers are searching for the specific genes responsible for AMD, with the goal of developing early detection and prevention programs. By studying a large family with a history of AMD, geneticists have identified *Hemicentin-1* as the gene where a mutation occurs in people with AMD. Future research will lead to animal models where the mutation can be created and treated, with the eventual goal of modifying the gene in humans before it manifests as AMD

(Schultz et al., 2003). Studies that have supplemented older people's diets with carotenoid-rich foods or used zinc supplements have found positive effects on visual activity of AMD patients, but no cure for AMD currently exists (Allikmets et al., 1997; Stuen, 2006).

The early stages of macular degeneration typically begin with a loss of detail vision; then central vision gradually becomes worse. Total blindness rarely occurs, but reading and driving may become impossible. Older persons with this condition may compensate by using their remaining peripheral vision. They may then appear to be looking at the shoulder of someone they are addressing while actually relying on peripheral vision to see the person's face. Laser treatment in the early stages of this disease is effective, but it carries a risk of burning away the center of the retina entirely. A new form of therapy combines a light-activated drug treatment (Visudyne) with a low-power laser light to activate the drug. This procedure is effective in destroying the abnormal blood vessels and scar tissue in the eye without damaging the retina. Although macular degeneration cannot be cured, this treatment can slow retinal damage and improve central vision.

Some older people, most often postmenopausal women, experience reduced secretion of tears. They may complain of "dry eyes" that cause irritation and discomfort. Unfortunately, this condition has no known cure, but it does not cause blindness and can be managed with artificial tears to prevent redness and irritation.

The muscles that support the eyes—similar to muscles in other parts of the body—deteriorate with age. In particular, two key muscles atrophy. These are the elevator muscles, which move the eyeball up and down within its socket, and the ciliary muscle, which aids the lens in changing its shape. Deterioration of the elevator muscles results in a reduced range of upward gaze. This may cause problems with reading overhead signs and seeing objects that are placed above eye level, such as on high kitchen shelves.

Assisting Adaptation and Active Aging Through Environmental Modifications

As suggested above, many older adults as a result of vision changes report modest impairments in their activities of daily living, including reading small print, adjusting to dimly lit environments, tracking moving targets, and locating a sign in a cluttered background. Family and friends can help by improving the physical environment in ways, such as replacing existing lightbulbs with higher wattage, installing fluorescent lighting with color correction and three-way bulbs, moving low tables and footstools outside the traffic flow, and putting large-print labels on prescription bottles, spices, and cooking supplies. Older people can also benefit from:

- large-print newspapers and books
- audiotapes of books that are available in community libraries and bookstores
- playing cards with large letters
- larger fonts on flat-screen computer monitors that are designed to reduce glare
- voice-activated computer software

Local agencies serving the visually impaired often provide relatively low-tech, low-vision aids at minimal cost. These include:

- needle threaders for sewing
- templates for rotary telephones, irons, and other appliances
- large-print phone books, clocks, and calendars
- magnifying glasses for situations where large-print substitutes are unavailable

Families and designers can help make the home and work environments safer for elders with visual impairments by:

- placing contrasting color strips on stairs, especially on carpeted or slippery linoleum stairs, to aid the older person's depth perception
- coloring and light-coding ramps and other changes in elevation

- clearly marking changes in floor surfaces such as door sills
- increasing the number of light sources
- installing non-slip and non-glossy floor coverings
- using a flat paint instead of glossy finishes to reduce the problem of glare on walls
- installing venetian and vertical blinds to control glare throughout the day
- using indirect or task lighting (e.g., reading lamps, countertop lamps) rather than ceiling fixtures
- adding dimmer switches so that lighting levels can be adjusted

Other environmental modifications may be more costly or require a professional architect or designer.

In summary, age-related vision changes need not disadvantage people if they can be encouraged and provided with options to adapt their activities and environment to fit their level of visual functioning with their needs. An older adult who is having difficulty adjusting to vision-related losses may initially resist such modifications. One way to address this resistance is to involve the older person in decisions about such changes to provide a sense of control and choice.

Changes in Hearing

Vision and hearing are perhaps our most critical links to the world. Although vision is important for negotiating the physical environment, hearing is vital for interpersonal communication. Because hearing is closely associated with speech, its loss disrupts a person's understanding of others and even the recognition of one's own speech. An older person who is experiencing hearing declines learns to make changes in behavior and social interactions, so as to reduce the detrimental social impact of such loss. Many younger hearing-impaired persons learn sign language or lip-reading. Because these are complex skills requiring extensive training and practice, they are less likely to be mastered by older adults.

POINTS TO PONDER

Consider some ways in which we rely on our hearing ability in everyday life: in conversations with family, friends, and coworkers; in localizing the sound of approaching vehicles as we cross the street or drive; and in interpreting other people's emotions through their tone of voice and use of language. How does a person function if these abilities gradually deteriorate?

THE ANATOMY AND PHYSIOLOGY OF THE EAR   It is useful to review the anatomy of the ear to understand where and how auditory function deteriorates with age. The auditory system has three components, as illustrated in Figure 3.5. The outer ear begins at the pinna, the visible portion that is identified as the ear. The auditory canal is also part of the outer ear. Note the shape of the pinna and auditory canal; it is a most efficient design for localizing sounds.

The eardrum, or tympanic membrane, is a thin membrane that separates the outer ear from the middle ear. This membrane is sensitive to air pressure of varying degrees and vibrates in response to a range of loud and soft sounds. Three bones, or *ossicles*—the *malleus, incus,* and *stapes*—that transfer sound waves to the inner ear are located in the middle ear. These very finely positioned and interrelated bones carry sound vibrations from the middle ear to the inner ear—that snail-shaped circular structure called the *cochlea.*

Amplified sounds are converted in the cochlea to nerve impulses. These are then sent through the internal auditory canal and the cochlear nerve to the brain, where they are translated into meaningful sounds. The cochlea is a fluid-filled chamber with thousands of hair cells that vibrate two parallel membranes to move sound waves. The vibration of these hair cells is one of several factors involved in perceiving the pitch (or frequency) and loudness (intensity) of a sound.

AGE-RELATED CHANGES   The pinna appears somewhat elongated and rigid in some older adults. These changes in the outer ear, however, have no impact on hearing acuity. The supporting walls of the external auditory canals also deteriorate with age, as is true for many muscular structures. Arthritic conditions may affect the joints between the malleus and stapes, making it more difficult for these bones to perform their vibratory function. This is compounded by stiffening of the tympanic membrane, which also becomes thinner and less vascular with age. **Otosclerosis** is a condition in which the stapes becomes fixed and cannot vibrate. It is most likely to affect older persons.

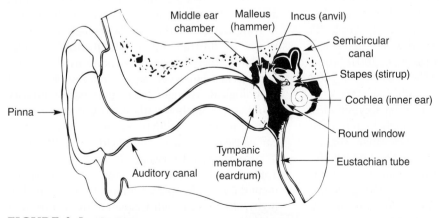

FIGURE 3.5   **The Ear**

The greatest decline with age occurs in the cochlea, where structural changes result in **presbycusis,** or sensorineural loss that accompanies aging. Changes in auditory thresholds can be detected by age 30, or even younger, but the degeneration of hair cells and membranes in the cochlea is not observed until much later. Age-related declines in the middle ear include:

- atrophy of hair cells
- vascular changes
- changes in the cochlear duct
- loss of auditory neurons
- deterioration of neural pathways between the ear and brain (Rees, 2000)

These alterations affect the older person's ability to detect and localize sounds, especially at lower volume and very high pitch or frequency. Tests of pure-tone thresholds (i.e., the level at which a tone of a single frequency can be detected) reveal a steady decline after age 60. Changes in the high-frequency range are about 1 dB per year. In the range of speech, changes are slow until age 60, then they accelerate to a rate of 1.3 dB per year after age 80 (Schneider & Pichora-Fuller, 2000). Estimates of the prevalence of hearing loss vary—in the range of speech, in the high-frequency range, and at the level of complete presbycusis—depending on tests used and whether self-reports or audiometric tests are used to assess hearing loss. Estimates range from 13 to 34 percent of people age 65 and older. In another epidemiological study, 17 percent of people 85 and older were deaf, compared with 5 percent of their peers age 70 to 74 (Desai et al., 2001; Stuen, 2006; Weinstein, 2000). More recently, a 2008 report of audiometric tests of adults age 20-69 in the National Health and Nutrition Examination Study (NHANES) found surprisingly high rates of hearing loss in the high frequency range, slightly lower in the range of speech. Hearing loss is more prevalent among men than women (approximately 5.5 times higher), more among whites than blacks (almost twice as much), and among heavy smokers, adults with hypertension or diabetes, who experience more hearing loss by age 40–49 than their peers without these risk factors (Agarwal, Platz, & Niparko, 2008).

Hearing loss in the high frequency range and in the range of speech were recorded among:

- 8.5 percent and 3.1 percent of adults respectively age 20–29;
- 34 percent and 15 percent of adults age 40–49 respectively;
- 77 percent and 49 percent of adults age 60–69 respectively;

High frequency hearing loss was found in 93 percent of this oldest group of white men and 65 percent of white women, compared with 74 percent of African American men and 46 percent of their female counterparts.

These findings provide new insights into risk factors for hearing loss, and possible environmental, gender, and race factors that affect rates of hearing loss. In addition, they point to the importance of conducting audiometric tests to assess hearing loss rather than relying on self-reports as many earlier national studies have done (Agarwal, et al., 2008).

As with studies regarding visual changes, some age-related alterations in the brain are responsible for the deterioration in auditory functioning. These alterations may include cellular deterioration and vascular changes in the major auditory pathways to the brain. Researchers have also found that genetic factors account for loss of hearing acuity in the middle-to-high frequency range. To illustrate, monozygotic twins are more similar in their hearing loss patterns than dizygotic twins. However, aging and disease-related pathological changes can aggravate auditory problems. Together with exposure to environmental noise over a lifetime, this range of factors can cause presbycusis (Wingfield et al., 2007).

In contrast to visual changes, hearing loss appears to be significantly affected by environmental causes. People who have been exposed to high-volume and high-frequency noise throughout their lives (e.g., urban dwellers, construction workers who use jack hammers and other power tools, and factory workers) experience more hearing decrements in middle and old age than do those from rural, low-noise environments. Some diseases and medications can also impair hearing acuity in middle-aged and older adults. As shown in Figure 3.6, women generally show less decline than men. Gender differences in hearing loss occur across the life course). Over the last four decades, hearing loss among people age

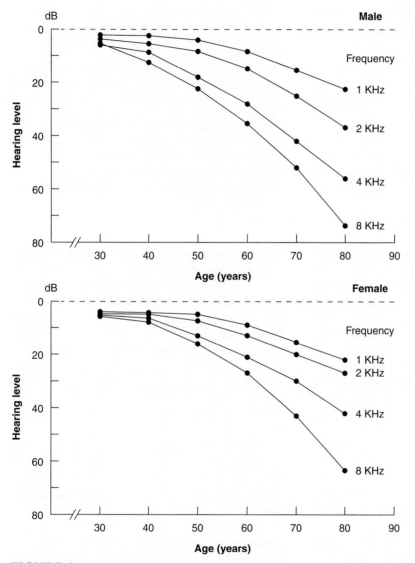

FIGURE 3.6   Gender Differences in Hearing Thresholds
SOURCE: J. M. Ordy, K. R. Brizzee, T. Beavers, and Medart, P, Age differences in the functional and structural organization of the auditory system in man. In J. M. Ordy and K. R. Brizzee (Eds.), *Sensory systems and communication in the elderly* (New York: Raven Press, 1979), p. 156. Reprinted with permission of the author and publisher.

18 to 44 has increased significantly. Given this pattern earlier in life, future cohorts are expected to include more elders with hearing loss that was environmentally induced earlier in their lives—perhaps from listening to loud music on MP3 players in adolescence and young adulthood!

Tinnitus, a high-pitched "ringing," is another problem that affects hearing in old age, although it can also occur earlier in life. It may occur bilaterally or in one ear only. The incidence increases threefold between youth and middle age, and fourfold between youth and old age, and may be aggravated by other types of hearing loss. Tinnitus may be related to occupational noise exposure; for example, men with tinnitus are more likely to have had exposure to noisy work environments. It cannot be cured, but people suffering from tinnitus can generally learn to manage it or try alternative approaches such as acupuncture (Micozzi, 1997).

COMPENSATION AND ADAPTATION As noted above, hearing loss can be of several types, involving limited volume and range or distortion of sounds perceived. Regardless of type, hearing loss results in some incongruence between the person and his or her environment. Older persons who have lost hearing acuity in the range of speech (500–3000 Hz) have particular difficulties distinguishing the sibilants or high-frequency consonants such as *z, s, sh, f, p, k, t,* and *g.* Their speech comprehension deteriorates as a result, which may be the first sign of hearing loss. In contrast, low-frequency hearing loss has minimal impact on speech comprehension. As Figure 3.6 illustrates, higher-frequency sounds can be heard better by raising the intensity. The recognition of some consonants such as *(p, t, k, b, d, g)* can be increased by 50 to 90 percent among older persons simply by raising their volume. An individual may compensate by raising the volume of the TV and radio, moving closer to the TV, or listening to other types of music made by lower-pitched instruments, such as an organ.

When an older adult starts raising the volume of the TV or radio, or increasingly asks people to repeat what they said, it is imperative to determine

RELUCTANCE TO USE HEARING AIDS

The social stigma associated with wearing a hearing aid is greater than with wearing glasses. These are undoubtedly some of the reasons why very few older people with hearing loss use them. After President Clinton was fitted with a new digital hearing aid in 1997, there was a dramatic increase in the number of hearing aids sold. Sales jumped by 25 percent between 1996 and 1997; many of these consumers were baby boomers like President Clinton who purchased a hearing aid for the first time. Nevertheless, a survey conducted in 1998 found that only 15 percent of older adults with hearing loss in the range of speech were using a hearing aid, and a 2003 study found rates lower than 12 percent (Crews & Campbell, 2004; National Academy, 1999; Popelka, Cruickshank, & Wiley, 1998). What might be some factors that would explain this slight decline in use of hearing aids, even though rates of hearing loss have increased?

whether a hearing loss exists, to identify the cause, and to fit the individual with an appropriate hearing aid, if affordable. A major difficulty with some of the less expensive types of hearing aids is that they merely raise the volume, so the volume of background noises is also raised. This may compensate for loss of higher-frequency sounds, but it cannot completely obliterate the problem of presbycusis. In fact, hearing aids may result in such major adaptation problems that older persons stop wearing them after several months, often to the frustration of their family members.

Fortunately, digital hearing aids are now available, which have tiny computer chips that filter sounds to match each user's hearing loss profile, without amplifying background noises. These newer designs are also less obtrusive and fit well inside the ear. However, they can cost about twice as much as conventional hearing aids and are not covered by Medicare or by most private health insurance plans. The cost, stigma, and adjustment problems with hearing aids may explain why proportionately so few older adults with reported hearing loss use a hearing aid.

Other means of compensating for hearing loss are to design environments that dampen background noises or to select such settings for communicating with older persons. Sound levels should not exceed 80 decibels. Soundproof rooms, while costly, are beneficial, particularly if housing for older people is built on busy streets or near freeways. Offices of health professionals should have at least one quiet area without the distraction of background noises. Older people with hearing impairments can also benefit from new designs in telephones with volume adjusters and lights that blink when the phone rings.

When conversing with people who are experiencing age-related hearing loss, the following hints can help both younger and older persons enjoy their communication:

- Face an older person directly and maintain eye contact.
- Sit somewhat close (3 feet away) and at eye level with the older person.
- Do not cover your face with hands or objects when speaking.
- Speak slowly and clearly, but without exaggerating speech.
- Do not shout.
- Avoid distracting background noises by selecting a quiet, relaxing place away from other people, machines, and traffic sounds.
- Speak in a lower, but not monotonic, tone of voice.
- Repeat key points in different ways and with different words.
- If specific information is to be transmitted (e.g., how to take medications), structure the message in a clear, systematic manner (Kawamoto & Kiyak, 2009; NIA, 2005).

Helping older people with hearing impairment compensate for this loss is essential to avoid harmful effects on interpersonal relationships, social engagement, and self-esteem. For some older adults, increasing levels of hearing impairment can disrupt functional abilities, resulting in social withdrawal

and even clinical depression (Dalton et al., 2003; Strawbridge et al., 2000). Older persons with significant hearing loss may also be at greater risk for falls. A study of 423 women age 63 to 76 measured their hearing threshold and postural stability (with eyes open), then followed them for 12 months to determine if and under what conditions they fell. Almost half experienced a fall. After adjusting for age, elders in the poorest-hearing quartile were 3.4 times more likely to fall as those in the best-hearing quartile. The researchers concluded that this higher risk for falls among elders with impaired hearing acuity may be related to their poorer postural stability, not their hearing loss per se (Viljanen et al., 2009).

The simultaneous deterioration of both hearing and vision can be particularly frustrating. Although it is relatively rare for both functions to decline significantly with age, family, friends, and professionals must learn to be versatile in using appropriate communication techniques, including those suggested earlier. For example, when talking with an older person who is impaired in both hearing and vision, touching a hand, arm, or shoulder may aid communication.

Sense Changes in Taste and Smell

Although older people may complain that food does not taste as good as it once did, these complaints are probably not due to an age-associated generalized loss of taste sensitivity. It was once thought that age brought dramatic decreases in the number of taste buds on the tongue, that such loss of receptor elements led to functional loss, which was experienced as a dulling of taste sensation, and that these changes accounted for older people's reduced enjoyment of food. Subsequent studies, however, have challenged each link in this chain of reasoning. Aging does appear to cause some loss of taste buds, but this does not affect taste thresholds. Furthermore, threshold loss almost never involves more than one of the four basic taste qualities (Cowart, 1989).

The notion that various functions decline differentially has replaced the belief that older people

Cooking with spices can enhance olfactory and taste sensitivity.

studies where older individuals' average taste performance is poorer than that of younger adults, some perform as well as, or better than, many younger persons.

Appreciation of food does not depend on taste alone. The sense of smell clearly is involved. We have all experienced changes in the way food "tastes" while ill with a head cold and a stuffy nose or suffering from allergies. These changes suggest that sensitivity to airborne stimuli plays a key role in the smell and taste of foods. Older people perceive airborne stimuli as less intense than younger persons, and they do less well on odor identification. External factors such as smoking and medications contribute to these differences, but even after accounting for these variables, age differences in odor identification and discriminations are dominant (Markovic et al., 2007; Stuen, 2006; Tuorila, Niskanen, & Maunuksela, 2001). When parallel assessments are made in the same subject, age-related declines for smell are greater than for taste. This suggests that one way to increase older people's enjoyment of eating is to provide them with enhanced food odors or opportunities for *olfactory hedonic experiences*. Hedonic evaluation of odor stimuli is generally an emotional, not an analytic, task. Research comparing young, middle-aged, and older persons' hedonic evaluations shows that ratings of the pleasantness of food odors increase after age 40. Research volunteers age 19 to 39 were significantly more negative in their ratings of lemon, garlic, and fish than those age 40 to 59 and those 60 and older (Dijksterhuis et al., 2002; Markovic et al., 2007). Classes in cooking with herbs and spices can be valuable for older people who are experiencing changes in their taste and olfactory abilities. These activities can also help older people in sharpening their sensitivity to tastes and odors, improving the palatability and intake of food, increasing salivary flow and immunity, and ultimately enhancing their quality of life (Schiffman & Graham, 2000).

Losing the ability to smell and taste is not just a matter of reduced enjoyment, but can foster risks such as unhealthy eating habits, social isolation,

experience a generalized taste loss. The research task now is to specify which aspects of taste function remain intact and which decline with normal aging or with disease. Although older people's taste function does not undergo a general decline in strength, it demonstrates specific changes. For example, while the relationship between taste intensity and stimulus strength is age-stable, older adults have more difficulty than younger people in discriminating between varying intensities of a flavor (tested by increasing the level of bitterness in coffee, the saltiness of food); however, discrimination occurs less often with a stimulus that varies in its sweetness. These differences have been observed across age groups, from teens to people in their 80s. It is also important to note that in and being unable to smell dangers like smoke or leaking gas. We have all known elders who keep adding salt and sugar to their food to enhance the taste, often doing the exact opposite of what their doctor recommends. Finding healthier ways to enhance the aroma and flavor of foods is important for both elders' nutrition and social engagement. In addition to cooking with herbs and spices, adding even a tablespoon of gravy or olive oil to food can dramatically improve its enjoyment by making the aroma and flavor chemicals more available to the taste buds without increasing fat content significantly. This is because fat in food is essential to flavor. Color in food also affects the perceived intensity of flavor, which suggests the importance of not overcooking food and attending to the visual presentation of a meal. As with all the age-associated sensory changes, families and health care providers need to be creative in modifying the environment and recommending appropriate tests. In fact, olfactory testing not only determines the level and type of loss in an elder's ability to taste and smell; it can also help with early diagnosis of neurodegenerative diseases such as Parkinson's and Alzheimer's (Muller, Mungersdorf, Reichan, Strehle, & Hummel, 2002; Peters et al., 2003).

Implications for the Future

New discoveries in genetics, pharmacology, biomedical technology, and surgical techniques hold great possibilities for enhancing the quality of life and extending the human life span. Today, scientists can already place embryonic stem cells in culture at an early stage and watch them maintain telomerase activity and indefinite replication. In the future, they will be able to transplant stem cells to human organs in a successful attempt to reverse the decline or disease processes in these organs.

Someday, people will know their predisposition to a wider array of genetically linked conditions, beyond a few that are currently predictable with genetic testing, such as Huntington's disease. The long-term impact of caloric restriction and the use of enzyme boosters and antioxidants throughout adulthood on pathogenic conditions in old age—as well as folic acid on atherosclerosis and heart disease—will become clearer. We will also learn the long-term effects of pharmacological and exercise interventions to prevent insulin resistance and coronary artery disease, osteopenia, and functional decline. Drug dosing will become more individualized so that physicians can assess each elder's ability to metabolize and excrete drugs before prescribing a particular medication at specific doses. In many ways, biological aging in the twenty-first century will move away from the treatment of disease and genetic disorders to their prevention. Trends in microbiological research suggest that an important focus will be on ways to extend the average length of life such as maintaining active lifestyles. Developments in technology and robotics will help older people remain in their own homes, with computers that monitor their activities (such as medication use) and robots that serve as "personal aides" if their mobility, vision, and hearing decline significantly.

Both scientific and technological advances in this field will result in the need for more skilled professionals to assist the aging population. These include scientists, such as microbiologists and geneticists, who focus on the basic mechanisms and genetics of aging, and researchers in computer sciences and engineering who can design external aids to reduce environmental press. Vision rehabilitation therapists are needed who can orient and help keep visually impaired elders active. It will also be important to encourage professionals such as occupational and physical therapists, as well as audiologists, to specialize in aging. These clinicians can test the aging individual and prescribe activities to maintain function. Health care providers must understand what is normal age-associated decline and what is disease, in order to help older adults who are experiencing significant loss of physiological functions. These experts also need skills to modify the environment and enhance elders' competence to accommodate such physiological changes. A significant barrier to the expansion of this necessary pool of professionals is that Medicare and many other health insurance policies do not reimburse for such specialized services to older adults.

Summary

As shown by this review of physiological systems, the aging process is gradual, beginning in some organ systems as early as the 20s and 30s and progressing more rapidly after age 70, or even 80, in others. Even with 50 percent deterioration in many organ systems, an individual can still function adequately. The ability of human beings to compensate for age-related changes attests to their significant amount of excess reserve capacity. In most instances, the normal physical changes of aging need not diminish a person's quality of life if person–environment congruence can be maintained. Since many of the decrements are gradual and slight, older people can learn to modify their activities to adapt to their environments—for example, by pacing the amount of physical exertion throughout the day. Family members and professionals can be supportive by encouraging home modifications, such as minimizing the use of stairs, moving the older person's daily activities to the main floor of the home, and reinforcing their efforts to cope creatively with common vision or hearing impairments.

The rate and severity of decline in various organ systems vary substantially, with the greatest deterioration in functions that require coordination among multiple systems, muscles, and nerves. Similarly, wide variations across individuals in the aging process spring from differences in heredity, diet, exercise, culture, and living conditions. Many of the physiological functions that were once assumed to deteriorate and to be irreversible with normal aging are being reevaluated by researchers in basic and clinical physiology as well as by health educators. Examples of master athletes who continue their swimming, running, and other competitive physical activities throughout life show that age-related declines are not always dramatic. Even people

who begin a regular exercise program late in life have experienced significant improvements in their heart and lung capacity. The role of preventive maintenance and health-enhancement programs in the aging process is discussed in Chapter 4.

Sleep patterns change with normal aging. Lab studies reveal changes in EEG patterns, sleep stages, and circadian rhythms with advancing years. However, true sleep disturbances are associated with physical and psychological disorders; with some medications used to treat these conditions; they are not due to aging per se. Sedative-hypnotic drugs are widely used by older people who complain of sleep disturbance. However, improving sleep hygiene by increasing daytime physical exercise and exposure to light; reducing daytime naps and the intake of alcohol, caffeine, and some medications; and modifying the sleep environment are generally more effective in the long-term than pharmacological approaches. This is particularly true for older persons with dementia. Medications are useful only in the case of true sleep disorders, such as sleep apnea and twitching legs during sleep.

Changes in sensory function with age do not occur at a consistent rate in all senses and for all people. Some people show rapid declines in vision while maintaining their hearing and other sensory abilities. Others experience an early deterioration in olfactory sensation but not in other areas. All of us experience some loss in these functions with age, but interindividual differences are quite pronounced. Normal age-related declines in vision reduce the ability to respond to differing light levels; function in low-light situations; see in places with high levels of glare; discern color tones, especially in the green-blue-violet range; and judge distances and depth. Peripheral vision becomes somewhat narrowed with age, as does upward and downward gaze. Older people have more diseases of the eye, including glaucoma, cataracts, and macular degeneration; if these diseases are not treated, blindness can result. Older persons who experience significant age-related declines in visual function can generally maintain former levels of activity if they adapt the environment to fit changing needs or substitute new activities for those that have become more difficult. Unfortunately, some older people prefer to withdraw from previous activities, thereby becoming more isolated and at risk of depression and deteriorating quality of life.

Decline in auditory function generally starts earlier than visual problems and affects more people. Significant impairments in speech comprehension often result. Although hearing aids can frequently improve hearing by raising the intensity of speech that is in the high-frequency range, they require time for the elder to adapt and to distinguish the focal sound from background noises that are also increased by the hearing aid; additionally, many older people feel uncomfortable and even stigmatized when using them. Hence, the solutions for communicating with hearing-impaired elders may lie mostly in the environment, not within older persons themselves. These include changes in communication styles, such as speaking directly at an older person in a clear voice but not shouting; talking in a lower tone; repeating key points; and sitting closer to a hearing-impaired person. Environmental aids such as soundproof or quiet rooms and modified telephones can also be invaluable for older people with significant hearing deterioration.

Although many older people complain that food does not taste as good as it once did, changes with age in taste acuity are minimal, whereas the hedonic evaluation of food is more emotional and unrelated to threshold detection and discrimination. The decline in olfactory receptors with age is more significant than in taste receptors, and may be responsible for the perception of reduced taste acuity. These changes are more pronounced in people who smoke or drink heavily, but the use of medications has only modest effects. There is less change in people who have sharpened their taste and olfactory sensitivity, such as professional winemakers and perfumers. This pattern emphasizes the importance of participating in activities that enhance elders' taste and olfactory functions.

As we learn more from studies of normal physiological changes with aging, reports that

once appeared definitive are found to be less so, and a complete understanding of some changes is shown to be lacking. This is particularly true in the areas of taste, smell, and pain perception. Research is needed to distinguish normal changes in these areas from those that are related to disease and those that can be prevented. Longitudinal research would help to answer many of these questions. Finally, research that examines the impact of sensory deterioration on the older person's interactions with the environment is also needed.

GLOSSARY

accommodation   ability of the lens of the eye to change shape from rounded to flat in order to see objects that are closer or farther from the lens

age-related cataract   clouding of the lens of the eye, reducing sight and sometimes leading to blindness; requires surgical extraction of the lens

age-related macular degeneration (AMD)   loss of vision in the center of the visual field caused by insufficient oxygen reaching the macula

atherosclerosis   accumulation of fats in the arteries and veins, blocking circulation of the blood

atrophic gastritis   chronic inflammation of the stomach lining

cellular aging theory   the hypothesis that aging occurs as cells slow their number of replications, based on the observation that cells grown in controlled laboratory environments are able to replicate only a finite number of times

dementia   diminished ability to remember, make accurate judgments, etc.

diastolic blood pressure   the level of blood pressure during the time when the chambers of the heart are filling with blood

estrogen   a female sex hormone that declines significantly with aging; can be replaced alone (estrogen replacement therapy) or in combination with progesterone, another female sex hormone (hormone replacement therapy)

free radical theory   a special case of the cross-linkage theory of aging that posits that free radicals (highly reactive molecules) may produce DNA mutations

functional (or reserve) capacity the ability of a given organ to perform its normal function, compared with its function under conditions of illness, disability, and aging

glaucoma a disease in which there is insufficient drainage or excessive production of aqueous humor, the fluid in the front portion of the eye

glucose a type of sugar found in plants and animals, serves as a major energy source and circulates in blood

healthy life span the number of years in good health and with quality of life

hyperthermia body temperatures several degrees above normal for prolonged periods

hypothermia body temperatures several degrees below normal for prolonged periods

immunological theory focuses on the deteriorating efficiency of the immune system as the cause of many normal age-related declines and chronic diseases associated with aging

kinesthetic system the body system that signals one's position in space

kyphosis stoop-shouldered or hunched condition caused by collapsed vertebrae as bone mass is lost

master athletes individuals who have continued to participate in competitive, aerobic exercise into the later years

melanin skin pigmentation

menopause one event during the climacteric in a woman's life when there is a gradual cessation of the menstrual cycle, which is related to the loss of ovarian function; considered to have occurred after 12 consecutive months without a menstrual period

mitochondrial DNA mutation theory the hypothesis that aging is caused by damage or mutation of DNA in the mitochondria of cells.

neurons nerve cells in the brain

orthopedic injuries injuries to the bones, muscles, and joints

osteoporosis a dramatic loss in calcium and bone mass resulting in increased brittleness of the bones and increased risk of fracture, more frequently found in white, small-stature women

otosclerosis loss of hearing caused by hardening of the stapes and its inability to vibrate; not normal aging

periodic limb movement disorder (PLMD) neuromuscular disturbance resulting in uncontrolled movement of legs during sleep (also known as *nocturnal myoclonus*)

presbycusis age-related hearing loss

prolongevity research aimed at increasing average life expectancy by reducing the burden of disease but not disrupting fundamental aging processes

renal function kidney function, defined by the rate at which blood is filtered through the kidneys

senescence biological aging; i.e., the gradual accumulation of irreversible functional losses to which the average person tries to accommodate in some socially acceptable way

sleep apnea 5- to 10-second cessation of breathing, which disturbs sleep in some older persons

sleep hygiene behaviors associated with sleep—e.g., location, lighting, regular versus irregular bedtime, use of drugs that promote or hinder sleep

systolic blood pressure the level of blood pressure during the contraction phase of the heart

telomerase the enzyme responsible for rebuilding telomeres

telomeres protective DNA structures at ends of each chromosome, lost as cells replicate

tinnitus high-pitched ringing in the ear

urinary incontinence diminished ability to retain urine; loss of bladder control

varicosities abnormal swelling in the veins, especially the legs

vital capacity the maximum volume of oxygen intake through the lungs with a single breath

wear and tear theory one of the biological theories of aging; states that aging occurs because of the system simply wearing out over time

RESOURCES

Log on to MySocKit (www.mysockit.com) for information about the following:

- AARP Andrus Foundation publication, "Lighting the Way" (2002)
- American Foundation for the Blind, Unit on Aging
- American Printing House for the Blind
- American Speech-Language-Hearing Association
- Better Hearing Institute
- International Hearing Aid Helpline of the International Hearing Society

- International Longevity Center
- Library of Congress, Blind and Physically Handicapped Division
- National Association for Continence
- National Sleep Foundation
- Self-Help for Hard of Hearing People (SHHH)

REFERENCES

Aldwin, C. M. & Gilmer, D. F. (2004). *Health, illness and optimal aging*. Thousand Oaks, CA: Sage.

Allikmets, R., Shroyer, N. F., Singh, N., Seddon, J. M., & Lewis, R. A. (1997). Mutation of the Stargardt disease gene (ABCR) in age-related macular degeneration. *Science, 277*, 1805–1807.

Asbell, P. A., Dualan, I., Mindel, J., Brooks, D., Ahmad, M., Epstein, S. (2005). Age-related cataract. *Lancet, 365*, 599–609.

Bauer, J., Pearson, K., Price, N., Jamieson, H., Lerin, C., et al. (2006). Resveratrol improves health and survival of mice on a high-calorie diet. *Nature, 10*, 1038–1040.

Beckman, K. B. & Ames, B. N. (1998). The free radical theory of aging matures. *Physiological Reviews, 78*, 547–581.

Bengtson, V. L., Gans, D., Putney, N. M., Silverstein, M. (Eds.). (2009). *Handbook of theories of aging* (2nd ed.). NY: Springer Publishing.

Bodnar, A. G., Kim, N. W., Effros, R. B., & Chiu, C. P. (1996). Mechanisms of telomerase induction during T cell activation. *Experimental Cell Research, 228*, 58–64.

Bodnar, A. G., Ouelette, M., Frolkis, M., Holt, S. E., Chiu, C. P., Morin, G. B., et al. (1998). Extension of life-span by introduction of telomerase into normal human cells. *Science, 279*, 349–352.

Braille Institute. (2004). *Statistics on sight loss.* Retrieved 2004, from http://www.brailleinstitute.org/Education-Statistics.html

Campisi, J. & Vijg, J. (2009) Does damage to DNA and other macromolecules play a role in aging? *Journal of Gerontology: Biological Sciences, 64A*, 175–178.

Carpenter, M. K., Cui, X., Hu, Z. Y., Jackson, J., Sherman, S., Seiger, A., et al. (1999). In vitro expansion of a multipotent population of human neural progenitor cells. *Experimental Neurology, 158*, 265–278.

Chang, E. & Harley, C. B. (1995). Telomere length as a measure of replicative histories in human vascular tissues. *Proceedings of the National Academy of Sciences, 92*, 11190–11194.

Coffey, C. E., Lucke, J. F., Saxton, J. A., Ratcliff, G., Unitas, L. J., Billig, B., et al. (1998). Sex differences in brain aging. *Archives of Neurology, 55*, 169–179.

Colman, R. J., Beasley, T. M., Allison, D. B. & Weindruch, R. (2008). Attenuation of sarcopenia by dietary restriction in rhesus monkeys. *Journal of Gerontology: Biological Sciences, 63A*, 556–559.

Cowart, B. J. (1989). Relationships between taste and smell across the life span. In C. Murphy, W. S. Cain, & D. M. Hegsted (Eds.). Nutrition and the chemical senses in aging: Recent advances and current research needs. *Annals of the New York Academy of Sciences.* New York: New York Academy of Sciences.

Crews, J. E. & Campbell, V. A. (2004). Vision impairment and hearing loss among community-dwelling older Americans: Implications for health and functioning. *American Journal of Public Health, 94*, 823–829.

Dagarag, M. D., Evazyan, T., Rao, N., & Effros, R. B. (2004). Genetic manipulation of telomerase in HIV-specific CD8 & T cells. *Journal of Immunology, 2004, 173*, 6303–6311.

Dalton, D. S., Cruickshanks, K. J., Klein, B. E. K., Wiley, T. L., & Nondahl, D. M. (2003). The impact of hearing loss on quality of life in older adults. *The Gerontologist, 43*, 661–668.

Desai, M., Pratt, L. A., Lentzner, H., & Robinson, K. N. (2001). Trends in vision and hearing among older Americans. *Aging Trends, vol. 2.* Hyattsville, MD: National Center for Health Statistics.

Dhatariya, K. K. & Nair, K. S. (2003). Dehydroepiandrosterone: Is there a role for replacement? *Mayo Clinic Proceedings, 78*, 1257–1273.

Dijksterhuis, G. B., Moller, P., Bredie, W. L., Rasmussen, G., & Martens, M. (2002). Gender and handedness effects on hedonicity of laterally presented odours. *Brain and Cognition, 50*, 272–281.

Effros, R. B. (2001). Immune system activity. In E. J. Masoro & S. N. Austad (Eds.). *Handbook of the biology of aging* (5th ed.). San Diego: Academic Press.

Effros, R. B. (2009a). The immunological theory of aging revisited. In V. L. Bengtson, D. Gans, N. M. Putney, & M. Silverstein (Eds.). *Handbook of theories of aging* (2nd ed.). NY: Springer Publishing.

Effros, R. B. (2009b). Kleemeier award lecture 2008: The canary in the coal mine: Telomeres and human healthspan. *Journal of Gerontology: Biological Sciences, 64A,* 511–515.

Endeshaw, Y. W., Ouslander, J. G., Schnelle, J. F., & Bliwise, D. L. (2007). Polysomnographic and clinical correlates of behaviorally observed daytime sleep in nursing home residents. *Journal of Gerontology: Biological Sciences, 62A,* 55–61.

Finch, C. E. (1990). *Longevity, senescence and the genome.* Chicago: University of Chicago Press.

Fishman, J. R., Binstock, R. H., & Lambrix, M. A. (2008). Anti-aging science: The emergence, maintenance, and enhancement of a discipline. *Journal of Aging Studies, 22,* 295–303.

Fontana, L., Meyer, T. E., Klein, S., & Holloszy, J. O. (2004). Long-term calorie restriction is highly effective in reducing the risk for atherosclerosis in humans. *Proceedings of the National Academy of Sciences of the U.S.A., 101,* 6659–6663.

Fontana, L., Villareal, D. T., Weiss, E. P., Racette, S. B., Steger-May, K., Klein, S., et al. (2007). Calorie restriction or exercise: Effects on coronary heart disease risk factors. *American Journal of Physiology Endocrinology and Metabolism, 293,* E197–E202.

Fozard, J. L. & Gordon-Salant, S. (2001). Changes in vision and hearing with aging. In J. E. Birren & K. W. Schaie (Eds.). *Handbook of the psychology of aging* (5th ed.). San Diego: Academic Press.

Grune, T. & Davies, K. J. A. (2001). Oxidative processes in aging. In E. J. Masaro and S. N. Austad (Eds.). *Handbook of the biology of aging* (5th ed.). San Diego: Academic Press.

Harman, D. (1956). Aging: A theory based on free radical and radiation chemistry. *Journal of Gerontology, 2,* 298–300.

Harman, D. (1972). The biological clock: The mitochondria? *Journal of the American Geriatrics Society, 20,* 145–147.

Harman, D. (1993). Free radical involvement in aging: Pathophysiology and therapeutic implications. *Drugs and Aging, 3,* 60–80.

Hayflick, L. (1996). *How and why we age.* New York: Ballantine Books.

Hayflick, L. (2000). The illusion of cell immortality. *British Journal of Cancer, 83,* 841–846.

Hayflick, L. (2004a). Anti-aging is an oxymoron. *Journal of Gerontology: Biological Sciences, 59A,* B573–578.

Hayflick, L. (2004b). From here to immortality. *Public Policy and Aging Report, 14,* 1–7.

Hayflick, L. & Moorehead, P. S. (1961). The serial cultivation of human diploid cell strains. *Experimental Cell Research, 25,* 285–621.

Hill, E. L., Cumming, R. G., Lewis, R., Carrington, S., & LeCouteur, D. G. (2007). Sleep disturbances and falls in older people. *Journal of Gerontology: Medical Sciences, 62A,* 62–66.

Holloszy, J. O. & Fontana, L. (2007). Caloric restriction in humans. *Experimental Gerontology, 42,* 709–712.

Hornsby, P. J. (2001). Cell proliferation in mammalian aging. In E. J. Masoro & S. N. Austad (Eds.). *Handbook of the biology of aging* (5th ed.). San Diego: Academic Press.

Horowitz, A. & Higgins, K. E. (2000). Older drivers and failing vision: Time to surrender the keys! *Consultant, 40,* 1310–1316.

Howitz, K. T., Bitterman, K. J., Cohen, H. Y., Lamming, D. W., Lavu, S., Wood-Zipkin, R. E., et al. (2003). Small molecule activators of sirtuins extend *Saccharomyces cerevisiae* lifespan. *Nature, 425,* 191–196.

In France, nothing gets in the way of vacation. (2003). *The New York Times,* August 24, p. 5.

Ingram, D. K., Anson, R. M., deCabo, R., Mamczarz, J., Zhu, M., Mattison, J, et al. (2004). Development of calorie restriction mimetics as a prolongevity strategy. *Annals of the New York Academy of Science, 1019,* 412–423.

Kawamoto, K. & Kiyak, H. A. (2009). Sensory changes and communication in the practitioner-aged patient relationship. In P. Holm-Pedersen, A. Walls, & J. Ship (Eds.). *Textbook of Geriatric Dentistry*, 3rd ed. (In press)

Kinouchi, Y., Hiwatashi, N., Chida, M., Nagashima, F., Takagi, S., Maekawa, H., & Toyota, T. (1998). Telomere shortening in the colonic mucosa of patients with ulcerative colitis. *Journal of Gastroenterology, 33*, 343–348.

Kirkland, J. L. & Peterson, C. (2009). Healthspan, translation, and new outcomes for animal studies of aging. *Journal of Gerontology: Biological Sciences, 64A*, 209–213.

Kujoth, G. C., Hiona, A., Pugh, T. D., Someya S., Panzer, K., Wohlgemuth, S. E. (2005). Mitochondrial DNA mutations, oxidative stress, and apoptosis in mammalian aging. *Science, 309*, 481–484.

Lane, M. A., Ingram, D. K., & Roth, G. S. (2002). The serious search for an anti-aging pill. *Scientific American, 287*, 36–41.

Lefevre, M., Redman, L. M., Heilbronn, L. K., Smith, J. V., Martin, C. K., Rood, J. C., et al. (2009). Caloric restriction alone and with exercise improves CVD risk in healthy non-obese individuals. *Atherosclerosis, 203*, 206–213.

Lesage, S. & Scharf, S. M. (2007). Beyond the usual suspects: Approaching sleep in elderly people. *Journal of Gerontology: Biological Sciences, 62A*, 53–54.

Markovic, K., Reulbach, U., Vassiliadu, A., Lunkenheimer, J., Lunkenheimer, B., Spannenberger, R., et al. (2007). Good news for elderly persons: Olfactory pleasure increases at later stages of the life span. *Journal of Gerontology: Medical Sciences, 62A*, 1287–1293.

Martin, J. L., Marler, M. R., Harker, J. O., Josephson, K. R., & Alessi, C. A. (2007). A multicomponent nonpharmacological intervention improves activity rhythms among nursing home residents with disrupted sleep/wake patterns. *Journal of Gerontology: Biological Sciences, 62A*, 67–72.

Martini, C., Pallottini, V., DeMarinis, E., Marino, M., Cavallini, G., Donati, A., et al. (2008). Omega-3 as well as caloric restriction prevent the age-related modifications of cholesterol metabolism. *Mechanisms of Ageing and Development, 129*, 722–727.

Masoro, E. J. (2001). Dietary restriction: An experimental approach to the study of the biology of aging. In E. J. Masoro and S. N. Austad (Eds.).

Handbook of the biology of aging (5th ed.). San Diego: Academic Press.

Masoro, E. J. (2003). Caloric restriction, slowing aging, and extending life. *Science of aging knowledge environment, 8*, RE2.

Mattison, J. A., Lane, M. A., Roth, G. S., & Ingram, D. K. (2003). Calorie restriction in rhesus monkeys. *Experimental Gerontology, 38*, 35–46.

McCurry, S. M., Reynolds, F., Ancoli-Israel, S., Teri, L., & Vitiello, M. V. (2000). Treatment of sleep disturbance in Alzheimer's disease. *Sleep Medicine Reviews, 4*, 603–628.

McShane, T. M., Wilson, M. E., & Wise, P. M. (1999). Effects of lifelong moderate caloric restriction. *Journal of Gerontology: Biological Sciences, 54A*, B14–B21.

Melov, S., Ravenscroft, J., Malik, S., Gill, M. S., Walker, D. W., Clayton, P. E., et al. (2000). Extension of life-span with superoxide dismutase/catalase mimetics. *Science, 287*, 1567–1569.

Messaoudi, I., Warner, J., Fischer, M., Park, B., Hill, B., Mattison, J., et al. (2006). Delay of T cell senescence by caloric restriction in aged long-lived nonhuman primates. *Proceedings of the National Academy of Sciences, 103*, 19448–19453.

Micozzi, M. (1997). Exploring alternative health approaches for elders. *Aging Today, 18*, 9–12.

Miller, R. A. (2009). "Dividends" from research on aging—Can biogerontologists, at long last, find something useful to do? *Journal of Gerontology: Biological Sciences, 64A*, 157–160.

Milton, R. C. & Sperduto, R. D. (1991). Incidence of age-related cataract: 13.6 year follow-up in the Framingham eye study. *Investigations in Ophthalmic Vision Science, 32*, 1243–1250.

Muller, A., Mungersdorf, M, Reichmann, H., Strehle, G., & Hummel, T. (2002). Olfactory function in Parkinsonian syndromes. *Journal of Clinical Neuroscience, 9*, 521–524.

Nair, K. S., Rizza, R. A., O'Brien, P., Dhatariay, K. K., Short, K. R., Nehra, A., et al. (2006). DHEA in elderly women and DHEA or testosterone in elderly men. *New England Journal of Medicine, 355*, 1647–1659.

National Institute on Aging (NIA). (2005). *Hearing loss age page*. Retrieved March 2005, from http://niapublications.org/engagepages/hearing.asp

National Institutes of Health (NIH). (2006). Hypothermia: A cold weather hazard for seniors. *NIH News*, February.

Newman, A. B., Spiekerman, C. F., Enright, P., Lefkowitz, D., Manolio, T., Reynolds, C. F., et al. (2000). Daytime sleepiness predicts mortality and CVD in older adults. *Journal of the American Geriatrics Society, 48,* 115–123.

Nikolaus, T. & Bach, M. (2003). Preventing falls in community-dwelling frail older people using a home intervention team (HIT): Results from the randomized Falls-HIT trial. *Journal of the American Geriatrics Society, 51,* 300–305.

Oberdoerffer, P., Michan, S., McVay, M., Mostoslavsky, R., Vann, J., Park, S. K., et al. (2008). SIRT1 redistribution on chromatin promotes genomic stability but alters gene expression during aging. *Cell, 135,* 907–918.

Ohayon, M. M., Carskadon, M. A., Guilleminault, C., & Vitiello, M. V. (2004). Meta-analysis of quantitative sleep parameters from childhood to old age in healthy individuals: Developing normative sleep values across the human lifespan. *Sleep, 27,* 1255–1273.

Olshansky, S. J., Hayflick, L., & Carnes, B. A. (2002). No truth to the fountain of youth. *Scientific American, 286,* 92–95.

Pearson, K. J., Baur, J. A., Lewis, K. N., Peshkin, L., Price, N. L., Labinsky, N., et al. (2008). Resveratrol delays age-related deterioration and mimics transcriptional aspects of dietary restriction without extending life span. *Cell Metabolism, 8,* 157–168.

Peters, J. M., Hummel, T., Kratzsch, T., Lotsch, J., Skarke, C., Frolich, L. (2003). Olfactory function in mild cognitive impairment and Alzheimer's disease. *American Journal of Psychiatry, 160,* 1995–2002.

Pringle-Specht, J. K. (2005). Nine myths of incontinence in older adults. *American Journal of Nursing, 105,* 58–68.

Ramirez, R. & Schneider, J. (2003). Practical guide to sun protection. *Surgical Clinics of North America, 83,* 97–107.

Rattan, S. I. S. & Clark, B. F. C. (2005). *Understanding and modulating ageing. UBMB Life, 57,* 297–304.

Rees, T. (2000). Health promotion for older adults: Age-related hearing loss. *Northwest Geriatric Education Center Curriculum Modules.* Seattle: University of Washington NWGEC.

Rincon, M., Muzumdar, R., & Barzilai, N. (2006). Aging, body fat, and carbohydrate metabolism. In E. J. Masoro & S. N. Austad (Eds.). *Handbook of the biology of aging* (6th ed.). Amsterdam: Elsevier Academic Press.

Robman, L. & Taylor, H. (2005). External factors in the development of cataract. *Eye, 19,* 1074-1082.

Rogers, M. A., Hagberg, J. M., Martin, W. H., Ehsani, A. A., & Holloszy, J. O. (1990). Decline in VO2 max with aging in master athletes and sedentary men. *Journal of Applied Physiology, 68,* 2195–2199.

Roth, G. S., Ingram, D. K., & Lane, M. A. (2001). Caloric restriction in primates and relevance to humans. *Annals of the New York Academy of Sciences, 298,* 305–315.

Rudman, D., Drinka, P. J., Wilson, C. R., Mattson, D. E., Scherman, F., Cuisinier, M. C., et al. (1991). Relations of endogenous anabolic hormones and physical activity to bone mineral density in elderly men. *Clinical Endocrinology, 40,* 653–661.

Rudolph, K. L., Chang, S., Millard, M., Schreiber-Agus, N., & DePinho, R. A. (2000). Inhibition of experimental liver cirrhosis in mice by telomerase gene delivery. *Science, 287,* 1253–1258.

Schiffman, S. S. & Graham, B. G. (2000). Taste and smell perception affect appetite and immunity in the elderly. *European Journal of Clinical Nutrition, 54,* S54–S63.

Schneider, B. A. & Pichora-Fuller, M. (2000). Implications of perceptual deterioration for cognitive aging research. In F.I.M. Craik, T. A. Salthouse (Eds.). Handbook of aging and cognition (2nd ed.). Mahwah, NJ: Erlbaum.

Schultz, D. W., Klein, M. L., Humbert, A. J., Luzier, C. W., Persun, V., et al. (2003). Analysis of the ARMD1 locus: Evidence that a mutation in *HEMICENTIN-1* is associated with age-related macular degeneration in a large family. *Human Molecular Genetics.* Retrieved February 2003, from http://hmg.oupjournals.org/content/abstract/ddg348v1

Shock, N. W. (1962). The physiology of aging. *Scientific American, 206,* 100–110.

Solana, R. (2003). *Immunosenescence in centenarians and the old-old.* Symposium presented at the

International Association of Gerontology, Barcelona, July.

Strawbridge, W. J., Wallhagen, M. I., Shema, S. J., & Kaplan, G. A. (2000). Negative consequences of hearing impairment in old age: A longitudinal analysis. *The Gerontologist, 40,* 320–326.

Stuen, C. (2006). Older adults with age-related sensory loss. In B. Berkman (Ed.), *Handbook of Social Work in Health and Aging.* New York: Oxford.

Sutton, D. A., Moldofsky, H., & Badley, E. M. (2001). Insomnia and health problems in Canadians. *Sleep, 24,* 665–670.

Swain, S. L. & Nikolich-Zugich, J. (2009). Key research opportunities in immune system aging. *Journal of Gerontology: Biological Sciences, 64A,* 183–186.

Tatar, M. (2009). Can we develop genetically tractable models to assess healthspan (rather than life span) in animal models? *Journal of Gerontology: Biological Sciences, 64A,* 161–163.

Terry, D. F., Nolan, V. G., Andersen, S. L., Perls, T. T., Cawthon, R. M. (2008). Association of longer telomeres with better health in centenarians. *Journal of Gerontology: Biological Sciences, 63A,* 809–812.

Thavanati, P. K. R, Kanala, K. R., deDios, A. E., Garza, J. M. C. (2008). Age-related correlation between antioxidant enzymes and DNA damage with smoking and body mass index. *Journal of Gerontology: Biological Sciences, 63A,* 360–364.

Thom, D. H. & Brown, J. S. (1998). Reproductive and hormonal risk factors for urinary incontinence in later life: A review of the clinical and epidemiological literature. *Journal of the American Geriatrics Society, 46,* 1411–1417.

Thomas, T., Thomas, G., McLendon, C., Sutton, T., & Mullan, M. (1996). Beta-amyloid-mediated vasoactivity and vascular endothelial damage. *Nature, 380,* 168–171.

Trifunovic, A., Wredenberg, A., Falkenberg, M. Spelbrink, J. N., Rovio, A. T., Bruder, C. E., et al. (2004). Premature ageing in mice expressing defective mitochondrial DNA polymerase. *Nature, 2004, 429,* 417–423.

Truscott, R. J. W. (2005). Age-related nuclear cataract: Oxidation is the key. *Experimental Eye Research, 80,* 709–725.

Tuorila, H., Niskanen, N., & Maunuksela, E. (2001). Perception and pleasantness of a food with varying odor among the elderly and young. *Journal of Nutrition, Health and Aging, 5,* 266–268.

Vijg, J. (2007). *Aging of the genome.* Oxford, UK: Oxford University Press.

Viljanen, A., Kaprio, J., Pyykko, I., Sorri, M., Pajala, S., & Kauppinen, M., et al. (2009). Hearing as a predictor of falls and postural balance in older female twins. *Journal of Gerontology: Biological Sciences, 64A,* 312–317.

Vincent, K. R., Braith, R. W., Feldman, R. A., Kallas, H. E., & Lowenthal, D. T. (2002). Improved cardiorespiratory endurance following 6 months of resistance exercise in elderly men and women. *Archives of Internal Medicine, 162,* 673–678.

Vitiello, M. V. (2000). Effective treatment of sleep disturbances in older adults. *Clinical Cornerstone, 2,* 16–27.

Vitiello, M. V. & Borson, S. (2001). Sleep disturbances in patients with Alzheimer's disease. *CNS Drugs, 15,* 777–796.

Vitiello, M. V., Larsen, L. H., & Moe, K. E. (2004). Age-related sleep change: Gender and estrogen effects on the subjective-objective sleep quality of healthy, noncomplaining men and women. *Journal of Psychosomatic Research, 56,* 503–510.

Vitiello, M. V., Moe, K. E., & Prinz, P. N. (2002). Sleep complaints cosegregate with illness in older adults. *Journal of Psychosomatic Research, 53,* 555–559.

Walford, R. L. (1969). The immunologic theory of aging. Copenhagen: Munksgaard.

Weinstein, B. E. (2000). *Geriatric Audiology.* New York: Thieme Medical Publishers.

Wikby, A., Nilsson, B. O., Forsey, R., Thompson, J., Strindhall, J., Lofgren, S., et al. (2006). The immune risk phenotype is associated with with IL-6 in the terminal decline stage: Findings from the Swedish NONA immune longitudinal study of very late life functioning. *Mechanisms of Ageing and Development, 127,* 695–704.

Wilson, D. L. (1974). The programmed theory of aging. In M. Rockstein, M. L. Sussman, & J. Chesky (Eds.). *Theoretical aspects of aging.* New York: Academic Press.

Wingfield, A., Panizzon, M., Grant, M. D., Toomey, R., Kremen, W. S., Franz, C. E., et al. (2007). A twin study of genetic contributions to hearing acuity in late middle age. *Journal of Gerontology: Medical Sciences, 62A,* 1294–1299.

Wolf, S. L., Barnhart, H. X., Kutner, N. G., McNeely, E., Coogler, C., Xu, T., et al. (2003). Reducing frailty and falls in older persons: An investigation of Tai Chi and computerized balance training. *Journal of the American Geriatrics Society, 51,* 1794–1803.

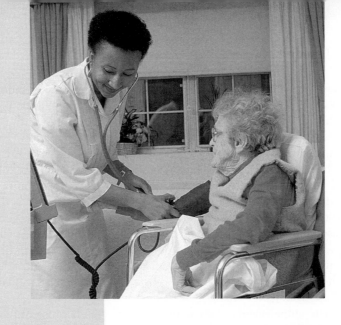

Chapter

4

Managing Chronic Diseases and Promoting Well-Being in Old Age

No aspect of old age is more alarming to many of us than the thought of losing our health. Our fears center not only on the pain and inconvenience of illness, but also on its social-psychological consequences, such as loss of personal autonomy and economic security. Poor health, more than other changes commonly associated with aging, can reduce a person's competence in mastering his or her environment.

Defining Health

Good health is more than merely the absence of disease or disability. As defined by the World Health Organization, **good health** is a state of complete physical, mental, and social well-being. The concept of health implies an

117

interaction and integration of body, mind, and spirit—a perspective that is reflected in the growth of health promotion programs and alternative medicine, and one that is congruent with the concept of active aging highlighted throughout this text.

As used by health care providers and researchers, the term **health status** refers to: (1) the presence or absence of disease, and (2) the degree of disability in an individual's level of functioning. Thus, activities that older people can do, or think they can do, are useful indicators of both how healthy they are and the services and environmental changes needed to cope with their impairments. Older people's ability to function as independently as possible is of primary concern. The concepts that capture this functional ability—**Activities of Daily Living (ADLs)** and **Instrumental Activities of Daily Living (IADLs)**—are described in the box on page 119.

The World Health Organization (2002) defines **disability** as impairments in the ability to complete multiple daily tasks. About 18 percent of older people are estimated to have a mild degree of disability in their ADLs, but only 2.5 percent are so disabled that they need help

with five or more ADLs (Federal Interagency Forum, 2008). Older adults who are disabled report limitations in multiple types of major activities and mobility, such as eating, dressing, bathing, or toiletry, and they require assistance from family or paid caregivers. Generally, the level of disability an older person experiences depends on whether they exercise, smoke, and maintain average weight (CDC & Merck Foundation, 2007; Christ & Divan, 2009). The extent of disabilities and need for help in personal care activities increase with age and differ by gender, race, and poverty status, as shown in Figure 4.1.

Because of their greater likelihood of coping with multiple chronic conditions, the old-old report more problems in performing ADLs, three times as many as the young-old. Women age 90 and older are twice as likely to be disabled and to require assistance than those age 70 to 74. Even though women on average live longer than men, men in both age groups are less likely to have IADL and ADL limits and show a smaller increase in disability with age. For example, only about half as many community-dwelling men over age 65 report ADL limitations as their female counterparts. This may be because men

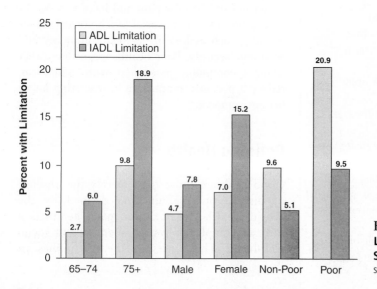

FIGURE 4.1 **Comparing ADL and IADL Limitations, 2002: Age, Gender, Poverty Status**
SOURCE: *Health, United States,* 2004a.

who survive to this age have a genetic advantage and are hardier than men who die at a younger age. African Americans are almost twice as likely as whites to report problems with ADLs and IADLs, and they have higher rates of disability, especially among low-income and less-educated elders (Federal Interagency Forum, 2008; Ferraro & Kelley-Moore, 2005; Kelley-Moore & Ferraro, 2004; NCHHHS, 2007).

Although disablity rates increase among some groups of older adults, overall they have declined in the population age 65 and older, especially among the oldest-old. The proportion of older adults who report any problems with IADLs or ADLs, has dropped from 14 percent and 20 percent, respectively, in 1992 to 12 percent and 18 percent in 2006. These figures reflect a decline in functional problems among successive cohorts of elders. They suggest that

people are not only living longer today but they are more likely to manage their chronic diseases without resulting in frailty or physical disability. These trends also reflect the growing emphasis on prevention and health promotion. Reductions in smoking, effective treatment of major circulatory diseases, and advances in chemotherapy are all health improvements that have reduced disability rates (AARP, 2003; AOA, 2008; Federal Interagency Forum, 2008; Manton, Gu & Lamb, 2006; Manton, Gu & Lowrimore, 2008).

Frailty is one way of describing such severe limitations in ADL. It generally includes problems in five areas (a person must exhibit at least three of these to be defined as frail): unintended weight loss, slow walking speed, low physical activity levels, weak grip strength, and chronic exhaustion. In many instances, frailty is complicated by **comorbidity**, defined as the coexistence of two or more chronic systemic or psychiatric conditions. For example, an older person's physical strength may be impaired by heart disease and the effects compounded by diabetes, depression, or arthritis. Frailty and comorbidity increase the risk of hospitalization, nursing home placement, and falls (Fried et al., 2001; Levers, Estabrooks, Ross-Kerr, 2006).

Quality of Life in Health and Illness

As noted in Chapter 1, the concept of active aging implies that aging need not be a time of decline or dependency. For most older adults, being able to do the things that they want at home and in the community is a primary component of active aging (Menec, 2003; Phelan et al., 2004). Even those who experience chronic diseases can usually maintain some degree of autonomy and avoid disability that impedes their daily functioning. As we will illustrate in this chapter, social and health behaviors throughout life—such as diet, smoking, alcohol consumption, and physical activity, as well as the physical

---

ASSESSING FUNCTIONAL HEALTH

The most commonly used measure of *functional health,* termed the *Activities of Daily Living (ADLs),* summarizes an individual's ability to perform basic personal care tasks such as:

- eating
- bathing
- dressing
- using the toilet
- getting in or out of a bed or chair
- caring for a bowel-control device
- walking (the most common ADL limitation for older adults)

Instrumental Activities of Daily Living (IADL) summarize an individual's ability to perform more complex, multidimensional activities and interact effectively with the environment:

- home management
- managing money
- meal preparation
- making a phone call
- grocery shopping (the most common IADL problem)

environment where we live and work—all play a role in the development and progression of chronic diseases. Health and wellness include a range of factors, such as health behaviors, social contributions, and access to health care (Putnam et al., 2003). To the extent that people practice health-enhancing habits and an active lifestyle in their younger years, many chronic conditions can be prevented, while others can be managed so they do not result in a severe disability that prevents active aging. However, medical care for chronic diseases results in high costs for society. Almost 95 percent of health care expenditures for older adults are spent on managing chronic diseases. Those with five or more chronic conditions (23 percent of all Medicare beneficiaries) account for 68 percent of all Medicare expenditures, a disproportionate rate that highlights the

Regular swimming can relieve the pain of arthritis.

importance of self-care through health promotion programs (Anderson, 2005; CDC & Merck Foundation, 2007; Lawlor, 2008).

Even though disability rates are declining, chronic illnesses often accompany old age, and societal values affect our attitudes toward loss of health. The importance placed by our culture on being independent and highly active may underlie our relative inability to accept illness graciously. It may also help account for the relatively high rates of depression experienced by elders with chronic illnesses, especially those with cardiovascular disease and diabetes. American values of independence may also partially explain why healthy older people often do not want to share housing or recreational activities with those who have mental or physical disabilities.

A reliable evaluation of health takes into account not only a physician's assessment of an older person's physical condition, but also elders' self-perceptions, observable behaviors, and life circumstances. **Quality of life** may be defined as this combination of an individual's functional health, feelings of competence, autonomy in performing ADLs, and satisfaction with one's social circumstances. Most older people appear to adjust their perceptions of their health in response to the aging process. In the 2004–2006 National Health Interview Survey (NHIS), 76 percent of non-Hispanic whites, 60 percent of African Americans, and 63 percent of Latinos age 65 and older rated their health as good to excellent. Self-ratings were slightly lower among those 85 and older; in this survey, 67 percent of whites, 54 percent of African Americans, and 47 percent of Latinos gave high self-ratings (Figure 4.2). Not surprisingly, higher household income is also associated with positive self-assessments of good health. Self-ratings are less positive among those with severe disability (AOA, 2008; Federal Interagency Forum, 2008; NCHS, 2009). More objective assessments by family and health care providers may differ from the elder's self-assessment of health. Even older persons in nursing homes tend to rate their health positively; often because they compare themselves to others who are more impaired than they are.

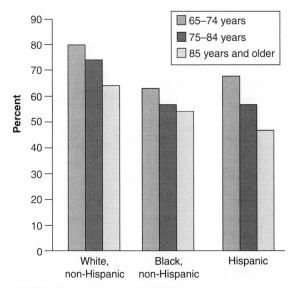

FIGURE 4.2 **Good to Excellent Health Among Noninstitutionalized Persons 65 and Older, by Age, Race, and Hispanic Origin: United States, 2004–2006**
SOURCE: Federal Interagency Forum on Aging-Related Statistics. *Older Americans Update 2008: Key Indicators of Well-Being.* Federal Interagency Forum on Aging-Related Statistics. Washington, DC: U.S. Government Printing Office, March 2008.

Older people who must take multiple medications, experience chronic pain, struggle with depression, or have financial and ADL limitations are most likely to report lower quality of life (Merck Institute, 2004). On the other hand, those who have recently had a successful medical or surgical intervention to alleviate the symptoms of their chronic conditions are more likely to report improved quality of life than elders who have not undergone successful health interventions.

It is noteworthy that physicians rate the quality of life of older persons with diabetes, arthritis, or even ischemic heart disease lower than do the elders themselves. This may indicate patients' greater adaptation to disabling conditions than physicians expect, or that medical professionals' definitions of quality of life are more constrained by objective health factors than are patients' own perceptions. The concept of resilience, described in Chapters 1 and 6, may also help explain the generally positive

POINTS TO PONDER

Think about you perceive your own health. To what extent do you compare your health to others of your age or gender? How does your ability to perform various ADLs affect your health perceptions? How does your day-to-day health affect your overall quality of life?

evaluations of their health by many older adults with chronic illness and disabilities. In general, older women rate their health more positively than men, even though they have more chronic diseases and are more likely to live in long-term care facilities (Federal Interagency Forum, 2008). The reasons for such gender differences are unclear.

Perceptions of good health are generally associated with other measures of well-being—particularly life satisfaction. Older persons who view themselves as reasonably healthy tend to be happier, more satisfied, more involved in social activities, and less lonely. In turn, lower-life satisfaction is associated with lower levels of self-perceived health. It has also been found that self-ratings of health are correlated with mortality. That is, older people who report poorer health, especially poorer functional abilities, are more likely to die in the next three years than those who perceive their functional health to be good (Benyamini, Blumstein, Lusky, & Modan, 2003).

WHY OLDER ADULTS RATE THEIR HEALTH POSITIVELY

- They compare themselves with peers.
- They have a sense of accomplishment from having survived to old age.
- They perceive themselves competent to meet environmental demands.
- They define quality of life broadly, to include meaning and life satisfaction, not just physical activity.

Chronic and Acute Diseases

As noted in Chapter 3, the risk of disease and impairment increases with age. However, the extreme variability observed in older people's health status suggests that poor health does not always accompany aging. The incidence of **acute** (or temporary) **conditions,** such as infections or the common cold, actually decreases with age. Those acute conditions that do occur, however, are more debilitating and require more care, especially for older women.

- The average number of days of restricted activity due to acute conditions is nearly three times greater for people age 65 and older than it is for those 17–44 years old.
- Older people report, on average, 33 days per year of restricted activity, of which 14 are spent in bed (NCHS, 2003).

An older person who gets a cold, for example, faces a greater risk of pneumonia or bronchitis because of changes in organ systems (described in Chapter 3) that reduce his or her resistance and recuperative capacities. Thus, older people are more likely than their younger counterparts to suffer restricted social activities as a result of temporary health problems.

In some cases, an acute condition that merely inconveniences a younger person may result in death for an older person. For example, respiratory infection rates are similar in young and old, but people age 65 and older account for 90 percent of all deaths due to pneumonia and influenza. Hospitalization for influenza-associated respiratory problems occurs much more frequently for older adults, increasing from less than 100 per 100,000 at age 50 to 64, to more than 400 at age 75 to 79, and 1,200 per 100,000 among those 85 and older (Thompson et al., 2004). This is why it is important for older people to be vaccinated against pneumonia and influenza. These vaccines can reduce the risk of pneumonia by 67 percent and of flu by 50 percent among older people, saving medical costs and increasing days of healthy living. Even if older adults develop pneumonia

after receiving a vaccine, the consequences are less severe. For example, their hospital stays are shorter, they are one-third less likely to have respiratory failure, and they are half as likely to die during hospitalization than elders who do not obtain the pneumococcal vaccine (Fisman et al., 2006). The proportion of older adults who obtained a pneumonia vaccine (57 percent) and flu vaccine (64 percent) in 2006 increased from less than 50 percent and 63 percent, respectively, in 1999. Rates are lower for African Americans and Latinos than for whites: 47 percent, 45 percent, and 67 percent, respectively, received flu vaccines in 2006; comparable figures for pneumonia vaccines were 36 percent, 33 percent, and 62 percent, respectively (Federal Interagency Forum, 2008). Even though Medicare Part B reimburses for these vaccines, older adults who rely only on Medicare for their health insurance are less likely to obtain flu shots than those with private insurance.

What is of greatest concern in terms of quality of life is that older people are much more likely than the young to suffer from **chronic conditions.** Chronic health conditions are:

- long-term (more than 3 months)
- often permanent, leaving a residual disability that may require long-term management or care rather than a cure

More than 80 percent of persons age 70 and over have at least one chronic condition, with multiple health problems occurring in 50 percent of the older population. Chronic problems are often accompanied by continuous pain and/or distress. At the very least, the individual is inconvenienced by the need to monitor health and daily activities, although ADLs may not always be limited. About 37 percent of older persons with chronic diseases report limitations in their ability to perform basic ADLs. Only about 2 percent of those age 65 and over are confined to bed by their chronic illness or disability, and most older people with chronic conditions are not dependent on others for managing their daily routines (AOA, 2008). On the other hand,

CHRONIC DISEASES AMONG ELDERS OF COLOR

Among those 70 and older:

- African American and Latino elders are more likely to suffer from diabetes than non-Hispanic whites.
- Diabetes is twice as common among women of color as in white women.
- Hypertension is 1.5 times more likely in African Americans than in whites.
- Rates of stroke are also higher among the former groups, but only when comparing black versus white women.
- In contrast, white men age 70 and older are more likely to report heart disease than their Latino or African American counterparts (Federal Interagency Forum, 2008).

Although one can live a satisfying life with multiple chronic conditions, these diseases may influence the decision to continue working or to retire. In a 2005 national survey, 25 percent of retirees ages 50 to 58, and 35 percent of those ages 59 to 61, cited chronic health problems as their reason for retiring. This varied by type of disease, and heart conditions were mentioned most frequently (He et al., 2005). Early retirement because of poor health can profoundly affect economic well-being in old age, as discussed more fully in Chapter 12.

The most frequently reported chronic conditions causing limitation of activity in persons age 65 and over are shown in Figure 4.3. Hypertension, arthritis, and heart disease are the leading chronic diseases, but older women are less likely to suffer from heart disease than older men; however their rates of heart disease are increasing dramatically, especially among the oldest-old, and approximating rates for men. The most common heart condition for both men and women is ischemic heart disease. Older women are more likely than men to

the small percentage who do need assistance with care have placed enormous pressures on health and long-term care services as well as on informal caregivers, as discussed in Chapters 10 and 17.

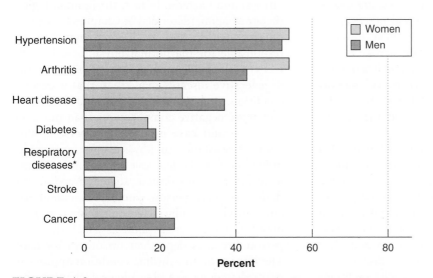

FIGURE 4.3   Percent of Persons 65 Years and Older Who Reported Selected Chronic Conditions by Gender: United States, 2005–2006
***(Includes emphysema, asthma, chronic bronchitis)**
SOURCE: Federal Interagency Forum on Aging-Related Statistics, 2008.

report arthritis and hypertension. Not surprisingly, most chronic conditions increase in prevalence with age. For example, almost twice as many people age 65 and older report that they have arthritis as those aged 45 to 64. The oldest-old suffer more than twice the strokes and one-third more heart attacks and heart disease than the young-old (CDC, 2009; Federal Interagency Forum, 2008).

Disabling chronic diseases tend to occur earlier among African Americans, Latinos, and American Indians than among whites. In the 2001–2002 National Health Interview Survey, 66 percent of African Americans age 65 and older had hypertension, compared with 48.5 percent of whites, and 48 percent of Latinos. Diabetes rates also varied by race and ethnicity: 23 percent of blacks, 14 percent of whites, and 24 percent of Latinos. These conditions result in higher rates of hospitalization, longer hospital stays, and shorter life expectancy. Therefore, it is not surprising that older persons of color with chronic conditions are less likely to describe their health as good or excellent than whites in every age group after age 65, as shown in Figure 4.2 (Federal Interagency Forum, 2008). Health disparities, such as poorer self-assessments of health and lower life expectancies, are due, in part, to discriminatory policies and practices earlier in life, causing nonwhites to have lower incomes and inadequate nutrition across the life course. An additional factor is that elders of color, because of past negative experiences with and distrust of formal services, may be less likely to utilize the health care system. These patterns are discussed further in Chapter 14.

As noted above, comorbidity, or the problem of coping with two or more chronic conditions, is another concept central to understanding health status and its secondary consequences, such as depression, anxiety, and social isolation. Comorbidity is more common in older women than in men. Among women age 65 and older, 50 percent have at least two chronic diseases, and 25 percent have three or more such conditions. Older women of color, especially in the lower socioeconomic range, have a higher prevalence of multiple chronic illnesses, functional limits on their ADLs, and disability, which reflects a lifetime of health and economic disparities (Clancey & Bierman, 2000).

Interactive Effects

Even though the majority of chronic conditions are not severely limiting, they can nevertheless make life difficult and lower older people's resistance to other illnesses. As noted earlier, the functional limits imposed by a chronic illness interact with the social constraints set by others' perceptions of illness to influence an older person's daily functioning and quality of life. Therefore, it is important to look beyond the statistics on the frequency of chronic conditions to the nature of chronic illness, the interaction of physical changes with emotional and sociocultural factors, and the physiological differences between young and old that may make the older person more susceptible to health problems.

Certain types of chronic diseases (e.g., cancer, anemia, and toxic conditions) may be related to older people's declining **immunity**: that is, reduced resistance to environmental carcinogens, viruses, and bacteria. In fact, the immunological theory of aging (described in Chapter 3) is based on the premise that declines in immunity are responsible for the normal physiological decrements with age. The accumulation of long-term, degenerative diseases may mean that a chronic condition, such as bronchitis, can have different and more negative complications than the same disease would have in a younger person. With reduced resistance to physical stress, an older individual may be less able to respond to treatment for any acute disease, such as a cold or flu, than a younger person would. The cumulative effect of chronic illness with an acute condition may become the crisis point at which the older person becomes dependent on others for care. The impact of any chronic condition appears to be mediated by the physiological changes that occur with age, the sociocultural context, and the person's mental and emotional outlook. This represents varying levels of P–E fit.

In sum, disabling health changes occur at different rates in different individuals and are not inevitable with age. We turn now to an examination of the chronic conditions that are the most common causes of death in older people.

Causes of Death in Old Age

Heart disease, cancer, and strokes accounted for 62 percent of all deaths among people age 65 and older in 2004 (Federal Interagency Forum, 2008). Declines in elders' deaths due to diseases of the heart since 1981—from 2,600 per 100,000 to about 1,500 per 100,000 in 2003—demonstrate progress in this area over the past 30 years (Hayflick, 1996; NCHS, 2003). Even so, heart disease remains the major cause of death among both men and women, killing 35 percent more people than all forms of cancer combined and resulting in 20 percent of adult disabilities. Heart disease accounts for 18 percent of hospital admissions and 33 percent of deaths that occur among older people, with the highest rates among the oldest-old and among African Americans (American Heart Association, 2005; OMHRC, 2006).

While stroke is also decreasing as a leading cause of death among the oldest-old; it is still the third leading cause for women over age 65 and fourth for men. This is slightly less than chronic obstructive pulmonary diseases (COPD) such as asthma and emphysema. Dramatic differences in the rates of death due to heart disease and stroke are found across ethnic and racial groups and by gender. Overall death rates are significantly higher among African Americans than whites until age 64 (by 80 percent), but lower among Latinos (by 20 percent) and Asian-Pacific Islanders (by 50 percent). These differences are less dramatic after age 75 (Williams, 2005). As Figure 4.4 demonstrates for 55- to 64-year-olds, African American men are at highest risk for death due to heart disease and cerebrovascular accidents (CVAs). Among women, African Americans are most likely to die of heart disease

and CVAs, but have about the same death rates as Latinas for cancer. Lower death rates among whites are attributable to greater access to quality health care across the life course, which allows early detection and management of these conditions so that they become chronic diseases among whites rather than causes of death. Likewise, Asian American adults are more likely to survive strokes and cancer, because these conditions are detected earlier than among African Americans, Latinos, and American Indians. Asian Americans also have the lowest incidence of heart diseases (NCHS, 2003). For older African American women and Latinas diabetes is the fourth major cause of death. It accounts for more than twice the rate of deaths as COPD, which is sixth in this population group (NCHS, 2003).

Educational achievement moderates the effect of race on chronic disease and disability, especially among older women. While African American women who have completed 0 to 8 years of school can expect 18.4 years of unhealthy life, their counterparts with 13 or more years of school can anticipate 12.9 years. Among white women, the difference is 17.5 versus 11.8 years of unhealthy life, respectively. Variations between more- and less-educated men are less dramatic; African American men with 0 to 8 years of education can expect 13.4 years of unhealthy life versus 9.0 for those with 13 or more years of education. The patterns for white men are comparable: 14.1 versus 10.0 years. Thus, education benefits people into old age, especially women, by enhancing their awareness of and access to preventive health services (Crimmins & Saito, 2001).

Men have higher rates of heart disease and cancer than women. In fact, gender differences in mortality are due mainly to the greater incidence of the principal fatal chronic diseases among men. However, women experience more nonfatal chronic conditions, including arthritis, incontinence, osteoarthritis, osteoporosis, and cataracts than do men. These diseases are less likely to result in death than cancer and heart disease, but they may lead to nearly as many days spent in bed. In

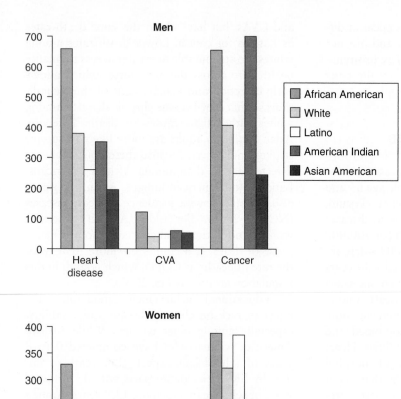

FIGURE 4.4 **Death Rates for Selected Diseases at Age 55 to 64 (per 100,000)**
SOURCE: NCHS, 2003b.

other words, older women are more likely to be bothered by chronic conditions, many of which can cause functional disability and impair their quality of life and daily interactions. However, they are less likely to die of such chronic conditions than are older men.

When examining rates of chronic diseases among low-income persons and elders of color, a life course perspective highlights the interplay among generational influences and economic and health inequalities. For example, in both developing and developed countries, chronic diseases are linked to poor health status and lower levels of quality of life. Poor people of all ages face an increased risk of health problems and disabilities. Although the likelihood of chronic illness increases with age, research increasingly shows that the origins of risk for chronic health conditions begin in early childhood. The intergenerational transmission of specific health-risk behaviors and lifestyles, including eating behaviors, depression, and family functioning, has been identified (Jacob & Johnson, 2001; Lawson & Brossart, 2001). Furthermore, risk continues to be influenced by factors such as socioeconomic status across the life course. For example, childhood conditions explain a substantial portion of the difference in men's mortality by race, operating indirectly through adult socioeconomic achievement (Warner & Hayward, 2002). At the same time, however, improvements in socioeconomic status help people live longer and healthier lives (Lynch et al., 2000; Whitfield & Hayward, 2003). Thus, any analysis of chronic conditions in old age needs to consider the role of racial, gender, and class inequities across the life course. We turn next to describing more fully the most common chronic illnesses and conditions in old age.

Common Chronic Conditions

Heart Disease and the Cardiovascular System

As noted above, cardiovascular diseases (CVD), which include coronary heart disease (CHD) and stroke, are the leading cause of death among older adults. Each year, CVD claims as many lives as the next five leading causes of death combined (Ai & Carrigan, 2006).

Coronary heart disease is a condition in which blood to the heart is deficient because of a narrowing or constricting of the cardiac vessels that supply it. This narrowing may be due to **atherosclerosis,*** in which fatty deposits (plaque formation) begin early in life and accumulate to reduce the size of the passageway of the large arteries. People in industrialized nations have higher levels of atherosclerosis than those in developing countries, which may be due to differences in diet and lifestyle. However, this pattern is shifting with globalization, with the incidence

---

HEART DISEASE AS A CHRONIC CONDITION

The dramatic decline in deaths due to heart attacks and strokes in the United States became front-page news in *The New York Times* in 2003: "The stereotypical heart attack patient is no longer a man in his 50s who suddenly falls dead. Instead, the typical patient is a man or woman of 70 or older who survives." The article addressed the growing challenge of maintaining heart attack survivors who must cope with chronic heart disease, including congestive heart failure, that can impair functional health.

SOURCE: *The New York Times*, January 19, 2003, pp. 1, 16.

---

of cardiovascular disease higher in India and China than in all developed countries combined (American Heart Association, 2003).

HEALTH AND BEHAVIORAL FACTORS THAT INCREASE THE RISK OF ATHEROSCLEROSIS

- hypertension or high blood pressure
- elevated blood lipids (resulting from a dietary intake of animal products high in cholesterol)
- cigarette smoking
- diabetes mellitus
- obesity
- inactivity
- stress
- family history of heart attack

---

*The terms **atherosclerosis** and **arteriosclerosis** are often used interchangeably, causing confusion regarding their distinction. Arteriosclerosis, a generic term, sometimes called hardening of the arteries, refers to the loss of elasticity of the arterial walls. This condition occurs in all populations and can contribute to reduced blood flow to an area. In atherosclerosis, the passageways of the large arteries narrow as a result of the development of plaques on their interior walls; atherosclerosis has been found to be age-related and has a higher incidence in industrialized populations. Arteriosclerosis and atherosclerosis can be superimposed, but there is not a causative relationship between the degree of atherosclerosis and the loss of elasticity (arteriosclerosis).

As the reduced blood flow caused by atherosclerosis becomes significant, angina pectoris may result. The symptoms of angina are shortness of breath and pain from beneath the breastbone, in the neck, and down the left arm. For older individuals, these symptoms may be absent or may be confused with signs of other disorders, such as indigestion or gallbladder diseases. In such instances, elders may delay seeking timely medical care. Treatment includes rest and nitroglycerine, which serves to dilate the blood vessels.

If deficient blood supply to the heart persists, heart tissue will die, producing a dead area known as an *infarct*. In other words, coronary artery disease can lead to a myocardial infarction (MI), or heart attack. The average age of a person experiencing a heart attack is 65.8 for men and 70.4 for women. After suffering an MI, 25 percent of men and 38 percent of women will die within a year. African American elders are more likely to die of heart disease than their white counterparts, a difference that is increasing. Among survivors, nearly 22 percent of men and 46 percent of women will be disabled within 6 years. Accordingly, about 50 percent of older adults with heart disease report limitations in their ADLs, compared with 26 percent of their age peers who do not have this condition (American Heart Association, 2005).

Acute myocardial infarction results from blockage of an artery supplying blood to a portion of the heart muscle. The extent of heart tissue involved determines the severity of the episode. Heart attacks may be more difficult to diagnose in older people, because their symptoms are often different from those in younger victims. These include:

- a generalized state of weakness
- dizziness
- confusion
- shortness of breath

These are dissimilar from the chest and back pain or numbness in the arms that characterizes heart attacks in younger people. Symptoms in older people may also merge with other problems, so that a heart attack may not be reported or treated until it is too late for effective help.

The term *congestive heart failure,* or heart failure, indicates a set of symptoms related to the impaired pumping performance of the heart, so that one or more chambers of the heart do not empty adequately during the heart's contractions. Heart failure does not mean that the heart has stopped beating. But decreased pumping efficiency results in shortness of breath, reduced blood flow to vital body parts (including the kidneys), and a greater volume of blood accumulating in the body tissues, causing edema (swelling). Treatment involves drugs, dietary modifications (e.g., salt reduction), and rest. Depression is a common complication of coronary heart disease and can affect the outcomes of cardiac surgery; this points to the importance of health care providers also treating depression (Ai Carrigan, 2006).

Most cardiovascular problems are treatable and preventable through diet, exercise, and medications. In fact, preventive steps are essential for most chronic diseases. For example, *hypertension,* or high blood pressure (defined as levels higher than 140 mm Hg for

---

PREVENTIVE MEASURES TO REDUCE CARDIOVASCULAR DISEASE RISK

- control weight
- engage in daily physical activity
- manage diabetes
- reduce intake of salt, saturated fat, processed carbohydrates
- increase intake of fruits rich in potassium (e.g., bananas, oranges) and vegetables rich in magnesium
- increase intake of foods high in calcium
- replace animal fat with olive oil
- avoid partially hydrogenated oils
- prevent cigarette smoking
- avoid excessive alcohol intake

systolic or 90 mm Hg for diastolic pressure) is the major risk factor in the development of cardiovascular complications and can be prevented, as illustrated in the box on page 128. As shown in Figure 4.3, the risk of hypertension is greater for women than men after age 65 (Federal Interagency Forum, 2008). This may partially explain why the incidence of coronary heart disease and strokes increases with age among women, although women with these conditions, on average, live longer than men. Older adults with the preventable conditions of hypertension and high cholesterol, and who are obese (body mass index greater than 30) are at greatest risk of coronary heart disease and stroke (NCHS, 2005). These modifiable lifestyle risk factors are more common among low-income individuals.

The prevalence of hypertension is significantly higher among older African Americans than whites (66 percent vs. 48.5 percent, respectively), but whether this difference is due to lifestyle or genetic factors is unclear. Significant increases in blood pressure should never be considered normal. For example, in some isolated primitive populations, a rise in blood pressure with age does not occur. Although genetic factors may come into play, this difference suggests that lifestyle can affect vulnerability to high blood pressure. Poverty is one risk factor associated with this condition; 50 percent of older adults with private insurance have hypertension, compared with 63 percent who are on Medicaid, a government-paid insurance plan for very low-income persons (Merck Institute, 2004; Schoenborn et al., 2006).

Most people can control their hypertension by improving health habits, although some must also use antihypertensive medications. Older adults who have been prescribed an antihypertensive must continue using it consistently and correctly. Because hypertension is not easily recognized by laypersons, older people may stop taking their medications if symptoms such as dizziness and headaches disappear. Some older adults discontinue their antihypertensive medications because they cannot afford the cost. This

COMMONLY PRESCRIBED CLASSES OF MEDICATIONS TO CONTROL HYPERTENSION

- *diuretics* (also known as "water pills"), which reduce excess water
- *beta blockers,* which reduce heart rate
- *ACE inhibitors*, which block an enzyme that constricts blood vessels
- *calcium channel blockers,* which work by preventing calcium from causing muscle contractions in the heart and inside blood vessels

can lead to significant elevations in blood pressure, as well as strokes or aneurysms.

Another cardiovascular problem, which is less frequently addressed than hypertension, is *hypotension,* or low blood pressure. Yet hypotension, characterized by dizziness and faintness from exertion after a period of inactivity and frequently related to anemia, is actually very common among older adults. Problems with hypotension may be more pronounced after sitting or lying down (postural hypotension) or suddenly standing, after which a person may appear to lose balance and sway. Hypotension is not dangerous in itself, but can increase the risk of falls. Older people who have a history of low blood pressure or who are taking some types of antihypertensive medications need to change positions slowly.

Strokes and Other Cerebrovascular Problems

We have seen how heart tissue can be denied adequate nourishment because of changes in the blood vessels that supply it. Similarly, arteriosclerotic and atherosclerotic changes in blood vessels that serve the brain can reduce its nourishment and result in the disruption of blood flow to brain tissue and malfunction or death of brain cells. This impaired brain tissue circulation is called *cerebrovascular disease.* When a portion of the brain is completely denied blood, a cerebrovascular accident (CVA), or stroke, occurs. The severity of the stroke depends on the particular areas as well as the total amount of brain tissue involved. Many older adults who have heart problems are also at risk for strokes.

CVAs represent one of the top four causes of death and the primary cause of disability for older men and women. Of the nearly 150,000 deaths from strokes in 2005, about 75 percent occurred among persons age 65 and older. African American elders and men in general are at greater risk of experiencing strokes than whites or other populations of color in the middle years, but after age 75, the incidence is higher among women across all races (CDC, 2009). African American men and women have almost twice the incidence of strokes as white men and women, and they are more likely to die of stroke. In 2005, strokes accounted for 70.5 deaths per 100,000 among black men vs. 44.7 for white men; 60.7 deaths per 100,000 for black women vs. 44 for white women. Death rates due to stroke are slightly lower for Latino and Asian American elders than for whites (NCHS, 2007). The rate of CVA incidents, disability, and deaths increases with age. The young-old stroke victim is twice as likely as the oldest-old to be discharged to home after recovery (63 percent and 32 percent, respectively). Conversely, the oldest-old stroke victim is twice as likely to die as the young-old (12.5 percent and 6.4 percent, respectively) (CDC, 2003a).

Atherosclerotic changes, in which fatty deposits gradually obstruct an artery in the brain or neck, are a common underlying condition. The most frequent cause of strokes in older persons is *cerebral thrombosis*, a blood clot that either diminishes or closes off the blood flow in an artery of the brain or neck. Cerebral hemorrhage, in which a weak spot in a blood vessel of the brain bursts, is another cause of strokes. Although less common in older adults, it is more likely to cause death when it does occur. The risk of stroke appears to be related most prominently to hypertension, but also to social and personal factors:

- age
- previous lifestyle
- diet
- exercise patterns
- socioeconomic status
- access to and utilization of health care

Regular sustained exercise and low-fat diets are associated with the reduction of fatty particles that clog the bloodstream. The use of such over-the-counter drugs as aspirin and warfarin in preventing blood clots also reduces the risk of strokes. Indeed, the death rate from strokes has dropped by 30 percent in the past 10 years, especially among the older population, because of these preventive measures and improved and immediate treatment (AHA, 2009). The area of the brain that is damaged by a stroke dictates which body functions may be affected. Results of stroke can include:

- *aphasia,* or inability of the stroke victim to speak or understand speech if the speech center of the brain dies
- *hemiplegia,* or paralysis of one side of the body
- *heminanopsia,* or blindness in half of the victim's visual field

The treatment for stroke is similar to that for heart attack and hypertension: modulated activity and supervised schedules of exercise and drugs, along with interventions to address depression. The FDA has approved new drugs to dissolve blood clots within three hours of the stroke. However, many victims do not receive this treatment because it generally takes longer than three hours to reach a diagnosis of the stroke and the location of the clot. An alternative method is to deliver the clot-dissolving drug directly with a long, fine tube through the artery; this can be effective within six hours after symptoms begin. These newer techniques offer great hope for patients and their families, but do not entirely prevent the neurological losses caused by a stroke.

Stroke survivors often require physical, occupational, and speech therapies, and the recovery process can be slow, frustrating, and emotionally draining for the patient and family. It is important to carefully assess the effects of a stroke and determine what functions can be relearned. Newer, more aggressive and immediate rehabilitation methods are effective in reducing the rates of residual impairments following a stroke. Within a year, about 50 percent of stroke victims have regained most of their motor function, but many report residual non-motor impairments such as problems with vision, speech, cognitive abilities, memory, and balance that can result in placement in a long-term care facility (Gubrium et al., 2003; Kugler et al., 2003; Mauk, 2006).

Rehabilitation must address not only physical conditions but also mental health issues such as depression, anxiety, and the psychosocial needs for support and respite of their family caregivers. The recognition of this wider range of rehabilitation has led to the creation of stroke support groups and Internet sites for both the survivor and family members.

Cancer

Almost 60 percent of all new cancers and 70 percent of cancer-related deaths occur in people age 65 and older. For that reason, cancer is often described as a disease of older adults (Christ, 2009; Marimaldi & Lee, 2006). Among those 65 and over, about 22 percent of deaths are due to cancer, especially cancers of the lungs, breast, colon, and pancreas. In fact, these malignancies in old age are the leading cause of death among women age 65 to 74 and are roughly equal to heart disease among men. However, the incidence of cancer decreases among those who reach age 90 (Masoro, 2006). In 2001, 3.5 percent of the U.S. adult population was a survivor of cancer; among these, 14 percent had survived for 20 years or longer. For those who survive into old age, cancer takes on the dimensions of a chronic disease rather than a life-threatening one (Institute of Medicine, 2007).

Breast cancer is the most common malignancy in older women, as is prostate cancer among older men. Lung cancer has its highest incidence in men age 65 and older, but appears to be associated more with smoking than with age. Cancer of the colon is more common in women, whereas colorectal cancer is more frequent in men. Breast cancer is the second leading cause of cancer death in women age 65 and older, who account for as much as 67 percent of breast cancer mortality (Ershler, 2003). Both the incidence and mortality rates due to cervical and breast cancer are greater in older African American women than in older white women, primarily because of lower use of cancer screening services (SEER, 2004). However, when screenings are regularly performed and the time between screening and diagnosis is minimized, both groups experience a similarly favorable prognosis (ACS, 2001). The greater risk of cancer with age may be due to a number of factors:

- the effects of a slow-acting carcinogen
- prolonged development time necessary for growth to be observable
- extended pre-exposure time
- failing immune capacity that is characteristic of increased age
- an accumulation of senescent cells with aging (Campisi, 2005)

Some cancers that have a high prevalence in the middle years and again in old age may have a different etiology with age. For example, breast cancer in premenopausal women appears to have a genetic basis and is related to family history, while it may have external or environmental causes in postmenopausal women. Certain dietary and lifestyle factors along with socioeconomic status and where one lives may also be related to cancer in older people. Diagnosing cancer in old age is often more difficult than at earlier life stages because of the existence of other chronic diseases and because symptoms of cancer, such as weight loss, weakness, or fatigue, may be inaccurately attributed to aging, depression, or dementia. In addition, some older people may not get regular cancer screenings. Because of racial differences in screening and early diagnosis, described previously, cancer is more likely to be a chronic disease in whites age 70 and older (21 percent) than among Latinos (10.5 percent) and African Americans (9.1 percent) (Merck Institute, 2004). Although future cohorts are more likely to participate in cancer screening as well as preventive measures, the numbers of people with cancer will continue to increase simply because of the higher incidence of cancer among the rapidly growing population of older adults (Marimaldi Lee, 2006). Nevertheless, many older adults today are cancer survivors and report cancer as a chronic rather than a life-threatening condition.

Arthritis

Although not a leading cause of death, arthritis is the second most common chronic condition affecting older people after hypertension and is a major cause of limited activity. In fact, 50 percent of those over age 65 and 58 percent over 70 report this problem (Federal Interagency Forum, 2008). Because arthritis is so common and the symptoms are so closely identified with the normal aging process, older people may accept arthritis as inevitable. If so, they may fail to seek treatment or to learn strategies to reduce pain and support their autonomous functioning. Although many treatments are used to control arthritic symptoms, little is known about ways to postpone or eliminate these disorders.

Arthritis is not a single entity, but includes over 100 different conditions of inflammations and degenerative changes of bones and joints. **Rheumatoid arthritis,** a chronic inflammation of the membranes lining joints and tendons, is characterized by pain, swelling, bone dislocation, and limited range of motion. It afflicts two to three times more women than men and can cause severe crippling. Rheumatoid arthritis is not associated with aging per se; many young people also have this condition, with initial symptoms most commonly appearing between 20 and 50 years of age.

Rheumatoid arthritis is characterized by acute episodes followed by periods of relative inactivity. Its cause is unknown; treatment includes

a combination of rest, exercise, and use of aspirin, which provides relief from pain, fever, and inflammation. Use of other anti-inflammatory agents, antimalarials, and corticosteroids, as well as surgical procedures to repair joints and correct various deformities, are effective for some people. There are extensive new developments in drug therapy for rheumatoid arthritis.

Osteoarthritis, which is presumed to be a universal corollary of aging, is a gradual degeneration of the joints that are most subject to stress—those of the hands, knees, hips, and shoulders. Pain and disfigurement in the fingers are manifestations of osteoarthritis but are generally not disabling. Osteoarthritis of the lower limbs, however, can limit mobility, reduce social activities, and increase the need for long-term care. Heredity as well as environmental or lifestyle factors are identified as causes of osteoarthritis, particularly:

- obesity
- occupational stresses
- wear and tear on the joints

Because of the increasing prevalence of obesity among U.S. adults, arthritis is expected to be more common among future cohorts of elders. Women are more likely to be affected by arthritis, especially after age 65. The condition is most prevalent among women age 85 and older (60 percent vs. 44 percent of their male counterparts). Compared to their male counterparts, this group reports more limitations in their ADLs, more

---

SYMPTOMS OF RHEUMATOID ARTHRITIS

- malaise
- fatigue
- loss of weight
- fever
- joint pain
- redness
- swelling
- stiffness affecting many joints

THERAPIES FOR OSTEOARTHRITIS

- anti-inflammatory drugs
- steroids
- regular exercise
- heat and cold
- reducing strain on weight-bearing joints through weight loss and the use of weight-bearing appliances
- surgical procedures that restore function to the hips and knees

psychological distress, and more joint pain than any other age group (CDC, 2008; Freedman, Hootman, & Helmick, 2007; Theist, Helmick, & Hootman, 2007).

Some progress has been made in minimizing inflammation and pain through the use of several types of therapy. A natural supplement (chondroitin sulfate, or CS) is effective in managing the pain associated with osteoarthritis without significant side effects (Leeb et al., 2000). Unfortunately, however, none of these techniques can reverse or cure the disease.

An estimated 50 percent of adults age 70 and older who have arthritis need help with ADLs, compared with 23 percent of their peers without arthritis. Not surprisingly, the former group uses health services (physicians, hospitals, medications, physical therapy, and nursing homes) and social services at a higher rate than the latter. Even though African Americans experience more limitations in activity, they are less likely to use medical services and physical or occupational therapy (Mikuls et al., 2003). Because of the constant pain and discomfort experienced by elders with arthritis, it is highly associated with self-reports of poor health. To illustrate, correlates of poor subjective health among people in their 60s include:

- arthritis
- poor vision
- few social resources

Among people in their 80s, subjective reports of poor health are associated with:

- arthritis
- heart disease
- low education
- poor mental health (Quinn et al., 1999)

It is noteworthy that arthritis is the only variable that appears as a central component of subjective health for both age groups.

The prime danger for people with arthritis is reducing their physical activity in response to pain. The adage "use it or lose it" has special meaning to a person with arthritis. Movement stimulates the secretion of synovial fluid, the substance that lubricates the surfaces between joints and increases blood flow to joint areas. Movement also tones the muscles that hold joints in place and that shield joints from excessive stress. When someone tries to avoid pain by sitting still as much as possible, the losses in lubricating fluid and muscular protection make movement even more painful. Eventually, the muscles surrounding immobilized areas lose their flexibility, and affected joints freeze into rigid positions called *contractures*. For these reasons, older people need to be encouraged to maintain physical activity in spite of pain. Researchers who tested a 6-month physical activity program for older adults with osteoarthritis in the knee and hip joints demonstrated significant improvements in lower extremity stiffness, pain, and walking speed (Hughes et al., 2004). Tai Chi, aerobics, and resistance training and fitness walking all show promise in decreasing the pain and stiffness associated with arthritis. The Centers for Disease Control and Prevention (CDC) recommends several programs that focus on educating patients on self-management, education, and physical activity programs on its website. Many of these are coordinated by the National Arthritis Foundation and its state chapters. Despite the proven effectiveness of these programs for relieving pain and improving ADLs, only about 11 percent of people with arthritis participate (CDC, 2008; Gallagher et al., 2003; Hughes et al., 2004; Rizzo, 2009).

The pervasive and unpredictable nature of the pain of arthritis can also result in social isolation and depression. A program to teach African American elders about managing their arthritis pain resulted in fewer symptoms of depression up to two years later than in elders who received no training (Phillips, 2000). Conversely, treating depression can reduce symptoms associated with arthritis. In a study testing antidepressant medications and psychotherapy with depressed older adults, 56 percent reported arthritis as a coexisting medical condition. Elders in the treatment group experienced a significant reduction in pain intensity and interference with ADLs due to arthritis compared with those not receiving any treatment. They also gave higher subjective ratings of health and quality of life. These indirect benefits of treating depression illustrate the importance of psychological factors in a systemic condition like arthritis (Lin et al., 2003).

Congruent with the person–environment perspective and the concept of active aging, the environment may need to be restructured so that a person with arthritis is able to walk around and keep up with daily activities but is not burdened by extreme press or demands. For example, a smaller home on one level can reduce environmental press. Despite the relatively low cost of physically modifying private homes, this is not widely done. A national survey revealed that only 17 percent of women and 12 percent of men age 70 and older have installed railings; 13 percent and 11 percent, respectively, have built ramps in their homes. Even the most frequently reported home modification—bathroom bars and shower seats—were made by only 43 percent of women and 36 percent of men (National Academy, 2000). Families and health care providers can be instrumental in recommending such modifications and helping elders locate programs, such as minor home repair, to reduce costs.

Osteoporosis

The human body is constantly forming and losing bone through the metabolism of calcium. As noted in Chapter 3, osteoporosis involves a more dramatic loss in bone mass. The increased brittleness of the bones associated with this condition can result in diminished height, slumped posture, backache, and a reduction in the structural strength of bones, making them susceptible to fracture. Compressed or collapsed vertebrae are the major cause of *kyphosis,* or "dowager's hump," the stooped look that many of us associate with the oldest-old.

Osteoporosis, together with its less serious counterpart, **osteopenia** (a significant loss of calcium and reduced bone density but without the risk of fractures), affects about 25 million Americans, 80 percent of whom are women. Caucasian and Asian American women are more likely to develop it than African American women; estimates are that 20 percent of white and Asian women age 50 and older have this condition, compared with 5 percent of African American and 10 percent of Latina women

Even severe osteoporosis does not inevitably limit elders' mobility.

(NIA, 2008). The causes of osteoporosis are unclear, although risk factors include:

- small stature and low body weight
- loss of calcium and estrogen in menopausal women
- sedentary lifestyle
- cigarette smoking
- excessive alcohol and caffeine consumption
- long-term dieting or fasting
- inadequate fluoride intake
- genetic factors that determine bone density
- family history of a hip fracture in a close relative (e.g., mother or sister)

The primary risk posed by osteoporosis is a fracture of the neck of the femur, or thigh. Many of the falls and associated hip fractures of old age actually represent an osteoporotic femoral neck that broke from bearing weight, causing the individual to fall. Many older people have undiagnosed osteoporosis, often showing no symptoms until a fall or fracture occurs. Typically, no immediate precipitating event can be identified as the cause of the fracture. Those at greatest risk for hip fractures are white women, the oldest-old who have functional health problems, diabetics, and elders with a history of hip fractures or stroke (Braithwaite, Col, Wong, 2003). Osteoporosis results in 1.5 million fractures per year; one in two women will have an osteoporosis-related fracture in their lifetime. Some 20 percent of white women experience fractures by age 65, increasing to more than 30 percent by age 90. Although both men and women lose bone mass at the same rate after age 65, men rarely develop symptomatic osteoporosis before age 70. White men are far less likely than white women to experience hip fractures; African American men and women have even lower rates of fractures than white men (Penrod et al., 2008). Gains in life expectancy are expected to double the number of hip fractures within the next 50 years.

The most common sites of fractures are:

- 20 percent hip
- 47 percent vertebrae

- 17 percent wrist
- 16 percent other sites (NIH, 2003)

Hip fractures are of great concern because of their impact on morbidity and mortality; about 24 percent of elders die within a year after a hip fracture. Even when death does not occur, falls can cause long-term disability and are responsible for more days of restricted activity than any other health problem. Those at greatest risk of dying within 6 months of a hip fracture are elders with dementia, stroke, Parkinson's, COPD, and congestive heart failure. The costs to society are also high because of hospitalizations and long-term care; in 2006, the cost of treating elders with hip fractures was $20 billion. With the growth of the older population and inflation in health-care costs, some estimate annual costs as high as $47 billion to care for victims of hip fractures by 2040. Therefore, it is not surprising that one of the health goals for older adults in the Surgeon General's report, *Healthy People 2010*, is to reduce annual hip fracture rates from 2006 rates of 11.1 per thousand to 4.2 among women, and from 5.6 per thousand to 4.7 among men. (*Healthy People 2010*; Wolinsky et al., 2009)

Not all falls and fractures among older people result from osteoporosis, however. Cardiovascular disease underlies approximately 50 percent of them. Others are due to a decline in postural control, produced by impairments of the senses and the central nervous system, changes previously discussed in Chapter 3. Table 4.1 (page 136) lists some of these risk factors.

PREVENTING OSTEOPOROSIS: THE CASE FOR AND AGAINST ESTROGEN Osteoporosis starts well before old age, perhaps as young as age 35. In the years immediately following menopause, the rate of bone loss can be as high as 5 percent, compared to a normal rate of 1 or 2 percent. Reduced estrogen—not calcium—is the primary cause of bone loss in the first 5 years after menopause. The goal in treating osteoporosis is to prevent further bone loss. Hormone replacement therapy (HRT), combining

TABLE 4.1   **Risk Factors for Falls**

RISK FACTOR	RELATIVE RISK**	
	FOR WOMEN	FOR MEN
Body mass index* less than 23.1 (i.e., a thin frame)	2.0	1.5
Daily alcohol consumption per day greater than 27 grams	2.9	1.9
No load-bearing exercise	2.0	3.4
No vigorous exercise in young adulthood	7.2	2.4
Two or more falls in past 12 months	3.0	3.4
History of stroke	3.8	3.6
Cigarette smoker (current or past)	1.5	not tested
Regularly uses sedatives	2.5	3.0
Regularly uses thyroid drugs	7.1	11.8

*Body mass index (BMI) is calculated by dividing weight (in kilograms) by height (in meters) squared: kg/m2. To calculate your own BMI, check the website: www.nhlbi.nih.gov/guidelines/obesity/bmi_tbl.htm.

**Increased risk relative to elders without these conditions

SOURCE: Lau et al., 2001.

estrogen with progesterone, or using estrogen alone (ERT), had been used for many years to prevent osteoporosis and bone fractures. This was because both HRT and ERT can decrease the risk of hip fractures and of spinal crush fractures. Since estrogen blocks the process of bone reabsorption, it can help the bones absorb dietary calcium and thereby increase bone mineral density (BMD) 3 to 5 percent. However, the effects may not be permanent, and benefits may be lost after discontinuing HRT.

Findings from the Women's Health Initiative (WHI) raised serious questions about the risks of HRT and resulted in fewer women using HRT. As part of this large (more than 100,000 women age 65 and older) national randomized controlled trial of exercise, diet, and HRT for preventing osteoporosis, heart disease, and cancer, one arm of the study tested the effects of a combined estrogen with progesterone intervention (HRT) against a placebo pill. Women enrolled in this arm did not know which drug they were using. Although the study was designed to measure health outcomes after 8.5 years of HRT or placebo use, it was stopped in 2002 after 5.6 years. This was because the

research team found no benefits of HRT on their primary outcomes, and in fact showed that HRT had several adverse effects. The relative risk of coronary heart disease, breast cancer, and stroke was *higher* among women in the HRT group compared to those in the placebo condition, although this translated to a slightly higher absolute risk (i.e., the number of women who actually developed these conditions). It should be noted that women using HRT were at much *lower* relative risk of developing colorectal cancer and hip fractures. In fact, their total bone and mineral density in the hip increased by 3.7 percent. These relative and absolute risks are shown in Table 4.2 (Cauley et al., 2003; WHI, 2002).

A SUMMARY OF PREVENTIVE STRATEGIES AGAINST OSTEOPOROSIS

- increased intake of calcium and vitamin D daily
- moderate weight-bearing exercise such as vigorous walking and strength training
- possibly fluoride
- possibly natural estrogens (phytoestrogens)

TABLE 4.2   **Risks and Benefits of Combined Estrogen Plus Progestin for Some Diseases**

COMPARED TO PLACEBO	RELATIVE RISK	ABSOLUTE RISK
Blood clot	111% increase	18 more cases per 10,000 women
Stroke	41% increase	8 more cases
Heart attack	29% increase	7 more cases
Breast cancer	26% increase	8 more cases
Colorectal cancer	37% *decrease*	6 fewer cases
Hip fractures	33% *decrease*	5 fewer cases

SOURCE: WHI, 2002.

On the basis of these findings, most physicians today do not recommend using HRT to prevent chronic diseases, especially coronary heart disease. In early 2004, the WHI director instructed all participants in the estrogen-only (ERT) arm of this clinical trial to stop using their pills as well. After 6.8 years, women using estrogen had a higher incidence of strokes than women on a placebo (12 more per 10,000). No differences were found in heart disease incidence or in breast or colorectal cancers. However, ERT did reduce the risk of hip fractures by 6 cases per 10,000 (WHI, 2003). Women coping with menopausal symptoms and attempting to prevent osteoporosis need to weigh the risks and benefits of HRT and ERT for their own health profile. Table 4.3 summarizes these findings.

As a result of these warnings, more women and health care providers are turning to natural remedies during menopause, such as soy or red clover iofavone extracts, or to nonhormonal prescription drugs, including antidepressants. However, an analysis of several clinical trials found that none of the nonhormonal therapies used to relieve hot flashes were as effective as estrogen or progesterone. The researchers concluded that the lowest effective dose of hormones for the shortest time possible should be used by women whose menopausal symptoms interfere with functioning (Nelson et al., 2006).

For women who cannot or choose not to use ERT or HRT, and because of their potential risks, new drugs such as Fosamax are approved by the Food and Drug Administration (FDA). Some of

TABLE 4.3   **Risks and Benefits of HRT**

ADVANTAGES	DISADVANTAGES
COMBINED HRT • can reduce risk of osteoporosis and hip fractures • can increase bone mineral density • can relieve hot flashes and night sweats • can relieve vaginal dryness • can improve cholesterol levels • can reduce risk of colon cancer	**COMBINED HRT** • can increase risk of blood clots • can increase heart attack and stroke risk • can increase risk of breast cancer • may contribute to gallbladder disease (pill form only)
Estrogen Only • can reduce risk of hip fractures	**Estrogen Only** • can increase risk of strokes

SOURCES: NIA, 2001; WHI, 2002.

these drugs can slow the rate of bone loss and prevent vertebral fractures. These medications may also cause adverse effects such as *osteonecrosis* (or bone death) of the jaw bone in some women, which can complicate tooth extractions in older women who are using these drugs but need to have a tooth removed. None of these medications eliminates the need for increased intake of calcium and vitamin D among older women. Combinations of fluoride and calcium treatments are sometimes given, but these may have negative side effects of gastrointestinal and rheumatic complaints. Researchers are also testing the effectiveness of phytoestrogenic or "natural" estrogens that are found in some foods such as wild yams.

Scientists are working on new forms of estrogen that will have the benefits of current forms without the risks. These "designer estrogens," or *selective estrogen receptor modulators,* appear to improve bone density and reduce levels of low-density lipoprotein (LDL) (bad) cholesterol while increasing the levels of high-density lipoprotein (HDL) (good) cholesterol. They do not have the adverse effects associated with HRT. Other researchers are exploring the effects of parathyroid hormone on advanced osteoporosis.

CALCIUM AND EXERCISE TO PREVENT OSTEOPOROSIS
Certain dietary and exercise habits may help prevent osteoporosis, especially increasing the amount of one's calcium intake after age 50. The National Institute on Aging (2008) recommends that women over age 50 consume 1,200 to 1,500 mg of calcium daily. This is higher than what was previously recommended; 1,500 mg of calcium is equivalent to five 8-ounce glasses of milk daily, far more than most women are accustomed to taking. In fact, some studies have recommended doses as high as 2,000 mg per day for older post-menopausal women. Given the difficulty of obtaining this much calcium from dietary sources, supplements are often the most effective way to increase calcium levels. Despite concerns about side effects related to high intake, such as kidney stones, there is little evidence that such supplementation harms older women.

Calcium is absorbed better when combined with vitamin D. For this reason, milk in the U.S. is fortified with vitamin D. Yet many older women do not consume enough milk or milk products to obtain vitamin D in that manner. It is also produced by the human body after 15 to 20 minutes of exposure to sunlight each day, but many older women use sun screen, avoid the sun or are unable to get outside every day, especially in the winter or in cloudy climates. Older women who do not obtain an adequate intake of fortified milk or exposure to sunshine should take daily multivitamins with at least 400 international units (IUs) of vitamin D (600 IUs for those over age 70) (NIA, 2008). It is noteworthy that regular intake of calcium and vitamin D supplements (at least 4 days per week) has been found to reduce hip fractures by 29 percent (WHI, 2003).

Although increased calcium appears to be an essential preventive measure, low dietary calcium may be only partly responsible for osteoporosis. Therefore, increasing calcium intake may not prevent fracturing after bone loss has occurred. One reason is that an estimated 40 percent of osteoporotic women have a deficiency of the enzyme that is needed to metabolize calcium (lactose), thus making it difficult for them to absorb calcium. An additional problem is that once one fracture is present, an individual has a 70 to 80 percent chance of developing another.

A combination of calcium and exercise (both aerobic and weight-bearing) appears to prevent bone loss. Researchers found that simple, vigorous walking on a daily basis for one year prevents bone loss in older women with osteopenia and osteoporosis. However, they concluded that this daily exercise program must continue longer to improve bone mineral density (BMD) levels (Yamazaki et al., 2004). On the other hand, new forms of exercise are found to increase BMD in the hip after just 8 months (Gusi, Raimundo, & Leal, 2006).

Because of the increased attention to osteoporosis today, many entrepreneurial clinics are offering bone-density testing to postmenopausal women. The small, portable machines generally used test bone density only at the wrist or ankle. This makes them less reliable and accurate than the large whole-body machines known as *DEXA*. Tests with portable machines show the obvious results: that most women over 50 have less bone mass than younger women. A major limitation is that such tests do not provide a comparison with any baseline data for a specific individual. Women should have a comprehensive baseline bone-density test before they undergo menopause and then be retested when they are in their 60s, 70s, and 80s. In fact, a committee of osteoporosis experts, convened by the U.S. Preventive Services Task Force in 2002, concluded that DEXA bone-density testing should be targeted at the hip where many fractures occur, and primarily for women 65 years and older, as well as women over 60 who weigh less than 127 pounds. These recommendations and other preventive suggestions can be found at http://www.ahrq.gov/clinic/uspstfix.htm.

Chronic Obstructive Pulmonary Disease or Respiratory Problems

Chronic bronchitis, fibrosis, asthma, and emphysema are manifestations of chronic obstructive pulmonary diseases (COPD) that damage lung tissue. They increase with age, develop slowly and insidiously, and are progressive and debilitating, often resulting in frequent hospitalizations, major lifestyle changes, and death. In fact, by age 90, most people are likely to have some signs of emphysema, with shortness of breath and prolonged and difficult exhalation. Getting through daily activities can be extremely exhausting under such conditions. Causes of COPD are both genetic and environmental, especially prolonged exposure to various dusts, fumes, or cigarette smoke. Three to four times as many men as women have these diseases, probably due to a combination of normal age changes in the lung and a greater likelihood of smoking and exposure to airborne pollutants. This is especially true in cohorts age 85 and older; men in the oldest-old group are three times more

likely to die of COPD than their female counterparts. This pattern may shift over time with more women exposed to pollutants. Treatment is usually continuous and includes:

- drugs
- respiratory therapy
- breathing exercises to compensate for damage
- avoidance of respiratory infections, smoking, pollution, and other irritants

Allergic reactions to bacterial products, drugs, pollutants, and even foods increase with age. The greater incidence of drug allergies may be a function of decreases in physiological capacities and the increased use of many drugs, such as sedatives, tranquilizers, antidepressants, and antibiotics.

Diabetes

Compared with other systems of the body, the endocrine glands do not show consistent and predictable age-related changes, other than the gradual slowing of functioning. However, insufficient insulin, produced and secreted by the pancreas, can lead to **diabetes mellitus.** Diabetes mellitus is characterized by hyperglycemia or above-normal amounts of glucose (sugar) in the blood and urine, resulting from an inability to use carbohydrates. Diabetics may go into a coma when their blood glucose levels get very high. Low blood glucose (hypoglycemia) can also lead to unconsciousness. Older diabetics include people who:

SYMPTOMS OF DIABETES

- excessive thirst
- increased appetite
- more frequent urination
- fatigue
- weakness
- loss of weight
- slower wound healing
- blurred vision
- irritability

- have had the disease since youth or had juvenile onset diabetes (Type I);
- develop it in middle age (adult onset diabetes)—most often between 40 and 50—and incur related cardiovascular problems (Type II)
- develop it late in life and generally show mild pathologic conditions (Type II)

Type II diabetes is most common in older adults, accounting for 90 to 95 percent of all diagnosed cases, and can generally be managed without insulin through careful diet and a strict exercise regimen (ADA, 2009). Although diabetes can occur at any age, diabetic problems related to the body's lessened capability to metabolize carbohydrates can be particularly severe in older adults. Older age, obesity, and race are among the most significant risk factors for Type II diabetes (ADA, 2004). Obesity is a primary risk factor due to changes in fat/muscle ratio and slower metabolism with aging. This is especially the case among older African American, American Indian, and Latina women, who have a higher rate of obesity and diabetes than do older white women. On average, African Americans, Latinos, and American Indians are 1.6, 1.5, and 2.2 times more likely, respectively, to have diabetes than non-Hispanic whites, 14 percent of whom have this condition (CDC, 2003b; OMHRC, 2006; Schoenborn et al., 2006). Glucose tolerance and the action of insulin are often compromised by poor diet, physical inactivity, and coexistent diseases, placing the individual at greater risk of diabetes. Poorly controlled diabetes can result in kidney failure and diabetic retinopathy, a disease that can cause blindness through lack of oxygen to the retina. These conditions are more common among African Americans with diabetes than among their white counterparts.

The prevalence of diabetes has increased dramatically among all age groups, from just under 6 million in 1980 to 18 million in 2005. Among adults age 60 and older, 21.2 percent have diabetes (National Institute of Diabetes, Digestive and Kidney Disease, 2007). However, the greatest increase is among 30- to 39-year-olds, which has disturbing implications for future cohorts of older adults. By 2050, diabetes prevalence is expected to increase three-fold among today's middle-aged adults who will then be 75 years or older. It is estimated that 4 million in this age group will have diabetes in 2050, compared with 1 million today (CDC, 2003b; Francoeur & Elkins, 2006). When rates are compared across racial groups in this middle-aged population, Latinos show the greatest increase in diabetes prevalence, followed by whites and African Americans. These increases in rates of diabetes over a 20-year period are attributed to a rise in obesity during this same interval, from 12 to 20 percent. As noted earlier, this growing rate of obesity, which is associated with low income, raises concerns about health risks for future cohorts of elders.

The symptoms of diabetes shown in the box above may not be present in older people, however. Instead, diabetes among the older population is generally detected incidentally through eye examinations, hospitalization, and testing for other disorders. Older people may experience fatigue, a sign of this disease, but attribute it to a slowing down often assumed to be normal with aging. Since blood glucose may be temporarily elevated under the stress of illnesses such as stroke, myocardial infarction, or infection, people should not be labeled as diabetic unless the high glucose level persists under conditions of reduced stress.

The cumulative effect of high blood glucose levels can lead to complications for some diabetics, especially if they cannot control their glucose levels. These complications include:

- high blood pressure
- infections
- painful nerves in the feet, legs, and hands
- blindness associated with diabetic retinopathy
- kidney disease or failure
- stroke
- cognitive impairment
- harm to the coronary arteries
- skin problems
- poor circulation in the extremities, leading to gangrene and amputations

Comorbidity of diabetes with other age-related physical problems such as hypertension can result in serious health difficulties, ADL and IADL limitations, and if left undetected or untreated can have life-threatening consequences. Approximately 2 out of every 3 people with diabetes die from heart disease or stroke associated with their diabetic condition (CDC, 2003b; NIDDK, 2007). Because they are more susceptible to most illnesses such as influenza or pneumonia, diabetics are more likely to die than are nondiabetics. Recent research suggests a possible link between diabetes and Alzheimer's disease, another leading cause of death among older adults (ADA, 2009b). Depression also appears to be associated with the development of Type II diabetes, but the direction of causality remains unclear (Golden et al., 2008). On average, life expectancy among diabetics is 15 years less than in the population without diabetes. Even when not life-threatening, adults age 60 and older who have diabetes are two to three times more likely to report an inability to walk a quarter of a mile, climb stairs, do housework, or use a mobility aid compared with their age peers without diabetes (NIDDK, 2007). Diabetes cannot be cured, but it can generally be managed at home primarily through changes in lifestyle and health behaviors. These include:

- a diet of reduced carbohydrates and calories
- regular exercise
- proper care of feet, skin, teeth, and gums
- monitored insulin intake for those who require it

Several studies in the U.S. and Europe have tested the impact of diet and exercise among middle-aged adults at risk for diabetes (i.e. overweight or obese, with impaired glucose tolerance). Reducing fat intake and calories, dietary counseling, increasing physical activity to 30 minutes per day for five days per week in combination can reduce the development of diabetes by lowering weight and improving glucose levels, especially among those age 60 and older. These beneficial effects of improved diet and exercise are found in as little as six months (Palmer, 2009).

To minimize forgetfulness and treatment errors, older people, especially those who acquire diabetes late in life, may need reminders from health care providers and family members regarding:

- the importance of diet
- daily examination of their skin
- urine testing
- the correct dosage of insulin or other drugs

Obesity

Although we generally hear about the health impact of obesity on middle-aged persons, the problem is also increasing among older adults. For most adults, weight increases until about age 60, then gradually decreases. However, an estimated 40 percent of adults age 60–69 and 30 percent of those 70–79 are obese. As noted earlier, this puts them at greater risk for disability and chronic diseases such as type II diabetes, heart disease, stroke, hypertension, osteoarthritis, sleep apnea, and some forms of cancer. Weight loss programs that minimize muscle and bone loss are important for older persons because aging itself is associated with a decline in muscle mass and an increase in fat mass. For this reason, one of the goals for older adults' health in *Healthy People 2010* is to reduce their rate of obesity to 15 percent (Alley et al, 2008; CDC & Merck Foundation, 2008; Elder obesity, 2009; NCHS Dataline, 2008; Villareal, Apovian, Kushner & Klein, 2005).

Problems with the Kidneys and Urinary Tract

The various diseases and disorders of the urinary system characteristic of old age tend to be either acute infections or chronic problems resulting from the gradual deterioration of the structure and function of the excretory system with age. As seen in Chapter 3, the kidneys shrink in size, and their capacity to perform basic filtration tasks declines, leading to a higher probability of disease or infection. One of the most common age-related problems for women is the inability of the bladder to empty completely. This often results in cystitis, an acute inflammatory state accompanied by pain and irritation that can generally be treated with antibiotics.

Older men face an increased risk of diseases of the prostate gland, with cancer of the prostate being the most frequent malignancy; After age 40, the risk doubles every decade, and the mortality rate among men age 65 and older is 100 times greater than for those under age 65; African American men have the highest rate (Coleman, Hutchins, & Goodwin, 2004, SEER, 2004). For these reasons, the American Cancer Society and the American Urological Association recommend annual prostate evaluations for men age 50 and older by both a digital rectal exam and a test to determine levels of prostate-specific antigen (PSA) in the blood. Cancer of the prostate frequently spreads to the bones, but surgery is rarely recommended for men over age 70 because the disease usually progresses slowly in this age group. Instead, more conservative treatment, such as hormonal therapy and more frequent monitoring are usually recommended. Treatment of prostate cancer and its effects on men's sexual functioning are described more fully in Chapter 7. A more common problem for older men is **benign prostatic hypertrophy,** a condition in which the prostate gland becomes enlarged and causes discomfort, but is not associated with prostate cancer.

INCONTINENCE **Incontinence,** or the inability to control urine or feces, is a chronic urinary problem that can profoundly alter an older person's social and living situations. It has been estimated to occur in at least 17 percent of men and more than 35 percent of women over age 65 and living in the community (Thom, Nygaard, Calhoun, 2005; Stothers, Thom, Calhoun, 2005). Because older people and their families often consider incontinence a taboo topic, they tend to be unaware of methods to treat it. Older adults generally do not discuss the problem with their doctors, and only a small percentage use any

protective devices, such as absorbent pads that can be purchased in drug stores. Many health care providers, in turn, do not ask their older patients about incontinence. This widespread reluctance to acknowledge incontinence as a problem can have serious psychological and social implications, especialy when precipitating the decision for nursing home placement. For many families, frequent incontinence is often the "breaking point" in their ability to provide in-home care. As a result, up to 10 percent of nursing home admissions are attributed to incontinence. This has significant cost and quality-of-life implications (Morrison & Levy, 2006). There are two primary types of incontinence:

- *urge incontinence,* where the person has a strong urge to urinate due to irregular bladder contractions and is unable to hold urine long enough to reach a toilet
- *stress incontinence,* where leakage occurs during physical exertion or when sneezing or coughing because of weakened pelvic floor muscles. This phenomenon can also occur among younger women

Many cases of incontinence represent a combination of these two types, referred to as *mixed incontinence.* Incontinence sometimes results from a specific precipitating factor, such as acute illness, infection, or even a change in residence. It can be treated if the cause is known. For example, temporary incontinence can be caused by bladder or urinary tract infections, which may be treated with antibiotics. Prescribed medications can also cause urgent and frequent urination. If informed of the detrimental effects of medication, a physician may reduce the drug dosage. With age, the bladder and urethra in women commonly descend, resulting in stress incontinence; leaking then occurs with the increased abdominal pressure brought on by coughing, sneezing, laughing, lifting, or physical exercise. Another type of incontinence, known as *functional incontinence,* often results from neurological changes and accompanies other health problems, such as Parkinson's disease and dementia. Other physical causes that should be investigated medically are prostate problems, pernicious anemia, diabetic neuropathy, and various cancers. Because the types and causes of incontinence vary widely, thorough diagnosis and individualized treatment programs are critical. Even habitual incontinence should not be assumed to be irreversible.

Although some physicians prescribe medications to increase bladder capacity or reduce urine production, these often have unpleasant side effects such as blurred vision and dry mouth. Noninvasive behavioral management techniques, such as frequent access to toilet facilities, restriction of fluid intake before bedtime, and systematic exercise of the pelvic muscle, are often just as effective. Even incurable problems can be managed through protective products (e.g., absorbent pads) and catheters (tubes draining the bladder) to reduce complications, anxiety, and embarrassment. Only a small proportion of older persons with incontinence, however, are so severely disabled that they are unlikely to regain continence and require a catheter or other external appliances to cope with the conditions. Physical exercise, known as *Kegels,* designed to promote and maintain sphincter muscle tone, can also prevent or reduce age-related incontinence, particularly among older women. All possible treatments, especially behavioral techniques, exercise, and biofeedback,

should be explored, because older people's embarrassment and humiliation may result in their avoiding social gatherings out of fear of having their incontinence detected. Support groups, such as those sponsored by the National Association for Incontinence, exist nationwide.

Problems with the Intestinal System

Many older people experience problems in digestion and continuing gastrointestinal distress, due particularly to age-related slowing down of the digestive process. Most intestinal difficulties are, in fact, related to unbalanced diets or diets with limited fiber content. **Diverticulitis** is one of the most common problems, affecting as many as two-thirds of the oldest-old, especially women (Korzenik, 2006). It is a condition in which pouches or sacs (diverticula) in the intestines (especially in the colon) result from weakness of the intestinal wall; these sacs become inflamed and infected, leading to symptoms of nausea, abdominal discomfort, bleeding, and changes in bowel function. Diverticulitis, which is increasing in industrialized nations, may be associated with a highly refined diet lacking in fiber. Self-management includes a high-fiber diet and antibiotic therapy.

Many older people worry about constipation, but this is not an inevitable outcome of aging, as noted in Chapter 3. It is more prevalent among elders in long-term care facilities but is also reported by approximately 26 percent of community-dwelling elders and accounts for about 2.5 million physician visits annually (Hsieh, 2005). Constipation may be a symptom of an underlying disease or obstruction. If this is not the case, treatment commonly includes:

- physical activity
- increased fiber intake
- increased fluid intake
- bowel training
- biofeedback
- laxatives and stool softeners

MANAGEMENT OF INCONTINENCE

- medications to increase bladder capacity
- surgery
- dietary changes
- Kegel exercises (at least 100 times per day)
- behavioral management techniques, such as reducing fluid intake when bathroom access is limited
- reduction in the intake of caffeine (e.g., coffee, tea, cola, even chocolate) can prevent the stimulation of the kidneys to excrete fluids
- weight loss can also help, as obesity is found to cause urine leakage

CAUSES OF CONSTIPATION

- overuse of cathartics
- lack of exercise
- psychological stress
- gastrointestinal disease
- an unbalanced diet with respect to bulk

Because many older people are overly concerned about having regular bowel movements, they may become dependent on laxatives. Data from more than 5,000 white and African American elders found that 10.2 percent of both groups used laxatives, with higher use among women, those taking four or more prescriptions, those with four or more physician visits per year, and those with ADL problems (Ruby et al., 2003). Over time, laxatives can cause other health problems, such as irritating the colon and decreasing the absorption of certain vitamins.

Hiatus hernia appears to be increasing in incidence, especially among obese women; this occurs when a small portion of the stomach slides up through the diaphragm. Symptoms include indigestion, difficulty in swallowing, and chest pain that may be confused with a heart attack. Medical management includes weight reduction, elevation of the upper body when sleeping, changes in the size and frequency of meals, and medication. Although hiatus hernia in itself is not especially severe, it may mask the symptoms of more serious intestinal disorders, such as stomach cancer.

The incidence of gallbladder disease, especially gallstones, also increases with age and is indicated by pain, nausea, and vomiting, with attacks increasing in number and severity. Most cases in older adults are asymptomatic, and physicians debate whether to perform surgery or follow a more conservative course of medical management. Medical treatment usually involves a combination of weight loss, avoiding high-fat foods, and using antacids as needed.

Oral Diseases

Because of developments in preventive dentistry, newer cohorts of older people have better oral health than any preceding cohort. Only 27 percent of adults over age 65 today are completely **edentulous** (i.e., no natural teeth remaining). As one might expect, edentulism increases with age.

- 24 percent of the young-old are edentulous
- 39 percent of the oldest-old are edentulous (Schoenborn et al., 2006)

This change is due entirely to historical differences in dental care delivery; not because of the aging process.

The common problems of tooth decay and periodontal diseases also appear to increase with age, although the evidence is limited and less clear. In national epidemiological surveys such as the National Health and Nutrition Examination Survey (NHANES III), the rate of root caries (cavities that develop on exposed root surfaces) was found to be more than three times greater among people over age 65 than in those under age 45. Rates of decay on the enamel surfaces of teeth, however, are not much higher among 65- to 74-year-olds compared with 35- to 44-year-olds. Differences are much greater when the older group is compared with people age 18 to 24, who have only about 10 percent of their tooth surfaces decayed or filled compared with 31 percent of people age 65 to 74 (Lamster & Northridge, 2008). These differences reflect changes over time in preventive dental care, such as the widespread use of water fluoridation. NHANES III also found an age-related increase in the incidence of periodontitis or gum disease, especially after age 45. As a result, 25 percent of older adults have poor bone support of existing teeth (CDC, 2005; Lamster & Northridge, 2008). Data from the Baltimore Longitudinal Study (described in Chapter 1) showed that older adults who are edentulous or have fewer than 20 teeth are more likely to die within a 15-year period—independent of age, systemic health, and smoking—compared with elders who have more teeth. These higher death rates may be associated with periodontal disease, which is a major cause of tooth loss but also impairs the immune system, or with poor nutrition caused by tooth loss (Padilla et al., 2008).

Cancers of the lip, tongue, mouth, gum, pharynx, and salivary glands increase with advanced age. In North America and Western Europe, cancer of the lip is the most frequent type of oral cancer and has a high survival rate (between 65 and 90 percent over a five-year period). Smoking and heavy alcohol use are strongly linked to oral cancer (USDHHS, 2000).

HIV/AIDS in the Older Population

While it cannot be classified as a chronic disease in the same way as diabetes or chronic obstructive pulmonary disease, the growing number of older adults with HIV (human immunodeficiency virus) or AIDS (acquired immune deficiency syndrome) and the increasing time between infection, diagnosis, and death make this an important public health issue in gerontology. In years to come, HIV/AIDS will place greater demands on long-term care, especially on home-based services and informal caregiving networks. Since it is mandatory to report AIDS cases, the Centers for Disease Control and Prevention (CDC) receive reports from all state and territorial health departments on all diagnosed cases of AIDS. Because of stereotypes that AIDS only affects younger populations and that older people are not sexually active, many physicians and HIV-testing programs do not routinely test older adults for HIV/AIDS. Cases often go undiagnosed because older people do not report symptoms, or symptoms such as nerve pain and vision problems are simply attributed to aging.

Almost one million Americans are living with HIV/AIDS. Although it is difficult to guess the actual prevalence, including undiagnosed cases, 24 percent of people with HIV/AIDS are estimated to be age 50 and older (considered "older adults" by the CDC). Additionally, persons age 50 and older account for 15 percent of new HIV/AIDS

diagnoses. Because medical interventions have extended the lives of those with HIV/AIDS, this age group is predicted to account for 50 percent of all HIV/AIDS cases by 2015. This will include people who were diagnosed earlier in life but have survived because of medical interventions, as well as those who contract the disease in old age. Men are at far higher risk than women, ranging from 86 percent of diagnosed AIDS cases among 50- to 54-year-olds to 79 percent among those 65 and older. More than half of all cases among the population 50 and older are African Americans and Latinos (52 percent). Rates among persons age 50 and older are 12 times as high among blacks and five times as high among Latinos compared with whites. Women of color are at greater risk than their white counterparts in this age group, representing 70 percent of women living with HIV/AIDS. The number of new HIV/AIDS cases in older women has risen sharply by 40 percent, due primarily to women becoming infected through unprotected sex with infected male partners. Approximately 17 percent obtained the virus by sharing needles for drug use. In 2005, 66 percent of all women diagnosed with AIDS had been exposed to the virus through heterosexual contact, and only 33 percent through intravenous drug use. The risk of exposure through unprotected sex is greatest for older women of color (CDC, 2008; HRSA, 2001; Nguyen & Holodniy, 2008; Stark, 2006; Vosvick et al., 2003; Zablotsky & Kennedy, 2003).

These prevalence rates may be underestimates because older adults are not routinely tested for HIV/AIDS. Physicians are often uncomfortable discussing sexuality with their older patients, and HIV/AIDS prevention programs for older adults are rare. Similarly, older people do not seek medical attention during the early stages of this disease because they assume many of the symptoms are merely signs of normal aging or chronic diseases that they are already managing. These symptoms include:

- general aches and pains
- headache
- chronic cough

- lack of energy
- loss of appetite and weight
- problems with short-term memory

Because of such misunderstandings, older people who become infected with the HIV/AIDS virus are often unaware that they are at risk and may not suspect their sexual partners. Detection may be even more difficult because conditions such as arthritis and dementia can also be caused by HIV, and they may not seem unusual in older adults. One reason for the significant rise of this disease among older women is that, after menopause, they may assume that they do not need to have their male partner use a condom and practice safe sex because they need not fear pregnancy. Menopause can also cause vaginal dryness and thinning of the vaginal lining. This may result in small abrasions and tears in the vaginal walls where the virus can penetrate.

Older men may be at risk because of unprotected sex with male partners and paid sex workers. The latter may be male or female, and some may use injected heroin or crack cocaine with shared needles. The growing rates of divorce among older adults have increased the numbers of newly single people engaging in unsafe sex. In fact, 38 percent of sexually active older adults infected with HIV are estimated to have unprotected sex, which highlights the importance of targeted prevention initiatives (Barrow, 2008; CDC, 2008; HRSA, 2001; Radda et al., 2003; *Science Daily,* 2007).

Older adults may also be at greater risk because already-low levels of T cells, part of the immune system, are lost more rapidly in older people with this infection. In elders with compromised immune systems, the HIV virus is more likely to attack than in younger people or in other older people who have a fully functioning immune system. This may also explain why the incubation period for HIV is shorter in older adults, an average of 5.7 years versus 7.3 years in people under age 50. Poorer immune reactions may also account for the shorter time

Grace was a happily married woman with a family and a career until her husband of 30 years left her. After her divorce, she began dating George, a close family friend she had known for many years. Because she was beyond childbearing years, she was not worried about pregnancy and never thought about using condoms. And because she knew George, it did not occur to her to ask about his sexual history or if he had been tested for HIV. At age 55, she had a routine checkup. Her blood tested positive for HIV. George had infected her. She will spend the rest of her life worrying that the virus might develop into life-threatening AIDS, that any cough, sneeze, rash or flu could indicate AIDS and perhaps the beginning of the end of her life (NIA, 2009).

between diagnosis and death for people over age 50, although this may also result from their being infected for years before being tested for the virus (Emlet & Farkas, 2002).

HIV/AIDS is not a major cause of death for older people compared to heart disease, cancer, stroke, and diabetes. Nevertheless, it accounted for 2.2 per 100,000 deaths among people age 65 to 74 and 0.7 per 100,000 for those age 75 to 84. As with younger populations, the availability of antiretroviral drugs has reduced death rates due to HIV/AIDS among older populations from a high of 3.6 per 100,000 in 1995 to 2.2 in 2000, which results in all age groups living longer with HIV/AIDS as a chronic rather than terminal illness. Most older adults take their antiretroviral medications more regularly and adhere better to treatment regimens than younger patients (CDC, 2008; NCHS, 2003).

Researchers question whether older adults with HIV/AIDS are more or less likely than younger people to use health services. An analysis of 571 cases in California compared 63 AIDS patients who were age 60 and older with 190 age 50 to 59 and 318 age 30 to 49. In addition to age, functional status and diagnosis were hypothesized to be predictors of inpatient and outpatient medical care, in-home services, and mental health services. Age was not associated with functional health or service utilization. Both younger and older patients were more likely to use all types of services as their ADL limitations increased. Among all types of health care, mental health services were least likely to be used by all age groups (Emlet & Farkas, 2002). These findings demonstrate that older adults with HIV/AIDS do not seek health services at a higher rate than younger patients unless their functional health has deteriorated significantly. However, another study identified age differences in perceptions of the importance of community-based services. Older patients age 50 and over rated home-delivered meals, adult day care, home-chore services, and physical therapy as more important than did their younger counterparts (20 to 39 years). Both groups rated drug programs to treat HIV/AIDS plus dental and primary medical care as a priority. These results suggest that older HIV/AIDS patients highly value long-term care services to improve their quality of life (Emlet & Berghuis, 2002). Recent federal and state budget cuts, however, are limiting the availability of prevention initiatives and community-based and home-care services. Some long-term care facilities still deny that any of their residents may have HIV/AIDS. In addition, older HIV-positive persons may not seek services because of real or perceived homophobia, HIV-associated stigma, and ageism, which create feelings of embarrassment, shame, and rejection (Emlet, 2006).

Unfortunately, many older persons with HIV/AIDS do not have an adequate social safety net to replace these needed community services. One survey of adults age 50 to 68 living with HIV/AIDS in New York City found that 42 percent perceived a lack of emotional support and 27 percent reported inadequate practical assistance. Those with a more advanced stage of the disease, who should have had *more* support, actually reported *less* emotional and practical help in coping with their activities of daily living (Schrimshaw & Siegel, 2003). In another survey of older adults with HIV/AIDS in New York, 71

> **WHEN SHOULD OLDER ADULTS BE TESTED FOR HIV/AIDS?**
>
> - If sexually active and not using a male latex condom
> - If unaware of partner's sexual and drug use history
> - If they inject drugs or share needles and syringes with other people (drug users are not the only people who share needles—for example, those with diabetes may share needles)
> - If they have had a blood transfusion between 1978 and 1985 when blood was not tested for HIV in the U.S., or if they had surgery in a developing country at any time

percent lived alone and only about 33 percent had a partner. Most had lost contact with their families (Shippy & Karpiak, 2005). In general, older HIV-positive persons are more likely to be socially isolated and to suffer from depression than their younger counterparts, which has implications for their caregiving and service needs to manage their condition (CDC, 2008; Poindexter & Emlet, 2006).

For all the reasons just described, it is essential to educate older adults about *their* risk for HIV/AIDS. Even those who know something about this disease may feel that it cannot affect them if they are not engaging in homosexual activity or intravenous drug use. Many older people have relied on the media for their knowledge in this area. If they were monogamous earlier in life, they may have ignored HIV prevention messages as irrelevant to them. Unfortunately, the media rarely reports on *older* adults contracting AIDS through heterosexual intercourse or blood transfusions. It is therefore not surprising that many older people are unaware that they may be infected. They are also less willing to be tested for the virus, and once diagnosed, are less likely to seek out AIDS support groups or other forms of emotional support. At the same time, ageist attitudes may prevent health providers from offering prevention programs for older adults, encouraging sexually active elders to use condoms or be tested for this virus, or even asking questions about their sexual history as part of a routine health screening (Jacquescoley, 2008).

Accidents Among Older People

Although mortality statistics suggest that older people are less likely than the young to die of accidents (only 7 per 10,000 deaths compared with 10 per 10,000 among people 21 and younger), these numbers mask the true incidence of deaths due to accident-related injuries. For example, if an older person breaks a hip after falling down a flight of stairs or fractures a leg in an auto accident, she enters a hospital, often is discharged to a nursing home, and soon after may die from pneumonia. Pneumonia is then listed as the cause of death, when in fact this acute condition was brought on by the patient's problems in recovering from the accident. Despite this underestimate, the risk of death from physical injuries is about four times greater for 80-year-olds than for 20-year-olds.

Older Drivers

Almost 90 percent of people who are age 65 and older continue to drive. These numbers will grow as baby boomers age and more people live into their 80s and 90s and want to continue driving. Between 2000 and 2020, the proportion of people age 65 and over who continue to drive will double. Many older people view driving as an important part of maintaining their autonomy and active aging. Loss of this ability often results in a decreased sense of control and can worsen preexisting symptoms of depression. Older drivers' reluctance to give up the car keys can have profound repercussions, because they have more accidents per mile driven. Older drivers and passengers are now three times more likely to die than younger people following an auto crash. They made up 10 percent of all auto fatalities in 1975, 17 percent in 1998, and are projected to represent 27 percent of auto fatalities in 2015 as more baby boomers reach old age (Ackerman et al., 2008; NHTSA, 2001; Windsor

et al., 2007). A U-shaped pattern of fatal crashes has been observed, from a high rate among 17-year-olds to a low at ages 30 to 64 to an increased rate among 75-year-olds. For drivers age 65 to 74, motor vehicle accidents are the leading cause of injury-related deaths. For those age 74 to 84, this is the second leading cause of injury-related deaths after falls (Arfin, 2006). Given these statistics, it is not surprising that many elders take refresher courses offered by AARP ("55 Alive Driver Safety Program") and the Automobile Association of America ("Safe Driving for Mature Operators"). Increasingly, insurance companies are requiring drivers over age 80 to take driving courses and tests.

The higher rate of accidents and fatalities in older drivers may be attributed to:

- changes in eye-hand coordination
- slower reaction time
- impaired vision (especially diminished night vision, sensitivity to glare, and poor peripheral vision)
- hearing impairments
- slower information processing and declining attention skills, especially divided attention
- problems with visual-spatial skills
- declines in physical strength, resulting in greater physical vulnerability

Even though most accidents by older drivers occur at low speeds, age-related declines in organ systems and brittle bones make the older person more vulnerable to injuries and death. Older drivers are more likely to sustain rib and pelvic fractures and thoracic injuries but fewer head and brain injuries in an auto accident. Regardless of their injuries, older adults, especially those age 75 and older, have longer hospital stays, more pulmonary, cardiovascular, and renal complications, and greater need for rehabilitation services following trauma. Some medications, especially those given for insomnia or anxiety that have a long half-life in the bloodstream, increase the risk of motor vehicle crashes in older adults by as much as 45 percent (Li, Braver, & Chen, 2003; Salen et al., 2003).

RETRAINING OLDER DRIVERS

It may be useful for state licensing departments to test all adults annually on some of the relevant physiological and cognitive abilities and to retrain older drivers who are experiencing significant declines in these areas. The AARP, National Safety Council, and the Automobile Association of America (AAA) have developed such courses. For example, AARP estimates that some 500,000 older drivers enroll in their "Mature Driver Safety" program each year. This 8-hour course is offered through retirement homes, senior centers, shopping malls, libraries, and religious institutions. Older persons can obtain discounts of 5 to 10 percent on their auto insurance in many states after completing such courses. A driver retraining program with 8 hours of classroom and 2 hours of on-road instruction significantly improved driving performance and knowledge of adults with a mean age of 80 (Marottoli, et al., 2007).

A tragic accident in July 2003 attracted national attention to the issues raised by older drivers. In that accident, an 86-year-old driver in California mistakenly stepped on the accelerator instead of the brake, causing the deaths of 10 people and many injuries in a crowded market area. This unfortunate event raised many questions about the need for mandatory tests and restrictions on driving after a certain age. A growing number of states have special license requirements for older drivers. Some include:

1. Cannot renew licenses by mail after age 70: Alaska, California, and Louisiana
2. More frequent renewals (hence, more regular testing) required for older people than for younger drivers: Arizona, Colorado, Hawaii, Idaho, Illinois, Indiana, Iowa, Kansas, Maine, Missouri, Montana, New Mexico, and Rhode Island
3. More frequent vision tests for older drivers: Arizona, Florida, Maine, Oregon, and Utah

4. A required road test for older drivers before they can renew their license: Illinois and New Hampshire
5. Medical report required for drivers 70 and older: Nevada

Older drivers are less likely to drive in bad weather, at night, in freeway traffic, or during rush hour. They generally select familiar routes of travel and drive fewer miles per year than younger drivers. They are also less prone to speeding or to driving while drunk than younger age groups.

Older adults diagnosed with Alzheimer's disease or other dementias on average drive 2.5 years after diagnosis. In fact, almost 4 percent of American men age 75 and older who drive have dementia (Foley et al., 2000; Kennard, 2006). Many older adults with cognitive impairments restrict their driving to the communities where they reside. However, city driving may actually pose more hazards than highways because of multiple intersections, traffic congestion, and other driving demands that require rapid information processing and reaction time. A national survey of more than 5,000 older men and women revealed that 75.6 percent of women with cognitive impairment do not drive compared to 43 percent of their male counterparts, which may reflect traditional gender roles characteristic of the cohort age 75 and older where driving has been associated with masculinity. Men with mild and severe cognitive impairments apparently cope by avoiding long-distance driving. As one might expect, both men and women with dementia who have another driver in their household are more likely to stop driving themselves. In this same survey, elders with impaired vision (including poor night vision, sensitivity to glare, glaucoma, and macular degeneration) and limitations in their ADLs were less likely to drive, but having heart disease, diabetes, or arthritis did not cause them to restrict their driving. Reduced cognitive processing speed, problems performing some IADLs that require cognitive processing, and poor balance increase the likelihood that elders will stop driving but also predict the possibility of car accidents caused by older adults (Ackerman et al., 2005; Freund & Szinovacz, 2002; Ross et al., 2009).

Improved environmental design can help some older drivers. For example, older people have more accidents while making left turns; these could be avoided by designing better left-turn intersections with special lanes and left arrow lights. Road signs that are clearer and well lighted could reduce the high number of violations received by older drivers for improperly changing lanes or entering and exiting highways. For drivers who are prone to falling asleep at the wheel, a device inserted behind their ears could sound an alarm if they start to drift off.

Another approach to reducing person–environment discrepancies for older drivers is to install in cars air bags that have lower power; of 68 adults killed by air bags between 1991 and 2000, 40 percent were age 70 or older. The Ford Motor Company has installed "force limiters" in some models. These are part of a personal safety system using sensors to adjust air bags and seatbelts according to the weight of the driver and passenger and according to how close the driver is to the steering wheel. Other design options to modify the environment are summarized in the box below. No matter how much automobile designs are modified and alarms added, however, families sometimes must initiate a difficult conversation about stopping driving, especially if

they notice that their older relative is experiencing increasing problems with vision, cognitive speed, reaction time, and has difficulty performing ADLs and IADLs.

Falls and Their Prevention

As noted earlier, older people are at a greater risk of falls than the young. Falls are the leading cause of injuries and injury-related deaths for people over age 65 in the U.S. and account for 95 percent of all hip fractures. Young people who fall can generally catch themselves and, at worst, break a wrist when they fall. But older adults' slower reaction time and reduced upper-body strength cause them to fall more on their hips, often resulting in fractures among those with osteoporosis. Up to 30 percent of older adults in the community, and even more in long-term care settings, experience a fall in a given year. Many older people who fall become more fearful of falling and therefore restrict their activity levels (Fletcher & Hirdes, 2004; NCHS, 2009). They may also become more rigid or overly cautious in walking. This may, in turn, increase the likelihood of subsequent falls. In fact, 65 percent of those who fall do so again within 6 months (CDC 2006c). The majority of elders who experience fall-related fractures have not recovered their pre-fall functional level one year later. Therefore, it is important to identify risk factors for falls and try to prevent them. The most common risk factors are lack of balance control, impaired gait, arthritis, cognitive impairment, increased age, use of four or more medications that cause blood pressure to drop or affect balance, use of multiple drugs that affect the central nervous system (including drugs for sleep and anxiety disorders, depression, and pain—taking 3 or more increase their risk threefold), visual impairment, and **sarcopenia** (Hanlon et al., 2009; Huang et al., 2003; Moreland et al., 2004). Sarcopenia refers to the atrophy of muscles and can affect all muscle groups, weakening the upper body and arms. It can impair balance and

> **DESIGN CHANGES THAT COULD HELP OLDER DRIVERS**
> - wider rearview mirrors
> - pedal extensions
> - less complicated and legible instrument panels
> - electronic detectors in front and back that signal when the car is too close to other cars
> - better protection on doors
> - booster cushions for shorter-stature drivers

RISK FACTORS FOR FALLS

- inactivity that weakens muscles and reduces leg and upper-body strength
- visual impairment
- fear of falling and lack of confidence
- gait disorders
- poor balance when standing
- multiple diseases
- medications used for cardiac conditions and others that cause postural hypotension
- Use of multiple medications that affect the central nervous system (e.g. for sleep, anxiety, depression)
- low lighting levels
- hazards in the environment such as slippery floors, loose area rugs, poorly demarcated stairs, and slick surfaces in showers and tubs
- unfamiliar environments

---

cause difficulties in rising from a chair, bathtub, or toilet and in maintaining elders' functional ability. Both men and women are at increased risk for sarcopenia after age 75, especially if they do not exercise.

Despite national and local public health efforts to prevent falls among older people, fall-related deaths and hip fractures due to falls have not declined dramatically, and falls continue to be the leading cause of accident mortality (Miltiades & Kaye, 2006). Between 1993 and 2003, there was an *increase* in the rate of deaths caused by falls, from 24 to 37 per 100,000. In fact, both hip fractures and fall-related deaths have actually increased since 1990, in contrast to other health problems that have shown a gradual decline (CDC, 2006; Merck Institute, 2004). The high medical cost of falls—$19 billion annually in the U.S.—is one reason why states and the federal government promote fall prevention efforts.

Most falls are preventable. As noted above, education and exercise training for older adults and their caregivers along with preventive medications and environmental interventions are needed

to reduce the risk of falls (see examples of intervention recommendations in the box above). New drugs can prevent fractures by strengthening bone. For example, alendronate (brand name, Fosamax) was found to be effective in reducing fractures of the spine and femoral neck by 50 percent in one study and 44 percent in another. Other effective medications are risedronate (brand name, Actonel) and raloxifene (brand name, Evista); the latter drug has been particularly useful in preventing spinal fractures (Cranney et al., 2002). Findings from a study in the Netherlands suggest that thiazide diuretics used to treat hypertension may indirectly prevent bone loss. Older adults using any one of many brands of thiazide diuretics for their hypertension for more than 1 year also lowered their risk for hip fractures by 50 percent, but the benefits diminished within 4 months of discontinuing the drug (Schoofs et al., 2003).

Informal social support, especially family networks and friendly visiting by volunteers, are also associated with reducing the risks of falling (Fletcher & Hirdes, 2004). In addition to the guidelines for fall prevention established by the American Geriatrics Society (2001), comprehensive checklists and measures of physical ability are available to assess the risk of falls. The Get Up and Go Test is recommended as an initial

---

INTERVENTIONS TO PREVENT FALLS

- Environmental modifications of the homes of older people who have experienced multiple falls in the past can significantly decrease falls.
- An investment in home modifications and assistive devices saves health care costs for an older person.
- Training older women how to control their balance can prevent falls.
- Exercise, such as Tai Chi, that promotes balance stability and postural control provide core body strength.
- Modifications to the physical environment of nursing homes along with wheelchair safety, and careful use of psychotropic medications.

assessment tool; older adults are asked by a health care provider to get up from a chair, walk 10 meters, return, and sit down in the chair. Creating a slip-free, clutter-free home environment can also reduce falls. The Home Fall Hazard Assessment Tool evaluates environmental conditions in the home that could contribute to falls (Wolf et al., 2003).

Use of Physician Services by Older People

The increased incidence of many chronic diseases among the older population would seem to predict a striking growth with age in the use of health care services. There is some support for a differential pattern of utilization among age groups. The probability of seeing a doctor at least once in the previous year increases slightly with age. For example, 91 percent of 55- to 64-year-old women reported visiting a physician in the past 12 months in the 2002 NHIS, compared with 94 percent of those age 65 to 74, 95 percent at age 75 to 84, and 95.5 percent of those 85 and older (Schoenborn et al., 2006). However, the major variation across age groups is in *frequency* of use annually:

- 1.3 physician visits per person among those 25 to 44
- 7.3 visits for people 45 to 64
- 11.4 visits for people 65 to 84
- 15.0 visits for those 85 and older
- On average, 13 visits per person among all persons 65 and older (Federal Interagency Forum, 2008).

Both younger and older people who visit physicians do so primarily for acute symptoms and to receive diagnostic and therapeutic services. However, the larger number of yearly visits by older persons may indicate that they are also seeking care for chronic conditions. It is noteworthy that only a small proportion of older

adults are high users of all health services. Low use, however, does not necessarily mean that all health needs are being met. For example, even with Medicare, low-income older adults report more unmet health needs than middle- or high-income elders, even though they pay more out-of-pocket for health care compared to their higher income peers (29 percent compared to 8 percent) (Federal Interagency Forum, 2008). Despite paying from their personal funds for care, low-income elders, especially elders of color, identify more unmet health needs. African American elders report more outpatient visits than whites but are also less likely to follow treatment recommendations, including medication use.

As baby boomers reach old age, health care spending in the U.S. could reach $4.4 trillion by 2018, or 20.3 percent of the nation's gross domestic product, compared with 17.6 percent in 2009 (CMS, 2009). This is based on projections from the current cohort of persons 65 and older, who on average have three times as many hospital days as younger persons. Because 62 percent of the current cohort age 50 to 64 have at least one chronic disease described in this chapter, many will develop other conditions, and many will survive longer. As a result, health care spending by state and federal governments for Medicaid and Medicare and by older persons themselves will escalate in the future. The problem will be compounded by the growing number of employers who are reducing health care benefits to their retirees (Medical News Today, 2008; Pathman, Fowler-Brown, & Corbie-Smith, 2006).

Use of Other Health Services

HOSPITALS Hospital utilization may reflect older people's need for health care more accurately than do elective visits to physicians' offices. Older people on average have three times as many hospital days and for longer periods of time than younger populations, accounting for about 38 percent of all short-stay hospital days of care. Although the rate of hospitalizations has declined among younger populations, it has increased steadily since the 1980s for older adults, especially those 75 and older (DeFrancis, Lucas, Buie, Golosinskiy, 2008). However, the average *length of stay* for all age groups has become shorter since the introduction of **diagnosis-related groupings (DRGs)** for Medicare patients in 1983, which have resulted in earlier discharge from inpatient hospitals to outpatient settings such as rehabilitation facilities and home care (see Chapter 17). In addition, hospital utilization may be declining because of the growing number of procedures that are performed in community-based settings. Hospital emergency rooms (ERs) are used for medical care more often among low-income populations. In the 2002 NHIS, 29 percent of elders classified as poor reported ER use in the past 12 months, compared with 22 percent of the nonpoor (Schoenborn et al., 2006). ER users tend to be people without a regular physician and private health insurance. Regardless of income, however, the use of hospital emergency rooms as the entry to health care is expanding as a result of the global economic crisis and the growing numbers of middle-aged and young old adults who lack health insurance.

MEDICATION USE   The use of prescription and nonprescription medications, including vitamins and

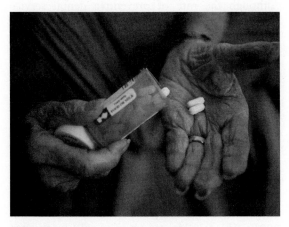

Older adults use more medications than other age groups.

mineral supplements, reflect the growth of pharmacotherapy for older adults' health conditions. Although they represent just under 13 percent of the population, older adults use 34 percent of all prescriptions and 30 percent of all nonprescription medications (NIDA, 2007). In a national survey of 2,590 adults conducted in 2001, 94 percent of older women and 90 percent of older men reported taking at least one medication; 57 percent of the former took five or more. Prescription drugs represented 25 percent of these. Older women, especially white women, were most likely to report using both prescription and nonprescription drugs, Asians and Pacific Islanders least likely. The most common prescription medications used by older and middle-aged respondents were antihypertensives, heart medications, and diuretics (reflecting the high prevalence of hypertension and heart disease that these drugs are intended to treat). Aspirin was the most commonly used over-the-counter (OTC) drug, reported by 58 percent of older men and 51 percent of older women who took it to prevent heart attacks. Older adults were second only to middle-aged adults in their use of multivitamins and some nutritional supplements, including herbal alternatives. An analysis of national data concluded that 25 percent of Asian and Latino elders used herbal remedies, compared with 10 percent of white and African American elders (Alcury et al., 2007; Kaufman et al., 2002).

An average older person living in the community takes 5.3 prescription medicines per day (Gurnack, Atkinson, & Osgood, 2002). Some older people take as many as 12 to 15 different medications (prescription and nonprescription) simultaneously. The financial burden falls especially hard on older women, who are most likely to experience chronic diseases and have the lowest incomes. Average costs for prescription drugs nearly tripled between 1994 and 2004 (Federal Interagency Forum, 2008). Although Prescription Drug Reform in 2003 expanded drug coverage for older adults, drug costs have continued to grow dramatically, a pattern discussed in detail in Chapter 17. Not surprisingly, nursing home residents take more prescription drugs than do community-dwelling elders. It is estimated that the average nursing home resident uses 8.8 medications per day, and 32 percent use nine or more (Doshi, Shaffer, Briesacher, 2005). Accordingly, adverse drug reactions are common among nursing home residents (Handler et al., 2006).

Many older people take either too many medications or inappropriate drugs, making medication misuse, whether intentional or not, a primary concern. This is risky because the less-efficient excretion of drugs by the kidney and liver and the changing proportions of fat and muscle tissue (as discussed in Chapter 3) may prolong the effects of some drugs. Furthermore, combinations of medications can cause adverse drug reactions. Numerous hospital admissions of older people result from such adverse reactions, and many falls and sudden impairments in cognitive function may be due to inappropriate medication use or overmedication. Older people who are discharged from hospitals with a large number of medications are more likely to be rehospitalized because of drug complications, especially if they are using seven or more medications. This pattern occurs independent of the elder's diagnosis and type of medication. In a study of almost 400 elders, average age 79, as many as 32 percent of this group discharged from a hospital experienced adverse drug reactions. Elders on multiple medications prior to their hospitalization were at greater risk for such complications (Page Ruscin, 2006). The higher rate of medication use among older adults may also result in reporting errors and incorrect use. Older people admitted to a hospital often give inconsistent medication reports. In some instances, older adults may deliberately misuse medications by "doctor shopping" or stockpiling medications, but this abuse is qualitatively and quantitatively different from that among younger adults (Bartels, Brockman, & Van Critters, 2006). Given the complexities surrounding medication use, health and social service providers must exercise caution in relying on elders' self-reports of medication use, perform a careful home-based medication review (including assessment of the elder's ability to use medications), and identify strategies to ensure medication adherence. Any interventions must take into account elders' language skills and health literacy. Not surprisingly, family members often find that their loved ones' medication misuse becomes a reason for in-home help or a move to a long-term facility where medications can be monitored.

Fortunately, increasing empirical evidence indicates that most medication-related problems are predictable and thus potentially preventable. Interventions identified as effective include home visit teaching sessions, computer-based reminder systems, electronic monitoring instructions organized in lists rather than paragraphs with pictorial icons, and use of calendar blister packs compared to a standard bottle. For example, the Self-Medication Program (SMP) gives patients increasing responsibility for administering their own medications while in the hospital; this results in fewer medication errors and improved compliance. Such interventions, however, do not substantially reduce morbidity, mortality and health care costs (Blow et al., 2006).

DENTAL SERVICES The use of professional dental services is an area of elective health care that is ignored even more than routine medical care. Although the rate of preventive dental service utilization has risen significantly over the past 20 years among younger cohorts, the utilization of dental services by older adults has increased only slightly. In the latest National Health Interview Survey, older persons continued to be the lowest users of professional dental care; 44 percent had not seen a dentist in the past year and 33 percent had not obtained care in the past 5 years. Elders of color are far less likely to visit a dentist; 65 percent of African Americans and 57 percent of Latino elders reported that they had not seen a dentist in 2004, compared with 40 percent of whites (NHIS, 2006; Schoenborn et al., 2006). This rate is incongruent with the level of oral diseases that require professional attention.

Yet once older adults enter the dental care system, their average number of visits is similar to that of younger people. The current state of Medicare reimbursement, where physician visits are covered but dental care is not, plays an important role in this differential pattern of utilization. Therefore, it is not surprising that older adults who are not poor are twice as likely to make preventive dental visits as those who are poor (67 percent vs. 32 percent, respectively). Elders with private health insurance that covers dental care are also twice as likely to make annual dental visits than those on Medicare only (Kiyak & Reichmuth, 2005; Schoenborn et al., 2006).

Health Promotion with Older People

Health promotion is defined as a combination of health education and related organizational, political, and economic changes aimed at enhancing an individual's control over and ability to improve their health, not just manage their diseases. Some programs emphasize the "health enhancement" or "wellness" aspects of their health promotion efforts. This contrasts with disease prevention, which is focused on avoiding diseases that can result in impairment and disability. Health promotion encompasses a variety of interventions, recognizing the complex social, biological, cultural, and economic factors that influence health and health behavior. Accordingly, this definition includes altering individual health practices such as diet and exercise, as well as creating healthier environments and changing cultural attitudes and expectations about health. Health promotion represents a shift from a biomedical model, where the physician is responsible to treat disease, to a model that emphasizes responsibility for one's health in an effort to improve physical well-being and quality of life. Health promotion thus makes explicit the importance of people's *environments* and *lifestyles* as determinants of good health.

The primary rationale for health promotion programs for older adults is to reduce the incidence

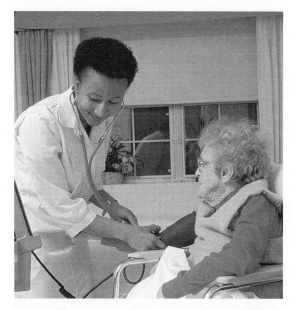

Frequent blood pressure checks are essential preventive behaviors into advanced old age.

of *disabling chronic diseases*. This can enhance the older person's functional ability and overall quality of life, not merely prolong life. Health promotion also recognizes that chronic conditions cannot be cured but can be prevented from causing functional disability. As suggested in our earlier discussion of disease, as many as 80 percent of the chronic illnesses that afflict older individuals may be related to social, environmental, and behavioral factors, particularly poor exercise and nutritional habits. In addition, 90 percent of fatal and near-fatal episodes of strokes and heart attacks are believed to be preventable.

A viable health care goal, as noted in Chapter 1, is compression of morbidity, delaying the age at which chronic illness and possible disabilities begin (Fries, 1980, 2003). This goal of delaying the onset of serious chronic diseases seems feasible. Longitudinal studies identify several healthy behaviors that increase chances of living longer than statistically expected. A study of older adults age 70 to 90 found that those who consumed a healthy diet, exercised 30 minutes daily, avoided smoking, and consumed alcohol in moderation were 50 percent less likely to die within the next 10 years than elders who did not practice these health-promoting lifestyles (Knoops et al., 2004). Research with older runners provides further evidence on the effectiveness of health promotion in delaying the onset of chronic disease and mortality. A 21-year longitudinal study compared runners and non-runners (average age 58 at the start) on rates of disability and death. Non-runners did worse on every annual assessment of functional disability, and group differences increased over time. Runners remained lean, were less likely to smoke, and were more likely to participate in other exercises. They were also less likely to die over this period than non-runners (15 percent vs. 34 percent, respectively), not only from cardiovascular causes but from cancer and neurological disorders (Chakravarty, Hubert, Lingala, & Fries, 2008). Even moderate exercise performed regularly, together with healthy eating and not smoking, can delay the onset of disability by as much as 10 years (CDC, 2008; Stepnick & Whitelaw, 2006).

Preventive health behaviors can save the individual and society significant amounts of money for treating more advanced disease. For example, influenza vaccines can save $118 in treatment costs per $1.50 spent on the vaccine itself (Rothberg, Ballantonio, & Rose, 2003). As another example, health care costs can be significantly reduced by increasing physical activity levels from sedentary to participation in 30 minutes of exercise, even for 2 days per week. In a study of more than 2,000 adults whose average age was 63, the greatest decline ($2,200) was identified for elders who increased their physical activity levels to 3 or more days per week from none or once a week, a relatively minor change (Martinson et al., 2003).

Despite the fiscal savings provided by health promotion, only a small percentage of national health care dollars are spent on prevention, early detection, and wellness services. Medicare and many private health insurance plans do not typically pay for prevention services. An

---

HEALTH PROMOTION CAN REDUCE HEALTH CARE COSTS

Several health promotion programs have concluded that healthy lifestyles can reduce health care costs.

- A community-based, peer-led program for elders with chronic disease found that exercise and dietary interventions resulted in fewer hospitalizations and in health care savings up to $520 over 2 years.
- An individualized intervention program to reduce risks for falls resulted in a $2,000 reduction in health care costs among participants compared to elders in the control group (Stepnick & Whitelaw, 2006).

---

encouraging sign, however, is the increasing number of hospitals, health care clinics, universities, local governments, and corporations that offer health promotion programs. For example, some county governments offer insurance incentives for people who engage in healthy behaviors, while those who choose not to participate pay higher premiums. Many of these programs

---

HEALTHY PEOPLE 2010

Two major goals of *Healthy People 2010,* prepared by the Secretary of Health and Human Services, are:

- to increase quality and years of healthy life for all Americans
- to eliminate health disparities among segments of the U.S. population

Although the 26 focus areas of *Healthy People 2010* do not specifically address elders or any particular age group, the health topics are relevant for current cohorts of older adults, as well as younger and middle-aged people today, who could improve their quality of life as they live longer. For example, by promoting healthy behaviors such as increasing levels of physical activity and fitness, improving nutrition, and reducing tobacco use (focus areas #1–3), future cohorts will not only increase their life expectancy but will improve the quality of those years.

SOURCE: *Healthy People 2010* (http://www.health.gov, 2000).

have been carried into senior centers, adult day health care sites, and assisted living, retirement, and nursing homes. The dramatic impact of self-care behaviors on reducing health care costs and hospital and physician use is a primary indicator of the benefits for both individuals and society of a healthy lifestyle in the later years. Fortunately, a growing number of older adults now obtain preventive services, in some cases higher than targets set by *Healthy People 2010*.

The Relationship Between Health Practices and Health Outcomes

Considerable research demonstrates the relationship of personal health habits to active aging or aging well. Factors that are related to good health outcomes encompass:

- consuming more vegetables and fruits, less saturated fats and refined carbohydrates
- maintaining a regular exercise schedule
- not smoking
- limiting alcohol consumption
- maintaining one's weight in the ideal range
- sleeping 7 to 8 hours per night

The relationship between these behaviors and healthy aging appear to be cumulative and independent of age, sex, race, and socioeconomic status. Additional epidemiological evidence demonstrates links between specific health habits and decreased longevity and increased health risks. These specific lifestyle factors, discussed briefly below, include

alcohol consumption, cigarette smoking, diet, and exercise.

ALCOHOL The relationship between drinking alcohol and physical health in old age is U-shaped; the least healthy are those who drink heavily and those who abstain, although abstainers may include former heavy drinkers who have damaged their systems. Excessive drinking (five or more drinks at a single sitting) contributes to poor physical health, more frequent hospitalizations, decreased cognitive function, poorer metabolism of prescription medications, and premature death.

While excessive alcohol use can cause significant health problems, moderate use is shown to have beneficial effects for cardiovascular functioning. As discussed in Chapter 3, consuming one to two servings of red wine with dinner two to four times per week appears to increase levels of HDL, the "good" cholesterol, in the blood while preventing oxidation of LDL. Polyphenols found in abundance in red wine (and less so in white wine) also reduce blood clotting and may lower the incidence of heart attacks. It is important to note that all these benefits derive from *moderate*, not excessive, consumption of wine (Bauer, et al, 2006).

SMOKING The effects of cigarette smoking, especially in interaction with other risk factors, on heart disease, emphysema, and lung cancer are extensively documented and widely recognized. Smokers who use oral contraceptives, are exposed to asbestos, have excessive alcohol consumption, or are at risk for hypertension have a greater chance of experiencing a nonfatal myocardial infarction and are at significant risk for cancers of the oral cavity and lung. Smoking can reduce bone density and musculoskeletal strength and interfere with the absorption of some medications. The longer one is exposed to tobacco, the greater these risks. However, quitting smoking can gradually reduce some of these health risks. For example, people who quit smoking 5 or more years earlier can reduce their risk of stroke to the same level as those who never smoked, and

---

POINTS TO PONDER

Identify healthy and unhealthy behaviors in your lifestyle. Have you ever tried to modify these behaviors? If so, what techniques worked for you? What were some obstacles? To what extent do you think that lifestyle changes after age 65 can overcome the effects of poor health habits acquired earlier in life?

15 years after quitting, they have the same life expectancy as their age peers who never smoked (Ostbyte & Taylor, 2004).

DIET Poor diet is related to obesity, cancer, and heart disease, among other conditions. Clinical studies have identified the effects of specific dietary behaviors on health outcomes. A moderate reduction in dietary fat consumption, to 26 percent of total calories, may be more beneficial than a severe reduction (18 percent fat) in reducing cholesterol levels. Indeed, among men with high levels of LDL (bad cholesterol) and triglycerides (a type of fat found in blood), those who reduced their fat intake to 26 percent while maintaining their HDL (good cholesterol) levels showed the greatest reduction in LDL and triglycerides. When fat intake decreases to 18 percent or less, HDL levels also decline (Stone, 2006). In another study, 50- to 89-year-old adults who modified their fat intake to include two-thirds from vegetable sources and only one-third from animal fats demonstrated a decrease in cholesterol and a reduction in risk of death from coronary heart disease (Chernoff, 2001).

Insufficient intake of certain nutrients is another problem of older adults. As many as 40 percent of older people have diets that are deficient in three or more nutrients. Up to 15 percent may have vitamin B_{12} deficiency.

BENEFITS OF ANTIOXIDANTS IN THE DIET

Antioxidants bind with free radicals and prevent them from damaging cells. They are abundant in fruits and vegetables that are colorful, such as blueberries, cherries, grapes, cranberries, broccoli, kale, and spinach. These foods are high in vitamins A, C, and E and in zinc and selenium. Dark chocolate and red wine are also high in antioxidants. Antioxidants are shown to improve brain function because free radicals cause so much damage in this organ. Rats fed a diet rich in antioxidants show significant improvement in their learning ability and observable changes in neuronal function (Wang et al., 2005).

Vitamin B_{12} is necessary for the production of blood cells and healthy functioning of the nervous system. These deficiencies are in part due to inadequate intake of milk, eggs, vegetables, fruit, and other sources of nutrients. They may also result from poorer absorption of nutrients by the gastrointestinal (GI) system in older adults, especially in those on multiple medications that affect GI absorption. By following the National Cancer Institute's "Five-a-Day" campaign to consume at least five servings of fruits and vegetables per day, older adults can reduce their chances of developing colon and other types of cancer. In fact, *Healthy People 2010* and MyPyramid.gov recommend even higher intakes—seven to nine servings per day—for older adults. Consumption studies show that older people generally eat more fruits and vegetables than younger persons—on average 3.5 to four servings per day, with about 37 percent of women 75 and older eating five servings per day. However, it is difficult for many to exceed higher levels because of barriers such as the cost of fresh fruits and vegetables, medication regimens, and the need to manage multiple chronic diseases that take their focus off of preparing healthy meals (CDC & Merck, 2007; Gray et al., 2003; Greeene et al., 2008; USDA, 2008).

Exercise as Central to Health Promotion

Up to 50 percent of physical changes in older people that are mistakenly attributed to aging may be due to being physically unfit. Physically inactive people age faster and look older than physically fit persons of the same age, in part because of what has been termed **hypokinesia,** a disease of "disuse," or the degeneration and functional loss of muscle and bone tissue. Exercise can slow this loss of muscle mass or lean body mass. Older people who participate in high-intensity resistance training 30 minutes per day can improve muscle mass and strength. Strength-training programs have been successful even with the oldest-old in nursing homes, improving their muscle strength, gait velocity (walking speed), and stair-climbing ability after just 8 to 12 weeks (DiPietro, 2001; Haber, 2003; Hewitt, 2003).

Moderate exercise is found to increase life expectancy by 1.3 to 3.7 years longer than for those who do not exercise. Rigorous exercise, equivalent to running 30 minutes per day 5 days a week, extended life by 3.5 to 3.7 years, based on adults examined in the Framingham Heart Study over 40 years (Franco et al., 2005). Researchers note that exercise efficiency and capacity can be improved in older adults through regularly occurring physical training. Older adults (ages 65 to 79) had lower exercise capacity and cardiovascular efficiency than 20- to 30-year-olds before training, but 3 to 6 months of aerobic training resulted in greater improvements on indicators of exercise efficiency among older adults than among the young (Woo et al., 2006).

Regardless of the types of chronic illness, most older adults experience health benefits from exercise. There is also considerable evidence of the relationship between regular, vigorous exercise

Older people with all levels of ability can benefit from physical exercise.

and the reduction in a person's chances of dying from heart disease and cancer, as well as lower hospital admissions for serious illness (Manini et al., 2006; Lee, Sheso, Ogumi, and Paffenbarger, 2004). People diagnosed with heart disease who participate in a regular, moderate exercise program can reduce their risk of cardiac death by 20 to 25 percent, as well as the possibility of disability. Both low- and high-intensity exercise programs can improve aerobic capacity and physical strength among the oldest-old. They can alleviate the problem of "stiff joints" and lower back pain by improving elders' flexibility and range of motion. Aerobic exercise and strength training are also shown to enhance the functional health of older adults with Type II diabetes. Physical activity can even reduce the risk of falls among older people, thereby preventing disability and the high costs of treatment and long-term care associated with falls. Regular exercise also reduces or slows the development of frailty; elders (average age 73.6 at the start) who participated in regular moderate physical activity were almost three times less likely to show signs of frailty five years after beginning the exercise regimen than those who were sedentary or only reported some household activities as their exercise (Peterson et al., 2009; Vincent et al., 2002; Wolf et al., 2003). Some older adults choose Tai Chi or yoga or pilates as a gentler form of exercise that strengthens muscles without injuring joints. These mind-body therapies reduce chronic pain associated with arthritis and improve leg and core body strength, flexibility, balance, and stability while walking, thereby diminishing the risk of falls and providing overall exercise (Morone and Greco, 2007; Reid et al., 2008).

Regular exercise may also reduce the risk of breast cancer. A study of almost 75,000 women age 50 to 79 who were enrolled in the Women's Health Initiative (described earlier) compared women who walked at least 10 hours per week with their counterparts who were sedentary. The former lowered their risk of developing breast cancer by 30 percent over the sedentary group. The greatest benefit was obtained by lighter-weight women, followed by women of normal weight and

EXERCISE AND HEALTHY AGING

Researchers report that strength-training exercises 20 minutes a day for just two to three times per week can help older adults gain three pounds of muscle and replace fat in just 10 to 12 weeks. Increased muscle tissue level improves metabolism and efficient use of glucose, reduces blood pressure, increases bone mass, and helps the gastrointestinal system function more efficiently (Crandell, 2006).

BENEFITS OF A DAILY, BRISK, 30-MINUTE WALK FOR OLDER ADULTS

- avoids obesity
- controls blood pressure
- boosts HDL cholesterol in blood
- boosts metabolic rate
- reduces body fat, improves lean muscle mass
- reduces risk of blood clots, heart attacks, strokes
- helps manage Type II diabetes
- reduces risk of osteoporosis
- improves long-term recovery from depression
- improves balance and prevents falls
- increases joint mobility for people with osteoarthritis

those who were slightly overweight. No racial or age differences emerged in the benefits of exercise. No additional gains were accrued from more vigorous exercise such as jogging or tennis, suggesting that a simple but regular routine of walking daily can play an important role in preventing breast cancer (McTiernan et al., 2003). The box above summarizes some of the health benefits of a regular walking regimen, but it should be noted that the gains are greatest if people begin this exercise habit during young adulthood or middle age and not wait until their 60s or 70s. Nevertheless, initiating regular exercise at any age, even after age 80, has beneficial effects (CDC & Merck, 2007).

Exercise needs to occur regularly, not just once a week or less. For example, in the Physicians' Health Study with 21,481 men, those who exercised less than once a week were 74 times more likely to die during exertion than men who exercised five or more times per week. This study concluded that exercise should be vigorous and last at least 30 to 60 minutes each time (Albert et al., 2000). National objectives for regular exercise state that adults and children over age six should engage in moderate physical activity at least 30 minutes each day (*Healthy People 2010*).

Such national recommendations have made only a modest impact on older people. Despite the known benefits of exercise, only about 22 percent of older Americans participate in *regular* physical activity (defined as 30 minutes or more at least five times per week). In the 2003–2004 National Health Interview Survey, 27.5 percent of those age 65 to 74 reported participating in regular physical activities,

compared with 19.4 percent of the old-old and 8.4 percent of the oldest-old. Even fewer—12 percent—engaged in strength training exercises. Older non-Hispanic whites are more likely to report regular physical activity (23 percent) than are African American (13 percent) and Latino (14 percent) elders. In contrast, 47 percent of older white women and 61 percent of older African American women report that they do not engage in *any* physical activity. A national survey conducted in 2002 found that the average proportion of a day spent on any form of exercise was only 4 percent among the young-old and only 2 percent among respondents age 75 and older. For some older people, a typical day consists of sitting for hours and even avoiding daily physical activities. Such extreme sedentary habits can result in deteriorating skin and muscle, blood volume, and metabolic rates. A longitudinal study of community-dwelling elders (age 80-98) found the lowest activity levels among men and both genders in the oldest group. Death rates were highest for the least active elders; sedentary men were more likely to die than sedentary women (29 percent vs. 10.5 percent), even after controlling for age and health status (CDC, 2004b; Chipperfield, 2008; Federal Interagency Forum, 2008).

A significant barrier to exercise participation may be attitudinal. Elders who have low expectations about health-related quality of life in old age are less likely to value exercise and do not believe it can help them. Elders with high expectations are more likely to engage in moderate to vigorous exercise than those with low expectations (Sarkinsian et al., 2005). Other barriers may be low income, living in communities that lack elder-friendly and affordable exercise opportunities (e.g., safe places to walk, low-cost gyms), limited encouragement from informal social networks, misinformation about exercise programs, and lack of time because of caregiving or employment demands.

Successful strategies to increase physical activity include goal-setting, self-monitoring, ongoing reminders and group support, regular telephone counseling with individualized motivational messages, and support of home-based activity programs. Some research suggests that older adults adhere better to individualized home-based exercise programs than to classes, while other studies point to the advantages of peer social interaction with other elders. Programs organized by Parks and Recreation departments are an example of accessible, low-cost exercise programs that build on peer support (Castro & King, 2002; Cattan, White, Bond, and Learmouth, 2005; Center for the Advancement of Health, 2006; Stepnick & Whitelaw, 2006).

SUSTAINING THE MOTIVATION TO CHANGE HEALTH BEHAVIORS

Motivating adults of any age to make and sustain changes in their health behaviors is a challenge. One program for older adults, Enhance Wellness, focuses on motivation first. A team of two professionals, typically a nurse and social worker, assess an individual's strengths and risks, then develops a plan in which the participant, not the professional, chooses the health behaviors they want to work on. As participants implement their individualized plan, a volunteer health mentor offers ongoing encouragement, feedback, and monitoring. Allowing elders to set their own goals and providing peer support are vital components of this program. It has reduced length of hospital stays, lowered medication use, alleviated symptoms of mood disorders, and enhanced elders' sense of self-efficacy. The Enhanced Fitness programs, part of Project Enhance, provides low-cost, evidence-based exercise programs that focus on stretching, flexibility, balance, low-impact aerobics, and strength-training exercises under the direction of a certified fitness instructor. Implemented at more than 200 sites nationwide, Enhanced Fitness provides a structured exercise program without requiring expensive equipment or a large space (Enhance Fitness, 2009).

BABY BOOMERS: THE MARATHON GENERATION

Future cohorts of older adults will include a growing number who participate in strenuous exercise. For example, in the United States, 43 percent of all marathoners in 2004 were age 40 and older, compared with 26 percent in 1980. In 2005, the average age of marathon runners was 36 for women and 40.5 for men. In the 2005 New York City Marathon, which requires minimum times to qualify, several participants were in their 70s. Among finishers, 16 percent were age 50 and older, compared with 4 percent in 1976. In the Boston Marathon that same year, 20 percent were over age 50.

source: Based on Kadlec, D., *Time,* June 26, 2006.

Improving the Impact of Health Promotion Programs

Modest gains have been made in reducing unhealthy behaviors among middle-aged and older adults. For example, smoking rates among older white and African American women have declined to less than 8 percent, and for white men to 9.4 percent. However, older African American men still exceed the target set by *Healthy People 2010;* 19.4 percent are current smokers (CDC, 2004a; NCHS, 2003).

In contrast to gains in smoking reduction, nutritional and exercise habits have not improved to levels envisioned by *Healthy People 2000,* so the same goals set in that document are specified in *Healthy People 2010.* Some healthier nutritional patterns are reflected in the decreased consumption

POINTS TO PONDER

Think about people you know who are between ages 75 to 85. What makes some of them look older, while others look younger than their chronological age? Compare their diets, smoking history, and exercise habits. Are there differences in their diets? Are any of them currently smokers, or have they smoked in the past? What physical activities are they participating in, and what did they do in the past?

of saturated and trans-fats and increased intake of vegetables, fruits, and complex carbohydrates during the past decade, particularly among middle- and upper-income older adults. Although 32 percent of older adults have improved their nutritional intake, this is considerably lower than the target of 50 percent set by *Healthy People 2010*. Similarly, activity levels among older adults are so low that meeting the Healthy People 2010 objectives will require significant behavioral changes among at least 59 percent of people 65 and older (Stepnick & Whitelaw, 2006). Although obesity is less common among older Americans than in other age groups, rates have increased among older adults, even among the old-old (Cole & Fox, 2004; Villareal et al., 2005).

Older people most likely to participate in organized health promotion are those with a preventive attitude (i.e., regular users of physicians and dentists for checkups, nonsmokers, exercisers, and users of seat belts and smoke alarms) and those with higher participation rates in community activities generally. Other factors that can enhance the effectiveness of health promotion programs include:

- utilizing social support, such as exercise groups or buddies, and neighborhood walking programs
- opportunities for intergenerational activities (e.g., healthy eating programs for grandparents and grandchildren)
- utilization of available resources such as outdoor paths or malls for walking programs

- culturally competent nutritional and exercise interventions with written and oral materials in the elders' native language
- outreach to older adults through senior centers, religious institutions, and doctor's offices
- availability and affordability of fresh produce in local grocery stores. For example, some inner city areas lack affordable food markets to purchase healthy food

Overall, health promotion programs must be designed to take account of structural factors such as income, living arrangements, social supports and cultural values of older adults who are the targets of such efforts.

Limitations of Health Promotion

Health promotion programs are sometimes criticized for their emphasis on individual responsibility for change, which minimizes the societal health and economic disparities (such as poverty) that underlie individual health practices. Community- and organizational-level changes are needed that consider the roles of policy makers, health care providers, food manufacturers, and the mass media in creating social and economic environments that may counter health promotion interventions. In addition to educating individuals to adopt healthy habits, the broader physical and social environments must be changed to support health promotion activities. For example, encouraging older adults to exercise may be counterproductive if they live in cities with high levels of pollution or near industrial sites contaminated by toxic waste.

Another limitation is that although the value of health promotion is widely publicized, individuals often do not act on this information to change their behavior. Think about the number of people who continue to smoke despite the empirical evidence linking smoking to lung cancer, or the fact that 33 percent of white women and 50 percent of women of color do not get regular mammograms (Federal Interagency Forum, 2008). In general,

LIFESTYLE AND LONGEVITY

Arthur is a 97-year-old who may be described as a "paragon of good living." He has never smoked and has maintained his ideal body weight throughout adulthood—mostly by eating a diet rich in vegetables, fruit, and nuts and by walking two miles daily in his hilly neighborhood. Arthur has no chronic diseases. Although he still grieves over the death of his wife of 60 years 5 years ago, Arthur's spiritual beliefs and strong family network of children, grandchildren, and great grandchildren who live nearby have all helped him cope with his loss. His lifestyle exemplifies the link between longevity and healthy habits (maintaining an ideal weight, eating a healthy diet, not smoking, regular exercise, strong support network, and spiritual values). Many of these individual behaviors were also found to predict survival in a 40-year study of Japanese men (Willcox et al., 2006).

organized health promotion programs have difficulty recruiting more than 50 percent of the target population. This is true even for programs focused on people with a potentially deadly condition, such as post-myocardial infarct patients and those with high blood pressure. Attrition is also high, with rates of 30 to 60 percent. The gap between health knowledge and health practices can be very wide. Even when individual behavior change is a legitimate goal, sustaining health practices over time is difficult in the face of years of habit. More longitudinal research is needed to assess the long-range (10 years or more) consequences of health promotion interventions for individuals and for health care costs, especially because programs may

POINTS TO PONDER

Think about a health habit that you have tried to change, such as increasing your daily exercise and intake of fruits and vegetables. What difficulties did you face in making the desired changes? What are some strategies that worked for you? Could these same methods be used to help older adults change lifelong habits?

initially be very costly before significant savings emerge (Christ & Diwan, 2009).

Health promotion is clearly a growing area, especially with the current focus on reducing rising health care costs for older adults. However, it requires collaboration among individuals and local, state, and federal organizations and governments. In 2001, 55 national organizations such as AARP, the American Geriatrics Society, and the National Council on the Aging joined forces with government agencies (including the CDC and NIA) and with foundations concerned about health care and aging. They developed *The National Blueprint: Increasing Physical Activity Among Adults Age 50 and Older*, with 18 priority areas that recommended strategies at the individual, community, and policy levels. Community efforts included developing exercise programs in neighborhoods with large populations of color and building safe walking trails. This partnership also promoted efforts to provide low-income elders with low-cost, healthy meals and fresh produce (Active Aging Partnership, 2006). *Building Healthy Communities for Active Aging*, designed by the Environmental Protection Agency (EPA), is another example of an effective community-level program. Ten strategies at both the macro and individual level help communities implement community-wide changes that effectively support older adults becoming more physically active. These include strategies to identify community-wide health indicators, strengths-based approaches to motivate change, public campaigns and special promotions, working with mass media, offering both structured programs and self-directed activities such as fitness trails and ongoing evaluation (EPA, 2007). The Administration on Aging created a national campaign, *You Can! Steps to Healthier Aging*, which enlists hospitals, area agencies on aging, parks departments and faith-based groups nationwide to provide information and activities that promote physical activity and healthy nutritional decisions (Loughrey, 2004). These research and demonstration programs provide ample evidence for the effectiveness of such a multi-pronged approach to health promotion in delaying the onset of chronic diseases, reducing disability and health care costs, and even extending life expectancy.

Implications for the Future

As baby boomers age, several trends may emerge. First, this cohort includes more informed, health-conscious consumers than their predecessors. As a result, they will make more demands on the health care system, not just for themselves but for those for whom they are caregivers. A greater proportion than among previous cohorts will continue their self-care and wellness focus. Many will attain *Healthy People 2010* objectives that their parents have not been able to achieve. At the same time, however, a significant minority of baby boomers, particularly smokers and those who have lived a lifetime in poverty with little access to preventive services, will cope with multiple chronic diseases as their life expectancy increases.

HEALTHY AGING AMONG BABY BOOMERS

"Healthy aging" has become a goal of many middle-aged adults today. As noted in this and previous chapters, newer cohorts of adults are avoiding smoking, watching their weight, eating a healthy diet, and increasing their exercise frequency and level. It is no longer surprising to see midlife and young-old men and women competing in marathons and race walks. A popular phrase is "age 60 today is the old 50," with many 60 and older taking on new challenges. Some examples of baby boomers who have made the most of turning 60:

- A businessman who recently became a part-time certified meditation teacher
- A pilot and motorcycle rider who celebrated his 60th birthday by riding his motorcycle 4,000 miles from Seattle, Washington to North Carolina
- An educator who assumed the position of vice president for a *Fortune 500* company at age 60

SOURCE: *Seattle Times*, 2005.

Changes in the health care system will also influence future cohorts' access to and use of health services. For example, because of increased cost containment efforts (described in Chapter 17), more adults are enrolled—often not by choice—in managed care for their health care. To the extent that these health care systems are focused on maintaining and enhancing health behaviors, elders will have opportunities to participate in health promotion activities. However, if services are limited and preventive programs such as exercise, smoking cessation, and nutritional counseling are not offered, future cohorts of elders will not have ready access to health-enhancement programs. The growth of health technology—including telemedicine and home-based medication dispensers that prevent undermedication or overmedication—education about health literacy can help future elders manage their own health. The impact of technologies on older adults' ability to age in place in their own homes is discussed in Chapter 11.

Because of improved health status and survival with multiple chronic diseases among the older population, there is a critical need for health care providers trained in gerontology and clinical geriatrics who can communicate successfully with an increasingly diverse older population. Geriatricians (physicians who specialize in geriatric medicine)—as well as dentists, pharmacists, nurses and nurse practitioners, social workers, health educators, physical therapists, and occu-pational therapists who have been trained in geriatrics and gerontology—are critical to helping future cohorts of elders manage their chronic conditions and maximize their functional abilities. The shortage of physicians and pharmacists trained in geriatrics is one reason why many older Americans experience adverse reactions to medications and high rates of emergency room and inpatient hospital visits. Health care providers who are trained in geriatrics are more likely to encourage exercise programs, smoking cessation, and dietary interventions for older people and less likely to endorse stereotypes of aging as a time of decline. Indeed, there is evidence for better health outcomes for older adults who receive specialized geriatric nursing and physician care (Kovner, Mezey, Harrington, 2002).

The increasing need for geriatric nurse specialists comes at a time when the nursing profession is experiencing a shortage in all specialties and the median age of nurses today, 45, is higher than in all other health professions. Over 1 million new and replacement nurses will be needed by 2012 (Rieder, 2006). These trends do not bode well for the field of geriatric nursing care. Only about 10,000 of the 2.56 million registered nurses are certified in gerontological nursing, while only 3 percent of the 111,000 advanced practice nurses are certified in geriatrics (American Association of Colleges of Nursing, 2004). Likewise, the number of physicians specializing in geriatrics is far from adequate. In 2005, there was one geriatrician for every 5,000 adults age 65 and older. This is less than half the projected need for the current patient pool, and only one-fourth of the number needed by 2030. A primary reason for this gap in workforce needs is that only 9 of the 145 medical schools in the United States have departments of geriatrics, few schools require geriatric courses, and teaching hospitals graduate internists with as little as 6 hours of geriatric training (Gross, 2006). The situation in pharmacy is especially dire, with only 720 of 200,000 pharmacists who have received certification in geriatrics (Alliance for Aging Research, 2002; Scharlach, Simon, Dal Santo, 2002).

Social workers, who are key members of interdisciplinary health care teams, are not yet prepared to meet the growing demand for geriatric social work. The National Institute on Aging has projected a need for 60,000 to 70,000 geriatric social workers by 2020. In 2001, only 3 percent of the 150,000 members of the National Association of Social Workers (NASW) identified their primary area of social work practice as geriatric. By 2005, this had increased somewhat to 9 percent of a sample of licensed NASW members who identified aging

as their specific field of practice. Among these, fewer than 5 percent had received training in gerontological social work (Bureau of Labor Statistics, 2004; NASW, 2005; Rosen, Zlotnik, & Singer, 2002; Whitaker, Weismuller, & Clark, 2006). Unless health professions schools become more proactive in recruiting faculty to develop geriatric curricula and in encouraging students to specialize in geriatrics or gerontology, the current situation will grow into a crisis. The federal government took an important first step by passing the Geriatric Care Act in 2001, aimed at improving Medicare reimbursement for geriatric care and offering incentives for health professionals to obtain training in this field. In addition, the John A. Hartford Foundation in New York City remains the primary source of funding for professional development and mentoring in geriatric medicine, nursing, and social work.

Summary

Although older adults are at risk for more diseases than younger people, most rate their own health as satisfactory. Health status refers not only to an individual's physical condition, but also to her or his functional ability in various social and psychological domains. It is affected by a person's social surroundings, especially the degree of environmental stress and available social support. Although stress increases the risk of certain illnesses such as cardiovascular disease, older people are generally less negatively affected by it; this may reflect maturity, resiliency, self-control, or a lifetime of developing coping skills.

Older people have lower rates of acute conditions as younger people but are more likely to suffer from chronic or long-term diseases. The majority of older persons, however, are not limited in their daily activities by chronic conditions. The impact of such conditions apparently varies with the physiological changes that occur with age, the individual's adaptive resources, and his or her gender, race, ethnicity, and mental and emotional perspective. The type and incidence of chronic illnesses also vary by gender, and socioeconomic status.

The leading causes of death among persons over age 65 are heart disease, cancer, stroke, and accidents. Diseases of the heart and blood vessels are the most prevalent. Because hypertension (or high blood pressure) is a major risk in the development of cardiovascular problems, preventive actions are critical, especially weight control, dietary changes, appropriate exercise, and avoidance of cigarette smoking. Cancers—especially lung, bowel, breast and colon cancers—are the second most frequent cause of death among older people; the risk of cancer increases with age. Cerebrovascular accident, or stroke, is the third leading cause of death among older persons. It may be caused by cerebral thrombosis, or blood clots, and by cerebral hemorrhage. Healthy lifestyle practices are important in preventing these deaths. Indeed, death rates due to heart disease and stroke have declined for older adults, while deaths attributable to cancer have declined among middle-aged adults. This is because of more preventive health care and early detection of cancer in the middle years. Similarly, accidents, particularly those associated with driving and falls, are often preventable through changes in environmental design as well as exercise.

Arthritis, although not fatal, is a major cause of limited daily activity and, to some extent, affects most older persons. Osteoporosis, or loss of bone mass and the resultant increased brittleness of the bones, is most common among older women and may result in fractures of the hip, spine, and wrist. New research supports the benefits of physical exercise for preventing fractures and falls and managing arthritis. Chronic respiratory problems, particularly emphysema, increase with age, especially among men. Diabetes mellitus is a frequent problem in old age and is particularly troubling because of

comorbidity or the many related illnesses that may result. Problems with the intestinal tract include diverticulitis, constipation, and hiatus hernia. Cystitis and incontinence are frequently occurring problems of the kidneys and urinary system, especially among older women. Although the majority of older persons have some type of incontinence, most kinds can be treated and controlled.

The growth of the older population, combined with the increase in major chronic illnesses, has placed greater demands on the health care system. Nevertheless, older people seek outpatient medical, dental, and mental health services at a slightly lower rate than their incidence of chronic illnesses would predict. Like younger people, the older population is most likely to seek health services for acute problems, not for checkups on chronic conditions or for preventive care. Perceptions that physicians, dentists, and mental health professionals cannot cure their chronic problems may deter many older people from seeking needed care. The problem may be compounded by ageist beliefs of some health care providers and by cultural and linguistic barriers that result in health care disparities among historically underserved groups. More training in geriatrics and gerontology is needed for health care providers in order to improve their attitudes toward and competencies for working with older people and their families.

Health promotion is effective in improving the well-being and enhancing the quality of life of older people. The elimination or postponement of the chronic diseases that are associated with old age is a major goal for specialists in wellness and health enhancement, as well as biomedical researchers interested in delaying the aging process. Treatment methods for all these diseases are changing rapidly with the growth in medical technology and the increasing recognition given to such environmental factors as stress, nutrition, and exercise in disease prevention. If health promotion efforts to modify lifestyles are successful, and if aging research progresses substantially, the chronic illnesses that we have discussed will undoubtedly be postponed, and disability or loss of functional status may rarely happen to future cohorts.

GLOSSARY

Activities of Daily Living (ADLs)   summarize an individual's performance in personal care tasks such as bathing or dressing, as well as such home-management activities such as shopping, meal preparation, and taking medications

acute condition   short-term disease or infection, often debilitating to older than younger persons

acute myocardial infarction   loss of blood flow to a specific region of the heart, resulting in damage of the myocardium

arteriosclerosis   loss of elasticity of the arterial walls because of fatty deposits

atherosclerosis   narrowing of large arteries because of plague deposits

benign prostatic hypertrophy (BPH)   enlargement of the prostate gland in older men, without signs of cancer or other serious disease; may cause discomfort

chronic condition   long-term (more than three months), often permanent, and leaving a residual disability that may require long-term management or care rather than cure

comorbidity   simultaneously experiencing multiple health problems, both acute and chronic

diabetes mellitus   a disease that impairs the ability of the pancreas to produce insulin, a hormone that enables glucose from the blood to cells and accumulates in the blood (type II is most common among adults, associated with obesity)

diagnosis-related groups (DRGs)   a system of classifying medical cases for payment on the basis of diagnoses; used under Medicare's prospective payment system (PPS) for inpatient hospital services

disability   an impairment in the ability to complete multiple daily tasks

diverticulitis   a condition in which pouches or sacs (diverticula) in the intestinal wall become inflamed and infected

edentulous   the absence of natural teeth

frailty   severe limitations in ADL

good health   more than the mere absence of infirmity, a state of complete physical, mental, and social well-being

health promotion   a model in which individuals are responsible for and in control of their own health, combined with health education and related organizational, political, and economic changes conducive to health

health status   the presence or absence of disease, as well as the degree of disability in an individual's level of functioning

hiatus hernia   a condition in which a small portion of the stomach slides up through the diaphragm

hypokinesia   the degeneration and functional loss of muscle and bone due to physical inactivity

immunity   ability of the organism to resist pathogens (viruses and bacteria)

Instrumental Activities of Daily Living (IADLs) summarize an individual's ability to interact in complex, multidimensional ways with the environment daily activities involving use of the environment

incontinence   the inability to control urine and feces. Of two types: urge incontinence, where a person is not able to hold urine long enough to reach a toilet, and stress incontinence, where leakage occurs during physical exertion, laughing, sneezing, or coughing

osteoarthritis   gradual degeneration of joints that are subject to physical stress

osteopenia   a significant loss of calcium and reduced bone density not associated with increased risk of fractures

quality of life   going beyond health status alone, this concept considers the individual's sense of competence, ability to perform activities of daily living, and satisfaction with social interactions in addition to functional health

rheumatoid arthritis a chronic inflammation of the membranes lining joints and tendons, characterized by pain, swelling, bone dislocation, and limited range of motion; can occur at any age

sarcopenia atrophy of skeletal muscle mass, generally resulting from a sedentary lifestyle and some chronic diseases

REFERENCES

AARP. (2003). Beyond 50. *A report to the nation on independent living and disability.* Washington, DC: AARP Public Policy Institute.

Ackerman, M. L., Edwards, J. D., Ross, L. A., Ball, K.K., Lundsman, M. (2008). Examination of cognitive and instrumental functional performance as indicators for driving cessation risk across 3 years. *The Gerontologist, 48,* 802–810.

Active Aging Partnership. (2006). National Blueprint: Increasing physical activity among adults aged 50 and older. Retrieved February 2006, from http://www.agingblueprint.org

Ai, A. & Carrigan, L. (2006). Older adults with age-related cardiovascular disease. In B. Berkman (Ed.), *Handbook of Social Work in Health and Aging.* New York: Oxford.

Albert, C. M., Mittleman, M. A., Chae, C. U., Lee, I. M., Hennekens, C. H., & Manson, J. E. (2000). Triggering of sudden death from cardiac causes by vigorous exertion. *New England Journal of Medicine, 343,* 1355–1361.

Alley, D. E., Ferrucci, L., Barbagallo, M., Studenski, S. A., Harris, T. B. (2008). A research agenda: The changing relationship between body weight and health in aging. *Journal of Gerontology: Medical Sciences,* 2008, *63A,* 1257–1259.

Alliance for Aging Research. (2002). *Medical never-never land: Ten reasons why America is not ready for the coming age boom.* Washington, DC: Alliance for Aging Research.

American Association of Colleges of Nursing. (2004). *Nursing practitioner and clinical nurse specialists competencies for older adult care.* Washington, DC.

American Cancer Society (ACS). (2001). *Breast cancer questions and answers; Cancer facts for men.* ACS.

American Diabetes Association (ADA). (2009a). *Type 2 Diabetes.* Retrieved May 2009, from http://www.diabetes.org/type-2-diabetes.jsp

American Diabetes Association. (2009b). *The Alzheimer's-Diabetes Link.* Retrieved May 2009, from http://www.diabetes.org/diabetes-research/hottopics.jsp

American Geriatrics Society. (2001). Guideline for the prevention of falls in older persons. *Journal of the American Geriatrics Society, 49,* 664–672.

American Heart Association. (2003). *Heart disease and stroke statistics 2003 update.* Dallas, TX: American Heart Association.

American Heart Association. (2005). *Heart disease and stroke statistics 2005 update.* Dallas, TX: American Heart Association.

Anderson, G. (2005) Medicare and chronic conditions. *New England Journal of Medicine, 353,* 305–309.

Arcury, T. A., Grzywacz, J. G., Bell, R. A., Neiberg, R. H., Lang, W., Quandt, S. A. (2007). Herbal remedy use as health self-management among older adults. *Journal of Gerontology: Social Sciences, 62B,* S142–S149.

Arfin, F. (2006). Older drivers turning to AAA, AARP for advice on road safety. *About: Senior Travel.* Retrieved December 2006, from http://seniortravel.about.com

Barrow, K. (2008). Speaking out for a group once unheard-of: Aging with AIDs. *The New York Times.*

Benyamini, Y., Blumstein, T., Lusky, A., Modan, B. (2003). Gender differences in the self-rated health-mortality association. *The Gerontologist, 43,* 396–405.

Blow, F., Bartels, S., Brockmann, L., & Van Citters, A. (2005). Evidence-based practices for preventing substance abuse and mental health problems in older adults. Older Americans Substance Abuse and Mental Health Technical Assistance Center: U.S. Department of Health and Human Services, Substance Abuse and Mental Health Services Administration, Center for Substance Abuse Prevention. Retrieved

February 2008, from http://www.samhsa.gov/OlderAdultsTAC

Blow, F., Serras, A., & Barry, K. (2007). Late-life depression and alcoholism. *Current Psychiatry Reports, 9,* 14–19

Braithwaite, R. S., Col, N. F., & Wong, J. B. (2003). Estimating hip fracture morbidity, mortality and costs. *Journal of the American Geriatrics Society, 51,* 364–370.

Campisi, J. (2005). Aging, tumor suppression and cancer: High-wire act. *Mechanics of Aging and Development, 126,* 51–58.

Castro, C. M. & King, A. C. (2002). Telephone-assisted counseling for physical activity. *Exercise and Sport Sciences, 30,* 64–68.

Cattan, M., White, M., Bond, J., & Learmouth, A. (2005). Preventing social isolation and loneliness among older people: A systematic review of health promotion interventions. *Ageing and Society, 25,* 41–67.

Cauley, J. A., Robbins, J., Chen, Z., Cummings, S. R., Jackson, R. D., LaCroix, A. Z., LeBoff, M., Lewis, C. E., et al. (2003). Effects of estrogen plus progestin on risk of fracture and bone mineral density. *Journal of the American Medical Association, 290,* 1729–1738.

Center for the Advancement of Health. (2008). *A new vision of aging: Helping older adults make healthier choices.* Issue briefing No. 2. Washington, DC. Retrieved March 2008, from http://www.cfah.org/pdfs/agingreport.pdf

Centers for Disease Control and Prevention (CDC). (2003a). Hospitalizations for stroke among adults aged ≥65 years: U.S., 2000. *MMWR Public Health Report, 52,* 586–589.

Centers for Disease Control and Prevention (CDC). (2003b). *National diabetes fact sheet:* General information and national estimates of diabetes in the United States.

Centers for Disease Control and Prevention (CDC). (2004a). *Health, United States, 2004. Special excerpt: Trend tables on 65 and older population.* Atlanta, GA: CDC.

Centers for Disease Control and Prevention (CDC). (2004b). Strength training among adults aged 65 and older—U.S. 2001. *Morbidity and Mortality Weekly Report, 53,* 25–26.

Centers for Disease Control and Prevention (CDC). (2006). Tips for preventing falls. Retrieved December 2006, from http://www.cdc.gov/ncipc/duip/fallsmaterial.htm

Centers for Disease Control and Prevention (CDC). (2008a). Chronic disease: Arthritis at a glance. Retrieved January 2008, from http://www.cdc.gov/arthritis/intervention/index.htm

Centers for Disease Control and Prevention (CDC). (2008b). Arthritis intervention programs. Retrieved January 2008, from http://www.cdc.gov/arthritis/intervention/lists.htm

Centers for Disease Control and Prevention (CDC). (2008c). *Healthy aging: Preserving function and improving quality of life among older adults.* Retrieved December 2008, from http://www.cdc.gov?nccdphp/publications/aag;pdf/healthy_aging.pdf

Centers for Disease Control and Prevention (CDC). (2009). *HIV/AIDS: Persons age 60 and older.* Retrieved May 2009, from http://www.cdc.gov/hiv/topics/over50/print/index.htm

Centers for Disease Control and Prevention (CDC), Division of Oral health (2009). *Oral health for older Americans.* Retrieved October 2009, from www.cdc.gov/oralhealth/publications/factsheets/adult_older.htm

Centers for Disease Control and Prevention and the Merck Foundation. (2008). *The state of aging and health in America 2008.* Whitehouse Station, NJ: The Merck Company Foundation.

Chakravarty, E. F., Hubert, H. B., Lingala, V .B., Fries, J. F. (2008). Reduced disability and mortality among aging runners: A 21-year longitudinal study. *Archives of Internal Medicine, 168,* 1638–1646.

Chernoff, R. (2001). Nutrition and health promotion in older adults. *Journals of Gerontology, 56A, Special Issue II,* 47–53.

Chipperfield, J. G. (2008). Everyday physical activity as a predictor of late-life mortality. *The Gerontologist, 48,* 349–357.

Christ, G. (2008). *Chronic illness and aging: Cancer as a chronic life threatening condition.* Council on Social Work Education, Section 4.

Christ, G. & Diwan, S. (2008) *Chronic illness and aging: The demographics of aging and chronic diseases.* Council on Social Work Education, Section 1.

Clancey, C. M. & Bierman, A. S. (2000). Quality and outcomes of care for older women with chronic disease. *Women's Health Issues, 10,* 178–192.

Cole, N. & Fox, M. K. (2004). *Nutrition and health characteristics of low-income populations: Older Adults.* (Vol. IV). U.S. Dept. of Agriculture Economic Research Service, Food Assistance and Nutrition Research Program.

Coleman, E. A., Hutchins, L., & Goodwin, J. (2004). An overview of cancer in older adults. *MEDSURG Nursing, 13,* 75–109.

Crandell, S. (2006). Living longer: Exercise. *AARP Magazine, 49,* 90–93.

Cranney, A., Tugwell, P., Wells, G., & Guyatt, G. (2002). Osteoporosis Methodology Group and the Osteoporosis Research Advisory Group. Meta-analyses of therapies for postmenopausal osteoporosis. Systematic reviews of randomized trials in osteoporosis: Introduction and methodology. *Endocrine Reviews, 23,* 496–507.

Crimmins, E. M. & Saito, Y. (2001). Trends in healthy life expectancy in the United States: Gender, racial and educational differences. *Social Science and Medicine, 52,* 1629–1641.

Doshi, J. A., Shaffer, T., & Briesacher, B. A. (2005). National estimates of medication use in nursing homes. *Journal of the American Geriatrics Society, 53,* 438–443.

Elder obesity lacks treatment options. (2009). *Gerontology News.* February, 1–11

Emlet, C. A. (2006). "You're awfully old to have this disease:" Experiences of stigma and ageism in adults 50 years and older living with HIV/AIDS. *The Gerontologist, 46,* 781–790

Emlet, C. A. & Berghuis, J. P. (2002). Service priorities, use and needs: Views of older and younger consumers living with HIV/AIDS. *Journal of Mental Health and Aging, 8,* 307–318.

Emlet, C. A. & Farkas, K. J. (2002). Correlates of service utilization among midlife and older adults with HIV/AIDS. *Journal of Aging and Health, 14,* 315–335.

Ershler, W. B. (2003). Cancer: A disease of the elderly. *Journal of Supportive Oncology, 1,* 5–10.

Federal Interagency Forum on Aging-Related Statistics. (2008). *Older Americans update 2008: Key Indicators of Well-Being.* Hyattsville, MD.

Ferraro, K. & Kelley-Moore, M. (2005). Are racial disparities in health conditional on socioeconomic status? *Social Science and Medicine, 60,* 191–204.

Fisman, D. N., Abrutyn, E., Spaude, K. A., Kim, A., Kirchner, C., & Daley, J. (2006). Prior pneumococcal vaccination is associated with reduced death, complications, and length of stay among hospitalized adults with community-acquired pneumonia. *Clinical Infectious Diseases, 42,* 1093–1101.

Fletcher, P. C. & Hirdes, J. P. (2004). Restriction in activity associated with fear of falling among community-based seniors using home care services. *Age and Ageing, 33,* 273–279.

Foley, D. J., Masak, K. H. G., Ross, W., & White, L. R. (2000). Driving cessation in older men with incident dementia. *Journal of the American Geriatrics Society, 48,* 928–930.

Franco, O. H., deLaet, C., Peeters, A., Jonker, J., Mackenbach, J., & Nusselder, W. (2005). Effects of physical activity on life expectancy with cardiovascular disease. *Archives of Internal Medicine, 165,* 2355–2360.

Francoeur, R. & Elkins, J. (2006). Older adults with diabetes and complications. In B. Berkman (Ed.). *Handbook of Social Work in Health and Aging.* New York: Oxford.

Freedman, M., Hootman, J., Helmick, C. (2007). Projected state-specific increases in self-reported, doctor-diagnosed arthritis and arthritis-attributable activity limitations: United States 2005-2030. *Mortality and Morbidity Weekly Report, 56,* 423–425.

Freund, B. & Szinovacz, M. (2002). Effects of cognition on driving involvement among the oldest old. *The Gerontologist, 42,* 621–633.

Fried, L. P., Tangen, C. M., Walston, J., Newman, A. B., Hirsch, C., Seeman, T., et al. (2001). Frailty in older adults: Evidence for a phenotype. *Journals of Gerontology: Medical Sciences, 56A,* M146–M156.

Fries, J. F. (2003). Measuring and monitoring success in compressing morbidity. *Annals of Internal Medicine, 139,* 455–459.

Gallagher, B., Tai Chi Chuan, & Qigong. (2003). Physical and mental practice for functional mobility. *Topics in Geriatric Rehabilitation, 19,* 172–182.

Golden, S. H., Lazo, M., Carnethon, M., Bertoni, A. G., Schriner, P. J., et al. (2008). Examining a bidirectional association between depressive symptoms and diabetes. *Journal of the American Medical Association, 23,* 2751–2159.

Gray, S. L., Hanlon, J. T., Landerman, L. R., Artz, M., Schmeder, K. E., & Fillenbaum, G. G. (2003). Is antioxidant use protective of cognitive function in community-dwelling elderly? *American Journal of Geriatric Pharmacotherapy, 1,* 3–10.

Gross, J. (2006). Geriatrics lags in age of high-tech medicine. *The New York Times.* Retrieved October 2006, from http://www.nytimes.com/2006/10/18/health/18aged

Gubrium, J., Rittman, M., Williams, C., & Boylstein, C. (2003). Benchmarking as everyday functional assessment in stroke recovery. *The Journal of Gerontology: Medical Sciences, 58A,* M203–M211.

Gurnack, A. M., Atkinson, R., & Osgood, N. (Eds.). (2002). *Treating alcohol and drug abuse in the elderly.* New York: Springer.

Gusi, N., Raimundo, A., & Leal, A. (2006). Low-frequency vibratory exercise reduces the risk of bone fracture more than walking. *BMC Musculoskeletal Disorders, 7,* 92–98.

Haber, D. (2003). *Health promotion and aging: Practical applications for health professionals* (3rd ed.). New York: Springer.

Handler, S. M., Wright, R. M., Rudy, C. M., & Hanlon, J. T. (2006). Epidemiology of medication-related adverse events in nursing homes. *American Journal of Geriatric Pharmacotherapy, 4,* 264–272.

Hanlon, J. T., Boudreau, R. M., Roumani, Y. F., Newman, A.B., Ruby, C.M., Wright, R.M., et al (2009). Number and dosage of central nervous system medications on recurrent falls in community elders. *Journal of Gerontology: Medical Sciences, 64A,* M492–M498.

Hayflick, L. (1996). *How and why we age.* New York: Ballantine Books.

He, W., Sengupta, M., Velkoff, V., & DeBerros, K. (2005). *65+ in the United States.* Washington, DC: U.S. Department of Health and Human Services.

Health Resources and Services Administration (HRSA). (2001). HIV disease in individuals ages 50 and above. *HRSA Care Action,* 1–3.

Healthy People 2010. (2000). *Understanding and improving health.* U. S. Government Printing Office. No. 017-001-00547-9.

Hewitt, M. J. (2003). *Growing older, staying strong: Preventing sarcopenia through strength training.* New York: International Longevity Center.

Hsieh, C. (2005). Treatment of constipation in older adults. *American Family Physician, 74,* 715–718.

Huang, G., Gau, M., Lin, W., & Kernoham, G. (2003). Assessing risk of falling in older adults. *Public Health Nursing, 20,* 399–411.

Hughes, S. L., Seymour, R. B., Campbell, R., Pollak, N., Huber, G., & Sharma, L. (2004). Impact of the fit and strong intervention on older adults with osteoarthritis. *The Gerontologist, 44,* 217–228.

Institute of Medicine. (2008). Cancer in elderly people: Workshop proceedings. Washington, DC: National Academies Press. Retrieved August 2008, from http://www.iom.edu/?ID= 53452

Jacob, T. & Johnson, S. L. (2001). Sequential interactions in the parent-child communications of depressed fathers and depressed mothers. *Journal of Family Psychology, 15,* 38–52.

Jacquescoley, E. (2008). Behavioral prevention study gauges HIV/AIDS and depression in the older U.S. population. *AIDS Care, 20,* 1152–1153.

Kaufman, D. W., Kelly, J. P., Rosenberg, L., Anderson, T. E., & Mitchell, A. A. (2002). Recent patterns of medication use in the ambulatory adult population of the United States. *Journal of the American Medical Association, 287,* 337–344.

Kelley-Moore, M. & Ferraro, K. (2004). The black-white disability gap: Persistent inequality in later life? *Journal of Gerontology: Social Sciences, 59,* S34–S43.

Kennard, C. (2009). Driving with Alzheimer's disease. About.com/Alzheimer's Disease, 2006. Retrieved May 2009, from http://alzheimers.about.com/cs/diagnosisissues/a/Driving.htm

Kiyak, H. A. & Reichmuth, M. (2005). Barriers to and enablers of older adults' use of dental services. *Journal of Dental Education, 69,* 975–986.

Knoops, K. T. B. (2004). Mediterranean diet, lifestyle factors and 10-year mortality in elderly European men and women. *Journal of the American Medical Association, 292,* 1433–1439.

Korzenik, J. R. (2006). Case closed? Diverticulitis: Epidemiology and fiber. *Journal of Clinical Gastroenterology, 40, Supplement 3,* S112–S116.

Kovner, C. T., Mezey, M., & Harrington, C. (2002). Who cares for older adults? *Health Affairs, 21,* 78–89.

Kugler, C., Altenhoner, T., Lochner, P., & Ferbert, A. (2003). Does age influence early recovery from ischemic stroke? A study from the Hession Stroke Data Bank. *Journal of Neurology, 250,* 676–681.

Lau, E. M. C., Suriwongpaisal, P., Lee, J. K., Das De, S., Festin, M. R., Saw, S. M., et al. (2001). Risk factors for hip fracture in Asian men and women: The Asian Osteoporosis Study. *Journal of Bone and Mineral Research, 16,* 572–580.

Lawson, D. M. & Brossart, D. F. (2001). Intergenerational transmission: Individuation and intimacy across three generations. *Family Process, 40,* 429–442.

Leeb, B. F., Schweitzer, H., Montag, K., & Smolen, J. S. (2000). A meta-analysis of chondroitin sulfate in the treatment of osteoarthritis. *Journal of Rheumatology, 27,* 205–211.

Li, G., Braver, E. R., & Chen, L. H. (2003). Fragility versus excessive crash involvement as determinants of high death rates per vehicle-mile of travel among older drivers. *Accident Analysis and Prevention, 35,* 227–235.

Lin, E. H. B., Katon, W., VonKorff, M., et al. (2003). Effect of improving depression on pain and functional outcomes among older adults with arthritis. *Journal of the American Medical Association, 290,* 2428–2434.

Loughrey, K. (2004). You can! Steps to healthier aging: AOA nationwide campaign. *Generations, 28,* 95–96.

Lynch, J. W., Smith, G. D., Kaplan, G. A., & House, J. S. (2008). Income inequality and mortality: Importance to health of individual income, psychosocial environment and material conditions. *British Medical Journal, 320,* 1200–1204.

Manton, K. G., Gu, X., & Lamb, V. L. (2006). Change in chronic disability from 1982 to 2004/2005 as measured by long-term changes in function and health in the U.S. elderly population. *Proceedings of the National Academy of Sciences, 103,* 18374–18379.

Manton, K. G., Gu, X., & Lowrimore, G. R. (2008). Cohort changes in active life expectancy in the U.S. elderly populating: Experiences from the 1982-2004 National Long-Term Care Survey. *Journal of Gerontology: Social Sciences, 63B,* S269–S282.

Marimaldi, P. & Lee, J. (2006). Older adults with cancer. In B. Berkman (Ed.). *Handbook of Social Work in Health and Aging.* New York: Oxford.

Marottoli, R. A., VanNess, P. H., Araujo, K. L. B., Iannone, L.P., Acampora, D., et al. (2007). A randomized trial of an education program to enhance older driver performance. *Journal of Gerontology: Medical Sciences, 62A,* 1113–1119.

Martinson, B. C., Crain, A. L., Pronk, N. P., O'Conner, P. J., & Maciosek, M. V. (2003). Changes in physical activity and short-term changes in health care. *Preventive Medicine, 37,* 319–326.

Masoro, E. J. (2006). Are age-associated diseases an integral part of aging? In E. J. Masoro & S. N. Austad (Eds.). *Handbook of the Biology of Aging* (6th ed.). Amsterdam: Elsevier Academic Press.

Mauk, K. (2006). Nursing interventions within the Mauk model of poststroke recovery. *Rehabilitation Nursing, 31,* 257–263.

McTiernan, A., Kooperberg, C., White, E., Wilcox, S., Coates, R., Adams-Campbell, L., et al. (2003). Recreational physical activity and the risk of breast cancer in postmenopausal women: The Women's Health Initiative Cohort Study. *Journal of the American Medical Association, 290,* 1331–1336.

Medical News Today. (2008). New study: Aging baby boomers could overwhelm U.S. health care system by 2017. Retrieved March 2008, from http://www.medicalnewstoday.com

Menec, V. (2003). The relation between everyday activities and successful aging: A 6-year longitudinal study. *Journal of Gerontology: Social Sciences, 58B,* S74–S82.

Mikuls, T. R., Mudano, A. S., Pulley, L. V., & Saag, K. G. (2003). Association of race/ethnicity with the receipt of traditional and alternative arthritis-specific health care. *Medical Care, 41,* 1233–1239.

Miltiades, H. & Kaye, L. (2006). Older adults with orthopedic and mobility limitations. In B. Berkman (Ed.). *Handbook of Social Work in Health and Aging.* New York: Oxford.

Moreland, J. D., Richardson, J. A., Goldsmith, C. H., & Clase, C. M. (2004). Muscle weakness and falls in older adults: A systematic review of the literature. *Journal of the American Geriatrics Society, 52,* 1121–1129.

Morrison, A. & Levy, R. (2006). Fraction of nursing home admissions attributable to urinary incontinence. *Value Health, 9,* 272–274.

National Association of Social Workers. (2005). *Assuring the sufficiency of a frontline workforce: A national study of licensed social workers.* Preliminary report. Center for Workforce Studies, NASW.

National Cancer Institute. (2005). *Facts about Office of Cancer Survivorship.* Retrieved February 2005, from http://dccps.nci.nih.gov/ocs/ocs_factsheet.pdf

National Center for Health Statistics (NCHS). (2003). *Trends in health and aging.* Retrieved 2003, from http://www.cdc.gov/nchs/about/otheract/aging/trendsoverview.htm

National Center for Health Statistics (NCHS). (2005). *Health, United States, 2005.* Retrieved 2005, from http://www.cdc.gov/nchs/data/hus/hus05pdf

National Center for Health Statistics (NCHS). (2007). *Health, United States, 2007.* Hyattsville, MD: NCHS.

National Center for Health Statistics (NCHS). (2009). *Beyond 20/20 WDS–Chronic conditions U.S.* 1999–2007. National Health Interview Survey. Retrieved May 2009, from http://205.207.175.HDI/Tableviewer

National Highway Traffic Safety Administration (NHTSA). (2001). *Traffic safety facts 2000: Older population.* Washington, DC: U.S. Department of Transportation.

National Institute on Aging. (2008). *Menopause,* Washington, DC: author. 2008. Retrieved May 2009, from http://www.nia.nih.gov/Health Information/Publications/menopause.htm

National Institute on Aging (NIA). (2008). *Osteoporosis: The bone thief.* Bethesda, MD: NIH/NIA.

National Institute on Aging (NIA). (2009a). *Exercise and physical activity: Getting fit for life.* Bethesda, MD: NIH/NIA.

National Institute on Aging (NIA). (2009b). *HIV/ AIDS and older people.* Bethesda, MD: NIH/NIA, 2008. Retrieved May 2009, from http//: www.nia.nih.gov/HealthInformation/Publications/ hiv-aids.htm

National Institute of Diabetes, Digestive and Kidney Disease (NIDDK). (2007). *National Diabetes Statistics.* Retrieved 2009, from http://diabetes .niddk.nih.gov/

National Institute on Drug Abuse (NIDA). (2007). *Research Report Series—Prescription drugs: Abuse and addition. Trends in prescrtipon drug use.* Retrieved 2007, from http://www.nida.nih.gov/ ResearchReports/Prescription/prescription5.html

NCHS Dataline. (2008) *Public Health Reports. 123,* 390–392.

Nelson, H. D., Vesco, K. K., Haney, E., Fu, R., Nedrow, A., Miller, J., et al. (2006). Nonhormonal therapies for menopausal hot flashes: Systematic review and meta-analysis. *Journal of the American Medical Association, 295,* 2057–2071.

Nguyen, N. & Holodniy, M. (2008). HIV infection in the elderly. *Clinical Interventions and Aging, 3,* 453–72.

Office of Minority Health Research (OMHRC). (2006). *HHS fact sheet: Minority health disparities at a glance.* Retrieved December 2006, from http://www.omhrc.gov/templates/content.as px?ID=2139

Ostbyte, T. & Taylor, D. H. (2004). Effect of smoking on years of healthy life lost among middle-aged and older Americans. *Health Services Research,* *39,* 531–551.

Palmer, S. (2009). Diabetes prevention: The best medicine. *Aging Well, 2,* 22–25.

Pathman, D. E., Fowler-Brown, A., & Corbie-Smith, G. (2006). Differences in access to outpatient medical care for black and white adults in the rural South. *Medical Care, 44,* 429–438.

Penrod, J. D., Litke, A., Hawkes, W. G., Magaziner, J., Doucette, T., et al. (2008). The association of race, gender, and comorbidity with mortality and function after hip fracture. *Journal of Gerontology: Medical Sciences, 63A,* 867-872.

Peterson, M. J., Giuliani, C., Morey, M. C., Pieper, C. F., Evenson, K. R., Mercer, V. et al. (2009). Physical activity as a preventive factor for frailty. *Journal of Gerontology: Medical Sciences, 64A,* 61-68.

Phelan, E., Anderson, L., LaCroix, A., & Larson, A. (2004). Older adults' views of "successful aging:" How do they compare with researchers' definitions? *Journal of the American Geriatrics Society, 53,* 211–216.

Phillips, R. S. (2000). Preventing depression: A program for African American elders with chronic pain. *Family and Community Health, 22,* 57–65.

Poindexter, C. & Emlet, C. (2006). HIV-infected and HIV-affected older adults. In B. Berkman (Ed.). *Handbook of Social Work in Health and Aging.* New York: Oxford.

Putnam, M., Greenen, S., Powers, L., Saxton, M., Finney, S., & Dautel, P. (2003). Health and wellness: People with disabilities discuss barriers and facilitators to well being. *Journal of Rehabilitation, 69,* 37–45.

Quinn, M. E., Johnson, M. A., Poon, L. W., & Martin, P. (1999). Psychosocial correlates of subjective mental health in sexagenarians, octogenarians, and centenarians. *Issues in Mental Health Nursing, 20,* 151–171.

Radda, K. E., Schensul, J. J., Disch, W. B., Levy, J. A., & Reyes, C. Y. (2003). Assessing human immunodeficiency virus (HIV) risk among older urban adults. *Family and Community Health, 26,* 203–213.

Rieder, C. (2006). Building academic geriatric nursing capacity: The JAHN/AAN Partnership. *Nursing Outlook, 54,* 169–171.

Rizzo, V. (2008). *Chronic illness and aging: Osteoarthritis.* Council on Social Work Education, Section 5.

Rosen, A. L., Zlotnik, J. L., & Singer, T. (2002). Basic gerontological competence for all social workers: The need to "gerontologize" social work education. *Journal of Gerontological Social Work, 39,* 25–36.

Ross, L. A., Clay, O. J., Edwards, J. D., Ball, K. K., Wadley, V. G., et al. (2009). Do older drivers at-risk for crashes modify their driving over time? *Journal of Gerontology: Psychological Sciences, 64B,* 163–170.

Rothberg, M. B., Bellantonio, S., & Rose, D. N. (2003). Management of influenza in adults older than 65 years of age: Cost-effectiveness of rapid testing and antiviral therapy. *Annals of Internal Medicine, 139,* 321–329.

Ruby, C. M., Fillenbaum, G. G., Kuchibhatla, M. N., & Hanlon, J. T. (2003). Laxative use in thecommunity-dwelling elderly. *American Journal of Geriatric Pharmacotherapy, 1,* 11–17.

Salen, P. N., Kellwell, K., Baumgratz, W., Eberhardt, M., & Reed, J. (2003). How does octogenarian status affect mobility, mortality, and functional outcomes of elderly drivers in motor vehicle crashes in Pennsylvania? *Academy of Emergency Medicine, 10,* 477–478.

Scharlach, A., Simon, J., & Dal Santo, T. (2002). Who is providing social services to today's older adults? *Journal of Gerontological Social Work, 38,* 5–17.

Schoofs, M., van der Klift, M., Hofman, A., de Laet, C., Herings, R., Stijnen, T., et al. (2003). Thiazide diuretics and the risk for hip fracture. *Annals of Internal Medicine, 139,* 476–482.

Schrimshaw, E. W. & Siegel, K. (2003). Perceived barriers to social support from family and friends among older adults with HIV/ AIDS. *Journal of Health Psychology, 8,* 738–752.

Science Daily. (2009). One-third of sexually active older adults with HIV/AIDS has unprotected sex. Retrieved May 2009, from http://www .sciencedaily.com/releases/200704/0704251221 57.htm

Shippy, R. A. & Karpiak, S. E. (2005). The aging HIV/AIDS population: Fragile social networks. *Aging and Mental Health, 9,* 246–254.

Stepnick, L. & Whitelaw, N. A. (2006). *A new vision of aging: Helping older adults make healthier choices.* Washington, DC: Center for the Advancement of Health.

Stark, S. W. (2006). HIV after age 55. *Nursing Clinics of North America, 41,* 469–479.

Stothers, L., Thom, D. H., & Calhoun, E. (2005). Urologic diseases in America project: Urinary incontinence in males. *Journal of Urology, 173,* 1302–1308.

Theis, T., Helmick, C., & Hootman, J. (2007). Arthritis burden and impact are greater among U.S. women than men: Intervention opportunities. *Journal of Women's Health, 16,* 441–453.

Thom, D. H., Nygaard, I. E., & Calhoun, E. (2005). Urologic diseases in America project: Urinary incontinence in women. *Journal of Urology, 173,* 1295–1301.

Thompson, W. W., Shay, D. K., Weintraub, E., Brammer, L., Bridges, C. B., & Cox, N. J. (2004). Influenza-associated hospitalizations in the U.S. *Journal of the American Medical Association, 292,* 1333–1340.

U.S. Department of Health and Human Services (USDHHS). (2000). *Oral Health in America: A Report of the Surgeon General.* Bethesda, MD: NIDCR/NIH.

Villareal, D.T., Apovian, C.M., Kushner, R.F., Klein, S. (2005). Obesity in older adults. *America Journal of Clinical Nutrition, 82,* 923–934.

Vincent, K. R., Braith, R. W., Feldman, R. A., & Lowenthal, D. T. (2002). Improved cardio-respiratory endurance following 6 months of resistance exercise in elderly men and women. *Archives of Internal Medicine, 162,* 673–678.

Vosvick, M., Koopman, C., Gore-Felton, C., Thoresen, C., Krumboltz, J., & Spiegel, D. (2003). Relationship of functional quality of life to strategies for coping with the stress of living with HIV/AIDS. *Psychosomatics: Journal of Consultation Liaison Psychiatry, 44,* 51–58.

Wang, Y., Chang, C. F., Chou, J., Chen, H. L., Harvey, B. K., et al. (2005). Dietary supplementation with blueberries, spinach or spirulina reduces ischemic brain damage. *Experimental Neurology, 193,* 75–84.

Warner, D. F. & Hayward, M. D. (2002). *Race disparities in men's mortality: The role of childhood social conditions in a process of cumulative disadvantage.* University of Pennsylvania, unpublished manuscript.

Whitaker, T., Weismiller, T., & Clark, E. (2008). *Assuring the sufficiency of a frontline workforce: A national study of licensed social workers.* Retrieved January 2008, from http://workforce.socialworkers.org/studies/aging/aging.pdf

Whitfield, K. E. & Hayward, M. (2003). The landscape of health disparities among older adults. *Public Policy and Aging Report, 13,* 1–7.

Willcox, B. J., He, Q., Chen, R., Yano, K., Masaki, K. H., Grove, J. S., et al. (2006). Midlife risk factors and healthy survival in men. *Journal of the American Medical Association, 296,* 2343–2350.

Williams, D. R. (2005). The health of U.S. racial and ethnic populations. *Journals of Gerontology, 60B, Special Issue II,* 53–62.

Windsor, T. D., Anstey, K. J., Butterworth, P., Luszcz, M. A., & Andrews, G. A. (2007). The role of perceived control in explaining depressive symptoms associated with driving cessation in a longitudinal study. *The Gerontologist, 47,* 215–223.

Wolf, S. L., Barnhart, H. X., Kutner, N. G., McNely, E., Coogler, C., Xu, T., et al. (2003). Reducing frailty and falls in older persons: An investigation of Tai Chi and computerized balance training. *Journal of the American Geriatrics Society, 51,* 1794–1803.

Women's Health Initiative Investigators (WHI). (2002). Risks and benefits of estrogen plus progestin in healthy postmenopausal women. *Journal of the American Medical Association, 288,* 321–333.

Women's Health Initiative Investigators (WHI). (2003). Effects of estrogen plus progestin on gynecologic cancers and associated diagnostic procedures: The Women's Health Initiative randomized trials. *Journal of the American Medical Association, 290,* 1739–1748.

Woo, J. S., Derleth, C., Stratton, J. R., & Levy, W. C. (2006). The influence of age, gender, and training on exercise efficiency. *Journal of the American College of Cardiology, 47,* 1049–1057.

World Health Organization (WHO). (2002). *Active aging: A policy framework.* Spain: Paper presented at the Second United Nations World Assembly on Aging.

Yamazaki, S., Ichimura, S., Iwamoto, J., Takeda, T., & Toyama, Y. (2004). Effect of walking exercise on bone metabolism in postmenopausal women with osteopenia/osteoporosis. *Journal of Bone and Mineral Metabolism, 22,* 500–508.

Zablotsky, D. & Kennedy, M. (2003). Risk factors and HIV transmission to midlife and older women: Knowledge, options and the initiation of safer sexual practices. *Journal of Acquired Immune Deficiency Syndrome, 33,* Supplement #2, S122–S130.

three

The Psychological Context of Social Aging

In part one we examined the dynamic interactions between people as they age and their environments, the population trends that make gerontology a growing field for practice, research, and policy, and patterns of aging in other countries. Part Two focused on the normal biological and physiological changes that take place with aging and our growing understanding of how biological aging may be altered. The most common chronic health problems associated with aging and how they may influence social functioning were presented. The older population's use of physician, hospital, and dentist services and prescription medications was reviewed. Part Two concluded with a discussion of the growing field of health promotion and how changes in health behaviors can help people experience active aging.

In this section, the focus is on psychological changes with aging—both normal and abnormal—that influence older people's social behavior and dynamic relationships with their physical and social environments. As we have already seen, many changes take place in the aging organism that may make it more difficult to perform activities of daily living and to respond as readily to external demands as in youth. Many older people have multiple chronic health problems that compound the normal changes that cause them to slow down. In a similar manner, some changes in cognitive functioning, personality, and sexuality are a function of normal aging. Other psychological changes may be due to the secondary effects of diseases.

Researchers have examined changes in intelligence, learning, and memory with aging. The literature in this area, reviewed in Chapter 5, suggests that normal aging does not result in significant declines, nor in all areas of intelligence, learning, and memory. Although older participants in the studies described do not perform as well as younger people, their scores are not so low as to indicate significant impairments in social functioning. Research on ways to improve memory in the later years is discussed, as well as how computers and the Internet affect cognitive functioning. The chapter concludes with a discussion of wisdom and creativity in old age, and how these abilities change with aging.

Chapter 6 describes personality development in the later years, the expression and regulation of basic and complex emotions, and the importance of maintaining self-esteem. The concept of successful aging and it how it differs from active aging is discussed. It is a concept that has drawn considerable research attention and debate, particularly because it may not be salient for low-income elders from historically underserved groups. Successful aging requires both high levels of physical and functional health and remaining active in cognitive and social functions, a lifestyle that may not be an option for those with limited financial and health care resources.

Certain forms of psychological disorders, such as schizophrenia, are more common in young adults than in old age. However, as will be described in Chapter 6, some older people are at high risk for anxiety disorders, depression, paranoia, and dementia. In the case of dementia, memory and problem-solving abilities decline quite dramatically—sometimes within a few years, other times over many years. Older individuals with a diagnosis of dementia experience significant impairments in their ability to interact with others and to control their physical and social environments. To the extent that older people do not seek mental health services for treatable disorders such as depression, their social interactions will deteriorate as well. Some may become reclusive and, in the case of severely depressed older white men, at greater risk of suicide. Despite the growing number of studies that document the benefits of therapeutic interventions for older adults, they use mental health services less than do younger persons. This is particularly true among elders of color. Most of the mental health care given to older adults takes place in hospitals, not in community mental health centers or in private practice. Furthermore, most therapy is provided by family doctors who generally do not have expertise in geriatric medicine or psychiatry.

An important aspect of personality is sexuality: the individual's ability to express intimate feelings through a wide range of loving and pleasurable experiences. Chapter 7 addresses the influence of social attitudes and beliefs, normal physiological changes, and diseases on older adults' sexuality. Contrary to popular belief, age-associated physiological changes do not necessarily reduce sexual pleasure and capacity. More often, both heterosexual and gay older people withdraw from sexual activity because of societal expectations, stereotypes and lack of available partners. As people become better informed about aging and sexuality, as sexual taboos are reduced, and as lesbian, gay, bisexual, and transgender (LGBT) elders are more integrated into society, aging baby boomers will more easily express their sexuality and need for intimacy.

As with physical aging, the material in Part Three suggests that aging does not affect all people's psychological functions in the same way. Normal cognitive changes, such as mild forgetfulness, generally do not impair older people's social functions. A relatively small segment of the older population experiences Alzheimer's disease or other types of dementia, but the incidence increases with age. Personality and patterns of coping also do not change so dramatically as to impair social functioning. Coping and adaptation skills do not become impaired with normal aging, although styles of coping vary widely. Similar to physical aging, increasing differences in psychological functioning among people are observed as they age. Some elders experience active aging despite chronic diseases and deterioration in cognitive function, while others adapt poorly to these normal and secondary changes of aging.

The next three chapters describe how the aging process influences cognitive abilities, personality styles, mental health, intimacy, and sexuality, as well as responses to major life events. They emphasize the wide variations in these processes as we age.

5

Cognitive Changes
with Aging

This chapter discusses

- Research on cognitive functions with normal aging
- Measurement of intelligence in older adults
- Individual and environmental factors that influence intelligence
- How we learn, and how aging affects the learning process
- The importance of learning and memory for everyday life
- Attention and its centrality for learning
- Individual and environmental factors that affect how older people learn
- Tip-of-the-tongue states as an example of difficulty in retrieval
- Cognitive retraining and other ways to help older adults improve their learning and memory skills
- What is required to achieve wisdom and creativity in old age

One of the most important and most studied aspects of aging is cognitive functioning; that is, intelligence, learning, and memory. These are critical to an individual's performance in every aspect of life, including work and leisure activities, social relationships, and productive roles. Older people who have problems in cognitive functioning will eventually experience stress in these other areas as well, along with an increasing incongruence between their competence levels and the demands of the environment. Researchers have attempted to determine whether normal aging is associated with a decline in the three areas of cognitive functioning and, if so, to what extent such a decline is due to age-related physiological changes. Much of the research on these issues has evolved from studies of cognitive development across the life course. Other studies have been undertaken in response to concerns expressed by older persons or their families that they cannot learn as easily as they used to or that they have more trouble remembering names, dates, and places than previously.

Intelligence and Aging

Intelligence is difficult to both define and to measure. Of all the elements of cognition, it is the least verifiable. We can only infer its existence and can only indirectly measure individual levels. **Intelligence** is generally defined as the "theoretical limit of an individual's performance" (Jones, 1959, p. 700). While the limit is determined by biological and genetic factors, the ability to achieve this limit is influenced by environmental opportunities such as challenging learning experiences as well as by environmental constraints (e.g., the absence of books or other intellectual stimulation). Intelligence encompasses a range of capabilities, including the ability to deal with symbols and abstractions, acquire and comprehend new information, adapt to new situations, and understand and create new ideas. Alfred Binet, who developed the first test of intelligence, emphasized the operational aspects of intelligence: "to judge well, to comprehend well, to reason well, these are the essentials of intel-ligence" (Binet & Simon, 1905, p. 106). In general, both experts and laypersons agree that intelligence consists of three major sets of abilities: problem-solving, verbal, and social competence (Cavanaugh & Blanchard-Fields, 2006). **Intelligence quotient (IQ)** refers to an individual's relative abilities in some of these areas compared to other people of the same chronological age.

A multidimensional structure of intelligence is assumed by most contemporary tests. Such tests measure a subset of intellectual skills known as **primary mental abilities (PMAs),** which include:

- number or mathematical reasoning
- word fluency, or the ability to use appropriate words to describe the world
- verbal meaning or vocabulary level
- inductive reasoning, or the ability to generalize from specific facts to concepts
- spatial relations, or the capacity to orient oneself in a three-dimensional space
- verbal memory, or the ability to retain and recall words, sentences, and passages from readings
- perceptual speed

A useful distinction is made between **fluid intelligence** and **crystallized intelligence** (Cattell, 1963; Horn, 1970, 1982; Horn & Donaldson, 1980). These two types of intelligence include some of the primary mental abilities described above. Fluid intelligence consists of skills that are biologically determined, independent of experience or learning, and may be similar to what is popularly called "native intelligence." It involves processing information that is not embedded in a context of existing information for the individual and thus requires flexibility in thinking. Crystallized intelligence refers to the knowledge and abilities that the individual acquires through education and lifelong experiences. It includes social judgment and the ability to understand subtle meanings in verbal communication. These two types of intelligence show different patterns with aging, as discussed in the next section.

MEASURES OF FLUID INTELLIGENCE

- spatial orientation
- abstract reasoning
- word fluency
- inductive reasoning

MEASURES OF CRYSTALLIZED INTELLIGENCE

- verbal meaning
- word association
- social judgment
- number skills

There has been considerable controversy regarding intelligence in the later years. Many researchers have identified significant differences between young and old persons on intelligence tests in cross-sectional studies, with older persons performing at a much lower level. Even when the same cohort is followed longitudinally, there is a decline in some intelligence tests that is independent of generational differences (Schaie, 1996a, 1996b). Others conclude that aging is not really associated with decrements in intelligence. However, standardized IQ tests and the time limits on test-takers may be more detrimental to older persons than to the young.

Many older persons are concerned that their intelligence has declined. This concern may loom so large for them that merely taking part in a study intended to "test their intelligence" may provoke sufficient anxiety to affect their performance. Such anxieties may also influence daily functioning. Older people who are told by friends, family, test-givers, or society in general that they should not expect to perform as well on intellectual tasks because aging causes a decline in intelligence may, in fact, perform more poorly.

The most widely used measure of adult intelligence is the Wechsler Adult Intelligence Scale (WAIS). It consists of 11 subtests, 6 of which are Verbal Scales (which measure, to some extent, crystallized intelligence) and 5 are Performance Scales (providing some indication of fluid intelligence). The performance tests on the WAIS are generally timed; the verbal tests are not.

Verbal scores are obtained by measuring an individual's ability to:

- define the meaning of words
- interpret proverbs
- explain similarities between words and concepts

In this way, accumulated knowledge and abstract reasoning can be tested.

Performance tests focus on an individual's ability to manipulate unfamiliar objects and words, often in unusual ways:

- tests of spatial relations
- abstract reasoning
- putting puzzles together to match a picture
- matching pictures with symbols or numbers
- arranging pictures in a particular pattern

Both psychomotor and perceptual skills are needed in performing these tasks. A consistent pattern of scores on these two components of the WAIS is labeled the **Classic Aging Pattern.** People age 65 and older in some studies, and even earlier in others, perform significantly worse on Performance Scales (i.e., fluid intelligence), but their scores on Verbal Scales (i.e., crystallized intelligence) remain stable. This tendency to do worse on performance tasks may reflect age-related changes in noncognitive functions, such as sensory and perceptual abilities, and in psychomotor skills. These changes, in turn, may make the older person more susceptible to interference during the learning or performance process (Hasher et al., 2002). As seen in Chapters 3 and 4, aging results in a slowing of the neural pathways and of the visual and auditory functions. This slower reaction time, and the delay in receiving and transmitting messages through the sense organs, explains poorer performance on subtests requiring such capabilities. Some researchers therefore argue for the elimination of time constraints in performance tasks. Studies that have not measured speed of performance have still found significant age differences in these subtests, however (Salthouse, 1996). Performance-related aspects of intellectual function appear to decline independent of psychomotor or sensory factors. Speed of cognitive processing, such as the time to perform simple math problems, also declines with age and, in turn, slows an individual's responses on tests of performance.

Turning to verbal skills, the Classic Aging Pattern suggests that the ability to recall stored

SUMMARY OF AGE-RELATED CHANGES IN INTELLIGENCE

- Peak performance varies by test, usually between the late 30s and early 40s.
- Performance on timed tests declines more than on non-timed tests.
- Performance on non-timed tests remains stable until the 80s.
- People rarely decline in all five PMAs.
- High scorers continue to do well even among the oldest-old.
- Declines in tests of fluid intelligence begin earlier than in crystallized intelligence ("classic aging pattern").

verbal information and to use abstract reasoning tends to remain constant throughout life. Declines, where they exist, typically do not show up until advanced old age, or, in the case of cognitive impairment such as the dementias, they tend to begin early in the course of the disease.

Problems in the Measurement of Cognitive Function

A major shortcoming of many studies of intelligence in aging is their use of cross-sectional research designs rather than longitudinal approaches. Age differences that are obtained in cross-sectional studies may reflect cohort or generational differences rather than actual age changes. In particular, modifications in educational systems, increasing levels of education, and the widespread access to the Internet and digital media have profoundly influenced the experiences of today's youth when compared with those of people who grew up in the early to mid-twentieth century. These cohort and historical factors may then have a greater effect on intelligence scores than age per se (Schaie, 2005).

Subject attrition, or dropout from longitudinal studies of intelligence, is another problem. There is a pattern of *selective attrition,* whereby the people who drop out tend to be those who have performed less well, who perceive their performance to be poor, or whose health status and functional abilities are worse than average. The people who remain in the study (i.e., "the survivors") performed better in the initial tests than did dropouts. This is consistent with our earlier observation that older persons often become unduly anxious about poor performance on tests of intellectual function. Hence, the results become biased in favor of the superior performers, indicating stability or improvement over time. They do not represent the wider population of older adults, whose performance might have shown a decline in intelligence (Schaie, 1996a, 2005).

Longitudinal Studies of Intelligence

Several major classic longitudinal studies have examined changes in intellectual function from youth to old age. Perhaps the best known and longest-lasting of these is the Seattle Longitudinal Study (SLS), which began in 1956 and has collected data on Thurstone's primary mental abilities every 7 years for more than 50 years (Schaie, 1996a, 1996b, 2005). At each follow-up assessment, individuals who are still available from the original sample are retested, along with a new, randomly selected sample

Intellectual stimulation can help sustain higher-level cognitive skills.

from the same population. This study has provided the basis for the development of sequential research models, described in Chapter 1. Peak performance varies across tests and between men and women, ranging from age 32 on the test of numbers for men and age 39 on the test of reasoning for women. Age decrements that become progressively worse in later years are observed after age 60 on tests of word fluency, numbers, and spatial orientation. Tests of spatial orientation and inductive reasoning—both indicators of fluid intelligence—show greater decline with age. Men experience earlier declines in spatial abilities than in other tests, whereas women slow down earlier on tests of word fluency than in other areas. However, other primary mental abilities, such as verbal meaning and numerical skills, show only minimal declines until the mid-70s. These results are supported by other, shorter longitudinal studies that have found little change over three years (Christensen et al., 1999; Zelinski, Gilewski, and Schaie, 1993).

The findings suggest that the Classic Aging Pattern holds up in both cross-sectional and longitudinal studies, and that some performance aspects of intelligence may begin to deteriorate after age 60, although substantial changes are generally rare until the 80s (Schaie, 2005, 2006).

In all these studies, most of the significant declines occur in intellectual abilities that are less practiced and require speed. Schaie (1996a, 1996b, 2005) concludes that the changes observed in the SLS indicate a normative developmental transition from stability in general intelligence in the middle years to a gradual decline that begins around age 60. Most people in the SLS maintained their abilities in one or more areas well into their advanced years, as shown in Figure 5.1. Only about 33 percent of participants showed decrements between ages 60 and 67. About 40 percent declined between ages 67 and 74, and even between ages 74 and 81 only 50 percent experienced significant diminishment. Notably, Schaie and his colleagues found no linear decline in all

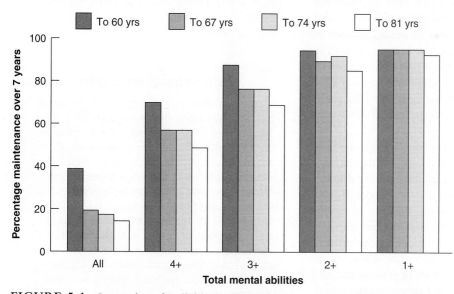

FIGURE 5.1 **Proportion of Individuals Who Maintain Scores on Multiple Abilities**

SOURCE: K. W. Schaie, The hazards of cognitive aging, *The Gerontologist* 29 (1989): 484–493. Copyright 1989 by Oxford University Press–Journals. Reproduced with permission of Oxford University Press–Journals in the format textbook and other book via Copyright Clearance Center.

five primary mental abilities for any participants as old as age 88. Declines during the middle years (ages 46–60) on delayed recall and word fluency tests and on tests of psychomotor speed may predict cognitive impairment in old age (Schaie, 1996a, 1996b, 2005, 2006).

Factors That May Influence Intelligence in Adulthood

Researchers who have compared intelligence test scores of older and younger persons have found wide variations in the scores of both groups. Older test-takers generally obtain poorer scores, but age per se is only one factor in explaining differences.

There is also a biological factor in intelligence, such that some people are innately more intelligent than others. However, it is difficult to determine the relative influence of biological factors, because it is impossible to measure the specific mechanisms of the brain that account for intelligence. Structural changes in the brain and in neural pathways occur with aging, as seen in Chapter 3. These changes, however, are generally diffused and not focused in a particular region of the brain. It is therefore impossible to determine what specific changes in the brain and its pathways may account for the age-related deterioration that is observed.

Other variables that have been examined are educational attainment, involvement in complex versus mechanistic work, cardiovascular disease, hypertension, and sensory deficits. Some studies have found cohort differences on tests of intelligence, with newer cohorts of older people performing better than previous cohorts who took the same test at about the same age. These variations emerge primarily on tests of crystallized and less on fluid intelligence and psychomotor speed, even when comparing adult children their parents (Schaie et al., 1992; Schaie & Willis, 1995; Willis & Schaie, 2006). Newer cohorts' advantage has been attributed to higher educational

attainment. Therefore, it is important to control statistically for educational differences when analyzing the relationship between age and intelligence. Significant positive effects of education were found on all tests of cognitive function when comparing healthy adults age 70 to 79 with different educational levels. In particular, participants with the highest level of education (12+ years) did three times better on a test of abstract thinking than did people with 7 or fewer years of education (Inouye et al., 1993).

Occupational level, which is generally associated with education, also influences intelligence test scores. Older people who still use their cognitive abilities in jobs or activities that require thinking and problem-solving show less decline on cognitive tests than those who do not use these skills. This is because most of the observed decrements in intellectual abilities occur in highly challenging, complex tasks. In addition, people whose occupations demand more verbal skills (e.g., lawyers and teachers) may continue to perform very well on these aspects of intelligence tests. Those who use more abstract and

INTELLECTUALLY ACTIVE ELDERS

Increasingly, more older adults continue to participate in intellectually challenging jobs well beyond their 60s and 70s. For example, college campuses are full of retired faculty who retain emeritus status and who continue to teach or conduct research well into their 80s. One of the Poet Laureates of the United States was Stanley Kunitz, appointed at age 95. He continued to write poetry in his 90s and died at age 100. Another active nanogenarian is Dr. Hilary Koprowski, whose research in 1948 led to the widespread adoption of a live vaccine to immunize children against polio. Koprowski, now age 93, continues to conduct medical research at Thomas Jefferson University in Philadelphia and is a linguist and an active music composer. Likewise, James Wiggins continued to edit a weekly newspaper in Ellsworth, Maine well into his 90s.

fluid skills in their occupations (e.g., architects and engineers) are more likely to do well on the performance tests of the WAIS well into their 70s and 80s. In general, older people who do not participate in any intellectual pursuits perform worse on intelligence tests than do their peers who are "cognitively engaged." The nature of intellectual activities is also important; those who participate in complex work and leisure activities with more opportunities for self-direction show consistently higher scores, even among the oldest-old (Mackinnon et al., 2003; Schooler & Mulatu, 2001; Schooler, Mulatu, Oates, 2004).

The effects of declining physical health and sensory losses on intelligence become more severe in the later years and may displace any positive influence due to education and occupation for people who are 75 years and older. Several studies have identified poorer performance on intelligence tests by older people with conditions such as diabetes, hypertension, and cardiovascular disease, particularly in tests that demand psychomotor speed (Elias et al., 2004; Hassing et al., 2004; Knopman et al., 2000; Rosnick et al., 2004). In the Seattle Longitudinal Study, participants with cardiovascular disease declined at younger ages on all tests of mental abilities than did those with no disease (Schaie, 1996a, 2006). Participants in the Baltimore Longitudinal Study were tested on working memory, nonverbal memory, and naming tests. Cognitive decline was greatest in people with higher systolic blood pressure, but even more among less educated volunteers (i.e., 12 years of education or less). Research examining how day-to-day changes in blood pressure affect cognitive functioning showed that older adults with high blood pressure perform worse on tests of verbal learning and numerical skills when their blood pressure exceeds their personal average. Use of antihypertensive medications to control high blood pressure attenuates this decline (Gamaldo, Weatherbee, & Allaire, 2008; Murray et al., 2002; Waldstein, Giggey, Thayer, & Zonderman, 2005).

Nutritional deficits may also impair an older person's cognitive functioning. One study of community-dwelling, healthy older persons (ages 66–90) examined their performance on multiple tests of cognitive functioning and nutritional status longitudinally. Older people with low intake of vitamins E, A, B_6, and B_{12} at baseline performed worse on visiospatial and abstraction tasks six years later; those who used vitamin supplements did better (Larue et al., 1997). These findings reinforce the results of research on the impact of nutritional deficiencies on physical performance, described in Chapter 4.

As noted in Chapter 3, hearing loss is common in older persons, especially in the lower frequency range, so that it affects their ability to comprehend speech. Visual deficits become more severe in advanced old age. Poorer performance by some test-takers who are very old may be due primarily to these sensory losses, not to a central cognitive decline. Older persons with hearing or vision loss do especially poorly on tests of verbal meaning and spatial relations (Lindenberger & Baltes, 1994).

An apparent and rapid decline in cognitive function within five years of death is another physical health factor that appears to be related to intelligence test scores. This phenomenon is known as the *terminal drop*, or **terminal decline hypothesis**, first tested by Kleemeier (1962). In longitudinal studies of intelligence, older subjects who decline more sharply are found to die sooner than good performers. This has been observed on many different tests, especially in verbal meaning, spatial and reasoning ability, and psychomotor speed (Bosworth et al., 1999). This suggests that the time elapsed since birth (i.e., age) is not as significant in intellectual decline as is proximity to death.

Finally, anxiety may negatively affect older people's intelligence test scores. As noted earlier, older test-takers are more likely than the young to express high test anxiety and cautiousness in responding. These same reactions may occur in older people taking intelligence tests, especially if they think that the test really measures how

HEALTH CONDITIONS THAT AFFECT PERFORMANCE

- cardiovascular disease
- hypertension
- nutritional deficits
- depression
- hearing loss
- terminal drop

"intelligent" they are. Anxieties about cognitive decline and concerns about dementia may make older people even more cautious, and hence result in poorer performance on intelligence tests.

The Process of Learning and Memory

Learning and *memory* are two cognitive processes that must be considered together. That is, learning is assumed to occur when an individual is able to *retrieve* information accurately from his or her memory store. Conversely, if an individual cannot retrieve information from memory, it is presumed that learning has not adequately taken place. Thus, *learning* is the process by which new information (verbal or nonverbal) or skills are *encoded,* or put into one's memory. The specific parts of the brain involved in this process are the hippocampus, which first receives and processes new stimuli, and the cerebral cortex, where memories are stored. Some of the most exciting research in this field is focused on the process of neuronal development as learning occurs. *Memory* is the process of retrieving or recalling the information that was once *stored*; it also refers to a part of the brain that retains what has been learned throughout a person's lifetime. Researchers distinguish three separate types of memory: sensory, primary or short-term, and secondary or long-term.

Sensory memory, as its name implies, is the first step in receiving information through the sense organs and passing it on to primary or secondary memory. It is stored for only a few tenths of a second, although there is some evidence that it lasts longer in older persons because of the slower reaction times of the senses. Sensory memory is further subdivided into **iconic** (or visual) and **echoic** (or auditory) **memory.** Examples of iconic memory are:

- words or letters that we see
- faces of people with whom we have contact
- landscapes that we experience through our eyes

Of course, words can be received through echoic memory as well, such as when we hear others say a specific word or when we repeat words aloud to ourselves. A landscape can also enter our sensory memory through our ears (e.g., the sound of the ocean), our skin (the feel of a cold spray from the ocean), and our nose (the smell of salt water). To the extent that we focus on or rehearse information that we receive from our sense organs, it is more likely to be passed into our primary and secondary memories.

Despite significant changes in the visual system with aging (as described in Chapter 3), studies of iconic memory find only small age differences in the ability to identify stimuli presented briefly. Such modest declines in iconic memory would not be expected to influence observed decrements in secondary, or long-term, memory. Although research on iconic memory is limited, there has been even less with echoic memory and less still that has compared older persons with younger. We have all experienced the long-term storage of memories gained through touch, taste, or smell. For example, the aroma of freshly baked bread often evokes memories of early childhood. However, these sensory memories are more difficult to test. As a result, very little is known about changes with other modes of sensory memory.

Working, or **primary memory** is a temporary stage of holding, processing, and organizing information and does not necessarily refer to a storage area in the brain. Despite its temporary nature, working memory is critical for our ability to process new information. We all experience situations where we hear or read a bit of information such as a phone number or someone's name, use that name or number immediately, then forget it. In fact, most adults can recall seven, plus or minus two pieces, of information (e.g., digits, letters, or words) for 60 seconds or less. It is not surprising, therefore, that local phone numbers in most countries are seven digits or fewer, although the addition of area codes for local dialing makes it more difficult to retain this information in our permanent memory store (**secondary, or long-term, memory**). In order to retrieve information later, it must first be rehearsed or "processed" actively. This is why primary memory is described as a form of "working memory" that decides what information should be attended to or ignored—which is most important—and how best to store it. If we are distracted while trying to retain the information for the 60 seconds that it is stored in short-term memory, we immediately forget it, even if it consists of only two or three bits of information. This happens because the rehearsal of such material is interrupted by the reception of newer information in our sensory memory. Most studies of primary memory have found minimal age differences in its storage capacity, but the encoding process which occurs in primary memory declines. This requires some organization or elaboration of the information received. Older persons are less likely than young people to process new information in this manner. Indeed, some argue that aging leads to a decline in "attentional resources," or mental energy, to organize and elaborate newly acquired information in order to retain it in secondary memory (Bopp & Verhagen, 2005; Zacks, Hasher, & Li, 2000). In fact, many of the age-related changes observed in different components of attention may explain these problems with working memory.

RETRIEVING OLD MEMORIES

A person may have learned many years ago how to ride a bicycle. If this skill has been encoded well through practice, the person can retrieve it many years later from his or her memory store, even if he or she has not ridden a bicycle in years. This applies to many other skills learned early in life, from remembering childhood prayers to diapering a baby.

Another explanation for this slowing process is that **perceptual speed**—the time required to recognize a stimulus and respond to it—deteriorates with aging. According to this theory, older people have more problems holding information in their working memory while receiving new stimuli through sensory memory ("simultaneity"). This is compounded by the possibility that it takes longer for older people to ignore irrelevant stimuli and complete working memory tasks (Salthouse, 1996). For example, if an older driver is trying to locate a street address that was just given but is also listening to news on the radio, the driver is less likely to remember the street address than would a younger driver in the same situation.

True learning implies that the material we acquire through our sensory and primary memories has been stored in "secondary memory." For example, looking up a telephone number and immediately dialing it does not guarantee that the number will be learned. In fact, only with considerable rehearsal can information from primary memory be passed into secondary memory. Secondary memory is the part of the memory store in which everything we have learned throughout our lives is kept; unlike primary memory, it has an unlimited capacity. The different components of secondary memory are described in Table 5.1 (page 188). Researchers have demonstrated significant declines in some components, but very little or no change in others.

TABLE 5.1   Types of Secondary Memory

It is important to recognize that secondary memory is not unilateral but has several components. The types of memory listed here (and many others) appear to be influenced differently by the aging process.

MEMORY TYPE	DESCRIPTION
Episodic memory	Consciously recalling specific events or episodes
Explicit memory	Consciously attempting to keep a stimulus in one's mind, in a specific order (e.g., a poem, a mental "to do" list)
Flashbulb memory	Remembering specific events that have personal relevance, and the emotions triggered by the events (e.g., remembering where one was and how one reacted to the September 11, 2001, terrorist attacks on the World Trade Center)
Implicit memory	Unintentionally remembering stimuli that were acquired without paying attention (e.g., words or music to an old song that one did not even realize one knew)
Procedural memory	Often nonverbal, this type of memory relies on motor functions, such as riding a bike or playing a piece on the piano without reading the music.
Semantic memory	The storehouse of words and facts that have accumulated over one's lifetime
Source memory	Remembering where one saw or heard a new piece of information (e.g., source of an article read on healthy aging)
Prospective memory	The task of remembering to do something in the future (e.g., remembering to keep a medical appointment)

Older adults consistently recall less information than younger people in paired-associates tests with retention intervals as brief as one hour or as long as eight months. Age differences in secondary memory appear to be more pronounced than in sensory or primary memory and are often frustrating to older people and their families. Indeed, middle-aged and older people are frequently concerned that they cannot remember and retrieve information from secondary memory. The perception of oneself as having a poor memory can seriously harm older adults' self-concept and performance on many tasks, and may even result in depression. Such concern, growing out of a fear of dementia, is generally out of proportion to the actual level of decline (Pearman & Storandt, 2004; Verhaeghen, Geraerts, & Marcoen, 2000). Older individuals can benefit significantly from methods to help organize their learning, such as imagery and the use of mnemonics. Examples of such techniques to improve learning and memory are discussed later in this chapter.

The Information-Processing Model

The **information-processing model** of memory is presented in Figure 5.2. As a conceptual model, it provides a framework for understanding how the processes of learning and memory take place. It is not necessarily what goes on in the neural pathways between the sense organs and the secondary memory store. Having described each of the components in this model, we next review the steps involved in processing some information that we want to retain. One example is the experience of learning new names at a social gathering. Sensory memory aids in hearing the name spoken, preferably several times by other people, and seeing the face that is associated with that name. Primary memory is used to store the information temporarily so that a person can speak to others and address them by name (an excellent method of rehearsing this information), or manipulate the information in order to pass it on to secondary memory. This may include repeating the name

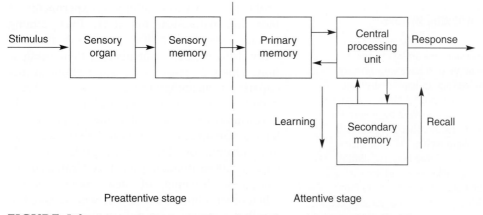

Stimulus → Sensory organ → Sensory memory → Primary memory → Central processing unit → Response

Learning

Secondary memory

Recall

Preattentive stage | Attentive stage

FIGURE 5.2 **Schematic Representation of the Information-Processing Model**

several times, trying to isolate some aspect of the person's physical features and relate it to the name, and associating the name with other people one has known in the past who have similar names. In the last type of mental manipulation, information from secondary memory (i.e., names of other people) is linked with the new information. This is a useful method because the material in secondary memory is permanent, and associating the new information with well-learned information aids in its storage and subsequent recall.

During any stage of this cognitive processing, the newly obtained information can be lost. This may occur if the sensory memory is flooded with similar information; in this case, if a person is being introduced to multiple new names and faces at a party, it is almost impossible to distinguish the names or to associate each name with a face. Information may also be lost during the primary memory stage. In our example, if a person is trying to use a newly heard name and is distracted by other names and faces or receives unrelated information (e.g., a telephone call) while rehearsing the new name, the name has not been sufficiently processed in working memory to pass into secondary memory.

The learning process may also be disrupted because of the inability to retrieve information efficiently from secondary memory. For example, a person may associate the newly heard name with someone known in the past; if he or she has difficulty retrieving the stored name from secondary memory, however, this may be so frustrating as to redirect the individual's attention from the new name to the old name. How often have you ignored everything around you to concentrate on remembering a name that is "on the tip of the tongue" (i.e., in secondary memory) but not easily retrievable? As noted above, aging appears to reduce the efficiency of *processing* information in sensory and primary memory (i.e. encoding), and has less effect on retrieval from secondary memory. It does *not* influence the storage capacity of primary or secondary memories. That is, contrary to popular opinion, these memory stores are not physical spaces that become overloaded with information as we age. Table 5.1 lists some key types of secondary memories. Although researchers have linked some types of memory to specific regions of the brain (e.g., episodic memory occurs in the medial temporal lobe, while procedural memory takes place in the striatum), this does not mean that they take up physical space in these areas. Episodic memory has been shown to decline the most with aging, especially after age 60. Nevertheless, more educated older adults and those given more practice opportunities during the learning process show less deterioration. These advantages have been demonstrated for

AIDS TO WORKING MEMORY

The popularity of phones with digital memory for storing multiple phone numbers attests to the problem that people of all ages have with primary memory. Rather than looking up important phone numbers or attempting to memorize them, we can store these in the phone and retrieve them with the push of one or two buttons. Another technological development that can help reduce the information we must store in our minds is the personal digital assistant (PDA). These handheld devices are useful for storing phone numbers, addresses, and memos and even helping with orientation to physical space via a global positioning system (GPS). As older adults become more comfortable with these new technologies, they may experience less stress about retaining newly acquired information.

both episodic and semantic memory (Hoyer & Verhaeghen, 2006; Rönnlund et al., 2005). Not surprisingly, semantic memory shows the least decline with aging because it is stimulated by words and concepts learned throughout one's lifetime. Procedural memory is also retained into advanced old age; even people who have not ridden a bike in 50 years can get on and start pedaling, albeit, perhaps, somewhat wobbly at first. Some age-related decline occurs in procedural memory where the elder is asked to remember a future event or time, but the effect is less dramatic than for episodic memory. Some researchers have demonstrated that source memory is not independent, but a component of episodic memory (Hoyer & Verhaeghen, 2006; Johnson, 2005; Siedlecki, Salthouse, & Berish, 2005).

The Importance of Learning and Memory in Everyday Life

As noted above, one of older adults' most common complaints is their difficulty when attempting to learn and remember new names. Researchers find that older learners have more problems than young adults in experiments of face and name learning tests. Even among younger people, recalling a person's name is more difficult than remembering their occupation. This is because information about an occupation is meaningful (e.g., we can visualize a person "doing" or "performing" a job or relate it to our own work), but names often do not have a semantic association to help process the new information (Fraas et al., 2002; Reese & Cherry, 2004; Rendell, Castel, & Craik, 2005). The best learning of new names occurs when older adults are told they will be asked to recall the names later. Information about the name to be recalled (e.g., facial features, a link between face and name) can help older learners, whether they are given this information or they generate the descriptors themselves (Troyer et al., 2006).

Executive Function in Older Adults

An important component of learning is **executive function,** which is the ability to organize one's learning. It includes planning, decision-making, avoiding interference or distraction from other stimuli while using one's working memory and learning new content, and the ability to shift attention from one task to another and to modify cognitive and spatial sets as new information is received. Normal aging is associated with mild declines in executive function, but older adults with dementia—as well as younger and older adults with depression or obsessive compulsive disorders—experience significant impairment in this ability to organize their learning (Brooks, Weaver, & Scialfa, 2006; Gunstad et al., 2006; Watkins et al., 2005). Elders who exhibit decrements in executive function over time also show signs of decline in instrumental activities of daily living (IADL), described in Chapter 4 as the functional ability to perform daily self-care activities (Royall et al., 2004). Problems with executive function and working memory may predict difficulties an elder will have with medication adherence. Scores on executive function and working memory explained more variance in elders' ability to take their drugs as prescribed than did their age, level of education, or illness severity. Executive function was even better than total memory scores in predicting medication adherence (Insel et al., 2006).

Can executive function be improved? Recent studies suggest that this may be possible with intensive cognitive intervention. An innovative study examined elders in Experience Corps, a high-intensity volunteer program that assigns older adults to work with schoolchildren. Elders who were trained to help primary schoolchildren with reading, behavior management, and in parent outreach were compared with their counterparts who did not receive any training. After 4 to 8 weeks of involvement in this program, elders who were trained scored higher on tests of executive function and memory compared to their baseline scores and compared with control group elders. Improvements by 44 to 51 percent were particularly dramatic for older adults with impaired executive function at baseline. In contrast, elders in the control group with impaired executive function showed a decline from baseline levels to follow-up. The researchers attribute these gains in executive function among volunteers to the complex environment of schools, with their cognitive challenges and diverse stimuli that Executive Corps volunteers must master (Carlson et al., 2008).

Factors That Affect Learning in Old Age

The Importance of Attention

Attention is a critical component of cognition, especially in the learning process. Researchers address three components of attention as central to people's ability to perform many different functions, including learning new skills and facts. These include selection, vigilance (or sustained attention), and attentional control under conditions of divided attention (Parasuraman, 1998).

Selective attention requires both conscious and unconscious skills; the learner must be able to select information relevant to a task while ignoring irrelevant information. Researchers who have tested age differences in selective attention have used visual search tasks, in which subjects must search for a target item in an array of items shown under different conditions. Older people do somewhat worse than young research subjects in such studies, but only under more complex conditions. **Vigilance,** or **sustained attention,** requires the individual to look out for a specific stimulus over time. This is the type of attention that air traffic controllers must use when watching for blips (each one representing an airplane) on a radar screen. In complex tasks in which each signal requires some decision (e.g., directing a plane to change its flight course upon seeing the blip), older people do worse than young adults. However, few differences between young and old are found when the task is simple or does not place significant demands on memory, or when participants have had practice with that type of vigilance or are told to ignore irrelevant information. Age effects emerge when an event to be attended to shows up in an unpredictable pattern (Einstein, Earles, & Collins, 2002; Rogers & Fisk, 2001). **Attentional control** is the individual's ability to determine how much attention should be directed at specific stimuli and when to shift focus to other stimuli. This is particularly important under conditions of **divided attention.** In such cases, the individual attempts to perform multiple tasks at the same time, such as listening to the radio or conversing on a cell phone when driving, or speaking on the phone in the kitchen while cooking a multicourse dinner. Experiments with divided attention tasks have used stimuli in the same sensory mode (e.g., listening to two channels of music or words simultaneously) or different sensory systems (e.g., listening to spoken words while reading a different set of words). As with the other two components of attention, age differences are not as dramatic as once thought. If the older person has had practice with managing multiple tasks (e.g., an experienced cook who can prepare multiple dishes simultaneously), it is just as easy for old and young subjects to shift their attention. To the extent that a task becomes practiced or "automatic," even if these skills were developed many years ago, an older person can perform them without any more attentional control than a young person. However, the more complex the activities demanded by each task, the more it affects an older person's ability to perform the tasks simultaneously. Furthermore, if the individual is anxious while taking tests that require divided attention, older adults do worse than do younger test-takers (Hogan, 2003; Whiting, 2003).

Practical Implications of Attention Changes with Aging

A better understanding of what causes age-related changes in attention and the nature of such changes can improve the person–environment (P–E) interface and competence for older people and their responses for maintaining active aging. For example, by examining each step of the task of driving under different conditions, researchers can focus on specific elements of selective attention, vigilance, and attentional control. Drivers must attend to important cues such as changes in traffic signals, traffic flow, and the speed of other cars. Vigilance plays an important role in long-distance driving, especially on monotonous stretches of interstate highways. By breaking down each component of driving and determining which conditions help or hinder older drivers, designers of traffic systems can place warning signs or traffic lights in the most complex locations in order to prevent accidents. Concurrently, classes aimed at older drivers can take advantage of this knowledge to improve students' selective attention and vigilance skills under diverse driving conditions. As described in Chapter 4, older adults are disproportionately involved in motor vehicle accidents.

A better understanding of age-related attention changes can reduce their high accident rates.

Environmental and Personal Factors

One problem with assessing learning ability is that it is not possible to measure the process that occurs in the brain while an individual is acquiring new information. Instead, we must rely on an individual's performance on tests that presumably measure what was learned. This may be particularly disadvantageous to older persons, whose performance on a test of learning may be poor because of inadequate or inappropriate conditions for expressing what was learned (Hess, Rosenberg, & Waters, 2001). For example, an older person may in fact have learned many new concepts in reading a passage from a novel, but not necessarily the specific concepts that are called for on a test of learning. Certain physical conditions may affect performance and thus lead to underestimates of what the older person has actually learned. These include:

- an unfamiliar learning environment
- poor lighting levels and small font size
- tone and volume of the test-giver's voice in an oral exam
- time constraints placed on the test-taker

The learning environment can be improved, however. Some ways to do this include:

- glare-free and direct lighting
- lettering of good quality
- larger fonts
- color contrast
- a comfortable test-taking situation with minimal background noise
- a relaxed and articulate test-giver

As noted above, time constraints are particularly detrimental to older people. Although the ability to encode new information quickly is a sign of learning ability, it is difficult to measure. Instead, response time is generally measured. As we have already seen, psychomotor and sensory slowing with

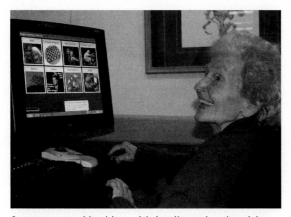

Computers provide elders with intellectual and social opportunities.

age has a significant impact on elders' response speed. Declines in perceptual speed, which can be measured separately from memory skills per se, may be a major reason why older people do worse on memory tests. Researchers have shown that perceptual speed accounts for a significant part of the observed age-related variance in memory performance. Even when older research subjects are given more time to complete tests of memory, their perceptual speed still plays a significant role in their performance (Ratcliff, Spieler, & McKoon, 2000; Salthouse, 1996).

The **general slowing hypothesis** proposed by Salthouse (1996) suggests that processing of information slows down in the nervous system with aging. This results in more problems with responding to complex tasks, with older subjects doing worse on tests involving more decisions than do younger people. This hypothesis also implies that older people perform worse under multitasking conditions (e.g., working on a computer while speaking on the phone and listening to the radio) than do younger people. Research on paired-associates tasks has demonstrated that older persons make more *errors of omission* than *errors of commission*. That is, older persons are more likely not to give an answer than to guess and risk being wrong. This phenomenon was first recognized in middle-aged and older adults in tests of psychomotor functioning. The older

the respondent, the more likely that the person has to work for accuracy at the expense of speed. This occurs even when the older learner is encouraged to guess and is told that it is acceptable to give wrong answers (i.e., commission errors). Conditions of uncertainty and high risk are particularly difficult for older persons, where they are far more cautious than the young. Low-risk situations elicit less caution from older adults and greater willingness to give responses in a learning task. The aging process may create an increased need to review multiple aspects of a problem, probably because of past experiences with similar dilemmas. Errors of omission may be reduced somewhat by giving rewards for both right and wrong answers, thereby forcing an answer.

Verbal ability and educational level are important factors in learning verbal information. Studies that entail learning prose passages show age deficits among those with average vocabulary abilities and minimal or no college education. In contrast, older persons with high verbal ability and a college education perform as well as younger subjects in such experiments. This may be due to greater practice and facility with such tasks on the part of more educated persons and those with good vocabulary skills. It may also reflect differences in the ability to organize new information, a skill that is honed through years of education and one that assists in the learning of large quantities of new material.

Stability in performing familiar perceptual-motor tasks may also occur because the accomplished performer of a specific task makes more efficient moves than does a less-skilled person. Such differences are evident in many areas demanding skill, from typing and driving to playing a musical instrument or operating a lathe. Therefore, older workers can overcome the effects of slower psychomotor speed and declines in learning skills by their greater experience in most occupations. As described above with respect to divided attention, older people who are experienced in performing specific tasks show no age decrements in these activities.

The conditions under which learning takes place affect the old more than the young, just as test conditions are more critical. Older persons respond differently to varied testing situations; people tested under challenging conditions ("this is a test of your intelligence") are likely to do worse than those in supportive conditions ("the researcher needs your help"). Positive feedback appears to be a valuable tool for eliciting responses from older adults in both learning and test situations. Fatigue may also play a role. Older adults perform better on tests of working memory in the morning when they are more alert. They perform worse than young adults on these same tasks in the evening (West et al., 2002).

Pacing the rate of information flow makes it suitable to learners of any age and gives them opportunities to practice the new information (e.g., writing down or spelling aloud newly learned words). Self-pacing is most beneficial for older learners, followed by a moderate pace set by the test-giver. Older adults do much worse than younger adults when information is presented in a fast-paced manner. Another condition that supports learning is the presentation of familiar and relevant material compared to information perceived by the older learner to be unimportant. Older people do worse in recalling recently acquired information than do younger people when the new material is unfamiliar or confusing. Age differences also emerge when the material to be learned has low meaning and personal significance to the learner. Laboratory studies of cognitive functioning often seem artificial and meaningless to older adults who are unaccustomed to such research methods, and even more so to those with little academic experience. Many people will complain that such tests are trivial, nonsense, or that the tasks have no connection to the "real world."

Spatial memory—that is, the ability to recall where objects are in relationship to each other in space (e.g., using a map or finding one's way back to where the car is parked)—also appears to decline with aging. It is unclear, however, if older people do worse than the young because they have difficulty encoding and processing the information or if the problem is in retrieval. It appears that there is an age-related decline in encoding ability for spatial information. Older people have more difficulty than younger persons in reading maps that are misaligned relative to the user. For example, when older people stand in front of a "You are here" map that is aligned 180 degrees away from their orientation, they take up to 50 percent more time and make 30 percent more errors than younger persons in the same condition. However, when the map is aligned directly with the user, no age differences are observed. This may be attributable to increased problems with mental rotation of external images and with perspective-taking as we age. Older adults also perform less well than younger people when they are shown a set of items in a certain arrangement, then the items are removed, and they are asked to reconstruct the objects in the same arrangement (Aubrey, Li, & Dobbs, 1994; Das & Agarwai, 2000).

Age-Related Changes in Memory

As we have seen, learning involves encoding information and storing it into secondary or long-term memory so that it can be retrieved and used later. Studies of this process have focused on two

---

EXAMPLES OF RETRIEVAL

Recall

Free recall "List the capitals of each state." "Describe how to repair a bicycle tire."

Cued recall "The capital of New York begins with the letter 'A'; what is it?"

Recognition

"Which of these three cities is the capital of New York?"

"All but one of the following is a type of memory. Select the one that is not."

types of retrieval: recall and recognition. **Recall** is the process of searching through the vast store of information in secondary memory, perhaps with a cue or a specific, orienting question. **Recognition** requires less search. The information in secondary memory must be matched with the stimulus information in the environment. Recall is demanded in essay exams, recognition in multiple-choice tests.

Not surprisingly, most researchers identify age-related deficiencies in recall but few differences in recognition. This may be due to the context in which multiple stimuli are presented, triggering cues for the test-taker. Recall tasks have been further divided into *free recall* and *cued recall* situations. In the former, no aids or hints are provided for retrieving information from secondary memory. In the latter case, the individual is given some information to aid in the search (e.g., category labels and the first letter of a word). Older people tend to do less well than the young in tests of free recall but are aided significantly by cueing. In particular, use of category labels (semantic cues) at the learning stage is found to be more helpful to older persons than the use of structural cues—for example, giving the respondent the first letter of a word to be recalled. However, cued recall tests are not as helpful as recognition tests for older learners.

The question of whether older people have better recall of events that occurred in the distant past than recent situations is unclear. Many events are firmly embedded in secondary memory because they are unique or so important that subsequent experiences do not interfere with the ability to recall them. The birth of a child, one's wedding ceremony, or the death of a parent, partner, or sibling are events that most people can recall in detail 40 or more years later. This may be because the situation had great personal significance or—in the case of world events, such as the bombing of Hiroshima or the terrorist attacks of 9/11/01—had a profound impact on world history. Some distant events may be better recalled because they have greater personal relevance for the individual's social development than recent experiences, or because they have been rehearsed or thought about more. Another

possibility is that cues that helped the older person recall events in the past are less effective with recalling recent occasions because of "cue-overload." That is, the same cues that were once helpful in remembering certain information are also used to recall many recent events, but the cues are so strongly associated with one's earlier life experiences that the newer information becomes more difficult to retrieve. For example, older people may have difficulty memorizing new phone numbers because the cues that helped them recall phone numbers in the past may be so closely associated with previous ones that they confuse recent phone numbers with old ones.

One problem in determining whether recall of distant situations is really better than recall of recent events is the difficulty in validating an older person's memories. In many cases, there are no sources that can be checked to determine the accuracy of such recollections. We can all identify with the process of asking an old friend or family member "Do you remember the time when...?" If others have no recollection of the event, it may make us wonder if the situation really took place, or it may mean that the event was so obscure that it made no impact on other people. Hence, such memories are difficult to measure accurately.

Several theories are offered to explain *why* older people may have problems with retrieving information from secondary memory. One explanation is that not using the information results in its loss (the **disuse theory**). This theory suggests that information can fade away or decay unless it is exercised, as in the adage "use it or lose it." However, this explanation fails to account for the many facts that are deeply embedded in a person's memory store and that can be retrieved even after years of disuse.

A more widely accepted explanation is that new information interferes with the material that has been stored over many years. As we have noted earlier, interference is a problem in the learning or encoding stage. When the older person is distracted while trying to learn new information, this information does not become stored in memory. Poor retrieval may be due to a combination of such distraction during the learning stage and interference by similar or new information with the material being searched in the retrieval stage. Although researchers in this area have not conclusively agreed on any of these explanations, the **interference theory** appears to hold more promise than others for explaining observed problems with retrieval.

Tip-of-the-Tongue States

Tip-of-the-tongue states (TOTs) represent a specific type of difficulty in retrieval. We all experience situations when we know the name of a place or person but cannot immediately recall it. This might be the name of a favorite restaurant or park or a famous actor, character in a story, or an acquaintance we have not seen in many years. Features of TOTs are that the target word is familiar and will be recalled by searching through one's memory, drawing associations from similar names, or mentally focusing on an image of the place or person. TOTs are also distinguished by a feeling of *imminence*—the sense that one can "almost" remember it or that it is on the "tip of one's tongue" (Schwartz, 2002).

Although all people experience TOTs, both anecdotal evidence and cross-sectional studies show that TOTs increase with age. Two different theories have been offered to explain this. The *decrement model* suggests that memory networks deteriorate with aging and TOTs are a manifestation of these impaired networks (Brown & Nix, 1996). The second model focuses on *incremental knowledge gain* with aging, whereby the cumulative knowledge and vocabulary of older adults can cause more names in secondary memory to interfere with the name to be recalled (Dahlgren, 1998). When we experience a TOT, most of us can rely on:

1. spontaneous retrieval of the name (i.e., letting it pop into our primary memory later, when we are removed from the immediate pressure to remember the words),

2. using specific search strategies such as cues (e.g., listing similar names or going through the alphabet), or

3. using other sources to aid recall, such as asking another person or looking in a dictionary or thesaurus.

Older people seem to utilize spontaneous recall more often and search strategies of any type less often than young adults. These differences may be explained by the decrement model and incremental knowledge model. The former would posit that aging causes deterioration in one's efficient use of cues; the latter attributes it to a larger bank of names in one's memory that makes it difficult to search for a specific word (Schwartz, 2002).

The Positivity Effect in Information-Processing

Recent studies have pointed to a **"positivity effect"** in older adults' attention skills and their learning and memory processes. Comparisons between older and younger adults show that the former recall twice as much information with positive emotional content than negative or neutral information. In contrast, younger adults recall positive and negative information equally well. Using functional magnetic resonance imaging (fMRI), researchers have observed this process by noting areas activated in the brain when attending to various stimuli. The amygdala is active when older adults respond to positive stimuli but not when faced with negative stimuli. Younger persons' amygdala is activated under both conditions. The same pattern appears when testing attention speed: older adults respond faster to positive images than to negative, whereas younger adults attend at the same speed to negative and positive images. These findings demonstrate a "positivity bias" with aging, such that older adults tend to regulate their emotional experience by focusing on positive information. The aging process may slow some learning and memory skills, but the type of information to be attended to, learned, and retained in memory affects the level of decline (Carstensen, 2007). However, one downside to this process is that older adults are less likely to detect deception and lying by others because their positivity bias results in an expectation that most people are honest. This may be a factor in how often older adults are victims of scams and financial exploitation (Blanchard-Fields & Kalinauskas, 2009; Stanley & Blanchard-Fields, 2008).

Improving Cognitive Abilities in Old Age

Cognitive Retraining

In the Seattle Longitudinal Study (SLS) described earlier in this chapter, the researchers tested the effects of **cognitive retraining**—teaching research participants how to use various techniques to keep their minds active and maintain good memory skills. This approach to retraining is based on the premise of maximizing one's remaining potential, a widely accepted concept in physical aging but only recently applied to cognitive aging. In the SLS, cognitive retraining resulted in a reversal of declines that had been observed over the preceding 14 years in 40 percent of research participants. Many elders maintained these gains over the next testing period, and up to five years in some retraining experiments (Willis, 2001; Willis et al, 2006). However, cognitive training in some areas may be more effective than others. Elders in the SLS trained in reasoning ability demonstrated more long-term gains than those trained in spatial orientation, especially 14 years later (Boron, Willis, & Schaie, 2007). Teaching older adults strategies for remembering lists of words, themes, and details in stories by using practice and performance feedback can significantly improve their memory. In one large-scale study, a 10-session memory-training intervention resulted in 26 percent of elders improving their memory immediately after the intervention, and the effects continued for 2 years (Ball et al.,

2002). This same study assessed the impact of memory retraining on IADLs up to 5 years later. Elders who received inductive reasoning training showed the greatest improvement in IADLs such as reading road signs, following directions on a medication bottle, and looking up telephone numbers. Booster sessions at 11 and 35 months improved skills even more. Training in memorization and speed of processing was less beneficial (Willis et al., 2006).

Most cognitive retraining programs focus on specific areas of cognition—including memory, speed of processing, and reasoning—because these functions all show some declines with aging. In the ACTIVE trial (Advanced Cognitive Training for Independent and Vital Elderly), older adults were randomly assigned to complete cognitive training in three areas simultaneously: memory, inductive reasoning and speed of processing, or to a control group with no interventions. More than 90 percent of the elders who completed memory training improved on at least one test of memory, regardless of the specific strategies they chose to help them remember. Those with a college degree or higher performed best, followed by elders who had completed high school. Young-old and old-old learners improved much more than the oldest-old (Langbaum et al., 2009). In another study that compared learners age 70–79 with those 80–90 on tests of perceptual-motor speed, reasoning and visual attention, the former group generally performed better, but both age groups retained 50 percent of what they had learned in the original retraining program eight months earlier (Yang & Krampe, 2009). Besides age and educational level, the effectiveness of cognitive retraining programs depends on the mental status and physical health of participating elders (Nyberg, 2005).

There has been considerable experimentation with chemical interventions to improve memory. Researchers have tested products that enhance the chemical messengers in neurons or improve the function of neural receptors. A natural extract derived from leaves of the *ginkgo*

LIFELONG LEARNING

Continuing education is an excellent way to maintain intellectual skills in old age. Elderhostel is a popular international program that offers older adults learning options located on college campuses and through tours to educational and historic sites. "Summer College for Seniors" is a program offered by Shoreline Community College in Seattle. Each summer, more than 100 elders participate in week-long college classes on topics as wide-ranging as constitutional law and classical music. College faculty who teach these older students enjoy the perspectives they bring and praise their maturity, both intellectually and emotionally. As one 65-year-old Summer College student noted, "The people here may be gray on top, but they're not dull between the ears." Another participant, age 75, added, "I think, as a senior, mental stimulation is as important as physical exercise."

SOURCE: *Seattle Times,* July 25, 2000, p. B1 (F. Vinluan, staff reporter).

---

biloba or maidenhair tree has received attention because it seems to improve memory by improving circulation in the brain. Systematic research on the effects of ginkgo biloba for mild memory loss, as well as for people with Alzheimer's disease, has not shown significant benefits, however (van Dongen et al., 2003). Vitamin E is an antioxidant (described in Chapter 3) that may help enhance memory by reducing oxidative damage resulting from normal aging. No long-term human studies are yet available to support these claims for the benefits of vitamin E or other possible supplements such as lecithin, vitamin B_{12}, and folic acid. It is also important to recognize that therapeutic doses of these and other supplements (i.e., levels that are high enough to show improved memory function) can cause harmful side effects such as internal bleeding, and megadoses may even increase mortality (Bjelakovic, et al., 2007).

Other research has examined the benefits of practical memory-enhancing methods, such as cognitive aids. Although useful at any age, cognitive aids may be particularly helpful for an older person who is experiencing increased problems with real-world cognitive abilities, such as recalling names, words, phone numbers, and daily chores. However, elders are more likely to use external aids such as notes and lists than cognitive aids. That is, they are more likely to reduce environmental press to enhance their competence in learning as a means of improving P–E congruence. One way of improving personal competence may be to enhance cardiovascular fitness. An intervention to increase physical activity among sedentary elders found that improving physical performance, gait, speed, and balance resulted in higher scores on a test of working memory and psychomotor speed. This finding suggests that, by steadily increasing the physical activity levels of sedentary elders, their cognitive skills can also be improved (Williamson et al., 2009). One explanation for the positive effects of cardiovascular fitness on learning and memory may be that exercise improves blood flow to the brain. Another factor may be that synaptic connections in the frontal lobes increase with cardiovascular activity (Colcombe & Kramer, 2003; Kramer, Erickson, & Colcombe, 2006).

DIET AND COGNITIVE CHANGE

The results of a large cohort study of almost 4,000 community-dwelling elders found that vegetable consumption may reduce the rate of cognitive decline with aging. Older adults who averaged 2.8 servings per day of vegetables (especially leafy greens, broccoli, squash, and collards) had a 40 percent slower decline over 6 years on tests of immediate and delayed recall, perceptual speed, attention, and short-term memory than did elders who consumed an average of 0.9 servings per day. High levels of fruit intake or use of vitamin supplements did not affect cognitive scores over time. The benefits of higher vegetable intake were greater for the old-old in this study. These results support the findings of a national study of women (the Nurses Study), which showed that high intake of vegetables, but not fruit, slowed cognitive decline (Kang, Ascherio, and Grodstein, 2005; Morris et al., 2006).

Older adults who are most concerned about declining memory use external and cognitive aids as a way of coping with the problem. This is particularly true for elders with a strong internal locus of control—that is, a belief that they have control over their well-being rather than attributing their problems to external forces (Verhaeghen et al., 2000). Similarly, older adults who believe they have good memory actually do better on tests of memory than their peers who lack confidence in their memory skills (Zelinski & Gilewski, 2004). Recognizing that low self-efficacy can affect older people's learning ability, researchers have used cognitive restructuring techniques to convince older learners to change their views of aging and memory. By focusing on their strengths and believing that they could control how much they retain of newly acquired information, elders in one study improved their scores on memory tests more than their counterparts who did not receive self-efficacy training (Caprio-Prevette & Fry, 1996).

Memory Mediators

Most memory improvement techniques are based on the concept of **mediators,** that is, the use of visual and verbal links between information to be encoded and information that is already in secondary memory. Mediators may be visual (e.g., the method of locations) or verbal (e.g. the use of mnemonics). **Visual mediators**—in particular, the method of locations (or loci)—are useful for learning a list of new words, names, or concepts. Each word is associated with a specific location in a familiar environment. For example, the individual is instructed to "walk through" his or her own home mentally. As the person walks through the rooms in succession, each item on the list is associated with a particular space along the way. Older persons using this technique are found to recall more words on a list than when they use no mediators. One advantage of the method of loci is that learners can visualize the new information within a familiar

setting and can decide for themselves what new concept should be linked with what specific part of the environment. Imaging is a useful technique in everyday recall situations as well. For example, an older person can remember what he or she needs to buy at the grocery store by visualizing using these items in preparing dinner. Another example of visual mediators is the use of visual images to recall names (e.g. recalling the name "John Doe" by visualizing him as making dough). This type of exercise to strengthen memory in one task can help improve performance on other memory tasks (Colcombe & Kramer, 2003).

Another way of organizing material to be learned and to ensure its storage in secondary memory is to use **mnemonics,** or verbal riddles, rhymes, and codes associated with the new information. Many teachers use such rhymes to teach their students multiplication, spelling (e.g., "*i* before *e* except after *c*"), and the calendar ("30 days hath September, April, June, and November..."). Many other mnemonics are acquired through experience as well as our own efforts to devise ways to learn a new concept (e.g., making up a word to remember the three components of cognition—intelligence, learning, memory—might become "IntLeMe"). These can assist older people to learn more efficiently, especially if the mnemonics are specific to the memory task at hand. Older people with mild or moderate dementia can also benefit from visual methods of recall but less from list-making. Whatever method is used, however, it is important to train the older adult in the use of a specific mnemonic and to provide easy strategies to help the person apply these techniques to everyday learning events. In one study, researchers provided half the sample with a "memory handbook" and 30 minutes of practical instruction; the other half were given just a pamphlet that provided examples of useful mnemonics (but no face-to-face instruction in their use). The former group demonstrated significant improvements in two subsequent memory tests; the pamphlet group did not

(Andrewes, Kinsella, Murphy, 1996). Other mediators to aid memory include:

1. using the new word or concept in a sentence,
2. associating the digits in a phone number with symbols or putting them into a mathematical formula (e.g., "the first digit is 4, the second and third are multiplied to produce the first"),
3. placing the information into categories,
4. using multiple sensory memories, and
5. combining sensory with motor function.

In this last technique, one can write the word (iconic memory), repeat it aloud to oneself (echoic memory), or "feel" the letters or digits by outlining them with one's hand. Unfortunately, many older persons do not practice the use of newly learned memory mediators. They may not be motivated to use the techniques, which often

---

LOOK, SNAP, AND CONNECT

A practical method for retaining information efficiently in order to recall it later is the "Look, Snap and Connect" technique, recommended by Small (2002), who suggests that we can improve our memory at every age by using an encoding and retrieval system that is personally meaningful. The components of this method are:

Look: Actively focus on what you want to learn in order to take in the information, and record the information received through multiple senses.

Snap: Create a mental snapshot or image of the object or person or word(s) to be remembered; the more bizarre or unusual the image, the better it will be recalled (e.g., remembering Mr. Brown's name by visualizing him covered with brown paint).

Connect: Visualize a link to associate the images created through mental snapshots, thereby retaining the information through its link with existing memories (e.g., remembering a grocery list by connecting items together, such as *flour* poured over *apples* that are swimming in a bowl of *milk*).

SOURCE: From G. Small, *The memory bible,* New York: Hyperion, 2002.

---

seem awkward, or they may forget and need to be reminded. Perhaps the major problem is that these are unfamiliar approaches to the current cohort of older adults. As future cohorts become more practiced in these memory techniques through their educational experiences, the use of such strategies in old age may increase.

The most important aspect of memory enhancement may be the ability to relax and to avoid feeling anxious or stressed during the learning stage. As noted earlier, many older people become overly concerned about occasional memory lapses, viewing them as a sign of deterioration and possible onset of dementia. Thus, a young person may be annoyed when a familiar name is forgotten, but will probably not interpret the memory lapse as loss of cognitive function as an older person is likely to do. Unfortunately, society reinforces this belief. How often are we told that we are "getting old" when we forget a trivial matter? How often do adult children become concerned that their parent sometimes forgets to turn off the stove, when in fact they may frequently do so themselves? Chronic stress can also impair older people's memory performance. Research with animals and humans has shown that some hormones released under high-stress conditions (e.g., cortisol and corticosterone) cause the subject to make more errors in memory tests (McGaugh, 2000).

In addition to mediators, **external aids** or devices are often used by older people to keep track of the time or dates, or to remember to turn the stove on or off. Simple methods such as list-making can significantly improve an older person's recall and recognition memory, even if the list is not used subsequently. A list that is organized by topic or type of item (e.g., a chronological "to-do" list or a grocery list that groups produce, meats, and dry goods) is also found to aid older people's memory significantly. Older adults with higher educational attainment and better vocabulary skills—which will be true of baby boomers compared to the current cohort of elders—benefit even more from list-making methods (Burack & Lackman, 1996). Older people can develop the habit of associating

A MEMORY EXERCISE

Use the method of loci to help you remember *seven* items that you need to buy at the grocery store. Go to the store without a list, but imagine yourself walking through the kitchen at home after your trip to the grocery store, placing each of the seven items in a specific location.

medication regimens with specific activities of daily living, such as using marked pill boxes and taking the first pill in the morning before their daily shower or just before or after breakfast, taking the second pill with lunch or before their noontime walk, and so on. These behaviors need to be associated with activities that occur every day at a particular time so that the pill-taking becomes linked with that routine. Charts listing an individual's daily or weekly routine can be posted throughout the house. Alarm clocks and kitchen timers also can be placed near an older person while the oven or stove is in operation. This will help in remembering that the appliance is on without the person's needing to stay in the kitchen. With the increased availability of home computers, daily activities and prescription reminders can be programmed into an older person's computer. Finally, for older people who have serious memory problems and a tendency to get lost while walking outdoors, a bracelet or necklace imprinted with the person's name, address, phone number, and relevant medical information can be a lifesaver.

Cognitive and Neural Plasticity

Although most reviews of change in cognitive abilities focus on declines with aging, there is growing evidence that gains also occur. The theory of **Selection, Optimization, and Compensation (SOC)** focuses on adapting and regulating individual resources, including cognitive abilities. The individual may *select* specific cognitive domains in which to adapt. However, because of age-related loss in some domains, older adults are more restricted in their selections. *Optimization* involves maximizing one's abilities in these selected areas, whereas *compensation* occurs when losses in some areas require the enhancement of skills in other areas, or acquiring new behaviors or knowledge to make up for lost abilities. **Cognitive plasticity** refers to the ability to accomplish these three mechanisms of SOC and to recognize where one must compensate for these deficits in cognitive abilities. For example, an older woman who acknowledges that she no longer has the executive function to organize a large family holiday party as she has done for many years utilizes her cognitive plasticity by inviting everyone from her invitation list to a dinner at a local restaurant. Older adults who cope best appear to have the most cognitive plasticity, perhaps indicating an ability to read their environment and adapt to its changing demands. Prior learning experiences can help this process, while stimulating environments and activities are useful for enhancing cognitive plasticity. The social context is also important in assisting or hindering this ability. Memory retraining studies appear to enhance cognitive plasticity in older adults, even among the very old, with long-term success in using newly acquired skills to achieve SOC (Kramer et al, 2004; Willis, Schaie, & Martin, 2009; Yang & Kraspe, 2009).

Part of the process of cognitive plasticity is **neural plasticity,** or changes in brain structure and function that occur as a result of the addition of new neurons and synaptic connections between neurons, activating specific regions of the brain. For example, the brains of professional musicians have more gray matter in the areas of the brain responsible for finger movements, while athletes' brains have more neuronal density in areas where eye–hand coordination is controlled. A growing body of research with computer and Internet users suggests that regular use of the Internet activates more brain regions, especially where decision making and complex reasoning occur. People who are tech-savvy may develop a stronger working memory (i.e., they can store and retrieve more information for immediate

PLAYING BRIDGE TO KEEP THE MIND ACTIVE

The 90+ Study, conducted by researchers at USC and UC-Davis, has examined longitudinally more than 1,000 people age 90 and older. Their behavioral, cognitive, and blood tests show that the oldest-old who spend several hours each day engrossed in mentally challenging activities such as puzzles and games are more likely to maintain their cognitive abilities than their less engaged peers. However, social connectedness is an important component. Those who play contact bridge and other activities in a group are most successful in retaining high levels of cognitive functioning well into their 90s.

SOURCE: Corey, *The New York Times*, May 2009.

processing). Research with middle-aged and older Internet users shows promise for aging computer users who learned to use the Internet earlier in their lives. Young adults today who grew up with e-mail, text messaging, and video games may show even greater neural plasticity as they age (Small, Moody, Siddarth, & Bookheimer, 2009; Small & Vorgan, 2008). Although neural plasticity continues throughout life, it is less efficient in old age, and the link between these changes and cognitive plasticity is unclear.

Benefits of Computers and the Internet for Older Adults

The use of computers and the Internet can improve older persons' cognitive functions and ability to maintain active aging. It can encourage learning and give them information about their health and their social and health care providers in the community, thereby enhancing autonomy and self-efficacy. As part of a "brain fitness" movement, a variety of electronic brain games are targeted to middle-aged and older adults, including those on Nintendo such as Wii (Cohen, 2009). Several cognitive and demographic variables affect older adults' performance on the computer. Crystallized intelligence, visual memory, and perceptual speed, as well as age and educational level, are important predictors of older

adults' ability to complete computer-related tasks and train for jobs using the computer (Czaja et al., 2001; Ownby, Czaja, Loewenstein, & Ruipert, 2008). Use of the computer and the Internet may also facilitate social interactions and communication. Although access to computers and the Internet enhances elders' sense of mastery and control over their environment, it does not necessarily improve their quality of life (Czaja & Lee, 2001; 2003; Slegers, van Boxtel, & Jolles, 2008).

However, given the significant growth in the number of older adults learning to use the computer and the Internet, it behooves Web designers to consider older users' special needs (Mead, Lamson, Rogers, 2002; Morrell, Mayhorn, Bennett, 2000). In addition to the changes in attention processes, Web and software designers must recognize that many older people experience problems with language comprehension, fine motor movement, and reading small print. Some suggestions for Web designers are presented in the following box.

IMPROVING WEB PAGES FOR OLDER USERS

- Avoid a patterned background behind text material.
- Use dark type or graphics against a light background.
- Avoid excess graphics and animation.
- Avoid pop-up menus that can confuse the main text.
- Use a consistent layout in different sections of the website.
- Limit how much information is presented on each page.
- Distinctly identify all links with a specific convention, such as underlining or a unique graphic.
- Clearly identify the content that is included under each heading.
- If animation or video is used, select short segments to reduce download time.
- Provide a telephone number and e-mail address for users who want direct contact.

SOURCES: Adapted from Mead, Lamson, and Rogers, 2002, and National Library of Medicine, 2002.

Wisdom and Creativity

Wisdom and creativity are difficult to define and measure, even though most people have an image of what it means to be wise or creative. *Wisdom* seems to require the cognitive development and self-knowledge that come with age (Cohen, 2005; Levitt, 1999). Wisdom is a combination of experience, introspection, reflection, intuition, and empathy; these are qualities that are honed over many years and that can be integrated through people's interactions with their environments. Thus, younger people may have any one of these skills individually, but their integration requires more maturity. Based on research with older adults who had been nominated as "wise" by other people, the following five criteria can be used to assess if the indivi-dual demonstrates wise behavior (Baltes & Kunzmann, 2003; Baltes & Staudinger, 2000; Staudinger, 1999):

- *Factual knowledge*—possessing both general and specific information about life conditions and relevant issues
- *Procedural knowledge*—using decision-making strategies, planning, and interpretation of life experiences to a given situation
- *Life-span contextualism*—considering the context in which events are occurring and the relationship among them
- *Value relativism*—considering and respecting values and priorities brought to the situation by other participants
- *Managing uncertainty*—developing backup plans or alternative strategies if one's performance is hampered by external factors.

Wisdom is achieved by transcending the limitations of basic needs such as health, income, and housing but is not limited to those with social and economic resources. Regardless of class or educational level, an individual who has continued opportunities for growth and creativity can develop wisdom (Ardelt, 1997). Wisdom implies that the individual does not act impulsively, has good

insights, and can reflect on all aspects of a given situation objectively. This makes the wise older person better at conflict resolution. In many cultures, as noted in Chapter 2, older persons are respected for their years of experience and ability to mediate conflicts, and the role of "wise elder" is a desired status. One perspective on wisdom is that it requires such lifelong experiences, insights, and emotional maturity in order to impart to younger generations skills, family and cultural values, and community traditions (Cohen, 2000, 2005). This approach combines the focus on emotional maturity and regulation of feelings that is typical of Eastern concepts of wisdom with the emphasis on cognitive maturity that is characteristic of Western perspectives, as shown by the five criteria in the previous column (Takahashi & Overton, 2002). The *balance theory* of wisdom suggests that a wise individual is one who can balance different components of intelligence—practical, analytical, and creative—and use them to solve problems that will benefit society, rather than focusing on using one's intelligence for personal gain. Developmental intelligence manifests as wisdom, with emotional and social intelligence, cognition, life experience, and spirituality becoming better integrated with age and favoring positive emotions (Cohen, 2009; Sternberg & Lubart, 2001).

Younger generations can benefit from the wisdom of elder scholars.

Not all older people achieve wisdom, however. Wisdom suggests the ability to interpret knowledge or to understand the world in a deeper and more profound manner. Such reflectiveness and the reduced self-centeredness that this requires allow older people to take charge of their lives and become more accepting of their own and others' weaknesses. Indeed, among older men and women in the Berkeley Guidance Study, those who scored high on the three components of wisdom (cognitive, reflective, affective thinking) also ranked high on a measure of life satisfaction (Ardelt, 1997). This suggests that active aging (described in Chapters 1 and 6) is enhanced when wisdom has been attained. Older people who have achieved this level of wisdom can play productive roles in many settings, where their years of experience and ability to move beyond the constraints presumed by others could help such organizations. (Such functions are discussed in more detail in Chapter 12.)

Creativity refers to the ability to bring something new into existence that is valued, such as applying unique and feasible solutions to new situations and coming up with original ideas or material products; this occurs because of changes in the aging brain, not despite them. We generally think of creativity in terms of extraordinary products that have been created (e.g., public creativity by composers or artists). However, people who come up with unique but smaller-scale products (e.g., personal creativity, such as an attractive garden, beautiful quilts or a delicious meal) are also displaying their creativity (Cohen, 2000, 2005, 2009). A person may be creative in science, the arts, or technology. Although we can point to well-known creative people in each of these areas (e.g., Albert Einstein in science, Wolfgang Amadeus Mozart and Georgia O'Keeffe in the arts, and Thomas Edison in technology), it is difficult to determine the specific characteristics that make such persons creative. As with intelligence in general, creativity is inferred from the individual's output but cannot really be quantified or predicted. One measure of creativity is a test of *divergent thinking*, which is part of Guilford's

(1967) structural model of intelligence. This is measured by asking a person to devise multiple solutions to an unfamiliar mental task (e.g., naming some different uses for a flower). Later still, Torrance (1988) developed a test of creativity that also measures divergent thinking. Children who scored high on this test were found to be creative achievers as young adults (i.e., the test has good predictive and construct validity), but the test has not been used to predict changes in creativity across the life course.

Divergent thinking may be only one component of creativity, however. A creative person must also know a great deal about a particular body of knowledge, such as music or art, before he or she can make creative contributions to it. However, this neglects the contributions to scientific problem solving or the arts by people who may have expertise in one area and bring a fresh perspective to a different field. To date, there have been no systematic studies of divergent thinking among people who are generally considered to be creative. Much of the research on creativity has been performed as analyses of the *products* of artists and writers, not on their creative *process* directly. Indeed, no studies have compared the cognitive functioning of artists, scientists, technologists, and others who are widely regarded as creative with that of persons not similarly endowed. Researchers who have examined the *quantity* of creative output by artists, poets, and scientists have identified that the average rate of output at age 70 to 80 drops to approximately half that of age 30 to 40. However, a secondary peak of productivity often occurs in the 60s, although not as high as the first peak. The second peak of creativity may produce even better works. Indeed, Simonton's analysis of the last works of 172 classical composers in their final years revealed compositions that were judged highly by musicologists in terms of aesthetics, melody, and comprehensibility (Simonton, 1989, 1991, 1999).

Some have suggested that creativity actually increases with age because the individual becomes more self-confident, experienced, and free from social constraints—what Cohen refers to as

CREATIVITY IN LATE LIFE

In his insightful book, *The Creative Age,* Dr. Gene Cohen examines how creativity and creative expression can expand with aging. He provides numerous examples of scientists, artists, writers, and composers who produced their most innovative works in their later years. These include:

- Sir Isaac Newton (1642–1727), the father of calculus, revised his influential book describing the three laws of motion at age 71 and again at age 84.
- The German mathematician Carl Friedrich Gauss (1777–1855) made many discoveries well into old age. He updated his fundamental theory of algebra at age 71.
- The Renaissance painter Titian painted several masterpieces between age 78 and 83, and began experimenting with an impressionistic style in his later years.
- Hanya Holm (1893–1992) choreographed popular Broadway plays in her young-old stage, including *My Fair Lady* when she was 63 and *Camelot* at age 67.
- Three early leaders of the women's rights movement started the six-volume *History of Women's Suffrage* in 1875. Elizabeth Cady Stanton was 72, Susan B. Anthony was 67, and Matilda Gage was 61 when the book was published.

the "liberation phase" of psychological growth (2009). This results in the ability to make novel decisions to solve problems. Indeed, older adults with high physical and cognitive functioning are found to use both hemispheres of the brain more equally than do younger adults (operating in "all-wheel drive"), and have a greater density of synapses accruing from a lifetime of learning and experiences. As a result of this increased capacity of the brain, combined with a feeling of being liberated from the commitments and expectations of younger years, older adults can explore and express their creativity in multiple ways. These have been categorized as continuing creativity with aging, changing creativity with age, commencing creativity, and creativity in

connection with loss. In fact, Cohen (2009) argues that the term "senior moment" should be used to refer to creative moments that increase with age, not to forgetfulness that adults of all ages experience (Cabeza et al., 2002; Cohen, 2000, 2005, 2009).

Opportunities for creative expression can have other significant benefits, as illustrated by a study of the impact of a structured and sustained arts program on elders' physical and emotional well-being. Older adults were randomly assigned to a 35-week arts education and activity program or to a control condition. When these elders were assessed again one year later, those in the arts and activity program had made fewer physician visits, used fewer medications, scored lower on a measure of depression, and experienced higher morale than did elders in the control group (Cohen, 2005). This suggests the value of encouraging elders' creativity in a wide range of forms.

Implications for the Future

Advances in neuroscience will eventually uncover the specific changes in the brain that account for age-related changes in memory, attention, and learning ability. New techniques of brain research are evolving with the use of functional magnetic resonance imaging (fMRI) and positron emission tomography (PET) that can determine which areas of the brain are responsible for different types of attention, learning, and memory. These noninvasive techniques adopted from the medical diagnostic field are already being used to study differences in attention tasks between young and old subjects, and between older persons with different types of dementia. As described in this chapter, fMRI can even be used to ascertain which parts of the brain are activated when an individual is told to attend to specific stimuli and under different learning conditions. PET scans can reveal differences in brain activity among people with varying educational levels and in the early stages of Alzheimer's disease (Carstensen, 2007; Greenwood & Parasuraman, 1999; Parasuraman &

Greenwood, 1998; Silverman, Small, Chang, & 2001; Small, 1999).

From a practical or diagnostic perspective, however, these high-tech methods to detect cognitive impairment may not be accessible to all people as they age because of their high cost. Without insurance coverage, these techniques will be limited to research and diagnosis tests for older adults who can afford to pay for them. This is true for other computer-assisted devices and systems that can be used in older adults' homes to help them maintain person–environment competence, as well as electronic games to stimulate memory, as will be described in Chapter 11.

Many career opportunities are emerging for students interested in the interface of cognitive psychology, education, technology, and gerontology. Especially among future cohorts, older adults will increasingly search for opportunities to learn and become retrained, using computer and digital technology. With the extension of life expectancy and changes in retirement patterns (as discussed in Chapter 12), many people will seek second and third careers that will require new cognitive and motor skills. Educators and software designers can apply the concepts presented in this chapter to respond to the needs of older learners, whether focused on creative aging or computer games.

Summary

This chapter presented an overview of major longitudinal studies of cognitive functioning. Researchers have examined age-related changes in intelligence, learning, and memory and what factors in the individual and the environment affect the degree of change in these three areas of cognitive functioning.

Of all the cognitive functions, intelligence in older adults has received the greatest attention and is most controversial. It is also the area of most concern for many older persons. One problem with this area of research is the difficulty of defining and measuring what is

generally agreed to be intelligence. In examining the components of intelligence measured by the Wechsler Adult Intelligence Scale (WAIS), fluid intelligence (as measured by performance scales) has been shown to decline more with aging than verbal, or crystallized, intelligence. This may be due partly to the fact that the former tests are generally timed, while the latter are not. However, age differences emerge even when tests are not timed and when variations in motor and sensory function are taken into account. This decline in fluid intelligence and maintenance of verbal intelligence is known as the Classic Aging Pattern. To the extent that older persons practice their fluid intelligence by using their problem-solving skills, they will experience fewer decrements in this area. In contrast, aging does not appear to impair the ability for remembering word and symbol meanings. This does not imply that the ability to recall words is unimpaired, but when asked for definitions of words, older people can remember their meanings quite readily.

One problem with studying intelligence in aging is that of distinguishing age *changes* from age *differences*. To determine changes with age, people must be examined longitudinally. The problems of selective attrition and terminal drop make it difficult to interpret the findings of longitudinal studies of intelligence. These factors may result in an underestimate of the decline in intelligence with aging. The problem of cross-sectional studies of intelligence is primarily that of cohort differences. Even if subjects are matched on educational level, older persons have not had the exposure to computers and early childhood learning opportunities that are available to recent cohorts. The Seattle Longitudinal Study, which initiated the approach of testing multiple cohorts longitudinally, provides valuable insights into the impact of cohort differences in education and health on intelligence. This study also determined that changes on some tests of cognitive function in the middle years can predict cognitive impairment in the later years. Occupation, educational achievement, sensory decline, poor physical health, and uncontrolled hypertension may also have a significant impact on intelligence test scores.

Learning and memory are cognitive functions that are usually examined because tests of memory are actually tests of what a person has learned. According to the information-processing model, learning begins when information reaches sensory memory and then is directed via one or more sensory stores to primary memory. It is in primary memory that information must be organized and processed if it is to be retained and passed into secondary memory. Information is permanently stored in this latter region. Studies of recall and recognition provide evidence that aging does not affect the capacity of either primary or secondary memory. Instead, it appears that the aging process makes us less efficient in "reaching into" our secondary memory and retrieving material that was stored years ago. Tip-of-the-tongue states are an example of problems in remembering familiar names and words, and the role of stress in the retrieval process. Recognition tasks, in which a person is provided with a cue to associate with an item in secondary memory, are easier than pure recall for most people, especially those who are older. Some types of memory, such as semantic and procedural memory, are retained into advanced old age. Others, like episodic memory, show significant age-related decrements. There appears to be a "positivity effect" in older adults' ability to attend to, learn, and retain new information. They can recall twice as much information with positive emotional content than negative or neutral information, compared with younger adults who can recall positive and negative information equally well.

The learning process can be enhanced for older people by reducing time constraints, making the learning task more relevant for them, improving the physical conditions by using bright but glare-free lights and large letters, and providing visual and verbal mediators for learning new information. Helping the older learner to relax and not feel threatened by the learning task also ensures better learning. Such

modifications are consistent with the goal of achieving greater congruence between older people and their environment.

Significant age-related declines in intelligence, learning, and memory are not inevitable. Older people who continue to perform well on tests of intelligence, learning, and memory are characterized by higher levels of education, good sensory functioning, maintenance of physical activities and good nutrition, and employment and leisure activities that require complex problem-solving skills. People who do not have serious cardiovascular disease or severe hypertension also perform well, although there is some slowing of cognitive processing and response speed. Even such slowing is not a problem for older people whose crystallized knowledge in the targeted area is high. Older adults should be cautious, however, of taking natural products and vitamins that may improve memory in older people but whose benefits are not proven.

Although most reviews of change in cognitive abilities focus on declines with aging, there is growing evidence of gains as well. Cognitive plasticity refers to the ability to select, optimize, and compensate for lost skills. Older adults who cope best appear to have the most cognitive plasticity, perhaps indicating an ability to read their environment and adapt to its changing demands. Memory retraining studies may be effective in improving cognitive plasticity in older adults. A growing body of research with computer and Internet users suggests that regular use of the Internet activates more brain regions, especially where decision making and complex reasoning occurs. Computer and Internet use can enhance cognitive processes in older persons, thereby improving their autonomy and sense of control over their environment.

Although wisdom and creativity appear to be enhanced by changes in the aging brain, there has been less research emphasis in these areas. Indeed, these concepts are more difficult to measure in young and old persons. These and other issues in cognition must be studied more fully with measures that have good construct validity before gerontologists can describe with certainty positive cognitive changes that are attributable to normal aging.

GLOSSARY

attentional control   ability to allocate one's attention among multiple stimuli simultaneously

Classic Aging Pattern   the decline observed with aging on some performance scales of intelligence tests versus consistency on verbal scales of the same tests

cognitive plasticity   ability to compensate for declines in cognitive abilities by selecting areas of deficits, making accommodations to optimize one's remaining capacities as needed

cognitive retraining   teaching research participants how to use various techniques to keep their minds active and maintain good memory skills

crystallized intelligence   knowledge and abilities one gains through education and experience

disuse theory   the view that memory fades or is lost because one fails to use the information

divided attention   ability to focus on multiple stimuli simultaneously

echoic memory   auditory memory; a brief period when new information received through the ears is stored

executive function   cognitive skills required to organize one's learning function

external aids   simple devices such as list-making used by older people to keep track of the time, dates, etc.

fluid intelligence   skills that are biologically determined, independent of experience or learning; similar to "native intelligence," requiring flexibility in thinking

general slowing hypothesis   physiological changes that cause slower transmission of information through the nervous system with aging

iconic memory   visual memory; a brief period when new information received through the eyes is stored

information-processing model   a conceptual model of how learning and memory take place

intelligence   the theoretical limit of an individual's performance

intelligence quotient (IQ)   an individual's abilities relative to population standards in making judgments, in comprehension, and in reasoning

interference theory   the view that memory fades or is lost because of distractions experienced during learning or interference from similar or new information to the item to be recalled

mediators   visual and verbal links between information to be memorized and information that is already in secondary memory

mnemonics   the method of using verbal cues such as riddles or rhymes as aids to memory

neural plasticity   physical changes in brain structure in the form of more neurons and synaptic connections between neurons as a result of practice and activation of specific regions of the brain

perceptual speed   time, in milliseconds, required to perceive and react to a stimulus

positivity effect   Process whereby older adults attend to, learn from, and retain positive information better than neutral or negative stimuli, because it helps them regulate emotional experiences by focusing on positive information

primary mental abilities (PMAs)   the basic set of intellectual skills, including mathematical reasoning, word fluency, verbal meaning, inductive reasoning, and spatial orientation

recall   the process of searching through secondary memory in response to a specific external cue

recognition   matching information in secondary memory with the stimulus information

secondary (long-term) memory   permanent memory store; requires processing of new information to be stored and cues to retrieve stored information

selective attention   being able to focus on information relevant to a task while ignoring irrelevant information

selection, optimization, and compensation (SOC)   a theory that focuses on elders' ability to adapt and regulate one's cognitive resources by selecting cognitive domains to improve, optimizing one's abilities in these areas and compensating when losses in those areas require enhancement of other skills or acquiring new behaviors or knowledge to make up for these lost abilities

sensory memory   the first step in receiving information through the sense organs and passing it on to primary or secondary memory

spatial memory   the ability to recall where objects are in relationship to each other in space

terminal decline hypothesis   the hypothesis that persons close to death decline in cognitive abilities

tip-of-the-tongue states (TOTs)   difficulty retrieving names from secondary memory but often spontaneously recalled later

vigilance (sustained attention)   keeping alert to focus on a specific stimulus over time

visual mediators   use of visual images to assist recall

working (primary) memory   holding newly acquired information in storage; a maximum of 7 ± 2 stimuli before processing into secondary memory or discarding

REFERENCES

Andrewes, D. G., Kinsella, G., & Murphy, M. (1996). Using a memory handbook to improve everyday memory in community-dwelling older adults with memory complaints. *Experimental Aging Research, 22,* 305–322.

Ardelt, M. (1997). Wisdom and life satisfaction in old age. *Journals of Gerontology, 52B,* P15–P27.

Aubrey, J. B., Li, K. Z. H., & Dobbs, A. R. (1994). Age and sex differences in the interpretation of misaligned "You-are-Here" maps. *Journals of Gerontology, 49,* P29–P31.

Ball, K., Berch, D. B., Hemers, K. F., Jobe, J. B., Leveck, M. D., Mariske, M., et al. (2002). Effects of cognitive training interventions with older adults. *Journal of the American Medical Association, 288,* 2271–2281.

Baltes, P. B. & Kunzmann, U. (2003). Wisdom. *Psychologist, 16,* 131–133.

Baltes, P. B. & Staudinger. U. M. (2000). Wisdom: A metaheuristic to orchestrate mind and virtue toward excellence. *American Psychologist, 55,* 122–126.

Binet, A. & Simon, T. (1905). Méthodes nouvelles pour le diagnostique du niveau intellectuel des anormaux. *Année Psychologique, 11,* 102–191.

Bjelakovic, G., Nikolova, D., Gluud, L. L., Simonetti, R. G., & Gluud, C. (2007). Mortality in randomized trials of antioxidant supplements for primary and secondary prevention. *Journal of the American Medical Association, 297,* 842–857.

Blanchard-Fields, F. & Kalinauskas, A. (2009) Theore- tical perspectives on social context, cognition and aging. In V. L. Bengtson, D. Gans, N. M. Putney, & M. Silverstein (Eds.). *Handbook of theories of aging* (2nd ed.), New York: Springer, Chapter 15.

Bopp, K. L. & Verhaeghen, P. (2005). Aging and verbal memory span: A meta-analysis. *Journal of Gerontology: Psychological Sciences, 60B,* P223–P233.

Boron, J. B., Willis, S. L., & Schaie, K. W. (2007). Cognitive training gain as a predictor of mental status. *Journal of Gerontology: Psychological Sciences, 62B,* P45–P52.

Bosworth, H. B., Schaie, K. W., & Willis, S. L. (1999). Cognitive and sociodemographic risk factors for mortality in the Seattle Longitudinal Study. *Journal of Gerontology: Psychological and Social Sciences, 54B,* 273–282.

Brooks, B. L., Weaver, L. E., & Scialfa, C. T. (2006). Does impaired executive functioning differentially impact verbal memory measure in older adults with suspected dementia? *The Clinical Neuropsychologist, 20,* 230–242.

Brown, A. S. & Nix, L. A. (1996). Age-related changes in the tip-of-the-tongue experience. *American Journal of Psychology, 109,* 79–91.

Burack, O. R. & Lackman, M. E. (1996). The effects of list-making on recall in young and elderly adults. *Journal of Gerontology: Psychological Sciences, 51B,* P226–P233.

Cabeza, R., Anderson, N. D., Locantore, J. K., & McIntosh, A. R. (2002). Aging gracefully: Compensatory brain activity in high-performing older adults. *Neuroimage, 17,* 1394–1402.

Carey, B. (2009). Card sharps: Bridge club holds clues to lucid aging. *The New York Times,* May 22.

Carlson, M. C., Saczynski, J. S., Rebok, G. W., Seeman, T., Glass, T. A., et al. (2008). Exploring the effects of an "everyday" activity program on executive function and memory in older adults: Experience Corps. *The Gerontologist, 48,* 793–801.

Carstensen, L. L. (2007). Growing old or living long: A new perspective on the aging brain. *Public Policy and Aging Report, 17,* 13–17.

Cattell, R. B. (1963). Theory of fluid and crystallized intelligence: A critical experiment. *Journal of Educational Psychology, 54,* 1–22.

Cavanaugh, J. C. & Blanchard-Fields, F. (2006). *Adult development and aging* (5th ed.). Belmont, CA: Thomson Wadsworth.

Christensen, H., Mackinnon, A. J., Korten, A. E., Jorm, A. F., Henderson, A. S., Jacomb, P., et al. (1999). An analysis of cognitive performance of elderly community dwellers: Individual differences in change scores as a function of age. *Psychology and Aging, 14,* 365–379.

Cohen, G. D. (2000). *The creative age.* New York: Aron Books.

Cohen, G. D. (2005). *The mature mind: The positive power of the aging brain.* Cambridge, MA: Perseus Books.

Cohen G. D. (2009). *Mirror, mirror on the wall: What is aging after all? Creative capacity and psychological growth in the second half of life. Positive brain and behavior changes that occur because of aging, not despite it.* Public Lecture, University of Washington, Seattle, WA May 27.

Colcombe, S. J. & Kramer, A. F. (2003). Fitness effects on the cognitive function of older adults: A meta-analytic study. *Psychological Science, 14,* 125–130.

Czaja, S. J. & Lee, C. C. (2001). The Internet and older adults: Design challenges and opportunities. In N. Charness, D. C. Parks, & B. A. Sabel (Eds.). *Communication, technology and aging.* New York: Springer.

Czaja, S. J. & Lee, C. C. (2003). Designing computer systems for older adults. In J. Jacko & A. Sears (Eds.). *The human-computer interaction handbook.* Mahwah, NJ: Erlbaum.

Czaja, S. J., Sharit, J., Ownby, R. L., Roth, D. L. & Nair, S. (2001). Examining age differences in performance of a complex information search and retrieval task. *Psychology and Aging, 16,* 564–579.

Dahlgren, D. J. (1998). Impact of knowledge and age on tip-of-the-tongue rates. *Experimental Aging Research, 24,* 139–153.

Das, I. & Agarwai, S. (2000). Effect of aging on memory for spatial locations of objects. *Psycho-Lingua, 30,* 17–20.

Einstein, G. O., Earles, J. L., & Collins, H. M. (2002). Gaze aversion: Spared inhibition for visual distraction in older adults. *Journal of Gerontology: Psychological Sciences, 57B,* P65–P73.

Elias, P. K., Elias, M. F., Robbins, M. A., & Budge, M. M. (2004). Blood pressure-related cognitive decline: Does age make a difference? *Hypertension, 44,* 1–6.

Fraas, M., Lockwood, J., Neils, S., Trunjas, J. Shidler, M., Krikorian, R., et al. (2002). "What's his name?" A comparison of elderly participants' and undergraduate students' misnamings. *Archives of Gerontology and Geriatrics, 34,* 155–165.

Gamaldo, A. A., Weatherbee, S. R., and Allaire, J. C. (2008). Exploring the within-person coupling of blood pressure and cognition in elders. *Journal of Gerontology: Psychological Sciences, 63B,* P386–P389.

Greenwood, P. M. & Parasuraman, R. (1999). Scale of attention focus in visual search. *Perception and Psychophysics, 1,* 837–859.

Guilford, J. P. (1967). *The nature of human intelligence.* New York: McGraw-Hill.

Gunstad, J., Paul, R. H., Brickman, A. M., Cohen, R. A., Arns, M., Roe, D., et al. (2006). Patterns of cognitive performance in middle-aged and older adults. *Journal of Geriatric Psychiatry and Neurology, 19,* 59–64.

Hasher, L., Chung, C., May, C. P., & Foong, N. (2002). Age, time of testing, and proactive interference. *Canadian Journal of Experimental Psychology, 56,* 200–207.

Hassing, L. B., Grant, M. D., Hofer, S. M., Pedersen, N. L., Nilsson, S. E., Berg, S., et al. (2004). Type 2 diabetes mellitus contributes to cognitive change in the oldest old. *Journal of the International Neuropsychological Society, 4,* 599–607.

Hess, T. M., Rosenberg, D. C., & Waters, S. J. (2001). Motivation and representational processes in adulthood: The effects of social accountability and information relevance. *Psychology and Aging, 16,* 629–642.

Hogan, M. J. (2003). Divided attention in older but not younger adults is impaired by anxiety. *Experimental Aging Research, 29,* 111–136.

Horn, J. L. (1970). Organization of data on life-span development of human abilities. In L. R. Goulet & P. B. Baltes (Eds.). *Life-span developmental psychology: Research and theory.* New York: Academic Press.

Horn, J. L. (1982). The aging of human abilities. In B. B. Wolman (Ed.). *Handbook of developmental psychology.* Upper Saddle River, NJ: Prentice-Hall.

Horn, J. L. & Donaldson, G. (1980). Cognitive development in adulthood. In O. G. Brim & J. Kagan (Eds.). *Constancy and change in human development.* Cambridge, MA: Harvard University Press.

Hoyer, W. J. & Verhaeghen, P. (2006). Memory Aging. In J. E. Birren & K. W. Schaie (Eds.). *Handbook of the Psychology of Aging* (6th ed.). Burlington, MA: Elsevier Academic Press.

Inouye, S. K., Albert, M. S., Mohs, R., & Sun-Kolie, R. (1993). Cognitive performance in a high-functioning, community-dwelling elderly population. *Journals of Gerontology, 48,* M146–M151.

Insel, K., Morrow, D., Brewer, B., & Figueredo, A. (2006). Executive function, working memory, and medication adherence among older adults. *Journal of Gerontology: Psychological Sciences,* 61B, P102–P107.

Johnson, M. K. (2005). The relation between source memory and episodic memory: Comment on Siedleckie et al. *Psychology and Aging, 20,* 529–531.

Jones, H. E. (1959). Intelligence and problem-solving. In J. E. Birren (Ed.). *Handbook of aging and the individual: Psychological and biological aspects.* Chicago: University of Chicago Press.

Kang, J. H., Ascherio, A., & Grodstein, F. (2005). Fruit and vegetable consumption and cognitive decline in aging women. *Annals of Neurology, 57,* 713–720.

Kleemeier, R. W. (1962). Intellectual change in the senium. *Proceedings of the Social Science Statistics Section of the American Statistical Association, 1,* 290–295.

Knopman, D. S., Boland, L. L., Folsom, A. R., Mosley, T. H., McGovern, P. G., Howard, G., et al. (2000). Cardiovascular risk factors and longitudinal cognitive changes in middle age adults. *Neurology, 54,* Supplement.

Kramer, A. F., Bherer, L., Colcombe, S. J., Dong, W., & Greenough, W. T. (2004). Environmental influences on cognitive and brain plasticity during aging. *Journal of Gerontology: Medical Sciences, 59,* 940–957.

Kramer, A. F., Erickson, K. I., & Colcombe, S. J. (2006). Exercise, cognition, and the aging brain. *Journal of Applied Physiology, 101,* 1237–1242.

Langbaum, J. B. S., Rebok, G. W., Bandeen-Roche, K., Carlson, M. C. (2009). Predicting memory training response patterns: Results from ACTIVE. *Journal of Gerontology: Psychological Sciences, 64B,* P14–P23.

Larue, A., Koehler, K. M., Wayne, S. J., Chiulli, S. J., Haaland, K. Y., & Garry, P. J. (1997). Nutritional status and cognitive functioning in a normally aging sample: A 6-year reassessment. *American Journal of Clinical Nutrition, 65,* 20–29.

Levitt, H. M. (1999). The development of wisdom: An analysis of Tibetan Buddhist experience. *Journal of Humanistic Psychology, 39,* 86–105.

Lindenberger, U. & Baltes, P. B. (1994). Sensory functioning and intelligence in old age. *Psychology and Aging, 9,* 339–355.

Mackinnon, A., Christensen, H., Hofer, S. M., Korten, A. E., & Jorm, A. F. (2003). Use it and still lose it? The association between activity and cognitive performance established using latent growth curve techniques in a community sample. *Aging, Neuropsychology and Cognition, 10,* 215–229.

McGaugh, J. L. (2000). Memory: A century of consolidation. *Science, 287,* 248–251.

Mead, S. E., Lamson, N., & Rogers, W. A. (2002). Human factors guidelines for web site usability: Health-oriented web sites for older adults. In R. W. Morrell (Ed.). *Older adults, health information, and the World Wide Web.* Mahwah, NJ: Erlbaum.

Morrell, R. W., Mayhorn, C. B., & Bennett, J. A. (2000). Survey of World Wide Web use in middle-aged and older adults. *Human Factors, 42,* 175–182.

Morris, M. C., Evans, A., Tangney, C. C., Bienias, J. L., & Wilson, R. S. (2006). Associations of vegetable and fruit consumption with age-related cognitive change. *Neurology, 67,* 1370–1376.

Murray, M. D., Lane, K. A., Gao, S., Evans, R. M., Unverzagt, F. W., et al. (2002). Preservation of cognitive function with antihypertensive medications. *Archives of Internal Medicine, 162,* 2090–2096.

National Library of Medicine. (2002). *Making your web site senior friendly: A checklist.* Bethesda, MD: NIH/NLM.

Nyberg, L. (2005). Cognitive training in healthy aging: A cognitive neuroscience perspective. In R. Cabeza, L. Nyberg, & D. Park (Eds.). *Cognitive neuroscience of aging: Linking cognitive and cerebral aging.* New York: Oxford University Press.

Ownby, R. L., Czaja, S. J., Loewenstein, D. & Rubert, M. (2008). Cognitive abilities that predict success in a computer-based training program. *The Gerontologist, 48,* 170–180.

Parasuraman, R. (1998). The attentive brain: Issues and prospects. In R. Parasuraman (Ed.). *The attentive brain.* Cambridge, MA: MIT Press.

Parasuraman, R. & Greenwood, P. M. (1998). Selective attention in aging and dementia. In R. Parasuraman (Ed.). *The attentive brain.* Cambridge, MA: MIT Press.

Pearman, A. & Storandt, M. (2004). Predictors of subjective memory in older adults. *Journal of Gerontology: Psychological Sciences, 59,* P4–P6.

Ratcliff, R., Spieler, D., & McKoon, G. (2000). Explicitly modeling the effects of aging on response time. *Psychonomic Bulletin and Review, 7,* 1–25.

Reese, C. M. & Cherry, K. E. (2004). Practical memory concerns across the lifespan. *International Journal of Aging and Human Development, 59,* 237–255.

Rendell, P. G., Castel, A. D., & Craik, F. I. M. (2005). Memory for proper names in old age: A disproportional impairment? *Quarterly Journal of Experimental Psychology, 58,* 54–71.

Rogers, W. A. & Fisk, A. D. (2001). Attention in cognitive aging research. In J. E. Birren & K. W. Schaie (Eds.). *Handbook of the psychology of aging* (5th ed.). San Diego: Academic Press.

Rönnlund, M., Nyberg, L., Bäckman, L., & Nillson, L. G. (2005). Stability, growth, and decline in adult life span development of declarative memory. *Psychology and Aging, 20,* 3–18.

Rosnick, C. B., Small, B. J., Graves, A. B., & Mortimer, J. A. (2004). The association between health and cognitive performance in a population-based study of older adults. *Aging Neuropsychology and Cognition, 11,* 89–99.

Royall, D. R., Palmer, R., Chiodo, L. K., & Polk, M. J. (2004). Declining executive control in normal aging predicts change in functional status. *Journal of the American Geriatrics Society, 51,* 346–352.

Salthouse, T. A. (1996). The processing speed theory of adult age differences in cognition. *Psychological Review, 103,* 403–428.

Schaie, K. W. (1996a). Intellectual development in adulthood. In J. E. Birren & K. W. Schaie (Eds.). *Handbook of the psychology of aging* (4th ed.). San Diego: Academic Press.

Schaie, K. W. (1996b). *Intellectual development in adulthood: The Seattle Longitudinal Study.* Cambridge: Cambridge University Press.

Schaie, K. W. (2005). *Developmental influences on adult intelligence: The Seattle Longitudinal Study.* New York: Oxford University Press.

Schaie, K. W. (2006). Intelligence. In R. Schulz (Ed.). *Encyclopedia of aging* (4th ed.). New York: Springer.

Schaie, K. W., Plomin, R., Willis, S. L., Gruber-Baldini, A., & Dutta, R. (1992). Natural cohorts: Family similarity in adult cognition. In T. Sonderegger (Ed.). *Psychology and aging: Nebraska symposium on motivation.* Lincoln: University of Nebraska Press.

Schaie, K. W. & Willis, S. L. (1995). Perceived family environments across generations. In V. L. Bengston, K. W. Schaie, & L. Burton (Eds.). *Societal impact on aging: Intergenerational perspectives.* New York: Springer.

Schooler, C. & Mulatu, M. S. (2001). The reciprocal effects of leisure time activities and intellectual functioning in older people: A longitudinal analysis. *Psychology and Aging, 16,* 466–482.

Schooler, C., Mulatu, M. S., & Oates, G. (2004). Occupational self-direction in older workers: Findings and implications for individuals and society. *American Journal of Sociology, 110,* 161–197.

Schwartz, B. L. (2002). *Tip-of-the-tongue states.* Mahwah, NJ: Lawrence Erlbaum Associates.

Siedlecki, K. L., Salthouse, T. A., & Berish, D. E. (2005). Is there anything special about the aging of source memory? *Psychology and Aging, 20,* 19–32.

Silverman, D. H. S., Small, G. W., & Chang, C. Y. (2001). Evaluation of dementia with positron emission tomography: Regional brain metabolism and long-term outcome. *Journal of the American Medical Association, 286,* 2120–2127.

Slegers, K., van Boxtel, M. P. J., & Jolles, J. (2008). Effects of computer training and internet usage on the well-being and quality of life of older adults. *Journal of Gerontology: Psychological Sciences, 63B,* P176–P184.

Small, G. W. (1999). Positron emission tomography scanning for the early diagnosis of dementia. *Western Journal of Medicine, 171,* 293–294.

Small, G. W. (2002). *The memory bible.* New York: Hyperion.

Small, G. W., Moody, T. D., Siddharth, P., Bookheimer, S. Y. (2009). Your brain on Google: Patterns of cerebral activation during internet searching. *American Journal of Geriatric Psychiatry, 17,* 116–126.

Small, G. W. & Vorgan, G. (2008). *iBrain: Surviving the technological alteration of the modern mind.* New York: Harper Collins.

Stanley, J. T. & Blanchard-Fields, F. (2008). Challenges older adults face in detecting deceit: The role of emotion recognition. *Psychology and Aging, 23,* 24–32.

Staudinger, U. M. (1999). Older and wiser? Integrating results on the relationship between age and wisdom-related performance. *International Journal of Behavioral Development, 23,* 641–664.

Sternberg, R. J. & Lubert, T. I. (2001). Wisdom and creativity. In J. E. Birren & K. W. Schaie (Eds.). *Handbook of the psychology of aging* (5th ed.). San Diego: Academic Press.

Takahashi, M. & Overton, W. F. (2002). Wisdom: A culturally inclusive developmental perspective. *International Journal of Behavioral Development, 26,* 269–277.

Torrance, E. P. (1988). The nature of creativity as manifest in its testing. In R. J. Sternberg (Ed.). *The nature of creativity: Contemporary psychological perspectives.* Cambridge: Cambridge University Press.

Troyer, A. K., Hafliger, A., Cadieux, M. J., & Craik, F. I. M. (2006). Name and face learning in older adults: Effects of level processing, self-generation, and intention to learn. *Journal of Gerontology: Psychological Sciences, 61B,* P67–P74.

van Dongen, M., van Rossum, E., Kessels, A., Sielhorst, H., & Knipscheld, P. G. (2003). Ginkgo for elderly people with dementia and age-associated memory impairment: A randomized clinical trial. *Journal of Clinical Epidemiology, 56,* 367–376.

Verhaeghen, P., Geraerts, N., & Marcoen, A. (2000). Memory complaints, coping and well-being in old age: A systematic approach. *The Gerontologist, 40,* 540–548.

Waldstein, S. R., Giggey, P. P., Thayer, J. F. & Zonderman, A. B. (2005). Nonlinear relations of blood pressure to cognitive function. *Hypertension, 45,* 374–379.

Watkins, L. H., Sahakian, B. J., Robertson, M. M., Veale, D. M., Rogers, R. D., Pickard, K. M., et al. (2005). Executive function in Tourette's syndrome and obsessive-compulsive disorder. *Psychological Medicine, 35,* 571–582.

West, R., Murphy, K. J., Armilio, M. L., Craik, F. I. M., & Stuss, D. T. (2002). Effects of time of day on age differences in working memory. *Journal of Gerontology: Psychological Sciences, 57,* P3–P10.

Whiting, W. L. (2003). Adult age differences in divided attention: Effects of elaboration. *Aging, Neuropsychology, and Cognition, 10,* 141–157.

Williamson, J. D., Espeland, M., Kritchevsky, S. B., Newman, A. B., King, A. C., et al. (2009). Changes in cognitive function in a randomized trial of physical activity. *Journal of Gerontology: Medical Sciences, 64A,* 688–694.

Willis, S. L. (2001). Methodological issues in behavioral intervention research with the elderly. In J. E. Birren & K. W. Schaie (Eds.). *Handbook of the psychology of aging* (5th ed.). San Diego: Academic Press.

Willis, S. L. & Schaie, K. W. (2006). A co-constructionist view of the third age: The case of cognition. *Annual Review of Gerontology and Geriatrics, 26,* 131–151.

Willis, S. L., Schaie, K. W. & Martin, M. (2009). Cognitive plasticity. In V. L. Bengtson, D. Gans,

N. M. Putney, & M. Silverstein (Eds.). *Handbook of theories of aging* (2nd ed.), New York: Springer.

Willis, S. L., Tennstedt, S. L., Marsiske, M., Ball, K., Elias, J., Koepke, K. M., et al. (2006). Long-term effects of cognitive training on everyday functional outcomes in older adults. *Journal of the American Medical Association, 296,* 2805–2814.

Zacks, R. T., Hasher, L., & Li, K. Z. H. (2000). Human memory. In F. I. M. Craik & T. A. Salthouse (Eds.). *The handbook of aging and cognition* (2nd ed.). Mahway, NJ: Erlbaum.

Zelinski, E. M. & Gilewski, M. J. (2004). 10-item Rasch modeled memory self-efficacy scale. *Aging and Mental Health, 8,* 293–306.

Zelinski, E. M., Gilewski, M. J., & Schaie, K. W. (1993). Individual differences in cross-sectional and 3-year longitudinal memory performance across the adult life span. *Psychology and Aging, 8,* 176–186.

6

Personality and Mental Health in Old Age

This chapter examines

- Normal developmental changes and stability in personality across the life course
- Stage and trait theories of personality that describe change or stability with aging
- Person–environment interactions that affect personality development
- Emotional expression and regulation in older and younger adults
- Stability versus change in self-concept and self-esteem with aging
- Evolution and critique of successful aging theories
- Active or robust aging/resilience
- Major mental disorders in old age:
  Depression, anxiety, schizophrenia, and paranoia
  Alzheimer's disease and other dementias
- Successful psychotherapeutic approaches with older persons
- Older people's use of mental health services

We have all had the experience of watching different people respond to the same event in varied ways. For example, you probably know some students who are extremely anxious about completing papers and exams, while others spend very little time and energy on assignments; and some students who express their opinions strongly and confidently, while others rarely speak in class at all. All these characteristics are part of an individual's personality.

Defining Personality

Personality can be defined as a unique pattern of innate and learned behaviors, thoughts, and emotions that influence how each person responds and interacts with the environment. An individual may be described in terms of several personality traits, such as passive or aggressive, introverted or extroverted, independent or dependent. Personality can

215

be evaluated with regard to particular standards of behavior; for example, an individual may be described as being adapted or maladapted, resilient or feeling hopeless. Personality styles influence how we cope with and adapt to the changes that occur as we age. The process of aging generally involves some stressful life experiences. How an older person attempts to alleviate such stress has an influence on that individual's long-term well-being. The person–environment congruence model presented in Chapter 1 suggests that our behavior is influenced and modified by the environment in interaction with our competence in multiple areas, and that we shape the environment around us. An individual's behavior is often quite different from one situation to another, and depends both on each situation's social norms and expectations as well as on that person's needs and motives.

Although personality remains relatively stable with normal aging, some older people who showed no signs of psychopathology earlier in their lives may experience some types of mental disorders in late life. For other older people, psychiatric disorders experienced in their younger years may continue or reemerge. In some individuals, the stresses of old age may compound any existing predisposition to **psychological disorders.** These stresses may be internal (resulting from physiological and cognitive changes) or external (a function of role losses and the deaths of partners, friends, or children). Such conditions may significantly impair older people's competence, so that they become more vulnerable to environmental press and less able to function at an optimal level.

Stage Theories of Personality

Most theories of personality emphasize the developmental **stages** (or phases) **of personality** and posit that the social environment influences development. We review these stages of adult development because of the significant impact that many of these classic theories have had on old age and programs for older adults. However,

it is important to avoid the image of rigid, immutable stages and inevitable transitions with no room for individual differences. In fact, people *do* make choices regarding their specific responses to common life changes. This results in diverse expressions of behavior under similar life experiences such as adolescence, parenting, midlife caregiving, retirement, and even the management of chronic diseases. There has been disagreement about whether this pattern of development continues through adulthood. Sigmund Freud's focus on psychosexual stages of development through adolescence has had a major influence on developmental psychology. In most of his writings, Freud suggests that personality achieves stability by adolescence. Accordingly, Freud views adult behavior as a reflection of unconscious motives and unsuccessful resolution of early childhood stages. Freud's work subsequently shaped the stage theories of personality developed by Jung and Erikson in the mid-twentieth century.

Jung's Psychoanalytic Perspective

Carl Jung's model of personality assumes changes throughout life, as expressed in the following statement from one of his early writings:

> We cannot live the afternoon of life according to the program of life's morning, for what was great in the morning will be little at evening, and what in the morning was true will at evening have become a lie (1933, p. 108).

Jung suggests that the ego moves from *extraversion*—or a focus on the external world in youth

---

JUNG'S PERSPECTIVE ON INTROVERSION WITH AGING

In contrast to the young, older persons have:

a duty and a necessity to devote serious attention to (themselves). After having lavished its light upon the world, the sun withdraws its rays in order to illuminate itself

SOURCE: (Jung, 1933, p. 109).

and middle age when the individual progresses through school, work, and marriage—to *introversion,* a focus on one's inner world in old age. Like Erikson, described below, Jung examined the individual's confrontation with death in the last stage of life. He suggested that life for the aging person must naturally contract, and that the individual in this stage must find meaning in inner exploration and an afterlife.

Jung (1959) also focused on changes in archetypes with age. That is, according to Jung, all humans have both a feminine and a masculine side. An **archetype** is the feminine side of a man's personality (the anima) and the masculine side of a woman's personality (the animus). As they age, people begin to adopt psychological traits more commonly associated with the opposite sex. For example, older men may show more signs of passivity and nurturance, while women may become more assertive as they age. This allows the individual to express oneself more fully and to satisfy their personal needs rather than being constrained by society's stereotypes of masculine versus feminine qualities. These concepts have influenced subsequent theories of personality development.

Erikson's Psychosocial Model

Although trained in psychoanalytic theory, Erikson moved away from this approach and focused on psychosocial development throughout the life cycle. According to his model (Erikson, 1963, 1968, 1982, 1997; Erikson, Erikson, & Kivnick, 1986), the individual undergoes eight stages of development, with the unconscious goal of achieving *ego identity*. Three of these stages are beyond adolescence, with the final one occurring in mature adulthood. At each stage, the individual experiences a major task to be accomplished and a conflict to be resolved; the conflicts of each stage of development are the foundations of successive stages. Depending on the outcome of the crisis associated with a particular stage, the individual proceeds to the next stage of development in alternative ways. Erikson also emphasized the

interactions between genetics and the environment in determining personality development. His concept of the *epigenetic principle* assumed an innate plan of development in which people proceed through stages as they become cognitively and emotionally more capable of interacting within a wider social radius. Hence, each subsequent stage requires additional cognitive and emotional development before it can be experienced.

The individual in the last stage of life is confronted with the task of **ego integrity versus despair.** According to Erikson, the individual accepts the inevitability of mortality and achieves wisdom and perspective, or despairs because he or she has not come to grips with death and lacks ego integrity. A major task associated with this last stage is to look inward in order to integrate the experiences of earlier stages and to realize that one's life has had meaning, whether or not it was "successful" in the traditional sense. Older people who achieve ego integrity feel a sense of connectedness with younger generations, and share their experiences and wisdom with them. In fact, **generativity,** or the desire to help and mentor younger persons, may be the most critical variable for achieving ego integrity. The commitment to mentor and nurture younger generations continues well into old age (Chang, 2009; James & Zarrett, 2006; Sheldon & Kasser, 2001). Generativity may take the form of:

- informal visiting
- counseling
- mentoring
- sponsoring an individual or group of younger people
- focusing on one's legacy
- writing memoirs or letters or sharing oral traditions
- assuming a leadership role in one's community
- conducting life review

The process of sharing one's memories and experiences with others (orally or written) is described as **life review,** and it is a useful form of

ERIKSON'S PSYCHOSOCIAL STAGES

	Stage	Goal
I	Basic trust vs. mistrust	To establish basic trust in the world through trust in the parent
II	Autonomy vs. shame and doubt	To establish a sense of autonomy and self as distinct from the parent; to establish self-control vs. doubt in one's abilities
III	Initiative vs. guilt	To establish a sense of initiative within parental limits without feeling guilty about emotional needs
IV	Industry vs. inferiority	To establish a sense of industry within the school setting; to learn necessary skills without feelings of inferiority or fear of failure
V	Ego identity vs. role diffusion	To establish identity, self-concept, and role within the larger community without confusion about the self and about social roles.
VI	Intimacy vs. isolation	To establish intimacy and affiliation with one or more others without fearing loss of identity in the process that may result in isolation
VII	Generativity vs. stagnation	To establish a sense of care and concern for the well-being of future generations; to look toward the future and not stagnate in the past
VIII	Ego integrity vs. despair	To establish a sense of meaning in one's life rather than feeling despair or bitterness that life was wasted; to accept oneself and one's life without despair

psychotherapy with older adults. Life satisfaction, or the feeling that life is worth living, may be achieved through these tasks of adopting a wider historical perspective on one's life, accepting one's mortality, sharing experiences with the young, and leaving a legacy to future generations. Erikson's theory is a widely accepted framework for studying personality in late life because it suggests that personality is dynamic throughout the life cycle. Indeed, this theory fits the person–environment model; we interact with a variety of other people in different settings, and our personality is affected accordingly. Both longitudinal and sequential research methods support the developmental stages postulated by Erikson. Standardized measures of personality demonstrate developmental growth in self-confidence, dependability, identity, and generativity (Ryff, Kwan, & Singer, 2001).

Jane Loevinger extended Erikson's theory by expanding the stages of ego development in adulthood (1976, 1997, 1998). According to her theory,

one's interactions with the environment shape one's thoughts and values. Instead of two stages occurring in adulthood, as Erikson's model proposes, Loevinger describes six. The individual must successfully progress through the preceding one to reach the next one, although most people remain at the second one. These stages are:

- conformist
- conscientious conformist
- conscientious
- individualistic
- autonomous
- integrated

Each stage requires a transition in several domains, including the individual's personal standards and life goals, interpersonal style, primary preoccupations in life, and cognitive style. Loevinger's last stage, labeled *integrated*, resembles that of Erikson, because in both cases, individuals integrate their identity, personal conflicts, and values.

Qualitative research with older adults reveals that progress from one stage to another is not always linear and that *phases* may be a term that better captures this process than *stages* (Cohen, 2005, 2009). Interviews with older people demonstrate that many have experienced setbacks in some aspects of their lives while moving forward in others. For example, some elders may have achieved integrity of their intellectual and spiritual selves, but may not have been successful with the generativity stage. Cohen suggests that these older adults can resolve the conflicts of an earlier stage even as they proceed through subsequent phases of development.

Empirical Testing of These Perspectives

In testing the validity of stage theories, subsequent research has contributed to our understanding of personality development in late adulthood. Many of these studies are cross-sectional; that is, they derive information on age *differences*, not age changes. There are notable exceptions to this approach, including the Baltimore Longitudinal Studies (described in Chapter 1) and the Kansas City Studies, which examined changes in physiological, cognitive, and personality functions in the same individuals over a period of several years. Research on personality characteristics in the Baltimore Longitudinal Studies is related to Erikson's work, because it identifies changes in *adjustment* with age but stability in specific *traits* (described later in this chapter). Cross-sectional studies by De St. Aubin and McAdams (1995) and by Peterson and Klohnen (1995) examined age differences in generativity, Erikson's seventh stage. These researchers consistently found that middle-aged and older adults express more generative concerns (i.e., attribute more importance to the care of younger generations than to self-development) than young adults. "Generative adults" exhibit concerns not just toward their own children, but toward the younger population in general.

The Grant Study of Harvard University Graduates is a longitudinal investigation that followed 268 men, beginning in 1938 when they were students, through age 65 when 173 of the men were still available to take part in these life reviews and qualitative interviews. This unique research has identified support for stage theories of personality (Vaillant, 1977, 1994, 2002). The men who remained for long-term follow-ups were observed to follow a common pattern of stages:

- having establishment of a professional identity in their 20s and 30s
- begin career consolidation in their 40s
- exploration of their inner worlds in midlife (a major transition similar to the stage of ego integrity versus despair that Erikson described as occurring in late life)

Men who were most emotionally stable and well adjusted in their 50s and 60s were characterized as:

- having higher levels of generativity (i.e., responsibility for and care of coworkers, children, charity)
- being less gender stereotyped in their social inter- actions
- more nurturant and expressive

These changes observed in men as they moved from youth to middle age to old age have implications for contemporary family care responsibilities, as discussed in Chapters 9 and 10.

POINTS TO PONDER

Think about an older person you know who appears to have achieved the stage of ego integrity. What adjectives would you use to describe this individual? How would you describe your interactions with this person?

LEVINSON'S "SEASONS" OF LIFE

Era I   Preadulthood (Age 0–22)
(An era when the family provides
protection, socialization, and support of
personal growth)
Early Adult Transition (Age 17–22)*

Era II   Early Adulthood (Age 17–45)
(An era of peak biological functioning,
development of adult identity)
Entering the adult world, entry life
structure for early adulthood
Age 30 transition*
Settling down, culminating life
structure for early adulthood
Mid-Life Transition (Age 40–45)*

Era III Middle Adulthood (Age 40–65)
(Goals become more other-oriented,
compassionate roles, mentor roles assumed;
peak effectiveness as a leader)
Entering life structure for middle adulthood
Age 50 transition*
Culmination of middle adulthood
Late Adulthood Transition (Age 60–65)*

Era IV   Late Adulthood (Age 60+)
(An era when declining capacities are
recognized; anxieties about aging, loss of
power and status begin)
Acceptance of death's inevitability

*Indicates major transitions to a new developmental era.

SOURCE: D. Levinson, C. M. Darrow, E. B. Klein, M. H. Levinson, & B. McKee, *The seasons of a man's life* (New York: Alfred A. Knopf, 1978). Reprinted with permission of the author and publisher.

Dialectical Models of Adult Personality

In contrast to Erikson's focus on stages of ego development, Levinson and colleagues (1977, 1978, 1986, 1996) have examined developmental stages in terms of **life structures,** or the underlying characteristics of a person's life at a particular period of time. Of all stage theories of adult development, this model is the most explicit in linking each stage with a specific range of chronological age. Each period in the life structure (defined as four "eras" by Levinson) represents developmental stages, each one lasting about 20 years. These are separated by *transitions* of about 5 years, each of which generally occurs as the individual perceives changes in the self, or as external events such as childbirth and retirement create new demands on one's social relationships with others (see the box above).

Levinson's model represents an example of a *dialectical approach* to personality development that is consistent with the person–environment model; it proposes that growth occurs because of interactions between a person who is changing

biologically *and* psychologically, and a dynamic environment. To the extent that an individual is sensitive to the changing self, he or she can respond to shifting external conditions by altering something within the self or by modifying environmental expectations. This process thereby reestablishes equilibrium with the environment. For example, an older person experiencing normal declines in cardiovascular function that is aggravated by heart disease may decide to shift from downhill to cross-country skiing while still maintaining her role as mentor to young skiers. In this manner, she can modify her lifestyle to meet her declining health without giving up her need for generativity.

Trait Theories of Personality

Another approach to studying personality is to examine characteristic behaviors specific within individuals that reflect **trait theories.** Traits are relatively stable personality dispositions; together

Maintaining an active lifestyle can enhance an older person's self-esteem.

they make up a constellation that distinguishes each individual. For example, we can describe people along a continuum of personality attributes such as extroverted to introverted, passive to aggressive, and optimistic to pessimistic, as well as high or low on need for achievement and affiliation. Most personality theorists agree that traits do not change unless the individual makes a conscious effort to do so—for example, undergoing psychological counseling to become more nurturant or more assertive.

This assumption of stability has led trait researchers to examine personality traits longitudinally in the middle and later years. Proponents of this approach are McCrae (2002) and Costa (1997, 2003), who measured specific traits of participants in the Baltimore Longitudinal Studies (described in Chapter 1). They propose a *five-factor model of personality traits,* consisting of five primary, independent dimensions:

- neuroticism
- extraversion
- openness to experience
- agreeableness
- conscientiousness

Within each component are six *facets,* or subcategories, of traits listed above; people who score high on the primary trait would demonstrate higher tendencies toward these behaviors and emotions.

Standardized tests such as the Guilford-Zimmerman Temperament Survey (GZTS) are used to compare individuals with population norms on these traits. By administering the GZTS to the same research subjects three times over 12 years in the Baltimore Longitudinal Studies, researchers found stability in the five traits described above, independent of environmental influences. Using a cross-sectional approach, they also identified consistency in these traits in middle-aged and older adults. Both groups differed from young adults on some personality factors, especially in neuroticism, extraversion, and openness to experience. Their research supports the idea of lifelong stability, and even heritability, of some personality traits. Subsequent studies by McCrae and Costa (with collaborators from diverse countries) demonstrate universal patterns of linear declines with age in neuroticism, extraversion, and openness, and an increase in agreeableness and conscientiousness. Although not all age differences were significant, the greatest difference was consistently between the youngest and oldest cohorts (Costa & McCrae, 1994, 1995; McCrae et al., 1999, 2000; McCrae & Terracciano, 2005; McCrae et al., 2004).

Life events play an important role in the pattern of these changes in personality traits. Negative life events occurring in the late 70s are associated with significant declines in extraversion and an increase in neuroticism. On the other hand, positive life events such as remarriage after age 70 are followed by increased extraversion (Maiden et al., 2003; Mroczek & Spiro, 2003; Mroczek, Spiro, & Griffin, 2006). When the Baltimore Longitudinal Studies tracked personality scores for as long as 42 years, the pattern of decline in neuroticism, extraversion, and openness and the increase in agreeableness and conscientiousness observed in cross-sectional and shorter longitudinal observations was supported.

However, the researchers also identified significant individual variability in these changes as well as in specific facets of the extraversion factor (Terracciano, McCrae, & Costa, 2006).

Cohort and cultural influences on some personality traits have also been identified. Using a cross-sequential research design, Schaie and Willis (1991) found few changes in specific traits of the same individuals over 7 years in the Seattle Longitudinal Study (described in Chapter 5), but they did find cohort differences. That is, the oldest participants in the first wave were less flexible and adaptable than were persons of the same age in the second wave of testing 7 years later. Cultural factors may also play a role in the development of certain traits. For example, traditional societies, including the United States before the feminist movement of the 1960s, reinforced "agreeableness" as a trait in women. Several facets of this trait—such as altruism, compliance, modesty, and tendermindedness—are viewed in traditional societies as important "feminine" traits. However, as women have moved into more diverse roles and entered occupations that were once considered "masculine," there is less gender stereotyping of traits, although women may still be expected to perform traditional caring roles.

Emotional Expression and Regulation

Basic emotions such as fear, anger, happiness, and shame are hardwired, or part of the core personality of every human being. However, as the individual matures, feelings may become more cognitively complex and expressed differently. For example, a young child often expresses any emotion under any circumstance, but with socialization and a lifetime of interpersonal experiences, older adults know how to regulate their emotional expression, including not expressing feelings like anger or fear. Studies reveal that negative affect declines and positive affect increases or remains stable over the life course. Experiences throughout life also help adults anticipate others' emotional responses.

Some personality theorists have suggested that emotion regulation and social expertise help elders achieve and sustain meaningful interpersonal relationships and minimize conflict. This allows them to maintain a positive emotional state by refocusing their negative or angry feelings (Carstensen, Mikels, & Mather, 2006; Charles & Cartensen, 2007; Phillips et al., 2008). However, older adults show greater emotional reactivity than younger persons when viewing acts of injustice, suffering, and loss (Birditt, Fingerman, & Almeida, 2005; Charles, 2005; Kliegel, Jager, & Phillips, 2007; Kunzmann & Gruhn, 2005). Overall, healthy emotional aging—characterized by an overall enhancement of emotional experience across the life course—is part of normal human development (Kryla-Lighthall & Mather, 2009; Zarit, 2009).

The role of family and culture on emotional expression and regulation has also been examined. People in the same age cohort may differ in their ability to express or deny emotions, based on the social conditioning they received from their parents and the cultural milieu regarding how, when, and where emotions can be expressed. Parents who discourage their children from crying in public or verbally expressing anger often set the stage for a lifetime of controlling one's emotions. Thus, emotional development depends not just on physiological and cognitive maturation, but also on familial and cultural influences (Magai, 2001; Magai et al., 2001). These early familial and cultural expectations that can influence emotional expression across the life course remain powerful messages in old age and need to be considered by social and health care providers working with older adults.

Self-Concept and Self-Esteem

A major adjustment required in old age is the ability to redefine one's **self-concept,** or one's cognitive image of the self, as some previous social roles shift and as new roles are assumed. Our

PERSONALITY FACTORS IMPORTANT FOR MAINTAINING SELF-ESTEEM

- *Reinterpretation of the meaning of self*, such that an individual's self-concept and self-worth are independent of any roles he or she has played ("I am a unique individual" rather than "I am a doctor/teacher/wife").
- *Acceptance of the aging process*, its limitations, and possibilities. That is, individuals who realize that they have less energy and respond more slowly than in the past, but that they can still participate in life, will adapt more readily to the social and health losses of old age.
- *Reevaluation of one's goals and expectations* throughout life. Too often people establish life goals at an early age and are constantly disappointed as circumstances change. The capacity to respond to internal and external pressures by modifying life goals appropriately reflects flexibility and harmony with one's environment.
- *The ability to look back objectively* on one's past and to review one's failures and successes. *Life review* entails an objective review and evaluation of one's life. An older person who has this capability to reminisce about past experiences and how these have influenced subsequent personality development, behavior, and interpersonal relationships can call upon coping strategies that have been effective in the past and adapt them to changed circumstances. As noted above, life review can also help the older person come to terms with unresolved conflicts from one's past, resulting in greater ego integrity.

self-concept emerges from our interactions with the social environment, our social roles, and our accomplishments. Through continuous interactions with the environment, people can confirm or revise these self-images. They do so either by:

- *assimilating* new experiences into their self-concept, or
- *accommodating* or adjusting their self-concept to fit the new reality.

Accommodation is more difficult and requires greater adaptive skills (Whitbourne & Primus, 1996). For example, how does a retired teacher identify himself or herself after giving up the work that has been that individual's central focus for the past 40 or 50 years? How does a woman whose self-concept is closely associated with her role as a wife express her identity after her husband dies?

Many older persons continue to identify with the role that they have lost (think of those who continue to introduce themselves as a "teacher" or "doctor" long after retiring from those careers). This would represent a type of *identity assimilation*. Others experience *role confusion*, particularly in the early stages of retirement, when cues from other people are inconsistent with an individual's self-concept. This may require *identity accommodation*. Still others may undergo a period of depression and major readjustment to the changes associated with role loss. To the extent that a person's self-concept is defined independently of particular social roles, one adapts more readily to the role losses that may accompany old age. Both assimilation of new social roles to a stable self-concept and some accommodation to changing realities are indicators of successful adaptation of one's self-concept. Older adults who have not been able to develop a sense of self as differentiated from their past roles are more likely to experience negative outcomes. However, research with the oldest-old demonstrates that self-concept remains essentially unchanged among most elders. Even with declining health and loss of significant others, those who survive to advanced old age generally maintain their long-held identity (Diehl, Hastings, & Stanton, 2001).

For an older person whose self-concept is based on social roles and others' expectations, role losses have a particularly significant impact on that individual's **self-esteem**—defined as an evaluation or feeling about his or her identity relative to some ideal or standard.

- *Self-concept* is the cognitive definition or self-perception of one's identity.
- *Self-esteem* is based on an emotional assessment of the self.

The affective quality of self-esteem makes it more dynamic and more easily influenced by such external forces as retirement, widowhood, poverty, health status, and both positive and negative reinforcements from others (e.g., respect, deference, or ostracism—treating the person as invisible). Social roles integrate the individual into society and add meaning to one's life. As a result, alterations in social roles and the loss of status that accompanies some of these changes often have a negative impact on an older person's self-esteem. Think, for example, of an older woman whose social roles have emphasized that of caregiver to her family. If she herself becomes dependent on others for care because of a major debilitating illness such as a stroke or dementia, she is unwittingly robbed of this "ideal self," and her self-esteem may suffer.

An individual who experiences multiple role losses must not only adapt to the lifestyle changes associated with aging (e.g., financial insecurity or shrinking social networks), but also must integrate the new roles with his or her "ideal self" or learn to modify this definition of "ideal." Older persons who experience major physical and cognitive disabilities simultaneously with role losses—or worse yet, whose role losses are precipitated by an illness (e.g., early retirement due to stroke or nursing home placement because of Alzheimer's)—must cope with multiple challenges at a time in their lives when they have the fewest resources to resolve them successfully. Grief and depression are common reactions to such losses.

Some studies have shown a generalized decrease in self-esteem from age 50 to 80, although many others have found improvement from adolescence through the young-old period. These varied findings may be attributed to the cross-sectional nature of research on self-esteem and age. An analysis of 50 published studies of self-esteem among people ranging in age from 6 to 83 found a common pattern of stability in self-esteem between midlife and old age. This pattern resembles the stability of personality traits described earlier in this chapter (Trzesniewski, Donallen, & Robins, 2003). Stressful life events and disabilities, such as severe hearing loss, can impair older adults' self-esteem. For example, older people who are socially isolated and have significant physical disabilities often have the poorest self-esteem. In contrast, those who practice active aging by maintaining a strong social network and participating in volunteer or civic activities tend to do better psychologically, experiencing a sense of personal competence (Ryff, Kwan, & Singer, 2001; Windsor, Anstey, & Rogers, 2008).

Successful Aging

Early gerontological studies focused on quality of life and subjective well-being, concepts that no longer dominate gerontological research. Instead, researchers and clinicians are increasingly interested in the concepts of successful, robust, vital, or positive aging and resilience, with the most attention given to defining and measuring **successful aging** (Danner, Snowden, & Friesen, 2001; George, 2006; Hendricks & Hatch, 2006; Rowe & Kahn, 1987, 1997, 1998). This interest has been sparked by the growing number of older people who have avoided disabling chronic health problems and declining cognitive skills and have managed to cope effectively in their daily lives. What are the characteristics of such elders who age successfully that distinguish them from their less hardy peers? Successful aging is defined as a combination of:

- physical and functional health
- high cognitive functioning
- active involvement with society

This definition implies that the successful older person has low risk of disease and disability (i.e., healthy lifestyle factors such as good nutrition, not smoking, physical activity); is actively using problem-solving, conceptualization, and language skills to ensure mental stimulation; is maintaining meaningful social contacts; exhibits emotional optimism; and is participating in activities that contribute to society (e.g., volunteering, paid or unpaid work). Consistent with the person–environment model, individuals who age successfully are choosing and seeking positive social experiences and relationships, and improving the fit of their social environment (Rohr & Lang, 2009). The concept of personal agency—individual choices and behaviors—is also central. The model of successful aging proposed by Rowe and Kahn (1997, 1998), shown in Figure 6.1, integrates these components.

The MacArthur Studies of Successful Aging, on which this model is based, examined longitudinally a cohort of men and women (aged 70–79 at baseline) in three East Coast communities. They were selected because they represented the top third of their age group in cognitive and physical functioning. Within this selective group of "robust" older persons, more specific tests of cognitive and physical abilities, as well as physiological parameters, were conducted in 1988 and 1991. Those with the highest performance scores in this group at follow-up and those who survived 3 years

Intergenerational celebrations provide opportunities for social engagement.

later had fewer chronic conditions (especially cardiovascular diseases), better self-rated health, and higher educational and income levels. The majority of these robust older adults reported no problems with daily physical activities such as walking, crouching, and stooping without help, and 55 percent maintained their baseline performance levels after 3 years. Although 23 percent showed a decline on the performance tests, 22 percent actually *improved*. Those who declined or died in the interim had greater weekly variability in their physical performance, blood pressure, balance, and gait, and had entered the study with some chronic diseases. Participants in the MacArthur Studies were also assessed on their physical functioning over 7 years. Those with a strong support system showed less deterioration in their functional health than elders without positive networks.

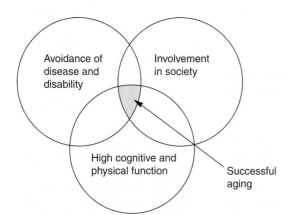

FIGURE 6.1   A Model of Successful Aging
This model assumes that all three components must exist for successful aging to occur.
SOURCE: Successful Aging in *The Gerontologist* by Rowe, J. W. and Kahn, R. L. Copyright 1997 by Oxford University Press—Journals. Reproduced with permission of Oxford University Press—Journals in the format textbook and other book via Copyright Clearance Center.

Such social supports were particularly valuable for men and those who had poorer physical health at baseline. Based on these findings, the MacArthur Studies researchers recommend that people remain actively engaged with life and connected to others as they age.

As noted on page 225, successful aging also implies maintenance of cognitive functioning. In the MacArthur Studies, *educational level* was the best predictor of continued high levels of cognitive ability. Rather than innate intelligence, higher educational achievement in those who aged successfully was most likely due to lifelong interest in intellectual activities as well as a beneficial effect of education on the development of complex networks in the brain. Other predictors of maintaining cognitive abilities were *involvement in strenuous physical activity*. A higher level of **self-efficacy**, that is, a feeling of competence in one's ability to deal with new situations, was also a significant predictor of high physical and cognitive functioning at follow-up (Seeman et al., 1999). A later review of 28 studies that examined correlates of successful aging confirmed that cognitive activity, absence of disability, more physical activity, not smoking, and absence of depression, diabetes, and debilitating arthritis were significantly correlated with objective measures of this concept (Depp & Jeste, 2006; Depp, Ipsit, & Jeste, 2007).

The concept of "robust aging" represents a broader perspective on successful aging, one that considers exceptional functioning on measures of physical health, cognitive abilities, and emotional well-being even among the oldest-old (Garfein & Herzog, 1995). Instead of focusing on decline, the emphasis is on trying to promote optimal aging in which emotional well-being is maintained or even enhanced (Kryla-Lighthall & Mather, 2009). Four important characteristics distinguish robust older adults from their less-robust peers:

- productive involvement (defined as 1,500 hours or more of paid or unpaid work, home maintenance, or volunteer activity in the past year)

- absence of depressive symptoms (i.e., high affective well-being)
- high physical functioning
- no cognitive impairment (Garfein & Herzog, 1995)

Robust elders reported more social contacts, better physical health and vision, and fewer significant life events (e.g., death of partner, child, close friend) in the past 3 years than did poorly functioning elders. For the oldest-old, robust aging also implies the ability to perform basic activities of daily living, higher-level work, and leisure and social activities (Horgas, Wilms, & Baltes, 1998).

A related concept is **resilience,** or the ability to thrive under adversity or multiple life challenges, turning adversity into a catalyst for growth and development. The concept of resilience takes account of background characteristics (e.g., gender, social class, race, sexual orientation, and age) and personal, family, cultural, and community capacities that can protect against or moderate adversity and influence meaning and well-being in later life. For example, people who have positive interpersonal relationships, strong cultural values, and a supportive community can enhance their resilience even in the face of chronic health problems and economic adversity. Paradoxically, older adults have lower rates of mental disorders than other adult age-groups and generally report higher emotional well-being and positive affect (Kahn, 2003; Neimeyer, 2001; Ryff & Singer, 2009; Ryff et al., 2001; Zarit, 2009).

A comparison of three large longitudinal studies provides insights into personality and coping styles that result in what some researchers call "positive aging" (i.e., actively responding to changes in one's health and interpersonal relations). The Grant Study of Harvard Graduates studied a cohort of men born in the 1920s from their student days through old age. The Glueck Study of Inner City Adolescent Boys followed a cohort born in the 1930s, while the Terman Study of Gifted Children examined both males and females starting in 1922. Vaillant continued to interview survivors of these three groups during their middle and older years, starting with the Grant sample in 1967, the Glueck men in 1970, and the surviving 90 women in the Terman study after 1987 (Vaillant, 1977, 1994, 2002). Important commonalities were identified across these diverse samples of men and women, despite their different childhood and family experiences and socioeconomic status during their youth and middle years. Vaillant concluded from these studies that:

- personality and coping strategies in youth and during college years predict adaptive ability in old age if the person does not have a psychological disorder
- childhood social class and parental problems had little impact on outcomes during these participants' old age
- self-confidence evolves with age

Vaillant observed that those who had aged "positively" shared the quality of resilience, which he defined as adaptability and taking life in stride. This trait was expressed by one of the Grant study subjects whose closest friends and relatives had died: "Life is like a book filled with many chapters. When one chapter is finished, you must go on to the next chapter" (Vaillant, 2002, p. 9). Based on his analysis of the early childhood and young adulthood experiences of surviving elders, Vaillant summarized qualities that predicted positive aging:

1. long-term "healing relationships" in which elders help others and accept help from close friends and family members
2. a supportive marriage or long-term partnership
3. continued involvement with life, making new friends to replace those lost through death or relocation, as well as the ability to accept the inevitability of death
4. mature defense mechanisms and active coping responses rather than passive acceptance when faced with crises in health and interpersonal relations (Vaillant, 2002)

Other researchers emphasize that a sense of purpose, meaning, or contribution to society is a critical element of successful aging. This sense of purpose is more than reflection, acceptance, and ego integrity (as Erikson describes in his eighth stage of adult development). It requires that older persons continue giving back to society, often through volunteering, which is the hallmark of the seventh stage—generativity. For example, participants in the Foster Grandparents Program believe they have achieved higher-order needs (such as helping children), are making a difference in others' lives, and that their lives have a purpose. These are elements of both generativity and ego integrity, and support the importance of both types of developmental tasks for successful aging. As discussed in Chapter 12, older adults who volunteer generally experience greater life satisfaction than their peers who do not, a pattern that underlies the current emphasis on civic engagement (Hudson, 2006). Even elders who do not volunteer but maintain social ties can increase their chances of life satisfaction in old age. In a study of community-dwelling older adults, greater activity levels, resilience, and the number of close friends were all associated with subjective reports of successful aging, but having multiple chronic illnesses or a disability was not (Montross et al., 2006).

A Critique of the Successful Aging Paradigm

One of the challenges in research on successful aging is the wide variation in defining and measuring successful aging, with one critical review noting 29 different definitions of successful aging, several of which include disability and mental disorders (Depp & Jeste, 2006). The concept of successful aging has also been widely critiqued for conveying a white, middle-aged, middle-class norm of remaining active as a way to show that one is an exception to their age peers—that is, "not really old, not aging."

The unspecified but clearly preferred method of successful aging is, by most accounts, not to age at all, or at least to minimize the extent to which it is apparent that one is ageing, both internally and externally. (Andrews, 1999, p. 305)

Since normal physical decrements do occur with age, an implicit message of successful aging is to develop strategies (or "lifestyle industries") to preserve "youthfulness" in order not to be seen as old. The focus on physical and mental activity is reinforced by mass marketing and advertising of exceptionally fit and physically attractive older adults who have the resources to slow decline (Hendricks & Hatch, 2006; Katz, 2000; McHugh, 2000). In such instances, successful aging assumes that everyone has autonomy and lifestyle options. But such opportunities across the life course may not be available to low-income and historically underserved elders who lack the resources or supports to engage in the lifestyle associated with successful aging. Instead, assumptions about appropriate lifestyles for happiness and successful aging are often class-based and may unintentionally overlook or blame older adults who have not had such lifestyle and genetic advantages (Wray, 2003). The concept of successful aging also minimizes the extent to which physical and social environments are structured to limit choices to engage in an active lifestyle (Hendricks & Hatch, 2006; Holstein & Minkler, 2003). Admonitions to choose healthy lifestyles do not generally resonate with low-income elders who are preoccupied with having enough to eat (Grzywacz & Marks, 2001). Based on these concerns, the MacArthur Studies researchers later emphasized the importance of structural factors and altering policies (e.g., funding prevention under Medicare) and environments (e.g., free public exercise areas) to increase opportunities to age successfully (Hendricks & Hatch, 2006; Kahn, 2003).

Another limitation of the successful aging model is its emphasis on activity and productivity characteristics of mainstream Western culture. This overlooks elders—often from other cultures—who are contemplative and engage in spiritual activities

and may experience a high degree of subjective well-being. Others have questioned the assumption that health is a necessary component of successful aging, because many older adults with chronic illness remain productive (Zarit, 2009). Similarly, some studies suggest that cognitive and emotional health are more important components of successful aging than physical well-being (Depp et al., 2007). A narrow definition of successful aging can also be stigmatizing to older adults with chronic illnesses who develop strategies to compensate for their functional disabilities and are able to experience a high level of a subjective well-being or quality of life even though they do not fit "successful aging" in terms of Rowe and Kahn's criteria (Minkler & Fadem, 2002; Moody, 2005). Instead, the focus might be on how to create conditions that allow elders to enjoy a good quality of life even if they have a chronic illness (Zarit, 2009). In effect, the concept of successful aging is an ambiguous and controversial one. As such, it raises questions about whose standards define "success," and overlooks the fact that older adults may perceive their quality of life to be high, even though they would not be classified as such by the theoretical models of successful aging (George, 2006). Indeed, in a study of 867 community-dwelling elders, 50.3 percent rated themselves as aging successfully, but when objectively assessed with Rowe and Kahn's three criteria, only 18.8 percent were classified in this manner (Strawbridge, Wallhagen, & Cohen, 2002). Similarly, a study of low-income older women found that they developed strategies to remain involved in personally meaningful activities and to experience quality of life even though their lives did not fit the prevailing models of successful aging (Wray, 2003).

It is important to note that "success" in the Rowe and Kahn model should not be viewed as a dichotomous state, but rather a continuous variable where elders may be more successful in one of the three criteria than in others and still be viewed as having aged well (Kahn, 2003). Nevertheless, because of some of the class, race, and gender biases implicit in successful aging and the role of social and economic structures in limiting opportunities for successful aging, the concept of active aging or resilience may be more applicable to historically underserved populations that display remarkable strengths despite adversities in their lives. Their strengths may derive from internal resources (e.g., spirituality, religiosity, self-concept, and sense of mastery) and from social and cultural resources (e.g., social supports, community resources, and cultural values). Resilience was described earlier in our review of longitudinal studies of personality and adaptability across the life course (Vaillant, 2002) and is discussed in Chapters 14 and 15 in the context of aging among elders of color and women.

Mental Disorders Among Older Persons

As shown in Chapter 5 and in the earlier sections of this chapter, normal psychological development with aging includes some changes in cognitive processes as well as maturation of coping responses, stability in personality traits, and a natural progression through different stages of personality development. The majority of older adults experience such changes without major disruptions in their behavior or mental health. In fact, older adults have a lower prevalence of mental disorders than do young and middle-aged adults, and most of these are chronic and recurring conditions across the life course—not due to aging (Zarit, 2009). However, some older people experience more severe problems in cognitive function, coping ability, emotional stability, or interpersonal behavior. In such instances of psychiatric or mental disorders, the individual's interpersonal and self-care behaviors are impaired and often result in feelings of distress and loss of autonomy. These conditions are not unique to older adults and are found across the life course. However, they may be more difficult to diagnose among older people due to comorbidities such as chronic systemic diseases and impaired sensory

function. The major forms of mental disorders in older adults include mood disorders, particularly depression; anxiety disorders (including phobias and panic disorders); schizophrenia; and substance abuse.

Depression, one of the primary mood disorders of old age, often coexists with other diseases, and accounts for a significant number of suicides, especially among older men. Anxiety, paranoid disorders, and schizophrenia are conditions that are typically first diagnosed in youth or middle age. Alcoholism and drug abuse is less common in older individuals, although their effect on older people's physical health and cognitive functioning is more detrimental than on younger persons. Alzheimer's disease and other dementias are cognitive disorders that are more likely to affect the oldest-old. Each of these conditions is reviewed in the following sections.

The prevalence of mental disorders among older persons who are living in the community ranges from 15 to 25 percent, depending on the population studied and the categories of disorders examined. Although the rates among community-dwelling elders are generally lower than other adult groups, higher rates are found in long-term care settings, with estimates of 10 to 40 percent of older residents who have mild-to-moderate impairments, and an additional 5 to 10 percent with significant disorders. Twenty percent of all first admissions to psychiatric hospitals are persons over age 65. Older psychiatric patients are more likely to have chronic conditions and to require longer periods of inpatient treatment than are younger patients, as evidenced by the fact that 25 percent of all beds in these hospitals are occupied by older persons, even though older adults comprise just over 12 percent of the U.S. population. However, most older patients with chronic psychiatric conditions live in the community; fewer live in nursing homes or psychiatric institutions. Overall, less than 25 percent of older adults who need mental health services ever receive treatment, a pattern that is true across all service areas. Older patients comprise only 4 percent of outpatient clients of mental health centers, and less than 2 percent of those served by private practitioners. A major barrier to treatment is a shortage of geriatric mental health professionals and adequate reimbursement for mental health services (Gatz & Smyer, 2001; Kaskie & Estes, 2001; Rosen, 2006).

One problem with describing the prevalence of mental disorders of older people is the lack of criteria distinguishing conditions that emerge in old age from those that continue throughout adulthood. In fact, the major classification system for psychiatric disorders according to the *Diagnostic and Statistical Manual of Mental Disorders,* fourth edition with text revisions (*DSM-IV-TR* 2000) makes such a distinction only for dementias that begin in late life. No other mental disorders are differentiated for old age, although other diagnostic categories are described specifically for adulthood as separate from childhood or adolescence. The problem of inadequate criteria for late-life psychological disorders is compounded by the lack of age-appropriate psychological tests for diagnosing these conditions. However, an increasing number of tests are being developed, especially for diagnosing depression and dementia in older people. For example, it is recommended that screening instruments, such the Cornell Scale for Depression in Dementia (CSDD) or the Short Geriatric Depression Scale (GDS-15 item), be implemented every 6 months.

Depression

Depression, anxiety, and personality disorders, such as, paranoia are the three most prevalent forms of late-life mental disorders. Of these, **depression** is the most common. It is important to distinguish *unipolar* depression from *bipolar* disorders (that is, ranging from a depressed to a manic state), as well as from sadness, grief reactions, and other types of affective disorders. Most of the depressions of old age are unipolar; of these, most are *minor* or *reactive* depressions, which arise in response to a significant life event with which an individual

cannot cope. For example, physical illness and the loss of loved ones through death and relocation may trigger depressive reactions in older people.

Bipolar disorders are rare, with major depressive disorders more common. Psychiatric symptoms that persist beyond 6 months in older persons may indicate the development of a major depressive episode. The vegetative signs, suicidal thoughts, weight loss, and mood variations from morning to night that are observed in major depression are not found in minor depression. Studies of older individuals in community settings and in nursing homes suggest that the prevalence of major depression is generally lower than the rates of minor or reactive depression. **Dysthymic disorder** is a less acute type of

Untreated depression in older men is a risk factor for suicide.

depression but with symptoms that last longer than major depression.

Estimates of depression for community-dwelling elders are:

- 10–30 percent for minor depression
- 1–4 percent for major depression
- 2 percent for dysthymic disorder
- 0.1 percent for bipolar disorder (Blazer, 2002; Hybels & Blazer, 2003; Kessler, Berglund, Demler, Jin, et al., 2003; Zalaquett & Stens, 2006; Zarit, 2009)

Rates are even higher for older persons with serious chronic diseases (10 to 12 percent are estimated to have major depression, 10 to 43 percent display depressive symptoms) and those receiving home health care (13.5 percent are estimated to have major depression, 27.5 percent with significant symptoms). These higher rates may be attributable to factors such as social isolation and co-occurring medical conditions and disability. Depression in hospital patients and nursing home residents is often misdiagnosed. Rates for minor depression and dysthymia as high as 20 to 50 percent and for major depression of 6 to 24 percent have been found among nursing home residents. Rates of major depression among hospital inpatients range from 6 to 44 percent, depending on the individual's medical condition (Gellis, 2006; Gellis & McCracken, 2008; Harralson et al., 2002; Jones, Marcantonio, & Rabinowitz, 2003; Zarit, 2009). Moderate (30 percent) to high (96 percent) rates of depressive symptoms are found among persons with dementia. The occurrence of depression in persons with dementia is associated with increased general severity of cognitive deficits and risk of death (Armore, Tagariello, Laterza, & Savoia, 2007). Since symptoms of depression may overlap with those of dementia, detection and assessment can be challenging. In fact, some studies suggest that depression may be a predictor or risk factor for dementia (Gellis & McCracken, 2008).

Relatively slight variations by race and gender have been identified. Clinically relevant depressive symptoms are more common among women younger than 85 and among both men and women 85 and older (19 percent) compared with men and women ages 65 to 74 (10 percent and 16 percent, respectively) (Health and Retirement Study, 2008). These rates are about the same for whites and African Americans. However, depression is more likely to be undetected or misdiagnosed in elders of color, in part because of cultural barriers to diagnosis and treatment (Das, Olfson, McCurtis, & Weissman, 2006; Larson, Belue, Schlundt, & McClellan, 2006a; Lincoln, 2003). Asian American elders, for example, attach a strong stigma to mental illness, which can result in an underdiagnosis (Surgeon General, 2001). Rates of depression among Latinos tend to be higher than among whites, especially among Mexican Americans (25.6 percent). This is explained partially by the following sociodemographic and health-related correlates of depression: lack of insurance, financial strain, low locus of control regarding health, and co-occurrence of chronic health conditions and functional disability. In addition, cultural factors—such as immigrant status, recency of immigration, and low levels of acculturation—are all associated with increased risk of depressive symptomatology (Aranda, Lee, & Wilson, 2001; Mui & Kang, 2006). Health care providers need to recognize such risk factors and be sensitive to cultural variations in order to diagnose accurately and treat depression effectively. Despite these risk factors, differences by race or ethnicity in prevalence rates for depression are not statistically significant (Zalaquett & Stens, 2006; Zarit & McCracken, 2008).

As noted earlier in this chapter, most role *gains* (e.g., paid worker, driver, voter, partner, or parent) occur in the earlier years, whereas role *losses* may multiply in the later years. As we have seen, loss of social roles may be compounded by decrements in sensory abilities, physical strength, and health. These role losses often result in grief, which may be misdiagnosed as depression or may be discounted by health care providers as a normal part of old age. Although depression usually does not result from any one of these losses alone, the combination of several losses in close sequence may trigger a reactive depressive episode. This may be due to changes in the brain caused by multiple stressors that affect the production of mood-regulating chemicals. Physical limitations in performing activities of daily living may also trigger symptoms of depression, possibly because of pain and perceived discrimination among elders experiencing significant difficulties with ADLs (Gayman, Turner, & Cui, 2008). It appears that acute life events can lead to a recurrence of major depression, but do not necessarily trigger its initial onset. Instead, major depressive disorders are likely to have originated earlier in life (Kessler et al., 2003; Zarit, 2009). Older people with chronic illnesses such as stroke, cancer, diabetes, or chronic pain and those who do not have a supportive social network are at greatest risk. In addition, older persons who have experienced depression in the past are at greater risk for a recurrence than those whose first episode occurs in old age, especially if the depression is triggered by a major life event (Mitchell & Subramaniam, 2005; Zarit, 2009). Risk factors for depression in older adults include:

- female gender
- unmarried
- comorbidity (i.e., multiple chronic diseases)
- chronic financial strain/poverty
- family history of depressive illness
- lack of social support (Aranda et al., 2001; Zarit, 2009)

The *Diagnostic and Statistical Manual (DSM-IV-R)* of the American Psychiatric Association (2000) lists the following criteria for major depression:

1. depressed mood most of day, nearly every day
2. markedly diminished interest or pleasure in activities, apathy
3. significant weight loss or weight gain, or appetite change
4. sleep disturbance (insomnia or hypersomnia) nearly every day

5. agitation or lack of activity nearly every day
6. low energy level or fatigue nearly every day
7. self-blame, guilt, worthlessness
8. poor concentration, indecisiveness
9. recurrent thoughts of death, suicide

At least five of these symptoms are present during the same two-week period and represent a change from a previous function. Among these, number 1 or 2 on the list should be at least one of the symptoms.*

Below are some symptoms of depression that may be confused with normal aging and therefore be overlooked by health care providers:

- reports or evidence of sadness
- feelings of emptiness or detachment with no precipitating major life event, such as bereavement
- expressions of anxiety or panic for no apparent cause
- loss of interest in the environment
- neglect of self-care
- changes in eating and sleeping patterns

The depressed person may complain of vague aches and pains, either generally or in a specific part of the body. Occasional symptoms or symptoms associated with a specific medication, physical illness, or alcoholism need to be distinguished from the somatic complaints associated with depression. When multiple symptoms appear together and persist *for at least two weeks,* an elder and his or her family should suspect major depression, especially if an older person speaks frequently of death or suicide.

One obstacle to detecting depression in older people is that they may be more successful than their younger counterparts at masking or hiding symptoms. In fact, many cases of depression in older persons are not diagnosed because

---

*Reprinted with permission from the *Diagnostic and Statistical Manual of Mental Disorders*, Text Revision, Fourth Edition, (Copyright 2000). American Psychiatric Association.

the individual either does not express changes in mood or denies them in the clinical interview. A *masked depression* is one in which few mood changes are reported. Instead, the patient complains of a vague pain, bodily discomfort, and sleep disturbance; reports problems with memory; is apathetic; and withdraws from others. These symptoms may be mistaken for typical physical and functional health problems associated with aging, making it more difficult to diagnose the depression (Blazer, 2003; Dunlop et al., 2005). This is a common condition in current cohorts of elders, especially Asian immigrants, because many of them were raised in environments that discouraged open expression of feelings.

Health care professionals and family members must distinguish depression from medical conditions and changes due to normal aging or from grief. For example, an older woman with arthritis who complains of increasing pain may actually be seeking a reason for vague physical discomfort that is related to a depressive episode. People with masked depression are more likely to complain of problems with memory or problem solving. Their denial or masking of symptoms may lead the physician to assume that the individual is experiencing dementia, a condition that is generally irreversible. It is for this reason that depression in older persons is often labeled *pseudodementia*.

Because of such likelihood of denial, a physician's first goal with an older patient who has vague somatic and memory complaints should be to conduct a thorough physical exam and lab tests. This is important in order to determine if an individual is depressed or has a physical disorder or symptoms of dementia. Standardized rating scales for assessing the presence and severity of depression, especially in long-term care settings, include the Geriatric Depression Scale (GDS), Beck Depression Inventory (BDI), the Hamilton Rating Scale for Depression (HAM-D), and the Cornell Scale for Depression in Dementia (CSDD). If the cognitive dysfunction is due to depression, it will improve when the depression is treated. On the other hand, some medical conditions may produce depressive symptoms. These include:

- Parkinson's disease
- rheumatoid arthritis
- thyroid dysfunction
- diseases of the adrenal glands

As noted earlier, depression can coexist with medical conditions such as heart disease, stroke, arthritis, cancer, diabetes, chronic lung disease, and Alzheimer's disease, compounding the dysfunction associated with these medical problems and delaying the recovery process. Certain medications may also lead to feelings of depression. In fact, any medication that has a depressant effect on the central nervous system can produce depressive symptoms, specifically lethargy and loss of interest in the environment. For these reasons, older adults with depressive symptoms should be examined thoroughly for underlying physical illness, hypothyroidism, vitamin deficiencies, chronic infections, and reactions to medications. Physicians must frequently conduct medication reviews to determine if their older patients begin to show side effects to a drug, even after using it for several months or years. Death rates are higher among older persons with a diagnosis of depression, almost twice that for nondepressed people within 1 year of diagnosis. Depressed older adults, especially if they have cognitive impairment, have a significantly higher mortality risk. The more severe a patient's depressive symptoms, the greater their risk of

---

MEDICATIONS THAT MAY PRODUCE SYMPTOMS OF DEPRESSION

- antihypertensives
- digoxin (used for some heart conditions)
- corticosteroids (used for preventing joint inflammation)
- estrogen
- some antipsychotic drugs
- anti-Parkinson's drugs such as L-dopa

premature death (Blazer, Hybels, & Pieper, 2001; Schulz et al., 2000; Unutzer et al., 2003). Medical hospital stays are often twice as long and health care costs in general are higher for those with depression. In addition, depressed older adults take longer to recover from a hip fracture or stroke, or from a cardiovascular disease episode (Ai & Carrigan, 2006; Chiles, Lambert, & Hatch, 1999). This may occur because older persons with depression are more apathetic, less motivated to improve their health, and more likely to entertain thoughts of suicide than younger depressives.

Late-life depression is costly not just for the individual's well-being, but it also exacts a large economic toll. The interaction of symptoms of depression with many somatic conditions results in more visits to primary care physicians and emergency rooms as well as longer hospital stays for older adults. Because elders with depression are most likely to be seen in these settings than in community mental health clinics, primary care physicians and emergency room personnel should be trained to detect signs of depression (Unutzer et al., 2003).

THERAPEUTIC INTERVENTIONS Consistent with the approach of person–environment fit, environmental and social interventions, as well as psychotherapy, are more effective than antidepressant medications for minor depression. However, medications and sometimes electroconvulsive therapy are necessary to treat major depression and prevent suicide, as described later in this chapter. It is important to treat both major and secondary depressions upon diagnosis, because the older depressed person is at higher risk of self-destructive behavior and suicide. Older adults are more likely to seek help for depressive symptoms from their family doctor than from mental health professionals. Primary care physicians who diagnose depression in an older person must provide psychological support for acute symptoms, including empathy, attentive listening, and encouragement of active coping skills and problem solving. For patients with minor depression, this may help to decrease

symptoms. For more severely depressed elders, alternative therapies may be required, as described below. There is some disagreement, however, about the efficacy of such therapies. Although short-term improvements may be achieved through treatment, the long-range prognosis is not always successful, and some older people will experience a relapse (Mitchell & Subramaniam, 2005).

The most common therapeutic intervention with depressed older individuals is pharmacological (*pharmacotherapy* or use of medications to treat the condition), which is particularly useful for those experiencing a major depression or bipolar depression (Frazer, Christensen, & Griffiths, 2005; Wilson et al., 2004). Among community-dwelling older adults, antidepressant use increased from 9 percent in 1997 to 13 percent in 2002 (Stagnitti, 2005). Therapy with antidepressants is generally long-term because the higher doses used during the acute episode must be followed by a maintenance dose in order to reduce the risk of relapse. Although antidepressants work well for some older persons, many cannot use these drugs because of other medications they are taking, such as antihypertensives, or because the side effects are more detrimental than the depression itself. These effects include postural hypotension (i.e., a sudden drop in blood pressure when rising from a prone position), increased vulnerability to falls and fractures, cardiac arrhythmias, urinary retention, constipation, disorientation, skin rash, and dry mouth (Ensrud et al., 2003; Richards et al., 2007). Because of these potentially dangerous reactions, it is important to start antidepressant therapy at a much lower dose (perhaps 50 percent lower) in older than in younger patients and to monitor its effects regularly.

Many older persons who turn to their primary care provider for treatment often receive antidepressants as a first line of attack rather than psychotherapy. As many as 10 percent of older patients in primary care practices suffer from depression. However, these settings do not have the necessary experts or time to provide lengthy psychotherapy (Arean & Unutzer, 2003; Mojtabi & Olfson, 2004). One effective

COMBINED THERAPIES MAY BE MOST EFFECTIVE WITH OLDER ADULTS

In the 6 months since the death of his wife of 52 years, Mr. Simon has lost interest in all the activities that he and his wife enjoyed together. He has lost weight and sleeps irregularly. His complaints of poor memory and loss of energy have alarmed his adult children, who insisted he see his family physician. The doctor prescribed an antidepressant upon recognizing the symptoms of depression. However, Mr. Simon stopped taking these medications after 2 weeks because they made him feel dizzy and caused dry mouth. The physician spent time discussing the immediate benefits from medications, but also arranged for Mr. Simon to participate in one-on-one psychotherapy sessions with an expert in geriatric psychotherapy. After 2 months, Mr. Simon has already seen the benefits of combining these two therapies for his condition. He now attends a local senior center daily and has begun a regular exercise program of walking for one hour every day.

solution is *problem-solving therapy for primary care* (PST-PC), a psychotherapeutic intervention created specifically for primary care settings. It consists of four to eight sessions that can be administered by health care providers without mental health training. Older adults receiving PST-PC were compared with elders receiving usual forms of psychotherapy. Those treated with PST-PC had more depression-free days and better functioning at the 12-month follow-up; benefits of PST-PC were even greater for elders on antidepressant medications. At 24 months, the PST-PC and usual therapy groups did not differ on depression or functional health status scores, but the former experienced several more months of depression-free days, especially if they also took antidepressants. The number of sessions and participation/nonparticipation in a monthly group therapy session did not alter the benefit of PST-PC (Arean et al., 2008).

PST has also been tested with depressed elders in home care. Significant reductions in depression

scores were achieved three months and six months later when the therapy ended, compared with a usual care group. Quality of life and problem-solving skills also improved with PST (Gellis et al., 2007). Another experimental intervention testing treatment in primary care settings, the PROSPECT study (Prevention of Suicide in Primary Care Elderly Collaborative Trial) demonstrated that older adults who were treated by depression care managers had fewer depressive symptoms and greater remission rates at 4-, 8-, and 12-month follow-ups than did elders who received "usual care" from their primary care providers (Bruce et al., 2004; Alexopoulos et al., 2005).

A combination of well-monitored pharmacotherapy and counseling has been found to reduce symptoms in up to 80 percent of older adults with chronic depression, even in the oldest-old (Blazer, 2003; Gellis & McCracken, 2008). Older adults with clinically diagnosed major depression showed the least recurrence of symptoms if they were treated with an antidepressant and psychotherapy (35 percent recurrence) rather than medication alone (37 percent recurrence) or psychotherapy alone (68 percent recurrence). Recurrence was 2.4 times more likely among those given a placebo rather than an antidepressant (Reynolds et al., 2006). Therapy lasting at least one year has also been shown to stabilize bouts of mania and depression in adults with bipolar disorder. This suggests that patients with major depression can benefit from combined therapeutic interventions. Furthermore, older adults rate the combination of cognitive therapy (a form of psychotherapy) and antidepressants more acceptable for treating depression than either method alone. This may be because they recognize the benefits of antidepressants for providing quick relief of symptoms, combined with gaining skills via cognitive therapy to fight depression (Hanson & Scogin, 2008; Keller et al., 2000).

Older people are just as likely as younger persons to benefit from the insight and empathy provided by a therapist trained in geriatric psychotherapy. In particular, secondary depression responds well to supportive therapy that allows the patient to review and come to terms with the stresses of late life and reestablish control. Depressed elders appear to benefit from short-term, client-centered, problem-solving directive therapy more than from therapy that is nondirective or uses free association to uncover long-standing personality conflicts. **Reminiscence therapy** allows older people with depression to work through difficult memories and process their loss and grief, but requires more sessions than other forms of psychotherapy with a cognitive orientation (Bohlmeijer, Smit, & Cuijpers, 2003; Cully, LaVoie, & Gfeller, 2001; Zarit, 2009).

Cognitive-behavioral interventions (CBI) use active, time-limited approaches to change the thinking and behavior that affect depression, such as self-monitoring of moods and negative thoughts about oneself, and increased participation in pleasant events for depressed elders who are caring for a frail spouse or partner. CBI is more effective than pharmacotherapy only and other therapies such as reminiscence (Frazer, Christensen, & Griffiths, 2005; Zalaquett & Stens, 2006). *Problem-solving therapy,* which is one type of cognitive behavioral therapy, teaches patients effective techniques for coping with their concerns related to their depression, and has been found to be especially effective among men and women of color (Gellis & McCracken, 2008; Gellis, Mcginty, Horowitz et al., 2007). In a systematic testing of this approach in elders with minor depression or dysthymia, researchers combined problem-solving therapy with social and physical activities, and antidepressants as needed. Elders in the intervention, Program to Encourage Active, Rewarding Lives for Seniors (PEARLS), described in the following box, experienced a 50 percent reduction in depressive symptoms and better quality of life than those treated by more conventional methods (Ciechanowski et al., 2004). Despite these benefits of some forms of psychosocial treatment for older adults with depression, primary care physicians are more likely to prescribe antidepressants and less likely to refer elders for counseling. In many cases, they receive only limited

> ## EVIDENCE-BASED THERAPY FOR MINOR DEPRESSION
>
> The Program to Encourage Active, Rewarding Lives for Seniors (PEARLS) is an innovative and effective therapy for minor depression. It was developed by researchers at the University of Washington Health Promotion Center with funds from the CDC. It consists of eight in-home visits by a counselor over 8 months. Older adults diagnosed with *minor depression* (characterized by loss of interest, feelings of sadness, or hopelessness) are helped by this structured behavior therapy and positive event scheduling. Together with their counselors, PEARLS clients develop and evaluate solutions to their depression. This technique has been found to be effective in eliminating depression completely for about a third of elders and reduced depressive symptoms by half in another 43 percent. PEARLS also lowers hospitalization rates compared to a control group (http://apps.nccd.cdc.gov).

counseling sessions because of the cost; this is especially the case among older men, Latinos, and African Americans (Unutzer et al., 2003).

Because older adults with depression are more likely to be seen in hospital settings than community mental health centers, hospital-based interventions need to be developed. One such intervention—Improving Mood-Promoting Access to Collaborative Treatment for Late-Life Depression (IMPACT) in

> ## SUMMARY OF THERAPEUTIC INTERVENTIONS FOR OLDER ADULTS WITH DEPRESSION
>
> Pharmacotherapy (antidepressants)
>
> Electroconvulsive therapy
>
> Psychotherapy
> - supportive
> - directive
> - cognitive-behavioral
> - problem-solving
>
> Combination of therapies

Washington State—designed a model of care coordination for patients with concurrent depression and mental illness. A depression care manager (who is a psychologist, psychiatric nurse, or social worker) provides patient education in the hospital with follow-up, treatment support, and brief psychotherapy after discharge. In a randomized control of 400 providers and 1,802 patients, those receiving the IMPACT intervention showed a greater reduction in depression and more depression-free days than those receiving usual care. Re-engineering Systems for Primary Care Treatment (RESPECT) in Colorado uses a similar coordinated care intervention involving patient and provider education, and close collaboration with the primary care physician. Patients with the care coordination intervention showed significant improvements in depres- sion symptoms. Both care coordination models have been implemented in hospitals across the country (Capers, 2004).

As noted above, therapy must be accompanied by **pharmacotherapy** or electroconvulsive therapy for elders with major depression. Despite past controversy about its use, **electroconvulsive, or electroshock, therapy (ECT)** is sometimes used in cases of severe depression. Delivering a brief electric current to the brain can be a quick and effective method, even in patients age 80 and older, for treating major depression in patients who:

- have not responded to medications
- have a higher risk of suicide
- refuse to eat
- are severely agitated
- show vegetative symptoms
- express feelings of hopelessness, helplessness, or worthlessness
- have experienced delusions
- cannot tolerate or are unresponsive to medication

Unilateral nondominant hemisphere ECT is often preferred because it is capable of alleviating depression without impairing cognitive functioning.

In fact, for some older adults, ECT can improve cognitive dysfunction associated with the depression. However, older adults with a recent history of a myocardial infarct, irregular heartbeat, or other heart conditions must be treated with caution because ECT can place a significant load on the cardiovascular system. Maintenance treatment with ECT may be necessary for older depressed persons (as often as once a month). In some cases, antidepressants are used after a course of ECT to prevent relapse. ECT remains a major form of treatment for severe depression, but not as commonly used as pharmacotherapy (Bosboom & Deijen, 2006; Rapaport, Mamdani, & Herrman, 2006; van der Wurff et al., 2004).

Depression in Nursing Homes

The 2004 Nursing Home Survey revealed that psychiatric disorders are the second most prevalent diagnosis among nursing home residents, increasing from 18 percent in 1999 to 22 percent in 2004 (NCHS, 2009). Estimates for depression range from 6 percent to 24 percent for major depression, and 30–50 percent for dysthymia and minor depression (Blazer, 2002; Hyer et al, 2005). Antidepressant medications are the most common treatment; approximately 43 percent of residents in an average facility take antidepressants (American Society of Consulting Pharmacists, 2006). In general, depression is inadequately treated in nursing homes (Brown, Lapane & Luisi, 2002). However, an innovative psychotherapeutic approach – Behavioral Activities Intervention (BE-ACTIV) has demonstrated success with depressed nursing home residents. It includes weekly meetings between the depressed resident and a mental health consultant, training staff to work with depressed elders, increasing the number of pleasant events, and removing barriers to residents' activities. After completing 10 sessions, depression scores, positive affect, and observed activity levels improved significantly (Meeks, Looney, Van Haitsma & Teri, 2008).

Suicide Among Older People

Older people are at greater risk of suicide than any other age group, often because of depression. It has been estimated that 17 to 20 percent of all *completed* suicides occur in persons aged 65 and older. In 2003, the national rate was 11.0 suicides per 100,000 population. The rate increased from 13.5 per 100,000 for persons 65 and older to 18 per 100,000 among those over age 85 (CDC, 2006a, 2006b). The highest suicide rates are among white males age 85 and older. The prevalence of suicide in this group, 51.6 per 100,000, is more than:

- twice the rate for white men age 65 to 74 (23.1 per 100,000)
- 6 times the rate for white women age 85 and older
- 4.5 times the rate for African American men age 85 and older (Gellis & McCracken, 2008; Hoyert, Kung, & Smith, 2005).

Note that these statistics reflect direct or clearly identifiable suicides. There are probably a significant number of indirect suicides that appear to be accidents or natural deaths (e.g., starvation or gas poisoning), and cases where family members and physicians do not list suicide as the cause of death; therefore, these rates may underrepresent the actual incidence of suicides.

One explanation for the higher rates of suicide among older white males is that they generally experience the greatest incongruence between their ideal self-image (that of worker, decision maker, or holder of relatively high status) and the realities of advancing age. With age, the role of paid worker is generally lost, chronic illness may diminish one's sense of control, and an individual may feel a loss of status. Social isolation also appears to be a salient factor; suicide rates among older widowed men are more than five times greater than for married men, but no differences are found between married and widowed women. This is because older widowed Caucasian men

are most likely to lack strong social support networks. In contrast, African American, Latino, and Chinese men are less likely to commit suicide because of more extensive family support systems, spiritual beliefs, and the importance of religious institutions in their lives. In fact, suicide rates peak for African Americans in young adulthood, with a slight rise at ages 50 to 55, then decline significantly (Oquendo, 2001).

Suicide risk is greatest among white males who are widowed, age 85 and older, with recurrent major depression, and with chronic pain, cardiopulmonary diseases, and cancer who are socially isolated and sometimes abusing drugs and alcohol (Gellis & McCracken, 2008). However, contrary to popular belief, older suicide victims are no more likely than other older people to have been diagnosed with a terminal illness prior to the suicide (Joe, et al., 2006; Yin, 2006). There are fewer nonfatal suicide attempts in older men compared to their younger counterparts. That is, the rate of completed suicides is far greater among older men—one for every eight attempts, compared with one completed suicide for every 100 to 200 attempts by the young. This difference may be due to the use of more lethal methods of suicide, such as shotguns. Firearms were used in 73 percent of suicides committed by older adults, compared with 54 percent of suicides committed by

---

RISK FACTORS FOR SUICIDE IN OLDER ADULTS

- a serious physical illness with severe pain
- the sudden death of a loved one
- a major loss of autonomy
- financial instability
- statements that indicate frustration with life and a desire to end it
- a sudden decision to give away one's most important possessions
- a general loss of interest in one's social and physical environment
- isolation and a feeling of being cut off from others

15- to 24-year-olds (Anderson & Smith, 2003; CDC, 2006a).

Because attempts at suicide are likely to end in death for older white men, family members and health care providers need to be sensitive to clues of an impending suicide. Approximately 70 percent of older persons who commit suicide had seen a primary care physician in the preceding month, but their psychological disturbances had not been detected or were inadequately treated. In most cases, these older persons had not sought psychiatric care (NIMH, 2006). For these reasons, the Surgeon General in 1999 issued a "Call to Action to Prevent Suicide." This effort, aimed at mental health providers and the older population directly, focused on increasing awareness of depression, its symptoms, and potential outcomes. However, it is crucial for primary care physicians to recognize symptoms of depression in their older patients and know how to refer them to mental health professionals *before* the older person demonstrates suicidal intentions (Surgeon General, 1999). Unfortunately, this rarely happens because the average visit to a primary care physician is only 17 minutes, providing little time for elders to express their concerns about depression (Heisel & Duberstein, 2005).

Watching for subtle cues is also important, because older people are less likely to make threats or to announce their intentions to commit suicide than are young people. Clearly, not all older people displaying such symptoms will attempt suicide, but recognizing changes in an older family member's or client's behavior and moods can alleviate a potential disaster.

Anxiety

Anxiety disorders—another type of psychological disorder with no obvious physiologic cause—are almost as common in later life as depression, but have received comparatively little attention. About 10 to 15 percent of older adults are coping with at least one anxiety disorder, with 9 percent suffering from significant levels of anxiety. Generalized anxiety disorders and phobias account for most anxiety disorders in later life (Gellis & McCracken, 2008; Kessler et al., 2005; Zarit, 2009).

- phobias in 0.7 percent to 12.0 percent
- obsessive-compulsive disorder in 0.1 percent to 1.5 percent
- panic disorders in up to 0.3 percent of elders (Krasucki, Howard, & Mann, 1998)

Although more common than schizophrenia and paranoid disorders, anxiety disorders are not diagnosed as frequently in older populations as they are in the young. This may be because the older person develops more tolerance and better ability to manage stressful events. More likely, however, it may be that clinicians cannot diagnose anxiety disorders as accurately in older adults because they are often masked by physical health complaints, behavior changes such as aggression, other medical conditions such as dementia, or symptoms of depression (Gellis & McCracken, 2008).

Anxiety often coexists with depression. Up to 25 percent of older adults with anxiety also have major depression, with rates of anxiety increasing for elders with bipolar disorder (Gellis & McCracken, 2008). In one study of 182 older adults who had been diagnosed with depression, 35 percent had also been diagnosed with an anxiety disorder at some point in their lives. A significant proportion (23 percent) had a current diagnosis of panic disorder or specific phobias (Lenze et al., 2000). Anxiety more often precedes depression than vise versa. Comorbid anxiety in late life depression is of concern because of its association with poor treatment response, worsened medical conditions and rates of disability, suicidality, reduced social supports, and lower life satisfaction (Gellis & McCracken, 2008; Jeste, Hays, & Steffens, 2006; Lenze, et al., 2005).

Older adults tend to minimize or underreport anxiety symptoms. As with other mental health disorders that can be masked by physical symptoms or somatic symptoms with no medical cause, primary care providers must probe further when older patients complain of diffuse pain, fast or irregular heart rate, fatigue, sleep disturbance, and restlessness. Once anxiety is diagnosed, older people can benefit from cognitive-behavioral therapy, relaxation training, psychosocial support, and in some cases, pharmacotherapy. More older than younger adults take benzodiazepines for anxiety, but there are increased risks of accidents and negative side effects associated with this drug. Cognitive-behavioral therapy—such as problem-solving skills, behavioral activation, and memory aids that challenge the elder's dysfunctional beliefs and maladaptive behaviors—is found to be more effective in reducing anxiety symptoms than supportive counseling and medication (Barrowclough et al., 2001; Gellis 2006; Gellis & McCracken, 2008).

Paranoid Disorders and Schizophrenia

Paranoia, defined as an irrational suspiciousness of other people, takes several forms. It may result from:

- social isolation
- a sense of powerlessness
- progressive sensory decline
- problems with the normal "checks and balances" of daily life

Still other changes in the aging individual, such as memory loss, may result in paranoid reactions. Some suspicious attitudes of older persons, however, represent accurate readings of their experiences. For example, an older person's children may in fact be trying to institutionalize him or her in order to take over an estate; a nurse's aide may really be stealing from an older patient; and neighborhood children may be making fun of the older adult. It is therefore important to distinguish actual threats to the individual from unfounded suspicions. To the extent that the individual has some control over his or her environment, the older person's perception of a threatening situation is reduced. The diagnosis of paranoid disorders in older people is similar to that in younger patients; the symptoms should have a duration of at least one week, with no signs of schizophrenia, no prominent hallucinations, and no association with signs of dementia (APA, 2000).

As with depression, counseling can be useful for paranoid older persons. In particular, cognitive behavioral approaches, in which an individual focuses on changing negative, self-defeating beliefs or misconceptions, may be useful in treating paranoid older adults who often attribute causality to external factors (e.g., the belief that someone took their pocketbook, that they themselves did not misplace it). Therapy with paranoid older persons may be effective in redirecting beliefs about causality to the individuals themselves.

Schizophrenia is considerably less prevalent than depression or dementia in old age. It is highest among adults age 18 to 54, declining to an estimated 1 percent in people age 65 and older. Alternatively, about 13.6 percent of adults with schizophrenia are age 65 or older (Cohen, 2003; Gellis & McCracken, 2008). Most older persons with this condition were first diagnosed in adolescence or middle age and continue to display behavior symptomatic of schizophrenia. However, the severity of symptoms appears to decrease and to change with age. Older schizophrenics are less likely to manifest thought disorders, loss of emotional expression, and problems with learning and abstraction; and more likely than younger schizophrenics to experience cognitive decline, depression, and social isolation. They also require lower doses of antipsychotic medications to manage their symptoms (Harvey, 2005).

Schizophrenics of any age, but especially older patients, need monitoring of their medication regimens and structured living arrangements. This is because pharmacotherapy with antipsychotic medications is the most effective treatment for older schizophrenic patients. However, many are unable to manage their medications or choose to discontinue them because of adverse side effects. This often results in repeated hospitalizations and ER visits. Elders of color, especially those with limited English proficiency, have even more problems with medication adherence; as many as 60 percent do not adhere to their medication regimens (Gilmer et al., 2009). Many older schizophrenics have lost contact with family and lack a social support system. Although less is known about the effectiveness of psychosocial interventions, cognitive behavioral treatment, social skills training, combined skills training and health management interventions are found to reduce symptoms and depression and improve social functioning and independent living skills. Training in the use of public transportation and individual placement and support (IPS) are identified as effective in supporting paid and volunteer work among older veterans with schizophrenia. Overall, older adults with schizophrenia are able to learn to control symptoms, manage medications, and learn independent living skills (Gellis & McCracken, 2008; Patterson, et al., 2005; Van Citters, Pratt, Bartels, & Jeste, 2005).

Older Adults Who Are Chronically Mentally Ill

The plight of older persons who are chronically mentally ill has not been addressed widely by mental health providers and advocates. This population is defined as people who suffer mental or emotional disorders throughout life that impair their ADL performance, self-direction, interpersonal relations, social interactions, and learning. Many have been in and out of hospitals as their conditions have become exacerbated. They have survived major upheavals and social neglect in their lives under marginally functional conditions. About half have substance abuse problems (Drake et al., 2002). The social disruption and years of treatment with psychotropic drugs have taken their toll; many are physiologically old in their 50s and 60s.

Their average life expectancy is 25 years less than their healthy peers. The cause of death is often cardiovascular and other systemic diseases that are not treated in a timely manner; and poor compliance with treatment regimens for these chronic conditions (O'Connell, 2005). Obtaining medical care for purely physical symptoms may be difficult because health care providers may attribute these to the patient's psychiatric disorder. Health professionals in this situation need to perform a thorough exam to exclude conditions caused by the mental disorder or by aging per se, and to treat any systemic diseases that are diagnosed.

Dementia

Normal aging does not result in significant declines in intelligence, memory, and learning ability, as described in Chapter 5. Mild impairments do not necessarily signal a major loss, but often represent a mild form of memory dysfunction known as **mild cognitive impairment (MCI)**. Some people with MCI eventually develop dementia; the majority do not. Only in the case of the diseases known collectively as *the dementias* does cognitive function show marked deterioration. **Dementia** includes a variety of conditions that are caused by or associated with damage of brain tissue, resulting in impaired memory and at least one of the following abilities:

- producing coherent speech or understanding language
- recognizing or identifying objects
- executing and comprehending motor tasks
- thinking abstractly and performing executive functions (Alzheimer's Association, 2009)

In more advanced stages, behavior and personality are also impaired. Such changes in the brain result in progressive deterioration of an individual's ability to learn and recall items from the past. Previously, it was assumed that all these syndromes were associated with cerebral

---

DEMENTIA AS A WORLDWIDE EPIDEMIC

A 2009 report by Alzheimer's Disease International estimates a dementia prevalence rate of 35.6 million people worldwide, and projects the rate to nearly double every 20 years. Thus, 65.7 million elders with this condition are predicted by 2030, 115.4 million by 2050. They attribute much of this increase to improved recognition and diagnosis of dementia in low- and middle-income countries, as well as significant growth in their oldest old populations (200 percent between 1990 and 2020 vs. 68 percent in higher income countries). The prevalence of dementia is estimated to increase by 44 percent in Western Europe and 63 percent in North America between 2010 and 2030, compared with 114 percent in Southeast Asia and 125 percent in North Africa and the Middle East. This report raises concerns about the imperative for more gerontological health care providers with expertise in dementia in developing countries (Alzheimer's Disease International, 2009).

arteriosclerosis ("hardening of the arteries"). In fact, we now know that a number of these conditions occur independently of arteriosclerosis. Some features are unique to each type of dementia, but all dementias have the following characteristics:

- a change in an individual's ability to recall events in recent memory
- problems with comprehension, attention span, and judgment
- disorientation to time, place, and person

The individual with dementia may have problems in understanding abstract thought or symbolic language (e.g., be unable to interpret a proverb), particularly in the later stages of the disease. Although not part of normal aging, the likelihood of experiencing dementia does increase with advancing age. It is estimated that as many as 7 million Americans over age 85 have some type of dementia; almost 2 million have severe dementia, and up to 5 million are mildly to moderately

impaired. Based on the 1999–2001 National Health Interview Survey (NHIS) and the 2004 National Nursing Home Survey (NNHS), 1 percent of the population age 65 to 84 and 9 percent of those age 85 and older are estimated to have memory loss that can be categorized as dementia. These national surveys suggest that 2.3 million elders have problems with ADLs due to dementia. Rates are even higher in nursing home populations; according to the NNHS, almost 30 percent of residents age 65 to 74 and 45 percent of those age 85 and older have dementia (NCHS, 2009). Because of problems in differentially diagnosis and variations in the criteria used by available tests and classification systems, prevalence rates are only estimates. Nevertheless, there is general agreement among epidemiological studies that the incidence of dementias increases with age, especially between ages 75 and 90. For example, it is estimated that:

- 12 percent of the 75-to-79 age group have some dementia
- 54 percent of 85- to 89-year-olds have signs of dementia
- 84 percent of people over age 90 have some symptoms (Kukull et al., 2002)

However, as noted in Chapter 1, rates of dementia among "hardy" centenarians may actually be lower than among 85- to 90-year-olds because of genetic advantages experienced by those who live to age 100 and beyond. Recent data from the Health and Retirement Study identify a decline in the prevalence of dementia, from 12.2 percent of adults age 70 and older in 1993 to 8.7 percent in the 2002 survey (Langa et al., 2008). This large sample of more than 7,000 older adults representing diverse populations included more elders with a high school diploma and more with a college degree than the 1990 Health and Retirement Study. The researchers attribute these lower rates of dementia in the recent survey to the benefits of higher education levels. Higher education is associated with greater brain development and mental stimulation, better control of cardiovascular and cerebrovascular risk factors, and more access to health care.

ACTIVE AGING MAY WARD OFF DEMENTIA

Eighty-seven-year-old Mr. Lawton is a retired engineer who still skis in the winter and hikes in the summer with his dog. He continues to run a small business and maintains a healthy diet and average weight. The only medication he takes is baby aspirin to prevent a heart attack. He attributes his excellent cognitive skills and mental health to his work, volunteer activities, physically active lifestyle, and being responsible for a pet.

The major types of dementias are shown below. Note the distinction between *reversible* and *irreversible* dementias.

Reversible	Irreversible
Drugs	Alzheimer's
Alcohol	Vascular
Nutritional deficiencies	Lewy body
Normal pressure	Huntington's
hydrocephalus	Pick's disease
Brain tumors	Creutzfeldt-Jacob
Hypothyroidism	Kuru
Hyperthyroidism	Korsakoff
Neurosyphilis	
Depression (pseudodementia)	

The first category refers to cognitive decline that may be caused by drug toxicity, hormonal or nutritional disorders, and other diseases that may be reversible. Sources of potentially reversible dementias include tumors in and trauma to the brain, toxins, metabolic disorders such as hypothyroidism or hyperthyroidism, diabetes, hypocalcemia or hypercalcemia, infections, vascular lesions, and hydrocephalus. Severe depression may produce confusion and memory problems in some older people. Some medications may also cause dementia-like symptoms. This problem is aggravated if the individual is taking multiple medications or is on a dosage that is higher than can be metabolized by the older kidney or liver. An individual who appears to be suffering from such reactions should be referred promptly for medical screening.

Irreversible dementias are those that have no discernible environmental cause and cannot yet be cured. Although there is considerable research on the causes and treatments for these conditions, they must be labeled irreversible at the present time. Some of these are more common than others; some have identifiable causes, while others do not. Pick's disease is one of the rarest; in this type, the frontal and temporal lobes of the brain atrophy. Of all the dementias, it is most likely to occur in younger persons (age of onset is usually 40–50), and to result in significant personality changes. Creutzfeldt-Jacob and Kuru diseases have been traced to a slow-acting virus that can strike at any age. In the former type of dementia, decline in memory and coordination occurs quite rapidly, as seen in the epidemics of "mad cow disease" in the past 15 years that were attributed to consuming tainted beef in Great Britain, Europe, and the U.S. Kuru disease is quite rare. Huntington's disease is a genetically transmitted condition that usually appears in people in their 30s and 40s. It results in more neuromuscular changes than do the other dementias. Attention and judgment declines in the earlier stages, but memory remains intact until the later stages when dementia symptoms become more severe. Korsakoff syndrome is associated with long-term alcoholism and a deficiency of vitamin B_1. This form of dementia results in severe loss of memory.

Vascular dementia is the second most common form of irreversible dementias. In the past it was labeled "multi-infarct dementia." In this type, blood vessels leading to the brain become occluded, with the result that several areas of the brain show infarcts, or small strokes. The primary risk factor for vascular dementia is the same as for strokes—that is, hypertension. Because of this, vascular dementia may be prevented by controlling hypertension. Nevertheless, once it occurs, this type of dementia is irreversible. Recent research suggests that the onset of vascular dementia may be predicted by abnormal walking patterns or gaits. In fact, elders with one of three types of abnormal gaits were 3.5 times more likely to develop vascular dementia (but no other type of dementia) in one study. Older people who walked with their legs swinging outward in a semicircle, took short steps with minimal lifting of their feet, or had an unsteady, swaying gait and no physical condition that would have caused this problem were eventually found to have vascular dementia. These movement patterns may reflect changes in the brain that trigger this condition (Verghese et al., 2002). *Lewy body dementia* is often confused with Alzheimer's disease because of similar patterns of decline, including impaired memory and judgment. In later stages, behavior also changes. However, it differs from Alzheimer's in its greater fluctuations in cognitive symptoms and alertness. Neuromuscular changes such as muscle rigidity and tremors occur in those with Lewy body dementias, but not in Alzheimer's. Brain changes include distinctive protein deposits inside nerve cells, known as Lewy bodies.

Delirium

Delirium is a reversible dementia that has a more rapid onset than other types of dementia. Signs of delirium are:

- abrupt changes in behavior
- fluctuations in behavior throughout the day
- worse symptoms at night and when first awake
- inability to focus attention on a task
- problems with short-term memory
- hallucinations
- speech that makes no sense or is irrational
- disturbance in sleep patterns

Delirium is usually caused by some external variables such as a reaction to an injury (especially head injury) or infection, malnutrition, reaction to alcohol or prescription medications, high fever, or even a fecal impaction or urinary problems. Up to 50 percent of older adults show symptoms of delirium after major surgery, possibly due to general anesthesia. A thorough medical assessment can help diagnose and reverse delirium and its symptoms by determining its causes. The condition generally resolves within 2 weeks, but those who take longer than 2 weeks and never return to pre-delirium functioning are elders who had more cognitive impairment, more comorbid conditions, and lower functional ability before the onset of delirium (Kiely et al., 2006; Speciale et al., 2007).

Alzheimer's Disease

Alzheimer's disease (AD) is the most common irreversible dementia in late life, accounting for 60 to 80 percent of all dementias. Prevalence rates are difficult to obtain, but it is estimated that about 5.3 million Americans, or 14 percent of all persons age 65 and over and 29 percent of those age 85 and older, have clinical symptoms of AD (Alzheimer's Association, 2009; Hebert et al., 2003). With the increased survival of older adults beyond age 85, it is estimated that as many as 11 to 16 million Americans will be diagnosed with AD by 2050. Although the prevalence rates may decline, as noted above from the Health and Retirement Study, the sheer increase in the population age 65 and over accounts for this increase in the U.S. and for most regions of the world. For example, in China and India, the *number* of elders with dementia is expected to double between 2005 and 2025, and to triple by 2050 (Alzheimer's Disease International, 2006). The dramatic rise in projected rates of AD underlies much of the research focus on the causes of and therapies for AD. This may also explain why the general public is more aware of Alzheimer's disease, its signs and symptoms, but knows very little about other irreversible dementias. Although most surveys have found awareness among the public about this specific form of dementia, there is limited information about progress in Alzheimer's disease research and current treatments (Anderson, Day, Beard, Reed & Wu, 2009).

Although a distinction was made in the past between pre-senile (i.e., before age 65) and senile dementia, there is now agreement that these are the same disease. Researchers do, however, make a distinction between the more common, late-onset form of AD and a rarer, early-onset form that appears in multiple generations of the same family, usually when the individual is in middle age (40s, even 30s). This is known as "familial AD." The rate of decline for those who are diagnosed with early-onset AD is faster and their lives often more severely affected than for the late-onset form, but it represents a very small proportion of all AD cases.

POTENTIAL CAUSES OF AND RISK FACTORS FOR ALZHEIMER'S DISEASE AND OTHER DEMENTIAS   Several hypotheses are proposed to explain the causes of Alzheimer's disease. Case control studies that

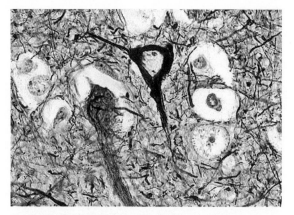

The dark patches in this brain section are neuritic plaques with a core of amyloid protein, characteristic of Alzheimer's disease.

focused on the incidence or development of AD have not found support for environmental hypotheses, such as a previous head injury, thyroid disease, exposure to therapeutic radiation, anesthesia, or the accumulation of metals such as aluminum in the brain.

Researchers have examined the impact of activity patterns during ages 20 to 60 among 193 older persons with AD and 358 healthy controls in their 60s and 70s. These activities included nonoccupational pastimes that could be classified as intellectual, physical, or passive. Elders with no signs of dementia had participated in more intellectual and physical recreational activities during their middle years than did those with AD. The greatest effect was for intellectual pastimes such as learning a new language, taking challenging courses, or learning a new activity; the more such activities an individual participated in, the lower the probability of AD. This was true regardless of educational level, gender, and current age. Although the findings must be interpreted with some caution, the dramatic differences observed suggest that participation in intellectual activities may have a protective effect against AD (Friedland et al., 2000).

Another research group tracked the physical activity levels of 1,740 older adults for 6 years who had no signs of dementia at the start of the

---

ALZHEIMER'S DISEASE VERSUS NORMAL CHANGES IN MEMORY

Many people in middle and old age become alarmed that they may have Alzheimer's disease at the first signs of forgetting. Here are some distinctions between *normal*, age-related changes in memory (as described in Chapter 5) and AD:

Normal Aging
- Forgetting to set the alarm clock
- Forgetting someone's name and remembering it later
- Forgetting where you left your keys and finding them after searching
- Having to retrace steps to remember a task
- Forgetting where you parked your car

Possible AD
- Forgetting *how* to set the alarm clock
- Forgetting a name and never remembering it, even when told
- Forgetting places where you might find your keys
- Forgetting how you came to be at a particular location
- Forgetting that you drove and parked car

THE EXPERIENCE OF DEMENTIA

Thomas DeBaggio, a writer, describes what it feels like to experience Alzheimer's disease firsthand:

> I thought I was breaking into pieces. Shards of memory kept disappearing. When, after the tests, the doctor told me I had Alzheimer's disease, the statement exploded in my head. There was no cure, only the hope that my brain's eager course of self-destruction could be slowed for awhile.... Now writing is like walking through a dark room. Sometimes I have to get down on my knees and crawl. Words slice through my mind so fast that I cannot catch them. I will soon be stripped of language and memory. I am on the cusp of a new world, a place I will be unable to describe. It is the last hidden place, and marked with a headstone (DeBaggio, 2002)

A daughter writes about her father's experiences with dementia:

> His memory is blank; words float by him in a soup. He can't button a shirt or negotiate a toilet. Yet when I look at him—at his body, his face—I see ... him. Warm, enraged, rejecting, beseeching, profane, silly; much of his mind is gone, but his self is still there.... There may be no drug (yet) to cure Alzheimer's but relationships are always possible, as long as the person of sounder mind holds up his or her end (Levine, 2004).

study. During this period, almost 10 percent began to show symptoms of dementia. The incidence rate of dementia for people who exercised three or more times per week (including walking, swimming, weight training, and stretching) was 13.0 per 1,000 person–years, compared with 19.7 per 1,000 person–years among elders who developed dementia. The researchers suggest that regular exercise may delay or prevent dementia by stimulating blood flow to the brain (Larson et al., 2006b). These findings are consistent with earlier studies that found that regular exercise can decrease the risk for AD

(50 percent) and any dementia (36 percent), and more varied physical activities further reduce the risk (Laurin et al., 2001; Podewils et al., 2005). This same longitudinal study also found that participants with poor physical functioning (poor standing balance, slower walking speed, and weak handgrip) were three times more likely to develop dementia, including Alzheimer's disease, than elders with good physical functioning. Regular physical activity can improve these functions. Walking speed may also be a good predictor of cognitive decline. In a study of over 3,000 elders, volunteers were asked to walk at their usual pace and at a rapid pace. Cognitive functioning scores were worst among elders in the lowest quartile of rapid-paced walking. They were twice as likely to have a poor score on the cognitive test as elders who were in the fastest quartile of rapid-paced walking. Those whose usual-paced walking was in the lowest quartile scored somewhat lower, but the differences were less dramatic (Fitzpatrick et al., 2007; Larson et al., 2006b). A unique opportunity to test the impact of physical activity at midlife and its association with dementia 3 decades later was presented by the Swedish Twin Registry. This population-based study has tracked health and activity levels for numerous cohorts of twins since 1967. A comparison of participants over age 70 with and without dementia 30 years later revealed that light exercise and participation in sports during middle age were associated with significantly lower rates of dementia in old age (Andel et al., 2008).

The Nun Study offers insights into the association between education, lifestyle, and cognitive and physical aging without the bias of socioeconomic status, diet, and health care that is a problem with many other studies of aging among the general population. The 678 members of the School Sisters of Notre Dame who participated in this longitudinal study, including the analysis of their brains at autopsy, shared an adulthood of identical lifestyles. Therefore, the differences seen among the nuns are attributable primarily to their educational levels and intellectual and physical activities throughout their lives. By analyzing the autobiographies these nuns had written at age 22, researchers found an association between linguistic skills in youth and the risk of dementia 50 to 70 years later. Greater atrophy and more plaques and tangles were found in the brains of women whose writings during their youth had fewer complex ideas, a simpler vocabulary, and lower "idea density" (Riley et al., 2005; Snowdon, Greiner, & Markesbery, 2000). The emotional content of these early autobiographies was also examined for their positive, negative, or neutral tone. By adjusting statistically for age and education, the researchers found a significant link between positive emotions and mortality; those in the highest quartile of positive emotional content in their early writings decreased their risk of death in old age by a factor of 2.5 compared with nuns whose writings lacked much positive expression. This may be because positive emotions triggered a lifetime of positive behaviors in the survivors. In addition, early samples of written language appear to be better than oral samples at distinguishing between high and low functioning (Danner, Snowdon, & Friesen, 2001; Mitzner & Kemper, 2003). The Nun Study also demonstrated that clinical manifestations of dementia may not always parallel the neuropathological changes experienced in these conditions. That is, many of the nuns at autopsy had the hallmarks of advanced dementia in their brain samples (e.g., neurofibrillary tangles in the neocortex), but they did not demonstrate any clinical symptoms of dementia before their death (e.g., disorientation to time, place, person) (Snowdon, 2001, 2003).

Physical health may also be related to AD. A recent study points to obesity as a risk factor for AD in women but not in men. Women who were overweight at age 70, 75, and 79 were more likely to develop dementia by age 88. The researchers suggest that being overweight may raise blood pressure and restrict blood flow to the brain, thereby indirectly increasing women's risk for AD, although a parallel effect was not observed in men (Gustafson et al., 2004). Experiencing a stroke may also increase an elder's risk for AD, and having a stroke during the course of AD can

accelerate the decline of cognitive function in AD patients (DeCarli, 2006). There is some evidence that a severe head injury during one's younger years (resulting in unconsciousness lasting more than 24 hours) can increase the risk of AD in old age. A study of more than 2000 veterans of World War II with documented head injuries revealed a four times greater likelihood of AD in severe head injury victims, and twice the risk in victims of a moderate head injury (Plassman et al., 2000).

Lack of estrogen is another potential risk factor that has drawn research interest. As estrogen secretion declines with aging, proteins associated with neuronal growth decrease, resulting in the synaptic impairments typical of AD. However, estrogen replacement therapy (ERT) does not appear to be an effective treatment or preventive mechanism against AD. The Women's Health Initiative Memory Study (ancillary to the WHI Study described in Chapter 4) found that, among more than 4,500 women who were placed on a combination of estrogen and progestin or a placebo for 5 years, there was no difference in the rates of developing mild cognitive impairment. In fact, twice as many women using the combination hormone developed dementia—40 versus 21—in this large sample (Shumaker et al., 2003).

The brains of AD patients experience a reduction in the number of cholinergic nerve cells (up to 80 percent loss in some key areas). These brain cells are important for learning and memory because they release an important chemical "messenger," *acetylcholine*, that transfers information from one cell to another (i.e., neurotransmitters). Their loss reduces the acetylcholine available for this important function. The noradrenergic system is another chemical messenger system that becomes impaired with AD, further complicating our understanding of why and how these neurochemical systems appear to break down in this disease.

Still another neurochemical change observed in Alzheimer's brains is the accumulation of *amyloid*, a protein. It appears that there may be a genetic defect in one of the normal proteins located in brain regions responsible for memory, emotions, and thinking. Amyloid is actually a group of proteins found in the neurofibrillary tangles that characterize an Alzheimer's brain. The precursor protein to amyloid, *beta-amyloid*, is coded by a gene located in chromosome 21, which is also the chromosome responsible for Down syndrome. This may explain why AD appears with greater frequency in families with a member who has Down syndrome. Deposits of amyloid or its precursor beta-amyloid have been found in the brains of Down patients as young as age 8 and in those who die later with AD. Beta-amyloid may be responsible for the death of brain cells in these patients. In fact, many Down patients have the characteristic brain changes of AD, but not the clinical symptoms. As with other changes observed in the brains of AD patients, it is not yet clear whether these beta-amyloid deposits are the *cause* of AD or secondary to other structural or biochemical changes (Mrak & Griffin, 2004).

Genes on at least four different chromosomes may be involved in the development of AD. In addition to mutations of the gene-encoding amyloid precursor protein on chromosome 21, presenilin 1 on chromosome 14, presenilin 2 on chromosome 1, and the apolipoprotein E gene on chromosome 19 have been implicated in this disease. While the mutations on chromosomes 1, 14, and 21 are associated with familial or early-onset AD, the more common late-onset form of AD appears to be linked to a genetic mutation on chromosome 19. Subsequent researchers have focused on a protein called *apolipoprotein,* or *APOE,* on this chromosome. APOE is responsible for transporting cholesterol in the blood and beta-amyloid in the brain. There are three genes associated with APOE: E2, E3, E4. The risk for Alzheimer's disease is associated with the E4 gene; people who inherit this gene from one parent have three times the risk of developing AD, and those who inherit one from each parent have eight times the risk (Olichney, 1997).

Characteristics of Alzheimer's Disease

Alzheimer's disease is characterized by deficits in attention, learning, memory, language skills, and—in some instances—problems in judgment, abstraction, and orientation. Early stages are marked by difficulty in remembering new information, confusion, problems in expressing themselves, and thinking clearly. Disorientation to time, place, and person occurs in the intermediate stages of AD. These changes in cognitive function appear to be related to structural changes in the brain. They include:

- a premature loss of nerve cells in some areas of the brain
- a loss of synapses
- deterioration of the free radical metabolism process described in Chapter 3
- impaired neurotransmitter function such as the cholinergic system, resulting in plaques and tangles throughout these areas

The *hippocampus* is a region in the limbic system deep inside the brain that is involved in learning new information and retrieving old information (see Chapter 5). It is one of the first regions where plaques and tangles occur, so it is not surprising that patients in the earlier stages of the disease often have difficulties with verbal memory, attention span, and orientation to the environment, as well as increased anxiety, restlessness, and unpredictable changes in mood. Researchers examined the volume of the hippocampus and severity of neurofibrillary tangles at autopsy of 56 women in the Nun Study. Those with the greatest hippocampal atrophy and the most tangles had performed worse on a test of delayed verbal recall 1 year before death (Mortimer et al., 2004). Family members may complain about personality changes such as the older person becoming more aggressive or, in some cases, more passive than in the past. Depression may set in as the individual realizes that he or she is experiencing these problems. In the more advanced stages of the disease, as it spreads to the *neocortex,* which controls higher-level brain functions and links new stimuli with information stored in the brain, the elder may experience problems recalling appropriate words and labels, perseveration (i.e., continually repeating the same phrase and thoughts), apathy, and problems with comprehension. Alzheimer's victims at this stage may not recognize their partners, children, and long-time friends. However, some patients in the intermediate stages of AD may describe quite articulately and vividly events that took place many years ago. In the advanced phases, as the neurons in the motor cortex die, the patient may need assistance with bodily functions such as eating and toileting. At autopsy, there is a generalized deterioration of cortical tissue, which appears to be tangled and covered with plaque. These plaques and tangles appear first in a region near the base of the skull (entorhinal cortex), and move higher and deeper to the hippocampus and eventually to the neocortex as the disease advances (Snowdon, 2001).

DESCRIBING STAGES OF ALZHEIMER'S DISEASE   There have been some attempts to determine if AD proceeds through a series of stages, such that symptoms become more prevalent and severe over time. This is a difficult task, because the course of AD varies so widely. Some patients may experience a rapid decline in memory, while their orientation to time, place, and people may remain relatively intact. Other patients may experience mood and personality changes early, whereas still others maintain their pre-morbid personality for many years after the symptoms first appear.

A broad distinction is often made among early, middle, and advanced stages of AD. These categories are based on the patient's levels of decline in memory, orientation, and activities of daily living. Frequently used assessment tools, such as, the Mini-Mental Status Exam (MMSE) and the Dementia Rating Scale (DRS) can help in categorizing levels of decline, although they contain an education/language bias (Brodaty, Withall, Altendorf, & Sachdev, 2007; Folstein, Folstein, & McHugh, 1975; Mattis, 1976). These give clues to the patients' levels of deterioration on the basis of their test scores, but are too long to be administered in primary care settings. The Mini-Cog (Borson et al., 2000) can be administered in under

GLOBAL DETERIORATION SCALE

Stage 1:   No cognitive or functional decrements

Stage 2:   Complaints of very mild forgetfulness and some work difficulties

Stage 3:   Mild cognitive impairment on cognitive battery; concentration problems; some difficulty at work and in traveling alone

Stage 4:   Late confusional stage; increased problems in planning, handling finances; increased denial of symptoms; withdrawal

Stage 5:   Poor recall of recent events; may need to be reminded about proper clothing and bathing

Stage 6:   More advanced memory orientation problems; need assistance with activities of daily living; more personality changes

Stage 7:   Late dementia with loss of verbal abilities; incontinence, loss of ability to walk; may become comatose

SOURCE: B. Reisberg, S. H. Ferris, M. J. De Leon, & T. Crook. (1982). The Global Deterioration Scale for assessment of primary degenerative dementia, *American Journal of Psychiatry* 139. 1136–1139. Copyright © 1982, American Psychiatric Association. Reprinted by permission.

five minutes and is often used in primary care settings. The widely used Global Deterioration Scale delineates seven stages of the disease, as shown in the box above (Agronin, 2008; Reisberg et al., 1982).

Because of attention on Alzheimer's disease by the media and by researchers, there is some tendency to overestimate its occurrence and to assume that it is the cause of all dementias. In many ways, it has replaced vascular dementia as a label given without a thorough diagnosis. The most confirmatory diagnosis of Alzheimer's disease today can still be made only at autopsy, when the areas and nature of damaged brain tissue can be identified. However, psychological measures of cognitive functioning such as the MMSE and DRS and a thorough physical exam can provide clues to its existence in the earlier stages. Or they may indicate that the observed changes in behavior

DIAGNOSING ALZHEIMER'S DISEASE

- a medical and nutritional history
- laboratory tests of blood, urine, and stool
- tests for thyroid function
- a thorough physical and psychological examination
- in some cases, a CT (computerized tomography) scan, a PET (positron emission tomography) scan, or MRI (magnetic resonance imaging) in order to detect any tumors, strokes, blood clots, or hydrocephalus, and to test the response of specific areas of the brain

and/or personality are due to a reversible condition. Early diagnosis can be made with some certainty after an extensive patient workup. In fact, it is primarily through a process of elimination of other conditions that some dementias such as AD may be diagnosed. In such diagnoses, it is particularly important to rule out depression, prolonged grief, drug toxicity, and nutritional deficiencies because, as stated earlier, these conditions may be reversed. Recent findings using protein biomarkers in cerebrospinal fluid show that these new techniques may be useful in diagnosing and distinguishing between Alzheimer's, Parkinson's, and Lewy body dementia (Zhang, Goodlett, & Montine, 2005).

THERAPY FOR PATIENTS WITH ALZHEIMER'S DISEASE
Unfortunately, no completely successful treatment for AD is yet available. If the evidence for high levels of certain abnormal proteins in Alzheimer's brains proves correct, future treatment might involve the use of drugs that interrupt the production of those proteins and their precursors so they cannot accumulate in brain tissue. Some researchers have focused on a nerve growth factor, a naturally occurring protein that replenishes and maintains the health of nerve cells. Animal studies show remarkable success in repairing damaged brain cells.

Currently, only a few drugs are approved for treating AD. Other medications in the testing

phase include some drugs that restore the activity of neurotransmitters in the brain and some that even replace lost neurochemicals. In the last several years, one drug has been found to slow the decline of memory loss by about 5 percent in the early-to-moderate stages of AD. This medication, donepezil (marketed as Aricept), is a cholinesterase inhibitor and slows the loss of acetylcholine in the brains of AD patients. More recently, two other cholinesterase inhibitors, rivastigmine (marketed as Exelon) and galantamine (Razadyne), were approved for use in AD. These drugs also prevent the breakdown of acetylcholine and slow the decline in cognitive ability, ADLs, and normal behavior; some studies have found modest improvements for up to 36 months (Feldman, 2002; Raskind et al., 2004; Seltzer, 2006). Another drug used to manage symptoms of AD is memantine (Namenda). This drug is designed to treat patients in the moderate-to-severe stages of AD. It works by lowering levels of the neurotransmitter glutamate, which can damage neurons at high levels (Reisberg et al., 2003; Tariot et al., 2004). However, none of these drugs reverses the destruction of brain tissue by plaques and tangles. They must be used with caution, or avoided altogether, in patients with liver disease, peptic ulcers, severe COPD, and bradycardia.

Some researchers are exploring the possibility that AD may be related to inflammation of brain tissue. This has led to the hypothesis that nonsteroidal anti-inflammatory drugs (NSAIDs), such as ibuprofen, can prevent or delay the onset of AD. Although many older people currently use low doses of NSAIDs to prevent heart attacks, few controlled clinical trials have tested whether NSAIDs have similar benefits for AD. A review of studies that followed NSAID users found that regular use for 2 or more years reduces the risk of AD by 40 to 50 percent (Szekely et al., 2004). Animal studies demonstrate that a daily dose of ibuprofen reduced inflammation in the brain, and resulted in about half the number of plaques and half the amyloid deposits as in the mice that were not given NSAIDs (Lim et al., 2000). The drug may act as a preventive by improving the production of chemicals that control amyloid buildup or by clearing amyloid more efficiently. Another promising pharmacotherapy for AD may be a combination of vitamin E (described in Chapter 3 as an antioxidant that appears to prevent or reduce the symptoms of other chronic diseases) and selegiline hydrochloride (marketed as Eldepryl and generally prescribed for Parkinson's disease). In one clinical trial, patients in the moderate stage of AD who were given this combination did not decline as rapidly as those given a placebo (Sano et al., 1997). Vitamin E may also be effective in reducing the risk of AD. In one study that examined almost 5,000 older adults for 5 years, the incidence of AD was lower among elders who used vitamin E supplements in combination with vitamin C than among those who did not use any vitamin supplements or only

one of these vitamins alone (Zandi et al., 2004). However, it is important to review AD patients' medications with their physicians to confirm that vitamin E will not interact with their other medications, in particular with blood thinners.

Some families report that regular use of an extract from the dried leaves of the ginkgo biloba or maidenhair tree improves the memory of AD patients in the early-to-intermediate stages. However, a study in the Netherlands casts some doubt on the benefits of this treatment. Researchers studied 214 nursing home residents with mild-to-moderate AD or vascular dementia. Each person was given a usual dose of ginkgo biloba (84 elders) or an elevated dose (82 elders), and compared with a group (48 elders) that used a placebo over 24 weeks. No effects were observed on tests of memory or depression, but those using ginkgo performed slightly better on self-reported ADLs (van Dongen et al., 2000).

Researchers have made dramatic strides toward understanding the neurochemical basis of this disease and are rapidly moving toward its treatment. There is even some promise of a vaccine that can help the immune system produce antibodies against amyloid proteins and clear amyloid deposits from the brain. Successful research with mice gives scientists hope that such a vaccine may be effective with humans (Schenk et al., 1999).

Medications are often prescribed to manage behavioral problems in some AD patients, including agitation, hallucinations, physical aggressiveness, and wandering. In particular, risperidone, a drug used to treat psychotic symptoms in schizophrenic patients, appears to calm aggressive, delusional behaviors in a significant segment of this population (Goldberg & Goldberg, 1997). Because of their potential side effects, however, it is important to weigh the harm caused by these patient behaviors against the possible side effects of medications. Furthermore, the prescribing physician must regularly reevaluate the need to continue or reduce the dosage of any drugs used for behavior management, perhaps as frequently as every 3 to 4 months.

HEALTH CARE COSTS OF DEMENTIA

Health care costs for patients with AD and other dementias are much higher than for adults in the same age range without dementia. Average annual costs for AD patients were almost $8,000 in 2004, and for those with vascular dementia almost $14,000. Medicare payments for AD patients' health and long-term care are almost three times higher than for elders without dementia; Medicaid payments are nine times higher (Alzheimer's Association, 2009; Hill et al., 2005). These higher costs are partly due to comorbidity, or the presence of other medical problems along with dementia. One study found that 35 percent of AD patients also had cardiovascular disease, compared with 10 percent of a control group of elders without AD; 25 percent had congestive heart failure, compared with 15 percent of controls. This results in greater expenditures for visits to physicians' offices and for hospital and home health care, but the greatest difference between AD patients and controls is for skilled nursing care at three times the rate for controls (Fillit et al., 2002). By preventing AD and other dementias, researchers can help to improve the quality of life for older adults and their families while reducing these skyrocketing health and long-term care costs.

Behavioral Treatment and Environmental Interventions

As noted earlier, new medications that are being approved by the FDA show some promise of slowing the rate of decline with AD. To date, however, neither these medications nor psychotherapy can restore the cognitive functions lost with most irreversible forms of dementia. Nevertheless, many older persons can benefit from behavioral and exercise therapies, and from some environmental modifications. For example, exercise training combined with behavioral management training for family caregivers can help both the AD patient and their caregivers. One study tested the effects of a 3-month exercise program for AD patients, together with teaching behavioral management to their caregivers. Compared with AD patients who received only routine medical care, those in the exercise program had significantly fewer days of restricted activity, lower scores on a measure of depression, and less likelihood of nursing home placement up to 2 years later (Teri et al., 2003).

Individual competence can be enhanced somewhat and the social and home environments simplified considerably in an effort to maintain P–E congruence and maintain some independent functioning. Simple changes, such as removing sources of glare and making lighting levels consistent throughout the house, can prevent confusion and "sundowning," a condition that affects some AD patients as natural light levels change and they become more fatigued later in the day. It is important to maintain a regular schedule, to keep the patient moderately active, and to prevent withdrawal from daily interactions. Written schedules of activities, simplified routes from room to room, and written directions for cooking, bathing, and taking medications can aid a person in finding his or her way around and prevent the frustration of getting lost or not recognizing once-familiar people and places. AD patients can be encouraged to perform more ADLs if their grooming supplies (e.g., toothbrush, toothpaste, comb) are kept visible and in a familiar sequence of use. These items can also help AD patients recognize their own bathroom or bedroom as the disease progresses. A useful device for some patients in the intermediate stages of Alzheimer's is a "memory box" that contains photos from the individual's past on the outside and mementos on the inside, placed on his or her door to identify the bedroom. Physical activity during the day can also help the patient sleep better through the night. Productive activities such as setting the table, folding laundry, and raking leaves in a secure backyard can also help patients maintain a sense of continuity with their past lives and use their excess energy. However, the frequency and intensity of such activities should not overwhelm or confuse the patient.

CARING FOR AD PATIENTS AT EACH STAGE OF THE DISEASE

Depending on the stage of the disease, caregivers of elders with AD can help them in different ways. Using the Global Deterioration Scale described in the box on page 249, families can try the following ways of helping the patient:

Stages 1–3 (Mild dementia)
- Set up an orientation area in the home where the patient's critical items (e.g., wallet, keys, glasses) can always be found.
- Watch for signs of driving problems.
- Encourage physical and social activities.

Stages 4–5 (Moderate dementia)
- Make changes in home environment to assure safety and autonomy, but maintain familiarity (e.g., improved, constant light levels).
- Put labels on important doors (e.g., patient's bedroom, bathroom) and drawers.
- Keep in visible areas photos of family and close friends taken with patient, with names clearly written on photos.

Stages 6–7 (Advanced dementia)
- Visit alternative long-term care facilities that fit P–E needs of the particular patient.
- Simplify daily routines but still encourage some physical activity (e.g., walks in fenced-in yard).
- Try alternative means of communication (e.g., touch, sharing old family photos).

Wandering is another problem that can be prevented with some environmental changes. These can be restrictive, such as locking all exterior doors, or more protective, such as providing a safe backyard or garden area for the AD patient to explore, within easy sight of the home's windows and doors to orient the patient. ID bracelets with silent or audible alarms that can help locate the AD patient are becoming more common for use in the home, given their demonstrated benefits in nursing homes. One company has even developed a model where family or close friends can record a message on a tape attached to the bracelet to guide the wandering person back home. Some local chapters of the Alzheimer's Association offer the "safe return" program, which provides ID bracelets for AD patients, maintains records, and assists emergency teams in locating, identifying, and returning the AD patient who becomes lost in the community. Agitation may also accompany AD; elders may display irritable behavior, pacing, restlessness, and general expressions of distress. These behaviors are not a normal outcome of AD but are triggered by environmental changes, fear, fatigue, loss of control, or medical conditions such as infections or adverse reactions to medications. The patient displaying signs of agitation should first be evaluated and treated for possible underlying medical conditions. If no systemic conditions are found, behavioral and environmental interventions can be used, such as

adapting the home environment to the older person's needs and providing stability in ADLs.

Ultimately, the goal of managing these dementias is to slow the rate of deterioration and to prevent nursing home placement for as long as possible. For the AD patient who does enter a nursing home, it is important to find a facility that can maximize the individual's remaining abilities as the disease progresses (i.e., environments that can maintain the patient's P–E congruence). During the 1990s, the number of special care units (SCUs) in nursing homes grew. These units are generally designed for residents with advanced dementia, especially AD, and staffed by nurses and therapists with special training in this field. Many provide a higher staff-to-resident ratio, a safe environment where patients can move about without getting lost, and special services aimed at maintaining the patients' remaining cognitive capacities. They are less likely to use chemical and physical restraints with disruptive residents. However, because there are no national licensing regulations for SCUs, the nature of services and quality of care provided vary widely. That is, the designation of a nursing home unit as a SCU does not necessarily imply richer or more tailored services than non-SCU units that also house AD and other dementia patients (Day, Carreon, & Stump, 2000).

Newer options include assisted living facilities, adult family homes, and adult day care (described in Chapter 11). However, like SCUs, families must determine if these alternative housing options can provide a safe and supportive environment for AD patients, especially as the disease progresses.

CAREGIVER NEEDS One of the most important considerations with Alzheimer's disease and other dementias is to provide social and emotional support to the family as well as the patient. It is estimated that about 70 percent of all people with AD are cared for by family. In fact, about 19 million family caregivers provide basic instrumental ADLs for their relatives with AD. It has been estimated that these informal caregivers provide as much as $94 billion in care. The typical

---

NEW WAYS OF HELPING AD PATIENTS

Until a few years ago, reality orientation was a popular therapeutic method that was used in nursing homes and by many families caring for AD patients. The emphasis was on reorienting confused older adults to the present and correcting them when they referred to a dead partner as being alive now or talked about getting to work despite being retired for over 20 years. However, these techniques can frustrate and agitate the patient. Most experts today agree that it is better to acknowledge the patient's memories of the past and not argue with them about the accuracy of these memories.

caregiver of an AD patient is a 46-year-old woman, employed full-time, and caring for a 77-year-old mother. On average, they provide care for 4.5 years (Alzheimer's Association, 2009; Bloom, de Pouvourville, & Straus, 2003). Chapter 10 describes the challenges faced by these caregivers as they balance the role of caregiver to their loved ones with the need to maintain their jobs, family, and personal life.

Parkinson's Disease

Parkinson's is a neurodegenerative disorder that begins as a loss of muscle control, impaired balance, and coordination, with tremors in the feet and hands, gradually progressing to slow and limited movements. Speech can become impaired, muscles become rigid, and the person moves more slowly and with a shuffling gait. In its later stages, Parkinson's can manifest dementia-like symptoms. Today, about one million Americans have this condition, projected to double by 2040 as the older population increases. It usually strikes people over age 60, although some people—such as the actor Michael J. Fox—are first diagnosed in their 30s.

Parkinson's differs from AD in many ways. First, the degeneration and loss of cells in the brain occurs mostly in the *substantia nigra*, located in the center of the brain. This is the region where dopamine is produced, the brain chemical responsible for initiating voluntary movement. This is why Levodopa (L-dopa) is the drug of choice for most people with Parkinson's, as a way of replacing dopamine. However, in some people, L-dopa can cause such side effects as hallucinations, agitation, and uncontrollable movement. Newer drugs known as *dopamine agonists* have been developed as an alternative for such patients.

Deep-brain stimulation helps some Parkinson's patients. Neurosurgeons place an electrode in the brain, which receives pulses from a pacemaker implanted in the chest. Electrical stimulation produced by the pacemaker reduces the tremor and rigidity of Parkinson's so that many patients can reduce the dosage of their medications or discontinue

it altogether. However, deep-brain stimulation cannot prevent the progress of Parkinson's (Lozano & Kalia, 2005). One of the most exciting research developments in this area is the possibility of implanting stem cells (described in Chapter 3) into the brain of Parkinson's patients. These cells appear to revitalize damaged regions and resume production of dopamine in the substantia nigra. The Parkinson's Association has actively lobbied for the harvesting of stem cells. Behavioral techniques such as meditation, biofeedback, and dietary modification are also recommended. The Parkinson's Association provides e-tutorials on the Internet about the characteristics and stages of this disease, advances in treatment, mobility and safety, digestion and bladder problems, communication, sleep, and mood changes. Gender differences have been found in how patients cope with Parkinson's. Older women focus on how it affects their ability to organize and maintain relationships, while men are more concerned with its impact on their physical strength and appearance (Solimeo, 2008).

Alcoholism

For most older people, alcohol use is associated with socializing and occurs in moderation (i.e., less than once a week, and no more than two drinks each time). As discussed in Chapters 3 and 4, moderate alcohol consumption (averaging one glass per day) can have cardiovascular health benefits. Using data from a national survey of almost 7,000 adults age 65 and older, researchers found that older women who are current drinkers (defined as consuming at least 12 drinks in the past year) reported better general and cardiovascular health and had fewer hospitalizations and ER visits than women who were former drinkers and lifelong abstainers. These differences were less evident among older men. Note that these findings are based on self-reports, not on hospital or physician records (Balsa et al., 2008).

Unhealthy drinking patterns are defined as four or more drinks in any single day during a typical month (Merrick, et al., 2008). Older adults who consume four or more drinks per occasion and do so frequently and routinely are more likely to use alcohol as a way to cope with stressful life events and to relax, although stresses per se are not necessarily triggers for late-onset alcoholism (Gomberg, 2003). Obtaining accurate statistics on the prevalence of alcoholism in older adults is difficult because of the stigma associated with this condition among older cohorts. Additionally, most statistics on alcohol use are for adults age 50 and older, and definitions of alcohol abuse vary. Estimates of problem drinking among community-dwelling older adults vary from 1 to over 15 percent (Farkas & Drabble, 2008; Project Mainstream, 2005). In general, alcohol consumption declines sharply with age, from 63.5 percent among 26- to 29-year-olds (2.9 drinks per day among men, 1.5 among women) to 48 percent among those 60 to 64 years old, to 28.4 percent among adults age 65 and older (1.02 drinks per day among men and 0.5 drinks among women) (Chan et al., 2007; Farkas & Drabble, 2008; SAMHSA, 2006). This means that about 40 percent of the current cohort of older adults is abstinent, and older adults have lower rates of heavy alcohol use than any other age-group, even when compared with middle-aged adults (DHHS, 2005; Hasin & Grant, 2005). The expected increase in alcohol dependence among baby boomers is of concern, however. Researchers from the Substance Abuse and Mental Health Services Administration (SAMHSA, 2001) estimate a 50 percent increase in the number of older adults with substance abuse problems (both alcohol and drugs) and a 70 percent increase in the rate of treatment need among older adults between 2001 and 2020. One indicator of this trend is the growing numbers of older patients in methadone treatment programs (Bartels, 2006; Bartels et al., 2006; Farkas & Drabble, 2008; Office of Applied Studies, 2008; Rosen, Smith, & Reynolds, 2008).

Alcoholism in older adults is accompanied by depression in 30 percent of cases and by dementia in 20 percent, although the direction of causality is not always clear. Alcohol can exacerbate depression, and depression can exacerbate alcohol use, creating a complex assessment process (Bartels et al., 2006; Blow, Serras, & Barry, 2007; Conway et al., 2006). Those at greatest risk are widowers and well-educated white men who have never married. Older men are four times more likely to have alcohol problems than are older women. Women at greatest risk of alcohol abuse are those who are smokers, not married, not religious, and with little social support. Findings on the extent of alcohol abuse among elders of color are mixed, with some studies noting no differences by race and others identifying higher prevalence rates for African American and Native American elders than for Caucasians. The lowest rates for alcohol abuse are found in older Latina women (Cummings, Bride, & Rawlins-Shaw, 2006; Gurnack & Johnson-Wendell, 2002; Hasin & Grant, 2004). Although general population studies do not differentiate by sexual orientation, studies among gay populations have found that rates do not decline with age and, in fact, tend to be higher than for heterosexual men (Drabble, Trocki, & Midanik, 2005).

It is important to distinguish lifelong abusers of alcohol from those who began drinking later in life. Alcoholics are less likely to be found among the ranks of persons over age 65 because of higher alcohol-related death rates at a young age. Those who continue to drink in old age tend to decrease their consumption. Some studies identified increased rates of concurrent mental health disorders with early-onset drinking (Farkas and Drabble, 2008). Surveys of alcoholism rates among older persons have revealed that approximately two-thirds began to drink heavily before age 40 (Shibusawa, 2006). Some older persons who are diagnosed as alcoholics have had this problem since middle age, but increasing age may exacerbate the condition for two reasons:

- The central nervous system (CNS), liver, and kidneys become less tolerant of alcohol with age because of the physiological changes described in Chapter 3 (e.g., loss of muscle tissue, reduction in body mass, and decreased efficiency of liver and kidney functions). For this reason, a smaller dose of alcohol can be more deleterious in the later years. In fact, current thinking is that people age 60 and older who drink should consume about half the amount acceptable for younger persons; that is, about one four-ounce glass of alcoholic beverage per day for men and somewhat less for women.

- An individual who has been drinking heavily for many years has already produced irreversible damage to the CNS, liver, and kidneys, creating more problems than those due to normal aging alone. Chronic diseases common in older adults and the medications used to manage them can exaggerate the effects of alcohol. Bone density is lower in older alcoholics than in their non-drinking peers, while sleep disorders, dementia, and (liver and GI) conditions are more common (Yuan et al, 2001; Onen et al, 2005).

Perhaps because of the damage to their central nervous system, men who drank heavily before age 40 are more likely to experience depression, restlessness, sleeplessness, and tension than those who started later. It is difficult to determine the incidence of alcoholism among older persons who have no previous history of this disease. Physiological evidence is lacking, and drinking is often hidden from friends, relatives, and physicians. The older person may justify overconsumption of alcohol on the grounds that it relieves sadness and isolation. Even when family members are aware of the situation, they may rationalize that alcohol is one of the older person's few remaining pleasures. Denial is a common problem among many alcoholics, young or old; some older people may feel that they should be able to cope with their alcoholism on their own and not have to rely on health professionals or even on support groups such as Alcoholics Anonymous.

Physicians may overlook the possibility that alcohol is creating a health problem, because the adverse effects of alcohol resemble some physical diseases or psychiatric and cognitive disorders that are associated with old age. For example, older alcoholics may complain of confusion, disorientation, irritability, insomnia or restless sleep patterns, heart palpitations, weight loss, depression, or a dry cough. Beliefs held by health care providers that alcoholism rarely occurs in older people may also prevent its detection. Because of the problems caused by heavy alcohol use in old age, primary care physicians must screen their older patients by asking questions about the quantity, frequency, and context of drinking. This can help in the diagnosis and referral of older alcoholics to treatment programs, which currently are underutilized by older adults. This can also reduce the emotional, physical, and cognitive deterioration caused by alcoholism in older people and the subsequent hospitalizations and use of emergency medical services for conditions that are secondary to heavy alcohol consumption (Shibusawa, 2006). The Screening, Brief Intervention and Referral to Treatment initiative of SAMHSA is found to be a useful approach; even 10–15 minute educational interventions by health care providers may be effective in reducing alcohol consumption. The Michigan Alcoholism Screening Test-Geriatric Version (MAST-G) is a screening tool developed specifically for use with older adults (Farkas & Drabble, 2008).

Treatment for older alcoholics has generally not been differentiated from that for younger alcoholics, and findings are mixed about the benefits of age-specific compared to age-integrated programs. However, it is probably more important to focus on older alcoholics' medical conditions because of physical declines that make them more vulnerable to the secondary effects of alcohol. As with younger alcoholics, counseling and occupational and recreational therapy are important for treating older people experiencing alcoholism. Motivational interviewing strategies as part of a multidimensional treatment and case-management approach are found to be effective

(D'Agostino et al., 2006; Zanjani et al., 2006). Recovery rates for older alcoholics are as high as for younger alcoholics, especially if the problem began in late life, and women tend to have more favorable outcomes than men. More research on gender and racial differences in substance use, on the relationship between alcohol consumption and disability risk, and on treatment outcomes for older adults are needed, however (Cummins, Bride, & Rawlins-Shaw, 2006; Farkas & Drabble, 2008; Lang et al., 2007). Prevention initiatives as part of health promotion programs are also critical, given the projected alcohol use of baby boomers.

Drug Abuse

As noted in Chapter 4, older persons use a disproportionately large number of prescription and over-the-counter (OTC) drugs, representing approximately 36 percent of outpatient prescription drug expenditures (Sambamoorthi, Shea, & Crystal, 2003; National Institute on Drug Abuse, 2007). In particular, older adults are more likely than the young to use tranquilizers, sedatives, and hypnotics, all of which have potentially dangerous side effects. They also are at risk of abusing aspirin compounds, laxatives, and sleeping pills, often because of misinformation about the adverse effects of too high a dosage or too many pills. It is not unusual to hear older patients state that they took two or three times as much aspirin as they were prescribed because they did not feel that their pain was being alleviated with the lower dose. Yet changes in body composition and renal and liver functions that occur with age, combined with the use of multiple medications make older persons more likely to experience adverse drug reactions. Noncompliance with therapeutic drug regimens is often unintentional; older patients may take too much or too little of a drug because of nonspecific or complicated instructions by the physician, and they may use OTC drugs without reading warning labels about side effects and interactions with other drugs they are using. Intentional noncompliance generally takes the form of older patients deciding that they no longer need the medication or that it is not working for them. Such noncompliance is a major cause of ER visits among elders. Assessment for medication misuse often begins with the "Brown Bag review," where an older adult is asked to bring all medications, including over-the-counter ones, in their original containers, in a bag, for a health care provider to review (Meadows, 2008).

Both health care providers and older people themselves are more aware of the effects of "polypharmacy" today, although research on illicit drug use is limited and no tools have been designed to assess drug abuse specifically among older adults (Zarowitz, 2006). Older persons do not abuse drugs to the extent that younger populations do, nor are they as likely to use illicit drugs such as heroin, cocaine, and marijuana. Among adults age 50 to 59, use of illegal drugs increased between 2002 and 2005, but remained unchanged in 2006, with 1.8 percent of older adults having used an illicit drug in the past month. Marijuana was the most commonly used illicit drug, followed by nonmedical use of prescription

---

MEDICATION MISMANAGEMENT CAN THREATEN ELDERS' AUTONOMY

Inability to manage their medications can be a threat to older people's autonomy. Families often cannot be present at every medication administration, and neighbors may help only intermittently. Even assisted living facilities cannot provide the daily help with medications that is needed, unless the older adult pays an additional fee. Some elders use plastic pillboxes with the days of the week printed on each section, or egg cartons or other small cups that the family has labeled with instructions. However, these devices cannot help an older person remember the time of day he or she must take the medication and are not effective at all for someone with dementia. Newer systems using digital technology that remind users when they must take their medications and that dispose the correct dose as needed have been developed and are still being tested.

drugs and cocaine. Older adults also are far less likely to use hallucinogens, amphetamines, or mood-enhancing inhalants. However, it is expected that the rate of drug abuse will increase by 50 percent between 2001 and 2020. These patterns reflect the aging of the baby boomers whose illicit drug use throughout their lives—especially marijuana—is higher than those of earlier cohorts (NSDUH, 2006; SAMHSA, 2006). Illicit drug use is greater among LGBT adults and Native Americans, African Americans, Puerto Ricans, and Mexicans than among white heterosexual populations (Cochran, et al., 2004; Gurnack & Johnson-Weendell, 2002). It is recommended that health care providers ask questions about previous drug use because of the strong correlation of current use with lifetime patterns of use (Simony-Wastila & Yang, 2006).

Psychotherapy with Older Persons

Despite early doubts by Freud (1924) and others about the value of psychotherapy for older patients, many researchers and therapists have developed and tested psychotherapeutic interventions specifically for this population or have modified existing approaches. One challenge in working with older individuals is to overcome misconceptions about psychotherapy. For this reason, short-term, goal-oriented therapies may be most effective with older patients because they can begin to experience benefits immediately. Several different types of therapy have been explored with this population.

As noted earlier, *life review* is one therapeutic approach that has been successfully used with older adults. Such therapy encourages introspection through active reminiscence of past achievements and failures, and may reestablish ego integrity in depressed older persons. This method may also be used effectively by social service providers without extensive training in psychotherapy. Life review can reduce symptoms of depression and increase life satisfaction and self-esteem in nursing

home residents (Haight, Michel, & Hendrix, 2000). An alternative form of life review, known as *reminiscence therapy*, has short-term benefits for depressed older people (Cully et al., 2001).

Group therapy is often advocated for older persons experiencing psychiatric disorders. Groups offer the opportunity for peer support, social interaction, and role modeling. Life review may be used effectively as part of group therapy. The opportunity to share life experiences and to learn that others have had similar challenges in their lives seems to enhance insight, self-esteem, and a feeling of catharsis.

Cognitive-behavioral (i.e., active, structured, and time-limited therapy) and *brief psychodynamic therapy* (i.e., helping the patient develop ego strength and feelings of control) both appear to be equally effective in alleviating minor depression, even up to 12 months following treatment. Psychodynamic therapy uses psychoanalytic concepts such as insight, transference, and the unconscious to relieve symptoms of depression and to prevent its recurrence by attempting to understand why the individual behaves in self-defeating ways.

Remotivation therapy has been used successfully with older persons who have some cognitive impairment and are withdrawn from social activities. They meet under the guidance of a trained group leader, discussing current events and experiences by bringing all group members into the discussion, emphasizing the event's relevance for each member, and encouraging them to share what they have gained from the session. This approach is found to be effective in psychiatric hospitals and nursing homes as well as in adult day health centers.

Despite these positive reports about the benefits of psychotherapy with older adults, they are more likely to relapse if treatment is discontinued or no booster sessions are offered. Relapse, or at least fading of treatment effects, is observed 6 to 12 months after these therapeutic interventions are discontinued (Reynolds et al., 2006).

Use of Mental Health Services

As noted in Chapter 4, older persons use physician services and inpatient hospital care more than do young adults. In contrast, mental health services are significantly underutilized by older people, especially elders of color and those who are low-income. Community-based mental health services are used by older people at a lower rate than inpatient hospital treatment, far below their representation in the U.S. population and less than the estimated prevalence of mental disorders in this group. In fact, fewer than 25 percent of older adults who need mental health care ever receive treatment; in addition, this lack of treatment provision to older adults is found across all service settings—community-based, inpatient hospitals, residential care, and nursing facilities (Kaskie & Estes, 2001). One major barrier to treatment is a serious shortage of mental health professionals with adequate training to meet the mental health, substance abuse, and psychosocial needs of older adults and their family caregivers (Rosen, 2006).

As noted above for depression, older persons may be more likely to seek help for psychiatric problems from their primary care providers. This may be because medical care does not carry the stigma of mental health services, especially for older adults of color. For example, Asians and Pacific Islanders tend to view psychiatric disorders with shame. A disproportionate number of older persons represent the population of patients in state mental hospitals that house the chronically mentally ill. Despite the deinstitutionalization movement of the 1960s, the great majority of all psychiatric services to older people are in hospital settings.

BARRIERS TO OLDER PERSONS' USE OF MENTAL HEALTH SERVICES   Older adults are generally unwilling to interpret their problems as psychological, preferring instead to attribute them to physical or social conditions or to normal aging. In addition,

many older adults have limited knowledge about mental disorders and lack confidence in mental health workers. This requires a good "psychological ear" on the part of the older person's health and social services providers. Therefore, these professionals must be attuned to the underlying emotional distress of the physical symptoms presented by their older clients.

Accessibility is perhaps the greatest barrier to older individuals obtaining mental health services. In addition to physical access issues, there are significant problems of fragmented services and older people's lack of knowledge about seeking mental health services on their own or obtaining appropriate referrals from physicians and social service providers. Cultural barriers, including communication problems, underlie the low utilization rates

---

OVERCOMING BARRIERS TO USING MENTAL HEALTH SERVICES

- Home visits by a psychiatrist, social worker, and a nurse are made to low-income, isolated older people in Baltimore through the Psychogeriatric Assessment and Treatment in City Housing (or PATCH) program.
- Rural elders in Iowa are served by mental health professionals through the Elderly Outreach Program (or EOP) of the community mental health system.
- The Family Services Program of greater Boston offers a community mental health program aimed especially at elders of color, entitled Services for Older People (or SOP).
- In Seattle, a mental health team from the community mental health network provides on-site evaluation and therapy to area nursing homes on a regular basis.
- In many communities, "gatekeepers" (nontraditional referral sources such as meter readers, postal carriers, and apartment and mobile home managers who have contact with isolated older people in the community) are trained to identify older persons who may require psychiatric care. These isolated older adults are typically chronically mentally ill.

of mental health services by elders of color. These barriers are discussed in greater detail in Chapter 14. Fortunately, many innovative programs have arisen to overcome these barriers and respond to the mental health needs of older adults, as highlighted in the box on the previous page. For example, many senior centers employ social workers trained in geriatrics to conduct support groups, education programs, and individualized counseling sessions on coping with grief, loss, and loneliness, and on methods to improve memory. Such programs reduce the stigma of psychotherapy by their informal structure in a familiar environment.

Reimbursement for psychological services is a major barrier. For example, Medicare Part A pays for no outpatient mental health expenditures, and only for a limited number of days for inpatient treatment. Furthermore, copayment by the subscriber for mental health services is greater than for physical health services. It should be noted that this lack of parity for mental health services occurs in many health insurance programs used by younger persons as well. However, elders' attitudes toward psychiatric disorders translate into these reimbursement issues being greater barriers to older persons' use of mental health services than they are for the young. In contrast, baby boomers may be more likely to seek such services in community mental health centers because of their increased awareness of mental disorders and treatment modalities.

Implications for the Future

During the past 25 years, there has been more research emphasis on normal, age-related changes in personality, as well as psychological disorders such as depression and dementia. Larger, cross-national, and longitudinal studies are providing insights into the universality of stability in some personality traits and change in others. The inclusion of larger samples of women and persons of color in more recent studies offers valuable information on gender and racial differences in psychological processes with aging. Researchers have

identified slight differences in rates and symptoms of some psychiatric disorders by gender and race. This information can help health and social service providers who work with older adults recognize signs of depression, anxiety disorders, dementia, and other conditions and help elders obtain the treatment they need.

With the growth of the older population and increased numbers of elders who live well beyond age 80, the sheer numbers of people with psychological disorders will expand over the next 30 years. Additionally, with the aging of the baby boomers, more older adults are likely to have been lifelong users of alcohol and illicit drugs. More emphasis will be placed on alternatives to medications to treat these conditions, as well as culturally competent methods of psychotherapy, such as problem-solving and cognitive-behavioral interventions and communication with older adults and their families. Support groups for elders and their families who are coping with psychological disorders will continue to grow. New research on the biochemistry of Alzheimer's disease and Parkinson's may offer hope for victims of these diseases, including early diagnosis and, potentially, stem cell transplants to repair affected areas of the brain. The Internet has already proven to be a valuable resource for older adults and their families as a means of learning more about their medical diagnoses, and even offers possibilities for group support and counseling by mental health professionals.

The discussion of normal personality development with aging and psychological disorders in this chapter should encourage students interested in pursuing psychological research and clinical careers. There is a great need for evidence-based psychosocial care by psychologists, social workers, psychiatrists, and nurses to work in direct mental health services with older adults and, in the case of elders with dementia, to provide therapeutic services to their caregivers. Geriatricians are needed who can understand the difference between normal and abnormal psychological functioning in older adults, and who can distinguish dementia and depression from adverse reactions to medications and from grief responses to losses associated with aging. Even nurses and physicians who elect to go into primary care should develop these skills; as seen from the research described in this chapter, many older people with mood disorders and dementia seek a diagnosis and treatment for these conditions from their primary care provider, not from a mental health specialist. Prevention initiatives are also critical to promoting successful, robust—or active—aging.

There is also a need for more researchers in gerontology who can advance the field of basic personality development and geriatric mental health. Whether you are interested in social or behavioral, biological, pharmacology, or technology sciences, there are many opportunities to test interventions to improve older persons' quality of life, both those who are healthy and those experiencing psychological disorders. In an era of limited resources for mental health services, it is essential to know what interventions are most effective with different groups of older adults.

Summary

Personality development in adulthood and old age has received increasing attention over the past 25 years. Earlier theories of personality suggested that development takes place only during childhood and adolescence, and stabilizes by early adulthood. Beginning with Erik Erikson, however, several theorists have suggested that personality continues to change and evolve into old age. According to Erikson's theory of psychosocial development, the individual experiences crises or conflicts at each stage of development, and the outcome of each has an impact on ego development in the next stage. The seventh stage, generativity versus stagnation, takes place mostly during the middle years, but researchers increasingly find that continued generativity in old age is important for active aging. Programs such as Foster Grandparents encourage older people to experience ongoing generativity, or giving back to society by working with young children. The eighth and last stage of personality development occurs in old age and poses the conflict of ego integrity versus despair in dealing with one's impending death. Both cross-sectional and longitudinal studies have found evidence for these last two stages of development, particularly using Loevinger's model of ego development, which expands Erikson's stage theory.

The work of Carl Jung also emphasizes the growth of personality across the life span, but does not specify stages of development. Jung's model, like Erikson's, focuses on the individual's confrontation with death in this last stage. In addition, Jung described a decrease in sex-typed behavior with aging. Researchers have found that men become more accepting of their nurturant and affiliative characteristics as they age, whereas women learn to accept their egocentric and aggressive impulses. Levinson's life structures model examines personality from a developmental stage perspective as well, but also represents a dialectical approach to personality change. This model is consistent with the person–environment approach in emphasizing the interaction between the individual and his or her environment as the impetus for change.

Trait theories of personality have been tested systematically in the Baltimore Longitudinal Studies of Aging, using the five-factor model of personality that consists of five primary traits (neuroticism, extroversion, openness to experience, agreeableness, and conscientiousness) and several subcategories of traits. Costa, McCrae, and their colleagues have found considerable stability in these traits from middle age to old age when tested longitudinally and internationally, and age differences between young and old when tested cross-sectionally. It is recognized that older persons' self-concept must be redefined as they move from traditional roles of worker, partner, and parent to less well-differentiated roles such as retiree or widow. But the process by which such changes take place and, more importantly, how they influence life satisfaction and self-esteem in old age is unclear.

Successful or active aging may be defined as the ability to avoid disease and disability, to function at a high level cognitively, to remain involved in society, and to cope effectively with life events and chronic hassles. An individual who has survived to the age of 75 or older has proved to be adaptable to new situations. Hence, older people who remain physically, cognitively, and socially active are the most resilient of their cohort. The concept of successful aging is often criticized for overlooking class, racial, and gender barriers to adopting healthy lifestyles.

The prevalence of psychological disorders in old age is difficult to determine, although estimates range from 5 to 45 percent of the older population. Research in long-term care settings gives higher estimates than epidemiological studies conducted in the community. This is because older persons with dementia and depression are more likely to live in long-term care settings and to be treated by primary care physicians than through community mental health services.

Depression is the most common mental disorder in late life, although estimates of its prevalence also vary widely depending on the criteria used to diagnose it. Bipolar disorders are rare in old age; major depression is more common. Reactive or minor depression that is secondary to major life changes is found frequently in older persons. This condition responds well to environmental and psychosocial interventions, whereas antidepressant medications combined with psychotherapy such as problem-solving and cognitive-behavioral therapies are more effective for major depression. Research has demonstrated that a combined approach of problem-solving therapy and antidepressants are successful in reducing symptoms of depression even when the therapist is not extensively trained in mental health counseling. Electroconvulsive therapy has been found to be effective for severe depression in older people who do not respond to other forms of therapy. Diagnosing depression in older people is often difficult. Both older adults and some health care providers deny it and accept "feeling blue" as a normal part of growing old, while others attribute it to medical conditions. On the other hand, it is important to screen for medical conditions and medications that may produce depressive symptoms as a side effect. Some studies have identified rates of anxiety disorders to be as high or higher than depression, and both conditions are often co-occurring.

Paranoia and schizophrenia are far less common than depression and anxiety in older persons. Most elders with these conditions first developed them in their younger years these become aggravated with chronic diseases associated with aging. Medications for these conditions also interact with antipsychotics and other prescriptions used for their psychiatric condition. Life changes such as relocation and confusion that result from dementia may trigger paranoid reactions in old age and may aggravate preexisting schizophrenic symptoms. Psychotherapy, especially using cognitive-behavioral strategies, may be effective in treating paranoia, although it is important first to determine and to verify the underlying causes of the condition.

Depression is a risk factor for suicide in older people, particularly for white men over age 85. Life changes that result in a loss of social status and increased isolation may explain why this group is more likely to commit suicide than other segments of the population. The increased risk of suicide in older adults highlights the need for family members and service providers to be sensitized to clues of an impending suicide.

Dementia includes numerous reversible and irreversible conditions that result in impaired cognitive function, especially recall of recent events, comprehension, learning, attention, and orientation to time, place, and person. It is essential to perform a complete diagnostic workup of older people who have symptoms of dementia. A medical history, physical examination, assessment of medications, lab tests, psychological and cognitive testing, as well as neurological testing will aid in distinguishing reversible dementias that can be treated from the irreversible dementias (such as Alzheimer's disease), which currently can be managed but not cured. The biological basis of Alzheimer's disease is receiving much more research attention today. Future treatments may involve medications that replace or prevent the loss of brain chemicals, as well as vaccines and even gene therapy. Family members and service providers should be aware of changes in the older person's cognitive functioning and behavior that may signal dementia, and must avoid labeling such changes as normal aging or as the catchall phrase "senility." The Nun Study has provided useful insights into early life experiences and activities that may prevent or delay the onset of dementia.

Although cognitive functioning cannot be restored in irreversible dementias, older persons in the early stages of these conditions often benefit from the newer medications, memory retraining, education, and counseling or psychotherapy to cope with the changes they are experiencing. Environmental modifications that simplify tasks and aid in orienting the patient may slow the rate of deterioration and postpone placement in a long-term care facility. It is also important to provide emotional and social support to family caregivers of elders with AD and other dementias. Support groups, education, adult day care, and other such respite programs are valuable for partners and other caregivers who assume full-time care for these patients at home, although they are limited by funding constraints.

Alcoholism and drug abuse are less common in older persons than in the young, although accurate estimates of prevalence are difficult to obtain. Physical health and cognitive function are significantly impaired in older alcoholics. Older men with a history of alcohol abuse also have a greater risk of suicide than do younger men or young and older women who are alcoholics. Drug abuse in older persons is rarely associated with illicit drugs but often takes the form of inappropriate use or overuse of some prescription and over-the-counter drugs. Adverse reactions are more likely to occur in older persons because of age-related physiological changes that impair the ability to metabolize many medications and because of the greater likelihood of polypharmacy. Rates of illicit

drug use are project to grow with the aging of baby boomers with drug-abuse histories.

Many researchers have explored the feasibility of psychotherapy with older patients. Both short-term, goal-oriented therapy and long-term approaches have been advocated. Specific modes of therapy with older patients include life review, reminiscence, and cognitive-behavioral techniques. Short-term interventions are particularly effective with depressed older people in community settings who seek care from their primary care providers. Nursing homes are ideal settings for long-term intense therapies using groups, but staff may not have the time or training to implement them. Behavior change and milieu therapy have resulted in significant improvements in the mental well-being of elders who participate in short-term experimental interventions.

Despite the demonstrated efficacy of many forms of therapy with older persons, they significantly underutilize mental health services. Most treatments for psychological problems in this population take place in hospitals. Many older people prefer to seek treatment for depression and other mental disorders from their primary care provider. This may result in an overuse of pharmacological treatment and an underutilization of counseling in cases where the latter may be more effective. Such behavior may be attributed to reluctance among the current cohort of elders to admit that they have a psychological disorder, a lack of knowledge about such conditions and their treatment, and access problems. Barriers include attitudes of mental health and social service providers about the value of counseling for older persons, as well as the shortage of geriatric mental health services. As discussed in Chapter 14, cultural competence among mental health providers is needed to improve access for historically underserved groups. As more programs evolve that integrate services and as future cohorts become aware of mental disorders and their treatment, acceptance and use of mental health services by older people will increase.

anxiety disorder functional psychological disorder often triggered by external stress; accompanied by physiological reactivity such as increased heart rate and sleep disorders

archetypes masculine and feminine aspects of personality, present in both men and women

delirium a reversible dementia characterized by sudden onset, generally caused by environmental factors

dementia progressive, marked decline in cognitive functions associated with damage to brain tissue; may affect personality and behavior; may be reversible or irreversible type

depression (major versus minor or reactive) the most common psychiatric disorder in old age, diagnosed if several behavioral and affective symptoms (e.g., sleep and eating disturbances) are present for at least 2 weeks; bipolar disorders are less common in older people than reactive (or minor) and major depression

dysthymic disorder a less acute type of depression, but often lasts longer than major depression

ego integrity versus despair the eighth and last stage of psychosocial development in Erikson's model; aging individual achieves wisdom and perspective, or despairs because he or she views one's life as lacking meaning

electroconvulsive, or **electroshock, therapy (ECT)** a form of therapy for severely depressed patients in which a mild electrical current is applied to one or both sides of the brain

generativity the seventh stage of psychosocial development in Erikson's model; goal of middle-aged and older persons is to care for and mentor younger generations, look toward the future, and not stagnate in the past

life review a form of psychotherapy that encourages discussion of past successes and failures

life structures in Levinson's model, specific developmental stages consisting of eras and transitions

mild cognitive impairment (MCI) a mild form of cognitive dysfunction; most cases do not develop into full dementia

paranoia a psychiatric disorder characterized by irrational suspiciousness of other people

pharmacotherapy use of medications to treat symptoms of physical or psychiatric disorders

psychological disorders abnormal changes in personality and behavior that may be caused or triggered by a genetic predisposition, environmental stress, and/or systemic diseases

reminiscence therapy a type of psychotherapy used with depressed, anxious, sometimes confused older adults, stimulating the older person's memory of successful coping experiences and past positive events

resilience the ability to cope with life challenges and maintain one's optimism and psychological well-being

schizophrenia a psychiatric disorder characterized by thought disorders and hallucinations, psychotic behavior, loss of emotional expression

self-concept cognitive representation of the self; emerges from interactions with social environment, social roles, and accomplishments

self-efficacy perceived confidence in one's own ability to know how to cope with a stressor and to resolve it

self-esteem evaluation or feeling about one's identity relative to an "ideal self" differs from self-concept in being more of an emotional, not cognitive, assessment of self

stage theories of personality development of an individual through various levels, each level necessary for adaptation and for psychological adjustment

successful aging achievement of good physical and functional health and cognitive and emotional well-being in old age, often accompanied by strong social support and productive activity

trait theories personality theories that describe individuals in terms of characteristics or "typical" attributes that remain relatively stable with age

RESOURCES

Log on to MySocKit (www.mysockit.com) for information about the following:

- Alzheimer's Disease Education and Referral Center (ADEAR)

- Alzheimer's Disease and Related Disorders Association Inc. (ADRDA)

- Alzheimer's Research Forum
- American Association for Geriatric Psychiatry
- American Parkinson's Disease Association, Inc.
- Eldercare Web
- Elder Care Locator
- National Family Caregivers Association
- National Institute of Neurological Disorders and Stroke

REFERENCES

Agronin, M. E. (2008). *Alzheimer's disease and other dementias.* (2nd ed.). Philadelphia, PA: Lippincott, Williams and Wilkins.

Alexopoulos, G., Katz, I., Bruce, M., Heo, T., Ten Have, T., Raue, P., et al. (2005). Remission in depressed geriatric primary care patients: A report from the PROSPECT Study. *American Journal of Psychiatry, 162,* 718–724.

Alzheimer's Association. (2009). Alzheimer's disease facts and figures. Retrieved April 2009, from http://www.alz.org

Alzheimer's Disease International. (2006). Dementia in the Asia Pacific region: The epidemic is here. Retrieved December 2006, from http://www.alz.co.uk/research/files/apreport

Alzheimer's Disease International. (2009). World Alzheimer Report. Retrieved September 2009, from http://www.alz.co.uk/research/worldreport

American Psychiatric Association. (2000). *Diagnostic and statistical manual of mental disorders.* Task Force on DSM-IV-TR. (4th ed.). Washington, DC: APA.

Andel, R., Crowe, M., Pedersen, N.L., Fratiglioni, L, Johansson, B., Gatz, M. (2008). Physical exercise at midlife and risk of dementia three decades later. *Journal of Gerontology: Medical Sciences, 63A,* 62–66.

Anderson, R. N. & Smith, B. L. (2003). Deaths: Leading causes for 2001. *National Vital Statistics Report 52:* 1–86. American Society of Consulting Pharmacists.

Andrews, M. (1999). The seductiveness of agelessness. *Ageing and Society, 19,* 301–318.

Aranda, M. P., Lee, P. J., & Wilson, S. (2000). Correlates of depression in older Latinos. *Home Health Care Services Quarterly, 20,* 1–20.

Arean, P. A., Hegel, M., Vannoy, S., Fan, M. Y., & Unutzer, J. (2008). Effectiveness of problem-solving therapy for older primary care patients with depression. *The Gerontologist, 48,* 311–323.

Arean, P. A. & Unutzer, J. (2003). Inequities in depression management in low-income, minority and old-old adults. *Journal of the American Geriatric Society, 51,* 1808–1809.

Balsa, A. I., Homer, J. F., Fleming, M. F., & French, M.T. (2008). Alcohol consumption and health among elders. *The Gerontologist, 48,* 622–636.

Barrowclough, C., King, P., Colville, J., Russell, E., Burns, A., & Tarrier, N. (2001). A randomized trial of the effectiveness of cognitive-behavioral therapy and supportive counseling for anxiety symptoms in older adults. *Journal of Consulting and Clinical Psychology, 69,* 756–762.

Bartels, S. (2006). The aging tsunami and geriatric mental Health and substance use disorders. *Journal of Dual Diagnosis, 2,* 5–7.

Bartels, S., Blow, F., Van Citters, A., & Brockmann, L. (2006). Dual diagnosis among older adults: Co-occurring substance abuse and psychiatric illness. *Journal of Dual Diagnosis, 2,* 9–30.

Birditt, K. S., Fingerman, K. L., & Almeida, D. M. (2005). Age differences in exposure and reactions to interpersonal tensions: A daily diary study. *Psychology and Aging, 20,* 330–340.

Blazer, D. G. (2002). *Depression in late life* (3rd ed.). New York: Springer

Blazer, D. G. (2003). Depression in late life: Review and commentary. *Journal of Gerontology: Medical Sciences, 58A,* M249–M265.

Blazer, D. G., Hybels, C. F., & Pieper, C. F. (2001). The association of depression and mortality in elderly persons: A case for multiple independent pathways. *Journal of Gerontology: Medical Sciences, 56A,* M505–M509.

Bloom, B. S., de Pouvourville, N., & Straus, W. L. (2003). Cost of illness of Alzheimer's disease: How useful are current estimates? *The Gerontologist, 43,* 158–164.

Blow, F., Serras A., & Barry, K. (2007). Late-life depression and alcoholism. *Current Psychiatry Reports, 1,* 14–19.

Bohlmeijer, E., Smit, F., & Cuijpers, P. (2003). Effects of reminiscence and life review on late-life depression: A meta-analysis. *International Journal of Geriatric Psychiatry, 18,* 1088–1094.

Borson, S., Scanlan, J. M., Brush, M., Vitalliano, P., & Dokmak, A. (2000). The Mini-Cog. A cognitive 'vital signs' measure for dementia screening in multi-lingual elderly. *International Journal of Geriatric Psychiatry, 15,* 1021–1027.

Bosboom, P. R. & Deijen, J. B. (2006). Age-related cognitive effects of ECT and ECT-induced mood improvement in depressive patients. *Depression and Anxiety, 23,* 93–101.

Brown, M., Lapane, K. & Luisi, A. (2002). The management of depression in older nursing home residents. *Journal of the American Geriatrics Society, 50,* 69–76.

Bruce, M., Ten Have, T., Reynolds, C., Katz, I., Schulberg, H., Mulsant, B., et al. (2004). Reducing suicidal ideation and depressive symptoms in depressed older primary care patients: A randomized controlled trial. *Journal of the American Medical Association, 291,* 1081–1091.

Capers, M. (2004). Conference Panel: Depression and illness: Coordinating care. *SMHSA News 12.* Retrieved February 2007, from http://www.SAMHSA_News/index.html

Carstensen, L. L., Mikels, J. A., Mather, M. (2006). Aging and the intersection of cognition, motivation and emotion. In J. Birren & K. W. Schaie (Eds.). *Handbook of the Psychology of Aging,* San Diego: Academic Press, 6th ed.

Chan, K. K., Neighbors, C., Gilson, M., Larimer, M. E., & Marlatt, A. (2007). Epidemiological trends in drinking by age and gender: Providing normative feedback to adults. *Addictive Behaviors, 32,* 967–976.

Charles, S. T. (2005). Viewing injustice: Greater emotional heterogeneity with age. *Psychology and Aging, 20,* 159–164.

Charles, S. T. & Carstensen, L. L. (2008). Unpleasant situations elicit different emotional responses in younger and older adults. *Psychology and Aging, 23,* 495–504.

Chiles, J. A., Lambert, M. J., & Hatch, A. L. (1999). The impact of psychological interventions on medical cost offset: A meta-analytic review. *Clinical Psychology: Science and Practice, 6,* 204–220.

Cochran, S. D., Ackerman, D., Mays, V. M., & Ross, M. W. (2004). Prevalence of non-medical drug use and dependence among homosexually active men and women in the U.S. population. *Addiction, 99,* 989–998.

Cohen, C. I. (Ed.). (2003). *Schizophrenia in later life: Treatment, research and policy.* Washington, D.C.: American Psychiatric Publishing.

Cohen, G. D. (2005). *The mature mind: The positive power of the aging brain.* Cambridge, MA: Perseus Books.

Costa, P. T. & McCrae, R. R. (1994). Stability and change in personality from adolescence through adulthood. In C. F. Halverson, G. A. Kohnstamm, & R. P. Martin (Eds.). *The developing structure of temperament and personality from infancy to adulthood.* Hillsdale, NJ: Erlbaum.

Costa, P. T. & McCrae, R. R. (1995). Solid ground in the wetlands of personality: A reply to Block. *Psychological Bulletin, 117,* 216–220.

Cully, J. A., LaVoie, D., & Gfeller, J. D. (2001). Reminiscence, personality, and psychological functioning in older adults. *The Gerontologist, 41,* 89–95.

Cummings, S., Bride, B., & Rawlins-Shaw, A. (2006). Alcohol abuse treatment for older adults: A review of recent empirical research. *Journal of Evidence-Based Social Work, 1,* 77–99.

D'Agostino, C., Barry, K., Blow, F., & Podgorski, C. (2006). Community interventions for older adults with comorbid substance abuse: The geriatric addictions program. *Journal of Dual Diagnosis, 3,* 31–45.

Danner, D. D., Snowdon, D. A & Friesen, W. V. (2001). Positive emotions in early life and longevity: Findings from the Nun Study. *Journal of Personality and Social Psychology, 80,* 804–813.

Das, A. K., Olfson, M., McCurtis, H. L., & Weissman, M. M. (2006). Depression in African Americans: Breaking barriers to detection and treatment. *The Journal of Family Practice, 55,* 30–43.

Day, K., Carreon, D. & Stump, C. (2000). The therapeutic design of environments for people with dementia: A review of the empirical research. *The Gerontologist, 40,* 397–406.

DeBaggio, T. (2002). *Losing my mind*. New York: The Free Press.

DeCarli, C. S. (2006). When two are worse than one: Stroke and Alzheimer disease. *Neurology, 67,* 1326–1328.

De St. Aubin, E. & McAdams, D. P. (1995). The relations of generative concern and generative action to personality traits, satisfaction/happiness with life, and ego development. *Journal of Adult Development, 2,* 99–112.

Department of Health and Human Services (DHHS), Office of Applied Studies (2005). *Substance use among older adults: 2002 and 2003 update. The National Survey on Drug Use and Health Report*. Rockville, MD: Substance Abuse and Mental Health Services Administration. Retrieved 2006, from http://oas.samhsa.gov/2k5/olderadults/olderadults.htm

Depp, C. A. & Jeste, D. V. (2006). Definitions and predictors of successful aging: A comprehensive review of larger quantitative studies. *American Journal of Geriatric Psychiatry, 13,* 6–20.

Depp, C. A., Ipsit, V. & Jeste, D. V. (2007). The intersection of mental health and successful aging. *Psychiatric Times*, 20–28.

Diehl, M., Hastings, C. T., & Stanton, J. M. (2001). Self-concept differentiation across the adult life span. *Psychology and Aging, 10,* 478–491.

Drabble, L., Trocki, K. F. & Madanik, L. T. (2005). Reports of alcohol consumption and alcohol-related problems among homosexual, bisexual and heterosexual respondents: Results from the 2000 National Alcohol Survey. *Journal of Studies on Alcohol, 66,* 111–120.

Drake, R. E., Wallach, M. A., Alverson, H. S., & Mueser, K. T. (2002). Psychosocial aspects of substance abuse by clients with severe mental illness. *Journal of Nervous and Mental Disease, 190,* 100–106.

Dunlop, D. D., Manheim, L. M., Song, J., Lyons, J. S., Chang, R. W. (2005). Incidence of disability among preretirement adults: The impact of depression. *American Journal of Public Health, 95,* 2003–2008.

Ensrud, K. E., Blackwell, T., Mangione, C. M., Bowman, P. J., Bauer, D. C., Schwartz, A., et al. (2003). Central nervous system active medications and risk for fractures in older women. *Archives of Internal Medicine, 163,* 949–957.

Erikson, E. H. (1963). *Childhood and society* (2nd ed.). New York: Norton.

Erikson, E. H. (1968). *Identity, youth and crisis*. New York: Norton.

Erickson, E. H. (1997). *The life cycle completed: Extended version with new chapters on the ninth stage of development by Joan M. Erickson*. New York: Norton.

Erikson, E. H. (1982). *The life cycle completed: A review*. New York: Norton.

Erikson, E. H., Erikson, J. M., & Kivnick, H. Q. (1986). *Vital involvement in old age*. New York: Norton.

Farkas, K. & Drabble, L. (2008). Substance use and older adults resource review. In S. Diwan (Ed.). Resource Reviews. Washington, DC: CSWE Gero-ed Center, Master's Advanced Curriculum Project. Retrieved August 2009, from http://depts.washington.edu/geroctr/mac/14substance.html

Feldman, H. H. (2002). Treating Alzheimer's disease with cholinesterase inhibitors: What have we learned so far? *International Psychogeriatrics, 14,* (Supp.) 3–5.

Fillit, H., Hill, J. W., Futterman, R., Loyd, J. R., & Mastey. V. (2002). *Costs of comorbid medical conditions are increased in Alzheimer's disease*. Paper presented at annual meeting of the American Association for Geriatric Psychiatry.

Folstein, M., Folstein, S. & McHugh, P. R. (1975). Mini-mental state: A practical method for grading the cognitive state of patients for the clinician. *Journal of Psychiatric Research, 12,* 189–198.

Frazer, C. J., Christensen, H., & Griffiths, K. M. (2005). Effectiveness of treatments for depression in older people. *Medical Journal of Australia, 182,* 627–632.

Freud, S. (1924). *Collected papers, Volume I*. London: Hogarth Press.

Friedland, R. P., Fritsch,T., Smyth, K., Koss, E., Lerner, A. J., Chen, C. H., et al. (2000). Participation in nonocupational activities in midlife is protective against the development of Alzheimer's disease: Results from a case-control study. *Neurology, 54,* Abstract #P05.076.

Garfein, A. J. & Herzog, A. R. (1995). Robust aging among the young-old, old-old, and oldest-old. *Journal of Gerontology, 50B,* S77–S87.

Gatz, M. & Smyer, M. A. (2001). Mental health and aging at the outset of the 21st century. In J. E. Birren & K. W. Schaie (Eds.). *Handbook of the psychology of aging* (5th ed.). San Diego: Academic Press.

Gayman, M. D., Turner, R. J., & Cui, M. (2008). Physical limitations and depressive symptoms: Exploring the nature of the association. *Journal of Gerontology: Social Sciences, 63B,* S219–S227.

George, L. K. (2006). Perceived quality of life. In R. Binstock & L. K. George (Eds.). *Handbook of aging and the social sciences* (6th ed.). New York: Academic Press.

Gellis, Z. D. (2006). Older adults with mental and emotional problems. In B. Berkman & S. D'Ambruoso (Eds.), *Handbook of social work in health and aging.* New York: Oxford University Press.

Gellis, Z. D. & McCracken, S. G. (2008). Depressive disorders in older adults. In S. Diwan (Ed.). Mental health. Washington, D.C. In: CSWE Gero-Ed Center. Master's Advanced Curriculum Project. Retrieved August 2009, from http://depts.washington.edu/geroctr/mac/14substance.html

Gellis, Z. D., McGinty, J., Horowitz, A., Bruce, M., & Misener, E. (2007). Problem solving therapy for late life depression in home care elderly: A randomized controlled trial. *American Journal of Geriatric Phychiatry, 15* (11), 968–978.

Gilmer, T. P., Ojeda, V. D., Barrio, C., Fuentes, D., et al. (2009). Adherence to antipsychotics among Latinos and Asians with schizophrenia and limited English proficiency. *Psychiatric Services, 60,* 175–182.

Goldberg, R. J. & Goldberg, J. (1997). Risperidone for dementia-related disturbed behavior in nursing home residents. *International Psychogeriatrics, 9,* 65–68.

Gomberg, E. (2003). Treatment for alcohol-related problems. *Special Populations: Research Activities. Recent Developments in Alcoholism, 16,* 313–333.

Grzywacz, J. G. & Marks, N. E. (2001). Social inequalities and exercise during adulthood: Toward an ecological perspective. *Journal of Health and Social Behavior, 42,* 202–220.

Gurnack, A. & Johnson-Wendell, A. (2002). Elderly drug use and racial/ethnic populations. *Journal of Ethnicity in Substance Abuse, 1,* 55–71.

Gustafson, D., Rothenberg, E., Blennow, K., Steen, B., & Skoog, I. (2004). An 18-year follow-up of overweight and risk of Alzheimer disease. *Archives of Internal Medicine, 163,* 1524–1528.

Haight, B., Michel, K., Y., & Hendrix, S. (2000). The extended effects of the life review in nursing home residents. *International Journal of Aging and Human Development, 50,* 151–168.

Hanson, A. E. & Scogin, F. (2008). Older adults' acceptance of psychological, pharmacological, and combination treatments for geriatric depression. *Journal of Gerontology: Psychological Sciences, 63B,* P245–P248.

Harralson, T. L., White, T. M., Regenberg, A. C., Kallan, M. J., & Have, T. T. (2002). Similarities and differences in depression among black and white nursing home residents. *American Journal of Geriatric Psychiatry, 10,* 175–184.

Harvey, P. D. (2005). *Schizophrenia in late life: Aging effects on symptoms and course of illness.* Washington, D.C.: American Psychological Association, 2005.

Hasin, D. S. & Grant, B. F. (2004). Co-occurrence of DSM-IV alcohol abuse in DSM-IV alcohol dependence. *Archives of General Psychiatry, 61,* 891–896.

Health and Retirement Study. (2008). *A longitudinal study of health, retirement, and aging.* Retrieved December 2009, from http://hrsonline.s.umich.edu

Hebert, L. E., Scherr, P. A., Bienias, J. L., Bennett, D. A., & Evans, D. A. (2003). Alzheimer disease in the U.S. population: Prevalence estimates using the 2000 census. *Archives of Neurology, 60,* 1119–1122.

Heisel, M. J. & Duberstein, P. R. (2005). Suicide prevention in older adults. *Clinical Psychology, 12,* 243.

Hendricks, J. & L. R. Hatch. (2006). Lifestyle and aging. In R. Binstock & L. George (Eds.). *Handbook of aging and the social sciences.* New York: Academic Press, 301–319.

Hill, J. W., Fillit, H., Shah, S. N., del Valle, M. C., & Futterman, R. (2005). Patterns of healthcare utilization and costs for vascular dementia in a community-dwelling population. *Journal of Alzheimer's Disease, 8,* 43–50.

Holstein, M. & Minkler, M. (2003). Self, society and the "new gerontology." *The Gerontologist, 43,* 787–796.

Horgas, A. L., Wilms, H. U., & Baltes, M. M. (1998). Daily life in very old age: Everyday activities as an expression of successful living. *The Gerontologist, 38,* 556–568.

Hudson, R. (2006). Terms of engagement: The right and left look at elder civic activism. *Public Policy and Aging Report, 16,* 13–18.

Hybels, C. & Blazer, D. (2003). Epidemiology of late life mental disorders. *Clinical Geriatric Medicine, 19,* 663–696.

Hyer, L., Carpenter, B., Bishmann, D., & Wu, H. S. (2005). Depression in long-term care. *Clinical Psychology: Science and Practice, 12,* 280–299.

Jeste, N. D., Hays, J. C., & Steffens, D. C. (2006). Clinical correlates of anxious depression among elderly patients with depression. *Journal of Affective Disorders, 90,* 37–41.

Joe, S., R. Baser, E. G., Breeden, Neighbors, H. W., & Jackson, J. S. (2006). Prevalence of and risk factors for lifetime suicide attempts among Blacks in the United States. *Journal of the American Medical Association, 296,* 2112–2123.

Jones, R. N., Marcantonio, E. R., & Rabinowitz, T. (2003). Prevalence and correlates of recognized depression in U.S. nursing homes. *Journal of the American Geriatrics Society, 51,* 1404–1409.

Jung, C. G. (1933). *Modern man in search of a soul.* San Diego: Harcourt Brace and World.

Jung, C. G. (1959). Concerning the archetypes, with special reference to the anima concept. In *C. G. Jung, Collected Works,* (Vol. 9, Part I). Princeton, NJ: Princeton University Press.

Kahn, R. L. (2003). Successful aging: Intended and unintended consequences of a concept. In L. W. Poon, S. H. Gueldner, & B. M. Sprouse (Eds.). *Successful aging and adaptation with chronic diseases.* New York: Springer.

Kaskie, B. & Estes, C. L. (2001). Mental health services policy and the aging. *Journal of Gerontological Social Work, 36,* 99–114.

Katz, S. (2000). Busy bodies: Activity, aging and the management of everyday life. *Journal of Aging Studies, 14,* 135–152.

Keller, M. B., McCullough, J. P., Klein, D. N., Arnow, B., Dunner, D. L., Gelenberg, A. J., et al. (2000). A comparison of nefazodone, the cognitive-behavioral analysis system of psychotherapy, and their combination for the treatment of chronic depression. *New England Journal of Medicine, 342,* 1462–1470.

Kessler, R., Berglund, P., Demler, O., Jin, R., Merikangas, K. R., & Walters, E. E. (2005). Lifetime prevalence and age of onset distributions of DSM-IV disorders in the national co-morbidity survey replication. *Archives of General Psychiatry, 62,* 593–602.

Kiely, D. K., Jones, R. N., Bergmann, M. A., Murphy, K. M., Orav, E. J., & Marcantonio, E. R. (2006). Association between delirium resolution and functional recovery among newly admitted postacute facilities patients. *Journal of Gerontology: Medical Sciences, 61A,* 204–208.

Kliegel, M., Jager, T., & Phillips, L. H. (2007). Emotional development across adulthood. *International Journal of Aging and Human Development, 64,* 217–244.

Krasucki, C., Howard, R., & Mann, A. (1998). The relationship between anxiety disorders and age. *International Journal of Geriatric Psychiatry, 13,* 79–99.

Kukull, W. A., Higdon, R., Bowen, J. D., McCormick, W. C., Teri, L., Schellenberg, G., van Belle, G., et al. (2002). Dementia and Alzheimer disease incidence: A prospective cohort study. *Archives of Neurology, 59,* 1737–1746.

Kunzmann, U. & Gruhn, D. (2005) Age differences in emotional reactivity: The sample case of sadness. *Psychology and Aging, 20,* 47–59.

Lang, I., Guralnic, K. J., Wallace, R., & Melzer, D. (2007). What level of alcohol consumption is hazardous for older people: Functioning and mortality in U.S. and English national cohorts. *Journal of the American Geriatrics Society, 1,* 49–57.

Langa, K. M., Larson, E. B., Karlawish, J. H., Cutler, D. M., Kabeto, M. U., Kim, S. Y., et al. (2008). Trends in the prevalence and mortality of cognitive impairment in the United States. *Alzheimer's and Dementia, 4,* 134–144.

Larson, C., Bele, R., Schlundt, D. G., and McClellan, L. (2006a). Relationship between symptoms of depression, functional health status and chronic disease among a residential samle of African Americans. *Journal of Ambulatory Care Management. 29,* 133–140.

Larson, E. B., Wang, L., Bowen, J. D., McCormick, W. C., Teri, L., Crane, P., & Kukull, W. (2006b). Exercise is associated with reduced risk for incident dementia among persons 65 years of age and older. *Annals of Internal Medicine, 144:* 73–81.

Laurin, D., Verreault, R., Lindsay, J., Mactherson, K. & Rockwood, K. (2001). Physical activity and risk of cognitive impairment and dementia in elderly persons. *Archives of Neurology, 58,* 498–504.

Lazarus, R. S. (1999). *Stress and emotion: A new synthesis.* New York: Springer.

Lenze, E. J., Mulsant, B. H., Shear, M. K., Schulberg, H. C., Dew, M. A., Begley, A. E., Pollock, B. G. & Reynolds, C. F. (2000). Comorbid anxiety disorders in depressed elderly patients. *American Journal of Psychiatry, 157,* 722–728.

Lenze, E. J., Mulsant, B. H., Dew, M., Shear, K., Houck, P., & Pollock, B. G., et al. (2005). Good treatment outcomes in late-life depression with co-morbid anxiety. *Journal of Affective Disorders,* 247–254.

Levine, J. (2004). *Do you remember me? A father, a daughter, and a search for self.* New York: Free Press.

Levinson, D. J. (1977). Middle adulthood in modern society: A sociopsychological view. In G. DiRenzo (Ed.), *We the people: Social change and social character.* Westport, CT: Greenwood Press.

Levinson, D. J. (1986). A conception of adult development. *American Psychologist, 41,* 3–13.

Levinson, D. J. (1996). *Seasons of a woman's life.* New York: Knopf.

Levinson, D. J., Darrow, C. M., Klein, E. B., Levinson, M. H., & McKee, B. (1978). *The seasons of a man's life.* New York: Knopf.

Lim, G. P., Yang, F., Chu, T., Chen, P., Beech, W., et al. (2000). Ibuprofen suppresses plaque pathology and inflammation in a mouse model for Alzheimer's disease. *Journal of Neuroscience, 20,* 5709–5714.

Lincoln, K. (2003). *Race differences in social relations and depression among older adults.* Paper presented at the Hartford Foundation Scholars Orientation, Washington, DC.

Loevinger, J. (1976). *Ego development.* San Francisco: Jossey-Bass.

Loevinger, J. (1997). Stages of personality development. In R. Hogan & J. A. Johnson (Eds.), *Handbook of personality psychology.* St. Louis: Washington University.

Loevinger, J. (1998). Sentence completion test. In J. Loevinger (Ed.). *Technical foundations for measuring ego development.* Mahwah, NJ: Erlbaum.

Lozano, A. M. & Kalia, S. K. (2005). New movement in Parkinson's. *Scientific American, 293,* 68–75.

Magai, C. (2001). Emotions over the life span. In J. E. Birren & K. W. Schaie (Eds.). *Handbook of the psychology of aging* (5th ed.). San Diego: Academic Press.

Magai, C., Cohen, C., Milburn, N., Thorpe, B., McPherson, R., & Peralta, D. (2001). Attachment styles in older European American and African American adults. *Journal of Gerontology: Psychological Sciences, 56A,* S28–S35.

Maiden, R. J., Peterson, S. A., Caya, M., & Hayslip, B. (2003). Personality changes in the old-old. *Journal of Adult Development, 10,* 31–39.

Mattis, S. (1976). Mental status examination for organic mental syndrome in the elderly patient. In R. Bellack & B. Karask (Eds.).

Geriatric psychiatry. New York: Grune and Stratton.

McCrae, R. R. & P. T. Costa. (1997). Personality trait structure as a human universal. *American Psychologist, 52*, 509–516.

McCrae, R. R., Costa, P. T., deLima, M. P., Simoes, A. Ostendorf, F., Angleitner, A., et al. (1999). Age differences in personality across the adult life span: Parallels in five cultures. *Developmental Psychology, 35*, 466–477.

McCrae, R. R., Costa, P. T., Hrebickova, M., Urbánek, T., Martin, T. A., Oryol, V. E., et al. (2004). Age differences in personality traits across cultures: Self-report and observer perspectives. *European Journal of Personality, 18*, 143–157.

McCrae, R. R., Costa, P. T., Ostendorf, F., Angleitner, A., Hrebickova, M., & Avia, M.D., et al. (2000). Nature over nurture: Temperament, personality and life span development. *Journal of Personality and Social Psychology, 78*, 173–186.

McCrae, R. R. & Terracciano, A. (2005). Universal features of personality traits from the observer's perspective: Data from 50 cultures. *Journal of Personality and Social Psychology, 88*, 547–561.

McHugh, K. (2000). The "ageless self:" Emplacement of identities in Sun Belt retirement communities. *Journal of Aging Studies, 14*, 103–115.

Meadows, M. (2008). Medication use and older adults. *FDA Consumer Magazine*, Rockville, MD: Food and Drug Administration. Retrieved August 2008, from http://www.fda.gov/fdac/features/200/406olderadults.html

Meeks, S. (2000). Schizophrenia and related disorders. In S. K. Whitbourne (Ed.). *Psychopathology in later life*. New York: Wiley.

Meeks, S., Looney, S. W., VanHaitsma, K. & Teri, L. (2008). BE-ACTIV: A staff-assisted behavioral intervention for depression in nursing homes. *The Gerontologist, 48*, 105–114.

Merrick, E., Horgan, C., Hodgkin, D., Houghton, S., Panas, L., et al. (2008). Unhealthy drinking patterns in older adults: Prevalence and associated characteristics. *Journal of the American Geriatrics Society, 56*, 214–223.

Minkler, M. & Fadem, P. (2002). Successful aging: A disability perspective. *Journal of Disability Policy Studies, 12*, 229.

Mitchell, A. J. & Subramaniam, H. (2005). Prognosis of depression in old age compared to middle age: A systematic review of comparative studies. *American Journal of Psychiatry, 162*, 1588–1601.

Mitzner, T. L. & Kemper, S. (2003). Oral and written language in late adulthood, Findings from the Nun Study. *Experimental Aging Research, 29*, 457–474.

Mojtabi, R. & Olfson, M. (2004). Major depression in community-dwelling middle-aged and older adults. *Psychological Medicine*, 2004, *34*, 623–634.

Montross, L. P., Depp, C., Daly, J., Reichstadt, J., Golshan, S., Moore, D., et al. (2006). Correlates of self-rated successful aging among community-dwelling older adults. *American Journal of Geriatric Psychiatry, 14*, 43–51.

Moody, H. (2004). From successful aging to conscious aging. In M. Wykle, P. Whitehouse, & D. Morris (Eds.). *Successful aging through the lifespan*. New York: Springer, 55–69.

Mortimer, J. A., Gosche, K. M., Riley, K. P., Markesbery, W. R., & Snowdon, D. A. (2004). Delayed recall, hippocampal volume and Alzheimer neuropathology: Findings from the Nun Study. *Neurology, 62*, 428–432.

Mrack, R. E. & Griffin, W. S. (2004). Trisomy 21 and the brain. *Journal of Neuropathology and Explorational Neurology, 63*, 679–685.

Mroczek, D. K. & Spiro, A. (2003). Modeling intraindividual change in personality traits: Findings from the Normative Aging Study. *Journal of Gerontology: Psychological Sciences, 58B*, P153–P165.

Mroczek, D. K., Spiro, A., & Griffin, P. W. (2006). Personality and aging. In J. E. Birren & K. W Schaie. (Eds.). *Handbook of the psychology of aging* (6th ed.). Burlington, MA: Elsevier Academic Press.

Mui, A. C. & Kang, S. Y. (2006). Acculturation stress and depression among Asian immigrant elders. *Social Work, 51*, 243–250.

National Institute of Mental Health (NIMH). (2006). *Research on mental illnesses in older adults.* Retrieved February 2006, from http://grants.nih.gov/grants/guide/pa-files/PA-03-014.html

National Institute on Drug Abuse. (2007). *Research report services–Prescription drugs: Abuse and addiction.* Retrieved September 2007, from http://www.nida.nih.gov/ResearchReorts/Prescriptons/prescription5.html

Neimeyer, R. A. (Ed.). (2001). *Meaning reconstruction and the experience of loss.* Washington, DC: American Psychological Association.

O'Connell, J. J. (2005). *Premature mortality in homeless populations: A review of the literature.* Nashville, TN: National Health Care for the Homeless Council.

Office of Applied Studies. (2008). *The NSDUH Report: Substance use among older adults: 2002 and 2003.* Retrieved March 2008 from, http://www.oas.samhsa.gov

Olichney, J. M., Sabbagh, M. N., Hofstetter, C. R., Galasko, D., Grundman, M., Katzman, R., Thal, L. J., et al. (1997). The impact of apolipoprotein E4 on cause of death in Alzheimer's disease. *Neurology, 49,* 76–81.

Oquendo, M. A. (2001). Ethnic and sex differences in suicide rates relative to major depression in the United States. *American Journal of Psychiatry, 158,* 1656.

Patterson, T. L, Bucardo, J., McKibbin, C. L., Mausbach, B. T., Moore, D., Barrio, C., et al., (2005). Development and pilot testing of a new psychosocial intervention for older Latinos with chronic psychosis. *Schizophrenia Bulletin, 31,* 922–930.

Peterson, B. E. & Klohnen, E. C. (1995). Realization of generativity in two samples of women at midlife. *Psychology and Aging, 10,* 20–29.

Phillips, L. H., Henry, J. D., Hosie, J. A., & Milne, A. B. (2008). Effective regulation of the experience and expression of negative affect in old age. *Journal of Gerontology: Psychological Sciences, 63B,* P138–P145.

Plassman, B. L., Havlik, R. J., Steffens, D. C., Helms, M. J., Newman, T. N., Drosdick, D., et al. (2000). Documented head injury in early adulthood and risk of Alzheimer's disease and other dementias. *Neurology, 55,* 1158–1166.

Podewils, L. J., Guallar, E. L., Kuller, H., Fried, L. P., Lopez, O. L., & Carlson, M. (2005). Physical activity, APOE genotype, and dementia risk. *American Journal of Epidemiology, 161,* 639–651.

Project Mainstream. (2005). *Interdisciplinary faculty development in substance abuse education. Module VII: Substance use/misuse/abuse among older adults.* Providence, RI: AMERSA.

Rapaport, M. J., Mamdani, M., & Herrman, N. (2006). Electroconvulsive therapy in older adults: 13-year trends. *Canadian Journal of Psychiatry, 51,* 616–619.

Reisberg, B., Doody, R., Stoffler, A., F. Schmitt, S. Ferris, & H. J. Mobius. (2003). Memantine in moderate-to-severe Alzheimer's disease. *New England Journal of Medicine, 348,* 1333–1341.

Reisberg, B., Ferris, S. H., De Leon, M. J., & Crook, T. (1982). The Global Deterioration Scale for assessment of primary degenerative dementia. *American Journal of Psychiatry, 139,* 1136–1139.

Reynolds, C. F., Dew, M. A., Pollock, B. G., Mulsant, B. H., Franks, E., Miller, M. D., et al. (2006). Maintenance treatment of major depression in old age. *New England Journal of Medicine, 354,* 1130–1138.

Richards, J. B., Papaioannou, A., Adachi, J. D., Joseph, L., Whitson, H. E., Prior, J. C., et al. (2007). Effect of selective serotonin reuptake inhibitors on the risk of fracture. *Archives of Internal Medicine, 167,* 188–194.

Riley, K. P., Snowdon, D. A., Desrosiers, M. F., & Markesbery, W. R. (2005). Early life linguistic ability, late in life cognitive function and neuropathology: Findings from the Nun Study. *Neurobiology of Aging, 26,* 341–347.

Rohr, M. K. & Lang, F. R. (2009). Aging well together–A mini-review. *Gerontology, 55,* 333–343.

Rosen, D., Smith, M., & Reynolds, C. (2008). The prevalence of mental and physical health disorders among older methadone patients. *The American Journal of Geriatric Psychiatry, 16,* 488–497.

Rowe, J. W. & Kahn, R. L. (1987). Human aging: Usual and successful. *Science, 237,* 143–149.

Rowe, J. W. & Kahn, R. L. (1997). Successful aging. *The Gerontologist, 37,* 433–440.

Rowe, J. W. & Kahn, R. L. (1998). *Successful aging.* New York: Pantheon Books.

Ryff, C. D. & Singer, B. (2009). Understanding healthy aging: Key components and their integration. In V. L. Bengtson, M. Silverstein, N. M. Putney, & D. Gans (Eds.). *Handbook of Theories of Aging.* New York: Springer.

Ryff, C. D., Kwan, C. M. L., & Singer, B. H. (2001). Personality and aging: Flourishing agendas and future challenges. In J. E. Birren & K. W. Schaie (Eds.). *Handbook of the psychology of aging* (5th ed.). San Diego: Academic Press.

Sambamoorthi, U., Shea, D., & Crystal, S. (2003). Total and out-of-pocket expenditures for prescription drugs among older persons. *The Gerontologist, 43,* 345–359.

Sano, M., Ernesto, C., Thomas, R. G., Klauber, M. R., Schafer, K., & Grundman, M. (1997). A controlled clinical trial of selegiline, alpha-tocopherol or both as treatment for Alzheimer's disease. *New England Journal of Medicine, 336,* 1216–1222.

Schaie, K. W. & Willis, S. L. (1991). Adult personality and psychomotor performance. *Journals of Gerontology, 46B,* P275–P284.

Schenk, D., Barbour, R., Dunn, W., Gordon, G., Grajeda, H., Guido, T., Hu, K., et al. (1999). Immunization with amyloid-B attenuates Alzheimer-disease-like pathology in the PDAPP mouse. *Nature, 400,* 173–177.

Schulz, R., Beach, S. R., Ives, D. G., Martire, L. M., Ariyo, A. A., & Kop, W. J. (2000). Association between depression and mortality in older adults. *Archives of Internal Medicine, 160,* 1761–1768.

Seeman, T. E., Unger, J. B., McAvay, G., & Mendes de Leon, D. (1999). Self-efficacy beliefs and perceived declines in functional ability. *Journals of Gerontology: 54B,* P214–P222.

Seltzer, B. (2006). Cholinesterase inhibitors in the clinical management of Alzheimer's disease: Importance of early and persistent treatment. *Journal of International Medical Research, 34,* 339–347.

Sheldon, K. M. & Kasser, T. (2001). Getting older, getting better? Personal strivings and psychological maturity across the life span. *Developmental Psychology, 37,* 491–501.

Shibusawa, T. (2006). Older adults with substance/alcohol abuse problems. In B. Berkman & S. D'Ambruoso (Eds.), *Handbook of social work in health and aging.* New York: Oxford University Press.

Shumaker, S. A., Legault, C., Rapp, S. R., et al. (2003). Estrogen plus progestin and the incidence of dementia and mild cognitive impairment in postmenopausal women. *Journal of the American Medical Association, 289,* 2651–2662.

Snowdon, D. (2001). *Aging with grace: What the Nun Study teaches us about leading longer, healthier, and more meaningful lives.* New York: Bantam.

Snowdon, D. (2003). Healthy aging and dementia: Findings from the Nun Study. *Annals of Internal Medicine, 139,* 450–454.

Snowdon, D., Greiner, L. H., & Markesbery, W. R. (2000). Linguistic ability in early life and the neuropathology of Alzheimer's disease: Findings from the Nun Study. In R. N. Kalaria & P. Ince (Eds.), *Annals of New York Academy of Sciences.* New York: New York Academy of Sciences.

Solimeo, S. (2008). Sex and gender in older adults' experience of Parkinson's disease. *Journal of Gerontology: Social Sciences, 63B,* S42–S48.

Speciale, S., Bellelli, G., Lucchi, E., Trabucchi, M. (2007). Delirium and functional recovery in elderly patients. *Journal of Gerontology: Medical Sciences, 62A,* 107–108.

Strawbridge, W., Wallhagen, M., & Cohen, R. D. (2002). Successful aging and well-being: Self-rated compared with Rowe and Kahn. *The Gerontologist, 42,* 727–733.

Substance Abuse and Mental Health Services Administration (SAMHSA). (2001). *Summary of the findings from the National Household Survey on Drug Abuse.* NHSDA Series H-13, DHHS Publication SMA 01-3549. Rockville, MD: NHSDA.

Surgeon General. (1999). *The Surgeon General's Call to Action to Prevent Suicide.* Retrieved 1999, from http://www.surgeongeneral.gov/library/calltoaction/fact2.htm

Surgeon General. (2001). *Mental health: Culture, Race, Ethnicity Supplement to "Mental health: Report of the Surgeon General."* Retrieved 2001, from http://www.mentalhealth.org/cre

Szekely, C. A., Thorne, J. E., Zandi, P., Ek, M., Messias, E., Breitner, J. C. S., et al. (2004). Nonsteroidal anti-inflammatory drugs for the prevention of Alzheimer's disease: A systematic review. *Neuroepidemiology, 23,* 153–169.

Tariot, P. N., Farlow, M. R., Grossberg, G. T., Graham, S. M., McDonald, S., & Gergel, I. (2004). Memantine treatment in patients with moderate to severe Alzheimer's disease already receiving donepezil. *Journal of the American Medical Association, 291,* 317–324.

Teri, L., Gibbons, L. E., McCurry, S. M., Logsdon, R. G., Buchner, D. M., Barlow, W. E., Kukull, W. A., et al. (2003). Exercise plus behavioral management in patients with Alzheimer disease, *Journal of the American Medical Association, 290,* 2015–2022.

Terracciano, A., McCrae, R. R., & Costa, P. T. (2006). Longitudinal trajectories in Guilford-Zimmerman Temperament survey data: Results from the Baltimore Longitudinal Study of Aging. *Journal of Gerontology: Psychological Sciences, 61B,* P108–P116.

Trzesniewski, K. H., Donellan, M. B., & Robins, R. W. (2003). Stability of self-esteem across the life span. *Journal of Personality and Social Psychology, 84,* 205–206.

Unutzer, J., Katon, W., Callahan, C. M., Williams, J. W., Hunkeler, E., Harpole, L., et al. (2003). Depression treatment in a sample of 1801 depressed older adults in primary care. *Journal of the American Geriatrics Society, 51,* 505–514.

Vaillant, G. E. (1977). *Adaptation to life.* Boston: Little, Brown.

Vaillant, G. E. (1994). Ego mechanisms of defense and personality psychopathology. *Journal of Abnormal Psychology, 103,* 44–50.

Vaillant, G. E. (2002). *Aging well.* Boston: Little, Brown.

Van Citters, A. D., Pratt, S. I., Bartels, S. J., and Jeste, D. V. (2005). Evidence-based review or pharmacologic and nonpharmacologic treatment for older adults with schizophrenia.

Psychiatric Clinics of North America, 28, 913–939.

Van der Wurff, F. B., Stek, M. L., Hoogendijk, W. L., & Beekman, A. T. (2004). Electroconvulsive therapy for depressed elderly (Cochrane review). *The Cochrane Library,* 1.

Van Dongen, M. C., van Rossum, E., Kessels, A. G. H., Sielhorst, H. J. G., & Knipschild, P. G. (2000). The efficacy of ginkgo for elderly people with dementia and age-associated memory impairment: New results of a randomized clinical trial. *Journal of the American Geriatrics Society, 48,* 1183–1194.

Verghese, J., Lipton, R. B., Hall, C. B., Kuslansky, G., Katz, M. J., & Buschke, H. (2002). Abnormality of gait as a predictor of non-Alzheimer's dementia. *New England Journal of Medicine, 347,* 1761–1768.

Whitbourne, S. K. & Primu, L. A. (1996). Physical identity. In J. E. Birren (Ed.). *Encyclopedia of Gerontology.* San Diego: Academic Press.

Windsor, T. D., Anstey, K. J., & Rodgers, B. (2008). Volunteering and psychological well-being among young-old adults: How much is too much? *The Gerontologist, 48,* 59-70.

Windsor, T. D., Coleman, Y., Yaffee, R., & Casimir, G. (2008). Volunteering and psychological well-being among young-old adults: How much is too much? *The Gerontologist, 48,* 59–70.

Wray, S. (2003). Women growing older: Agency, ethnicity and culture. *Sociology, 37,* 511–527.

Yin, S. (2006). *Elderly white men afflicted by high suicide rates.* Washington, DC: Population Reference Bureau.

Zalaquett, C. & Stens, A. (2006). Psychosocial treatments for major depression and dysthymia in older adults. *Journal of Counseling and Development, 84,* 192–201.

Zandi, P. P., Anthony, J. C., Khachaturian, A. S., Stone, S. V., Gustafson, D., Tschantz, J. T., et al. (2004). Reduced risk of Alzheimer's disease in users of antioxidant vitamin supplements. *Archives of Neurology, 61,* 82–88.

Zanjani, R., Zubrtitsky, C., Mullahy, M., and Oslin, D. (2006). Predictors of adherence within an intervention research study of the at-risk older drinker. PRISM-E. *Journal of*

Geriatric Psychiatry and Neurology, 19, 231–238.

Zarit, S. H. (2009). A good old age: Theories of mental health and aging. In Bengtson, V. L., Silverstein, M., Putney, N. M., & Gans, D. (Eds.). *Handbook of Theories of Aging.* New York: Springer.

Zarowitz, B. (2006). Medication overuse and misuse. *Geriatric Nursing, 27,* 204–205.

Zhang, J., Goodlett, D. R., & Montine, T. J. (2005). Proteomic biomarker discovery in cerebrospinal fluid for neurodegenerative diseases. *Journal of Alzheimer's Disease, 8,* 377–386.

7

Love, Intimacy, and Sexuality in Old Age

The previous chapter focused on personality: who one is and how one feels about oneself. An important aspect of one's personality is sexuality. In fact, **sexuality** encompasses many aspects of one's being as a man or a woman, including one's self-concept, gender-role identity, body image, and relationships. Sexuality is different from **sex**, which is defined as a biological function involving genital intercourse, and from the sexual excitement of **orgasm.** Sexuality also includes the expression of feelings—love, loyalty, passion, affection, esteem, and affirmation of one's body and its functioning—as well as **intimacy** or the freedom to express and respond to human closeness through feelings of deep mutual regard, affection and trust; these are part of healthy and active aging. A person's speech and movement, vitality, and ability to enjoy life are involved in sexuality. As with other aspects of aging discussed throughout this text, sexuality encompasses physiological, emotional, intellectual, spiritual, behavioral, and sociocultural components. Patterns of sexual expression vary widely among older populations, just as they do at all ages.

Overall, sexual behavior in old age is influenced by

- physiological changes often associated with aging
- the individual's personal sexual history, self-concept, and self-esteem
- the person's sexual orientation
- the psychological meaning attached to one's sexual experiences
- chronic illness; the degree of physical fitness and functional ability
- the physical and social environment, such as living arrangements, the availability of sexual partners and opportunities for intimacy
- others' attitudes and practices (e.g., family, health care providers, long-term care staff)

In many instances, dynamic contextual factors may exert greater influence than physiological changes.

Attitudes and Beliefs about Sexuality in Later Life

It is striking that, at a time when safe sex for nearly every segment of our population is publicly discussed, outdated ideas related to sex and aging persist, and research on sexuality and aging is still relatively limited (Bancroft, 2007; Lindau, Schumm, Laumann, et al., 2007). Despite its powerful role in many elders' lives, sexuality remains one of the least understood and visible aspects of active aging (Henry & McNab, 2003; Pangman & Seguire, 2000). Widespread stereotypes, misconceptions, and jokes about old age and sexuality can powerfully and negatively affect older people's sexual experience. Such biases stem in part from ageism and ableism (a form of discrimination against persons who are disabled and in favor of those who appear able-bodied), such as perceptions that older people, especially women and those with chronic physical or mental disabilities, are unattractive and therefore asexual. Another example of ageism is the stereotype that elders lack energy and are devoid of sexual feeling, and therefore are not interested in sex. Since sexuality in our society tends to be equated with youthful standards of attractiveness, older women and individuals with chronic illness and disability may experience the most negative consequences from ageist and sexist definitions. Even more deleterious effects may be experienced when sexual interaction between older persons is viewed as socially unacceptable or even physically harmful (e.g., a health care provider who advises a person with a terminal illness against engaging in sexual activity). It is noteworthy that research and education on loss, grief and aging are widely available, but very rarely are the topics of love and aging broached (DeLamater & Friedrich, 2002; Pangman & Seguire, 2000; Zeiss & Kasl-Godley, 2001).

These attitudes and beliefs may stem from misinformation, such as the perception that sexual activity and desire do and should decline with old age. Alternatively, older people who speak of enjoying sexuality or express caring and physical affection for one another may be infantilized, defined as "cute," and teased by professionals, their age peers, and family members. Such public scrutiny and ridicule frequently occur among residents and staff of long-term care facilities. Surrounded by societal stereotypes and fearing negative judgments, older people may unnecessarily withdraw from all forms of sexual expression, thereby depriving themselves and their partners of the energy and vitality inherent in sexuality. On the other hand, some elders genuinely do not

> **POINTS TO PONDER**
>
> Think about jokes or stories you have heard about older adults and sexuality or messages on birthday cards. What have they conveyed? How did they affect your understanding of sexuality and aging?

desire to engage in the physical aspects of sexual behavior. Since our sexual nature goes far beyond whether we are sexually active at any particular point in life, elders need to be comfortable with their decisions regarding expression of their sexuality. Accor- dingly, professionals need to respect older adults' choices and values.

Yet for many older adults, sexual activity, in the broadest sense of encompassing both physical and emotional interaction, is necessary for them to feel alive, affirm their identity, and communicate with their partners. It can also enhance their well-being (Henry & McNab, 2003; Trudel, Turgeon, & Piche, 2000; Zeiss & Kasl-Godley, 2001). Fortunately, the media, gerontologists, and other professionals are beginning to convey the message that sex is acceptable—even desirable—in old age. This is especially true among aging baby boomers, who experienced the sexual revolution of the 60s and who will redefine sexuality in old age. One sign of change is that the young-old appear more accepting of and permissive in their attitudes toward sexuality and intimacy than in the past (AARP, 2004). An increase in the frequency and range of sexual activity from 1999 to 2004 is illustrated in Figure 7.1 on the next page.

Myths and Reality about Physiological Changes and Frequency of Sexual Activity

One of the most prevalent societal myths is that age-related physiological changes detrimentally affect sexual functioning. Such misconceptions were shaped by early studies on sexuality, where questions about older adults' sexual behavior were rarely raised.

Other early studies included questions about sexuality but focused only on the frequency of sexual intercourse between a man and a woman. These researchers overlooked the

Sexuality and intimacy are important throughout the later years.

subjective or qualitative aspects of sexuality in old age, as well as the experience of LGBT individuals. For example, from 1938 to 1948, Kinsey and his colleagues studied primarily 16- to 55-year-olds, and their discussion of respondents over age 60 only focused on the incidence of sexual intercourse, not its quality. In fact, their 735-page report devoted only three pages to the topic of sex and aging (Schiavi, 1996). Using the number of orgasms or ejaculations as the measure of good sex, Kinsey and his colleagues found that by age 70, 25 percent of men experienced sexual dysfunction. Women were portrayed as reaching the peak of their sexual activity in their late 20s or 30s, then remaining on that plateau through their 60s, after which they showed a slight decline in sexual response capability (Kinsey, Pomeroy, & Martin, 1948, 1953). Because Kinsey and colleagues minimized the broader psychological aspects of sexuality, they failed to address the subjective meaning of sex at different ages. Older individuals may have sexual intercourse less often, but it may be as or more satisfying than at younger ages. In fact, few age-related physiological changes prevent continued sexual enjoyment and activity in old age.

One reason that sexual activity and pleasure may appear to decline with age is because of the cross-sectional research designs used. Studies of

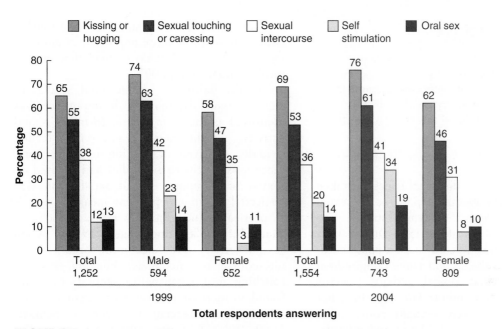

FIGURE 7.1 Sexual Activities Engaged in Once a Week or More Often in Past Six Months: 1999 vs. 2004

SOURCE: American Association of Retired Persons, 2004

sexuality in old age often reflect the methodological limitations, described in Chapter 1, when younger and older cohorts are compared at one point in time. For example, the 1954 Duke Longitudinal Study concluded that there are gradual age-related declines in frequency of sexual activity for older adults compared to their young and middle-aged counterparts, especially for women and unmarried individuals. The median age for stopping intercourse was 68 in men and 60 in women (Pfeiffer & Davis, 1972). This study had several additional limitations. The definition of sexual activity was confined to heterosexual intercourse, and the respondents constituted a cohort of individuals raised during a period of strict sexual conservatism. As discussed in Chapter 1, such cross-sectional data fail to give a lifetime picture of an individual's sexual behavior. The low levels of sexual activity reported may be related to the cohort effect of elders who grew up in an era still influenced by conservative Victorian values, rather than any age-related physiological changes in sexual functioning. For this cohort, sex was

typically viewed as intercourse primarily for reproductive purposes between a man and women, (Schiavi & Rehman, 1995). Another limitation is that study participants were primarily Caucasian, well-educated, and healthy older adults who self-identified as heterosexual (Zeiss & Kasl-Godley, 2001).

THE INVISIBILITY OF OLDER ADULTS IN EARLY SEXUALITY RESEARCH

- Kinsey, 1948, 1953: 126 men and 56 women over age 60; 4 men over age 80
- Masters and Johnson, 1966, 1970: 20 older males
- Hite Report on Female Sexuality, 1976: 19 women out of a total of 1,844 were age 60 or older
- Janus Report on Sexual Behavior, 1993: 34 percent were age 51 and over
- National Health and Social Life Survey, 1994: excluded those age 60 and over

POINTS TO PONDER

Is older adults' sexuality largely invisible to you? Or have you heard about it mostly through jokes, the media, the Internet, or birthday greeting cards? If so, what did these images convey? How did they affect your understanding of sexuality and aging?

When such methodological issues are taken into account, the identified patterns of sexual activity differ from these early studies. For example, a reanalysis of the 1954 Duke Longitudinal Study data—to control for a possible cohort effect—and the second Duke Longitudinal Study showed that sexual activity patterns remain stable from mid-to-late life. In other words, those who were sexually conservative and inactive in young adulthood and mid-life, perhaps because of their social upbringing, sustained that pattern as they aged. Similarly, those who were more sexually involved in young adulthood and middle age remained active in old age. A later analysis of the Duke data also found older women to be more interested in sex than older men. However, the rate of sexual activity among older women declined, partly because of the absence of partners or because husbands tended to curtail or discontinue sexual

activities. In fact, marital status and relationship issues appear to be more important in influencing women's sexual behavior than they are for men's (Lindau et al., 2007).

In the Baltimore Longitudinal Studies of Aging, sexual dysfunction or impotence was identified as the main barrier to men's sexual activity. Yet the men did not report feeling sexually deprived or lacking in self-esteem. Since most of the early studies had focused on sexual performance, sexual satisfaction was neglected as an independent measure that is theoretically and clinically relevant (Schiavi, Mandeli, & Schreiner-Engel, 1999). When sexual activity is defined more broadly than intercourse to encompass hugging, kissing, touching, and masturbation, activity rates are found to increase to over 80 percent for men and over 60 percent for women (Schiavi, 1999; Wiley & Bortz, 1996). Recent studies that include open-ended questions identify the excitement, enjoyment, and pleasure—the passion and romance—of late-life sexuality and the value older adults place on the quality and meaning of intimate relationships. Accordingly, sexual activity and satisfaction are found to be related to 53 percent of older men's and 37 percent of older women's sense of self-worth, competence, and quality of life (AARP, 2004).

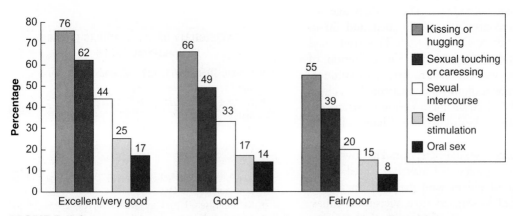

FIGURE 7.2 **Engaged in Sexual Activity at Least Once per Week by Overall Health Status**
SOURCE: American Association of Retired Persons, 2004

One of the first large-scale studies that provided evidence for continued sexual satisfaction in old age was the work of Masters and Johnson (1981). In their classic study of sexual responsiveness across the life course, Masters and Johnson determined that the capacity for both functioning and fulfillment does not disappear with age, even though physiological changes occur. They concluded that age-based limits to sexual behavior do not exist. Similarly, 75 percent of the respondents in the classic Starr and Weiner study (1981), which explored the meaning and significance of sexuality in old age, stated that sex is the same or better than when they were younger. Although the majority of female respondents considered orgasm as essential to a good sexual experience, they also emphasized mutuality, love, and caring as central to their enjoyment and willingly varied their sexual practices to achieve satisfaction. Male respondents stated that not only was the physical stimulation of sex important, but that it was necessary for them to feel alive and reaffirm their identity.

Later studies, with predominantly white heterosexual samples, reported that many older adults, especially men, and even among those over age 80, remain sexually active. As with most behaviors, there is a wide range. Some individuals after age 55 experience an increase in sexual activity, perhaps because of the absence of children in the home (Matthias et al., 1997; Schiavi & Rehman, 1995; Weg, 1996). For others, sexual activity in old age may represent a continuation of activity earlier in life (Willert & Semans, 2000). Overall, sexual inactivity appears to depend on life circumstances, such as illness or mobility problems, not lack of interest or desire (Zeiss & Kasl-Godley, 2001). The methodological limitations of most studies of older adults and sexuality are summarized in the box in the next column.

In the National Social Life, Health and Aging Project (NSHAP)—a community-based survey of 3,005 adults—73 percent of respondents age 57 to 64, 53 percent among those

> ## METHODOLOGICAL LIMITS OF RESEARCH ON SEXUALITY AND OLDER ADULTS
>
> - Emphasis on frequency of intercourse, not its meaning or quality or on other types of sexual activity
> - Small sample size, low response rates, and associated selection bias in most studies
> - Nonrandom and nonrepresentative samples, including lack of elders of color and of LGBT elders
> - Because of social taboos against sexuality in old age, respondents may overestimate or underestimate sexual activity, or provide socially acceptable responses
> - The cohort age 70 and older today is less forthcoming than baby boomers will be because of their socialization not to discuss private issues, such as sex
> - Researchers' discomfort or biases about sex and aging may influence the nature of their questions and interactions with respondents
> - Primarily self-reports of sexual activity

65 to 74 years of age, and 25 percent among the age-group 75 to 85 years reported that they were sexually active. Among the oldest-old adults who were sexually active, 23 percent indicated they had sex once a week or more. Women were significantly less likely to report sexual activity; this gender difference increased with age, primarily because of lack of partners. Rates of sexual activity declined and reported sexual problems increased among those who rated their health as poor (Bancroft, 2007; Lindau et al., 2007).

A 2004 AARP phone survey of 2,930 men and women over age 45 sought to understand the factors affecting sexuality and quality of life of midlife and older adults, and to compare the results to those of a 1999 AARP survey. A major advantage of the later survey was the addition of Latino (3 percent), Native American (1 percent), African American (8 percent), and Asian (1 percent) respondents. The following

POINTS TO PONDER

When you were growing up, how did you perceive your parents' and grandparents' sexuality? What were your sources of information about older adults and sexuality? How did these affect your thinking? Have your views changed?

patterns were identified among the subgroup age 70 and older:

- 87 percent of men and 63 percent of women had engaged in various forms of sexual expression (kissing, hugging, sexual touching or caressing, intercourse, self-stimulation, or oral sex) in the past 6 months.
- 85 percent of men and 55 percent of women indicated that they always or usually have an orgasm when engaging in sexual intercourse.
- Of those with a partner, 85 percent of men and 81 percent of women reported moderate to extreme physical pleasure from their relationship.
- Of those with a partner, a similarly high proportion, 88 percent of men and 83 percent of women, reported moderate to extreme emotional satisfaction from their relationship with their partner.
- Sexual activity and satisfaction were related to 53 percent of older men's and 37 percent of older women's sense of self-worth, quality of life, and competence.
- Patterns of sexual activity and satisfaction were similar across ethnic and racial groups (AARP, 2004).

The following is a summary of recent studies about older people and sexuality:

- As our biological clocks change with age, the frequency or the nature of sexual experience does not change for better or worse. Older people who remain sexually active do not change significantly in their frequency of sexual relations (longitudinal data). Rather, sexual activity appears to be much lower when older people are compared with younger persons at the same point in time (cross-sectional data).
- When a partner is available, the rate of sexual behavior is fairly stable throughout life. Individuals who have been sexually active all their lives continue to enjoy sexual satisfaction in their later years, although their experience may differ subjectively from earlier in life (DeLamater & Friedrich, 2002; Zeiss & Kasl-Godley, 2001). Such changes can be positive.
- Although good physical and mental health are predictors of sexual activity and satisfaction, even older people with chronic health problems, depression, and cognitive dysfunction can achieve sexual satisfaction. On the other hand, undiagnosed or untreated sexual problems can lead to or can be accompanied by depression or sexual withdrawal.
- Relationships are more important than sexual activity per se. Regardless of the length or nature of a late-life relationship, its quality is enhanced by emotional intimacy and mutually respectful sexual interactions (AARP, 2004; Lindau et al., 2007; Pangman & Seguire, 2000; Willert & Semans, 2000; Zeiss & Kasl-Godley, 2001).

SEEKING NEW LOVE

Contrary to stereotypes of lack of intimacy and sexuality among older adults, two AARP surveys found that many adults over age 50 are eager to date and form new relationships. The most common ways for meeting new people are religious organizations, outdoor clubs, speed dating, the Internet, personal ads, special interest services (to meet others with similar interests), and matchmakers. And for many older adults (as is true for younger adults), informal networks or just being in the right place at the right time are key to forming new and intimate relationships (Mahoney, 2003; AARP, 2004).

Lesbian, Gay, Bisexual, and Transgender (LGBT) Partners in Old Age

Even though many examples of sexual activity in this chapter are presented in terms of heterosexual marital relationships, this is not always the case. Although the U.S. Census or other large-scale data collection instruments do not ask about sexual orientation and gender identity, gay men and lesbians are estimated to comprise about 8 percent of the total population, with a similar proportion among older adults (Sperber, 2006). Research on LGBT elders is limited. A 2002 comprehensive MEDLINE search showed that only 0.1 percent of the 3.8 million articles focused on LGBT populations addressed LGBT elders' sexuality (Boehmer, 2002). In the 2004 AARP national survey, 5 percent of men and 1 percent of women age 70 and older reported having current same-sex partners (AARP, 2004). In the NSHAP study described above, less than 2 percent of respondents indicated that their relationship was with someone of the same sex (Lindau et al., 2007). It is important to note that same-sex relationships may be underreported because of beliefs among adults age 65 and older and their families that homosexuality is wrong (Bennett & Gates, 2004). The sociohistorical context and cohort effect profoundly affected the oldest-old experiences of being gay, sexually active, and developing intimate relationships (deVries & Blando, 2004; Wierzalis et al., 2006). Coming of age following World War II and before the New York City Stonewall riots in 1969 and the emergence of Gay Liberation, they were more likely to remain closeted to family, friends, employers, and even to themselves. It is critical that health and social service professionals are sensitive to homosexual relationships, primarily by discarding stereotypical views of the nature of LGBT relationships. Contrary to commonly held images, the varieties of gay and lesbian bonding are similar to heterosexual relationships—ranging from monogamous life partners and

Many lesbian and gay couples maintain long-term commitments to each other.

nonmonogamous primary relationships to serial monogamy and episodic liaisons. LGBT life partners face many of the issues that confront long-term heterosexual couples, such as fears about the loss of sexuality, the death or illness of a sexual partner, or diminished interest in sex because of chronic disease. On the other hand, after a lifetime of ostracism, many older LGBT couples face not only overt discrimination from health and service providers, but also "an atmosphere of silence" and invisibility related to their expression of intimacy and sexuality (Brotman, Ryan, & Cormier, 2003; Butler, 2006; Blank, 2006; deVries & Blando, 2004; Sperber, 2006).

Although sexual activity for LGBT elders varies as much as it does for heterosexuals, there is also a consistent pattern of relatively high life satisfaction with being gay, positive adjustment to aging, and ongoing sexual interest and activity. Both lesbians and gay men are more likely to report a high level of life satisfaction if they are happily partnered and communicating effectively with one another. Satisfaction is also high if they have a strong informal social support system,

REDEFINING SEXUAL ORIENTATION IN LATER LIFE

After her husband left her for a younger woman, a bout with breast cancer, and the death of her 26-year-old daughter, Isabel found herself increasingly drawn to spending time only with women: in a mothers' support group, in a group of midlife women coping with divorce, and through her work. She started attending workshops and lectures through the local college's Women's Information Center. At one of those courses, she met Carla, also recovering from a bitter divorce. They began to spend nearly all their free time together, enjoying the equality and closeness in their relationship. Within a year, Carla moved in with Isabel. Although their adult children were initially shocked by their mothers' behavior, they soon saw the value of the loving support and intimacy that their mothers experienced for the next 26 years.

often defined as family and friends of choice, and have reconstituted what it means to be queer into a positive source of identity (deVries & Blando, 2004; Garnets & Peplau, 2006; Healy, 2002; Hostetler, 2004; Orel, 2004; Wierzalis, Barret, Pope, & Rankins, 2006).

Lesbians age 65 and older, often closeted about their sexual orientation, have generally practiced serial monogamy throughout their lives. However, nearly 50 percent had been married at some point and over 75 percent had had heterosexual intercourse (Garnets & Peplau, 2006). For many of the current cohort of older lesbians, they first became involved in a lesbian relationship at midlife. Even among older women who have hidden their sexual orientation throughout their lives, most usually report a positive self-image and a high degree of sexual satisfaction as they age (Clunis et al., 2005; Garnets & Peplau, 2006; Goldberg, Sickler, & Dibble, 2005; Konik, 2005; Martin & Lyon, 2001; Weinstock, 2004). Older lesbians generally do not fear changes in physical appearance, loneliness, or isolation in old age as much as some heterosexual women do. This may

be because of the strong friendship networks that characterize many lesbian relationships or flexibility in gender roles that allow them to adjust more effectively to the socially constructed beliefs of aging and being old. Most lesbians remain sexually active and attracted to their own age-group, but sexual frequency generally declines. The extent to which sexual activity is considered to be an integral part of a lesbian relationship varies, although sexuality in a broader sense of intimacy and female interdependence continues to be essential to a positive self-identity in old age (Jones & Nystrom, 2002; Weinstock, 2004).

The number of gay men with partners increases with age and peaks among those age 46 to 55. After age 60, the percent of gay couples and the frequency of sexual activity decreases because of death, illness, cautiousness, or rejection of the notion of having a single, lifelong partner. But most gay men report that they are sexually active and are satisfied with their partners and their sex lives. They are more likely to be in long-term relationships (with an average length of 10 years) or none at all, rather than in brief relationships of a year or less. However, unlike lesbians, older gay men are often devalued in youth-oriented gay communities for their graying hair, wrinkles, or added weight. Looking fit and youthful—that is, "not your age"—tends to increase a gay man's acceptability as a partner, with some believing that they are no longer attractive after age 35 (Cohler, 2004; deVries & Blando, 2004; Hostetler, 2004; Wierzalis et al., 2006). Nevertheless, gay men typically maintain positive feelings about themselves and their appearance in old age. Most report a positive sense of self-esteem, well-being, and contentment. Despite societal assumptions of loneliness and social isolation, most gay men have closer friendships in old age than do heterosexual men. For many who have faced societal rejection, intimacy assumes greater importance than sexual activity compared to heterosexuals, and friendships may replace family ties disrupted by the declaration of their homosexuality (Berger & Kelley, 2001; Cruz, 2003; Morrow, 2001; Wierzalis et al., 2006). Overall, older gay men are generally as involved in the gay network and satisfied with their social lives and sexual preference as their younger counterparts (Blank, 2006; MetLife, 2006; Murray & Adam, 2001). On the other hand, compared with younger homosexuals, gay men in today's older cohort tend to:

- fear exposure of their homosexuality
- hide their sexual orientation
- view their relatives, friends, and employers as less accepting of their homosexuality
- see their sexual preference as outside their personal control

However, these differences largely reflect cohort effects, rather than the aging process per se.

As noted in Chapter 4, the increase in HIV/AIDS among the older population is a growing concern. Despite the risks, many older gay men engage in unprotected sex, although less frequently in one-night encounters, and they are more knowledgeable about safe sex than heterosexual age peers. Of additional concern is the increase in high-risk sexual behavior among younger gay men who may be partners with older gay men or who will grow old with HIV. Therefore, ongoing, accessible, and culturally relevant public education about the prevention of HIV/AIDS and safe sex is essential. Older persons with HIV/AIDS are found to be less likely to use emotional support and mental health services than younger people. Such services may need to be reconfigured to meet the emotional needs of elders diagnosed with HIV/AIDS. Preventive and support interventions need also to be culturally congruent (Emlet, 2006; Gorman & Nelson, 2004).

Recommendations for working effectively and respectfully with LGBT elders include:

- Address issues in a matter-of-fact, nonjudgmental manner.
- Be comfortable talking about sexual orientation and behavior.

- Check assumptions and language. For example, ask "do you have a companion or sexual partner" rather than "are you married?"
- Assess the stage of development of sexual identity (e.g., the extent to which the older adult is open about and comfortable with their sexual orientation).
- Be aware of the gay culture and local and national organizations that can provide resources to gay elders.
- View sexual activity for the aging gay, lesbian, or bisexual elder as positive (Wierzalis et al., 2006).

Overall, health care providers, especially staff in long-term care facilities, must recognize LGBT elders' relationships and modify the environment to support their desire for intimacy (Kean, 2006). Similarly, it is vital to affirm LGBT caregivers in their role and to offer them services and support (Hash, 2006).

For both heterosexual and homosexual partners, numerous age-related physiological changes can affect the nature of the sexual response, as we next explain.

Staff in long-term care facilities can provide emotional support through touch.

SENSITIVITY OF STAFF TO LGBT RESIDENTS

In a nursing home in San Francisco, a chronically ill, wheelchair-bound African American man who had become depressed and withdrawn, confided to a psychiatrist that "he liked men." That clue was the catalyst for a collaborative project between concerned staff and local gay and lesbian leaders to develop a social support system to draw out presumed closeted and lonely LGBT residents. Staff participated in sensitivity training, and a LGBT Rainbow group was formed. Social workers and nursing staff sensitively and discretely directed invitations to individuals who might be interested in coming to a Halloween party. Fifteen LGBT residents came, danced in wheelchairs, laughed, and sang. A year later, the Rainbow group had become the largest social support group at the facility (Martin & Lyon, 2001).

Women and Age-Related Physiological Changes

With the growing numbers of women in the 45- to 54-year-old age-group, increasing attention is being given to menopause. As noted in Chapter 4, the major changes for women as they grow older are associated with the reduction in estrogen and progesterone, the predominant hormones produced by the ovaries during menopause. The **climacteric**—loss of reproductive ability—takes place in three phases: perimenopause, menopause, and post-menopause, and may extend over many years.

Perimenopause, also known as the menopausal transition, is marked by a decline in ovarian function when a woman's ovaries stop producing eggs and significantly decrease their monthly production of estrogen, resulting in widely fluctuating estrogen levels and unpredictable menstrual cycles. This can occur as long as 10 years before menopause, starting as young as age 35. Only recently have researchers and health care providers recognized that perimenopause brings hot flashes around the head and upper body, lapses in concentration and memory, mood swings, sleep troubles, irritability, and

migraines typically associated with menopause. Unfortunately, some health care providers dismiss these early symptoms as being "all in her head." **Menopause** is a period in a woman's life when there is a gradual cessation of the menstrual cycle, including irregular cycles and menses, which are related to the loss of ovarian function. Menopause is considered to have occurred when 12 consecutive months have passed without a menstrual period (**postmenopause**). The average age of menopause is 51 years, although it can begin as early as age 40 and as late as age 58. Smoking can lead to early menopause. Surgical removal of the uterus—hysterectomy—also brings an end to menstruation (NIA, 2008).

Physiological changes related to the decrease in estrogen in menopause and postmenopause include:

- hot flashes
- urogenital atrophy, which can make intercourse painful
- urinary tract changes
- bone changes (osteoporosis)

Hot flashes are caused by vasomotor instability, when the nerves overrespond to decreases in hormone levels. This affects the hypothalamus (the part of the brain that regulates body temperature), causing the blood vessels to dilate or constrict. Blood then rushes to the skin surface, causing perspiration, flushing, and increased pulse rate and temperature. Hot flashes are characterized by a sudden sensation of heat in the upper body, often accompanied by a drenching sweat and sometimes followed by chills. Gradually diminishing in frequency, hot flashes generally disappear within a few years.

Hormonal changes and vasomotor instability such as hot flashes and sweats can disrupt sleep (e.g., night sweats), with sleep deprivation leading to irritability and moodiness that are often associated with menopause. Most women do not experience hot flashes or night sweats sufficiently severe to warrant treatment. Nor do they generally interfere with a woman's sexual functioning or cause psychological difficulties. More Caucasian women report symptoms such as hot flashes and insomnia than Asian American and Latina women, but the reasons for this are probably cultural or social rather than physiological. For example, African American women are generally more positive than other older adults about this life phase. Such wide variability in symptoms and responses suggests that there is no inevitable "menopausal syndrome." Nor is there a scientific explanation for why symptoms such as hot flashes occur in some women and not in others (NIA, 2008).

Estrogen loss combined with the normal biological changes of aging leads to **urogenital atrophy**—a reduction in the elasticity and lubricating abilities of the vagina approximately 5 years after menopause. As the vagina becomes drier and the layer of cell walls thinner, the amount of lubricants secreted during sexual arousal is reduced. Although vaginal lubrication takes longer, these changes have little impact on the quality of orgasms and do not result in an appreciable loss in sensation or feeling. Nevertheless, discomfort associated with urogenital atrophy is a frequent complaint and often contributes to a decline in sexual activity (NIA, 2008; Zeiss & Kasl-Godley, 2001). Artificial lubricants such as KY jellies and vaginal creams can help minimize discomfort. In addition, regular and consistent sexual activity, including masturbation, maintains vaginal lubricating ability and muscle tone, thereby reducing discomfort during intercourse (Gelfand, 2000; Pangman & Seguire, 2000).

Because of the thinning of vaginal walls, which results from estrogen degeneration and offers less protection to the bladder and the urethra, lower urinary tract infections such as cystitis and burning urination may occur more frequently (NIA, 2008). These problems can be treated, however. Incontinence is found to inhibit sexual desire and response; unfortunately, older women may be reluctant to discuss incontinence with others, which precludes their finding ways to prevent its negative impact on sexual activity.

The primary medical response to the symptoms of hot flashes and vaginal atrophy has been hormone replacement therapy (HRT), using estrogen alone (ERT) or in combination with progestin (EPT), which restores women's hormones to levels similar to those before menopause. As noted in Chapter 3, estrogen can alleviate hot flashes and vaginal changes, including atrophy, dryness, itching, pain during intercourse, urinary tract problems, and frequent urination (NIA, 2006, 2008). However, the risk of breast cancer, blood clots, heart attacks, and strokes with long-term HRT may be substantially greater than previous research indicated, as described in Chapter 4. For these reasons, women who choose to use HRT for menopausal symptoms should receive the lowest effective dose (Nelson et al., 2006; NIA, 2006).

Because of the risks of HRT, many women have turned to alternative therapies. Some therapies appear to help moderate the symptoms of menopause and perimenopause; these include eating foods that are high in calcium, vitamin E, and fiber, and lower in fat; weight-bearing and aerobic exercise; acupuncture; biofeedback; and herbal or naturopathic treatments, as shown in the box below (NIA, 2008; Phillip, 2003). Phytoestrogens are estrogen-like substances found in cereal, vegetables, soy, and herbs, but whether they relieve menopausal symptoms or carry risks is not yet known (NIA, 2008). Overall, women need to be cautious about the use of alternative therapies not yet scientifically proven to be effective.

In many non-Western cultures, menopause is viewed as a time of respect and status for women. The Western cultural view is that women are expected to have difficulty at this period of life, although this too has shifted as baby boomers have redefined menopause. The incidence of insomnia, depression, and anxiety may be traced to the meaning or psychosocial significance that women attach to menopause, the cultural value placed on body image and on women's maternal role, or other stresses such as caregiving for parents. Other symptoms, such as headaches, dizziness, palpitations, and weight gain, are not necessarily caused by menopause itself, but may be due to underlying psychosocial reasons.

A growing number of women view menopause as a potentially positive transition characterized by relief rather than as a loss of fertility or a cause for depression. It can be a fulfilling time of opportunities, new accomplishments,

> **NONMEDICAL STRATEGIES TO RELIEVE HOT FLASHES**
> - Avoid spicy foods, caffeine, and alcohol.
> - Drink cold water or juice as a hot flash comes on.
> - Wear breathable clothing (e.g., cotton), not synthetics.
> - Dress in layers of clothing that can be gradually removed.
> - Sleep in a cool room.

meaning, and greater autonomy (Brice, 2003 Gonyea, 1998). In sum, like other transitions experienced by women, menopause is affected not only by physiological and health factors, but also by personality, self-esteem, and culture.

Despite some uncomfortable symptoms, menopause does not physiologically impede full sexual activity. In fact, many women, freed of worries about pregnancy and birth control, report greater sexual satisfaction after menopause, including after a hysterectomy (NIA, 2008). Generally, an older woman's sexual response cycle has all the dimensions of her younger response, but the time it takes for her to respond to sexual stimulation gradually increases. The subjective levels of sexual tension initiated or elaborated by clitoral stimulation do not differ for older and younger women, nor for heterosexual and homosexual partners. In fact, the **preorgasmic plateau phase**, during which sexual tension is at its height, is extended in duration. Older women's capacity for orgasms may be slowed, but not impaired. The orgasm is experienced more rapidly, somewhat less intensely, and more spasmodically. The resolution phase, during which the body returns to its baseline prearousal state, occurs more rapidly than in younger women (Blonna & Levitan, 2000; Zeiss & Kasl-Godley, 2001).

As noted above, lesbian partners are more likely to conceptualize sexuality broadly in terms of whole-body stimulation (kissing, hugging,

> **ALTERNATIVES TO HORMONE REPLACEMENT THERAPY**
> - herbal remedies, including soy, wild yams, beans, and black cohosh—a folk medicine made from a shrub root—but their effectiveness is unproven
> - drugs already proven for other conditions that may reduce hot flashes (e.g., some antihypertensives; certain antidepressants; Neurontin, an antiseizure drug)
> - combination of fluoride and calcium, but these may have gastrointestinal side effects

touching, and holding) than are heterosexual women, who tend to be more focused on genital contact and orgasm. However, in some studies, lesbians report having orgasms easily and more frequently than their heterosexual counterparts. This difference may reflect the pattern that women in general attach greater importance than men to emotional closeness than to sexual activity per se; as a result, sexual satisfaction is more strongly associated with the quality of the relationship than with physical sexual variables, such as frequency of sexual interactions. Accordingly, lesbians who have had both male and female relationships often view the latter as less demanding and more sexually gratifying. Commitment, compatibility, emotional sharing, affection, and enduring tenderness are terms used to describe their female relationships. Similar to their heterosexual counterparts, sexual frequency declines over time in lesbian relationships, but this may be a function of the length of the relationship rather than age. Those who are happy with their sex lives tend to be happier in general (Garnets & Peplau, 2006; Matthews, Tartaro, & Hughes, 2003).

In the NSHAP survey described earlier, 14 percent of men and 1 percent of women reported taking medication or supplements to improve sexual function within the past 12 months (Lindau et al., 2007). With more men turning to **sexupharmaceuticals,** such as, Viagra to treat erectile difficulties, little is known about the experiences of their female partners and possible detrimental effects for them. Although the publicity surrounding Viagra—and its wide availability—may facilitate more positive attitudes to sexuality in old age, it may also create a societal expectation that a healthy and "normal" life for older adults requires the continuation of "youthful" (frequent) sexual activity focused on intercourse. When prescribing these drugs, health care providers should be sensitive to both partners' perspectives and desires, as well as to the dynamics of the relationship (Potts et al., 2003).

In summary, no physiological impediment exists to full sexual activity for postmenopausal women. Changes such as the thinning of vaginal

---

VIAGRA: UNINTENDED EFFECTS FOR WOMEN

Viagra has been touted as a wonder drug for men, with flashy ads typically featuring a romantic man and woman. The benefits described by the ads have been empirically supported. For example, a 1998 study of over 500 men reported in the *New England Journal of Medicine* confirmed Viagra's effectiveness. The most common side effects were headache, flushing, and disturbed digestion. For men and their partners who have been frustrated by impotence, the side effects are undoubtedly viewed as minor irritants. About 20 percent of men, however, do not experience any benefits from taking Viagra. Newer drugs such as Levitra and Cialis are advertised to be more vigorous and longer-lasting. Viagra is sometimes prescribed for women, and has resulted in marked improvement in arousal, orgasm, and sexual enjoyment. However, Viagra does not alter women's sexual desire, which is a key factor in older women's sexuality and sexual satisfaction (American Federation for Aging Research, 2000).

---

walls and loss of vaginal elasticity may render intercourse somewhat more painful, but these effects can be minimized by sexual regularity and use of lubricants. Instead, older women's sexuality tends to be influenced more by sociocultural expectations than by physiological changes—by the limited number of available male partners for heterosexual women, societal stigma associated with lesbian relations, and Western cultural definitions of older women as asexual and unattractive, especially to younger partners. These psycho-social barriers are discussed more fully later in this chapter.

Men and Age-Related Physiological Changes

Relatively little attention has been given to men's hormonal rhythms compared to women's. One reason for this is that men generally maintain their fertility and their capacity to father children as they age, making hormonal and sexual changes less abrupt and visible. There is, however, increasing evidence that **male menopause,** or **viropause,** occurs and can affect the psychological, interpersonal, social, and spiritual dimensions of a man's life. Nevertheless, the male climacteric differs from women's in two significant ways: it occurs 8 to 10 years later than for women, and it progresses at a more gradual rate. This is because the loss of testosterone (approximately 1 percent per year on average), while varying widely among men, is not as dramatic or as abrupt as the estrogen depletion for menopausal women. Effects of this loss of testosterone include:

- loss of erection during sexual activity
- reduced muscle size and strength
- decreased levels of calcium in the bones
- declining response by the immune system
- lessened sexual response, particularly inability to climax
- reduced desire for sex, along with increased anxiety and fear about sexual performance
- fatigue, irritability, indecisiveness, depression, loss of self-confidence, listlessness, poor appetite, and problems of concentration
- increased relationship problems and arguments with partners over sex, love, intimacy, and use of medications (Diamond, 1997; Lindau et al., 2007)

These changes, which occur in varying degrees, require some adaptation. But they do not necessarily interfere with sexual performance nor intrinsically reduce sexual enjoyment.

The normal physiological changes that characterize men's aging can alter the nature of the sexual response. The preorgasmic plateau phase, or excitement stage, increases in length, so that response to sexual stimulation is slower. An **erection** may take longer to achieve and may require more direct stimulation. For example, in 18-year-old males, full erection is achieved on stimulation in an average of 3 seconds. At age 45, the average time is 18 to 20 seconds, while it may take a 75-year-old man 5 minutes or more. Erections tend to be less full and firm with age. The two-stage orgasm—the

---

POINTS TO PONDER

Imagine the appeal of a typical Internet ad to some older men:

> Internet Advertising of Herbal Viagra—No prescription, no doctor, less than $1 a pill

> Welcome to the new sexual revolution. It's the all-natural male potency and pleasure pill that men everywhere are buzzing about. Herbal V is safe, natural, and specifically formulated to help support male sexual function and pleasure. You just take two easy-to-swallow tablets one hour before sexual activity. . . Herbal V—bringing back the magic.

---

sense of ejaculation followed by actual semen expulsion that is experienced by younger males—often blurs into a one-stage ejaculation for older men. Yet these erectile changes do not necessarily alter a man's sexual satisfaction (Blonna & Levitan, 2000; DeLamater & Friedrich, 2002; Lindau et al., 2007).

AGE-RELATED PHYSIOLOGICAL CHANGES IN SEXUAL FUNCTION

Normal Changes in Aging Women

- Reduction in vaginal elasticity and lubrication
- Thinning of vaginal walls
- Slower response to sexual stimulation
- Longer preorgasmic plateau phase
- Fewer and less intense orgasmic contractions
- Rapid return to prearousal state after orgasm

Normal Changes in Aging Men

- Erection may require more direct stimulation
- Erection is slower, less full, and disappears quickly after orgasm
- Orgasm is experienced more rapidly, less intensely, and more spasmodically
- Decreased volume and force of ejaculation
- Increased length of time between orgasm and subsequent erections (longer refractory period)
- Occasional lack of orgasm during intercourse
- More seepage or retrograde ejaculation

Another physiological change is that orgasm is experienced less intensely and more spasmodically and rapidly by older men, occurring every second or third act of intercourse rather than every time. The length of time between orgasm and subsequent erections increases (i.e., the **refractory period** after ejaculation, before a second ejaculation is possible, is longer). Although these changes may alter the nature of the sexual experience, none of them causes sexual inactivity or impotence. As a result, the subjectively appreciated levels of sensual pleasure may not diminish (Bortz & Wallace, 1999a, 1990b; Masters & Johnson, 1981). In recent years, as noted in Chapter 3, there has been increasing attention to hormones such as DHEA, which are produced by the adrenal glands, the brain, and the skin, to revive men's sexual interest.

Older gay men experience many of the same physiological factors that affect sexual functions as their heterosexual counterparts, but these changes do not eliminate the need and desire for sexual intimacy with another man. As they age, gay men tend to focus more on their partner, less on experiencing an orgasm, and while sexual frequency declines, sexual activity becomes more satisfying and relaxed (Wierzalis et al., 2006).

Although not an inevitable consequence of aging, **erectile dysfunction**, or **impotence** (i.e., an inability to get and sustain an erection), is the chief sexual problem experienced by older men. (Note that *erectile dysfunction* is a more accurate medical term than *impotence*, although the two terms are used interchangeably here.) In the NSHAP survey, 37 percent of men reported difficulty in achieving or maintaining an erection, while 90 percent were bothered by erectile dysfunction (Lindau et al., 2007). In the 2004 AARP survey, 24 percent of older male respondents had been diagnosed with erectile dysfunction. Most dysfunction is caused by disease or by age-induced deterioration of the blood vessels. Other causes are low testosterone levels and excess tobacco, drug or alcohol use. Older men and their partners need to be informed that erectile dysfunctions are both common and treatable.

Although impotence and lowered testosterone levels are not significantly correlated, declines in DHEA levels with aging appear to be associated with erectile dysfunction (American Prostate Society, 2003).

Despite the underlying pathologies frequently associated with impotence, it tends to be underdiagnosed because of the embarrassment and reluctance of some older men and their health care providers to discuss sexual matters candidly. Since medical treatments can be effective in altering erectile dysfunction, health care providers must rule out any physiological reasons for impotence, which tend to be more important than psychosocial factors (NIA, 2009). Physical risk factors include cardiovascular disease, the effects of drugs (especially antihypertensives, antidepressants, and tranquilizers), diabetes, hypertension, endocrine or metabolic disorders, neurological disorders, depression, alcohol, or prostate disorders. Most types of prostate surgery do not cause impotence, as discussed in the next section. In recent years, new ways to treat impotence have drawn increased attention. The marketing of a wide range of products reflects, in part, drug companies' awareness of baby boomers' buying power and their greater openness to talking about and wanting to experience sexual pleasure than prior cohorts of older men.

Clinical trials of sexupharmaceuticals, such as Sildenafil or Viagra, found that 60 to 80 percent of the men with varying degrees of impotence who participated benefited in terms of increased sexual satisfaction and improved relationships with their partners. However, only 8 percent of men and 2 percent of women age 65 and older reported that they had taken any medicine, hormone, or other treatment to enhance sexual performance (AARP, 2004). This suggests that more attention should be given to the psychological factors related to intimacy and sexual enjoyment in old age, not just to medical solutions. As noted earlier, one potential negative impact of Viagra and other erectile dysfunction drugs is reinforcing the cultural expectations that aging men are required to retain their youthful virility (Gross & Blundo, 2005). A theme of this chapter is that sexuality for older men must be expanded to include more than erection and ejaculation during intercourse, and both partners' needs must be considered. For example, health care providers and counselors must encourage couples to communicate their fears about impotence and suggest how they can openly enjoy fulfilling sexual experiences and intimacy without an erection, including:

- oral medications that cause erections
- pellets inserted into the urethra with an applicator that dilate the arteries and relax the erectile tissues, thereby triggering involuntary erections
- injection therapy
- vacuum pumps
- penile implants
- vascular surgery

However, fewer than 50 percent of men with erectile dysfunction/impotence obtain treatment for this condition (AARP, 2004).

Chronic Diseases and Sexuality

Sexuality is generally associated with physical and psychological well-being, including being physically active and fit. Since sexual response requires the coordination of multiple systems of the body—hormonal, circulatory, and nervous systems—if any of these are disrupted, sexual functioning can be affected. As a result, chronic diseases can play a major role in the decline of sexual function, and are often cited as a reason for refraining from sexual activity (Nusbaum, Hamilton, & Lenahan, 2003). Even when illness and functional disability do not directly affect the sexual organs themselves, systemic diseases can influence sexual functioning for the following reasons:

- their effects on mediating physiological mechanisms such as hypertension and arrhythmia
- chronic pain
- complications from medications, especially from antihypertensive drugs

- negative effects on well-being and self-perceptions
- the all-consuming distraction of the illness or functional disability may deplete the emotional energy needed for sexual interest and responsiveness (NIA, 2002)

Given these factors, it is not surprising that 30 percent of older men and 16 percent of older women cite better health as something that would improve their satisfaction with their sex lives (AARP, 2004). In the NHSAP survey, poor health was a primary factor affecting sexual activity. Respondents who rated their health as fair or poor had a higher prevalence of sexual problems, such as difficulty with erection or lubrication, pain, and lack of pleasure compared to those who rated their health as excellent to good. The most commonly reported reason for sexual inactivity was the man's physical health (Lindau et al., 2007). As is true across the life course, elders' personal characteristics combined with the specific challenges imposed by an illness influence how they adjust to disease and respond to treatment. Accordingly, how individuals appraise threats to sexual identity, sexual intimacy, body image, and control over bodily functions determines the nature of their adaptive responses (Shiavi, 1999). How older people approach sexual losses entailed by chronic illness probably reflects how they have coped with other losses throughout their lives. Fortunately, health care providers now know more about how adults can compensate for disease and disability to maintain sexually satisfying lives, as shown in the box on page 293 regarding psychological treatment of sexual problems.

There is also growing recognition that sexual activity can be an important part of recovery from a major illness or surgery and is a minimal risk to a person's health (Nusbaum et al., 2003; Pangman & Seguire, 2000). In this section, the chronic illnesses that commonly affect sexual functioning—diseases of the prostate or heart, diabetes, strokes, degenerative and rheumatoid arthritis, depression and dementia—are briefly discussed.

> ### NONMEDICAL APPROACHES TO SEXUAL LIMITATIONS ASSOCIATED WITH CHRONIC ILLNESS: SUGGESTIONS FOR HEALTH CARE PROVIDERS
>
> - Provide information about normal sexual responses and the impact of the illness on sexual function.
> - Create a welcoming, open atmosphere, encouraging elders to talk about sexual concerns.
> - Emphasize acceptance of a wide range of sexual behaviors that enhance mutual pleasure and intimacy, rather than focusing on intercourse.
> - Review medications that may interfere with sexual fulfillment.
> - Increase mutual communication about sexual preferences and needs.
> - Facilitate the elder's patient's accommodation to the limitations imposed by the chronic illness.
> - Create living arrangements that support sexual intimacy between partners, including rooms with doors that can be closed.

More than 50 percent of men age 65 and older have some degree of **prostate enlargement,** known as *benign prostatic hypertrophy (BPH),* and experience some prostate difficulties, usually inflammation or enlargement of the prostate gland, pain in the urogenital area, and urinary flow dysfunction (Bostwick, MacLennan, & Larson, 1996; Diamond, 1997). Infections can be successfully treated with antibiotics, and new drugs are available to shrink the prostate. Some prostate problems can be reduced through simple treatments such as warm baths and gentle massage or antibiotics. However, when urination is severely restricted or painful, surgery is necessary. After surgery, semen is no longer ejaculated through the penis, but is pushed back into the bladder and later discharged in the urine. After healing occurs, the capacity to ejaculate and fertility may return in some men. The feeling of orgasm or climax can still be present, and sexual pleasure is not inevitably lessened.

Prostate cancer, the most common male cancer, affects one in eight American men. The rate at which this cancer kills men is similar to that of breast cancer in women. About 80 percent of all prostate cancers are found in men age 65 and older. Because men who have a family history of prostate cancer and African American men are at increased risk of developing it, these two groups should have more frequent screening exams. A major problem in diagnosis is that prostate cancer may have no symptoms in its early and middle stages while it is confined to the prostate gland and more likely to be amenable to treatment. After it spreads, symptoms include pain or stiffness in the lower back, hips, or upper thighs. Because the early symptoms are often masked, the American Cancer Society recommends that all men 40 years of age and older have an annual rectal exam, and that men age 50 and older receive an annual prostate specific antigen (PSA) test (American Federation for Aging Research, 2000; Gallagher & Gapstur, 2006).

The most extreme but effective treatment for prostate cancer is radical perineal prostatectomy, which includes cutting nerves. Although most prostate cancer treatments do not cause impotence, irreversible erectile dysfunction and incontinence can result from radical prostatectomy. Some researchers have found that potency and continence outcomes from surgery may be similar to other forms of treatment for prostate cancer (Han et al., 2004; Peschel & Colberg, 2003). Nerve-sparing surgery has also been developed and may reduce the incidence of impotence among some men who undergo radical prostatectomy. Of course, the urologist's priority is to rid the patient of cancer tissue, and nerves very close to the prostate gland must often be severed. Nevertheless, even in these cases, men who have lost their normal physiologic response can still achieve orgasm (Donatucci & Greenfield, 2006; Harris, Weiss, & Blaivas, 2004; Rogers et al., 2006; Saranchuk et al., 2005).

Fortunately, there are an increasing number of alternatives for early prostate cancer, such as radioactive pellet implantation, cryotherapy, other forms of radiation therapy, and microwave energy (to produce heat that can destroy cancer cells). Other promising developments are the clinical testing of a variety of vaccinations; brachytherapy, which precisely places radioactive seeds into the prostate gland to kill cancer cells and reduces the rates of impotence and incontinence; and new chemotherapy regimens that have improved survival rates (Doust et al., 2004; Gallagher & Gapstur, 2006; Han et al., 2004; Peschel & Colberg, 2003; Swanson, 2006). More research is needed on the effectiveness of new options to restore sexual functioning after treatment of the cancer such as **penile implants** and smooth muscle relaxants that are injected into the penis to reverse the period after impotence. Health care providers must offer older men as much information as possible about the implications of prostate surgery, radiation, and hormonal treatments for sexual functioning. In some instances, men with prostate cancer place more weight on quality-of-life considerations than on improving survival through aggressive treatment, even though survival rates are greater for men who choose a definitive therapy (Afrin & Ergul, 2000; McNeel & Disis, 2000; Tward et al., 2006; Van Tol-Geerdink et al., 2006).

Although prostate surgery does not cause impotence in the majority of cases, between 5 and 40 percent of men who have undergone such surgery can no longer achieve an erection In addition, because treatment of prostate cancer often involves methods that lower testosterone levels or block the effects of testosterone, a large percent of men undergoing such treatment lose their sexual desire, and up to 40 percent actually experience hot flashes (Gotay, Holup, & Muraoka, 2002). In some instances, a man's postoperative "impotence" may be a convenient excuse for not engaging in sexual activity or may represent fears of additional illness. When this occurs, psychological factors need to be addressed through counseling, and couples should be encouraged to try alternate methods of sexual satisfaction. When impotence is irreversible, partners need to be supported to pursue such alternatives or to consider a penile implant or vacuum pump. Masturbation, more

leisurely precoital stimulation, and use of artificial lubricants can all provide pleasurable sexual experiences for partners dealing with erectile dysfunction.

While most older men fear that prostate surgery will interfere with their sexual functioning and satisfaction, women may worry that a hysterectomy (surgical removal of the uterus), an ovariectomy (surgical removal of both ovaries), or a mastectomy (surgical removal of one or both breasts) will negatively affect their sexuality. In most instances, however, women's sexual satisfaction and long-term functioning are not affected by these surgeries, particularly if their partners are sensitive and supportive. On the other hand, some hormonal changes associated with a complete hysterectomy may affect sex drive. When women experience menopause as a result of a hysterectomy—perhaps earlier than the average age of onset for menopause—short-term, low dose hormone replacement therapy is advisable except when the hysterectomy resulted from cancer.

More common medical causes of male impotence than prostate surgery are arteriosclerosis—the vascular hardening that leads to heart attacks and strokes and diabetes, particularly for lifelong diabetics. Anything that damages the circulatory system—smoking, inactivity, poor diet—can cause erectile dysfunction. Older people who have experienced a heart attack or heart surgery may assume that sexual activity will endanger their lives and therefore must give it up. Unfortunately, many health care providers are not sensitive to such fears and fail to reassure individuals that sexual activity can be resumed after they undergo a stress test without pain or arrhythmia (Nusbaum et al., 2003). People who have had a stroke may also feel compelled to abstain because of an unfounded fear that sex could cause another occurrence. Generally, strokes do not harm the physiology of sexual functioning or the ability to experience arousal. However, some antihypertensive drugs can cause impotence or inhibit ejaculation. Fortunately, ACE inhibitors are a class of antihypertensive drugs that are reported to cause fewer side effects on sexual function.

Among the many side effects described in Chapter 4, diabetes may be associated with a higher likelihood of difficulty with erection (Lindau et al., 2007). Impotence in lifelong diabetics occurs because diabetes interferes with the circulatory and neurologic mechanisms responsible for the supply of blood flowing to the penis for erection. In such instances, a penile implant may be an option. With late-onset diabetes, impotence may be the first observable symptom of the disease. When the diabetes is under control, however, potency generally returns. The sexual functioning of women diabetics appears to be relatively unimpaired. When diabetes is controlled through balanced blood chemistry, sexual problems other than impotence that are attributable to the disease should disappear or become less severe. Other less common diseases that may cause erectile dysfunction are illnesses that affect the vascular and endocrine systems, kidney diseases, and neurological lesions in the brain or spinal cord (Schiavi, 1999; Zeiss & Kasl-Godley, 2001).

Arthritis does not directly interfere with sexual functioning but can make sexual activity painful. Some medications used to control arthritis pain may also impede sexual desire and performance. Yet sexual behavior can serve to maintain some range of motion of the limbs and joints and thereby reduce soreness; it can also stimulate the body's production of cortisone, which is one of the substances used to treat the symptoms of rheumatoid arthritis. Experimenting with alternative positions can minimize pain during sexual intercourse. A warm bath, massage of painful joints, and timing the use of painkilling medications may also help to control arthritic pain. As with most chronic diseases, communication with the partner about what is comfortable and pleasurable is essential. Unfortunately, the majority of older adults with arthritis do not receive treatment that could minimize its negative effects on sexual activity (AARP, 2004; Nusbaum et al., 2003).

Up to 70 percent of patients with depression, especially men, are estimated to experience sexual dysfunction. Depression also has differential effects on sexual interest, activity, and satisfaction. On the other hand, it is not clear that depression *causes* erectile dysfunction; it may be that the depression is a *reaction* to difficulties in sexual functioning. An alternative explanation is that sexual dysfunction is a side effect of antidepressants and therefore may be prevented or treated (Balon, 2006; Lindau, 2007; Werneke, Northey, & Bhugra, 2006). Although reasons for this association of depression with sexual dysfunction are unclear, health care providers should ask about sexual function to identify problems early among patients who exhibit depressive symptoms, as well as those who are taking antidepressants. Tailoring therapy for depression to minimize adverse effects on sexual function can improve patients' treatment compliance and quality of life (Phillips & Slaughter, 2000).

Despite the high prevalence of Alzheimer's disease and other dementias, along with concerns expressed by partners and caregivers, there is limited empirical data about the impact of these disorders on sexual function. Partners faced with early-stage dementia may find that sexual intimacy remains a vital means of communication and support. As the dementia progresses, however, changes in functional capacity and sexual expression can be extremely distressing to partners. Erectile problems commonly occur among men with Alzheimer's disease. Other sources of distress are awkward sequencing of sexual activity, requests for activities outside of the couple's sexual repertoire, and lack of regard for the healthy partner's sexual satisfaction. Healthy partners are often troubled by changes in the perceived nature of the relationship and their own loss of sexual desire as the disease progresses, furthered by their exhaustion from being full-time caregivers. Health care providers need to help couples deal with losses in the relationship and changes in communication, sexuality, and intimacy (Kuhn, 2002; LoboPraabhu et al., 2005). Although concerns have been raised about whether sexual activity with a partner who has dementia and cannot consent is unethical and in some instances abusive, it can be argued that

LOVING AND LETTING GO

When former Supreme Court Justice Sandra Day O'Connor's husband of 55 years fell in love with another nursing home resident, she and her adult children responded with compassion and selflessness. After her husband's years of anguish and depression associated with his dementia, she was grateful that he could find some solace and happiness in his final days.

from a relationship-centered perspective, sexual activity between loving spouses is morally permissible, even if the partner lacks the cognitive ability to consent (Lingler, 2003). On the other hand, some caregivers of partners with advanced dementia, longing for their intimacy needs to be met, may develop other close relationships (Castle, 2001). In such instances, health care professionals and family members should validate the healthy partner's need for intimacy. Alternatively, some long-term residents with dementia may discover love among other residents, as occurred with the husband of former Supreme Court Justice Sandra Day O'Connor.

Issues of competency also arise when a patient with dementia attempts to initiate a relationship with a new sexual partner, which may occur in long-term care facilities. Although such behavior may be disturbing to health care providers and families, it raises concerns about individuals' rights as well as the difficult task of determining a person's capacity to make informed judgments regarding new relationships. Staff in such facilities often express fears about inappropriate sexual behavior by patients with dementia. However, the incidence of sexually aggressive behaviors toward staff or other patients is actually quite low. This suggests that the same degree of skill needed by health care staff to manage other symptoms of dementia is required to address inappropriate or ambiguous sexual behaviors if they occur. Training in sexual matters may enable health care providers to assist family members, as well as patients themselves, in dealing with this

often-overlooked aspect of Alzheimer's disease and other dementias (LoboPraabhu et al., 2005; Loue, 2005).

Closely related to the effects of chronic illness on sexuality are those of drugs, including alcohol. Diagnosing the effects of substance use on sexuality may be particularly difficult, because drugs affect individuals differently, and drug interactions frequently occur. Drugs that inhibit the performance of any organ system can alter sexual response. For men, some medications that are prescribed for chronic conditions may cause impotence, decrease sexual drive, delay ejaculation, or result in an inability to ejaculate. Medications such as SSRIs that are used to treat depression and psychosis are particularly likely to impair erectile functioning (Balon, 2006). Of patients taking antipsychotics such as thioridazine, up to 49 percent will experience impaired ejaculation, and 44 percent impotence. Yet this is one of the first drugs that physicians prescribe for older persons who are agitated, depressed, schizophrenic, or anxious. Similarly, erectile dysfunction occurs in 40 percent of cases involving the antidepressant amoxapine. As noted above, other types of medications likely to affect sexual functioning are antihypertensives used to treat high blood pressure, drugs to control diabetes, and steroids. As a whole, medication use and the rate of adverse effects of drug therapy are consistently higher in older women than in men (Gelfand, 2000). For women, drugs can be associated with decreased vaginal lubrication, reduced sexual drive, and a delay or inability to achieve orgasm. Fortunately, both physicians and older people are now more aware of potential negative effects of drug regimens on sexual functioning. Likewise, more drugs are available that do not have negative side effects on sexual desire and ability. These include ACE inhibitors among the antihypertensives; fluoxetine, trazodone, and maprotiline among the antidepressants; desipramine among the tricyclic antidepressants; and lorazepam, alprazolam, and buspirone among antianxiety agents (Balon, 2006).

Alcohol use can act as a depressant on sexual ability and desire (Johnson, Phelps, & Cottler,

2004). Alcohol consumption affects male sexual performance at any age by making both erection and ejaculation difficult to attain; consequently, a man's anxiety about performance may increase and result in temporary impotence. Prolonged alcoholism may lead to erectile dysfunction as a result of irreversible damage to the nervous system. Although there is little research on the effects of alcohol on women's sexual performance, some women who misuse alcohol are found to experience less sexual desire and no orgasms. More research is needed to differentiate the extent to which alcohol may be a means of coping with sexual problems or whether concerns about sexual performance are a consequence of alcohol misuse and contribute to sustaining the addiction (Schiavi, 1999).

Psychosocial Factors and Late-Life Affection, Love, and Intimacy

In addition to the effects of normal physiological changes and chronic disease on sexual activity and enjoyment, a number of psychosocial factors affect how older people express their sexuality and their self-concept as a sexually attractive and interesting partner. These include:

- Past history of sexual activity and availability of a partner
- Fear of trying new ways of expressing intimacy other than intercourse—such as kissing, holding and being held, dancing, massage, and masturbation.
- Emotional reactions to physiological changes and to illness- or doctor-induced changes
- Responses to others' attitudes, including the societal norm that one is "too old" for sex
- Societal misconceptions regarding sexuality in later life.
- Living arrangements. For example, residents in long-term care facilities may face structural barriers to sexual expression, including lack of privacy and available partners, and negative attitudes among staff and family.

Even in facilities with rooms for partners, staff may keep the doors open or enter without knocking.

A primary psychosocial factor, especially for women, is the availability of a partner, as illustrated in Figure 7.3 on p. 298. For women in heterosexual relationships, a central problem is differential life expectancy and the fact that most women have married men older than themselves. Because of older women's lower marriage and remarriage rates, their opportuni- ties for sexual activity within heterosexual relationships are dramatically reduced with age. The current cohort of older women, for whom sexual activity was generally tied to marriage, has relatively few options for sexual relationships. Unfortunately, these options are even more constrained by the lack of socially approved models of sexuality for older women. For many women, their only models for sexuality may be the young. In addition, the pairing of older women

Older adults find numerous ways to express intimacy.

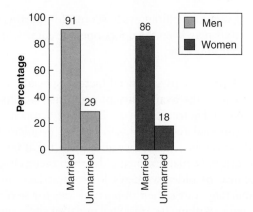

FIGURE 7.3   Presence of a Regular Sex Partner by Marital Status
SOURCE: American Association of Retired Persons, 2004

with younger men is still relatively rare. Women are also more likely than men to face socioeconomic barriers to meeting new partners. When a woman is preoccupied with financial or health worries, sexual activity may be a low priority.

Gender differences in sexual interest and parti- cipation may also be a barrier to finding satisfying intimate heterosexual relationships. Women generally report that the relational aspects of sexual activities—having long conversations, taking leisurely walks together, making oneself more attractive, and saying loving words—are more important to them than to men. Men, however, often view sexual activities such as erotic movies and magazines, sexual daydreams, and physically intimate activities such as body caressing, intercourse, and masturbation, as more important than do women. Men tend to perceive women more sexually than women perceive men, although women who rate their partners as physically attractive also attribute positive qualities to their partner and to the sexual interaction (Johnson, 1997; Levesque, Nave, & Lowe, 2006).

A man who has not had sexual intercourse for a long time following the loss or illness of a partner may experience what has been called **widower's syndrome.** He may have both the desire and opportunities for sexual activity, but his phys-

iological system may not respond and he may be unable to maintain an erection. Because fear and performance anxiety tend to block sexual interest and response, he may be caught in a bind—the more he is concerned about performing well, the harder he tries and the more difficult it becomes. Unhurried, nondemanding sexual interaction with an understanding partner can help resolve anxieties associated with widower's syndrome.

Similarly, women may face **widow's syndrome.** After a year or more of sexual inactivity, women are likely to experience reduced elasticity of the vaginal walls. With less response to sexual stimulation, vaginal lubrication is slowed. Although these are all symptoms that arise from estrogen deficiency, they become more severe after a long period of sexual abstinence. For men and women, frequent contact is important to ensure sexual responsiveness and comfort. However, older adults grieving the loss of a partner are initially unlikely to have the energy or the interest in anyone else—both essential features of successful sexual activity.

Another critical factor in the physical and social environment is whether living arrangements in residential care facilities provide opportunities for expression of intimacy. Lack of privacy, small single beds, negative staff

THE IMPORTANCE OF CONTINUED INTIMACY

When 95 year-old Gene and 82-year-old Doris, both with dementia, developed a sexual relationship in a nursing home, Gene's son was outraged, believing that his father didn't understand what was going on and was not acting his age. The staff, however, tried to honor the relationship and saw the benefits for both partners—how they lit up when seeing each other, how they paid greater attention to their appearance, and how they sat for hours playing the piano and singing together. Nevertheless, the son decided his father should be moved and neither adult be told of this plan. Doris has now retreated to her room, barely eats or drinks, and no longer plays the piano and sings.

attitudes, administrative rules, and the unromantic atmosphere of many facilities reduce the opportunities for residents to be sexually attracted or involved. On the other hand, when conjugal rooms are set aside, some residents may be uncomfortable using them, partially because of critical staff or family attitudes (Hu & Za, 2006; Loue, 2005).

Staff biases that older adults no longer need sexual intimacy may be the greatest barrier in long-term care facilities. If older residents express a desire for sexual activity, staff may ignore, infantilize, tease, or ridicule them—or report it to administrators or family members, thereby adding to a sense of embarrassment. Other staff may believe that chronic illness makes sexual activities impossible or harmful. Despite such obstacles, some residents in these settings are sexually active, and others would be if opportunities were available. The placement of older persons in long-term care facilities does not mean the end of their sexual interest. As noted earlier, even older people with dementia in nursing homes may maintain the competency to initiate sexual relationships (Hu & Za, 2006). Although there are significant legal and ethical issues in establishing institutional policies and procedures to address residents' intimacy needs, more long-term care facilities are moving in this direction. These policies encompass residents' rights to privacy, conjugal rooms or home visits, evaluation of residents' concerns about sexual functioning, encouragement of varied forms of sexual expression, and education for both staff and residents about sexuality and aging (Loue 2005).

POINTS TO PONDER

On the website for your state's Long-Term Care Ombudsman, review the Resident Bill of Rights. To what extent does it honor elders' desire for sexual intimacy? How well does it protect the rights of LGBT elders?

To summarize, the psychological and social factors that may affect sexual activity and satisfaction among older people include:

- past history of sexual activity
- attitudes toward sexual activities other than intercourse
- responses to physiological or illness-induced changes
- reactions to others' attitudes
- availability of a partner, especially for women
- performance anxiety, which is often exacerbated for widows and widowers
- opportunities for privacy
- staff attitudes, including heterosexism, ageism, and institutional policies

Facilitating Older Adults' Intimacy and Sexuality

As noted throughout this chapter, professionals play vital roles in conveying to older individuals that sexuality and affection may be expressed in ways other than only through sexual activity. Similarly, **intimacy**—love, attachment, and friendship—are cherished aspects of life, vital to an older person's well-being, quality of life, and active aging. Avenues for expressing intimacy are sensory, sensual, and sexual. Intimacy can involve flirting, laughing, smiling, communicating love through words, singing, touching, holding each other, as well as genital expression (Genevay, 1999).

Touch is an essential aspect of most intimate relationships. The need to be touched is lifelong; physical contact through touching and caressing is as powerful in old age as in infancy, childhood, and early adulthood. Since the sense of touch is the most basic sense, older individuals may rely on it to a greater extent in their social interactions than other age groups (Weil, 2005). The desire to be touched may lie just beneath an older person's expression of loneliness or grief. A handclasp or a hand laid gently on the shoulder or arm, a child's hug, or a massage can all be vital to addressing elders' needs for affection and can increase their responsiveness. Staff in residential settings must be sensitive to the life-affirming role of touch for most elders, including those with dementia and those who are withdrawn or disoriented. On the other hand, health care providers must respect cultural and religious differences regarding the meaning and appropriateness of touch.

Given the importance of intimacy, sexuality, and sexual satisfaction to elders' well-being, any clinical assessment or evaluation should address such issues. When an older person raises concerns about sexual functioning such as impotence, physicians must first differentiate potential physical causes, including medications, from psychological and relational ones. This can occur through a careful medical and social history, a thorough physical assessment, and basic hormone tests. Such an approach helps to distinguish short-term problems that some individuals experience—such as transitory erectile dysfunction—from problems that persist under all circumstances with different sexual partners over a prolonged time period. It is important for health care providers to be aware of their own biases related to aging and sexuality and to learn to recognize that the loss of

intimacy may underlie other medical disorders such as depression.

During a psychosocial evaluation, concerns about sexuality may surface when health care professionals initiate discussion of multiple

---

QUESTIONS FOR HEALTH PROVIDERS TO ELICIT ELDERS' CONCERNS REGARDING SEXUALITY

- Many people have unanswered questions or need information about sexual functioning. Would you like to discuss any questions or problems related to sex?
- What do you consider satisfactory sexual function?
- Are you currently sexually active with men, women, or both? Was this true in the past as well?
- If active, how often are you having sexual activity?
- How long ago did you last engage in any sexual activity?
- Are you satisfied with your sex life? If not, why not? (Determine whether the patient's expectations are reasonable.)
- What types of intimate relationships are most pleasurable for you (touching, physical closeness, stroking, petting, intercourse, masturbation, or oral sex)?
- What types of intimate relationships do you now engage in?
- At some time in their lives, most people experience a sexual problem. What physical concerns or medical or emotional problems that affect sexual functioning have you or your partner had?
- Have any of your partners had sexual relations with someone engaging in high-risk behaviors (such as using intravenous drugs or having sex with a prostitute)?
- Do you have any anxieties about your sexual performance?
- If you have had disfiguring surgery, do you have any concerns about body image? Does your partner have any concerns about it?
- How often do you masturbate? What, if any, were your previous masturbatory practices?
- Do you have any fear of illness or death during sexual intercourse?

THE IMPORTANCE OF TOUCH

Val, a widow for 12 years, lives in a central Boston neighborhood. Her son and daughters live on the West Coast and rarely see her. Fortunately, her neighborhood is a close-knit one, and younger neighbors keep an eye on her. They are accustomed to seeing her out walking her three small dogs, talking to the dogs, and giving them lots of affection. Last week, she was out walking her dogs for the first time in 3 weeks after a severe bout of flu. One of her 35-year-old male neighbors came up to her, said how glad he was to see her, and hugged her. She began to cry in response to the human warmth of the hug. It had been nearly 2 years since someone had hugged her like that.

losses and loneliness, what older people miss in terms of intimacy, their history of loving relationships, and their interest in establishing new intimate relationships. Establishing a safe place for such discussions is a vital first step. Unfortunately, many health care providers may be uncomfortable or ill-informed when addressing the lifelong intimacy needs of people as old as their own parents or grandparents. They may face time constraints in talking with older adults because of reimbursement mechanisms tied to the number of patients seen in a day. As a result, they may be more likely to prescribe medications for physical symptoms such as vaginal dryness than to respond to the older person's emotional concerns or need for information and reassurance. In the NSHAP study of older adults' sexual behaviors, only 38 percent of men and 22 percent of women reported having discussed sex with a physician since the age of 50 (Landeau et al., 2007). If health professionals are not knowledgeable about sexuality in the later years in order to respond to concerns expressed by older patients, referral to appropriate experts is critical.

Increased knowledge of sexuality and aging among older adults tends to be associated with more accepting attitudes and enhanced sexual activity (Willert & Semans, 2000; Zeiss & Kasl-Godley, 2001). Sex education and opportunities for group discussion and support can broaden older adults' awareness, interest, and enjoyment of a range of sexual activities. Alex Comfort (1980), one of the first health professionals to address these issues, noted that sexual responsiveness should be fostered but not preached. Health care providers should use clear and easy-to-understand terms; be open-minded, respectful, and nonjudgmental; and encourage discussion. An older person who raises sexual concerns may want support, acceptance, and a sympathetic ear more than anything else. Elders who are concerned about their sexual functioning should be advised to focus on giving and receiving pleasure rather than on genital sex. As noted earlier, professionals should

convey that there is no prescribed way for sex to proceed, but that instead elders can select from many options. Many older people need to be "given permission" to develop alternative definitions of sexual activity in order to gain intimacy, joy, and fulfillment through a broad spectrum of sensual interactions. When a partner is not available, masturbation may be an acceptable approach. Explicit discussion of masturbation with older people may relieve anxiety caused by earlier prohibitions during their adolescence and young adulthood. Alternatively, professionals need to be sensitive to the fact that some elders do not want to engage in any sexual activity and must not put undue pressure on them to take part in or even discuss sexuality. Taking account of an older person's values, culture, religious beliefs, life experiences, and right to autonomy as they make choices about their sexual behavior and sexuality is critical.

As noted above, sex education is also essential for other staff who work directly with elders. For example, long-term care workers must recognize that the desire for intimacy and closeness continues throughout life among

---

SEX THERAPY WITH OLDER PERSONS

- Eliminate or manage medical problems, including medication side effects, that may directly impair genital functions or indirectly affect sexual functioning.
- Include practical behavioral techniques in the form of specifically structured sexual interactions that the couple can conduct in the privacy of their home.
- Emphasize activities that encompass intimacy, giving pleasure, communicating with the partner, and letting the partner know when pleasure or pain or discomfort is experienced.
- Provide opportunities to discuss problems encountered as well as concerns about performance.
- Employ a holistic approach that includes exercise, nutrition, and interventions to build self-esteem (Kingsberg, 2000).

heterosexual and LGBT adults, even those with chronic disabilities. With older people who are experiencing memory loss or disorientation, the staff need to evaluate the elder's competence when developing a care plan that allows the expression of appropriate sexual behavior. This includes assessing the older person's awareness of the relationship, ability to avoid exploitation, and understanding of potential risks, including family members' disapproving attitudes (Hu & Za, 2006).

Implications for the Future

Compared to other areas, gerontological research on sexuality remains relatively limited, suggesting that myths and discomfort regarding sexuality among older adults may still persist. However, baby boomers are likely to influence these attitudes as they age, just as they are affecting nearly every aspect of our society. One primary factor is that more boomers are single than any previous cohort of adults age 40 to 60, largely because of divorce or never marrying. And many of them date regularly, although men are more likely to be looking for someone to live with than women, who tend to place a higher value on personal freedom and want to avoid additional caregiving roles. Older boomers are also likely to be more comfortable expressing their sexuality than prior cohorts who were influenced by Victorian-era values and norms (Henry & McNab, 2003; Kingsberg, 2000). Boomers' attitudes toward sexuality were strongly colored by the open, permissive atmosphere of the 1960s. The "sexual revolution," along with increased options for birth control, especially influenced women, giving them permission to express their sexual needs and desires and to be more assertive in relationships. Baby boomers' preoccupation with physical fitness, antiaging treatments, and cosmetic surgery will also affect their views of sexuality in old age. Aging boomers may press for more

research on sexual dysfunction and ways to manage the negative effects of chronic illness, disability, and medications on sexuality. They will view sexuality as a quality-of-life issue that is central to wellness and active aging (Henry & McNab, 2003). Recognizing the wide range of ways in which sexuality and intimacy can be expressed, they will probably expect health care providers to consider the sexual side effects of medications or other treatments for health problems. Additionally, they are likely to ask for drugs such as Viagra that can improve their sexual function and to buy products to enhance their sexual pleasure.

Boomers are more likely than current cohorts of elders to search online as a way to meet others, with some websites catering specifically to those over age 50. A long-range health concern, however, is that the majority of boomers who have sex regularly do not use any protection. This is particularly problematic for women who are at risk of developing HIV from heterosexual sex because their thinner vaginal walls are more susceptible to cuts and tears. The sexual needs of baby boomer LGBT partners are likely to be discussed more openly; but the incidence of unprotected sex is increasing. Overall, senior boomers are likely to dramatically alter our images of sexuality in old age, push for more opportunities to form intimate relationships, and accept sexuality as a continuation of normal lifelong pleasures.

These trends point to the importance of mental health counselors, medical personnel, and social workers acquiring basic knowledge and skills regarding older adults' sexuality. Such training needs to encompass attitudes and values as well, so that professionals are more comfortable and sensitive in discussing sexual issues with elders, including LGBT partners. Increased professional knowledge and understanding are essential because older adults, like younger adults, are more likely to be treated by primary care providers or internists in a wide range of clinical setting rather than be seen by a specialist such as a sex therapist.

Summary

As highlighted throughout this chapter, sexuality is affected by physical, psychological, social, and disease-related changes. The normal physiological changes that men and women experience in their sexual organs as they age do not necessarily affect their sexual pleasure or lead to sexual dysfunction. Even chronic disease and disability do not necessarily eliminate sexual capacity. For example, many older persons, after adequate medical consultation, can resume sexual activity following a heart attack or stroke. Contrary to some myths about sexuality in old age, many people in their 70s and 80s enjoy sexual activities, and an even larger number express their sexuality in a wide range of intimate behaviors.

Older couples can adapt to age-related changes in sexual functioning in a variety of ways. Simply knowing that such changes are normal may help older people maintain their sexual self-esteem. For both older men and women, long, leisurely foreplay can enhance sexual response. Avoiding alcohol prior to sexual activity can be helpful, because while alcohol increases desire it also decreases sexual ability. Health professionals need to be alert to medications that adversely affect sexual functioning, such as antihypertensives, tranquilizers, and antidepressants.

This chapter emphasizes how psychosocial factors can have the greatest influence on elders' sexual behavior. Myths, stereotypes, and jokes pervade views of sexuality in old age. Unfortunately, societal expectations about reduced sexual interest may mean that older people stop sexual activity long before they need to. In future years, these myths may change as the media, gerontologists, and other professionals convey the message that sex is not only permissible but desirable in old age.

In professional work with older partners, definitions of sexuality need to be broadened beyond sexual intercourse. A variety of behaviors—such as touching, kissing, hugging, massage, and lying side by side—can contribute to sexual intimacy and satisfaction, even for older persons in long-term care facilities and those with dementia. Touching older people—a handclasp or a back rub, for example—is especially important in homebound and institutional settings but needs to be tempered with awareness of cultural differences. Professionals and family members also need to be attentive to barriers to expressions of sexuality within long-term care facilities.

Practitioners need to be sensitive to their clients' values and life experiences, and to support them in making their own choices about their sexual behavior and expressions of sexuality, including the choice not to engage in sexual activity. Many of the current cohort of oldest-old grew up with taboos relating not only to intercourse but also to other forms of sexual activity, such as masturbation. Hence, such older individuals are likely to need encouragement from professionals and family members if they are to be free to affirm their sexuality and to experience intimacy with others. This pattern is shifting, however, with the aging of the young-old and the baby boomers who are more open in their sexual attitudes and behaviors.

GLOSSARY

climacteric in women, the decline in estrogen production and the loss of reproductive ability; in men, the decline in testosterone

erection the swelling of the penis or clitoris in sexual excitement

erectile dysfunction inability to get and sustain an erection

hot flash a sudden sensation of heat in the upper body caused by vasomotor instability as nerves over-respond to decreases in hormone level during menopause

impotence the inability to have or maintain an erection

intimacy freedom to express and respond to human closeness

male menopause a term that suggests a significant change experienced by men as their production of testosterone decreases in later life; although male fertility is maintained, some men experience both psychological and physiological changes

menopause   cessation of the menstrual cycle

orgasm   climax of sexual excitement

penile implant   a device surgically implanted in the penis to reverse impotence and allow an erection

perimenopause   unpredictable menstrual cycles—up to 10 years before menopause

postmenopause   when 12 months have passed without a menstrual cycle

preorgasmic plateau phase   in men and women, the phase of lovemaking prior to orgasm and in which sexual tension is at its height

prostate cancer   the most common cancer among men age 65 and older

prostate enlargement   growth of the prostate due to changes in prostatic cells with age, which can result in pain and difficult urination

refractory period   in men, the time between ejaculation and another erection

sex   in the narrowest sense, a biological function involving genital intercourse or orgasm; in a broader sense, expressing oneself in an intimate way through a wide-ranging language of love and pleasure in relationships

sexuality   feelings of sexual desire, expression, and intimacy, not only sexual activity

sexupharmaceuticals   prescribed medications, such as Viagra, to treat men's erectile difficulties

urogenital atrophy   reductions in the elasticity and lubricating abilities of the vagina approximately 5 years after menopause

viropause   male menopause

widow(er)'s syndrome   a term coined by Masters and Johnson describing sexual dysfunction following a long period of abstinence due to a partner's illness and/or death

REFERENCES

Afrin, L. B. & Ergul, S. M. (2000). Medical therapy of prostrate cancer. *Journal of South Carolina Medical Association 26*, 77–84.

American Association of Retired Persons (AARP). (2004). *2004 Update of attitudes and behavior: Sexuality at midlife and beyond.* Washington, DC: American Association of Retired Persons.

American Federation for Aging Research. (2000). Research news on older men's health. *Lifelong Briefs.*

American Prostate Society. (2003). *Impotence.* Washington, DC: American Prostate Society.

Balon, R. (2006). SSRI—associated sexual dysfunction. *The American Journal of Psychiatry 163*, 1504–1509.

Bancroft, J. (2007). Sex and aging. *The New England Journal of Medicine, 357*, 820–822.

Bennett, L. & Gates, G. (2004). *The cost of marriage inequality to gay, lesbian and bisexual seniors.* Washington, DC: Human Rights Campaign.

Berger, R. & Kelly, J. J. (2001). The older gay man. In B. Berzon (Ed.). *Positively gay: New approaches to gay and lesbian life.* Berkeley, CA: Celestial Arts.

Blank, T. O. (2006). Gay and lesbian aging: Research and future directions. *Educational Gerontology 32*, 241–243.

Blonna, R. & Levitan, J. (2000). *Healthy sexuality.* Englewood, CO: Morton.

Boehmer, U. (2002). Twenty years of public health research: Inclusion of lesbian, gay, bisexual and transgender populations. *American Journal of Public Health, 92*, 1125–1130.

Bortz, W. M. & Wallace, D. H. (1999a). Physical fitness, aging and sexuality. *Western Journal of Medicine, 170*, 167–169.

Bortz, W. M. & Wallace, D. H. (1999b). Sexual function in 1202 aging males: Differentiating aspects. *Journals of Gerontology 54B*, M237–M241.

Bostwick, D. G., MacLennan, G. T., & Larson, T. (1996). *Prostate cancer: What every man—and his family—needs to know.* New York: Villard.

Brice, C. (2003). *Age ain't nothing but a number: Black women explore midlife.* Boston: Beacon Press.

Brotman, S., Ryan, B., & Cormier, R. (2003). The health and social service needs of gay and lesbian elders and their families: An exploration in four Canadian cities. *The Gerontologist, 43*, 192–202.

Butler, S. (2006). Older gays, lesbians, bisexuals and transgender persons. In B. Berkman (Ed.). *Handbook of social work in health and aging.* New York: Oxford.

Castle, E. (2001). A couple's journey with Alzheimer's disease: The many faces of intimacy. *Generations, 25*, 81–86.

Clunis, M., Fredriksen-Goldsen, K., Freeman, P., & Nystrom, N. (Eds.). (2005). *Lives of lesbian elders. Looking back, looking forward.* Binghamton, NY: Haworth Press.

Cohler, B. (2004). Saturday night at the tubs: Age cohort and social life at the urban gay bath. In G. Herdt & B. deVries (Eds.). *Gay and lesbian aging: Research and future directions.* New York: Springer.

Comfort, A. (1980). Sexuality in later life. In J. E. Birren & R. B. Sloane (Eds.). *Handbook of mental health and aging.* New York: Van Nostrand Reinhold.

Cruz, J. M. (2003). *Sociological analysis of aging: The gay male experience.* New York: Haworth Press.

DeLamater, J. & Friedrich, W. N. (2002). Human sexual development. *Journal of Sex Research, 39,* 10–14.

deVries, B. & Blando, J. (2004). The study of gay and lesbian aging: Lessons for social gerontology. In G. Herdt & B. deVries (Eds.). *Gay and lesbian aging: Research and future directions.* New York: Springer.

Diamond, J. (1997). *Male menopause.* Naperville, IL: Sourcebooks.

Donatucci, C. F. & Greenfield, J. M. (2006). Recovery of sexual function after prostate cancer treatment. *Current Opinion in Urology, 16,* 444–448.

Doust, J., Miller, E., Duchesne, G., Kitchener, M., & Weller, D. (2004). A systematic review of brachytherapy: Is it an effective and safe treatment for localized prostate cancer? *Australian Family Physician, 33,* 1–4.

Emlet, C. A. (2006). "You're awfully old to have this disease:" Experiences of stigma and ageism in adults 50 years and older living with HIV/AIDS. *The Gerontologist, 46,* 781–790

Gallagher, E. & Gapstur, R. (2006). Hormone-refractory prostate cancer: A shifting paradigm in treatment. *Clinical Journal of Oncology Nursing, 10,* 233–240.

Garnets, L. & Peplau, L. A. (2006). Sexuality in the lives of aging lesbian and bisexual women. In D. Kimmel, T. Rose, & S. David (Eds.). *Lesbian, gay, bisexual and transgender aging.* New York: Columbia University Press.

Gelfand, M. M. (2000). Sexuality among older women. *Journal of Women's Health and Gender-Based Medicine 9,* S15–20.

Genevay, B. (1999). Intimacy and older people: Much more than sex. *Dimensions 1,* 7.

Goldberg, S., Sickler, J., & Dibble, S. L. (2005). Lesbians over sixty: The consistency of findings from twenty years of survey data. *Journal of Lesbian Studies, 9,* 195–213.

Gorman, E. M., Nelson, K. R., Applegate, T., & Scrol, A. (2004). Club drug and poly-substance abuse and HIV among Gay/Bisexual men: Lessons gleaned from a community study. (cover story). *Journal of Gay & Lesbian Social Services, 12(2),* 1–17.

Gonyea, J. (1998). Midlife and menopause: Uncharted territories for baby boomer women. *Generations,* 87–89.

Gotay, C. C., Holup, J. L., & Muraoka, M. Y. (2002). The challenges of prostate cancer: A major men's health issue. *International Journal of Men's Health, 1,* 59–72.

Gross, G. & Blundo, R. (2005). Viagra: Medical technology constructing aging masculinity. *Journal of Sociology and Social Welfare, 32,* 85–97.

Han, M., Nadler, R. B., Catalona, W. J., Thrasher, J. B., Tewari, A., & Menon, M. (2004). Point and counterpoint. Radical prostatectomy: Should the retropubic approach remain the standard of care? *Contemporary Urology, 16,* 38–50.

Harris, M. J., Weiss, J. P., & Blaivas, J. G. (2004). The renaissance of nerve-sparing radical perineal prostatectomy. *Contemporary Urology, 16,* 16–22.

Hash, K. (2006). Caregiving and post-caregiving experiences of midlife and older gay men and lesbians. *Journal of Gerontological Social Work, 47,* 121–138.

Healy, T. (2002). Culturally competent practice with elderly lesbians. *Geriatric Care Management Journal, 12,* 9–13.

Henry, J. & McNab, W. (2003). Forever young: A health promotion focus on sexuality and aging. *Gerontology and Geriatrics Education, 23,* 57–74.

Hite, S. (1976). *The Hite report: A nationwide study on female sexuality.* New York: Macmillan.

Hostetler, A. (2004). Old, gay and alone? The ecology of well-being among middle-aged and older single gay men. In G. Herdt & B. deVries (Eds.). *Gay and lesbian aging: Research and future directions,* 143–176. New York: Springer.

Hu, L. & Za, A. (2006). Sexual expression among the institutionalized elderly with dementia and strategies for sexual care. *Archives of Internal Medicine, 53,* 73–78.

Jacobson, S. (2000). Menopause. *The Seattle Times* 2B.

Janus, S. S. & Janus, C. L. (1993). *The Janus Report on sexual behavior*. New York: John Wiley and Sons.

Johnson, B. (1997). Older adults' suggestions for health care providers regarding discussions of sex. *Geriatric Nursing, 18,* 65–66.

Johnson, S. D., Phelps, D. L., & Cottler, L. B. (2004). The association of sexual dysfunction and substance use among a community epidemiological sample. *Archives of Sexual Behavior, 33,* 55–63.

Jones, T. & Nystrom, N. (2002). Looking back...looking forward: Addressing the lives of lesbians 55 and older. *Journal of Women and Aging, 14,* 59–73.

Kean, R. (2006). Understanding the lives of older gay people. *Nursing Older People, 18,* 31–36.

Kingsberg, S. A. (1998). Postmenopausal sexual functioning: A case study. *International Journal of Fertility and Women's Medicine, 43,* 122–128.

Kingsberg, S. A. (2000). The psychological impact of aging on sexuality and relationships. *Journal of Women's Health and Gender-Based Medicine, 9,* S33–38.

Kinsey, A., Pomeroy, B., & Martin, E. (1948). *Sexual behavior in the human male*. Philadelphia: W. B. Saunders.

Kinsey, A., Pomeroy, B., & Martin, E. (1953). *Sexual behavior in the human female*. Philadelphia: W. B. Saunders.

Konik, J. (2005). Exploring the lives of older lesbians. *Psychology of Women Quarterly, 29,* 447.

Kuhn, D. (2002). Nursing home residents with Alzheimer's: Addressing the need for intimacy. *Dimensions, 6,* 4–5.

Levesque, M., Nave, C., & Lowe, C. (2006). Toward an understanding of gender differences in inferring sexual interest. *Psychology of Women Quarterly, 30,* 150–158.

Lindau, S. T., Schumm, P., Laumann, E., Levinson, W., Muircheartaigh, C., & Waite L. (2007). A study of sexuality and health among older adults in the United States. *The New England Journal of Medicine, 357,* 762–774.

Lingler, J. H. (2003). Ethical issues in distinguishing sexual activity from sexual maltreatment among women with dementia. *Journal of Elder Abuse and Neglect, 15,* 85–102.

LoboPraabhu, S., Mollinari, V., Arlinghaus, K., Barr, E., & Lomax, E. (2005). Spouses of patients with dementia: How do they stay together 'till death do us part'? *Journal of Gerontological Social Work, 44,* 161–174.

Loue, S. (2005). Intimacy and institutionalized cognitive impaired elderly. *Care Management Journals, 6,* 185–190.

Mahoney, S. (2003). Seeking love. *AARP Magazine, 85,* 59–67.

Martin, D. & Lyon, P. (2001). Positively gay: New approaches to gay and lesbian life. In B. Berzon (Ed.). *Positively gay: New approaches to gay and lesbian life*. Berkeley, CA: Celestial Arts.

Masters, W. & Johnson, V. (1966). *Human sexual response*. Boston: Little Brown.

Masters, W. & Johnson, V. (1970). *Human sexual inadequacy*. Boston: Little Brown.

Masters, W. H. & Johnson, V. E. (1981). Sex and the aging process. *Journal of the American Geriatrics Society, 29,* 385–390.

Matthews, A., Tartaro, J., & Hughes, T. (2003). A comparative study of lesbian and heterosexual women in committed relationships. *Journal of Lesbian Studies, 7,* 101–114.

Matthias, R. E., Lubben, J. E., Atcheson, K. B., & Schweitzer, S. O. (1997). Sexual activity and satisfaction among very old adults: Results from a community-dwelling Medicare population survey. *The Gerontologist, 37,* 6–14.

McNeel, D. G. & Disis, M. L. (2000). Tumor vaccines for the management of prostate cancer. *Archives, 48,* 85–93.

MetLife Mature Market Institute. (2006). *Out and aging: The MetLife study of lesbian and gay baby boomers*. Westport, CT: MetLife.

Morrow, D. F. (2001). Older gays and lesbians: Surviving a generation of hate and violence. *Journal of Gay and Lesbian Social Services, 13,* 151–169.

Murray, J. & Adam, B. D. (2001). Aging, sexuality and HIV issues among older gay men. *The Canadian Journal of Human Sexuality, 10,* 75–90.

National Health and Social Life Survey. (1994). *The social organization of sexuality*. Chicago: The National Organization for Research.

National Institute on Aging (NIA). (2006). *Hormones and menopause*. Washington, DC: NIA. Retrieved August 2009, from http:// www.nia.nih.gov/ HealthInformation/Publications/hormones.htm

National Institute on Aging (NIA). (2008). *Age page: Menopause.* Washington, DC: NIA. Retrieved August 2009, from http://www.nia.nih.gov/HealthInformation/Publications/menopause.htm

National Institute on Aging (NIA). (2009). *Sexuality in later life.* Washington, DC: NIA. Retrieved August 2009, from http://www.nia.nih.gov/HealthInformation/Publications/sexuality.htm

Nelson, H. D., Vesco, K. K., Haney, E., Fu, R., Nedrow, A., Miller, J., et al. (2006). Nonhormonal therapies for menopausal hot flashes: Systematic review and meta-analysis. *Journal of the American Medical Association, 295,* 2057–2071.

Nusbaum, M. R. H., Hamilton, C., & Lenahan, P. (2003). Chronic illness and sexual functioning. *American Family Physician, 67,* 347–354.

Orel, N. A. (2004). Gay, lesbian and bisexual elders: Expressed needs and concerns across focus groups. *Journal of Gerontological Social Work, 43,* 57–77.

Pangman, V. & Seguire, M. (2000). Sexuality and the chronically ill older adult: A social justice issue. *Sexuality and Disability, 18,* 49–59.

Peschel, R. E. & Colberg, J. W. (2003). Surgery, brachytherapy and external-beam radiotherapy for early prostrate cancer. *Lancet Oncology, 4,* 233–241.

Pfeiffer, E. & Davis, G. C. (1972). Determinants of sexual behavior in middle and old age. *Journal of the American Geriatrics Society, 20,* 151–158.

Phillip, H. A. (2003). Hot flashes—a review of the literature on alternative and complementary treatment approaches. *Alternative Medicine Review, 8,* 284–302.

Phillips, R. L. & Slaughter, J. R. (2000). Depression and sexual desire. *American Family Physician, 64,* 782–786.

Potts, A., Gavey, N., Grace, V. M., & Vares, T. (2003). The downside of Viagra: Women's experiences and concerns. *Sociology of Health and Illness, 25,* 697–719.

Rogers, J., Su, L. M., Link, R. E., Sullivan, W., Wagner, A., & Pavlovich, C. P. (2006). Age stratified functional outcomes after laparoscopic radical prostatectomy. *Journal of Urology, 176,* 2448–2452.

Saranchuk, J. W., Kattan, M. W., Elkin, E., Touijer, A. K., Scardino, P. T., & Eastham, J. A. (2005). Achieving optimal outcomes after radical prostatectomy. *Journal of Clinical Oncology, 23,* 4146–4151.

Schiavi, R. C. (1996). Sexuality and male aging: From performance to satisfaction. *Journal of Sex and Marital Therapy, 11,* 9–13.

Schiavi, R. C. (1999). *Aging and male sexuality.* Cambridge, UK: Cambridge University Press.

Schiavi, R. C., Mandeli, J., & Schreiner-Engel, P. (1994). Sexual satisfaction in healthy aging men. *Journal of Sex and Marital Therapy, 20,* 3–13.

Schiavi, R. C. & Rehman, J. (1995). Sexuality and aging. *Urologic Clinics of North America, 22,* 711–726.

Sperber, J. (2006). As time goes by: An introduction to the needs of lesbian, gay, bisexual and transgender elders. In M. Shankle (Ed.). *The handbook of lesbian, gay, bisexual and transgender public health.* New York: Haworth Press.

Starr, B. D. & Weiner, M. B. (1981). *The Star-Weiner report on sex and sexuality in the mature years.* New York: Stein and Day.

Swanson, G. P. (2006). Management of locally advanced prostate cancer: Past, present, future. *Journal of Urology, 176,* S34–41.

Trudel, G., Turgeon, L., & Piche, L. (2000). Marital and sexual aspects of old age. *Sexual and Relationship Therapy, 15,* 381–406.

Tward, J. D., Lee, C. M., Pappas, L. M., Szabo, A., Gaffney, D. K., & Shrieve, D. C. (2006). Survival of men with clinically located prostate cancer treated with prostatectomy, brachytherapy, or no definitive treatment: Impact of age at diagnosis. *Cancer, 107,* 2392–2400.

Van Tol-Geerdink, J. J., Stalmeier, P. F., van Lin, E. N., Schimmel, E. C., Huizenga, H., van Daal, W. A., et al. (2006). Do patients with localized prostate cancer treatment really want more aggressive treatment? *Journal of Clinical Oncology, 24,* 4581–4586.

Weil, A. (2005). *Healthy aging.* New York: Knopf.

Weinstock, J. S. (2004). Lesbian friendship at and beyond midlife: Patterns and possibilities for the 21st century. In G. Herdt & B. deVries (Eds.). *Gay and lesbian aging: Research and future directions.* New York: Springer.

Werneke, U., Northey, S., & Bhugra, D. (2006). Antidepressants and sexual dysfunction. *Acta Psychiatrica Scandinavica, 114,* 384–397.

Wierzalis, E., Barret, B., Pope, M., & Rankins, M. (2006). Gay men and aging: Sex and intimacy. In D. Kimmel, T. Rose, & S. David (Eds.). *Lesbian, gay, bisexual and transgender aging.* New York: Columbia University Press.

Wiley, D. & Bortz, W. M. (1996). Sexuality and aging— Usual and successful. *Journals of Gerontology, 51A,* M142–M146.

Willert, A. & Semans, M. (2000). Knowledge and attitudes about later life sexuality: What clinicians need to know about helping the elderly. *Contemporary Family Therapy, 22,* 415–435.

Zeiss, A. M. & Kasl-Godley, J. (2001). Sexuality in older adult's relationships. *Generations, 25,* 18–25.

Part four
The Social Context of Aging

Throughout the previous three sections, we have identified how changes in the physical and psychological aspects of aging have numerous consequences for older people's cognitive and personality functioning, sexuality, and mental health. We have also seen how social factors (e.g., family and friendship ties) can affect physical changes (e.g., being at risk for certain chronic illnesses) as well as psychological experiences (e.g., the likelihood of depression and suicide). Within this framework of the dynamic interactions among physical, psychological, and social factors, we turn now to a more detailed discussion of the social environment of aging and its congruence with older people's level of functioning.

We begin with a review in Chapter 8 of the major social theories of aging—explanations of changes in social relationships that occur in late adulthood. Consistent with the person–environment perspective, these theories address alternative ways in which people relate to their changing functional capacity and social and physical environments as they age. The early positivist social gerontological theories, such as role, activity, and disengagement, were concerned with adaptation to age-related changes. These differ substantially from later theories, including continuity, age stratification, and exchange theory, which recognize the diverse and dynamic nature of the aging experience. The most recent theories are described as taking a "qualitative leap" over prior theories; these include social phenomenology, social constructionism, feminist theory, critical theory, and postmodernism. All of these represent a paradigmatic shift away from positivist or empirical approaches to studying

aging and toward an emphasis on the highly subjective nature of the aging experience. These social gerontological theories or perspectives provide the basis for examining the primary dimensions of older people's social environments in subsequent chapters: family, friends, and other social supports; housing and community; paid and nonpaid productive roles and activities; and changes in social networks through death and loss. These later theoretical approaches, in particular, recognize how older people's experiences, along with their social environments, vary by race, ethnicity, social class, functional ability, gender, and sexual orientation.

Chapter 9 begins by examining the vital contribution of informal social supports, particularly family and friends, to quality of life and well-being. Chapter 1 identified how longer life expectancies, combined with earlier marriages and childbearing in previous cohorts, have reduced the average span in years between generations. This has also increased the number of three-, four-, and sometimes five-generation families. The growth of the multigenerational family has numerous ramifications for relationships between partners, including LGBT and heterosexual partners who choose cohabitation rather than marriage; grandparents and grandchildren; adult children and older relatives; and siblings and extended family members. Generally, these relationships are characterized by reciprocity, with older family members providing resources to younger generations and trying to remain as autonomous as possible. The normal physical and psychological changes of aging are generally not detrimental to family relationships, although caring for an older relative with a long-term illness can burden family members. Compared to the earlier years, later-life family relationships are more often characterized by losses that demand role shifts and adjustments. A widower may cope with the loss of his wife by remarrying, whereas a widow tends to turn to adult children and friends.

Although some older people live alone—including a growing number who are homeless—friends, neighbors, and even acquaintances often perform family-like functions for them. More conducive to reciprocal and spontaneous exchanges, non-kin may be an even more important source of support for an older person than one's family, especially if family relationships are conflicted. As gerontologists have recognized the importance of informal social networks for older people's well-being, programmatic interventions—including intergenerational programming and age-friendly communities—have been designed specifically to strengthen these ties, which are described briefly in Chapters 9 and 11.

Although most families and friends willingly provide support, informal caregiving to frail elders can become burdensome. The positive and negative impacts of informal caregiving on both the care recipient and the caregiver are examined in Chapter 10. Elder mistreatment, although infrequent, can occur when caregivers feel extremely stressed and lacking in social supports. Generally, however, abuse happens because of the abuser's own behavioral problems, such as substance use or mental illness, not because of care demands per se.

Where people live—the type of living arrangement, urban-suburban location, and safety of the community—affects their social interactions. Chapter 11 illustrates the importance of achieving congruence between older people's social, psychological, and physical needs and their physical environments, particularly what they call home. Relocation is an example of a disruption of this congruence, or fit, between the environment and the older person. Characteristics of the neighborhood can enhance older persons' social interactions and, in some instances, their feelings of safety. Elder-friendly communities, planned housing, cohousing, assisted living facilities with multiple levels of care, adult family homes, and skilled nursing facilities are alternative forms of housing that support older people's changing and diverse needs. Chapter 11 also includes a discussion of housing policies and community-based social and health services that affect older people's ability to be autonomous, as well as an analysis homelessness among older adults and the health care needs of older prisoners.

Throughout our examination of the social context of aging, the effects of socioeconomic status on types of interactions and activities are readily apparent. This status is largely determined by past and current employment patterns, the changing economic marketplace and the resulting retirement benefits. Chapter 12 shows changing rates of labor-force participation and retirement among both men and women age 65 and older. Since the 1950s, most adults have chosen to retire early, provided their public or private pensions enabled them to enjoy economic security. But the global economic downturn has resulted in more people working longer because they cannot afford to retire. Although most older adults apparently do not want to work full-time, many enjoy the option of flexible part-time jobs, increasingly for economic reasons. For most people, retirement is not a crisis, although for those without good health, adequate finances, or prior planning, retirement can be a difficult transition. Accordingly, women, elders of color, and unskilled workers are most vulnerable to experiencing poverty or near-poverty in old age.

Chapter 12 also examines how people's interactions change with age in terms of their nonpaid productive roles, including involvement in community, organizational, religious, and political activities. The extent and type of civic engagement are influenced not only by age but also by gender, race, sexual orientation, functional ability, social class, and educational level. Therefore, declines in participation in other productive roles may not necessarily be caused by age-related changes but instead represent the interaction of these variables. Generally, involvement tends to be fairly stable across the life course; leisure, volunteer and community activities, and roles formed in early and middle adulthood are maintained into later life. This does not mean, however, that older people do not develop new interests and skills. Many people initiate new forms of productivity through senior centers, volunteering, civic organizations, political activism, and education programs. Think about the reports of older athletes who complete their first marathon or mountain ascent in their 70s, or become Peace Corps volunteers in their 80s. Given older adults' extensive knowledge and skills, they contribute to families, communities,

and society in numerous ways, even when they are not compensated financially. These are all ways in which people can maintain active aging.

Chapter 13 examines attitudes toward death and dying, the process of dying, and the importance of palliative or end-of-life care. The impacts of social and cultural values, as well as individual factors such as the relationship between the dying person and caregivers, are discussed in reviewing research on grief and mourning. An individual's right to die, the legal and ethical debates about assisted suicide, and the role of advance directives are also reviewed in this chapter. It concludes by examining the process of widowhood and how adults cope with this major life event.

Because of the predominance of challenges faced by older women and elders of color, their distinctive needs and relevant practice and policy interventions are discussed in Chapters 14 and 15. Economic and health disparities experienced in young and middle adulthood by these groups tend to be perpetuated across the life course and into old age. These are not isolated problems, but rather patterns of increasing concern to gerontologists and policy makers. This is because women over age 65 form the majority of older people, and the number of older persons of color is growing more rapidly than the older Caucasian population. These chapters illustrate how both women and elders of color display considerable strength and resilience in the face of a lifetime of inequities.

Chapter

8

Social Theories of Aging

This chapter discusses

- The theoretical question of what is the optimal way for older people to adapt to their changing functional capacity and social and physical environments
- Major social theories of aging
- Some important factors related to aging or age-related issues that serve as a guide for further inquiry and suggest possible interventions in the aging process
- Different theoretical lenses through which to view and explain the phenomenon of aging, such as social phenomenology, feminism, social constructionism, and constructivism

The Importance of Social Theories of Aging

All of us develop interpretive frameworks or lenses, based on our experiences, by which we attempt to explain the aging process and answer questions we may wonder about:

- What makes for successful, active, or vital aging?
- Who defines what is active aging?
- What are governmental roles and responsibilities toward older people in our society?
- What enhances older people's life satisfaction and well-being?

We observe older people in our families and communities and make generalizations about them. For example, some of our stereotypes of older people may be the result of unconscious theorizing about the meaning of growing old. Or, we may devise our own recommendations for policies or programs based on our informal and implicit theories. In effect, we all develop theories based on our own experiences.

In contrast to our personal observations about age changes, the scientific approach to theory development is a systematic attempt to explain *why* and *how* an age change or event occurs. *Theory building*—the cumulative development of explaining and understanding observations and findings—represents the core of the foundation of scientific inquiry and knowledge (Bengtson, Gans, Putney, & Silverstein, 2009). By using scientific methods, researchers seek to understand phenomena in a manner that is reliable and valid across observations, and then to account for what they have observed in the context of previous knowledge in the field. Scientists never entirely prove or disprove a theory. Instead, through both quantitative and qualitative research, they gather evidence that may strengthen their confidence in, or move them closer to rejecting the theory by demonstrating that parts of it are not supported. Scientific theories not only lead to the accumulation of knowledge, they also point to unanswered questions for further research and suggest directions for practical interventions. In fact, a good theory is practical! For example, some of the biological theories of aging discussed in Chapter 3 are useful in guiding people's health behaviors and health care services and policies. If the theory is inadequate, the research, the intervention, or public policy may fail by not achieving their intended goals (Bengtson et al., 2009).

As noted in Chapter 1, the biomedical study of aging, with its emphasis on disease and decline, has dominated the disciplinary development of gerontology since the beginning of the twentieth century. This chapter focuses on social theories of aging—explanations of changes in social relationships that occur in late adulthood—which are less well developed than biological explanatory frameworks but

are evolving (Bengtson et al., 2009; Powell, 2006; Powell & Longino, 2002). Most social gerontological theories have been formulated only since the 1950s and 1960s, and some have not been adequately tested. In fact, some social theorists assert that the theoretical interpretations of aging are in their infancy (Estes, Biggs, & Phillipson, 2003). One reason for what has been called gerontology's theoretically sterile nature is that early research in the field tended to be applied rather than theoretical; it attempted to solve problems facing older people. Researchers were concerned with individual life satisfaction and older people's adjustment to the presumably "natural" conditions of old age—retirement, ill health, or poverty—which resulted in the definition of aging itself as a problem (Biggs & Powell, 2001; George, 1995; Powell, 2006). Despite their relatively recent development, social theories of aging can be classified into first, second, and third generations, first and second *transformations of theoretical development*, or evolution of new modes of consciousness. Others categorize early theories as modernist, later ones as postmodernist (Bengtson et al., 2009; Lynott & Lynott, 1996; Powell, 2006). The order in which theories are presented in this chapter basically reflects the temporal dimensions of this intellectual history. Although there is some overlap of the central theoretical concepts across time, the later social theories are distinguished by a shift from:

- a focus on the individual to structural factors (e.g., societal institutions and social ranks) and interactive processes that affect aging, and
- largely quantitative methods in the positivist scientific tradition of seeking to understand "objective" reality to a range of more qualitative methodologies that aim to understand the individual interpretations and meanings of age-related changes among those experiencing them.

Social Gerontological Theory before 1961: Role and Activity

Early social gerontological research tended to be organized around the concept of adjustment, with the term "theory" largely absent from the literature (Lynott & Lynott, 1996). The perspectives on roles and activities, however, later came to be called *theories*. Identified as *functionalist gerontology* because of its emphasis on the consequences of role loss, theories of adjustment focused on personal characteristics (e.g., health, personality, etc.) as well as society's demands on and expectations of the aging individual. "Growing old" was conceptualized as the person encountering problems of adjustment due to role changes in later life. Role and activity theories not only postulated how individual behavior changes with aging, but also implied how it *should* change (Powell, 2006). These early classic theories are described here because of their influence on the field, even though some of them are no longer salient nor supported by empirical evidence.

Role Theory

One of the earliest attempts to explain how individuals adjust to aging involved an application of **role theory** (Cottrell, 1942). In fact, this theory has endured partly because of its applicable and self-evident nature. Individuals play a variety of social roles across the life course, such as student, mother, wife, daughter, businesswoman, and grandmother. Such roles identify and describe a person as a social being and are the basis of self-concept and identity. They are typically organized sequentially, so that each role is associated with a certain age or stage of life. In most societies, especially Western ones, chronological age is used to determine eligibility for various positions, to evaluate the suitability of different roles, and to shape expectations of people in social situations. Some roles have a reasonable biological basis related to age (e.g., the role of mother), but many can be filled by individuals of a wider age range (e.g., the role of volunteer, employee or student). Age alters not only the roles expected of people, but also the manner in which they are expected to play them. For example, a family's expectations of a 32-year-old mother are quite different from those of the same woman at age 82. How well individuals adjust to aging is assumed to depend on how well they accept the role changes presumed to be typical of the later years.

Age norms serve to open up or close off the roles that people of a given chronological age can play. Age norms are assumptions of age-related capacities and limitations—beliefs that a person of a given age can and ought to do certain things. As an illustration, a 79-year-old widow who starts dating a younger man may be told by family members that she should "act her age." Her behavior is viewed as not *age appropriate*. Norms may be formally expressed through social policies and laws (e.g., mandatory retirement policies that have been mostly eliminated in the U.S. but still exist for some jobs). Typically however, they operate

---

ROLE LOSS: GIVING UP THE CAR KEYS

A major role loss for many older people, especially older men, is that of driver. Families often worry about an older relative's driving, especially if he or she has had a minor accident or some near collisions. They fear that their older relative will cause a major accident as a result of slow driving or abrupt shifting of lanes without first signaling. Yet the older driver often refuses to stop driving, blaming close calls on other drivers, poor brakes, or road conditions. The driver may deny the problem and resist giving up the keys, because the loss of the driver role carries many consequences: loss of independence, identity, personal satisfaction, the ability to carry out daily tasks, and the sense of personal power and control. For most older people, losing one's ability to drive—to go where they want when they want—is a major role transition, symbolizing loss of autonomy. Any efforts to convince an older driver to give up the car keys must take account of what such loss of the driver role subjectively means to that individual.

informally. For example, even though employers cannot legally refuse to hire an older woman because of her age, they can assume that she is too old to train for a new position. Individuals also hold norms about the appropriateness of their own behavior at any particular age, so that social clocks become internalized and age norms operate to keep people on a time track (Hagestad & Neugarten, 1985). Most people in American society, for example, have *age-normative expectations* about the appropriate age at which to graduate from school, start working, marry, have a family, reach the peak of their career, and retire. These expectations have been markedly shifting among baby boomers and their children however, with more persons marrying later, more entering second or third careers in middle age, and more adult children facing difficulties in "launching."

Every society conveys age norms through *socialization*, a lifelong process by which individuals learn to perform new roles, adjust to changing roles, relinquish old ones, learn a "social clock" of what is age appropriate, and thereby become integrated into society. Older adults become socialized to new roles, such as grandparenting. In addition, they must learn to deal with *role losses*, such as the loss of the spouse or partner role by widowhood or divorce, or the worker role with

retirement. These losses can lead to an erosion of identity and self-esteem (Rosow, 1985). Older people may also experience *role discontinuity*, whereby what is learned at one age may be useless or conflict with role expectations at a later age. For example, learning to be highly productive in the workplace may be antithetical to adjusting to more ambiguous and undefined roles in retirement. Nevertheless, older adults often display considerable flexibility in creating or substituting roles in the face of major life changes. In fact, a process of *role exit* has been identified, whereby individuals discard roles that have been central to their identity, such as the employee role. Interventions such as retirement planning can encourage a process of gradually ceasing to identify with the worker role, shifting to civic engagement or a different career (Ekerdt & DeViney, 1993).

Some older people lack desirable role options. Until recently, few positive role models existed; those in the media and the public realm have tended to be youthful in appearance and behavior, maintaining middle-age standards that can hinder adapting to old age, especially for those who have chronic health conditions. In addition, some groups, particularly women and elders of color, may lack the resources to move into new roles or to emulate younger, physically fit models. Fortunately,

---

POINTS TO PONDER

Within a 5-year age range, how would you respond to the following questions *for most people, for your parents, and for yourself*? If your responses differ across these three groups, reflect upon why there are disparities. What does this tell you about how you view aging?

	For Most People	For Your Parents	For Yourself
Best age for a man to marry	_____	_____	_____
Best age for a woman to marry	_____	_____	_____
When most people should become grandparents	_____	_____	_____
When most men should be settled into a career	_____	_____	_____
When most women should be settled into a career	_____	_____	_____
When most people should retire	_____	_____	_____
When a man accomplishes the most	_____	_____	_____
When a woman accomplishes the most	_____	_____	_____

with the growth, visibility and improved health of the older population, more models of role gains and active aging as well as alternative roles exist than in the past. There is also wider recognition that the role of "dependent person" is not inevitable with age. Rather, the life course is characterized by varying periods of greater or lesser dependency in social relationships, with most people interdependent on others regardless of age. Even a physically impaired elder may still continue to support others financially and emotionally and may devise creative adaptations to ensure competence at home and a sense of meaning. For example, older people who volunteer as "phone pals" in a telephone reassurance program for latchkey children provide valuable emotional support.

Activity Theory

Activity theory also attempts to answer how individuals adjust to age-related changes such as retirement, chronic illness, and role loss. Successful aging is viewed largely as an extension of middle age, in which older people seek to maintain roles, relationships, and status in later life. Based on Robert Havighurst's (1963, 1968) analyses of the Kansas City Studies of Adult Life, it was believed that the well-adjusted older person takes on age-appropriate replacements for past roles through **productive roles** in voluntary, faith-based, and leisure associations. It was assumed that the more active the older person, the greater his or her life satisfaction, positive self-concept, and adjustment. Accordingly, age-based policies and programs are conceptualized as ways to develop new roles and activities, often consistent with middle-aged behaviors, and to encourage social integration. To a large extent, activity theory is consistent with the value placed by our society on paid work, individual responsibility, and productivity (Powell, 2000; 2001). Losing any of these characteristics is viewed as evidence of decline. Many older people have themselves internalized this perspective and believe that keeping active helps them maintain life satisfaction, as illustrated by the vignettes in the boxes on this page.

POINTS TO PONDER

Flip through a popular magazine or newspaper, noting how older adults are portrayed in ads and news stories. What roles do older people play in the print media? Are there differences between magazines aimed at younger versus older audiences (e.g., *Wired* vs. *Time*)? Are the roles mostly positive or negative images? Exceptional or realistic? To what extent is diversity portrayed in terms of race/ethnicity, gender, age, social class, sexual orientation, or disability? Or are the images mostly homogeneous? Reflect on how these images fit with or contradict your own perspectives on others' aging as well as your own. We encourage you to develop a critical eye with regard to the role models for older adults portrayed in the media.

KEEPING ACTIVE

The following two cases illustrate the possible link between activity theory and life satisfaction:

- Bob lives in the Pacific Northwest. He retired at age 62 after 30 years of work as a manager in an aerospace company. He and his wife of 40 years carefully saved money so that they could be very active in their retirement. They spent their winters as "snowbirds," traveling in their mobile home to the Sun Belt. Now, at age 69, they have spent 7 years in the same community in Arizona, where they have a network of good friends from many parts of the U.S., who are also retired. In the summer, they usually take one extended trip to the mountains. They enjoy good health and believe that keeping active is the key to their zest for life.

- Rose was a nurse for 30 years. In her career in direct patient care and teaching, she held positions of authority. She has always liked learning new things. Now 74 and retired, she is very active in her church and directs the adult education program. She has participated in Elderhostel four times and has traveled to Asia and Europe. She has taken two trips with her teenage grandchildren as well. Staying active means always learning and expanding her knowledge, so Rose consistently looks forward to new challenges. She has completed several photography classes at a community college and loves showing her travel photos to others.

Activity theory, however, fails to take account of how personality, social class, and lifestyle—particularly health and economic disparities—may be more salient than maturational issues in the associations found between activity and life satisfaction, health, and well-being (Bengtson et al., 2009). In fact, the value placed by older people on being active varies with these other factors in their life experiences. Activity theory defines aging as a social problem that can be addressed by trying to retain status, roles, and activities similar to those of earlier life stages. In contrast, the concept of active aging discussed throughout this book does not define aging as a problem, and it places greater emphasis on health, cognitive well-being, and social supports than does activity theory.

A challenge to the perspective of activity theory was formulated in 1961 as *disengagement theory*, which shifted attention away from the individual to the social system as an explanation for successful adjustment to aging.

The First Transformation of Theory

Disengagement Theory

The development of **disengagement theory** represents a critical juncture—as the first public statement wherein social aging theory is treated as a form of objective scientific inquiry using surveys and questionnaire methods separate from policy and practice applications (Lynott & Lynott, 1996). In fact, disengagement theory was the first comprehensive, explicit, and multidisciplinary theory advanced in social gerontology (Achenbaum & Bengtson, 1994). Cumming and Henry, in their classic work, *Growing Old* (1961), argued that aging cannot be understood separate from the characteristics of the social system in which it is experienced. All societies need orderly ways to transfer power from older to younger generations, and to prepare for the disruption entailed by the death of its oldest members. Therefore, the social system deals with the problem of aging, or "slowing down", by

institutionalizing mechanisms of disengagement or separation from society. Disengaging was assumed to benefit older adults as well through their decreased activity levels, more passive roles, less frequent social interaction, and preoccupation with their inner lives. *Disengagement* is thus viewed as inevitable and adaptive, allowing older people to maintain a sense of self-worth while adjusting through withdrawal to the loss of prior roles, such as occupational or parenting roles, and ultimately preparing for death (Powell, 2000, 2001). Since disengagement is presumed to have positive consequences for both society and the individual, this theory challenges assumptions that older people must be actively engaged in order to be well-adjusted. In contrast to activity theory, it views old age as a separate period of life, not as an extension of middle age.

Disengagement theory is now widely discounted by most gerontologists. While attempting to explain both system- and individual-level change with one grand theory, it has generally not been supported by later empirical research (Achenbaum & Bengtson, 1994). Elders, especially in certain cultures, may move into new roles of prestige and power. Even in cultures in which disengagement is normative, not all elders disengage, as evidenced by the growing numbers of older people who remain employed, healthy, and politically and socially active (Bengtson et al., 2009). As demonstrated by the MacArthur Studies described in Chapter 6, successful or active aging is more likely to be achieved by people who remain socially involved and integrated. Disengagement theory also fails to account for variability in individual preferences, personality, culture, and environmental opportunities within the aging population (Estes & Associates, 2001). Likewise, it cannot be assumed that older people's withdrawal from useful roles is necessarily good for society. For example, policies to encourage retirement have resulted in the loss of older workers' skills and knowledge in the workplace, and altered the dependency ratio described in Chapter 1. Although disengagement theory has largely disappeared from empirical literature, it nevertheless had a profound impact on the field as the first attempt to define an explicit multidisciplinary theory of aging.

Gerotranscendence Theory

Gerotranscendence theory, to some extent, parallels disengagement theory in its aim of developing a metatheory of the universal phenomenon of normal aging. This theory views greater focus on the inner self as a positive characte-ristic of old age, however. Gerotranscendence represents a shift in the elder's perspective from a materialistic, rational view of the world to a more cosmic and transcendent one, in which older adults explore their inner selves, are less interested in material goods, become more selective in their meaningful

relationships and, consistent with Erikson's work, are less self-centered, instead searching for ego integrity (Tornstam, 2000, 2005). This connection with the cosmic world may be expressed as wisdom, spirituality, and one's "inner world," and entails a shift away from activity, materialism, rationality, superficial social contacts, and preoccupation with the physical body. Like disengagement theory, gerotranscendence values contemplation and solitude in old age. The aging experience may cause elders to feel increased affinity to prior generations, smaller time gaps between historical periods, and a lesser divide between life and death. Gerotrans cendence, characterized by wisdom, self-acceptance, purpose, and a shift from judgments implicit in "successful aging," is viewed as the highest level of human development but it is not a universal or culture-free process. For example, Western culture—with its emphasis on consumerism, independence, productivity, and physical attractiveness—creates barriers to achieving gerotranscendence (Cruikshank, 2009; Moody, 2005; Tornstam, 1994, 1996a). This theory is criticized for not considering the historical and cultural context in which aging occurs, and for postulating a universal aging process. Critics contend that a theoretical perspective is needed that encompasses elders

Golf is a lifelong leisure activity for many elders.

who are active or passive, participating or withdrawn, cosmic or worldly, angry or cheerful (Thorsen, 1998). Nevertheless, gerotranscendence theory has profound implications for both elders and service providers working with older adults. It is reflected in the practice of life review, reminiscence therapy (described in Chapter 6), and increased attention to spiritu-ality and meaning in life (Johnson, 2009; Tornstam, 1996b, 2005; Wadensten, 2005; Wadensten & Carlsson, 2003).

Continuity Theory

While challenging both activity and disengagement theories, **continuity theory** maintains the focus on social-psychological theories of adaptation that were developed from the Kansas City Studies. According to continuity theory, individuals tend to maintain a *consistent* pattern of behavior as they age, substituting similar types of roles for lost ones and keeping typical ways of adapting to the environment. In other words, individuals do not change dramatically as they age, and their personalities remain similar throughout their adult lives, unless impacted by illness or other major life events. Life satisfaction is determined by the consistency between current activities or lifestyles with one's lifetime experiences (Neugarten, Havighurst, & Tobin, 1968). This perspective essentially states that, with age, we become more of what we already were when younger. Central

personality characteristics become more pronounced, and core values more salient with age. For example, people who have always been passive or withdrawn are unlikely to become active upon retirement. In contrast, people who were involved in many organizations, sports, or religious groups are likely to continue these activities, or to substitute new ones for those that are lost with retirement or relocation. An individual ages successfully and "normally" if she or he maintains a mature, integrated personality while growing old.

Continuity theory has some face validity because it seems reasonable. However, it is difficult to test empirically, because an individual's reaction to aging is explained through the interrelationships among biological and psychological changes and the continuation of lifelong patterns. Another limitation is that by focusing on the individual, it

---

CONTINUITY AND ADAPTATION

The following two cases illustrate the benefits of continuity for some elders:

At age 80, Rabbi Green, who has taught rabbinical students for 40 years, still makes the trip from his suburban home into the city to work with students one day per week. He speaks with considerable excitement about his reciprocal relationships with his students, how much he learns from them, and how he enjoys mentoring. When students talk about their relationship with him, it becomes clear how much they value him as a mentor. Being a teacher is who he is now, and who he has always been.

Mary, 70, was always the "cookie jar" mother to her children and their friends. She was there to offer goodies and a listening ear. Now her children and the generation of young persons who were their friends live far away. But a new generation of children has moved into the neighborhood in the small town where she lives. She has become acquainted with many of them and their parents as they stop to talk with her while she works in her beloved yard. Now many of the children stop by for a cookie and a glass of milk after school. She is fondly called the "cookie jar grandma." The children say that, along with giving them cookies, she always listens to them.

overlooks the role of external social, economic, and political factors that influence the aging process. Thus, it could rationalize a laissez-faire, or "live and let live," approach to addressing problems facing older people (Bengtson et al., 2009).

Alternative Theoretical Perspectives

Activity, disengagement, and continuity theories have often been framed as directly challenging one another, even though they differ only in the extent to which they focus on individual behavior or social structure (Lynott & Lynott, 1996; Marshall, 1996). None fully explains successful or active aging, nor adequately addresses the social structure or the cultural and historical contexts in which the aging process occurs. During this early period of theory development, the factors found to be associated with optimal aging were, for the most part, individualistic—keeping active, withdrawing, "settling" into old age. When macro-level phenomena were considered, they were not conceptualized as structurally linked between the individual and society. Nor were race, ethnicity, gender, sexual orientation, and class explicitly identified as social structural variables. A number of alternative theoretical viewpoints have emerged since the 1960s, each attempting to explain "the facts" of aging better than another, or to take account of its subjective meaning (Bengtson et al., 2009; Powell, 2006). Perspectives that emphasized a macro level of structural analysis include symbolic interactionism, age stratification, social exchange, and political economy.

Symbolic Interactionism

Consistent with the person–environment perspective outlined in Chapter 1, these **interactionist theories** focus on the person–environment transaction process as the dynamic interplay between older individuals and their social world. When confronted with change, whether in the process of relocating to a long-term care facility or learning to use a computer, elders are expected to try to master the new situation while extracting from the larger environment what they need to retain a positive self-concept.

Attempting to bridge the gap between the activity and disengagement points of view, the **symbolic interaction perspective** posits that interactions between individuals and their environment significantly affect people's experience of the aging process and themselves. People reflect on their lives and design ways of understanding their position in the social system (Bengtson et al., 2009; Gubrium, 1973). This viewpoint emphasizes the importance of considering the meaning of the activity for the individuals concerned, since the extent to which an activity is valued varies with the environment. Symbolic interactionists view both the self and society as able to create new alternatives. Therefore, withdrawal from social networks is not inevitable with aging. Policies and programs based on the symbolic interactionist framework optimistically assume that both environmental constraints and individual needs can be modified.

Although the symbolic interactionist perspective has implications for how to restructure environments, primary attention focuses on how individuals react to aging rather than on the broader sociostructural factors that shape its experience and meaning in our society. Most people move into and out of a succession of different roles and statuses as they age. These are determined by structural factors, a perspective congruent with age stratification theory.

Age Stratification Theory

Just as societies are stratified in terms of social class, gender, and race, every society divides people into categories or strata according to age— "young," "middle-aged," and "old." Age stratification is defined in terms of differential age cohorts. This means that individuals' experiences with aging, and therefore their roles, vary with their age strata. Structural changes in the system of age stratification influence how a person's

Age stratification theory and the subculture of aging suggest that older people prefer socializing within their own cohorts.

experiences affect life satisfaction (Lynott & Lynott, 1996).

Age stratification theory, first conceptualized by Matilda White Riley (Riley, 1971; Riley, Johnson, & Foner, 1972; Riley, Foner, & Riley, 1999), challenges the focus of activity and disengagement theories on individual adjustment. This theory adds a structured time component in which cohorts pass through an age-graded system of expectations and rewards (Riley et al., 1972). It recognizes that the members of one stratum differ from each other in both their stage of life (young, middle-aged, or old) and in the historical periods they have experienced. Both the life course and the historical dimensions explain differences in how people behave, think, and, in turn, contribute to society. Differences due to the historical dimension are referred to as cohort flow. As we saw in our discussion of research designs in gerontology (Chapter 1), people born at the same time period (cohort) share a common historical and environmental past, present, and future. They

have been exposed to similar events and changes, and therefore come to see the world in comparable ways (Riley, 1971). For exam-ple, the oldest-old today—who were children and young adults during the Depression—have generally valued economic self-sufficiency and "saving for a rainy day," compared to their children and grandchildren who experienced periods of economic prosperity during early adulthood.

Because of their particular relationship to historical events, people in the old-age stratum today are very different from older persons in the past or in the future, and they experience the aging process differently. This also means that cohorts collectively influence age stratification as they age. When there is a lack of fit in terms of available roles, cohort members may challenge the existing patterns of age stratification. For example, aging baby boomers are likely to alter the age stratification as they age system profoundly, given their sheer size, higher education and income levels, and the social structural changes that they have experienced in their lifetimes.

INTERGENERATIONAL CONFLICT AND AGE STRATIFICATION

Edna is a 90-year-old retired teacher who grew up during the Great Depression, and was a young bride during World War II. These two major historical events have shaped her life, because she learned to make do with whatever resources were available to her. As a result, she has always been frugal with her spending, to the point of saving a large nest egg to pass on to her grandchildren when she dies. However, she is often critical about the way her grandchildren seem to spend every penny they earn. Even worse, they use credit cards freely and don't worry about carrying debt. She has expressed her concerns to her daughter, telling her that these young people have not learned to save for a rainy day. Her daughter listens patiently but does not agree with what she considers her mother's penny-pinching ways. And her grandchildren try to explain to her that being in debt is a good way to build up credit for when they need a loan. She responds that she and her husband never took out a loan for anything, but always paid in cash.

Consider how the baby boomers who are retiring today differ from the cohort that retired in the 1950s. Although heterogeneous, this later cohort will tend to:

- view retirement and leisure more positively
- be physically active and healthier, although growing numbers of baby boomers and younger cohorts are obese
- be more likely to challenge restrictions on their roles through age discrimination lawsuits, legislative action, and political organization
- live long enough to become great-grand-parents
- be more planful and proactive about the aging and dying processes and end-of-life choices

These variations, in turn, will affect the experiences and expectations of future cohorts as they age. In other words, as successive cohorts move through the age strata, they alter conditions to such a degree that later groups never encounter the world in exactly the same way, and therefore they age differently.

The concept of **structural lag** emerged from the age stratification perspective. Structural lag occurs when social structures cannot keep pace with population changes (Riley, Kahn, & Foner, 1994; Riley & Loscocco, 1994; Riley & Riley, 1994). For example, with the increase in life expectancy, most workplaces, religious institutions, and voluntary associations are inadequately prepared to build on older adults' assets. Proponents argue that an age-integrated society would compensate for structural lag by developing policies—such as extended time off for education across the life course or new career options in old age—to bring social structures into balance with individuals' lives (Estes & Associates, 2001).

Social Exchange Theory

Social exchange theory also challenges activity and disengagement theories. Drawing on economic cost-benefit models of social participation, Dowd (1980) attempts to answer why social interaction

and activity often decrease with age. He maintains that withdrawal and social isolation result from an unequal exchange process of "investments and returns" between older persons and other members of society. The balance of interactions—the costs and benefits—between older people and others determines personal satisfaction. Because of the shift in opportunity structures, roles, and skills that accompanies aging, some elders have fewer resources with which to exert power in their relationships, and their status declines accordingly (Lynott & Lynott, 1996).

However, most older adults seek to maintain reciprocity and to be active agents in the

Our personal experiences with older family members affect our perceptions of aging and elders.

management of their lives. In the social exchange model, adaptability is a dual process of influencing one's environment as well as adjusting to it. This is consistent with the dialectical models of adult personality described in Chapter 6. Although older individuals may have fewer economic and material resources to bring to interactions, they often have nonmaterial assets, such as respect, approval, love, wisdom, and time for giving back to society. Similarly, policies and services can serve to increase opportunity structures for elders to contribute nonmaterial resources. For example, intergenerational programs recognize the knowledge and skills that older adults can share with youth. Exchange theory is also relevant to debates about intergenerational transfers through Social Security and within family caregiving relationships (Silverstein et al., 2002).

FOSTER GRANDPARENT PROGRAMS: INTERGENERATIONAL EXCHANGE

Ten-year-old Ann lives with her mother and older brother in a public housing high-rise apartment. Her mother has to work two jobs in order to make ends meet. This means that Ann is often left at home alone after school. Through the Foster Grandparent Program administered by the local senior services and available in Ann's school, Ann has someone to call after school if she is lonely or needs help with homework. And twice a week, her foster grandmother comes to visit her, taking her on neighborhood outings, making clothes for her favorite doll, buying a special treat, or tutoring her. Ann benefits from her foster grandmother's attention and love. And her foster grandmother, a widow in her mid-70s, feels a sense of satisfaction, accomplishment, and responsibility in her relationship with Ann. She looks forward to her time with Ann and speaks with pride to her friends about Ann's achievements as if she were her real granddaughter. Most of all, the young girl and the older woman love each other—an emotional component of exchange relationships that may be even more salient to quality of life than economic exchanges.

Political Economy of Aging

The focus of exchange theory on power and opportunity structures is related to the development of the **political economy of aging.** This is a macroanalysis of structural characteristics of capitalism that determines how scarce social resources are allocated in old age and serves to marginalize older people. Political economy theorists reject biomedical, activity, and disengagement models of aging. Instead, the attention is on social class as the primary determinant of older people's position, with dominant groups trying to sustain their own interests by perpetuating class inequities (Estes, 2001; Estes & Associates 2001; Kail, Quadagno, & Keene, 2009; Minkler & Estes, 1998). Thus, socioeconomic and political constraints, not individual factors, shape the experience of aging and are patterned not only by age and class but also by gender, sexual orientation, functional ability, and race. These structural factors—often institutionalized and reinforced by public policy—limit the opportunities and choices of later life, resulting in cumulative disadvantages in old age, which are further exacerbated by retirement. In other words, the cumulative effects of disadvantage are linked to mechanisms of social stratification (Ferraro & Kelly-Moore, 2003; Kail et al., 2009). Contrary to those who warn that older adults are bankrupting our society, the process of aging and how individuals adapt are not problems. Rather, the major problems faced by older people are socially constructed, often by structural limitations of income maintenance and health and long-term care policies. (Estes & Associates, 2001; 2004). Accordingly, policies that focus on personal responsibility are critiqued for socializing elders to adapt to their status, rather than altering the structural inequities that underlie challenges facing them (Harrington Meyer, Wolf, & Himes, 2005; Walker, 2009).

Political economy theory generated considerable research on inequality in old age and continues to influence gerontological theorizing. But it has generally been reframed as "critical gerontology," which remains concerned with structural disparities but also aims to confront the marginalization of elders (Baars, Dannefer, Phillipson, & Walker, 2006; Powell, 2006; Phillipson, 1996; Walker, 2009). Additionally, feminist theorists have added a gender dimension to the political economy perspective regarding how institutionalized mechanisms disadvantage women across the life course by limiting their labor market opportunities. The ways in which both racial and gender stratification are embedded in social institutions, resulting in inequality in old age, are captured by the example below of older women of color (Kail et al., 2009).

More recently, political economy theorists have criticized the emphasis on civic engagement for implicitly devaluing the worth of elders who cannot or choose not to participate in such community programs (Biggs, 2001; Martinson & Minkler, 2006). They view the growing call for civic engagement as a way to meet service gaps created by reduced public funding for health and social services, and the federal deficit. Despite the benefits of volunteerism and productivity for

successful aging (described in Chapter 6), political economists and critical theorists critique the implicit assumption that older people have an *obligation* to give back to their communities. From a political economy perspective, social and structural factors affect the older person's choices related to productivity. For example, caregivers of a partner with dementia, or custodial grandparents of young children, often cannot take on the additional role of a volunteer. An emphasis on civic engagement and productive aging can also divert the aging person from gerotranscendence, described earlier, in which contemplation allows the elder to find coherence and meaning in life (Biggs, 2001; Johnson, 2009). Even though proponents of the civic engagement movement for older adults recognize the dangers of a "one-size-fits-all" approach to healthy aging, a paradigm of aging that primarily values productivity and civic engagement can disempower elders who cannot contribute to their communities because of illness, disability, family caregiving, or poverty (Holstein & Minkler, 2003; Moody, 2005).

A POLITICAL ECONOMY PERSPECTIVE ON OLDER WOMEN OF COLOR: LIFE-COURSE INEQUITIES

Discrimination during their younger years and lack of opportunity throughout life have placed today's cohort of older African American women at an economic disadvantage. Because of racial and gender discrimination in education and employment throughout the life course, many did not have access to good jobs with retirement and health benefits. As a result, today many subsist on minimum Social Security benefits as their only source of income and Medicaid as their primary form of health insurance. This means that their health care options are structurally limited to providers who will accept Medicaid. And because of past encounters with institutionalized racism, they may be wary of other age-based services such as Supplemental Security Income (SSI). Subsisting on a limited income and often busy caring for grandchildren, admonishments from care providers to keep active and volunteer do not take into account the demands that these women face daily just to get by.

Life-Course Perspective

The **life-course perspective** is not necessarily a theory but a framework pointing to a set of issues that require explanation (George, 1996; 2007). As noted in Chapter 1, it attempts to bridge sociological and psychological constructs about processes at both the macro (population) and micro (individual) levels of analysis. The life-course perspective proposes that aging and its meaning are shaped by structural influences of cohort, history, culture, and location, as well as individual developmental factors such as the sequence of life events, interrlatedness with others, and human agency. The cohort is the fundamental unit of social organization that creates the context for human development and for structured access to opportunity. Accordingly, future cohorts of elders (Generations X and Y, with their consumerism and electronic communications) will adapt to their own aging in the context of different patterns of social ties than previous cohorts (e.g., the World War II cohort and its ethic of hard work and thrift). As noted in Chapter 7, the concept of cohort is also critical to understanding the different experiences of LGBT elders, according to the historical period in which they first self-identified as gay (Blaikie, 2006; Dannefer & Miklowski, 2006; Ferraro, Shippee, & Schafer, 2009; George, 2007; Heaphy, 2007).

The four principles of life-course theory are:

- Historical time and place (e.g., social context and cohort effects)
- Timing in lives
- Linked lives (intergenerational transmission and shared experiences)
- Human agency to make choices (Elder, 1994, 1998)

The life-course perspective expands on Erikson's stage-based model of psychosocial development by emphasizing that human development cannot be solely equated with steady incremental growth. Instead, it is an multidirectional, interactive, fluid, and nonlinear process characterized by the simultaneous appearance of gains and losses in roles and functions, as well as structured advantage and disadvantage within a particular social context. Accordingly, the social roles in which a person participates create and express the social context (Vincent, Phillipson, & Downs, 2006). In addition, patterns of development are not the same in all individuals, as reflected by the considerable heterogeneity of life transitions among older adults. The life-course perspective can provide a critical analysis of how caregiving for older relatives is now a standardized and "on-time" part of the life trajectory for growing numbers of adult children because of increased life expectancy among their parents' generation. Additionally, it examines how caregiving roles across the life course affect well-being in old age (Blieszner, 2006).

As noted in Chapter 1, growing research on health disparities takes into account how social systems, stratified by gender, race/ethnicity and social class, structure the life course and can generate inequality in old age (Ferraro et al., 2009). For example, because of care responsibilities, women have

---

LIFE-COURSE ADVANTAGE: OPPORTUNITY IN OLD AGE

James is a 72-year-old civil engineer who retired from the Army Corps of Engineers at age 66. But his expertise in designing large bridges has resulted in a second career as a consultant to state and federal projects where he is asked to assess the safety of bridges and to evaluate them after natural disasters. He is doing so well in his consulting job that he withdraws only the minimum from his pension benefits. He enjoys the respect and friendship of his new colleagues as well as the opportunities to use his professional skills in this second career. The chance to still feel useful is more important to him than what he gets paid to consult.

---

limited opportunities to accumulate savings across their lives, resulting in lower income and higher rates of poverty in old age compared to men (O'Rand, 2006). The life-course perspective also considers the role of "human agency," or individual decisions that affect one's future, along with the accumulation of risk and resources. Disadvantage increases exposure to risk, but advantage magnifies exposure to opportunity. For example, dropping out of high school or graduating as valedictorian have lifelong consequences on economic and social well-being (George, 2007). Last, it considers the intergenerational transmission of inequality and how childhood conditions structure the life course through both demographic and developmental processes (Ferraro et al., 2009).

Recent Developments in Social Gerontological Theory: The Second Transformation

Social Phenomenology, Social Constructivism, and Social Constructionism

The "second transformation" in theoretical development, distinguished by social phenomenology, is described as a qualitative leap in gerontological thought occurring since the early 1980s (Bengtson et al., 2009; Lynott & Lynott, 1996; Powell, 2006). **Social phenomenology** uses an interpretive approach to knowledge and focuses on understanding the human meanings of social life in the context of everyday life rather than explanation of facts. Taking issue with the presumed "facts of aging," phenomenological theorists question the nature of age, how it is described, and whose interests are served by thinking of aging in particular ways. Accordingly, the emphasis is on understanding individual processes of aging that are influenced by social definitions and social structures (Bengtson et al., 1997; 2009; Longino & Powell, 2009). People actively participate in their everyday lives, creating and maintaining social meanings for themselves and those around them. These then influence what we each call "reality." No one, including researchers, directly or objectively "sees" a fixed reality. For phenomenologists, it is not the objects or facts, but rather the assumptions and interpretations of these purported facts that are critical. For example, this theoretical perspective attempts to understand how policy makers interpret the growth of the older population when debating whether to increase or decrease Medicare or Social Security benefits (Estes & Associates, 2001). If they perceive the aging population to be economically homogeneous, then policy solutions will not distinguish elders who have achieved a comfortable retirement from those who have experienced a lifetime of disadvantages. The resulting policies will continue to perpetuate such inequities because of their focus on individual interactions to understand the multifaceted aging experience. They claim that the data or facts of aging cannot be separated from researchers' perceptions about time, space, and self—or those of the individuals being studied. Gubrium (1993) used life narratives to discern the subjective meanings of quality of care and quality of life for nursing home residents—meanings that cannot be uncovered by predefined measurement scales. Simi- larly, Diamond (1992) utilized participant observation techniques as a nursing assistant to learn about the social world of nursing homes. He described how the meanings of care are constantly negotiated as the invisible work of caring for older residents' emotional needs clashes with the daily physical tasks of a nursing assistant. Such approaches contrast with the **positivism** (or *quantitative approach*) of earlier theories. To positivists, phenomenological theories may seem impossible to test and closer to assumptions about meanings than propositions that can be proved or disproved (Bengtson et al., 1997).

Phenomenology provides the epistemological underpinning of social constructivism, social constructionism, feminist theories, critical theory, and postmodern perspectives. Although both social constructionism and social constructivism are phenomenological approaches that address ways in which social phenomena develop, they are distinct concepts. **Social constructionism** refers to the structural development of phenomena relative to social contexts, while **social constructivism** refers to an individual's making meaning of knowledge within a social context. For this reason, social constructionism is typically described as a sociological construct, and social constructivism as a psychological one. We use social constructionism when referring to how aging is defined as a problem more by culture and society than by biology, more by beliefs, customs, and traditions than by bodily changes, while *social constructivism* refers to how individuals experience and make meaning of the aging process.

As noted, social constructivism is one element of the phenomenological approach to knowledge (Bengtson et al. 2009). Instead of asking how factors such as age cohorts, life stages, or system needs organize and determine one's experience,

POINTS TO PONDER

A debate before Congress in 2003 was whether or not to differentially allocate Medicare drug benefits according to income. What assumptions did this debate make about the older population as a whole? About upper- versus lower-income elders? What is your position on differential allocation of Medicare's prescription drug benefits? What theoretical perspective guides your thinking?

social constructionists reverse the question and ask how individuals—whether professionals or laypersons—draw on age-related explanations and justifications in the ways that they relate to and interact with one another. Individual behavior produces a "reality," which in turn structures individual lives. In other words, the realities of age and age-related concepts are socially constructed through interpersonal interactions. We learn to be old in response to the way we are treated by others (Cruikshank, 2009). For example, labeling older people as dependent, asexual, frail, or marginal is defined through social interactions by health care providers, family members, and society in general. As another example, the "social constructivism perspective" of relationships maintains that an individual's subjective view of social ties is what matters for well-being, not the objective nature of the relationships (Dykstra & Mandemakres, 2007). Accordingly, social reality and the meaning of being old shift over time, reflecting the differing life situations and social roles that occur with individual maturation. Additionally, what is considered to be old age varies with the economic, cultural, historical, and societal contexts and, thus, is socially constructed.

As noted in Chapter 1, chronological age is a poor predictor of social, physical, and cognitive abilities. Yet most of us, even gerontological scholars, may make positive or negative assumptions about someone simply on the basis of chronological age. Many depictions of old age present it as a negative experience, something to be avoided, a disease to be dealt with by medical interventions. Older adults may shun the label "old," reserving it for those with obvious physical or mental decline (e.g., "I don't want anything to do with those old people"). Even the current preoccupation with healthy, successful aging and advertisements for beauty products still portray aging as something to be forestalled as long as possible. In addition, the visual images associated with many of these anti-aging activities are unattainable by the majority of Americans.

From the perspective of social constructionism, the negative ways in which age is socially

> ### SOCIAL CONSTRUCTIVISM OF THE CONCEPT OF "OLD"
>
> At age 85, Martha enjoys a brisk, daily 30-minute walk around the park near her home. She manages her household on her own, participates in exercise classes at the local senior center, and enrolls in one history class each semester at the local community college. Nevertheless, the young people she meets at the park and in her college classes are always amazed at her vigor and intellectual curiosity. They often express surprise that she can do all she does "at her age" and ask her about her "secret to aging well." Martha tells them they need to expand their view of aging, discard their ageist stereotypes of growing older as an illness, and stop viewing active older people as "exceptional." She views herself as an healthy adult, just as capable at age 85 as she was at 45. But many of these young adults rely on the negative images of aging that they have seen on TV or in popular magazines.
>
> James is an 80-year-old retired dentist who was diagnosed with dementia 20 years ago and now lives in a skilled nursing facility. His personal funds ran out long ago, so his long-term care is covered by Medicaid. His family visits him regularly and tries to contribute as much as possible to his financial needs. But they marginalize him by referring to him in the third person and focusing on his dependence and losses, rather than the fact that his strengths coexist. As a result, he increasingly doubts his capabilities and is giving up even going to the dining area or any social events.

constructed has numerous consequences for social policy, employer practices, and public perception (Estes, 2001; Kail, Quadagno, & Keene, 2009). Consider how public resources, particularly Medicaid, are disproportionately allocated toward skilled nursing home care rather than toward supplementing the personal assistance provided by families and low-wage workers. Accordingly, the majority of public funds go toward medical care, not psychosocial and personal care services that might enhance elders' autonomy, quality of life, and active aging. Similarly, the general public tends to think of old age as a homogenous physical condition, overlooking the tremendous diversity that exists across at least one third of our lifetimes. Yet no one refers to childhood or adolescence solely as a physical condition (Cruikshank, 2009).

From the perspective of social constructionism, we need to deconstruct the concept *old*, and recognize how one's socially structured position or location (gender, race/ethnicity, social class, sexual orientation, functional ability) creates lifelong disparities that shape the experiences of old age. This also suggests that gerontologists focus not only on the problems facing the old, but also on eliminating structural barriers that may impede elders' strengths,

---

A SOCIAL CONSTRUCTIONIST PERSPECTIVE ON NURSING HOMES

Nursing homes have traditionally been based on a hierarchical medical model in which professional health care providers believe that they know what is "best." The medicalization of nursing homes has meant that most such facilities are viewed as places to die, not to live. Rules and regulations tend to be oriented to efficiencies and staff needs, not those of residents. When to get up and go to bed, when to eat meals, and when to have baths are all typically determined by administrative staff and licensing requirements. In addition, staff members are assigned particular tasks (such as the medication nurse or the bathing aide), without taking into account the needs or preferences of the residents. In contrast, recent efforts to transform nursing home organizational culture have encompassed resident-directed care, whereby the residents choose when to get up, when to eat breakfast, and the timing of all other daily activities (described in more detail in Chapter 11). Past assumptions, and even licensing requirements are questioned, and creative approaches to regulations implemented. Services are decentralized and task-focused roles eliminated so that staff can work with the same residents over time and build relationships. While the traditional nursing home has tended to be a microcosm of how our society has viewed elders, these new options typically put older adults in central decision-making roles, thus representing how socially constructed roles and positions can change.

---

resilience, and capacities to overcome adversity (Bengtston, 2009; Calasanti & Slevin, 2006; Olson, 2003, Ryff & Singer, 2009).

Critical Theory and Feminist Perspectives

Phenomenology has also influenced other contemporary social gerontology theories, especially **critical** and **feminist theories.** Critical theory, encompassing critical gerontology, deconstructs the biomedical model of aging and examines how structural and institutional factors, especially social class, create disparities in the aging experience. Critical theorists are concerned with how positivist conceptualizations of aging represent a language that serves to reify experiences as something separate from adults experiencing aging—as is illustrated by health care providers who direct their questions to a family member rather than including the older patient (Lynott & Lynott, 1996). They contend that a more critical and humane approach, drawing upon the humanities and social sciences, would allow older people to define the research questions themselves and would better capture the multiplicity and diversity of the aging experience. Arguing for humanistic discourse in gerontology, Moody (1988, 2002) identifies four goals of critical gerontology:

1. to theorize subjective and interpretive dimensions of aging
2. to focus not on technical advancement but on "praxis," defined as active involvement in practical change, whether making decisions about care or influencing public policy
3. to link academics and practitioners through praxis
4. to produce "emancipatory knowledge"—a positive vision of how things might be different, or what a rationally defensible vision of a "good old age" might be (e.g., an older adult might "reinvent" him/herself after losing his/her job, or forcefully declare self-worth in the face of irreversible physical decline) (Cruikshank, 2009; Moody 2002).

Older feminists are often role models for younger women.

To achieve such knowledge requires moving beyond the conventional confines of gerontology to explore contributions toward theory development from more reflective modes of thought that are derived from the humanities (Cole et al., 1993). What is yet unknown is what "a good old age" means, how it can be attained, and what type of "emancipatory knowledge" is possible. More recently, critical gerontology has not merely critiqued existing theory, but aimed to create positive models of aging that emphasize strengths and diversity. For example, critical gerontologists now question traditional positivistic measures to try to understand the multiple dimensions of retirement, including retirement as a freeing stage in the life course and a chance to "reinvent" oneself (Minkler, 1996; Moody, 2002;

Phillipson, 1996; Powell, 2006). By questioning traditions in mainstream social gerontology, critical theory calls attention to other perspectives relevant to understanding aging, such as the humanistic dimension, and has influenced feminist theories of aging (Gullette, 1998; Woodward, 1998). In addition, the self-reflexive nature of critical theory constantly challenges gerontologists to understand the impact of social research and policy on older individuals. Critical thinking expands the field of social gerontology by providing insight into, and critical self-reflection on, the continuing effort to understand the aging experience. With growing attention to ethnographic and other qualitative methodologies, the interpretive approach of critical theory is increasingly brought to bear on empirical observations of aging.

Feminist theories are guided by social constructivism, constructionism, and critical gerontology, but they differ by making women's issues central to the discourse (Bengtson et al., 2009). The feminist perspective contends that the current theories of aging are insufficient by their failure to include gender relations and women's experiences as central to the aging experience (Calasanti, 2009; Cruikshank, 2009; Estes, 2001). Feminist theories attempt to integrate micro and macro approaches to aging through linkages between individuals and social structures, or between personal problems and public responses. In particular, they make explicit how women's and men's experiences are influenced by structural, gender-based inequities across the life course (Bengtson et al., 2009; Calasanti, 2009; Estes & Associates, 2001; Moody, 2002).

From a feminist perspective, simply adding women to research samples, models, and theories derived from men's experience is inadequate, because conceptually, such approaches still consider gender an individual attribute, and men are viewed as the implicit standard for assessing women's lives. Instead, feminist theorists contend that gender should be a primary consideration in attempts to understand aging, not just one variable, particularly since women form the majority of the older population. Because gender is an organizing principle and is institutionalized by processes through which people assume "masculine" and "feminine" to be natural, men and women experience aging differently. For example, feminists move beyond documenting that women have lower retirement benefits to ask why this exists and why it is viewed as "natural." Conventional gerontology may frame studies of women's retirement in terms of individual financial responsibility, while a feminist perspective questions what social and economic structures and policies make it difficult for women to accumulate savings despite decades of employment (Cruikshank, 2009). The gender identities that emerge in social interactions across the life course serve to privilege men and generally disadvantage women. Those who are privileged use their greater resources to justify gender-based inequities as "natural" or based on social necessity, such as the implicit assumption that women will be the primary family caregivers (Calasanti & Slevin, 2006; King, 2006).

The intersecting inequalities of gender with race, social class, sexual orientation, and disability are also examined by feminist theorists. For example, gender inequities underlie the fact that more older women than men are poor. But when intersections with race are examined, both African American men and women have higher poverty rates than white women. Feminist gerontologists also theorize old age itself to be a social location that intersects with gender. More recently, feminist gerontologists have pointed to the intersection of gender with sexual identity, and how these affect both men's and women's well-being. In sum, feminist gerontologists take into account how intersections of age relations with other social locations reveal multiple "old ages" (Acker, 2008; Calasanti, 2004; 2009).

Feminist theorists draw upon the political economy perspective to understand women's aging experiences in light of macro-level social,

economic, and political forces rather than as isolated results of individual choices. Women's caregiving, retirement, health, and poverty across the life-course are examined in terms of women's differential access to power in the paid labor force, in child rearing, and in unpaid housework throughout their lives. Social policies are criticized for defining the problems facing women as private responsibilities rather than taking account of how existing structural arrangements create women's limited choices in old age. For example, the lack of public and private pensions for a lifelong career as homemaker and caregiver leaves older women economically vulnerable. Feminists also point to society's failure to take domestic labor seriously in life-course analyses of work and in the unpaid nature of family leave policies. From a feminist view, work in the home is integral to economic productivity but is devalued. When postmodern and feminist theories are integrated, for example, the primary deconstructionist task is to critique language, discourse, and research practices that constrict knowledge about older women. To illustrate, caregiving is viewed not as the result of women's natural tendencies toward nurturing, but as the outcome of socialization processes and policies that reinforce gendered patterns of care and depend on the unpaid labor of women as cost-effective for society (Calasanti & Slevin, 2001; Hooyman et al., 2002).

Similarly, feminists contend that the consequences of caregiving should not be evaluated on the basis of individual characteristics such as burden. Instead, the underlying problem for women of all ages is not personal stress levels, but inadequate and gender-based public policies that fail to support their care work. They suggest that the long-range solution is reorganizing work, including the work of caregiving, as a societal rather than an individual responsibility. Feminists argue that unpaid caring by families and underpaid work by direct care workers are interconnected and must be fundamentally changed to be more equitable and humane for both the givers and the recipients of care, in order to improve elders' well-being (Calasanti, 2009; Gonyea & Hooyman, 2005; Hooyman et al., 2002).

Addressing issues that are relevant to women's lives, feminist gerontologists draw explicit linkages to practice and policy changes, such as economic rewards for women's caregiving. In addition, they provide models for integrating micro (personal) and macro (political) levels of analysis. Thus, they encompass both structural and individual levels of theory and change in order to improve the social and economic positions of all women as they age. Lastly, they challenge "mainstream" feminist theories, which typically have focused on issues pertaining to younger women, to take account of age. The merging of feminist and aging scholarship has the potential for formulating politically sustainable solutions related to employment and caregiving that can benefit both men and women, young and old (Calasanti, 2009; Moen, 2001; Powell, 2006).

A FEMINIST PERSPECTIVE ON CAREGIVING

Maria grew up with the expectation that she would marry, have children, and take care of her family. She fulfilled this expectation, raising four children, caring for her husband when he suffered a heart attack in his early 60s, and later caring for both her mother and her mother-in-law. She never held a full-time job outside the home; instead, she occasionally worked part-time in order to supplement her husband's income. When he died at age 65, she was left with only his Social Security income. All her years of caregiving work, which had contributed to her family's well-being and to the economy, were not compensated in any way. She feels that she is being penalized for following the "rules" expected of her throughout her life. If her caregiving work were valued by our society and viewed as legitimate, Social Security would be altered to provide benefits for such in-home care. This would mean that caregivers such as Maria would receive Social Security benefits in their own right in old age.

Postmodernist Theories of Aging

Postmodernist theory (or deconstructionism, which in itself is atheoretical) represents a decisive break with modernity or a positivist scientific approach to an "objective" truth. Similar to social constructivist theories, postmodernists contend that knowledge is socially constructed and social life highly improvisational. As a result, all forms of meaning and "knowledge" are not to be taken for granted. According to this perspective, constructs such as "social class" and "gender" relegate individual elders to socially constructed categories and overlook human agency to organize changes in political and economic systems and life conditions. Even the political economy perspective is critiqued by postmodernists for treating aging as a problem, and for assuming an industrial economy with structured mass production. In contrast with political economy theorists, postmodernists point to the shift to a service economy—which is more flexible, fluid, and alterable, and promotes consumer choice among a wide array of options. For example, with the changing nature of labor, older adults have far more time for leisure, travel, and personal enrichment. Communities are redefined as collectives of individuals who share similar beliefs and interests and are brought together through associations or in virtual contexts (Bass, 2007, 2009; Powell, 2006; Powell & Longino, 2002).

Themes of the postmodern movement are summarized by Powell (2006):

- Objective truth is unlikely or impossible; truth is variable, depending on the situation and circumstances.
- Decentralized power and authority are preferable to centrally held power, especially at the federal government level.
- Reality and truth should be questioned.
- Individual choice dominates postmodern society, which focuses on individual consumption of goods and services.

Central to postmodernists is the intent to describe the changed and changing world, not in an idealized way but as it appears today. They contend that the ideas of critical gerontologists, represented by the political economy and to some extent feminist perspectives, are no longer relevant to this changed world. Instead, new frameworks are necessary to interpret the society in which we are aging. Similarly, understanding the uniqueness and diversity of the aging experience replaces interest in conformity and universality (Bass, 2009).

Some postmodernists emphasize the cultural interaction between the complexity of the aging body and the social context in shaping people's "lived experience" across the life course. The notion of the aging body not as a medical or biological phenomenon but as a social and cultural practice of everyday life is an important narrative in the construction of the aging identity of individuals and the subjective sense of self and meaning. In other words, we are insidiously aged by Western culture (Gullette, 1997, 1998; 2004; Longino & Powell, 2009). Yet, while one's external physical appearance changes with age, a person's essential identity does not. Consider how we often hear older adults state that they don't feel old until they see themselves in a mirror and are surprised by their own image. The body is not passive material that is only acted upon; instead, it is always in the process of becoming (Longino & Powell, 2004, 2009; Powell, 2006). At the same time, the aging body is exploited by popular culture, especially by glamorized representations of old age in advertisements oriented to foster consumption and a continual flight from the "symptoms" of aging to "aging successfully" and "finding the perfect body." Despite the discontinuity between the experience of living in an aging body and images of aging, most older adults maintain their sense of identity, derived from their past achievements and what they hope to attain in the future, not stereotypical attributes of old age (Biggs, 1999; Gilleard & Higgs, 2000; Longino & Powell, 2009; Powell & Longino, 2001).

Postmodernism also addresses biotechnology and the reconstruction of aging bodies to reinvent aging through biomedical and

POSTMODERN IMAGES OF "SUCCESSFUL AGING"

Many older adults today are faced with the dilemma of "looking young," while portraying the image of the "wise elder." Some have turned to plastic surgery, expensive cosmetics, and monthly injections of human growth hormones to maintain a youthful appearance, while others spend several hours per day to maintain their bodies' firmness despite the effects of aging. When asked why they spend so much time and money on maintaining their physical appearance, many older men confess that it is necessary to be accepted in the upper echelons of management. Women focus on both these concerns and the social stigma of looking old in American society.

information technologies. In fact, biotechnology can sell a dream of "not growing old" to people who have the resources to afford such technology (Longino & Powell, 2004). While advances in biomedicine and computer technology can provide new options for persons with chronic illness or disability, they also mean that some aspects of the human body can be reconstructed to prevent, hide, or slow the aging process (Powell & Wahidin, 2007). Closely related to the active adoption of consumer practices such as biotechnology is a growing emphasis on personal responsibility for one's health, whereby those who do not engage in adequate self-care may not be deserving of societal resources to address their illnesses (Powell & Biggs, 2004).

Summary and Implications for the Future

This review of theoretical perspectives has highlighted the multiplicity of lenses through which to understand the aging process. Although we have emphasized the utilization of explicit theoretical perspectives to build, revise, and interpret how and why phenomena occur, it is apparent that no single theory can explain all aging phenomena. Instead, these theories—or conceptual frameworks—vary widely in their emphasis on individual adjustment to age-related changes; their attention to social structure, power, economic conditions, and life-course inequities; the methodologies utilized; and their reflective nature on the meaning of the aging experience. As noted early in the chapter, they represent different times or historical periods in the development of social theories. Some, such as disengagement theory, have been largely rejected by empirical data, while others, such as social phenomenology and feminist theory, are evolving and capturing the attention of a new generation of gerontological researchers. Other earlier perspectives, such as social exchange and symbolic interactionism still influence research questions as well as social policy and practice. As a whole, these theoretical perspectives point to new ways of seeing and new modes of analyzing aging phenomena laying the groundwork for future research directions. As the social, economic, and political conditions affecting older people change, new theoretical perspectives must develop or former ones must be revised through the gathering of information from diverse cultures, contexts, and circumstances. The theme of for the 2006 Gerontological Society annual meeting, "the gerontological imagination," reflected the growing interest in alternative perspectives across a wide range of disciplines. Given the increasing heterogeneity of the aging process, interdisciplinary research and theory building are essential. Such research must take into account both individual and macro-level changes. It must encompass the role of gender, race, class, sexual orientation, and functional ability, and allow for the dynamic nature and meaning of the aging experience. We turn next to the social context and relationships addressed by many of the social theories of aging: the vital role of social supports in old age; how physical living arrangements affect

social interactions; the concept of productive aging, which encompasses both paid and nonpaid roles and activities; and coping with loss through death, bereavement, and widowhood.

GLOSSARY

activity theory a theory of aging based on the hypothesis that (1) active older people are more satisfied and better adjusted than those who are not active, and (2) an older person's self-concept is validated through participation in roles characteristic of middle age and therefore older people should replace lost roles with new ones to maintain their place in society

age stratification theory a theoretical perspective that the societal age structure affects roles, self-concepts, and life satisfaction

continuity theory a theory based on the hypothesis that central personality characteristics become more pronounced with age, or are retained through life with little change; people age successfully if they maintain their lifelong roles and adaptation techniques

critical theory the perspective that genuine knowledge is based on the involvement of the "objects" of study in its definition, which results in a positive vision of how things might be better, rather than only an understanding of how things are

disengagement theory a theory of aging based on the hypothesis that older people, because of the inevitable decline with age, become less active with the outer world and increasingly preoccupied with their inner lives, thereby shifting an orderly transfer of power from older to younger people

feminist theory the view that the experiences of women are often ignored in understanding the human condition, together with efforts to attend critically to those experiences

gerotranscendence theory a theory which places greater emphasis on the inner self; as people age, they move away from a focus on materialism and productivity to contemplation, spirituality, and place greater value on close relationships

interactionist theory a perspective that emphasizes the reciprocal actions of persons and their social environment in shaping perceptions, attitudes, and behavior

life-course perspective a view of human development that focuses on changes with age and life experiences in the larger social, historical, and political context

political economy of aging a theory based on the hypothesis that social class and other structural variables determine a person's access to resources and that dominant groups within society try to sustain their own interests by perpetuating class inequities

positivism the perspective that knowledge is based solely on observable facts and their relation to one another (cause and effect, or correlation);

postmodernist theory a theory that contends that knowledge is socially constructed so that no forms of meaning and "knowledge" are to be taken for granted.

productive roles a concept central to activity theory; values activities in voluntary associations, employment, politics, and faith-based organizations

role theory a theory based on the belief that roles define us and our self-concept and shape our behavior

social constructivism a psychological construct within the phenomenological approach, which refers to an individual's making meaning of knowledge within a social context

social constructionism a sociological construct within the phenomenological approach, which refers to the structural development of phenomena relative to social contexts

social exchange theory a theory based on the hypothesis that personal status is defined by the balance between people's contributions to society and the costs of supporting them

social phenomenology a point of view in studying social life that emphasizes the assumptions and meanings of experience rather than the "objective" facts, with a focus on understanding rather than explaining

structural lag the inability of social structures (patterns of behavior, attitude, ideas, and policies)

to adapt to changes in population and individual lives

symbolic interaction perspective a theoretical perspective that posits that interactions between individuals and their environment affect their experience of the aging process

REFERENCES

Achenbaum, W. A. & Bengtson, V. C. (1994). Re-engaging the disengagement theory of aging: Or the history and assessment of theory development in gerontology. *The Gerontologist, 34,* 756–763.

Acker, J. (2008). Feminist theory's unfinished business: Comment on Andersen. *Gender and Society, 22,* 120–125.

Baars, J. Dannefer, D. Phillipson, C., & Walker, A. (Eds.). (2006). Aging, globalization and inequality. Amityville, NY: Baywood Publishing.

Bass, S. A. (2007). The emergence of the golden age of social gerontology? *The Gerontologist, 46,* 406–412.

Bass, S. A. (2009). Toward an integrative theory of social gerontology. In V. L., Bengtson, D. Gans, N. M. Putney, & M. Silverstein, M. (Eds.), *Handbook of theories of aging.* (2nd ed). New York: Springer Publishing.

Bengtson, V. L., Burgess, E. O., & Parrott, T. M. (1997). Theory, explanation and a third generation of theoretical development in social gerontology. *Journals of Gerontology, 52B,* S72–S88.

Bengtson, V. L., Gans, D., Putney, N. M., & Silverstein, M. (Eds.). (2009). *Handbook of theories of aging.* (2nd ed). New York: Springer Publishing.

Biggs, S. (1999). *The mature imagination.* Milton Keynes, UK: Oxford University Press.

Biggs, S. (2001). Toward a critical narrativity: Stories of aging in contemporary social policy. *Journal of Aging Studies, 15,* 303–316.

Biggs, S. & Powell, J. L. (2001). A Foucauldian analysis of old age and the power of social welfare. *Journal of Aging and Social Policy, 12,* 93–111.

Blaikie, A. (2006). Visions of later life: Golden cohort to generation z. In J. A. Vincent, C. R., Phillipson, & M. Downs, M. (Eds.). *The futures of old age*. London: Sage Publications.

Calasanti, T. M. (2004). Feminist gerontology and old men. *Journal of Gerontology: Social Sciences, 59*, S305–314.

Calasanti, T. M. & Slevin, K. (Eds.). (2006). *Age matters: Re-aligning feminist thinking*. New York: Routledge.

Cole, T. R., Achenbaum, W. A., Jacobi, P. L., & Kastenbaum, R. (1993). *Voices and visions of aging: Toward a critical gerontology*. New York: Springer.

Cottrell, L. (1942). The adjustment of the individual to his age and sex roles. *American Sociological Review, 7*, 617–620.

Cruikshank, M. (2009). *Learning to be old*. Lanham, MD: Rowman & Littlefield.

Cumming, E. & Henry, W. E. (1961). *Growing old*. New York: Basic Books.

Dannefer, D. & Miklowski, C. (2006). Developments in the life course. In J. A. Vincent, C. R., Phillipson, & M. Downs, M. (Eds.). *The futures of old age*. London: Sage Publications.

Diamond, T. (1992). *Making grey gold: Narratives of nursing home care*. Chicago: University of Chicago Press.

Dowd, J. J. (1980). *Stratification among the aged*. Monterey, CA: Brooks Cole.

Dykstra, P. A. & Mandemakers, J. J. (2007). *Parent-child consensus and parental well-being in mid and late life*. Paper presented at the annual meeting of the Gerontological Society of America, San Francisco.

Ekerdt, D. J. & DeViney, S. (1993). Evidence for a preretirement process among older male workers. *Journal of Gerontology, 48*(2), S35–S43.

Elder, G. H. Jr. (1994). Time, human agency and social change: Perspectives on the life course. *Social Psychology Quarterly, 57*, 4–15.

Elder, G. H. Jr., (1998). The life course and human development. In R. M. Lerner (Ed.). *Handbook of child psychology, Vol 1: Theoretical models of human development* (5th ed). New York: Wiley

Estes, C. L. (2001). From gender to the political economy of ageing. *European Journal of Social Quality, 2*, 28–46.

Estes, C. L. (2004). Social Security privatization and older women: A feminist political economy perspective. *Journal of Aging Studies, 18*, 9–26.

Estes, C. L. & Associates. (2001). *Social policy and aging: A critical perspective*. Thousand Oaks, CA: Sage.

Estes, C. L., Biggs, S. & Phillipson, C. (2003). *Social theory, social policy and ageing*. Milton Keynes, UK: Oxford University Press.

Ferraro, K. F. & Kelley-Moore, J. A. (2003). Cumulative disadvantage and health: Long-term consequences of obesity? *American Sociological Review, 68*, 707–729.

Ferraro, K. F., Shippee, T. P., and Schafer, M. H. (2009). Cumulative inequality theory for research on aging and the life course. In V. L. Bengtson, D. Gans, N. M. Putney, & M. Silverstein. (Eds.). *Handbook of theories of aging*. (2nd ed). New York: Springer Publishing.

George, L. K. (1995). The last half century of aging research—and thoughts for the future. *Journals of Gerontology 50B*, S1–3.

George, L. K. (1996). Missing links: The case for a social psychology of the life course. *The Gerontologist, 36*, 248–255.

George, L. K. (2007). Age structures, aging, and the life course. In J. M. Wilmoth & K. F. Ferraro (Eds.). *Gerontology: Perspectives and issues* (3rd ed.). New York: Springer.

Gilleard, C. & Higgs, P. (2000). *Culture of ageing*. London: Prentice Hall.

Gonyea, J. & Hooyman, N. (2005). Reducing poverty among older women: The importance of Social Security. *Families in Society, 86*, 338–346.

Gubrium, J. F. (1973). *The myth of the golden years*. Springfield, IL: Charles C. Thomas.

Gubrium, J. F. (1993). *Speaking of life: Horizons of meaning for nursing home residents*. New York: Aldine de Gruyter.

Gullette, M. M. (1997). *Declining to decline: Cultural combat and the politics of midlife*. Charlottesville, VA: University Press of Virginia.

Gullette, M. M. (1998). Midlife discourse in twentieth-century North America: An essay on the sexuality, ideology, and politics of midlife aging. In R. K. Shweder (Ed.). *Welcome to middle age! and other cultural fictions.* (pp. 3–44). Chicago: University of Chicago Press.

Gullette, M. M. (2004). *Aged by culture.* Chicago, University of Chicago Press.

Hagestad, G. & Neugarten, B. (1985). Age and the life course. In R. H. Binstock & E. Shanas (Eds.). *Handbook of aging and the social sciences* (2nd ed.). New York: Van Nostrand.

Harrington Meyer, M. Wolf, D. A., & Himes, C. L. (2005). Linking benefits to marital status: Race and Social Security in the U.S. *Feminist Economics,* 11, 145–162.

Havighurst, R. J. (1963). Successful aging. In R. Williams, C. Tibbits, & W. Donahue (Eds.). *Processes of aging* (Vol. 1). New York: Atherton Press.

Havighurst, R. J. (1968). Personality and patterns of aging. *The Gerontologist,* 38, 20–23.

Heaphy, B. (2007). Sexualities, gender and ageing: Resources and social change. *Current Sociology,* 55, 193–210.

Holstein, M. & Minkler, M. (2003). Self, society, and the "new gerontology." *The Gerontologist,* 43, 787–796.

Hooyman, N. R., Brown, C., Raye, R., & Richardson, V. (2002). Feminist gerontology and the life course: Policy, research and teaching issues. *Gerontology and Geriatrics Education,* 22, 3–26.

Johnson, M. L. (2009). Spirituality, finitiude and theories of the life span. In V. L. Bengtson, D. Gans, N. M. Putney, & M. Silverstein, (Eds.). *Handbook of theories of aging.* (2nd ed). New York: Springer Publishing.

Kail, B. L, Quadagno, J., & Keene, J. R. (2009). The political economy perspective of aging In V. L. Bengtson, D. Gans, N. M. Putney, M. Silverstein, (Eds.). *Handbook of theories of aging.* (2nd ed). New York: Springer Publishing.

King, N. (2006). The lengthening list of oppressions: Age relations and the feminist study of inequality. In T. Calasanti & K. Slevin (Eds.). *Age matters.* New York: Routledge.

Longino, C. F. & Powell, J. L. (2004). Embodiment and the study of aging. In V. Berdayes (Ed.). *The body in human inquiry: Interdisciplinary explorations of embodiment.* New York: Hampton Press.

Longino, C. F. & Powell, J. L. (2009). Toward a phenomenologists of aging. In V. L. Bengtson, M. Silverstein, N. M. Putney, & D. Gans (Eds.). *Handbook of theories of aging.* (2nd ed.) New York: Springer Publishing.

Lynott, R. J. & Lynott, P. P. (1996). Tracing the course of theoretical development in the sociology of aging. *The Gerontologist,* 36, 749–760.

Marshall, V. W. (1996). The state of theory in aging and the social sciences. In R. H. Binstock & L. K. George (Eds.). *Handbook of aging and the social sciences* (4th ed.). San Diego: Academic Press.

Martinson, M. & Minkler, M. (2006). Civic engagement and older adults: A critical perspective. *The Gerontologists,* 46, 318–324.

Minkler, M. (1996). Critical perspectives on aging: New challenges for gerontology. *Aging and Society,* 16, 467–487.

Minkler, M., & Estes, C. (Eds.). (1998). *Critical gerontology: Perspectives from political and moral economy.* New York: Baywood.

Moen, P. (2001). The gendered life course. In R. Binstock & L. K. George (Eds.). *Handbook of aging and the social sciences* (5th ed.). San Diego: Academic Press.

Moody, H. R. (1988). Toward a critical gerontology: The contribution of the humanities to theories of aging. In J. E. Birren & V. L. Bengtson (Eds.). *Emergent theories of aging.* New York: Springer.

Moody, H. R. (2002). *Aging: Concepts and controversies* (4th ed.). Thousand Oaks, CA: Sage.

Moody, H. R. (2005). From successful aging to conscious aging. In M. Wykle, P. Whitehouse, & D. Morris (Eds.). *Successful aging through the life span.* New York: Springer.

Neugarten, B., Havighurst, R. J., & Tobin, S. S. (1968). Personality and patterns of aging. In B. L. Neugarten (Ed.). *Middle age and aging.* Chicago: University of Chicago Press.

Olson, L. K. (2003). *The not so golden years: Caregiving, the frail elderly, and the long-term care establishment.* Lanham, MD: Rowman & Littlefield.

O'Rand, A. M. (2006). Stratification and the life course. Life course capital, life course risks and social inequality. In R. Binstock & L. K. George (Eds.). *Handbook of aging and the social sciences* (6th ed.). San Diego: Academic Press.

Phillipson, C. (1996). Interpretations of aging: Perspectives from humanistic gerontology. *Aging and Society, 16*, 359–369.

Powell, J. L. (2000). The importance of a "critical" sociology of old age. *Social Science Paper Publisher, 3*, 105.

Powell, J. L. (2001). Aging and social theory: A sociological review. *Social Science Paper Publisher, 4*, 1–12.

Powell, J. L. (2006). *Social theory and aging.* Lanham, MD: Rowman and Littlefield.

Powell, J. L. & Biggs, S. (2004). Aging, technologies of self and bio-medicine. A Foucauldian excursion. *International Journal of Sociology and Social Policy, 25*, 96–115.

Powell, J. L. & Longino, C. F. (2001). Toward the postmodernization of aging: The body and social theory. *Journal of Aging and Identity, 6*, 20–34.

Powell, J. L. & Longino, C. F. (2002). Modernism vs. postmodernism. Rethinking theoretical tensions in social gerontology. *Journal of Aging Studies, 7*, 115–25.

Powell, J. L. & Wahidin, A. (2007). Understanding aging bodies: A postmodern dialogue. In J. Powell & T. Owen (Eds.). *Reconstructing postmodernism.* New York: Nova Science.

Riley, M. W. (1971). Social gerontology and the age stratification of society. *The Gerontologist, 11*, 79–87.

Riley, M. W., Foner, A., & Riley, J. W. (1999). The aging and society paradigm. In V. L. Bengtson & K. W. Schaie (Eds.). *Handbook of theories of aging.* New York: Springer.

Riley, M. W., Johnson, J., & Foner, A. (1972). *Aging and society: A sociology of age stratification* (vol. 3). New York: Russell Sage Foundation.

Riley, M. W., Kahn, R. L., & Foner, A. (Eds.). (1994). *Age and structural lag: Society's failure to provide meaningful opportunities in work, family and leisure.* New York: John Wiley.

Riley, M. W. & Loscocco, K. A. (1994). The changing structure of work opportunities: Toward an age-integrated society. In R. P. Abeles, H. C. Gift, & M. G. Ory (Eds.). *Aging and quality of life.* New York: Springer.

Riley, M. W. & Riley, J. W. (1994). Age integration and the lives of older people. *The Gerontologist, 34*, 110–115.

Rosow, J. (1985). Status and role change through the life cycle. In R. H. Binstock & E. Shanas (Eds.). *Handbook of aging and the social sciences* (2nd ed.). New York: Van Nostrand.

Ryff, C. D. & Singer, B. (2009). Understanding healthy aging: Key components and their integration. In V. L. Bengtson, M. Silverstein, N. M. Putney, & D. Gans (Eds.). *Handbook of theories of aging.* (2nd ed.) New York: Springer Publishing.

Silverstein, M., Conroy, S. J., Wang, H., Giarusso, R., & Bengtson, V. L. (2002). Reciprocity in parent-child relations over the life course. *Journal of Gerontology: Social Sciences, 57B*, S3–S13.

Thorsen, K. (1998). The paradoxes of gerotranscendence: The theory of gerotranscendence in a cultural gerontological and post-modernist perspective. *Norwegian Journal of Epidemiology, 8*, 165–176.

Tornstam, L. (1989). Gero-transcendence: A metatheoretical reformulation of the disengagement theory. *Aging: Clinical and Experimental Research, 1*, 55–64.

Tornstam, L. (1994). Gerotranscendence—A theoretical and empirical exploration. In L. E. Thomas & S. A. Eisenhandler (Eds.). *Aging and the religious dimension.* Westport: Greenwood.

Tornstam, L. (1996a). Gero-transcendence—A theory about maturing into old age. *Journal of Aging and Identity 1*, 37–50.

Tornstam, L. (1996b). Caring for the elderly: Introducing the theory of gerotranscendnece as a supplementary frame of reference for the care of the elderly. *Scandinavian Journal of Careing Sciences, 10*, 144–150.

Tornstam, L. (2000). Transcendence in later life. *Generations, 23*, 1014.

Tornstam, L. (2005). *Gerotranscendence: A developmental theory of positive aging.* New York: Springer Publisher.

Vincent, J. A., Phillipson, C. R., and Downs, M. (2006). The futures of old age. London: Sage Publications.

Wadensten, B. (2005). Introducing older people to the theory of gerotranscendence. *Journal of Advanced Nursing, 42,* 381–388.

Walker, A. (2009). Aging and social policy: Theorizing the social. In V. L. Bengtson, D. Gans, N. M. Putney, & M. Silverstein, (Eds.). *Handbook of theories of aging.* (2nd ed). New York: Springer Publishing.

9

The Importance of Social Supports: Family, Friends, Neighbors, and Communities

This chapter focuses on informal social support systems, including

- Social networks, social engagement, and their importance for health and active aging
- Multigenerational families
- Different types of family relationships
  LGBT families
  Grandparents and great-grandparents and grandchildren
  Grandparents as primary caregivers to grandchildren
- Friends, neighbors, and acquaintances as social supports
- Social support interventions
- Intergenerational programming
- Pets as social support

As people age, their social roles and relationships change. Earlier chapters have noted that physiological, social, and psychological changes, as well as opportunities for social engagement in the larger environment, affect how older people interact with others. For example, after having raised their children and without daily contacts with coworkers, older people may lose a critical context for social integration. At the same time, their need for social support may increase because of changes in health, cognitive, and emotional status. Such incongruence between needs and environmental opportunities can negatively influence elders' well-being.

The Nature and Function of Informal Supports

A common myth is that many older adults are lonely and isolated from family and friends. Contrary to this misperception, even older people who appear isolated are generally able to turn to an informal network for advice, emotional reassurance, or concrete services. **Social networks** encompass interrelationships among individuals that affect the flow of resources and opportunities. Families, friends, neighbors, and acquaintances such as postal carriers and grocery clerks, can be powerful antidotes to some of the negative social consequences of the aging process. Elders can draw on these informal networks as a source of **social support** that may be informational, emotional, or instrumental (e.g., assistance with tasks of daily living). Older adults first turn to informal networks for support before seeking formal assistance. As suggested by the person–environment model, elders draw on their informal networks as a way to enhance their competence (Moren-Cross & Lin, 2006). Definitions and measures of social support vary widely. Most research on social supports differentiates social networks, social integration, and social capital; support that is assistance-related and nonassistance-related (e.g., feelings of worth, emotional closeness, and belonging); and the importance of *perceived* social support. In fact, perceptions of support may be more important than the actual support received (Antonucci, Birditt, & Akiyama, 2009; Lyyra & Heikkinen, 2006).

POTENTIAL OUTCOMES OF SOCIAL SUPPORTS

- Physical and mental well-being (increased morale and self-confidence, reduced depression)
- Feelings of personal control, autonomy, and competence
- Improved cognitive abilities
- Active aging and resilience
- Diminished negative effects of stressful life events (bereavement, widowhood)
- Reduced disability and mortality risk

Social integration, which encompasses both social networks and support, refers to the degree to which an individual is involved with others in the larger social structure and community. This concept captures the degree of emotional closeness, the availability of support when needed, and the perception of oneself as a person actively engaged in social exchanges (such as volunteering). The social structure shapes the individual, but the individual may also affect the social structure (Antonucci et al., 2009; Antonucci, Sherman, & Akimaya, 1996; Berkman, 2000; Moren-Cross & Lin, 2006). Both of these concepts, social support and social integration, take account of (1) the specific types of assistance exchanged within networks; (2) the frequency of contact; (3) how a person assesses the adequacy of supportive exchanges; and (4) anticipated support or the belief that help is available if needed. Social integration, however, tends to emphasize the giving as well as the receiving of support, and thus takes account of cross-generational interdependence.

Consistent with theories of social exchange described in Chapter 8, most older adults try to maintain **reciprocal exchanges**—being able to help others who help them. Even frail elders who require personal care from their families may still contribute through financial assistance or child care. The meaningful role of helping others also benefits the helper, and is associated with positive affect, self-esteem, a sense of purpose, life satisfaction, and physical and mental health (Keyes, 2002; Krause & Shaw, 2000; Morrow-Howell et al., 2001; Kawachi & Berkman, 2001; Temkin-Greener et al., 2006; Uchino, 2004). The **social convoy model** captures how close social relationships that surround an individual can provide a protective, secure base, but also how personal and situational characteristics of age, gender, race, sexual orientation, and social class influence the type and extent of support needed (Anotonucci, et al., 2009; Ajrouch, Blandon, & Antonucci, 2005). As noted in Chapter 6, supportive networks generally foster active aging and characterize resilient elders.

> ### SOCIAL SUPPORT AMONG FRIENDS
>
> After 40 years of marriage, Nan was devastated by her husband's decision to divorce her. Her children lived across the country, and she had no close relatives in the town where they had raised their children. Nan turned to two women whom she had confided in for more than 30 years of child rearing and the ups and downs of their marriages. These other women, both divorced, provided emotional support as Nan grieved the loss of her marriage and a life of economic security. They helped her find a good divorce attorney and financial advisor, who in turn helped her obtain an adequate settlement from her husband. Most importantly, the friends were available 24/7 to help her cope with this unexpected phase in her life, giving her more strength than her children or other relatives could have.

The Impact of Informal Networks and Social Supports on Well-Being

As noted above, informal reciprocal relationships are crucial for older adults' physical and mental well-being, cognitive functioning, feelings of personal control, sense of meaning, morale, and even for preventing disability and delaying mortality (Berkman & Harootyan, 2002; Krause, 2006; Lubben & Gironda, 2003a, 2003b; Lubben et al., 2006; Lyyra & Heikkinen, 2006; Uchino, 2004). In fact, one study found that older adults with limited social support were 3.6 times more likely to die within the next five years than those with extensive support (Blazer, 2006). Provision of support, like its receipt, contributes to elders' perceptions of support availability, which is generally linked with physical and mental health. Face-to-face interactions and the size of informal networks are also associated with improved cognitive functioning. Social support can mediate the effects of adversity and other stressful life circumstances, such as retirement, widowhood, illness, or relocation. It is unclear, however, whether such supports act as buffers against the negative impact of life events on health, or whether they have a more direct effect, independent of the presence or absence of major life events. The extent of perceived control or self-efficacy may also mediate the relationships between social support and health (Antonucci et al., 2009; Cohen, 2004; Cohen, Gottlieb, & Underwood, 2001; DuPertuis, Aldwin, & Bosse, 2001; Eng et al., 2002; Fiori, Antonucci, & Akiyama, 2008; Holtzman et al., 2004; Liang, Krause, & Bennett, 2001; Moren-Cross & Lin, 2006; Seeman et al., 2002).

Alternatively, loss of social support through divorce, widowhood, or the death of loved ones may contribute to health problems. For example, older adults who live alone and are not regularly tied into informal networks are more likely to use formal services and to be placed in residential care settings. Their self-reported well-being tends to be lower. Similarly, social isolation may increase the risk of disability, poor recovery from illness, and earlier death. Although several longitudinal studies identified an association between social support structures and reduced mortality risk, findings are mixed on whether such support actually diminishes the risk of mortality (Findlay, 2003; Lyyra & Heikkinen, 2006; Moren-Cross & Lin, 2006). The Lubben Social Network Scale, a widely applied to assess social integration and to screen for social isolation among community-dwelling elders, has been used with culturally diverse elders in many countries. Low scores on this scale—indicating social isolation—are correlated with a wide range of health problems (Lubben et al., 2006). Living alone, however, does not necessarily mean social isolation, especially for women who tend to maintain active social ties (Antonucci et al., 2009; Jeon et al., 2007; Michael, Berkman, Colditz, & Kawaski, 2001).

The extent to which networks vary with age is not clear-cut. While some studies identify a decline in friendship networks, others report that changes occur primarily in network composition (e.g., less contact with couples, more with informal helpers) or in the role played by this network (e.g., increased need for instrumental support) (Antonucci et al., 2009; Jeon et al., 2007; Kalmijn, 2003). In fact, elders active in voluntary associations or retirement communities may actually expand and diversify their networks. A process of social selection may occur whereby healthy people are more likely to have supportive social relationships precisely because they are healthy. Conversely, poor health may hinder them from initiating or sustaining social relationships (Wethington et al., 2000). In some cases, negative interactions with one's informal networks can have adverse effects on health. In addition to conflictual relationships, other types of negative interactions may be due to incongruence between an older person's needs and competence level, such as disappointment that one's children are not visiting often enough or that relatives are giving unsolicited advice or criticism. The concept of ambivalence conveys that close relationships can have both positive and negative features (Antonucci et al., 2009; Krause, 2004, 2006).

The family—the basic unit of social relationships—is the first topic considered here. We examine the rapid growth of the multigenerational family and how relationships with spouses, partners, adult children, parents, grandparents, and siblings shift with age.

Changing Family Structure

Contrary to commonly held perceptions of elders as separate from families, the lives of young and old, even at a geographic distance, are intertwined through cross-generational support. The family is the primary source of such support for older adults; nearly 94 percent have living family members. These include partners, adult children, grandchildren or great-grandchildren, and siblings. Approximately 80 percent of adults over age 65 have children, but this percentage is declining because of reduced fertility rates (Cruikshank, 2009; Uhlenberg, 2004).

About 66 percent of older adults live in a family setting—with a partner, child, or sibling—although not necessarily in a multigenerational household (Figure 9.1). Given the higher rates of widowhood among women than men, older men

Long-term married couples generally express satisfaction with their marriages.

are more likely to live in a family setting, typically with a spouse or partner than are women (81 and 61 percent, respectively). Only about 6 percent of older men and 17 percent of older women live with children, siblings, or other relatives instead of a spouse or partner (Federal Interagency Forum, 2008). However, the majority have at least one child living close by who sees them regularly but older adults typically do not want to live with their adult children (Davidson, 2006). Nevertheless, declining health, loss of a former caregiver or partner, desire for companionship, and lower income often precipitate the move to a shared residence. Widowed mothers are more likely to live with a child than are divorced, single, or married mothers (Wilmouth, 2000). In a growing number of households, adult children are moving back into the family home, typically for financial reasons or following a divorce or unemployment; such arrangements may strain family relations (Calasanti & Kiecolot, 2007).

Factors associated with geographic proximity to the nearest child are:

- parents' health: as health declines, parents tend to move closer to an adult child
- parents' age: parents over age 80 live closer to adult children
- parents' socioeconomic status: higher social class tends to be associated with greater geographic distance

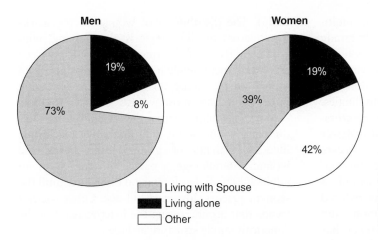

Men

73%

19%

8%

Women

39%

19%

42%

- Living with Spouse
- Living alone
- Other

FIGURE 9.1 **Living Arrangements of Persons 65+, 2008**

SOURCE: Administration on Aging (AOA). (2008). *A Profile of Older Americans.* Washington, DC.

- marital status: widowed mothers live closest to daughters; remarried parents tend to live at a greater geographic distance than parents who remain married to each other

Geographic distance in itself does not impair the quality of parent-adult child relationships. In fact, as described in Chapter 10, adult children often provide care to parents at a considerable distance.

The Growth of the Multigenerational Family

The term **multigenerational family** encompasses the growing reciprocity across three or more generations, both in the United States and

Family gatherings help maintain multigenerational ties.

globally. Since 1990, the number of multigenerational households has grown by approximately 60 percent. Nearly four million American households consist of three or more generations living together, with about 78,000 households nationwide consisting of four generations (Generations United, 2009). For individuals born in 1900, the chances of both parents dying before the child reached age 18 were 18 percent; by age 30, only 21 percent had any grandparents alive. In contrast, 68 percent of individuals born in 2000 will have four grandparents alive when they reach age 18; and 76 percent will have at least one grandparent at age 30—almost four times that of the cohort born in 1900. In fact, 20-year-olds today are more likely to have a grandmother living (92 percent) than 20-year-olds in 1900 were to have their mother alive (83 percent) (Kleyman, 2006). Another indicator of changing multigenerational dynamics is that increasing numbers of people over age 65 have a child who is also over 65, who may then be both a child and a grandparent at the same time. In sum, persons at all stages of life are more likely to have kinship networks involving older people than in the past. This has resulted in parents and children now sharing five decades of life; siblings perhaps sharing eight decades; and the grandparent–grandchild bond lasting three or more decades. Multigenerational families cut across race, ethnicity, and social class.

Increased life expectancy may create multi-generational kinship networks to provide family continuity, along with instrumental or emotional support when needed. Yet increased longevity may also mean extended years of family dysfunction and caring for relatives with chronic disabilities. Although families are experiencing more cross-generational relationships, paradoxically, fewer people within each generation are available to care for older family members. Demographic and societal trends that underlie this paradox include a decrease in overall fertility rates that have reduced family size, an increase in family dissolutions, and more women employed. As life expectancy has grown and the birthrate has declined, delaying the age of childbearing has become common, and resulted in a shift in the age structure for most families from a "pyramid" to a "beanpole." This means that American families are smaller today (averaging 2.6 people in the nuclear family) than ever before, with the age of first births now 25 years, and first births to women age 35 years and older increasing nearly eight times since 1970 (United Press International, 2009). Nevertheless, cross-generational obligations and exchanges have remained relatively stable across time (Bengtson, 2001; Bengtson & Putney, 2006; Harper, 2006).

The number of women entering the paid workforce has increased dramatically in the past 50 years; over 60 percent compared to 33 percent of women in the 1950s (Bureau of Labor Statistics,

2006). The distribution of women in the workforce across the life-course is also striking, with women in their childbearing years most likely to be employed, increasingly for economic reasons. Even though many family relationships are becoming more egalitarian, most women still face multiple care responsibilities across the life-course: for children and young adults with disabilities or chronic illnesses, parents or grandparents during the woman's middle age, a partner in old age, or an adult child with developmental disabilities until the woman reaches advanced old age. Other societal trends that are increasing the heterogeneity of the American family structure include:

- a growth in divorce and **blended families** (e.g., families reconstituted by divorce and remarriage)
- more people living alone
- more single-parent households
- never-married individuals living together as **nontraditional families** (e.g., LGBT families, cohabitation of heterosexual couples, and single parents choosing to raise children on their own)
- more egalitarian relationships in younger generations
- more emphasis on affective bonds and choice, less on normative prescriptive relationships
- more grandparents and great grandparents with primary responsibilities for grandchildren.

For the first time, only 23.5 percent of U.S. households are composed of nuclear families. Similarly, the number of children living in single-parent households grew from about 12 percent in 1950 to about 32 percent today. As a result, the pattern of first marriage and nuclear family is no longer the societal norm, but one of numerous family structures. In fact, the blended family may soon outnumber other forms (Doodson & Morley, 2006).

Defining Multigenerational Families

Consistent with social constructionism theory described in Chapter 8, definitions of families are

Multigenerational families often provide reciprocal support.

socially constructed and vary by culture and socioeconomic class. In this text, *family* is broadly defined by interactional and emotional quality, not necessarily by members living together, by birth, or marriage. Kinship is a matter of social definition, particularly within families of color, as reflected in the role of fictive kin within populations of color: grandparents as primary caregivers to grandchildren, "play relatives," godparents, and friends. Among gays and lesbians, chosen or "friendship" families are common. Gerontological practitioners and policy makers must be sensitive to the ways in which elders and their networks define family in order to work effectively and respectfully with family members.

A life-course and multigenerational perspective on families captures the interdependence of lives in three ways: the interdependence of cohorts in societies, that of generations in families, and individual life paths in relation to these interdependencies. It also takes account of individual, family, and historical time (Bliezsner, 2006; Hagestad, 2003). Multigenerational families are characterized by cross-generational reciprocity and interdependence rather than dependence or independence. None of us, no matter what our age, is ever totally independent. Generations are interdependent across the life-course; each contributes to the other, through families and nontraditional informal supports (e.g., friends, neighbors, "community gatekeepers"). In fact, the global economic crisis may be reducing social mobility between generations and enhancing obligations felt toward one another as families increasingly help each other out (Bengtson & Putney, 2006). Contrary to stereotypes of selfish older adults, most exchanges of time and financial assistance are from the older to younger generations, unless older adults require caregiving help (Silverstein et al., 2002). Overall, older adults perform vital unacknowledged functions within families as role models for socialization, economic transfers, bearers of family history, and daily assistance (Bengtson & Putney, 2006; Blieszner, 2006; Harper, 2006).

Regardless of the particular family structure, family relationships inevitably involve a social contract characterized by both solidarity and conflict. Cohesion appears to be based on sharing across generations, including the extent of common activities, the degree of positive sentiment, consensus on lifestyle choices, and the exchange of assistance. Less is known about tensions, disagreements, or conflicts across generations over the life-course (Bengtson & Putney, 2006; Bleiszner, 2006; Giarrusso et al., 2006; Hagestad, 2003; Hummert & Morgan, 2001). Gerontological practitioners increasingly assess and work with more than one generation within families, and need to locate services to support families. As noted in the box below, they can also encourage families to value their elder relatives' histories and the sharing of stories across the generations as a way to contribute to solidarity.

FAMILY HISTORIES: PRESERVING THE LEGACY OF AN OLDER RELATIVE

Along with the growth of multiple generations within families, younger family members are encouraging their older relatives to write their family history or record it on DVD or CD-ROM. Life stories are typically not just about one older person, but that individual in the context of the whole family history. In fact, websites that assist with writing personal histories advertise journalistic or service professionals for this age-old task. While families have always passed stories across generations, baby boomers are "professionalizing" storytelling, sometimes paying up to $30,000 for a written record of their ancestry. Multimedia legacies can include mementos, photos, and music and provide archived material from the relevant historical period. Such storytelling not only leaves a legacy for younger generations, but the process of life review can have psychological and physical health benefits for older adults. Perhaps most important to families who are often separated by geographic and psychological distance, future generations will continue to benefit from the full, rich lives of their predecessors.

SOURCE: Based on S. S. Stitch (2002). Family lore: Stories to keep, *Time*, November 11, A3.

Cultural Variations in Multigenerational Families

Due to the significant aging of the global population, as described in Chapter 2, other countries are also experiencing an increase in multigenerational families. In contrast to the U.S., three- and four-generation families are more likely to live together in countries such as Japan, Korea, India, and Mexico. Within the U.S., multigenerational families living together are more common among populations of color than among Caucasians; they have been a source of strength historically. For example, grandparents and "fictive kin" of friends or other relatives among African American households have traditionally played a central role in caring for children. Even when controlling for need, families of color are more likely to live in multigenerational contexts, or to depend on non-kin (e.g., friends and neighbors) who provide both social and instrumental support, especially for unmarried children and parents. Indeed, the world is watching a maternal grandmother play a vital support function in President Obama's family (Dilworth-Anderson, Williams, & Gibson, 2002).

This greater incidence of cross-generational households in communities of color may underlie the higher levels of assistance to elders and the generally positive parent-adult child relationships reported by African American, Latino, and Asian American families compared with their Caucasian counterparts (Dilworth-Anderson et al., 2002). On the other hand, the existence of extended family arrangements and fictive kin may grow out of economic necessity, especially because older African American women are less likely to be married than any other group among the older population. Additionally, these arrangements may carry financial and emotional costs and divert elders from accessing formal supports. These patterns may shift over time with increased economic and geographic mobility and levels of acculturation by younger generations.

By contrast, American values and economic pressures often weaken multigenerational support networks within immigrant and refugee populations. Among Asian American immigrants, grandparents frequently provide child care to enable both parents to work outside the home, but younger generations' sense of filial responsibility toward older relatives may be eroded by their upward mobility, as described in Chapter 2. Latino immigrant families typically have strong cross-generational cohesion, but smaller family size, increased employment of women, and economic pressures may compromise such supportive interactions (Beyene, Becker, & Mayen, 2002). As an example, Cuban American elders place a high value on extended family relationships, but those now residing in Florida tend to live alone, in part because of declining family size related to their immigration history. Nevertheless, they often compensate for the lack of large, geographically close family supports by engaging in social networks through religious organizations or senior centers (Martinez, 2003).

Despite pressures for assimilation and rapid economic and social changes, cultural variations remain salient in how multigenerational relations are defined and experienced. Even when behaviors such as dress, appearance, and material goods differ markedly across generations, some cultural values may nevertheless be shared. Cultural notions of "family" are strong, but are reinterpreted in rapidly changing economic and social conditions. As a result, living arrangements for elders often represent a balance of cultural convictions, functional ability, and actual choices. What is most important to elders, however, is not the structural makeup of family exchanges, but the subjective or emotional quality of the relationships (Martinez, 2003). Regardless of the particular family structure or nature of relationships, practitioners must be sensitive to cultural variants.

THE STRENGTH OF MULTIGENERATIONAL TIES

During the summer of 2000, the governments of North and South Korea agreed to an unprecedented reunion of families that had been torn apart during the Korean War. Siblings who had not seen each other since their teens, and parents now in their 80s and 90s were reunited with their children who were themselves in their 60s. The fortunate 100 families were selected by lottery from the citizens of North Korea and flown to South Korea for a brief visit. This bittersweet reunion lasted only one week, after which those from North Korea were required to return home. Nevertheless, the stories shared by these families provided a dramatic illustration of the endurance of family bonds across generations and over time.

Older Partners*

The marital or partnered relationship plays a crucial support function in most older people's lives, especially men's. Of all family members, partners are most likely to serve as confidants, offer support, facilitate social interaction, foster emotional well-being, and guard against loneliness (Davidson, 2006; Russell & Taylor, 2009; Walker & Luszcz, 2009). Nearly 55 percent of the population age 65 and older is married and lives with a spouse in an independent household. Marriage rates are highest among Asian and Pacific Islanders, then whites, followed by Latinos and African Americans (American Community Survey, 2007; Calasanti & Kiecolt, 2007). Less is known about the percentage living with a gay or lesbian partner, as discussed below. Significant differences exist, however, in living arrangements by gender and age. Because of women's longer life expectancy, higher rates of widowhood, and fewer options for

remarriage, only 42 percent of women age 65 and older are married and living with a spouse, as compared to 73 percent of men. These percentages decline dramatically with age for women, with only 15 percent of women age 85 and older married versus 60 percent of men, as shown in Figure 9.2. (page 348). Accordingly, almost 30 percent of community-dwelling elders live alone, with women representing 80 percent of those individuals. (AOA, 2008; Connidis, 2006; DHHS, 2006; Federal Interagency Forum, 2008).

Marital status affects socioeconomic well-being, living arrangements, and the nature of care that is readily available in case of illness. Older men living alone, particularly Latino males, are found to have higher levels of clinical depression, loneliness, and social isolation, and are more likely to use formal social services compared to those living with a partner. Married people, especially men, are found to be healthier and to live longer than their unmarried counterparts. They seem to benefit from social support, health monitoring, economic resources, and the stress reduction of the marital relationship. In fact, marital status and its supportive functions appear to be related to physical and psychological health, life satisfaction, happiness, and well-being, especially for men—although we can all think of exceptions to these associations (Bookwala, 2005; Bookwala & Franks, 2005; Davidson, 2006; Lyyra & Heikkinen, 2006; Russell & Taylor, 2009). While generally not having the legal option of marriage, LGBT elders who are in committed relationships tend to be less lonely and enjoy better physical and mental health than their counterparts who live alone (Cruikshank, 2009; Heaphy, 2007).

Marital Satisfaction

Marital quality tends to vary by gender, life course, and, to some extent, race. Men consistently experience increased levels of marital satisfaction over time than do women (Calasanti & Slevin, 2001; Umberson, Williams, Powers, Chen & Campbell, 2005; Umberson et al., 2006).

*Research on gay, lesbian, bisexual, and transgender partners is relatively limited. Although we use the term *partner* throughout the text where relevant, in some instances data are only available on married heterosexual couples.

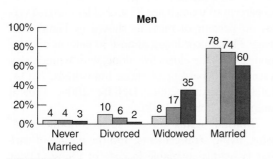
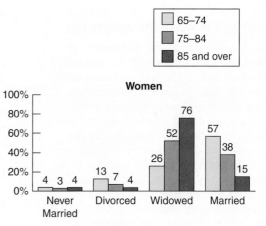

FIGURE 9.2 **Marital Status of Persons 65+**
SOURCE: Federal Interagency Forum on Aging, 2008.

Although older African Americans typically report lower marital satisfaction than do whites, and older African American women less satisfaction than white women, marriage still promotes well-being for African American women (Connidis & Kiecolt, 2007). Marital satisfaction is high among those recently married, lower among those in the child-rearing period—especially in middle age—and higher in the later stages, when children typically leave home and household division of labor may equalize with age (Frisco & Williams, 2003; Ward & Spitze, 2004). Contrary to stereotypes, most women are not upset when their children leave home, but rather view the **empty nest** as an opportunity for new activities. However, children today are leaving the nest later and are more likely to return home, often for financial reasons (known as "boomerang children," who leave and come back multiple times), which can negatively affect marital satisfaction. Retirement can be a difficult transition, especially if the couple was already dissatisfied before retirement. Some retired partners experience changes in the emotional quality of their relationship, along with conflicts over too much time together and the loss of personal space. On the other hand, increased time together in shared activities and with friends during retirement can positively impact marital satisfaction (Blieszner, 2006).

As partners modify roles through retirement, post-parenthood, illness, or disability, they face the strain of relinquishing previous roles and adapting to new ones. Older partners' ability to negotiate such role transitions depends, in large part, on their prior flexibility and satisfaction in their marital relationship. Marital satisfaction may increase in middle age to early old age, with couples becoming more similar in their attitudes, beliefs, roles, and behaviors (Davey & Szinovacz, 2004). Sex-role expectations and behaviors are often relaxed in old age, with the marital relationship becoming more central to men's lives as they age. In fact, marital quality may be more important for older men than age, health, life expectancy, education, or retirement in predicting life satisfaction and well-being (Davidson, 2006; George, 2006). Happy marriages in old age are characterized by adequate communication, gender equality, and joint decision making through a gradual relaxation of boundaries and a decreasing division of labor based on traditional male/female roles. Nevertheless, women still carry primary responsibility for domestic tasks and elder care (Calasanti & Kiecolt, 2007; Kaufman & Taniguchi, 2006). Failure to negotiate role expectations, such as the division of household tasks after retirement, can result in disagreements and divergent paths. In a study of gender ideology among individuals age 51 to 92, men who held egalitarian attitudes reported significantly higher levels of marital happiness than did those with more traditional attitudes. Overall, feeling equitably treated in a marriage tends to reduce marital stress (Hagedoorn, Van Yperen, Coyne et al., 2006; Kaufman & Taniguchi, 2006). Accordingly, with more opportunities for companionship, older partners may discover common interests and a greater sense of interdependence. As a consequence, expressive aspects of the marriage—affection and companionship—may emerge more fully across time.

When marital strain occurs, it is heightened by the fact that long-lived relationships are a contemporary phenonenon with few role models for how to negotiate 40 to 50 years of marriage. At the beginning of the twentieth century, the average length of marriage at the time of a spouse's death was about 28 years, peaking at over 45 years late in that century. Never before in history have the lives of so many couples remained interwoven long enough to encounter the variety of life-changing events that later stages of marriage now bring. Marital strain tends to affect older adults' health status and self-ratings of health negatively (Umberson et al., 2005; Wallace & Luszcz, 2009). One reason may be that marital conflict may precipitate physiological changes, which can impair immune response and increase cardiovascular reactivity (Robles & Kiecolt-Glaser, 2003; Umberson & Williams, 2005). One study found that over 20 percent of couples experience moderate or strong emotional and social loneliness in their marriage. Such marriages were characterized by a spouse with health problems, limited emotional support from the spouse, infrequent conversations or being in disagreement, or evaluating their current sex life as relatively unpleasant or nonexistent. Emotional loneliness was stronger among women in second marriages, whereas marked social loneliness was acute for older men with

wives who had a disability (Gierveld, van Grownou, Hoogendoom, & Smit, 2009).

Divorce in Old Age

The pattern of long-term marriages is declining, however. Although the percentage divorced is lower for those over age 65 than for all age groups under 65, more elders in future cohorts will be divorced and single. Just one in five marriages of late-life couples will survive 50 years, with four of five ending in divorce or widowhood. Additionally, the estimated 11 percent of adults in the current cohort age 65 and older who are divorced or separated is almost double that of 1980, and is expected to grow to 13 percent by 2021. This increased dissolution rate results in part from baby boomers' permissive attitudes about divorce and priority on personal self-fulfillment. Accordingly, this cohort experienced a decline in first-marriage rates and an increase in never-marrying rates, later age of first marriage, divorce, and cohabitation Increased emphasis on individualism combined with the realization that an adult may live another 25 to 30 years after retirement appears incompatible with lifelong marriage. Boomers who enter old age as single after experiencing multiple marital transitions may find their well-being in old age is affected. These trends also demonstrate the growing societal acceptance of separation as an option among all age and racial groups (AOA, 2008; Wu & Schimmele, 2007; Zhang & Hayward, 2006).

Late-life divorce tends to be the dissolution of long-term marriages (over 10 years). Such long duration contributes to postponement of divorce, coupled with fears and uncertainties about postmarital life. Such concerns include facing old age alone, the threat of economic hardship, inability to establish new partnerships, and psychological distress. The desire for a happier life, however, tends to outweigh such concerns. The primary reasons for divorce among adults age 65 and over are "falling out of love," "growing apart," boredom with stale relationships, or personal change—not interpersonal conflict per se. Contrary to the commonly held image of men seeking divorce because of younger women, women are more likely to initiate late-life divorce than men, in some instances to escape an abusive relationship (Bair, 2007; Clift, 2005; Montenegro, 2004; Wu & Schimmele, 2007).

Older divorcees are more likely to experience psychological distress, loneliness, depression, financial difficulties, and social isolation than are younger divorced women (Montenegro, 2004; Wu & Schimmele, 2007). Being divorced in old age typically means economic hardships and diminished interactions with adult children for women, although divorced mothers receive more advice, financial help, emotional support, and service assistance from their adult children than do divorced fathers. Divorced men tend to lose the "kin-keeping" and intimacy functions performed by their wives, relocate away from neighbors and friends, and have less contact with and support from their children and grandchildren than do divorced mothers. As a result, they have the greatest need for formal supports in old age. The increase in the divorce rate affects all ages and generations, both directly and indirectly. Nevertheless, most older divorced persons do not express regret about their decision and generally experience a sense of relief (Bair, 2007; Calasanti & Kiecolt, 2007; Daatland, 2007; Davidson, 2006; Kreider, 2005; Lin, 2008).

Remarriage and Other Late-Life Romantic Relationships

For both men and women, increasing age decreases the likelihood of remarriage following divorce, making rates of remarriage in old age relatively low (Calasanti & Kiecolt, 2007; Kreider, 2005). The smaller pool of potential partners partially explains gender differences in remarriage. Women have fewer options to remarry, because they generally outlive their male peers, and men tend to marry women younger than themselves. As a result, the likelihood that widowed men—who are more likely to experience depressive symptoms in widowhood than women—will remarry is seven times greater than for widowed

women (Calasanti & Kiecolot, 2007; Moorman, Booth & Fingerman, 2006). Moreover, divorced people are more likely to remarry than are the widowed. Socioeconomic status affects the chances of remarriage among divorced women but not divorced men. Women who remain divorced as they age are more likely to experience financial difficulties. On the other hand, the desire to remarry tends to be lower among divorced than among widowed women. Such reluctance is probably related to past negative experiences with marriage (Wu & Schmille, 2007).

A desire for companionship and having sufficient economic resources are central considerations in remarriage, while declining health, financial problems, a desire to protect one's inheritance, concerns about providing care for someone else, and disinclination to relocate are common reasons not to remarry. Factors that appear to be related to successful late-life remarriages are long prior friendship, family and friends' approval, adequate pooled financial resources, and personal adaptability to life changes. Among the approximately 75 percent of men and 60 percent of women across all ages who remarry, more than 40 percent are estimated to divorce again, creating complex stepfamily relationships in old age (Calasanti & Kiecolt, 2007; Sherman & Boss, 2007).

An increasing number of older couples choose to live together in intimate heterosexual relationships but not to marry, generally for economic and inheritance reasons. More than 1 million older adults, comprising 3.7 percent of unmarried men and 0.9 percent of unmarried women, are estimated to cohabitate, reflecting greater flexibility in lifestyle choices than in the past. About 90 percent of these individuals were previously married. Some research has identified that older cohabiters are less likely to be lonely than single elders, and tend to view their relationship as an alternative to marriage. The stability and relationship quality of these arrangements are as high as for younger adults for whom cohabitation is often a prelude to marriage. Other studies point to greater disadvantages in such arrangements compared to married couples, such as fewer economic resources, poorer physical health, higher levels of depression, and weakened relationships with adult children as well as legal barriers in states that do not have domestic partner benefits (Blieszner, 2006; Brown, Bulanda, & Lee, 2005; Brown, Lee, and Bulanda, 2006; Calasanti and Kiecolt, 2007; Connidis, 2006; Daatland, 2007; King & Scott, 2005; De Jong Gierveld, & Peeters, 2003). These mixed findings point to the need for more research on the benefits and costs of cohabitation in old age.

Another trend, especially in Western European countries, is identified as "living apart together," or LAT relationships. Older couples maintain separate homes but visit each other, including overnights; they socialize together and carry out daily routines. This allows couples to enjoy intimacy while maintaining personal autonomy and protecting their children's inheritance. Often, such arrangements result from women's desires to remain independent financially and domestically, and not be burdened with care responsibilities (Calasanti & Kiecolt, 2007; Davidson, 2006; Davidson & Fennell, 2004; Ghazanfareeon Karlsson & Borell, 2005).

Lesbian, Gay, Bisexual, and Transgender (LGBT) Partners

Although gerontological family research has traditionally focused on spouses in heterosexual couples, the concept of families in old age needs to be broadened to include LGBT individuals. More than 25 percent of same-sex partners include a partner age 55 or older, and more than 10 percent a partner over age 65; however, the proportion may be higher because these relationships may have been hidden over the years or because of the taboo of identifying as LGBT in an interview or survey (Bennett & Gates, 2004; Lambert, 2005). LGBT elders are referred to as the "twice hidden" and the "most invisible of an already invisible minority" (Blando, 2001). Research on LGBT aging is relatively new; no longitudinal studies of LGBT adults are available; and studies of aging transgender and bisexual persons are rare (Barker, 2004; Cruikshank, 2009; Smith, 2002). In addition, little attention has been given to the intersections of race, ethnicity, culture, age, and social class with sexual orientation that influence the life course and produce distinctive and diverse experiences (Connidis, 2006; Heaphy, 2007). Some studies suggest that the aging experience of gay men and lesbians is qualitatively different as a result of their sexual orientation and identity, in part because of a double stigma from the interaction of age and sexual orientation. Transgender elders who are transitioning to the other sex in late life face distinctive challenges, especially since few states have laws that forbid gender-based discrimination (Butler, 2006; Cook-Daniels, 2007; Cruikshank, 2009).

DATING IN OLD AGE

Divorce, widowhood, and increased life expectancy of adults who chose to remain single earlier in life have created growing numbers of single older adults engaged in a "dating game"—although the incidence of dating is lower than in younger age-groups (Calasanti & Kiecolt, 2007). As is true among younger couples, they are motivated by the desire for companionship and intimacy. With being single in later life becoming the norm, the stigma of looking for a new partner is diminishing, although women still face more barriers than men. In fact, baby boomers, accustomed to dating services, personal ads, and Club Med singles vacations, are redefining dating and turning to creative ways of finding a partner. Already accustomed to the Internet for a range of services, they are generally comfortable with Internet dating services tailored to specific interests (adventure travel, hiking, science and nature, religious affiliation, environmental issues, vegetarianism, to name a few). Aware of the higher rate of divorce among remarried partners, older singles are often more interested in companionship—someone to do things with—than in marriage, especially when their children may be critical of potential partners or they fear needing to care for an older spouse.

SOURCE: AARP, 2003.

Although the majority of gays and lesbians are part of a live-in couple at any one time, as older adults they are more likely to live alone (66 percent), less likely to be living with life partners, and less likely to have children than their heterosexual counterparts (Hecht, 2004; Kurdek, 2005). However, their higher rates of living alone do not necessarily translate to being lonely and isolated. Instead, LGBT elders, especially lesbians, tend to have well-developed mutually helpful social networks of choice—partners and friends, members of their family of origin, and the larger community (Cruikshank, 2009; Healy, 2002; Heaphy, 2007; Hostetler, 2004; Orel, 2004).

Older LGBT individuals share concerns similar to those of other older adults—health, income, caregiving, living arrangements—but what is unique is that they have lived the majority of their lives through historical periods actively hostile and oppressive toward homosexuality. Some LGBT elders, especially those in their 70s and 80s, remain concerned with "passing" or "being invisible" in a heterosexual society, because being "out" was far riskier for them than for current cohorts. "Coming out" to family may be more difficult for people of color and for working-class men (Connidis, 2001; Cruikshank, 2009). In one study, African American older gay men reported experiencing higher levels of ageism than older white gay men and higher levels of perceived racism than younger black gay men. Despite evidence that perceived stigmatization has been associated with negative mental health outcomes, older black gay men do not necessarily experience worse mental health than older white gay men or younger African American gay men (David & Knight, 2008).

From a life-course perspective, the choice of some LGBT elders to remain silent about their sexual orientation is understandable. As noted in Chapter 7, the current cohort of older LGBT adults did not benefit from the 1969 clash between the New York City police and gay and transgender persons (known as the "Stonewall riots"), which was a watershed for gay pride.

They also lived through the McCarthy era when homosexuality and subversion were linked. Coming out was viewed as failing to successfully manage identity disclosure, and typically resulted in loss of social support (Rosenfeld, 2003). Homosexuality was often a reason to be institutionalized. For example, until 1973, homosexuality was classified as a mental illness by the American Psychiatric Association, and it was not removed from the *Diagnostic and Statistical Manual of Mental Disorders* (DSM) until 1986.

Accordingly, the experience of LGBT elders who have come out in middle age or late adulthood is likely to be different from those who identified as LGBT in their youth (Butler, 2006). Unlike their younger counterparts, older LGBT persons have generally not benefited from antidiscrimination laws and supports for same-sex partners. They may even encounter ageism by and feel excluded from the primarily youth-oriented gay community. Health care professionals need to be aware of the significance of identity cohort membership or the historical period when LGBT individuals first identified as such, because this has profound implications for how they experience aging (Porche & Purvin, 2008; Rosenfeld, 2003)

If LGBT adults reveal their sexual orientation later in life, they must integrate their past lives with children, friends, and other partners into the coming-out process. While an estimated 33 percent of lesbians have children, those who came out in old age may be ostracized at the stage when they most need support (Barker, 2004). They may also encounter heterosexist attitudes and practices from health care providers. For example, the partners of LGBT elders who are hospitalized or in a long-term care residential facility may be denied access to intensive care units and to medical records; staff may limit their visits as well as expressions of affection. In a survey of 1,100 self-identified LGBT adults age 40 to 61, 32 percent of gay men and 26 percent of lesbians cited their greatest concern about aging as discrimination due to their sexual orientation. And 19 percent of the respondents had little or no confidence that health care professionals would treat them with dignity and respect (MetLife, 2006). A survey of LGBT adults in small- to medium-sized cities identified that a majority of the respondents believed that LGBT residents in long-term care facilities are victims of discrimination and assumed they would have to hide their sexual orientation if admitted to a residential facility (Jackson, Johnson, & Roberts, 2008).

LGBT elders face other legal and policy barriers. To illustrate, domestic partners do not qualify for bereavement or sick leave in most companies, or for family leave under the 1993 Family and Medical Leave Act. When a partner is hospitalized or relocates to a nursing home, if a durable power of attorney for health care is not in place, blood relatives can control visitation, treatment options, and discharge planning in jurisdictions that do not provide legal recognition of these rights for married or registered same-sex couples. They can exclude gay partners from decision making and any rights to an inheritance (McFarland & Sanders, 2003; Orel, 2004). Because the federal government does not recognize marriage for same-sex couples, even in states that issue marriage licenses to same-sex couples, Social Security's treatment of LGBT partners (they are ineligible for benefits) may be the most blatant and costly instance of discrimination based on sexual orientation. When LGBT adults are able to participate in health benefit plans provided by their partners' employers, unlike married heterosexual couples, these benefits are counted as taxable income by the Internal Revenue Service (Badgett, 2007). In addition, LGBT surviving partners are charged an estate tax on a jointly owned home and may accrue taxes after inheriting a retirement plan—negative financial consequences that do not apply to heterosexual married couples (Cahill et al., 2000; Hecht, 2004).

Fortunately, many families are more accepting of LGBT partners today than in the past, with groups such as Parents and Friends of Lesbians and Gays supporting families in the process of

Gays and lesbians often create families of choice.

coming to terms with a relative's sexual orientation. In addition, recent civil union legislation and legalized marriage in some states are gradually addressing some local legal and health care barriers faced by earlier cohorts of gay men and lesbians, but these do not impact federal policies such as Social Security. As of 2009, three states (Iowa, Massachu- setts and Connecticut) issue marriage licenses to same-sex couples with full equality of

CARE NETWORKS OF OLDER LESBIANS

A group of seven lesbians with varying backgrounds took turns caring for an 84-year-old, terminally ill, single lesbian, providing transport to medical appointments and leisure activities, coordinating her access to needed services, and talking with her about her life, politics, and dying. The primary physician, a woman with a specialty in geriatrics, became part of the network by responding to calls from the group, making home visits, and supporting their role as caregivers. As death neared, one year later than expected, the woman felt supported in making arrangements to die where and how she wanted.

state-level marriage benefits and obligations (NGLTF, 2008). Six states and the District of Columbia maintain legal recognition of same-sex relationships with broad access to many of the benefits and obligations of marriage. Although some states' policies and legislation help to overcome lack of access to legal protections for same-sex couples, this does not address federal policies. Furthermore, LGBT adults in the 26 states that have amended their constitutions to prevent the legal recognition of same-sex marriages face additional challenges negotiating between self-protection and self-efficacy within hostile political environments (Levitt et al., 2009).

On the other hand, lifelong marginalization because of sexual orientation may stimulate adaptive strategies to meet the challenges of aging. In a 2006 MetLife survey, about 40 percent of respondents believed that negotiating nonheterosexual identities facilitated their preparation for aging through positive character traits, greater resilience, or better support networks. Latino and African American respondents were more likely than the sample as a whole to agree that their LGBT identities had helped them approach midlife, and they anticipated a relatively easy transition to old age. A successful transition to one stigmatized status (being queer) may contribute to resilience and competence in adjusting to another stigmatized status (being old), thereby buffering other normative age changes such as

---

FINALLY ABLE TO MARRY... BUT NOT FOR LONG

The first couple to be married in San Francisco when same-sex marriages became legal in California in 2008 were ages 87 and 84. When California voters supported Proposition 8 against same-sex marriages later that year, their marital status was in jeopardy. In 2009, the California Supreme Court upheld Proposition 8 that marriage is only between a man and a woman but allowed couples who had married during the brief time period when same-sex marriage was allowed to remain married in the eyes of the law.

---

friends and family moving away or dying. (Clunis et al., 2005; Cruikshank, 2009; Gabbay & Wahler, 2002; Heaphy, Yip, & Thompson, 2004; Hostetler, 2004; MetLife, 2006). This may occur because LGBT elders have learned coping skills through the "crisis" management of their sexual orientation and dealing on a daily basis with homophobia throughout their lives. Having experienced greater blurring of gender-role definitions throughout their lives, gays and lesbians are often more egalitarian in their relationships than heterosexual couples, particularly in terms of household tasks. But they also tend to be comfortable with being single. Overall, older LGBT individuals, especially among the young-old, generally emphasize positive aspects about aging, experience self-acceptance and high self-esteem, and have satisfying long-term relationships (Clunis et al., 2005; Heaphy, 2007; Hostetler, 2004; Weeks, Heaphy, & Donovan, 2001). On the other hand, if they have not developed supportive networks, LGBT elders may be at greater risk for loneliness and social isolation in old age. Not surprisingly, the meanings attached to aging by LGBT individuals tend to be as dependent on the social context and are as fluid as they are for heterosexual adults (Heaphy, 2007).

By having confronted real or potential loss of family support earlier in life, LGBT elders are also less prone to assume that their biological families, including their adult children, will provide for them in old age and are more likely to plan for their own financial security and health care arrangements. Having learned self-reliance and other skills that serve them well in old age, they may more readily adjust to care tasks. Most gay men now approaching old age have experienced multiple losses through deaths of friends and lovers to AIDS. Their accumulated grief may paradoxically enhance their acceptance of other losses associated with age, including the loss of friends to help care for them.

Since approximately 90 percent of the current cohort of LGBT elders are childless, they typically build a "surrogate family" through a strong mixed-age network of friends and significant others, which either complements or replaces supports within their family of origin. A national survey of LGBT persons in New Zealand discovered complex relationships between biological and chosen family systems, with significant variation between and among men and women (Neville & Henrickson, 2009). In effect, they create "friendship families" or "families of choice" (Calasanti & Slevin, 2001; MetLife, 2006). In such instances, the caring and emotional qualities of gay male friendships tend to distinguish them from the "doing" friendships of their heterosexual peers. Some gays and lesbians design innovative housing arrangements and empowering communities deliberately framed in terms of politics and the ethics of care (Heaphy, 2007). Support and advocacy organizations include Senior Action in a Gay Environment (SAGE), New Leaf Outreach to Elders, Open House in San Francisco, Older Lesbians Organizing for Change, and the National Association of Lesbian and Gay Gerontologists, organized by the American Society on Aging. SAGE, for example, has chapters nationwide that sponsor intergenerational friendly visitors' services, housing and legal advocacy, professional counseling, as well as SAGE Net, a consortium of groups offering similar services around the nation (Butler, 2006). Although the growing number of gay retirement communities cannot discriminate against heterosexual individuals, they nevertheless convey a welcoming message to LGBT elders. Those who have such support through informal networks, social organizations, and housing tend to be characterized by high self-esteem and life satisfaction, less fear of aging, and greater effectiveness in managing age-associated changes (Hecht, 2004).

The growing number of LGBT elders has implications for health care providers, who must be cautious not to assume that all clients are heterosexual. Assessment, psychosocial histories, and care-planning practices must recognize that older LGBT individuals may have distinctive needs related to their sexual orientation and a lifetime of dealing with stigma and discrimination that may deter them from seeking services. In addition, LGBT elders who are

THE AGING OF LESBIAN COMMUNITIES

In the 1960s and 1970s, lesbians who chose to withdraw from heterosexual society formed matriarchal communities of "womyn's land," mostly in rural areas. They believed that such separatism was necessary in order to draw on their own strength and empowerment. Such utopian communities have lost their appeal to younger lesbians, so that recruiting new members is difficult. Nevertheless, lesbians who have valued the cooperation and safety of such communities are working to raise funds for assisted living facilities and to set up hospice care within them (Kershaw, 2009).

concerned with maintaining privacy may be uncomfortable with allowing formal caregivers into their homes (Cook-Daniels, 1997; Neville & Henrickson, 2009; Zodikoff, 2006). Staff committed to enhancing the quality of life in long-term care settings also need to advocate for non-homophobic policies and practices that allow LGBT partners to be together and to participate in critical end-of-life decisions. Fortunately, such needs are being recognized by some service providers, and agency culture is being modified to be more inclusive of LGBT elders, often through staff training. The inclusion of LGBT elders through an expanded definition of minority populations in the Report of the 2005 White House Conference on Aging is a tangible recognition of their distinctive needs (Hecht, 2004).

POINTS TO PONDER

Imagine being a gay or lesbian elder who attends an adult day health or senior center daily. Because of fear of ostracism, you need to respond to every question without mentioning a lifelong partner— either a partner at home or your grief over a partner's death. And imagine maintaining that silence day after day, perhaps year after year. This is what life is like for many older LGBT adults.

Never-Married Older People

Approximately 4 percent of the older population has never married (Federal Interagency Forum, 2008). Contrary to a commonly held image of loneliness and isolation, the majority of never-married older persons typically develop reciprocal relationships with other kin, especially siblings, and with friends and neighbors. While living alone in old age is often interpreted as a risk factor, it may not harm health, emotional well-being, and social integration when an older person is accustomed to living autonomously. Elders who have lived alone all their lives may not feel lonely or isolated. Families and health care providers often assume that co-residence is desirable; but simply living with others tells little about the quality of relationships and life satisfaction. It may be that lack of social support most negatively affects mental and physical well-being when the loss of a partner or other relatives occurs later in life, rather than representing a lifelong pattern. Therefore, social service providers must avoid making assumptions about preferred living arrangements in old age (Connidis, 2001).

As another example of resilience among those who have lived alone most of their adult lives, never-married adults, who typically have had lifelong employment, tend to enjoy greater financial security in old age. In addition, they may be more socially active and resourceful, with more diversity in their social networks—especially more interactions with younger persons, friends, neighbors, and siblings—than their married counterparts. This pattern of greater social and economic resilience tends to differentiate never-married women from their married, divorced, or widowed counterparts. Compared with widowed peers, they generally are more satisfied with their lives and self-reliant. When they do need others' assistance, they are more likely to turn to siblings, friends, neighbors, and paid helpers than are their married peers (Barrett & Lynch, 1999; Tennstedt, 1999).

Organizations aimed specifically at single people are growing, although many of these are for younger singles. Alternative living arrangements, such as cross-generational home-sharing programs and cooperative housing, may appeal to single older adults who choose not to live alone. The proportion of single older adults is likely to increase in the future, because singlehood is increasingly common (approximately 28 percent currently) at earlier life stages, and because of baby boomers' decisions about marriage and divorce, described earlier.

Childless Older Adults

Although most elders have living children, approximately 20 percent of those age 85 and older are childless. These older adults lack the natural support system of children and grandchildren; they tend to have smaller social networks and are less socially integrated. Childless elders are not necessarily socially isolated, however (Pearl, 2006). When faced with health problems and need for instrumental support, childless elders turn first to their partners/ spouses (if available), then to siblings, then to nieces and nephews, and last to friends. Research findings are mixed regarding whether marital or parenting history is more conducive to social integration and life satisfaction (Dykstra & Wagner, 2007; Pearl, 2006). Childlessness does not appear to affect the developmental task of generativity or contributing to younger generations, however (Rothrauff & Cooney, 2008). It is not surprising that unmarried childless elders, lacking informal support systems, tend to utilize services and nursing homes more than do married childless persons (Connidis, 2001; Uhlenberg, 2004). On the other hand, simply having children does not guarantee adequate care in old age or satisfaction with the parenting role. From a practice perspective, it is important to differentiate lifelong childlessness from outliving one's children.

Some childless unmarried elders, particularly women, develop kin-like or "sisterly" non-kin relations and may be quite satisfied with their lives. Yet they may not want these relationships to be a source of care, fearing the change from voluntary mutuality into dependency (Wu & Pollard, 1998). The growing number of childless and unmarried older individuals may affect the proportion of older people who will seek formal supports and develop alternative living arrangements in the future. The numbers of elders who have no grandchildren will also increase proportionately. The percentage of women age 60 to 64 who never experience grandparenthood will increase from the current 13 percent to over 20 percent by 2020 (Uhlenberg, 2004).

Sibling Relationships

Sibling relationships represent the one family bond with the potential to last a lifetime. The likelihood of having a sibling in old age has increased most dramatically since the early twentieth century. Given current life expectancy, most persons will not experience the death of a sibling until they are past age 70. About 80 percent of older people have at least one sibling, and approximately 33 percent of these elders see a sibling monthly, although yearly visits are most typical. As with other kin-keeping responsibilities, sisters are more likely than brothers to maintain frequent contact with same-sex siblings, whether by phone, e-mail, or face-to-face interaction (Connidis, 2001; Uhlenberg, 2004).

The sibling relationship in old age is characterized by a shared history, egalitarianism, and increasing feelings of closeness and affection, particularly among sisters. Although the sibling relationship is relatively stable across the life course, as they age, siblings often renew past ties, forgive prior conflicts, reduce verbally aggressive behavior toward one another, and become more trusting, affectionate,

emotionally committed and supportive of each other (sometimes through shared reminiscence) (Blieszner, 2006; Myers & Goodboy, 2006; Rittenour, Myers, & Brann, 2007). Siblings are particularly vital sources of psychological support in the lives of never-married older persons, widowed persons, and those without children, although their ability to provide instrumental support often declines with age (Lu, 2007). Assistance generally increases after a spouse's death and enhances the widowed person's psychological well-being. Although siblings are less frequently caregivers to each other than are partners and adult children (with the exception of caring for the never-married), they do supplement the efforts of others during times of crisis or special need. The very existence of siblings as a possible source of help may be important, even if such assistance is rarely used. Given these strong ties, it is not surprising that bereaved siblings may suffer from depression, feel more personally vulnerable, and fear death more than bereaved spouses or friends (Cicirelli, 2009).

The increasing rate of divorce and remarriage will undoubtedly affect sibling relationships. The growth in blended families through remarriage will result in more half siblings and stepsiblings. For divorced older people who do not remarry, interactions with siblings may become more important than when they were married. The sibling relationship is also vital to LGBT elders, presuming their siblings have accepted their sexual orientation (Connidis, 2001).

POINTS TO PONDER

If you have a brother or sister, try to imagine what your relationship will be like in old age. If you are an only child, have you created other networks that can replace the sibling relationship and support you as you grow older?

Other Kin

Interaction with secondary kin—cousins, aunts, uncles, nieces, and nephews—appears to depend on geographic proximity, availability of closer relatives, and preference. Extended kin can replace or substitute for missing relatives, especially during family rituals and holidays. For example, compared to their white counterparts, African American childless elders often turn to nieces and nephews when siblings are not available. Accordingly, family reunions are a vital source of connections among African American extended kin in both rural and urban areas (Chadiha et al., 2005). Personal or historical connections that allow for remembering pleasurable events may be more critical than closeness of kinship in determining such interactions.

Intergenerational Relationships: Adult Children

After spouses/partners, adult children are the most important source of informal support and social interaction in old age. As noted earlier, the flow of instrumental and emotional support is typically not unidirectional from adult child to older parent, but largely from parent to child. Adult children who are not married are more likely to transfer resources to parents. Contrary to stereotypes, most adult children who assist their parents are not motivated by the expectation of an inheritance (Blieszner, 2006; Silverstein et al., 2002). In a study of support patterns and relationship quality over a four-year period, even when parents' instrumental support to adult children decreased, their emotional support increased. Overall, the degree of support exchanged was less critical to adult children's well-being than the quality of the intergenerational relationship (Giarrusso et al., 2006).

Over 80 percent of persons age 65 and older have surviving children, although the number of children in most families has decreased—a trend expected to continue. The majority of older adults live near at least one adult child, sharing a social life but not a home (Connidis & Kiecolt, 2007). Most older people state that they prefer not to live with their children, seeking to maintain their autonomy. As a result, only 6 percent live in their children's homes (American Community Survey, 2007). As stated earlier in this chapter, the percentage of older persons who live in their children's households increases with advancing age, extent of functional disability, and among those who are widowed, separated, and divorced. Most older adults who need long-term care generally prefer to live with their children than in a skilled nursing facility, although children are often less willing than their parents to share a residence. When older parents do live with their children, they usually choose to live with the one who has the greatest potential to provide support, typically a daughter. Less than 14 percent of the young-old and 4 percent of the oldest-old live in multigenerational households composed of parents, children, and grandchildren. These proportions are higher, however, among some families of color, especially African Americans (Connidis, 2001; Connidis & Kiecolt, 2007; Dilworth-Anderson et al., 2002).

Although not necessarily living together, the majority of parents and adult children see each other frequently, as illustrated by the following patterns of interaction:

- Approximately 50 percent of older people have daily contact with their adult children.
- Nearly 80 percent see an adult child at least once a week.
- More than 75 percent talk on the phone at least weekly with an adult child. (AOA, 2008)

Geographic separation of family members is generally due to adult children's mobility. Older parents who live closer to their children have more contact, feel greater affection for them, and are more involved with grandchildren; however, geographic separation does not necessarily weaken emotional bonds, and **intimacy at a distance** can occur (Silverstein & Angelelli, 1998).

Less is known about the quality than about the frequency of these interactions. Most cross-generational relationships inherently involve some conflict, with parents concerned about their children's lifestyle choices and children noting differences in communication and interaction styles. Nevertheless, most families report affection, mutual support, and a desire for more satisfying cross-generational relations. This reflects the theory of intergenerational ambivalence, in which solidarity and conflict, support and obligation fluctuate over the life course (Blieszner, 2006; Fingerman, Pitzer, Lefkowitz, et al., 2008; Pillemer & Luscher, 2004). Social and health care providers need to recognize how each generation faces its own developmental transitions as well as complex cross-generational issues.

Patterns of Intergenerational Assistance Are Reversed

In some instances, parents continue to provide care to adult children beyond normative expectations of "launching" them to be more independent. For example, caregiving remains a central role late in life for parents of adult children with developmental or physical disabilities or chronic mental illness. The life expectancy for persons with developmental disabilities has been extended by medical advances, and deinstitutionalization means that most individuals live in the community, typically with family. This increased life expectancy has brought new challenges to the person with developmental disabilities due to age-associated changes. For example, dementia is more likely to occur among people with Down syndrome than the average person, strikes sooner, presents different symptoms, and progress more rapidly. Longer life expectancy also challenges their families who care for them. For the first time in history, persons with developmental disabilities are outliving their parents. Parental caregivers often face their own age-associated declines in functional ability, energy, and financial resources, which can affect their caregiving ability.

The history and cumulative nature of care demands can make their situation particularly stressful. A major worry is how their child will be cared for after their own deaths or after developing a debilitating illness. Despite such concerns, most caregiving parents do not make long-term plans about where their children will eventually live. For example, when parental caregivers of adult children with psychiatric disorders die, their children often experience housing disruptions and potentially traumatic transitions. Fortunately, the Planned Lifetime Assistance Network (PLAN) is now available in some states through the National Alliance for the Mentally Ill. PLAN provides lifetime assistance to individuals with disabilities whose parents or other family members are deceased or can no longer provide care. As the population of adults with chronic illnesses and developmental disabilities grows, the aging, mental health, and disability service networks are initiating new support systems to maintain persons with developmental disabilities in the community. These include respite care, day programs, more residential alternatives, and assistance with permanency planning (e.g., designing plans for permanent housing in the community) (McCallion, 2006). Increased coordination between the Aging Network and the developmental disability system is essential, along with more staff and training to provide community-based care and housing for persons with increasingly complex needs. In some states, the Alzheimer's Association has initiated education and support programs specifically for people with developmental disabilities who also have dementia. Some group homes and smaller nursing homes are opening for people who have both developmental disabilities and limitations related to aging. In addition to supervision and care coordination, many of these offer fitness classes, physical therapy, and music therapy (Swingle, 2007).

Grandparenthood and Great-Grandparenthood

At the turn of the twentieth century, three-generation families were less common, with only 6 percent of 10-year-olds having all four grandparents alive compared to 41 percent in 2000. Today, more older people are experiencing the role of grandparent and, increasingly, of great-grandparent, although they have proportionately fewer grandchildren than preceding generations. Among parents age 90 and older, 90 percent are grandparents and nearly 50 percent are great-grandparents, with some women experiencing grandmotherhood for more than 40 years. This is because the transition to grandparenthood typically occurs in middle age, not old age, with about 50 percent of all grandparents under the age of 60. As a result, grandparents vary in age from their late 30s to over 100-years-old, and their grandchildren range from newborns to retirees (Reitzes & Mutran, 2004a). A 40-year-old woman and a 2-year-old boy may form a grandparent-grandchild dyad, as may a 90-year-old man and a 70-year-old woman. The issues faced by each generation vary by their life-course position, as well as the historical and spatial context for cohorts.

The grandchild experience is another way of grasping the significance of increased years spent in grandparenting. For example, the proportion of 30-year-olds with a grandparent alive tripled between 1900 and 2000—from 21 to 75 percent (Silverstein & Marenco, 2001; Uhlenberg, 2004). Contrary to stereotypes, most emotional and social interactions involving reciprocal exchanges

Great-grandparents provide time and attention to young children.

between grandchildren and grandparents are with adolescents and young adults, not with young children.

The vast majority of grandparents do not live with their grandchildren, but approximately 80 percent see a grandchild at least monthly, and nearly 50 percent do so weekly. Geographic proximity and the nature of the grandparents' relationship with their adult child are major factors that determine frequency of visits. On the other hand, geographic distance does not markedly affect the quality of the grandchild-grandparents emotional bonds. Parents primarily determine the degree of interaction when grandchildren are young. The parental, or middle generation, shapes their children's ties to grandparents by modeling behaviors, expressing their own attitudes toward grandparents, and providing means for contact, although adult grandchildren's ties to grandparents depend less on the middle generation. Because women traditionally have stronger ties to their family of origin than do men, bonds between aging mothers and adult daughters tend to be closest. While both grandmothers and grandfathers perceive ties to daughters as stronger and closer than to sons, relationships are generally closest between grandmothers and granddaughters. Family size also affects these relationships. Grandparents with many children and grandchildren tend to be less invested in any particular grandchild (Davies & Williams, 2002; Dubas, 2001; Fingerman, 2004).

Multiple grandparenting roles and meanings exist, given the wide variation within this phase of the life course that can encompass more than 40 years. Grandparent/grandchild ages and life-course position, frequency of contact, and parental influences all affect grandparents' satisfaction with the role. Early research found this role to be peripheral and not a primary source of identity, meaning, or satisfaction for older adults (Neugarten, 1964; Wood & Robertson, 1976). The prime significance of grandparenthood was reported to be biological renewal and/or continuity (e.g., seeing oneself extended

PELOSI CHANGES THE IMAGE OF GRANDMOTHERS

Immediately after the 2006 election, Nancy Pelosi, the first female Speaker of the House, was on the phone with her daughter—about to give birth to Pelosi's sixth grandchild—while a White House aide tried to connect her with President Bush. Pelosi believes that "everything stops" when a grandchild is coming. The grandmother story reflects the profound changes in our society—with people living longer and healthier lives and, as grandparents, wanting influence in the political discourse. Pelosi has made it chic to be a grandma (Trafford, 2006).

into the future), and emotional self-fulfillment, especially the opportunity to be a better grandparent than parent. In terms of style, older grandparents were more apt to be formal and distant, whereas younger ones emphasized mutuality, informality, and playfulness. Surprisingly, about 30 percent of respondents in the early grandparent research did not derive satisfaction from the role, describing it as difficult, disappointing, and unpleasant. Satisfaction tended to be higher among grandmothers than grandfathers (Neugarten & Weinstein, 1964).

More recent research concludes that grandparents generally derive great emotional satisfaction from interacting with their grandchildren and observing their development and activities. With declining fertility rates resulting in fewer grandchildren, they have more time and resources to invest in those who are available (Bengtson & Putney, 2006). They want to have an influence on their grandchildren, typically to encourage moral standards, integrity, a commitment to succeed, and religious beliefs and values. Age influences the types of grandparent-grandchild interactions; younger grandparents, especially grandmothers, generally live closer and have more frequent contact through child care and shared recreational activities, while older grandparents with higher incomes provide financial and other types of instrumental assistance (Davies & Williams, 2002; Musil, 2006; Reitzes & Mutran,

2004a; Silverstein & Marenco, 2001; Uhlenberg, 2004). These age differences may shift, however, as baby boom grandparents re- main employed longer or choose to travel more during retirement than past cohorts. More grandparents are turning to e-mail and social networking sites for communication with their computer-savvy grandchildren. Consistent with role theory, grandparenthood provides opportunities for older adults to experience a sense of meaning, morale, and positive role identity, to relive their lives through their grandchildren, and to indulge them with unconditional love. Overall, grandparent identity tends to be associated with embeddedness in the family, along with life satisfaction and psychological well-being. Additionally, grandparents' involvement with their grandchildren is compatible with the concept of active aging (Drew & Silverstein, 2004; Mueller & Elder, 2003; Reitzes & Mutran, 2004a, 2004b; Soliz & Harwood, 2006; Uhlenberg, 2004). The box on page 362 illustrates the diversity of grandparenting styles.

THE INTERNET AS A TOOL FOR INTERGENERATIONAL COMMUNICATION

Grandparents at a geographic distance who have the financial means and are computer savvy are discovering that they can stay in touch with their grandchildren of any age through webcams, such as Skype. In a way that e-mailed photos never could, the webcam video capability promises to transcend distance and the inability of toddlers to hold up their end of a conversation. Instead, grandparents can participate in "tea parties," sing favorite songs, make faces together, or read stories to their grandchildren. For some grandparents, they feel like they are actually interacting face-to-face with the younger generation and thus need to travel less to have that experience. For others, the illusion of proximity makes them ache for the real thing. How such internet-based interaction will affect long-term grandparent/grandchild relationships is unknown (Harmon, 2008).

The **intergenerational stake hypothesis** refers to a societal level pattern whereby the older generation tends to be more invested in imbuing future generations with their values, and therefore is more committed to relationships with younger generations. In contrast, younger generations, as a whole, place a higher value on establishing autonomy from older generations and thus report lower levels of intergenerational solidarity (Reitzes & Mutran, 2004a). Consistent with social exchange theory, described in Chapter 8, this differential stake may reflect the greater investment by elders in raising younger generations, often viewing their relationship with their grandchildren as closer and more positive than do their grandchildren. On the other hand, grandchildren may perceive the relationship as an active, supportive one and less authoritarian than their relationships with their parents. For the most part, young adult children, whose relationships with their grandparents are no longer mediated by their parents, view their grandparents as "helping them out" and emotionally supporting and investing in them (Harwood, 2001). When young adults develop open communication patterns with their grandparents—telling stories, chatting on the phone or internet—both generations recognize the mutual benefits that foster shared family identity with and positive attitudes toward grandparents.

Gender also influences grandparenting. Grandmothers generally emphasize closeness, open communication, warmth, and fun (i.e., an expressive approach) and attribute greater importance to family relationships. Grandfathers place higher priority on their role as advisors (i.e., an instrumental approach) and their sense of obligation to grandchildren (Roberto, Allen, & Bleiszner, 2001).

Some studies point to greater interactions among populations of color through an extended kin network and more grandparent responsibility for childrearing. African American grandparenting tends to be characterized as authoritative or influential. In Asian immigrant families, grandparents who offer child care help support the family's economic success.

STYLES OF GRANDPARENTING

Companionate, Friend, or Apportionate Style
Grandparent feels close and affectionate to grandchildren without taking on a particular role, gives advice informally, talks about family history, serves as confidant, and occasionally indulges the grandchild

Remote Style
Grandparent is less involved, often because of geographic distance

Involved Style
Grandparent is geographically close, often assumes parent-like responsibilities in response to a family crisis (e.g., separation or divorce), or to enable the parents to work outside the home

Individualized Style
This grandparent is emotionally closer than the remote grandparent, but does not contribute substantially to the lives of grandchildren.

Authoritative or Influential
Grandparents, typically grandmothers, provide extensive support, sometimes assuming parental responsibilities; this style is more characteristic of African American families.

SOURCE: Adapted from Davies and Williams (2002); Roberto and Stroes (1995).

Mexican American families tend to have strong grandparent-grandchild ties, with the financial assistance flowing from older to young generations. Historically, grandparent-grandchildren relationships were characterized by norms of noninterference, with grandparents assuming only occasional or short-term responsibility in responding to emergencies. The dramatic increase in the number of grandparents as primary caregivers to grandchildren reflects a profound shift in this pattern, with more grandparents taking on full-time responsibility for their grandchildren today. The most common reasons are their adult children's substance abuse or incarceration (Bengtson & Putney, 2006; Hayslip & Kaminski, 2005).

Grandparents as Primary Caregivers of Grandchildren

Grandparents and other extended family members have traditionally cared for grandchildren across families of color and in many other countries and cultures, as described in Chapter 2 (Cox, 2002). Such care by grandparents in three-generation households generally supplemented parental care or supported the young parents while they worked outside the home or faced short-term disruptions. However, over the past three decades there has been a rapid growth of grandparents (or great-grandparents) who are the primary or sole caregivers for grandchildren because their adult children are unable or unwilling to provide care. With over 2.5 million grandparents giving primary care, such **skipped-generation households** are currently the fastest-growing type in the U.S. Characterized by the absence of the parental generation; this structure is also referred to as **downward-extended households.** At the same time, the number of children living in a home with both a parent and grandparent present has declined (Casper & Bianchi, 2002; Generations United, 2007; Simmons & Dye, 2003). These shifts represent an increase of over 30 percent in custodial grandparenting (i.e., those who have legal custody) since 1990 (Bryson & Casper, 2007; U.S. Bureau of the Census, 2006b).

Over 6 percent of all children live in grandparent-headed households. Of these, an estimated 30 percent are in such households without either of their parents for more than 6 months at a time and where grandparents have assumed sole care responsibility. More than 10 percent of grandparents raise a grandchild for at least 6 months, but typically for far longer periods—in some cases for more than a decade. Although grandparent caregiving crosscuts social class, sexual orientation, race, and ethnicity, African American children are more likely to live in a skipped-generation household than their white counterparts. Approximately 4 percent of Caucasian children, 6.5 percent of Latino, and 13.5 percent of African American children live with grandparents

CHALLENGES FACING GRANDPARENT CAREGIVERS

In Washington state, a 56-year-old woman who is blind cares for her severely disabled 13-year-old grandson who was violently shaken, struck, and thrown as a baby, suffering brain damage that left him with cerebral palsy and unable to walk, talk, drink, or eat solid food. Blind since age 16, she relies on Braille, a guide dog, and a few close friends to try to provide as full a life as possible for him. A case aide provides some daily assistance and can drive the teenager to school and other activities, but has an old, unreliable car. The woman survives on disability for both herself and her grandson, which does not cover additional costs entailed by the intensity of the level of care that she must provide. Both grandmother and grandson dreamed of owning a van so that friends could drive them to sports events, church, and other activities that bring some joy into both of their lives. Fortunately, after her moving story ran in the *The Seattle Times*, local contributors helped them realize their dream of an accessible van.

or other relatives. Although most **custodial grandparents** are under age 65, 20 percent are age 65 and older. Often they are facing their own age-related changes and chronic diseases, as well as dealing with age-appropriate developmental tasks (Hayslip & Kaminski, 2005; Kropf & Yoon, 2006). Grandparents younger than 60 do not qualify for age-based services, however (Generations United, 2007).

The majority of custodial grandparents are female, married, and live in the South. However, unmarried women and African Americans tend to predominate among grandparents who do not have legal custody (informal kinship care) (Hayslip & Kaminscki, 2005). Even among older couples, women still predominate as the primary caregivers of their grandchildren. Although national studies indicate that the majority of sole grandparent caregivers are white (62 percent), Latinos (10 percent), and African Americans (over 30 percent) are disproportionately represented, given their percentage in the total population (Fuller-Thompson & Minkler, 2001; Hayslip & Kaminscki, 2005). Latino households differ from other populations of color because relatives such as aunts and siblings provide similar amounts of care as do grandparents. Latino caregivers face the additional burden of anti-immigration sentiments and their legal manifestations, making them less likely to seek formal assistance with care tasks even if they hold legal status (Cox, 2002; Cox, Brooks, & Valcarcei, 2000). Interventions to support grandparent caregivers need to take account of their wide diversity in terms of race, culture, age, sexual identity, and social class.

GRANDPARENTS AS CAREGIVERS

Mary long ago earned her stripes as a mom. She raised five children alone, in a tough Los Angeles neighborhood, and managed to put them through college or vocational training. She had looked forward to retirement and being a loving grandmother, to spoiling her grandchildren on visits and then sending them home. But her life has not turned out as expected. Instead, she's raising her 8-year-old grandson, James, alone, since the incarceration of her daughter and the boy's father for selling drugs.

When Mary's daughter was charged with possession of drugs, Mary could not bear the thought of her grandson being raised by strangers in the foster care system. She petitioned the courts to become his guardian. Her daughter has only contacted her son twice in the past four years. This has made the adjustment difficult for Mary and James, who often lashes out at his grandmother. Mary tries to provide as much love and stability for him as possible, helping him with his homework, assisting with his Cub Scout troop, and attending all his school events. She derives some emotional rewards from these activities with James, but misses activities with her peers. Many of her friends have disappeared as they have more freedom to "take off and do things." She also struggles with guilt about her daughter and her situation. She has turned her anger and grief into organizing local support groups for others like herself and pressuring legislators to recognize caregiving grandparents' needs.

FACTORS ASSOCIATED WITH THE INCREASE IN GRANDPARENT CAREGIVING   One factor underlying the dramatic increase in grandparent caregivers is a 2003 Supreme Court decision, which upheld a lower court's decision that federal foster care benefits could not be denied to relatives who were otherwise eligible. This resulted in the practice of **formal kinship care**—the placement of children with relatives by the state—as opposed to the widespread **informal kinship care** arrangements that do not involve state foster care or adoption systems. The majority of states now require that preference be given to relatives for placement of foster children. However, federal and state laws and policies that promote kinship care do not explain the concomitant growth in the number of informal arrangements of children living with grandparents (Cuddeback, 2004). In fact, grandparents' intent to keep a grandchild out of the state foster care system is a primary reason that they assume the care role informally, typically well before any legal custody relationship is established. Ironically, the only way that grandparents can be partially compensated for their care is by meeting the state requirements for foster parents. Contrary to conservative arguments that grandparent caregivers take in grandchildren for financial gain, caring for grandchildren typically exacerbates already difficult economic circumstances. Even if grandparents do qualify for foster kinship care payments, they may experience delays and eligibility problems, and their payment is substantially lower than that for nonrelative foster parents (Goodman et al., 2004).

Rather than financial motivation, the predominant reasons underlying increased grandparent caregiving are the parents' drug and alcohol abuse, especially the meth epidemic, HIV/AIDS, unemployment, divorce, incarceration, teen pregnancy, death, and issues of safety and child welfare. Many of these factors will continue to expand the number of grandparent caregivers in the future (Hayslip & Kaminski, 2005; Joslin, 2002). It is important to note that all of these conditions are tied in fundamental ways to institutionalized racism and the growing inequities between rich and poor, Caucasians and populations of color (although many grandparent caregivers are not low-income). Nevertheless, policy changes to address the factors contributing to the rise in skipped-generation households cannot be made without a commitment to confronting the underlying structural causes of class and racial inequities (Haglund, 2000).

THE GAINS AND COSTS OF CARE As with care responsibility across the life course, women predominate in the grandparent caregiving role and experience both gains and costs. Although some grandparents enjoy emotional closeness and pleasure with grandchildren and a sense of being productive and needed (i.e., keeping the "family together and out of foster care"), they also experience significant costs (Giarrusso, Silverstein, & Feng, 2000; Kropf & Yoon, 2006). Not surprisingly, stress is greatest with older grandchildren because of social, behavioral, and academic difficulties faced by some preteens and adolescents (Musil et al., 2002).

The economic costs of custodial grandparenting are significant. Compared to noncustodial grandmothers, they are more likely to live in poverty. As many as 50 percent of grandparent caregivers live on a limited income and are not employed, even though the majority are age 45 to 64 and therefore not the typical retirement age (Hayslip & Kaminski, 2005; Park, 2006). Those who are employed may need to reduce their hours or quit their jobs in order to care for their grandchild. Others may have to remain employed to cover basic costs entailed in raising a child. Such financial stress can exacerbate other types of distress, intensify feelings of being overwhelmed by multiple roles, and compromise their health. Grandparents who are sole caregivers are found to have higher levels of psychological distress compared with those who provide only supplemental care to grandchildren. This distress, often with symptoms of depression, increases when they are caring for grandchildren with behavioral or emotional problems. They also tend to rate their health poorly, experience multiple chronic health problems, and avoid seeking care for themselves, especially for mental or emotional health conditions. Some recent studies, however, suggest that demographic and socioeconomic characteristics may be more salient to poor health outcomes than caregiving responsibilities per se (Baker & Silverstein, 2008; Hinterlong & Ryan, 2008; Hughes, Waite, LaPierre, & Luo, 2007; Simmons & Dye, 2003). These mental and physical problems tend to be magnified for grandparents who are raising a chronically ill or special-needs child; approximately twice as many children cared for by a custodial grandparent have emotional or behavioral problems, often due to past traumatic family circumstances, compared with those in two-parent families (Kolomer, McCallion & Janicki, 2002; Musil et al., 2006; Trute, 2003).

INFORMAL AND FORMAL SUPPORTS Caregiving by grandparents also carries social costs. About 30 percent of grandmother caregivers are not married and therefore lack a partner's support. The nonnormative nature of grandparent caregiving can intensify feelings of loneliness and loss from their own age peers who do not share similar responsibilities. Grandparents may grieve the loss of the adult children whom they knew as children and young adults (Waldrop & Weber, 2001). Adult children who are incarcerated, drug addicted, or mentally ill are described as being "present but not present." Regardless of the reasons for the adult child's absence, most grandparents experience disappointment, embarrassment, shame, resentment, and guilt over their failure as parents who raised an adult child who relinquished their children. In this manner, grandparents may experience loss of identity and self-esteem as good parents, along with alienation from their children. Society may reinforce this negative self-judgment because of common misconceptions of grandmothers as nondeserving poor (e.g., "they could not have been good parents or their children would not have turned out the way they did"). Grandparent distress is further intensified by the loss of anticipated retirement time or income, loss of dreams about their family and their life as an older adult, and envy of friends who are free to pursue travel and enjoy their child-free old age (Goodman, 2003; Hayslip & Kaminski, 2005).

Nevertheless, most grandparents assume the role willingly, often acting out of a deep sense of duty and obligation (Testa & Slack, 2002). Their grandchildren, however, may repeatedly long for their parents, further intensifying the grandparent's sense of loss. What can be especially painful is when other family members, particularly other adult children and friends, pull away and fail to help out, intensifying feelings of alienation, isolation, and loneliness. Custodial grandparents also report more strain and conflict with other family members than their peers who are not providing daily care. Such strains and resultant loneliness are often worse among those who assumed the care role because of their adult child's substance abuse, incarceration, or AIDS. Not surprisingly, custodial grandmothers perceive less support from others than other grandmothers. Even their grandchildren and their adult children may not appreciate their sacrifice. In a study of children at risk born to unmarried mothers, grandparents were never mentioned by the mothers as a critical support to their children (McLanahan et al., 2003; Musil et al., 2006).

Despite the burdens of unanticipated caregiving, most custodial grandparents do not seek help for themselves, which increases their vulnerability, and most believe that they would take responsibility for their grandchildren again, despite the costs (Baird, 2003; Hayslip & Kaminski, 2005; Wohl, Lahner, & Jooste, 2003). Some grandparents may experience the cumulative effects of lifelong structural inequities due to race, gender, or disability, exacerbating the problems they face as primary caregivers, as illustrated in the box on page 367 summarizing challenges and options. To outsiders, grandparent caregivers may be invisible, largely because of their age and gender (i.e., most are women), even though they may be the primary caregivers for the majority of their

grandchild's life. Service systems, such as public child welfare, community mental health, and schools, are often ill-prepared to support grandparents or to recognize the losses faced by the grandchild (Wallace, 2001).

Although grandparents are eligible for the Temporary Assistance for Needy Families Program (TANF), its employment requirements and 5-year lifetime benefit limits create obstacles for grandparents in accessing services and financial support through the public welfare system (Minkler, Berrick, & Needell, 1999). Most grandparents receive the child-only benefit through TANF, with no financial support for themselves and no funds for child care. Although foster care payments are higher than welfare benefits, grandparents can qualify for such payments only by transferring custody of the children to the state. In other words, they cede their own parental authority and become "foster parents" to their own grandchildren. Some grandparent caregivers, especially among immigrants, may be unable to meet foster care regulations for home size, even though child welfare experts agree that relative placement is preferable. Several studies suggest that the state's reliance on kinship caregivers for low- or no-cost out-of-home foster placements results in an inequitable burden on informal support systems (Hayslip & Kawarski, 2005; Smith, 2000). In addition, informal kinship caregivers—for example, those who have chosen not to transfer custody to the state— do not qualify for any state-funded services.

Fortunately, child welfare policy makers are beginning to recognize the need to develop services to support grandparent caregivers outside the traditional foster care or TANF programs. Education and support groups as well as Internet resources are available to help grandparents, including Kinship Care Navigators and 1-800 information and assistance. Support groups tend to be most effective when they offer information on how to access resources, enhance parenting skills, build on strengths, use a constructive problem-solving focus, and are combined with respite care. While social support is vital, the major need remains economic. Advocates for kinship care providers maintain that, at a minimum, grandparents should receive full foster care rates as well as other benefits accorded to unrelated foster parents, and should have the possibility of kinship adoption with federal

CHALLENGES AND OPTIONS FOR GRANDPARENTS IN RAISING THEIR GRANDCHILDREN

Legal Options
- Guardianship and custody, which grant parental authority to grandparents but allow parental visitation rights
- Adoption, which gives grandparents all authority
- Foster parenthood, informal or formal: if the latter, grandparent qualifies for foster care payment, though at a lesser amount than non-relative foster parents

Financial Options
- Temporary Assistance for Needy Families (TANF): benefits only for children
- Food stamps
- Supplemental Security Income (SSI)
- Public housing/age-segregated retirement communities
- Foster care payment
- Adoption assistance

Child Care (day care, preschool, babysitters, respite)

Medical Insurance
- Medicaid but not Medicare
- Private insurance

Schooling
- Legal custody is necessary for grandchild to:
  attend a public school
  be tested for learning disabilities
  qualify for remedial education

Psychological/Emotional Challenges for the Child
- Loss and grief, confusion, anger

Psychological/Emotional Challenges for the Grandparent
- Loss and grief over adult child, retirement plans, or employment
- Social isolation from age peers
- Concern about own health affecting child care responsiblites.

subsidies for low-income families. In an effort to encourage permanent family placements, the Kinship Caregiver Support Act of 2005 gives states the option to use federal funds for subsidized guardianship payments to relative caregivers of children in foster care. This also made it easier for grandparents to become legal guardians and reduced barriers to services (Hayslip & Kawaski, 2005; Kelley, Whitley, & Sipe, & Yorker, 2000; Wohl et al., 2003).

An area for further multigenerational research and practice is to understand the needs of the "invisible" middle generation of parents who are unwilling or unable to raise their offspring and how this affects cross-generational exchanges across a family's life cycle. The lack of attention to this middle generation reflects, in part, our societal values on who is "deserving" of public benefits; but such neglect will have long-term consequences in terms of the middle generation's ability to be contributing members of society and to care for their parents in old age. Programs are needed that foster the relationship between grandmothers and their daughters, not only the parent to child (Engstrom, 2008). Health care providers, teachers, pediatricians, and social workers in child welfare settings, correctional facilities, schools, mental health clinics, hospitals, and senior centers can play pivotal roles in offering education and support to grandparent caregivers, advocating for economic resources and meeting the treatment needs of parents.

Great-Grandparents

The role of great-grandparent has expanded with increased life expectancy, although the associated expectations and responsibilities are ambiguous (Drew & Silverstein 2004). Two predominant styles of great-grandparenthood are identified. The most common, which tends to characterize generations separated by physical distance, is remote, involving only occasional and somewhat ritualistic contact on special occasions such as holidays and birthdays. Despite the irregular nature of contacts, however, great-grandparents derive considerable emotional satisfaction and a sense of personal and familial renewal from seeing a fourth generation as representing family continuity. The other common style occurs when great-grandparents are geographically close (within 25 miles) to the fourth generation, and thus have frequent opportunities for physical and emotional closeness to great-grandchildren. Even great-grandparents who are in their 70s and 80s may serve as babysitters or take their great-grandchildren shopping or on trips. These activities provide meaning in their lives and can enhance psychological well-being. Such positive interactions will undoubtedly be more common in the future, when great-grandparenthood is the norm and the oldest-old generations are healthier than current cohorts. Consistent with the reciprocal nature of most intergenerational relationships, growing numbers of adult grandchildren today help care for frail great-grandparents.

The Effects of Divorce and Changing Marital Patterns on Grandparenthood

A number of social trends affect the role of grandparent. Since 1950, marriage and remarriage rates have declined, while rates of divorce, cohabitation, and births occurring to unmarried mothers have markedly increased. A growing proportion of unmarried mothers are in a cohabiting relationship with the biological father. But 75 percent of the children born into such informal arrangements experience a single-family household before reaching age 15 (Heuveline, Timberlake, & Furstenberg, 2003). The decline in the proportion of available fathers negatively affects paternal grandparents' roles while often increasing the involvement of maternal grandmothers in their grandchildren's lives. Compared to grandparents of children in two-parent families, maternal grandparents often provide a safety net and protect their grandchildren from some of the risks of family disruptions when the father is absent (Elder & Conger, 2000; Uhlenberg, 2004).

The growing divorce rate profoundly affects the meaning of the grandparenthood experience. As noted earlier, at least 50 percent of

all persons marrying today will face divorce. The fact that over 30 percent of children live in one-parent families or with neither parent will affect the nature of grandchild-grandparent relationships (Uhlenberg, 2004; U.S. Bureau of the Census, 2006b). Because the tie between young grandchildren and their grandparents is mediated by the grandchildren's parents, divorce disrupts these links, changes the balance of resources within the extended family, and requires renegotiating existing bonds. Who has custody affects the frequency of interaction with grandchildren; the grandparents whose adult child is awarded custody have more contact. Generally, grandmothers maintain more contact with their grandchildren than do grandfathers after an adult child's divorce, although emotional bonds, a sense of biological connection, and grandparents' feelings of responsibility toward grandchildren may endure even without frequent interaction (Copen & Silverstein, 2004; Ehrenberg & Smith, 2003; Uhlenberg, 2004).

Controversies regarding **grandparents' rights** for visitation and proposed state legislation to ensure such rights highlight the issues faced by grandparents when the parent who is not their adult child is awarded custody, thereby reducing grandchild-grandparent interactions. Complex issues have also emerged concerning the liability of grandparents and step-grandparents for support of grandchildren in the absence of responsible parents. When parents divorce, the norm of noninterference by grandparents generally disappears. Instead, many grandparents, especially those related to the custodial parent, give substantial assistance to their grandchildren, function as surrogate parents, and mediate tensions.

Since the mid-1960s, all states have passed laws granting grandparents the right to petition a court to legally obtain visitation privileges with their grandchildren. This resulted from the passage of a 1983 uniform nationwide statute to ensure grandparents visitation rights even if parents object. However, in June 2000, the U.S. Supreme Court ruled by a 6–3 vote that the right of responsible parents to raise their children as they see fit takes precedence over prior state laws that give grandparents visitation rights. Any state law must respect the parents' wishes, although grandparents have the right to petition in cases of parental death or divorce. It is rare for grandparents to successfully petition for visitation rights when their grandchildren reside with both parents, however (Davitt, 2006). These rulings raise complex issues and may place children at the center of an intergenerational conflict played out in the courts. The long-term effects for grandchildren from visiting noncustodial grandparents over their parents' objections are unclear.

Despite the dramatic growth of blended families and thus of nonbiological grandparents, research on stepgrandparenting relationships is limited. Based on marriage and divorce patterns during the 1990s, it is estimated that by 2030 the population age 70 to 85 may have 1 stepgrandchild for every 1.7 biological grandchildren. A grandchild may have stepgrandparents, ex-stepgrandparents, parents of a cohabiting partner of a parent, or LGBT grandparents (Uhlenberg, 2004). Not surprisingly, grandparents' sense of responsibility toward biological grandchildren is greater than toward stepgrandchildren (Ganong & Coleman, 2006). From a grandparent's perspective, the growing pattern of divorce-remarriage means sharing grandchildren with their newly acquired relatives under conditions in which grandchildren will be scarcer because of declining birthrates. Grandchildren, in turn, may find themselves with eight or more grandparents. Kinship systems are further complicated by the fact that, with the increased divorce rate after 20 or more years of marriage, grandparents may no longer be married to one another. With the aging of cohorts that have experienced high divorce rates, a growing proportion of grandparents will be divorced.

Divorce among grandparents may have negative repercussions on the grandparent-grandchild relationship; divorced elders, especially grandfathers, have less interaction with their grandchildren because of weaker ties with their adult children (King, 2003). Groups such as the Foundation for Grandparenting and the National Committee of Grandparents for Children's Rights play important roles in disseminating up-to-date resources to grandparents regarding the complexities created by divorce in either generation and by stepgrandparenting.

Friends and Neighbors as Social Supports

Although the majority of older people live with others, approximately 16 percent of men and 30 percent of women age 65 to 74 live alone. After age 75, these rates increase to 23 percent of men and 50 percent of women. In fact, the incidence of older persons living alone increased by 1.5 times the growth rate for older people in general since 1970. Those living alone are most likely to be women, elders of color, the oldest-old, low-income adults, and those in rural areas. Older men, widowed and childless elders living alone are especially vulnerable to lack of social supports, as well

GRANDPARENTING AND LEGAL ISSUES

Laura and David's son was killed in an auto accident. He left behind two girls, ages 3 and 5, and their biological mother, who was his girlfriend, but who had left the relationship after the birth of the second child. David and Laura had always been close to the grandchildren and involved in their care. After their son's death, his girlfriend returned to assume responsibility for the girls. In her grief and anger, the girlfriend claimed the paternal grandparents had no legal right to visit the girls and refused to allow contact. She later married, and her new husband felt even more strongly that Laura and David should not be allowed to visit the girls. The grandparents took their case to court, but the court ruled in favor of the mother.

as to increased risk of health problems and placement in a long-term care facility. (Federal Interagency Forum, 2008).

Although time with friends may decline, the majority of older adults have at least one close friend with whom they are interact frequently, and to whom they can turn in emergencies. Even older adults who have kin may nevertheless turn first to friends and neighbors for assistance, partially because friendship involves voluntary and reciprocal exchanges between equals (Barker, 2002; Davidson, 2006). The average friendship network is from 5 to 10 persons, which typically declines after age 85 when the need for assistance with personal care increases (Kalmijn, 2003; Litwin, 2003). Older adults who refuse to leave their own communities to live with or near adult children may recognize the importance of friends as essential to their well-being. On the other hand, many older people steadily make new friends, including younger adults, and relationships generally get closer with age, particularly among women. Some friendship networks may even expand and become more fluid in old age, such as when an elder moves to a retirement community or becomes more engaged in civic activities. Baby boomers' friendship networks are likely to be more diverse than those of past cohorts of elders because of greater cross-race and cross-gender relationships in young and middle adulthood (Blieszner, 2006).

According to socioemotional selectivity theory, individuals over the life course are surrounded by an informal social network of family, friends, and neighbors. With age and awareness that time is limited, they may choose deliberately to narrow their social networks to devote more time and energy to fewer relationships with people they care about most (Ajrouch, Blandon, & Antonucci, 2005; Blieszner, 2006). Such selective engagement, which is captured in the theory of gerotranscendence described in Chapter 8, is not the same as disengagement from social relationships. Instead, older adults may prefer to derive emotional comfort and meaning from familiar or intimate social interactions—or even from solitude—rather than expending the effort required to create and maintain a wide network of acquaintances that may offer less meaning to their lives. Careful selection of social network members can be viewed as an indicator of resilience, because it determines the degree to which elders have access to social resources that can satisfy their socioemotional needs. Which informal networks become involved appears to vary with the type of task to be performed, as well as the helper's characteristics, such as proximity, extent of long-term commitment, and degree of interaction. Friends and neighbors are well suited for providing emotional support (e.g., stopping by to chat) and to assist spontaneously and occasionally (e.g., "checking in," providing transportation, and running errands), while families are best equipped for long-term personal care. Even friends facing chronic health problems may still be able to assist others, such as by listening and offering advice and emotional support. Among populations of color, friends often link older persons to needed community services. In fact, African American peers are more likely than whites to give and receive both instrumental and emotional support, often through the church (Barker, 2002; Nocon & Pearson, 2000; Porter, Ganong, & Armer, 2000).

FRIENDSHIPS AMONG OLDER WOMEN

Five women had gone to high school together, married their high school sweethearts, and remained in the same Midwestern town raising their children, volunteering, and working part-time. They met occasionally to play bridge, helped watch each other's children, and shared in the joys and sadness of family life. Within an 8-year time period, all became widows. They began to meet more often than when their husbands were alive—joining each other for meals, shopping trips, and bridge. When one of the women, Marge, suffered a stroke, the other four became her primary caregivers—bringing her food, accompanying her to the doctor, visiting with her daily, and helping to clean her home. This friendship network greatly relieved the caregiving burden for Marge's daughter.

Friends are critical for intimacy and the sharing of confidences, especially when compared to relatives other than marital partners, and after major role transitions such as widowhood or retirement. For example, an older widow generally prefers help from confidants because relatives may reinforce her loss of identity as "wife," may be overly protective, or alternatively may minimize her loss. To the extent that friendships are reciprocal and satisfy social and instrumental needs, they can compensate for the absence of a partner and help mitigate loneliness (Stevens et al., 2006).

The role of friend can be maintained long after that of worker, organization member, or partner is lost. The extent of reciprocity, intimacy, and quality rather than quantity of interactions appears to be the critical factors in maintaining friendship networks. Friendship quality may be related to psychological well-being and happiness (Adams, Blieszner, & de Vries, 2000; Hogan, Linden, & Najarian, 2002; Shaw, Krause, Liang, & Bennett, 2007). In one study, depressive symptomatology was highest for elders without friend networks; and the absence of family in the context of friends was found to be less detrimental for mental health than the absence of friends in the context of family (Fiori, Antonucci, & Cortina, 2006). Given the centrality of friendships to well-being, professionals need to encourage older adults to sustain such relationships or assist them with building new ones.

Gender differences in informal supports are more pronounced than life-course variations, with men showing greater declines than women in the number of new friends, their desire for close friendships, the intimate nature of friendships, and involvement in activities beyond the family (Blieszner, 2006). Women generally have more emotionally intimate, diverse, and intensive friendships than men. For many men, their wives are their only confidants, a circumstance that may make widowhood or divorce devastating for them. In contrast, women tend to satisfy their needs for intimacy throughout their lives by establishing close friendships with other women and therefore are less emotionally dependent on the marital relationship. When faced with widowhood, divorce, or separation, they often turn to these friends. The resilience of some older women, in fact, may be rooted in their ability to form close reciprocal friendships (Moen, Erickson, & Dempster-McClain, 2000; Stevens et al., 2006).

Both men and women tend to select friends from among their social peers—those who are similar in age, sex, marital status, sexual orientation, and social class. Most choose age peers as their friends, even though common sense would suggest that cross-generational friendship networks could reduce their vulnerability to losses as they age. Age homogeneity plays a strong role in facilitating friendships in later life, in part because of shared life transitions, reduced cross-generational ties with children and work associates, and possible parity of exchange. Although friends are vital resources, their helping efforts usually do not approach those of family members in duration or intensity, and do not fully compensate for the loss of a partner or children, especially for low-income elders with chronic illnesses. Friendships can also be characterized by negative interactions, such as unwanted advice or assistance, or by responses that minimize the challenges facing elders, and may become strained by excessive demands for assistance (Hogan et al., 2002; Litwin, 2003).

Interventions to Strengthen or Build Social Supports

Because of the importance of peer-group interactions for well-being, initiatives exist to strengthen existing social ties or to create new ones. Consistent with the person–environment model, such interventions can promote a more supportive environment for elders. They can be categorized as personal network building, volunteer linking, mutual help networks, and neighborhood and community development. Despite extensive literature on the benefits of social supports, empirical evidence is limited about how—and how well—social support interventions work (Hogan et al., 2002).

Personal network building aims to strengthen existing ties, often through **natural helpers**—nonfamily members to turn to because of their concern, interest, and understanding. Such natural helpers provide emotional support, assist with problem solving, offer concrete services, and act as advocates. Neighbors often perform natural helping roles, and may strengthen these activities through organized block programs and block watches (Subramanian et al., 2006). Even people in service positions, often referred to as **gatekeepers**, can fulfill natural helping functions because of the visibility of their positions and the regularity of their interactions with elders. For example, postal alert systems, whereby postal carriers observe whether an older person is taking in the mail each day, build on routine everyday interactions. Pharmacists, ministers, bus drivers, local merchants, hair stylists, and housing managers are frequently in situations to provide companionship, advice, and referrals. In high-crime areas, local businesses, bars, and restaurants may have a "safe house" decal in their windows, indicating where residents of all ages can go in times of danger or medical emergencies. These and other community-based supports are further described in Chapter 11.

Religious or faith-based institutions may also serve to strengthen and build personal networks, in some cases creating a surrogate family for older people. Members of religious institutions can help with transportation, friendly visiting, housework, home repair, and meal preparation, as well as offer psychological support. At the same time, older members may take on leadership and teaching roles within the church, synagogue, or mosque, thereby enhancing their sense of belonging and self-worth. In many private and public programs, volunteers are commonly used to develop new networks or expand existing ones for older persons. For example, older volunteers deliver meals, offer peer counseling, information, and assistance, and serve as friendly visitors to

INFORMATION TECHNOLOGY AND COMMUNITY BUILDING

When the public library in a small Massachusetts town began to offer computer training, they expected the classes to be filled with teenagers and young adults. Instead, the classes were filled with adults over age 55, eager to learn how to e-mail their friends and families around the country and to use the Internet to search for health information and facts about their town's history.

other older adults. The value of voluntarism and social support is discussed fully in Chapter 12.

By providing access to online support groups, blogs and social networking sites, referral links and informational support, and e-mail, the Internet offers new opportunities for network building with peers and across generations for those with access to such information technology (Segrist, 2004; Willis, 2006). Over 72 percent of adults ages 50 to 64 use the Internet, a percentage that is likely to grow and that suggests more Internet users among the oldest-old in the future (Pew Trust, 2009). A growing number of websites targeted to older adults—with music, news clips or information on career changes, leisure opportunities and caregiving—aim to build virtual community connections and exchange information,

OLDER ADULTS AND THE INTERNET

A 78-year-old British man was the first older adult to upload a video on YouTube in August 2006. His first video begins with the streaming text "geriatric gripes and grumbles," but he does not fit that stereotype. Not only is he enthusiastically embracing this medium typically used by 20-somethings, he is an avid blues and motorcycle enthusiast. His first five YouTube videos received more than 154,000 hits in less than two weeks, and he received about 4,000 messages via YouTube in a single morning. He represents the new reality, where baby boomers use the Internet for entertainment, shopping, and communication.

which may reduce social isolation. Chat rooms or discussion boards are modeled upon community members' interests. People may be drawn to such virtual communities as a way to readily connect with others in the anonymity of their home or office. Creating an electronic community, however, is obviously limited to older people who can access computers and the Internet. "Computer support" holds promise for elders with debilitating illnesses that present physical barriers to attending support groups, for rural and other isolated populations, and for those who desire anonymity (Czaja et al., 2006).

As described in Chapter 5, some studies suggest that computer and Internet use can improve cognitive functioning and promote active aging, as evidenced by the growing number of "brain games" designed specifically for older adults (Charness & Holley, 2004; Miller, 2009; Yange et al., 2006). Other studies have found that using computers and the Internet neither positively nor negatively influences everyday functioning, well-being and mood, or social networks (Slegers, van Bostel, & Jolles, 2008).

Another approach creates or promotes the supportive capacities of mutual help networks through joint problem solving and the reciprocal exchange of resources. Mutual assistance may occur spontaneously as neighbors watch out for each other, or it may be facilitated by professionals. Networks may also be formed on the basis of neighborhood ties or around shared problems, such as widow-to-widow programs and support groups for family caregivers. Interacting with peers who share experiences may reduce elders' loneliness and expand problem-solving capacities, but may also inadvertently increase stress when groups lack a professional facilitator and participants share primarily negative or widely varying experiences. Support that does not meet the recipients' needs or is perceived as critical or dismissive of problems can inadvertently magnify negative effects. Self-help groups tend to be most effective for diseases considered stigmatizing (e.g., substance use mental illness, HIV/AIDS). Overall, the kind of support, who provides it, and contextual

issues all play roles in determining whether support interventions are perceived as beneficial (Davison et al., 2000; Hogan et al., 2002).

Increasingly, boomers are creating their own communities and support systems, sometimes called Circles of Caring, to meet their emotional, spiritual, and physical needs as they age. A group called Fiercely Independent Seniors in a rural area of Washington State meets weekly; members reciprocate by assisting each other with tasks like writing advance directives and regularly checking up on each other. It is not surprising that the cohort who engaged in consciousness-raising during the 1960s is fostering movements identified as "conscious aging," "proactive aging," or "aging on your own terms." Such an approach is consistent with research findings that both the recipients of peer support and those who provide it benefit (King, 2006; Trenshaw, 2004). Neighborhood and community building is another approach to strengthening a community's self-help and problem-solving capabilities and may involve advocacy through lobbying and legislative activities. Such initiatives aim to build upon the strengths and resources of local communities, including communities of color, and many include an intergenerational component. The Tenderloin Project, which has existed for over 30 years in a low-income area of single-room occupancy units in San Francisco, is a model of neighborhood development. Nearby residents worked cross-generationally on the immediate problem of crime and victimization of older people and then dealt with community-wide issues such as nutrition, child care, and prostitution. In the process, social networks were strengthened and weekly support groups formed. Neighborhood-based intergenerational helping networks connect the formal service system to provide personal care services to frail elders. Similarly, social supports can buffer the effects of neighborhood stressors, such as crime or traffic congestion on elders (Schieman & Meersman, 2004). Targeted senior center activities can also promote community-based support and advocacy that extends outside the center (Kehow & Farney, 2006).

Intergenerational Programming

Intergenerational programs linking older people with schoolchildren, high-risk youth, children with special needs, and young families are a rapidly growing type of mutual help. This can also be extended to address cross-generational neighborhood and community problems such as safety and the environment, with environmentalism increasingly conceptualized as an aging issue (Moody, 2008). The most common type of intergenerational programming involves older adults serving children and youth. For example, after-school telephone support, pen pal projects, tutoring, and assistance at day care programs are provided through Retired Senior Volunteer Programs (RSVP). The Foster Grandparents Program offers tutoring and mentoring, generally to low-income youth. The Computer Pals Program fosters e-mail partnerships between youth and elders, with adolescents often teaching computer skills to older adults. Big Brothers and Big Sisters now pairs older adults (the "Bigs") as mentors with youth. Some programs involve elders and youth in social action projects, such as Caring Communities, that seek to improve society through environmental activism, gardening, music, and art. Older adults can also assist young families with parenting skills, literacy training, social support, and job hunting and create supportive communities for foster and adoptive families and other families with high-risk children. Residential facilities for high-risk youth sometimes involve older adults as mentors and "surrogate" grandparents. Adolescents, even those who are marginalized, can in turn assist older neighbors with yard work, home maintenance, and friendly visiting (Butts & Lent, 2009; Eheart, Power, & Hoping, 2003).

Sharing physical space can also encourage intergenerational contact, such as child care programs housed in skilled nursing homes or assisted living facilities, or offering senior center activities within public schools. In such instances, however, it is essential to respect the needs of

Tutoring young children benefits both the older tutor and the young child.

both elders and children; for example, some older adults in long-term care facilities may not want to interact daily with children and may resent an environment that is too child-centered. Careful planning is necessary to ensure that interactions are age and developmentally appropriate and allow elders to have choice and autonomy (Hayes, 2003; Salari, 2002). One program that took account of these factors implemented Montessori-based activities for both children and adults with dementia in an adult day care setting, which had positive outcomes for both age groups (Camp et al., 2005). Both young and old generations may benefit from training on how to interact successfully; for example, young children are more spontaneous and comfortable with elders with disabilities, while teenagers may need some tips on ways to interact with a person in a wheelchair. Successful programs are characterized by reciprocal benefits for both young and old, and understanding of human development and differences in communication styles. They typically enhance the self-esteem and social engagement of both young and old and may in some instances foster empathy and positive attitudes toward aging (Lewis, 2006). Older participants in some intergenerational programs have experienced health benefits as well as increased social interaction (Butts & Lent, 2009). This is the case in an intergenerational school in a center serving older adults, where elders serve as reading mentors and computer pals in the classroom, and students volunteer in affiliated nursing homes—each generation valuing their shared educational experiences (Whitehouse, Fallcreek, & Whitehouse, 2005).

Increasingly, intergenerational community-based programs bring long-term older residents into planned activities with their new immigrant neighbors where they can discover commonalities despite cultural and often language differences (Brown, 2007). Some programs and cities, making intergenerational interaction a public policy goal, are seeking to transform communities in a way that explicitly promotes cross-age interactions and systems responsive to all their residents across the life course (Butts & Lent, 2009; Henkin, Holmes, Walter, Greenberg, & Schwartz, 2005).

Consistent with the broad concept of productivity discussed in Chapter 12, intergenerational programs are likely to grow in the future as a way to match elders' resources with the needs of younger generations. This is also congruent with President Obama's emphasis on community service by all age groups and his expansion of Americorps and Peace Corps for Seniors. Practitioners in schools, senior centers, long-term care facilities, and other community-based settings can play pivotal roles in fostering cross-generational interactions that benefit young and old. On the other hand, because public funding tends to be based on age, ongoing fiscal support for intergenerational projects is limited, and many depend on volunteers to sustain the program. Nearly everyone will agree that intergenerational programs are a good idea, but neither the government nor private funders in the past have provided adequate support. The Association of Gerontology in Higher Education, Generations United, and Generations Together are national groups that promote intergenerational policy and practice.

Relationships with Pets

Many older adults talk to and confide in their pets, and believe that animals are sensitive to their moods and feelings. Having a pet to feed, groom, or walk can provide structure, a sense of purpose, and an anchor on days that might otherwise lack meaning—and may even serve to reduce depression. Wives caring for husbands with dementia note increased feelings of attachment with their dogs, but pets may also be a burden for such caregivers (Connell, Janevic, Solway, & McLaughlin, 2007). With their unconditional love, pets may compensate for lack of family members in the home. In some studies, pet owners score higher than their peers without pets on measures of happiness, self-confidence, morale, self-care, alertness, responsiveness, dependability, and sense of control (Johnson et al., 2003; LeRoux & Kemp, 2009; Watt & Pachana, 2007). Owning a pet in itself does not appear to reduce loneliness, however. Other factors such as moderate religious participation and interactions with other people may

AN INTERGENERATIONAL GRAN PAL PROJECT

A second-grade public school teacher involves his class in regularly visiting with their "Gran Pals" in a nearby skilled nursing care facility. In preparation for their visits, he first has them participate in a simulation of what it feels like to be "old and frail" by wearing glasses with Vaseline on the lens, being pushed in a wheelchair, wearing gloves while opening a bottle, learning to speak clearly and directly to someone while wearing earplugs, and so on. Such simulations are frequently created for undergraduate students, but this program involves 6- and 7-year-olds, who then write and talk about what they experience when their usual activities are restricted. Each visit to the skilled care facility begins with the teacher talking with the children about what they might experience, and this is then followed by the children writing and discussing what they learned. The teacher is motivated not only by the social benefits for the older residents, but also by the recognition that by the time his second graders enter the job market, 20 percent of the population will be older adults.

be more salient (Nunnelee, 2007). Similarly, some benefits may be partially explained by the fact that pet owners are more likely to be younger, physically active, and married or living with someone. On the other hand, one of the few longitudinal studies on the benefits of pet ownership found that people who continuously owned a pet were healthier than those who had never had one or who had ceased owning a pet (Headey & Grabka, 2007). The mobility benefits from walking a dog and preventing further health deterioration are also identified (Giles-Corti, Knuiman, & Burke, 2007; Thorpe et al., 2006).

The perceived benefits of pets has led to an increase in pet-facilitated programs for older adults in long-term care settings, as well as loan-a-pet or pet day care programs for elders in their own homes. A study of pets in skilled nursing facilities identified significant benefits, particularly in terms of reduced depressive symptoms and improved perceptions of quality of life. Pet visitation with nursing home residents is found to improve health, self-concept, life satisfaction, and mental functioning (Columbo et al., 2006; Ross & Kemp, 2009). Some residential care facilities, particularly those using the Eden Alternative (described in Chapter 11), create a more homelike setting by having pets (Coleman et al., 2002). Facilities that have concerns about pet maintenance are using robotic pets that also have benefits in terms of well-being (Kramer, Friedmann & Bernstein, 2009). However, a pet—real or robotic—should not be viewed as a substitute for human relationships; in fact, some cases of self-neglect involve homes filled with pets but lacking food, hygiene, and other social interaction for the elder. Nevertheless, pet ownership can enhance well-being and enrich elders' quality of life. In recognition of these benefits, the National Institute of Health's definition of complementary/alternative medicine (CAM) includes human-animal interaction as pet ownership, animal-assisted activity (e.g., pet visitation), or animal-assisted

therapy (structured sessions with treatment goals) (Johnson et al., 2003).

Given the apparent benefits of this relationship, the loss of a pet can result in intense grief, especially when this grief is minimized by others suggesting to the bereaved pet owner that "it was just a cat" (Doka, 2001; Johnson et al., 2003). Hurricane Katrina survivors who had to hurriedly flee their homes grieved the loss of pets left behind, with negative effects on their mental well-being (Campbell, 2007). Pet ownership for elders, however, can require constant attention as well as expenses of food, veterinary care, and training. The global economic downturn has resulted in some pet owners giving up their pets because they can no longer afford to care for them In some instances, temporary visits by a pet may still have therapeutic benefits, but without the costs. More longitudinal studies of the benefits of pet ownership and its effects on loneliness are critical (Banks & Banks, 2002; Saito et al., 2001). Differentiating pet ownership from occasional interactions with a pet in long-term care settings is also important in future research and practice interventions with pets and elders. More research is also needed on differences in pet ownership patterns, attachment to pets, health beliefs, and health practices to determine the relevance of animal-assisted techniques with culturally diverse elders (Johnson & Meadows, 2002).

Implications for the Future

Increases in life expectancy and declining family size will continue to produce more diverse and complex family structures. The vertical, or "beanpole," family structure will grow—that is, an increasing number of living generations in a family, accompanied by decreasing numbers of family members within the same generation due to declining fertility rates. These trends, combined with growth in the number of unmarried persons and childless partners, will mean that future cohorts of adult children will have a greater number of aging parents and grandparents to care for, but fewer siblings to assist them. Top-heavy kin networks will raise caregiving challenges for both families and society, along with questions of intergenerational equity and reciprocity.

Delayed childbearing and smaller family size will also result in greater age differences between each generation and the blurring of demarcations between generations, especially among Caucasian families. Active involvement in the daily demands of raising children will be fully completed by the time women are grandmothers, although some grandmothers will then become primary caregivers of grandchildren. More women will simultaneously be both grandmothers and granddaughters. But baby boomers will have, on average, fewer grandchildren than the prior cohort who gave birth to the baby boomers. Growing proportions of parents, children, grandchildren, and even great-grandchildren will share such critical adulthood experiences as school, work, parenthood, retirement, and widowhood. On the other hand, generational differences of 30 years, along with geographic mobility, may contribute to difficulties in building affective bonds across multiple generations due to dissimilar values or lifestyles. The increasing divorce rate may mean that multiple generations will invest time in building reconstituted or blended families, which later may be dissolved. How these changes translate into new forms of family structure in the future remains unclear, because the extent to which acculturation and economic conditions will modify more traditional family arrangements is unknown. For both Caucasians and families of color, life-course variations will grow as longer-lived men and women move in and out of various relationships, including cohabitation, divorce and remarriage, and same-sex relationships; caregiving arrangements; living and employment situations; and communities.

All of these changes highlight the need for gerontological practitioners in a wide range of settings to gain skills in assessing and intervening with families, not only with the older person. Providers need to be sensitive to the wide variation of family forms, including grandparents as caregivers, LGBT partners, mothers who have delayed childbearing and are simultaneously caring for a toddler, and widowed, divorced, childless, or never-married older adults with extensive friendship networks, and elders of color with fictive kin networks. Patterns of social ties, particularly friends and neighbors, will become more diverse and remain vital sources of support.

Health and human service providers in schools, community clinics, public child welfare systems, hospitals, and mental health centers—regardless of their area of expertise—will increasingly encounter multigenerational families. This trend suggests the need for all such professionals to have basic knowledge and skills in working effectively with older adults and their increasingly complex families. In times of shrinking resources, professional creativity regarding intergenerational and multigenerational programs is needed to build on the resources and contributions of multiple generations to address social problems. Such collaborations are ways for both younger and older adults to engage in meaningful roles, such as cross-generational environmental activism. In addition, service systems may shift from categorical, age-based services to ones that meet human needs across the life course. For example, the Lifespan Respite Bill passed by Congress in 2006 and programs such as the National Family Caregiver Support Program and the federal Family and Medical Leave Act address caregiving demands across the life course, not just for a particular age group. Given the dramatic growth in multigenerational families and the complexity of family forms, professionals will be challenged to think outside traditional age-based silos and models of service delivery and develop new ways to utilize older adults as a civic resource.

Summary

The importance of informal social support networks for older people's physical and mental well-being is widely documented. Contrary to stereotypes, very few older people are socially isolated. The majority have family members with whom they are in regular contact, although they are unlikely to live with them. Their families serve as critical sources of support, especially when older members become impaired by chronic illness. The marital relationship is most important, with more than half of all persons age 65 and over married and living with a partner. Most older couples are satisfied with their marriages, which influences their life satisfaction generally. Older couples freed from childrearing demands, have more opportunities to pursue new roles and types of relationships.

Less is known about sibling, grandparent, and other types of family interactions in old age, although the importance of their support is likely to increase in the future. Also, comparatively little research has been conducted on LGBT relationships in old age and on never-married older persons who may rely primarily on friendship networks to cope. Siblings can be crucial in providing emotional support, physical care, and a home. Interaction with secondary kin depends on geographic proximity and whether more immediate family members are available.

Contrary to the myth that adult children are alienated from their parents, the majority of older persons are in frequent contact with their children, either face-to-face or by phone. Filial relationships are characterized by patterns of reciprocal aid throughout the life course, until the older generation becomes physically or mentally disabled. At that point, adult children—generally women—are faced with providing financial, emotional, and physical assistance to older relatives, oftentimes with little support from others for their caregiving responsibilities. In low-income families and families of color, older relatives are most likely to receive daily help from younger relatives and to be involved in caring for grandchildren.

Most families, regardless of social class, race, ethnicity, or sexual orientation, attempt to provide care for their older members, and use long-term care facilities only when they have exhausted other resources. Such caregiving responsibilities are affected by a number of social trends, most notable among them the increasing percentage of middle-aged women who are more likely to be employed and the number of reconstituted families resulting from divorce and remarriage. The needs of caregivers are clearly a growing concern for social and health care providers and policy makers, and are discussed in Chapter 10.

With the growth of three- and four-generation families, more older persons are experiencing the status of grandparenthood and great-grandparenthood. Most grandparents are in relatively frequent contact with their grandchildren, and derive considerable satisfaction from the grandparent role. The demands of grandparenthood are changing, however, as a result of divorce and remarriage. Perhaps the most dramatic shift in the past decade has been the increase in the number of grandparents who are the primary or custodial caregivers to young grandchildren because their adult children are unable or unwilling to provide care.

For many older persons, friends and neighbors can be even more helpful than family members in maintaining morale and quality of life. Generally, women interact more with friends than do men. In recognition of the importance of informal networks to physical and mental well-being, mutual support, neighborhood and community-based interventions have been designed to strengthen friendship and neighborhood ties. In recent years, many of these programs have attempted to foster intergenerational contacts. In sum, the majority of older persons continue to play a variety of social roles—partner, parent, grandparent, friend, and neighbor—and to derive feelings of satisfaction and self-worth from these interactions.

GLOSSARY

blended families families whose memberships comprise blood and non-blood relationships through divorce or remarriage

custodial grandparents grandparents who have legal custody of their grandchildren when adult children are unable to provide adequate care

empty nest normative for middle-aged parents when adult children leave home for college or employment

formal kinship care placement of children with relatives by the state child foster care

gatekeepers people in formal (e.g., physicians, nurses) or informal (e.g., friends and neighbors) service roles who regularly interact with older adults and can watch for signs indicating a need for assistance

grandparents' rights legal rights of grandparents to interact with grandchildren following divorce of the grandchildren's parents; liabilities of grandparent and stepgrandparents as custodians of grandchildren in the absence of responsible parents

informal kinship care relatives, especially grandparents, provide care without any formal child welfare involvement or benefits

intergenerational programs services that facilitate the interaction of people across generations; typically young and old

intergenerational stake hypothesis pattern whereby the older generation tends to be more invested in future generations around transmission of values and resources

intimacy at a distance strong emotional ties among family members even though they do not live near each other

multigenerational family a family with three or more generations alive at the same time; considers the needs of middle generation, not just young and old

natural helpers people who assist others because of their concern, interest, and innate understanding

nontraditional families new family structures derived through gay and lesbian partnerships, cohabitation, informal adoption, etc.

reciprocal exchange sharing resources and assistance among individuals

skipped-generation household where the parent generation is absent

social convoy model close social relationships that surround an individual and can provide a protective, secure base, but personal and situational characteristics influence the type and extent of support needed

social integration encompasses both social networks and support; degree to which a person is involved with others in the larger social structure and community

social networks the interrelationships and interactions among individuals that affect the flow of resources and support

social support informational, emotional, or instrumental (e.g., help with tasks of daily living) assistance from social networks

RESOURCES

Log on to MySocKit at (www.mysockit.com) for information about the following:

- AARP Grandparent Information Center
- Association for Gerontology in Higher Education (AGHE)
- Child Welfare League of America
- Foster Grandparents
- Foundation for Grandparenting
- Gatekeeper Program
- Generations Together, University of Pittsburgh
- Generations United
- National Center on Grandparents and other Relatives Raising Grandchildren
- National Center for Resource Family Support, the Casey Family Program
- National Coalition of Grandparents (NCOG)
- National Center for Grandparents Children's Rights

REFERENCES

Adams, R. G., Blieszner, R., & de Vries, B. (2000). Definitions of friendship in the third age: Age, gender, and study location effects. *Journal of Aging Studies, 14,* 117–133.

Administration on Aging (AOA). (2008). *Profile of Older Americans.* Washington, DC.

Ajrouch, K. J., Blandon, A. Y. & Antonucci, T. C. (2005). Social networks among men and women: The effects of age and socioeconomic status. *Journals of Gerontology: Social Sciences,* 6-. 311–317.

American Association of Retired Persons (AARP). (2003). *AARP's Singles Survey.* Washington, DC: Author.

American Community Survey. (2007). *The Marriage Measures Guide of State-Level Statistics.* Retrieved November 2009, from http://aspa.hhs.gov/hsp/07/marriagemeasures .html

Antonucci, T., Birditt, K. & Akiyama, H., (2009). Convoys of social relations: An interdisciplinary approach. In V. B. Bengtson, D. Gans, N. M. Putney & M. Silverstein (Eds.). *Handbook of theories of aging* (2nd ed). New York: Springer.

Antonucci, T. C., Sherman, A. M., & Akimaya, H. (1996). Social networks, support, and integration. In J. E. Birren (Ed.). *Encyclopedia of gerontology* (Vol. 2). New York: Academic Press.

Badgett, M. V. L. (2007). *Unequal taxes on equal benefits: The taxation of domestic partner benefits.* Center for American Progress. Retrieved March 2009, from http:// americanprogress.org/issues/2007/12/ pdf/domestic_partners.pdf

Bair, D. (2007). *Calling it quits: Late-life divorce and starting over.* New York: Random House.

Baird, A. (2003). Through my eyes: Service needs of grandparents who raise their grandchildren from the perspective of a custodial grandmother. In B. Hayslip & J. Patrick (Eds.). *Working with custodial grandparents.* New York: Springer.

Baker, L. A. & Silverstein, M. (2008). Preventive health behaviors among grandmothers raising grandchildren. *Journal of Gerontolooy: Social Sciences, 63B,* S304-S311.

Banks, M. R. & Banks, W. A. (2002). The effects of animal-assisted therapy on loneliness in an elderly population in long-term care facilities. *Journal of Gerontology: Medicine, 57A,* M428–M432.

Barker, J. (2002). Neighbors, friends and other non-kin caregivers of community-living dependent elders. *Journal of Gerontology: Social Sciences, 57B,* S158–S167.

Barker, J. (2004). Lesbian aging: An agenda for social research. In G. Herdt & B. de Vries (Eds.). *Lesbian and gay aging: Research and future directions.* New York: Springer.

Barrett, A. E. & Lynch, S. M. (1999). Caregiving networks of elderly persons: Variation by marital status. *The Gerontologist,* 695–704.

Bengtson, V. C. (2001). Beyond the nuclear family: The increasing importance of multigenerational bonds. *Journal of Marriage and the Family, 63,* 1–16.

Bengtson, V. C. & Putney, N. M. (2006). Future "conflicts" across generations and cohorts. In J. Vincent, C. Phillipson, & M. Downs (Eds.). *The futures of old age.* London: Sage.

Bennett, L. & Gates, G. (2004). *The cost of marriage inequality to gay, lesbian and bisexual seniors.* Washington, DC: Human Rights Campaign.

Berkman, B. & Harootyan, L. (2002). *Social work and health care in an aging society: Education, policy, practice and research.* New York: Springer.

Berkman, L. F. (2000). Social support, social networks, social cohesion, and health. *Social Work and Health Care, 31,* 3–14.

Beyene, Y., Becker, G., & Mayen, N. (2002). Perception of aging and sense of well-being among Latino elderly. *Journal of Cross-Cultural Gerontology, 17,* 155–172.

Blando, J. A. (2001). Twice hidden: Older gay and lesbian couples, friends and intimacy. *Generations, 25,* 87–89.

Blazer, D. (2006). *How do you feel about …?* Self perceptions of health and health outcomes in late life. Kleemeier Award lecture delivered at Annual Meeting of the Gerontological Society of America, Dallas, Texas.

Blieszner, R. A (2006). lifetime of caring: Dimensions and dynamics in late-life close relationships. *Personal Relationships, 13,* 1–18.

Bogard, R. & Spilka, B. (1996). Self-disclosure and marital satisfaction in mid-life and late-life remarriages. *International Journal of Aging and Human Development, 42,* 161–172.

Bookwala, J. (2005). The role of marital quality in physical health during the mature years, *Journal of Aging and Health, 17,* 85–104.

Bookwala, J. & Franks, M. M. (2005). The moderating of marital quality in older adults' depressed affect: Beyond the 'main effects' model. *Journal of Gerontology: Psychological Sciences, 60,* 338–341.

Brown, G. (2007). Susan Langford. In G. Brown (Ed.), *Britain's everyday heroes.* Edinburgh, Mainstream.

Brown, L. B., Alley, G. R., Sarosy, S., Quarto, G., & Cook, T. (2001). Gay men: Aging well. *Journal of Gay and Lesbian Social Services, 13,* 41–54.

Brown, S. L., Bulanda, J. R., & Lee, G. R. (2005). The significance of nonmarital cohabitation: Marital status and mental health benefits among middle-aged and older adults. *Journal of Gerontology: Social Sciences, 60,* S21–S29.

Brown, S. L., Lee, G. R., & Bulanda, J. R. (2006). Cohabitation among older adults: A national portrait. *Journal of Gerontology: Social Sciences, 61,* S71–S79.

Bryson, K. & Casper, L. M. (2007). *Current populations reports.* Washington, DC: U.S. Bureau of the Census. Retrieved April 2007, from http://www.census.gov

Bureau of Labor Statistics. (2006). *The employment situation:* September 2006. Washington, DC: U.S. Department of Labor.

Butler, S. (2006). Older gays, lesbians, bisexuals and transgender persons. In B. Berkman (Ed.). *Handbook of social work in health and aging.* New York: Oxford.

Butts, D. M. & Lent, J. P. (2009). Better together: Generational reciprocity in the real world. In R. Hudson (Ed.). *Boomer Bust? (Vol. 2). The boomers and their future.* Westport, CT: Praeger.

Cahill, S., South, K., & Spade, J. (2000). *Public policy issues affecting gay, lesbian, bisexual and transgender elders.* New York: The Policy Institute of the National Gay and Lesbian Task Force.

Calasanti, T. & Kiecolt, K. J. (2007). Diversity among late-life couples. *Generations, 31,* 10–17.

Calasanti, T. & Slevin, K. (2001). *Gender, Social inequalities and aging.* Walnut Creek, CA: Altima.

Camp, C., Orsulic-Jeras, S., Lee, M., & Judge, K. (2005). Effects of a Montessori-based intergenerational program on engagement and affect for adult day care clients with dementia. In M. Wykle, P. Whitehouse, & D. Morris (Eds.). *Successful aging through the life span: Intergenerational issues in health.* New York: Springer.

Casper, L. M. & Bianchi, S. M. (2002). *Continuity and change in the American family.* Thousand Oaks, CA: Sage.

Charness, N. & Holley, P. (2004). The new media and older adults: Usable and useful? *American Behavioral Scientist, 48,* 416–433.

Cicirelli, V. G. (2009). Sibling death and death fear in relation to depressive symptomatology in older adults. *Journal of Gerontology: Psychological Sciences, 64,* P24–P29.

Clift, E. (2005). Grey divorce on the rise. *Financial Express.*

Clunis, M., Fredriksen-Goldsen, K., Freeman, P. & Nystrom, N. (Eds.). (2005). *Lives of lesbian elders. Looking back, looking forward.* Binghamton, NY: Haworth Press.

Cohen, S. (2004). Social relationships and health. *American Psychologist, 59*, 676–684.

Cohen, S., Gottlieb, B. H., & Underwood, L. G. (2001). Social relationships and health: Challenges for measurement and intervention. *Advanced Mind Body Medicine, 17*, 129–41.

Coleman, M. T., Looney, S., O'Brien, J., Ziegler, C., Pastorino, C. A., & Tumer, C. (2002). The "Eden Alternative." Findings after one year of implementation. *Journal of Gerontology: Medicine, 57A*, M419–M421.

Columbo, G, Buono, M., Smania, K., Raviola, R., & De Leo, D. (2006). Pet therapy and institutionalized elderly: A study on 144 cognitively unimpaired subjects. *Archives of Gerontology and Geriatrics, 42*(2), 207–216.

Connell, C. M., Janevic, M. R., Solway, E., & McLaughlin, S. J. (2007). Are pets a source of support or added burden for married couples facing dementia? *Journal of Applied Gerontology, 26*(5), 472–485.

Connidis, I. A. (2001). *Family ties and aging.* Thousand Oaks, CA: Sage.

Connidis, I. A. (2006). Intimate relationships: Learning from later life experience. In T. Calsanti & K. Slevin (Eds.). *Age matters.* New York: Routledge.

Cook-Daniels, L. (1997). Lesbian, gay male, bisexual and transgendered elders: Elder abuse and neglect issues. *Journal of Elder Abuse and Neglect, 9*, 35–49.

Cook-Daniels, L. (2007). Planning for late life: Transgender people. *Age Concern.* Retrieved November 2009, from http://www.ace.org/uk

Copen, C. & Silverstein, M. (2004). Predictors of grandparent-grandchild closeness after parental divorce. *The Gerontologist, 44*, 91–92.

Cox, C. (2002). Empowering African American custodial grandparents. *Social Work, 47*, 262–267.

Cox, C., Brooks, L. R., & Valcarcel, C. (2000). Culture and caregiving: A study of Latino grandparents. In C. Cox (Ed.). *To grandmother's house we go and stay: Perspectives on custodial grandparents.* New York: Springer.

Cruikshank, M. (2009). *Learning to be old: Gender, culture and aging.* New York: Rowman & Littlefield.

Cuddeback, G. S. (2004). Kinship family foster care: A methodological and substantive synthesis of research. *Children and Youth Services Review, 26*, 623–639.

Cutt, H., Giles-Corti, B., Knuiman, M., & Burke, V. (2007). Dog ownership, health and physical activity: A critical review of the literature. *Health and Place, 63*, 261–272.

Czaja, S., Charness, N., Fisk, A., Hertzog, C., Nair, S., et al. (2006). Factors predicting the use of technology: Findings from the Center for Research and Education on Aging and Technology Enhancement (CREATE). *Psychology and Aging, 21*, 333–352.

Daatland, S. O. (2007). Marital history and intergenerational solidarity: The impact of divorce and unmarried cohabitation. *Journal of Social Issues, 63*, 809–825.

Davey, A. & Szinovacz, M. E. (2004). Dimensions of marital quality and retirement. *Journal of Family Issues, 25*, 431–464.

David, S. & Knight, B. G. (2008). Stress and coping among gay men: Age and ethnic differences. *Psychology and Aging, 23*, 62–69.

Davidson, K. (2006). Flying solo in old age: Widowed and divorced men and women in later life. In J. Vincent, C. Phillipson, & M. Downs (Eds.). *The futures of old age.* London: Sage.

Davidson, K. & Fennell, G. (Eds.) (2004) *Intimacy in Later Life,* New Brunswick, NJ: Transaction Publishers.

Davies, C. & Williams, D. (2002). *Grandparent study.* Washington, DC: American Association of Retired Persons.

Davies, C. & Williams, D. (2002). *Grandparent study.* Washington DC: American Association of Retired Persons.

Davison, K. P., Pennebaker, J. W., & Dickerson, S. W. (2000). Who talks: The social psychology of illness support groups. *American Psychologist, 55,* 205–217.

Davitt, J. (2006). Policy to protect the rights of older adults. In B. Berkman (Ed.). *Handbook of social work in health and aging,* 923–934. New York: Oxford Press.

De Jong Gierveld, J. & Peeters, A. (2003). The interweaving of repartnered older adults' lives with their children and siblings. *Ageing and Society, 23,* 187–205.

Department of Health and Human Services. (2006). *Trends in health and aging.* Washington, DC.

Dilworth-Anderson, P., Williams, I. C., & Gibson, B. E. (2002). Issues of race, ethnicity, and culture in caregiving research: A 20-year review. *The Gerontologist, 42,* 237–272.

Doka, K. J. (2001). *Caregiving and loss: Family needs, professional responses.* Washington, DC: Hospice Foundation of America.

Doodson, L. & Morley, D. (2006). Understanding the roles of non-residential stepmothers. *Journal of Divorce and Remarriage, 45,* 109–130.

Drew, L. & Silverstein, M. (2004). Intergenerational role investments of great-grandparents: Consequences for psychological well-being. *Ageing and Society, 24,* 95–111.

Dubas, J. S. (2001). How gender moderates the grandparent-grandchild relationship. *Journal of Family Issues, 22,* 407.

DuPertuis, L. L., Aldwin, C. M., & Basse, R. (2001). Does the source of support matter for different health outcomes? *Journal of Aging and Health, 13,* 494–510.

Dykstra, P. A. & Wagner, M. (2007). Pathways to childlessness and later-life outcomes. *Journal of Family Issues, 28,* 1487–1517.

Eheart, B. K., Power, M. B., & Hoping, D. E. (2003). Intergenerational programming for foster-adoptive families: Creating community at Hope Meadows. *Intergenerational Relationships, 1,* 17–28.

Ehrenberg, M. & Smith, S. (2003). Grandmother-grandchild contacts before and after an adult daughter's divorce. *Journal of Divorce and Remarriage, 39,* 27.

Elder, G. H. & Conger, R. D. (2000). *Children of the land: Adversity and success in rural America.* Chicago: University of Chicago Press.

Eng, P. M., Rimm, E. B., Fitzmaurice, G., & Kawachi, I. (2002). Social ties and change in social ties in relation to subsequent total and cause-specific mortality and coronary heart disease incidence in men. *American Journal of Epidemiology, 155,* 700–709.

Engstrom, M. (2008). Involving caregiving grandmothers in family interventions when mothers with substance use problems are incarcerated. *Family Process, 47,* 357–371.

Federal Interagency Forum on Aging. (2008). *Older Americans 2008: Key indicators of well-being.* Washington, DC: Federal Interagency Forum on Aging.

Fields, J. & Casper, L. M. (2001). America's families and living arrangements. *Current Population Reports.* Washington, DC: U.S. Census Bureau.

Findlay, R. A. (2003). Interventions to reduce social isolation among older people: Where is the evidence? *Ageing and Society, 23,* 647–658.

Fingerman, K. (2004). The role of offspring and in-laws in grandparents' ties to their grandchildren. *Journal of Family Issues, 25,* 1026–1049.

Fingerman, K. Pitzer, L., Lefkowitz, E.S., Birtditt, K. S., & Mroczek, D. Ambivalent relationship qualities between adults and their parents: Implications for the well-being of both parties. *Journal of Gerontology: Psychological Sciences,* 2008, *63B,* P362–372.

Fiori, K. L., Antonucci, T. C., & Akiyama, H. (2008). Profiles of social relationships among older adults: A cross-cultural approach. *Ageing and Society, 28,* 203–231.

Frisco, M. L. & Williams, K. (2003). Perceived housework equity, marital happiness and divorce in dual-earner households. *Journal of Family Issues, 24,* 51–73.

Fuller-Thompson, E. & Minkler, M. (2001). American grandparents providing extensive child care to their grandchildren: Prevalence and profile. *The Gerontologist, 41,* 201–209.

Gabbay, S. & Wahler, J. (2002). Lesbian aging: Review of a growing literature. *Journal of Gay and Lesbian Social Services, 14,* 1–21.

Ganong, L. & Coleman, M. (2006). Patterns of exchange and intergenerational responsibilities after divorce and remarriage. *Journal of Aging Studies, 20,* 265.

Generations United. (2007). *Defintion of grand-families.* Washington, D.C.: Retrieved May 2009, from http://ipath/gu.org/Grand8101303.asp

Generations United. (2009). *Numbers of multigenerational families on the rise.* Retrieved May 2009, from http://www.pbs.org/americanfamily/gap/multi.html

George, L. K. (2006). Perceived quality of life. In R. Binstock & L. K. George (Eds.). *Handbook of aging and the social sciences.* New York: Academic Press.

Ghazanfareeon Karlsson, S. & Borell, K. (2005). A home of their own: Women's boundary work in LAT relationships. *Journal of Aging Studies, 19,* 73–84.

Giarrusso, R., Silverstein, M., & Feng, D. (2000). Psychological costs and benefits of raising grandchildren: Evidence from a National Survey of Grandparents. In C. B. Cox (Ed.). *To grandmother's house we go and stay: Perspectives on custodial grandparenting.* New York: Springer.

Giarrusso, R., Silverstein, M., Gans, D., & Bengston, V. L. (2006). Aging parents and adult children: New perspectives on intergenerational relationships. In M. Johnson (Ed.). *The Cambridge handbook on age and aging,* Cambridge University Press.

Gierveld, J. D. J., van Grownou, M. B., Hoogendoorn, A. W., & Smit, J. H. (2009). Quality of marriages in later life and emotional and social loneliness. *Journal of Gerontology: Psychological Sciences Social Sciences,* 64B, 497–506.

Goodman, C. (2003). Multigenerational triads in grandparent-headed families. *Journal of Gerontology: Social Sciences, 58B,* S281–S289.

Goodman, C., Potts, M., Pasztor, E., & Scorzo, D. (2004). Grandmothers as kinship caregivers: Private arrangements as compared to public child welfare oversight. *Children and Youth Services Review, 26,* 287–305.

Hagedoorn, M., Van Yperen, N. Q., Coyne, J. C., van Jaarsveld, C. H. M., Ranchor, A. V., van Sonderen, E., et al. (2006). Does marriage protect older people from distress? The role of equity and recency of bereavement. *Psychology and Aging, 21,* 611–20.

Hagestad, G. O. (2003). Interdependent lives and relationships in changing times: A life course view of families and aging. In R. A. Settersten, Jr. (Ed.). *Invitation to the life course: Toward new understandings of later life.* Amityville, NY: Baywood.

Haglund, K. (2000). Parenting a second time around: Ethnography of African American grandmothers parenting grandchildren due to parental cocaine abuse. *Journal of Family Nursing, 6*, 120–135.

Harmon, A. (2008). Granny cam tightens family bonds. *The Seattle Times,* A16.

Harper, S. (2006). The ageing of family life transitions. In J. Vincent, C. Phillipson, & M. Downs (Eds.). *The futures of old age.* London, Sage.

Harwood, J. (2001). Comparing grandchildren's and grandparent's stake in their relationship. *Interna- tional Journal of Aging and Human Develop- ment, 53*, 195–210.

Hayes, C. (2003). An observational study in developing an intergenerational shared site program: Challenges and insights. *Journal of Intergenerational Relations, 1*, 113–132.

Hays, J. C., Gold, D. T., & Peiper, C. F. (1997). Sibling bereavement in late life. *Journal of Death and Dying, 35*, 25–42.

Hayslip, B. & Kaminski, P. (2005). Grandparents raising their grandchildren. In R. K. Caputo (Ed.). *Challenges of aging in U.S. families: Policy and practice implications.* Binghamton, NY: The Haworth Press.

Hayslip, B. & Shore, R. J. (2000). Custodial grandparenting and mental health services. *Journal of Mental Health and Aging, 6*, 367–384.

Headey, B. & Grabka, M. M. (2007). Pets and human health in Germany and Australia: National longitudinal results. *Social Indicators Research, 80*, 297–311.

Healy, T. (2002). Culturally competent practice with elderly lesbians. *Geriatric Care Management Journal, 12*, 9–13.

Heaphy, B. (2007). Sexualities, gender and ageing: Resources and social change. *Current Sociology, 55*, 193–201.

Heaphy, B., Yip, A. K., & Thompson, D. (2004). Ageing in a non-heterosexual context. *Ageing and Society, 24*, 881–902.

Hecht, R. (2004). No straight answers. *AARP The Magazine.* Retrieved November 2006, from www.aarpmagazine.org/people/Articles

Henkin, N. A., Holmes, B., Walter, B. Greenberg, R., & Schwarz, J. (2005). *Communities for all ages: Planning across generations—Intergenerational strategies series.* Baltimore, Annie E. Casey Foundation. Retrieved June 2009, from http://www.aecf.org/upload/publicationfiles/cfaa.pdf

Heuveline, P., Timberlake, J. M., & Furstenberg, Jr., F. F. (2003). Shifting childbearing to single mothers: Results from 17 Western countries. *Population and Development Review, 29*, 47–71.

Hinterlong, J. & Ryan, S. (2008). Creating grander families: Older adults adopting younger kin and nonkin. *The Gerontologist, 48*, 527–536.

Hogan, B., Linden, W., & Najarian, B. (2002). Social support interventions: Do they work? *Clinical Psychology Review, 22*, 381–440.

Holtzman, R. E., Rebok, G. W., Saczynski, J. S., Kouzis, A. C., Doyle, K. W., & Eaton W. W. (2004). Social network characteristics and cognition in middle-aged older adults. *Journal of Gerontology: Psychological Sciences, 59B*, P278–P283.

Hostetler, A. J. (2004). Supportive Housing for LGBT Elders. *Generations, 29*, 64–9.

Hummert, M. L. & Morgan, M. (2001). Negotiating decisions in the aging family. In M. L. Hummert & J. F. Nussbaum (Eds.). *Aging, communication and health*. Mahwah, NJ: Lawrence Erlbaum Associates.

Hughes, M., Waite, L., LaPierre, T. & Luo, Y. (2007). All in the family: The impact of caring for grandchildren on grandparents' health. *Journal of Gerontology: Social Sciences, 62B*, S108–119.

Jackson, N. C., Johnson, M. J., & Roberts, R. (2008). The potential impact of discrimination fears of older gays, lesbians, bisexuals and transgender individuals living in small- to moderate-sized cities on long-term health care. *Journal of Homosexuality, 54*, 325–339.

Jeon, G. S., Jang, S. N., Rhee, S. J., Kawachi, I., & Cho, S. I. (2007). Gender differences in correlates among elder Koreans. *Journal of Gerontology: Social Sciences, 62B*, S323–329.

Johnson, R., Meadows, R., Haubner, J., & Sevedge, K. (2003). Human–animal interaction: A complementary/alternative medical intervention for cancer patients. *American Behavioral Scientist, 47*, 55–69.

Johnson, R. A. & Meadows, R. G. (2002). Older Latinos, pets and health. *Western Journal of Nursing Research, 24*, 609–620.

Joslin, D. (2002). *Invisible caregivers: Older adults raising children in the wake of HIV/AIDS*. New York: Columbia University Press.

Kalmijn, M. (2003). Shared friendship networks and the life course: Analysis of survey data on married and cohabiting couples. *Social Networks, 25*, 232–249.

Kaufman, G. & Taniguchi, H. (2006). Gender and marital happiness in later life. *Journal of Family Issues, 27*, 735–757.

Kawachi, I. & Berkman, L. F. (2001). Social ties and mental health. *Journal of Urban Health: Bulletin of the New York Academy of Medicine, 78*, 458–467.

Kelley, S. J., Whitley, D. M., Sipe, T. A., & Yorker, B. (2000). Psychological distress in grandmother kinship care providers: The role of resources, social support and physical health. *Child Abuse and Neglect, 24*, 311–321.

Kershaw, S. (2009). My sister's keeper. *The New York Times*. Retrieved February 2009, from http://www .nytimes.com

Keyes, C. L. (2002). The exchange of emotional support with age and its relationship with emotional well-being by age. *Journal of Gerontology: Psychological Sciences, 57B*, 518–525.

King, M. (2006). Elderly seek to grow old together, form new support groups. *Seattle Times*, A1, A11.

King, V. (2003). The legacy of a grandparent's divorce: Consequences for ties between grandparents and grandchildren. *Journal of Marriage and the Family, 65*, 170–183.

King, V. & Scott, M. (2005). A comparison of cohabiting relationships among older and younger adults. *Journal of Marriage and the Family, 67*, 271–85.

Kleyman, P. (2006). Families for the 21st century: A multigenerational affair. *Aging Today*, San Francisco: American Society on Aging.

Kolomer, S., McCallion, P., & Janicki, M. (2002). African American grandmother carers of children with disabilities: Predictors of depressive symptoms. *Journal of Gerontological Social Work, 37*, 45–64.

Kramer, S. C., Friedmann, E., & Bernstein, P. L. (2009). Comparison of the effect of human interaction, animal-assisted therapy, and AIBO-assisted therapy on long-term care residents with dementia. *Anthrozoos: A Multidisciplinary Journal of The Interactions of People & Animals, 22*, 43–57.

Krause, N. (2004). Stressors in highly valued roles, meaning in life and the physical health status of older adults. *Journal of Gerontology: Social Sciences, 59B*, S87–S117.

Krause, N. (2006). Social relationships in late life. In R. Binstock & L. George (Eds.). *Handbook of aging and the social sciences* (6th ed.). New York: Academic Press.

Krause, N. & Shaw, B. (2000). Giving social support to others, socioeconomic status and changes in self-esteem in late life. *Journal of Gerontology: Social Sciences, 55B,* S323–S333.

Kreider, R. (2005). Number, timing and duration of marriages and divorces: 2001. *Current Population Reports.* Washington, DC: U.S. Bureau of the Census.

Kropf, N. & Yoon, E. (2006). Grandparents raising grandchildren. Who are they? In B. Berkman (Ed.), *Handbook of social work in health and aging.* New York: Oxford Press.

Kurdek, L. A. (2005). What do we know about gay and lesbian couples? *Current Directions in Psychological Science, 14,* 251.

Lambert, S. (2005). Lesbian and gay families: What we know and where to go from here. *The Family Journal: Counseling and Therapy for Couples and Families, 13,* 43–51.

LeRoux, M. C. & Kemp, R. (2009). Effect of a companion dog on depression and anxiety levels of elderly residents in a long-term care facility. *Psychogeriatrics, 9,* 23–26.

Levitt, H. M., Ovrebo, E., Anderson-Cleveland, M. B., Leone, C., Jeong, J. Y., et al. (2009). Balancing dangers: GLBT experience in a time of anti-GLBT legislation. *Journal of Counseling Psychology, 56,* 67–81.

Lewis, L. (2006). Intergenerational programs that really work. *Caring for the ages,* 1–7. Columbia, MD: American Medical Directors Association.

Liang, J., Krause, N., & Bennett, J. (2001). Is giving better than receiving? *Psychology and Aging, 16,* 511–523.

Lin, I. F. (2008). Consequences of parental divorce for adult children's support of their frail parents. *Journal of Marriage and Family, 70,* 113–128.

Litwin, H. (2003). The association of disability, sociodemographic background, and social network type in later life. *Journal of Aging and Health, 15,* 391–408.

Lu, P. C. (2007). Sibling relationships in adulthood and old age. *Current Sociology, 55,* 621–638.

Lubben, J., Blozik, E., Gillmann, G., Iliffe, S., Kruse, W., Beck, J., et al. (2006). Performance of an abbreviated version of the Lubben Social Network Scale among three European community-dwelling older adult populations. *The Gerontologist, 46,* 505–513.

Lubben, J. E. & Gironda, M. W. (2003a). *Centrality of social ties to the health and well-being of older adults.* New York: Springer.

Lubben, J. E. & Gironda, M. W. (2003b). Measuring social networks and assessing their benefits. In C. Phillipson, G. Allan, & D. Morgan (Eds.), *Social networks and social exclusion.* Hants, England: Ashgate.

Lyyra, T. M. & Heikkinen, R. L. (2006). Perceived social support and mortality in older people. *Journal of Gerontology: Social Sciences, 61B,* S147–S153.

Martinez, I. L. (2003). The elder in the Cuban American family: Making sense of the real and ideal. *Journal of Comparative Family Studies, 33,* 359–370.

McCallion, P. (2006). Older adults as caregivers to persons with developmental disabilities. In B. Berkman (Ed.). *Handbook of social work in health and aging.* New York: Oxford Press.

McFarland, P. L. & Sanders, S. A. (2003). A pilot study about the needs of older gays and lesbians: What social workers need to know. *Journal of Gerontological Social Work, 40,* 67–80.

McLanahan, S., Garfinkel, I., Reichman, N., Teitler, J., Carlson, M., & Audiger, C. N. (2003). *The fragile families and child well-being study: Baseline national report.* Princeton, NJ: Princeton University.

MetLife Mature Market Institute. (2006). *Out and aging: The MetLife study of lesbian and gay baby boomers.* Westport, CT: Metropolitan Life Insurance.

Michael, Y. L., Berkman, L. F., Colditz, G. A., & Kawachi, I. (2001). Living arrangements, social integration, and change in functional health status. *American Journal of Epidemiology, 153,* 2, 123–131.

Miller, L. C. (2009). Brain games put noggin to work. *Star-Bulletin.* Retrieved November 2009, from www.starbulletin.com/features/20090117_brain_games_put_noggin_to_work.htm

Minkler, M., Berrick, J. D., & Needell B. (1999). Impacts of welfare reform on California grandparents raising grandchildren: Reflections from the field. *Journal of Aging and Social Policy, 10,* 45–63.

Moen, P., Erickson, M. A., & Dempster-McClain D. (2000). Social role identities among older adults in a continuing care retirement community. *Research on Aging, 22,* 559–579.

Montenegro, X. P. (2004). *The divorce experience: A study of divorce at midlife and beyond.* Washington, DC: AARP.

Moody, H. R. (2008). Environmentalism as an aging issue. *Public Policy and Aging Report, 18,* 1, 3–7.

Moorman, S. M., Booth, A., & Fingerman, K. L. (2006). Women's romantic relationships after widowhood. *Journal of Family Issues, 27,* 1281–1304.

Moren-Cross, J. & Lin, N. (2006). Social networks and health. In R. Binstock & L. George (Eds.). *Handbook of aging and the social sciences* (6th ed.). New York: Academic Press.

Morrow-Howell, N., Sherraden, M., Hinterlong, J., & Rozario, P. A. (2001). *The productive engagement of older adults: Impact on later-life well-being.* St. Louis: Longer Life Foundation.

Mueller, M. & Elder, G. (2003). Family contingencies across the generations: Grandparent-grandchild relationships in holistic perspective. *Journal of Marriage and Family, 65,* 404–417.

Musil, C. M., Warner, C., Zauszniewski, J., Jeanblanc, A., & Kercher, K. (2006). Grandmothers, caregiving and family functioning. *Journal of Gerontology: Social Sciences, 69B,* 89–98.

Musil, C. M., Youngblut, J., Ahn, S., & Curry, V. (2002). Parenting stress: A comparison of grandmother caretakers and mothers. *Journal of Mental Health and Aging, 8,* 197–210.

Myers, S. A. & Goodboy, A. K. (2006). Perceived sibling use of verbally aggressive messages across the lifespan. *Communication Research Reports, 23,* 1–11.

National Gay and Lesbian Task Force (NGLTF). (2008). *Relationship recognition map for same-sex couples in the United States.* Retrieved March 2009, from http://www.thetaskforce.org/reports_and_research/relationship_recognition

Neugarten, B. (1964). *Personality in middle and late life: Empirical studies* by Bernice L. Neugarten in collaboration with Howard Berkowitz and others. New York: Atherton Press.

Neugarten, B. & Weinstein, K. (1964). The changing American grandparent. *Journal of Marriage and the Family, 26,* 199–204.

Neville, S. & Henrickson, M. (2009). The constitution of 'lavender families:' A LGB perspective. *Journal of Clinical Nursing, 18,* 849–856.

Nocon, A. & Pearson, M. (2000). The roles of friends and neighbors in providing support for older people. *Ageing and Society, 20,* 341–367.

Orel, N. A. (2004). Gay, lesbian and bisexual elders: Expressed needs and concerns across focus groups. *Journal of Gerontological Social Work, 43,* 57–77.

Park, H. O. (2006). The economic well-being of households headed by a grandmother as caregiver. *Social Services Review, 80,* 264–295.

Pearl, A. (2006). Off the beaten track. *Research on Aging, 28,* 749–767.

Pew Trust. (2009). Pew Internet and American Life Study. Adults and Social Network Websites. Retrieved November 2009, from http://www.pewinternet.org/Report?2009/Adults-and-Social-NetworkWebsites.aspx

Pienta, A., Hayward, M. D., & Jenkins, K. R. (2000). Health and marriage in later life. *Journal of Family Issues, 21,* 559–586.

Pillemer K. & Luscher, K. (Eds.). (2004). *Intergenerational ambivalencies: New perspectives of parent-child relations in later life.* Amsterdam, Elsevier.

Porche, M. V. & Purvin, D. M. (2008). 'Never in our lifetime': Legal marriage for same-sex couples in long-term relationships. *Family Relations, 57,* 144–159.

Porter, E. J., Ganong, L. H., & Armer, J. M. (2000). The church, family and kin: An older rural black woman's support network and preferences for care providers. *Qualitative Health Research, 10,* 452–470.

Reitzes, D. C. & Mutran, E. J. (2004a). Grandparent identity, intergenerational identity and well-being. *Journal of Gerontology: Social Sciences, 59B,* S213–S220.

Reitzes, D. C. & Mutran, E. J. (2004b). Grandparenthood: Factors influencing frequency of grandparent-grandchildren contact and grandparent role satisfaction. *Journal of Gerontology: Social Sciences, 59B,* S9–S16.

Rittenour, C. E., Myers, S. M., & Brann M. (2007). Commitment and emotional closeness in the sibling relationship. *Southern Communication Journal, 72,* 169–183.

Roberto, K. A., Allen, K. R., & Blieszner, R. (2001). Grandfathers' perceptions and expectations of relationships with their adult grandchildren. *Journal of Family Issues, 22,* 407–426.

Roberto, K. A. & Stroes, S. J. (1995). Grandchildren and grandparents: Roles, influences, and relationships. In J. Hendricks (Ed.). *The ties of later life.* Amityville, NY: Baywood.

Robles, T. F. & Kiecolt-Glaser, J. K. (2003). The physiology of marriage: Pathways to health. *Physiology and Behavior, 79,* 409–416.

Rosenfeld, D. (2003). *The changing of the guard: Lesbian and gay elders, identity and social change.* Philadelphia, PA: Temple University Press.

Russell, D. & Taylor, J. (2009). Living alone and depressive symptoms: the influence of gender, physical disability, and social support among Hisanic and non-Hisanic older adults. *Journal of Gerontology: Social Sciences,* 95–104.

Rothrauff, T. & Cooney, S. (2008). The role of generativity in psychological well-being: Does it differ for childless adults and parents? *Journal of Adult Development, 15,* 148–159.

Saito, T., Okada, M., Ueji, M., Kikuchi, K., & Kano, K. (2001). Relationship between keeping a companion animal and instrumental activity of daily living: A study of Japanese elderly living at home in Satomi Village. *Nippon Koshu Eisei Zasshi, 48,* 47–55.

Salari, S. M. (2002). Intergenerational partnerships in adult day centers: Importance of age-appropriate environments and behaviors. *The Gerontologist, 42,* 321–333.

Schieman, S. & Meersman, S. (2004). Neighborhood problems and health among older adults: Received and donated social support and the sense of mastery as effect modifiers. *Journal of Gerontology: Social Sciences, 59B,* S89–S97.

Seeman, T. E., Singer, B. H., Ryff, C. D., Love, G. D., & Levy-Storms, L. (2002). Social relationships, gender and allostatic load across two age cohorts. *Psychosomatic Medicine, 64,* 395–406.

Segrist, K. (2004). A computer training program for older adults: Identifying and overcoming barriers to continued computer usage. *Activities, Adaptation and Aging, 28,* 13–26.

Shaw, B. A., Krause, N., Liang, J., & Bennett, J. (2007). Tracking changes in social relations throughout late life. *The Journals of Gerontology: Psychological Sciences and Social Sciences, 62*(2): S90–9.

Sherman, C. W. & Boss, P. (2007). Spousal dementia caregiving in the context of late-life remarriage. *Dementia, 6,* 245–270.

Silverstein, M. & Angelli, J. (1998). Older parents' expectations of moving closer to their children. *Journals of Gerontology, 53B,* S153–S163.

Silverstein, M., Conroy, S. J., Wang, H., Giarrusso, R., & Bengtson, V. (2002). Reciprocity in parent-child relations over the adult life course. *Journal of Gerontology: Social Sciences, 57B,* S3–S13.

Silverstein, M. & Marenco, A. (2001). How Americans enact the grandparent role across the family life course. *Journal of Family Issues, 22,* 493–522.

Simmons, T. & Dye, J. (2003). *Grandparents living with grandchildren: 2000.* Washington, DC: US Census Bureau.

Slegers, K., van Boxtel, M. P., & Jolles, J. (2008). Effects of computer training and internet usage on the well-being and quality of life of older adults: A randomized controlled study. *Journal of Gerontology: Psychological Sciences, 63B,* P176–P185.

Smith, H. & Calvert, J. (2001). *Opening doors: Working with older lesbians and gay men.* London: Aging Concern.

Smith, P. R. (2002). Bisexuality: Reviewing the basics, debunking the stereotypes of professionals in aging. *Outward: Newsletter of LGAIN, 8,* 2, 8.

Soliz, J. & Harwood, J. (2006). Shared family identity, age salience and intergroup contact: Investigation of the grandparent-grandchild relationships. *Commu-nication Monographs, 73,* 87–107.

Stevens, N. L., Camille, M. S., Martina, M. A., & Westerhof, G. J. (2006). Meeting the need to belong: Predicting effects of a friendship enrichment program for older women. *The Gerontologist, 46,* 495–502.

Stitch, S. S. (2002). Stories to keep. *Newsweek,* A3.

Subramanian, S. V., Kubzansky, L., Berkman, L., Fay, M., & Kawachi, I. (2006). Neighborhood effects on the self-rated health of elders: Uncovering the relative importance of structural and service-related neighborhood environments. *Journal of Gerontology: Social Sciences, 61B,* S153–S160.

Swingle, C. (2007). *Aging presents challenges for disabled, providers.* Retrieved September 2008, from http://www.democratandchronicle.com/apps/pbcs.dll/aticle?AID=200808

Temkin-Greener, H., Bajorska, A., Peterson, D. R., Kunitz, S. J., Gross, D., Williams, T. F., et al. (2006). Social support and risk-adjusted mortality in a frail older population. *Medical Care, 42,* 779–788.

Tennstedt, S. (1999). *Family caregiving in an aging society.* Washington DC: Administration on Aging.

Testa, M. F. & Slack, K. S. (2002). The gift of kinship foster care. *Children and Youth Services Review, 24,* 79–108.

Thorpe, R. J., Simonsick, M., Ayonayon, H. Satterfield, S., et al. (2006). Dog walking behavior and maintaining mobility in later life. *Journal of the American Geriatrics Society, 54,* 1419.

Trafford, A. (2006). Power to the grandparents. *Washington Post*, 1.

Trenshaw, C. (2004). *A harvest of years: A PeerSpirit guide for proactive agin g circles.* Langley, WA: PeerSpirit.

Trute, B. (2003). Grandparents of children with developmental disabilities: Intergenerational support and family well-being. *Families in Society, 84,* 119–126.

Uchino, B. N. (2004). *Social support and physical health: Understanding the health consequences of relationships.* New Haven, CT: Yale University Press.

Uhlenberg, P. & Kirby, J. B. (1998). Grandparenthood over time: Historical and demographic trends. In M. E. Szinovacz (Ed.). *Handbook on grandparenthood.* Westport, CT: Greenwood Press.

Umberson, D. & Williams, K. (2005). Marital quality, health and aging: Gender equity? *Journal of Gerontology: Social Sciences, 60B,* 109–113.

Umberson, D., Williams, K., Powers, D. A., Chen, M. D., & Campbell, A. (2005). As good as it gets? A life course perspective on marital quality. *Social Forces, 84,* 493–511.

Umberson, D., Williams, K., Powers, D. A., Liu, H., & Needham, B. (2006). You make me sick: Marital quality and health over the life course. *Journal of Health and Social Behavior, 47,* 1–16.

U.S. Bureau of the Census. (2006). *Median age of the total population: 2005.* Retrieved October 2006, from http://www. factfinder .census.gov

U.S. Bureau of the Census. (2006). *Statistical Abstract of the United States.* Washington, DC: U.S. Government Printing Office.

Van Tilburg, T. (1998). Losing and gaining in old age: Changes in personal network size and social support in a four-year longitudinal study. *Journals of Gerontology, 53B,* S313–S323.

Walker, R. B. & Luszcz, M. A. (2009). The health and relationship dynamics of late-life couples: A systematic review of the literature. *Ageing and Society, 29,* 455–480.

Wallace, G. (2001). Grandparent caregivers: Emerging issues in elder law and social work practice. *Journal of Gerontological Social Work, 34,* 127–134.

Ward, R. A. & Spitze, G. D. (2004). Marital implications of parent-adult child coresidence: A longitudinal view. *Journal of Gerontology: Social Sciences, 59B,* S2–S8.

Watt, D. & Pachana, N. A. (2007). The role of pet ownership and attachment in older adults. Australian *Journal of Rehabilitation Counseling, 13*(1), 32–43.

Weeks, J., Heaphy, B., & Donovan, D. (2001). *Same-sex intimacies: Families of choice and other life experiments.* New York: London Routledge.

Wethington, E., Moen, P., Glasgow, N., & Pillemer, K. (2000). Multiple roles, social integration, and health. In P. Moon, K. Pillemer, E. Wethington, & N. Glasgow (Eds.). *Social integration in the second half of life.* Baltimore: Johns Hopkins University Press.

Whitehouse, C., Fallcreek, S., & Whitehouse, P. (2005). Using a learning environment to promote intergenerational relationships and successful aging. In M. Wykle, P. Whitehouse, & D. Morris (Eds.). *Successful aging through the life span: Intergenerational issues in health.* New York: Springer.

Willis, S. (2006): Technology and learning in current and future generations of elders. *Generations,* 44–48.

Wilmouth, J. M. (2000). Unbalanced social exchanges and living arrangement transitions among older adults. *The Gerontologist, 40,* 64–74.

Wohl, E., Lahner, J., & Jooste, J. (2003). Group process among grandparents raising grandchildren. In B. Hayslip & J. Patrick (Eds.). *Working with custodial grandparents.* New York: Springer.

Wood, V. & Robertson, J. (1976). The significance of grandparenthood. In J. Gubruim (Ed.). *Time, roles and self in old age.* New York: Human Sciences Press.

Wu, Z. & Pollard, M. S. (1998). Social support among unmarried childless elderly persons. *Journals of Gerontology, 53B,* S324–S335.

Wu, Z. & Schimmele, C. M. (2007). Uncoupling in late life. *Generations, 31,* 41–46.

Yange, L., Krampe, R. T., & Baltes, P. B. (2006). Basic forms of cognitive plasticity extended into the oldest-old: Retest learning, age and cognitive functioning. *Psychology and Aging, 21,* 372–378.

Zhang, Z. & Hayward, M. (2006). Gender, the marital life course, and cardiovascular disease in late life. *Journal of Marriage and Family, 68*(4), 639–657.

Zodikoff, B. D. (2006). Services for lesbian, gay, bisexual and transgender older adults. In B. Berkman (Ed.). *Handbook of social work in health and aging.* New York: Oxford Press.

10

Opportunities and Challenges of Informal Caregiving

As noted in Chapter 9, the majority of long-term care to adults age 65 and older is provided not in long-term care facilities, but informally and privately, at little or no public cost, within elders' homes or other community-based settings. Over 80 percent of older adults with limitations in three or more activities of daily living (ADL) are able to live in the community primarily because of informal assistance. Among elders in the community, about 9 percent rely exclusively on formal care, while nearly 70 percent receive care solely from family, friends, and neighbors. The availability of such supports helps determine whether elders can remain at home rather than be placed in a long-term facility; older adults who have an informal caregiver are five times more likely to remain in their own homes than those without informal supports (AOA, 2008; Family Caregiving Alliance, 2006b; Gonyea, 2008; Hargrave, 2008;

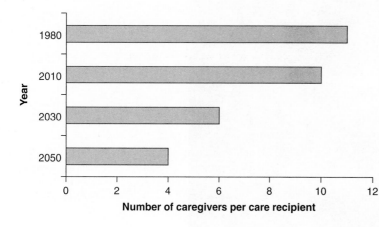

FIGURE 10.1   **The Shrinking Pool of Potential Caregivers**
SOURCE: U.S. Census Bureau, 2006.

Raphael & Cornwell, 2008; Schmieding, 2006; Van Houtven & Norton, 2008). Projected declines in the availability of such informal assistance is illustrated in Figure 10.1.

Who Are Informal Caregivers?

The terms *family* and **informal caregiving** are often used interchangeably, although informal caregivers also include friends, neighbors, and even acquaintances. Throughout this chapter, we intermix the term *care recipient* to recognize the care of nonrelatives as well. **Caregiving,** whether informal or formal, denotes supportive, nonmedical, mostly low-tech services, such as help with bathing or eating, and some medical services, such as administering medications and attending to surgical wounds (Schmieding, 2006). The primary forms of care provided by families are:

- emotional support
- instrumental activities inside and outside the home (e.g., transportation, meal preparation, shopping)
- personal care (e.g., bathing, feeding, dressing)
- contacting and monitoring agencies for services and coordinating such services

The vast majority of family caregivers help older relatives daily; 50 percent assist with one or more ADLs, such as getting in and out of bed and chairs and getting dressed, and 80 percent help with three or more IADLs, primarily with transportation, grocery shopping, and housework. A focus on ADLs and IADLs, however, fails to capture the complexity and intensity of caregiving work (Bookman & Harrington, 2007; National Alliance for Family Caregiving and AARP, 2004, 2008). The type and extent of family care is largely influenced by the older adult's functional status, intensity of needed care, coresidence, and the caregiver's gender.

Family members, whether related by birth and marriage or friends, neighbors or "family of choice" (among gay and lesbian populations), are central to long-term care delivery in the United States. The number of family caregivers giving personal assistance to adults age 50 and older with disabilities or chronic illness is estimated at 34 million (16 percent of the population). Among these, almost 7 million care for persons age 65 and older. On average, family caregivers devote approximately 25 hours per week and more than four years to caregiving, with over 40 percent giving care for five years or longer Not surprisingly, the number of hours of care each week and the length of care increase with the age of the care recipients and for persons with dementia, regardless of age. The average caregiver is age 47, female, married, and working outside the home. However, caregiving for elders occurs across the life course; a growing number of young caregivers ages 8 to 18 are helping parents or grandparents, while adult children in their 60s or 70s may be caring for parents in their 90s (Arno, 2006; Family Caregiver Alliance, 2006b, 2009; Gonyea, 2008; Johnson & Wiener, 2006; Lewis, 2008; National Alliance for Caregiving and United Hospital Funds, 2005).

Even though families have always been the primary caregivers of elders, family care was perceived by policy makers as nonexistent and by researchers as largely invisible until the mid-1980s. Although Shanas's groundbreaking research (1979) refuted the prevailing social myth of families' alienation from their elders, policy makers and frequently the general public still assumed that many families abandoned their elders to institutional care. After three decades of caregiver research and numerous testimonials regarding care demands, the central role played by families in the lives of elders with chronic illness is now widely documented, and the term *family caregiver* is used by policy makers and the popular press. Nevertheless, the family's significant contributions to elder care are still largely unrecognized by many policy makers, creating a "shadow workforce" in geriatric health care (Bookman & Harrington, 2007; Gonyea, 2008).

The complexity and diversity of family support vary by geographic proximity, gender, race, social class, sexual orientation, family structure, and the history and nature of the relationship between caregiver and care recipient. Distance—both geographic and emotional—often inhibits family members' provision of care. Among primary family caregivers, 42 percent live within 20 minutes of the elder and nearly 65 percent of them visit care recipients at least an hour a week. But among the remainder, an estimated 5 to 7 million caregivers live more than an hour away. Not surprisingly, caregivers at a geographic distance are more likely to spend their time arranging for services, checking that care is provided, and managing finances than providing hands-on personal care (Family Caregiver Alliance, 2009; Parker, Church, & Toseland, 2006). Emotional distance in the caregiving dyad may have a greater impact on quality of care than physical distance, however. It

may occur when caring for a partner or parent after years of conflictual relationships and family disruption, neglect, abuse, or separation. With growing rates of divorce, more adult children will be faced with caring for parents who did not care for them as children. As noted in Chapter 9, changes in family relationships through divorce and remarriage can negatively affect interactions with children—especially for men—and limit the availability of both biological children and stepchildren as potential sources of support in old age (Davey, 2007; Gonyea, 2008). The effects of the nature of the care dyad, gender, race, and sexual orientation on caregiving are discussed more fully below.

Costs and Benefits of Informal Care

For Society

Because of the many hours of unpaid family care provided, it is not surprising that informal caregiving saves the American health care system substantial dollars; the economic value contributed by family caregivers to society is estimated to be $350 billion, exceeding the total amount spent in 2005 by either Medicare ($342 billion) or Medicaid ($300 billion). Additionally, the value of informal care consistently exceeds the costs of paid home care (Gibson & Houser, 2007). If informal supports were unavailable, total long-term care costs are estimated to more than double (Arno, 2006).

While informal care is not a new phenomenon, demographic and social changes are intensifying demands on families to provide more complex care for longer periods of time and for multiple relatives (Bengtson et al., 2009; Gonyea, 2008). These changes include the rapid growth of the oldest-old with chronic illness, more women employed outside the home, more complex family structures (e.g., multigenerational, single-parent, LGBT "families of choice," blended families, and skipped-generation households), and increasing racial and class inequities. These are compounded by cost-cutting health care measures, particularly to Medicaid. In addition, families are increasingly expected to provide both high-tech and "high-touch" care because of policies that provide fiscal incentives to discharge Medicare patients quickly from hospitals. As a result, families, who typically are unprepared for caregiving and may not even consult with each other about care plans, often have to provide medically oriented acute care along with post-acute and rehabilitative care (such as intravenous drug therapy and ventilator assistance). Yet the majority of families lack the necessary knowledge about the aging process or available resources, let alone such technical skills. The range of factors affecting caregiving stress are captured in the box to the right (Given, Sherwood, & Given, 2008; Iecovich, 2008; Kelly, Reinhard, & Brooks-Danso, 2008; Zarit & Femia, 2008).

Yoga is an excellent way to reduce caregiver stress.

SOURCES OF CAREGIVER STRESS

Financial
- direct costs of care, such as home care equipment and medicine
- travel costs for long-distance caregivers
- reduced hours (and income) at work
- absenteeism and disruptions at work
- reduced productivity at work
- missed career opportunities
- lack of flexible, family-friendly workplace policies
- early retirement

Physical
- health problems (headaches, stomach disturbances, and weight changes)
- use/misuse of prescription drugs and health services
- sleep disorders and exhaustion
- neglect of self and others
- higher rates of morbidity and mortality
- increased use of emergency rooms and inpatient hospitalization

Emotional
- grief and hopelessness
- guilt, anger, resentment, and denial
- giving up time for oneself and family
- strained social and family relationships
- social isolation
- worry and anxiety
- feelings of being alone
- negative attitudes or behaviors toward care recipient
- depression

For Informal Caregivers

The negative consequences experienced by caregivers are conceptualized as primary and secondary stressors that typically result in objective and subjective burden. **Primary stressors** are events that derive directly from the elder's illness, such as cognitive impairments and associated behavioral problems. **Secondary stressors** are not secondary in terms of their importance, but are so called because they do not arise directly from the older person's illness. Common secondary stressors are role strains and deterioration of the caregivers' sense of mastery, self-esteem, and competence (Family Caregiver Alliance, 2006b, 2009). These stressors create a sense of **caregiver burden:**

> **Objective burden** refers to the daily physical demands, tasks, and behavioral phenomena of caregiving: the older care recipient's symptomatic behaviors; disruption of family life and roles; and legal, employment, health, and mental health problems.
>
> **Subjective burden** encompasses the family caregivers' feelings about their role, such as grief, anger, guilt, worry, loneliness, and sadness.

The caregiver's individual appraisal of the situation or subjective burden appears to be more salient than the objective burden or the actual tasks performed. This is consistent with findings presented in Chapter 9 on how perceptions of social support are more important to the quality of life than the actual support given. Similarly, caregiving stress is multidimensional and not assessed or modified by focusing only on one cause or manifestation of such strain (Family Caregiver Alliance, 2006b; Zarit & Femier, 2008). On the other hand, living with the care recipient, being a woman, coping with the elder's behavioral problems—especially those associated with dementia—long hours of intensive levels of care without any break, and declines in the care recipient's status over time rather tend to be associated with increased caregiver stress (Chappel & Reid, 2002; Nelson et al., 2008; Savundranagam, Hummert, & Montgomery, 2005; Schulz & Sherwood, 2008). Families experience costs or burdens in three primary areas:

1. *Physical and mental health outcomes:* A growing body of evidence documents that increases in caregiving stress are related to poor health outcomes (Beach et al., 2005; Family Caregiver Alliance, 2009; Kiecolt-Glaser & Glaser, 2003; Lee, Colditz, Berkman, & Kawachi, 2003; Schmieding, 2006; Schulz & Sherwood, 2008; Vitaliano, Zhang, & Scanland, 2003). Physical health problems affect 25 to 30 percent of caregivers, most often among African American, female, unemployed, and middle-aged caregivers and those providing the most intensive levels of care, such as for persons with dementia. These problems include headaches, exhaustion, pain, arthritis, back troubles, sleep disorders, intestinal disturbances, weight changes, inappropriate use of prescription drugs, elevated blood pressure, and poorer-functioning immune systems (which results in more colds and other viral illnesses) (Family Caregiver Alliance, 2006c; Mittelman, 2002; Schulz & Sherwood, 2008). In one study, women who spent 9 or more hours a week caring for a spouse increased their coronary heart disease risk twofold (Lee et al., 2003). Not surprisingly, caregivers whose health is compromised by care-related stress may face an increased risk of mortality. In fact, an 8-year study of over 500,000 couples enrolled in Medicare found that hospitalization of a spouse or partner for serious illness, especially one that interferes with the patient's physical or mental ability, also increases their partner's risk of death, with the biggest impact on wives (Christakis & Allison, 2006).

   Poorer physical health and lower physical stamina are associated with emotional distress and mental health problems, especially depression and anxiety (Beach et al., 2005; Schulz & Sherwood, 2008). Among caregivers, 40 to 60 percent are estimated to have clinical depression; 25 to 50 percent suffer from major depression (Family Caregiver Alliance, 2006b). One 4-year study found that women caring for a spouse with a chronic illness were almost six times more likely to suffer symptoms of depression or anxiety than those who had no care responsibilities, and those caring for parents rather than other relatives were twice as likely to manifest such symptoms (Cannuscio et al., 2002). Depression is found to increase with the length of caregiving and the amount of time (36 hours or more) devoted to weekly care (Bookwala, 2009). It appears that a threshold of time involvement exists beyond which the likelihood of negative mental health consequences rapidly escalates. Levels of depression and loneliness remain high for caregivers even after the daily caregiving ends, such as when the care recipient is placed in a long-term care setting (Whitlatch, 2008).

THE FINANCIAL BURDEN OF PARENTAL CAREGIVING

For some adult children, the costs of accessible housing, medical supplies, and other care-related expenses that are not covered by Medicare or private insurance can deplete their savings. Unlike spousal caregivers, they cannot even claim expenses on their income tax unless they pay more than half of the parent's support. This may force the middle-aged child to work beyond their preferred retirement age. In some cases, this financial devastation occurs because they are reluctant to use their parents' savings; in many cases the elder does not have sufficient savings or does not qualify for Medicaid. As one example, a bank vice president borrowed against her 401(k) retirement plan, sold her house, and depleted 20 years of savings to care for her 97-year-old father. She spent $50,000 for lawyers' fees to win a contested guardianship, $3,000 for home care equipment, $400 a month for home-delivered meals, $330 per trip for a wheelchair accessible van, and $1,600 each month to rent an apartment large enough for herself, her dad, and a home aide. She does not worry about what she spends, stating that you "just have to buy what you have to buy." In the 2009 recession, middle-income caregivers who have lost their jobs often struggle to make ends meet, and may be unaware of government services that could help them (Konrad, 2009; Gross, 2006).

2. *Financial:* These encompass the direct costs for medical care, adaptive equipment, or hired help as well as indirect opportunity costs from lost income, missed promotions, or unemployment. Excluding those who care for a spouse/partner, more than 30 percent of informal caregivers contribute $2400 a year to care of the care recipient. With more caregivers employed full time, the greater the burden of care responsibilities, the higher the probability of negative work-related adjustments; caregivers of elders with dementia must make the most changes in their jobs. Among such caregivers, more than 80 percent go to work later or leave earlier than scheduled; nearly 40 percent move from full-time to part-time jobs, which may be a transitional step to leaving the labor force (Conrad, 2009; Gonyea, 2008). Compared to their Caucasian counterparts, African American caregivers are more likely to continue in the labor force, often out of financial necessity (Bullock, Crawford, & Tennstedt,

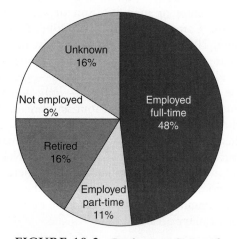

FIGURE 10.2 **Employment Status of Caregivers: 2005**

SOURCE: Family Caregiver Alliance (2005). *Selected Caregiver Statistics.* San Francisco: Author.

SELF-CARE NEEDS

- Learn to accept help.
- Take time for relaxing and pleasurable activities by asking others for help or by utilizing respite/adult day care.
- Find ways to incorporate exercise into your daily routine.
- Take time to eat healthy food.
- Set limits on the care recipient's demands.
- Attend to your spiritual needs.
- Participate in caregiver support groups.

2003). Averaging 12 years out of the paid workforce to care for children or elders, women suffer long-term economic costs of caregiving, including lower retirement income and higher rates of poverty in old age (Gonyea, 2008; Wakabayashi & Donato, 2004). These costs are discussed more fully in Chapter 15. Disruptions and absenteeism due to caregiver responsibilities not only affect the employee financially, but also cost employers up to $33.6 billion per year in lost productivity (MetLife, 2006a).

3. *Emotional:* Subjective burdens tend to be of greatest concern. They encompass worry, anxiety, and feelings of being alone, isolated, and disconnected from others; "erosion of self" with one's identity completely submerged in the care role; and feeling overwhelmed, out of control, inadequate, and fearful over the unpredictability of the future. Loss of time for oneself, family, and friends; giving up vacations, hobbies, and social activities; and getting less exercise than before are frequently cited by caregivers as the most negative impacts (Braithwaite, 2000; Moen, Erickson, and Dempster-McClain, 2000; National Alliance for Caregiving and AARP, 2004). Emotional costs tend to increase with difficult levels of care and are experienced by

women more than men. Caregivers who feel trapped in the role are at risk of neglect, burnout, or "compassion fatigue" (Family Caregiver Alliance, 2009).

Caregivers

Given the problem-focused nature of gerontological research, most caregiving studies have examined stress, burden, and the losses entailed. However, caregiving is multidimensional and includes both negative and positive experiences (Family Caregiver Alliance, 2006b; Gonyea, 2008; Schumacher et al., 2006; Naylor & Keating, 2009). Similar to other types of adversity throughout the life course, caregiving can be lonely, stressful, moving, and satisfying all at the same time. In other words, psychological well-being can coexist with distress under adverse life circumstances for both caregivers and care recipients. This means that caregivers may experience losses of identity, privacy, and time for self, while simultaneously experiencing personal benefits, such as self-efficacy, confidence, self-affirmation, pride, and greater closeness with the care recipient and other family members. These gains can buffer some of the adverse effects of care-related stressors. And for parents and children who have had a conflictual relationship, caregiving may offer an opportunity to work through these issues (Carroll, 2009; Narayn et al., 2001; Richards, 2009).

Some caregivers find personal meaning in their role, such as preserving values and ideals, and feelings of giving back to older generations. In fact, a greater sense of meaning in life can enhance caregiver well-being. These findings regarding caregiver gains reflect its qualitative or subjective nature and the role of individual appraisal; for example, what one caregiver experiences as stressful, another may find to be a source of satisfaction. In addition, benefits and costs vary over time in the caregiving process, especially when beginning and leaving the role.

POWERFUL TOOLS FOR CAREGIVERS

Powerful Tools for Caregivers (PTC), available in over 20 states, is based on a self-efficacy model that teaches caregivers to manage their emotions, engage in self-care behaviors (e.g., take time to relax), and communicate assertively and effectively. For example, caregivers learn and rehearse changing "You" messages into "I" messages to communicate their thoughts and feelings. They enact plans to take time for themselves without feeling guilty. Caregivers learn emotion-focused coping skills to help them reframe difficult care situations and view self-care as essential to being a good caregiver. Caregivers create weekly action plans for self-care. After taking part in PTC, caregivers, spouses, and adult children report significant improvements on all outcome measures, especially participation in relaxation activities and physical exercise. Most of these gains in physical and mental health are sustained 6 months later (Boise, Congelton, & Shannon, 2005; Kuhn, 2004; Schmall, Cleland, & Sturdevent, 2000).

These patterns also point to the need for practitioners to recognize both role gains and strains as intervening processes in understanding caregiver well-being outcomes and designing caregiver interventions (Narayn et al., 2001; Richards, 2009; Seltzer & Li, 2000; Sherrell, Buckwalter, & Morhardt, 2001).

Caregivers' well-being and costs of care (and the interaction between gains and costs) are thus affected by two clusters of factors: *contextual* (e.g., level of care, care recipient's behavior and symptoms, quality of relationship with care recipient, socioeconomic status) and *dynamic* (e.g., the caregiver's internal capacities and social, cultural, and spiritual resources). The following variables, which are often more important than the elder's disability status or the amount or type of care provided, influence whether caregivers experience primarily costs or gains:

1. The nature of the relationship between the caregiver and recipient dyad (e.g., the degree of closeness, past history of conflict/neglect between them; the recipient being unappreciative, making unreasonable demands, adopting manipulative behavior). A good relationship prior to caregiving can minimize stress, even in the face of heavy care demands and may in some instances even slow decline in dementia (Norton, et al., 2009).

2. Family support or disharmony, coresidence or geographic distance, financial resources

3. The salience and timing in the caregiver's life course (e.g., when faced with multiple demands at midlife)

4. Gender (women typically experience caregiving as more stressful than men)

5. Race and ethnicity, with caregivers of color generally using fewer formal services but experiencing less depression and stress

6. Social networks and degree of reciprocity between caregiver and care recipient (Sebern, 2005; Whitlatch, 2008).

Caregiving research has focused on outcomes for the family caregiver. Yet both the stress of care and reciprocity in the caregiving dyad can affect the well-being of both the caregiver and care recipient. The importance of such reciprocity across the life course suggests the value of studying family care from the perspective of both members of the care dyad. Even caregivers of elders with dementia may experience reciprocity in the relationship, especially when there is a history of solidarity, deeply established attachments, and rich memories. To illustrate, a care recipient who can no longer manage daily chores can nevertheless entertain the caregiver with stories of family history. Similarly, interventions should address both the caregiver and the care recipient in the dyad, facilitate communication and decision making, and provide elders with no more assistance than what is required to help them maintain competence and self-efficacy. Since many caregivers misperceive the care recipients' preferences for care, involving the older person in decision making tends to benefit both members of the care dyad. Project ANSWERS (Acquiring New Skills

While Enhancing Remaining Strengths) trains dyad partners in communication related to care values and preferences and decision making to benefit both the care giver and care recipient (Judge, 2007). Unfortunately, relatively few programs employ a dyadic approach that seeks to improve outcomes for both care partners (Beach et al., 2005; Menne et al., 2008 Whitlatch; Piiparinen & Feinberg, 2009; Whitlatch et al., 2006; Whitlatch, 2008).

The Gendered Nature of Family Care

Primary caregivers (i.e., the one family member who assumes most of the responsibility) are generally adult children (41 percent), followed by partners or spouses (38.4 percent), and other family members and friends (20.4 percent) (Wolff & Kasper, 2006). This division of labor is due in part to high rates of widowhood among older adults. Along with multiple siblings sharing care responsibilities, children outnumber spouses as active carers. Regardless of the type of care relationship, women form approximately 75 percent of primary family caregivers. Although gender roles are changing and the number of sons providing care is growing, women are still the primary nurturers and kin keepers. Daughters are twice as likely as sons to become the primary caregiver. Of those who give constant care—40 or more hours per week—the vast majority are women (Calasanti, 2006; 2009). In fact, 50 percent of all women provide elder care at some point in the life course, whether as partners, daughters, or daughters-in-law (Family Caregiver Alliance, 2006c; Gonyea, 2008; Johnson & Wiener, 2006; Wolff & Kasper, 2006). Among all types of caregivers (primary and secondary), approximately 36 percent are wives, 29 percent are daughters, 20 percent are other females (nieces, daughters-in-law, granddaughters, etc.), and the remainder are male relatives. When men are primary caregivers, they are usually husbands, secondarily sons, and least often sons-in-law (Family Caregiver Alliance, 2006c, 2009).

Growing numbers of younger women will assume both elder-care and employment responsibilities.

The average woman today can expect to spend more years caring for an older family member than for her children. From the feminist theory perspective discussed in Chapter 8, women predominate not only because they are socialized to be carers, but also because society devalues a woman's unreimbursed responsibilities in the home as well as their paid work through employment. That is, because women typically earn less than men, an implicit assumption is that they can more readily give up paid employment to provide care (Calasanti, 2009; Cruikshank, 2009; Gonyea, 2008). Types of care also vary by family relationship. Daughters predominate as the primary caregivers for older

LOSS OF SELF IN THE CAREGIVING ROLE

"By definition, caregiving does not affect your life; it becomes your life. Outside activities disappear. In eight years, I have been to the movies three times" (McLeod, 1999, p. 81). As noted by a daughter, "It is culturally expected to care for a parent in the home, yet it is viewed as women's work, and we don't value that very much in our society. Society thinks 'it's just an old person,' and 'it's just a woman.' So there are no benefits—no unemployment insurance, no vacations. It's insulting, and yet this is important work" (McLeod, 1999, p. 36).

widowed women and older unmarried men, and they are the secondary caregivers in situations where the partner of an older person is still alive and able to provide care. Daughters are more likely than sons to be involved in *caring for* (i.e., help with daily personal care tasks that are physically draining, such as bathing, dressing, and eating, involve daily interruptions, and entail intimate contact), as well as *caring about* the care recipient (i.e., relational aspects of care that involve trust, rapport, compassion, comfort, communication, and a sense of psychological responsibility). On the other hand, men are most often the primary caregivers of people with HIV/AIDS, where they often provide personal care (Greenberg, Seltzer, & Brewer, 2006; Russell, 2004; Thompson, 2002).

Some researchers contend that men as caregivers and their distinctive needs have been marginalized and overlooked in caregiving studies (Greenberg et al., 2006; Russell, 2004). As a whole, sons tend to focus on more circumscribed, instrumental, and sporadic tasks, such as house and yard maintenance, financial management, and occasional shopping, although this pattern is changing as more men assume the primary caregiver role. Sons are more likely to adopt an attitude of "you do what you have to do" and use a "work" paradigm in approaching caregiving (Calasanti, 2006; Family Caregiver Alliance, 2009; Greenberg, Seltzer, & Brewer, 2006). They provide less personal care, especially to mothers, although they are more likely to perform "nontraditional" tasks (e.g., bathing, meals, dressing) when they are

---

SONS AS CAREGIVERS

When Peter Nicholson's mother suffered a series of strokes last winter, he did something women have done for generations: he quit his job and moved into her West Hollywood home to care for her full time. Since then, he has lost 45 pounds and is running out of money. But the most difficult adjustment has been the emotional toll. "The single toughest moment was when she said to me, 'And now who are you?' That was the pinnacle of despair." For Mr. Nicholson, the whole experience has been a journey into the surreal, but especially at bath time when the "weirdness of this permeates our relationship. I'm always asking myself. Am I even qualified for this? Just because I love her a lot doesn't mean that I have any idea if I'm doing the right thing or doing what's best for her." (Leland, 2008).

---

the primary caregiver for a parent in the home. In addition, sons place less importance on emotional well-being and more on completing care goals. In other words, women more often approach caregiving with empathy, feel responsible for the care recipient's physical *and* psychological well-being, and perceive caregiving demands as more disruptive of their emotional and social lives than do men. In contrast, male caregivers are more likely to separate boundaries of employment and caregiving, to compartmentalize the loss of marital reciprocity, and to engage in task-oriented self-care (such as exercise) than female careers (Calasanti, 2006, 2009; Kramer & Thompson, 2002; Russell, 2004; Thompson, 2002).

Middle-aged adult children, particularly daughters and daughters-in-law, are often referred to as the This is called the "sandwiched generation" because of competing responsibilities of parental and child care. In many instances, **women in the middle** may be juggling extensive family responsibilities along with employment and their own age-related transitions. This latter issue is particularly important because the age-group 35 to 64 is most likely to be providing parent care (Brody, 2004). Women in the middle generation are also centrally involved in maintaining family communication and cohesion across generations.

CHARACTERISTICS OF WOMEN AS CAREGIVERS

- form the majority of caregivers, even when male family members are available (except for spouses)
- feel more psychological responsibility
- are more likely to give up or modify their employment status
- face multiple demands and roles from employment and/or dependent children
- caregiving is often a "career" over the life course and affects economic well-being in old age

Health professionals should seek signs of stress in the caregiving process.

Juggling multiple roles, however, may not always be a primary source of stress. In fact, women who lack any meaningful social roles may experience greater stress compared with women with multiple roles. Others' support for the caregiving role may be more important than the multiplicity of roles per se.

Compared to adult sons, daughters are more likely to give up employment, which can result in a loss of income (both current and in retirement) and a source of identity and self-esteem. More recent data, however, indicate that daughters caring for older parents typically do not have dependent children (under age 18) for whom they are responsible. This means that they are more likely to face the competing demands of parental care and paid employment than the dual responsibilities of child and elder care (Gonyea, 2008). Nevertheless, middle-aged women may still feel psychologically and financially responsible for their young adult children, who frequently return home to the "empty nest" out of economic necessity or because of divorce. Even if the empty nest is not refilled, parents may be actively engaged in tangibly or emotionally assisting their adult children during a prolonged period of "emerging adulthood," leading to what is called "permaparenting" or "helicopter parenting" (Arnett, 2000; Dettinger & Clarkberg, 2002; Gonyea, 2008; Paul, 2003).

SANDWICH GENERATION INCLUDES DAUGHTERS-IN-LAW

A woman in her mid-50s with teenage children and a full-time job, Annette cared for both her parents. Her mother, disabled with rheumatoid arthritis, and her father, who had suffered a major stroke, lived with Annette's family for over 5 years. Annette's teenagers resented the amount of time she devoted to her parents, and her husband also became impatient with her focus on her parents. They had not had a vacation in 5 years. Since family and friends were not interested in helping her with the care of her parents, Annette and her husband rarely even had a night out alone together. As an employed caregiver, Annette frequently missed work and was distracted on the job whenever she had to consult doctors or take her parents for therapy during normal business hours. She felt alone, isolated, and overwhelmed by the stress. She was physically and mentally exhausted from trying to meet too many demands—unaware that some support services were available in her community—and feeling that she had to handle these responsibilities on her own. When her mother-in-law became too frail to live alone, Annette knew her family and job would suffer once again if she tried to balance household duties, a full-time job, and the care of both older and younger relatives. She began to explore assisted living options for her mother-in-law.

Given these deeply rooted gender-based differences and the distinction between caring for and caring about, daughters are found to experience more stress and feelings of psychological burden than sons, even when both are performing similar tasks across comparable time periods (Calasanti, 2006; Family Caregiver Alliance, 2009; Navaie-Waliser et al., 2002). Accordingly, women caregivers report higher levels of depression, anxiety, psychiatric symptomatology, and lower life satisfaction than their male counterparts, although these mental health problems are probably not due only to caregiving strain. A meta-analysis of 229 caregiver studies suggests that while female caregivers have higher rates of depression and health problems than their male counterparts, this difference may be associated with depression and poor health among women in general and not a result of caregiver stress alone (Pinquart & Sorensen, 2006). Another limitation is that most studies of gender differences are cross-sectional and thus do not capture how caregiving stress changes over time for both men and women. Nevertheless, gender-based patterns are identifiable and generally consistent across cultures. For example, as noted in, Chapter 2, although norms of filial support are weakening in Asian countries, daughters-in-law are still expected to provide care, without emotional or tangible support from their husbands (Navaie-Waliser et al., 2001; Yee & Schulz, 2000).

Increasingly, researchers are exploring not only how men and women differ in performing the caregiving role, but also how gender influences the meaning, social context, and consequences of caring (Cruikshank, 2009; Leland, 2008; Pinquart & Sorensen, 2006). Women, for example, generally have more extensive social networks than do men, who are more likely to feel socially isolated. Although social networks may be useful resources, they may also be sources of stress if they are characterized by conflict or other negative interactions. Of greatest concern is that women experience greater

economic costs from the undervalued work of caregiving across the life course than do men (Calasanti, 2006, 2009; Gonyea, 2008; Russell, 2004). These economic inequities are discussed more fully in Chapter 15.

WOMEN IN THE MIDDLE

A woman in her early 40s had left a rewarding career to care for her mother-in-law with Alzheimer's disease, her 11-year-old daughter, and 8-year-old son. Her husband's siblings, who had no children, provided only occasional financial assistance, refusing to help by giving her respite or time off. Her husband worked two jobs, and although he was emotionally supportive, he was rarely present to help. Caring for her mother-in-law dominated her life, and she had little time to attend her children's special events or sports. Her son had had to give up his room for his grandmother, and her daughter complained about how her mother never spent time with her. In the 2 years of caring for her mother-in-law, she had not had a day just for herself. When she learned about the availability of respite services, she started to sob, recognizing how much she had been grieving over her loss of time with her husband and children.

CULTURAL EXPECTATIONS OF WOMEN AS CAREGIVERS

A researcher in Seoul, Korea who studies women's labor market issues has cared for her mother-in-law for 22 years. Although her husband and in-laws help pay for a personal assistant to care for her mother-in-law during the day, the middle-aged professional assumes all the care after her 8- to 10-hour workday and on weekends, without any assistance from her husband. She has had only one vacation during that time period, has little social life, but rarely questions her obligation to her mother-in-law.

Spouses/Partners as Caregivers

The most frequent caregiving pattern is between spouses/partners, who perform up to 80 percent of all care tasks, spending 40 to 60 hours per week on household chores and personal care. For those assisting someone age 65 and older, the average age is 63 years, with 33 percent of these caregivers in fair to poor health. Because of differences in life expectancy, more wives than husbands over age 65 care for a partner with chronic illness. Men receive more care on average, typically from only one person—their wife. In contrast, women are helped by a larger number of caregivers, including children and grandchildren (Family Caregiver Alliance, 2006b, 2006c, 2009; Johnson & Wiener, 2006). Since most caregiving studies have focused on heterosexual couples, the term *spouse* is used most frequently in this discussion; nevertheless, it is important to recognize the distinctive structural challenges faced by gay and lesbian partner caregivers, as discussed in Chapter 9.

Within the gender-based differences described above, husbands, who are more likely to provide care than are sons or sons-in-law, predominate among the approximately 30 percent of caregivers who are male. In fact, husbands of women with functional disability are more likely to provide care than are other relatives. As a result, husbands comprise nearly 40 percent of spousal caregivers and are predicted to grow in the future because of gains in men's life expectancy. Husbands tend to be the first person called on to care for their wives, reflecting the marital contract "in sickness or in health," to be the oldest subgroup of caregivers, and to spend the greatest number of hours in this role compared with other caregivers.

> **POINTS TO PONDER**
>
> Spouses/partners account for:
>
> - 28 percent of caregivers of Caucasian elders
> - 20 percent of caregivers of Latinos
> - 15 percent of African American caregivers
>
> What factors do you think may account for these differences?

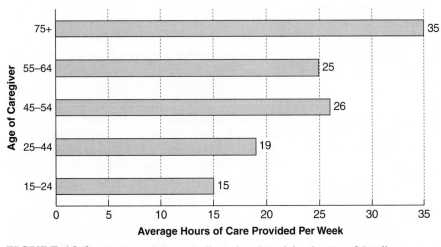

FIGURE 10.3   Number of Hours Dedicated to Caregiving by Age of Family Caregiver, 2005

SOURCE: Family Caregiver Alliance. (2005). *Selected Caregiver Statistics*. San Francisco: Author.

As noted above in our discussion of career stress, these men tend to report less distress because they redefine the relationship in terms of task accomplishment. They are more likely to experience instrumental difficulties of care, not affective challenges. Because caregiving work is not part of their self-concept, care difficulties are less likely to detract from their identities as husbands and men (Calasanti, 2006, 2009; Leland, 2008; Russell, 2004).

Older spouses generally experience more negative consequences from caregiving than do younger adult children (Ory, Tennstedt, & Schulz, 2000). Both husband and wife caregivers report considerable stress and feelings of grief and loss. These problems may be exacerbated because spousal caregivers are also facing their own aging-related changes, physical illnesses, or reduced finances. Emotional stress, particularly depression, tends to be highest among spouses caring for partners with cognitive impairment. The nature of the relationship also affects the consequences of care. For example, caregiving is found to be more stressful for wives than daughters, since wives more frequently experience losses in marital and family relationships and social involvement. Wives' sense of well-being, however, may increase when a husband dies, especially after a long period of caregiving (Seltzer & Li, 2000). As a whole, spousal caregivers experience more negative consequences than do adult children.

LGBT partners' caregiving experiences are made more difficult by legal and structural barriers in most societies. For example, they may be denied visitation rights in the hospital or nursing home, overlooked by health care providers as the primary support, and excluded from decision making about end-of-life care (Zodikoff, 2006). In a national survey of 1,000 self-identified LGBT baby boomers, 25 percent of respondents had provided care for a friend or family member within the past 6 months. Of these, 36 percent were caregivers for parents, 18 percent for partners, and 26 percent for

friends and other nonrelatives. In contrast with heterosexual caregivers, about the same proportion of gay men and lesbians serve as caregivers. In addition, both perform care-management and care-provider tasks, which suggest greater role flexibility and egalitarian relationships than in the heterosexual population (Calasanti, 2009; Heaphy, 2007). LGBT caregivers' time commitment is also found to be greater than in the population as a whole (MetLife, 2006b). The extent to which these greater time demands result from caring for persons with HIV/AIDS is not clear.

Adult Children/Grandchildren as Caregivers

The importance of the parent-child bond across the life course is underscored by the fact that adult children represent the largest group of primary carers for aging parents with chronic illness or disability. Parent care has become a predictable and nearly universal experience across the life course, yet many adults are typically thrust into the role with little advance warning and thus are not adequately prepared for it. Although often referred to as a "role reversal," an adult child never becomes a parent's parent. Instead, caring for parents involves letting go of outmoded patterns to meet current family needs, a process that can lead to feelings of loss and grief among adult children caregivers and that persist even after a parent's death (Given et al., 2008). Additionally, adult children often experience sibling and parental conflict around caregiving decisions, or past conflicts may resurface (Connidis & Kemp, 2008; Satow, 2005; Whitlatch, 2008). Given the gendered nature of care described above, it is not surprising that daughters predominate among adult children caring for their parents. Adult children as caregivers are discussed more fully above under the Gendered Nature of Care.

More sons today are caregivers to aging parents than in the past.

Family Caregivers of Color

Because caregiving research has focused on U.S.-born whites, less is known about care in communities of color or other cultures. African Americans and Latinos are more likely to be providing informal care than other populations of color. For both African Americans and Latinos, caregivers are less likely to be spouses and more likely to be another family member or a friend. Both groups tend to experience more physical health problems compared to their white counterparts (Haley et al., 2004; National Alliance for Caregiving and AARP, 2004; Pinquart & Sorenson, 2006; Weiss et al., 2005). African

American caregivers tend to provide higher levels of care, to be more likely to assist extended family members, and to be more economically disadvantaged than their white counterparts. They are also less likely to have alternative caregivers to assist them on an ongoing basis and use formal supports even though they often face more severe care situations. Despite these objective burdens, African American caregivers typically report less stress, anxiety, feelings of "bother," and depression; higher levels of self-efficacy; and greater rewards compared to other groups. Their greater satisfaction and perceived gains (e.g., pride, belief that they will be rewarded by God) may be partially due to the mediating effects of religion, spirituality, prayer, and faith; to strong cultural beliefs about filial support and familism; and to more positive, respectful views of elders (Chadiha, Brown, & Aranda, 2006; Dilworth-Anderson, Williams, & Gibson, 2002; Dilworth-Anderson, Brummett, Goodwin et al., 2005; Foley, Tung, & Mutran, 2002; Haley et al., 2004; Roff et al., 2004). On the other hand, younger African American caregivers who are facing financial and other pressures may experience a contradiction between cultural expectations about what they *should* do for care recipients and what they can *actually* do. In some instances, holding strong beliefs of familism may predispose some African American women caregivers to higher levels of psychological distress (Rozario & DeRienzis, 2008; Dilworth-Anderson et al., 2005).

Latinos are identified as experiencing greater burden and rates of depression and less positive appraisals and feelings of competence than whites or African Americans, despite strong norms of filial responsibility. This pattern may occur because of Latinos' high rates of poverty, poor health, and limited access to insurance and other services (Adams et al., 2002; Magana, 2006). Cultural values of familism and collectivism mean that Latinos typically feel obligated to provide care and are at high risk for putting the needs of family and community above their own well-being.

Among Chinese and Korean immigrant families, older members often experience shifts in their expectations of filial piety. While parents typically sacrificed for their children's education and economic advancement, their adult children in the United States—who may not live in close physical proximity—may not perceive a filial obligation to care for their parents as strongly as adult children in Korea and China. As daughters-in-law enter the paid workforce and sons develop financial independence in the United States, they may feel less obligated to provide care. Yet seeking help within the family remains a strong Asian American value, reducing the likelihood that elders will turn to services for support to reduce their social isolation (McCormick et al., 2002; Wong, Yoo, & Stewart, 2006).

Among American Indians, providing care for elders is a core cultural value, which may place a strain on the community as a whole, not only on individual caregivers. American Indian caregivers face additional stressors, including poverty, lack of access to support services, limited systemic understanding of care recipients' needs, and caring for elders with high levels of functional disability (Goins, Moss, Buchwald, & Guralnik, 2007; Jervis & Manson, 2002; John, Hennessy, Dyeson, & Garrett, 2001). A complementary and alternative medicine therapy that uses the gentle pressure of touch on energy points was found to be more effective at reducing American Indian caregivers' stress, depression and pain than was enhanced respite; this points to the value of culturally competent caregiver interventions (Korn, Logsdon, Polissar et al., 2009).

Caregiving experiences among families of color are explored more fully in Chapter 15. Inconsistent findings related to caregiving consequences among families of color are partially due to methodological limitations, such as using a "grouping variable" by race/ethnicity, culture, or national origin to attribute differences between groups of caregivers. Whether identified differences are largely due to cultural factors (e.g., language, values, beliefs, or norms) or to racial status (with the latter implying the effects of inequality and discrimination across the life course) requires further research. What is clear is that sociodemographic variables (i.e., gender, race, marital status, sexual orientation) per se are not the primary causes of caregiver outcomes. It is also known that adults of color are at higher risk of morbidity and mortality across the life course. The greater incidence of health problems does not, however, translate into higher rates of institutional care; a smaller percentage of elders of color (3 percent) than Caucasian elders (4.2 percent) live in skilled nursing facilities. Yet, even among populations of color with strong norms of filial piety and familism, economic and social forces increasingly influence their abilities and willingness to care for aging family members, and rates of skilled nursing home care are likely to increase (NCHS, 2008; Ness, Ahmed, & Aronow, 2004).

Caregiving for Persons with Dementia

The demands and losses associated with caregiving tend to be intensified when caring for an elder with dementia (Family Caregiver Alliance, 2005, 2009; Prigerson, 2003). Almost 70 percent of adults with Alzheimer's disease (AD) are

Caregiving is an intergenerational responsibility in many cultures.

cared for at home by family for the entire duration of the disease (Ginzler, 2009). This translates into families providing up to 80 percent of
the care for older adults with AD. In a national
survey that compared caregivers of care recipients with dementia to other caregivers, the former were found to provide the most difficult
kinds of personal care (bathing, feeding, dealing
with incontinence), to spend more hours per
week providing care ("constant care"), and to
do so for longer periods of time. Not surprisingly, they are at higher risk of strain, mental
and physical health problems, and family conflicts (Belle, Burgio, Burns, et al., 2006). In one
study, over 40 percent of caregivers of a relative
with dementia report high levels of emotional
stress compared to 30 percent of all caregivers,
20 percent rate their health as fair or poor, and
18 percent state that caregiving has made their
health worse (Mittelman et al., 2004b). Another
study found greater risk of death among spousal
caregivers: The spouse's diagnosis with dementia
or cognitive impairment increased the caregiver
husband's death risk by 22 percent and wives'
risk by 28 percent—which is higher than for
those caring for elders with less-debilitating illnesses (Christakis & Allison, 2006). This may be
due, in part, to an immune system diminished by
stress (Li, Cowden, King et al., 2007). Physical
health indicators, such as blood lipids and
glucose levels, are also higher among caregivers
of elders with dementia than among other caregiving older partners. Caregivers of elders with
dementia must live with behavior problems,
such as marked confusion, anxiety and agitation,
suspicion, and sleep disturbances (Alzheimer's
Association and National Alliance for Caregiving, 2004). Rates of depression in caregivers
of persons with dementia range from 25 to
87 percent, along with a high incidence of anger,
grief, and anxiety (Covinsky Newcomer, Rox,
et al., 2003; Mittelman, 2002; Mittelman et al.,
2004b; Ory et al., 2000; Schulz et al., 2003a,
Vitaliano et al., 2002). Given these patterns, it is
not surprising that 25 percent of caregivers of
Alzheimer's patients have at least one emergency

INTENSIFICATION OF PAST BEHAVIORS WITH ALZHEIMER'S DISEASE

In *Elder Rage: or Take my Father . . . Please!*,
Marcell (2000) tells of caring for her father, who
had always had a bad temper and was a controlling,
dominating, explosive, and verbally abusive husband
and father. Afflicted with Alzheimer's disease at age
83, he constantly raged and cursed at his daughter
and his wife, threatened physical violence, and
refused to take his medications.

room visit or hospitalization every 6 months
(Schubert, Boustani, Callahan, Perkins, Hui,
et al., 2008).

The concept of "learning to bend without
breaking" refers to the high level of unpredictability and continual changes faced by families of AD
patients (Gwyther, 1998). For long-term partners,
their roles and relationships are profoundly redefined by the pervasiveness of care responsibilities
and the perception of no end in sight. When care
recipients with AD are no longer psychologically
present or when their personalities are markedly
changed, new disruptive behaviors may emerge
(e.g., emotional and verbal abuse, greater
aggressive or violent behavior) that increase their
caregivers' sense of loss. Adult children typically
grieve the loss of their relationship with their parent and of opportunities missed because of care
responsibilities. A particularly painful situation is
when the person with AD no longer recognizes
their adult child. Older partners, on the other
hand, may experience a loss of couple identity and
intimacy and an increase of uncertainty and
aloneness. In such instances, caregivers are experiencing **disenfranchised grief**, which is not publicly
recognized by others as a loss (Meuser & Marwit
2001).

Caregivers of elders with AD who tolerate
an ambiguous situation for long periods of time
often experience **anticipatory grief**. They refer
to their loved one as having died twice: first the
psychological death of the person they knew
and loved, and then the physical death. This can

result in multiple waves of grief—denial, anger, guilt, resentment, and depression. Similarly, older adult caregivers for partners with brain injury or a stroke that has affected the loved one's personality, or who are comatose experience their partner's psychological death years before the physical death. These emotional responses are similar to the feelings of loss and grief that occur when a loved one dies, and may contribute to increased feelings of burden. For example, one study found that anticipatory grief explained an additional 14 to 22 percent of the variance in burden, beyond the effects of background characteristics, care recipient behavior problems, and depressive symptoms (Holley & Mast, 2009). The Marwit and Meuser Caregiver Grief Inventory is recommended for health care providers to screen for high levels of grief among caregivers of care recipients with AD (Adams & Sanders, 2004; Dupuis, 2002; Marwit & Meuser, 2005; Ott, Sanders, & Kelber, 2007).

Such instances of prolonged stress from caring for a loved one with dementia, as illustrated by the daughter and husband caregivers in the two boxes on this page, can create a sense of desperation over lacking control of a difficult situation. This **chronic sorrow** or "long good-bye" can negatively affect caregivers' physical and mental health and increase their risk of mortality, with grief often misdiagnosed as clinical depression. Fortunately, more education and social supports are now

---

THE "ABSENCE" OF ALZHEIMER'S PATIENTS

As described by a 36-year-old daughter, "She is not the way she used to be as my mother. Just looking in her bedroom at home, it is feeling like she is gone. Yet she's still alive. Her things are still where they have been for years, even when she was well. She sits and looks at the things that once made up her life and to her that life never existed. I ask myself daily, 'Is my mother alive or dead?'" (Sanders & Corley, 2003).

DAILY GRIEVING BY THE AD CAREGIVER

According to a 71-year-old husband, "being married to someone for 50 years and seeing her with this disease, I am daily grieving over her loss. Upon death, you will grieve for a while, but your life goes on. Seeing your loved one daily die for over 6 years just makes your feelings stronger. I just wish I could have killed her and myself and just got this whole thing over really quickly" (Sanders & Corley, 2003).

---

available to caregivers of care recipients with dementia. These include interventions that utilize in-person, telephone, and Internet support groups to teach effective strategies to change behaviors of both the caregiver and care recipient. It is essential that such interventions take account of anticipatory and disenfranchised grief and cultural differences, however (Bourgeois et al., 2002; Holley & Mast, 2009; Logsdon et al., 2005). The growth of adult day health care is another response to the need to maintain persons with dementia in the community, to help them remain active and retain learned skills, and to provide respite for caregivers—although Medicaid funding for adult day health has been sharply reduced with the downturn in the economy (Zarit & Femia, 2008). The need for well-funded adult day-centers, respite, and support groups is greater than the availability of services, especially during the 2009 economic downturn. However, caregivers of AD elders are less likely to use such services to address their sense of burden than other types of caregivers (Brodaty et al., 2005).

Policies relating to work and family balance typically focus on parents of young children and on child care, not elder care. During the 2008 Presidential campaign, Hillary Rodham Clinton called for grants to encourage states to develop paid family leave programs referring to "kids, mothers and fathers," and "nurturing the next generation" with no mention of caregivers of elders or to an aging society. (Wisensale, 2009).

Legislation to Support Family Caregivers

Two major federal policy initiatives to support families include caregivers of older adults: the **Family and Medical Leave Act** of 1993 (FMLA) and the **National Family Caregiver Support Program** of 2000 (NFCSP). Under the FMLA, businesses with 50 or more employees are required to grant up to 12 weeks of unpaid leave annually when a child is born or adopted, when a child, spouse, or parent (not in-laws) with a serious health condition needs care, or when the employee is unable to work because of a serious health condition. Employers must provide health coverage and reinstate employment after the leave.

Because the FMLA does not apply to small employers, less than 10 percent of private sector worksites are covered, since small businesses employ almost 60 percent of American workers. Additionally not all workers of covered employers are eligible for FMLA benefits because of requirements related to duration and amount of work. When these eligibility criteria are applied, only about 40 percent of private sector employees are eligible for leave. Other barriers to using FMLA are lack of knowledge about the Act and the unpaid nature of the leave. From a political economy perspective (described in Chapter 8), FMLA only benefits those who can afford to forgo income while on leave. Workers who cannot manage the loss of wages entailed by family care leave are more likely to be African Americans, hourly wage earners (who are predominantly women), and those with lower household incomes (Wisensale, 2001, 2009). The FMLA also does not recognize extended family members, a characteristic of many families of color, or LGBT caregivers.

The biggest gap of FMLA is that the leave is unpaid. All industrialized countries except Australia and the United States, have some form of wage replacement for those who take leave. Additionally, no state or federal laws require employers to provide paid sick days, although the Healthy Families Act (HFA) introduced in 2009 by Senator Ted Kennedy and Representative DeLaoura (but not yet passed), would require employers with 15 or more employees to provide 7 paid sick days to care for their own and their families' medical needs. Another barrier to family-friendly employment is that most workers in the U.S. have little paid vacation time, and increasing numbers are expected to work even on paid holidays (Wisensale, 2009).

Proposals for paid leave continue to be debated along partisan lines in the U.S. Congress. From 2000 to 2002, more than half of the states introduced legislation to provide paid leave to family caregivers through the use of state unemployment insurance trust funds, but only 5 of the 26 state initiatives included care of an older parent in their coverage; the rest limited benefits to "baby care." The original intergenerational structure of FMLA is threatened by state legislators focused on care of children (Wisensale, 2009). California was the first state to expand its state disability insurance program from maternal to family care, including care for an older parent or a domestic partner. Washington State was the second state to adopt paid leave, but it does not include elder care. Proponents of paid leave contend that employers would actually save money when factoring in less turnover and fewer paid sick days. Under the Medicaid waiver system, described more fully in Chapter 17, some states now allow relatives (with the exception of spouses and same-sex partners) to be paid as personal care providers.

The National Family Caregiver Support Program (NFCSP) was funded by the Administration on Aging in 2000. For the first time in the history of the Older Americans Act, state units on aging and area agencies on aging are required to serve not only older adults but also family caregivers. These include caregivers of elders and grandparents, and older-kin caregivers of children/grandchildren. The NFCSP gives a higher priority to services for low-income, older caregivers and for those caring for persons with developmental disabilities.

In recognition of the growing phenomenon of grandparents as sole caregivers for grandchildren, each state may use up to 10 percent of its total funds to help grandparents and other family caregivers over age 60. Funds are also designated for American Indian caregivers. The primary service funded to date is information and referral (AOA, 2004). Although the NFCSP is important as public policy recognition of the central role of informal elder care, the program has had only modest impact. This is because of insufficient funding, the shift in thinking required by providers to conceptualize caregivers as clients, inadequate attention by health care providers to assessing caregivers' needs, and lack of consensus among states on "best practices." Overall, most federal and state policies continue to focus on the care recipient rather than supporting the caregiver (Family Caregiver Allowance and the National Conference on State Legislatures, 2004; Feder & Levine, 2004; Feinberg, 2008; Feinberg et al., 2004).

Flexible work hour policies for family caregivers of elders are also needed. Both federal and state governments could promote such policies by offering tax incentives to family-friendly corporations that offer generous leave policies, flexible work hours, and resource and referral to services to support elders and their family caregivers. Great Britain has adopted a soft-touch law that promotes employee–employer dialogue by legally empowering employees to request a flexible work schedule to address family care

---

FORMAL SUPPORTS FOR CAREGIVERS

- adult day care
- respite care
- home health care
- counseling in person or by phone
- psychoeducational groups
- training programs/skill development
- self-care techniques
- support groups
- Internet resources, chat rooms

---

needs. Through funding demonstration projects, the federal government could stimulate states to implement paid leave laws, flex work and soft-touch policies and other family-friendly initiatives (Wisensale, 2009).

Use of Services

Consistent with the person–environment (P–E) model, interventions to support caregivers aim to increase their care capacities and reduce the environmental press created by the elder's needs. Such supports to caregivers can help sustain care of their older relative at home and thereby reduce costly nursing home care. Ideally, services are provided to both members of the care dyad. For example, adult day health care offers socialization and health services for older adults, but also gives their caregivers a break from care. Services targeted to older adults in general are discussed in Chapter 11 and 16. This next section focuses on services primarily for informal caregivers.

Supportive Services for Family Caregivers

Caregiver Assessment

In the past, health care providers focused primarily on the care recipient, overlooking family caregivers as the "hidden patients" needing care

---

SERVICES UNDER THE NATIONAL FAMILY CAREGIVER SUPPORT PROGRAM

- information and assistance
- individual counseling
- support groups and caregiver training
- respite care
- supplemental services to complement family care

themselves (Family Caregiver Alliance, 2006a; Levine et al., 2004). Fortunately, leaders in both health care and long-term care are now emphasizing the importance of assessing caregiver needs. In a 2005 National Consensus Development conference hosted by the Family Caregiver Alliance, attendees reached agreement about basic principles and practice guidelines, strategies to change the field of practice, and reimbursement to carry out caregiver assessment across disciplines. These principles recognize that family caregivers are a core part of health and long-term care and that the field of geriatrics needs to shift to a family-centered perspective (Family Caregiver Alliance, 2006). Family caregivers require their own care plan to provide quality care and to maintain their own well-being. In programs where caregivers are assessed, they are more likely to feel acknowledged and valued as part of the health care team. Caregiver assessment can also identify family members most at risk of negative mental health effects and determine eligibility for additional support. Caregiver assessment should be multidimensional and reflect culturally competent practice. Most importantly, government and third-party payors must reimburse caregiver assessment (Family Caregiver Alliance, 2006a; Feinberg, 2004, 2008; Pickard, 2004).

A thorough assessment considers the caregiving context, the caregiver's health, knowledge, and skills; the care recipient's functional level; and the nature of care tasks. The Caregiver Burden Interview (CBI) and the Revised Memory and Behavior Problems Checklist (RMBPC) are two of the most frequently used assessment instruments. The RMBPC also assesses subjective burden. However, both scales should be used cautiously with families of color (Gottlieb, Thompson, & Bourgeois, 2003; Richardson & Barusch, 2006). Most caregiver assessments are not culturally sensitive because they were developed for research purposes, with small, primarily white, middle-class samples (Feinberg, 2003–2004; Gaugler et al., 2000a, 2000b). Home assessments are shown to be better than clinic-based ones at identifying

potentially serious caregiving issues (Ramsdell et al., 2004). In general, caregivers are first preoccupied with having their loved one's needs evaluated, which suggests that caregiver assessment is most likely to be effective if it takes place after this process is complete (Family Caregiver Alliance, 2006a). Outcomes of caregiver assessment include maintenance of health and well-being, prevention of social isolation, and identification of appropriate supportive services (Nicholas, 2003). Unfortunately, fewer than 50 percent of programs funded by the National Family Caregiver Support Program and Medicaid waiver programs uniformly assess caregiver needs (Feinberg, 2008; Feinberg & Newman, 2004).

Service Utilization

Although the Aging Network, especially through the National Family Caregiver Support Program, now provides more support for caregivers, increased service availability does not in itself enhance the caregiver or care recipient's well-being. Most family caregivers do not use services, or they do so selectively to supplement informal care for limited time periods, or wait until services are absolutely necessary (Zarit & Femia, 2008). Whether reliance on informal networks results in or causes underutilization of formal services is unclear. To some extent, patterns of lower service use may persist because families are unaware of services, unwilling to accept them, or lack the time and resources to access them. Yet services tend to be underutilized even by caregivers who perceive a need for greater formal support (Family Caregiver Alliance, 2006b; Montgomery & Kwak, 2008; Montgomery & Kosloski, 2000). Another reason formal services are underutilized is that family members may not identify themselves as caregivers needing support. For example, a daughter who begins by assisting her mother with shopping may not think of herself as a caregiver when she starts providing more intensive levels of care. When her identity changes to that of caregiver, she may be more open to accepting services. The caregiver identity theory helps to explain why some interventions, such as respite, are not uniformly beneficial (Brodie & Gadling-Cole, 2003; Dobrof & Ebenstein, 2003–2004; Montgomery & Kwak, 2008; Franks, Pierce, & Dwyer, 2003).

Gender and race affect service utilization, with women and caregivers of color the least likely to turn to formal supports. Some caregivers of color may not utilize services because of economic, religious, insurance, and other barriers to access, or because of discriminatory experiences that cause them to feel like unwelcome outsiders to agencies (Dilworth-Anderson et al., 2002; Magana, 2006). On the other hand, the Resources for Enhancing Alzheimer's Caregiver Health (REACH) trials found that African American caregivers responded more positively than whites to a behavior management intervention, and Cuban American husbands and daughters were more likely to benefit from a combined family systems and technology intervention (Burgio et al., 2003; Eisdorfer et al., 2003; Zarit & Femia, 2008).

Even when formal services are used, the overall effects are relatively modest in terms of caregiver abilities, knowledge, and emotional well-being (Gallagher-Thompson & Coon, 2007; Pinquart & Sorenson, 2006; Zarit & Femia, 2008; Zarit & Zarit, 2007). This pattern may occur if services prolong the duration of caregiving but not necessarily reduce subjective burden. Interventions may occur too late in the caregiving cycle after stress has already spilled over into other aspects of caregivers' lives (e.g., secondary stressors) or problems have become too complex to solve through short-term strategies. More likely, services may not meet what caregivers perceive to be their needs (i.e., their subjective appraisal of their situation). For example, many services are oriented toward crisis intervention, short-term support, and residential care rather than in-home and long-term personal care to assist with daily tasks. In other instances, families do not have the resources to purchase private pay services but are not low-income enough to be eligible for Medicaid-reimbursed services.

Compared to narrowly focused interventions, multi-component interventions are most effective; these incorporate several strategies and services (respite, adult day health, counseling, education, and support groups), are targeted to specific needs, are 8 to 12 weeks in duration, and are tailored or adapted to fit the care context. Multiple relatively comprehensive support services (e.g., they address psychological barriers to service use as well as access through case management) are effective because at least one of the supports probably will be appropriate at some point in time and they are likely to meet caregivers' needs as they change over time. Effective treatments are also characterized by a psychosocial rather than a purely educational approach, flexibility, and sufficiency of the amount or dosage of the treatment (Belle et al., 2006; Zarit & Femia, 2008). An example of a flexible intervention is the protocol used by Mittelman and colleagues (2004), whereby the counselor draws upon a set of approaches but has flexibility in allocating time to different problems. Such interventions, which require active participation by the caregiver and promote their sense of mastery, realistic appraisals of their situations, and skills to manage the situation, are found to reduce depression and burden, and to lengthen the time before relocating to a long-term care facility. The Mittelman program refers caregivers to ongoing support groups and individual counseling after completing the 6-week treatment core program (Given et al., 2008; Mittelman et al., 2004a, 2004b; Pinquart & Sorensen, 2006).

The largest six-site multicomponent intervention program, Resources for Enhancing Alzheimer's Caregiver Health (REACH), aims to reduce depression and burden among caregivers of relatives with AD. REACH attempts to change the nature of specific stressors along with caregivers' appraisal of and response to them. In REACH II, a follow-up to the original REACH program, an adaptive approach tailored the intervention based on the caregiver's scores on risk and protective factors in the initial assessment;

> ### TAILORED CAREGIVER ASSESSMENT AND REFERRAL (TCARE)
>
> The TCARE protocol utilizes: (1) an assessment tool that is clear, specific, reasonably short, and easy to use; and (2) decision maps or algorithms that guide care managers through a decision process (e.g., choice of appropriate intervention goals and strategies). It consists of a six-step caregiver assessment and referral process.
>
> 1. Assess caregiver needs using the TCARE Caregiver Assessment.
> 2. Complete an Assessment Summary Sheet on key measures such as depression and burden.
> 3. Select one of the six decision maps to identify goals and appropriate strategies and services.
> 4. Develop a Care Plan Consultation Worksheet using Guides for Selecting Support Services.
> 5. Discuss with the caregiver the outcomes of the assessment process and the options for obtaining support services.
> 6. Write a care plan that includes decisions made with the caregiver during consultation. (Montgomery & Kwak, 2008)

then assigned participants to specific treatment components according to their risk factors. This was found to improve caregivers' quality of life and depressive symptoms (Belle, Burgio, Burns, et al., 2006; Wisniewski et al., 2003; Zarit & Femia, 2008). On the other hand, multicomponent interventions may not uncover the relative impact of specific problems, making it difficult to target particular services. For instance, counseling may reduce emotional stress but typically requires that the caregiver travel for this service; in such instances, telephone-based assistance may better address time and geographic barriers (Coon, Ory, & Schulz, 2003; Pinquart & Sorensen, 2003; Sorensen, Pinquart, & Duberstein, 2002). Health and social service providers need to be attuned to the fact that caregiving is a dynamic process, changing as the care recipient's needs shift, and thus the types of

supports required also vary over time. We turn now to describing some specific family caregiver interventions.

Support Groups

Although findings are somewhat contradictory, support groups for caregivers are generally effective, especially if organized around particular illnesses or needs. For example, posttest measures of a support group for early-stage caregivers indicated a significant increase in preparedness for the caring role, competence, use of positive coping strategies, and a decrease in their levels of perceived strain (subjective burden). This suggests that during the early phase of caregiving, families can promote their wellness and enhance their ability to manage challenges through increased emotional strength and coping skills. Support group participation is also associated with decreased depression and increased morale, lower rates of nursing home placement, greater knowledge of illness and resources, and increased informal support. In contrast to these benefits, some studies report that support groups are less effective than individualized cognitive behavior counseling and skills training for reducing strain and improving well-being (Gallagher-Thompson, 2007). In some instances, support groups may be perceived as an additional burden by caregivers who have to travel and arrange respite care for their elder in order to attend—or if the groups focus primarily on the negative aspects of caregiving. Support group facilitators should take into account the different needs of spouses/partners and adult children caregivers and the fact that men typically prefer to talk to other men. In one study involving Cuban Americans, telephone support groups were found to be effective in overcoming logistical problems (e.g., transportation, scheduling, respite care) faced by both English- and Spanish-speaking caregivers, and offered benefits similar to those of face-to-face groups (Bank et al., 2006; Gartska,

McCallion, & Toseland, 2001; Harris, 2002; Toseland & Smith, 2003).

Psychoeducational Groups and Skills Training

Psychoeducational groups, which usually combine education and social support, are found to enhance caregiver well-being, delay nursing home placement, and increase use of supportive services (Bourgeois et al., 2002; Burgio et al., 2003b; Kuhn & Fulton, 2004; Mittelman et al., 2004a, 2004b). Since caregivers often do not know how to access services, they benefit from understanding the nature of the illness and learning about relevant resources. Some groups educate and empower caregivers to advocate for policy and programmatic changes (Morano, 2002; Schulz et al., 2002).

Family caregivers require both knowledge and skills in order to reduce their perceived burden and stress (Gallagher, Thompson & Coon, 2007; Given, Sherwood, & Given, 2008). Definitions of caregiver skills encompass goal-directed behaviors acquired through practice and performed with economy of effort (Farran et al., 2007) Examples are monitoring care, making decisions, adjusting to changing needs, managing medications, comforting with hands-on care, accessing resources, communicating with health care providers, and negotiating the health care system. They also need to know how to adjust their skills and knowledge to accommodate changes in the care recipients' condition and treatment plans and complexity of care (Given et al., 2008). A formal skills assessment provides the basis for determining what training is needed. To illustrate, an intervention known as the Environmental Skill-Building Program assesses caregivers' needs and then teaches them how to use environmental and personal resources to modify the care recipient's behavioral problems. Caregivers are also taught distraction techniques and how to enhance communication with their care recipient. Such skill-building benefits male caregivers in particular, who may be less likely to attend

support groups that emphasize expressing their feelings. Skills training programs that focus on management of behavior, depression, and anger are identified as particularly effective (Gallgher-Thompson & Coon, 2007; Richardson & Barusch, 2006; Femiano & Coonerty-Femiano, 2002; Gitlin & Gwyther, 2003).

Psychoeducational Treatment: Individual and Group Counseling

In psychoeducational treatments, a therapist uses psychotherapeutic techniques to encourage behavior change and overcome barriers to change (Zarit & Zarit, 2007) In group treatment, the leader uses group processes to build cohesion and model new behavior (Zarit & Femia, 2008). Individual therapeutic interventions tend to be more effective than groups in addressing issues such as family conflict, emotional reactions, and challenges resulting from a care recipient's cognitive or emotional disorders (Barusch & Richardson, 2006; Mittelman et al., 2003; Toseland & Smith, 2003). Family-level interventions should address not only how much other members do, but the manner by which assistance is given. For example, other family members may increase the caregiver's subjective burden by giving too much advice or criticism. Mittelman et al., 2004a, 2004b; Zarit & Zarit, 2007). The effectiveness of individual and family counseling generally varies with the caregiver's gender, race, education, and social class. Overall, cognitive behavioral therapy with caregivers tends to be most effective (Gallagher-Thompson & Coon, 2007).

Electronic Supports

Toll-free information and referral lines are vital, such as a national elder-care locator service sponsored by the Administration on Aging. The Internet has emerged as a way for caregivers to acquire information and share their experiences with others facing similar burdens. Some websites include advice and updated information from experts (such as the Alzheimer's Association's suggestions for managing behavioral issues and educational materials for caregivers), while others encourage caregivers to offer support to their caregiver peer. A growing number of websites through AARP, AOA, and the Assisted Living Federation of America (ALFA) allow caregivers to complete an interactive assessment online to determine the services they need most. Teleconferencing is being used to create virtual support groups among caregivers and can be accessed through caregiver websites. The opportunity to log on to a chat room on the Internet avoids the need to find alternative care or respite for the care recipient at home while the caregiver attends support groups or trainings in person. Outcomes from accessing the Internet include caregivers' increased sense of control, confidence, and support as well as greater involvement of distant family members (Smith, 2008; Czaja & Schultz, 2006). Use of the Internet for accessing services and support is likely to increase with computer-savvy baby boomers and their adult children. Although Internet usage is expanding among older adults and their caregivers, a "digital divide" still persists, with less Internet availability for and fewer studies of use by historically underserved populations (Kaufman & Rockoff, 2006).

Respite Care

Respite care is planned or emergency short-term relief for caregivers from the demands of ongoing care. Accessible and affordable respite and adult day care can provide caregivers with a break from their daily demands, thereby reducing both caregiver distress and nursing home placement. Respite encompasses a range of services and may be in- or out-of-home care—for example, through adult day health or overnight care in a long-term care facility. As noted by one caregiver interviewed for an AOA study, "Respite is my number one need. I've been caring for Mom for seven years ... in that time, I have had one vacation for three days" (AOA, 2003). Many

caregivers state that they would like respite services, but often face barriers to their use, including their own unwillingness to entrust their relative's care to someone else or guilt over taking a much-needed break. The amount of respite provided appears to be a critical variable in whether its use makes a difference. When respite is used at least twice a week for 3 months, caregiver depression, role overload, and strain are reduced, and nursing home admission may be delayed (Gaugler et al., 2003; Kagan, 2006; Zarit & Femia, 2008).

The Lifespan Respite Act, passed by Congress in 2006, authorizes competitive grants to Aging and Disability Resource Centers (in collaboration with a public or private nonprofit state coalition or organization) to make quality respite available and accessible to family caregivers regardless of age or disability. Giving one agency authority to integrate funds, ensure care coordination, control costs, and identify gaps is intended to make respite more accessible. This integrated approach recognizes the fragmentation and insufficient funding for respite services based on categorical age-groups (Kagan, 2003, 2006). The 2009 federal Omni-bus Appropriations Bill provided significant funding for respite care, a marked change from past years.

Future Service Directions

Regardless of the specific service configuration, support services should be culturally competent and accessible, such as in faith-based institutions, schools, primary care clinics, the workplace, and senior and community centers. Ideally, assistance is provided early in the caregiving cycle or even before it begins. This enables caregivers to plan before they are abruptly thrust into a burdensome role. Unfortunately, it is human nature that most people do not seek out information and assistance until they need it. General information sessions about services and supports for older adults and their caregivers are typically not well attended, often because few people like to think about these late-life challenges. An effective early preventive strategy would engage the caregiver in planning shortly after experiencing the first acute incident or receiving the diagnosis of a chronic disease.

Self-care for caregivers is an essential component in reducing stress and preventing out-of-home placement. A goal of self-care is to prevent the onset of stress and, if such signs do occur, to reduce care demands. Learning how to accept limits and ask others to help, attending to one's physical and spiritual needs (such as through exercise, meditation, or time for reflection), and creating moments of joy with friends or family are critical to both self-care and to giving effective care over the long haul. Organizations such as the Family Caregiver Alliance have developed Caregiver Bills of Rights as a way to encourage caregivers to take care of their own health in order to sustain quality care for their loved ones. Yet the demands of caregiving that underlie stress often interfere with finding the time and resources for self-care. Self-care activities are most realistic when they can be integrated with other daily routines. The need for a grass-roots caregiver movement to make caregiver voices heard by policy-makers and press for caregiver-focused legislation is increasingly recognized by advocates for families. The obvious barriers to such mobilization are the multiple demands on caregivers that reduce their time for such activities. In some instances, caregivers have turned to activism after the death of their loved one. For example, caregivers of persons with AD have become advocates for more federal money for research on dementia. In the current economic downturn, caregiver activists may need to frame their messages in terms of effectiveness and cost reduction.

Placement in Long-Term Care Facilities

Although living alone is a major predictor of admission to long-term care facilities, the decision to seek nursing home placement is frequently precipitated by the family caregiver's illness or death, or by severe family strain. In most cases, families turn to nursing homes only after exhausting their own resources, although adult daughters and husbands resort to out-of-home placement earlier than do other family members. Placement is thus often the result of a breakdown in the balance between the older person's care needs and self-care abilities; the primary caregiver's internal and external resources; and the larger support network. For example, characteristics of the caregiving context—especially perceived burden, negative family relationships, and low confidence in care—are stronger predictors of whether an Alzheimer's patient will enter a nursing home than are the illness characteristics or symptoms of the care recipient (Gaugler et al., 2005; LoSasso & Johnson, 2002).

Most people hold negative attitudes toward nursing homes, even though the quality of care in many facilities is excellent. Given such attitudes, moving an older relative to a nursing home is typically a stressful family event, especially for wives who vowed to care for their husbands "in sickness and in health" and for families of color where family members view elder care as part of their duty (Seltzer & Li, 2000). Accordingly, the placement decision often arouses feelings of grief, loss, guilt, and fear, and may renew past family conflicts. However, some families experience improved relationships with their relatives and continue to visit and assist with hands-on care in long-term care facilities. In other words, the role of "caregiver" does not cease after out-of-home placement, but the nature of tasks and stressors

---

PRECIPITANTS TO LONG-TERM CARE PLACEMENT

Caregiving stress becomes intensified when older adults experience the following, often resulting in nursing home placement:

- Falls
- Incontinence that cannot be managed
- Aggressiveness
- Sleep problems

change (Gaugler, Kane, & Kane, 2002; Polivka, 2005). Families typically still feel psychologically responsible, even though they must relinquish control over daily care decisions to staff and learn how to be "visitors" rather than primary caregivers (Schulz et al., 2003b). These role changes can initially trigger the family's dissatisfaction with their elder's care. However, when staff-family partnerships develop, families generally experience less stress and are more satisfied with the care received by their elder.

With the growth of the oldest-old population, placement in a long-term care setting may come to be viewed as a natural transition in the life cycle. Geriatric care managers can assist with the timing of this transition and with negotiating a positive role for the caregiver's continued involvement in the facility. To ease the transition to the post-placement phase, many nursing homes have developed support and educational groups for families and special training for staff. Internet-based services can also assist families with locating an appropriate long-term care facility.

Elder Mistreatment

In some cases, informal caregivers may mistreat older care recipients, although this is not typically due to caregiver stress. Instead, it is most often connected to caregivers' own emotional or behavioral problems and to power inequities between the caregiver and care recipient. Elder mistreatment, often invisible, became a public issue only after the 1987 Amendments to the Older Americans Act provided guidelines for identifying mistreatment, and as a result of the visible advocacy of the National Center for the Prevention of Elder Abuse.

Elder mistreatment encompasses any knowing, intentional, or negligent act by a caregiver or other person that harms or causes risk of harm to a vulnerable adult (National Center on Elder Abuse, 2007). Our focus here is on domestic abuse in the home, but elder abuse also occurs in long-term care settings (e.g., nursing homes,

adult family homes, group homes). Types of mistreatment range from physical, sexual, or emotional to financial or material exploitation and neglect/abandonment (either self-imposed or by another person) that result in unnecessary suffering. Self-neglect is distinguisheed from types of elder abuse where there is a perpetrator. Although findings on the incidence of abuse vary because of methodological problems, an estimated 2 to 10 percent of older adults are abused by someone who lives with them, and the rate increases among those over age 85 (Lachs & Pillemer, 2004; National Center on Elder Abuse, 2006; Taylor et al., 2006; Tomita, 2006). In the National Social Life, Health and Aging Project—the first population-based nationally representative study to ask older adults about their experiences with mistreatment—9 percent of elders reported verbal mistreatment, 3.5 percent financial exploitation, and 0.2 percent physical abuse by family members (Laumann, Leitsch, & Waite, 2008). A comprehensive review of

TYPES AND SIGNS OF ELDER MISTREATMENT

- *Physical:* willful infliction of pain and injury, such as restraining, slapping, hitting, malnutrition
- *Emotional:* verbal assault, threats, insults, humiliation, infantilization, isolation, exclusion from activities
- *Sexual:* nonconsensual sexual contact
- *Material or financial:* theft; misuse or concealment of the elder's funds, property, or estate; telemarketing fraud; investment schemes; usurious home loans; home repair scams
- *Medical:* withholding or improperly administering needed medications, aids such as dentures, glasses, or hearing aids, and visits to physicians
- *Neglect:* refusal or failure to fulfill any part of a person's obligations to an elder; withholding of food, medications, funds, or medical care
- *Violation of rights:* removal from home or placement in a long-term care setting without elder's consent
- *Abandonment:* desertion of elder by someone responsible for the elder's care

49 studies on abuse concluded that one in four vulnerable elders are at risk of abuse, with only a small proportion of this detected (Cooper, Selwood, & Livingston, 2008). For every case of mistreatment that is reported to authorities, there may be as many as five unreported cases (APA, 2006). In a large longitudinal study, elders who were mistreated were 3.1 times more likely to die within a 3-year period than those who had not experienced abuse (Lachs & Pillemer, 2004). Almost 66 percent of elder abuse reports involve family members as perpetrators (usually adult children or spouses), and over half represent self-neglect and neglect. Abusers are primarily men (National Center on Elder Abuse, 2006; Teaster et al, 2005).

Although financial and emotional abuse and self-neglect are most common, neglect and physical abuse (e.g., slapping, hitting, bruising) are reported most frequently. Emotional mistreatment, neglect, sexual assault, and abandonment are harder to document and often unreported (Schofield & Mishra, 2003; Teaster & Roberto, 2004). Underreporting also occurs because some abusive behavior is enmeshed within complicated familial relationships (e.g., a family that has always yelled at one another) and because elders who are dependent on their abusers fear retaliation if they report mistreatment. Psychological and financial abuse is even further complicated by the victim's dependency on the abuser or the perpetrator's economic dependency on the victim (Muehlbauer & Crane, 2006).

Financial Abuse and Exploitation

Financial abuse is the improper use of an elder's funds, property, or assets, often resulting from a distorted sense of entitlement in managing elder's finances.

Three common types of financial exploitation are

- Door-to-door scams: Scammers represent themselves as repairmen, skilled workers, or representatives of charities. They contract for services they do not provide, double-bill for services, or collect money for false charities.
- Professional swindles by insurance or investment agents who promise wealth and security in exchange for a bogus financial investment
- Caregiver, relative, or acquaintance abuse. As noted above, this is the most prevalent and predatory type, and encompasses psychological abuse, including deceit, intimidation, threats, and insults to establish power and control over the elder.

Financial abuse is frequently the underlying motive for other forms of abuse as well (Jayawardena & Liao, 2006; Sutterlund, Tilse, Wilson, McCawley, & Rosenman, 2007).

PROSECUTING ELDER NEGLECT

Neglect cases are generally extremely difficult to prosecute because of the challenge of proving "failure to act." Investigating cases of elder neglect can also be complicated by the victim's underlying disease: Was the disease or neglect responsible for the person's death? When King County prosecutors in Washington State charged a daughter with killing her mother through reckless neglect, the case broke new ground. It was the first time the county medical examiner had declared a death to be homicide by elder neglect, and it sent an aggressive new message that crimes of neglect would no longer be ignored. A fire department aid crew found the mother in her garbage-littered, foul-smelling suburban home. The mother was lying in the fetal position, her head and body covered with feces. She was taken to the hospital, where she died a week later of dehydration and hypothermia. Her daughter, who had called 911 and reported that her mother had fallen, was charged with first-degree manslaughter. The daughter said she had brought her mother shampoo, assumed she was bathing, and had not noticed any unusual smells about her mother.

BEWARE OF PREDATORS PREYING ON OLDER ADULTS

Betsy was a 78-year-old widow living alone in her own home in the suburbs. For most of the 10 years since her husband died, Betsy had been able to maintain her home and yard. However in the last couple of years, her property had been showing signs of neglect. The house was overdue for a painting. A fence in the backyard needed to be repaired. The yard was no longer a source of pride as it had once been.

Although it was not evident to Betsy's grown children—who were living away from home and had busy lives of their own—Betsy was beginning to show early signs of dementia. Her short-term memory was poor, and she had problems managing her finances. She knew her property needed fixing up but was reluctant to "bother" her children with it.

One day a man knocked on her door and said that it appeared she needed some work done around the house. He spoke kindly to her and quickly won her confidence. She thought he was the answer to her prayers. He realized that Betsy had some cognitive problems and told her not to worry, that he would help her with things that needed to get done and would give her a special deal. Taking advantage of her confusion and trust, he had her sign a contract and began asking for money right away so that he could buy supplies and get started. He asked Betsy to write him a check made out to "cash," which she did.

Over the next week, this man politely asked Betsy for more checks. He always had a reason for needing more money, and Betsy believed him. To avoid raising suspicion, he did not ask for a large sum at one time. Instead, he had her write a series of checks on different days. Betsy became confused about what she was paying for, but it never crossed her mind that this nice man was swindling her until he stopped showing up to complete the work. By the time Betsy's daughter became involved, the man was nowhere to be found and had cashed all of her checks. A police investigator told Betsy and her daughter that he had seen an increase of cases in recent years in which vulnerable older adults are victims of fraud. Betsy's children finally realized that their mother needed more of their support, and they have worked out a system in which Betsy remains in her own home while allowing her children to help with specific tasks like, check-writing and decision making.

Undue influence is an abusive behavior that is especially difficult to detect. It occurs when a person uses his or her role and power to exploit the trust, dependency, and fear of another, often isolating and creating a world controlled by the abuser. If the abuser is a family member, older victims have trouble separating their feelings of care and love from the loss and trauma experienced at the hands of the abuser. The abusive situation becomes more complicated when the abuser is dependent on the older victim financially, emotionally, and for housing. A web of mutual dependency is created when both the abuser and the victim rely on each other for a portion of their livelihood. Abuser dependency occurs more often than the reverse; for example, the dependent caregiver relies on the elder's financial resources, but the older person accepts such exploitation over being placed in a nursing home (Wilber & Nielsen, 2002; Sutterland et al., 2007).

Elder neglect or deprivation, whether deliberate or unintentional, accounts for 60 to 70 percent of all reported elder mistreatment cases (Fulmer et al., 2005). It occurs when the caregiver does not provide assistance, goods, or services necessary to avoid physical harm or mental anguish of the care recipient, such as denying food or health-related services to the elder. It can range from withholding appropriate attention to intentionally failing to meet the elders' needs, including not managing older adults' money responsibly (Muehlbauer & Crane, 2006). The elder's personality, childhood trauma experiences, and cognitive status are identified as risk factors for neglect. Some research on the relationship between self-reported childhood trauma and later-life neglect found that elders who suffered from neglect or abuse in childhood are more likely to tolerate poor care in later life because they view it as normative (Fulmer et al., 2005).

Self-neglect is three times more likely to occur than physical abuse or caregiver neglect, and it is becoming more widespread as older adults stay in their homes longer (Pavlik et al., 2001). It occurs when the older adult engages in behavior

RECOMMENDED ACTIONS FOR PROFESSIONALS SUSPECTING FINANCIAL EXPLOITATION

I. Interview the elder alone, although caregiver may resist leaving the room.
  A. Inquire about various financial transactions—including cash, income checks, checking accounts, credit cards, securities, home ownership, wills, and payments for services—that include the caregiver. Consider the following concerns:
    1. Who manages monthly income checks?
    2. Who signs checks and other documents?
    3. If the elder signs documents, are they read before signing?
    4. If an attorney is involved, who hired him/her?
  B. Inquire about relationships with family members, caregivers, insurance and investment advisors, friends, and new acquaintances. Consider the following:
    1. Who lives with the elder?
    2. Who cares for the elder's needs?
    3. Are relatives, friends, or acquaintances intrusive?
    4. Who initiated contact involving insurance and investment advisors?
  C. Perform a cognitive assessment, evaluating the elder's ability to make financial decisions.
  D. Conduct a geriatric psychiatry assessment to uncover psychological vulnerabilities that might impair judgment and decision-making ability.
  E. Ask the following specific questions:
    1. What is your approximate net financial worth?
    2. Has anyone been treating you badly?
    3. Has anyone forced you to do anything against your will?
    4. Has anyone coerced you to transfer money or sign any document?
    5. Has anyone hurt you?
    6. Are you afraid of anyone?
II. Interview with suspected perpetrator (if available)
  A. Present a relaxed, nonconfrontational demeanor.
  B. Ask about their relationship with the older adult.
  C. Discuss the elder's activities, daily routines, and special needs.
  D. Look for the following behaviors:
    1. Demeaning comments about the older person
    2. Defensive, suspicious attitude
    3. Hostility about your inquiries
    4. Threat to change doctors
III. Other suggested actions:
  A. Contact supportive family members regarding your concerns.
  B. Recommend that a nurse or social worker visit the home.
  C. Contact your state Office of Protective Services. Since each state's reporting laws are different, be sure you understand and follow the laws of your state.

that threatens his or her safety, even though he or she is mentally competent and understands the consequences of decisions. In some instances, the inability to perform essential self-care activities (e.g., providing for food, shelter, medical care, and general safety) may reflect a lifelong lifestyle choice and a way of preserving identity and remaining in preferred environments. **Hoarding** is an extreme case of self-neglect that may threaten elders' health, safety, and dignity, particulary because its private nature means it may remain unseen by others (Poythress et al, 2006). Elders who save everything may be trying to maintain control of their space. Yet such self-preservation behaviors are typically socially unacceptable (Bozinovski, 2000; Tomita, 2006). Self-neglect is also associated with mental impairment such as dementia, isolation, depression, and alcohol abuse. The incidence of self-neglect is highest among women living alone (Heath et al., 2005). Professional interventions—typically by social workers or nurses—generally focus on building trust with the elder to allow some services to reduce dangerously unhealthy living situations while still protecting the elder's autonomy regarding his or

> ### SIGNS AND SYMPTOMS OF SELF-NEGLECT
> - dehydration, malnutrition, untreated or improperly managed medical conditions, poor personal hygiene
> - hazardous or unsafe living conditions (e.g., improper electrical wiring, no indoor plumbing, no heat, no running water)
> - unsanitary or unclean living quarters (e.g., animal/insect infestation, no functioning toilet, fecal/urine smells)
> - inappropriate and/or inadequate clothing, lack of necessary medical aids (e.g., eyeglasses, hearing aids, dentures)
> - grossly inadequate housing or homelessness

her living situation. In some instances, however, professionals need to accept that there is nothing they can do to change the situation (Otto, 2002; Wilber & Nielsen, 2002).

Whether a behavior is labeled as abusive or neglectful depends on its frequency, duration, intensity, and severity, and varies across states. Lacking a national policy on elder mistreatment, each state determines standards for what constitutes abuse, who should be protected, and how. Regardless of state statutory definitions, however, the older person's perception of the action and the sociocultural context of the mistreatment also affect its identification and consequences.

Although ethnic and cultural groups vary in their opinions about what constitutes abuse, cultural differences should never be used as a justification for harming an older person. Nevertheless, culture, degree of acculturation, and filial values and beliefs can influence the definition of abuse and the elder's response to it as normal or not (Lachs & Pillemer, 2004). Professionals must take account of cultural differences when reporting mistreatment. In Korean families, for example, an elder may tolerate financial abuse because of the traditional patriarchal property transfer system, where sons enjoy exclusive family inheritance

rights. Korean elders are also less likely to report mistreatment out of shame or fear of creating conflict (Moon, Tomita, & Jung-Kamei, 2001; Tomita, 2006). Underreporting of abuse among communities of color, especially among Asian Americans, may also reflect language barriers or mistrust of the legal and health care systems. Prevention and outreach strategies are needed to address both general and culture-specific risk factors that contribute to elder abuse (Patterson & Malley-Morrison, 2006).

The extent of elder mistreatment among LGBT relationships is unknown. Many in the current cohort who are uneasy being "out" about their sexual orientation might have a difficult time admitting that they are abuse victims. However, this may improve in the future with greater societal acceptance of same-sex partnerships (MetLife, 2006b). With the increasing numbers of grandparents as primary caregivers for grandchildren, the hidden problem of mistreatment of grandparents by older grandchildren may also become more visible and appropriate interventions may be developed (Brownell & Berman, 2000; Bullock, 2007).

As noted earlier, while caregiver burden and the elder's limited functional ability may be contributing factors, caregiving stress does not in itself lead to abuse or explain its occurrence. In fact, assumptions that such stress is the cause of mistreatment can lead to inappropriate interventions for the caregiver rather than a criminal investigation (Anetzberger, 2000; Quinn & Heisler, 2002). Consistent with the P–E model, causes result from interplay of individual characteristics of the abuser and the victim within familial, cultural, and social contexts that result in adaptive or maladaptive behaviors. Consistent with feminist and social exchange theories discussed in Chapter 8, power inequities are more plausible explanations than family stress. There is growing recognition that elder mistreatment should be viewed largely from the perspective of power and control, and

MR. JONES' EMERGENCY ROOM VISIT

As an intern in a regional hospital, you have been called into the emergency room by a nurse supervisor to talk with Mr. Jones, an 80-year-old widower. The nurse, while leaving to respond to another emergency, asks you to "deal with this senile patient." Mr. Jones is sitting in a chair beside a 65-year-old man, Mr. Sloan, who brought Mr. Jones to the emergency room.

The two men have been living together for the past 16 years, after Mr. Jones became widowed. Mr. Sloan has a history of mental illness and heavy drinking, and has been unable to hold a steady job for the past 10 years. Nevertheless, the two men appear to care for one another and Mr. Sloan says that he cooks, cleans, and cares for Mr. Jones's needs. Mr. Sloan keeps repeating that he "doesn't know how much longer he can do this" and just does not understand what is wrong with Mr. Jones.

Mr. Jones is disheveled and has visible bruises on his face and arms. You learn from the nurse that he is waiting to have his broken right wrist set. You greet Mr. Jones and ask him what happened, and Mr. Sloan answers for him. He says he found Mr. Jones after he had fallen off a chair when trying to change a lightbulb. As he describes this, Mr. Jones is silent and unresponsive. Mr. Sloan tells you that both the hospital intake worker and emergency room nurse admonished Mr. Jones for climbing on a chair, saying he should know better. Mr. Sloan says that he just can't control Mr. Jones every minute to prevent accidents from happening. Mr. Jones looks away. He is confused and tells you that he couldn't find his Medicare card when the intake worker asked for it. He says he can't remember whether he took his wallet with him when he left home.

When Mr. Jones is taken into an examining room, Mr. Sloan insists on accompanying him. Mr. Jones begins an agitated monologue that does not seem to make sense. Mr. Sloan explains to you that his behavior is typical and that there is no point in talking with him. Mr. Sloan says that he will answer any questions. Mr. Jones becomes increasingly agitated and starts to cry. As the intake provider in the emergency room, what information would you want to gather from these two men?

WARNING SIGNS OF ABUSE AND NEGLECT

- depression, fear, or anxiety on the part of the elder
- discrepancy in psychosocial and medical history between elder and possible abuser
- vague, implausible explanations of illness or injuries
- illness that does not appear to be responding to treatment; lab findings inconsistent with history provided
- frequent visits to the emergency room; unexplained injuries or illnesses

thus treated as a criminal matter, whereas neglect may be a crisis in caregiving and therefore a health and social issue (Fulmer, Paveza, & Quadagno, 2002). In fact, case descriptions of abusers and victims reflect such power dynamics and marginalization of elders (especially women and the oldest-old), with the abuser exerting control over the vulnerable elder. In some instances, power and control dynamics are most salient in cases of nonphysical abuse, which may be more difficult to endure and may have more lasting negative effects than actual physical violence (Seff, Beaulaurier, & Newman, 2008). The elder's lack of adequate resources to pay for essential services and inadequate social supports also increase the risk of mistreatment (Choi, Kim, & Asseff, 2009). Given gender inequities and the role of victim dependency, it is not surprising that older women are mistreated at higher rates than men, comprising approximately 70 percent of reported victims. Nor should we be surprised that those over age 85 are abused at two to three times their population representation. Power differentials may also underlie the fact that sexual abuse is the least acknowledged, detected, and reported type of elder mistreatment (National Center on Elder Abuse, 2006; Teaster & Roberto, 2004). Recent research suggests that mistreatment of older men is often invisible, under-studied and undertreated. Increasing attention is being given to the abuse of older men, particularly abandonment of those who have "fractured relationships" with their families (Kosberg, 2007; Stratton & Moore, 2007; Thompson et al., 2007).

Research on **intimate partner violence** among older couples is relatively limited compared to that of younger populations. Yet partner violence may have more adverse effects on physical and mental health, and may be more severe than among younger partners. Although men are also victims of abuse, women are most frequently the victims of spousal or partner violence. In general, older women underreport partner abuse compared to older men (Logan et al., 2006). In one study, more than 50 percent of older women victims experienced multiple types of abuse during their lives (Bonomi et al, 2007). Violence among older partners, often reflecting lifelong patterns of "domestic violence grown old," is not an isolated one-time occurrence or a new crisis in old age. In such instances, older women may stay in an abusive relationship for years, hoping the situation will get better or is unaware of any other options. They may cope by redefining the situation as unchangeable while focusing on their other roles, setting limits with their abusive partners, and reaching out to others to survive and maintain an appearance of conjugal unity (Zink et al, 2006). Women who silently endure violence into their 70s or 80s tend to become increasingly isolated and "fall between the cracks"—too old to go to domestic violence shelters designed for younger women and invisible to providers of age-based services (Coker et al., 2002; Fisher & Regan, 2006; Kosberg 2008). Partner violence may also occur in new, first-time relationships or may be "late-onset" domestic violence, perhaps triggered by retirement, illness, reduced income, cognitive decline, and dementia. Few shelters promote themselves to older women or are equipped to handle their distinctive needs; but even when such shelters exist, they are underutilized by older women. As noted by one advocate, "When we advertised an elder-domestic violence support group, no one came. But when we relaunched it as a quilt-making group, women felt comfortable to come forward" (France, 2006, p. 82). Professionals in the domestic violence and aging networks should be trained to look for signs of intimate-partner violence to ensure that older victims' needs are addressed (Demaris & Reeves, 2007).

As noted earlier, abuser impairment is one of the strongest explanations for elder mistreatment. Abusers typically have more mental or physical health problems, alcohol or drug dependence, financial troubles and resentment toward and social isolation from the older person

---

THE COMPLEXITIES OF DOMESTIC VIOLENCE GROWN OLD

Married for 41 years, Audrey was first abused 2 months after their wedding. Her husband's attacks increased in frequency and cruelty. Once he caught her fingers in his car window and let her loose only when her screams drew a crowd. She camouflaged her bruises. But her psychological wounds were painfully visible. He made her believe she was dumb and fat, though she slimmed down to a fashion model's stature, and made her totally dependent on him. He refused to let her see family and friends alone and had the telephone removed from the house. She prayed that time would temper his moods, though it never did. Retirement seemed to make him angrier. Even when he sank into a feeble old age, he would strike at her with his cane. Only a few years ago, a doctor, alerted by her sad demeanor, asked if she was experiencing trouble at home. Unloading her secret brought Audrey a sense of liberation she hadn't felt in years. Although the doctor introduced her to a domestic abuse intervention program and she attended weekly meetings, she remained with her husband. Even when her husband was totally reliant on her because of his heart disease, high blood pressure, and diabetes, the physical abuse never ebbed. Right before he died, he put his arm around her and told Audrey he loved her. When he died, she was finally free of his abuse (France, 2006).

compared to nonabusers (Lachs & Pillemer, 2004; Schofield & Mishra, 2003; Tomita, 2006). The history of the relationship is also salient; for example, a history of alcoholism, financial problems, child abuse and neglect, conflict, and violence in the relationship are risk factors (Barusch & Richardson 2006). The following behavioral characteristics of the care recipient are associated with greater probability of being abused: being aggressive, critical, complaining, combative, and excessively dependent or expressing unrealistic expectations. Given these factors, it is not surprising that older adults who are socially isolated—and those with dementia, who may display aggressive, unpredictable behavior and who are typically less able to report abuse and access services—are the most vulnerable to mistreatment (Anetzberger et al., 2000; National Center on Elder Abuse, 2006; Wilber & Nielsen, 2002).

Assessment, Interventions, and Reporting

Families and health care providers must be alert to signs of potential mistreatment, although it may still be difficult for the abused to talk openly about their experiences. Additionally, abusers are typically effective at presenting themselves as overly concerned about their older victim and thus at masking signs. A range of screening and assessment tools for professionals to evaluate both caregivers and care recipients for risk of elder mistreatment are available. Two with excellent psychometric properties are the Elder Assessment

> **CHARACTERISTICS THAT REFLECT POWER INEQUITIES**
> - being male
> - dependent on the elder for housing, finances, or other services (e.g., meals, laundry)
> - mental illness, substance abuse, a history of problem behaviors, and lack of empathy for those with disabilities

Instrument (EAI), used by clinicians (Fulmer, 2003), and an index of risk factors as part of a comprehensive geriatric assessment (Shugarman, et al., 2003). Primary care physicians tend to underreport abuse, in part because of concerns about physician-patient rapport, patient quality of life, and physician control to decide what is in the patient's best interest (Rodriguez et al., 2006). The Elder Abuse Suspicion Index (EASI) is being tested with physicians as a user-friendly tool to facilitate referrals of possible abuse victims to specialized professionals (Wolfson, Lithwick, & Weiss, 2008). The use of elder abuse screening tools with family caregivers is problematic, since families are reluctant to report risk factors. For this reason, some researchers recommend the use of self-report measures with elders, such as the Vulnerability to Abuse Screening Tool (VAT) (Schofield & Mishra, 2003). Others argue for a comprehensive assessment that takes account of the caregiver, care recipient, environmental, housing, and community factors (Anetzberger, 2005). Valid, reliable measures and consensus on what constitutes an adequate standard for validity of abuse measures are needed (Cooper, Selwood, & Livingston, 2008).

Multilevel interventions aim to take account of such person–environment characteristics. One intervention program successfully coordinated the work of adult protective services and the Alzheimer's Association in educating caregivers to prevent mistreatment (Anetzberger et al., 2000). Another model focused on empowerment and strengthening the elder's resources and educating the caregiver; it also included home care interventions, support groups for elders, and caregiver support groups (Nahmiash & Reis, 2000). Because of the high incidence of behavioral and emotional problems of abusers, targeted individual interventions with caregivers are also important (Reay & Brown, 2002).

All 50 states have procedures for reporting domestic abuse (including 24-hour toll-free numbers for receiving confidential reports of abuse), and all but six have made such reporting mandatory for health care providers. This means that providers' failure to report elder abuse to public agencies is a criminal offense. In fact, eight states require "any person"—not just professionals—to report suspicion of mistreatment. All states have established APS programs, which generally have the authority to investigate reported cases or to refer them to appropriate legal authorities such as district attorneys. Every state also has a long-term care ombudsman to investigate and resolve complaints about nursing homes, but only 37 states require Adult Protective Services (APS) investigation in institutional settings (Teaster & Roberto, 2004).

Adult Protective Services is the state or county system that evaluates risk, assesses the elder's capacity to agree to services, develops and implements care plans, and monitor ongoing service delivery (Otto, 2002). Since mandatory reporting laws require that APS accept all reports, heavy caseloads typically are filled with complex and difficult cases that other agencies are unwilling or unable to accept (Wilber & Nielsen, 2002). Another barrier is that few community-based living options and in-home supports exist for elders removed from high-risk situations. In addition, professionals are often biased toward home care and resist placing the elder in a long-term care facility, even when the latter would be safer for the abused elder than remaining at home with a suspected abuser.

Only about 16 percent of cases of mistreatment are reported; of these, over 60 percent are substantiated after investigation, but relatively few are prosecuted, often because witnesses or victims are unable or unwilling to testify (Choi & Mayer, 2000; Fulmer et al., 2002; Wilber & Nielsen, 2002). Other reasons for underreporting include social isolation and our society's value on family privacy (which make concealment possible), lack of uniform reporting laws, and professionals' reluctance to report suspected cases. Screening measures for abuse typically assume that the alleged victim has the cognitive ability to respond to questions. In addition, the unknown consequences from reporting abuse (e.g., removal from the home,

nursing home placement, abuser's anger) may be more traumatic to the abused than remaining in the negative situation. Reporting abuse may make visible to others the emotionally painful reality that a child can abuse a parent. If the abuser is arrested, restrained by court order from the home, or abandons the elder, the older adult suffers the loss of a caregiver and companion, no matter how harmful the relationship may be. The elder may grieve the loss of the family member who was abusive as well as the other multifaceted losses entailed by abuse (Bergeron, 2000).

Since reports of abuse to APS appear to be only the "tip of the iceberg," large, rigorous probability samples of community-dwelling older adults' self-reports are needed. In addition, it is essential to conduct longitudinal follow-ups of APS use. Such information would help clarify the magnitude of the problem (Branch, 2002; Otto, 2002; Thomas, 2000).

Ethical issues typically emerge in instances of elder mistreatment. Elders' rights to self-determination and to refuse treatment—which are difficult to assess in ambiguous situations—are central to any systems to prevent mistreatment. In addition, professional ethics places a high value on confidentiality and protection of client's rights and autonomy. As a result, less than 10 percent of APS clients receive services without the client's consent

---

PRINCIPLES THAT SHAPE ADULT PROTECTIVE SERVICES PRACTICE

- the client's right to self-determination and autonomy
- the use of the least restrictive alternative
- the maintenance of the family unit whenever possible
- the use of community-based services rather than nursing homes
- the avoidance of ascribing blame
- the presumption that inadequate or inappropriate services are worse than none (Otto, 2000)

(Otto, 2002). In contrast to cases of child abuse, an older person has the right to refuse assistance even if he or she is found to be incompetent. In such instances, however, APS would move to have a guardian appointed who would assume authority over the elder's personal financial and estate affairs and could authorize nursing home placement against the elder's wishes (Lachs et al., 2002). However, a court-appointed guardian may also mistreat the elder, typically through financial exploitation. Issues of confidentiality are salient in caregiver support groups where caregivers self-disclose abuse, but the health care provider is mandated to report this information (Bergeron & Gray, 2003).

Cases of mistreatment have become criminalized under state statutes in the last two decades. This means that law enforcement may conduct a criminal investigation while APS supports the victim with counseling and services designed to provide safe medical and physical care. Some intervention models include teaming law enforcement professionals (e.g., police, district attorneys) with social workers and other health and human service professionals from a wide range of agencies to address the needs of both the victim and the abuser (Brownell, 2002). Elder Justice Act legislation has been introduced for the past several sessions of Congress to provide more funds to detect, prevent, and prosecute elder abuse, but has not yet been passed.

A MODEL FOR MULTIDISCIPLINARY COLLABORATION TO PREVENT AND PROSECUTE ABUSE

The first Elder Abuse Forensic Center (EAFC), instituted in 2003, was a collaboration of APS social workers, law enforcement, the district attorney's office, a medical response team, public guardians, ombudsmen, mental health services, a victim advocate, and a domestic violence expert who worked cooperatively on cases of elder and dependent adult mistreatment. This multidisciplinary model is being implemented nationwide (Wiglesworth et al., 2006). For example, a county-wide Elder Abuse Project in Seattle sponsors an elder abuse council that includes police, prosecutors, nurses, medical examiners, and social service workers. It meets monthly to determine how "the system" can better prevent, treat, and respond to the abuse of older and disabled adults. A criminal mistreatment review panel helps policy makers decide whether elder neglect cases can be prosecuted. The project also trains police, emergency room staff and medical technicians, and long-term care workers to detect signs of elder abuse and familiarize themselves with state laws. Recognizing that neglect is one of the most underreported crimes and one of the least understood by police and prosecutors, the project is currently focusing on adult neglect cases.

Underpaid Caregivers: Direct Care Workers

We turn now to the largest group of health care workers and the biggest component of the long-term care workforce—**direct care workers.** They are second only to families—the unpaid caregivers—as the primary providers of long-term care in both the community and in skilled nursing facilities. The direct care industry is comprised of three groups: 1) nurse aides, orderlies and attendants; 2) home health aides; and 3) personal and home care aides (Leutz, 2007). Of the total number of direct care jobs in long-term care, 56 percent are in nursing and personal care facilities, 17 percent in assisted living and other residential care settings, and the remaining 27 percent in home health care (either through an agency or as independent providers or employed by older adults through consumer-directed care programs) (Howes, 2004). As the "hands, voice, and face" and core of the long-term care system, direct or chronic care workers provide "high-touch" intimate, personal, and physically/emotionally challenging care (Harahan & Stone, 2009; Institute of Medicine, 2008). These hands-on providers are expected to be compassionate in their care, yet usually do not feel prepared, respected, or valued—similar to the experiences of many family caregivers.

The intersections of gender, race, and immigration status are reflected in the characteristics of direct care workers. Nine out of ten are women, oftentimes single mothers responsible for dependent children, with minimal education, frequently holding more than one job but still living in poverty or near-poverty, and increasingly dependent on food stamps and other public benefits to supplement their income. Many are women transitioning from welfare to work and facing significant barriers to employment. These conflicting pressures may affect their work performance. Racial inequities in terms of education and employment opportunities across the life course partially explain the predominance of African American, Asian, and Latina women (many of whom are immigrants) among such hands-on care providers. African Americans form 33 percent of the workforce and Latina or other workers of color comprise over 15 percent. Foreign-born women, generally educated in another country, comprise 20 to 25 percent of the direct care workforce and have the greatest likelihood of such employment, with the highest rates among immigrants from Mexico, Haiti, Puerto Rico, Jamaica, and the Philippines. Immigrant women are especially vulnerable to financial exploitation because such work is often paid under the table, which means local labor laws may not be enforced. The wide variation by race, ethnicity, and culture among direct care staff—reflected in language and cultural differences in communication—may result in miscommunication and conflict with other staff, older care recipients, and family members, which may interfere with meeting older persons' needs (Browne & Braun, 2008; Harahan & Stone, 2009; Leutz, 2007; Smith & Baughman, 2007; Stone & Dawson, 2008). Over 12 percent of nurses aides, for example, report that they speak English poorly or not at all (Redfoot & Houser, 2005).

Our society's lack of public recognition of the socially and economically important work of caregiving is, in turn, reflected in relatively negative working conditions. These include poverty-level wages and part-time employment with no or limited benefits (particularly health insurance); little training; inadequate supervision; and low status. As a result, 19 percent of home care aides and 16 percent of nurse's aides are poor by the U.S. Census definition (Browne & Braun, 2008; Harrahan & Stone, 2009; Stone & Dawson, 2008). In fact, the current direct care workforce has median hourly earnings that are more than 30 percent lower than that of the overall female workforce in the U.S., due in part to the high proportion of nonwhite and foreign-born workers and their lower education levels (Smith & Baughman, 2007).

Although many people are drawn to direct care work from a desire to help people (Squillace, Bercovitz, Rosenoff & Remsburg, 2008), such work is physically and emotionally draining. The heavy workload is often a repetition of single tasks, and the risk of personal injury from physical work is among the highest of any occupation, by one estimate second only to truck drivers (Stone & Dawson, 2008). The rate of depression among personal care workers is the highest across 21 occupational categories that were tracked (SAMHS, 2007). Workers of color may be treated disrespectfully, called "girl" or "maid," even verbally and physically abused, by some older care recipients. In addition, there are few incentives for such direct care workers to obtain more training or education to enhance quality of care. (Stone & Dawson, 2008).

The low societal value placed on caregiving within the long-term care system can create problems not only for the workers but also for older adults, family members, and formal providers of care. Quality of care is diminished when morale among direct care workers is low, turnover high, and labor shortages persistent (Howes, 2006). Not surprisingly, the turnover rate among direct care workers is high, with over 70 percent of certified nursing assistants replaced annually in nursing homes and 30 percent in home care. Turnover not only disrupts continuity of care but is expensive, costing providers from $1,400 to $3,900 per direct care worker for recruitment, training, and lost productivity. The total costs of turnover among direct care workers is estimated to exceed $4 billion annually (Harrahan & Stone, 2009; Wiener, Squillace, Anderson & Khatutsky, 2009). Over 66 percent of states face a shortage of direct care workers. To illustrate, a national study of nursing home staffing found that 97 percent had staffing levels below those recommended by the Institute of Medicine (Harrington, 2005). This raises concerns because a direct relationship between higher nursing home staffing levels and improved quality of care has been identified (Bostick et al, 2006). Additionally, consumer-direct care programs are often not able to provide adequate services because of staff shortages (Dale & Brown, 2007). Such labor shortages will be exacerbated as the population of older adults increases, with projections of a nearly 70 percent growth in long-term care workers required between 2000 and 2010 (Howes, 2004; Institute for the Future of Aging Services [IFAS], 2004; Montgomery et al., 2005; Moore, 2006). While hiring immigrants could be a way to ease the labor shortage, stringent immigration laws for direct care workers limit the numbers, and only temporary work visas are possible (Browne & Braun, 2008).

Fortunately, employers and policy makers are beginning to recognize the centrality of direct care workers to quality long-term care. Primary strategies include the need to expand wages and benefits, upgrade training programs and career ladders, improve organizational culture, and implement recruitment priorities. The 2001 Institute of Medicine report emphasized that the quality of long-term care depends on the performance of the caregiving workforce and recommended more attention to education, training, and supports for direct care workers This represented a shift from past reports' emphasis on regulations and staffing levels (Harrington, 2005; IOM, 2001; Stone & Dawson, 2008). The recruitment and retention of direct care workers qualified to provide patient-centered care is also recommended by the 2008 Institute of Medicine report (IOM, 2008). More recently, the improved quality of direct care jobs has been linked to the economic development of surrounding communities (Stone & Dawson, 2008). In California, Oregon, and Washington, home care workers have unionized; coalitions of organized labor, disabilities activists, senior citizens' lobbies, and community groups share the goal of changing the structure of employment in home health care. Because of unionization in California, roughly 25 percent of home care workers earn more than the minimum wage and have access to health, dental, and vision care insurance. As a result, being a home care worker has been considered a good job in California, although this may be shifting because of the state's severe budget cuts in 2009-10 (Howes, 2004). Nevertheless, a well-documented pattern exists in several states where recruitment and retention are improved when wages and health benefits are increased. Unfortunately, employers have limited ability to enhance wages and benefits because of constraints inherent in Medicaid and Medicare funding for long-term care (Harahan & Stone, 2009; Howes, 2005, 2006; Smith & Baughman, 2007; Wiener et al., 2009).

As a result, most direct care workers lack basic competencies essential to quality care, particularly effective interpersonal communication skills (Levy-Storms, 2005). In addition, few incentives exist for direct care workers to obtain more training or education (IOM, 2008). By keeping reimbursement rates low, the federal government sets the near-poverty-level wages and undervalued career paths of direct care staff in long-term care that may negatively affect frail elders' physical and mental health and well-being (Stone, 2004). As the predominant long-term care recipients, older women, who are frequently poor, are most often negatively impacted by the adverse work environments faced by their low-income female caregivers.

In addition to improved wages and benefits as a result of public funding, it is essential to provide direct care workers with more opportunities to be involved in decision making. This is because the staff often knows the older resident better than professional staff. When direct care workers feel valued by their supervisors who ask for their opinions, they generally experience higher levels of job satisfaction and are more likely to stay in their jobs (Harahan & Stone, 2009; IFAS, 2004; Wiener et al., 2009). The need to improve the recruitment and preparation of direct care workers is acute. While increases in wages, benefits, and particularly health insurance coverage are critical, the nature of the work environment is one of the most salient predictors of job satisfaction and turnover among direct care workers. This is shaped primarily by the management style and quality of supervision. The job satisfaction of direct care workers is likely to be enhanced by changes in the organizational environment that support worker autonomy and a sense of personal responsibility for one's work (e.g., involvement in care planning meetings), promote good relationships with older clients, and provide training and feedback from supervisors (Dawson, 2007; Leutz, 2007; Stone, 2004). The Institute for the Future of Aging Services administered "Better Jobs, Better Care—a national project funded by the Robert Wood Johnson Foundation to encourage policy and practice initiatives related to the recruitment and retention of a quality direct care workforce—recommended the following strategies (Stone & Dawson, 2008):

Organizational culture-change projects in skilled nursing facilities have also reduced turnover significantly and increased the satisfaction of direct care staff and family caregivers, as described in Chapter 11 (Dawson, 2007; Kane et al., 2007; Wiener et al., 2009). There are also recent positive developments in terms of organizing and unionizing direct care workers (e.g., state innovations to provide advancement opportunities or career ladders and changes in organizational

EFFECTIVE STRATEGIES FOR IMPROVING QUALITY OF DIRECT CARE

Supervision is the most important factor promoting job commitment and retention, staff camaraderie, and team building.

- Supportive services, such as full-time employment counselors and coaching supervision
- Retention specialist teams
- Enhanced training based on adult learning in communication and problem solving
- Opportunities for professional growth
- Worker participation in all decisions
- Career and education advancement
- Leadership development
- Organizational assessment for cultural competence and institutionalized racism
- Targeted recruitment through significant up-front assessment and screening
- Wage and benefit enhancements
- Worker empowerment and advocacy (Stone, 2004; Stone & Dawson, 2008)

culture to foster worker involvement in decision making). Training and hiring of low-income older workers as direct care staff are also proposed as solutions to the long-term workforce shortage and to increasing the economic well-being of elders who need to work. However, this direction may carry the risk of perpetuating a pattern of low-income older women being caregivers across the life course, without adequate compensation or recognition (Butler, 2009; Calasanti, 2004; Hwalek, Straub, & Kosniewski, 2008). National advocacy organizations, such as the *Direct Care Alliance*, are highly visible in policy arenas, working to increase salaries and occupational therapy to direct care workers. Another national organization, *PHI: Quality Care through Quality Jobs*, not only addresses policy issues, but provides technical assistance related to best practice for the direct care workforce. The *National Elder Care Workforce Alliance (EWA)*, a coalition of professionals and direct care workers, seeks to implement the 2008 IOM report recommendations related to direct care workers and quality of care through federal legislation. In some states, direct care workers and family caregivers collaborate to influence legislation with benefits for both types of caregivers.

Implications for the Future

With the aging of the baby boomers and increased longevity, family care of older adults will undoubtedly encompass a longer phase of the life course, with adults devoting 40 to 50 years to caring for older care recipients. Care networks will be larger and more complex because of the diversity of family structures and the effects of divorce, remarriage, blended families, more single parents, unmarried heterosexual couples, and LGBT families raising children. Women are likely to remain the primary caregivers for elders. Although 75 percent of married mothers work outside the home, women still assume primary responsibility for children. In fact, women devote nearly as much time to household tasks now as they did 50 years ago, even though the expectation and necessity for women to enter the paid workforce has grown. The persistence of this gender-based pattern in child care and household tasks thus tempers expectations that men will soon become the majority of primary care providers of frail elders, although the percent of male caregivers is already increasing (Family Caregiver Alliance, 2006b).

The workforce need for direct care workers in home health and residential care will outpace the supply among women ages 25 to 54. In fact, the job growth rate for direct care workers is projected to be twice as high as health care employment in general (45 percent vs. 25 percent) and three times as high as in all other industries (45 percent vs. 16 percent) (Montgomery et al., 2005). Possible solutions to this looming shortage are to recruit more workers from other countries (although this is more difficult with new immigration restrictions); expand the number of training programs; offer retraining for

older and displaced workers; improve worker safety, wages, and benefits; and utilize technology to assist with direct care monitoring, as described in Chapter 11 (Dawson, 2008).

The role of government in supporting family caregivers in the near future is unclear and will undoubtedly be affected by the escalating federal deficit. Current federal cutbacks, increased military spending, and the devolution of responsibility for services to the states suggest that public funding to support informal caregivers will probably be limited. More corporations may offer elder care services as an employee benefit because of the effects of family caregiving on worker productivity, although this is unlikely to occur until businesses see the economic gains of such programs Other private sector initiatives, such as faith-based programs, may offer incremental supports for families, but these are unlikely to reduce substantially the burdens faced by families who may be caring for persons with cognitive impairments for many years. For-profit geriatric care management businesses are likely to grow, especially to address issues of caregiving at a geographic distance. However, these services to locate and coordinate resources will be primarily accessible to upper-middle-class adult children. Unless patterns of public funding change dramatically, low-income families who are not poor enough to qualify for Medicaid-funded services will typically lack such supports.

Health care providers' assessments of older adults will increasingly include taking account of family caregivers' capacities. Nurses and social workers will play a key role in identifying supportive resources for families to enhance their caregiving capability and reduce stress. The issues of grief and loss inherent in family care, especially for an older adult with dementia, will need to be addressed by hospice workers, bereavement counselors, and other providers. The professional preparation of health care providers must include more information about how family history and relationships affect care, how to work effectively with family systems, and how to identify supportive resources for caregivers. Providers will also need training on detecting and reporting elder mistreatment.

The use of information technology to provide family caregivers with informal and mutual support will grow. Living in a networked society, senior boomers, facile with computers and the Internet throughout their adult lives, will be more comfortable than current cohorts in accessing information and support from others—including resources for family caregivers—through computer-based technology. The Internet already provides a wealth of information for family caregivers. These include free e-mail question-and-answer sites, bulletin board structures for sharing concerns and joint problem solving, digital photos of long-term care facilities, and links to national resources. Services such as these will continue to grow. Family caregivers will increasingly turn to other caregivers for 24-hour mutual support as well as accessing medical information via the Internet. The growth of assistive technology and computerized "smart homes," as described in Chapter 11, will enable more frail elders to remain safely in their own homes. However, such innovative supports will be more readily available to those who can privately purchase them than to low- or moderate-income elders and their families. Whether computer technology can, over time, reduce inequities and barriers to services among low-income elders of color remains unknown, and will probably mirror racial and class gaps among younger generations.

Summary

Most families, regardless of social class or race/ethnicity, attempt to provide care for their older members for as long as possible, and seek nursing home placement only when they have exhausted other resources. Without informal caregiving, the costs of long-term care to society would be staggering. Adult children—generally women—are faced with providing financial, emotional, and physical assistance to elders, oftentimes with little support from others. In low-income families and those of color, older adults are likely to receive daily care from younger caregivers and to be involved themselves in caring for grandchildren. But there are often numerous financial, physical, and emotional costs to caregiving. Elder mistreatment is one tragic outcome of a stressful caregiving situation, although most likely a result of caregivers' own behavioral problems. Responsibilities for caregiving are affected by a number of social trends, most notably the increasing percentage of middle-aged women (traditionally the caregivers, who are more likely to be employed) and the number of reconstituted families resulting from divorce and remarriage. The needs of caregivers are clearly a growing concern for social and health care providers and policy makers.

GLOSSARY

anticipatory grief   experienced before the death of the care recipient, often when there are cognitive and personality changes in persons with dementia, so that psychological death occurs before the physical one

caregiving   the act of assisting people with personal care, household chores, transportation, and other tasks associated with daily living; provided primarily by families without compensation or by direct care workers

caregiver burden   physical, emotional, and financial costs associated with assisting persons with long-term care needs

chronic sorrow   long term, seemingly never-ending grief that can impede physical and mental well-being

direct care workers   nurse aides, personal assistants, and home care staff who provide hands-on care in both home and long-term care settings; also referred to as *chronic care workers*

disenfranchised grief   grief that is not publicly recognized, such as the death of an LGBT partner, a lover, or a pet

elder mistreatment maltreatment of older adults, including physical, sexual, and psychological abuse, and financial exploitation and neglect

elder neglect deprivation of care necessary to maintain elders' health by those trusted to provide the care (e.g., neglect by others) or by older persons themselves (self-neglect)

Family and Medical Leave Act federal legislation passed in 1993 that provides job protection to workers requiring short-term leaves from their jobs for the care of a dependent parent, seriously ill newborn, or adopted child

hoarding a type of self-neglect in which the person excessively saves things, often putting themselves or others at risk

informal caregiving unpaid assistance provided by family, friends, and neighbors for persons requiring help with ADL and IADLs

intimate-partner violence domestic violence between partners/spouses

National Family Caregiver Support Program of 2000 requires state and area agencies on aging to provide services to support family caregivers

objective burden reality demands that caregivers face (income loss, job disruption, poor health)

primary stressors events that derive directly from the elder's illness, such as memory loss or wandering

respite care short-term relief for caregivers; may be provided in the home or out of the home (e.g., adult day health centers)

secondary stressors do not arise directly from the older person's illness, such as role strains and loss of time for self; however these are not secondary in terms of their importance

self-neglect the older adult engages in behavior that threatens their own safety, even though mentally competent

subjective burden the caregiver's experience of caregiver burden; differential appraisal of stress

undue influence abusive behavior when a person uses role and power to exploit the trust, dependency, and fear of another, often around financial matters

women in the middle women who have competing demands from older parents, partners, children, or employment

RESOURCES

Log on to MySocKit (www.mysockit.com) for information about the following:

- Administration on Aging, National Family Caregiver Support Program
- Alzheimer's Association
- Elders in Action
- Eldercare Locator
- Eldercare Web
- Family Caregiver Alliance
- The Home Care Page
- National Alliance for Caregiving
- National Association of Geriatric Care Managers
- National Center on Elder Abuse
- National Family Caregivers Association
- National Institute on Aging, Family and Professional Caregiver Programs
- National Respite Coalition Task Force: Lifespan Respite

REFERENCES

Adams, B., Aranda, M., Kemp, B., & Takagi, K. (2002). Ethnic and gender differences in distress among Anglo-American, African American, Japanese American and Mexican American spousal caregivers of persons with dementia. *Journal of Clinical Geropsychology, 8,* 279–301.

Adams, K. B. & Sanders, S. (2004). Alzheimer's caregiver differences in experience of loss, grief reactions and depressive symptoms across stage of disease. *Dementia, 3,* 195–210.

Administration on Aging (AOA). (2004). *The Older Americans Act: National Family Caregiver Support Program (Title III-E and Title VI-C): Compassion in Action.* Washington, DC: U.S. Department of Health and Human Services.

American Psychological Association (APA). (2006). *Elder abuse and neglect. In search of solutions.* Retrieved December 2006, from http://www.apa.org

Anetzberger, G. J. (2000, Summer). Caregiving: Primary cause of elder abuse? *Generations, 24,* 46–51.

Anetzberger, G. J. (2005). Clinical management of elder abuse: General considerations. *Clinical Gerontologist, 28,* 27–41.

Anetzberger, G. J., Palmisano, B. R., Sanders, M., Bass, D., Dayton, C., Eckert, S., et al. (2000). A model intervention for elder abuse and dementia. In E. S. McConnell (Ed.). Practice Concepts. *The Gerontologist, 40,* 492–497.

Arno, P. S. (2006). *Prevalence, hours and economic value of family caregiving.* Kensington, MD: National Family Caregivers Association & San Francisco, CA: Family Caregiver Alliance.

Bank, A. L., Soledad, A., Rubert, M., Eisdorfer, C, & Czaja, S. J. (2006). The value of telephone support groups among ethnically diverse caregivers of persons with dementia. *The Gerontologist, 46,* 134–138.

Beach, S., Schulz, R., Williamson, G., Miller, L., Weiner, M., et al. (2005). Risk factors for potentially harmful informal caregiver behavior. *Journal of the American Geriatrics Society, 53,* 255–261.

Belle, S. H., et al. (2006). Enhancing the quality of life of dementia caregivers from different ethnic or racial groups: a randomized, controlled trial. *Annals of Internal Medicine 145*(10), 727–738.

Belle, S. H., Burgio, L., Burns, R., Coon, D., Czaja, S. J., Gallagher-Thompson, D., et al. (2006). Enhancing the quality of life of dementia caregivers from different ethnic or racial groups: A randomized controlled trial. *Annals of Internal Medicine, 145,* 727–738.

Bengtson, V. L., Gans, D., Putney, N. M., & Silverstein, M. (2009). Setting the context of theories of aging. In V. L. Bengston, D. Gans, N. M. Putney and M. Silverstein (Eds.). *Handbook of theories of aging.* New York: Springer.

Bergeron, R. (2000). Serving the needs of elder abuse victims. *Policy and Practice of Public Human Services, 58,* 40–45.

Bergeron, R. & Gray, B. (2003). Ethical dilemmas of reporting suspected elder abuse. *Social Work, 48,* 96–105.

Boise, L., Congelton, L., & Shannon, K. (2005). Empowering family caregivers: The powerful tools for caregiving program. *Educational Gerontology, 31,* 1–14.

Bonomi, A. E., Anderson. M. L., Reid, R. J., Carrell, D., Fishman, P.A. Rivara, R. P. et al. (2007). Intimate partner violence in older women. *The Gerontologist, 47,* 34–41.

Bookman, A. & Harrington, M. (2007). Family caregivers: A shadow workforce in the geriatric health care system? *Journal of Health Politics, Policy and Law, 32,* 1005–41.

Bourgeois, M. S., Schulz, R., Burgio, L., & Beach, S. (2002). Skills training for spouses of patients with Alzheimer's disease: Outcomes of an intervention study. *Journal of Clinical Geropsychology, 8,* 53–73.

Bozinovski, S. (2000). Older self-neglectors: Interpersonal problems and the maintenance of self-continuity. *Journal of Elder Abuse and Neglect, 12,* 37–56.

Branch, L. (2002). The epidemiology of elder abuse and neglect. *Public Policy and Aging Report, 12,* 19–23.

Brodaty, H., Thompson, C., Thompson, C., & Fine, M. (2005). Why caregivers of people with dementia and memory loss don't use services. *International Journal of Geriatric Psychiatry, 20,* 537–546.

Brodie, K. & Gadling-Cole, C. (2003). The use of family decision meetings when addressing caregiver stress. *Journal of Gerontological Social Work, 41,* 89–100.

Brody, E. (2004). *Women in the middle.* New York: Springer.

Browne, C. V. & Braun, K. L. (2008). Globablization, women's migration and the long-term care workforce. *The Gerontologist, 48,* 16–24.

Brownell, P. (2002). *Project 2015: The future of aging in New York state.* New York: Department for the Aging.

Brownell, P. & Berman, J. (2000). Elder abuse and the kinship foster care system: Two generations at risk. In C. Cox (Ed.). *To grandmother's house we go and stay.* New York: Springer.

Bullock, K. (2007). The vulnerability of elder abuse among a sample of custodial grandfathers. *Journal of Elder Abuse and Neglect, 19*, 133–150.

Bullock, K., Crawford, S., & Tennstedt, S. (2003). Employment and caregiving: Exploration of African American caregivers. *Social Work, 48*, 150–162.

Burgio, L., Solano, N., Fisher, S., Stevens, A., & Gallagher-Thompson, D. (2003a). Skill-building: Psychoeducational strategies. In D. W. Coon, D. Gallagher-Thompson, & L. Thompson (Eds.). *Innovative interventions to reduce dementia caregiver distress: A clinical guide.* New York: Springer.

Burgio, L., Stevens, A., Guy, D., Roth, D. L., & Haley, W. E. (2003b). Impact of two psychosocial interventions on white and African American family caregivers of individuals with dementia. *The Gerontologist, 43*, 568–581.

Butler, S. (2009). Women still taking care: The experiences of older home care workers. *Journal of Gerontological Social Work, 52*, 277–293.

Calasanti, T. (2004). Feminist gerontology and old men. *Journal of Gerontology: Social Sciences, 59B*, S305–314.

Calasanti, T. (2006). Gender and old age: Lessons from spousal caregivers. In T. Calasanti & K. Slevin (Eds.). *Age matters: Re-aligning feminist thinking.* New York: Routledge.

Calasanti, T. (2009). Theorizing feminist gerontology, sexuality and beyond: An intersectional approach. In V. L Bengtson, D. Gans, N. M. Putney, & M. Silverstein (Eds.). *Handbook of theories of aging.* New York: Springer Publishing.

Cannuscio, C., Jones, C., Kawachi, I., Colditz, G., Berkman, L., & Rimm, E. (2002). Reverberations of family illness: A longitudinal assessment of informal caregiving and mental health status in the nurses' health study. *American Journal of Public Health, 92*, 1305–1311.

Chappell, N. L. & Reid, R. C. (2002). Burden and well-being among caregivers: Examining the distinction. *The Gerontologist, 42*, 772–80.

Choi, N. G., Kim, J. & Asseff, J. (2009). Self-neglect an neglect of vulnerable older adults. *Journal of Gerontological Social Work, 52*, 171–187.

Choi, N. G. & Mayer, J. (2000). Elder abuse, neglect and exploitation: Risk factors and prevention strategies. *Journal of Gerontological Social Work, 33*, 5–25.

Christakis, N. & Allison, P. (2006). Spouse's hospitalization increases partner's risk of death. *New England Journal of Medicine, 54*, 719–730.

Coker, A. L., Davis, K. E., Arias, I., Desai, D., Sanderson, M., & Brandt, H. M., et al. (2002). Physical and mental health effects on intimate partner violence for men and women. *American Journal of Preventive Medicine, 23*, 260–268.

Coon, D., Ory, M., & Schulz, R. (2003). Family caregivers: Enduring and emerging themes. In D. W. Coon, D. Gallagher-Thompson, & L. Thompson (Eds.). *Innovative interventions to reduce caregiver distress.* New York: Springer.

Cooper, C., Selwood, A., & Livingston, G. (2008). The prevalence of elder abuse and neglect: A systematic review. *Age and Ageing, 27*, 151–260.

Covinsky, K. E., Newcomer, R., Fox, P. Wood, J., Sanders, L, Dane, K. et al. (2003). Patient and caregiver characteristics associated with depression in caregivers of patients with dementia. *Journal of General Internal Medicine, 18*, 1006–1014.

Czaja, S. J. & Schultz, R. (2006). Innovations in technology and aging: Introduction. *Generations, 30*(2), 6–8.

Davey, A. (2007). Divorce foretells child's future care for elderly parent. *Science Daily.* Retrieved June 2009, from http://www.sciencedaily.com/releases/2007/09/070915081436.htm

Dilworth-Andersen, P., Brummett, B. H. Goodwin, P., Williams, S. W., Williams, R. B., & Siegler, I. C. (2005). Effects of race on cultural justification for caregiving. *Journal of Gerontology: Social Sciences, 60B*, S257–262.

Dobrof, J. & Ebenstein, H. (2003–2004). Family caregiver self-identification: Implications for healthcare and social service professionals. *Generations, 27*, 33–38.

Donorfio, L. M. & Sheehan, N. W. (2001). Relationship dynamics between aging mothers and caregiving daughters: Filial expectations and responsibilities. *Journal of Adult Development, 8,* 39–49.

Dupuis, S. (2002). Understanding ambiguous loss in the context of dementia care: Adult children's perspective. *Journal of Gerontological Social Work, 37,* 93–114.

Eisdorfer, C., Czaja, S. J., Loewenstein, D., Rubert, M., Arguelles, S., et al. (2003). The effect of a family therapy and technology-based intervention on caregiver depression. *The Gerontologist, 43,* 521–531.

Family Caregiver Alliance. (2005). *Fact sheet: Selected caregiver statistics.* Retrieved October 2008, from http:www.caregiver.org/caregiver/jsp/content-node.jsp?nodeid=368

Family Caregiver Alliance & National Center on Caregiving. (2006a). *Caregiver assessment: Principles, guidelines, and strategies for change.* Report from a National Consensus Development Conference. San Francisco.

Family Caregiver Alliance & National Center on Caregiving. (2006b). *Selected caregiver statistics.* San Francisco: Family Caregiver Alliance.

Family Caregiver Alliance & National Center on Caregiving. (2006c). *Women and caregiving: Facts and figures.* San Francisco: Family Caregiver Alliance.

Family Caregiver Alliance (2009). *Fact sheet: Caregiving.* San Francisco: Family Caregiver Alliance.

Farran, C. J., Gilley, D. W., McCann, J. J., Bienias, J. L., Lindeman, D. A., & Evans, D. A. (2007). Efficacy of behavioral interventions for dementia caregivers. *Western Journal of Nursing Research, 29,* 944–960.

Feder, J. & Levine, C. (2004). Explaining the paradox of long-term care policy. In C. Levine & T. Murray (Eds.). *The cultures of caregiving: Conflict and common ground among families, health care professionals and policy makers,* 103–112. Baltimore: Johns Hopkins University Press.

Feinberg, L. F. (2003–2004). The state of the art of caregiver assessment. *Generations, 27,* 24–32

Feinberg, L. F. (2008). Caregiver Assessment. *Journal of Social Work Education, 44,* 39–41.

Feinberg, L. F. & Newman, S. (2004). A study of 10 states since passage of the National Family Caregiver Support Program: Policies, perceptions and program development. *The Gerontologist, 44,* 760–769.

Feinberg, L. F., Newman, S., Gray, L., Kolb, K., & Fox-Grage, W. (2004). *The state of the states: A 50-state study.* San Francisco: Family Caregiver Alliance.

Femiano, S. & Coonerty-Femiano, A. (2002). Principles and interventions for working therapeutically with caregiving men: Responding to challenges. In E. Kramer & L. Thompson (Eds.). *Men as caregivers.* New York: Springer.

Fisher, B. S. & Regan, S. L. (2006). The extent and frequency of abuse in the lives of older women and their relationship with health outcomes. The *Gerontologist, 46*(2), 200–209.

Foley, K. L., Tung, H. J. & Mutran, E. J. (2002). Self-gain and self-loss among African American and white caregivers. *Journal of Gerontology: Social Sciences, 57,* S14–S22.

France, D. (2006). And then he hit me. *AARP Magazine,* 73–77.

Franks, M., Pierce, L. & Dwyer, J. (2003). Expected parent-care involvement of adult children. *Journal of Applied Gerontology, 22,* 104–117.

Fulmer, T. (2003). Try this: Elder abuse and neglect assessment. *Journal of Gerontological Nursing, 29,* 8–10.

Fulmer, T., Paveza, G., & Quadagno, L. (2002). Elder abuse and neglect: Policy issues for two very different problems. *Public Policy and Aging Report, 12,* 15–18.

Fulmer, T., Paveza, G., VandeWeerd, C., Fairchild, S., Guadagno, L., Bolton-Blatt, M., et al. (2005). Dyadic vulnerability and risk profiling for elder neglect. *The Gerontologist, 45,* 525–535.

Gallagher-Thompson, D., & Coon, D. W. (2007). Evidence-based psychological treatments for distress in family caregivers of older adults. *Psychology of Aging, 22,* 37–51.

Gartska, T., McCallion, P., & Toseland, R. (2001). Using support groups to improve caregiver health. In M. L. Hummert & J. F. Nussbaum (Eds.). *Aging, communication, and health*. Mahwah, NJ: Lawrence Erlbaum Associates.

Gaugler, J. E., Edwards, A., Femia, E., Zarit, S., Stephens, M., et al. (2000). Predictors of institutionalization of cognitively impaired elders: Family help and the timing of placements. *Journal of Gerontology: Psychological Sciences, 55B*, P247–255.

Gaugler, J. E., Jarrot, S., Zarit, S., Stephens, M., Townsend, A., & Greene, R. (2003). Adult day service use and reductions in caregiving hours: Effects on stress and psychological well-being for dementia caregivers. *International Journal of Geriatric Psychiatry, 18*, 55–62.

Gaugler, J. E., Kane, R. L., & Kane, R. A. (2002). Family care for older adults with disabilities: Toward more targeted and interpretable research. *International Journal of Aging and Human Development, 54*, 205–231.

Gaugler, J. E., Kane, R. L., Kane, R. A., Clay, T., & Newcomer, R. (2005). The effects of duration of caregiving on institutionalization. *The Gerontologist, 45*, 78–89

Gaugler, J. E., Leitsch, S. A., Zarit, S. H., & Pearlin, L. I. (2000). Caregiver involvement following institutionalization: Effects of preplacement stress. *Research on Aging, 22*, 337–360.

Gibson, M. J. & Houser, A. N. (2007). *Valuing the invaluable: A new look at the economic value of family caregiving*. Washington, DC: AARP Public Policy Institute (Issue Brief 82). Retrieved August 2009, from http://assets.aarp.org/rgcenter/il/ib82_caregiving.pdf

Ginzler, E. (2009). *Family caregiving, Alzheimer's and caring for loved ones*. Retrieved June 2009, from http://www.aarp.org/family/caregiving/articles/ginzler_alzheimers_caregiving.html?print=1

Gitlin, L. & Gwyther, L. (2003). In-home interventions. Helping caregivers where they live. In D. W. Coon, D. Gallagher-Thompson, & L. Thompson (Eds.). *Innovative interventions to reduce dementia caregiver distress*. New York: Springer.

Given, B. Sherwood, P., & Given, C. (2008). What knowledge and skills do caregivers need. *Journal of Social Work Education, 44*, 28–34.

Goins, R. T., Moss, M., Buchwald, D., & Guralnik, J. M. (2007). Disability among older American Indians and Alaska Natives: An analysis of the 2000 Census public use microdata sample. *The Gerontologist, 47*, 670–696.

Gonyea, J. (2008). Foreward: America's aging workforce: A critical business issue. *Journal of Workplace Behavioral Health, 23*(1/2), 1–14.

Gottlieb, B. H., Thompson, L., & Bourgeois, M. (2003). Monitoring and evaluating interventions. In D. W. Coon, D. Gallagher-Thompson, & L. Thompson. (Eds.). *Innovative interventions to reduce dementia caregiver distress*. New York: Springer.

Greenberg, J., Selzter, M., & Brewer, V. (2006). Caregivers to older adults. In B. Berkman (Ed.). *Handbook of social work in health and aging*. New York: Oxford.

Gross, J. (2006). Elder care costs deplete savings of a generation. *The New York Times*, pp. A1, A16.

Gwyther, L. (1998). Social issues of the Alzheimer's patient and family. *Neurological Clinics, 18*, 993–1010.

Haley, W. E., Gitlin, L., Wisniewski, S., Mahoney, D., Coon, D., Winter, L., Corcoran, M., et al. (2004). Well-being, appraisal and coping in African American and Caucasian dementia caregivers: Findings from the REACH study. *Aging and Mental Health, 8*, 316–329.

Harahan, M. & Stone, R. (2009). Who will care? Building the geriatric long-term care labor force. In R. B. Hudson (Ed.). Boomer bust, (Vol. 2). The boomers and their future. Westport, CT: Praeger.

Hargrave, T. H. (2008). The Worker's Point of View VIII. Working Conditions and Morale. *Human Factors [London], 6*(10), 382–384.

Harris, P. B. (2002). The voices of husbands and sons caring for a family member with dementia. In E. Kramer & L. Thompson, (Eds.). *Men as caregivers*. New York: Springer.

Harris-Kojetin, L., Lipson, D., Fielding, J., Kiefer, K., & Stone, R. (2004). *Recent findings on frontline* long-term care worker: A research synthesis 1999–2003. Retrieved December 2006, from http://aspe.hhs.gov/daltcp/reports/insight.pdf

Heaphy, B. (2007). Sexualities, gender and ageing: Resources and social change. *Current Sociology, 55*, 193–210.

Heath, J., Brown, M., Kobylarz, F., & Castano, S. (2005). The prevalence of undiagnosed geriatric health conditions among adult protective service clients. *The Gerontologist, 45*, 820–823.

Holley, C. K. & Mast, B. T. (2009). The impact of anticipatory grief on caregiver burden in dementia caregivers. *The Gerontologist, 49*, 388–397.

Howes, C. (2004). Upgrading California's home care workforce: The impact of political action and unionization. *The State of California's Labor*, 71–105.

Howes, C. (2005). Living wages and retention of homecare workers in San Francisco. *Industrial Relations, 44*, 139–162.

Howes, C. (2006). *Wages, benefits and flexibility matter: Building a high quality home care workforce, better jobs, better care*. Washington, D.C.: American Association of Homes and Services for the Aging.

Hwalek, M., Straub, V., & Kosniewski, K. (2008). Older workers: An opportunity to expand the long term care/direct care labor force. *The Gerontologist, 48*, 90–103.

Iecovich, E. (2000). Sources of stress and conflicts between elderly patients, their family members and personnel in care settings. *Journal of Gerontological Social Work, 34*, 73–88.

Iecovich, E. (2008). Caregiving burden, community services, and quality of life of primary caregivers of frail elderly persons. *Journal of Applied Gerontology, 27*(3), 309–330.

Institute for the Future of Aging Services (IFAS). (2004). *Better Jobs, Better Care*. Washington, DC.

Institute of Medicine. (2008). *Retooling for an Aging America: Building the Health Care Workforce*. Washington, DC: The National Academies Press.

Jayawardena, K. M. & Liao, S. (2006). Elder abuse at end of life. *Journal of Palliative Medicine, 9*(1), 127–136.

Jervis, L. L. & Manson, S. S. (2002). American Indians/Alaska Nataives and dementia. *Alzheimer Disease and Related Disorders, 16*, S 89–95.

John, R. Hennessy, C. H., Dyeson, T. B., & Garrett, M. D. (2001). Toward the conceptualization and measurement of caregiver burden among Pueblo Indian family caregivers. *The Gerontologist, 41*, 210–219.

Johnson, R. W. & Wiener, J. M. (2006). A profile of frail older Americans and their caregivers. Washington, D.C. The Urban Institute: The Retirement Project. Occasional Paper Number 8.

Judge, K. S. (2007). *Acquiring new skills while enhancing remaining strengths: Strength-based intervention for individuals with dementia and their care partners*. Symposium conducted at the Gerontological Society of America 60th Annual Scientific Meeting, San Francisco, November 16–20, 2007.

Kagan, J. (2003). *Lifespan respite. Fact sheet number 7*. Annandale, VA: National Respite Coalition.

Kagan, J. (2006). *Lifespan Respite Act now goes to President's desk to be signed into law*. Annandale, VA: National Respite Coalition. Press Release from Hilary Rodham Clinton.

Kane, R. A. Lum, T. Y., Cutler, L. J., Degenholtz, H. B., & Tu. T. C. (2007). Resident outcomes in small-house nursing homes: A longitudinal evaluation of the initial Green House program. *Journal of the American Geriatrics Society, 55*, 832–839.

Kaufman, D. R., & Rockoff, M. L. (2006). Increasing access to online information about health: A program for inner-city elders in community-based organizations. *Generations, 30*, 55–57.

Kelly, K., Reinhard, S. C., & Brooks-Danso, A. (2008). Executive summary: Professional partners supporting family caregivers. *Journal of Social Work Education, 44*, 5–15.

Kiecolt-Glaser, J. & Glaser, R. (2003). Chronic stress and age-related increases in the proinflammatory cytokine IL-6. *Proceedings of the National Academy of Sciences 100*, 9090–9095.

Konrad, W. (2009). Taking care of parents also means taking care of finances. *The New York Times*, B5.

Korn, L., Logsdon, R. G. Polissar, N. L., Gomez-Beloz, A., Waters, T., & Ryser, R. (2009). A randomized trial of a CAM therapy for stress reduction in American Indian and Alaskan Native family caregivers. *The Gerontologist*, 49, 368–377.

Kosberg, J. (2007). *Abuse of Older Men*. Binghamton, NY: Haworth Press.

Kramer, B. J. & Thompson, E. H. (2002). *Men as caregivers: Theory, research and service implications*. New York: Springer.

Kuhn, D. (2004). Empowering family caregivers. *Social Work Today*, 4, 38.

Kuhn, D. & Fulton, B. (2004). Efficacy of an educational program for relatives of persons in the early stages of Alzheimer's disease. *Journal of Gerontological Social Work*, 42, 109–130.

Lachs, M. & Pillemer, K. (2004). Elder abuse. *The Lancet*, 364, 1263–1272.

Lachs, M., Williams, C., O'Brien, S., & Pillemer, K. (2002). Adult protective service use and nursing home placement. *The Gerontologist*, 42, 734–739.

Laumann, E. D., Leitsch, S. A., & Waite, L. (2008). Elder mistreatment in the United States: Prevalence estimates from a nationally representative study. *Journal of Gerontology: Social Sciences*, 63B, S249–S254.

Lee, S., Colditz, G., Berkman, L., & Kawachi, I. (2003). Caregiving and risk of coronary heart disease in U.S. women: A prospective study. *American Journal of Preventive Medicine*, 24, 113–119.

Leland, J. (2008). More men take the lead role in caring for elderly parents. Retrieved December 2008, from http://www.nytimes.com/2008/11/29/us/29sons.html?_r=1&ref=health

Levine, C., Reinhard, S., Feinberg, L., Albert, S., & Hart, A. (2004). Family caregivers on the job: Moving beyond ADLS and IADLs. *Generations*, 27, 17–23.

Li, J., Cowden, L. G., King, J. D. Briles, D. A., Schroeder H. W. Stevens, A. B., et al. (2007). Effects of chronic stress and interleukin-10 gene polymorphisms on antibody response to tetanus vaccine in family caregivers of patients with Alzheimer's disease. *Psychosomatic Medicine*, 9, 551–559.

LoSasso, A. T. & Johnson, R. W. (2002). Does informal care from adult children reduce nursing home admissions for the elderly? *Inquiry*, 39, 279–297.

Logsdon, R., McCurry, S. M., & Jeri, L. (2005). STAR caregivers: A community-based approach for teaching family caregivers to use behavioral strategies to reduce affective disturbances in persons with dementia. *Alzheimer's Care Quarterly*, 6, 146–153.

Magana, S. (2006). Older Latino family caregivers. In B. Berkman (Ed.). *Handbook of social work in health and aging*. New York: Oxford University Press.

Marcell, J. (2000). *Elder rage or take my father...please!* Irvine, CA: Impressive Press.

Marwit, S. J. & Meuser, T. M. (2005). Development of a short form inventory to assess grief in caregivers of dementia patients. *Death Studies*, 29, 191–205.

McCormick, W. C., Ohata, C. Y., Uomoto, J., Young, H., & Graves, A. B. (2002). Similarities and differences in attitudes toward long-term care between Japanese Americans and Caucasian Americans. *Journal of the American Geriatrics Society*, 50, 1149–1155.

McLeod, B. W. (1999). *Caregiving: The spiritual journey of love, loss and renewal*. New York: John Wiley and Sons.

Menne, H. L., Tucke, S. S., Whitlatch, C. J., & Feinberg, L. F. (2008). Decision-making involvement scale for individuals with dementia and family caregivers. *American Journal of Alzheimer's Disease and Other Dementias*, 23, 23–29.

MetLife Mature Market Institute and the Lesbian and Gay Aging Issues Network of the American Society on Aging. (2006a). *Out and aging: The MetLife study of lesbian and gay baby boomers*. Westport, CT: MetLife Market Institute.

MetLife Mature Market Institute and National Alliance for Caregiving. (2006b). *The MetLife caregiving cost study: Productivity losses to U.S.*

business. Westport, CT: MetLife Mature Market Institute.

Meuser, T. M. & Marwit, S. J. (2001). A comprehensive stage sensitive model of grief in dementia caregiving. *The Gerontologist, 41,* 658–670.

Mittelman, M. (2002). Family caregiving for people with Alzheimer's disease: Results of the NYU Spouse Caregiver Intervention Study. *Generations, 3,* 104–106.

Mittelman, M., Roth, D., Coon, D., & Haley, W. (2004a). Sustained benefit of supportive intervention for depressive symptoms in caregivers of patients with Alzheimer's disease. *American Journal of Psychiatry, 161,* 850–856.

Mittelman, M., Roth, D. Haley, W., & Zarit, S. (2004b). Effects of a caregiver intervention on negative caregiver appraisals of behavior problems in patients with Alzheimer's disease. Results of a randomized trial. *Journal of Gerontology: Psychological Sciences, 59B,* P27–P34.

Mittelman, M., Zeiss, A., Davies, H., & Guy, D. (2003). Specific stressors of spousal caregivers: Difficult behaviors, loss of sexual intimacy and incontinence. In D. W. Coon, D. Gallagher-Thompson, & L. Thompson (Eds.). *Innovative interventions to reduce dementia caregiver distress.* New York: Springer.

Montgomery, R. & Kwak, J. (2008). TCARE: Tailored caregiver assessment and referral. *Journal of Social Work Education, 44*(3), 59–64.

Montgomery, R. J. V., Holley, L., Deichert, J., & Kosloski, K. (2005). A profile of home care workers from the 2000 census. *The Gerontologist, 45,* 593–600.

Montgomery, R. J. V. & Kosloski, K. (2000). Family caregiving: Change, continuity and diversity. In M. P. Lawston & R. L. Rubenstein (Eds.). *Alzheimer's disease and related dementias: Strategies in care and research.* New York: Springer.

Moon, A., Tomita, S. K., & Jung-Kamei, S. (2001). Elder mistreatment among four Asian-American groups: An exploratory study on tolerance, victim blaming and attitudes toward third party intervention. *Journal of Gerontological Social Work, 36,* 153–169.

Morano, C. (2002). A psycho-educational model for Hispanic Alzheimer's disease caregivers. *The Gerontologist, 42,* 122–126.

Muehlbauer, M. & Crane, P. (2006). Elder abuse and neglect. *Journal of Psychosocial Nursing, 44,* 43–48.

Nahmiash, D. & Reis, M. (2000). Most successful intervention strategies for abused older adults. *Journal of Elder Abuse and Neglect, 12,* 53–70.

Narayn, S., Lewis, M., Tornatore, J., Hepburn, K., & Corcoran-Perry, S. (2001). Subjective responses to caregiving for spouses with dementia. *Journal of Gerontological Nursing, 27,* 19–28.

National Alliance for Caregiving and AARP. (2004). *Caregiving in the U.S.* Bethesda: National Alliance for Caregiving and Washington, DC: AARP.

National Alliance for Caregiving and the United Hospital Fund. (2005). *Young caregivers in the U.S.: Findings from a national survey.*

National Center on Elder Abuse. (2007). *Major types of elder abuse.* Retrieved May 2009, from http://www.ncea.aoa.gov/ncearoot/Main_Site/FAQ/Basics/Types_Of_Abuse.aspx

National Center on Elder Abuse. (2006). *The 2004 Survey of State Adult Protective Services: Abuse of adults 60 years of age and older.* Washington, DC: National Center on Elder Abuse.

Navaie-Waliser, M., Feldman, P. H., Gould, D. A., Levine, C., Kuerbis, A. N., & Donelan, K. (2001). The experiences and challenges of informal caregivers: Common themes and differences among whites, blacks and Hispanics. *The Gerontologist, 41,* 733–741.

Navaie-Waliser, M., Feldman, P. H., Gould, D. A., Levine, C., Kuerbis, A. N., & Donelan, K. (2002). When the caregiver needs care: The plight of vulnerable caregivers. *American Journal of Public Health, 92,* 409–413.

Nelson, M. M., Smith, M., Martinson, B.C, Kind, A., & Luepker, R. V. (2008). Declining patient functioning and caregiver burden/health: The Minnesota Stroke Survey—Quality of Life After Stroke Study. *The Gerontologist, 48,* 573–583.

Ness, J., Ahmed, A., & Aronow, W. S. (2004). Demographics and payment characteristics of nursing home residents in the U.S.: A 23-year trend. *Journal of Gerontology: Social Sciences, 59,* S1213–S1217.

Nicholas, E. (2003). An outcomes focus in career assessment and review: Value and challenge. *British Journal of Social Work, 33,* 31–47.

Ory, M., Tennstedt, S. L., & Schulz, R. (2000). The extent and impact of dementia care: Unique challenges experienced by family caregivers. In R. Schulz (Ed.). *Handbook of dementia caregiving: Evidence-based interventions for family caregivers.* New York: Springer.

Ott., C. H., Sanders, S., & Kelber, S. T. (2007). Grief and personal growth experience of spouses and adult-child caregivers of individuals with Alzheimer's disease and related dementias. *The Gerontologist, 47,* 798–809.

Otto, J. M. (2002). Program and administrative issues affecting adult protective services. *Public Policy and Aging Report, 12,* 3–7.

Parker, M., Church, W., & Toseland, R. (2006). Caregiving at a distance. In B. Berkman (Ed.). *Handbook of social work in health and aging.* New York: Oxford Press.

Pavlik, V. N., Hyman, D. J., Festa, N. A., & Dyer, C. B. (2001). Quantifying the problem of abuse and neglect in adults: Analysis of a statewide database. *Journal of the American Geriatrics Society, 49,* 45–49.

Patterson, M. & Malley-Morrison, K. (2006). A cognitive-ecological approach to elder abuse in five culture: Human rights and education. *Educational Gerontology, 32,* 73–82.

Paul, P. (2003). The permaparent trap. *Psychology Today,* September/October 2003.

Pickard, L. (2004). *The effectiveness and cost-effectiveness of support and services for informal carers of older people.* London: Audit Commission.

Pinquart, M. & Sorensen, S. (2006). Gender differences in caregiver stressors, social resources and health: An updated meta-analysis. *Journal of Gerontology: Psychological Sciences, 61B,* P33–P45.

Pinquart, M., Sorensen, S., & Peak, T. (2003). Helping older adults and their families develop and implement care plans. *Journal of Gerontological Social Work, 43,* 3–23.

Polivka, L. (2005). Always on call: When illness turns families into caregivers/Caring for our elders. *The Gerontologist, 45,* 557–561.

Poythress, E. L., Burnett, J., Pickens, S., & Dyer, C. B. (2006). Severe self neglect: An epidemiological and historical perspective. *Journal of Elder Abuse and Neglect, 18,* 5–12.

Prigerson, H. G. (2003). Costs to society of family caregiving for patients with end-stage Alzheimer's disease. *New England Journal of Medicine, 20,* 1891–1892.

Quinn, M. J. & Heisler, C. J. (2002). The legal system: Civil and criminal responses to elder abuse and neglect. *Public Policy and Aging Report, 12,* 8–16.

Ramsdell, J., Jackson, J., Guy, H., & Renvall, M. (2004). Comparison of clinic-based home assessment to a home visit in demented elderly patients. *Alzheimer Disassociation Disorder, 18,* 145–153.

Raphael, C. & Cornwell, J. L. (2008). Influencing support for caregivers. *Journal of Social Work Education, 44,* 97–103.

Reay, A. & Brown, K. D. (2002). The effectiveness of psychological interventions with individuals who physically abuse or neglect their elderly dependents. *Journal of Interpersonal Violence, 17,* 416–431.

Richards, M. (2009). *Care sharing.* Woodstock Vermont: Skylight Paths.

Richardson, V. & Barusch, A. (2006). *Gerontological practice for the twenty-first century.* New York: Columbia University Press.

Rodriguez, M. A., Wallace, S. P., Woolf, N., & Mangione, C. M. (2006). Mandatory reporting of elder abuse: Between a rock and a hard place. *Annals of Family Medicine, 4,* 403–409.

Roff, L. L., Burgio, L., Gitlin, L. Nichols, L., Chaplin, W., et al. (2004). Positive aspects of Alzheimer's caregiving: The role of race. *Journals of Gerontology: Psychological Sciences, 59B,* P185–P190.

Rozario, P. A. & DeRienzis, D., (2008). Familism beliefs and psychological distress among African American women caregivers. *The Gerontologist, 48*, 772–780.

Russell, R. (2004). Social networks among elderly men caregivers. *Journal of Men's Studies, 13*, 121–143.

Sanders, S., & McFarland, P. (2002). Perceptions of caregiving role by son's caring for a parent with Alzheimer's disease. *Journal of Gerontological Social Work, 37*, 61–75.

Satow, R. (2005). *Doing the right thing: taking care of your elderly parents even if they didn't take care of you*. New York: Penguin Group.

Schmall, V., Cleland, M., & Sturdevent, M. (2000). *The caregiver help book*. Oregon Gerontological Association: Legacy Health System.

Schmieding, L. (2006). *Caregiving in America: At home there's always hope*. New York: International Longevity Center and Arkansas: Schmieding Center for Senior Health and Education of Northwest Arkansas.

Schofield, M. & Mishra, G. (2003). Validity of self-report screening for elder abuse: Women's Health Australia Study. *The Gerontologist, 43*, 110–120.

Schubert, C. C., Boustani, M., Callahan, C. M., Perkins, A. J., Hui, S., & Hendrie, H. C. (2008). Acute care utilization by dementia caregivers within urban primary care practices. *Journal of General Internal Medicine, 23*, 1736–1740.

Schulz, R., Burgio, L., Burns, R., Eisdorfer, C., Gallagher-Thompson, D., Gitlin, L., & Mahoney, D. (2003). Resources for enhancing Alzheimer's caregiver health (REACH): Overview, site-specific outcomes and future directions. *The Gerontologist, 43*, 514–520.

Schulz, R., Mendelsohn, A. B., Haley, W. E., Mahoney, D., Allen, R. S., Zhang, S., et al. (2003). End of life care and the effects of bereavement on family caregivers of persons with dementia. *The New England Journal of Medicine, 20*, 1936–1942.

Schulz, R., O'Brien, A., Czaja, S., Ory, M., Norris, R., Martire, L. M., et al. (2002). Dementia caregiver intervention research: In search of clinical significance. *The Gerontologist, 42*, 589–682.

Schulz, R. & Sherwood, P. R. (2008). Physical and mental health effects of family caregiving. *Journal of Social Work Education, 44*, 105–113.

Sebern, M. (2005). Psychometric evaluation of the shared care instrument in a sample of home health care family dyads. *Journal of Nursing Measurement, 13*, 175–191.

Seff, L., Beaulaurier, R., & Newman, F., (2008). Nonphysical abuse: Findings in domestic violence against older women study. *Journal of Emotional Abuse, 8*, 355–374.

Seltzer, M. & Li, L. W. (2000). The dynamics of caregiving: Transitions during a three-year prospective study. *The Gerontologist, 40*, 165–178.

Setterlund, D., Tilse, C., Wilson, J., Macawley, A. L., & Rosenman, L. (2007). Understanding financial elder abuse in families: The potential of routine activities theory. *Ageing and Society, 27*, 599–614.

Shanas, E. (1979). The family as a social support in old age. *The Gerontologist, 19*, 169–174.

Sherrell, K., Buckwalter, K., & Morhardt, D. (2001). Negotiating family relationships: Dementia care as a midlife developmental task. *Families in Society, 82*, 383–392.

Smith, C. (2008). Technology and web-based support. *Journal of Social Work Education, 44*, 75–82.

Smith, K. & Baughman, R. (2007). Caring for America's aging population: A profile of the direct care workforce. *Monthly Labor Review*, 20–26.

Squillace, M., Bercovitz, A., Rosenoff, E., & Remsburg, R. (2008). An exploratory study of certified nursing assitants' intent to leave. Washington, D.C.: U.S. Department of Health and Human Services. Retrieved August 2008, from http://aspe/hhs.gov/daltcp/reports/2008/intent.htm

Stone, R. I. (2000). *Long-term care for the elderly with disabilities: Current policy, emerging trends and implications for the 21st century*. New York: The Milbank Memorial Fund.

Stone, R. I. & Dawson, S. L. (2008). The orgins of Better Jobs Better Care. *The Gerontologoist, 48*, 5–13.

Taylor, D., Ghassan, B., Evans, J., & Jackson-Johnson, V. (2006). Assessing barriers to the identification of elder abuse and neglect: A community survey of primary care physicians. *Journal of the National Medical Association, 98,* 403–404.

Teaster, P. & Roberto, K. (2004). Sexual abuse of older adults: APS cases and outcomes. *The Gerontologist, 44,* 788–796.

Teaster, P. B., Dugar, T. A., Mendiondo, M. S., & Otto, J. M. (2005). *The 2004 Survey of State Adult Protective Services: Abuse of Adults 60 Years of Age and Older.* Washington, DC: National Center on Elder Abuse.

Thompson, L. (2004). *Long-term care: Support for family caregivers.* Washington, DC: Georgetown University, Long-Term Care Financing Project.

Tomita, S. (2006). Mistreated and neglected elders. In B. Berkman (Ed.). *Handbook of social work in health and aging.* New York: Oxford University Press.

Toseland, R. & Smith, G. (2003). *Supporting caregivers through education and training.* Washington, DC: National Family Caregiver Support Program, Administration on Aging.

Van Houtven, C. H. & Norton, E. C. (2008). Informal care and Medicare expenditures: Testing for heterogeneous treatment effects. *Journal of Health Economics, 27,* 134–156.

Vitaliano, P., Zhang, J., & Scanlan, J. (2003). Is caregiving hazardous to one's physical health? A meta analysis. *Psychological Bulletin, 129,* 946–972.

Vitaliano, P. P., Scanlan, J. M., Zhang, J., Savage, M. V., Hirsch, I. B., & Siegler, I. C. (2002). A path model of chronic stress, the metabolic syndrome, and coronary heart disease. *Psychomatic Medicine, 64,* 418–435.

Wakabayashi, C. & Donato, K. (2004). *The consequences of caregiving for economic well-being in women's later life.* Presented at the annual meeting of the American Sociological Association, San Francisco.

Weiss, C., Gonzalez, H., Kabeto, M., & Langa, K. (2005). Differences in the amount of informal care received by non-Hispanic whites and Latinos in a nationally representative sample of older Americans. *Journal of the American Geriatrics Society, 53,* 146–151.

Whitlatch, C. (2008). Informal caregivers: Communication and decision-making. *Journal of Social Work Education, 43,* 89–95.

Whitlatch, C., Judge, K., Zarit, S., & Femia, E. (2006). Dyadic counseling for family caregivers and care receivers in early stage dementia. *The Gerontologist, 46,* 688–694.

Whitlatch, C. J., Piiparinen, R., & Feinberg, L. F. (2009). How well do family caregivers know their relatives' care values and preferences? *Dementia, 8,* 223–243.

Wiener, J. M., Squillace, M. R., Anderson, W. L., & Khatutsky, G. (2009). Why do they stay? Job tenure among certified nursing assistants in nursing homes. *The Gerontologist, 49,* 198 – 210.

Wilber, K. H. & Nielsen, E. K. (2002). Elder abuse: New approaches to an age-old problem. *Public Policy and Aging Report, 12,* 24–26.

Wisensale, S. (2001). Federal initiatives in family leave policy: Formulation of the FMLA. In S. Wisendale (Ed.). *Family leave policy: The political economy of work and family in America.* New York: M.E. Sharpe.

Wisensale, S. (2009). Aging policy as family policy: Expanding family leave and improving flexible work policies. In R. Hudson (Ed.). *Boomer Bust: Vol. 1. Perspectives on the boomers.* Westport, CT: Praeger Publishing.

Wisniewski, S., Belle, S., Coon, D., Maracus, S., Ory, M., Burgio, L., et al. (2003). The Resources for Enhancing Alzheimer's Caregiver Health (REACH): Project design and baseline characteristics. *Psychology and Aging, 7,* 622–631.

Wong, S., Yoo, G., & Stewart, A. (2006). The changing meaning of family support among older Chinese and Korean immigrants. *Journal of Gerontology, 61B,* S4–S9.

Yee, J. L. & Schulz, R. (2000). Gender differences in psychiatric morbidity among family caregivers:

A review and analysis. *The Gerontologist, 40,* 147–164.

Zarit, S. & Femia, E. (2008). Behavioral and psychosocial interventions for family caregivers. *American Journal of Nursing, 108,* 47–53.

Zarit, S. H. & Zarit, J. M. (2007). *Mental disorders in older adults: Fundamentals of assessment and treatment* (2nd ed.). New York: Guilford Press.

Zink, T., Jacobson, J., Pabst, S., Regan, S., & Fisher, B., (2006). A lifetime of intimate partner violence. *Journal of Interpersonal Violence, 21,* 634–651.

Zodikoff, B. D. (2006). Services for lesbian, gay, bisexual and transgender older adults. In B. Berkman (Ed.). *Handbook of social work in health and aging.* New York: Oxford University Press.

Chapter

11

Living Arrangements and Social Interactions

In this chapter, we focus on

- P–E theories that describe how to maximize competence as we age
- The impact of the natural and built environment on older persons' social functioning
- The importance of planning elder-friendly and livable communities
- Options in housing and community-based long-term care
- Organizational cultural change in long-term care facilities
- Services to help elders remain as autonomous as possible in the community
- Universal design and new assistive technologies to promote aging in place
- Housing policy affecting older adults and the impact of federal policy changes on subsidized housing
- Homelessness among older adults
- Housing and health services for aging prisoners

Elders' interactions with their physical environment are examined in this chapter, from the community to the neighborhood and private home to alternative long-term care settings. Chapter 17 addresses the cost of and challenges facing long-term care facilities and services. As we have discussed, active aging depends on physical and functional health, cognitive and emotional well-being, spirituality, and a level of social engagement that is congruent with an individual's abilities and needs. Another critical element that affects the aging process is the environment, both social and physical, that serves as the context for activities as well as the stimulus that places demands on the individual. According to person–environment (P–E) theories of aging, an individual is more likely to experience high life satisfaction and quality of life in an environment that is congruent with his or her physical, cognitive, and emotional needs and level of competence.

Age-related changes and disease conditions tend to make older people more sensitive to characteristics of the physical environment that may have little effect on the typical younger person. They may impair the older person's ability to adapt to and interact with complex and changing environments. On the other hand, many older people function as well as younger persons in a wide range of physical surroundings. Observation of these differences in individual responses has led to the concept of *congruence* or *fit* between the environment and the individual.

Person–Environment Theories of Aging

The impact of the environment on human behavior and well-being is widely recognized in diverse disciplines. Environment as a complex variable entered the realm of psychology in the early work of Kurt Lewin and his associates (Lewin, 1935, 1951; Lewin, Lippitt, & White, 1939). Lewin's field theory (1935, 1951) emphasizes that any event is the result of multiple factors, individual and environmental; or, more simply stated, B = f(P,E) (i.e., behavior is a function of personal and environmental characteristics). Accordingly, any change in characteristics of either the person or the environment is likely to modify that individual's behavior. Optimal well-being is experienced when a person's needs are in equilibrium with environmental features. For example, an older woman who has lived on a farm will adjust more readily to a small nursing home in a rural area than to a large urban facility. In contrast, an older couple who are city-dwellers may be dissatisfied if they decide to retire to a small home on a lake far from town; adaptation may be more difficult and perhaps never fully achieved. To the extent that individual needs are not satisfied because of existing environmental characteristics and level of "press," P-E theories would predict that the person will experience frustration and strain.

The environment affects older people with ADL limitations the most because of their reduced capacity to control their surroundings, such as

> ### CONTROLLING P-E CONGRUENCE
>
> An older man who lives with his daughter and teenage grandchildren in a small home may feel overwhelmed and unable to control the high level of activity and noise by the younger family members and their friends. In contrast, an older man who lives alone in a quiet neighborhood has greater control over the level of activity in his home, even though the house may seem too quiet and boring to his grandchildren when they visit.

moving from an undesirable setting. Therefore, this perspective may be even more useful for understanding frail elders' behavior than the actions of healthier older adults and younger populations.

The *competence model*, described in Chapter 1, assumes that the impact of the environment is mediated by the individual's level of abilities and needs. Competence is defined as "the theoretical upper limit of the individual to function in areas of biological health, sensation-perception, motives, behavior, and cognition" (Lawton, 1975, p. 7). *Environmental press* refers to the potential of a given environmental feature to influence behavior (for example, the extent of stimulation, physical barriers, and lack of privacy). For older adults who experience a decline in function and ability to perform ADLs and IADLs, the environment must be simplified and more supportive. But when the environment is too demanding, an individual experiences P–E incongruence. However, a given environment is not inherently good or bad for all older users. Instead, one must examine a physical setting vis-à-vis each elder's competence. For example, an environment that enhances one older person's activity level and autonomy may pose risks for another, resulting in falls and accidents (Iwarsson, 2004; 2005; Iwarsson et al., 2007; Wahl et al., 2009).

The practical implications of the P–E model are illustrated by examples of older persons with Alzheimer's disease or other forms of dementia. Their cognitive deterioration may make them unable to recognize the incongruence between their needs and the environment, and certainly reduces their ability to reestablish congruence. Patients with dementia may become agitated unless others intervene to ensure environmental fit. Caregivers can simplify the environment to make it fit the individual's cognitive competence; for example, by providing cues and orienting devices in the home to help the person move around without becoming lost or disoriented. The ultimate goal of any modification should be to maximize the older person's ability to negotiate and control the situation, and to minimize the likelihood that the environment will overwhelm the individual's competence.

The concept of **life-space** relates to the interaction between an elder's competence and their physical environment. Defined as the distance a person travels to perform activities over a specified time (e.g., one week, one month), an individual's life-space can range from the immediate surroundings of one's bedroom to the home and neighborhood. For active elders, the usual pattern of mobility extends beyond the town where they live. Researchers who have created a tool to assess life-space note that the larger an elder's life-space, the better their functional abilities, health status, and psychological well-being. Similarly, their longitudinal studies reveal that older adults whose life-space constricts over time also experience declines in ADLs and IADLs (Allman, Sawyer, & Roseman, 2006; Brown et al., 2009; Crowe et al., 2008).

COPING WITH DECLINING COMPETENCE

As an example of modifying environmental press to be more congruent with declining levels of competence, grocery shopping in a large supermarket on a busy Saturday morning may become an overwhelming task for an older person who has difficulties with hearing and walking. To reestablish congruence, the older adult might decide to shop in a smaller store at non-peak hours, avoid supermarkets altogether and use a neighborhood grocery store, order groceries by phone or online, or ask friends and neighbors for assistance.

AN ENVIRONMENT THAT PLACES EXTREME DEMANDS ON ELDERS' COMPETENCE

In February 2006, 82-year-old Mayvis Coyle received a traffic ticket for the first time in her life. Her crime was jaywalking at a crosswalk on a busy five-lane boulevard in Los Angeles, where the pedestrian light is green for only 20 seconds. Mayvis was fined $114 for continuing to cross the street after the light had turned red. Others, including a 78-year-old woman using an electric cart, have complained that the light changes when they are only halfway across the boulevard. The policeman who issued the ticket defended his action by responding that his job was to assure pedestrian safety. Clearly, the timing of this light places unrealistic *environmental press* on people whose physical *competence* declines because of age or disability (Associated Press, 2006).

Geographic Distribution of the Older Population

The Aging Experience in Rural, Urban, and Suburban Areas

As the United States and other industrialized countries have become more urbanized, a smaller proportion of all population subgroups, including those age 65 and older, reside in rural communities. The great majority of older Americans (71.7 percent) live in metropolitan areas (i.e., urban and suburban communities), compared with only 5 percent in communities with fewer than 2,500 residents. Elders of color are more likely to live in central cities, placing them at greater risk for victimization and poor-quality housing (AOA, 2008).

There is also a "graying of the suburbs;" that is, a greater proportion of people who moved into suburban developments in the 1960s and 1970s have raised their children and remained in these communities after retirement. Since 1977, increasing numbers of older people are living in the suburbs rather than in central cities, as shown in Figure 11.1 on page 449. Compared to their urban counterparts, elders in suburban communities tend to have higher incomes, are less likely

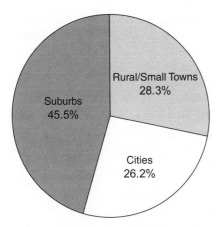

FIGURE 11.1 **Population of Older Americans Living in Urban, Suburban, Small Towns and Rural Areas**
SOURCE: U. S. Census Bureau, 2008.

to live alone, and report themselves to be in better functional health.

However, the lower density of housing, greater distance to social and health services, and fewer mass transit options make it difficult for older suburban dwellers to remain there if they become frail or unable to drive. Many suburban communities are responding to their changing resident needs by developing community transit programs (e.g., vans or special buses) to take older adults and persons with disabilities to social and health services, senior centers, shopping, restaurants, and places of worship. Future cohorts of older adults will expect more of these services to be located in the suburbs, in the same way that shopping centers and retirement housing options are now constructed in these population centers.

Older persons who live in nonmetropolitan areas generally have lower incomes (near the poverty level) and poorer health than those in metropolitan areas. A greater proportion, especially elders of color, relies on Social Security benefits for their primary source of income. Limitations in mobility and activity are greater among elders in rural communities and least among those in suburbs. This may be a function of income and cohort differences. The greater availability of services such as hospitals, clinics, senior centers, private physicians, and transportation in urban and suburban communities compared to rural settings may also

AN INNOVATIVE TRANSPORTATION PROGRAM: SOCIAL ENTREPRENEURSHIP AND OLDER ADULTS

Public transit is not always available or convenient, particularly for those who live outside of large cities; and it carries its own set of issues for this age group. Bus stops, for example, can be many blocks away and require standing out in bad weather. Bus schedules and routes do not provide the autonomy and mobility most people experience with their own private cars. Therefore many people continue to drive long after they really should because they think they have no alternative. The independent ITNAmerica, a nonprofit offering more than 30,000 door-to-door rides for elders in eight states, was designed to meet these challenges. Riders purchase an annual membership ($40 for individuals, $50 for family memberships) along with ride credits to be placed in a Personal Transportation Account™, based on an estimate of how much travel is needed. ITN uses an estimate of $9 per ride to guide consumers on how much to put in their accounts. Unlike publicly funded transportation for older adults, which provides trips only to doctors, churches, and grocery stores within restricted hours, ITNAmerica is available 24/7 and will arrange rides wherever its riders want to go. Among its innovations, older people can trade their own cars to pay for rides and volunteer drivers to store transportation credits for their own future transportation needs. Since riders do not pay cash and only private automobiles are used, riding ITN vehicles is more like riding with a friend than taking a taxi. ITN actively solicits business community support. Area retailers get involved through the Ride & Shop™ promotion, helping to pay for rides for shoppers who buy from them. And doctors' offices and clinics help out the program and their patients through the Healthy Miles™ donation program. The goal is to make each community program self-sustaining within a five-year period (http://www.itnamerica.org/).

explain these variations. Despite attempts to offset urban–rural differences in services, significant gaps remain in terms of access and availability. Transportation is a critical problem for older rural residents, both to take them to medical and social services and for providers to travel to their homes.

Despite their lower income and poorer health, older persons in small communities tend to interact more with neighbors and friends of the same and younger ages than do those in urban settings. Other positive features of smaller communities are greater proximity to neighbors, stability of residents, and shared values and lifestyles. Proportionately few rural elders live near their children or receive financial and social support from them. However, friendship ties appear to be stronger and more numerous among rural elders than among those in urban settings. In sum, older persons who remain in rural areas and small towns are more disadvantaged in terms of income, health, and service accessibility than are those in metropolitan areas. On the other hand, P–E fit considerations suggest that elders who have a high need for social interaction and have lived most of their lives in rural areas would be most satisfied in such settings and would experience severe adaptation problems in more anonymous urban environments.

Elder-Friendly/Livable Communities

An emerging concept in the physical environment for older adults—one that is consistent with the need for P–E congruence—is that of **elder-friendly,** or **livable, communities.** While P–E congruence focuses on the individual's level of competence, needs, and preferences, this concept examines environmental demands at the community level. Elder-friendly communities are defined as:

- Addressing basic needs of safe neighborhoods, affordable and accessible housing, and adequate mobility options
- Optimizing physical and mental health by providing access to social and health services, preventive and health promotion activities, chronic disease management, and end-of-life care
- Promoting social and civic engagement, including opportunities for employment, volunteering, and cross-generational interaction

- Maximizing autonomy for frail and disabled elders by providing accessible public transportation and resources to help them remain at home (Advantage and Age Initiative, 2007; Hanson & Emlet, 2006; Oberlink, 2008)

Elder friendly or livable communities benefit residents of all ages. To illustrate, these communities promote healthy activities by building walking or biking trails or curb cuts at every corner that are enjoyed by young parents with babies in strollers, active elders riding a bike, as well as persons with disabilities who use wheelchairs.

To determine if communities fulfill these criteria for elder-friendliness, researchers have conducted surveys of older residents in diverse areas. An AARP 2005 national survey of 1,000 adults age 50 and older found that the availability of community services such as dependable transportation, nearby grocery and drug stores, hospitals, and options for different types of affordable housing affected residents' satisfaction with their community. Urban dwellers were more satisfied than those in suburbs where these services were less available. Dissatisfied residents also felt isolated and disengaged from their neighbors and the larger community. Barriers to creating livable communities include inadequate housing type and supply as well as dispersed communities without good mobility options. Findings from surveys such as the one by AARP are useful for guiding city officials and leaders in the aging network to improve housing, services, and employment and volunteering opportunities for older citizens (AARP, 2005; Hanson & Emlet, 2006; Kochera & Bright, 2005–2006; Oberlink, 2008). Some organizations serving older adults are engaged in *asset mapping,* which refers to a range of approaches that work from the principle that a community is best built by focusing on the strengths and capacities of the citizens and associations that call a neighborhood, community, or county "home." Their mapping is guided by the goal of how community assets can be mobilized to ensure quality of life for their older residents.

Relocation

Relocation, or moving from one setting to another, also represents P–E incongruence or discontinuity between individual competence and environmental demands. Anyone who has moved from one city or one house to another has experienced the problems of adjusting to new surroundings and to different orientations, floor plans, and design features in the home. An older person who has lived in the same home for many years will require more time to adapt, even if the move is perceived as an improvement to a better, safer, or more comfortable home. This is because the older person has adjusted to a particular level of P–E fit over a long time. A relocation that entails extensive lifestyle changes, such as a move to a retirement community or a nursing home, requires more time to adapt. Older adults who move voluntarily often feel more stress before the move than after. Regardless of the nature of the move, many elders experience feelings of loss associated with giving up possessions and a familiar setting.

Older homeowners are far more likely than younger families to have lived in their current homes for at least 30 years (50 percent vs. 4 percent). This difference also occurs among renters (16 percent vs. 1 percent, respectively) and may explain why older people are less likely to relocate than younger persons. Furthermore, relocation rates continue to decline for the population age 65 and older (Sergeant, Ekerdt, & Chapin, 2008; Wolf & Longino, 2005). A national survey by AARP revealed an overwhelming desire by people

Relocation generally entails a loss of familiar surroundings and possessions.

age 50 and older to remain in their own homes and communities.

- 69 percent were very satisfied with their residence
- 73 percent preferred to remain in the same community (AARP, 2006c)

The great majority of moves by older people occur within the same state (AOA, 2008). In general, older people are less likely to move to a new community than are younger families, but they are more likely to move to a different type of housing within the same community. In their early life-course model of retirement migration, Litwak and Longino (1994) proposed that the large migrant stream of retirees to the Sunbelt from northern states was accompanied by a smaller counterstream in the opposite direction. In their subsequent work, these researchers suggest that older people generally relocate in response to changes in life conditions, such as retirement or functional disabilities, that make their existing home environments incongruent with their needs (Longino et al., 2008; Longino & Bradley, 2006). As a result, the type of housing chosen varies according to the reasons for the move.

ADAPTING TO P–E INCONGRUENCE IN ONE'S HOME

It may seem odd to family, friends, and service providers that an older person does not wish to leave a home that is too large and difficult to negotiate physically, especially if he or she is frail and mobility-impaired. The problem is compounded if the home needs extensive repairs that an older person cannot afford. Despite such seemingly obvious needs to relocate, it is essential to consider older people's preferences before encouraging them to sell a home that appears to be incongruent with their needs. Families should take account of the meaning of home to the older person as a symbol of self-identity, control, autonomy, and emotional and cognitive bonding with their social and physical environment (Oswald & Wahl, 2004).

Their three-stage model of migration is described as:

- Stage 1, known as *amenity or lifestyle-driven moves,* occurs most often among the young-old and recent retirees, generally to retirement communities in the Sunbelt—Florida, California, Arizona, or Texas. This may include "snow-birds" who spend their winters in the warmer climate and the remaining months in their home states. Both patterns have resulted in a significant increase in the population age 65 and older in Sunbelt states in the past 40 years. However, this pattern is shifting as more older adults are unable to sell existing homes to move to warmer climates and Sunbelt communities seek to attract younger families as a way to survive financially.
- Stage 2 is often precipitated by chronic illness that limits elders' abilities to perform ADLs. They may move to retirement communities or assisted living facilities nearby that offer some amenities (e.g., meals, housekeeping), but seek to promote as much autonomy as possible. Sometimes elders move closer to family members in Stage 2 (*assistance moves*).
- Stage 3 is not experienced by most elders but occurs when severe or sudden disability (e.g., stroke) makes it impossible to live even semi-independently. For example, a frail older person relocates from a Sunbelt community to a nursing home near family members. One indicator of this shift is that Florida has the highest population of people age 65 and older but ranks 24th in its proportion of oldest-old (Longino, 2004).

For many other elders, an intermediate stop may be an adult child's home before relocating to a long-term care facility. In other cases, older persons receive some home care, other types of community-based long-term care, or additional support services that allow them to remain in their homes. To the extent that older retirees who relocate to the Sunbelt have children and siblings living in their state of origin and the more visits they make back home, the more likely they are to create a "counterstream migration" by moving back to their home state. However, having children who live

RETIREES CAN REVITALIZE AMERICA'S SMALL TOWNS

New cohorts of active retirees have revitalized once-dying communities by relocating there, spending money for goods and services, sometimes continuing to work part-time, and creating jobs for other residents. One estimate is that a retiree who relocates to a community can have as great an economic impact as three to four factory workers because, in general, they are wealthier and have more disposable income. In 2000, new residents age 50 and older brought twice as much revenue to Florida as they cost the state in services (*The Seattle Times,* 2003). This pattern may be changing, however, with the 2009 recession.

nearby in the Sunbelt state where they have relocated and being satisfied with their new residences makes it less likely that retirees will return to their home states (Stoller & Longino, 2001).

The oldest-old are most likely to make *assistance moves,* often into or near their children's homes. Such moves are precipitated by widowhood, significant deterioration in health, or disability (Longino et al., 2008). Not surprisingly, relocation is more difficult for elders with multiple or severe physical or cognitive disabilities because they have problems coping with stressful life events, such as relocation. Unfortunately, they are often the very people who must relocate to skilled nursing facilities—environments that may be most incongruent with their needs. Relocation stress can be reduced if the older person has some control over the decision to move and is involved in the decision-making process, such as selecting the facility and what possessions to keep.

The stress of adapting to a new setting is one reason why many frail older people who can no longer maintain their own homes are reluctant to move, even though they may recognize that they "should" be in a safer environment. Indeed, the 2005 housing survey by AARP found overwhelming support for the statement "I'd like to stay in my home and never move." Among all respondents 50 and older, 89 percent agreed with the statement, and this preference increased with age.

- 84 percent among those 50–64
- 95 percent among those 75 years and older (AARP, 2006c)

A major reason for this large proportion of elders who prefer to remain in their own home, regardless of its condition, is the almost universal desire for **aging in place.** This is the preference to stay in their homes where the environment is familiar, neighbors can be relied on for assistance and socializing, and the aging person has control. As more adults live to their 80s or 90s, however, a growing number of services are likely to be required to allow aging in place. To the extent that these resources are accessible in the neighborhood or local community, people are more likely to remain there and to avoid or delay relocation to a long-term care facility. Examples of these support services are described later in this chapter.

Some older people may live in communities that were not planned for this population (unlike a Sun City or Leisure World, for example) but have become **naturally occurring retirement communities (NORCs).** Such settings have, over the years, attracted adults who have eventually "aged in place" there. As the population of older

WHAT TO DO WITH A LIFETIME OF POSSESSIONS?

Older adults who move to a smaller home—whether a condo, apartment, assisted living, or nursing home—are typically faced with the task of disposing of a lifetime of possessions. The memories associated with a favorite possession can result in wrenching decisions for elders and their families, intensifying the feelings of loss associated with a move. This task can be even more daunting for elders from the Depression-era cohort who have saved material items throughout their lives. For other elders who are classified as hoarders, their living spaces are so cluttered that they are not usable and can pose a fire risk. Another complicating factor in disposing of lifelong possessions is when family members live far from the elder or disagree over who should inherit which cherished possessions. To assist with this process, new services have recently emerged, including Senior Move Managers, Professional Organizers, consultants to help arrange home furnishings, and even support groups for hoarders.

Retirement communities offer opportunities for social interaction and physical activity.

adults with chronic care needs increases in NORCs, some state and local governments are offering expanded services. For example, city funds and philanthropic grants pay for an on-site team of social workers and nurses to care for elders in a Queens, New York, apartment complex where more than 60 percent of residents are age 60 and older. This program is a model for communities in 25 other states. Such programs typically encourage older residents to actively participate in shaping their NORC. Funding comes from federal, state, and local governments and from housing partners, philanthropies, and businesses. The paid staff includes older residents who work on community-building and identifying problems in the NORC's physical environment, such as inadequate bus routes and health clinics and home repair needs (Larson, 2006; United Hospital Fund, 2009).

Another type of community where people are aging in place is a collaborative neighborhood known as **cohousing** (Co-housing Association of the U.S., 2006; deLaGrange, 2006; Durrette, 2009; Greene, 2006; Vierck, 2005). Adapted from Denmark in the late 1980s, cohousing communities are clusters of 10 to 30 individually owned housing units (attached or single-family homes) where families of all ages, or older adults only, live somewhat independently but share a "common house" where social and recreational activities,

community meetings, and occasional group meals are shared. In most cases the private units are small, with the common house rather than individual homes serving as a center for social activities. Residents share cooking, cleaning the common house, and physical maintenance. A key element for achieving successful cohousing is that the planning and construction of the community is led by both owners and future residents. Most existing cohousing communities today are intergenerational and have only recently begun to deal with issues of aging residents with chronic diseases and dementia. In some cases, one or more guest rooms in the common house—designed for visiting friends and family members—are available as a residence for caregivers of cohousing members. Sometimes this caregiver provides full-time assistance to several residents and becomes part of the community. Such options are critical to avoid burdening cohousing neighbors with ongoing care for frail residents. Physical barriers such as inaccessible entries and multi-story dwellings become increasingly difficult for those with disabilities. The principles of participatory decision making and resident management that characterize cohousing may elude those experiencing cognitive decline. In recognition of the potential incongruence of age-integrated cohousing for frail older adults, that targets a new trend has emerged in cohousing, those 55 and older (deLaGrange, 2006; Durrette, 2009; ElderCohousing.org, 2006). Many of these neighborhoods are being built near intergenerational cohousing communities, but often with fewer homes (15 to 20 households) and more physical features and social services that take account of declines in physical and cognitive function.

Intentional communities are another more recent model of housing that encourages aging in place. These are communal housing projects, both intergenerational or targeted only at older adults, where people with common interests (e.g., religious, political, professional, or sexual orientation) collaborate in the construction of a community of apartments, townhouses, or detached single-family homes. Residents of intentional communities generally share more activities than those in cohousing (Christian, 2003; Yeoman, 2006).

The Impact of the Neighborhood

All of us live in a neighborhood, whether a college campus, a mobile home park, an apartment complex, or the several blocks surrounding our homes. Because of its smaller scale, the neighborhood represents a closer level of interaction and identification than does the community. Satisfaction with one's neighborhood increases if amenities such as a grocery store, bank, laundromat, or senior center are located nearby. These services also can provide a social network. For many older people, however, special vans or other types of transportation are necessary to access such services. Older adults are willing to travel farther for physician services, entertainment, family visits (although friends need to be nearby for regular visiting to occur), and club meetings, probably because these activities occur less frequently than grocery shopping and laundry. Because of the importance of family ties, visits to relatives may occur more often, regardless of proximity. Distance is less important if family members drive older relatives to various places, including their homes.

Proximity and frequent contact with families may not be as critical if neighbors and nearby friends can provide necessary social support. As discussed in Chapter 9, neighbors play critical roles in older people's social networks. When adult children are at a geographic distance, neighbors may help in emergencies and on a short-term basis, such as with minor home repairs, meal preparation, or transportation. It is often more convenient for neighbors than family to drive an older individual to stores and doctors' offices. This does not mean that neighbors can or should replace family support systems. Nevertheless, neighbors are a vital supplementary resource.

Victimization and Fear of Crime

A common stereotype is that crime affects the older population more than other age groups. However, national surveys by the U.S. Department of Justice's Bureau of Justice Statistics consistently show that people age 65 and older have the lowest rates of all types of victimization among all age groups over age 12. As Table 11.1 illustrates, when compared to people age 16 to 19, in 2007, people age 65 and older were:

- 23 times less likely to be victims of an assault
- 11 times less likely to experience a robbery
- half as likely to be attacked by a purse snatcher or pickpocketer (Bureau of Justice Statistics, 2008)

Nevertheless, some segments of the older population are at greater risk:

- The young-old are more likely than those age 75 and older to face all types of crime.
- African American elders are 25 percent more likely than whites to be assault victims

PRACTICAL HELP FROM NEIGHBORS

Neighbors can create a security net as partners in a Neighborhood Watch crime-prevention program or in informally arranged systems of signaling to each other. The older neighbor who lives alone might open her living room drapes every day by 9:00 AM to signal to her neighbors that all is well. Other neighbors might check in on the older person on a daily or weekly basis to make sure that home-delivered meals are being eaten regularly.

TABLE 11.1 Victimization Rates per 1,000 Persons or Households, 2005

AGE	VIOLENT CRIME	ROBBERY	ASSAULT	PURSE SNATCHING/ PICKPOCKETING
16–19	45.8	7.0	33.9	1.6
25–34	23.6	3.1	19.9	1.0
50–64	11.4	1.4	9.3	0.6
65+	2.4	0.6	1.9	0.4

SOURCE: Bureau of Justice Statistics, 2006.

and four times more likely to be victims of purse snatching and pickpocketing.

- Both young and old Americans with incomes less than $7,500 are most likely to become victims of property and violent crimes, including assault (1.4 times and 2.3 times the rate for those with incomes over $75,000, respectively).

- Not surprisingly, older people in urban centers are 1.6 times more likely than suburban or rural elders to experience violent crimes, 1.3 times more likely to be assaulted, and 1.5 times more likely to be victims of property crimes. African American elders in urban settings are more likely than their rural counterparts to experience all three types of crimes (Bureau of Justice Statistics, 2008).

Contrary to common beliefs, older white and African American women are at lowest risk for violent crimes:

- For all types of assault, 1.4 per 1,000 versus 2.2 for older white men and 5.6 for older African American men.

NEIGHBORHOOD CRIME PREVENTION PROGRAMS

In response to concerns about crime, Neighborhood Watch and other programs encourage neighbors to become acquainted and to look out for signs of crimes. Such crime-prevention programs increase older people's access to their neighbors. They break down the perception of neighbors as strangers and the apprehension of being isolated in a community, both of which foster fear of crime. Some large communities have established special police units to investigate and prevent crimes against older people. These units often train police to understand processes of aging and to communicate better with elders to help them overcome the trauma of a theft or physical assault. Improvements in community design can also create a sense of security. For example, brighter and more uniform street lighting, especially above sidewalks and in alleys, can deter many would-be criminals.

- For all crimes of violence, 1.8 per 1,000 among white women and less than 0.3 for older African American women, compared to 3.2 for older white men and 5.6 for black men. This compares with the highest-risk group, males age 20 to 24, who experience 58.8 violent crimes per 1,000 population (Bureau of Justice Statistics, 2006).

The conditions under which crimes are committed against older people differ from those of other age groups. For example, they tend to be victimized during the day, by strangers who more often attack alone, in or near their homes, and with less use of weapons. This pattern suggests that perpetrators of crimes feel that they can easily overtake the older victim without a struggle. The sense of helplessness against an attacker may make older persons more conscious of their need to protect themselves and produce levels of fear that are incongruent with the statistics about their relative vulnerability to violent crimes. Such fear of crime results in dissatisfaction with their neighborhoods. In the 2005 AARP housing survey, 87 percent of those 65 to 74 and 84 percent 75 and older were satisfied with the security of their neighborhoods. However, those in urban areas were twice as dissatisfied with the safety of their neighborhoods as their counterparts in suburbs and 50 percent more than elders in rural areas. Similarly, elders with household incomes less than $25,000 were much less satisfied with neighborhood safety than those with incomes over $50,000, mostly because they lived in areas with higher crime rates (AARP, 2006c).

It is not surprising that older adults in high-crime areas are concerned, given the potential adverse consequences of a physical attack or theft for an older person. Even a purse snatching can be traumatic because of the possibility of an injury or hip fracture during a struggle with the thief and the resulting economic loss. Experiencing a violent crime can even precipitate nursing home placement. In a study of over 2,300 older adults in New Haven, Connecticut, 5 percent had experienced a violent crime and 21 percent some type of victimization prior to their move to the nursing home. Over the next 10 years, 32 percent entered a nursing home other than for post-hospitalization rehabilitation. Those who had been victims of violent crimes were 2.1 times more likely to enter a nursing home than their nonvictimized counterparts (Lachs et al., 2006). Being a crime victim can also disrupt the individual's sense of competence and subjective well-being. Older women are particularly fearful of crime, although, as described above, they are even less likely to be victims. Although seemingly irrational, such fear of crime is an important determinant of older women's behavior that requires community-level interventions to empower and strengthen their environmental competence. For example, older women can benefit from self-defense education and from neighborhood support networks. Thus, the significance of the fear of crime is not whether it is warranted, but the effect it has on elders' psychological well-being. On the other hand, older persons report feeling safe going outdoors in urban neighborhoods with police nearby, with easy access to public transportation, with coexisting businesses and housing, and with "green features" such as trees and clean streets (Beard et al., 2009).

Although less likely to be victims of violent crime, older people are more susceptible to economically devastating crimes such as fraud and confidence games, as noted in Chapter 10. Police departments in major cities report higher rates of elder victimization by con artists and high-pressure salesmen. Medical quackery and insurance fraud are also more common, perhaps because many older people feel desperate for quick cures or overwhelmed by health care costs. They therefore become easy prey for unscrupulous people who exploit them by offering the "ultimate medical cure" or "low-cost, comprehensive long-term care insurance" coverage. Older adults are also more vulnerable to commercial fraud by funeral homes, real estate brokers, and investment salespeople. The negative impact of such fraud on elders' trust and self-confidence is perhaps more devastating than the financial consequences. Such feelings can prevent the older person from seeking appropriate

professional services for medical conditions, insurance, and other transactions. And families may perceive their older relatives as no longer competent to live autonomously. AARP's classes on how to prevent victimization by fraud are among their most popular educational offerings.

Housing Patterns of Older People

In this section, the residential arrangements of older persons are reviewed, including independent housing, planned housing, retirement communities, and residential long-term care. We also discuss newer models of long-term care, both community-based and residential. Policies that govern such long-term care options are described in Chapter 17.

By far the most common type of housing for older adults is traditional independent housing (93 percent of those 65 and older live in such housing), followed by long-term care (LTC) facilities (4 percent), and community housing with services, such as continuing care retirement communities (3 percent). However, for the oldest-old, these latter options are more common: 17 percent in LTC, and 8 percent in community housing with services although 75 percent still live in independent housing (Federal Interagency Forum, 2008).

Independent Housing

In 2008, of the 24 million total older households, 80 percent were homeowners and 20 percent were renters. Rates of home ownership were higher among married households than among single elders (91.5 percent and 69 percent, respectively) (U.S. Census Bureau, 2009). The former spent 35 percent of their income for housing, less than half that spent by renters (76 percent). Rather than indicating low mortgages, this difference may be explained by the fact that homeowners, on average, have higher median income levels than renters ($29,647 versus $15,130 in 2008). This variation may also be explained by the fact that older homeowners are more likely than any other

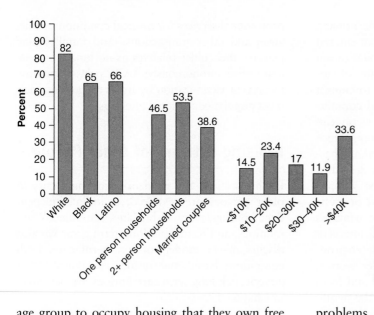

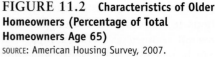

FIGURE 11.2   **Characteristics of Older Homeowners (Percentage of Total Homeowners Age 65)**
SOURCE: American Housing Survey, 2007.

age group to occupy housing that they own free and clear of a mortgage (68 percent in 2008) (U.S. Census Bureau, 2009). These include condominiums, mobile homes, and even congregate facilities that offer "life care" for retired persons; but single family homes are by far the greatest proportion of owned units. As shown in Figure 11.2, home ownership varies considerably among the older population. Married couples, non-Hispanic whites, especially those with an annual income of $40,000 or more, and those residing in rural communities are most likely to own their homes. However, the cost of utilities, taxes, insurance, and repair and maintenance can be financially devastating because their homes tend to be poorly constructed and in need of maintenance, resulting in a high level of environmental stress on the older person.

Many of the houses owned by elders are old; 36 percent were built before 1959, compared with 27 percent of homes in general. As a result, they have inadequate weatherproofing and other energy-saving features, with large indoor and outdoor spaces that are costly to maintain. Exposed wiring, lack of sufficient outlets, and worn-out oil furnaces can be hazards. The 2007 American Housing Survey revealed that 10 percent of homes occupied by older homeowners had moderate or severe physical

problems. Renter-occupied dwellings are twice as likely to need repairs as owner-occupied units (U.S. Census Bureau, 2009).

It is not unusual to hear news stories during winter months of fires in older homes that result from faulty wiring, overloaded circuits, and the use of space heaters because of an inadequate furnace. The latter situation is particularly troublesome for older persons who have difficulties in maintaining body heat and prefer warmer ambient temperatures (see Chapter 3). Many communities attempt to prevent these problems by offering free or low-cost home repairs for low-income elders and special assistance to all older persons to make their homes more energy efficient (e.g., no-interest loans for weatherproofing and installing storm windows). Some cities that have experienced sudden increases in their electricity and natural gas rates have also developed programs to aid low-income people of all ages, but this is becoming more difficult with current high energy costs and cuts in public services.

Reverse Mortgages

Since 1989, the U.S. Department of Housing and Urban Development (HUD) has had the authority to offer insurance for **home equity conversion**

mortgages (HECM, or reverse mortgages). With insurance from HUD, numerous lenders across the country provide reverse mortgages to homeowners age 62 and older with little or no mortgage debt remaining. The largest lender is the Federal Housing Administration (FHA), which limits HECMs to $417,000 (NRMLA, 2009). More than 40 percent of older adults have paid off their mortgages, and their average equity exceeds $55,000. A reverse mortgage is a useful option for people age 62 and older who are "house-rich but cash-poor." It can help people age in place and pay for needed repairs and maintenance. In effect, reverse mortgages lend the older person money based on the home's equity and remaining mortgage; interest and a fee are charged, and the title to the property is retained by the lender (or the lender puts a lien on the home). The older person receives a lump sum or monthly payment (or annuity) from the lender and still lives in the house. This can mean an additional $1,000 or more each month for many older homeowners. These funds can supplement their income, especially during economic downturns when stock portfolios and pensions lose value. When the older person dies or sells the house, the lender generally deducts the portion of the mortgage that has been paid, including interest, as well as a percentage (usually about 10 percent) of the home's appreciated value or equity since the date of the reverse mortgage. Reverse mortgages have become a popular source of funds for older adults; 112,000 reverse mortgage loans were completed in 2008, compared with only 157 in 1990. The economic downturn that started in 2008 has made reverse mortgages more attractive to older homeowners. For those with considerable equity in their homes but unable to sell their homes in the slow real estate market, reverse mortgages provide funds for in-home care or other services needed to help the elder age in place, at least until the house can be sold and assets used to buy into a continuing care retirement community or other congregate living facility.

Reverse mortgages may carry long-term risks for the lender and the federal government; currently, there are no guidelines for the duration of such mortgage plans. For example, what if the older homeowner outlives the home's equity? Lenders do not want to evict such a person, but at the same time they do not want to lose their investment. The FHA pays the lender up to a certain proportion of these losses, but recent cases of fraud and misleading ads for reverse mortgages by some unscrupulous lenders have resulted in Congressional actions for greater regulation of this industry. In addition, homeowners must consider the initial costs of such a mortgage, as well as the mandatory mortgage insurance fee, a loan origination fee, and standard closing costs. Together with interest, a borrower could pay an annualized credit-line rate of 13 to 17 percent for this type of loan. The FHA has developed a program to reduce these costs, especially for elders with small or no mortgages. Depending on the homeowner's age, they may be able to borrow up to 56 percent of their home's value at a reasonable interest rate (AARP, 2006b). For older people with other assets to use as collateral, other types of loans may be more cost effective than a reverse mortgage. HUD offers information about reverse mortgages on its website and its toll-free phone number.

On the other hand, many people in their 50s and 60s have considerable equity in their homes because of housing prices rising steeply since the early 1990s. As their children leave, some prefer to sell these homes and move to smaller dwellings. A trend in the past decade, however, is represented by upper-income aging baby boomers who want a large home with many amenities that will help them age in place. These include features such as master bedrooms and full bathrooms on the main floor, universal design in the kitchen and bathrooms accessible to people in wheelchairs and walkers, wireless computer systems, and "smart homes" (discussed later in this chapter). Builders and architects need to recognize that boomers will expect more options in the size and amenities of homes, and also in the ability to adapt their homes to allow aging in place than any previous generation, assuming that their retirement income can fund such arrangements (see Chapter 12 for a discussion of baby boomers' changing retirement finances).

AN URBAN HOUSING SOLUTION

Increased housing costs and a desire to live close to relatives have produced innovative housing options for some older adults. City and municipality ordinances are changing to allow detached cottages, also known as **accessory housing** or **mother-in-law units,** to be built behind single family homes. The Seattle City Council held hearings in 2009 to allow homeowners to build such units up to 800 square feet in their backyards, covering no more than 40 percent of the area. While some hailed this as an innovative solution for homeowners to create an inexpensive housing option for their younger or older family members, others decried them as increasing the density of urban neighborhoods (*The Seattle Times,* 2009).

Planned Housing

During the past 45 years, federal and local government agencies and some private organizations, such as faith-based groups, have developed planned housing projects specifically for older persons. These include subsidized housing for low-income elders and age-segregated housing for middle- and upper-income older persons. Gerontologists have attempted to understand the effects of the quality and type of housing on older persons' satisfaction level and behavior following relocation to such environments. It appears that planned housing can indeed improve older persons' quality of life.

"SUMMER CAMP FOR ADULTS"

Many housing developers are expanding their markets by building active retirement communities for newer cohorts of older adults. Unlike the huge developments of the past—such as Sun Cities in California and Arizona with over 9,000 homes—recent projects have less than 1,000 units and often in less populated areas such as small communities in Colorado, Oregon, and Washington. They offer golf courses, tennis courts, and swimming pools for active adults age 60 and older. Indeed, these developments have so many recreational amenities that some are marketed as "full-time summer camps for adults."

Where to locate planned housing projects raises a number of complex issues. Developers must consider such factors as how the area is zoned as well as access to social and health services. As stated earlier in the discussion of neighborhood characteristics, older adults are most likely to use services when they are on-site and public transportation is easily accessible. If a particular site is not already near a bus stop, residents and developers may be able to convince the local public transportation authority to place one nearby. Some larger developments provide van services for their older residents to obtain medical and social services, as well as planned excursions to theaters, museums, religious institutions, parks, senior centers, and shopping malls. There has also been an expansion of somewhat exclusive retirement communities with units costing nearly a million dollars and offering computer access, health spas and fitness centers, golf courses, hiking trails, and some communal services such as meal options. These are known as "active adult communities."

Continuing Care Retirement Communities

Another option for elders with financial resources is the growing number of **continuing care retirement communities (CCRCs).** They are also known as life-care communities and continuum of care facilities in some areas. These multilevel facilities offer a range of housing, social, and health services on the same campus, from independent-to-congregate living arrangements, and intermediate-to-skilled care. While more than 3,000 CCRCs exist today, they continue to be built at a faster rate than other types of senior housing. Such options are more widely available in housing that is purchased, less so for rental housing. A report by the American Association of Homes and Services for the Aging (AAHSA, 2006) estimates that 98 percent of CCRCs provide apartment style living, 81 percent assisted living or other types of intermediate care, and 95 percent have a nursing home on-site or nearby. When several levels of care are available at one site, older partners can feel assured that they can remain near each other, even if one needs to be placed in intermediate or skilled care. The extent to which LGBT partners feel that such options are available to them varies widely. Reasons for choosing a CCRC include:

- a desire to plan ahead if care is needed in the future
- not wanting to be a burden on family members
- guaranteed health care
- freedom from home maintenance
- availability of supportive services and social, educational, and exercise programs (Gilbert Guide, 2009)

Many housing plans with options in living arrangements also offer different types of contracts. Under these plans, an older person must pay an initial entry fee—often quite substantial—based on projections of life expectancy, extent of care, and size of the living quarters. At the highest level and for the most expensive buy-in fee, an individual who eventually requires increased care is provided nursing home care without paying more beyond the buy-in fee. Known as a *life care contract*, this is a form of long-term care insurance that provides care as needed. The higher buy-in fee is based on the assumption that the elder will need higher levels of care in the future and relieves the buyer of anxieties about skilled care costs. The individual is taking the chance that higher levels of care will eventually be required, so the costs are averaged out over a long period. In a second type of contract, a *modified* or *continuing care contract*, the buyer pays less and is guaranteed housing, services, or amenities, but if they need long-term health care, they are restricted to a specific number of days. Some contracts offer a discounted rate for additional days in the CCRC's health facility if needed. In a third type, known as a *fee for service contract*, access to long-term-care in the CCRC is guaranteed, but residents must pay its full cost. Although the buy-in fee for this type of contract is

> ### ADVANTAGES AND DISADVANTAGES OF CCRCs
>
> Considering the high cost of CCRCs with life care contracts, potential buyers should consider the pros and cons of these commitments. Their greatest advantages are access to services that permit one to live autonomously and, for married residents, the opportunity to continue to live together if one person needs nursing home care. A potential risk for older people who enter into a life care contract is that the facility could declare bankruptcy. In an attempt to avoid this, most states now require providers to establish a trust fund for long-term care expenses.

lower (in some cases they may not even charge an entry fee) and the older resident benefits from many CCRC services and amenities, it can become much more costly than a life care contract or a continuing care contract if long-term care is required for long periods (Gilbert Guide, 2009).

The variation in services guaranteed by CCRCs results in monthly payments for entry fees ranging from $200 to $2,500 (Netting & Wilson, 2006). For those who die soon after moving in or who decide this is not where they want to live out their lives, some facilities refund all or part of the entry fee. Obviously, the ability to purchase these contracts is limited to the small percentage of older people who have considerable cash assets. Indeed, older persons in these facilities are better educated and have greater financial resources than the general older population.

Long-Term Care

As noted earlier, most older adults prefer to live in their own homes. An international survey by AARP found older Americans second only to Australians in their preference for independent living (87 percent and 98 percent, respectively). Fewer than 10 percent of elders in the U.S. thought long-term care was the best living arrangement. In contrast, 58 percent of Japanese and 30 percent of Chinese believed independent living was ideal, and tended to prefer intergenerational living (AARP, 2007). However, whether the older person lives alone or with extended family, functional decline may impair an elder's competence so much that P–E congruence cannot be achieved and long-term care services are required. Traditionally, this has meant relocation to a nursing home, but as described in this section, home and community-based long-term care options have expanded in the past 30 years. Following a description of nursing homes and the cultural changes taking place in this industry, we discuss newer options in both residential and community-based long-term care.

Nursing Homes

People who are unfamiliar with the residential patterns of older people mistakenly assume that the majority live in **nursing homes**; however, the actual proportion is only 4 percent of the population 65 and older, or 1.5 million. This is a decline from 1985, when 5.4 percent resided in nursing homes (NCHS, 2008). The lifetime risk of admission to a nursing home increases with age, from 39 percent at age 65 to 49 percent at age 85. Approximately 47 percent of women and 33 percent of men age 65 and older use skilled nursing homes at some point in their lives, often for a short stay after hospitalization (Seperson, 2002; Spillman & Lubitz, 2002).

As shown in Figure 11.3, the oldest-old are most likely to live in nursing homes; when all ethnic and racial groups are combined, rates increase from just under 1 percent of the young-old, to 13 percent of the oldest-old, to almost 50 percent of those who are age 95 and older (Federal Interagency Forum 2008; NCHS, 2008). Each year more than one million older persons leave long-term care facilities—almost evenly divided among discharges to the community, transfers to other health facilities, and death. Therefore, the statistic of 4 percent is a static picture of the population in nursing homes that does not take account of movement into and out of such settings.

With the increase in alternative long-term care options such as assisted living and adult family homes (described later in this chapter), rates of nursing home admissions are declining substantially. More elders, even those with multiple physical and cognitive impairments, are selecting or

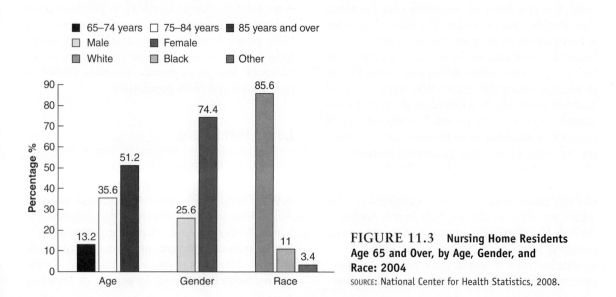

FIGURE 11.3 **Nursing Home Residents Age 65 and Over, by Age, Gender, and Race: 2004**
SOURCE: National Center for Health Statistics, 2008.

are placed in long-term care facilities other than nursing homes, while many others receive care in their own homes. This has resulted in a reduction in nursing homes, from 19,100 in 1985 to just over 16,000 today. These newer options in LTC have also reduced the proportion of elders in nursing homes, from 1.3 percent in 1985 to 1 percent among the young-old and from 22 to 13 percent among the oldest-old (Federal Interagency Forum 2008; NCHS, 2008). The total number of beds and the average number of beds per home have both expanded, however. This reflects a decline in the number of smaller nursing homes; only 14 percent have fewer than 50 beds, while almost 49 percent have 100 or more beds. The lower rates of nursing home admissions will probably continue, despite the significant growth of the oldest-old. This is because of increasing LTC options and a preference for remaining in one's own home. Nevertheless, skilled nursing homes are often the best choice for the oldest, most frail, and most vulnerable segments of the population. With the growth of community-based options, elders who use nursing homes today are generally more frail and require more intensive services than their counterparts 20 years ago. This greater intensity of services has raised the cost of living in a nursing home, not including specialized care, such as for dementia. In fact, 27 percent of skilled nursing homes today have specialized units for residents with dementia, indicating a high level of care for difficult patients (NCHS, 2008). The average age of nursing home residents is 84, and women are disproportionately represented. The typical nursing home:

- has 108 beds
- has 88 percent of its residents age 65 and older
- has 74 percent women residents
- 98 percent require assistance with at least one ADL
- 51 percent need help with five or more ADLs (NCHS, 2008)

The gender differential in nursing homes, shown in Figure 11.3, is due to women's longer life expectancy, their greater risk of multiple chronic and disabling illnesses, and their higher likelihood of being unmarried. The last factor is a critical one, since the absence of a partner or other caregiver is a major predictor of nursing home placement, as noted in Chapter 10.

In some instances, the demands of care become too great for families to manage. That is, if an adult child must help an increasingly frail parent, the likelihood of nursing home placement increases. Elders with incontinence, hallucinations, impaired communication, and severe ADL and IADL limitations are more likely to move to a nursing home, whether or not they have a family caregiver (Friedman et al., 2006). Almost 86 percent of nursing home residents are white, compared to 11 percent who are African American, and 3 percent who are Latino, American Indian, or Asian-Pacific Islander (NCHS, 2008). African Americans have historically been less likely to live in nursing homes, but since 1985, an increasing proportion are turning to skilled nursing home care (NCHS, 2006).

The under-representation of elders of color in nursing homes appears to reflect cultural differences in the willingness to place older persons in such facilities, greater availability of family supports, or institutionalized discrimination. For low-income elders of color, options are limited by the lack of an adequate number of Medicaid beds in nursing homes. This under-representation may also reflect the dearth of facilities that address the distinctive needs of elders of color, thereby forcing them to enter nursing homes that are incongruent with their cultural needs. In some communities with highly diverse populations, ethnic-specific nursing homes are now built under the auspices of nonprofit organizations or faith-based groups. For example, in San Francisco and Seattle, Japanese and Chinese American elders can enter nursing homes operated and staffed by people who speak their language and serve culturally specific foods. In most of the Chinese facilities, for example, employees can communicate with residents in many dialects of Chinese (*The New York Times*, 2003).

Most nursing homes (about 61.5 percent) are *proprietary,* or *for-profit,* and thus operate as a business that aims to make a profit for the owners or investors. Nursing homes owned by large multifacility chains are increasing (currently 54 percent). Another 7.7 percent are owned by federal, state, or local governments. *Nonprofit* homes (30.8 percent of the total) are generally sponsored by faith-based or fraternal groups (NCHS, 2008); while profit is not their goal, they must be self-supporting. Although instances of re-imbursement fraud by proprietary homes are highly publicized, the terms *proprietary* and *nonprofit* do not designate type or quality of care, but rather how the home is governed and how its earnings are distributed. The extent to which nurs-ing home care is shaped by federal funding mecha-nisms (e.g., Medicare, Medicaid) and regulations is discussed in Chapter 17.

Because of stereotypes and media stories about poor-quality facilities, few older people ini-tially choose to live in a nursing home. Most en-ter after receiving informal care from family members, formal home care services, and, in some cases, following a stay in facilities such as assisted living or adult family homes. African Americans are more likely than other groups to enter directly from a hospital and therefore have less control over the placement decision. Despite negative perceptions, nursing home life offers some advantages over other types of long-term care. These include:

- increased social interaction
- accessible social activities
- intensive rehabilitation services not provided by other long-term care alternatives
- relief from the stress of caregiving on family

Although the media report instances of abuse and violation of regulations, many excellent skilled nursing homes exist. Increased efforts to improve nursing homes and the development of innovative options signal an important change in skilled nursing facilities. Such options include sub-acute care for post-hospital discharge residents,

palliative and hospice care for terminally ill per-sons, and special care units (SCUs) or *memory care units* for residents with dementia (Gwyther & Kane, 2006; Vourlekis & Simons, 2006).

Increasingly, residents of nursing homes and their families have more influence over their lives through resident councils, patients' bills of rights, nursing home ombudsmen, and the advocacy of groups such as the National Citizens' Coalition for Nursing Home Reform (NCCNHR). In its resident surveys, this organization found that a major concern of cognitively intact older people is to be involved in decisions about their daily lives in the facility. Through such efforts, along with increased gerontological training, nursing home staff are also implementing ways to involve family, friends, and the larger community in their policies, procedures, and activities.

Congress enacted provisions in nursing home regulations of the Omnibus Budget Reconciliation Act (OBRA 1987) that were intended to recognize and respect residents' rights. This law requires every nursing home that participates in Medicare or Medicaid to respect residents' dignity, choice, and right of self-determination. Most states have a nursing home ombudsman or a complaint-resolution unit where residents and their families can report their concerns and grievances. An im-portant component of OBRA was to discourage pharmacological and physical restraints for man-aging behavior problems among residents with dementia. Research and demonstration initiatives to test alternative approaches to behavior manage-ment include training nurse aides in effective non-verbal and communication skills, as well as specific staff behaviors that can prevent the onset of problematic resident behaviors. Such training can reduce agitation and improves residents' com-munication skills up to 6 months after the inter-vention (Burgio et al., 2002).

Culture Change in Nursing Homes

New paradigms for the care of frail elders in skilled nursing homes are emerging. Since the 1990s, there has been a major **culture change** and a focus on **resident-centered care** in nursing homes. Culture change focuses not just on the physical environment, but also on decision making that encourages more input by residents, family members and staff, and also a less hierarchical organizational structure than the traditional nursing home model. Nursing homes that have adopted this paradigm shift focus on individualizing services to each resident's needs and preferences (i.e., resident-centered care), offering them choices in waking and eating times, and in some cases even selecting which staff members serve them. One of the first national efforts aimed at changing nursing home culture was labeled the **Eden Alternative** by its founder, Dr. Bill Thomas. This approach to nursing home policy and operations emphasizes the "home" aspect of nursing homes as a place where residents can continue to grow, rather than institutions where they come to die. According to the Eden paradigm, elders should continue to make decisions for themselves and engage in meaningful activities, including caring for plants and pets in the home or volunteering in a child care center if there is one on-site. Facilities that have adopted the Eden Alternative deemphasize strictly scheduled activities and focus on humanizing staff–elder interactions (Thomas, 1999). An initial period of educating residents, employees, and families is vital to the success of the Eden Alternative. All staff must receive some hands-on training, and those who are more extensively trained—Eden Associates—represent diverse levels and types of managers and staff. In one study of its impact on residents, overall quality of care had improved in a Canadian home that implemented the Eden Alternative (Schmidt & Beattie, 2005). In another study, elders in a home that adopted the Eden Alternative were assessed at baseline and one year after the program began, compared with elders in a typical nursing home. Lower levels of boredom and helplessness were found among residents in the Eden Alternative facility, but the groups did not differ in loneliness scores (Bergman-Evans, 2004). In another case where this model was implemented by a large facility (450 beds), residents became more involved in new activities and self-care. Job turnover among nurse aides declined while job satisfaction improved. However, not all managers underwent the necessary training, thereby causing problems with facility-wide adoption of Eden values and practices into resident care. Another challenge that can arise is that staff may become responsible for the home's companion animals, adding to their workload. Although it is assumed that residents will take on this role of caring for pets, there is no way to require them to do so (Sampsell, 2003).

Other paradigms of culture change are promoted by the **Pioneer Network,** a growing national coalition of long-term care administrators, practitioners, and advocates for improving the quality of care in nursing homes. The Pioneer Network also emphasizes the importance of "person-centered care" rather than rigid adherence to institutional regulations. Unlike the policy and operations focus of the Eden Alternative, this model modifies the physical environment to make nursing homes more homelike, create "neighborhoods," and offer residents more privacy. Organizational changes such as expanding staff roles, leadership, and decision making are also intended to create a resident-centered facility (Angelelli & Higbie, 2005; Grant, 2006; Yeatts, et al., 2004). One of the first nursing homes in the country to implement these physical and organizational changes was Mt. St. Vincent Home in Seattle. In this dramatic example, each floor is divided into "neighborhoods" of 20 residents per group, with their own small dining rooms, resident-directed care, integration of cognitively alert elders and those with dementia, and assignment of staff to each "neighborhood" (Boyd, 2003).

The **Green House** concept also focuses on de-institutionalizing long-term care by converting large nursing facilities into multiple intentional communities of 8 to 10 residents and by empowering direct care workers as well as residents with as much autonomy and choice as possible. These smaller houses are linked together organizationally, but residents remain part of the 8- to 10-person home. The community of residents interacts in a shared living and dining area, but residents have their private rooms and bathrooms. The homes do not have nursing stations, unlike the typical nursing home design. Each unit has a lower resident-to-staff ratio, and all staff are taught to provide direct or hands-on care. These **universal workers** perform multiple services, including meal preparation, personal care, and housekeeping, rather than specializing in one task. This allows greater opportunities for staff and residents to know each other. One licensed nurse is available for two to three houses, depending on the level of skilled care needed. Preliminary evaluations suggest less depression agitation and antipsychotic medication use among elders with dementia in Green House homes. Job satisfaction among staff appears to be higher and turnover lower than in traditional nursing homes (Green House Project, 2006; Lustbader & Williams, 2006; Rabig et al., 2006). This philosophy has been enhanced by the implementation of technology to assist universal workers and further improve the quality of life of frail residents at Oatfield Estates, near Portland, Oregon, as described in the box on this page.

Even without physical modifications, empowering direct-line workers (specifically certified nurse aides or CNAs) can improve resident care and enhance staff cooperation and job satisfaction. Modifying workloads and improving supervision and training can also reduce staff turnover, as discussed more fully in Chapter 10. Under the overall framework of the Pioneer Network, these significant paradigm shifts in organizational philosophy and structure, physical design, and staff caregiving practices are improving the quality of care for frail elders in nursing homes (Angelelli, 2006; Fagan, 2004; Yeatts & Cready, 2007).

Newer Options for Long-Term Care

Home and community-based services (HCBS) have also grown dramatically in the past 20 years. This LTC model is defined as group housing with additional services such as meals, basic health

---

IMPLEMENTING RESIDENT-CENTERED CARE IN ASSISTED LIVING

One facility that has combined technology with a resident-centered model of long-term care is Oatfield Estates, or Elite Care, located just outside Portland, Oregon. The campus is comprised of multiple houses with 12 private suites for up to 15 elders who eat and socialize with their housemates and the staff who are assigned to that house. Family members are encouraged to visit and volunteer, and they can monitor their elder's daily activities 24 hours a day (with the resident's permission). This is because residents wear an unobtrusive electronic monitoring device that can track their activities, where they are spending their time, and how well they are sleeping. Such monitoring also allows elders to wander throughout Oatfield Estates' gardens and houses without concerns about getting lost. This combination of technology and resident-centered care has allowed the facility to care for many elders with dementia who would ordinarily be placed in a nursing home. Elite Care has garnered international attention for this ability to combine technology and humanistic care for even the most frail elders.

---

care, and some personal assistance, as well as a wide range of other services (including home care) to assist elders in their own homes, as described below under in-home services. Examples of HCBS housing options include assisted living and board and care homes (also known as *adult family homes* and *adult foster care*), discussed more fully below. An HCBS housing option provides room and board, at least one meal per day, and 24-hour security, although not as extensively as nursing homes (Hawes, 2001). These alternatives in community residential care can help older people maintain their autonomy, even if they have multiple ADL limitations. Because HCBS facilities cost less to operate, more individuals and organizations are investing in this type of housing. Large health care systems, insurance companies, and nonprofit and for-profit corporations have built these alternative facilities or added new apartment or cottage units to their existing nursing home campuses. The majority of assisted living and adult family home residents are age 75 and older. Many would have been placed in nursing homes in the past, but they are now using HCBSs. Its lower cost has made HCBS housing a more desirable option for states with growing numbers of frail elders who need public assistance. One reason for this is the trend toward state licensure and Medicaid reimbursement, albeit at lower levels, for these alternatives. This increasing use of Medicaid waivers is discussed in Chapter 17. Currently the average share of Medicaid LTC spending allocated to HCBS is only 24 percent nationwide, but wide variation occurs because each state can determine its level of spending for nursing homes vs. HCBS. Washington state, for example, allocates 54 percent of its Medicaid funds for HCBS care and 70 percent of frail elders use HCBS programs. In contrast, only 15 percent of Michigan's Medicaid LTC funds are spent on HCBS and 56 percent of the state's frail elders are enrolled in HCBS (AARP, 2009).

Assisted Living

Assisted living (AL) is seen by its advocates as a more humane model of housing for elders who need assistance with personal care and with some ADLs, but who are not so severely impaired physically or cognitively that they require 24-hour skilled medical care. The Assisted Living Federation of America (ALFA) defines assisted living as "a special combination of housing, personalized supportive services, and healthcare" (www.alfa.org). It is based on a social model of long-term care rather than a medical model such as skilled nursing homes. As such, it is not necessarily a specific building type but a philosophy of care. Nevertheless, AL facilities usually provide private apartments, which typically include:

- a small kitchen
- a full bathroom
- in some, a bedroom, sitting room, and an additional partial bath

These features create a more homelike, less-institutional setting that encourages frail elders to maintain active aging and continuity with their previous lifestyles (National Center for Assisted Living, 2008; Marsden, 2005; Wilson, 2007). Some assisted living facilities offer shared units as a lower-cost alternative. Most provide congregate meals in a common dining room, as well as housekeeping, laundry, and help with some ADLs, such as medication use. Staff generally include at least one nurse, a social worker, and one or more people to provide case management services. Access to health care is offered to specific residents as needed (often contracting the services of physicians, physical therapists, mental health specialists). As a result, staffing costs are lower than in nursing homes, thereby keeping the average cost of AL lower. An extensive analysis of such facilities throughout the U.S. and northern Europe led Regnier (2002) to develop nine criteria for a successful assisted living project. According to these guidelines, AL facilities that want to achieve excellent resident outcomes should:

1. appear residential in character
2. be perceived as small in scale
3. provide residents with privacy
4. recognize each resident's uniqueness
5. encourage independence and interdependence
6. emphasize health maintenance, mental stimulation, and physical activity
7. support involvement by residents' families
8. maintain contact with the immediate community
9. serve frail elders

Assisted living facilities often develop individual service plans, based on each resident's functional abilities. Families considering these options must ask what the facility will provide when their older relatives decline physically or cognitively. Like nursing homes, AL providers that offer a variety of services generally charge "tiered" rates—that is, increasingly costly fees for elders who require more services. Therefore, even though AL on average costs half as much as a nursing home, some facilities with extensive amenities and health services can cost as much as a nursing home.

Assisted living generally offers residents more autonomy, privacy, and participation in care decisions than do nursing homes. The trade-off, of course, is that the individual may decide to participate in activities that are risky or that do not comply with health care regimens recommended by a professional. These may include choices such as refusing to use a walker or not following a specific diet. As a result of this conflict between assuring resident autonomy versus safety, many facilities have moved toward a policy of managed risk, or **negotiated risk.** Under such policies, residents (and often their family or guardian) must sign a written agreement that allows the resident to accept greater risk of personal injury in exchange for autonomy in decisions about lifestyle and privacy. Many elders and their families are willing to accept such risk, despite the fact that elders in AL today are more frail than was intended by this type of housing. Residents of AL have these common features:

- Their average age is 85
- A range of 40 to 67 percent have some form of dementia
- About 33 percent have a significant hearing impairment and/or visual impairments
- 72 percent need some help with bathing and 57 percent with dressing
- More than 75 percent need help with managing medications and money
- Only 20 percent can perform all ADLs independently (Hyde, Perez & Forester, 2007; Marsden, 2005)

When the AL model was first proposed (Wilson, 1993, 1995), the focus was on creating a homelike setting, smaller in scale than nursing homes, that allowed resident control and privacy. These facilities were intended to provide apartments with private baths, food preparation and storage areas, and doors that residents could lock. The goal was to allow elders to age in place

by offering services as needs changed, but with shared responsibility and negotiated risk, since AL could not provide all the medical services available in nursing homes. Over time, however, the concept has changed so that many facilities do not offer private apartments. In addition, the lack of state and federal legislation defining AL has resulted in diverse models of this concept, depending on ownership and location. Approximately 65,000 AL facilities today that care for over two million residents (National Center for Assisted Living, 2008). Some AL facilities can accommodate older people with multiple disabilities, many of whom traditionally would be placed in nursing homes. However, some have argued that many AL facilities are not good settings for aging in place because they do not provide adequate services as residents become more frail. Some states have policies against admitting elders with cognitive impairment or behavioral problems into AL unless staff receives special training, but exceptions are common (Hernandez, 2005–2006; Zimmerman, Munn, & Koenig, 2006).

Assisted living is most prominent in Oregon, where the concept was first introduced. Because of flexible regulations about residents' ADL limitations, only 20 percent have left AL for nursing homes, compared with 60 percent in other states (Phillips et al., 2003; Golant, 2004). Oregon currently has an equal mix of nursing home and AL beds (30 percent each) for elders who need long-term care. Most states and the District of Columbia have adopted the concept of assisted living. They provide **Medicaid waivers** for elders to use AL as an alternative to nursing homes for those who have fewer ADL limitations. Some, such as Oregon and Washington, have implemented programs that encourage the use of AL and other community-based long-term care options. Interest in AL is growing, but costs are prohibitive for many low- and middle-income elders, and many facilities do not accept elders who depend on Medicaid for their long-term care because reimbursement rates are lower than fees charged to private pay residents. In some cases, elders must

THE DOWNSIDE OF HCBSs

Despite its many advantages, housing for older adults that is based on a social model of long-term care can have its downside. These problems are aggravated in states that have few or no licensure requirements for assisted living or other HCBSs. For example, state officials and industry representatives in Alabama agreed to enforce stricter rules after reviewing complaints against 200 unlicensed facilities. Two particularly egregious examples are a 92-year-old man who climbed out of a window in the assisted living facility where he lived, walked away, and died of exposure; and a frail resident in another facility who became bedridden, lost 40 pounds, and died when no medical care was provided.

status (i.e., private vs. Medicaid) predicted whether or not they would relocate to higher levels of care. No differences emerged on these variables between the two types of facilities. These data suggest that older adults who need residential long-term care may do just as well in terms of health outcomes in the less restrictive and less costly AL setting as they would in a nursing home (Pruchno & Rose, 2000). These positive findings have led many housing policy advocates to promote the expansion of AL for lower-income elders. One result has been an allocation of funds from HUD to states to convert existing multifamily units into AL. Several states have received these funds to accommodate their low-income, frail elders who could not otherwise afford it (HUD, 2006a).

Private Homes That Provide Long-Term Care

Adult foster care (AFC) or **adult family homes (AFH)** are other options for older persons who do not need the 24-hour medical care of skilled nursing homes. In some states, they are known as *board and care homes* or *group homes*. AFC is generally provided in a private home (hence the term AFH) by the owners who may have some health care training but are not required to be professionals in the field. The owner and, in some cases, auxiliary staff provide housekeeping, help with some ADLs, personal care, and some delegated nursing functions, such as giving injections, distributing medications, and changing dressings on wounds if they have been trained and certified by a registered nurse. Like AL residents, older residents in AFHs can generally decide for themselves whether to take their medications or to exercise, unlike the more structured nursing home schedule. These homes are licensed to house up to five or six residents. Some specialize in caring for adults with physical disabilities or psychiatric disorders, others refuse to care for people with advanced dementia, while still others offer services to dementia patients only. Families and elders both tend to like the small family-like atmosphere of AFHs in contrast to larger

move out because they have run out of funds and must turn to nursing homes that accept Medicaid, even though they might benefit from the greater autonomy and self-care at AL facilities. As more states offer Medicaid waivers for assisted living as an alternative to nursing homes, greater P–E congruence can be achieved between needs of elders with fewer ADL limitations and available housing options (Hernandez, 2005–2006). Medicaid waivers are described in detail in Chapter 17.

Since most elders and their families prefer AL over nursing homes, there is growing research on whether these LTC options produce different resident outcomes. In a comparison of 76 elders living in a nursing home with 82 in an assisted living facility within the same CCRC campus, medical records were examined and residents were interviewed four times over a 12-month period. At the baseline assessment, cognitive status did not differ between groups, but nursing home residents had more symptoms of depression and poorer functional health than AL residents. During the 12-month follow-up, mortality rates and relocation to units or facilities with more assistance did not differ between the two sites. Residents' age was the best predictor of mortality, whereas their functional and cognitive ability, educational level, and payment institutional-like settings, even though quality among AFHs varies widely.

Medicaid reimbursement rates for AFC are one-third to one-half the rates paid to nursing homes. This works well for residents who do not require heavy care (e.g., those who are not bedridden or with severe behavioral problems due to dementia). However, for more frail elders or for those who have aged in place (i.e., have become more impaired while living in an AFC), the reimbursement rates do not reflect the time and effort required of the facilities' caregivers, which can negatively affect the overall quality of care.

This trend toward placing more impaired older persons in AFCs or AFHs is driven by states' efforts to control long-term care costs and most elders' and families' preferences for a social, rather than a medical, model of care. Similar to the study described above that compared residents' health outcomes in nursing homes versus assisted living facilities (Pruchno & Rose, 2000), Hedrick and colleagues (2003) compared health, relocation, and mortality over a 12-month period among residents of AL, adult family homes (AFH), and adult foster care (AFC) facilities. They followed 349 adults in 219 facilities (including AL, AFH, and AFC) from 3 months after the individual entered the facility to 12 months later.

At baseline, AFH residents were more likely than the other two groups to require help with multiple ADLs (especially bathing and dressing), even though the oldest group resided in AL settings. General health status was similar across the three types of settings, and cognitive impairment was more common in AFH and AL residents than among those in AFC (58, 43, and 23 percent, respectively). However, there were no significant differences across the three types of long-term care in mortality rates, declines in health, or relocation to different settings over the 12 months of follow-up.

These results support the findings of the study comparing nursing homes and AL—that a less restrictive and less costly LTC setting can accommodate frail elders just as well as the more expensive option. Furthermore, residents' health outcomes as measured by mortality, morbidity, and relocation are similar across these settings. Aging in place appears to be possible without relocating to the more expensive setting, whether that is AFH versus AL or AL versus nursing homes. To the extent that these HCBSs offer some help with ADLs, they can reduce the costs for elders and their families who pay out of pocket as well as Medicaid expenditures at the state level (Chapin & Dobbs-Kepper, 2001). The success of alternative long-term care models in providing high quality care, often at lower costs than nursing homes, has encouraged the Veterans Health Administration (VHA) to offer these HCBS options to its burgeoning population of veterans. With projections of a doubling of its veterans age 85 and older by 2013 and an increase in LTC needs by 20 to 25 percent, the VHA has expanded its LTC services. While 95 percent of all LTC care for veterans was provided by nursing homes in 1992, AL increased to 15 percent of LTC by 2007 (Kinosian, Stallard, & Wieland, 2007).

Outcomes across a range of residential LTC options—such as mortality, morbidity, and relocation—are often similar, despite wide variations in the costs and types of services offered. Given this, other outcomes also need to be considered. Improving the older person's quality of life, not just extending life, should become a primary goal for long-term care providers. Critical elements of quality of life to be considered by such facilities encompoass

- a sense of safety, security, and order
- physical comfort and freedom from pain
- enjoyment of daily life
- meaningful activities
- meaningful interpersonal relationships
- preserving functional competence (or "active aging" within the limits of the elder's capacities)
- enhancing dignity
- ensuring a sense of privacy
- opportunities for intimacy and expressing one's sexuality
- a sense of individuality, autonomy, and choice
- spiritual well-being

Services to Assist Aging in Place

As noted earlier, long-term care has evolved in the past 20 years from an emphasis on purely institutional care to a broad range of HCBSs to help older adults age in place in the least restrictive environment possible. Under this broader definition, homemaker services, nutrition programs, adult day care, and home health care are all long-term care services which can assist the older person in maintaining P–E congruence in the least restrictive setting. As shown in Figure 11.4, some of these services (e.g., home care) are brought to the older person's residence, whereas others (e.g., adult day health) require the individual to leave home to receive the services. We briefly describe home care and adult day care/adult health care in this chapter, with other services that are funded through the Aging Network illustrated in Chapter 16.

Chore workers and other home and community-based services can help older people remain in their homes.

Home Care

Most older adults prefer to age in place, ideally in their own homes for as long as possible, despite the increasing array of residential options available today (AARP, 2003, 2006a, 2006c). While some home care alternatives are motivated by elders' desire to age in place, cost concerns drive other changes. As third-party payers (e.g., Medicare) seek to reduce escalating hospital and nursing home costs, home care services, including hospice, have grown dramatically. Medicare reimburses *some* **home health care** services, defined as skilled nursing or

rehabilitation benefits that are provided in the patient's own home and prescribed by a physician. Not surprisingly, the average home health consumer is a woman age 70 and has 1.7 ADL impairments. The oldest-old generally receive more home health visits on average than any other age group—about four times as many as for among the young-old (Hughes & Pittard, 2001; Peng, Navaie-Waliser, & Feldman, 2003).

The number of agencies providing home health care or hospice care increased by almost 50 percent between 1992 and 2001, to more than 11,400 across the country (CDC, 2009). In addition, as demand has increased, home care

In Home
Home care
Home health services
Home-delivered meals
Home improvement

Older Adult at Home

In Community
Social services
Adult day care
Transportation
Shopping

FIGURE 11.4 Services Needed by Elders at Home with Long-Term Care Needs

agencies have expanded their services beyond health care to include a broad array of HCBSs to support aging in place:

- personal assistance, such as chore services to maintain the home
- personal care to help the person perform ADLs
- home-delivered meals
- home repair and modification to enhance P-E fit
- hospice care
- respite care, either in the home or in a facility that gives family caregivers a break
- automatic safety response systems

The checklist in the box below summarizes factors that families should consider when selecting home health care services.

Other options, such as adult day care and adult day health, are offered in community settings outside the home. These services provide

---

A CHECKLIST FOR CHOOSING HOME HEALTH CARE SERVICES

- Is the agency licensed, accredited, and certified to give home health care?
- Is the agency Medicare-certified/approved?
- Does it have a written statement about its services, eligibility, costs, and payment procedures?
- Does it do background checks on potential employees?
- Are homemakers and home health aides trained? For how long? By whom?
- How are employees supervised?
- Will the same person provide care on a regular basis?
- What are the hourly fees? Minimum hours required?
- How does the agency handle theft and other unacceptable and unethical behaviors?
- Will you be given a copy of the treatment/service plan?
- Does the agency have a Bill of Rights for clients?

---

respite to family caregivers and opportunities for social interaction for elders.

Adult Day Care and Adult Day Health Care

Adult day care (ADC) allows the older person to remain at home but receive some health and social services outside the home. In this case, users attend a local ADC center one or more times per week, for several hours each day. ADC goes beyond senior centers in providing structured health and social services for older people with cognitive and functional impairments. These facilities are smaller than most senior centers, with an average daily attendance of less than 25 elders; about 75 percent of the facilities are nonprofit. Some ADCs are based on a health rehabilitative model of long-term care with individualized care (**adult day health care**, or **ADHC**), while others fit into a social psychological model ("social day care"). Although both may provide recreation, meals, transportation to and from the facility, and memory-retraining programs, ADHCs are more likely to offer nursing care, physical and speech therapy, health monitoring, and scheduled medication distribution. The greatest advantage of ADHCs over home health care is bringing older people together for social interaction. Equally important, they provide respite and support for family caregivers, as noted in Chapter 10. Respite is an important function, especially since it can reduce caregivers' feelings of stress and enhance their self-efficacy (Gitlin et al., 2006). ADC can decrease agitation and nighttime sleep disturbance among elders with dementia (Femia et al., 2007). Users of ADCs may delay moving into a nursing home, but this depends largely on the characteristics and stress level of the elder's family caregiver (Cho, Zarit, & Chiriboga, 2009). Such services are not suitable for the most impaired or bedbound older person but are an invaluable resource for elders with moderate levels of dementia or with serious physical impairments and chronic illnesses who still benefit from living in the community.

PACE: AN INTEGRATED CARE MODEL: (An innovative model of community-based care is PACE (Program of All-Inclusive Care of the Elderly). Persons 55 and older who are state-certified as nursing home eligible enroll in this community alternative that includes adult day health care, medical services, home health and personal care, all necessary prescriptions, several specialty services (e.g. dentistry, audiology, podiatry), and hospital and nursing home care as needed. The average age of the nearly 18,000 users of 67 PACE sites around the country is 84; the typical user is a woman has 12.7 different diagnoses and needs help with 3.3 ADLs. These demographics could describe the typical nursing home resident, but PACE focuses on preventing nursing home placement, offering specific health and social services as needed, and maintaining frail elders in the community. Although PACE is very expensive to initially implement, it can cut costs over the long run (Dobell & Bloom, 2009).

Technology to Help Aging in Place

Designing housing that is adaptable to elders' changing competence levels is a central consideration in helping them to age in place. The areas of flexible housing, universal design, use of assistive technology, and gerotechnology are all exciting and rapidly changing developments to promote aging in place.

PLANNING FOR AGING IN PLACE

When Mr. and Mrs. Pond bought their last home, they were in their late 60s. They chose a house on one level and installed grab bars in the bathroom, nonslip surfaces, and other safety features. When Mr. Pond was 78, he had a stroke that restricted his mobility. Mrs. Pond's vision became more impaired. However, with help from a weekly chore worker, daily meals delivered to their home, and twice-weekly visits to an adult day care facility, they were able to remain in their home until they died, he at age 82, she at 85.

Even among middle-aged adults, new home buyers are requesting *flexible housing*. In response to this growing demand, the Master Builders Association has designed a training program to help contractors build and remodel homes that can be used throughout a lifetime. This interest on the part of home builders is clearly more than academic. It reflects the trend of first-time buyers to select neighborhoods where they will want to live for many years. As a result, architects and builders are already designing homes with movable walls that can expand or shrink a room as needs change, or plumbing that can convert a small room on the main floor of the house into a bathroom. Other options are modifiability in the number and size of bedrooms and using a cluster design so that multiple generations and even unrelated renters can live under the same roof while retaining their privacy. Builders and architects who are knowledgeable about the Americans with Disabilities Act (ADA) build main-floor hallways and doorways in private homes that are wide enough for wheelchair access. Even though the ADA does not require accessibility in private homes, these shifts are occurring because builders recognize the growing market for such housing features. All of these give families the flexibility to adapt their homes as they assume caregiving roles or if one of the current residents requires community-based, in-home care in the future.

Newer cohorts of elders are also benefiting from the **universal design** movement, first proposed by an activist for the rights of persons with disabilities. This concept of designing the environment to allow the widest range of users possible (i.e., inclusive design) and to facilitate active aging attracts the attention of architects, landscape architects, and interior and furniture designers. What began as an attempt to make street curbs and hallways and bathrooms in homes accessible to people in wheelchairs has grown to a movement that makes all environments—parks, wilderness areas, automobiles, and computer workstations—accommodate people who are able-bodied as well as those with limited mobility, vision, and hearing. Universal design can benefit all age groups, not only older adults. The principles behind universal design are to:

- maximize autonomy
- enhance personal dignity
- enable full participation in society
- provide opportunities for self-fulfillment (Preiser & Ostroff, 2001)

Some architects are working on cost-effective means of applying new technology to home and long-term care design. For example, systems that make a room light up through sensors in the floor can help prevent falls when an older person gets up at night. Bed sensors that detect weight change can be used to monitor how often the older person gets out of bed during the night. Remote controls for operating thermostats, windows, and their coverings can help an older adult change the room temperature as needed, as well as open and close windows and shades to manage the ambient temperature and to prevent glare. Other design features that can be built into housing to assist aging in place include:

- bathrooms with roll-in showers
- hands-free sensors on faucets
- nonskid flooring
- low-pile carpeting
- uniform lighting throughout the house
- elevator shafts that are built into the home and used as closets until they are needed as elevators
- computerized controls (portable keypads) for heat, artificial lighting, and window shades

Today nearly 35 percent of individuals age 75 and older use at least one assistive device or have had their home modified for accessibility. This proportion will increase dramatically in the future, especially among baby boomers. The most popular modification is to install grab bars in bathrooms (in about 30 percent of homes owned by adults 65 and older). Other changes are far less frequent, perhaps because of cost concerns.

The field of **gerontechnology** (or *gerotechnology*), where gerontologists and industrial and human factors engineers work together to create **assistive technology** has expanded in the past 15 years. Technology, is being built into housing and products to improve P–E congruence for older adults. Many of these products are designed to help people remember tasks such as medication schedules. One product already on the market uses verbal and tone reminders, as well as flashing lights and a single red button, to dispense medications on a predetermined schedule. Others use an automated system to call the patient after the scheduled medication time and ask if the pill has been taken; if the elder does not respond or does not recall taking the medication, phone alerts are sent to family members or other contact persons. Families or health providers can set up a prescription routine on a specific schedule for up to 11 different drugs for 30 days. Other devices can be attached to each prescription container; a prerecorded voice announces the schedule and dose needed for that particular medication. This technique is especially useful for older people with dementia who would benefit from hearing a family member's voice reminding them what medications to take. For older adults who are cognitively alert and use personal data assistants (PDAs), software is available to remind them when it is time to take their meds. These new technologies for medication management are not necessarily better than hands-on care by caregivers, but they may allow the elder to remain self-sufficient longer, reduce caregiver burden, and are often more cost effective than paid caregivers (Agree & Freedman, 2003; Rialle et al., 2002).

Computer programs have been designed to describe potential side effects of various medications and interactions among them. Currently, these software programs are aimed at physicians, pharmacists, and other health professionals. However, programs will soon be available, written in layman's language, where elders can type in the names and doses of medications they are taking and then obtain a printout of potential side effects and special precautions. This would be particularly useful to the many older adults who are using multiple prescriptions and over-the-counter medications. It is also technically possible to conduct remote monitoring between a patient's home and a local health care facility for such information as blood pressure and heart-rate measurement. Indeed, as Figure 11.5 illustrates, such monitoring consists of wearing a bracelet or arm cuff attached to a computer or a cell phone that transmits health data to a centralized database in a hospital or health provider's office. After paying for the necessary hardware and software, however, the costs of regular monitoring by a health care provider may be prohibitive for many older adults. In the future, more accurate monitoring devices may be implanted as tiny sensors inside the body. Health insurance plans may cover the costs if they see that these technologies will reduce health care expenditures by preventing hospitalizations and ER visits.

Assistive technology can include home monitoring for people with particular chronic illnesses, such as diabetes and hypertension. In this case, the patient's relevant health variables (e.g., weight, blood pressure, blood glucose, and cholesterol) are transmitted to a centralized health care database, as shown in Figure 11.5. Indeed, the field of **telehealth**, where health information is transmitted electronically from the patient's home to their physician's office, or from an ambulatory care setting such as a health clinic to a specialist's office, has grown 40 percent annually since 1997. These biometric, video phone, and telemonitoring systems can increase patients' compliance with medication regimens and reduce their hospitalization and nursing home placement rates. The VA health system has enrolled more than 35,000 veterans in its home telehealth program. Patients with chronic diseases monitor their vital signs regularly; clinicians at VA hospitals review these data that can be transmitted via regular phone lines. Telehealth is found to be cost effective because it reduces hospitalizations and ER visits, and it

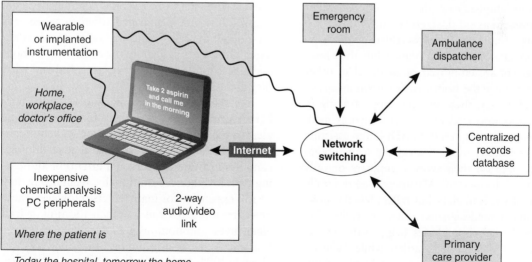

FIGURE 11.5 **Schematic Diagram of a Proposed Interface between the Patient and the Health Care System**
SOURCE: Reprinted with permission from Professor Paul Yager.

also improves patients' perceived control over their health. Information about the elder's health status can also be transmitted online to family members who live or work at a distance from the elder. This allows long-distance surveillance by caregivers (Department of Veterans Affairs, 2009; Lehmann, 2003; Utterback, 2005).

Telehealth, the use of assistive technology and other strategies for elders to take a greater role in managing their health assumes a level of **health literacy.** This refers to the degree to which individuals have the capacity to obtain, process and understand health information to make informed and appropriate decisions, reduce health risks and increase quality of life (Nielsen-Bohlman, Panzer & Kindig, 2004; USDHHS, 2000; Zarcadoolas, Pleasant & Greer, 2006) This capacity is affected by cultural, social and individual factors. The Department of Health and Human Services (2007) publishes a *Quick Guide to Health Literacy and Older Adults,* which addresses special issues such as older adults' strengths, visual and hearing impairments and normal cognitive changes. Strategies to address these changes include taking account of cultural beliefs and values, using plain language, minimizing distractions, and emphasizing desired actions rather than actions to avoid (USDHHS, 2007).

Monitoring systems allow elders with early-stage dementia to remain at home while their family caregivers are employed or involved in other activities outside the home. Also known as *aware home technology,* these systems support aging in place by monitoring daily activities such as medication use, mapping trends in ADLs, and assisting elders' communication. Caregivers can obtain real-time data on their work computers or only emergency information. Alarms can alert family members if the frail elder has fallen, left the stove on beyond a predesignated time, or walked beyond the home's boundaries (e.g., "safe" doors may lead to a protected garden while "alarm" doors lead to the street). Sensors can be placed under mattresses to determine if the older person is sleeping, restless, or out of bed during the night. Because they work by detecting weight on the bed,

---

ROBOTS FOR FRAIL ELDERS

Researchers at Waseda University in Tokyo have developed a bedside robot that can lift frail elders out of bed, carry them, and even serve them breakfast. Its delicate grip can hold a straw and bring it to an elder's lips. The software is being refined to respond to voice commands to bring medications and food. However, this type of robot may cost far more than individuals or even a long-term care facility can afford; developers project its price to be around $200,000 when the robot becomes available within a decade (Binns, 2009).

---

these sensors can also track the elder's weight and notify caregivers if significant weight loss occurs. Despite its potential benefits, some older caregivers reject home monitoring systems because they require learning technology and they have concerns about their reliability (Kinney & Kart, 2006; Rogers & Fisk, 2005).

Researchers and engineers at the Massachusetts Institute of Technology, Sony, Honda, and other Japanese companies are testing robots that can be used by frail elders to perform routine housework and personal services and even socialize with their owners. The Intel Corporation is designing a digital photo frame that is activated when someone calls the elder. If the caller's information is stored on the digital frame, it can identify the caller with a photo and a description of when they last called and what they discussed.

As the fields of gerontechnology and telehealth grow, elders and their families must be alert to the ethical issues of privacy and confidentiality. They also must recognize that technology cannot substitute for personal attention and caring by a loved one. Additionally, technology may be too expensive for many elders. However, these new developments can lengthen the time a frail elder lives autonomously and reduce caregiver burden (Agree & Freedman, 2003; Pew & Van Hemel, 2004; Rogers & Fisk, 2005). A 2009 report, *State of Technology in Aging Services,* by the Center for Aging Services Technologies (CAST) reviews some of these new technologies that are commercially available and in development, on its website, http://www.agingtech.org.

Technology can also be used to enhance options for older adults' recreation and enrichment. For example, computers are commonly used for obtaining information via the Web and for leisure (e.g., games linked by telecommunication channels, books read on a computer monitor with adjustable font size, programs that convert written to spoken text for visually impaired users). Interactive television, CD-ROM and DVD, closed-caption TV programming, and online education can greatly expand the social worlds of home-bound elders and stimulate intellectual functioning through active participation in learning. For example, Senior Net is a nationwide computer network that encourages discussion on diverse topics and offers hands-on classes in computer use. For a small membership fee, users can attend local classes on computer literacy, word processing, database management, and how to access useful sites on the Internet. Computer game companies such as Nintendo are marketing brainpower games specifically to older adults and even younger adults are purchasing them on the belief that this will enhance their memories as well.

Given trends toward Internet banking and shopping, future cohorts with computer skills may not need to leave their homes to obtain many services. More older adults are using computers for accessing the Web at home or in nearby libraries and senior centers. But cohort differences are evident: 40 percent of households headed by those age 70 to 79 had a computer in 2003, compared with 58 percent of households headed by adults age 60 to 69. Only 25 percent of the former and 44 percent of the latter group reported using the Internet (U.S. Census Bureau, 2005). However, expanding recognition of the scope of the Internet has resulted in a significant growth in its use by elders in the past few years, with an almost equal interest by men and women. In 2009, 41 percent of people age 65 and older reported using the Internet, compared with 72 percent of 50- to 64-year-olds—baby boomers who will enter their young-old years with far greater access to and

---

ELDERS WHO USE NEW COMMUNICATION TECHNOLOGIES

Lorrene is an 80-year-old blogger whose witty and acerbic view of the world has made her blog a popular site (www.petpeevesandotherrantings.blogspot.com). She has converted her love of letter-writing to blogging, with the encouragement of her grandchildren.

Other older adults use Facebook as a way to communicate with family members, especially grandchildren. The Pew Internet and American Life Project report that 7 percent of people older than 65 now have online social networking profiles. Baby boomers, especially women over age 55, are the fastest growing Facebook user group.

SOURCE: CNN.com, 2009; PewInternet.com, 2009; *The Seattle Times*, 2008

---

everyday use of the Internet. The majority of elders who use computers do so for e-mail communication, online social support, banking, shopping, and the latest health information. But increasing numbers of elders are utilizing social networking sites and websites (AOA, 2006, 2008; Fox, 2004; Morgan, 2004; PewInternet.org, 2009).

Housing Policy and Government Programs

Housing policy for older people is less well developed than in the areas of income security and health care. This is due, in part, to the influence of well-organized interest groups such as builders and real estate developers.

The major housing programs that benefit older adults involve subsidies to suppliers of housing to enable them to sell or rent housing for less than the prevailing market price. Since 1959, two special housing programs for very low-income older people and those with disabilities have given long-term loans for the construction of housing for these groups. *Section 202* grants are specifically for elders, while *Section 8* grants are for low-income families and people with disabilities, which may include elders. Both are administered by HUD. Section 202 provides housing for people age 62 and older whose incomes are less than 50 percent of the median income in their areas (HUD, 2006b). This program subsidizes rent for qualified elders, so that they pay only 30 percent of their adjusted gross income as rent, and the federal government covers the remainder. Section 202 grants also provide loans with no or low interest to private nonprofit organizations or consumer cooperatives for the financing, construction, or rehabilitation of housing for older people. These loans do not need to be repaid as long as the housing is available to very low-income elders for at least 40 years. These subsidized housing projects must provide some support services such as meals and transportation.

Section 8 housing programs represent an additional form of housing subsidy for very low-income families and individuals, regardless of age, as long as their income is less than 80 percent of the median income in that area. Qualifying elders or families of persons with disabilities receive rent vouchers to subsidize their rent in the private housing market. Landlords receive from federal and state governments the difference between the rental cost of a housing unit and 30 percent of the tenant's income available for rent. Fewer than 2 million households currently benefit from Section 8 vouchers and federal funding for new housing is almost nonexistent since 1997 (National Coalition for the Homeless, 2006).

Federal funds for Section 8 vouchers were markedly reduced under the Bush administration, and many owners have lost interest in the low-income housing market, especially in urban centers undergoing renewal or "gentrification." Some landlords have converted their buildings into higher-rent apartments or condominiums, hotels, or office spaces, or have sold the property outright to local developers. These changes in federal funding and local priorities have significantly reduced the supply of Section 8 housing. Some relief has come in the form of vouchers given directly to low-income renters to find

FEDERAL HOUSING PROGRAMS FOR OLDER ADULTS

HUD's mission is to increase home ownership, support community development, and expand access to affordable housing free from discrimination. Its broad mission affects many populations (e.g., very low-income families, younger persons with disabilities), not just older adults. HUD oversees five types of government-assisted housing-related programs for older adults. These five programs are as follows:

- Public housing makes available low-cost units in complexes that are available to low-income families, including older adults and people with disabilities. These units allow tenants to pay no more than 30 percent of their income for rent. Public housing is available to applicants who do not exceed specified income levels that vary based on household size.
- A limited number of Section 8 rental vouchers and certificates are available to very low-income families with incomes below 80 percent of the median income for the area.
- Section 202 housing is specifically for older adults, usually providing support services such as meals, transportation, and accommodations for persons with disabilities. Private nonprofit organizations and consumer cooperatives are eligible to offer this type of housing to elders with disabilities and to very low-income households that have at least one member 62 years or older.
- The Section 232 program supports construction and rehabilitation of nursing homes, assisted-living facilities, and board-and-care homes by providing mortgage insurance and long-term, fixed-rate financing.

market-rate housing, although they may pay more than 30 percent of their income in rent—higher than the traditional form of Section 8 units. Other policies that indirectly affect older homeowners are:

- property tax relief
- energy assistance
- home equity conversion, or reverse mortgages, described earlier in this chapter

- energy assistance for low-income homeowners to offset air-conditioning and heating costs under the federal government's allocation of block grant money to cities and states

Less than 5 percent, or 1.5 million older people, benefit from federally funded housing assistance programs. The numbers declined during the 2001 to 2008 Bush administration as HUD reduced its direct subsidies to older adults in the form of rent vouchers (Section 8 and 202). There was some increase in funding for Section 202 low-cost loans to builders of housing for low-income older people in 2006 and 2007, but this was insufficient to meet the growing need (Senior Journal, 2009). Most recent federal activity in the housing arena has maintained the programs and housing stock that currently exist, modifying programs only incrementally to serve larger numbers of older adults. The goal is to make better use of existing housing resources through accessory apartments and reverse mortgages, rather than to increase the overall housing supply for older adults. Another major need is for more home and community-based services (HCBS). As described earlier, HCBS is an important link in the long-term care network, enabling frail and low-income older people to maintain P–E congruence. Innovations are needed that modify existing communities and neighborhoods to meet elders' changing housing needs. This may include creating accessory housing or mother-in-law units as part of existing homes to accommodate older people in smaller units near family or close friends.

Although the federal government has recently started to increase the supply of subsidized housing for older adults, the demand far outpaces the planned development. For example, on average HUD has approved the construction of 3000 – 4500 units per year under Section 202. However, the projected need is for a total of 730,000 additional units by 2020, about 15 times the number expected to be available. In fact, a report to Congress by the Commission on Affordable Housing for Seniors noted that the current waiting list includes nine older people for each Section 202 unit, and the average wait is one year for a subsidized unit (Sainz, 2009). This has become a crisis for the many older persons who cannot afford market rate housing, and as a result, some become homeless in their later years.

Homelessness

Although this chapter focuses on elders' housing and community service options, a growing segment of the older population is homeless, often unable to afford or access funds for basic housing and unaware of services to which they are entitled. Homeless people generally include those who, "for whatever reason, do not have a fixed, regular, and adequate night-time residence" (McKinney, 1987). Today's homeless elders (defined as age 50 and older because they are often 10 to 20 years older physiologically than their chronological age) are largely the chronic homeless who have lived on the streets for many years and have lost contact with their families. People between ages 50 and 61 comprise 10.3 percent of the homeless population, but because they are more likely to be sick and frail, they are disproportionately likely to be victims of crime; in 2006, they made up 27 percent of all homeless persons who were victims of violent crime (National Coalition for the Homeless, 2009). The homeless older population includes an increasing number of women, although there are approximately four times more men in this population (U.S. Conference of Mayors, 2005). Older homeless men have generally lived this way longer than their female counterparts. Many suffer from psychiatric disorders, alcoholism, or dementia, and lack strong social supports. As a result, this vulnerable segment of the homeless population has a life expectancy of 42 to 52 years, far lower than the national average discussed in Chapter 1 (O'Connell, 2005). Unfortunately, the trend is toward increased homelessness among older adults. This is due primarily to the loss of affordable housing, reductions in HUD's housing assistance programs (Section 8 and Section 202) directed at persons 62 and older, and the rising number of home foreclosures and cost of living. Although most homeless adults receive Supplemental Security Income (SSI) (described in Chapter 17), the current monthly maximum SSI benefit is so low that is inadequate to cover a person's food, medicine, and health care costs. Most SSI recipients cannot find rental housing in major cities with their Section 8 or Section 202 vouchers, as noted above. Affordable housing for homeless elders is difficult to find even in communities with low housing costs. Another barrier is that homeless shelters are often ill prepared to deal with the distinctive needs of frail elders who are homeless, although some shelters specifically for this population are being developed (NLIHC, 2006; National Coalition for the Homeless, 2009). Homeless people who become redomiciled (i.e., find permanent housing) tend to be older women with some social support who attend community facilities (and become more familiar to service providers), and who do not display psychotic symptoms (Stergiopoulos & Herrmann, 2003).

Homeless people also lack food, clothing, medical care, and social supports. Such a disorganized lifestyle can magnify the usual age-related declines in biological and psychological processes described in earlier chapters. A life at the edge, in which the individual is constantly trying to fulfill basic human needs (food, shelter, safety from predators), does not leave much energy for these elders to maintain even a modicum of health and well-being. Their problems are compounded by chronic psychiatric disorders, alcoholism, drug abuse, and cognitive impairment (often a result of long-term alcohol abuse). Due to their unstable lifestyles and frequent disruptions to mental well-being, homeless elders with chronic health problems often do not have the physical, social, or psychological resources to seek regular medical care for these conditions, or even to follow the necessary medication schedules and dietary restrictions. The prevalence of chronic diseases in this group is higher than for other segments of the older population, yet their access to health services is inadequate and sporadic at best (Folsom et al., 2002). They generally obtain health care through public hospital emergency rooms; clinical appointments and follow-up visits are rarely kept. Thus, they often die because of diseases that are neglected, accidents, and victimization on the streets. The number of homeless elders is expected to double in the future due to an increase in the number of younger persons with risk factors of lifelong poverty, substance abuse, incarceration, marital disruption, and loss of family contacts (Crane et al., 2004).

The McKinney-Vento Homeless Assistance Act provides limited funds to respond to some of these needs. These funds, administered by HUD, are given as grants to communities to develop services that address the multiple problems of shelter, food, health care, and victimization faced by homeless adults and families. The grants are intended for programs that provide supportive and SRO housing with services, and for emergency shelters. Unfortunately, the available funds are inadequate for most communities to respond to the growing homeless population.

Homeless elders often provide support to each other.

THE INCREASING POPULATION OF HOMELESS ELDERS

The global economic crisis that emerged in late 2008 resulted in job losses and home foreclosures for many middle-class families. Older adults were not immune from this crisis. With their shrinking pensions and dependence on Social Security income, some older persons can no longer afford their homes or pay for apartments and have been relegated to living in their cars and pickups. The long waiting lists for public housing and homeless shelters that are filled to capacity cannot provide them with better housing options. Many churches and businesses have opened their parking lots to these homeless elders living in their cars. According to the executive director of the National Coalition for the Homeless, "The homeless population is graying along with the general population, and we're seeing more elderly people living out their final years on the streets."

SOURCE: Michael Stoops, *The Seattle Times,* April 8, 2009, p. 1.

Aging in Place Among Older Prisoners

The U.S. Department of Justice and state departments of corrections or criminal justice categorize prisoners 50 and older as "older." This is because of the small number of inmates over age 65 and because inmates generally age faster as a result of more chronic diseases and a history of drug and alcohol abuse. The cohort age 50 and older represents 8.6 percent of the total U.S. prison population, while those 55 and older make up about 5 percent. The average age among older prisoners is 57. This population is expanding, attributable to the large numbers who have aged in prison with life terms, mandatory minimum sentences with no parole, and older adults committing more serious crimes. In some cases, prison is a "haven" for those who intentionally commit new crimes to avoid life on the streets. As with younger populations of prisoners, African Americans are disproportionately represented among older inmates: about 700 per

100,000 African American adults 55 and older are in prison, compared with 420 per 100,000 Latinos and 130 per 100,000 whites (Aday, 2006; Harrison & Beck, 2006; Loeb & AbuDagga, 2006).

The rapidly increasing costs of health care for older inmates have gained the attention of correctional officials. Lifestyles and incarceration have accelerated the aging process for many inmates whose health problems and poor diet are compounded in prison. The most common chronic diseases among older prisoners are hypertension, arthritis, and chronic obstructive pulmonary disease. These are typical in the older population generally, but rates are 25 percent higher among prisoners and occur at younger ages. Psychiatric conditions, especially depression, are often lifelong and go untreated in as many as half of prisoners (Loeb & AbuDagga, 2006; Mitka, 2004; Regan, Alderson, & Regan, 2002; Williams et al., 2006).

Several recommendations have been offered to improve the health status of older prisoners and reduce state and federal corrections systems' health care costs. These include reallocating budgets to provide more health services to older inmates (currently prison budgets are determined on a per-inmate basis, although older prisoners' costs are three times higher than the general inmate population); providing separate geriatric health facilities and hospice services; making physical accommodations in older inmates' cells and in bathrooms (e.g., installing handrails, removing top bunks); and training younger inmates to be caregivers to older inmates with functional impairments (this would also provide job training for future parolees). A more controversial proposal is early release, known as **compassionate release,** for nonviolent older inmates. Efforts by the Project for Older Prisoners Program have led to the early release of over one hundred older prisoners without any subsequent recidivism (Aday, 2006; Mitka, 2004; Turley, 2006; Williams et al., 2006).

Implications for the Future

As baby boomers age, larger numbers of older adults will reside in suburbs and fewer in central cities. Future cohorts will create a demand for services in the suburbs rather than traveling to city centers for their health care, social, recreational, and shopping needs. These trends are already evident as more businesses, medical and dental providers, senior centers, and shopping malls relocate to suburbs. This will increase the demand for public transportation within suburbs at a time when public transit has become too expensive for most municipalities to provide. Boomers will be more likely than their parents' generation to continue driving or to use specialized transportation such as vans provided by community agencies.

Because of earlier experiences with relocation and more travel opportunities during their youth, baby boomers will feel more confident about relocating, including to less costly rural communities and small towns. Some will even choose to move to other countries such as Mexico, where their retirement income can buy more, or as a form of reverse migration to their homeland. These options may become more attractive to the growing number of retirees whose pensions have lost value during the economic downturn that began in 2008. Instead of large, isolated retirement communities, future cohorts of elders are more likely to select independent housing in the communities where they relocate, and become active participants in these settings, integrating by volunteering or obtaining paid employment. More cohousing and intentional communities, as well as *virtual communities* that do not require relocating but provide services to a network of elders for a small annual fee, will emerge as groups of older adults choose to live near people who share their interests and lifestyle, but where they can age in place in their own homes. Others will opt to live in continuing care retirement communities (CCRCs) that provide choices in housing and services if they become frail with age.

As the number of people living to age 85 and older increases and as the cost of nursing home care rises, demand for more choices in long-term care will also grow. Aging in place will become a more viable option than it is today, thanks to technological advances that can create more P–E congruence. Technology allows older people to communicate with family members and health and social service providers via the Internet and telehealth. These innovative technologies will offer control and choice for the older user, which will be even more critical for the boomer generation than for current cohorts of elders. New developments in this area can provide electronic reminders to take medications, exercise, and eat healthy meals, as well as record and transmit vital signs to health care providers. Families may find that caregiving burdens are reduced if they can safely leave the elder at home and monitor them from a distance. The use of technology will be aided by the growth in "flexible housing" that is being demanded by baby boomers today. Middle-aged adults who are building new homes or remodeling existing homes to accommodate their aging parents often find that the home can benefit them as they age in place. They are discovering that homes with elder-friendly home design—including bedroom, bath, and kitchen facilities on the entry floor, easy-to-operate mechanical and electronic devices, and temperature controls for each area of the home—is practical and can be built with minimal construction costs. Such homes can create a more supportive environment for aging baby boomers but will be limited to those who can afford them (Werner, 2009).

Although future cohorts of elders will have more options, these will depend on their financial resources. As a result, economic disparities will become greater than during their youth. Those who have adequate resources will be able to travel and relocate to more desirable communities. They can purchase services and technology that can help them age in place. If they eventually need long-term care services, they can select from among multiple options in types and quality. Middle-aged people today with adequate financial resources are also more likely to purchase long-term care insurance than in the past, creating a wider range of options for those who may need such services in their later years. Older adults who do not have adequate income—including those who have lost retirement income due to the recession—will have to retire on the limited options available to them through Medicaid and Social Security. These elders often have little choice in the type or quality of services they obtain.

Homelessness also is likely to rise among older people, especially for those who have severed ties from their families due to divorce, alcohol and drug abuse, and those who became unemployed during the economic downturn of 2008–2009, and as a result, lost their homes. As described further in Chapter 12, these trends suggest an increasing schism between the small percentage of extremely wealthy older adults and those who have faced adversity throughout their lives, including homeless adults and those growing old in prison, or baby boomers who have watched their retirement investments precipitously decline.

Health and social service providers who serve future cohorts of elders should be informed of the growing options in housing and long-term care and how to effectively utilize them to support older adults' aging in place and autonomy. These professionals must be sensitive to the impact of the home and neighborhood on elders' security, comfort, social engagement, and ultimately their quality of life. If these features are incongruent with elders' needs, knowledgeable experts can play a significant role in helping make necessary environmental changes, including relocating them to a setting that fits their needs. Long-term care providers, especially in nursing homes, must also change existing paradigms of caring for frail elders, from institutional models that focus on maintaining policies and regulations to more resident-centered care. Skilled nursing homes, in particular, are initiating culture change where many employees of the future will be trained as "universal workers."

These expanded roles for direct care workers can reduce staff turnover and improve quality of care for frail elders (Noelker & Ejaz, 2005; Pérez-Peña, 2003; Wiener, 2003).

Summary

This chapter presented ways in which environmental factors affect the physical and psychological well-being of older people, and the importance of achieving P–E congruence in living situations. Perhaps the most important lesson to be gained from this discussion is that a given environment is not inherently good or bad. Some environments are more conducive for achieving active aging among *some* people, while other older adults need an entirely different set of features. For example, an older person who has a high need for activity and stimulation and has always lived in an urban setting will be more satisfied with an assisted living facility in a metropolitan center than will the individual who has always lived in a single-family dwelling in a rural community. Most P–E models point to the necessity of examining each older person's specific needs, preferences, and abilities, and designing environments that can flexibly respond to these differences. Relocation represents a special case of P–E incongruence that can disturb the well-being of an impaired older person by raising the level of environmental press. To the degree that environmental press can be reduced to accommodate changing levels of competence and needs, the aging person can function more effectively and experience enhanced well-being. The growing home and community-based options provide one way of achieving P–E fit for elders with diverse preferences and needs.

Differences in housing quality and services for rural older residents are of concern. Current cohorts are more likely than previous ones to live in suburbs, although disproportionately more elders of color than whites live in urban centers.

The neighborhood and neighbors play a significant role in older adults' well-being. With retirement and declining health, the older person's physical life-space becomes more constricted. The neighborhood takes on greater significance as a source of social interactions, health and social services, grocery shopping, banking, and postal services. Neighbors represent an important component of older people's social and emotional network, especially when family is unavailable.

Fear of crime among older persons is widespread but is incongruent with actual victimization rates. Older people experience far lower rates than younger people for violent crimes and somewhat lower rates for other types of crime. Victimization rates have declined particularly for older women. African American men, however, are at greater risk for crimes than any other group of elders. The potential danger of injury and long-term disability, as well as the fear of economic loss, may contribute to this incongruence between elders' actual victimization rates and their relatively high levels of fear of crime.

The high rate of home ownership and long-term residence in their homes make it difficult for older people to relocate to different housing, even when the new situation improves the elder's P-E congruence. The poor condition of many older people's homes and the high costs of renovating and maintaining them sometimes make relocation necessary, even when an older homeowner is reluctant. Better living conditions and a safer neighborhood in which several other elders reside are found to improve older people's morale and sense of well-being, especially following a move to a planned housing project from substandard housing. The growth of planned and congregate housing for older adults raises the issue of site selection for such housing. It is especially important when designing housing that public transportation be located nearby and that facilities such as medical and social services, pharmacies, and groceries be within easy access. Services need to be integrated from the beginning, because many who move in as young adults continue to live there for many years and age in place.

As people live longer and healthier lives beyond retirement, the need for housing that provides a range of care options will continue to grow. The expansion in housing and long-term care alternatives benefits elders who can afford to pay for them, but they face limited choices if they cannot pay out of pocket or have not purchased long-term care insurance. Assisted living and adult foster care or adult family homes are rapidly becoming a cost-effective option to nursing homes for older people who need help with ADLs but not necessarily 24-hour care. Many of these home and community-based services provide greater autonomy and privacy, and less direct supervision than nursing homes. Home care is now the fastest-growing component of personal health care expenditures. It allows older people to age in place while bringing services such as skilled nursing care, rehabilitation, and personal and household care to the person's home. Adult day care or adult day health care, both as a social and rehabilitative model, provides social and health care opportunities for frail older people who are living at home alone or with a family caregiver. The older person can attend adult day health care for several hours each day and receive nursing and rehabilitation services, while the caregiver obtains respite from care tasks. Many adult day care programs also offer counseling and support groups for caregivers. Unfortunately, as states have faced the need to curtail Medicaid spending, adult day health has increasingly been a victim of budget cuts.

The growing number of older homeless people have chronic medical, psychiatric, and cognitive disorders that often go unattended because of inadequate access to health services. As a result, these homeless elders grow physiologically old more rapidly and have a shorter life expectancy than do their more stable peers. Another concern is increased numbers of elders in prisons, mostly because many have aged in place but also because of mandatory minimum sentences with no parole and older adults committing more serious crimes. By age 55, many of these prisoners have chronic diseases and disabilities found in chronologically older adults in the community. The escalating costs of care for this population, as well as the incongruence between prison environments and the needs of frail older persons, have stimulated discussions about the need for geriatric facilities in prisons, physical accommodations, and even early release.

GLOSSARY

accessory housing or **mother-in-law units**   a housing option where small units are added to an existing home or as a detached unit on the property

adult day care (ADC)   a community facility that frail older people living at home can attend several hours each day; those based on a social model focus on structured social and psychotherapeutic activities

adult day health care (ADHC)   Adult day care with a strong health rehabilitative component, provides several health services and help with medications, in addition to social programs

adult foster care (AFC)/adult family home (AFH)   a private home facility, licensed by the state, in which the owner of the home provides housekeeping, personal care, and some delegated nursing functions for the residents

aging in place   continuing to live in a private home or apartment, even when declining competence reduces P–E congruence and more assistance with ADL is needed

assisted living (AL)   a housing model aimed at elders who need assistance with personal care, e.g., bathing and taking medication, but who are not so physically or cognitively impaired as to need 24-hour attention

assistive technology   a range of electronic and computer technologies that assist people with disabilities to perform as many ADLs as possible without help from others

cohousing   a community of families and/or elders who share some activities in a common house but live independently, in intergenerational or elders-only housing

compassionate release   the controversial proposal of releasing nonviolent, older inmates early to improve prisoner health status and reduce health costs in correction systems

continuing care retirement community (CCRC)   a multilevel facility offering a range from independent to congregate living arrangements, including nursing home units; generally requires an initial entry fee to assure a place if skilled nursing care is needed in the future

culture change   new models of nursing home care that attempt to humanize these facilities and make them more home-like and less institutional

Eden Alternative   a paradigm for nursing home care that encourages active participation by residents and greater staff decision making

elder-friendly (livable) communities   cities, suburbs, and towns that offer transportation, social and health services, and safe and adaptable housing to help older residents age in place

gerontechnology (or gerotechnology)   a recent field of research and practice aimed at using technology to improve older adults' autonomy

Green House   an expansion of the Eden Alternative that focuses on smaller groups of residents served by a core group of workers who perform multiple tasks

health literacy   an individual's capacity to obtain, process and understand health information to make informed health decisions

home and community-based services (HCBS)   a general label for residential and community-based long-term care options other than nursing homes; includes adult foster care, adult family homes, assisted living, adult day care, adult day health, and various other services to support elders remaining in the community

home health care   a variety of nursing, rehabilitation, and other therapy services, as well as assistance with personal care and household maintenance, that are provided to people who are homebound and have difficulty performing multiple ADLs

intentional communities   a group of families or elders with common values (e.g., political, religious, lifestyle) who live relatively independently but share meals, activities, and some expenses

life-space the distance a person travels to perform activities over a specified time (e.g. one week, on month)

long-term care a broad range of services geared to helping frail older adults be autonomous as long as possible; offered in nursing homes and other types of facilities, or in their own home through nutritional programs, adult day care, and home health services

Medicaid waivers exceptions to state Medicaid rules that allow use of Medicaid funds for services that are traditionally not covered by Medicaid, such as chore services and home care

naturally occurring retirement community (NORC) a neighborhood or larger area occupied mostly by older people who have aged in place, but without having been planned specifically for this population

negotiated risk agreement between a resident, family, or guardian and facility administration that the resident in a CRC setting will assume risks if problems such as falls and accidents that result from maintaining autonomy

nursing homes facilities with three or more beds staffed 24 hours per day by health professionals who provide nursing and personal-care services to residents who cannot remain in their own homes due to chronic disease, functional disabilities, or significant cognitive impairments

Pioneer Network a coalition of nursing home administrators and LTC advocates focused on improving quality of care and residents' quality of life by making organizational changes

resident-centered care a model of long-term care in which frail elders have the right and ability to determine their own needs and how these should be met

reverse mortgages or **home equity conversion mortgages (HECM)** Banks lend the older person money on his or her property based on its equity; interest and a fee are charged, and the title is retained by the lender (or the lender puts a lien on the home) until the house is sold or the elder dies

telehealth transmitting a patient's health status and vital signs via computer or telephone lines directly to a health provider

universal design designing a product, building, or landscape to make it accessible to and usable by the broadest range of users

universal worker nursing home staff who perform multiple services, including meal preparation, personal care, and housekeeping, rather than specializing in one task

RESOURCES

Log on to MySockit (www.mysockit.com) for information about the following:

- Advantage Age Initiative
- AgeNet, LLC
- American Association of Homes and Services for the Aging (AAHSA)
- American Association of Retired Persons (AARP)
- American College of Health Care Administrators (ACHCA)
- American Health Care Association (AHCA).
- American Seniors Housing Association
- Assisted Living Federation of America (ALFA)
- Caring Concepts
- Citizens for the Improvement of Nursing Homes (CINH)
- Gatekeeper Program
- Department of Housing and Urban Development (HUD)
- National Adult Day Services Association (NADSA)
- National Association for Home Care (NAHC)
- National Association of Directors of Nursing in Long Term Care (NADONAILTC)

- National Association of Senior Move Managers (NASMM)
- National Citizens Coalition for Nursing Home Reform (NCCNHR)
- National Coalition for the Homeless (NCH)
- National Institute on Adult Day Care
- National Low Income Housing Coalition (NLIHC)

REFERENCES

AARP. (2003). *These four walls: Americans 45-plus talk about home and community.* Washington, DC: AARP Public Policy Institute.

AARP. (2005). *Beyond 50.03: A report to the nation on independent living and disability.* Washington DC: AARP Public Policy Institute.

AARP. (2006a). *Across the states: Profiles of long-term care and independent living.* Washington, DC: AARP Public Policy Institute.

AARP. (2006b). *Federally insured loans.* Retrieved December 2006, from http://www.aarp.org/money/revmort/revmort_federal

AARP. (2006c). *The state of 50+ America 2006.* Washington, DC: AARP Public Policy Institute.

AARP. (2007). Aging in Asia and Oceania. Washington DC: AARP Public Policy Institute.

AARP. (2009). A balancing act: State long-term care reform. Retrieved July 2009, from http://www.aarp.org/research/longtermcare/programfunding/2008_10_ltc

Aday, R.H. (2006). Aging prisoners. In B. Berkman & S. D'Ambruoso (Eds.). *Handbook of social work in health and aging.* New York: Oxford Press.

Administration on Aging (AOA). (2008). *A profile of older Americans: 2005.* Retrieved November 2008, from http://www.aoa.gov/stats/profile

Agree, E. M. & Freedman, V. A. (2003). A comparison of assistive technology and personal care in alleviating disability and unmet need. *The Gerontologist, 43,* 335–344.

Allman, R. M., Sawyer, P. & Roseman, J. M. (2006). The UAB study of aging: Background and prospects for insights into life-space mobility among older African Americans and whites in rural and urban settings. *Aging and Health, 2,* 417–428.

American Association of Homes and Services for the Aging (AAHSA). (2006). *Continuing care retirement communities.* Retrieved November 2006, from http://www.aahsa.org/consumer_info/homes_ svcs_ directory

Angelelli, J. (2006). Promising models for transforming long term care. *The Gerontologist, 46,* 428–430.

Angelelli, J. & Higbie, I. (2005). Unfolding the culture change map and locating ourselves together. *Journal of Social Work in Long-Term Care, 3,* 121–135.

Associated Press. (2006). *Woman, 82, gets ticket for slow crossing.*

Beard, J. R., Blaney, S., Cerda, M., Freye, V., Lovasi, G. S., Ompad, D. et al. (2009). Neighborhood characteristics and disability in older adults. *Journal of Gerontology: Social Sciences, 64B,* 252–257.

Bergman-Evans, B. (2004). Beyond the basics: Effects of the Eden Alternative model on quality of life issues. *Journal of Gerontological Nursing, 30,* 27–34.

Binns, C. (2009). Machines that heal. *Popular Science, 275,* 62–63.

Boyd, C. (2003). The Providence Mt. St. Vincent Experience. *Journal of Social Work in Long Term Care, 2,* 245–268.

Brown, C. J., Roth, D. L., Allman, R. M., Sawyer, P., Ritchie, C. S., & Roseman, J. M. (2009). Trajectories of life-space mobility after hospitalization. *Annals of Internal Medicine, 150,* 372–378.

Bureau of Justice Statistics. (2006a). *Criminal victimization in the United States 2005: Statistical tables.* Washington DC: U.S. Department of Justice.

Bureau of Justice Statistics. (2008). *Criminal victimization in the United States 2007: Statistical tables.* Washington DC: U.S. Department of Justice.

Burgio, L. D., Stevens, A., Burgio, K. L., Roth, D. L., Paul, P., & Gerstle, J. (2002). Teaching and maintaining behavior management skills in the nursing home. *The Gerontologist, 42,* 487–496.

Centers for Disease Control and Prevention (CDC) (2009). *National home health aide survey.* Retrieved July 2009, from http://www.cdc.gov/nchs/nhhas.htm

Christian, D. L. (2003). *Creating a life together.* New York: New Society.

CNN.com. (2009). *All in the facebook family: Older generations join social networks.* Retrieved April 2009, from http://www.CNN.com

Co-housing Association of the U.S. (2006). *What is co-housing?* Retrieved December 2006, from http://www.cohousing.org/overview.aspx

Crane, M., Byrne, K., Fu, R., Lipmann, B., Mirabelli, F., Bartelink, A., et al. (2004). *Causes of homelessness in later life: Findings from a 3-nation study.* Washington, DC: Committee to End Elder Homelessness.

Crowe, M., Andel, R., Okonkwo, O., Wadley, V., Sawyer, P. & Allman, R. M. (2008). Life-space and cognitive decline in a community-based sample of African American and Caucasian older adults. *Journal of Gerontology: Medical Sciences, 63,* 1241–1245.

deLaGrange, K. (2006). Elder cohousing: How viable is cohousing for an aging population? Retrieved December 2006, from http://www.cohousing.org/livingincoho_seniors.aspx

Department of Veterans Affairs. (2009). *Care coordination services: Telehealth.* Retrieved May 2009, from http://www.carecoordination.va.gov/telehealth/

Dobell, G. & Bloom, S. (2009). *Integrated care for frail elders: The PACE example.* Presentation to Institute for Research on Public.

Durrette, C. (2009). *The senior cohousing handbook.* Gabriola Island, B. C.: New Society Publishers.

ElderCohousing.org. (2006). *Getting started workshops for elder cohousing.*

Fagan, R. M. (2004). Culture change in long-term care: Creating true independence for elders. *Maximizing Human Potential, 11,* 1–6.

Federal Interagency Forum on Aging-Related Statistics. (2008). *Older Americans: 2008.* Washington DC: Government Printing Office.

Femia, E. E., Zarit, S. H., Stephens, M. A. P., & Greene, R. (2007). Impact of adult day services on behavioral and psychological symptoms of dementia. *The Gerontologist, 47,* 775–788.

Folsom, D. P., McCahill, M., Bartels, S. J., Lindamer, L. A., Ganiats, T. G., & Jeste, D.V. (2002). Medical comorbidity and receipt of medical care by older homeless people with schizophrenia or depression. *Psychiatric Services, 53,* 1456–1460.

Friedman, S. M., Steinwachs, D. M., Temkin-Greener, H., & Mukamel, D. B. (2006). Informal caregivers and the risk of nursing home admission among individuals enrolled in PACE. *The Gerontologist, 46,* 456–463.

Gilbert Guide. (2009). *CCRC vs. life care: Which contract is right for you?* Retrieved July 2009, from http://www.gilbertguide.com/articles/ccrc-vs-life-care-which-contract-is-right-for-you

Gitlin, L.N., Reever, K., Dennis, M.P., Mathieu, E., & Hauck, W. W. (2006). Enhancing quality of life of families who use adult day services. *The Gerontologist, 46,* 630–639.

Golant, S. M. (2004). Do impaired older persons with health care needs occupy U.S. assisted living facilities? *Journal of Gerontology: Social Sciences, 59B,* S68–S79.

Grant, L. (2006). *Culture change in for-profit nursing homes.* The Commonwealth Fund. Retrieved November 2006, from http://www.cmwf.org/spotlights/spotlights_show.htm?doc

Green House Project. (2006). Described in http://www.edenalt.com

Greene, K. (2006). When it comes to finding a new place to live, today's retirees are looking for something completely different. *The Wall Street Journal.*

Gwyther, L. P. & Kane, R. A. (2006). Dementia special care units in residential care. In B. Berkman & S. D'Ambruoso (Eds.). *Handbook of social work in health and aging.* New York: Oxford Press.

Hanson, D. & Emlet, C. A. (2006). Assessing a community's elder friendliness. *Family and Community Health, 29,* 266–278.

Harrison, P. M. & Beck, A. J. (2006). Prisoners in 2005. *Bureau of Justice Statistics Bulletin,* NCJ 215092, 7–8.

Hedrick, S. C., Sales, A. E. B., Sullivan, J. H., Gray, S. L., Tornatore, J., Curtis, M., et al. (2003). Resident outcomes of Medicaid-funded community residential care. *The Gerontologist, 43,* 473–482.

Hernandez, M. (2005–2006). Assisted living in all its guises. *Generations, 29,* 16–23.

Hughes, S. L. & Pittard, M. A. (2001). Home health. In C. J. Evashwick (Ed.). *The continuum of long-term care* (2nd ed.). Albany, NY: Delmar.

Hyde, J., Perez, R., & Forester, B. (2007). Dementia and assisted living. *The Gerontologist, 47* (Special Issue), 51-67.

Iwarsson, S. (2004). Assessing the fit between older people and their physical home environments: An occupational therapy research perspective. In H-W. Wahl, R.J. Scheidt, & P.G. Windley (Eds.). *Annual Review of Gerontology and Geriatrics: Socio-Physical Environments.* New York: Springer.

Iwarsson, S. (2005). A long-term perspective on person-environment fit and ADL dependence among older Swedish adults. *The Gerontologist, 45,* 327–336.

Iwarsson, S., Wahl, H. W., Nygren, C., Oswald, F., Sixsmith, A., Sixsmith, J., et al. (2007). Importance of the home environment for healthy aging. *The Gerontologist, 47,* 78–84.

Kinney, J. M. & Kart, C. S. (2006). Somewhere between panacea and impossibility: Assessing the place of technology in facilitating caregiving to a relative with dementia. *Generations, 30,* 64–66.

Kinosian, B., Stallard, E., & Wieland, D. (2007). Projected use of long-term care services by enrolled veterans. *The Gerontologist, 47,* 356–364.

Kochera, A. & Bright, K. (2005–2006, Winter). Livable communities for older people. *Generations, 29,* 32–36.

Lachs, M., Bachman, R., Williams, C. S., Kossack, A., Bove, C., & O'Leary, J. R. (2006). Violent crime victimization increases risk of nursing home placement in older adults. *The Gerontologist, 46,* 583–589.

Larson, C. (2006). Finding a good home: Taking care of your parents. *U.S. News and World Report.*

Lawton, M. P. (1975). Competence, environmental press, and the adaptation of older people. In P. G. Windley & G. Ernst (Eds.). *Theory development in environment and aging.* Washington, DC: Gerontological Society.

Lehmann, C. A. (2003). *Economic benefits of telehealth in managing diabetes patients in ambulatory settings.* Paper presented at SPRY Foundation Conference on Technology and Aging, Bethesda, MD.

Lewin, K. (1935). *Dynamic theory of personality.* New York: McGraw-Hill.

Lewin, K. (1951). *Field theory in social science.* New York: Harper & Row.

Lewin, K., Lippitt, R., & White, R. (1939). Patterns of aggressive behavior in experimentally created social climates. *Journal of Social Psychology, 10,* 271–299.

Loeb, S. J. & AbuDagga, A. (2006). Health-related research on older inmates. *Research in Nursing and Health, 29,* 556–565.

Longino, C. F. (2004). Socio-physical environments at the macro level: The impact of population migration. In H. W. Wahl, R. J. Scheidt & P. G. Windley (Eds.). *Annual Review of Gerontology and Geriatrics, 23,* 110–129.

Longino, C. F. & Bradley, D. E. (2006). Internal and international migration. In R. H. Binstock & L. K. George (Eds.). *Handbook of aging and the social sciences* (6th ed). San Diego: Academic Press.

Longino, C. F. Bradley, D. E., Stoller, E. P. & Haas, W. H. (2008). Predictors of non-local moves among older adults: A prospective study. *Journal of Gerontology: Social Sciences, 63B,* S7–S14.

Lustbader, W. & Williams, C. C. (2006). Culture change in long-term care. In B. Berkman & S. D'Ambruoso (Eds.). *Handbook of social work in health and aging.* New York: Oxford Press.

Marsden, J. P. (2005). *Humanistic design of assisted living.* Baltimore: Johns Hopkins University Press.

McKinney, S. B. (1987). *Homeless Assistance Act,* P.L. 100–77.

Mitka, M. (2004). Aging prisoners stressing health care system. *Journal of the American Medical Association, 292,* 423–424.

Morgan, R. (2004). Computer-based technology and caregiving for older adults. *Public Policy and Aging Report, 14,* 1–5.

National Center for Assisted Living. (2008). *Fact sheet.* Washington DC: NCAL.

National Center for Health Statistics (NCHS). (2008). 2004 National Nursing Home Survey. Hyattsville, MD: NCHS.

National Center for Health Statistics (NCHS). (2006). *Health, United States.* Retrieved December 2006, from http://www.cdc.gov/nchs/hus.htm

National Coalition for the Homeless (NCH). (2006). *Federal housing assistance programs.* Retrieved December 2006, from http://www.nationalhomeless.org

National Coalition for the Homeless (NCH). (2009). *Homelessness among elderly persons.* Retrieved July 2009, from http://www.nationalhomeless.org

National Low Income Housing Coalition (NLIHC). (2006). Out of reach. Retrieved December 2006, from http://www.nlihc.org

National Reverse Mortgage Lenders Association (NRMLA). (2009). *Information on reverse mortgages.* Retrieved July 2009, from http://www.nrmla.org

Netting, F. E. & Wilson, C. C. (2006). Continuing care retirement communities. In B. Berkman & S. D'Ambruoso (Eds.). *Handbook of social work in health and aging.* New York: Oxford Press.

Noelker, L. S. & Ejaz, F. K. (2005). Training direct-care workers for person-centered care. *Public Policy and Aging Report, 15,* 17–19.

Oberlink, M. R. (2008). *Opportunities for creating livable communities.* Washington DC: AARP Public Policy Institute.

O'Connell, J. J. (2005). *Premature mortality in homeless populations. A review of the literature.* Retrieved September 2009, from http://www.nhchc.org

Peng, T. R., Navaie-Waliser, M., & Feldman, P. H. (2003). Social support, home health service use, and outcomes among four racial-ethnic groups. *The Gerontologist, 43,* 503–513.

Nielsen-Bohlman, L., Panzer, A. M. & Kindig, D. A. (Eds.). (2004). Institute of Medicine Report Health literacy: *A prescription to end confusion.* Retrieved January 2009, from http://search.nap.edu/nap-cgi/skimchap.cgi?recid=10883&chap=1–18

Perez-Pena, R. (2003). Overwhelmed and under-staffed, nursing home workers vent anger. *The New York Times,* p. 1.

Phillips, C. D., Munoz, Y., Sherman, M., Rose, M., Spector, W., & Hawes, C. (2003). Effects of facility characteristics on departures from assisted living. *The Gerontologist, 43,* 690–696.

Preiser, W. & Ostroff, E. (Eds.). (2001). *Universal design handbook.* New York: McGraw Hill.

Pruchno, R. A. & Rose, M. S. (2000). Effect of long-term care environments on health outcomes. *The Gerontologist, 40,* 429–436.

Rabig, J., Thomas, W., Kane, R. A., Cutler, L. J., & McAlilly, S. (2006). Radical redesign of nursing homes: Applying the Green House concept in Tupelo, Mississippi. *The Gerontologist, 46,* 533–539.

Regan, J. J., Alderson, A., & Regan, W. M. (2002). Psychiatric disorders in aging prisoners. *Clinical Gerontologist, 26,* 8–13.

Regnier, V. (2002). *Design for assisted living.* Hoboken, NJ: John Wiley & Sons.

Rialle, V., Duchene, F., Noury, N., Bajolle, L., & Demongeot, J. (2002). Health "smart" homes: Information technology for patients at home. *Telemedicine Journal and e-Health, 8,* 395–409.

Rogers, W. A. & Fisk, A. D. (2005). Aware home technology: Potential benefits for older adults. *Public Policy and Aging Report, 15,* 28–30.

Sainz, A. (2009). Senior housing need grows. *Seattle Times,* pp. E1–3.

Sampsell, B. G. (2003). *The promise, practice and problems of the Eden Alternative.* Nursing Homes.

Schmidt, K. & Beatty, S. (2005). Quality improvement: The pursuit of excellence. *Quality Management in Health Care, 14,* 196–198.

Seattle Times. (2003). Retirees gaining popularity in towns yearning for growth, p. A5.

Seattle Times. (2008). Yakima grandmother is a rarity: A blogging octogenarian., p. B2.

Seattle Times. (2009). Backyard houses in Seattle. p. B1 and B9.

Sergeant, J. F., Ekerdt, D. J., & Chapin, R. (2008). Measurement of late-life residential relocation: Why are rates for such a manifest event so varied? *Journal of Gerontology: Social Sciences, 63B,* S92–S98.

Seperson, S. B. (2002). Demographics about aging. In S. B. Seperson & C. Hegeman (Eds.). *Elder care and service learning: A handbook.* Westport, CT: Auburn House.

Spillman, B. C. & Lubitz, J. (2002). New estimates of lifetime nursing home use. *Medical Care, 40,* 965–975.

Stergiopoulos, V. & Herrmann, N. (2003). Old and homeless: A review and survey of older adults who use shelters in an urban setting. *Canadian Journal of Psychiatry, 48,* 374–380.

Stoller, E. P. & Longino, C.F. (2001). "Going home" or "leaving home"? The impact of person and place ties on anticipated counterstream migration. *The Gerontologist, 41,* 96–102.

The New York Times. (2003). Immigrants now embrace homes for elderly, pp. A1, A10.

Thomas, W. H. (1999). *The Eden alternative handbook.* Sherburne, NY: Eden Alternative Foundation.

Turley, J. (2006). Release elderly inmates. Retrieved December 2006, from http://www.LATimes.com/news/opinion/commentary

United Hospital Fund. *What is a NORC?* Retrieved July 2009, from http://www.norcblueprint.org

U.S. Census Bureau. (2005). Computer and internet use in the U.S.: 2003. *Current Population Reports.* Series P23-208. Washington DC: U.S. Government Printing Office.

U.S. Census Bureau. (2008). American housing survey for the U.S.: 2007. *Current Housing Reports.* Series H150–07. Washington DC: U.S. Government Printing Office.

U.S. Conference of Mayors. (2005). *Hunger and homelessness survey: A status report on hunger and homelessness in America's cities.* Retrieved December 2005, from http://www.usmayors.org/uscm/hungersurvey/2005/HH2005final.pdf

U.S. Department of Health and Human Services (2007). *The quick guide to health literacy and older adults.* Retrieved August 2009, from: http://www.health.gov/communication/literacy/olderadults/default.htm

Vierck, B. (2005). Cohousing comes of age. *Aging Today, 27,* 1–5.

Vourlekis, B. & Simons, K. (2006). Nursing homes. In B. Berkman & S. D'Ambruoso (Eds.). *Handbook of social work in health and aging.* New York: Oxford Press.

Wahl, H. W., Fange, A., Oswald, F., Gitlin, L.N., & Iwarsson, S. (2009). The home environment and disability-related outcomes in aging individuals. *The Gerontologist, 49,* 355–367.

Werner, C. (2009). One to grow on. *Seattle Metropolitan,* 73–76.

Wiener, J. M. (2003). An assessment of strategies for improving quality of care in nursing homes [Special Issue]. *The Gerontologist, 43,* 19–27.

Williams, B. A., Lindquist, K., Sudore, R. L., Strupp, H. M., Wilmott, D. J., & Walter, L.C. (2006). Being old and doing time: Functional impairment and adverse experiences of geriatric female prisoners. *Journal of the American Geriatrics Society, 54,* 702–707.

Wilson, K. B. (1993). Developing a viable model of assisted living. In P. Katz, R. L. Kane, & M. Mazey (Eds.). *Advances in long-term care.* New York: Springer.

Wilson, K. B. (1995). Redefining quality in assisted living. *Provider,* 73–74.

Wilson, K. B. (2007). Historical evolution of assisted living in the U.S.: 1979 to the present. *The Gerontologist, 47* (Special Issue), 8–22.

Wolf, D. A. & Longino, C. M. (2005). Our increasingly mobile society? The curious persistence of a false belief. *The Gerontologist, 45,* 5–11.

Yeatts, D. E. & Cready, C. M. (2007). Consequences of empowered CAN teams in nursing home settings. *The Gerontologist, 47,* 323–339.

Yeatts, D. E., Cready, C. M., Ray, B., DeWitt, A., & Queen, C. (2004). Self-managed work teams in nursing homes: Implementing and empowering nurse aide teams. *The Gerontologist, 44,* 256–261.

Yeoman, B. (2006). Rethinking the commune. *AARP Magazine.* Retrieved December 2006, from http://www.aarpmagazine.org/lifestyle/rethinking_the_commune.html

Zarcadoolas, C., Pleasant, A., & Greer, D. S. (2006). *Advancing health literacy: A framework for understanding and action.* San Francisco, CA: Jossey-Bass/Wiley.

Zimmerman, S., Munn, S., & Koenig, T. (2006). *Assisted living settings.* In B. Berkman & S. D'Ambruoso (Eds.). *Handbook of social work in health and aging.* New York: Oxford Press.

12

Productive Aging: Paid and Nonpaid Roles and Activities

What Do We Mean by Productive Aging? Definitions and Critique

Productivity is typically thought of as paid work. In fact, as noted in Chapter 8, disengagement and role theories focus on the losses associated with withdrawal from employment. Many older adults, however, are productive without being employed or engaged in obligatory activities. In fact, older adults across history have always been productive in families and communities, often as a means to survive (Achenbaum, 2008). As described in Chapters 1 and 6, the model of successful, robust, or active aging implies that productivity is broader than paid work. As used here, it includes any paid or unpaid activity that produces goods and services for the benefit of society—such as household tasks, child care, volunteerism, and contributing to family, friends, neighbors, and community members—and which reciprocally benefits both elders and society. The concept of productivity views older adults individually and collectively as a resource to meet their own and society's needs, while successful aging focuses on individual aging, especially life satisfaction and efforts to prolong healthy aging. Engagement in productive activity is assumed to have a positive influence on older adults' mental and physical well-being, but also to benefit others, with civic engagement defined as a retirement role (Gerontological Society of America, 2005; Hinterlong & Williamson, 2006–2007; Kaskie et al., 2008; Morrow-Howell, Hong, & Tang, 2009; Windsor, Anstey, & Rodgers, 2008; Hao, 2009).

The concept of productivity is subject to criticisms similar to those leveled at successful aging (see Chapter 6 for a critique of successful aging). From the perspectives of feminist gerontology, political economy, social constructionist, and critical theories, an emphasis on productivity may lead to further marginalization and blaming of low-income women and elders of color who cannot attain middle-class standards of productive activity. If such groups are unable to do so, are they then defined as failures? Similarly, are those with disabilities or those who prefer to be contemplative a problem for society (Estes & Mahakian, 2001; Martinson, 2006–2007; Martinson & Minkler, 2006; Moody, 2005)? For example, an individual may sit and think about an idea that can lead to tremendous productivity in gains to society but that cannot be readily quantified, and thus they may not appear to be engaged in "productive behavior" (Achenbaum, 2008). Likewise, cognitive and emotional exchanges, such as Erikson's concept of generativity or giving back to younger generations (as described in Chapter 6), cannot always be measured quantitatively.

Critical gerontology theorists maintain that the concept of producti- vity has class, race, and gender biases because of implicit middle-class norms of what is considered a "productive" way to spend time and the growing number of entrepreneurial initiatives to create new "productive" roles for older adults. They caution against "prescribing" active engagement for elders and instead emphasize fostering

opportunity and choice. Accordingly, inequities by class, race, ethnicity, gender, sexual identity, and functional ability across the life course all affect an older adult's ability to engage in meaningful and productive experiences. The meaning of productive aging is shaped by increasing inequalities in our society and among the aging population, which create different life opportunities for elders. Overall, critics of the concept of productive aging urge caution regarding who defines productive aging, which segments of the older population this concept applies to, and who benefits (Achenbaum, 2008; Cruikshank, 2009; Holstein, 2007; Moody, 2001).

Given this context, we use the concept of productivity in this text in the broadest sense of engagement with and contributions to others—family, neighbors, friends, and community. But the contributions need not be "goods and services" in a traditional sense. The active aging model, described in Chapter 1, suggests that productivity can benefit society, the community, the family, or even just the individual. It can include social, psychological, and spiritual dimensions, such as self-improvement through learning, personal fulfillment, and searching for life's meaning. Productivity is not the same as "staying busy," because a contemplative elder who meditates daily may nevertheless be contributing to his or her own or others' well-being. This broad definition recognizes that even a homebound elder with disabilities may be productive by teaching others how to age with dignity, placing phone calls to check up on neighbors, reading to a young child, listening to a grieving friend, or providing encouragement and life lessons to a confused adolescent. The older woman who prefers to spend hours working alone in her garden may be contributing to the "common good" by creating beauty for neighbors to enjoy, even though she may not view herself as contributing directly to the community. Regardless of our life circumstances, there is a universal human need to be of use, and reaching out and giving to others in a wide variety of ways can be a powerful antidote to loneliness, isolation, and depression.

DEFINING PRODUCTIVE AGING

A 67-year-old retired mathematics teacher and immigrant from Eastern Europe, Yakov volunteers in the Senior Companion program. He spends a day each week with Harry, a postman who is legally blind, assisting with daily tasks that enable Harry to remain in his own home. Theirs is a reciprocal relationship: Each is convinced that he is the helper and the other is the recipient of the help. Harry helps Yakov with his English, correcting grammatical errors, while Yakov receives a stipend to help with household tasks. They often go out to lunch at the local Burger King, their favorite restaurant. The waiter who takes their order looks to be about their age, but he is wearing an orange and blue polyester outfit and a Burger King beanie and working alongside giggling 15-year-olds acquiring their first job experience. Which of these three older adults is "productive"?

SOURCE: Adapted from Freedman, 2001, p. 246.

An assumption throughout this text is that older adults represent our society's greatest underutilized asset. They bring the resilience and hardiness of survivors and the wisdom of life experiences and lessons learned. As such, elders are a civic treasure that can provide leadership in community and religious organizations, volunteer formally or informally, and influence decision-making and legislative processes. What is critical is for older adults to be able to exercise choice over how they spend their time. Although the concept of productive aging may imply that older adults *should* be outwardly productive and that society should exert pressures on them to engage in activities that they would prefer not to undertake, the greater danger appears to be that our society offers limited opportunities for older adults to remain engaged and make meaningful contributions. Consistent with the person–environment (P–E) framework, older adults need chances to choose actions to maintain a sense of competence in a changing environment. Accordingly, modifications are needed in public

policy and societal institutions to allow older adults to contribute to others and to play meaningful leadership roles (Freedman, 2001, 2002).

Race, ethnicity, gender, social class, sexual orientation, cohort experiences, living arrangements, and neighborhoods are structural or societal factors that influence older adults' choices. Personal capacities—such as the normal physical and psychological changes of aging, health status, personality, cognitive capacity, and values—also influence how individuals choose to spend their time in old age. Self-esteem and self-concept are powerful factors. Some older adults may believe that they are "too old" or lack the capacity to perform certain activities, even though they have objective resources such as finances and a supportive family or lifestyle. Others with limited objective resources (e.g., in poor health or poverty) may nevertheless possess the inner resources to seek out new opportunities because of their zest for living and learning new things. In other words, people's use of time and areas of involvement all vary with the options provided by the larger environment, as well as with their personal capacities at each phase in the life course. Nevertheless, the meanings, options, and outcomes for productive aging and engagement vary among different populations.

Social class appears to be the most salient structural factor in shaping what is possible in old age, because class is related to every measure of health, illness, and disability (Estes & Mahakian, 2001). As illustrated in this text, poor health, reduced income, transportation difficulties, and social isolation across the life course often disrupt and reduce choices in old age and lead to cumulative disadvantages. Nevertheless, as noted by Cohen (2005; 2009) and discussed in Chapter 6, elders of diverse social backgrounds pursue new activities, including art, music, running, hiking, meditating, or teaching for the first time in old age. Even with decreased competence in health and physical functioning, older people can enjoy active aging by modifying their activities to establish congruence between their needs and abilities and environmental demands. Having the option to decide how one spends time is a salient factor that distinguishes retirement from earlier life phases of obligatory school, employment, or dependent care.

This chapter reviews the opportunities as well as the constraints that older adults face related to productivity: retirement, employment, economic well-being, leisure, religious participation and spirituality, membership in community associations and volunteerism, education, and political action. It concludes by recognizing how societal institutions need to create more options for older adults to choose how they wish to remain engaged and contributing to others. Community and societal responsibility, including policy changes and resource commitments, are essential to promote productive aging and to reduce inequities in options for active engagement. We turn now to retirement, which removes older adults from paid forms of productivity and shapes chances for engagement in nonpaid activities. Our discussion of employment and retirement first summarizes patterns for the current cohort age 65 and older. We then present two contrasting retirement scenarios likely for baby boomers, the first of whom reached retirement age 62, when they could collect Social Security on January 1, 2008.

Retirement

With increased longevity and changing work patterns, **retirement** has often defined a third or more of the life course and is as much an expected phase as raising children, completing school, or working outside the home. Adults hold age-related expectations about the rhythm of their careers—when they should start working, when they should be at their career peak, and when to retire. They typically assess whether or not they are "on time" according to these socially defined schedules. Their thinking shifts from how much time has passed to how much time is left (Cartensen, 2006).

The value placed on work and paid productivity in our society shapes how individuals approach employment and retirement. Those over age 75 today—the World War II generation—were socialized to a traditional view of hard work, job loyalty, and occupational stability. Current demographic trends, the global economic crisis, and declining investments and retirement income mean that expectations about work and retirement are markedly changing. Many of the young-old are exiting the workforce involuntarily and trying to reenter through partial employment or new careers. As individuals live longer, a smaller proportion of their lifetime is typically devoted to paid employment, even though the number of years worked is longer (Urban Institute, 2007). However, the growing number of employed older adults, often out of financial necessary, suggests that this pattern is changing.

Conceptions of work and leisure took on new meanings in the industrialized world, with the institutionalization of retirement a relatively recent phenomenon in Western society. Retirement developed as a twentieth-century social institution, along with industrialization, surplus labor, and a rising standard of living. **Social Security** legislation, passed in 1935, established the right to financial protection in old age and thus served to institutionalize retirement. Based on income deferred during years of employment, Social Security was viewed as a reward for past economic contributions to society and a

---

POINTS TO PONDER

How does your view of work and retirement differ from that of your parents and/or grandparents? What does retirement mean to you and how can you assure a successful retirement, including enough income? At what age do you see yourself retired, and what type of planning should you do to achieve that goal? Will you even want to retire? How many careers do you anticipate having? It's never too early to be thinking about these issues.

way to support people unable to work because of illness or disability. At the same time, Social Security created jobs for younger people by "removing" adults age 65 and over from the labor force. From the perspective of critical gerontology theory, retirement serves a variety of institutional functions in our society. It can stimulate and reward worker loyalty, or remove older workers and replace them with younger, lower-wage employees who are assumed to be more productive (Hardy, 2002; Moen, 2003).

Nevertheless, some societal and individual consequences of retirement are negative. Earlier retirement, combined with longer life expectancies, has prolonged elders' dependence on Social Security and other retirement benefits as well as contributed to a loss of older workers' skills and knowledge. Because retirement is associated in the public mind with the chronological age of 65 (the age of eligibility for full Social Security and Medicare benefits in the past), it also carries the connotation of being "old" and no longer physically or cognitively capable of full-time employment. Since society tends to associate aging with decreased employment capacity, this may limit implementation of flexible work arrangements and retraining opportunities for older adults.

The Timing of Retirement

Retirement policies, labor market conditions, and individual characteristics all converge on the decision to retire and affect its timing. Federal laws influenced the retirement age prior to 1986, when mandatory retirement for most jobs was eliminated. Even so, financial incentives were more salient, because less than 10 percent of employees had been forced to retire due to legal requirements (Quinn & Burkhauser, 1993). The arbitrary nature of a specific age for retirement is illustrated by the pattern that, since World War II and until the twenty-first century, most people retired between the ages of 60 and 64, and very few continued to work past age 70. In fact, during this time period, age 65 was not the "normal" retirement age,

mostly because chronological age alone does not explain the diversity of health status, disability, and economic factors. Instead, in 2000—14 years after mandatory retirement laws disappeared—the average age for retirement was 61.5 years compared to 74 years in 1910, largely due to employer incentives to move older workers out of the labor force. Each year, 75 percent of all new Social Security beneficiaries retired before their 65th birthday, and most began collecting reduced benefits at age 62.5. This five-decade trend toward early retirement was not markedly slowed by the 1983 amendments to the Social Security Act, which delayed the age of eligibility for full benefits and increased the financial penalty for retiring at age 62 (Rix, 2006, 2008).

A noticeable shift to these patterns is now occurring, however. The average age of retirement is rising and participation in the labor force is increasing, suggesting an emphasis on both the desire and financial necessity to remain on the job or to change careers (Federal Interagency Forum, 2008). A number of factors underlie this shift:

- the reduction in defined benefits and early retirement benefits of private pension plans
- changes to Social Security that allow older adults to continue to work and still receive partial Social Security benefits
- the scheduled increase in age for receiving full Social Security benefits (age 67 by 2022)
- improvements in health and longevity

In addition, modifying the terms of pension eligibility, increasing the taxation of Social Security benefits, and reducing employer-sponsored health insurance have increased the proportion of older workers who are employed primarily for financial reasons, especially among women and persons of color. By contrast, in surveys prior to the 2008–2009 recession, 70 percent or more of respondents age 55 and older indicated that they planned to continue working during retirement, and a portion said they would work beyond age 70 or never retire, largely because of the meaning and sense of purpose they experienced in their jobs (AARP, 2004, 2006).

Over time, this shift to a later retirement age will have several societal benefits, because older adults will be contributing longer as taxpayers. In fact, it has been estimated that if every worker paid into the Social Security system for an additional five years, more than 50 percent of the projected Social Security shortfall would be offset (Urban Institute, 2006). Continuing to earn and postponing receipt of Social Security benefits until age 70 could nearly double payments for some older adults compared to what they would receive if they retired at age 62 (Rix, 2008; U.S. Congressional Budget Office, 2004). But later retirees will also receive larger monthly benefits that could offset these gains to the Social Security Trust Fund. Nevertheless, a later retirement age to qualify for benefits is not favored by most workers age 50 and older; workers may expect and even want to work in retirement, but they want to choose for themselves (Rix, 2006).

FACTORS THAT AFFECT THE TIMING OF RETIREMENT
This section discusses five P–E characteristics that affect retirement decisions:

1. an adequate retirement income based on Social Security, private investments, pensions and/or economic incentives from employers to retire
2. health status, functional limitations, and access to health insurance other than Medicare
3. the nature of the job, employee morale, and organizational commitment
4. gender, class, and race
5. family roles and responsibilities

An *adequate income* through Social Security, a private pension with a defined benefit schedule, or interest income is the major factor affecting retirement timing. Similarly, financial adequacy, followed by access to health care, is the single most important variable in decisions to keep working rather than retire (Rix, 2008). Until 10 to 15 years ago, employment and retirement/pension policies since the 1900s encouraged early retirement. For example, 9 out of 10 U.S. pension plans, particularly for white-collar workers, provided financial incentives for early retirement along with employer-sponsored health insurance, creating the "pension elites" of the 1980s (O'Rand, 2005). Even employees who were not planning to retire were offered benefits too attractive to turn down. Workers accumulated a significant proportion of their retirement funds in the decade preceding retirement, presumably when their earnings were the highest. As noted above, changes in the eligibility age for Social Security, a shift from defined-benefit pension plans toward defined contribution plans—such as 401(k)s—and the global economic downturn have now increased the number of older adults remaining employed or seeking a job out of financial necessity.

Functional limitations and access to health insurance are also important factors in the retirement decision. Poor health, when combined with an adequate retirement income and health insurance, usually results in early retirement. In contrast, poor health, an inadequate income, and lack of health insurance generally delay retirement, as is often the case with low-income workers and employees of color. What remains unclear, however, is whether those in poorer health and with disabilities are more likely to lose their jobs because of unemployment, job displacement, or plant closures, or conversely whether job loss itself leads to poorer health, or both. But once a person is not employed, poor health often acts as a barrier to reentering the labor force (Mandal & Roe, 2008; O'Rand, 2005).

A third factor affecting timing is the *nature of one's job,* including job satisfaction, employee morale, and organizational commitment. Some workers retire to escape boring, repetitive jobs such as assembly line and service positions or stressful working conditions. In the past, workers who had a positive attitude toward retirement and leisure but a negative view of their jobs were likely to retire early. But with the economic downturn, sustaining an income has become more important than job satisfaction in remaining employed.

While *gender and race* can exacerbate economic inequities in old age, their effects on the timing of retirement are not clear-cut. Current income and receipt of a pension other than Social Security are primary factors in both men and women's retirement decisions. Although both men and women have chosen early retirement in the past, women of retirement age are less likely to be fully retired than their male counterparts. Women's decision making may also be determined by variables such as marital status and years devoted to childrearing. Women who entered the labor force in middle age or later, after performing family caregiving roles or because of divorce or widowhood, often had to remain in low-wage jobs without pensions to get by financially. In fact, unmarried women face the most negative economic prospects for retirement now and for at least the next 20 years (Havemann et al., 2005; Holden, 2008). African American women are more likely to have been employed steadily most of their adult lives but also more likely to retire later than their white counterparts, primarily for economic reasons.

To a large extent, the retirement system exacerbates the inequalities of the labor market earlier in life. Employment histories that fit the expectation of lifelong work with few disruptions tend to be associated with a smoother transition to retire- ment. In contrast, the timing of retirement for women and for persons of color, particularly African Americans and Latinos, differs from the traditional pattern for white males. Lifetime employment patterns of low-income adults of color often create an unclear line between paid work and nonwork. Additionally, lengthy periods of unemployment or underemployment at an earlier age limit their access to retirement benefits. Yet job reductions may have "pushed" adults of color into retirement (Flippen 2005; James & Wink, 2007). Furthermore, their greater likelihood of chronic illness and disability

(discussed in Chapters 4 and 14) makes declining health a more salient reason for retirement among African Americans than among whites (Angel & Angel, 2006).

In some cases, retirement due to poor health and adverse work conditions results in older adults perceiving their early retirement as forced—that is, needing to leave the workforce earlier than they had planned or wanted to. Nearly 33 percent of retirees in an analysis of the Health and Retirement Survey felt their choices had been restricted by health limitations, job displacement, layoffs or downsizing, and caregiving obligations (Prisuta, 2004). In other studies, race and ethnicity did not affect perceptions of involuntary retirement among men, but did so among women. Single African American women tend to remain underemployed and caught in a situation in which they lack adequate resources to retire but receive only a low income from work, suggesting a pattern of growing cumulative inequities (James & Wink, 2008; Szinovacz & Davey, 2005). The experience of lacking choice about retirement age is undoubtedly growing as jobs disappear and income declines.

Satisfaction with Retirement

Early gerontological studies emphasized the negative impacts of retirement as a life crisis due to loss (Atchley, 1976; Streib & Schneider, 1971). Later research identifies the positive effects of retirement on life satisfaction and health. Similar factors (e.g., financial security and health status) also influence the degree of satisfaction with retirement as well as its timing. In general, control over the timing of retirement, financial security, and health appear to be the major determinants of retirees' satisfaction. Not surprisingly, retirees with higher incomes report being more satisfied and having a more positive retirement identity than those with lower incomes. Regardless of social class, however, most retirees remain engaged in some type of productive activity other than paid work. As discussed further under civic engagement, activities that provide autonomy, a sense of control, and a chance to learn new things are all related to retirement satisfaction (Drentea, 2002; Fast, Dosman, & Moran, 2006).

It is useful to examine retirement as a *process* or *transition* that affects people's life satisfaction and self-identity in multiple ways. This concept encompasses not only the timing and type of retirement as a life stage, but also the phases of developing a retiree identity. Similarly, an individual's degree of satisfaction with the outcome depends to some extent on how the retirement process is experienced, especially the extent of choice preparation and planning, and congruence with prior employment roles. Overall, whether individuals adopt a retiree identity (i.e., what they make of the retiree role) depends on their prior employment status, amount of retirement income, and extent of disability (Szinovacz & Davey, 2004b). While it is a major transition, overall the majority of retirees experience minimal stress and report being relatively satisfied with their lives.

Retirement does not *cause* poor physical or mental health (e.g., depression) or death, although involuntary job loss does have negative effects on mental health (Bidisha & Roe, 2008). For retirees who have chosen this transition, their physical and mental health generally improves, perhaps because they are no longer subject to stressful, unhealthy,

Many older adults discover their artistic side with retirement.

or high-risk work conditions. People who die shortly after retiring were probably in poor health before they retired. In fact, deteriorating health is more likely to cause someone to retire than vice versa. The misconception that people become ill, depressed, or die as a *consequence* of retirement undoubtedly persists on the basis of findings from cross-sectional data, as well as anecdotal reports of isolated instances of such deaths. In addition, traditional American ideology that life's meaning is derived from paid work may reinforce the stereotype that retirement has primarily negative consequences. Retirees may also be motivated to exaggerate their health limitations to justify their retirement. In fact, health status is interconnected with other factors such as the normative acceptability of not working and the desire for a retirement lifestyle. Overall, whether retirement is chosen or forced appears to be the primary factor influencing the extent of functional health impairment and symptoms of depression by retirees (Fondon, 2007; Bidisha & Roe, 2008; Stephan, Fouquereau, & Fernandez, 2008).

Personal and *social characteristics* that contribute to satisfaction in retirement encompass:

- perceptions of daily activities as useful
- internal locus of control and self-determination
- a sense of having chosen the timing of retirement
- access to adequate informal social support systems
- marital or partner relationships that are supportive of the retiree role

Consistent with continuity theory, *preretirement self-esteem* and *identity* influence postretirement mental well-being. Individuals whose primary source of meaning was not their employment may adjust to a satisfying routine more readily than do those with strong work ethics who did not develop leisure activities when employed. Conversely, retirees who do not adapt well typically have poor health, inadequate finances, marital problems, and difficulties making transitions across the life course. Those who retire early because of poor health or lack of job opportunities or who feel pushed out of their jobs are less satisfied with retirement. But they are also generally dissatisfied with other aspects of their lives, such as their housing, standard of living, and leisure (Butrica & Shaner, 2005; Smith & Moen, 2004).

Occupational status, which is frequently associated with educational level, is also a predictor of retirement satisfaction. Not surprisingly, lower-status workers have more health and financial problems and are therefore less satisfied than higher-level white-collar workers. The more meaningful work characteristics of higher-status occupations may "spill over" to a variety of satisfying nonemployment pursuits throughout life. These are conducive to more social contacts and structured opportunities during retirement. For example, a college professor may have a work and social routine that is more readily transferable to retirement than that of a construction worker. Differences between retirees in upper- and lower-status occupations do not develop with retirement, but rather reflect inequality and differentiated opportunities throughout the life course (Henrette, 2008).

The nature of the *spouse/partner relationship* and the partner's role in the decision-making process affect retirement satisfaction in a range of ways. In one study of retirement satisfaction by gender, couples who reported both individual and joint satisfaction were those where the wives felt that their husbands did not influence their retirement decision (Smith & Moen, 2004). Having control over the timing of retirement along with the nature of the marital relationship—such as a partner's disability—influence post-retirement well-being, with effects differing by gender. Women caring for a partner with a disability who also perceived that they had been forced into an abrupt or too-early retirement because of caregiving reported more depressive symptoms than others. Another study found that women experienced more depressive symptoms than men when their spouses were already retired while the woman continued to be employed. A wife's continued employment tended to cause greater conflicts in the marital

relationship than men's employment, because of the impact on joint time together (Davey & Szinovacz, 2004a, 2004b). These examples of the nature of the partner relationship and how it affects retirement illustrate the common saying "I married you for life, but not for lunch." Quite simply, conflicts are more likely when partners do not enjoy spending leisure time together and when wives feel they did not control the timing of their retirement.

Gender and *race* markedly influence retirement satisfaction. Women's retirement plans and well-being, like men's, are influenced by their own finances and health, not by their husbands'. Their slightly reduced levels of retirement satisfaction seem related to their lower incomes, typically because of the lack of private pensions and more years out of the paid labor force spent giving dependent care. For women who enjoy the routine, rewards, and sociability of paid employment, adjusting to a full-time stay-at-home role can be difficult. Those who entered the workforce in midlife, after raising their children, may not be ready to retire when their husbands are (Moen et al., 2001).

Reentry to the labor force (or "unretirement") is distinct from "partial" retirement (reducing hours worked per week or weeks worked per year). As noted above, retirement for African Americans and Latinos is not a single, irreversible event that represents the culmination of career employment. Instead, those who experienced discontinuous work patterns and ongoing financial problems generally do not define themselves as retired. As "unretired-retired," they spend a greater percentage of their lives employed intermittently and in temporary jobs after retirement because of their low wage base. Elders of color are more vulnerable to job displacement and more adversely affected by it than any other group. Their reemployment rates, personal and household income, and health insurance coverage following displacement are lower than that of white workers. Accordingly, displaced older workers must often move into lower-paying jobs to bridge the years to retirement. In addition, African American men tend to have higher rates of disability across the

> **SUMMARY OF FACTORS AFFECTING RETIREMENT SATISFACTION**
>
> - financial security
> - good health
> - a retirement process that involves choice, autonomy, adequate preparation and planning, and congruence with prior job roles
> - retirement activities that offer autonomy, sense of control, and chances to learn and feel useful
> - a suitable living environment
> - a strong social support system characterized by reciprocal relationships
> - a higher-status occupation prior to retirement
> - personal capacities, such as a positive outlook and sense of mastery

life course and especially in the years preceding retirement, which intensify retirement inequities (Flippen, 2005; Hardy, 2006; James & Wink, 2008; Mutchler & Burr, 2009).

For all retirees, however, retirement is now less a single phase in a person's life course and more a dynamic process with several stages where the retired/nonretired roles overlap and individuals move in and out of the workforce. Instead of a "crisp" or unidirectional one-step shift, blurred transitions often involve complex patterns such as returning to employment, flexible hours and part-time options, "unretirements," and later, second or third partial or full retirements. About 50 percent of older workers currently pass through a period of partial retirement on the way to complete retirement, or reverse the process by reentering the labor force (Hardy, 2006). This means that the end of a career often differs from the end of a working life. The propensity to work on a part-time or part-year basis—exiting and reentering the workforce—is primarily for economic reasons and is not specific to a particular job. Those who change jobs shortly before retirement are the most likely to work afterward, suggesting that "unretirement" is part of a repertoire of adaptive behaviors in the later years.

Money is not the only reason why older adults move from retirement to employment, however; many of them generally enjoy work and see it as a way to remain active, socialize, and experience psychological benefits (Calvo, 2006; Li & Rerraro, 2005, 2006; Holden, 2008). As noted above, the first boomers turned 62 in 2008, enabling them to retire and receive partial Social Security benefits. As a whole, boomers are healthier, better educated, and seeking "successful aging" more than prior cohorts during their pre-retirement years. (The image of retirement held by many boomers presumes good health, combined with disposable income to pursue meaningful activities, such as education, leisure, travel and civic engagement and a time for creativity. The life course of boomers has been more fluid than prior generations, with many of them entering and exiting education, work and leisure at different points. Boomer women in particular see this phase of life as time of additional career development, community involvement and continued personal growth (Piktialis, 2008; Smyer, Besen & Pitt-Catsouphes, 2008).

For some boomers, a job represents a new career, a continuation of earlier work, or a way to learn new skills and form new friendships. They implicitly recognize the benefits of continued employment in terms of higher morale, happiness, and longevity (Chen & Scott, 2006). Most workers would like to retire gradually, phasing down from full-time to part-time work with *bridge jobs* (e.g., new full- or part-time jobs that "bridge" the transition from work to retirement (Harvard/MetLife, 2004). This preference for bridge jobs reflects financial, health insurance, and social needs, as well as a desire for creative and challenging opportunities after years in a traditional worker role. Such options are contingent on whether employers will retrain them for a new job, make pension contributions after age 65, or transfer them to jobs with less responsibility, fewer hours, and less pay as a transition to full retirement. Not surprisingly, these options are most readily available to higher-income workers.

However, with the economic recession, bridge jobs and other formal phased retirement programs are now unrealistic for many employers because of their potential added cost (Hutchens, 2003; Piktialis, 2008). Today it will

Part-time work can provide both income and satisfaction.

take the typical 55-year-old employee at least 2 extra years in the full-time workforce to recoup 2008's market losses (Brandon, 2009; Smyer et al., 2008). In an AARP survey prior to the recession, only 33 percent of respondents said the only reason they continued to work was that they needed the income. But financial reasons have become more salient with time (Johnson, 2009; Rix, 2008). When boomers were asked about retirement prior to the current recession, only 13 percent of respondents in a national survey felt economically secure and looking forward to retirement and the leisure they believed they had earned. In contrast, 32 percent were classified as "strugglers" and "anxious," primarily women who feared retirement as a time of financial hardship and worried about health care costs

(Prisuta, 2004). Ironically, this latter group, typically lower-income workers, is also the least likely to have access to resources to plan for retirement or quit working. During the current economic downturn and job insecurity, one would expect far more than 32 percent to report anxiety about their pending retirement. Government employees and older men with more years of education, higher occupational status, and private pensions have more retirement planning opportunities, thereby perpetuating inequities in old age.

Although boomers have been seen as a prosperous generation, 33 percent do not own assets and have little in savings or projected retirement income beyond Social Security (Rix, 2008). This stems in part from their employment record, which resulted in the highest wage inequality at midlife of all recent cohorts (Smyer et al., 2008). Many would like to shift to other jobs or careers, but few firms actively recruit older workers (Manpower, 2007). Boomers increasingly face the prospect of working longer for higher retirement benefits or making do with less. But given past consumerism and lifestyle choices, they will probably work longer (Rix, 2008).

RETIREES' INCREASING ECONOMIC WORRIES

Mary O'Connell, 75, and husband S. F., age 78, retired without pensions and with meager benefits from Social Security, counting on income from four stocks. But the bulk of it was in Bank of America, whose stocks have declined dramatically. So they don't want to sell any stocks whose value is deteriorating. Their "safe investments" of certificates of deposit now have a lower interest rate, reducing a reliable income stream. She says she doesn't follow her stocks too closely because it would only make her depressed. "We figured we worked all our lives. This is something we wanted to enjoy. But now that's taken away from us" (Leland & Uchitelle, 2008).

Employment Status

As described above, some older adults never fully retire, and employment remains their primary means of productivity. In 2008, 6.6 million Americans age 65 and over (16 percent) were in the labor force working or actively seeking work, including 3.2 million men (20.5 percent) and 2.6 million women (12.6 percent), while the numbers of employed young adults age 16 to 24 has declined. Older adults comprised 3.8 percent of the U.S. labor force. About 3.3 percent were unemployed. Labor force participation of men 65 and older decreased steadily from 66 percent in 1900 to 15.8 percent in 1985, then stayed at 16 to 18 percent until 2002; it has been increasing since then to over 20 percent. The participation rate for women 65 years and older rose slightly from 8 percent in 1900 to 10.8 percent in 1956, fell to 7.3 percent in 1985, and was around 7 to 9 percent from 1986

to 2002. However, since 2000, labor force participation of older women has been gradually rising. This increase is especially noticeable among the population age 65 to 69 (AOA, 2008; Federal Interagency Forum, 2008; Greenhouse, 2009). As noted by Schulz and Binstock (2006), the "economics of population aging" necessitates that people work longer in the future (Schulz & Binstock, 2006, p. 151). These changes are illustrated in Figure 12.1

Individuals who continue to be employed past age 55 remain almost as likely to work full-time as their younger counterparts until about age 62. After that, most prefer part-time work, which has increased more than full-time employment. Women are more likely to work part-time than their male counterparts, especially after age 70 (Purcell & Whitman, 2006; Wan et al., 2005). (See Figure 12.2.) As noted above, part-time work that

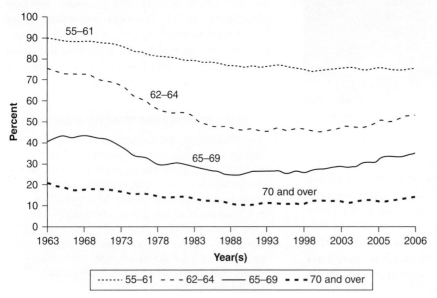

Note: Data for 1994 and later years are not strictly comparable with data for 1993 and earlier years due to a redesign of the survey and methodology of the Current Population Survey. Beginning in 2000, data incorporate population controls from Census 2000.

Reference population: These data refer to the civilian noninstitutionalized population.

Source: Bureau of Labor Statistics, Current Population Survey.

FIGURE 12.1   **Labor Force Participation Rates of Men Age 55 and Over, By Age Group, Annual Averages, 1963–2006**

SOURCE: Federal Interagency Forum on Aging-Related Statistics, 2006.

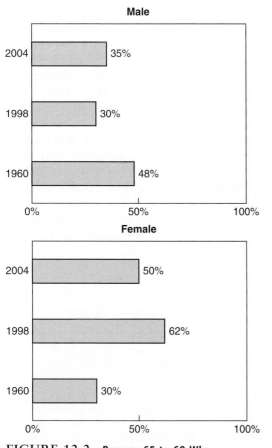

FIGURE 12.2   Persons 65 to 69 Who Work Part-Time
SOURCE: Based on Purcell and Whitman, 2006.

- Employer policies may prevent part-time workers from drawing partial pensions, assuming pensions exist.
- Employers resist the additional administrative work and higher health insurance costs entailed in hiring part-time older employees. Those costs, however, may be tempered by the advantage of fewer employer-paid benefits for dependents among older workers.

In part because of such barriers to part-time work, older workers are more likely to be self-employed than younger workers (Wan et al., 2005).

More Older People Seek Employment

The unemployment rate for adults age 65 and older was 6.8 percent in February 2009, the highest level ever recorded. This increased proportion does not include the many older adults who call themselves retired simply because they have given up on finding a job (Brandon, 2009). The primary reasons why older people seek employment are similar to the ones that keep them from

allows gradual retirement is perceived by the working public of all ages as a desirable alternative, especially when a flexible work schedule is combined with the ability to draw partial pensions. It is unclear, however, to what extent part-time work represents underemployment of adults whose hours of work have been reduced because of job losses or company downsizing, feeling pressured to leave full-time work, or inability to find full-time employment. Furthermore, part-time work has some disadvantages

- Part-time work may not offer a wage level similar to full-time employment.

RETIREES WHO DON'T

The number of employees age 75 and older has increased more than 80 percent in the past 25 years. Marge, age 79, is one such employee. She still works 2 days a week as a waitress in a family restaurant. She states that she would rather work than go to a social club or senior center. Marge brings a strong work ethic and commitment to the job. A younger coworker maintains that "sometimes she runs us under the table" (Hollingsworth, 2002). Another is Waldo, who began working when he was 13, guiding a lead team of horses pulling a wheat thrasher. After a series of varied jobs, he started a business cleaning seeds for planting in the 1950s and ran it until he was 91 years old. He then took a decades-long hobby of beekeeping and went into the honey business, which he is still running at age 104 (Manning, 2006). And Arthur, who worked 72 years repairing Los Angeles buses, eventually retired at age 100.

retiring. Increasingly, retirees discover that it is harder than anticipated to live on a reduced income. This challenge has been exacerbated in the last few years as major companies have declared bankruptcy, pension plans have collapsed or shrunk, and the stock market plunged after 2000 and again in 2008, thereby depleting retirement investments and leaving retirees with a much smaller income than anticipated.

Barriers to Employment

Why do unemployed older workers have a difficult time with their job search? Several reasons have been identified:

- They may have been in one occupation for many years and therefore lack job-hunting skills.
- They are more vulnerable to skill obsolescence created by changes in the economy, including the shift away from product manufacturing and medium-wage manufacturing jobs toward low-wage positions in an information- and services-dominated economy.
- Jobs have shifted to the Southeast, Southwest, and West, leaving older workers in the Midwest and East with fewer options if they are not receptive to moving.
- The U.S. ranks last among all industrialized countries in terms of providing job retraining and assistance to the workforce across all ages (Schulz & Binstock, 2006).
- With rising unemployment levels at all ages, businesses are less likely to modify the work environment, such as allowing part-time work, to prepare older workers for rapid changes.
- Only a few programs, such as the federal **Senior Community Service Employment Program (SCSEP)**, specifically target low-income older adults through retraining, job placement, a stipend and part-time subsidized employment. It enrolls only a small proportion of elders a year and has numerous eligibility requirements.

- Age-based employment discrimination persists, often going "underground," even though mandatory retirement policies are illegal for most jobs. Age discrimination alleged as the basis for loss of employment is the fastest-growing form of unfair dismissal complaints submitted to the Equal Employment Opportunity Commission. Ageism in the workplace may also manifest by older adults being passed up for promotion or not receiving raises because of age. The **Age Discrimination in Employment Act (ADEA)** has reduced blatant forms of age discrimination (e.g., advertisements that restrict jobs to younger people) but has been less effective at promoting the hiring and

IS THIS AGE DISCRIMINATION?

A bank announces that it is opening a new branch and advertises for tellers. Jane Feld, age 53 with 22 years of banking experience, applies. The employment application includes an optional category for age. Rather than pausing to think about whether to indicate her age, she answers the question voluntarily and truthfully. The next week, Ms. Feld receives a polite letter from the bank complimenting her on her qualities but turning her down because she is overqualified. She later finds out that a 32-year-old woman with only 4 years' experience has been hired.

Sarah Nelson, age 55, is a manager with a large advertising company. For the past 5 years, she has received outstanding performance reviews. Two months after a strong review and pay increase, she was abruptly fired for "poor performance." Her replacement, age 35, started a week after she was fired.

A 65-year-old man, who had held a high-level managerial position in a bank before it closed, interviewed for a project manager position in a nonprofit. All the interviewers were in their late 20s. They told him that "people here work really hard and have a lot of energy," implying that they doubted his ability to work hard because of his age. Yet when employed at the bank, this man had worked 10-hour days, six days a week. When he told them that, they just looked past him.

LAWS TO PREVENT OR ADDRESS DISCRIMINATION BASED ON AGE

- The Age Discrimination in Employment Act (ADEA), passed in 1967, protects workers age 40 and over from denial of employment strictly because of age.
- This act was amended in 1978 to prohibit the use of pension plans as justification for not hiring older workers and to raise the mandatory retirement age to 70. In 1986, mandatory retirement was eliminated.
- In 1990, the Older Workers Benefit Protection Act prohibited employers from treating older workers differently than younger workers during a reduction in workforce.
- The Americans with Disabilities Act (ADA) of 1990 also offers protection to older adults. Employers are expected to make work-related adjustments and redesign jobs for workers with disabilities, including impairments in sensory, manual, or speaking skills.

POINTS TO PONDER

Next time you are talking socially to an employer, ask whether the firm has older workers and how they define "older worker," Is it those in their 50s, 60s, or older? How are their skills utilized? Are they given opportunities for training and promotions? What have the firm's experiences been with older workers in terms of absenteeism, productivity, and morale?

Economic Status: Sources of Income in Retirement

In terms of the P–E model, economic status in old age is largely influenced by societal conditions, especially the larger economy, past and current employment patterns, and resultant retirement income and benefits. Although financial resources in themselves do not guarantee satisfaction, they affect older people's daily opportunities and competence that can enable them to experience active and productive aging.

The median household income of people age 65 and older was $24,323 in 2008 for males and $14,171 for females. About one of every 14 (7.4 percent) family households with an older member had incomes less than $15,000, and 59.5 percent had incomes of $35,000 or more (AOA, 2008). These figures dispel the myth that all older adults are wealthy and benefiting at the expense of younger generations. Older adults are estimated to need 80 percent of their preretirement income to maintain their living standard in retirement. Since retirement can reduce individual incomes by one-third to one-half, retirees who do not fall into upper-income brackets must markedly adjust their standard of living downward—while their out-of-pocket spending for items such as health care typically increases.

Sources of income for the older population include Social Security earnings, savings, assets, and pensions (which comprise nearly 97 percent of all income received) (Federal Interagency Forum 2008). The sources of aggregate income

retraining of older workers. Overall, age discrimination laws may help older workers remain employed but have done little to help them be reemployed if they lose their jobs (Schulz & Binstock, 2006).

- Subtle forms of ageism endure, such as expectations of attractiveness in dress, makeup, and hairstyle, or making jobs undesirable to older workers by downgrading the title or salary.
- Negative stereotypes about aging and productivity persist. Despite decades of evidence to the contrary, some employers still assume that older workers will not perform as well as younger ones because of poor health, declining energy, diminished intellectual ability, or different work styles.
- Others perceive older workers as less cost effective (given their proximity to retirement), less adept in a changing, technology-oriented workplace, more expensive to train, and incurring higher health care costs (Schulz & Binstock, 2006; Hardy, 2006).

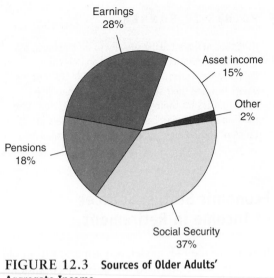

FIGURE 12.3 **Sources of Older Adults'**
Aggregate Income
SOURCE: Federal Interagency Forum, (2008).

for persons over age 65 are illustrated in Figure 12.3. The distribution of income sources varies widely, however, with women, elders of color, and the oldest-old being most likely to rely on Social Security and to lack pensions and other assets. Those at the bottom of the income range depend primarily on Social Security and/or Supplemental Security Income (SSI), as described below.

Social Security

Many older people depend on Social Security for their retirement income.

- Nearly 40 percent of all income received by older units (i.e., a married couple with one or both members age 65 and older and living together or a person age 65 or older not living with a spouse) is from Social Security.
- Approximately 95 percent of all older people receive Social Security, with women and the oldest-old most likely to have this as their only source of income.
- Social Security constitutes 90 percent or more of the income received by 32 percent of

beneficiaries (20 percent of married couples and 41 percent of unmarried recipients).
- Without Social Security, 48 to 55 percent of all older adults would live in poverty.
- Marital status often determines the extent of reliance on Social Security; for approximately 75 percent of single older women, Social Security represents more than 50 percent of their income compared to an estimated 50 percent of married couples.
- Among low-income households and the oldest-old, as much as 80 percent of their income is from Social Security (AOA, 2008; Federal Interagency Forum, 2008; Gist, 2007).

Social Security was never intended to provide an adequate retirement income, but only a floor of protection or the first tier of support. It was assumed that additional pensions and individual savings would help support people in their later years. This assumption has not been borne out, as reflected in the proportionately lower income received by retirees from savings and private pensions. Not surprisingly, older individuals with the lowest total income have Social Security as their *sole* source (AOA, 2008).

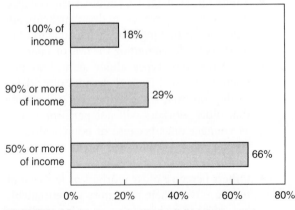

FIGURE 12.4 **Percent of Beneficiary Units with Social Security Benefits as a Major Source of Income, 2003**
SOURCE: National Center for Policy Analysis, 2003.

As described further in Chapter 16, the Social Security system is a public trust into which all workers pay and from which all are guaranteed an income floor in old age or disability. To be insured, a worker retiring now must be age 62.5 or older and must have been employed at least 10 years in a job covered by Social Security. The level of benefits received is based on a percentage of the retired worker's average monthly earnings that were subject to Social Security tax. Insured persons who were born before 1937 are eligible for full benefits at age 65, with the age rising from 65 to 67 by 2022, beginning with workers and spouses born in 1938, who must be 65 years and two months for full benefits. If workers choose to retire at age 62.5, their monthly benefits are permanently reduced (with the exception of 2009–2010). Since 1975, Social Security benefits are automatically increased annually whenever the Consumer Price Index goes up by 3 percent or more. This is known as the cost-of-living adjustment, or COLA, which protects benefits from inflation. Since benefits are related to a worker's wage and employment history, women and people of color with patterns of intermittent or part-time work tend to receive less than the average monthly benefit. Another inequity inherent within Social Security is that LGBT partners cannot qualify for benefits based on their partner's earnings. In addition, some of the oldest-old do not qualify for Social Security because they were employed in occupations such as domestic work not covered by the system. Future retirees who are immigrants or LGBT partners will not be covered, even in states that allow same-sex marriage, unless federal legislation broadens the definition of who is eligible.

The Social Security payroll tax is regressive (i.e., both the rich and the poor pay the same rate of 12.4 percent). This means that low-income workers, often women and people of color, pay a larger proportion of their monthly salary for the Social Security tax compared to higher-income workers. On the other hand, lower-income workers benefit proportionately more from Social Security when they retire, receiving benefits equal to 56 percent of their working wages, while high-income workers' benefits on average are only 28 percent of their prior salary. In addition, higher-income workers must now pay income tax on 50 percent of their Social Security benefits. Unfortunately, most low- and middle-income adults do not plan sufficiently for their retirement income because they assume that Social Security will be adequate, and they fail to assess the impact of inflation and reduced income levels. Some are able to supplement their Social Security income with assets, pensions, job earnings, and SSI.

Asset Income

Assets (e.g., savings, investments, home equity, and personal property) are the next most important source of income received by about 60 percent of older adults. This represents a decline since 1986, coinciding with a long period of falling interest rates and dividend yields. But assets comprise only 15 percent of the total income of all older people. Not surprisingly, the median income of those with assets is more than twice the median income of those without. Over 30 percent of older households—typically the oldest old, women, and persons of color—report no asset income (Federal Interagency Forum, 2008; Purcell & Whitman, 2006).

Home equity represents the major component of older people's assets and is about 50 percent of their net worth. Approximately 80 percent of older people own their homes, although this percentage declines among elders of color. Yet approximately 50 percent of older homeowners spend almost half of their incomes on property taxes, utilities, and maintenance and face higher maintenance costs than other age groups (Federal Interagency Forum, 2008). In contrast, boomers are unlikely to have paid off their mortgages and more likely to have refinanced multiple times as a way to reduce monthly expenses and to increase their cash flow, and therefore are at a high risk of foreclosure. In terms of quality of life, home equity is not liquid wealth or cash and cannot be relied on to cover daily expenses. Increasing numbers of older people participate in reverse mortgages, described in Chapter 11, as one way to convert the accumulated value of a home into regular monthly income. Other assets are primarily interest-bearing savings and checking accounts, although today most of these accounts generate very low earnings from interest.

Even though older adults with fixed incomes cannot depend on assets to meet current expenses, their net worth (all sources of income) tends to be greater than for those under age 35. As an indicator of vast income differences among older people, overall net worth is approximately $17,800 for African American households, but above $226,000 for white households. Education is a primary factor affecting total assets; across all groups, the net worth of those with no high school diploma is approximately $59,000, compared to $412,000 for those with some college or more (Federal Interagency Forum, 2008).

Pensions

Although nearly all jobholders are covered by Social Security as a general public pension, less than 50 percent of all private workers receive *job-specific pensions.* Pensions were a product of the nineteenth and twentieth centuries in order to provide secure, adequate funding for older adults and typically had rigid requirements (Schulz & Binstock, 2006). Pension benefits are generally based on earnings or a combination of earnings and years of service; they were traditionally intended to supplement Social Security. Pensions are available only through a specific employment position and are administered by a place of employment, union, or private insurance company. Relatively few workers are enrolled in private pension programs that provide the replacement rate of income necessary for retirement. Indeed, job-specific pensions comprise only 18 percent of the older population's aggregate income, and even less among the lowest-income elders. Only about

3 percent of pension plans provide cost-of-living increases, so most plans are adversely affected by inflation. The recession and escalating health care costs have also reduced pension assets. The marked decline of employee pension coverage is a problematic trend for older adults' future well-being (Federal Interagency Forum, 2008).

Until the late 1990s, there were **defined benefit pension plans,** in which a specified amount is guaranteed by the company as a lifetime annuity, and employees knew what they could count on as retirement income; this provided incentives for building seniority (typically 30 years) as well as disincentives for quitting mid-career and delaying retirement. Defined benefit pension plans were also used to encourage early retirement, especially connected with plant closures and a priority on retaining younger workers (Hardy, 2006). Now, pensions are typically **defined contribution plans,** such as 401(k) plans, in which the amount of the benefit varies depending on an individual's investment returns and thus carries greater financial risk for the employee. The proportion of private workers who participated in defined benefit plans decreased from 32 percent in 1992–1993 to 21 percent in 2005, while participation in defined contribution plans *increased* from 35 percent to 42 percent. These plans require workers to manage their own retirement portfolios. The risk is magnified because those saving for retirement report that they are doing only a fair or poor job of managing their investment portfolios (Schulz & Binstock, 2006; Lusardi, 2009). Of even greater significance is that fewer than 10 percent of all workers have enough disposable income to have IRAs (Verma, 2006). Lower-income workers generally cannot spare the money, and the tax benefit is considerably less for them. Ironically, then, the people who need retirement income the most cannot take advantage of IRAs. This shift has also been fostered by increased federal regulation of pensions, pension liabilities, and employers' desire for flexibility in making labor force adjustments. The growth of defined contribution plans influences retirement indirectly by removing penalties for delayed retirement and allowing more individualized timing of retirement, with some workers remaining employed longer in order to retire with a larger pension account balance (Hardy, 2006; Purcell & Whitman, 2006; Weller, 2009). Increasingly, employers have converted their defined benefit plans to **cash balance plans,** which combine elements of both types of plans. At the same time, more employers have eliminated health insurance for their employees. Not surprisingly, pension coverage varies by class, race, gender, and age. Women, workers of color, and lower-income workers in small nonunion plants and low-wage industries, such as retail sales and services, have the lowest rates of pension coverage (Older Women's League, 2009; Purcell & Whitman, 2006).

Maintaining employer-provided health insurance is increasingly a primary consideration for retirees. Less than 33 percent of large companies and only 4 percent of small firms offered retiree health benefits in 2008 (Brandon, 2009). Health insurance benefits have also been jeopardized by company bankruptcies. Think about airline pilots and flight attendants who have lost pensions and other benefits when their company declared bankruptcy. In such instances, a company can "shed" its union contracts by arguing that the financial burden of pension obligations makes it unattractive to prospective buyers. Once sold, companies can be reopened as nonunion operations (Hardy, 2006).

Earnings

Current job *earnings* form approximately 28 percent of the aggregate income of older units and are reported by about 18 percent of men and 13 percent of women. In fact, the proportion of income from earnings has already grown, partially because of increased employment among older people, as described earlier, and a drop in interest and dividend income (Purcell & Whitman, 2006). Not surprisingly, the percentage of income from earnings differs markedly by age and class; elders in the lowest fifth of aggregate incomes garner only 2 percent of their

income through earnings, while this comprises 41 percent of aggregate income among the highest fifth. Although earnings are an important income source to the young-old and to those with the highest income from assets and pensions, they diminish with age (Federal Interagency Forum, 2008).

Poverty Among Old and Young

The economic status of older adults has improved dramatically since the 1960s. In 1969, 35 percent of those ages 65 and older fell below the official poverty line. In 2007, 9.7 percent of older people were poor, compared with 11.3 percent of those under age 65 and 17.8 percent of children under age 18. However, this poverty rate is a statistically significant increase from the rate in 2006 (9.4 percent). It is noteworthy that while the *proportion* of poor people age 65 and older has fallen since 1950, the *number* of elders living in poverty has remained constant since the 1970s due to the growth in the total number of older adults (Federal Interagency Forum, 2008). A primary factor in reducing poverty among elders has been Social Security, including the 1972 increases in Social Security benefits and COLAs that began in 1975 (described earlier). Other factors include:

- the strong performance of the economy and labor productivity in the 1950s and 1960s
- the growth of real wages that the current cohort of older adults experienced during their working lives
- accumulation of home equity
- existence of Medicare
- pension protection, although this is now declining
- implementation of the SSI program
- changes in the definition of the poverty threshold for older adults

As a result of such gains, the public perception is that *all* older persons are financially better off than other age-groups. This perception is also fueled by the increase in poverty among children under age six, who are the poorest age-group. However, the decline in the income status of children is largely structural, caused by economic, political, and demographic forces—especially cuts in child welfare and income maintenance programs—not by the income growth of the older population.

Poverty Differentials Over Time

When viewed over time, many older people are not financially comfortable, despite their over-all improved income status. A larger proportion (6.4 percent) of older people than younger (4.5 percent) fall just above the poverty line (income between the poverty level and 125 percent of this level). They are considered "near poor" and at risk for poverty, making 16.1 percent of elders poor or near poor (AOA, 2008). A growing proportion of older adults are caught between upper-income and poor older people—not well enough off to be financially secure but not poor enough to qualify for the means-tested safety net of Medicaid and SSI. Paradoxically, the only way they can improve their economic well-being is to qualify for Medicaid and SSI by spending down (using up their assets). The proportion of subgroups that are poor, even with Social Security, and the percentage kept out of poverty by Social Security are illustrated in Figure 12.5 on page 514.

These figures do not reflect the fact that the federal poverty standard for a single adult age 65 and over is 8 to 10 percent lower than for younger adults. In setting this lower threshold to qualify for benefits as "poor," the Census Bureau assumes that the costs of food and other necessities are lower for older people, even though many have special nutritional needs and spend proportionately more on housing, transportation, and health care than do younger groups. If the same standard were applied to the older population as to the other age groups, the poverty rate for older people would increase to over 15 percent (AOA 2008). Another factor that increases the economic vulnerability of older adults

is that they are less likely to have reserve funds to cover emergencies such as catastrophic medical expenses. As a result, low-income elders often face impossible trade-offs, such as giving up medications or food in order to pay for housing. If older people are facing major health care needs or living alone in inadequate, poorly heated housing, they may have greater difficulty coping with economic hardship than younger adults (Richardson & Barusch, 2006).

Contrary to the static nature of poverty that is suggested by cross-sectional data at a single point in time, many older people move in and out of poverty over time, often because of health and long-term care costs. The uncertainty of economic hardship in itself can negatively affect elders' well-being. When such individual movements are identified, the risk of falling below the poverty line at some time during a specified period more than doubles the highest average risk for older couples, and by almost 30 percent for widows. For example, many women become poor for the first time in their lives after depleting their assets while caring for a dying partner. Once an older person moves into poverty, she or he is less likely to return to financial adequacy than are younger age groups. Many "hidden poor" among the older population are either living with relatives or in long-term care facilities and thus not counted in official census statistics. In sum, more elders are at marginal levels of income and at greater risk of poverty than the population 18 to 64 years; they

---

WHO ARE THE OLDER POOR?

- 7.4 percent of older whites
- 11.3 percent of older Asians and Pacific Islanders
- 17.1 percent of older Latinos
- 23 percent of older African Americans
- 29 percent of older American Indians
- 17.8 percent of older people living alone
- 14 percent of those over age 85
- 12.2 percent of those in central cities
- 10.8 percent of those in rural areas (AOA, 2008)

are also more likely to be trapped in long-term poverty. As noted throughout this text in discussions of disparities, wide socioeconomic diversity exists within the older population, with economic marginality most pronounced among older women, those who live alone or in rural areas, elders of color, and the oldest-old.

Poverty Differentials by Gender

Older women comprise one of the poorest groups in our society. In fact, the risk of poverty among couples and single men has fallen sharply, leaving poverty in old age a characteristic primarily of single frail women over age 85, especially women of color, in rural areas, and who have outlived their husbands. Slightly over 12 percent of older women are poor, compared to 6.6 percent of older men (AOA, 2008). As noted above, widows account for over 50 percent of all older poor, reflecting the loss of income with the death of a wage-earner spouse. In contrast, the wife's death *reduces* the risk of poverty for widowers (Purcell & Whitman, 2006). The reasons for these gender-based inequities are discussed in full in Chapter 15.

Poverty Differentials by Race

African American and Latino elders of both genders have substantially lower incomes than their white counterparts, as described earlier. Approximately 23.2 percent of older African Americans and 17.1 percent of older Latinos are poor, compared with 7.4 percent of older whites (AOA, 2008). The median income of older African American and Latino men living alone is about 33 percent lower than for older white men living alone. Although differences are less pronounced among women, the median incomes of older African American and Latina women are generally 25 to 33 percent lower than those of white women. Additionally, the average black or Latino household has no financial or liquid assets. Within each population of color, poverty is more common for women, especially divorced women,

than for men. The highest poverty rates are among Latina (39.5 percent) and African American (39 percent) women (Federal Interagency Forum, 2008). These higher rates of poverty among elders of color are discussed more fully in Chapter 14.

Poverty Differentials by Age and Living Status

Poverty rates among the young-old are lower, in part because many of them have some income from continued employment. In contrast, older cohorts continue to experience income loss as they age, and therefore greater economic deprivation than younger cohorts. The poverty rate for those 65 to 74 years is 9 percent; for those over age 85, nearly 15 percent (Federal Interagency Forum, 2008). The fact that median income declines with age is due in part to the disproportionate number of unmarried women among the oldest-old. The economic hardships of older cohorts are often compounded by a lifetime of discrimination, by historical factors such as working at jobs with no pension, and by recent events such as loss of a partner or declining health. Accordingly, older cohorts are more likely to live alone, which is associated with poverty. Of all older people living alone, nearly 18 percent are poor, compared with 6 percent of those living with others. When the poor and the near-poor are grouped together, 45 percent of older adults living alone fall into this category. In every successively older age-group, unmarried women have a lower median income than unmarried men or married couples (AOA, 2008; Federal Interagency Forum, 2008).

In sum, despite the overall improved financial situation of the older population, large pockets of poverty and near-poverty exist among women, elders of color, those over age 85, those who live alone, and elders in rural areas. As a result, economic inequities are actually greater among older people than among other age-groups. Aging advocates maintain that strategies to alleviate poverty among today's older Americans cannot rely on the labor market. Instead, immediate

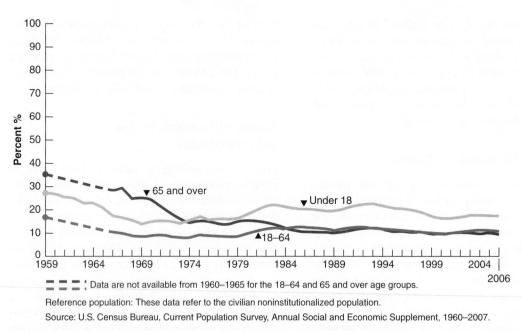

▬ ▬ ▬ ┊ Data are not available from 1960–1965 for the 18–64 and 65 and over age groups.

Reference population: These data refer to the civilian noninstitutionalized population.

Source: U.S. Census Bureau, Current Population Survey, Annual Social and Economic Supplement, 1960–2007.

FIGURE 12.5   **Poverty Rate of the Population, By Age Group, 1956—2006**
SOURCE: Social Security Administration, Social Security Bulletin Annual Statistical Supplement, 2000.

strategies are needed, such as increasing levels of Social Security for those with low lifetime earnings and ensuring that women and men have full access to benefits accrued by their spouses. Such changes are highly unlikely, given the current economic climate and lawmakers' resistance to adding to Social Security's costs.

Public Assistance

Only a small proportion of the older population receives some type of public assistance, primarily in the form of **Supplemental Security Income** (SSI). This percentage is greater among women and persons of color (U.S. Census Bureau, 2005). SSI was established in 1974 to provide a minimum guaranteed income for elders living on the margin of poverty, and for older adults and persons of all ages who are visually impaired or disabled. In contrast to Social Security, SSI does not require a history of covered employment contributions. Instead, eligibility is determined at the state level by a categorical requirement

that the recipient be 65 years of age, blind, or disabled, with a strict means-test based on monthly income and assets. Nevertheless, many eligible older poor do not participate in SSI, and others are denied benefits because they are immigrants. For those who do so, the federal SSI benefits fall substantially below the poverty line, especially for women who live alone, because benefit levels are higher for couples than for individuals. Only a few states have supplemented federal benefits; even in those instances, levels remain low, so that SSI supplies only about 14 percent of the income of poor older people. Those who receive SSI may also qualify for Medicaid and food stamps, but only about 20 percent of eligible elders receive food stamps despite the importance of good nutrition to their well-being (Fuller-Thomson & Redmond, 2008). The level of SSI benefits depends on income, assets, and gifts or contributions from family members for food, clothing, or housing. These gifts may be counted as income and may result in a reduction in benefits. Becoming eligible for

---

BARRIERS TO UTILIZATION OF PUBLIC SERVICES BY LOW-INCOME ELDERS

- Confusing information about program eligibility, benefits, and policies
- Enrollment obstacles, such as lack of access to welfare offices, misconceptions regarding the application process, its complexity, and language barriers for non-native English speakers
- Perceived stigma about public assistance
- Perceptions concerning lack of need or inadequate benefits

SSI is a time-consuming and often demeaning process, requiring extensive documentation and the ability to deal with conflicting criteria for benefits from SSI, Medicaid, and food stamps. Additionally, even legal immigrants are denied access to these programs. Of greatest concern is the number of states that have reduced SSI, food stamps, and Medicaid benefits during the current economic downturn, even though increasing numbers of "poor" or "near-poor" older adults are eligible for public assistance.

As noted earlier, along with health, living arrangements, and marital status, social class influences elders' nonpaid roles and activities. This is particularly important for organizational membership, volunteerism, religious participation and spirituality, and political involvement. We turn now to these other forms of productive aging.

Patterns and Functions of Nonpaid Roles and Activities

Leisure

Leisure can be defined as any activity characterized by the absence of obligation, which in itself is inherently satisfying. People's reactions to the concept of leisure are influenced by cultural values attached to paid work and a mistrust of nonwork time. Because of American values of productivity and hard work—especially among the World War II cohort of elders—many of the oldest-old have not experienced satisfying nonwork activities during earlier phases in their lives. Societal values are changing, however, with more legitimacy given to nonwork activities across the life course, as evidenced by the growing number of classes and businesses that specialize in leisure for middle-aged adults; additionally, the boomers will bring a stronger leisure orientation to retirement than past cohorts. For elders of color or those with low incomes, however, leisure may be a meaningless concept if they have to work long hours to survive, lack resources for satisfying recreational time, or must cope with functional disabilities.

Older adults' leisure time often involves teaching younger generations.

Disagreement regarding the value of leisure pursuits for older people is reflected historically in gerontological literature. An early perspective was that leisure roles could not substitute for employment because they were not legitimated by societal norms. Since work is a dominant value in U.S. society, it was argued that individuals cannot derive self-respect from leisure. A closely related view was that retirement is legitimated in our society by an ethic that esteems leisure that is earnest, occupied, and filled with activity—a "busy" ethic that is consistent with the activity theory of aging (Ekerdt, 1986). For those with strong work values, work-like activities were defined as important for achieving satisfaction in retirement. In fact, the prevalence of the "busy" ethic is reflected in a question commonly asked of retirees: "What do you do all day?" "Keeping busy" and engaging in productive activities analogous to work were presumed to ease the adjustment to retirement by adapting retired life to prevailing societal norms, even though the "busy" ethic is contrary to the definition of leisure as intrinsically satisfying. A prevailing counterargument is that leisure can replace the employment

role and provide personal satisfaction in later life, especially when the retired person has good health and an adequate income and their activities build upon preretirement skills and interests. In fact, leisure activities that challenge a person's cognitive and physical abilities, such as dancing, playing a musical instrument, using the computer, and playing board games, can enhance their sense of competence, control, and mastery (Cohen, 2005).

Although wide variations exist, there are common *patterns of meaningful nonpaid activity* among older individuals:

- Most activity changes are gradual, reflecting a consistency and a narrowing of the repertoire

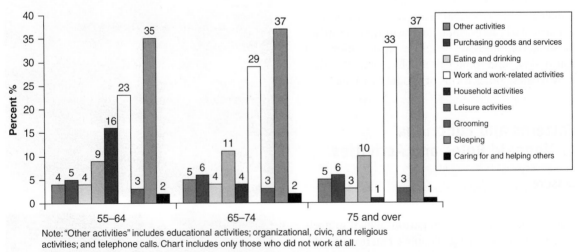

Note: "Other activities" includes educational activities; organizational, civic, and religious activities; and telephone calls. Chart includes only those who did not work at all.

Reference population: These data refer to the civilian noninstitutionalized population.

Source: Bureau of Labor Statistics, American Time Use Survey.

FIGURE 12.6 **Percentage of Day That People Age 55 and Over Spent Doing Selected Activities on an Average Day, By Age Group, 2006**

of activities, consistent with the theory of selective optimization of how we choose to spend time as we age.

- Compared to younger people, older adults are more likely to engage in solitary and sedentary pursuits, such as watching television, visiting with family and friends, and reading.
- The time spent on personal care, sleep and rest, hobbies, and "doing nothing in particular" composes a larger fraction of the oldest-old's days than among young-old and middle-aged individuals (Johnson & Schaner, 2005; Prisuta, 2004).

When judged by younger persons or by middle-class standards, these essential and universal activities may be viewed as "boring and nonproductive." Yet the ability to perform these more mundane nonwork activities—cooking, doing errands, puttering around the house or garden, checking e-mail, or sitting in quiet reflection—can be critical to maintaining older people's competence, self-esteem, and life satisfaction, especially among the oldest-old. Furthermore, these routines may represent realistic adjustments to declining energy levels and incomes. Such routine pursuits, consistent with the broader concept of productive aging, may thus reflect rational choices about ways to cope that are congruent with environmental changes and may also enhance quality of life, but do not always fit a narrow definition of leisure.

Nonwork activities also vary by gender and social class. Older men tend to do more household and yard maintenance, while older women perform more housework, child care, and other types of caregiving, as well as volunteering and participating in voluntary associations. Not surprisingly, higher-income older people, especially those living in planned retirement communities, tend to engage in more active leisure pursuits than low-income elders. Such differences in activities are attributable primarily to the costs of pursuing them, not necessarily to inherent differences by social class. As a result, a wide range of leisure-oriented businesses, including group travel and adventure programs, market services to higher-income older and middle-aged adults, especially baby boomers. Nevertheless, several age-based benefit programs are designed to reduce financial barriers to leisure. For instance, Golden Passports issued by federal agencies give older people reduced admission fees to national parks. Similar programs at the local or state level as well as AARP membership provide reduced admission to parks, museums, and cultural activities, and discounted prices from businesses and transportation services.

The major gains from leisure activities appear to be building social networks and creating new sources of personal meaning and competence. Not surprisingly, leisure activities enhance elders' positive identity and self-concept. Accordingly, activities that result in a sense of being valued are related to life satisfaction and mental well-being in retirement (Menec, 2003). This relationship does not mean, however, that leisure activity itself creates well-being, because active older people also tend to be healthier and of higher socioeconomic status. The quality of interactions with others in nonwork activities may be more salient for well-being than the number or frequency of interactions.

Religious Participation, Religiosity, and Spirituality

Of the various options for organizational participation, religious affiliation is the most common choice for older persons. After family and government, religious groups or denominations are an important source of instrumental and emotional support for elders. Despite a slight decline in participation among adults in their late 60s or early 70s, the level of organizational religious involvement for older adults exceeds that of other age-groups, with 50 percent of persons over age 65 attending a religious institution in an average week and many more attending less frequently. Additionally, the meaning and importance of religion are stronger in old age than in the earlier phases of life. In a 2006 Gallup Poll, more than 60 percent of adults age 65 and older indicated that religion was "very important" to them, compared to less than 50 percent of people 18 to 29 (Gallup, 2006). Furthermore, adults 65 and older are the most likely of any age group to belong to religiously affiliated groups that offer a loving, supportive community and a way to contribute.

DO WE BECOME MORE RELIGIOUS WITH AGE?

It remains unclear whether people become more religious with age or whether the observed increase in religiosity among some older adults is a cohort or period effect. Although no definitive data support either of these perspectives, consistent findings from Gallup Poll data tend to support the view that religiosity increases with age:

- In 1975, 45 percent of persons age 18 to 29 indicated their religious beliefs were "very important" to them, compared with 63 percent of those age 50 and older.
- In 2001, 58 to 60 percent of that same cohort (now age 44 to 55) stated their religious beliefs were "very important" to them, compared with 65 to 75 percent of those age 65 and older.
- In 1966, 38 percent of persons age 18 to 29 attended religious services in a typical week, compared to 51 percent of those age 50 and older.
- In 2001, 44 percent of persons in that cohort (now age 54 to 65) participated in religious services in a typical week, compared with 32 percent of 18- to 29-year-olds and 60 percent of those older than age 75.
- In 2006, more than 50 percent of adults age 65 and older indicated that religion was very important to them, compared to less than 50 percent of young adults age 18 to 29.

These data suggest that the young in previous generations also tended to be less religious than the old; however, as they have aged, they too have become more religious. On the other hand, if religiousness is related to better health, those who are less religious may be more likely to die at a younger age, leaving those who are more religious alive at a later age (i.e., a selection effect).

SOURCE: Gallup Poll, 2002, 2006; Idler, 2006; Koenig, 2002; Koenig & Brooks, 2002.

In contrast to other types of voluntary organizations, leadership positions in churches, temples, and synagogues are often concentrated among older members. Multidimensional in nature, religiosity can be differentiated in terms of organized religion, nonorganized religion, (e.g., the personal meaning of religion (private devotional activities) and intrinsic religiosity, (e.g., a person's experience in the context of organized religion). All three dimensions have benefits for mental and physical well-being, quality of end-of-life, and facing one's mortality (Parker et al., 2003).

Religion is a narrower concept than religiosity, referring to an organized system of spiritual beliefs, values, and behaviors shared by a community (a denomination) and transmitted over time. Religion encompasses communal ties and practices within formal religious institutions, rather than individual behavior (Nelson-Becker, 2004; Nelson-Becker, Nakashama, & Canda, 2006). Declines in rates of such formal participation after age 70 may reflect health and transportation difficulties and functional limitations more than lack of religiousness and spirituality per se. In fact, while attendance at formal services declines slightly with age, elders may compensate by increasing their internal religious practices—reading the Bible, Koran, or other religious books, listening to or watching religious broadcasts, praying and meditating, or studying religion, often in their homes. They also report higher levels of subjective religious experiences than other age-groups, such as life-changing religious events, daily spiritual experiences, relying on their faith to cope with adversity, and thinking of themselves as religious or spiritual persons (Canda, Nakashama, & Furman, 2004; Idler, 2006; Nelson-Becker, 2004; Nelson-Becker et al., 2006). For many elders, religiosity—which encompasses trust and faith in a power greater than oneself, prayer, and strength from a greater being—is an effective way to cope. Accordingly, older adults pray, asking help from a divine being, more often than other age-groups. The emotions of hope, gratitude, and forgiveness may represent significant components by which prayer exerts a salutary influence on elders' mental health. Religious beliefs, as contrasted with attendance at formal religious events, appear to be relatively stable from the late teens until age 60, and to increase thereafter. Thus, some older people who appear to be disengaged from religious organizations may be fully engaged nonorganizationally, experiencing a sense of spirituality and strong and meaningful subjective ties to religion (Idler, 2006; Nelson-Becker et al., 2006).

Most surveys on religiosity are limited by cross-sectional research, as discussed in Chapter 1. That is, they do not attempt to measure adults' past religious values and behaviors and changes with age. The few available longitudinal studies suggest that cohort differences (e.g., a strong period effect of a rise in church attendance in the 1950s and early 1960s) may be more important than the effects of age; they have produced mixed findings of increased, decreased, or stable religiousness over the life course (Hays et al., 2001; Ingersoll-Dayton, Krause, & Morgan, 2002). Thus, although religious convictions appear to become more salient over the years, this may be a generational phenomenon captured by the cross-sectional nature of most of the research. The current cohort of older persons, raised during a time of more widespread religious involvement, had their peak rates of attendance in the 1950s, when this country experienced a church revival. Despite the cross-sectional limitations of most studies in this field, religious involvement appears to increase with age and then decline among the oldest-old, but subjective religiousness does not diminish and may actually increase prior to death (Benjamin et al., 2003; Idler, 2006).

Studies of religious activity identify both gender and racial differences. Consistent with participation patterns in other organizations, women have higher rates of religious involvement than men (Miller & Stark, 2002; Taylor, Chatters, & Levin, 2004). Religion appears to be central to the lives of most older African Americans and Latinos, and related to their sense of meaning, life satisfaction, feelings of self-worth, personal well-being, and resilience and integration into the larger community,

although African Americans with reduced functional ability find attendance at religious services to be difficult (Idler, 2006; Krause, 2003; Roff et al., 2006; Taylor et al., 2004). The high esteem afforded African American elders in the church may partially underlie these positive associations. Historically, African Americans have had more autonomy in their religious lives than in their economic and political lives. The negative effects of life stress for older African Americans are found to be offset by increased religious involvement through prayer and other private religious activities, and a cognitive reframing of the situation in positive terms (e.g., "I have been through a lot before and I'll get through this too") (Mattis & Jagers, 2001; Taylor et al., 2004). For some African American caregivers, the church and God are considered part of their informal support and respite system (Idler, 2006; Parker et al., 2002). The church also provides social services such as in-home visitation, counseling, meals, household help, and transportation for older members, and links them with formal agencies. Such instrumental support reflects the African American church's historical responsibility for improving its parishioners' socioeconomic conditions.

Benefits of Religious Participation and Religiosity

The association between religion, religiosity and health is receiving growing attention by gerontological researchers, educators, and practitioners—along with increased visibility in the popular press. A primary reason for this increased attention is that the benefits of religion for physical and mental well-being appear to be significant and consistent. Perhaps the most compelling finding is that religious participation may reduce the risk of mortality and is associated with a lower prevalence of physical illness. For example, religious participation has been shown to reduce the risk of death and decrease time until recovery among patients undergoing cardiac surgery. Religious activity in later life is also found to be associated with better immune and cognitive functioning, lower blood pressure, greater longevity overall, as well as enhanced quality of life at the end-of-life (Atchley, 2008, 2009; Hill, 2008; Idler, 2006; Nelson-Becker, 2004; Powell, Shahabi, & Thoresen, 2003; Seeman, Dubin, & Seeman, 2003; Roff et al., 2008; Schaie, Krause, & Booth, 2004).

Religious participation (e.g., attending religious services) is also found to be associated with later onset of disability, and for those who experience functional limitations, increased likelihood of improving their physical functions. Although service attendance decreases with the onset of disability, it is often temporary, with attendance levels later returning to almost the level observed before the disability occurred. Accordingly, individuals who report that they turn to religion to cope with their problems exhibit better health outcomes. Because religion provides a world view that infuses the present with meaning and the future with hope, it may help people cope with health problems (Miller & Thoresen, 2003; Parker, et al., 2003; Roff et al., 2006; Smith, McCullough, & Poll, 2003).

Religion also has benefits for mental well-being, self-esteem, life satisfaction, a sense of usefulness, and morale. Religious participation is associated with decreased prevalence of mental disorders such as major depression and anxiety, substance use, and suicide. In instances of depression, religious involvement is linked with both a greater likelihood of recovery from depression and a shorter time until recovery. In fact, level of religious service attendance is a significant predictor of better and quicker recovery. As is the case with recovery from physical illness, religious coping is the facet of religious experience most strongly related to recovery from depression (Idler, 2002, 2006; Koenig, McCullough, & Larson, 2001; Koenig, 2002; Van Ness & Larson, 2002). Across all religions, the more devout members are usually less afraid of dying and less prone to depression and loneliness than the less devout. Accordingly, individuals for whom faith provides meaning in their lives experience greater feelings of internal control and a

more positive self-concept. The strong association between religion and physical and mental well-being does not imply that religious characteristics are the only or the primary factors causing good health. Religion has beneficial effects on health because there are so many different pathways to it: through the modification of known risk factors, the provision of social support and a sense of control over unhealthy behaviors such as substance use, and the availability of belief systems for coping with adverse circumstances. Regardless of its particular pathways, a growing body of evidence indicates that religious participation has protective effects on physical and mental well-being and helps older adults cope more effectively. In fact, the strength of these relationships between religious involvement and well-being increases over time (Bosworth et al., 2003; Idler, 2006).

Although religiousness itself is beneficial, the sense of belonging and social support derived from the organizational aspects also enhance well-being (Idler, 2006). Across the life course, religious groups' supportive interactions can reduce stress in people's lives. Congruent with the broad concept of productivity, religious institutions also provide innumerable opportunities to care for and serve others in need. The connection between religious activity and health appears to be especially strong among those who volunteer within religious settings. However, the growing numbers of oldest-old who experience functional limitations may have difficulties dealing with the demands of attendance, despite the social support it provided in their past. This suggests that religious institutions need to assess their accessibility and, if necessary, provide transportation, minimize physical barriers such as stairs, and organize healthier members to accompany elders to worship services (Cnaan, Boddie, & Kang, 2005; Benjamin, 2004; Nelson-Becker, 2005; Roff et al., 2006).

Fortunately, a growing number of religious institutions are now reaching out to their aging members by offering transportation, making large-print publications and hearing-assistance devices available, and visiting those who are homebound or in hospitals. Religious institutions are also distinctive for having memberships that cut across the entire life course, creating opportunities for intergenerational interaction and reciprocity. Yet religious institutions often encounter the paradox that as their congregation ages and faces increased need, fiscal resources diminish (Cnaan, 2002; Idler, 2006). In addition, as public social services continue to lose their funding, religious institutions are expected to play a greater role in providing counseling, referral to services, and illness prevention/health promotion. The role of faith-based services that receive federal support, however, raises complex issues regarding interactions between church and state that require ongoing dialogue among religious leaders, ethicists, constitutional scholars, and gerontological practitioners (Brooks & Koenig, 2002; Cnaan & Boddie, 2002).

The Value of Spiritual Well-Being

Spirituality, the belief in a relationship with a higher power, is a broader concept than religion or religiosity; it provides an interpretive framework for individuals to make sense of the world—who they are and how they should live. Definitions of spirituality emphasize an individual's personal experience, while religiosity refers to a person's experience within the context of organized religion (Crowther et al., 2002; Parker et al., 2003). Spirituality is defined in multiple ways:

- a human quest for meaning, sense of purpose, and moral principles in relation to one's deepest convictions and experiences about the nature of reality
- a relationship with that which is sacred in life and transcends the ordinary limits of the body, ego, linear space, and time
- wisdom in which the individual tries to achieve balance in life
- self-transcendence, or crossing a boundary beyond the self, being supported by some power greater than oneself

- achievement of meaning and purpose for one's continued existence
- sense of the wholeness of life and connectedness to the universe, nature, and a higher power
- awe or unconditional joy
- giving and receiving support through affiliation with others
- intuitive nonverbal understanding of how to cope with life's circumstances (Canda & Smith, 2001; Hodge, 2003; Nelson-Becker et al., 2006)

People express spiritual needs in both religious and nonreligious forms. Consistent with the theory of gerotranscendence described in Chapter 8, older adults are likely to communicate a sense of spirituality by seeking the meaning and purpose of life, examining the significance of past events, and wondering what will happen after death (Dalby, 2006; Tornstam, 2005). As they age, people may also turn to spirituality as they contemplate the legacy they hope to leave behind. Only small proportions of adults in national studies describe themselves as "spiritual but not religious," whereas the majority define themselves as both religious and spiritual, which makes it difficult to determine the unique effects of these two dimensions on physical and mental well-being. Those who view themselves as spiritual but not religious appear to be rejecting participation in organized religion, but emphasizing personal spiritual practices—praying or meditating, appreciating nature, applying spiritual principles to everyday life, and practicing positive emotions such as gratitude and forgiveness. Baby boomers are less likely than the pre-World War II cohort to say they are "religious and spiritual" or "religious only," but they are more likely to say "spiritual only." With increased spiritual diversity in our society, associated with the immigration of growing numbers of Muslims, Hindus, and Buddhists, boomers are likely to relate to a wider set of both religious and spiritual possibilities (Ardelt & Koenig, 2006; Marler & Hadaway, 2002; Nelson-Becker, 2004; Smith & Seokho, 2005).

High levels of spirituality, as measured by closeness to a supreme power, are associated with mental health indicators such as purpose and meaning in life, self-esteem, life satisfaction, and perceived quality of life. Similarly, spiritual beliefs influence definitions of health, prevention and self-management of illness, interactions with health care providers, and coping with physical illness, depression, and other life challenges (Atchley, 2008; Fry, 2000; Harvey & Silverman, 2007; Idler, 2006; Keyes & Reitzes, 2007; Koenig, 2007; Nelson-Becker, 2005; Yoon & Lee, 2007). Spirituality can serve as an effective coping strategy that provides mental and social support, and the ability to derive meaning from everyday lives. Such findings are consistent with the relationships between religiousness and health, because many of the private forms of religious participation (e.g., prayer, meditation, personal rituals) are similar, whether people define themselves as religious or spiritual (Ano & Vasconcelles, 2005; Okon, 2005; Shreve-Niger & Edelstein, 2004).

Aging can be characterized as a spiritual journey in which the person aims to achieve integration across a number of areas—biological, psychological, social, and spiritual. An ageless self—that is, a person who is not preoccupied or discouraged by his or her aging—has an identity that maintains continuity and is on a spiritual journey in time, despite age-related physical and social changes. For such an individual, being old per se is neither a central feature of the self nor the source of its meaning. Spiritual deepening can also come from confronting and working through doubt and uncertainty. For others, spirituality is a state of being rather than of doing— of approaching others with kindness, openness, forgiveness and grace to their unique way of manifesting their spirituality. It is a way to experience others authentically without judging or evaluating them. Confronting negative images of aging, loss, and death is believed to be essential for psychological-spiritual growth and healthy aging. In fact, dealing with loss can be one of the greatest spiritual challenges for elders. Autobiographical storytelling, journal keeping, and empathic interactions with others are useful in supporting older persons' spiritual wholeness.

The central role of spirituality in many older adults' lives, especially among women, elders of color, and immigrants, has numerous implications for professionals working with them. Many faith traditions emphasize the importance of silence in creating space to experience spirituality, with the silence of meditation or prayer as a way to nourish our spirituality. For example, Muslim elders need a private place to pray. In hospice programs, where a sense of purpose positively affects subjective well-being, patients, workers, and families can experience profound togetherness out of shared silence (Ardelt & Koenig, 2006). In long-term care facilities where spirituality may provide comfort, consolidation, hope, meaning and purpose, and a positive outlook, residents, staff, and families may also find that silence has value (Schwarz & Cottrell, 2007). Spiritual reflections and experiences can also be a source of insight for both practitioners and older clients. When practitioners are open to cultivating conversations about spirituality with older adults, they can create common experiential ground that transcends the confines of specific faith traditions, opens opportunities for incorporating spirituality into all aspects of everyday life, and allows treatment interventions that take account of spiritual variations.

MEDITATION AS A FORM OF SPIRITUALITY

Carl, age 68, is an active volunteer and employed part time. No matter how busy he is, however, he always manages to set aside a half hour in the morning to meditate. Since he started meditating at age 62, his blood pressure has decreased, he has fewer health problems and a calm, positive outlook on life. He describes his meditation to his friends as the center of his spiritual journey.

They are also better equipped to respect cultural norms and accommodate spiritual practices, such as Muslim ablutions, in health care settings. (Cullinane, 2008; Hodge, 2004a; Nelson-Becker et al., 2006; Snodgrass, 2009).

Historically, the medical profession has taken a predominantly biological perspective toward aging, overlooking psychological, emotional, and spiritual factors. There is increasing acceptance that physicians and other health care professions should introduce questions of religion or spirituality into patient care, particularly because failing to address spirituality can overlook a source of patient strength (Awara & Fasey, 2008; Idler, 2006; Miller & Thoresen, 2003). Practitioners who view spiritual well-being as important to older people's physical and mental health have developed instruments to assess spiritual interests and assets, such as personal values, philosophy, and sense of purpose (Larrimore, Parker, & Crowther, 2002; Nelson-Becker, 2005b; Nelson-Becker, Nakashima, & Canda, 2007). A spiritual assessment conducted in an open, inquiring manner would include questions such as:

- What helps you experience a deep sense of meaning, purpose, and moral perspective in your life?
- Do you consider yourself religious or a person of faith? Do you consider yourself to be spiritual?
- If so, what terms for referring to spirituality, religion, or faith do you prefer?
- Would you like to incorporate spirituality or religion in our work together?

> **POINTS TO PONDER**
>
> Ask an older person—a relative, neighbor, or close friend—whether he or she perceives himself or herself as spiritual. What does spirituality mean to the individual? How has that meaning developed over time?

Some health-promotion screening tools include questions on the individual's spiritual or philosophic values, life goal-setting, and approach to answering questions, such as: What is the meaning of my life? How can I increase the quality of my life? Depending on elders' responses to such questions, health care providers may encourage them to seek religious support or reconnect with a spiritual community (Hodge, 2003, 2004b; Nelson-Becker et al., 2006).

Civic Engagement

The **civic engagement** of elders is closely related to the concept of productive aging. Both perspectives emphasize individual responsibility, self-reliance, and contribution. Fueled by the concern that civil society is weakened by Americans' growing focus on private self-focused activities, increasing attention is given to tapping older adults' vast civic potential—a non-monetized form of activity. Baby boomers represent the first generation reaching retirement age in which a large proportion of men and women have amassed a lifetime of knowledge and skills that can be used to benefit communities and society as a whole. In this sense, civic engagement can be conceptualized as a retirement role for older adults (Kaskie et al., 2008; Wilson & Harlow-Rosentraub, 2008). According to Mark Freedman, whose national organization, **Civic Ventures** provides guidance to older adults seeking civic engagement opportunities, "older adults might produce a windfall for American communities in the twenty-first century...and along the way bring opportunities for greater fulfillment and purpose in later years" (Freedman, 2002; Freedman & Adler, 2005). Additionally, the Gerontological Society of America, American Society on Aging, and National Council on the Aging have major civic engagement initiatives that, over time, constitute a social change movement. For the first time, the reauthorization of the Older Americans Act (2006) called for strategies to utilize older adults to address critical local needs and national concerns.

Civic engagement is generally defined as the process in which individuals actively participate in the life of their communities through individual and collective activities, such as voting, joining community groups, and service volunteering, oftentimes in nonprofits. Civic engagement is thus viewed as a vital element in the maintenance of livable communities, described in Chapter 11 (Hinterlong & Williamson, 2006–2007; Morrow-Howell et al., 2009; Portney, 2005; Sampson et al., 2005). However, some studies equate civic engagement with volunteerism only and overlook other activities associated with civic life, such as voting, community leadership and political activism, cleaning up a local park, assisting a homebound friend or neighbor, joining in neighborhood mutual aid activities, staying informed about current events, and caregiving of young and old (Hinterlong & Williamson, 2006–2007); Kaskie et al., 2009; Martinson & Minkler, 2006).

Both political conservatives and progressives advocate civic engagement, but for different reasons. Conservatives distinguish between the civic and the political, and favor voluntary involvement as a way to address social problems rather than governmental solutions. Older adults as volunteers, often through faith-based organizations, are viewed as a way to fill gaps created by budgetary cuts in social service programs. Core concepts of governmental programs to protect elders, such as Social Security, are viewed as inconsistent with civic engagement. In contrast, progressives advocate for elders to be politically active to ensure that public policies safeguard the rights of vulnerable elders (Eberly & Streeter, 2002; Holstein & Minkler, 2003; Hudson, 2006–2007, 2007; Martinson, 2006–2007). The conservative definition of civic engagement overlooks organizations of elders that aim to foster social change and promote social justice, such as the Gray Panthers and the Older Women's League. This social justice perspective was often articulated by Maggie Kuhn, the founder of the Gray Panthers: "[the] old, having the benefit of life experience, the time to get things done and the least to lose by sticking their necks out, are in a perfect position to serve as advocates for the larger public good" (Kuhn, 1991). Progressives also contend that a narrow focus on volunteering and individual betterment devalues and detracts from grass-roots civic activism, promotes engagement as "social therapy," and minimizes the need for broader institutional and policy-level changes (Holstein, 2007; Martinson, 2006–2007; Martinson & Minkler, 2006). To illustrate this distincttion, "volunteering in a soup kitchen will help hungry individuals in a town, but will do nothing to address broader problems of homelessness and poverty" (Theiss-Morse & Hibbing, 2004, p. 237–238). This tension between individual and government responsibility for basic human needs, intertwined with civic engagement as political activism, was at the heart of the 2005 White House Conference on Aging, which emphasized individual, family, and community responsibilities over those of government and the need for systemic changes (Hudson, 2006; Martinson, 2006–2007; Moody, in press).

From a social constructionist perspective, as discussed in Chapter 8, the current focus on civic engagement—similar to productive and successful aging—may inadvertently devalue those for whom engagement is neither possible nor chosen, such as elders caring for partners with dementia or for grandchildren, or having to work minimum wage jobs to make ends meet. Civic engagement is also criticized for excluding low- and middle-income elders who cannot afford to volunteer and may have the highest rates of disability and poor health. As noted above, some programs—such as the SCSEP, funded by AOA, and **Foster Grandparents**—provide small stipends for elder volunteers and must be brought into the national discourse about civic engagement. While some might argue that such paid public service is not volunteerism in the pure sense (i.e., nonpaid work), policy makers need to recognize that the only way that some older adults, especially elders of color, can participate is to offset their costs by a modest stipend, child care, reimbursement for gas and transportation, and, if necessary, support for time away from employment or caregiving responsibilities. From a social justice perspective, such programmatic supports are essential to ensure that low-income elders' voices are heard by policy makers (Holstein, 2007; Morrow-Howell et al., 2009).

Advocates for civic engagement may also overlook other ways of attaining meaning and fulfillment in later life, as reflected in the concept of gerotranscendence. Social constructionists argue for defining civic engagement broadly as ways to flourish, grow, and live a good old age in whatever ways are possible and desired. They also contend that all elders should be honored and their dignity respected, regardless of whether or not they choose to be engaged in this manner (Holstein, 2007; Martinson, 2006–2007). From their viewpoint, civic engagement should be broadened to encompass a wide range of activities that foster social connectedness—or the "social capital of the community." Such community-level reciprocities—keeping an eye on each other's house or on the children in the neighborhood—may be more salient for both individual and community well-being than formal volunteering. In fact, what people do may matter less than the fact that they are involved in their community and experience a feeling of belonging (Putnam, 2002). Because most elders seek meaning and purpose—personal, spiritual, religious, artistic, political—in their lives, the challenge for modern society is to create purposeful roles for all older adults (Emerman, 2006).

Membership in Voluntary Associations

Given our societal emphasis on being active and productive, voluntary association membership as one form of civic engagement is often presumed to be a "good" leisure activity that positively affects physical and mental health. These benefits appear to be associated with having a sense of control and social engagement (Newson & Kemps, 2005; Verghese et al., 2003). For example, researchers found that participating in a formal community-based cultural program had positive effects on overall health, doctor visits, prescription use, loneliness, and morale among older adults whose mean age was 80 (Cohen, 2005; Cohen et al., 2006). Overall, older people tend to be more involved in voluntary organizations than are younger adults, although membership in faith-based organizations is the only type that actually increases with age (Prisuta, 2004). Membership is most closely tied to social class and varies among cultures. When social class is taken into account, older adults show considerable stability in their general level of voluntary association participation from middle age until their 60s (Cutler & Hendricks, 2000).

Similar to most retirement activities, characteristics that influence voluntary association membership include age, gender, race, ethnicity, prior activities and memberships, health, and social class. Older women are more active in voluntary associations than men, perhaps because of their multiple roles in earlier years that enhanced their social networks and opportunities to join organizations. Older African Americans have higher rates of organizational membership than do whites or other elders of color. Nevertheless, for both blacks and whites, membership is highest among those with better health and higher income and education levels. Some racial differences exist in the types of associations joined. Older African Americans are especially likely to belong to church-related groups and social and recreational clubs; older whites frequently are members of nationality organizations and senior citizen groups, while older Latinos participate in fraternal and service-oriented organizations, mutual aid societies, and "hometown" clubs.

Senior centers are one type of voluntary association. With over 16,000 such centers nationally, they vary widely in the type of services offered, ranging from purely recreational events to social action or the delivery of social and health services, including nutrition programs, health screening, health promotion, and support groups for caregivers and grandparents. The Older Americans Act identifies senior centers as preferred focal points for comprehensive, coordinated case management service delivery, especially social and nutritional supports to promote elders' autonomy and remaining in the community. In recent years, programs focused on "aging in place"—such as health promotion, adult day health, mental health services, caregiver support, and community ombudsman—have expanded, and are associated with improved physical and mental health, enhanced friendships, and increased health-promoting behaviors (Aday, 2003). Despite the range of activities and services offered, less than 20 percent of older persons participate in senior centers. Furthermore, centers typically draw from a relatively narrow population, reaching primarily healthy, lower- to middle-class individuals under age 85 with a lifetime of joining groups. Nationwide, individuals who are

generally less advantaged, but not the least advantaged, are most likely to join in senior center activities. Already socially active, they view centers as arenas for enhanced social interaction (Pardasani, 2004a).

Senior centers face programmatic challenges. Staff are concerned that rapidly aging participants are not being replaced by the young-old, and some centers are eliminating "senior" from their names, marketing and developing more inclusive language such as "community or intergenerational centers." They may offer new fee-based programs, such as fitness, to attract the young-old while trying to retain their current participants who are increasingly frail with more traditional programming (Pardasani, 2004a). The Older Americans Act requires that agencies receiving public funding concentrate on providing services to those most in need, who tend to be low-income, rural, people of color, or frail elders (Wacker, Roberto, & Piper, 2003). But elders of color are consistently underrepresented in senior centers, even in diverse communities (Pardasani, 2003). Lack of transportation, inadequate facilities, language differences, staff with limited cultural competence, and nonrelevant programming are barriers to senior center participation faced by elders of color. However, increasing the representation of culturally diverse and bilingual staff and culturally specific and linguistically appropriate programming can foster their participation.

When center programs do take account of specific needs and kinship and mutual aid networks by culture and social class, African American elders are slightly more likely than whites to attend. Similarly, Latino participation increases if staff speak Spanish and if centers serve ethnic-specific congregate meals on-site and offer socialization opportunities with members of their own communities (Pardasani, 2004b). Asian American elders are more likely to participate if they are in relatively good health and if the senior centers are located in their own neighborhood and offer programs in

---

REASONS FOR LOW LEVELS OF PARTICIPATION IN SENIOR CENTERS BY OLDER ADULTS

- lack of interest in the center's activities (i.e., poor fit between elder's needs and center services)
- programming that does not address the needs of young-old and oldest-old
- inadequate fluency in English
- poor health
- inadequate transportation to the center
- desire not to be with only old people
- not identifying self as a "senior"
- the small proportion of men in many centers
- the low percentage of elders of color in many centers

their native language (Lai, 2001). However, some observers contend that such targeting of services runs counter to the universal nature of the Older Americans Act and may reduce the participation and voluntary financial contributions of those relatively more advantaged older people who currently attend senior centers. The challenge for senior centers is to reach out to the broadest cross-section of the older population while expanding the participation of young-old and elders from culturally diverse backgrounds (Pardasani, 2004b).

In general, activity in community organizations such as senior centers is positively associated with well-being, improved functional and cognitive status and physical health, and expanded social interaction—all conducive to promoting active aging, although the benefits and protective effects may differ slightly by gender (Greenfield & Marks, 2004, 2007; Menec, 2003). Interactions with others who are similar in age and interests often result in friendships, higher morale, perceived well-being, a sense of belonging, mutual exchanges of resources, and collective activity, although some of these benefits may be attributed to greater levels of health, income, and education. Consistent with the broader concept of productivity, voluntary associations can also serve to maintain the social integration of elders, countering losses in roles and in social relationships. The most satisfied

members of organizations are those who become involved in order to have new experiences, achieve something, be creative, and help others. Such members, in turn, participate actively through planning and leadership. Opportunities for more active participation are found in senior advocacy groups such as the Older Women's League and AARP, or in organizations such as advisory boards to Area Agencies on Aging where older people must, by charter, be in leadership roles. Overall, voluntary association membership appears to be most satisfying when it provides options for active, intense involvement, and significant leadership roles.

Volunteer Work and NonProfit Organizations

Similar to participation in voluntary associations, volunteering is more characteristic of our society than others (Independent Sector, 2006a, 2006b). Volunteer work is distinguished by choosing to serve or help others, rather than by its unpaid nature or by formal activity, and can be formal (within an organization) or informal (such as time spent helping others in one's neighborhood or community). Volunteering thus has value both to the individual because of its association with autonomy and choice and to society because of its public service component. With cutbacks in public funding, nonprofit, service, educational, and religious organizations increasingly rely on volunteers to accomplish their missions and provide services. The Depression era cohort of older adults, parents of baby boomers, were generally actively engaged in community service and civic engagement in middle age, and have continued this pattern in old-old age. The boomers are different in terms of how they spend their time. They vote less, read newspapers less, are less likely to join religious or civic organizations, and tend to change activities abruptly. In addition, female baby boomers are more likely to be employed and therefore may have less time to volunteer than did their mothers (Morrow-Howell, Hinterlong, & Sherraden, 2001; Putnam, 2002, 2004).

VOLUNTEERING AS A SUBSTITUTE FOR PAST ROLES

Ted was a teacher of sixth-grade science in an inner-city public school for 35 years. When he retired at age 57, he began a successful second career selling real estate. Now, at age 72, he continues to work on average 2 days per week. He enjoys the contact with people and finds his work very different from teaching. Because he believes it is important to give back to his community, he also volunteers as a tutor in an after-school program run by his church for neighborhood "latchkey" children.

Volunteerism rates are highest among adults at midlife:

- 51 percent at age 34 to 44
- 48 percent of those age 45 to 54
- 41 percent from 65 to 74 years
- 9 percent among those age 75 and older

Higher volunteerism rates earlier in life are often associated with work or family roles, and thus with having more rather than fewer obligations and commitments (Prisuta, 2004). It may also reflect that younger adults are likely to volunteer in programs that benefit their children, such as in Parent-Teacher-Student Associations (PTSA). It is estimated that slightly more than 24 percent of all adults age 65 and older volunteer, a rate that is lower than adults as a whole (nearly 29 percent) (Rozario, 2006–2007).When volunteering is redefined to include informal contributions (e.g., helping neighbors), however, an additional 50 percent volunteer informally (Zedlweski & Schaner, 2005). Although volunteerism rates are slightly lower for adults age 65 and older than for adults in their 40s and 50s, their level of involvement in terms of time spent volunteering (approximately 96 hours a year) is greater than the younger age-group (about 50 hours a year) (Rozario, 2006–2007). Consistent with socioemotional selectivity theory, older volunteers place a higher value on meaningful relationships and derive satisfaction from helping others. They tend to reduce the number of volunteer organizations in which they participate, but the total time spent volunteering increases in a linear fashion until about age 80. For most retirees, volunteering is apparently not a work substitute, although it may protect them from negative effects of retirement. In fact, a growing number of young-old adults (about 29 percent) are volunteering while employed. In such instances, full-time work combined with low levels of volunteering enhances mental health (Hao, 2008). Most elders want roles that fully

AN ACTIVE VOLUNTEER AT AGE 80

Edna was an elementary school librarian forced to retire at age 62 to care for her sick husband. After his death, she was back in the local school working 4 or 5 days a week as a substitute librarian. She is universally loved by the kids, and the parents and teachers respect her ability to relate to a wide range of children, managing to hook them into "listening to reading."

engage their capacities and interests and in ways that are meaningful to them or matter to their communities (Wilson & Hawlow-Rosentraub, 2008; Wilson & Simson, 2006). Reasons for older adults not volunteering typically include that no organization or member of their social network has asked them to do so (Cartensen & Lockenhoff, 2003; Hendricks & Cutler, 2004; Windsor, Anstey, & Rodgers, 2008; Rozario, 2006–2007). The primary sites for volunteering among older adults are religious organizations, followed by social and community services and hospitals (U.S. Census Bureau, 2006).

DIFFERENCES IN VOLUNTEERISM BY GENDER AND RACE Studies that identified lower rates of volunteerism among women suggest that this may be a result of more women entering the paid workforce. On the other hand, higher rates of volunteerism are found among employed adults than those who are not (Rozario, 2006–2007). Elders of color are more likely to participate in informal than formal volunteering. In fact, the term "volunteering" and "community service" can have negative connotations in some communities of color, similar to court-ordered community service. Immigrant groups often value helping others, but the concept of volunteer is uniquely American and does not translate into their familiar concept of informal service. Nevertheless, volunteering as a way to help others through informal networks is frequent in communities of color, such as through African American churches and mutual aid associations. When informal volunteering is included in definitions, African American elders report slightly more hours of volunteering than whites (Carlton-LaNey, 2006–2007; Rozario, 2006–2007). Mutual aid (e.g., providing food and lodging to older persons) is common in American Indian communities. Volunteer activities among Asian and Pacific Islander elders reinforce the continuation of their value systems. Older Chinese, for example, often work through family associations or benevolent societies. Some Japanese elders participate in clubs that are an extension of the "family helping itself" concept rooted in traditional Japanese culture. The Latino community emphasizes informal volunteering, such as self-help, mutual aid, and neighborhood assistance, but has the lowest rate of formal volunteering (Zedlewski & Schaner, 2006).

Given these diverse meanings, organizations are changing how they define and promote volunteering by emphasizing "neighboring" and "community involvement." The Legacy Leadership Institute, which develops and tests models of meaningful civic engagement and leadership, does not use the word "volunteering" in their recruitment materials, but instead emphasizes "Are you ready for your next challenge?" (Wilson & Hawlow-Rosentraub, 2008). More programs are recognizing that they need to help volunteers in underserved communities address their economic needs. For example, in addition to SCSEP, **Experience Corps** sponsors school-based programs where older adults work one-on-one with young children, create before- and after-school programs, and receive a modest stipend for their service. The **Senior Companion Program** also offers low-income elders a stipend.

PROGRAMS TO EXPAND VOLUNTEERISM   Within the past 40 years, a number of public and private initiatives have increased community service

> ### VOLUNTEERING AS A SOURCE OF SUPPORT
>
> Mary, a homemaker and mother of four children, spent her early adult years involved with Scouts and PTA and teaching Sunday school. Her last child left home when Mary was 52, and she felt "lost" because there was no one to "need" her in the same ways her children had. At 53, she began volunteering, answering the phone for a community center that served children and elders, and found a new role. When she was widowed at age 70, she increased the hours of volunteering to fill the lonely hours when she especially missed her husband. Because she has never driven, she takes the bus one day a week to the community center. Now age 80, she was recently honored by the city at a special reception for her 8,000 hours of volunteer service.

and civic engagement by older persons, as summarized in the box on the next page. Other approaches have sought to expand volunteer involvement; for example, workplace volunteering allows companies to improve their communities while building teamwork skills and morale and enhancing their corporate public image. In some instances, employees use set hours of paid time each month to participate in community service and involvement in children's education. As a sign of the times, Single Volunteers, an organization with 18 chapters nationally, brings single adults together for service events and indirectly as a way to make new friendships.

BENEFITS OF VOLUNTEERISM   Volunteer programs serve *two major social benefits*: (1) provide individuals with meaningful social roles that enhance their well-being; and (2) furnish organizations with experienced, reliable workers at minimal cost.

Volunteering is increasingly viewed as a central component of active aging and healthy communities (O'Neill & Lindberg, 2005;

Wilson & Harlow-Rosentraub, 2008). As described above for elders active in voluntary community organizations, older volunteers generally experience psychological and physical health benefits, such as greater life satisfaction, self-rated health, sense of accomplishment, cognitive activity, and feelings of usefulness. They also have lower rates of functional disability and depression (Cartensen, 2006; Corporation for National and Community Service, 2007; Fried et al., 2004; Greenfield & Marks, 2004; Hendricks & Cutler, 2004; Lum & Lightfoot, 2005; Menec, 2003; Musick & Wilson, 2003). In fact, both moderate levels of physical fitness and volunteering are found to lower the risk of mortality. This relationship between volunteering and lower mortality rates may occur when volunteering provides older adults who lack other major sources of role identity with opportunities to develop more meaning and purpose in their lives, expand their social networks, and perceive that they have made a difference in others' lives. The direction of causality is unclear—whether volunteerism improves well-being or if individuals with better health and functioning are more likely to be engaged, with both relationships likely to be salient (Avlund et al., 2004; Fried et al., 2004; Greenfield & Marks, 2004, 2007; Harris & Thoresen, 2005; Hinterlong & Williamson, 2006–2007; Lum & Lightfoot, 2005; Morrow-Howell, Hong, & Tang, 2009; Shmotkin, Blumstein, & Modan, 2003; Zedlewski & Schaner, 2006).

In a recent study examining time spent volunteering and well-being, the psychosocial benefits were greatest for those who engaged in moderate levels of volunteering (at least 100 hours of volunteer activity per year, but fewer than 800 hours). Volunteering more than 800 hours per year was associated with lower levels of well-being, instead creating feelings of obligation, strain, and burden, especially for women (Windsor et al., 2008). This suggests that nonprofits utilizing volunteers should take account of what is realistic in terms of time commitments and resources, such as the costs of transportation to and from volunteer activities (Li & Ferraro, 2006; Morrow-Howell et al., 2003; Musick & Wilson, 2003). Furthermore, Morrow-Howell and colleagues (2009) found that volunteers who received a modest stipend and reported better training and support from agency staff experienced the most benefits from volunteering.

VOLUNTEER OPPORTUNITIES FOR OLDER ADULTS

- Ask a Friend Campaign: aims to increase the number of volunteers benefiting local communities
- Civic Ventures Experience Corps: tutors and mentors in public schools
- Civic Ventures: offers the Purpose Prize to recognize older individuals for exemplary service and the BreakThrough Award for innovative organizations
- Environmental Alliance for Senior Involvement: environmental protection activities
- Family Friends: advocates and mentors young children
- Foster Grandparents: offers support to children with special needs
- National Council on the Aging: RespectAbility provides technical assistance to nonprofits to more effectively utilize older volunteers
- Older Americans Act programs: assist at meal sites; offer escort and transportation services, home repair, counseling, legal aid
- Peace Corps: places older volunteers to meet needs in other countries
- Retired and Senior Volunteer Program (RSVP): funds volunteers in schools, hospitals, and other community settings
- Service Corps of Retired Executives (SCORE): retired executives and small business owners assist small businesses and first-time entrepreneurs
- Volunteers in Parks: volunteer programs with the National Parks Service
- Senior Companionship Program: gives financial support to low-income adults age 60 and older to provide in-home services to elders in need

The experiences of Edna and Ted (see boxes on pages 527 and 528) illustrate how some older adults achieve life satisfaction when volunteering builds on previous professional skills as teachers and mentors. Mary's activities, (page 529) portray how volunteering can support older adults in generative roles. A number of trends will influence the meaning and functions of volunteerism for older persons. Those who are critical of the growing emphasis on civic engagement see volunteerism as a way to fill gaps in services created by growing federal and state budget cuts (Holstein, 2007). With increased national attention on self-help and mutual aid, some people may choose to become more active in cross-generational neighborhood and community activities. Regardless of the type of volunteer and informal helping networks, the challenge remains one of whether and how to involve older people who are low-income, persons of color, living alone, frail and disabled, or from areas with inadequate public transportation. Volunteer programs in the future may need to expand outreach capacities to such elders, allow flexible schedules, provide accessible training, compensate them monetarily, or provide other benefits such as transportation and meals. Regardless of the type of volunteerism, the documented benefits suggest that more older persons should be encouraged to volunteer (Freedman, 2001, 2002; Menec, 2003; Morrow-Howell et al., 2003; Zedlewski & Schaner, 2006).

Lifelong Learning Programs

In the past 40 years, creative learning initiatives that are constructed around images of productive aging for midlife and older adults have developed nationally and internationally. Most of these are entrepreneurial, or part of the "silver industry" geared to the young-old with discretionary resources (Moody, 2004–2005). Lifelong Learning Institutes (LLI), typically linked with colleges and universities, are unique not only because members are in charge, but also because they are based on a financial model that requires participants to provide labor and leadership to pay for their own continuing education. Osher Lifelong Learning Institutes are a type of LLIs at colleges and universities. The nature of course offerings vary, with some programs hiring expert faculty and others utilizing volunteers and hosting a journal and national conferences to bring together members of diverse communities (Corley & Monnier, 2007; Manhiemer, 2008). LLIs are also affiliated with the Elderhostel Institute Network (EIN).

ELDERHOSTEL   One of the oldest and best known is **Elderhostel,** renamed Exploritas in 2009, where older learners attend "learning adventures" on campuses and affiliated locations throughout the country and the world. Each one has an educational component and is often associated with a university, whether the group is studying architecture in London, seals in Antarctica, monkeys in Belize, antiquities in Greece, or archaeology in the Southwest U.S. To date, Elderhostel has involved over 150,000 adults in 8,000 programs at over

Elderhostel (Exploritas) can include active learning experiences such as sailing.

1,500 different academic institutions. Offered in all 50 states and in 90 countries, the oldest participant to date is 103 (Elderhostel, 2007). To cater to the young-old and boomers, Exploritas, open to all adults who are curious, adventuresome and open to experiencing the world through travel, now offers more physically challenging tours than past Elderhostel programs.

Some gerontology certificate programs prepare significant numbers of older people for roles as advocates and service providers. Community colleges, because of their accessibility, are ideal settings in which to design human service programs that offer older adults ways to be of service. A few states recognize the market for lifelong learning and are funding a range of programs, including liberal arts education, peer learning groups, health promotion, training, and intergenerational service learning. A growing number of organizations now offer leadership training for older persons in advocacy and nonprofit organizational management. With the growth of distance learning and Web-based instruction, baby boomers provide a growing market for online educational programs.

As suggested in Chapter 5, educational programs need to take account of older learners' particular needs, such as self-paced learning and accommodation of hearing and vision decrements. As lifelong learning options increasingly become a function of the marketplace, strategies are needed to make such programs accessible to low-income and historically disadvantaged populations who may have had limited educational experiences earlier in life. Certificate programs and vocational education will also be in demand as older adults move into second and third careers, perhaps with an emphasis on technical and business-related training needs. Retirement communities associated with colleges and universities are likely to grow as well, along with the number of older adults taking advantage of tuition-free courses in a wide range of academic settings (Manheimer, 2008).

Lifelong learning programs for all elders represent an area ripe for further development and funding, especially as baby boomers seek new learning challenges.

Political Participation

Political acts range from voting to participation in a political party or a political action group, to grassroots campaign work, to running for or holding elective office. In examining older people's political behavior, three factors make interpretation of the relationship between age and political behavior complex:

1. stages in the life course
2. cohort effects
3. historical or period effects, as discussed in Chapter 1

Historical factors influence interpretations of older people's political behavior, particularly analyses of the extent of conservatism. Age differences in conservatism/liberalism are less a matter of people becoming more conservative or liberal than of their maintaining these values throughout life. Successive generations entering the electorate since World War II have become comparatively more liberal, with older people more likely in the past to identify with the Democratic Party since the mid-1980s. This shift may have been due in part to increases in low-income and retired blue-collar adults who were opposed to the Republican Party's stance on issues, such as Social Security and Medicare. More recently, older voters have appeared to be more conservative on policy issues and less supportive of the Democractic Party. On the other hand, voters age 50 and older—which includes the baby boomers—were the core of President Obama's winning coalition in 2008, delivering more votes than any other age demographic. The importance of voters age 50 and older to Obama's victory

Older and younger generations unite around environmental actions that will benefit future generations.

was especially evident in the battleground swing states (Bedard, 2008; Fisher, 2008).

Overall, various cohorts of older adults during the past 60 years have distributed their votes among presidential candidates in roughly the same proportions as other age-groups. In other words, voting differences are greater within than between age groups. Individuals of all ages are not ideologically consistent in their issue-specific preferences, such as Medicare, Social Security, or taxes. Furthermore, both older and younger people may hold beliefs on specific issues that contradict their views on more general principles. Given the older population's heterogeneity, differences of opinion on any political issue are likely to equal or exceed variations between age-groups and are due to social class and partisanship more than age (Binstock, 2006).

Voting Behavior

Older Americans are more likely than younger adults to vote. The voting rates of older adults have remained steady or have increased over the past 35 years, while those of other age-groups have declined. The participation rate of older people in the last eight presidential elections has been higher than the rates for all other age groups; although in the 2008 election, all age groups turned out in higher proportions than in previous decades (Binstock, 2006; Hudson, 2007, 2008).

- Older adults are more likely than younger age groups to pay attention to the news and to be more knowledgeable about politics and public affairs generally, demonstrating higher levels of "civic competence."
- They indicate the highest level of interest in political campaigns and public affairs generally
- Strong partisans are more likely to vote, and the current cohort of older people identifies with the major political parties more strongly than do younger persons.
- They make campaign contributions at higher rates than younger people and are active in contacting their representatives regarding proposed legislation
- They participate in a variety of political organizations (Binstock, 2006; 2006–2007).

In instances where voter turnout among older adults is low, factors other than aging are probably the reason, including gender, race, ethnicity, immigration status, education, and generational variables, as well as access to the polls. For example, the voter turnout among persons of color is lower than that of whites. The lack of political acculturation of some Latinos appears to influence their relatively low rates of participation; for example, Mexican American elders, some of whom lived under the fear of deportation, tend to be more cautious and conservative in their political involvement. On the other hand, older African

Americans who are active in their communities, with a strong sense of responsibility, a Democratic identity, and higher levels of education, are more likely to vote than other historically underserved groups. Similarly, Cuban American elders represent a strong voting bloc in Florida, where they have long influenced local, state, and national policies. These and earlier findings suggest that differences in political participation rates among older people of color do not reflect age or race per se, but rather lower educational levels, feelings of powerlessness, cohort and immigration experiences, and real or perceived barriers to voting and other political activities.

To public officials and the media, the older electorate is viewed as exerting substantial political influence beyond what their numbers and voting record might suggest, as reflected in the following perspectives on "senior power."

Senior Power

Research on senior power reflects an ongoing debate about whether age serves as a catalyst for a viable political movement.

PROPONENTS OF THE SENIOR-POWER MODEL OF POLITICS Older people are a powerful political constituency in the policy-making process because legislators and appointed officials are most influenced by those who vote and are political party leaders, as is the case with older people. Because of common values and experiences, older people develop a shared political consciousness that is translated into collective action on old-age-related issues. Better educated, healthier, and with higher incomes, baby boomers are presumed to have more resources essential to political power. The senior-power model also assumes that older cohorts in the future will experience increasing pride, dignity, and shared consciousness about old age and thus define problems collectively.

Although there is little evidence of old-age voting blocs, mass membership interest groups that cast themselves as "representatives" of older voters (e.g., AARP) generally have significant political influence. This occurs because policy makers find it useful and incumbent to invite them to participate in policy activities and thus to be "in touch with" older adults. In addition, AARP tends to heighten its members' political awareness through policy-focused articles in its various publications (Binstock, 2006–2007). The symbolic legitimacy of old-age organizations' participation in interest group politics gives them power in the following ways:

- They have relatively easy informal access to public officials, members of Congress and their staffs, and administrative officials.
- Their legitimacy enables them to obtain public platforms in the national media, congressional hearings, national conferences, and commissions dealing with issues affecting older adults.
- Mass membership groups can mobilize their members in large numbers to contact policy makers and register displeasure (Binstock, 2006–2007).

"Senior citizens" have traditionally been a prime target of campaign efforts in critical states with large blocs of electoral votes, as illustrated by presidential elections in Florida. Both political parties strategize about how to target older adults, given their aggregate numerical importance as voters. In fact, an important form of power available to old-age interest groups is "the electoral bluff"—the perception of being powerful is, in itself, a source of political influence, even though old-age organizations have been unable to swing a decisive bloc of older voters. Whether older people act as a unified bloc or not, many policy makers behave as if there were a "politics of age" founded on cohort-based interest groups, and politicians continue to court elders' votes. Even if older people cannot affect the passage of legislation, they are seen as blocking changes in existing policies, especially when programs such as Social Security and Medicare are threatened. Perceptions of such influence, then, affect the feasibility of major changes in policies on issues affecting elders, even though the political legitimacy of old-age interest groups has eroded over the past decade (Binstock, 2006–2007; Hudson, 2006, 2008).

COUNTERARGUMENT: OLDER PEOPLE ARE NOT A SIGNIFICANT AGE-BASED POLITICAL FORCE Critics of senior power argue that the heterogeneity of the older population precludes their having shared interests around which to coalesce. Most older people, especially the young-old, do not identify themselves as "aged," behave as an old-age-benefits voting bloc, or define problems as stemming from their age. Even though older adults participate in elections at a high rate, they do not appear to vote as a homogeneous group (Binstock, 2006–2007). They distribute their votes among candidates in roughly the same proportion as the electorate as a whole rather than act as a unified group. In fact, it is difficult for those who identify on the basis of age to determine differences between candidates' positions on old-age-policy issues, because no candidate wants to alienate "the senior vote." In addition, older voters are not captives of any single political philosophy, party, or mass organization. In fact, some argue that "the elderly" is really a category created by policy analysts, pension officials, key political figures, and outdated models of interest-group politics and not a sound basis for political mobilization. Since age is only one of many personal characteristics, it cannot predict political behavior or age-group consciousness based on differential access to resources. Nor are these self-interests or old-age policy issues the most important factors in elders' electoral decisions (Binstock, 2006–2007; Hudson, 2006, 2007).

Instead, differences by class, race, and religion increasingly influence older people's political interests (Hudson, 2006). For example, upper- and lower-income older adults are not unified on Social Security or Medicare. Nor do they typically vote as a bloc against increasing property taxes to support public schools. Instead, they generally recognize the importance of education for economic productivity in the future. This example suggests that old-age-related issues are not necessarily more important than other partisan attachments or the characteristics of specific candidates. In fact, it appears that older and younger people are more likely to form alliances along economic, racial, ethnic, sexual identity, gender, and ideological lines than to unite horizontally on the basis of age. **Generations United** is an umbrella organization composed of national, state, and local organizations of different age-groups and represents one such vertical intergenerational coalition. Such organizations acknowledge the mutual interdependence of generations, suggesting common ground on which to build a more inclusive sense of community (Prisuta, 2004).

As an example of cross-age collaborations, middle-income people of all ages may come together around issues of climate change and preserving the environment for future generations. Indeed, older adults are well poised to work with environmental groups around how issues of energy and the environment are vital to the future of younger generations, their communities, and the world. Acting as stewards of the environment, older adults' "legacy work" regarding what will outlive their individual lives is congruent with the theory of gerotranscendence and Erikson's concept of ego integrity. Generations United, for example, has launched environmental campaigns based on intergenerational cooperation (Kaplan & Lui, 2004; Moody, 2008). The Environmental Protection Agency (EPA) creates opportunities for elders to become environmental stewards. One successful project is the Legacy Leadership Institute of the Environmental Coalition, which involves a university-based center on aging with an environmental center (Sykes et al., 2008). As other examples of cross-generational political action, aging advocates increasingly act upon the shared goals with disability rights groups and with low-income groups related to health care reform.

HISTORY OF AGE-BASED GROUPS At first glance, the number, variety, and strength of age-based national organizations appear to support the perspective that older people are a powerful political force. Age-based organizations are effective at building memberships, conducting policy analyses, marshaling grassroots support, and utilizing direct mail and political action. The first age-based politically oriented interest group grew out of the Depression. The Townsend Movement proposed a tax on all business transactions to finance a $200-per-month pension for every pensioner over age 60. However, passage of the Social Security Act in 1935, in which groups of older people played a supporting but not a leading role, slowed the Townsend Movement's momentum, and the organization died out in the 1940s. Most political divisions during the turbulent period of the Depression were class- and labor-based rather than age-based. New Deal legislation on behalf of older people (e.g., Old Age Insurance of the Social Security Act) owed its birth to the hardships of the Great Depression, President Roosevelt's leadership, and reformers' invoking the plight of older people as a strategy for introducing social insurance, not to the influence of an organized bloc of older people (Hudson, 2007). The McClain Movement—another early, age-based organization—aimed to establish financial benefits for older persons through a referendum in the 1938 California elections but lost followers after economic conditions improved in the 1940s. These early groups nevertheless furnished older people with a collective voice and identity.

Organized interest groups of older people did not reemerge until the 1950s and 1960s. Even so, the passage of Medicare in 1965 was due more to the leadership of key politicians than to the political influence of older individuals. However, the presence of successful public policies served to galvanize elders into a self-identified political constituency and created the political base to advocate for later aging network services (Binstock, 2006–2007; Hudson, 2008). Over 1,000 separately organized groups for older adults now exist at the local, state, and national levels, with approximately 100 major national organizations involved in political action on behalf of older persons (Hudson, 2007; Walker, 2006). In many ways, the heterogeneity of the older population is reflected in the variety of organizations themselves, ranging from mass membership groups to nonmembership staff organizations and associations of professionals or service providers. Yet, the very diversity of these groups reduces their ability to act together as a unified bloc. For example, the National Caucus for the Black Aged, the National Hispanic Council on Aging, the National Asian-Pacific Center on Aging, and the National Indian Council on Aging were

created to address political inequities facing specific groups of elders of color. They do not always act in concert with each other or with organizations such as the AARP (formerly known as the American Association of Retired Persons) that have traditionally represented primarily a white, middle-class constituency. The Leadership Council of Aging Organizations (LCAO) consists of 54 member organizations that aim to represent older adults' interests, although recent activity has tended to focus on service providers rather than on older adults themselves (Hudson, 2008)

The best-known and largest national organization is **AARP,** which began in 1958 with a small number of older adults working to provide a special group health insurance program. It has now grown to a membership of over 40 million, encompassing almost 50 percent of the nation's population over age 50 and over 13 percent of the population generally. Now using only its acronym rather than its full name, AARP seeks to recruit the young-old and baby boomers who may not consider themselves to be retirees or old. In fact, the minimum age of membership has been lowered from 55 to 50. It has merged its two magazines—*My Generation* for adults ages 50 to 59 and *Modern Maturity* for those older than 60—into *The Magazine,* which does not make age explicit on the cover. An assumption of this merger is that both the young-old and the old-old (who may be their parents) share interests related to health, financial security, and travel. Nevertheless, AARP continues to publish three slightly different versions of *The Magazine* to appeal to cohorts in their 50s, 60s, and beyond. It is also published in Spanish to reach out to the rapidly growing young-old Latino population. In addition, AARP spends millions to advertise in popular magazines such as *Time* and *Newsweek* with ads displaying healthy, robust, and often physically attractive older adults. In a similar spirit, they now sponsor 10K runs, marathons, a wide range of fitness activities, and adventure travel. Such ads and "repackaging" reflect AARP's recognition of the huge market for their products with the baby boomers.

SERVICES OFFERED BY AARP

- free tax preparation services
- peer grief and loss counseling
- legal counsel for older adults
- driver safety courses
- classes on personal safety
- a money management program
- home, auto, and life insurance at reduced rates
- mobile home insurance
- Grandparent Information Center
- AARP Health Care Options (supplemental health insurance)
- fraud prevention courses

Members are attracted by the material benefits of lower-cost health insurance, credit cards, travel, rental car discounts, discount prescriptions by mail, and a myriad of other services available for the current membership fee of only $16.00 a year. The political arm of AARP has also played role in speaking out for or against bills that affect the health and social well-being of older adults. AARP has had an impact on policies and practices for older adults through its support of the 2003 Medicare Part D Prescription Drug Coverage Bill and, currently, health care reform and policy and programmatic supports for family caregivers. As noted in Chapter 17, AARP was seen as responding to drug company and insurance interests in their support of Part D, however. Critics contend that AARP has moved away from advocacy on behalf of the older population and has become a big business that markets products and services. In addition, AARP has joined with nonaging

A NEW IMAGE FOR AARP

AARP ads feature themes such as "Age is just a number, and life is what you make it" or "You're ready to make this the time of your life. We help make it happen." A cover of AARP's magazine promised "Great Sex" and carried a picture of actress Susan Sarandon wearing a deep V-necked sweater.

organizations, such as the Child Welfare League and Generations United, to address issues related to grandparenting and kinship care. They are committed to intergenerational programming as well, as demonstrated by their national partnership with Big Brothers/Big Sisters.

A wide range of trade associations, professional societies, and coalitions concerned with aging issues also exists. *Trade associations* include:

- American Association of Homes and Services for the Aged (AAHSA)
- American Nursing Home Association (ANHA)
- National Council of Health Care Services (NCHCS), consisting of commercial enterprises in the long-term care industry, such as a nursing home subsidiary of major hotel chains
- National Association of State Units in Aging (NASUA), which is composed of administrators of state and area agencies on aging

Trade associations work to obtain federal funds and influence the development of regulations for long-term care facilities and service delivery. Two multidisciplinary *professional associations* active in aging policy issues, the **Gerontological Society of America (GSA)** (which now also encompasses the **Association for Gerontology in Higher Education**) and the **American Society on Aging (ASA)**, are composed primarily of gerontological researchers, educators, and practitioners from many disciplines and professions. Accordingly, there are numerous other largely discipline-specific organizations, such as the American Geriatrics Society. The major confederation of social welfare agencies concerned with aging is the **National Council on Aging (NCOA)**, which encompasses over 3,500 affiliates, composed of senior centers, senior housing, faith-based groups, area agencies on aging, consumers, and leaders in academia, business, and the human services.

Several organizations that began at the grassroots level now have nationwide membership and recognition. The **Older Women's League**

POLITICAL ACTIVISM AND OLDER WOMEN

Tish Sommers is an example of older women's political activism. Sommers, a longtime homemaker, learned about the vulnerability of older women when she was divorced at age 57. She found that newly single homemakers her age had a hard time getting benefits that people who have been employed take for granted. She coined the term *displaced homemaker* and organized women to lobby successfully for centers where displaced homemakers had job training during the late 1970s. In 1980, she and Laurie Shields founded the Older Women's League (OWL). Her maxim was "Don't agonize, organize." Even at her death in 1986, she was still fighting, organizing groups nationally around the right to maintain control over end-of-life care.

(OWL), founded in 1981 and composed of 38 chapters, brings together people concerned about issues affecting older women, especially health care and insurance, Social Security, pensions, and caregiving. It advocates for older women both in the federal policy-making process and within the programs of national associations such as the GSA. The **Gray Panthers,** founded by the late Maggie Kuhn, aims to form grassroots intergenerational alliances around issues affecting all ages. Since Maggie Kuhn's death, the Gray Panthers' visibility has declined, but they are still involved in social change related to cross-generational issues.

Some national age-based organizations are viewed as being biased toward the interests of middle- and upper-working-class older people. AARP, for example, has been criticized for advancing only the interests of its primarily middle-class membership, for recruiting members largely on the basis of selective incentives and direct member services (e.g., insurance, drug discounts, and travel), and for imposing its policy agenda on its members. In recent years, however, age-based organizations have not only reached out to lower-income older persons, but also collaborated with other groups. This is reflected by the cross-age coalitions that have formed around

health and long-term care. In addition to national associations, a wide range of local and state organizations have mobilized around intergenerational and cross-class issues such as affordable public transportation, environmental issues, safe streets, and low-cost health care, or joined with other movements such as disability rights.

In sum, despite the growth of age-based organizations, the senior-power model appears to have little validity with respect to older adults' voting behavior and political attitudes. Old age per se is currently not a primary basis for political mobilization, despite images of homogenous senior groups put forth by politicians, the media, and age-based organizations. With regard to the future, we can predict that baby boomers will cast a higher total vote in national elections than voting rates today; on the other hand, the heterogeneity of the baby boom cohort suggests that age will not form the primary basis for political behavior (Binstock, 2006–2007; Hudson, 2006). Cross-generational alliances are likely to be most important in influencing policies and programs, as further discussed in Chapters 16 and 17.

Implications for the Future

As they have moved through life, boomers have continued to reshape many of the social conventions around marriage and family, sexuality, parenting, and workplace behavior and seek opportunities that provide them with a sense of meaning and purpose. Prior to the global economic crisis beginning in 2008, it had been assumed that the boomers would enter old age with greater economic resources than prior cohorts and would shape new paradigms of work, productivity, and retirement. Many baby boomers were able to earn six-figure salaries, a pattern resulting from economic and demographic shifts such as deferred marriage, reduced and later child-bearing, increased labor force participation of women, higher levels of educational attainment, and greater investments. They also acquired more real estate and invested in the stock market more than prior cohorts. Despite their greater lifetime earnings and more extensive equity in real estate than prior cohorts, 75 percent in a 2006 survey of baby boomers reported that they did not feel financially prepared to retire and that they expected to keep working, health permitting (Harney, 2006). Many planned to keep working to enjoy the sense of productivity and satisfaction. They anticipated the availability of bridge jobs, phased retirement, and flex time positions, giving them discretion to choose how much and where they worked.

However, with the global economic downturn and the U.S. recession, baby boomers now face a very different future. Most cannot retire because of financial necessity. And if they do retire or lose their jobs, they will face numerous barriers to finding work during a time period of high unemployment. Because they typically borrowed more and saved less than their parents, they hold fewer assets than prior cohorts and have seen their private investments, particularly their individual retirement accounts, decimated by the economic downturn. Many who acquired real estate now watch property values decline to levels below their current mortgage and the market glutted with homes and condominiums.

Retirement will continue not to be a single irreversible event. Instead, more adults will change careers multiple times throughout their lives and move in and out of the workforce, often out of financial necessity. They will cycle between periods of work and leisure well beyond age 65. Although more companies are beginning to modify the workplace in order to retain older workers longer, such workplace modifications do not adequately meet the growing interest in part-time employment. The economic downturn and high unemployment rates are likely to adversely affect efforts to retrain and retain older workers, as well as options such as flexible hours and telecommuting.

The numbers of economically vulnerable elders will not diminish dramatically. Instead, a permanent underclass of boomers is projected, with a disproportionate representation of African Americans and Latinos, those with a sporadic employment history, single women, and those with limited education. In fact, the baby boom cohort is characterized by more income inequality, including a disappearing middle class, than any prior cohort. Women continue to face more financial challenges in old age than men, despite the growing number who have entered the paid labor force. These inequities among the boomers are unlikely to change without interventions earlier in the life course to prevent poverty and chronic illness and ensure educational and employment opportunities in young adulthood and middle age.

From a societal perspective, a work-retirement continuum for a population with a longer life expectancy requires modifying our expectations regarding lifelong education and training. Changing societal values about the "appropriate age" for education, employment, retirement, and leisure demand a reexamination of employment policies and norms. The traditional linear life cycle of education for the young, employment for the middle aged, and retirement for the old is already undergoing major changes. This is occurring as more middle-aged and older persons enter college for the first time, move into new careers, or begin their studies for graduate or professional degrees. Educational opportunities will become more accessible through online learning formats. Such educational options benefit employees by allowing them to explore new careers, volunteer and pursue leisure interests. Many other countries are well ahead of the U.S. in fostering models for reconceptualizing work and retirement. A "gliding out" plan of phased retirement in Japan and some European countries permits a gradual shift into a part-time schedule. Some Scandinavian countries give workers year-long sabbaticals every 10 years as a time to reevaluate their careers or to take a break instead of working straight through to retirement. Jobs can also be restructured, gradually allowing longer vacations, shorter workdays, and more opportunities for community involvement during the preretirement working years. Barriers to such changes in our society, however, include the fact that Americans have fewer vacation days than any other Western industrialized society, and some do not even use their earned vacation days. In addition, the current climate of job losses and bankruptcy makes it unlikely that older workers will ask for alternative employment models.

New jobs are likely to be in the service sector (e.g., health and social services, food, and recreation) and information technology. But these types of jobs cannot provide older workers with financial security. Whether technological advances will produce new jobs or result in net job losses is also unknown. What is certain is greater labor market diversity among the older population and greater variations in the reasons for retirement, unemployment, and economic well-being. Definitions of the nature of work, family, careers, and retirement will gradually reshape cultural and organizational expectations about work life and retirement.

The concept of the *Third Age* moves beyond focusing only on employment roles; instead, it denotes the stage in life that occurs after middle age but before the final stage, and is conceptualized as a time of continued involvement and growth in areas of life beyond employment and family. This concept is congruent with the broad perspective of productivity, discussed throughout this chapter, which seeks new ways to expand and use our human potential in old age. The vitality of the older population must be built upon as a way to involve their skills and wisdom through both paid and unpaid positions for the benefit of society and of older adults themselves. Increasingly, questions will be raised about how work should be defined and contributions measured. Advocates of a productive aging society point to the need to place a real value on unpaid volunteer and caregiving activities. Volunteer effort may be perceived as contributing more to the common good than paid

work and therefore as deserving greater rewards than currently exist. However, flexible options for productive activity by older adults are unevenly distributed across all sectors of society. Therefore, initiatives to encourage volunteerism and other types of unpaid productive contributions must occur within a broader framework that seeks to eliminate economic inequities across the life course and in old age.

These changes in work, retirement, and productivity will require new skills and knowledge among social and health care providers and planners of services for older adults. Preretirement counseling, lifelong distance learning opportunities, career development and retraining projects, and expanded volunteer programs all pose new roles for gerontological practitioners and researchers. Professionals and laypersons alike will be challenged to reconceptualize the use of time and human resources, given reduced rates of disability and increased longevity.

Summary

Paid employment is typically associated with productivity in our society. While early retirement was the norm for the past five decades, older adults are increasingly remaining employed, often in multiple careers. Health status, income, and attitudes toward the job influence decisions about when to retire, with income increasingly the primary factor. Most retirees adjust well to this important transition and are satisfied with the quality of their lives. Those with good health, higher-status jobs, adequate income, and existing social networks and leisure interests are most likely to be satisfied. Not all retirement is desired, however; many older people would prefer the opportunity for part-time work, but are unable to find suitable and flexible options. Preparation for the retirement transition is beneficial, but planning assistance is generally not available to those who need it most—workers who have less education, lower job status, and lower retirement incomes. Retirement by itself does not cause poor health or loss of identity and self-esteem. Dissatisfaction in this stage of life is more often due to poor health and low income.

Although a smaller percentage of older people have incomes below the poverty line than was true in the past, more older than younger people live at marginal economic levels. In addition to older adults who are officially counted as living below the poverty line, many others live near this level, and many are "hidden" poor who live in nursing homes or with their families. Frail, unmarried older women—especially African American women—are the most likely to live in or near poverty. Public assistance programs such as SSI and food stamps have not removed the very serious financial problems of the older poor, in part because they are underutilized and are becoming more restrictive with state budget cuts. Social Security is the major source of retirement income for a large proportion of the older population; those who depend on Social Security alone are the poorest group. Private pensions—especially those with a defined benefit plan—tend to be small in relation to previous earnings, are subject to attrition through inflation, and have disappeared in many business settings. The most common asset of older people is their home, which typically provides no immediate income and may entail extensive maintenance costs.

As earlier chapters documented, changes in employment and parenting roles, income, and physical and cognitive capacities often have detrimental social consequences for older adults. Nevertheless, there are arenas in which older people may still experience meaningful involvement and develop new opportunities and skills, consistent with the broader definition of productive aging that includes nonpaid contributions to society. This chapter has considered seven of these arenas: leisure pursuits, civic engagement, voluntary association

membership, volunteering, education, formal and informal religious involvement, and political activity. Civic engagement has become akin to a social change movement, with proponents advocating for elders to help solve societal problems such as climate change, while critics worry that civic engagement, particularly volunteerism, can perpetuate reductions in publicly funded services. The meaning and functions of participation in these arenas are obviously highly individualized. Participation may be a means to strengthen and build informal social networks, influence wider social policies, serve other persons, substitute new roles, and acquire new sources of meaning and purpose. The extent of involvement is influenced not by age alone, but also by a variety of other salient factors including gender, race, ethnicity, health, social class, and educational level.

Because of the number of interacting variables, age-related patterns in participation are not clearly defined. There are some general age-associated differences in types of leisure pursuits; with increasing age, people tend to engage in more sedentary, inner-directed, and routine pursuits in their homes rather than social activities or obligations outside the home, although this pattern may shift with the baby boomers who are likely to travel more and seek out new adventures. Changes in organizational participation, such as senior centers and volunteering, are less clearly age-related. Participation in voluntary associations stabilizes or diminishes only slightly with old age; declines that do occur are associated with poor health, inadequate income, and transportation problems. Volunteering, which is higher among today's older population than among other age-groups, tends to represent a lifelong pattern of community service that peaks in middle age and then remains stable until after age 80.

Past research on religious and political participation has pointed inaccurately to declines in old age. Although formal religious participation such as church or synagogue attendance appears to diminish slightly, other activities such as reading religious texts, listening to religious broadcasts, and praying increase. Religiosity appears to be an effective way of coping, particularly among elders of color. Spirituality is differentiated from religion as a positive and broader factor in older people's physical and mental well-being and active aging. Health care providers now recognize the importance of conducting a spiritual assessment to ensure that treatment and services are congruent with elders' spirituality.

Voting by older people has increased since the 1980s. Declines in voting and political participation in the past may have been a function of low educational status or physical limitations, not age per se. In fact, older persons' skills and experiences may be more valued in the political arena than in other spheres. The extent to which older people form a unified political bloc that can influence politicians and public policy is debatable. Some argue that older adults are cohesive, with a strong collective consciousness; others point to their increasing diversity and differences on public policy. As a whole, it appears that older adults are not a homogeneous voting bloc and often react to policies rather than initiate them, but many politicians still court them as if they were.

Most forms of organizational involvement appear to represent stability across the life course; the knowledge and skills necessary for a varied set of activities in old age are generally developed in early or middle adulthood and maintained into later life. On the other hand, preretirement patterns of productivity are not fixed. Individuals can garner new interests and activities in later life, often with the assistance of senior centers, lifelong learning programs, and community organizations. Despite the economic challenges facing older adults, particularly baby boomers, they will find numerous opportunities to engage in mutually beneficial relationships, to contribute to society, or to pursue solitary creative activities.

GLOSSARY

Age Discrimination in Employment Act (ADEA) federal law that protects workers age 40 and over from denial of employment strictly because of age

AARP (formerly known as the American Association of Retired Persons),   a national organization open to all adults age 50 and over, offering a wide range of informational materials, discounted services and products, and a powerful political lobby

American Society on Aging (ASA) association of mostly practitioners interested in gerontology

assets an individual's savings, home equity, and personal property

Association for Gerontology in Higher Education the only national membership organization of colleges and other academic groups devoted primarily to gerontological education

cash balance plans a pension plan that combine elements of both defined benefit and defined contribution models

civic engagement active participation in one's community by voting, volunteering, joining community groups

Civic Ventures an organization that provides resources for civic engagement and awards to innovators and agencies working for the common good

defined benefit pension plans a specified amount is guaranteed by the company as a lifetime annuity, and employees know what they could count on as retirement income

defined contribution plans such as 401(k) plans, in which the amount of the benefit varies depending on an individual's investment returns and thus carries greater financial risk for the employee

Elderhostel renamed Exploritas in 2009, a program that offers adventures in learning and travel

Experience Corps sponsors school-based programs where older adults work one-on-one with children, create before- and after-school programs, and receive a modest stipend for their service

Foster Grandparents Program volunteer program pairing elders with children with special needs

Generations United a national intergenerational coalition of over 30 organizations, including AARP, the Child Welfare League, and the Children's Defense Fund

Gerontological Society of America (GSA) an association of researchers, educators, and practitioners interested in gerontology and geriatrics

Gray Panthers a national organization founded by Maggie Kuhn, which encourages intergenerational alliances around social and environmental issues

leisure any activity characterized by the absence of obligation, which in itself is inherently satisfying

National Council on the Aging (NCOA) national organization of over 2,000 social welfare agencies concerned with aging that provides technical consultation and is involved in federal legislative activities

Older Women's League (OWL) a national advocacy organization concerned about issues affecting older women

religion an organized formal system of spiritual beliefs, values, and behaviors shared by a community (a denomination), not an individual behavior

religiosity individual's personal experience in the context of organized religion, but does not necessarily require participation in a formal organized setting with others

Retired and Senior Volunteer Program (RSVP) federally sponsored program that places older adult volunteers in a wide range of service settings

retirement the period of life, usually starting between age 60 and 65, during which an individual stops working in the paid labor force

Senior Community Service Employment Program (SCSEP) program sponsored by the federal

government that provides subsidies for nonprofit groups and businesses to employ older workers

Senior Companion Program a volunteer program in which seniors receive a stipend to assist homebound elders

Social Security federal program into which workers contribute a portion of their income during adulthood and then, beginning sometime between age 62 and 67, receive a monthly check based on the amount they have earned and contributed

spirituality believing in one's relationship with a higher power without being religious in the sense of organized religion

Supplemental Security Income (SSI) federal program to provide a minimal income for low-income older people (and other age-groups with disabilities)

RESOURCES

Log on to MySocKit (www.mysockit.com) for information about the following:

- American Association of Retired Persons (AARP)
- American Society on Aging (ASA)
- Association for Gerontology in Higher Education (AGHE)
- Elderhostel (or Exploritas as of 2009)
- Generations United
- Gerontological Society of America (GSA)
- Gray Panthers
- National Association of Retired Federal Employees (NARFE)
- National Council on Aging (NCOA)
- National Council of Senior Citizens (NCSC)
- The Leadership Council of Aging Organizations

REFERENCES

AARP. (2004a). *Baby boomers envision retirement II: Survey of boomers' expectations for retirement.* Washington, DC: AARP.

AARP. (2004b). *Time and money: An in-depth look at 45+ volunteers and donors.* Washington, DC: AARP.

AARP. (2006). *Boomers turning 60.* Washington, DC: AARP.

Aday, R. H. (2003). *Identifying important linkages between successful aging and senior center participation.* Presented at the joint conference of the National Council on Aging and American Society of Aging, Chicago, Illinois.

Administration on Aging (AOA). (2008). *Profile of Older Americans: 2008.* Washington, DC.

Angel, R. & Angel, J. (2006). Diversity and aging in the United States. In R. Binstock and L. K. George (Eds.). *Handbook of aging and the social sciences* (6th ed.). New York: Academic Press.

Ano, F. F. & Vasconcelles, E. B. (2005). Religious coping and psychological adjustment to stress: A meta-analysis. *Journal of Clinical Psychology, 61,* 461–480.

Ardelt, M. & Koenig, C. S. (2006). The role of religion for hospice patients and relatively healthy older adults. *Research on Aging, 28,* 184–215.

Atchley, R. C. (1976). *The sociology of retirement.* New York: Wiley/Schenkman.

Atchley, R. C. (2008). Spirituality, meaning, and the experience of aging. *Generations, 32,* 12–16.

Atchley, R. C. (2009). *Spirituality and aging.* Baltimore: John Hopkins University Press.

Avlund, K., et al. (2004). The impact of structural and functional characteristics of social relations as determinants of functional decline. *Journal of Gerontology: Social Sciences, 59B,* S44–51.

Awara, M. & Fasey, C. (2008). Is spirituality worth exploring in psychiatric out-patient clinics? *Journal of Mental Health, 17,* 183–191.

Benjamin, M. R. (2004). Religion and functional health among the elderly: Is there a relationship and is it constant? *Journal of Aging and Health, 16,* 355–374.

Benjamin, M. R., Musick, M., Gold, D., & George, L. K. (2003). Age-related declines in activity level: The relationship between chronic illness and religious activities, *Journal of Gerontology: Social Sciences, 58B,* S377–S385.

Binstock, R. H. (2006). Older voters and the 2004 election. *The Gerontologist, 46,* 382–384.

Binstock, R. H. (2006–2007). Older people and political engagement: From avid voters to 'cooled-out marks.' *Generations, 30,* 24–30.

Bosworth, H., Park, K., McQuoid, D., Hays, J., & Steffens, D. (2003). The impact of religious practice and religious coping on geriatric depression. *International Journal of Geriatric Psychiatry, 18,* 905–914.

Brooks, R. G. & Koenig, H. G. (2002). Having faith in an aging health system: Policy perspectives. *Public Policy and Aging Report, 12,* 23–26.

Butrica, B. A. & Shaner, G. (2005). Satisfaction and engagement in retirement. *Perspectives on Productive Aging, 2.* Washington, DC: The Urban Institute, The Retirement Project.

Calvo, E. (2006). *Does working longer make people healthier and happier?* Retrieved June, 2007, from http://www.bc.edu/centers/crr/issues/wob_2.pdf

Canda, E. & Smith, E. (Eds.). (2001). *Transpersonal perspectives on spirituality in social work*. Binghamton, NY: Haworth Press.

Canda, E., Nakashama, M., & Furman, L. (2004). Ethical considerations about spirituality in social work: Insights from a national qualitative survey. *Families in Society*, *85*, 27–35.

Carlton-LaNey, I. (2006–2007). 'Doing the Lord's work': African American elders' civic engagement. *Generations*, *30*, 47–50.

Chen, Y. P. & Scott, J. (2006). *Phased retirement. Who opts for it and toward what end?* AARP. Retrieved February 2007, from http://assets .aarp.org/rgcenter/econ/2006

Cnaan, R. (2002). *The invisible caring hand*. New York: New York University Press.

Cnaan, R. & Boddie, S. (2002). Charitable choice and faith-based welfare: A call for social work. *Social Work*, *47*, 224–235.

Cohen, G. D. (2005). *The mature mind: The positive power of the aging brain*. New York: Avon Books.

Cohen, G. D., Perlstein, S., Chapline, J. Kelly, J., Firth, K., et al. (2006). The impact of professionally conducted cultural programs on the physical health, mental health and social functioning of older adults. *The Gerontologist*, *46*, 726–734.

Corporation for National and Community Service, Office of Research and Policy Development. (2007). *The health benefits of volunteering: A review of recent research*. Washington, DC: Corporation for National and Community Service.

Cullinane, B. D. (2008). Guest at the door: Spirit waiting to be invited. *Generations*, *32*, 17–19.

Cutler, S. J. & Hendricks, J. (2000). Age differences in voluntary association memberships: Fact or artifact. *Journals of Gerontology*, *55B*, S98–S107.

Dalby, P. (2006). Is there a process of spiritual change or development associated with aging? A critical review of research. *Aging and Mental Health*, *10*, 4–12.

Davey, A. & Szinovacz, M. E. (2004). Dimensions of marital quality and retirement. *Journal of Family Issues*, *25*, 431–464.

Eberly, D. & Streeter, R. (2002). *The soul of civil society: Voluntary associations and the public value of moral habits*. Lanham, MD: Lexington Books.

Ekerdt, D. J. (1986). The busy ethic: Moral continuity between work and retirement. *The Gerontologist*, *26*, 239–244.

Elderhostel. (2005). *Adventures in Lifelong Learning*. Retrieved February 2006, from http://www .elderhostel.org

Emerman, J. (2006). On life's new stage—and its challenge to the field of aging. *Aging Today*, 3–4.

Estes, C. & Mahakian, J. L. (2001). The political economy of productive aging. In N. Morrow-Howell, J. Hinterlong, & M. Sherraden (Eds.). *Productive aging: Concepts and challenges*. Baltimore: Johns Hopkins University Press.

Fast, J., Dosman, D., & Moran, L. (2006). Productive activity up in later life. *Research on Aging*, *28*, 691–712.

Federal Interagency Forum on Aging-related Statistics. (2008). *Older Americans 2008: Key indicators of well-being*. Washington, DC: Federal Interagency Forum on Aging.

Fisher, P. (2008). Is there an emerging age gap in U.S. politics? *Society*, *45*, 504–511.

Flippen, C. (2005). Minority workers and pathways to retirement. In R. Hudson (Ed.). *The new politics of old age policy.* Baltimore: John Hopkins University Press.

Freedman, M. (2001). Structural lead: Building new institutions for an aging America. In N. Morrow-Howell, J. Hinterlong, & M. Sherraden (Eds.). *Productive aging: Concepts and challenges.* Baltimore: Johns Hopkins University Press.

Freedman, M. (2002). Civic windfall? Realizing the promise in an aging America. *Generations, 26,* 86–89.

Freedman, M. & Adler, R. (2005). Capturing the windfall: Older adults in the social sector workforce. *Elders as resources: Intergenerational strategies series.* Baltimore: Annie E. Casey Foundation.

Fried, L., Carlson, M., Freedman, M., Frick, K., & Glass, T., et al. (2004). A social model for health promotion for an aging population: Initial evidence on the Experience Corps model. *Journal of Urban Health, 81,* 64–78.

Fry, P. S. (2000). Religious involvement, spirituality and personal meaning for life: Existential predictors of psychological wellbeing in community-residing and institutional care elders. *Aging & Mental Health, 4,* 375–387.

Fuller-Thomson, E. & Redmond, M. (2009). Falling through the social safety net: Food stamp use and nonuse among older impoverished Americans. *The Gerontologist, 48,* 235–244.

Gallup Poll. (2002). *Poll topics and trends: Religion.* Retrieved July 2002, from http://www.gallup.com/poll/topics/religion2.asp

Gallup Poll. (2006). *Religion most important to Blacks, women and older Americans.* Retrieved February 2007, from http://www.gallup.com/poll/topics

Gerontological Society of America. Press release: (2005). *The Gerontological Society of America announces initiative on civic engagement in older Americans.* Retrieved December 2005, from http://www.geron.org/press/engagement.htm

Gist, J. (2007). Population aging, entitlement growth and the economy. AARP. Retrieved February 2007, from http://assets/aarp.org/rgcenter/econ/2007_01_security.pdf

Greenfield, E. & Marks, N. (2004). Formal volunteering as a protective factor for older adults' psychological well-being. *Journal of Gerontology: Social Sciences, 59B,* S258–S264.

Greenfield, E. & Marks, N. (2007). Continuous participation in voluntary groups as a protective factor for the psychological well-being of adults who develop functional limitations: Evidence from the National Survey of Families and Households. *Journal of Gerontology: Social Sciences, 62B,* S60–S68.

Hao, Y. (2008). Productive activities and psychological well-being among older adults. *Journal of Gerontology: Social Sciences, 63B,* S64–S72.

Hardy, M. (2002). The transformation of retirement in 20th century America. *Generations, 26,* 9–16.

Hardy, M. (2006). Older workers. In R. Binstock & L. George (Eds.). *Handbook of aging and the social sciences* (6th ed.). New York: Academic Press.

Harney, K. (2006). Study finds boomers bigger on real estate. *The Seattle Times,* pp. E1, E6.

Harris, A. & Thoresen, C. (2005). Volunteering is associated with delayed mortality in older people: Analysis of the longitudinal study of aging. *Journal of Health Psychology, 10,* 739–752.

Harvard School of Public Health/MetLife Foundation. (2004). *Reinventing aging: Baby boomers and civic engagement.* Harvard School of Public Health, Center for Health Communication.

Harvey, I. S. & Silverman, M. (2007). The role of spirituality in the self-management of chronic illness among older African, Americans and whites. *Journal of Cross-Cultural Gerontology, 22,* 205–220.

Hays, J., Meador, K., Branch, P., & George, L. (2001). The Spiritual History Scale in four dimensions (SHS-4): Validity and reliability. *The Gerontologist, 41,* 239–249.

Hendricks, J. & Cutler, S. J. (2004). Volunteerism and socioemotional selectivity in later life. *Journal of Gerontology: Social Sciences, 59B,* S251–S257.

Hill, T. D. (2008). Religious involvement and healthy cognitive aging: Patterns, explanations, and future directions. *Journal of Gerontology: Psycho- logical Sciences, 63A,* P478–479.

Hinterlong, J. E. & Williamson, A. (2006–2007). The effects of civic engagement on current and future cohorts of older adults. *Generations, 30,* 10–17.

Hodge, D. R. (2003). The intrinsic spirituality scale: A new six-item instrument for assessing the salience of spirituality as a motivational construct. *Journal of Social Service Research, 31,* 41–61.

Hodge, D. R. (2004a). Social work practice with Muslims in the United States. In A. T. Morales & B.W. Sheafor (Eds.). *Social work: A profession of many faces* (10th ed.). Boston: Allyn & Bacon.

Holden, K. C. (2008). The boomers and their economic prospects. In R. B. Hudson (Ed.). *Boomer bust? Economic and political issues of the graying society* (Vol. 1). Westport, CT: Praeger.

Hollingsworth, B. (2002). Retirees who don't. *The Seattle Times,* p. H1.

Holstein, M. & Minkler, M. (2003). Self, society and the "new gerontology." *The Gerontologist, 43,* 787–796.

Holstein, M. (2007). A critical reflection on civic engagement. *Public Policy and Aging Report, 16,* 21–26.

Hudson, R. B. (2006). The 2005 White House Conference on Aging: No Time for Seniors. *Public Policy and Aging Report, 16,* 1–3.

Hudson, R. B. (2006–2007). Aging in a public space: The roles and functions of civic engagement. *Generations, 30,* 51–58.

Hudson, R. B. (2007). Terms of engagement: The right and left look at elder civic activism. *Public Policy and Aging Report, 16,* 17–18.

Hudson, R. B. (2008). Public policy and the boomers: An expanding scope of conflict. In R. B. Hudson (Ed.), *Boomer bust? Economic and political issues of the graying society* (Vol. 1). Westport, CT: Praeger.

Hutchens, R. (2003). *The Cornell Study of employer phased retirement policies: A report on key findings.* Ithaca, NY: Cornell University School of Industrial and Labor Relations.

Idler, E.L. (2002). The many causal pathways linking religion to health. *Public Policy and Aging Report, 12,* 7–12.

Idler, E. L. (2006). Religion and aging. In R. Binstock & L. K. George (Eds.). *Handbook of aging and the social sciences* (6th ed.). New York: Academic Press.

Independent Sector. (2006a). *Giving answers.* Retrieved December 2006, from http://www.givinganswers.com/nmrd/nonprofitsectoroverview/organizations/Independent

Independent Sector. (2006b). Research: *Value of volunteer time*. Retrieved December 2006, from http://www.independentsector.org/programs/research/volunteer_time.html

Ingersoll-Dayton, B., Krause, N., & Morgan, D. (2002). Religious trajectories and transitions over the life course. *International Journal of Aging and Human Development, 55*, 51–70.

James, J. B. & Wink, P. U. (2007). *The crown of life: Dynamics of the early post-retirement period*. New York: Springer Publishing.

Johnson, R. & Schaner, S. (2005). Value of unpaid activities by older Americans tops $160 billion per year. *Perspectives on Productive Aging*, Brief No. 4. Washington, DC: The Urban Institute.

Kaplan, M. & Liu, S. T. (2004). Generations united for environmental awareness and action. Washington DC: Generations United.

Keyes, C. L. M. & Reitzes, D. C. (2007). The role of religious identity in the mental health of older working and retired adults. *Aging and Mental Health, 11*, 434–443.

Koenig, H. G. (2002). An 83-year-old woman with chronic illness and strong religious beliefs. *Journal of the American Medical Association, 288*, 487–493.

Koenig, H. G. (2007a). *Spirituality in patient care* (2nd ed.). Philadelphia: Templeton Foundation Press.

Koenig, H. G. (2007b). Religion and depression in older medical inpatients. *American Journal of Geriatric Psychiatry, 15*, 282–291.

Koenig, H. G. & Brooks, R. G. (2002). Religion, health, and-aging: Implications for practice and public policy. *Public Policy and Aging Report, 12*, 13–19.

Koenig, H. G., McCullough, M. E., & Larson, D. B. (2001). *Handbook of religion and health*. New York: Oxford University Press.

Krause, N. (2003). Religious meaning and subjective well-being in late life. *Journal of Gerontology: Social Sciences, 58B*, S160–S170.

Kuhn, M. (1991). *No stone unturned*. New York: Ballatine Books.

Lai, D. (2001). Use of senior center services by elderly Chinese immigrants. *Journal of Gerontological Social Work, 35*, 59–79.

Larrimore, W., Parker, M., & Crowther, M. (2002). Should clinicians incorporate positive spirituality into their practices: What does the evidence say? *Annals of Behavioral Medicine, 24*, 69–73.

Li, Y. & Ferraro, K. F. (2006). Volunteering in middle and later life: Is health a benefit, barrier or both? *Social Forces, 85*, 498–519.

Lum, T. & Lightfoot, E. (2005). The effects of volunteering on the physical and mental health of older people. *Research on Aging, 27*, 31–55.

Lusardi, A. (2009). Planning for retirement: The importance of financial literacy. *Public Policy and Aging Report, 19*, 7–13.

Manheimer, R. J. (2008). Gearing up for the big show: Lifelong learning programs are coming of age. In R. B. Hudson (Ed.). *Boomer bust? Economic and political issues of the graying society* (Vol. 2). Westport, CT: Praeger.

Manpower. (2007). *The new agenda for an older workforce*. White paper GC-13. Milwaukee, WI: Manpower.

Marler, P. & Hadaway, C. (2002). 'Being religious' or 'being spiritual' in America: A zero sum proposition? *Journal for the Scientific Study of Religion, 41*, 289–300.

Martinson, M. (2006–2007). Opportunities or obligations? Civic engagement and older adults. *Generations, 30*, 59–65.

Martinson, M. & Minkler, M. (2006). Civic engagement and older adults: A critical perspective. *The Gerontologist*, 46, 318–324.

Mattis, J. & Jagers M. (2001). A relational framework for the study of religiosity and spirituality in the lives of African Americans. *Journal of Community Psychology*, 29, 519–539.

Menec, V. (2003). The relation between everyday activities and successful aging: A 6-year longitudinal study. *Journal of Gerontology: Social Sciences*, 58B, S74–S82.

Miller, A. & Stark, R. (2002). Gender and religiousness: Can socialization explanations be saved? *American Journal of Sociology*, 107, 1399–1423.

Miller, W. R. & Thoresen, C. E. (2003). Spirituality, religion, and health: An emerging research field. *American Psychologist*, 58, 3–66.

Moen, P. (2003). Midcourse: Reconfiguring careers and community service for a new life stage. *Contemporary Gerontology*, 9, 87–94.

Moen, P., Kim, J., & Hofmeister, H. (2001). Couples' work a status transitions, and marriage quality in late midlife. *Social Psychology Quarterly*, 64, 55–71.

Moody, H. R. (2001). Productive aging and the ideology of old age. In N. Morrow-Howell, J. Hinterlong, & M. Sherraden (Eds.). *Productive aging: Concepts and challenges*. Baltimore: Johns Hopkins University Press.

Moody, H. R. (2004–2005). Silver industries and the new aging enterprise. *Generations*, 28, 75–78.

Moody, H. R. (2005). From successful aging to conscious aging. In M. Wykle, P. Whitehouse, & D. Morris (Eds.). *Successful aging through the life span*. New York: Springer.

Moody, H. R. (2008). Environmentalism as an aging issue. *Public Policy and Aging Report*, 18, 1–7.

Moody, H. R. (in press). Productive aging and the ideology of old age. In N. Morrow-Howell (Ed.). *Perspectives on productive aging*. Baltimore: John Hopkins University Press.

Morrow-Howell, N., Hinterlong, J., Rozario, P., & Tang, F. (2003). The effects of volunteering on the well-being of older adults. *Journal of Gerontology: Social Sciences*, 58B, S137–S146.

Morrow-Howell, N., Hinterlong, J., & Sherraden, M. W. (2001). *Productive aging: Concepts and challenges*. Baltimore: Johns Hopkins University Press.

Morrow-Howell, N., Hong, S. I., & Tang, F. (2009). Who benefits from volunteering? Variations in perceived benefits. *The Gerontologist*, 49, 91–102.

Musick, M. A. & Wilson, J. (2003). Volunteering and depression: The role of psychological and social resources in different age groups. *Social Science & Medicine*, 56, 259–269.

National Center for Policy Analysis. (2003). *Annual Report of the Board of Trustees of the Federal Old-age and Survivors' Insurance Trust Funds*. Washington, DC.

Nelson-Becker, H. (2004). Meeting life challenges: A hierarchy of coping styles in African-American and Jewish elders. *Journal of Human Behavior in the Social Environment*, 10, 155–174.

Nelson-Becker, H. (2005a). Religion and coping in older adults: A social work perspective. *Journal of Gerontological Social Work*, 45, 51–68.

Nelson-Becker, H. (2005b). Development of a spiritual support scale for use with older adults.

Journal of Human Behavior in the Social Environment, 11, 195–212.

Nelson-Becker, H. (2005c). Religion and coping in older adults: A social work perspective. *Journal of Gerontological Social Work, 45*, 54–67.

Nelson-Becker, H., Nakashima, M., & Canda, E. R. (2006). Spirituality in professional helping interventions with older adults. In B. Berkman (Ed.). *Handbook of social work in health and aging.* New York: Oxford Press.

Nelson-Becker, H., Nakashima, M., & Canada, E. R. (2007). Spiritual assessment in aging: A framework for clinicians. *Journal of Gerontological Social Work, 48*, 331–347.

Newson, R. & Kemps, E. (2005). General lifestyle activities as a predictor of current cognition and cognitive change in older adults: A cross-sectional and longitudinal examination. *Journal of Gerontology: Psychology, 60B,* P113–P120.

Okon, T. R. (2005). Palliative care review: Spiritual, religious, and existential aspects of palliative care. *Journal of Palliative Medicine, 8,* 362–414.

O'Neill, G. & Lindberg, B. (2005). *Civic engagement in an older America.* Gerontological Society of America. Retrieved February 2007, from www.agingsociety.org/agingsociety/Pages%20from%20GeronNLSept05.pdf

O'Rand, A. M. (2005). When old age begins: Implications for health, work and retirement. In R. Hudson (Ed.). *The new politics of old age policy.* Baltimore: Johns Hopkins.

Pardasani, M. (2003). Senior Centers: Patterns of programs and services. *Dissertation Abstracts.* New York: Yeshiva University.

Pardasani, M. (2004a). Senior centers: Focal points of community-based services for the

elderly. *Activities, Adaptation and Aging, 28,* 27–44.

Pardasani, M. (2004b). Senior centers: Increasing minority participation through diversification. *Journal of Gerontological Social Work, 43,* 41–56.

Parker, M. W., Bellis, J. M., Bishop, P., Harper, M., Allman, R. M., Moore, C., & Thompson, P. (2002). A multidisciplinary model of health promotion incorporating spirituality into a successful aging intervention with African American and white elderly groups. *The Gerontologist, 42,* 406–415.

Parker, M., Roff, L. L., Klemmack, D. L., Koenig, H. G., Baker, P., & Allman, R. M. (2003). Religiosity and mental health in southern, community-dwelling older adults. *Aging & Mental Health, 7,* 390–397.

Piktialis, D. S. (2008). Redesigning work for an aging labor force: Employer and employee perspectives. In R. B. Hudson. (Ed). *Boomer bust? Economic and political issues of the graying society* (Vol. 2). Westport, CT: Praeger.

Portney, K. (2005). Civic engagement and sustainable cities in the United States. *Public Administration Review, 65,* 579–91.

Powell, L., Shahabi, L., & Thorsesen, C. (2003). Religion and spirituality: Linkages to physical health. *American Psychologist, 2003, 58,* 36–52.

Prisuta, R. (2004). Enhancing volunteerism among aging boomers. Harvard School of Public Health and MetLife. *Reinventing aging: Baby boomers and civic engagement.* Boston: Harvard School of Public health, Center for Health Communication.

Purcell, P. & Whitman, D. (2006). Income of Americans age 65 and older, 1969 to 2004. *Journal of Deferred Compensation, 12,* 1–41.

Putnam, R. (2002). Bowling together. *The American Prospect*, 13, 3.

Putnam, R. (2004). *Democracies in flux.* New York: Oxford University Press.

Richardson, V. E. & Barusch, A. S. (2006). Poverty and aging. In V. E. Richardson & A. S. Barusch (Ed.). *Gerontological practice for the twenty-first century* 338–354. New York: Columbia University Press.

Rix, S. E. (2006). Work in the new retirement. *Public Policy and Aging Report*, 16, 9–15.

Rix, S. E. (2008). Will the boomers revolutionize work and retirement? In R. Hudson (Ed.). Boomer bust? Economic and political issues of the graying society (Vol. 1). Westport, CT: Praeger.

Roff, L. L., Klemmack, D. L., Simon, C., Cho, G. W., Parker, M. W., Koenig, H. G., Sawyer-Baker, P., & Allman, R. M. (2006). Functional limitations and religious service attendance among African American and white older adults. *Health and Social Work*, 31.

Rozario, P. A. (2006–2007). Volunteering among current cohorts of older adults and baby boomers. *Generations*, 30, 31–36.

Sampson, R. J., et al. (2005). Civic society reconsidered: The durable nature and community structure of collective civic action. *American Journal of Sociology*, 3, 673–714.

Schaie, K., Krause, N., & Booth, A. (Eds.). (2004). *Religious influences on health and well-being in the elderly.* New York: Springer.

Schwarz, L. & Cottrell, R. F. (2007). The value of spirituality as perceived by elders in long-term care. *Physical & Occupational Therapy in Geriatrics*, 26, 43–62.

Seeman, T., Dubin, L., & Seeman, M. (2003). Religiosity/spirituality and health: A critical review of the evidence for biological pathways. *American Psychologist*, 58, 53–63.

Shmotkin, D., Blumstein, T., & Modan, B. (2003). Beyond keeping active: Concomitants of being a volunteer in old-old age. *Psychology and Aging*, 18, 602–607.

Shreve-Niger, A. K. & Edelstein, B.A. (2004). Religion and spirituality: A critical review of the literature. *Clinical Psychology Review*, 24, 379–397.

Smith, D. & Moen, P. (2004). Retirement satisfaction for retirees and their spouses: Do gender and the retirement decision-making process matter? *Journal of Family Issues*, 25, 262.

Smith, T., McCullough, M., & Poll, J. (2003). Religiousness and depression: Evidence for a main effect and the moderating influence of stressful life events. *Psychological Bulletin*, 129, 614–636.

Smith, T. W. & Seokho, K. (2005). The vanishing Protestant majority. *Journal for the Scientific Study of Religion*, 44, 211–223.

Smyer, M. A., Bensen, E., & Pitt-Catsouphes, M. (2008). Boomers and the many meanings of work. In R. B. Hudson (Ed.). *Boomer bust: Economic and political issues of the graying society* (Vol. 2). Westport, CT: Praeger.

Snodgrass, J. (2009). Toward holistic care: Integrating spirituality and cognitive behavior therapy for older adults. *Journal of Religion, Spirituality and Aging*, 21, 219–236.

Streib, G. & Schneider, C. J. (1971). *Retirement in American society. Impact and process.* Ithaca, NY: Cornell University Press.

Sykes, K., Manning, T., Campbell, P. A., & Schmeckpeper, B. J. (2008). To endow every child…*Public Policy and Aging Report*, 18, 14–18.

Szinovacz, M. E. & Davey, A. (2004a). Honeymoons and joint lunches: Effects of retirement and spouse's employment on depressive symptoms. *Journal of Gerontology: Social Sciences, 59B,* P233–P245.

Szinovacz, M. E. & Davey, A. (2004b). Retirement transitions and spouse disability: Effects on depressive symptoms. *Journal of Gerontology: Social Sciences, 59B,* S333–S342.

Szinovacz, M. E. & Davey, A. (2005). Predictors of perceptions of involuntary retirement. *The Gerontologist, 45,* 36–47.

Taylor, R., Chatters, L., & Levin, J. (2004). *Religion in the lives of African Americans.* Thousand Oaks, CA: Sage.

Theiss-Morse, E. & Hibbing, J. (2004). Citizenship and civic engagement. *Annual Review of Political Science, 8,* 227–249.

Tornstam, L. (2005). *Gerotranscendence: A developmental theory of positive aging.* New York: Springer Publishing.

Urban Institute. (2006). *Work and retirement: Facts and figures.* Washington, DC: Urban Institute.

U.S. Census Bureau. (2005a). *Reported voting and registration by race, Hispanic origin, sex and age groups: November 1964 to 2004.* Retrieved July 2005, from http://www.census.gov/population/www/socdemo/voting.html

U.S. Census Bureau. (2005b). *Current Population Survey, 2005 Annual Social and Economic Supplement.* Washington, DC: U.S. Census Bureau.

U.S. Census Bureau. (2006). *Current Population Survey, 2006 Annual Social and Economic Supplement.* Retrieved February 2007, from http://pubdb3.census.gov/macro/032006/pov/new01_100_01.htm

U.S Congressional Budget Office. (2004). *Retirement age and the need for saving.* Washington, DC: Congressional Budget Office.

Van Ness, P. & Larson, D. (2002). Religion, senescence and mental health. The end of life is the not the end of hope. *American Journal of Geriatric Psychiatry, 10,* 386–397.

Verghese, J., Lipton, R., Katz, M., Hall C., Derby, C., et al. (2003). Leisure activities and the risk of dementia in the elderly. *New England Journal of Medicine, 348,* 2508–2516.

Verma, S. K. (2006). *Retirement plan coverage of boomers. Analysis of 2003 SIPP data.* AARP. Retrieved February 2007, from http://assets/aarp.org/rgcenter/econ/sipp_cb_2006.pdf

Wacker, R., Roberto, K., & Piper, L. (2003). *Community resources for older adults* (2nd ed.). Thousand Oaks, CA: Pine Forge Press.

Walker, A. (2006). Aging and politics: An international perspective. In R. H. Binstock & L. K. George (Eds.). *Handbook of aging and the social sciences* (6th ed.). San Diego: Academic Press.

Wan, H., Sengupta, M., Velkoff, V., & DeBarros, K. (2005). U.S. Census Bureau, *Current Population Reports, P23–209, 65+ in the United States: 2005.* Washington, DC: U.S. Government Printing Office.

Weller, C. E. (2009). Pension design in the crisis. *Public Policy and Aging Report, 19,* 1, 3–6.

Wilson, L. B. & Harlow-Rosentraub, K. (2008). Providing new opportunities for volunteerism and civic engagement for boomers: Chaos theory redefined. In R. B. Hudson (Ed.). *Boomer bust: Economic and political issues of the graying society* (Vol. 2). Westport, CT: Praeger.

Wilson, L. & Simpson, S. (Eds.). (2006). *Civic engagement and the baby boomer generation. Research, policy and practice perspectives:* Binghamton, NY: Haworth Press.

Yoon, D. P. & Lee, E. K.O. (2007). The impact of religiousness, spirituality, and social support on psychological well-being among older adults in rural areas. *Journal of Gerontological Religion, Spirituality and Aging, 48,* 281–298.

Zedlewski, S. & Schaner, S. (2006). Older adults engaged as volunteers. *Perspectives on productive aging.* Washington, DC: Urban Institute, The Retirement Project.

c h a p t e r

13

Death, Dying, Bereavement, and Widowhood

You have probably heard of people who "lost their will to live" or "died when they were ready." Such ideas are not simply superstitions. Similar to other topics addressed throughout this book, death involves an interaction of physiological, social, and psychological factors. The social context is illustrated by the fact that all cultures develop beliefs and practices regarding death in order to minimize its disruptive effects on the social structure. These cultural practices influence how members of a particular society react to their own death and that of others. Although death is measured in physical terms, such as the absence of a heartbeat or brain waves, psychosocial factors, such as the will to live, can influence the biological event. For instance, people with terminal illnesses may die shortly after an important event, such as a child's wedding, a family reunion, or a holiday, suggesting that their social support systems, enthusiasm for life, and "will to live" prolonged life to that point. How people approach their own death and that of others is closely related to personality styles, sense of competence, coping skills, and informal social supports.

The Changing Context of Dying

In Western society, dying is associated primarily with old age. Although we all know that aging does not cause death and younger people also die, there are a number of reasons for this association. The major factors are medical advances and increased life expectancy. In preindustrial societies, death rates were high in childhood and youth, and parents could expect as many as half of their children to die before the age of 10. Most deaths now occur from chronic disease. This means that it is increasingly the old who die, making death a predictable function of age. Death in old age has thus come to be viewed as a timely event, the completion of the life cycle.

Others view death not only as the province of the old, but also as an unnatural event that is to be fought off as long as medically possible. In this sense, death has become medicalized, distorted from a natural event into the end point of untreatable or inadequately treated disease or injury. Prior to the 1900s, the period of time spent dying was relatively short, due to infectious diseases and catastrophic events. With improved diagnostic techniques and early detection, individuals are living longer with terminal and chronic illnesses. At the end of a prolonged illness, when medicine may care for but not cure the patient, dying may seem more unnatural than if the person had been allowed to die earlier in the progression of the disease. With expanded technological mastery over the conditions of dying, chronically ill people have often been kept alive long beyond the point at which they might have died naturally in the past. Achieving a peaceful death is more difficult today because of the complexity of drawing a clear line between living and dying—which is a result of both technology and societal and professional ambivalence about whether to fight or accept death.

The surroundings in which death occurs have also changed with increased medical interventions. In preindustrial societies, most people died at home, with the entire community often involved in rituals surrounding the death. Similarly, about 90 percent of adults today indicate that they want to die at home, without pain, surrounded by friends and family. Yet 80 percent of all deaths occur in institutions where aggressive treatment is common, generally in hospitals (60 percent) and nursing homes (approximately 20 percent), and with only a few relatives and friends present. African American and less educated older adults are even more likely to die in a hospital. Contrary to hopes for a peaceful death, the majority of dying patients of any age experience severe, undertreated pain, and spend a period of time in an intensive care unit (Gruneir et al., 2007; National Center for Health Statistics, 2003; Weitzen et al., 2003).

Attitudes Toward Death

More insulated from death than in the past, many Americans are uncomfortable discussing it—especially the prospect of their own death. This discomfort is shown even in the euphemisms people use—"sleep," "pass away," "rest"—instead of the word "death" itself. In fact, Freud recognized that although death was natural, undeniable, and unavoidable, people behaved as though it would occur only to others; that is, *they* will die, but not *me*. Fear and denial, even when facing a terminal illness, are natural responses to our inability to comprehend our own death and lack of physical existence. Such fear tends to make death a taboo topic in our society, and the association of aging with death also explains why many people are attracted to antiaging medicine and products. Although death has become a more legitimate topic for scientific and social discussion in recent years, most people talk about it on a rational, intellectual level, rather than discuss and prepare for their own deaths or those of loved ones (Cicirelli, 2006). Both acceptance and denial reflect the basic paradox surrounding death, in which we recognize

Spirituality is a source of strength for many elders facing death.

its universality but cannot comprehend or imagine our own dying. Dying is one of the few events in life certain to occur, but for which we rarely plan.

When asked what they fear most about death, adults mention suffering and pain, loss of their physical body and personality, giving up self-control, concern over an afterlife and the

unknown, their spiritual or mental annihilation, loneliness, and the effects of their death on survivors. In general, people fear the inability to predict what the future might bring and the process of dying, particularly a painful death (Cicirelli, 2006). Older patients tend to choose *quality* of life in their end-of-life decision making, although this may differ by age, race, and class. Older African Americans, however, are less likely than older whites to communicate their end-of-life care wishes informally or to make prior legal arrangements for such care (Gerst & Burr, 2008). Instead, they are more likely to want lifesaving technology and to die in hospitals rather than with hospice care compared to whites (Kwak, Haley, & Chiraboga, 2008). While health professionals use the term *end-of-life,* African Americans tend to use the term *passed* or *passed on* because of common beliefs that the immortal soul carries on a journey of life after death (Crawley, 2001). It is essential that health care providers take account of such cultural differences in order to ensure both a good life and a good death for all their patients.

Variation by Age and Gender

Multiple factors, particularly age, previous experience with the death of loved ones, and gender influence socioemotional responses to death and dying. Both men and women experience the highest level of death anxiety in their twenties, followed by gradual declines. For women, death anxiety spikes again in their fifties, and for both genders, anxiety remains stable and relatively low in older adulthood (Russac, Gatliff, Reese, & Spottswood, 2007). Older women more often report anxiety and fear of dying, but less fear of the unknown than their male counterparts, although this may reflect gender differences in religiosity and women's greater ability to express emotions, such as fear. In general, the oldest-old think and talk more about death and appear to be less afraid of their own death than midlife and young-old adults, who have "unfinished business" and goals they still want to accomplish. Regardless of age, a near-universal fear is the pain of dying and concern over an afterlife—the possibility of either no afterlife or a threatening one (Cicirelli, 2002, 2006; Fortner, Neimeyer, & Rybarczyk, 2000).

A number of factors may explain this apparent paradox of elders' lessened fear of death in the face of its proximity. Having internalized society's views, the current cohort of elders may see their lives as having ever-decreasing social value, thereby lowering their own positive expectation of the future. If they have lived past the age they expected to, they may view themselves as living on "borrowed time." A painless death tends to be preferred over physical or mental deterioration, becoming socially useless, or being a burden on family. In addition, dealing with their friends' deaths can help socialize older people toward an acceptance of their own. Experiencing "bereavement overload" through deaths of family and friends, they are more likely than younger people to think and talk in a matter-of-fact way about death on a regular basis and to develop effective means of coping, including humor (Lamberg, 2002; Thorson & Powell, 2000; Tomer & Eliason, 2000). On the other hand, having sustained contacts with younger family members and still having goals to accomplish creates a greater desire to prolong life (Cicirelli, 2006).

Older adults facing death often turn inward to contemplation, reminiscence, reading, or spiritual activities. The awareness of one's mortality can stimulate a need for the "legitimization of biography"—to find meaning in one's life and death through life review. Elders who engage in such review and achieve the developmental stage of ego integrity, as described in our discussion of Erikson in Chapter 6, are generally able to resolve conflicts and relieve anxiety,

becoming more accepting of death. People who successfully achieve such legitimization experience a new freedom and relaxation about the future and tend to hold favorable attitudes toward death. Older people generally consider a sudden death to be more tragic than a slow one, since they desire time to see loved ones, say good-bye, settle their affairs, and reminisce. In general, older adults accept the inevitability of their own death, even though they tend to be concerned about the impact of their death on relatives.

Religion may interact with age and cohort to affect attitudes toward death. For instance, in all age groups, the most religious persons who hold the strongest beliefs in an afterlife have less anxiety about dying. The religious are less fearful about the unknown and view death as the doorway to a better state of being. Those most fearful about death are irregular participants in formal religious activities or those intermediate in their religiosity whose belief systems may be confused and uncertain (Cicirelli, 2006). Religion can either comfort or create anxiety about an afterlife, but across cultures, it offers one way to try to make sense of death. The age of the person who has died is also a factor in how survivors react to death. Because the death of older people is often anticipated, it may be viewed as a "blessing" for someone whose "time has come" rather than as a tragic experience. Consider the different reactions you may have to the death of a child compared to that of a very old person who has suffered from chronic illness.

POINTS TO PONDER

We spend more time planning for a 2-week vacation than we will for our last 2 weeks of life. What factors might explain this?

POINTS TO PONDER

What thoughts, feelings, or images do you experience when you hear that a baby has died? What about the death of a young adult just graduating from college? A 50-year-old mother just starting her new career? An 85-year-old who has advanced dementia? A 79-year-old who is hit by a car while crossing the street? What variables or factors might explain differences in your reactions?

The Dying Process

As noted earlier, what older adults most fear is the painful process of dying. The stages of dying—one of the most widely known and classic frameworks for understanding the **dying process**—was advanced by Kübler-Ross (1969, 1981). Each stage represents a form of coping with the process of death.

1. shock and denial
2. anger ("why me?"), resentment, and guilt
3. bargaining, such as trying to make a deal with God
4. depression and withdrawal from others
5. adjustment/acceptance

Although Kübler-Ross cautioned that these stages were not invariant, immutable, or universal, she nevertheless implied that dying persons need to complete each stage before moving onto the next. She encouraged health care providers to help their patients advance through them to achieve the final stage. This widely debated perspective, sometimes misused with the dying and the bereaved, has been empirically rejected. Family members and health care providers must be cautious about implying that the dying person must move through these stages, and thus creating an illusion of control or what one "should do." Dying is more "messy" than sequential stages. Grieving over one's death does not proceed in a linear fashion, but reappears again and again to be reworked, and the emotional reactions to dying vary greatly (Neimeyer, 1998; Hooyman & Kramer, 2006; Walter, 2003). In fact, sequencing may not occur at all; instead, feelings of guilt, protest, anger, fearfulness, and despair can intermesh with humor, hope, acceptance, and gratitude, with the dying person moving back and forth between them. Alternatively, some people remain at one of the earlier stages of denial or anger, while others move readily into accommodating the reality of their death (Weiss, 2001).

Although there is now general agreement that there is no "typical," unidirectional way to

> "Once you learn how to die, you learn how to live" (Moyers & Moyers, 2000).

die through progressive stages, Kübler-Ross's controversial work was a pioneering catalyst; it increased public and professional awareness of death and the needs of the dying and their caregivers. Her framework can be a helpful cognitive grid or guideline, not a fixed sequence that determines a "good death." Another contribution was her emphasis on dying as a time of growth and profound spirituality. By accepting death's inevitability, dying persons can live meaningfully and productively and come to terms with who they really are. Since the dying are "our best teachers," those who work with them can learn from them and emerge with less anxiety about their own deaths (Kübler-Ross, 1969, 1975; Kubler-Ross & Kessler, 2001).

Other models conceptualize dying and grief as *tasks*, *phases*, or *processes* (Parkes, 1972; Stroebe et al., 2001; Weiss, 2001; Worden, 2002). As C. S. Lewis wrote, "sorrow turns out to be not a state, but a process. It needs not a map but a history…there is something new to be chronicled everyday" (Lews, 1961). A process perspective recognizes the alternating currents of emotion, thought, and behavior, which individuals move through at varying rates, oscillating through some emotions multiple times. Phases of the dying process, similar to those of grief, are conceptualized as:

1. *Avoidance:* shock, numbness, disbelief, and denial, all of which can function as buffers from the painful reality, especially when first learning that one is dying; fear, anxiety, and dread; feelings of unreality, disorganization, and not being able to comprehend the situation; trying to gain some control and understanding by gathering facts of what happened. Some dying individuals surround themselves with as many people as possible, while others isolate themselves or may even reject the presence of loved ones.

2. *Confrontation:* guilt; blaming self or others; rage; feelings of being overwhelmed and losing control; helplessness, panic, confusion, and powerlessness; the diffused energy of unfocused anger and despair, loss of faith, a sense of injustice or disillusionment; intense sadness

3. *Accommodation:* acceptance of the reality of death, saying good-byes, and gradually letting go of the physical world

To summarize, consistent with the framework of dynamic interactions discussed throughout this book, the process of dying is shaped by:

- an individual's own personality, resilience, and philosophy of life
- the specific illness
- the social context (e.g., whether at home surrounded by family who encourage the expression of feelings or isolated in a hospital)
- the cultural context: values, beliefs, shared meanings, and rituals

What is essential is for family and health care providers to create choices and supports for the dying person, without making judgments about "the right way to die." In all instances, cross-cultural variations in how dying is experienced and grief expressed need to be attended to by health care and social service providers.

End-of-Life Care: Palliative Care and Hospice

The concept of the dying process highlights the importance of how end-of-life care is provided. As noted earlier, although older people prefer to die at home, most deaths of elders occur in hospitals or nursing homes. Rather than happening suddenly from accident or infection, death is now most often the culmination of years with a chronic illness, such as dementia, congestive heart failure, or cancer. Most older people die of chronic diseases, and often suffer debilitating

symptoms such as nausea, delirium, or severe pain in the process. Since medicine focuses on treating the diseases, physicians and families may see death as a defeat, not an inevitable culmination. The traditional problem-oriented cure model of health care that emphasizes life-enhancing therapies falls short in guiding end-of-life care. Increasingly, adults express a preference for quality of life in the time they have remaining and a "good death." According to the Institute of Medicine, a "good death" is characterized by:

- knowledge that death is coming and an understanding of what to expect physically and emotionally
- the ability to maintain dignity and retain reasonable control over what happens
- adequate control of pain and other symptoms
- choice about where death occurs
- access to information and expertise of whatever kind is needed
- supports to minimize spiritual and emotional suffering
- access to hospice or palliative care in any location
- adequate time to say good-bye (DeSpelder & Strickland, 2002; Dula & Williams, 2005; Richardson & Barusch, 2006).

Because of traditional medicine's emphasis on curing disease, many patients and families find that care provided at the end of life is inappropriate or unwanted. SUPPORT (Study to Understand Prognoses and Preferences for Outcomes and Risks of Treatment), funded by the Robert Wood Johnson Foundation, is the largest

POINTS TO PONDER

If you have experienced the dying process of someone close to you or for whom you provided care, what phases did you observe? Did you observe the dying process as flowing, alternating between different stages, or unidirectional? Did the person reach the stage of acceptance? How did you know?

DECIDING TO FORGO MEDICAL TREATMENTS

Some terminally ill patients, both young and old, decide to forgo extraordinary or special treatments in order to live their remaining months, or even years, in ways they choose. Some opt out because they feel that the burdens of treatment outweigh the benefits; others do so because they are concerned that another round of chemotherapy treatment or another transplant will only add to their suffering with no chance of a cure. In some cases, these patients outlive their doctors' predictions, but for most, the primary gain is control over one's remaining life. A prominent example of such a patient is the columnist Art Buchwald, who died in 2007 after refusing kidney dialysis a year earlier. He outlived his doctors' predictions and made the most of his time remaining by visiting with family and friends across the country.

study ever to examine the care of seriously ill and dying patients. It found that patients and their physicians did not routinely make plans for end-of-life care or for how to address predictable complications and pain, nor did they discuss the overall course of dying and aims of care. Patients died in pain, often in intensive care units, with their families financially devastated by efforts to keep them alive. Even in illnesses with a predictable course, physicians considered an order to forgo resuscitation only in the patients' last few days (Christopher, 2003; Kaufmann, 2002; Schroepfer, 2006).

Medical experts agree that at least 90 percent of all serious pain can be effectively treated, yet at least 25 percent of dying patients do not receive adequate pain medication (Dula & Williams, 2005). The pain of dying is intensified by the fact that terminally ill patients often experience depression, delirium, anxiety, despair, helplessness, hopelessness, anticipatory grief, and guilt. As discussed in Chapter 6, the prevalence of depression increases with the severity of the illness, pain, and limitations related to symptoms or treatment. Yet depression is often dismissed as a natural reaction of sadness and grief from knowing that one's life is

ending. When left untreated, depression causes significant suffering, reduces patients' ability to fully participate in life and comply with medical treatments, and can contribute to other medical problems—in some instances, an earlier death (Adamek, 2003; Unutzer et al., 2003). The incidence of depression is not surprising, given findings that older patients with cancer, for example, have less symptom management than other age groups. One study found that 25 percent of cancer patients in a nursing home who reported daily pain received no analgesia; in addition, patients age 85 and older and elders of color were less likely to receive analgesia. Furthermore, older adults have often been excluded from research trials and studies on pain management (Bern-Klug, Gessert, & Forbes, 2001; Dula & Williams, 2005; Wilkinson & Lynn, 2001).

The **Dying Person's Bill of Rights,** developed nearly 40 years ago, states that individuals have the right to personal dignity and privacy; informed participation, including to have their end-of-life choices respected by health care professionals; and considerate, respectful service and competent care during their dying process. As highlighted in the next box, the **right to die** with dignity and without pain is currently supported by laws, public policies, and clinical practice more than it was at the time the Dying Person's Bill of Rights was introduced. Although controversy surrounds the use of life-sustaining technology, both sides agree that the dying person's self-determination and right to be free from physical pain are essential to humane care. As articulated by the American Geriatrics Society (2007), dying persons should be provided with opportunities to make the circumstances of their dying consistent with their preferences and values. The U.S. Supreme Court ruled in 1997 that Americans have a constitutional right to palliative care. **Palliative care** is both a philosophy and a program model. It focuses not on lifesaving measures, but on relief of pain and suffering by addressing the patient's emotional, social, and spiritual needs. Physicians, nurses, and social workers use both pharmacological and psychosocial approaches to cope with symptoms and needs, especially pain management. Palliative care is most effective when integrated into existing care settings, such as hospitals, skilled nursing facilities, or private homes, and is not necessarily tied to end-of-life care. Proponents of palliative care believe that it should be an integral part of comprehensive care for patients of all ages with life-limiting illnesses (National Consensus Project for Quality Palliative Care, 2009). The box on this page differentiates pain management, hospice care, and formalized palliative care, with pain management as a major component of both types of care.

With palliative care, both the patient and health care providers recognize that quality of life can be enhanced at any stage of an illness. Because of its emphasis on pain management, it may also be delivered in conjunction with active treatment to patients of all ages. Medical professionals increasingly think of pain as the "fifth vital sign." Although palliative care is a subspecialty within medicine and typically a program within hospitals, a holistic rather than a largely medical approach is increasingly advocated (Ferrel, et al., 2007; Jost, 2005; Schroepfer, 2006). Such care is characterized by respect for the patient's values and choices about privacy and type of care, candid and sensitive communication, encouragement to express feelings, social support from family and friends, and a multidisciplinary team approach. Music, art therapy, spiritual exploration, and reminiscence through photos and mementos may all be encouraged as a way to add pleasure and meaning to life. Medical professionals today are more open in talking about death with their patients and families than in the past. Increasingly, the pursuit of a peaceful, pain-free illness and death is viewed as the proper goal of medicine, even though there is less agreement on how to achieve this (e.g., how aggressively pain-killers should be used). This breaking of "professional silence" is in part a reaction to external pressures, including growing public support for physicians to provide aggressive pain control and palliative care with patients who insist on having some control over their dying.

The number of hospitals providing palliative care programs has grown from 632 in 2000 to 1,240 in 2007, including more than 50 percent

> **TYPES OF PAIN AND PALLIATIVE CARE SERVICES AS DEFINED BY THE AMERICAN HOSPITAL ASSOCIATION**
>
> - *Pain management:* a formal program that educates staff about how to manage chronic and acute pain based on accepted academic and clinical guidelines
> - *Hospice:* a program providing end-of-life care and supportive services, broader than but inclusive of pain management, which uses interdisciplinary teams to address the emotional, social, financial, and legal needs of terminally ill patients and their families. It is only available to persons with a diagnosis of less than six months to live, although palliative care services have recently been developed within community-based hospice programs to serve people who wish to continue curative treatment during the dying process.
> - *Palliative care:* a program providing specialized medical care, drugs, or therapies to manage acute or chronic pain and to control other symptoms, increasingly from diagnosis of serious illness to terminal phases. It differs from hospice because it may be delivered concurrently with curative or life-prolonging medical care and is not dependent on the patient's prognosis (e.g., expected time until death). The program, run by specially trained physicians and other clinicians, also provides services such as counseling about advance directives, spiritual care, and social services to seriously ill patients and their families. Palliative care programs typically refer patients to hospice when cure is no longer an option (Chris & Blacker, 2008).

of hospitals with more than 75 beds (Growth of hospital-care palliative care programs surges, 2007). Much of this growth is fueled by efforts to reduce costs (Morrison, Pendrod, Cassel, et al., 2008). However, such hospital-based programs are still far from the norm and do not easily fit into the coverage and payment policies of Medicare and private insurers. Funding for these programs often depends on piecing together resources from different funding streams, including short-term grants. This funding pattern jeopardizes the sustainability of formal palliative care programs (Kayser-Jones, 2006).

FACING DEATH ON YOUR OWN TERMS

Ruth, age 85, was diagnosed with incurable cancer. She told her family and doctor that she wanted to live long enough (5 months) to see her first granddaughter married. Her doctor arranged for low-dose chemotherapy that did not cause much discomfort, and she experienced a remission. After her granddaughter's wedding, the doctors found that the cancer had returned and spread. Her response was that she was now ready to die. She received excellent palliative care, lived 3 months without pain with the help of morphine, and was alert almost to the end, sharing memories and saying good-bye to her family.

Some physicians still wrongly assume that they will be censured or prosecuted for giving controlled substances to the terminally ill, even when the controlled drug is the approved treatment. In fact, the Supreme Court has cited two legal methods for more aggressive pain management:

1. the "morphine drip," a continuous administration of morphine at a dose that will abolish pain; and if that is not effective,
2. physician-prescribed "terminal sedation" with barbiturates an other drugs providing continuous anesthesia.

Despite the growth of websites dealing with "pain control" or "death and dying," many patients and their families are unaware that pain-killing narcotics are legally available. However, both professional and public awareness of these options is growing.

A groundbreaking 1997 report by the Institute of Medicine criticized health care providers for failing to provide competent palliative and supportive care, and it recommended ways to improve care, as summarized in the box on page 564 (Field & Cassel, 1997). Many of these principles were subsequently reflected in the 2004 Clinical Practice Guidelines for Quality Palliative Care. While certification in palliative care is now available

for physicians and nurses providers, specialty training to offer this care is essential. Although accreditation standards for medical schools now include the mandate to cover palliative care, the requirement contains no clear standards for teaching this topic (Last Acts, 2002). Nevertheless, there are many encouraging signs among the professional associations of medicine, nursing, and social work, including the following:

- The American Medical Association and the American College of Physicians: guidelines for quality pain-management technologies
- The American Medical Association: a profession-wide educational program on how to provide quality advance care planning and comprehensive palliative care
- The American Geriatrics Society: fosters the development and study of instruments that measure quality of care at the end of life, including physical and emotional symptoms, advance care planning, and aggressive care near death
- The American Board of Internal Medicine: educational resources to promote physician competency during internal medicine residency and subspecialty training
- The American Association of Colleges of Nursing: national education program to improve training in end-of-life care in nursing curricula
- The National Association of Social Workers: Standards for Social Work Practice in Palliative and End-of-Life Care: identifies specific practice behaviors for social workers providing end-of-life care
- Social Work Leaders in End-of-Life Care: priority agenda for the profession set at the Social Work Summit on End-of-Life and Palliative Care
- Institute for Health Care Improvement: breakthrough collaborative in quality improvement for end-of-life care, for advanced heart and lung disease, and for pain

- The Joint Commission for Accrediting Hospitals: requires hospitals to implement pain management plans for terminally ill patients
- The Department of Veterans Affairs: innovations aimed at better care of advanced illnesses; pain as a fifth vital sign; quality measures in advance care planning and pain management; and faculty development
- National Consensus Project on Palliative Care: sponsored by five national palliative care/hospice associations in 2004
- The Soros Foundation's Death in America Project: fellowships in end-of-life care are awarded to physicians and social workers
- Last Acts: a coalition of 72 organizations to enhance communication and decision-making

among health care providers, insurers, hospitals, nursing homes, and consumers. Although closed in 2005, publications from this task force are available on the Robert Wood Johnson Foundation website (http://www.rwjf.org).

We turn next to discussing the primary delivery system for end-of-life care—hospice.

Hospice Care

Another approach to being more responsive to dying patients and their families is the **hospice** model of caring for the terminally ill. Hospice is not always a "place" but a philosophy of, and approach to care that is offered primarily in the home, but also in hospital and long-term care settings, such as assisted living. In fact, availability of hospice care along with caregiver support and state funding for home care often determine whether an older person dies at home (Cantwell et al., 2000; Muramatsu,

---

AN INTEGRATED HOSPITAL-BASED PALLIATIVE CARE PROGRAM

One of the nation's premier hospital-based palliative care programs is the Lillian and Benjamin Hertzberg Palliative Care Institute at Mount Sinai Hospital in New York City. A consultation team is composed of a nurse, physicians, rotating fellows, and medical residents in training. This team advises hospital physicians who care for seriously ill patients on topics such as when to use comfort care, how to talk about treatment choices with patients and families, and pain and symptom management.

A four-bed inpatient unit is available for patients with complex emotional and physical symptoms and for those who need help in planning a course of care for their terminal illness. Nurses, social workers, interns, and residents staff this unit, working closely with the consultation team. Home care is available for seriously ill patients who are able to return home. All efforts are made to allow patients to go home, usually with hospice care, or to a nursing home rather than die in a hospital.

To ensure that palliative care is available to all patients in the hospital, new physicians are trained in palliative care through bedside teaching, clinical rotations, and lectures. All oncology and geriatric fellows at Mt. Sinai Hospital are required to complete a 1-month clinical palliative care rotation.

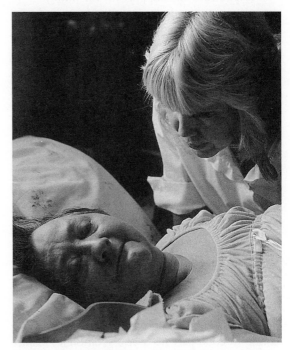

Hospice care can enhance quality of life for the dying person.

Hoyem, Yin, & Campbell, 2008). Hospice is a central component of palliative care by providing integrated physical, medical, emotional, and spiritual care not only to the patient but also to his or her support system. As one type of end-of-life care, hospice is dedicated to helping individuals who are beyond medicine's curative power to remain in familiar surroundings where pain is reduced and personal dignity and control over the dying process are maintained. Ensuring the patient's quality of life and the assessment and coordination of the physical, psychosocial, and spiritual needs of the patient and family are fundamental to the hospice approach. More nursing homes and hospitals, responsive to a changing market, are providing hospice care and pain management programs.

Most hospice programs share the following characteristics:

- focus on quality of life
- service availability 24 hours per day, 7 days per week, as needed
- respite care and support for the family
- management of physical symptoms and pain
- psychological, social, and spiritual counseling for patients and their families
- coordination of skilled and homemaker home care services and collaboration among providers (home health care, hospitals, nursing homes)
- physician direction of services by a multidisciplinary team
- use of volunteers as central to the team
- inpatient care when needed
- bereavement counseling for family and friends after the death

St. Christopher's Hospice, started in Great Britain in 1967, was the first formal hospice in the world, although TB asylums for younger people had informally performed similar functions before then. The first hospice in the U.S. was developed in 1974 in New Haven, Connecticut. Today there are over 4,700 hospices nationwide, serving about 900,000 patients a year (National Hospice and Palliative Care Organization, 2008). The majority of these are independent, free-standing

RECOMMENDATIONS OF THE INSTITUTE OF MEDICINE FOR IMPROVING END-OF-LIFE CARE

- People with advanced, potentially fatal illnesses and those close to them should be able to expect and receive reliable, skillful, and supportive care.
- Health care providers should commit themselves to improving care for dying patients and to use existing knowledge effectively to prevent and relieve pain and other symptoms.
- Policy makers, consumer groups, and purchasers of health care should work with health care practitioners, organizations, and researchers to:

  1. strengthen methods for measuring quality of life and other outcomes of care for dying patients and those close to them
  2. develop better tools and strategies for improving the quality of care and hold health care organizations accountable for care at the end of life
  3. modify mechanisms for funding care in order to encourage rather than impede good end-of-life care
  4. reform drug prescription laws, burdensome regulations, and state medical board policies and practices that impede effective use of opioids to relieve pain and suffering

- Educators of health professionals should initiate changes in undergraduate, graduate, and continuing education to ensure that practitioners develop empathy, knowledge, and skills to care for dying patients. Palliative care should become a defined area of expertise, education, and research.
- The nation's research establishment should define and implement priorities for strengthening the knowledge base for end-of-life care.
- Public discussion on end-of-life issues is needed to improve understanding of the experience of dying, the options available to patients and families, and the obligations of communities to those approaching death (Field & Cassel, 1997).

agencies that provide in-home services for cancer and HIV/AIDS patients with a prognosis of 6 months or less to live. In recent years, hospice has been extended to dying prisoners, with inmate volunteers trained to provide care.

In 1986, Congress passed legislation making hospice a permanent Medicare benefit, including reimbursement for prescriptions and granting a modest increase in reimbursement rates. Medicare's hospice benefit includes services that are not generally covered under Medicare, such as:

- home nursing care without homebound or skilled service requirements
- on-call availability of providers for crises 24 hours a day and 7 days a week
- interdisciplinary team management for comprehensiveness and continuity
- spiritual counseling, family support
- treatment for pain/symptoms, medications
- emergency acute medical care, equipment
- inpatient care when needed (e.g., for respite or symptom management)
- bereavement care for survivors.

Medicare pays a capitated, all-inclusive, prospectively set per-day rate for four categories of service; of these, routine home care accounts for the majority of all care delivered (Centers for Medicare and Medicaid Services, 2009).

Hospice professionals and volunteers, working as an interdisciplinary team, advocate for giving dying persons full and accurate information about their condition. They also try to design supportive environments in which people can tell their life stories, resolve and reconcile relationships, and find meaning in their deaths. Listening to and touching the dying person, enjoying music and art, family involvement, and ritual celebration of special events such as birthdays and weddings are all encouraged. For those who value spirituality, staff supports them in their quest for meaning and dignity in the last stage of life. In addition, hospice staff work directly with family and friends to help them deal with their loss, clarify expectations, relate effectively to the dying patient, and then provide bereavement counseling after the death. Hospice programs also offer counseling and support to staff members to help prevent "burnout."

Hospice care benefits the patient both financially and in terms of extending life. Hospice use in the final year of life reduces Medicare expenditures an average of $2,309 per patient (Taylor, et al., 2007). There is also increasing evidence that hospice provides better quality of life for both end-of-life patients and their caregivers than do hospitals. For example, a study of 8,700 Medicare patients with 16 different terminal diseases found that for all conditions, patients age 65 and older in hospice lived longer than those in other settings (Brink, 2007). Another study showed that the mean survival was 29 days longer for hospice patients than for non-hospice patients (Conner, et al., 2007). Approximately 38 percent of all deaths in the U.S. are under the care of a hospice program, even though it is estimated that twice as many patients probably should have received hospice. About 80 percent of hospice patients are age 65 and older, while the pediatric and young adult population accounts for less than 1 percent of hospice admissions (National Hospice and Palliative Care Organization, 2008). Hospice use is greatest for diseases that impose a heavy burden on the caregiver and have higher rates of an accurate prognosis—cancer, kidney diseases, and Alzheimer' disease. Hospice utilization is lower among all populations of color compared to whites. For example, 9 percent of dying African Americans use hospice compared to 80 percent of whites (Abelson, 2007; Cohen, 2008; National Hospice and Palliative Care Organization, 2008).

The reasons for a relatively low rate of participation are complex. One of the barriers to a "good death" is that doctors often refer patients to hospice too late. Approximately 31 percent of all hospice patients (82 percent of whom are over age 65) die within a week of admission. The median length (50th percentile) of stay in a hospice is about 20 days, far less than the 180 days of care covered by Medicare (National Hospice and Palliative Care Organization, 2008). Despite technological advances, it is still difficult for doctors to predict how long terminally ill patients will survive. In addition, some physicians remain uncomfortable with being honest with a dying person. Instead, they tend to convey an optimistic bias and to overestimate survival and future quality of life.

As a result of late referrals, most patients begin hospice during a period of rapid physical decline and often in crisis. At such times, the immediate management of symptoms and relieving the family overshadows the need to address the emotional and spiritual issues of remembering, forgiving, and bringing closure to a person's life. When more time is available, the dying person can participate in the process of validating the past and planning for the future, and this gives the family opportunities to address unresolved issues. Some hospice professionals view this short-term use of Medicare-covered services as a problem (Brickner et al., 2004). However, short periods of hospice utilization may actually represent an informed preference for delaying formal end-of-life care for families and patients unlikely to use hospice earlier. For them, 2 to 3 weeks may be just the right amount of time (Waldrop, 2006). And even short hospice stays in the last month of life can be less expensive than end-of-life care in other settings, depending on the acuity of needs at the end (National Hospice and Palliative Care Organizations, 2008). Nevertheless, the National Hospice Organization tries to educate physicians on how to predict appropriate entry points to hospice for various conditions so that patients are fully aware of their options and timing for palliative care.

Another barrier to hospice use is that the oldest-old are more likely to die from chronic illnesses, such as heart or lung disease, than cancer—the most common terminal condition among hospice patients. Unlike cancer, where a more definable process of decline can be projected, most elders die from the accumulation of conditions that actually may be more imminently terminal yet do not meet the hospice criterion of a prognosis of death in 6 months or less. In other instances, even patients with cancer do not receive an accurate diagnosis and are unlikely to be informed about or qualify for hospice benefits, including pain relief. Among those who do, a substantial percent resist hospice because it requires acknowledging that one is dying and abandoning hope of cure (Waldrop, 2006). In the past, hospice patients had to give up all

THE COMFORT PROVIDED BY HOSPICE CARE

Three months of chemotherapy followed by 6 weeks of radiation was not working for Mr. Frank. His last hope was a stem cell transplant, but those prospects were dimming each day as he became weaker and weaker. Mr. Frank decided that he did not want to spend his final days in a losing battle with his rapidly advancing and painful lymphoma. He preferred to be as comfortable as possible and to leave the hospital and return home.

Mr. Frank and his wife, Jean, contacted a local hospice that helped them set up a range of services at home that would assist both of them through the final months of his life. A nurse and physician were assigned to his care. The hospice staff also trained Jean, friends, and family in how to administer Mr. Frank's pain medications and to use tiny ice chips to help him deal with his extremely dry throat and mouth. The staff also taught Jean how to tell when Mr. Frank's pain was increasing, so that he could be given a high dose of morphine before it became unbearable.

Mr. Frank also received visits from the hospice team social worker, who talked with him about how to resolve some issues with his daughter, who held considerable anger toward her father. When the hospice team estimated that Mr. Frank would probably die in 3 days, they encouraged Jean to contact family and friends who lived at a distance so that they would have time to visit and say good-bye. In those last 3 days, Mr. Frank was lucid and able to talk, laugh, and cry with those who loved him, including his daughter.

His family and friends all commented later that they felt Mr. Frank had a "good death." They appreciated being able to be part of his peaceful death in the comfort and familiar surroundings of his home. The hospice social worker kept in touch with Jean for a year after her husband's death, encouraging her to express her grief and learn new coping skills. Mr. Frank's daughter was especially grateful for the opportunity to reconcile with her father before he died.

treatment to qualify for hospice. Therefore, those who did not choose hospice often spent their last days in a hospital receiving expensive medical care. However, a few insurance companies and some large hospice providers have instituted an "open access" approach that continues to cover advanced medical treatment—such as radiation, chemotherapy, and dialysis—for hospice patients. This approach recognizes that some more aggressive treatments have both a palliative and potentially curative effect, and are therefore consistent with the model of hospice care. Due to the potentially high cost of providing more aggressive treatments near end of life, open access remains the exception rather than the rule for all but the largest hospice and insurance providers (Wright & Katz, 2007). As a result of continued treatment and the supportive at-home approach of hospice, some patients have even been able to gain the weight and strength necessary to leave the program (Abelson, 2007). Hospice providers must recertify a patient's eligibility for hospice services at the end of each of two 90-day periods, then at the end of each subsequent 60-day recertification periods. Patients who show improvement in their primary hospice diagnosis often no longer meet eligibility requirements for hospice care. Patients whose health continues to decline and who meet criteria of having a terminal diagnosis and an anticipated 6-month prognosis can continue to be recertified for an unlimited time period.

Low-income individuals and persons of color appear to be underserved by hospice, even though, as described in Chapter 4, groups such as African Americans have a higher overall incidence of death from cancer, a greater likelihood of inadequate pain treatment, and intensified financial strain (Cone et al., 2003; Welch, Teno, & Mor, 2005). The reasons for this are complex and reflect historical, economic, cultural, and religious factors, suggesting that racial disparities persist into end-of-life care and death, particularly related to communication and family needs (Dula & Williams, 2005). African Americans and Latinos are less likely than other groups to complete advance directives, to see physicians who spend time talking with them about end-of-life care, or to participate in hospice (Cohen, 2008; Gert & Burr, 2008; Kwak, Haley, & Chiraboga, 2008). When death is inevitable and

imminent, African American families are twice as likely as whites to request aggressive life-sustaining treatments, including dialysis, artificial nutrition, surgery, and antibiotics, even if the patient is in a coma or permanent vegetative state, has little chance of survival, and will lose their life savings to pay their health care costs (Dula & Williams, 2005; Payne, Medina, & Hampton, 2003).

In some cases, this may occur because African Americans perceive advance directives and palliative care as "giving up hope" or not respecting their cultural and personal values. For example, African American elders are more likely than whites to believe that God is the ultimate decision maker regarding the time, manner, and place of death, and to have religious prohibitions against limiting life-sustaining treatment (Johnson, Elbert-Avila, & Tulsky, 2005). Some may fear that hospice or palliative care is being prescribed as a way to limit care or "trying to get rid of them" rather than a vehicle for increasing control or self-determination. The fear of not receiving needed medical care at the end of life is indeed based on the reality that various cardiovascular, cerebrovascular, cancer, and kidney transplant procedures are still less available to blacks than whites (Kressin & Peterson, 2001; Hampton, 2008; Condon, Miller, Quasem, & Looney, 2008). Perceptions of palliative care as a way to control African Americans' survival also stem from unethical research conducted on blacks in the past, along with health care disparities across the life course (Dula & Williams, 2005; Institute of Medicine, 2002; Washington, 2007).

Given African Americans' shorter life expectancy, it is also understandable that they would prefer treatments that may enable them to live as long as possible. In contrast to a peaceful death, aggressive medical treatment ("fighting while going down" as an expected part of life's ongoing struggle) is often viewed as a sign of respect among African Americans, even if it means feeding tubes, pain, and loss of life savings. Providers need to be sensitive to cultural differences in how patients choose to die and be able to discuss ways to give African

Americans the gift of a "good death" while not giving up hope. On a larger scale, palliative and end-of-life care is unlikely to be successful without addressing disparities in access to prevention, risk assessment, diagnosis, and evidence-based curative treatment across the life course (Crawley, 2001).

Despite the varied definitions of **death with dignity** among culturally diverse groups, underutilization of hospice may also stem from inadequate knowledge of this service and the lack of culturally competent providers who are trained to discuss end-of-life care with persons of color. Working through African American ministers and community centers may be a way to increase the availability of hospice information to black communities (Kurent, 2000). Culturally specific end-of-life care programs that originate in the African American community, such as the Harlem Palliative Care Network or the Seattle African American Comfort Care Program (described in the box on this page), are more likely to be trusted. In addition, medications for managing pain must be accessible in pharmacies in neighborhoods of color. Religious organizations in culturally diverse communities may be the best locus for discussing death, dying, and end-of-life care (Braun, Pietsch, & Blanchette, 2000; Crawley, 2001).

Although most research on end-of-life care focuses on Medicare utilization, Medicaid also funds end-of-life care, including hospice care, in the last 6 months of life. While Medicaid funding for hospice varies widely by states, Medicaid accounts for about 5 percent of total hospice revenues. Most of Medicaid's funding for long-term care for the dually eligible (those eligible for both Medicaid and Medicare), however, goes to nursing home care at the end of life. Although the proportion of hospice enrollees in nursing homes has increased from 9.9 percent in 1990 to nearly 29 percent in 2007, it is estimated that 45 to 85 percent of nursing home residents are in constant pain because of inadequate pain management or none at all (Duncan, Forbes-Thompson, & Bott, 2008; Miller, Teno, & Mor, 2004; National Hospice and Palliative Care Organization, 2008). The lack of pain management in

PALLIATIVE CARE PROGRAMS DEVELOPED BY AFRICAN AMERICAN COMMUNITIES

The mission of the Seattle African American Comfort Program (SAACP) is advocating, creating, and coordinating culturally respectful end-of-life services for African Americans. The program offers information about access to medical, psychosocial, spiritual, and legal services to African Americans who are facing end-of-life issues and considering hospice. Services are provided at no charge to individuals in the community at convenient locations, by telephone, and through the program's website. The program also provides training to health care providers.

The Balm of Gilead Project in Alabama's largest county was created to meet the palliative care needs of low-income African Americans. It aims to be responsive to the economic and social realities of the community, where dying patients often lack appropriate caregivers to remain at home and where distrust of the medical system is pervasive. The Balm of Gilead itself is an umbrella organization, providing an infrastructure for an array of services to address the holistic needs associated with terminal illness in each of its stages and treatment settings. These include:

- Hospital-based services—with a 10-bed inpatient palliative care unit, palliative care consultation, and educational efforts with hospital staff and students—all focus on pain management.
- Home care services
- Long-term residential care through a palliative care program at a local nursing home
- Community outreach and education involving care teams, civic groups, faith communities, and community education

The Harlem Palliative Care Network assumes that an effective palliative care program must come from, and be part of, the community. Organizers first established a base of expertise in palliative medicine at a community hospital and networked with community organizations—churches, social groups, and nursing homes. These networks helped to identify patients and families with advanced illnesses who could benefit from palliative interventions, including pain management early in the course of a disease to prevent emergency room care for an acute health crisis. The network also provides nonmedical services to support patients and families emotionally and spiritually.

nursing homes—even in those that have hospice care—is generally attributed to shortages of physicians in these settings and nurses without adequate time and training to provide analgesics when hospice staff is unavailable (Kayser-Jones et al., 2006). Given the projected growth in long-term care, it is essential that nursing home staff receive training and resources for palliative care.

The Right to Die or Hastened Death

Along with increased attention to the ways in which people choose to die, the right-to-die movement is growing. This has given rise to new ethical and legal debates regarding the right to a "good death." Advocates of the right to die increasingly use the term **hastened death** rather than **euthanasia**, because it speeds up the inevitable. Whether others have a right to help people die, and under what conditions, has been discussed throughout history (see the box on page 570 summarizing major events in the right-to-die movement). But recent debates about the ethical, social, and legal issues raised by hastened death have intensified with increased medical advances used to prolong life and the legal recognition of patients' autonomy. These issues revolve around three types of patients:

1. the terminally ill who are conscious
2. the irreversibly comatose
3. the brain-damaged or severely debilitated who have good chances for survival but have limited quality of life (e.g., patients with Alzheimer's or Lou Gehrig's disease)

Central to these debates is the doctrine of **informed consent,** which establishes competent patients' rights to accept or refuse medical treatment based on their understanding of its benefits and harms. Standard informed consent procedures work best in the acute care setting, where they involve treatment choices that lead to cure, significant improvement, or death. Decision-making for older people with chronic illness, often in

> "The good death: We only get one time to get it right."

long-term care settings, is much more ambiguous than in acute-care environments, and long-term care providers tend to disagree about patients' rights to end their lives. Findings are mixed regarding the acceptability of a range of end-of-life decision options among older people. Although increased age is generally associated with preferring quality over quantity of life, health care providers cannot always assume that this is the case, especially among elders of color (Dula & Williams, 2005).

The value of autonomy, articulated in informed consent and advance directives, may conflict with cultures that are more collectivist than individualist in nature. For example, decisions about end-of-life care in Asian and Pacific Islander cultures are influenced by the value placed on shared decision-making within families; filial piety; silent communication, whereby it is improper to discuss issues of death and dying with one's parents; and preservation of harmony, or the sense that family members should not share bad news if it disrupts family harmony. When patients have difficulty making health care decisions and defer to the family or doctor, they may unfortunately be labeled noncompliant by traditional Western medicine. To take account of such cultural variations, family-centered, shared, or negotiated models of medical decision-making recognize the legitimacy of multiple points of view. Similarly, African Americans' religious beliefs and historical experiences were discussed earlier as factors in their willingness to utilize hospice services and advance directives.

Passive Euthanasia (Voluntary Elective Death)

Euthanasia, which was originally referred to as a painless or peaceful death, can be passive (allowing death) or active (causing death). In **passive euthanasia,** treatment is withdrawn, and nothing is done to prolong the patient's life

HISTORY OF MAJOR EVENTS RELATED TO THE RIGHT-TO-DIE MOVEMENT IN THE UNITED STATES

1937   The Euthanasia Society of America is founded.

1967   The first living will is written.

1968   The first living will legislation is introduced in Florida.

1973   The American Hospital Association creates the Dying Persons' Bill of Rights, which includes informed consent and the right to refuse treatment.

1974   The first U.S. hospice opens in Connecticut.

1975   The New Jersey Supreme Court allows Karen Ann Quinlan's parents to disconnect the respirator that was keeping her alive.

The California Natural Death Act is passed—the first aid-in-dying statute—which gives legal standing to living wills and protects physicians from being sued for failing to treat incurable illnesses.

1980   The Hemlock Society is founded, distributing how-to-die information.

1987   The California State Bar Conference passes a resolution to become the first public body to approve of physician aid-in-dying.

1990   The American Medical Association adopts the position that, with informed consent, a physician can withhold or withdraw treatment from a patient who is close to death and may also discontinue life support of a patient in a permanent coma.

The Supreme Court decision in the Nancy Cruzan case rules that competent adults have a constitutionally protected right to refuse medical treatment and allows a state to impose procedural safeguards.

Congress passes the Patient Self-Determination Act, which requires hospitals that receive federal funds to tell patients about their state's legal options.

1991   Washington State voters reject Ballot Initiative 119 (54 to 45 percent), which would have legalized physician aid-in-dying.

The Federal Patient Self-Determination Act requires health care facilities that receive Medicare or Medicaid funds to inform patients of their right to refuse medical treatment and to sign advance directives.

1992   California voters defeated Proposition 161, a law similar to the Washington State initiative, and at a similar proportion (54 to 46 percent).

1993   Compassion in Dying is founded in Washington State.

Compassion in Dying files a lawsuit challenging the constitutionality of laws banning assisted dying in Washington State and New York. They win in the District Court in Washington State, but not in New York.

Oregon voters approve (51 to 49 percent) Measure 16, the Oregon Death with Dignity Act, which permits terminally ill patients, under proper safeguards, to obtain a physician's prescription to end life in a humane and dignified manner.

1995   Both Washington State's Compassion ruling and Oregon's Death with Dignity Act are ruled unconstitutional at the district court level.

1996   The Ninth Circuit Court of Appeals issues a landmark decision in *Compassion v. Washington State*, which upholds that assisted dying is protected by the liberty and privacy provisions of the U.S. Constitution.

1997   The U.S. Supreme Court reverses the circuit court decisions in Washington State and rules that state laws against assisted suicide are not unconstitutional. The Court also finds that patients have a right to aggressive treatment of pain and other symptoms, even if the treatment hastens death.

1997   Oregon citizens vote by a margin of 60 to 40 percent to retain the Oregon Death with Dignity Act.

Jack Kevorkian videotapes himself administering a lethal medication to a terminally ill man, which is broadcast on *60 Minutes*. He is charged with first-degree premeditated murder and incarcerated.

(Continued)

MAJOR EVENTS RELATED TO THE RIGHT-TO-DIE (Continued)

2005 The Schiavo case dominates national headlines, pitting her parents against her husband in federal and state courts, and disability rights versus right-to-die groups.

2005 Partially as a result of the highly visible Shiavo case, legislation is introduced before Congress to establish a stricter rule for withdrawing food and water from Medicare and Medicaid patients than for terminating other types of life support, but does not pass.

2005 Compassion and Choices is formed as a coalition of end-of-life organizations, encompassing Compassion in Dying and the Hemlock Society.

2008 Washington State passes citizens' Initiative 1000 (58 to 42 percent), known as the "Washington Death With Dignity Act," and similar to Oregon's law. It permits Washington State residents with a terminal diagnosis and less than 6 months to live to obtain a physician-prescribed lethal dose of medication.

artificially, such as using a feeding tube or ventilator. Suspension of medical interventions or physician aid in dying allows the natural dying process to occur, but no active steps are taken to bring about death. Medications to relieve pain are sometimes given that may hasten death, but the object is to relieve suffering, not to bring about death. Withholding or

POINTS TO PONDER

DEFINING END OF LIFE

How the end of life is defined has implications for quality of care and quality of life, when decisions need to be made about life-sustaining care, and eligibility for hospice. One definition of the end of life is the beginning of an illness that is characterized by any of the three dimensions of severity:

- diagnosis of a potentially fatal illness
- the beginning of a functional limitation in one's ability to perform any of the basic activities of daily living, or
- the advent of pain or physical symptoms that are a major distress to the patient and/or precursors to and resulting in death (Lawton, 2001).

What would you consider to be the end of life? What kind of care would you want at the end of your life? Would you want any measures taken to sustain life, even if you were in a coma or had advanced dementia?

withdrawing useless or unwanted medical treatments, or providing adequate pain relief, even if it hastens death, has been determined to be legal and ethical and is generally accepted. For example, 84 percent of Americans in a Pew 2005 poll approved of laws that let terminally ill patients make decisions about whether to be kept alive through medical treatment, even though the majority of Americans would favor doctors doing everything possible to save their lives (DiCamillo & Field, 2006). The legal context for this is the 1990 U.S. Supreme Court case of *Cruzan v. Director, Missouri Department of Health*, which recognized the right of a competent patient to refuse unwanted medical care, including artificial nutrition and hydration, as a "liberty" interest and therefore as constitutionally protected. The Supreme Court later delegated regulation of this constitutional right to the states.

Another indicator of changing legal interpretations is the position of the American Medical Association (AMA). Their 1984 statement on euthanasia presented two fundamental guidelines:

- The patient's role in decision-making is paramount.
- A decrease in aggressive treatment of the hopelessly ill patient is advisable when treatment would only prolong a difficult and uncomfortable process of dying.

Written in 1989 and most recently updated in 1996, the AMA concurred that, with informed consent, physicians could withhold or withdraw treatment from patients who are close to death. Most physicians agree that withholding and withdrawing nutrition and hydration are permissible in certain circumstances, and that it is the physician's duty to initiate discussion of these issues with patients and their families.

In contrast to passive euthanasia, where deliberate decisions are made about withholding or withdrawing treatment, there is also a form of hastened death whereby older people may voluntarily make decisions about their lives that are equivalent to choosing to die. For example, an older person may refuse extra help at home or insist on hospital discharge directly to the home, in spite of the need for skilled health care. When an older person commits suicide through the process of **self-neglect**, the effects of his or her decisions are subtle and gradual. If older people neglect their care needs or choose an inappropriate living situation because of impaired judgment, involuntary treatment laws can sometimes be used to move them to protected settings. If their "failure to care," however, is not immediately life-threatening, their right to self-determination must be respected, even if families or professionals disagree with their choices. If found to be incompetent, however, they can be legally compelled to comply with others' expectations for their care.

Active Euthanasia: Assisted Suicide

Active euthanasia refers to deliberate steps taken to bring about someone else's death, by administering a lethal injection or by some other means. It can be voluntary (at the dying person's request) or involuntary (without consent). Sometimes called *mercy killing*, the legality of active euthanasia has been tested by several highly controversial court cases, voter initiatives, and state legislation. As noted above, a subject of intense controversy is **assisted suicide** or **physician-assisted suicide (PAS)**—or the term **physician-assistance-in-dying** which removes the connotation of suicide. All three terms are used here. PAS occurs when someone else provides the means by which an individual who chooses to, can end his or her life. For example, a physician may prescribe medication, typically barbiturates, knowing that the individual intends to use it to end his or her life, but it is the dying person who decides when and whether to take it.

Those who argue against the legalization of assisted suicide, such as the U.S. Conference of Catholic Bishops and the National Right to Life Committee, fear a "culture of death" or "slippery slope" is being created, to the detriment of the oldest-old and persons with disabilities who could be pressured to feel that it is "their duty to die" (Jost, 2005). They fear that a law made to convey permission could come to be seen as prescriptive, with assisted suicide viewed as a solution to solve societal problems faced by the poor, persons of color, or individuals with disabilities. The public is nearly equally divided over legalizing PAS (45 to 46 percent) (DiCamillo & Field, 2006). However, when asked if physicians should be allowed to dispense life-ending prescriptions, 62 percent of physicians and 64 percent of the general public indicate that they should (*Journal of Pain and Palliative Care Pharmacotherapy*, 2006). The strongest supporters

---

POLITICIANS GET INVOLVED IN PRIVATE RIGHTS

The Terry Schiavo situation is the most visible recent case regarding the right to die, where the Supreme Court, Congress, and even President George W. Bush voiced opinions. Terry's husband believed, on the basis of comments she made to him in her 20s, that she would not have wanted to be kept alive by artificial means. Her parents, backed by right-to-life and disability rights groups, sought to prevent removal of her feeding tube. Congress passed a law that imposed federal jurisdiction over the case, but the state courts' decisions were upheld and the feeding tube was removed. Public opinion polls showed solid majorities in favor of withdrawing Schiavo's feeding tube and strong criticism of the frantic legal and political maneuvers to block the eventual outcome. Most Americans believe that the federal government should not be involved in such individual or state-level decisions (Jost, 2005).

of PAS are Japanese Americans, followed by Caucasians, with the least support among African Americans and Filipino Americans (Braun, Tanji, & Heck, 2001). The AMA, based on the historical role of physicians as advocates for healing, officially opposes physicians' prescribing lethal medications to directly assist their patients in ending their lives. However, a large majority of rank-and-file doctors support PAS and believe that it is ethical to assist an individual who has made a rational choice to die due to unbearable suffering. While supporting that right, almost 50 percent of AMA members would not personally participate in assisting any patient, and 54 percent believe that this should be a decision between patient and doctor, without government involvement (O'Reilly, 2005). Accordingly, the AMA advocates compassionate, high-quality palliative care in addressing fears about dying as a way to reduce the expressed need for PAS.

Citizen initiatives and recent legislation in several states reflect increasing public support for PAS. In fact, approximately 74 percent of adults in nationwide polls believe that doctors should be allowed to help terminally ill patients in severe pain take their own lives, even if this is not legalized (Lee, 2009a). The degree of support, however, diminishes among those with conservative religious affiliations. Most believe that forcing people to endure prolonged suffering is inhumane and cruel. *Compassion et al. v. Washington State* was the first case to challenge in a federal court the constitutionality of a state law on assisted suicide insofar as it applies to mentally competent, terminally ill patients seeking prescribed medications with which to hasten death. The complexity of legal and medical issues is captured by citizen votes and court rulings over a 17-year time period. An initiative in Washington State to permit physician aid in dying was only narrowly defeated in 1991. However, 4 months after the initiative's defeat at the polls, the legislature passed a bill giving comatose and dying people the right to have food and water withdrawn. In 1994, the federal district court ruled that the Washington State ban on PAS violated patients'

constitutional right to liberty, but this ruling did not protect physicians from prosecution if they assisted in a terminally ill patient's suicide. In 1996, a federal appeals court struck down Washington statutes banning PAS. The plaintiffs (near-death patients and physicians) argued that no public interest is served by prolonging pain in hopeless situations and that to do so is to subject patients to potential abuse. The courts linked the right to facilitate death with the right to refuse medical treatment. They argued that the Fourteenth Amendment protects the individual's decision to hasten death with physician-prescribed medication and that statutes prohibiting PAS deny equal protection guaranteed by this Amendment to competent terminally ill adults who are not on life support.

THE CONTROVERSIAL DR. KEVORKIAN

One of the states in which the legality of assisted suicide has been the focus of public attention is Michigan, where Dr. Jack Kevorkian assisted over 100 people to end their lives. In the first case, involving a woman with Alzheimer's disease, the court dismissed the murder charges on the grounds that no law in Michigan prohibited assisting in a death. Subsequently, the legislature passed a bill to stop Dr. Kevorkian's activities. While prior cases were dismissed on the grounds that the law against PAS is unconstitutional, Kevorkian was charged with second-degree murder in 1999. He was sentenced to 10 to 25 years in prison because he directly administered a lethal injection to an adult in the final stages of amyotrophic lateral sclerosis (ALS) rather than the dying individual taking the final action. Although controversial, Kevorkian's crusade to legalize active euthanasia pushed the debate on PAS to the forefront of public awareness. He was paroled in 2007 with the stipulation that he must abstain from assisting terminally ill patients and that he could not provide care for anyone age 62 or older, or anyone with a disability. Dr. Kevorkian has lectured widely since his parole, stating that he will now work to persuade states to change their assisted suicide laws.

A GOOD DEATH

Anne was a 68-year-old retiree who had battled breast cancer for over 4 years. She had received radiation and chemotherapy, but the cancer had metastasized and spread to other organs in her body. She had lost more than 40 pounds, had no appetite, and had difficulty breathing, even with the aid of an oxygen tank. Anne decided to end her suffering and wanted to die.

Her husband contacted the local office of Compassion and Choices. The case management staff arranged for a visit and included medical staff to verify the primary physician's diagnosis. Mentally alert, Anne assured the staff that she understood and met the requirements outlined in Compassion's Guidelines and Safeguards. She indicated that her physician had already prescribed half the necessary medications needed to hasten her death; the rest would be obtained within 2 weeks. The physician carefully reviewed with Anne the procedures for self-administering the required medications. She hoped for a hastened death within 6 weeks. Her husband, Ed, confirmed that he supported Anne's decision to choose when the end would come rather than watch her continue to suffer.

A month later, Ed phoned the Compassion staff and indicated that Anne was ready. Upon their arrival, the staff reminded Anne that she need only tell them if she had changed her mind. She was clear and adamant in her decision to proceed: "Today is the day." According to Compassion's protocol, she ate some food to be certain she had something in her stomach before taking the first dose of medications. Anne began to take the pills with a glass of orange juice, according to Compassion's guidelines that patients must be able to ingest all of the medications by themselves. As suggested in the protocol, Anne asked for some vodka to speed the effect of the drugs. She expressed her appreciation to the Compassion staff for their assistance, kissed her husband and two sons, laid her head back on the pillow, and looked as if she were going into a peaceful sleep. In about 15 minutes, she stopped breathing. She had died what Compassion calls "a good death."

These conflicting state rulings and pressure from right-to-die advocacy organizations brought the issue of assisted suicide to the U.S. Supreme Court. In June 1997, the Court ruled that there is no constitutional or fundamental "right to die." This Supreme Court ruling, however, did not preclude states from deciding on their own to pass laws allowing PAS. By returning the debate to the states, the justices apparently opened the way for other jurisdictions to follow Oregon, the first state to legalize the PAS choice for patients who are diagnosed by two doctors as having less than 6 months to live. The Supreme Court ruling also left open the possibility that the Court might extend federal constitutional protection in the future.

Nor did the 1997 Supreme Court ruling keep patients from seeking physicians to prescribe lethal medications or stop doctors from providing them illegally. The Court ruled that prescribing medication with the intent to relieve suffering is legal and acceptable, but presenting drugs with the intent to cause death is not. Because "intent" is difficult to determine, the Court gave significant discretion and latitude to physicians to use adequate pain medication and explicitly endorsed "terminal sedation." The Court concluded that a dying patient who is suffering and is in pain has no legal barriers to obtaining medication from qualified physicians to alleviate that suffering, even to the point of causing unconsciousness and hastening death. In many ways, this solution—known as the "double effect"—is an old one. In the Supreme Court's definition, this occurs when a physician, intending to relieve pain or suffering, gives a terminally ill patient medication that has the unintended—but foreseeable—side effect of hastening death. Often, this medication is morphine. Nevertheless, many physicians still incorrectly assume that they can be

POINTS TO PONDER

Have you and your loved ones ever discussed how to die, your preferences, and fears? If not, how could you initiate such a discussion with your parents, your partner, or your adult children?

IS THIS PHYSICIAN-ASSISTED SUICIDE?

An 89-year-old man was in tremendous pain from the end stages of pancreatic cancer. He had been diagnosed only 6 weeks earlier, and nothing could be done to halt the spread of this deadly cancer. His daughter flew him cross-country to her home in order to provide daily care and to have his beloved grandsons nearby. The day before his 90th birthday, he cried out for relief from the pain. His daughter called the hospice doctor, who delivered a bottle of morphine to her home. He advised the daughter to start a heavy dosage right after dinner. While leaving, he gently said to her, "and if he does not wake up, that may be a blessing." The next morning, her father did awaken, but he was very disoriented, appeared to have suffered a mild stroke during the night, and was crying from the pain. Anxious to relieve the pain, his loving daughter gave him another dose of morphine. Within a few hours, he was dead. Did the morphine hasten his death? What was the doctor's role? The daughter's?

undertreat pain can be charged with unprofessional conduct (see the box on this page).

It is also not surprising that Oregon's law has been under challenge almost constantly since it was approved by a 51 percent majority in 1994. Nevertheless, there are no documented incidents of the law being abused. The vast majority of the estimated 401 individuals who have ended their lives since 1997 had cancer. Physicians consistently report that concerns about loss of autonomy and dignity and decreased ability to participate in activities that make life enjoyable are the primary motivating factors in patient requests for lethal medication, a finding corroborated by families. While it may be common for patients with terminal illnesses to consider PAS, such a request can also serve as an opportunity for a medical provider to explore with the patient their fears and hopes around end-of-life care, and to make patients aware of other options. In most cases, once the provider has addressed a patient's concerns, he

censured or prosecuted for giving controlled substances to dying patients.

As noted above, Oregon, one of only two states that have legalized PAS, leads the nation in aggressive pain management. To use the Death with Dignity law, a patient must make three requests—two oral and one written—and be diagnosed by two doctors as terminal and expected to die within 6 months. The prescribing physician must inform the patient of feasible alternatives to suicide and must refer the patient for a psychological examination if needed. Oregon's Intractable Pain Act set rules to ease doctors' fears about prescribing controlled substances for pain management. In fact, the state's medical board shocked professionals around the country by disciplining a doctor for not prescribing enough pain medication! Not surprisingly, Oregon leads the country in the lowest rates of in-hospital deaths, better attention to advance planning, more referrals to hospice, fewer barriers to prescribing narcotics, and a smaller percentage of dying patients experiencing pain. California now has a similar law in which physicians who

UNDERTREATMENT OF PAIN SPARKS LEGISLATIVE CHANGE

At age 85, Mr. B was dying of lung cancer. He was admitted to a medical center in Northern California in 1998, complaining of intolerable pain. During a 5-day hospital stay, nurses charted Mr. B's pain level at 10—the worst rating on their pain-intensity scale. Despite his family's intention that his pain be addressed, Mr. B's internist sent him home—still in agony—with inadequate medication. Ultimately, his family contacted another physician who took a more aggressive approach, and Mr. B died at home without pain soon afterward.

The case inspired the California Legislature to pass Assembly Bill 487, signed into law in 2001. This law requires that physicians who fail to prescribe, administer, or dispense adequate pain medication be charged with unprofessional conduct and be investigated by the California Medical Board's Division of Licensing. Physicians found guilty of undertreating pain must complete a pain-management education program.

SOURCE: Copyright © 2002 Robert Wood Johnson Foundation. Used with permission from the Robert Wood Johnson Foundation in Princeton, New Jersey.

or she chooses not to pursue PAS (Jost, 2005; Oregon Department of Human Services, 2009).

Seventeen years after Washington State's citizens rejected an initiative to legalize PAS and 14 years after the passage of Oregon's Death with Dignity Act, Washington State in 2008 became the second state to legalize it. This time, 58 percent of voters supported the citizens' initiative modeled after Oregon's law. Debates among medical care providers, lawmakers, and patient rights advocates continue, but public opinion remains in support of physician-assistance-in dying (Tu, 2009).

HOW WE DIE: A DIVISIVE VOTE

The battle lines around initiatives for physician-assistance-in-dying are often very personal, colored by voters' memories, fears, and hopes about death. Because experiences with loved ones are so nuanced and intimate, even those who have seemingly similar circumstances may end up on opposing sides. In Washington State, one proponent of physician-assistance-in-dying watched her husband endure a lingering, ugly, painful death from brain cancer. When told that state laws prevented hospice workers from helping him hasten his death, he became angry, saying "They don't have the right to tell me how long I have to suffer." Promising him she would work to change the law, his wife gathered 1,700 signatures for the initiative because "This is about giving people options and choice, since none us knows how we're going to die." Another proponent had witnessed a man with terminal cancer shooting himself alone in his car to avoid the prolonged suffering. An opponent of the initiative, a nurse who had witnessed patient suffering and believed in patient self-determination, came to a different conclusion after her husband of 53 years died. In their case, patient-administered pain medication and pain teams allowed him to have a pain-free death and gave her extra months with her husband. With careful pain management, she did not think the initiative was necessary. Another opponent, paralyzed by a diving accident 42 years ago, feels that physician-assistance-in-dying would be extended to persons with disabilities as a way to "get rid of them."

SOURCE: Copyright © 2002 Robert Wood Johnson Foundation. Used with permission from the Robert Wood Johnson Foundation in Princeton, New Jersey.

Legal Options Regarding End-of-Life Care

While active euthanasia continues to be debated in courtrooms and the ballot box, all 50 states have laws authorizing the use of **advance directives** to avoid artificially prolonged death. These refer to patients' oral and written instructions about end-of-life care and someone to speak on their behalf if they become incompetent; it may include proxy directives. The most common type of advance directive is a **living will**. An individual's wishes about medical treatment are put into writing in the case of irreversible terminal illness or the prognosis of a permanent vegetative (unconscious) state. Under such conditions, living wills can direct physicians to withhold life-sustaining procedures and can assist family members in making decisions when they are unable to consult a comatose, or medically incompetent, relative.

Both federal and state laws govern the use of advance directives. The federal law passed in 1990, the **Patient Self-Determination Act,** requires health care facilities (hospitals, skilled nursing facilities, hospice, home health care agencies, and health maintenance organizations) that receive Medicaid and Medicare funds to inform patients in writing of their rights to execute advance directives regarding how they want to live or die. However, these facilities do not require the patient to make an advanced directive; the law specifies only that people must be informed of their right to do so. State regulations related to advance directives vary widely. State-specific advance directives can be ordered from the national organization Compassion and Choices or downloaded from their website.

The Patient Self-Determination Act assumes that increased awareness of advance directives will generate discussion between patients and their health care providers and result in more completed advance directives. Despite this act, less than 30 percent of the general population, primarily white and middle-to-upper class, has a written document stating their preferences about end-of-life care (DiCamillo & Field, 2006). African Americans are the least likely to have advance directives, such as, living wills or to have discussed end-of-life care with their doctors (Dula & Williams, 2005). As noted above under palliative care, African Americans often do not want to complete a written document that could be used to justify inadequate treatment, limit their autonomy, and needlessly hasten death. Many would prefer to have their families rather than health care professionals—whom they often do not trust—make the decision (Borum, Lynn,

---

ADVANCE DIRECTIVES

To what extent do patients participate in determining their care? Research conducted by the Agency for Healthcare Research and Quality (AHRQ) indicates:

- Fewer than 50 percent of the severely or terminally ill patients studied had an advance directive in their medical record.
- Only 12 percent of patients with an advance directive had received input from their physician in its development.
- Between 65 and 76 percent of physicians whose patients had an advance directive were not aware that it existed.
- Advance directives helped make end-of-life decisions in less than 50 percent of those cases where a directive existed.
- Providers and patient surrogates had difficulty knowing when to stop treatment and often waited until the patient had crossed a threshold into an actively dying state before the advance directive was invoked.
- Physicians were only about 65 percent accurate in predicting patient preferences and tended to undertreat, even after reviewing the patient's advance directive.
- Surrogates who were family members tended to make prediction errors of overtreatment, even if they had reviewed the advance directive with the patient or assisted in its development.
- Overall, care at the end of life appears to be inconsistent with patients' preferences to forgo life-sustaining treatment, and many dying patients receive life-sustaining care that they do not want.

SOURCE: Kass-Bartelmes & Hughes, 2003.

& Zhong, 2000; Dula & Williams, 2005; Smith, 2004). Among nursing home residents, 70 percent have advance directives (Institute for the Future of Aging Services, 2008). The primary reason for this higher rate compared to the general population may stem, in part, from the lower nursing home use by elders of color who resist advance (Troyer & McAuley, 2006). The box on this page summarizes the relatively limited impact of advance directives on end-of-life decision making (Kass-Bartlemas & Hughes, 2003).

In an attempt to resolve some of the problems with implementing the Patient Self-Determination Act, the **Uniform Health Care Decision Act** was passed in 1993 to provide uniformity and a minimum level of standards in statutes across state lines. This act promotes decision-making autonomy by acknowledging individuals' rights to make health care decisions in all circumstances, including the right to decline or discontinue health care. Providers, agents, surrogates, and guardians are mandated to comply with an individual's instructions. Even with such safeguards, compliance is not guaranteed, and, as noted above, a health care provider may decline to honor an advance directive: (1) for reasons of conscience if a directive conflicts with institution policy or values, and (2) if the instruction is contrary to accepted health care standards. However, according to the act, reasonable efforts must be made to transfer the patient to a facility that *can* honor the directive. In such situations, the act provides for court mechanisms to resolve disputes. A major limitation of this act is that each state may choose whether to replace its own advance directive mandates with the Uniform Health Care Decisions Act. Without federal mandates, the number of states that have done so is limited.

Although it is human nature to delay discussions about aging and dying, in many cases, families and patients may be confused about both their prognosis and their choices. Communication difficulties with health care providers are another common barrier to quality end-of-life care. Ironically, 33 percent of dying patients in a national study said they would discuss advance care planning if the physician brought up the subject, but 25 percent thought that such planning was only for people who were very ill or very old. On the other hand, only 5 percent of elders themselves stated that they found discussions about advance planning too difficult (Kass-Bartelmes & Hughes, 2003). A study of 203 critically ill patients with chronic diseases admitted to a hospital respiratory care unit found that only 21 percent had appointed a health care proxy and only 16 percent had expressed their preferences in advance directives (Camhi et al., 2009). In a study of women diagnosed with metastatic breast cancer, 66 percent of the patients had written advance directives, but health care providers were aware of these advance directives in only 14 percent of the cases (Ozanne et al., 2009). In a 2-year clinical intervention (SUPPORT) to improve doctor-patient communication, doctors still did not know what their patients wanted, often did not put preferences in medical records, or, if they did, frequently got them wrong (Dula & Williams, 2005; Phillips et al., 2000). For these reasons, it is crucial to encourage culturally appropriate communication between health care providers, patients, and their families about the process of end-of-life decision-making and advance directives.

STEPS TO TAKE TO HELP AVOID AN ARTIFICIALLY PROLONGED DEATH

- Download state-specific advance-directive documents from Compassion and Choices.
- Execute an advance directive, witnessed or notarized according to state laws.
- Give copies to your personal physician and family members.
- While healthy, make sure that your family understands your wishes.
- Be sure that your desires are also noted in your medical record.
- Begin this process while you are still healthy, your thought processes are clear, you are not in crisis, and time is available.

Some research indicates that adults of all ages, but particularly elders, do not like the standardized approach of advance care planning whereby preferences for specific life-sustaining treatments are documented and strictly followed near death. Instead, they preferred opportunities for ongoing discussion of their values and goals for care with their **surrogate decision maker** and flexibility in decision making (Hawkins et al., 2005). There is growing recognition of the value of appointing a health care proxy—someone known and trusted to make emotionally complex decisions, rather than depending only on a written document (Jost, 2005). A 2005 Pew poll shows that more Americans today are willing to talk about end-of-life issues with their loved ones and to let family members make decisions about continuing medical treatment (DiCamillo & Field, 2006). When advance care planning is discussed with family members (or a health care proxy) and physicians, patients' satisfaction, perceived ability to influence and direct their care, and belief that their physicians understand their wishes increase, while their fear and anxiety about dying decrease. Such conversations also help families, other designated surrogate decision makers, physicians, and patients to reconcile their differences about end-of-life care. These findings support the importance of physicians and other decision makers conducting advance care planning discussions with patients during routine outpatient office visits and hospitalization, and, when there are written documents, reviewing them on a regular basis and updating them to reflect patients' preferences at that time. The AMA's Advanced Care Planning Process is an ongoing series of discussions among the patient, physician, social worker, and family to clarify values and goals, and to agree on principles to guide these decisions (AMA, 2009).

Even when advance directives exist, other problems with implementation may arise. Older adults may fail to tell their doctors about the directive, instead trusting that their families know what to do. Or the advance directive may be in a safe-deposit box, unavailable to either family or health care providers. Additionally, those who are designated to make medical decisions may be unaware of their selection. When faced with the impending death of their loved one, family members may later change their minds about adhering to an advance directive, especially if the document has not been updated for years. In such instances, physicians are more likely to comply with the family's preference than with the written directive. In addition, federal law does not require health care providers to follow such directives, only that they adhere to state laws or court decisions that deal with advance directives. This means that, in some instances, the physician's decision may override both patient and family preferences. In one study, 65 percent of physicians stated that they would not follow a living will under certain circumstances (Jost, 2005). This highlights the importance of having a health care proxy as an advocate.

Patients and their families can access their state's particular law and forms through national organizations such as Compassion and Choices, local hospitals, state attorneys general's offices, or the Internet. **"Five Wishes"** is a document available in 23 languages and meets the legal requirements for an advance directive in 40 states. Unlike other advance directives, Five Wishes is written in everyday language and is designed to encourage conversation and consideration of broader questions related to health care decisions than those covered in most advance directive documents (Aging with Dignity, 2007). In situations where there is no living will, the family of an incompetent patient must go to court to obtain legal authority if they wish to refuse life support on the patient's behalf. This expensive and time-consuming process is viewed as necessary when doctors and health care facilities are unwilling to make decisions to remove life-sustaining treatment because of the perceived risk of liability. To obviate this court process, all states have some form of process for designating health care powers of attorney. Some states have adopted statutes that support the concept that the people closest to the patient are in the best position to know his or her wishes or to act in the patient's best interest. The

surrogate has a duty to act according to the patient's known wishes. If those are not known, the surrogate must act according to the patient's best interest. Each state's law requires a prioritized list of people connected to the patient. The doctor must approach these individuals, in order of priority, to find someone who is willing to make decisions about life support.

Durable power of attorney is another type of written advance directive, usually in addition to a living will. This authorizes someone to act on an individual's behalf with regard to property and financial matters. The individual does not relinquish control with a power of attorney, because it is granted only for the financial matters specifically set forth in the relevant document. An advantage of durable power of attorney is that a living will cannot anticipate what might be wanted in all possible circumstances.

A **medical power of attorney** (or durable power of attorney for health care) specifically allows for a health care surrogate to make decisions about medical care if the patient is unable to make them for him or herself. A durable power of attorney for healthcare may be used instead of, or in addition to, a living will because it is more broadly applicable to nearly any type of health care during periods when the patient is not competent to make decisions. *Durable* means that the arrangement continues even when the person is incapacitated and unable to make his or her own medical decisions. A durable power of attorney agreement may be written to go into effect upon its signing or only when the disability occurs. At that point, bills can continue to be paid and revenues can be collected while other more permanent arrangements are being made, such as the appointment of a conservator or guardian.

Conservatorship generally relates to control of financial matters. In this instance, a probate court appoints a person as a conservator to care for an individual's property and finances because that person is unable to do so due to advanced age, mental weakness, or physical incapacity. Such a condition must be attested to by a physician. Once appointed, the conservator will be required to file an inventory of all the assets and to report annually all income and expenses. The individual, however, loses control over his or her property and finances.

Guardianship is a legal tool that establishes control over a person's body as well as financial affairs. In a guardianship, a probate court appoints someone to care for the individual's person, property, and finances because of the individual's mental inability to care for him or herself. The guardian has the responsibility to direct the individual's medical treatment, housing, personal needs, finances, and property. To establish guardianship, a medical certificate from a physician must state that the individual is mentally incapable of caring for him or herself. As with conservatorships, the medical certificate by the physician must be made not more than 10 days before the probate court hearing; in this sense, guardianship cannot be arranged in advance of need. However, through a medical power of attorney, an individual may nominate someone he or she would like to act as guardian if such a need develops. Since the guardian manages all the individual's affairs, guardianship is generally considered a last resort. This is because the process essentially eliminates an individual's legal rights, since consent is not required, Additionally, guardianship is costly and rarely reversible.

Family members who are concerned about finances may move too quickly through these options. However, families and service providers should try for as long as possible to respect the older person's wishes regarding living arrangements, a legal will, and other financial decisions. In other words, the older person should be encouraged to exercise as much control as possible, to the extent that his or her cognitive status allows. In general, less restrictive approaches than guardianship that balance the need for protection with self-determination are needed.

Some nursing homes include a statement with their admissions packet that, unless otherwise noted in writing, there will be "no code" for the patient. This type of advance directive means that if the patient quits breathing or his or her heart stops, the staff will not "call a code" to initiate cardiopulmonary resuscitation (CPR). In other nursing homes or hospitals, this type of statement must be written on the patient's chart and signed by the patient and witnesses.

Seven Principles for Patient-Centered End-of-Life Care

Compassion and Choices has identified seven principles to guide policy makers and providers. If implemented, they would radically change how the health care system treats terminally ill patients (Lee, 2009a):

1. Focus on the person who has the disease, not on the disease.
2. Self-determination, particularly regarding pain management.
3. Autonomy: the answer to "who should decide" is "the patient decides."
4. Personal beliefs should be honored.
5. Informed consent: patients should be provided with adequate information to make decisions.
6. Balance: Patient should feel empowered to make decisions based on their assessment of quality versus quantity of life.
7. Notice: Patients should be informed of institutional or personal policies that could impact their end-of-life preferences.

Compassion and Choices is now the largest and most comprehensive end-of-life organization in the country, with over 60 chapters and 30,000 members. By consolidating several end-of-life organizations, some of which had existed since 1938, supporters of hastened death or assisted suicide dramatically increased their numbers, garnered influence and power, and attracted more donors. Compassion and Choices seeks to support, educate, and advocate for choice and care at the end of life, while pursuing legal reform to promote pain control, advance directives, and legalized physician-assistance-in-dying. Living wills for each state can be downloaded from their website, which provides up-to-date information about right-to-die legal and ethical issues and options nationwide. An organization that attempted to change laws in order to legalize assisted suicide for the terminally ill was the **Hemlock Society.** The society's popular publication, *Final Exit*, by its founder, Derek Humphry, is a manual on nonviolent methods to commit suicide with prescription barbiturates to assure a gentle, peaceful death. The Hemlock Society distinguished between "rational or responsible suicide" (i.e., the option of ending one's life for good and valid reasons) and suicide that is caused by a rejection of life because of depression or other psychological disorders. It viewed the right to request assistance in dying as merely an extension of the individual's right to control the kind of treatment he or she receives. The Hemlock Society no longer exists as a separate entity, but was grandfathered into Compassion and Choices.

Societal cost-benefit criteria inevitably come into play in discussions of active and passive euthanasia. Admittedly, a significant proportion of the money spent on medical care in a person's lifetime goes to services received during the last years and months of life; for example, the proportion of Medicare expenditures spent on elders in their last year of life is around 30 percent. Yet even if such end-of-life care were eliminated, Medicare expenditures would be reduced by only a small percentage. Additionally, Medicare costs for hospice care tend to be lower than for elders not receiving hospice (National Hospice and Palliative Care Organization, 2008). Instead, non-Medicare expenditures for long-term care for chronic illness in the last year of life are projected to increase. Nevertheless, the public and policy makers still misperceive the costs of medical technology to be prohibitively high in order to keep alive a comparatively small number of people.

Rapid improvements in medical technology are not matched by refinements in the law and the ethics of using those therapies. This is the case even though **bioethics**, or medical ethics—which focuses on procedural approaches to questions about death, dying, and medical decision making—has grown in the past 40 years. Assisted suicide raises not only complex ethical and legal dilemmas, but also resource allocation issues. Both policy makers and service providers face the challenge of how to balance an individual client's needs for personal autonomy with the community's demand to conserve resources. A fundamental question is whether the doctrine of personal privacy under the U.S. Constitution and related state laws extends to individuals' decisions about their physical care, even when those decisions involve life or death choices for themselves or others. Alternatively, as aging baby boomers seek to remain at home to die, what are equitable ways to allocate community services such as home care in the face of a growing distrust of public programs combined with shrinking federal resources? As noted by Holstein (1998), providers, policy makers, and families are taking ethics beyond autonomy and decision making into the broader realm of how we treat the terminally ill—how we look at them, what we expect of them, and how we talk to them.

ETHICAL DILEMMAS

"With the use of our moral imagination, we can reshape the way we behave toward people with any kind of disability. It goes back to Aristotle's question, How does one live a good life? How does ethical thinking help older people live a good life? Ethics is part of what we do every day. It's so much more than making a decision about putting in a feeding tube...." (Holstein, 1998, p. 4). On a personal and practical level, many dying people find that the medical technology that prolongs their lives may financially ruin their families. It is important that families discuss in advance who should assume medical care decision making on the patient's behalf, if necessary, or under what circumstances life support should be removed. Most families find it emotionally difficult to do such planning, especially if the older adult refuses to do so or cannot make a rational decision because of dementia.

Bereavement, Grief, and Mourning Rituals

Death affects the social structure through survivors, especially spouses and partners, who have social and emotional needs resulting from that death. How these needs are expressed and met varies across place, time, and culture. This is because grief is a highly individualized phenomenon with a complex and wide range of what is considered "normal" within different social and cultural environments.

Bereavement and the Grief Process

Bereavement is defined as the objective situation of having lost someone significant (e.g., being deprived) and the overall adaptation to loss (Stroebe et al., 2001; Stroebe, Hansson, Schut, & Stroebe, 2008). It usually refers to loss through death, although individuals can be bereaved through other types of losses such as divorce or relocation. The **grief process** is the complex emotional response to bereavement and, similar to the dying process, can encompass shock and disbelief, guilt, psychological numbness, depression, loneliness, fatigue, loss of appetite, sleeplessness, and anxiety about one's ability to carry on with life. **Mourning** signifies culturally patterned expectations about the expression of grief. What is believed about the meaning of death, how it should be faced, and what happens after physical death varies widely by culture and its associated religious and spiritual practices. Cultural variations are particularly marked with regard to beliefs about the meaning of loss through death, including the possibility of future reunion with the dead, the significance of various emotions, and what to say to oneself and others following a death. With the increasing diversity of American society and globalization, professionals must be sensitive to the influences of multiple cultures on elders and to the dying patient's generation and acculturation level. Even within a group such as Asian Americans, expressions of grief vary widely. For

AN INNOVATIVE GRIEF COUNSELING PROGRAM

Family members of patients dying in the intensive care unit (ICU) of hospitals often experience a grief process characterized by anxiety, depression, and even post-traumatic stress disorder (PTSD). The usual practice of most hospitals is for health professionals and trained grief counselors to hold a brief conference with families of patients in the ICU. The impact of a structured counseling session has been tested, using the guidelines of: *V*aluing what family members have to say, *A*cknowledging their emotions, *L*istening to their feelings, *U*nderstanding, and *E*liciting questions from participants ("VALUE"). Families receiving the structured counseling were compared with others who were given the typical, brief end-of-life conference. A follow-up 90 days later found that the VALUE approach reduced symptoms of anxiety, depression, and PTSD. These results point to the benefits of a proactive communication strategy with longer conferences that allow family members of the dying to express their feelings and acknowledge the importance of this process (Laureate et al., 2007).

example, Japanese Americans tend to be reluctant to talk about death; grief is kept within the family rather than expressed publicly, and the body is not to be moved nor organs removed for donation until the soul has had time to travel from it. In contrast, crying among bereaved Filipinos is sometimes uncontrollable, especially when viewing the body (Rosenblatt, 2008).

Although there are clusters or phases of **grief reactions**, the progression is more like a roller coaster—with overlapping responses and wide individual variability—rather than orderly stages or a fixed or universal sequence. As noted in the earlier discussion of Kübler-Ross's work, to expect grieving individuals to progress in some specified fashion is inappropriate and can be emotionally harmful to them. The highs and lows within broad phases can occur within minutes, days, months, or years, with grieving individuals moving back and forth among them. A person who is grieving may simultaneously experience mixed reactions within a matter of hours—anger, guilt, helplessness, loneliness, and uncontrolled crying—along with personal strength and pride in their coping. Emotions change rapidly, beginning with shock, numbness, and disbelief, followed by an all-encompassing sorrow. Early months following the loss are the most difficult. However, even when a grieving person has tried to work through early phases and to integrate the loss into his or her life, a picture, a favorite song of the deceased, or a personal object may evoke more intense grief reactions.

An intermediate phase of grief often involves an idealization and seeking the presence of the deceased person, as well as an obsessive review to find meaning in the death and to answer the inexplicable "why?" The grieving individual may experience anger toward the deceased, a supreme being, and caregivers, as well as guilt and regrets for what survivors did not do or say. When the permanence of the loss is acknowledged and yearning ceases, anguish, disorganization, and despair often result. The grieving person tends to experience a sense of confusion; feelings of aimlessness, loss of motivation, confidence, and interest; and inability to make decisions. Simply getting out of bed in the morning may require intense effort. These feelings may be exacerbated if the grieving person tries to live according to others' expectations, including those of the deceased. Instead, successful accommodation requires active coping strategies in which the bereaved individual finds his or her own best way to live with grief.

The final phase of grief—reorganization—is marked by a resumption of routine activities and social relationships while simultaneously recognizing that life will never be the same and still remembering and identifying with the deceased. The ability to effectively communicate one's thoughts and feelings to others, form new relationships, and learn new skills and competencies enhances this reorganization phase. Some older adults may also experience personal growth and meaning through multiple losses. *Integration of the loss into one's life* might be more appropriate than the term *recovery* to describe changes in the grieving person's identity and emotional reorganization to

ordinary levels of functioning. This concept also recognizes that for many elders, grief is never completely resolved and is always present (Niemeyer, 2001; Wordon, 2009; Wortman, 2002; Wortman & Silver, 2001).

When grief is not openly acknowledged, socially validated, or publicly mourned, "disenfranchised grief" may result in a more complicated or prolonged experience. People who are grieving socially discouraged relationships, such a same-sex partners or secret lovers or non-family relationships such as friends, neighbors or even pets, may be impeded in the process of moving through grief due to the lack of social validation of their grief (Doka, 2008).

Process of Mourning

A "six-R process of mourning" integrates much of what has been written about grief stages, phases, and tasks, and can provide guidelines for family members and professionals. These include:

- Recognize and accept the reality of the loss
- React to, experience, and express the pain of separation or active confrontation with the loss, including deep weeping and articulating feelings of guilt
- Reminisce: tell and retell memories, dreams and stories about the deceased
- Relinquish old attachments
- Readjust to an environment in which the dead person is missing, adapt to new roles, and form a new identity.
- Reinvests in new personal relationships and in acts of meaning rather than remaining tied to the past, while recognizing that the pain of the loss may continue throughout life (Stroebe et al., 2008; Weiss, 2001; Worden, 2009; Wortman, 2002; Wortman & Silver, 2001).

Grief theorists increasingly emphasize the importance of maintaining connections to the person who has died, but in ways different than in the past. This may occur when the bereaved engage in the following behaviors.

The classical paradigm of grief, derived from Freud's psychoanalytical perspective, assumed that grieving individuals needed to let go of their attachment to the deceased in order to complete their "grief work." Individuals who did not engage in grief work were assumed to be at risk of pathological grief and increased risk of physical and mental illness. Later postmodern and social constructionist theoretical perspectives do not presume the universality of responses to death. Instead, they acknowledge the tremendous diversity of healthy grieving and that the "grief work" model of actively confronting negative emotions is not always the best approach. For some elders, denial, distraction, and humor can also be effective ways to grieve. From the postmodern perspective, the process of vacillation between the dual goals of avoiding and engaging in grief work is fundamental to reconstructing meaning and a basic sense of self. Later theorists also emphasized that the goal of grieving is not to disengage completely from memories and bonds with the deceased. Instead, as noted above, bereaved individuals redefine their connection to the deceased in a way different from the past, and allow themselves to form new relationships. It is important to acknowledge that conflicting views about healthy grieving and resilience exist, and that we have too little knowledge to claim that we know the best way for older adults to grieve (Bonanno, Boerner, & Wortman, 2008; Carr, 2006; Lindenstrom, 2002; Walter, 2003).

Many people never fully resolve their loss or cease grieving but learn to live with the pain of loss for a lifetime and to integrate it into their lives. Older adults' experiences with grief may be even more complex than those of other age groups for several reasons. They are more likely to experience unrelated, multiple losses over relatively brief periods, at a time when their coping capacities and social supports may be diminished. The cumulative effects of loss may be

---

HOW PROFESSIONALS AND FAMILIES CAN SUPPORT THE GRIEVING PROCESS

- Listen, without judgment or giving advice, to the bereaved individual's expression of feelings including guilt, anger, and anxiety, rather than suggesting what he or she *should* feel or do.
- Realize that grieving is a natural response to loss that can be a lengthy and emotional rollercoaster, not a fixed progression.
- Be careful to avoid endless chatter or simplistic statements ("I know just how you feel." "She is happier now." "God loved him more than you did." "You should feel better in 6 months." "You can marry again/you'll meet someone else").
- Resist telling your own stories.
- Listen carefully to the silences, to what is not said as well as what is said.
- Encourage sharing of memories and stories.
- Sometimes the most helpful response is simply "to be there" for the bereaved and to encourage them to express their feelings.
- Time itself does not heal. Healing occurs through dealing with grief, which can be painful and exhausting. But some mourners never engage in "grief work."
- Do not tell the bereaved to stop crying or not be sad; provide time and space to cry; be aware that hugging or patting the crying person's hand may actually shut down crying.
- Identify concrete tasks by which to help—such as organizing meals, child care, yard work, and house cleaning—so the bereaved has time and space to grieve.
- Respect gender and cultural differences in grieving.
- Encourage meditation, deep breathing, self-care, and exercise.

---

greater, especially if the older person has not resolved earlier losses, such as a child's death, or interprets current losses as evidence of an inevitable continuing decline. Health care providers must be careful not to misdiagnose grief symptoms as physical illness, dementia, or hypochondria. On the other hand, prior losses can facilitate accommodation to a loved one's death, especially for older adults who are resilient. Personal capacities of resilience include previous experiences with handling losses, spirituality and religiosity, and ability to find meaning in life. How other losses have been interpreted as positive (i.e., leading to personal growth) and the degree to which relationships seem complete also appear to be critical factors in the grief process (Bonanano et al., 2008; Moss, Moss, & Hansson, 2001; Nadeau, 2008).

Whether grieving is more difficult when death is sudden or unexpected is unclear. In comparison to the young, older people may be less affected by a sudden death because they have rehearsed and planned for the death of a partner or spouse as natural, and widowhood as a life-stage task. They have also experienced it vicariously through the deaths of their friends or partners of friends. An expected death allows survivors to prepare for the changes through **anticipatory grief,** but it does not necessarily minimize the grief and emotional strain following the death. In fact, some studies indicate that a longer period of anticipatory grief, through lengthy caring for an individual with chronic illness such as Alzheimer's disease, can make adaptation difficult and increase the risk of anxiety, feelings of isolation, depression, and other psychiatric disorders. For example, if a dying partner suffered in pain, the bereaved caregiver tends to be more prone to depression, guilt, and feelings of helplessness, and to recover more slowly (Carr, 2003; Rando, 2000; Richardson, 2006; Schulz, Boerner, & Hebert, 2006).

In contrast, some studies identify a "relief model" of bereavement. Family members who have provided years of care often experience a death as a relief from long-term demands of caregiving and may become engaged in other activities more readily (Keene & Prokos, 2008). A central dynamic in caregiver bereavement is the support experienced while providing care, as well as the possibility of continued support through surviving confidants (Benkel et al., 2009). For example, widowers typically feel short-term relief after protracted caregiving, but those who experienced social isolation while providing care often suffer long-term consequences from

the lack of social interaction (Carr, 2004; Schulz et al., 2003; Schulz et al,. 2008).

The location of a partner's death—whether in a nursing home or at home—also affects bereavement, with less distress felt if a partner dies at home, particularly if the bereaved individual was present at the moment of death (Bennett & Vidal-Hall, 2002). However, bereaved persons in one study adjusted more quickly when their partners died in a nursing home, perhaps because they had grieved in anticipation when their partner moved there initially (Richardson, 2006). Other researchers have concluded that the overall grief process is similar whether the loss is expected or unexpected, although suddenness (i.e., being unprepared for death) may make a difference early in the process of bereavement (Barry, Kasl, & Prigerson, 2002). This similarity may occur because no matter when a partner dies or under what circumstances, the surviving partner has to shift from "we" to "I" (Carr, 2003; 2008).

When death is anticipated, some psychosocial interventions before the death can help prevent complications following the death. These include facilitating communication with the ill partner, preparing the survivor for the practical aspects of life without the partner, and enabling the surviving partner to deal with his or her own illness-related chronic stressors and losses. Health care providers now recognize the importance of attending to the bereaved's grief process and view grieving, often expressed in diverse ways, as a natural healing process. Overall, assistance in grieving, perhaps through life review and encouragement of new risk-taking, is especially important for older adults (Hooyman & Kramer, 2006).

Mourning involves cultural assumptions about appropriate behavior during bereavement. Mourning rituals develop in every culture as a way to channel the expression of grief, define the appropriate timing of bereavement, and encourage support for the bereaved among family and friends. Professionals must be sensitive to cultural, religious, and racial differences regarding the form and meaning of death and the burial or cremation of the dead. Grief rituals, such as sorting

Visiting the grave of a loved one provides solace for many elders.

where death is predominantly confined to the old. Money donations instead of flowers, memorial services and celebrations of the deceased person's life instead of formal funerals, and cremations instead of land burial signal the development of new and less costly kinds of death rituals. In addition to serving specific social functions, funerals and other mourning rituals frequently permit grievers to receive assurances within their religious traditions of the meaning of death and an afterlife. Specific funeral practices often straddle both religious and cultural traditions, as grievers are surrounded by a community of support and take comfort in a recitation of religious expectations for death and life after death.

Modern funeral ceremonies are criticized for being costly, for exploiting people who are vulnerable, and for elaborate cosmetic restorations of the body. Legislation has been enacted to control some of the excesses of the funeral industry; organizations such as the People's Memorial Association ensure lower funeral costs to its members. Despite criticisms of the funeral industry, however, most people approve of some type of ceremony to make the death more real to the survivors and to offer a meaningful way to cope with the initial grief.

and disposing of personal effects and visiting the gravesite, are often important in working through the grief process. The timing and means of interring a body, the expected duration of grieving behaviors such as wearing certain clothing, and the exchange of signs of consolation among grievers and their supporters are examples of the intersections of culture, religion, race, and ethnicity as they inform mourning (Kastenbaum, 2008).

The funeral or memorial service, for example, serves as a rite of passage for the deceased and a focal point for the expression of the survivors' grief. Funerals also allow the family to demonstrate cohesion through sharing rituals, food, and drink, and thus to minimize the disruptive effects of the death. Funerals and associated customs are more important in societies with high mortality rates throughout the life course than in societies

Widowhood

A spouse's death (or that of a partner, in the case of LGBT couples or unmarried heterosexual couples) may be the most catastrophic and stressful event experienced by older adults, altering one's self-concept to an "uncoupled identity." Widowhood for both men and women not only represents the obvious physical loss, but numerous other changes in the survivor's life that are experienced as losses. These include the end of:

- a shared past and a future
- the role or status of married partner
- a sexual partner
- companionship, social networks, and a confidant
- economic security, especially for women

Older widows generally have more extensive peer support than widowers.

The death of a partner tends to trigger "cascading effects:" one's grief interacts with or exacerbates other changes such as chronic illness, financial loss, or involuntary relocation (Cicirelli, 2002; Hooyman & Kramer, 2006).

As discussed in Chapter 15, among women age 65 and older, up to 42 percent are widowed, more than three times the rate among their male peers (13 percent). Among the oldest-old, these

THE EXPERIENCE OF WIDOWHOOD

Darlene became a widow at age 56. Although she was too young to qualify for her husband's Social Security, her dependent children received a monthly benefit of approximately $1,000 per child. A successful career woman, Darlene sought refuge in her work, her friends, and her children. She learned new skills, such as home and car repairs, and appeared to be self-sufficient and "moving on" to her friends and children. During the day, she functioned well. It was only at the end of the day, when other family members were asleep, that she would be overcome by feelings of intense loneliness, hopelessness, and regret. At times, she felt overwhelmed at the thought of all the years ahead when she would bear both responsibilities and pleasure alone, lacking a partner with whom to share joys and sorrows. For more than 2 years, she cried every night before she fell asleep.

rates increase to 76 percent of women and 34 percent of men (AOA, 2008; Federal Interagency Forum, 2008). Marital dissolution through widowhood is an example of an anticipated or normative life-course transition for older women, who may be better prepared for a spousal death than older men are. Of all wives, 85 percent outlive their husbands, because women generally marry men older than themselves, live longer than men, and experience widowhood earlier than men. They also spend more years as a widow and, in their later years, seldom remarry after the death of their husbands. Among people of color, the proportion of widows is twice that among whites. Women of color are also widowed earlier, which reflects the shorter life expectancy of men of color (Kreider, 2005). Older widows and widowers are more likely than younger adults to become sick or die in the short term, often within the first 6 months of the spouse's death. Their immune systems may weaken, and their chronic conditions and functional disabilities may become exacerbated. They visit physicians more often and are more likely to be hospitalized or spend time in a nursing home. Their health care utilization and costs increase, and they experience more depressive symptoms. The rates of physical and mental problems along with mortality are higher for widowers than widows. Physical symptoms include dry mouth, changes in appetite, muscle weakness, tightness in the chest, headaches, dizziness, insomnia, and physical exhaustion. Similarly, rates of depression, anxiety, substance use, mood alterations, obsessive thoughts of the deceased, disorientation, memory problems, and difficulties concentrating are nearly nine times as high among the newly bereaved, especially men, as among married individuals. These high rates of illness may result from hormonal responses to the stress of loss, which can lead to suppression of the body's immune system. However, over the long term (i.e., more than 2 years), the effects on physical and mental health are generally diminished (Hall & Irwin, 2001; Laditka & Laditka, 2003).

Despite the stress of widowhood, the course of spousal bereavement is often characterized by resilience and effective coping, which allows feelings of self-confidence, self-efficacy, and personal growth to follow short-term depression and illness. Nevertheless, the greatest problem faced by widows and widowers is loneliness and being alone, given disruptions in social relationships inherent in being a couple. In fact, the terms *widow* and *alone* are almost synonymous, at least during the early phases of widowhood (Utz et al., 2002; Worden, 2002).

The negative effects of widowhood can be attenuated through a number of psychosocial variables. The quality of the prior relationship affects how partners experience the death of a spouse. Grief tends to be less for those whose relationship was marked by conflict (Carr et al., 2000). In contrast, short-term grieving is more difficult for those whose relationships were harmonious and characterized by warmth, strong bonds, and emotional dependence, but over time, these qualities may bring solace and foster personal growth. In addition, harmonious marriages appear to have a protective effect in terms of the use and costs of health care when both partners are alive, but such costs are higher for widows and widowers from harmonious marriages than for survivors of discordant ones (Richardson, 2006; Worden, 2002).

Other variables that affect the long-term effects of widowhood are the adequacy of social support networks, including professional support, and one's closeness to children and intimate friends; the individual's characteristic ways of coping with stress; and religious commitment and cultural values and beliefs. Although family plays an important role following widowhood, friendships developed on the basis of marital relationships may not survive, with many widows initially lacking a confidant (Ha, 2008). In fact, the ability to make new friends is an indicator of how well an individual is coping with the loss of a spouse/partner.

The age, gender, and health status of the widowed person also affect the degree of stress. Age by itself, however, is found to have little effect on bereavement outcomes. Differences between younger and older widows can be explained largely by the relationship of age to employment status and income. Age is associated, however, with a greater need to learn new life skills, such as an older widow mastering financial-management tasks, or widowers learning housekeeping skills and managing social activities (van den Hoonaard, 2001). Social context and social connections clearly play a significant role in shaping outcomes for widows. For example, widows living in neighborhoods with a low concentration of widowed adults are at a higher risk for death than those living in neighborhoods with high concentrations of widowed persons (Subramanian, Elwert, & Christakis, 2008).

Whether the stress of bereavement through widowhood is greater for the young than for the old is unclear. As noted above, the intensity of psychological distress immediately post-death tends to be greater for younger widows than older ones, because of the unanticipated nature of the death. Although younger spouses are found to manifest more intense grief initially, a reverse trend is noted after 18 months; the emotional and physical distress associated with grief lasts longer for older partners. This may be because the end of a lifelong relationship results in greater disorganization of roles, commitments, and patterns of daily life (Moss et al., 2001). As noted earlier, this is compounded by the fact that older people are more likely to experience other losses simultaneously, or **bereavement overload** (Kastenbaum, 2004, 2008), which may intensify and prolong their grief. On the other hand, spousal bereavement in later life is an "on-time" or normative event, especially for older women. In such instances, widowhood may be less stressful, even among the oldest-old, and different death circumstances do not appear to have a significant impact on long-term accommodation (Van den Hoonaard, 2001; Vinokur, 2002).

Preventive psychoeducational interventions initiated pre-death, such as through hospice, can minimize problems in mourning, as opposed to interventions post-death, after problems have surfaced. Interventions post-death focus on assisting the surviving spouse to review and reflect on the loss, providing support for grieving, and

---

DEVELOPING NEW ROLES IN WIDOWHOOD

Martha had always seen her role as wife and mother and left the "business" aspects of family life to her husband. Her "job" was to keep the home a comfortable place for him and their daughter. Widowed at age 63, she felt ill prepared to take on paying the bills and budgeting. She sought the advice of her banker on the best way to set up a bookkeeping system. After paying the bills and taking care of the Medicare paperwork for the past few years, she now sees herself as being in the role of "manager" for herself (even arranging home repairs) and is pleased with what she has learned.

---

redefining the emotional attachment to the dead partner. Reviewing, evaluating, and perhaps reinterpreting prior experiences to resolve earlier conflicts can facilitate attaining a sense of meaning in the grief process (Corr, Nabe, & Corr, 2003). Since bereaved partners who have extensive contacts with friends and family and who belong to religious institutions and other voluntary associations are less likely to die soon after the death of a spouse, interventions need to encourage informal network building and organizational affiliations. Community mental health centers, primary care clinics, and senior centers are suitable venues for cost-effective support interventions.

Gender Differences in Widowhood

Whether widowhood is more difficult for women or men is unclear. Certainly, coping or adaptation to widowhood is related to income for both men and women. Adequate financial resources are necessary to maintain a sense of self-sufficiency and to continue participation in meaningful activities. As detailed in Chapter 15, older widows are generally worse off than widowers in terms of finances, years of education, legal problems, and prospects for remarriage. Women who have been economically dependent on their husbands often find their incomes drastically reduced. Financial hardships

may be especially great for women who have been caring for a spouse during a long chronic illness or who have depleted their joint resources during the spouse's relocation to a long-term care facility. Furthermore, older widows generally have few opportunities to augment their income through paid work. Insurance benefits, when they exist, tend to be exhausted within a few years of the husband's death. Not surprisingly, higher income is found to be associated with better bereavement outcomes, especially rates of depression that are lower post-death than immediately prior to death (Schulz et al., 2006).

Increasingly, women, especially among the baby boomers, do not want to depend on a man for economic or social support. Among women over age 70, the married woman is the unusual case. A widow may still have an extensive social support network formed across the life course and now largely composed of other widows. Such social connectedness can buffer some of the adverse effects of widowhood for recently bereaved women, including the risk of hospitalization and health problems (Laditka & Laditka, 2003; Miller, Smerglia, & Bouche, 2004). Even when their friends die, women generally establish new relationships, exchanging affection and material support outside their families, although they may not want to call on such relationships to care for them (Ajrouch, Blandon, & Antonucci, 2005). Friends may be more supportive than children, especially when friends accept the widow's emotional ambivalence, do not offer unwanted advice, and respond to what she defines as her needs. Adjusting to the loss of a partner is likely to be most difficult for women who are in poor health, have had limited resources throughout their lives, and perceive themselves as dependent.

The extent to which widows have strong friendship networks appears to vary with social class and race, whether they had a social network and satisfying roles before their partner's death and the prevalence of widowhood among aperson's own age, sex, and class peers. For example, Latina and Asian American widows are more likely to live with others and thus to have more active support systems than Caucasian widows (Moen, 2001). Coping with widowhood may be hardest for women whose identity as a wife is lost without the substitution of other viable roles and lifestyles. A closely related factor appears to be whether a gap exists between the extent to which a woman was socialized to be dependent on a man and how she must now be more self-reliant as a widow (van den Hoonaard, 2001). These recent findings of widows' extensive informal networks differ markedly from Lopata's (1973) classic study, where widows who did not have their own friends or who had only couple-based friendships before the husband's death generally had difficulty forming new friendships and developing satisfying roles. Because more women have entered the workforce in the past 40 years, the employment-associated social networks of future cohorts of older women may also enhance their capacity to live on their own, compared to the women in Lopata's early studies.

While older widowed men are seven times more likely than older widows to remarry, many widows have no interest in remarriage. For some women who have been restricted or even abused in their partner relationships or faced long-term care responsibilities, widowhood can bring opportunities to develop new interests. Although a husband's death is devastating, personal growth can be a positive result of the loss. Some widows redefine themselves, calling themselves "new women" (Walter, 2003). Personal characteristics of widows such as involvement with others, perceived control in their lives, and an attitude of learning from experience appear to decrease perceived stress and increase life satisfaction (Rossi et al., 2007). Overall, women living alone now, including widows, feel more positive about their autonomy than women did in the past (AARP, 2006; Cheng, 2006).

A woman's change in status inevitably affects her relationship with her children and other relatives. While most adult children try to support their widowed mothers, this tends to diminish over time. Although the children may view their widowed mother as "helpless" and urge her to move in with them, most widows do so only as a "last

resort." Older widows often grow closer to their daughters through patterns of mutual assistance, but sons tend to provide instrumental support (e.g., home repairs, yard work) for widowed mothers in their own homes. Nevertheless, although children offer both socioemotional support and task assistance, this may not necessarily reduce their widowed parent's loneliness. For example, interactions with an adult child are less reciprocal than with a partner, while friends and neighbors are better suited for sharing leisure activities and providing companionship. Such reciprocity tends to be associated with higher morale. What is clear is the importance of creating diverse social networks that include age-generational peers, whether family or nonfamily.

Less is known about the effects of widowhood on older men, for whom their wife's death tends to be unexpected (think about how many widowers say "I always thought I was the one who would go first"). Men more often complain of loneliness, experience lower life satisfaction, and make slower emotional recoveries than do women. As noted above, they are more likely to experience physical and mental health problems, particularly depression (Berg, et al., 2009). Compared to women's emotive patterns of coping, men tend to be more instrumental, although this is not determined by gender per se (Martin & Doka, 2000).

Other factors that affect men's grief process appear to be their lower degree of involvement in family and friendship roles across the life course, their lifelong patterns of restraining their emotions, their limited prior housekeeping experiences, and, among older cohorts, their greater likelihood of a double role loss as paid worker and spouse. In addition, older men in this current cohort have more difficulty in seeking informal support and in expressing their feelings. Although older widowers describe themselves as sad and think about their wives nearly constantly, they typically do not share these feelings with others (Martin & Doka, 2000; Miller & Golden, 1998). For men who focused largely on work outside the home, their wives' deaths may raise issues of self-identity and profoundly affect their social relationships. One reason is that men tend to have larger non-kin networks, perhaps as a result of employment, but are less resourceful in planning social get-togethers and building informal networks that substitute for the sociability they typically enjoyed in marriage (Ajrouch et al., 2005).

Given these factors, men may "need" remarriage more than women do, and appear to have been socialized to move more quickly into restructuring their lives through remarriage. Although the death of their wives may significantly impair older men's well-being, it is less likely to place men at an economic disadvantage. And in some instances, men experience pride and enhanced self-esteem from mastering new housekeeping skills. More research is needed on how men cope with the loss of their wives/partners, as well as greater professional sensitivity to men's problem-focused style of grieving (Doka, 2000; Walter, 2003). Even less is known about how older men's experience of widowhood varies by social class, race, or ethnicity.

As described in Chapter 9, informal social supports can significantly reduce the risk of illness and mortality (Krause, 2006; Lyra & Heikkenen, 2006). In order to provide such support for persons coping with loneliness and isolation, mutual help and bereavement groups are widely available in most communities, with women the most frequent participants. Such widow-to-widow groups are based on the principle of bringing together people who have the common experience of widowhood and who can help each other identify solutions to shared concerns. They recognize that a widowed person generally accepts help from other widowed people more readily than from professionals or family members. Support groups thus can provide widows with effective role models, help integrate them into a social network, and enhance their sense of competence. Similar groups also need to be developed for LGBT elders who are coping with the loss of a partner. Some studies, however, have suggested that a widowed person's sense of self-esteem, competence, and life satisfaction may be as important as the self-help

MEN AND WIDOWHOOD

George's first wife died in childbirth; his second wife, who suffered a long bout of cancer, died when he was 79, and his third wife died when he was 85. After the deaths of his first two wives, he quickly sought out someone else who could help fill the void left by their deaths. Each time, he looked for someone who would attend to his needs, listen to his stories, and join him on short outings and trips. He was seeking a companion, not a lover. After the death of his third wife, he became socially isolated and depressed. She had been the one who had kept their social life going. Without her, friends seemed to drop away.

intervention itself—or more so. One implication is that group interventions should focus on ways for the bereaved to draw on and enhance their internal resources, to increase their confidence, and to learn new skills, not just serve as a forum to address the disruptive effects of the loss. More research is needed on how support-group dynamics and structure relate to specific adjustment outcomes for women and men from diverse backgrounds.

The Death of Siblings and Friends

Although the likelihood of siblings dying increases with age, research on the effects of sibling death is relatively limited. Sibling relationships represent the one family bond that can last a lifetime. Yet the older person's grief over the death of siblings may be overlooked by other family members and health care professionals, and few social supports exist specifically for bereaved siblings. The death of a friend is also often minimized. For many older people, especially women, a friend may be a closer confidant than a partner. Lifelong friends share a history of memories and experiences that no one else can fully understand. With a friend's death—similar to that with siblings—older adults lose a past that can never be recaptured with anyone else. Relatively little is known about the cumulative effects of numerous friends' deaths in old age (Connidis, 2001; Hooyman & Kramer, 2006).

Implications for the Future

The right-to-die movement, death with dignity, palliative care, pain management, and use of advance directives all raise ethical dilemmas related to the prolongation and termination of life. These dilemmas are often framed within the context of escalating health care costs and the use of expensive technology to prolong life. Many older adults are now saved, often at considerable cost, from diseases that previously would have killed them, only to be guaranteed death from another disease at equally high or even greater cost. Physicians have traditionally been taught to spare no effort in keeping a patient alive. Nevertheless, health professionals and laypersons are increasingly questioning whether dying should be prolonged when there is no possibility of recovery.

The timing, place, and conditions of death are increasingly under medical control. For almost any life-threatening condition, some interventions can now delay the moment of death, but not its inevitability. As a sign of the increasing medicalization of aging, adults age 80 and over are the most rapidly growing group of surgical patients. In fact, three groups of medical procedures are becoming almost routine for the oldest-old: cardiac bypass, angioplasty, stent and other cardiovascular procedures; renal hemodialysis; and kidney transplants (Kaufman, Shim, & Russ, 2004). Doctors and nurses have always dealt with dying, but not until current higher use of technical advances have they had so much power and responsibility to control the medicalization of the end of life. Accordingly, adults of all ages are faced with greater challenges of saying no to life-extending interventions. These new medical capacities demand a new set of ethics and practices. The field of bioethics was born out of the dilemmas surrounding the introduction and withdrawal of invasive treatments, patients'

decision-making capacity to participate in treatment decisions, and their quality of life. Health care facilities are now required to have the capacity to address such bioethical issues, typically through ethics committees. With the medicalization of aging, bioethics will continue to grow in this century, encompassing a wider range of professionals in debates about end-of-life care. Three features of the new ethos of care are:

1. taking account of the ways the ways in which routine medical care overshadows choice
2. transforming the technological imperative to a moral imperative (e.g., caregiving and love are tied to clinical acts that either extend life in advanced old age or allow "letting go")
3. the coupling of hope for a cure and of "growing old without aging" with the normalization and routinization of life-extending interventions (Kaufman et al., 2004)

Concerns about when and whether treatment should be withheld frame debates regarding the rights to die and to assistance-in-dying. Proponents of the right to die and assisted suicide maintain that prolonging excruciating pain and threatening a person's dignity in a hopeless situation serve no public interests. These decisions become even more complex when the elder is mentally incompetent or comatose. Cross-cultural differences also affect how life-sustaining treatment and palliative care are interpreted and the value and respect accorded elders' lives.

The increased visibility of right-to-die legislation, court rulings, and individual cases means that more people know about their legal rights and have thought about what they might choose for themselves or other family members when faced with a terminal illness. There is general agreement that individuals should have the right to control how they die. However, disagreement persists about what is meant by terminal and medical finality, and under what circumstances decisions to cease life-sustaining treatment should be made. The 1997 Supreme Court decision put at the forefront the issue of aggressive pain management and how well health care providers are trained in end-of-life care. More and more professional organizations are seeking to ensure that providers are prepared to give palliative care.

Public support is relatively widespread for individual determination regarding life-sustaining treatment through advance directives, including living wills. Baby boomers, who will be better educated and accustomed to having control over their lives, are more likely to complete advance directives and to be outspoken about their end-of-life preferences than the current cohort of elders. Even though all 50 states have laws authorizing the use of advance directives, variability across states in their interpretation and implementation will probably continue. This also highlights the need for older adults, their surrogate decision makers, and their physicians to have opportunities to discuss end-of-life preferences rather than depend only on a standardized written document.

Divided votes on state legislation to legalize assisted suicide will probably persist in the future. Regardless of the laws, however, some elders and their families will continue to make decisions to hasten death, especially for terminal cancer patients in pain or for those with neurological disorders such as Lou Gehrig's disease. Internet resources on dying, including those that provide information on how to hasten death, foster the debates taking place at the grassroots level and empower families and their older relatives. The website of Compassion and Choices is a comprehensive resource for information and the right-to-die movement, and to download advance directive packages geared to the laws and regulations of a particular state. Such Internet resources, which once were unimaginable, will increase in number and detail in the future. Not surprisingly, the number of anti-euthanasia websites is also growing, such as Life WEB of the International Anti-Euthanasia Task Force. Internet resources articulating the pros and cons of the right to die and assisted suicide will undoubtedly proliferate. These legal and ethical debates—whether in courtrooms, ethics committees, or cyberspace—translate into daily practice and hard choices for those who are caring for chronically ill and dying elders. The questions of who should control decisions about life and death will continue to be argued philosophically and legally, but doctors, nurses, social workers, and families will be faced with the hard clinical decisions for timely practical solutions. As noted throughout this chapter, the professional preparation of a wide range of health care providers in the future must address such legal and ethical issues, as well as how to deliver culturally competent end-of-life care.

Summary

Although death and dying have been taboo topics for many people in our society, they have become more legitimate issues for scientific and social discussion in recent years. At the same time, there is a growing emphasis on preparing professionals to work effectively with the dying and their families, as well as a movement toward death with dignity. A major framework advanced for understanding the dying process is the concept of stages of dying. However, the stage model is only an inventory of possible sequences, not fixed steps.

Most people appear to accept and deny death simultaneously, are better able to discuss others' deaths than their own, and fear a painful dying process for themselves more than the event of death itself. Different attitudes toward dying exist among the old and the young. As a whole, older people are less fearful and anxious about their deaths than younger people and would prefer time to prepare for death. Likewise, survivors tend to view an older person's death as less tragic than a younger individual's.

Professionals and family members can address the dying person's fears, minimize the pain of the dying process, and help the individual to attain a "good death." One of the major developments in this regard is hospice, a philosophy of caring that can be implemented in both home and institutional settings, and which provides people with more control over how they die and the quality of their remaining days. However, hospice and other palliative care initiatives need to take account of cultural variations regarding the use of life-extending technology and advance directives.

The movement for a right to a dignified death has prompted new debates about euthanasia. Both passive and active euthanasia (or assisted death) raise complex moral and legal questions that have been only partially addressed by the passage of living will legislation and a growing number of judicial decisions, including the 1997 Supreme Court decision that ruled that there is no constitutional "right to die." Economic issues are also at stake; as costs for health care escalate, questions about how much public money should be spent on caring for patients at the end of life are likely to intensify. Bioethics, with its emphasis on informed consent, patient rights, and autonomy, addresses the moral issues raised by the health care of older people.

Regardless of how individuals die, their survivors experience grief and mourning. The intensity and duration of grief appear to vary by age and sex, although more research is needed regarding gender differences in the reaction to the loss of a spouse/partner and the adjustment to widowhood.

By age 70, the majority of older women are widows. A much smaller proportion of older men become widowers, generally not until after age 85. The status of widowhood has negative consequences for many women in terms of increased legal difficulties, reduced finances, and few remarriage prospects. Although men are less economically disadvantaged by widowhood, they may be lonelier and have more difficulty adjusting than women. As a result, men are more likely than women to remarry after the deaths of their wives. Social supports, particularly close friends or confidants, are important for both men and women's physical and mental well-being during widowhood. In addition to mourning rituals to help them cope with their grief, services such as widows' support groups are also needed. Comprehensive and diverse service formats are essential, given the variety of grief responses, and interventions should be available early in the bereavement process and continue over relatively long periods of time to ensure maximum effectiveness. Health and social service professionals can play a crucial role in developing services for the dying and their survivors that are sensitive to cultural, racial, sexual orientation, and gender differences.

GLOSSARY

active euthanasia   positive steps to hasten someone else's death, such as administering a lethal injection; assisted suicide, generally by a physician

advance directives   documents such as living wills, and durable powers of attorney for health care decisions that outline actions to be taken when an individual is no longer able to do so, often because of irreversible terminal illness

anticipatory grief   grief for a loved one prior to his or her death, usually occurring during the time that the loved one has a terminal illness that may allow survivors to prepare

assisted suicide/physician-assisted suicide (PAS)/ physician-assistance-in-dying considered active euthanasia when a physician actively aids a person who is dying, typically through the use of drugs

bereavement   state of being deprived of a loved one by death

bereavement overload   an experience of older adults who are exposed to the increased frequency of family and friends' deaths and may become desensitized to the impact of death

bioethics (medical ethics)   discipline of medicine dealing with procedural approaches to questions about death, dying, and medical decision making

Compassion and Choices   formed in 2005 when several national end-of-life organizations; merged to become the largest and most comprehensive organization of its type

conservatorship designation by a court to manage the affairs, either personal or fiscal or both, of persons unable to do so for themselves

death with dignity dying when one still has some autonomy and control over decisions about life

durable power of attorney legal document that conveys to another person, designated by the individual signing the document, the right to make decisions regarding either health and personal care or assets and income, or both, of the person giving the power; does not expire, as a power of attorney normally does, when a person becomes incompetent

Dying Person's Bill of Rights affirms dying person's right to dignity, privacy, informed participation, and competent care

dying process five stages that may be experienced by the dying person, as defined by Kübler-Ross: (1) denial and isolation, (2) anger and resentment, (3) bargaining and an attempt to postpone, (4) depression and sense of loss, and (5) acceptance

euthanasia the act or practice of killing (active euthanasia) or permitting the death of (passive euthanasia) hopelessly sick or injured individuals in a relatively painless way; mercy killing

"Five Wishes" an living wills in 23 languages and in 40 states designed to encourage consideration of broader questions related to health care decisions than those covered in most living wills

grief process intense emotional suffering caused by loss

grief reaction emotional and cognitive process following the death of a loved one or other major loss

guardianship establishes legal control over another person's body, finances, and all legal affairs

hastened death viewed as a more socially acceptable term than *euthanasia* because it speeds up the inevitable

Hemlock Society national organization that promoted the right to die for terminally ill persons, calling for legalizing assistance for those who decide to take their own lives, now merged with Compassion and Choices

hospice a program of care for dying persons that gives emphasis to the personal dignity of the dying person, reducing pain and sources of anxiety and family reconciliation when needed

informed consent written or oral document that states indications/reasons for treatment, its benefits, risks, and alternatives

living will legal document in which an individual's wishes about medical treatment are put in writing should he or she be unable to communicate at the end of life, directing physicians and hospitals to withhold life-sustaining procedures, take all measures to sustain life, or whatever seems appropriate to the person executing the document

medical power of attorney similar to *durable power of attorney*, but focuses on a health care surrogate to make decisions about the individual's *medical* care

mourning culturally patterned expressions of grief at someone's death

palliative care treatment designed to relieve pain provided to persons of all ages with a terminal illness

passive euthanasia voluntary elective death through the withdrawal of life-sustaining treatments or failure to treat life-threatening conditions

Patient Self-Determination Act federal law requiring that health care facilities inform their patients about their rights to decide how they want to live or die; for example, by providing them information on refusing treatment and on filing advance directives

right to die the belief that persons have a right to take their own lives, especially if they experience untreatable pain, often accompanied by the belief that persons have a right to physician assistance in the dying process

self-neglect a process by which a person voluntarily makes decisions that are equivalent to choosing to die (e.g., refusing help, not eating)

surrogate decision maker person legally designated to act according to patient's known wishes or "best interest;" also known as proxy

Uniform Health Care Decision Act mandates compliance with patients' health care decisions

RESOURCES

Web Resources on Grief and Loss are increasing in both quantity and quality. Sites offer information on the grief process and provide opportunities to share feelings, questions, and concerns with others. Below is a small sampling of some of these sites. Log on to MySocKit (www.mysockit.com) for information about the following:

- AARP Grief and Loss Programs
- American Academy of Hospice and Palliative Medicine
- American Hospice Foundation
- Center to Advance Palliative Care
- Compassion and Choices
- Death with Dignity National Center
- Five Wishes
- Hospice Foundation of America
- Last Acts Coalition
- National Hospice and Palliative Care Organization

REFERENCES

AARP. (2006). Looking at act II of women's lives: Thriving and striving from 45 on. *The AARP Foundation Women's Leadership Circle Study.*

Abelson, R. (2007, February 10). A chance to pick hospice and still hope to live. *The New York Times*, pp. A1, B4.

Adamek, M. (2003). Late life depression in nursing home residents: Social work opportunities to prevent, educate and alleviate. In B. Berkman and L. Harootyan (Eds.). *Social work and health care in an aging society.* New York: Springer.

Aging with Dignity. (2007). Five Wishes. Retrieved May 2009, from http://www.agingwithdignity .org/five-wishes.php

Ajrouch, K., Blandon, A., & Antonucci, T. (2005). Social networks among men and women: The effects of age and socioeconomic status. *Journal of Gerontology: Social Sciences, 60B*, S311–S317.

American Geriatrics Society. (2007). *The care of Dying Patients.* Washington DC.

Barry, L., Kasl, S., & Prigerson, H. (2002). Psychiatric disorders among bereaved persons: The role of perceived circumstances of death and preparedness for death. *American Journal of Geriatric Psychiatry, 10*, 447–457.

Benkel, I., Wijk, H., & Molander, U. (2009). Family and friends provide most social support for the bereaved. *Palliative Medicine, 23*, 141–149.

Bennett, K. M. & Vidal-Hall, S. (2000). Narratives of death: A qualitative study of widowhood in women in later life. *Ageing and Society, 20*, 413–428.

Berg, A. I., Hoffman, L., Hassing, L. B., McClearn, G. E., & Johansson, B. (2009). What matters, and what matters most, for change in life satisfaction in the oldest-old? A study over 6 years among individuals 80+, *Aging & Mental Health, 13*, 191–201.

Bern-Klug, M., Gessert, C., & Forbes, S. (2001). The need to revise assumptions about the end of life: Implications for social work practice. *Health and Social Work, 26*, 38–43.

Borum, M., Lynn, J., & Zhong, Z. (2000). The effects of patient race on outcomes in seriously ill patients in SUPPORT: An overview of economic impact, medical intervention and end-of-life decisions: Study to understand prognoses and preferences for outcomes and risks of treatments. *Journal of the American Geriatrics Society, 48*, S194–S198.

Braun, K. L., Pietsch, J. H., & Blanchette, P. L. (Eds.). (2000). An introduction to culture and its influence on end-of-life decision making. In *Cultural issues in end-of-life decision making.* Thousand Oaks, CA: Sage.

Braun, K. L., Tanji, V. M., & Heck, R. (2001). Support for physician-assisted suicide: Exploring the impact of ethnicity and attitudes toward planning for death. *The Gerontologist, 41*, 51–60.

Brickner, L., Scannell, K., Marquet, S., & Ackerson, L. (2004). Barriers to hospice care and referrals:

Survey of physicians' knowledge, attitudes and perceptions in a health maintenance organization. *Journal of Palliative Medicine, 7,* 411–418.

Brink, S. (2007). Saying no and moving on. *The Seattle Times,* pp. A3.

Camhi, S. L., Mercado, A. F., Morrison, R. S., Du, Q., Platt, D. M., et al. (2009). Deciding in the dark: Advance directives and continuation of treatment in chronic critical illness. *Critical Care Medicine, 37,* 919–925.

Cantwell, P., Turoc, S., Brenneis, C., & Hanson, J. (2000). Predictors of home death in palliative care cancer patients. *Journal of Palliative Care, 16,* 23–30.

Carr, D. (2003). A good death for whom? Quality of spouse's death and psychological distress among older widowed persons. *Journal of Health and Human Behavior, 44,* 215–232.

Carr, D. (2004). Gender, preloss martial dependence and older adults' adjustment to widowhood. *Journal of Marriage and the Family, 66,* 220–235.

Carr, D., House, J. S., Kessler, R. C., Nesse, R. M., Sonnega, J., et al. (2000). Marital quality and psychological adjustment to widowhood among older adults: A longitudinal analysis. *Journal of Gerontology: Social Sciences, 55B,* S197–S205.

Carr, D., Nesse, R., & Wortman, C. B. (Eds.). (2006). *Spousal Bereavement in Late Life.* New York: Springer Publishing.

Centers for Medicare and Medicaid Services. (2009). Hospice payment system. Retrieved 2009, from http://www.cms.hhs.gov/mlnproducts/downloads/hospice_pay_sys_fs.pdf

Cheng, C. (2006). Living alone: The choice and health of older women. *Journal of Gerontological Nursing, 32,* 24–25.

Christopher, M. J. (2003). The new place of end-of-life issues on the policy agenda. *Public Policy and Aging Report, 13,* 23–26.

Cicirelli, V. G. (2002). *Older adults' views on death.* New York: Springer.

Cicirelli, V. G. (2006). Fear of death in mid-old age. *Journal of Gerontology: Psychological Sciences, 61B,* P75–P81.

Cohen, L. L. (2008). Racial/ethnic disparities in hospice care: A systematic review. *Journal of Palliative Medicine, 11,* 763–768.

Condon, J. V., Miller, K. M., Le, A. H., Quasem, M., & Looney, S. W. (2008). Acute myocardial infarction and race, sex, and insurance types: Unequal processes of care. *The Health Care Manager, 27,* 212–222.

Cone, D., Richardson, L., Todd, D., & Betancourt, J. (2003). Health care disparities in emergency medicine. *Academic Emergency Medicine, 10,* 1176.

Connidis, I. A. (2001). *Family ties and aging.* Thousand Oaks, CA: Sage.

Corr, C., Nabe, C., & Corr, D. (2003). *Death and dying: Life and living.* Belmont, CA: Wadsworth.

Crawley, L. (2001). Palliative care in African American communities. *Innovations in end-of life care,* 3. Retrieved February 2007, from http://www2.edc.org/lastacts/archives/archivesSept01/editorial.asp

DeSpelder, L. & Stickland, A. (2002). *The last dance: Encountering death and dying* (6th ed.). Boston: McGraw Hill.

DiCamillo, M. & Field, M. (2006).*Continued support for doctor-assisted suicide. Most would want their physician to assist them if they were incurably ill and wanted to die.* San Francisco, CA: Field Research Corporation.

Doka, K. J. (2008). Disenfranchised grief in historical and cultural perspective. In M. S. Stroebe, R. O. Hansson, H. Schut, W. Stroebe, & E. Van den Blink (Eds.). Handbook of Bereavement Research and Practice: Advances in Theory and Intervention. Washington: American Psychological Association.

Dula, A. & Williams, S. (2005). When race matters. *Clinical Geriatric Medicine, 21,* 239–253.

Duncan, J. G., Forbes-Thompson, S., & Bott, M. J. (2008). Unmet symptom management needs of nursing home residents with cancer. *Cancer Nursing, 31,* 265–273.

Federal Interagency Forum on Aging. (2008). *Aging-related statistics. Older Americans 2008: Key indicators of well-being.* Washington, DC: U.S. Government Printing Office.

Field, M. J. & Cassel, C. K. (1997). *Approaching death: Improving care at the end of life.* Washington, DC: National Academy Press.

Fortner, B., Neimeyer, R. A., & Rybarczk, B. (2000). Correlates of death anxiety in older adults: A comprehensive review. In A. Tomer (Ed.). *Death attitudes and the older adult: Theories, concepts and applications.* Philadelphia: Taylor and Francis.

Gert, K. & Burr, J. A. (2008). Planning for end-of-life care: Black-white differences in the completion of advance directives. *Research on Aging, 30,* 428–449.

Growth of hospital-based palliative care programs surges. (2007). *Healthcare Benchmarks & Quality Improvement.* AHC Media.

Gruneir, A., Vincent, M., Weitzen, S., Truchil, R., Teno, J., & Roy, J. (2007). Where people die: A multilevel approach to understanding influence on site of death in America. *Medical Care Research & Review, 64,* 351–378.

Ha, J. (2008). Changes in support from confidants, children, and friends following widowhood. *Journal of Marriage and Family, 70,* 306–318.

Hall, M. & Irwin, M. (2001). Physiological indices of functioning in bereavement. In M. S. Stroebe, R. O. Hansson, W. Stroebe, & H. Schut (Eds.). *Handbook of bereavement: Consequences, coping and care.* Washington, DC: American Psychological Association.

Hampton, T. (2008). Studies address racial and geographic disparities in breast cancer treatment. *Journal of the American Medical Association, 300,* 1641.

Hawkins, N., Ditto, P., Danks, J., & Smucker, W. (2005). Micromanaging death: Process preferences, values, and goals in end of life decision-making. *The Gerontologist, 45,* 107–117.

Holstein, M. (1998). Ethics and aging: Bringing the issues home. *Generations, 22,* 4.

Hooyman, N. & Kramer, B. (2006). *Living through loss: Interventions across the lifespan.* New York: Columbia University Press.

Institute of Medicine. (2002). *Unequal treatment: Confronting racial and ethnic disparities in health care.* Washington, DC: National Academy Press.

Johnson, K., Elbert-Avila, K., & Tulsky, J. (2005). The influence of spiritual beliefs and practices on the treatment preferences of African Americans: A review of the literature. *Journal of the American Geriatrics Society, 53,* 711–719.

Journal of Pain & Palliative Care Pharmacotherapy. (2006). News and innovations: Physicians and general public support for physician-assisted suicide. *Journal of Pain and Palliative Care, 20,* 100.

Jost, K. (2005). Right to die. *The CQ Researcher,* 423–438.

Kass-Bartelmes, B. & Hughes, R. (2003). *Advance care planning: Preferences for care at the end of life. Research in action.* Washington, DC: Agency for Healthcare Research and Quality.

Kastenbaum, R. (2004). On our way: *The final passage through life and death.* Berkeley, CA: University of California Press.

Kastenbaum, R. (2008). Death, Society, and Human Experience. Addison-Wesley.

Kaufman, S. R. (2002). A commentary: Hospital experience and meaning at the end-of-life. *The Gerontologist, 42,* 34–39.

Kaufman, S. R., Shim, J., & Russ, A. (2004). Revisiting the biomedicalization of aging: Clinical trends and ethical challenges. *The Gerontologist, 44,* 731–738.

Kayser-Jones, J., Kris, A., Miaskowski, C., Lyons, W., et al. (2006). Hospice care in nursing homes: Does it contribute to higher quality pain management? *The Gerontologist, 46,* 325–333.

Keene, J. R. & Prokos, A. H. (2008). Widowhood and the end of spousal care-giving: Relief or wear and tear? *Ageing and Society*, 23, 551–570.

Krause, N. (2006). Social relationships in late life. In R. Binstock & L. George (Eds.). *Handbook of aging and the social sciences* (6th ed.). San Diego: Academic Press.

Kressin, N. & Peterson, L. (2001). Racial differences in the use of invasive cardiovascular procedures: Review of the literature and prescription for future research. *Annals of Internal Medicine*, 135, 352–366.

Kübler-Ross, E. (1969). *On death and dying*. New York: Macmillan.

Kübler-Ross, E. (Ed.). (1975). *Death: The final stage of growth*. Englewood Cliffs, NJ: Prentice-Hall.

Kübler-Ross, E. (1981). *Living with dying*. New York: Macmillan.

Kübler-Ross, E. & Kessler, D. (2001). *Life's lessons: Two experts on death and dying tell us about the mysteries of life and living*. New York: Scribner.

Kwak, J., Haley, W. E., & Chiraboga, D. A. (2008). Racial differences in hospice use and in-hospital death among Medicare and Medicaid dual-eligible nursing home residents. *The Gerontologist*, 48, 32–41.

Laditka, J. & Laditka, S. (2003). Increased hospitalization risk for recently widowed older women and protective effects of social contacts. *Journal of Women and Aging*, 15, 7–28.

Lamberg, L. (2002). "Palliative care" means "active care:" It aims to improve quality of life. *Journal of the American Medical Association*, 288, 943–944.

Last Acts. (2002). *Means to a better end: A report on dying in America today*. Washington, DC.

Lawton, M. P. (2001). Quality of life and the end of life. In J. Birren and K. W. Schaie (Eds.). *Handbook of the psychology of aging* (5th ed.). San Diego: Academic Press.

Lewis, C. S. (1961). *A grief observed* (1st ed.). New York: Seabury Press.

Lindenstrom, T. (2002). It ain't necessarily so: Challenging mainstream thinking about bereavement. *Family and Community Health*, 25, 11–21.

Lopata, H. Z. (1973). *Widowhood in an American city*. Cambridge, MA: Schenkman.

Martin, T. L. & Doka, K. J. (2000). *Men don't cry, women do*. Philadelphia: Brunner/Mazel.

Miller, J. & Goldman, T. (1998). When a man face grief: A man you know is grieving. Fort Wayne, IN: Willowgreen Press.

Miller, N., Smerglia, V., & Bouche, N. (2004). Women's adjustment to widowhood: Does social support matter? *Journal of Women and Aging*, 16, 149–167.

Miller, S., Teno, J., & Mor, V. (2004). Hospice and palliative care in nursing homes. *Clinics in Geriatric Medicine*, 20, 717–734.

Moen, P. (2001). The gendered life course. In R. H. Binstock & L. K. George (Eds.). *Handbook of aging and the social sciences* (5th ed.). San Diego, CA: Academic Press.

Morrison, R. S., Penrod, J. D., Cassel, J. B., Caust-Ellenbogen, M., Litke, A., Spragens, L., et al. (2008). Cost savings associated with US hospital palliative care consultation programs. *Archives of Internal Medicine*, 168, 1784–1790.

Moss, M., Moss, S., & Hansson, R. (2001). Bereavement in old age. In M. Stroebe, R. Hansson, W. Stroebe, and H. Schut (Eds.). *Handbook of bereavement research*. Washington, DC: American Psychological Association.

Muramatsu, N., Hoyem, R. L., Yin, H., & Campbell, R. T. (2008). Place of death among older Americans: Does state spending on home and community-based services promote home death? *Medical Care*, 46, 829–838.

National Center for Health Statistics. (2003). *National Mortality Followback Survey*, Hyattsville, MD: author.

National Consensus Project for Quality Palliative Care. (2009). *Clinical practice guidelines for quality palliative care.* Retrieved May, 2009, from http://www.nationalconsensus project.org

National Hospice and Palliative Care Organization Research Department. (2008). *Hospice facts and figures.* Retrieved May, 2009, from http://www .nhpco.org/files/public/Statistics_Research/NHPCO _facts-and-figures_2008.pdf

Neimeyer, R. A. (1998). Can there be a psychology of loss? In J. H. Harvey (Ed.), *Perspectives on loss.* Philadelphia: Taylor and Francis.

Oregon Department of Human Services. (2009). Death with Dignity Act Annual Reports – Year 11. Portland, OR: Office of Disease Prevention and Epidemiology. Retrieved June, 2009, from http://oregon.gov/DHS/ph/pas/ ar-index.shtml

O'Reilly, K. B. (2005). *Doctors favor physician-assisted sui-cide less than patients do. AMedNews.com.* Retrieved November, 2005, from http://www .compassionandchoices.org/documents/20051121 suicidepolls.pdf

Ozanne, E. M., Partridge, A., Moy, B., Ellis, K. J., & Sepucha, K. R. (2009). Doctor-patient communication about advance directives in metastatic breast cancer. *Journal of Palliative Medicine, 12,* 547–553.

Parkes, C. M. (1972). *Bereavement: Studies of grief in adult life.* New York: International University Press.

Payne, R., Medina, E., & Hampton, J. (2003). Quality of life concerns in patients with breast cancer, evidence of disparity outcomes and experiences in pain management and palliative care among African American women. *Cancer, 97,* 311–317.

Phillips, R., Hamel, M., Covinsky, K., & Lynn J. (2000). Findings from SUPPORT and HELP: An introductory study to understand prognoses and preferences for outcomes and risks of treatment: Hospitalized elderly longitudinal project. *Journal of the American Geriatrics Society, 48.*

Rando, T. (2000). *Clinical dimensions of anticipatory mourning: Theory and practice in working with the dying, their loved ones, and their caregivers.* Champaign, IL: Research Press.

Richardson, V. E. (2006). Bereavement in later life. In V. E. Richardson & A. S. Barusch (Eds.). *Social work practice with older adults.* New York: Columbia University Press.

Richardson, V. E. & Barusch, A. (2006). *Gerontological practice for the 21st century: A social work perspective.* New York: Columbia University Press.

Rosenblatt, P. C. (2008). Grief across cultures: A review and research agenda. In M. Stroebe, R. O. Hansson, H. Schut, & W. Stroebe (Eds.). *Handbook of bereavement research and practice: Advances in theory and intervention.* Washington DC: American Psychological Association Books.

Rossi, N. E., Bisconti, T. L., & Bergeman, C. S. (2007). The role of dispositional resilience in regaining life satisfaction after the loss of a spouse. *Death Studies, 31,* 863–883.

Russac, R. J., Gatliff, C., Reece, M., & Spottswood, D. (2007). Death anxiety across the adult years: An examination of age and gender effects. *Death Studies, 31,* 549–561.

Schulz, R., Boerner, K., Shear, K., Zhang, S., & Gitlin, L. N. (2006). Predictors of complicated grief among dementia caregivers: A prospective study of bereavement. *The American Journal of Geriatric Psychiatry, 14,* 650.

Schulz, R., Mendelsohn, A. B., Haley, W. E., Mahoney, D., Allen, R. S., et al. (2003). End of life care and the effects of bereavement on family caregivers of persons with dementia. *New England Journal of Medicine, 349,* 1936–1952.

Smith, S. H. (2004). End of life decision-making pro- cesses of African American families. *Ethnic and Cultural Diversity in Social Work, 13,* 1–23.

Stroebe, M. S., Hansson, R. O., Stroebe, W., & Schut, H. (2001). Future directions in bereavement research. In M. Stroebe, R. Hansson,

W. Stroebe, & H. Schut (Eds.). *Handbook of bereavement research.* Washington, DC: American Psychological Association.

Stroebe, M. S., Hansson, R. O., Schut, H., Stroebe, H. W., & Van den B. (2008). *Handbook of bereavement research and practice: Advances in theory and intervention.* Washington, DC: American Psychological Association.

Subramanian, S. V., Elwert, F., & Christakis, N. (2008). Widowhood and mortality among the elderly: The modifying role of neighborhood concentration of widowed individuals. *Social Science & Medicine, 66,* 873–884.

Taylor, D. H., Ostermann, J., Van Houtven, C. H., Tulsky, J. A., & Steinhauser, K. (2007). What length of hospice use maximizes reduction in medical expenditures near death in the US Medicare program? *Social Science & Medicine, 65,* 1466–1478.

Thorson, J. & Powell, F. C. (2000). Death anxiety in younger and older adults. In A. Tomer (Ed.). *Death attitudes and the older adult: Theories, concepts and applications.* Philadelphia: Taylor and Francis.

Tomer, A., & Ellison, G. (2000). Attitudes about life and death. Toward a comprehensive model of death anxiety. In A. Tomer (Ed.), *Death attitudes and the older adult: Theories, concepts and applications.* Philadelphia: Taylor and Francis.

Troyer, J. & McAuley, W. (2006). Environmental contexts of ultimate decisions: Why nursing home residents are twice as likely as African American residents to have an advance directive. *Journal of Gerontology: Social Sciences, 61B,* S194–S202.

Tu, J. I. (2009). Rules governing state's Death With Dignity law debated. *The Seattle Times.* Retrieved May 2009, from http://seattletimes.nwsource.com/html/localnews/2008730971_death11m0.html

Unutzer, J., Katon, W., Callahan, C. M., Williams, J. W., Hunkeler, E., Harpole, L., et al. (2003). Depression treatment in a sample of 1801 depressed older adults in primary care. *Journal of the American Geriatrics Society, 51,* 505–514.

Utz, R., Carr, D., Nesse, R., & Wortman, C. (2002). The effect of widowhood on older adults' social participation: An evaluation of activity, disengagement, and continuity theories. *The Gerontologis, 42,* 522–533.

van den Hoonaard, D. (2001). *The widowed self: Older women's journey through widowhood.* Waterloo, Ontario: Wilfred Laurier University Press.

Waldrop, D. P. (2006). At the eleventh hour: Psychosocial dynamics in short hospice stays. *The Gerontologist, 46,* 106–114.

Walter, T. (2003). *The loss of a life partner: Narratives of the bereaved.* New York: Columbia University Press.

Washington, H. (2007). *Medical apartheid: The dark history of medical experimentation on Black Americans from colonial times to the present.* New York: Doubleday.

Weiss, R. S. (2001). Grief, bonds and relationships. In M. Stroebe, R. Hansson, W. Stroebe, & H. Schut (Eds.). *Handbook of bereavement research: Consequences, coping and care.* Washington, DC: American Psychological Association.

Weitzen, S., Teno, J., Fennell, M., & Mor, V. (2003). Factors associated with site of death: A national study of where people die. *Medical Care, 41,* 323–335.

Welch, L. C., Teno, J. M., Mor, V. (2005). End-of-life care in black and white: Race matters for medical care of dying patients, and their families. *Journal of the American Geriatrics Society, 53,* 1145–1153.

Wilkinson, A. M. & Lynn, J. (2001). The end of life. In R. H. Binstock and L. K. George (Eds.). *Handbook of aging and the social sciences* (5th ed.). San Diego: Academic Press.

Worden J. W. (2002). *Grief counseling and grief therapy: A handbook for the mental health practitioner.* New York: Springer.

Worden, W. J. (2009). *Grief counseling and grief therapy: A handbook for the mental health practitioner* (4th ed.). New York: Springer Publishing.

Wortman, C. B. (2002). *Changing Lives of Older Couples Study.* Retrieved January 2002, from http://www.cloc. isr.umich.edu/index.htm

Wortman, C. & Silver, R. C. (2001). The myths of coping with loss revisited. In M. Stroebe, R. Hansson, W. Stroebe, & H. Schut (Eds.). *Handbook of*

bereavement research: Consequences, coping and caring. Washington, DC: American Psychological Association.

Wright, A. A. & Katz, I. T. (2007). Letting go of the rope: Aggressive treatment, hospice care, and open access. *New England Journal of Medicine, 357,* 324–327.

14

The Resilience of Elders of Color

When discussing the changes experienced by older adults, there is a tendency to speak about them as if they were a homogeneous group. Yet, as illustrated throughout this book, the older population is more heterogeneous than any other. Two primary variables in this heterogeneity are gender and race; both influence an individual's position in the social structure and experiences across the life course. To be an older person of color, or an older woman, is to experience environments substantially different from those of a white male across the life course. For example, both older women and older African Americans are twice as likely as white men to be poor and live alone, which places them at greater risk of poorer health status and social isolation. But African American women are more than twice as likely as white women to be poor (Kail, Quadagno, & Keene, 2009).

The intersections of gender, race, ethnicity, living arrangements, and social class are illustrated by the following examples of cumulative disadvantage across the life course, reflected in exposure to risk and resulting in health and economic disparities:

- The poverty rate for African American women who live alone is four to five times greater than for their married counterparts.
- African American and Latino households headed by women are more than twice as likely than non-Hispanic whites to be poor in old age.
- Older women of color are more likely to obtain health care from hospital outpatient units, emergency rooms, and neighborhood centers than from private physicians, generally because they lack adequate insurance.
- Older women of color who live alone form the poorest group in our society, with widowhood having more negative economic consequences than for their male counterparts.

(AARP, 2008; Angel & Hogan, 2004; Angel, Jimenez, & Angel, 2007; AOA, 2008, 2009; Federal Interagency Forum, 2008; Heinz, Lewis, & Hounsell, 2006; Mutchler & Burr, 2008).

Consistent with the *life-course perspective* described in Chapter 8, such disparities in old age are typically related not only to current conditions, but also to earlier experiences of disadvantage in education, labor force participation, income, health status, access to health care, and home ownership. Disadvantage can be conceptualized as exposure to risk, and advantage as exposure to opportunity (Ferraro & Shippee, 2009). Many elders of color bring to old age the cumulative effects of a lifetime of inequities because of their race. From a political economy perspective, racial inequality in old age reflects underlying processes of cumulative disadvantage, which is a product of institutional racism in the labor market and educational inequality. However, institutionalized racism may also affect genes, gestation, and exposure to early childhood infections (Ferraro, Shippee, & Schafer, 2009; Kail et al., 2009; HealthReform.gov, 2009; Mead et al., 2008; Whitfield, 2004). As noted in Chapter 12, early life inequities are usually intensified in old age. Increasingly gerontologists are recognizing the role of biological processes associated with adversity and early origins of health on old age (Ferraro & Shippee, 2009).

Relevant differences among older people arising from their racial status and gender are noted throughout this text. However, this chapter and the next focus specifically on these factors because of their interactive effects with age and the resulting higher incidence of poverty, poor health, barriers to health care, and inadequate living arrangements. In this sense, both older women in general and men and women of color are affected by environmental changes that are incongruent with their needs as they age. Socioeconomic status (SES) or social class is a primary factor, along with race and gender, which creates inequities across the life course. SES varies greatly within groups, not only between groups. For example, there is tremendous economic diversity within the Latino population in the U.S., often based on timing of immigration, home country, and length of time in the U.S. Despite the greater problems and patterns of discrimination faced by women in general and by people of color, both groups display strengths and resilience in old age.

The concept of resilience, or "hardiness," which was introduced in Chapter 6, encompasses the behavioral patterns, functional competence, and cultural capacities that individuals, families, and communities utilize under adverse circumstances, and their ability to integrate adversity as a catalyst for growth and development. Populations of color, despite experiencing great adversity, often have extensive resources that are personal (e.g., spirituality, sense of mastery, faith), cultural (e.g., beliefs, values, and traditions), and social (e.g., friends, extended family), helping them cope with negative life conditions and experience well-being

(Zauszniewski et al., 2005). By emphasizing resilience, we do not intend to minimize the growing economic and health inequities faced by populations of color within our society. However, a focus on resilience among elders of color recognizes their considerable strengths in the face of such adversity. As such, it moves beyond individual characteristics to include contextual or environmental factors and contrasts with earlier research that emphasized deficits among racial groups. It also recognizes the critical role of human agency and resource mobilization in how adversity is experienced and life trajectories are shaped. In other words, interventions that expand resources of groups exposed primarily to risk can alter a trajectory away from accumulated disadvantage and toward advantage (Ferraro & Shippee, 2009).

Defining Ethnicity and Culture

Ethnicity and culture are different concepts than race. Ethnicity encompasses a sense of "peoplehood" evolved from a group's common ancestry and history, social status that can determine how people eat, work, celebrate, care for each other, and die, as well as their informal social support systems. Accordingly, ethnicity patterns people's thinking, feeling, and behavior, although generally people are unaware of these effects. Accordingly, it can be a powerful influence on older people's roles and their adaptation to aging (McGoldrick, Giordano, & Garcia-Preto, 2005). Within the P–E model, ethnicity is central to the individual's sense of competence vis-à-vis environmental demands. Ethnicity may serve the following functions for elders:

- an integrating force when experiencing significant life changes and transitions
- a buffer to stresses of old age, especially when the surrounding community supports the expression of peoplehood and culture

- a filter to the aging process, influencing beliefs, behaviors, and interactions with informal and formal supports

Given these functions, social and health care providers need to understand ethnicity and how it influences behaviors such as help-seeking, family obligation, and mutual support.

People with a common ancestry and history have evolved shared values and customs that are passed on across generations. Their resulting *culture* is a complex system and process of shared knowledge, beliefs, traditions, symbols, language, art, spiritual orientation, and social organization. Culture is a lens through which individuals define their identity, perceive and interpret the world, provide coherence, and create meaning out of life events, including death (Lum, 2003). Cultural diversity refers to people's national origin, their language, and other features of their heritage that influence their daily behavior and world view (Angel & Angel, 2006). Of interest to gerontologists is how culture influences the definition and conceptualization of problems as well as the meaning, values, and experiences of aging, health, wellness, and healing. Based on its unique history and culture, each ethnic group develops its own methods of managing the inevitable conflicts between traditional and dominant westernized ways of life, leading to both vulnerabilities and strengths. Similarly, race is not a proxy for culture, since persons classified as the same race may belong to subpopulations with different cultural identities—such as African Americans whose ancestors were slaves from Ghana versus recent refugees from Somalia (Garroutte, et al., 2008; Kleinman & Benson, 2006).

For most immigrants to the United States from non-European countries, cultural values of cooperation and interdependence contrast with Western norms of competition, self-reliance, and efficiency. For example, many Chinese American elders emigrated as youth in the early part of the twentieth century from small farming villages where ancestor worship was practiced, reflecting the respect traditionally accorded the old. They have grown old in a country where youth and material success are more highly valued than age, and thus may experience conflicts between their views and those of their children and grandchildren. By identifying an elder's cultural values, gerontological practitioners and researchers can gain a better understanding of attitudes and behaviors that influence both their experience of aging and utilization of social and health services. A classic study of how groups of elders manage their chronic illnesses highlights the central role of cultural values. Researchers found that Filipino Americans felt a strong sense of responsibility for maintaining good health, but this was to their family and social group rather than for their own individual well-being. Similarly, the Western notion of individual responsibility for illness was foreign to Latino elders, who did not perceive themselves as responsible for making lifestyle changes such as exercise and diet, nor for developing self-care practices. Instead, they believed that medication alone would control their illnesses, although some also used alternative healing (e.g., herbal teas and roots) (Becker et al., 1998). Since people's cultural lens profoundly affects their behavior, social and health care providers must understand how cultural differences affect diverse elders' well-being, utilization of services, and interaction with them.

People of Color

For purposes of this text, older people of color belong to groups whose language, physical or cultural characteristics make them visible and identifiable, have experienced differential and unequal treatment, share a distinctive history and bonds among group members, and regard themselves as objects of collective discrimination and oppression *by reason of their race.* For people of color, race interacts with ethnicity and culture

to shape an individual's values, behaviors, distribution of resources, and interaction with social structural factors (such as SES) to affect the aging process. It is not only their ethnic and cultural traditions that influence this process, but also their experience of being a person of color within a white majority culture. Accordingly, the quality of life of elders of color is inevitably affected by a lifetime of racial discrimination and institutionalized racism (Angel & Hogan, 2004; Rook & Whitfield, 2004; Williams, 2004, 2005).

This chapter examines the life-course conditions and adaptation to aging among people of color who are defined by the federal government as protected groups—African Americans, Latinos* (including Mexican Americans/Chicanos, Puerto Ricans, Cubans, and Latin Americans), American Indians, and Asian/Pacific Islanders (API). The term *whites* will refer to non-Hispanic whites unless otherwise stated. Data are typically collected in terms of these designations, but this overlooks preferences such as *First Nations People,* increasingly used by American Indians (Weaver, 2005). Within these four federally protected groups, there are ethnic and cultural variations based on nationality and country of origin. For example, consider

---

*Over 3 decades after the federal government agreed on the use of the term *Hispanic* to identify persons with mixed Spanish heritage, debate regarding whether to use "Hispanic" or "Latino" continues. *Latino* refers to the Latin-based Romance languages of Spain, France, Italy, and Portugal. *Hispanic* is an American derivative from "Hispana," the Spanish-language term for the cultural diaspora created by Spain. People who are disturbed because the diaspora is the result of a bygone age of conquest prefer the term Latino. One survey found that a majority of Hispanics and Latinos—53 percent—have no preference for either term, instead identifying themselves by national origin (e.g., Cuban, Mexican, Puerto Rican). Students, intellectuals, and scholars tend to use the term Latino. Throughout this textbook, we use the term Latino because of the negative association of Hispanic with colonialism and because it appears to be most widely used in scholarly circles. Nevertheless, we recognize that both terms have limitations and that both are widely used (Fears, 2003).

the diversity among black populations: Ethiopian and Caribbean immigrants along with African Americans whose roots in the United States trace back to slavery. We also recognize how ethnicity or cultural homogeneity influences the aging process and the importance of ethnic identity for white populations, such as Jewish Americans. Our focus, however, is on *people of color* who have experienced oppression, discrimination, inequities, and disadvantage because of their race, and thus often face greater challenges in old age than white ethnic groups. The terms *historically underserved* and *historically disadvantaged populations* are also often utilized to refer to people of color and are used throughout this chapter.

Two distinct perspectives—one of strengths and resilience, the other of disadvantage—should be kept in mind in this discussion of elders of color:

1. The distinctive historical and cultural calendar of life events and their impact on aging, many of which are positive and are sources of strength and resilience.
2. The consequences of racism, ageism, oppression, discrimination, and prolonged poverty, most of which are negative and perpetuate socioeconomic and health inequities across the life course, beginning in childhood and continuing into old age.

The Dramatic Growth of Populations of Color

Among the current population age 65 and over, about 19 percent are elders of color; this is projected to increase to about 40 percent by 2050, as noted in Chapter 1 (Federal Interagency Forum, 2008.) Populations of color include a smaller proportion of older adults (7.1 percent) and a larger percent of younger adults than does the non-Hispanic white population (15.4 percent). This differential rate results primarily from patterns of immigration, higher fertility rates among younger persons of color, and higher mortality rates among those age 65 and older compared with their non-Hispanic white counterparts. The median age of each group compared to Caucasians

captures their relative youthfulness (U.S. Census Bureau, 2007):

General population	36.5 years
White	37.6
African American	30.9
American Indian	29.6
Asian	34.5
Latino	27.2

However, this pattern will shift dramatically by approximately 2050, as described below and illustrated in Table 14.1. As noted above, older populations of color will grow at an extraordinary rate, partially because of the large proportion of children who, unlike their parents and especially their grandparents, are expected to reach old age. What is unknown is the extent to which immigration laws and the loss of jobs will slow the growth of people of color.

Populations of color are of increasing concern to gerontologists because of: their disproportionately higher rate of population increase compared with whites: over 183 percent versus 74 percent between 1999 and 2030. The older Latino population is projected to grow the fastest of any population (from 2 to 15 million), followed by the Asian and Pacific Islander population (from 1 to 7 million) by 2050. As shown in Table 14.1 on page 610, elders of color are projected to comprise about 41 percent of the older population in 2050 (18 percent Latino, 12 percent African American, 8 percent Asian American, 3 percent American Indian or other races) (Federal Interagency Forum, 2008). In most instances, by the middle of the twenty-first century, groups that are currently numerical minorities will become the majority in many states. The greatest growth will occur in those age 85 and older: from 1 in 10 today to 1 in 5 by the year 2050, with the largest increase among Latino oldest-old (AOA, 2008). Despite their numerical majority, however, they may continue to face oppression and discrimination. For example, Latinos are the numerical majority in California but continue to be

TABLE 14.1   Distribution of the Older Population of Color

	% OF TOTAL POPULATION, 65+	% OF POPULATION OF COLOR, 65+	PROJECTED % IN 2050
Whites	84.3*	—	—
African Americans	8.1*	8.4	12.2
Asian/Pacific Islanders	2.4*	7.5	6.5
American Indians	0.4*	7.2	0.6
Latinos	5.6*	5.8	16.4

*The sum of the specific percentages reported here will never round off to approximately 100 percent if a Latino percentage is included. The reason for this anomaly is that the U.S. Census Bureau does not treat the Hispanic category (which includes Mexicans, Venezuelans, and Latinos who self-designate themselves as being white) as one that is mutually exclusive from the racial categories. Thus, the Hispanic data are also included within each of the racial categories. Persons of Hispanic origin may be of any race.

SOURCE: AOA, 2008.

poorer and less healthy than their Caucasian counterparts. The disproportionately higher number of inequities that they face relative to whites. For example, as noted in Figure 14.1, rates of poverty and near-poverty are highest among persons of color, which negatively affects their retirement, health status, living arrangements, and access to health care, social services, and long-term care.

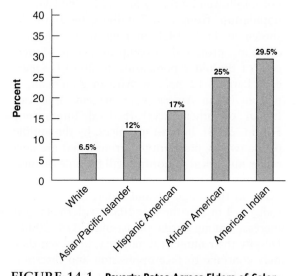

FIGURE 14.1   Poverty Rates Across Elders of Color
SOURCE: AOA, 2008.

For the past two decades, immigration from Asia and Latin America has altered the American landscape, especially in major metropolitan areas. Patterns of immigration to the U.S. (size, year of entry, cohort, age of arrival, and gender composition) have little effect on the white majority or on the distribution of African American and Native American populations, but profoundly shape the characteristics of immigrant groups from Asia, Mexico, Central America, and the Caribbean. As described in Chapter 2, immigrants tend to be predominantly younger families, but since the 1980s, *Family Reunification* laws have allowed these immigrants to bring their older parents and other relatives to the U.S. In numerous cases, these elders are culturally and linguistically isolated. However, given many immigrant groups' high fertility rate, the younger age strata nationwide will remain disproportionately persons of color and immigrants, while older cohorts will continue to be mostly non-Hispanic white, even in 2050. This is of societal concern because historically disadvantaged youth will still face lower educational levels and hold primarily low-wage jobs. Accordingly, such low-wage workers—concentrated among African Americans and Latinos—will not have the resources such as the taxes paid into Social Security to shoulder the burden of supporting a privileged non-Hispanic white older population, thus weakening the social contract between young and old (AARP, 2008; Angel & Angel, 2006).

Recurring themes in analyses of race, ethnicity, and aging are conflicts of cultural values with those of mainstream American society and barriers to use of social and health services. However, significant variations exist *within* as well as *among* these groups. Differences in immigration patterns, birthrates, region, social class, rural or urban location, gender, and acculturation level add to intragroup variations. Latinos, for example, who are defined by the Census Bureau as Spanish-speaking persons, include people from many different cultures and a high percentage of recent immigrants. Accordingly, no single term for persons of Spanish heritage is accepted by all. They can be from any of the following racial groups: Caucasians, Native American/Indian, and African. Mexican Americans are generally of Spanish-Caucasian/Indian descent, while Cubans and Puerto Ricans are of Spanish-Caucasian/African descent. American Indian refers to the indigenous peoples of North America, including Indians, Eskimos, and Aleuts, and over 500 recognized tribes, bands, or Alaskan Native villages. African Americans differ from one another in terms of cultural background, socioeconomic status, and geographic location—especially recent refugees from Ethiopia, Eritrea, Somalia, and immigrants from Haiti or the Caribbean Islands. Asian Americans remain highly diverse because of immigration status. For example, recent immigrants from Laos, Cambodia, and Vietnam have a higher proportion of elders than do other Asian/Pacific Islander groups, and thus face different challenges than individuals of Chinese, Japanese, and Filipino origin, who form the largest percentage of Asian American elders. Given this within-group diversity, generalizations about the health, economic, and social status of elders of color are limited, and numerous exceptions to the norm exist.

HURRICANE KATRINA: THE INTERSECTIONS OF RACE, CLASS, AND AGE

When Hurricane Katrina hit the Gulf Coast in August 2005, it exposed race and class disparities in the aftermath of the tragedy. What is often overlooked is that older people died in greater numbers. Of the 1,400 people who died in Louisiana as a result of the hurricane, 78 percent were age 51 and older, and 39 percent older than age 75; most were African American. These were residents, some in nursing homes but others in their own homes, who could not crawl out on roofs or set off walking on highways. Many of them had special needs neglected by disaster workers, such as untreated chronic illnesses, loss of crucial medications, or higher rates of dehydration. Ageism contributed to their tragic deaths. A lesson learned from this tragic experience is that, as part of their disaster preparedness, city agencies need to compile lists by neighborhood of frail elders and those with disabilities, and develop plans for how to help them if needed. Even more important is that neighbors need to be responsible for their older neighbors (Gullette, 2006).

Research History

Ethnogerontology, a field of social gerontology, is the study of the causes, processes, and consequences of race, national origin, and culture on individual and population aging. From 1940 to 1970, when both scholarly and political concern with older adults grew, little was written about the circumstances of elders of color. In part, this was due to their relatively small numerical size compared to that of Caucasian older adults and in part to racism inherent in many professions during that time period (Markides & Black, 1996). In 1956, Tally and Kaplan first raised the **double jeopardy hypothesis:** Does being both *minority* (a term that was widely used during that time) and old result in a double disadvantage to health and well-being in old age? That is, do lifetime factors of economic and racial discrimination make the aging experience more difficult for African Americans (and other persons of color) than for whites? Debates about double jeopardy—whether it exists and is related to socioeconomic status or to race per se—were central in research and policy discussions in ethnogerontology for many years. However, the growing empirical evidence on racial disparities in health status and health care indicates that such inequities exist across the life course.

A second but related position asserted that patterns of racial inequality are changing and that opportunities for populations of color throughout their lives are related more to their SES than to their race. This perspective maintained that education and social class, not racial status per se, jeopardize populations of color. The **multiple hierarchy stratification perspective** encompassed both views, defining race as one source of inequality along with class, gender, and age itself (Bengtson, 1979). A third widely tested hypothesis is that age is a leveler of differences in life expectancy. The mortality **crossover effect** refers to the fact that people of color experience poorer health and higher death rates than whites at all ages until old age. From age 75 to 85, the death rates for African Americans, Asian/Pacific Islanders, and American Indians are actually lower than for whites. Accordingly, life expectancy after age 75 for these survivors is greater, due to a combination of biological vigor, psychological strength, and resources for coping with stress, such as religious and spiritual practices that link individuals to communities. Thus, the oldest-old segment of populations of color may represent selective survival of the biologically more robust or "hardy" individuals. In fact, although people of color may experience increasing income and health disparities with age, they nevertheless display considerable strengths and resilience that may mitigate the effects of cumulative adversity earlier in the life course. As noted above, this resilience reflects both the role of human agency and the mobilization of resources to reduce exposure to risk. This apparent racial crossover may also be partially due to enumerative errors, such as misreporting age and a reliance on cross-sectional data to compare advantaged and disadvantaged populations (Beckett, 2000). Even if such errors do occur, however, there is increasing evidence of the reversal of health difference with advanced age (Alwin & Wray, 2005; Dannefer, 2003; House, Lantz, & Herd, 2005; Rook & Whitfield, 2004). The racial crossover effect also raises questions about the usefulness of chronological age as a measure of aging. Functional age seems to be a better measure for elders who have faced racial and socioeconomic inequities affecting their well-being across the life course.

As noted in Chapter 4, the concept of **health disparities**—class and racial/ethnic inequalities in health, mortality, and other adverse conditions across the life course—is a rapidly growing area of concern in health policy and gerontology. Removing health disparities is one of two overarching goals in *Healthy People 2010,* described in Chapter 4 (NCHS, 2009). **Health care disparities** are defined as differences in access, quality, or use of health care services, where populations of color have substantively lower rates. Such differences in utilization rates appear to be a function of both a lack of trust due to failures within the health care system (e.g., overexposure to medical errors, missed diagnoses, and inappropriate treatments) and the patient's underutilization of existing services, often because of barriers to access, intended or unintended discrimination, and patient-physician communication problems (Office of Minority Health, 2007; Yee-Melichar, 2004). The effects of social inequality and discrimination on health within populations of color appear to be compounded by age, leading to growing gaps in health status and access to health care (Angel & Hogan, 2004; Ferraro et al., 2006; Health CareReform.gov, 2009; House et al., 2005; Mead et al., 2008; Williams, 2004). The ultimate gauge of health disparities is health

ISSUES COMMON ACROSS ELDERS OF COLOR

1. Cumulative structural disadvantages beginning in childhood and often exacerbated in old age:
   - low-wage jobs with few or no benefits, such as health insurance, that limit their economic security and use of health services across the life course as well as their retirement income in old age
   - higher rates of poverty and near-poverty negatively impact nutrition and exercise patterns, resulting in health differences between people of color and whites
   - women outnumbering men and more likely to be widowed and living alone

2. Centrality of family/kin values affecting informal caregiving and use of long-term care services:
   - preference for in-home services
   - reluctance to use out-of-home services, especially nursing homes and end-of-life care
   - higher utilization of informal networks than formal ones, including grandparents as primary caregivers for grandchildren
   - expectations of adult children or grandchildren to provide care (filial responsibility)

3. Lower rates of health insurance coverage and health care utilization, especially preventive and health promoting services:
   - sociocultural and political barriers to health care (e.g., different communication styles, history of racism, discrimination, segregation, and language barriers)
   - lower utilization of preventive screenings such as mammograms and pap smears
   - preference for complementary medicine, such as non-Western methods of healing (especially among Asian/Pacific Islanders and American Indian elders)

4. Chronic illness:
   - higher rates of obesity, diabetes, and heart disease
   - greater number of functional disabilities (e.g., restricted activity and bed-disability days), although less so among API elders
   - social and functional age may be older than chronological age
   - greater likelihood of psychosocial distress and depression, especially among immigrants
   - misdiagnoses of mental health problems and treatment that is culturally inappropriate

outcomes, with elders of color experiencing higher rates of mortality and morbidity and lower rates of self-assessed health and functional status compared to whites, as described in Chapter 4. Increasing policy concerns about such disparities, led the National Institutes of Health (NIH) to fund research centers to address the reasons for and test interventions to reduce such inequities. The issue of health disparities has numerous policy implications for improving overall population health, compression of morbidity, and functional limitations, as well as for current health reform debates.

Elders of Color in Gerontology

The year 1971 marked a turning point in the recognition of elders of color as an area of gerontological study. In that year, the National Caucus on the Black Aged was formed (later becoming the National Center and Caucus on the Black Aged), and a session on "Aging and the Aged Black" was held at the White House Conference on Aging. This conference, especially important from a policy perspective, highlighted the need for income and health care supports for this population. Since 1971, the National Association for Hispanic Elderly, the National Indian Council on Aging, and the National Asian Pacific Center on Aging have been established. These associations function as advocacy groups for elders of color and as research and academic centers.

The census is the primary source of information on elders of color. Census data, however, are criticized for undercounting groups of color, misclassifying individuals, or merging data about various nonwhite groups. For example, the Census Bureau traditionally grouped people by race as "white," "black," or "other." However, the 2000 Census was the first to include multiracial categories. Another problem is the use of birth certificates and self-reports of age. Racial and ethnic classifications based on self-reports often fail to take account of the growing interracial/interethnic heterogeneity of individuals. In addition, the use of major racial and ethnic categories to define groups masks substantial within-group heterogeneity pertaining to cultural beliefs. Immigration dynamics (movements in and out of the country) and settlement patterns pose additional challenges for determining the morbidity and mortality experiences of diverse populations.

In addition to problems with census data, high-quality population-level mortality and disease data are limited. Early studies typically used small, nonrepresentative samples. Many national estimates have been limited to comparisons of blacks and whites and thus exclude other populations of color or within-group variations by ethnicity or immigration status (Whitfield & Hayward, 2003). Research on elders of color generally does not break down data by gender, and studies on older women do not cross-classify data by race. From the feminist perspective discussed in Chapter 8, it is difficult to determine how racism and sexism interact to produce gender-specific race effects and race-specific gender effects, which result in older women of color as the poorest group in our society. Fortunately, research methodology is improving, especially in the areas of cross-cultural measurement and sampling, as well as in participatory action research strategies to engage older adults of color in the research design.

Because of census data limitations and wide cultural variations, findings on one historically underserved group cannot be generalized to older populations of color as a whole. Using race per se as a variable may not lead to straightforward interpretations, because ethnicity, cultural values, education, patterns of immigration, and SES are interdependent and difficult to separate. Within the overall context of these limitations, we next briefly review the life conditions of each of the four major groups that have been historically disadvantaged in the United States.

Older African Americans

Although African Americans are the largest population of color, only about 8 percent of them are over 65 years of age, compared to 15 percent of the white population (AOA, 2008). The young outnumber the old, due primarily to the higher fertility of African American women and men's higher mortality in their younger years. African Americans' life expectancy is 71 years, compared to 78.1 years for all population groups. The difference is particularly striking among African American men, who have a life expectancy of only 70 years compared to the national average of 75.4 years for all men (U.S. Census Bureau, 2009). Cohort effects and succession must be considered in studies of African Americans. To illustrate, the current cohort of elders grew up in a "Jim Crow" environment of racial segregation, discrimination, low SES, and little access to physicians and hospitals within the dominant health systems available to whites. Although they have physically survived this disadvantaged social environment, its effects persist in terms of higher rates of mortality, morbidity, and poorer functional health. Additionally, this pattern is unlikely to change markedly in the future, because the gap in health status between African Americans and Caucasians has not narrowed in the past 50 years; in fact, it is now wider on some indicators, such as infant mortality (Mead et al., 2008; Rooks & Whitfield, 2004).

While these disparities in life expectancy reflect variations in childhood and youth

Older African American men can inspire their sons and grandsons.

mortality rates and socioeconomic status, differences in life expectancy after age 75 are less dramatic. African Americans have higher mortality rates than Caucasians up to age 75, after which they have a longer life expectancy than their Caucasian counterparts (Rooks & Whitfield, 2004). This narrowing of differences in life expectancy after age 75 (the crossover effect discussed earlier) may be explained by the fact that African Americans who survive to this age tend to be the most robust of their cohort. Although still a small percent of the African American population, adults age 65 and older form its fastest-growing segment and are projected to grow by 102 percent from 1990 to

2020 (AOA, 2009). The young-old comprise nearly 60 percent of the African American older population. However, as with other population subgroups, the oldest-old is the fastest-growing segment and is expected to triple in the next 40 years. The ratio of men to women age 65 to 75 is slightly lower than among whites because of the excess mortality that black men experience at every age. Oldest-old women are the most rapidly growing group of African American elders, and they have the longest average remaining life expectancy (AOA, 2009; Angel & Angel, 2006).

Economic Status

The poverty rate among older African Americans is 23 percent, compared to approximately 7 percent of whites, although this represents a significant decline from the rate of 65 percent in 1965. The poverty rate across groups is shown in Figure 14.1. on page 610. Poverty rates are high among households composed of unrelated black individuals, especially females age 65 and over. The median income of African American men age 65 and older is approximately $10,000 less per year than that of white men (U.S. Census Bureau, 2007). However, poverty rates are highest among women living alone and the oldest-old, with the rate of poor African American women age 85 and older approximately 10 times that of young-old (age 65 to 74) white women. Overall, the proportion of older African American female-headed families in poverty has increased in the past 40 years, despite declines in the poverty rates of African American elders as a whole (AOA, 2009, Holden & Hatcher, 2006).

The primary reasons for the lower socioeconomic status of older African Americans are tied to their history of disadvantage and discrimination in our society and include:

- limited access to educational opportunities in their younger years, although the percentage of the black population with a high school education increased from 9 percent in 1970 to over 57 percent in 2007 (which bodes well for future cohorts of African American elders)

- reduced employment opportunities and long periods of unemployment or underemployment throughout their lives
- concentration in low-wage, sporadic service jobs, without benefits or the option of savings and private pensions
- greater likelihood of retirement or leaving the workforce earlier—frequently because of health problems—and then reentering it later out of financial necessity
- greater reliance on Social Security benefits as their only income source
- greater dependence on Supplemental Security Income (SSI) and Medicaid (AARP, 2008; AOA, 2009; Angel & Angel, 2006; Kail, et al., 2009; Purcell & Whitman, 2006).

Differences in education, however, do not explain the gaps in socioeconomic status, which have persisted since 1985. Instead, these inequities are increasing due to growing unemployment and underemployment of blacks, no gains in real wages, declines in pension coverage, and reductions in public supports such as SSI and Medicaid.

As noted in Chapter 12, African Americans often return to work after retirement because of economic necessity, creating the phenomenon of "unretired-retired." In such instances, blacks spend a greater proportion of their lives working in low-paid jobs, with fewer years in retirement compared to their white peers (Schieman, Pearlin, & Nguyen, 2005). Other studies suggest that older African Americans face more difficulties in maintaining employment than whites and are often forced out of the labor market because of unemployment. This means that they are more likely to exit the labor market through pathways other than retirement and face difficulties in reentry. Compared with

whites, blacks not only have lower earnings at equivalent levels of education, but also less wealth at the same levels of income and less purchasing power due to higher costs in segregated urban communities. And if they are employed, they are less able to retire because of inadequate savings and pension benefits (Flippen, 2005).

Health

By most measures, the health of African American adults is worse than that of their white counterparts, again reflecting a lifetime of cumulative disadvantages from poverty and racism. As noted earlier, being either black or poor is a powerful predictor of higher rates of disability, illness, and mortality. A primary reason for continued health disparities among older African Americans is their lower SES and poorer access to health services at each stage of the life course. Fewer years of education, limited entry into high-paying occupations, lower income, and less wealth accumulated over time compound health difficulties into old age (LaVeist, 2003; Mead, et al., 2008; Rooks & Whitfield, 2004; Williams, 2004). The socioeconomic disadvantages experienced by African Americans explain many of the black–white differences in health status, health behaviors, and self-reports of health, as follows:

- less access to health care services, often entering the health care system through hospital emergency rooms
- lower utilization of health services, although the percentage of African American elders reporting that they have a usual source of health care is increasing slightly
- greater delays in obtaining health care and medications, often due to cost
- lower likelihood of having private health insurance, such as Medicap insurance

- greater likelihood that life-threatening diseases are diagnosed later and treated less aggressively
- higher rates of mortality from cancer, heart disease, diabetes, and strokes, as described in Chapter 4 (AARP, 2008; AOA, 2009; Angel & Angel, 2006; Office of Minority Health, 2007)

Among all African American adults, 48 percent suffer from chronic diseases compared to 39 percent of the general population. Not surprisingly, African Americans more often report problems with ADLs and IADLs, and more perceive themselves as being in poor health than do their white counterparts. While heart disease is decreasing among Caucasian men, it is increasing in African American males. As many as 100 black men develop heart failure before the age of 50—20 times the rate in their white counterparts. Although heart disease, stroke, and cancer are the leading causes of death for both African Americans and whites at age 65 and older, mortality rates for African Americans are higher for each of these conditions and occur at a younger age (average age of 39) than for non-Hispanic whites. Blacks experience higher rates of heart disease and stroke at ages 45 to 54 than those reported for all other groups at ages 55 to 64. These are often preceded by risk factors such as high blood pressure, obesity, and chronic kidney disease 10 to 20 years earlier (Bibbings-Domingo et al., 2009; Office of Minority Health, 2007).

This pattern of premature or accelerated aging among African Americans means that the level of mortality experienced by this group at ages 45 to 54 does not occur in other groups until many years later. Deaths from heart disease and stroke are associated with a clustering of risk factors, including obesity, high blood pressure, sedentary lifestyle, and diabetes (American Heart Association, 2005; Office of Minority Health, 2007).

As another example of the interactive effects of discrimination with health behavior, African Americans' higher rates of morbidity and mortality from certain cancers (e.g., stomach, prostate, and cervical) are an outcome of poorer health practices, quality of health care, and more risk factors, including greater occupational and residential exposure to cancer-causing substances, higher rates of obesity, greater prevalence of smoking, and less knowledge about cancer and its prevention. This intensified vulnerability is compounded by disparities in access to health care and higher rates of undetected diseases, so that many cancers are not diagnosed early enough to prevent metastasis. Blacks receive curative surgery for early-stage lung, colon, and breast cancer less often than whites, and are generally inadequately treated for cancer-related pain (Margolis et al., 2003; Mukamel, Weimer, & Mushlin, 2006; Harrington Meyer & Herd, 2008; Office of Minority Health, 2007).

As described in Chapter 4, African Americans also experience higher rates of Type II diabetes—typically associated with obesity—resulting in kidney failure, hypertension, diabetic retinopathy, and other complications. They are twice as likely as whites to die from diabetes (McDonald et al., 2004; Mead et al., 2008; Wen, Cagney, & Christakis, 2005). Similar to the patterns associated with both heart disease and cancer, lifestyle factors—particularly poor nutrition, high fat diets, and lack of exercise—are risk factors for diabetes.

African Americans not only have a shorter life expectancy but also a protracted period of dependent life expectancy and of managing chronic disabling conditions. They experience more rapid declines in functional ability, more days of functional bed disability (i.e., being confined to bed for at least half of the day), and more use of assistive devices for walking and at earlier ages than whites. Nearly twice as many African American elders as whites are completely incapacitated and unable to carry on any major activity (e.g., employment, keeping house), although still residing in the community (Angel & Angel, 2006). These higher rates of disability also have profound consequences for family caregivers.

Additionally, African American elders have less access to quality health care than their white counterparts and delayed access due to cost (Rooks & Whitfield, 2004; Williams, 2004; Mead et al., 2008). Unequal opportunities for good jobs limit access to health insurance as an employment benefit and, in turn, medical care during their working years, including preventive care and access to specialists. Across the life course and into old age, African Americans are more likely to use hospital emergency rooms for health care and to lack continuity in the health care they receive. Lower admission rates and untreated morbidity place African Americans at a higher risk than whites of being hospitalized for an extended stay and dying in hospitals (Ferraro et al., 2006; Kelley-Moore & Ferraro, 2004). In 2007, only 32 percent of African American older adults had both Medicare and supplementary private health insurance, while 53 percent of all older adults had both (U.S. Census, 2008).

Most health disparities research has focused on physical health issues (Alwin & Wray, 2005). Racial disparities, including daily experiences with discrimination, also affect the diagnosis and treatment of mental disorders, particularly depression. However, research findings on depression among African Americans are mixed and reasons for differences are unclear. When standardized clinical measures are used, African Americans typically have lower rates of depression than whites, but this may be due to the use of culturally biased instruments that lead to misdiagnosis (Kessler et al., 2003). In contrast, when culturally appropriate measures are used, African Americans have higher mean scores than whites on depression measures (Bernal, 2002; Dwight-Johnson et al., 2001; Jackson, 2005). Social support tends to be associated with lower rates of depressive symptoms but is unable to mediate the stress associated with financial strain and traumatic events (George & Lynch, 2003; Skarupski et al., 2005; Williams, 2004; Williams, Neighbors, & Jackson, 2003). Research on the association between cerebrovascular risk factors and depression among African Americans is important, because hypertension and congestive heart failure are significantly more common in African American older adults than in Caucasians (Yochim, Kerkar, & Licthtenberg, 2006). These patterns are of concern since, as stated in Chapter 6, higher rates of depression may lead to significant disability, impairment, and/or suicide (Adamson et al., 2005; Bartels, et al., 2005). More research is needed on depression among African Americans to disentangle the effects of discrimination, financial strain, gender, traumatic events, and social support. What is clear is that mental health issues among African Americans often go misdiagnosed, underdiagnosed, or untreated by health care professionals (Das et al., 2006; Larson et al., 2006). On the other hand, researchers who have tested various types of psychotherapy for older adults with depression have found cognitive-behavioral therapy through nontraditional delivery methods to be effective for historically underserved populations such as African Americans (Scogin et al, 2007).

Socioeconomic status is one of the strongest known determinants of variations in health, with persons of higher social status, regardless of race or ethnicity, enjoying better health than their lower SES counterparts (Alwin & Wray, 2005; Phelan & Link, 2005; Robert & Ruel, 2006; Williams, 2005). Gaps in mortality rates for blacks and whites are reduced to some extent when social class is controlled. In fact, marginal increases in income level and education generally have larger positive effects on the health of African Americans than on whites (Wen, Cagney, & Christakis, 2005). Similarly, high-income white and black men both live longer than their lower-income counterparts (Williams, 2004). The power of SES to shape differences in health for both whites and blacks is vividly apparent when low-income whites are compared with high-income African Americans, who have a life expectancy at age 65 that is almost 3 years longer than that of white men in the lowest income groups (Williams & Wilson, 2001). Similarly, education can be protective against years of life lost. African American women who have completed 0 to 8 years of school can expect 18.4 years of unhealthy life, while their counterparts with 13 or more years of education can anticipate just 12.9 years—two-thirds the length of disability experienced by less-educated elders (Crimmins & Saito, 2003).

Although SES is a significant predictor of health status, it cannot fully explain health differences by race (Alwin & Wray, 2005). For example, the incidence of chronic disease is often higher or roughly equivalent for African Americans with 16 years of education than for whites with 8 years of education. As another example that race and SES are related but not interchangeable systems of inequality, the highest SES group of African American women has equivalent or higher rates of hypertension and obesity than the lowest SES group of white women (Williams, 2004, 2005). This suggests that education and income do not fully overcome the disadvantages of being black in our society. In addition, some research suggests that perceptions of discrimination by elders of color, even among those in high-status occupations, incrementally contribute to racial disparities in health beyond that of SES (Williams, Neighbors, & Jackson, 2003). In sum, a growing body of evidence demonstrates that racial differences result from patterns of institutionalized racism that produce differential social pathways contributing to varied health outcomes (Alwin & Wray, 2005; Ferraro et al., 2006).

African American elders also face a wide range of social and political barriers to physical and mental health care that affect their general well-being:

- Given a history of discrimination in health care systems, especially in the South, providers may be perceived as unwelcoming. Additionally, most African Americans identify problems in communicating with health care providers (Mead et al., 2008).
- Residential segregation affects the health care facilities, providers, and pharmacists available to African Americans. They are more likely than whites to be treated at large inner-city hospitals, receive poorer quality medical care, and have less access to therapeutic medical procedures and physical and occupational therapy (Mead et al., 2008; Smedley, Stitch, & Nelson, 2003).
- Providers may be unaware of how skin color can affect the presentation or manifestation of a disease.
- Potentially significant conditions may not be detected until advanced stages, or benign conditions may be misdiagnosed as more serious than they are.
- Indirect communication styles and mistrust of whites may interfere with the sharing of information, increasing the probability of misdiagnoses (Currey, 2008).

Social Supports and Living Situations

Living arrangements affect blacks' health and socioeconomic status. The proportion of married African Americans is lower than that of any other population of color. This is because of black men's lower life expectancy, described above. This results in high rates of widowhood among black women (75 percent over age 65 are widowed compared to 42 percent of all women). Among African Americans over age 65, 55 percent of men and approximately 20 percent of women are married and living with their spouses. This compares with 75 percent and 42 percent, respectively, among whites. Widowhood, divorce, and separation account for the fact that over 40 percent of African American women live alone—a higher proportion than that of their white counterparts or of older black males (19 percent). Those who live alone are more likely to be impoverished, marginally housed, and even homeless (AOA, 2009). In addition, rates of remarriage are lower among African Americans than in other groups.

Even though most older African Americans do not live in extended families, approximately 32 percent compared to 13 percent of their white counterparts live with a family member other than their spouse (U.S. Census Bureau, 2007). They have larger, more extended families than do whites, a higher frequency of family-based households with their adult children, and greater levels of social support from their extended families. Accordingly, older African American women are more likely than white women to have their adult children and grandchildren living with them, frequently in interdependent relationships (Angel & Angel, 2006). These are often three- or four-generation households, with older women at the top of the family's hierarchy, playing an active role in the management of the family. As noted in Chapter 9, older African American women are more likely than their white counterparts to provide daily care for grandchildren, as well as children of other family members and friends. These cross-generational caregiving patterns are associated with higher rates of functional limitations and poverty, because no social insurance program protects them from the economic insecurity resulting from these responsibilities (Hayslip & Kaminski, 2005; Kail, et al., 2009; Minkler & Fuller-Thomson, 2005). Nevertheless, most African American grandmother caregivers exhibit considerable resilience and know how to seek and utilize support services (Cox, 2002; Gibson, 2002).

Similar to whites, adult children are a primary source of assistance and support for older African Americans. For childless older adults, siblings are the most important kin tie.

Intergenerational assistance, typically from older to younger, is a function not just of race, but also of age, marital and socioeconomic status, and level of functional disability. In some instances, multigenerational households may be a way to cope with low socioeconomic status rather than an indicator of a supportive extended family. Some social supports may be characterized by negative social interactions, especially when financial hardship can adversely affect elders' well-being (Antonucci et al., 2009). Indeed, an increasing number of older blacks are affected by stressors influencing members of their social networks, such as crime and substance abuse by children and grandchildren, and face caregiving responsibilities as a result. On the other hand, intergenerational households that develop out of financial necessity illustrate the resourcefulness of African American families whose domestic networks expand and contract according to economic resources. Even though social class partially explains race differences in intergenerational exchanges, there is strong adherence to norms of filial support and respect toward elders among African Americans across social classes. African Americans comprise more than 10 percent of all caregiving households and are more likely to live with the care recipient than their white counterparts (AOA, 2009).

The African American family tends to have flexible definitions of membership and more elastic boundaries that can potentially expand to include fictive kin, described in Chapter 9. This includes foster parents of children who function in the absence of blood relatives or when family relationships are unsatisfactory. Creation of fictive kin is another source of loving support. As an illustration, African American women active in church may turn to a variety of friends, fellow church members, and other nonrelative contacts in times of need, but these non-kin are considered part of an extended family network. Similarly, they are more likely than whites to have networks that include more distant family members among their pool of unpaid caregivers (Antonucci, 2009; Chadiha, Brown, & Aranda, 2006; Chadiha et al., 2002). By redefining distant kin and friends as primary kin, they may increase the number of close relationships. The process of enlarging their extended family beyond lineal ties thus expands their pool of supportive resources.

Overall, African American elders appear to have a broader range of informal instrumental and emotional supports than is characteristic of Caucasian older people. Social support can enhance a sense of mastery or self-confidence, which has positive effects on mental health (Lincoln et al., 2003, 2005). Norms of reciprocity are generally strong and have evolved from a cooperative lifestyle that served as a survival mechanism in earlier times and continues to be a source of both emotional and instrumental support. Such informal helpers often function as critical links to social services or meet immediate needs, such as providing housing or transportation (Lincoln, Taylor & Chatters, 2003; Lincoln, Chatters & Taylor, 2005; Taylor, Chatters & Celious, 2003).

On the other hand, health and social service providers must be cautious not to assume the existence of strong social supports, especially at the point of discharge to home care settings or in instances of chronic financial strain. Patterns of familial support vary within the African American population and are undoubtedly affected by economic pressures on younger family members. Such patterns should be carefully assessed because of their implications for greater isolation, home confinement, stress on family caregivers, and the need for additional health care services. It is also important to recognize that conflicts with members of support networks can occur, which may reduce the level of emotional support and result in negative mental health outcomes. In other words, not all

> **OUTREACH TO AFRICAN AMERICAN ELDERS**
>
> Scores of low-income African American older women live alone, with chronic illness and in substandard housing and apartments, often socially isolated and relatively invisible. The African American Elders program in Seattle, Washington, tries to find such isolated women. Many of these women moved from the Midwest as young adults, worked as poorly paid domestics without any benefits, and suffered from discrimination and poor-quality care in their younger years. They have nevertheless managed to survive. Since most of the women are members of local churches, the elders' program works through clergy and other church members to make connections with them, offering rides, meals, access to culturally competent social services programs, and companionship (King, 2006).

social relationships provide unambiguous health protection (Lincoln, 2000; Lincoln et al., 2005; McDonald & Wykle, 2003).

African American elders' psychological well-being and life satisfaction are often explained in terms of their spiritual orientation and religious participation, including a belief in a higher power and the role of prayer in healing. In fact, prayer is found to have positive health-related outcomes for African American elders and families (Decoster & Cummings, 2004; Pinquort & Sorenson, 2005). As noted in Chapter 12, spirituality and religiosity, which are important in the lives of many black elders for adaptation and support, are related to feelings of well-being, self-esteem, and personal control (Jang et al., 2003; Taylor, Lincoln, & Chatters, 2005). The church also provides a support network of spiritual help, companionship, advice, encouragement, and financial aid. For these reasons, some have suggested that the church should implement spiritually based community models of health promotion that are more likely to be accepted by African Americans than those through health care settings (Parker et al., 2002; Resnick et al., 2006; Townes, et al., 2009).

In the past, African Americans were less likely to enter nursing homes than whites, although they did so at higher rates than other historically underserved groups. As noted in Chapter 11, their nursing home placement is second after that of non-Hispanic whites. African American nursing home residents are found to be more limited in their ability to carry out activities of daily living and less likely to receive the appropriate level of care than are whites. They also are less likely to be discharged, largely because they are too impaired to live in the community and their informal resources have been exhausted (AARP, 2005; Angel & Hogan, 2004).

Older Latinos

As noted earlier, Latinos are the largest population of color (approximately 14 percent of the total population but only 6 percent of the population age 65 and older) and the fastest growing group in the U.S. The number of Latinos is expected to triple by 2050, representing nearly 30 percent of the total population and 18 percent of the older population if current trends continue (Aizenman, 2008; Matza, 2009). Latinos are a diverse population, encompassing native-born as well as legal and undocumented immigrants with varying lengths of residence in the U.S. Although bonded by a common language, each group differs substantially by geographic location, income, education, cultural heritage, national origin, history, dialect, and their racial designation by the majority—all differences that pose challenges in providing culturally competent services to Latino elders. The predominant groups of Latino elders are illustrated in Figure 14.2.

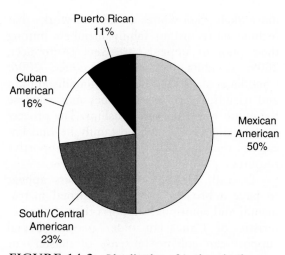

FIGURE 14.2 Distribution of Latinos in the United States by Country of Origin

Within each subgroup of Latinos, those 65 and older comprise a relatively small proportion (Angel & Hogan, 2004):

Mexican Americans	4%
Central and South Americans	5%
Puerto Ricans	6%
Cuban Americans	21%

Latinos are also widely dispersed geographically, with Mexican Americans in the five primarily rural southwestern states, Puerto Ricans in the east, and Cubans in Florida. Overall, 70 percent of Latino elders live in the four states of California, Texas, Florida, and New York (AOA, 2009). The largest proportion of Latinos—and also the poorest—are Mexican Americans. The history of some Mexican Americans predates colonial times and settlement by English-speaking groups, while other Mexican Americans who have immigrated to the U.S. since 1942 (the "bracero" period) were recruited primarily to fill the need for low-paid agricultural workers.

More recent immigrants—both documented and undocumented—have dramatically increased the size of the Mexican population in the U.S. In contrast to the early immigrants who are now the oldest-old, the more recent Mexican immigrants

Family celebrations are an important part of Latino culture.

are young. Their aging experiences will play a major role in the growth of the Latino older population in the future and fuel heated debates about whether and how to limit immigration from Mexico (Angel & Hogan, 2004; Matza, 2009). In contrast, Cubans who were political refugees created "Little Havana" in Miami, where they rapidly achieved economic success; they represent the wealthiest and most educated of Latinos. Puerto Rican elders are distinguished by their citizenship that provides full access to U.S. government services and their ability to travel freely between the mainland and Puerto Rico. Yet they have not achieved the degree of economic success that Cubans have. Elders from Central and South America face pressing needs for housing, assistance with the naturalization process, and help obtaining basic medical and social services. Latino elders' needs may be underestimated, because past studies typically included Latinos in either black or white categories. Furthermore, the Hispanic classification often fails to differentiate among the diverse subgroups.

Compared to other historically disadvantaged groups, the Spanish-speaking population is youthful, which may be due to several factors. One variable is lower average life expectancy, which may be partially explained by poor

economic and health status among Mexican Americans and Puerto Ricans. The most important contributing factor, however, is higher fertility rates among many Latino subgroups. The number of children born and the average family size among Latinos exceed the national average. High levels of net immigration and repatriation patterns are secondary factors, with the youngest (and often poorest) people most likely to move to a new country and some middle-aged and older Mexican Americans returning to Mexico. Despite its current relative youthfulness, the Latino population experienced the greatest increase in median age of all groups of color from 1960 to the late 1990s, with Latinas experiencing a larger gain in life expectancy than non-Hispanic white women during that time period. As noted earlier, these changes will likely result in Latinos age 65 and older growing from the current 6.6 percent to 19.8 percent of the Latino population by 2050. Accordingly, the parent-support rate is expected to triple by 2030, with more middle-aged and young-old Latinos faced with family care responsibilities (Angel & Hogan, 2006; AOA, 2009; Federal Interagency Forum, 2008).

Within the overall Latino population, the sex ratio varies because of the gender imbalance in previous immigration streams and women's greater survival rates. As a whole, there are proportionately more Latino men to women over age 65 than among the white older population:

- 76 men per 100 women age 65 to 74 among Puerto Ricans
- 78 men per 100 women among Cuban Americans
- 83 men per 100 women among Mexican Americans (Angel & Hogan, 2004)

This is due to the higher mortality rate of Latinas than white women at earlier ages, not to greater life expectancy among Latino men. Nevertheless, the overall gender patterns of this population are similar to those of other older people. Women live longer and outnumber men. They more often remain widowed and live alone than their male counterparts. Older Latino men marry or remarry more often than men in other groups of color, with over 65 percent of older Latino males married, compared to 39 percent of older Latinas. The proportion of older Latinas living alone is lower than that of the general population, while the percentage living with other relatives is almost twice that of the total population (AOA, 2009).

Economic Status

Sociocultural conditions underlie Latinos' poor educational and economic status. More than any other immigrant group, they have retained their native language, because of geographic proximity to their home countries combined with the availability of mass communication. Approximately 32 percent of older Latinos speak only Spanish, compared to about 17 percent of their grandchildren and great grandchildren (Wingett & Dempsey, 2006). Although this preserves their cultural identity, their inability to speak English is a major barrier to their education, employment, and access to health and social services. About 60 percent of older Latinos never completed high school, compared to 24 percent of the overall older population. Even when educational levels are the same, Latino elders often earn less than their white counterparts (AOA, 2009).

A barrier encountered by those who entered the country illegally is that they are unable to apply for Social Security, SSI, Medicare, or Medicaid. Even those who entered legally require a sponsor for five years before they can apply for such benefits. Mexican Americans or Puerto Ricans who immigrated in middle or old age typically worked for low pay in physically exhausting jobs in their home countries. As a result, they bring limited resources for finding better-paying jobs in their old age. This work pattern, combined with their ineligibilty for public programs, means that they are often dependent on their adult children (including their sponsors), who must provide support for five years (Angel & Angel, 2006). Not surprisingly, they are least likely to receive Social Security, but when they do, it typically represents their sole source of income. These employment and educational conditions contribute to the high rate of poverty among older Latinos. Slightly over 17 percent live below the poverty level, compared to 7.4 percent of older whites. Approximately twice as many Latino elders are classified as living in near-poverty, falling below 150% of the poverty line. The median personal income of Latino men age 65 and older is about 65 percent of white males' income; for Latinas, the median income is approximately 68 percent that of white females, with 16 percent reporting an income of less than $15,000. Households headed by Latina women are among the poorest in the U.S. (AOA, 2009; Aranda, 2006).

Health

As noted in our discussion of African Americans, low socioeconomic status is typically associated with poorer health across the life course, which then reduces chances for employment, education, and accumulation of income. However, despite their high-risk profiles, including higher rates of poverty, Latinos in general have lower mortality rates from both acute and chronic diseases than whites. In 2007, about 66 percent of older Latinos reported good, very good, or excellent health compared to over 77 percent of whites; twice as many reported problems with ADLs and IADLs. On the other hand, the health status of Latinos in the Southwest is more comparable to the health status of non-Hispanic whites than with African Americans, even though Latinos are socioeconomically similar to African Americans. The greatest mortality advantage is found among Mexican American men. This discrepancy between their socioeconomic risk profile and their relatively favorable health outcomes and self-assessments has been termed an **epidemiological paradox.** This paradox of the Latino population (or the "Hispanic paradox") is not readily explained (Angel & Angel, 2006;

Anderson, 2002; Markides & Eschbach, 2005). It may be partially due to personal health behaviors. Other studies suggest a protective health factor associated with Latino culture, including strong traditional family norms and supports from large extended families and community mutual aid. Some research posits that the Hispanic paradox is a result of the return migration of midlife and older Mexicans with health problems to Mexico (Palloni & Arias, 2004). Lastly, there is probably a genetic component to these differences in mortality and morbidity. More research is needed to disentangle this complex, interactive set of biological, cultural, and SES variables (Angel & Angel, 2006).

Immigration is a primary factor in the relatively good overall health profile of Latinos. In fact, across all racial and ethnic groups in the U.S. immigrants, even when they are lower in SES, tend to enjoy better health than the native born. Recent immigrants appear to bring some protective aspects of their culture of origin with them, including a strong spiritual orientation and healthier diets, and experience better health throughout their lives. As they become more culturally and behaviorally American, their morbidity and mortality profiles more closely resemble those of native-born Americans. Studies of Mexican Americans, for example, find that disease rates increase progressively with acculturation to the U.S.. As length of stay increases, fiber consumption and breast feeding decline, while the use of cigarettes, alcohol, and illicit drugs grows. Rates of infant mortality, low birth weight, cancer, high blood pressure, adolescent pregnancy, and mental health disorders also increase with length of residence in the U.S. This suggests that the increasing length of stay and greater acculturation of the Latino population to the dominant culture will lead to future trends in worsening health for those who came to the U.S. as young people and grew old here (Alegria et al., 2008; Angel & Angel, 2006; Keane et al., 2008; Uretsky & Mathiesen, 2007).

The primary exception to this profile of better health is that Latinos experience higher rates of adult onset (Type II) diabetes than whites, along with its potential complications, including amputation, vision loss, and mortality, even after controlling for demographic and SES factors. The 18.7 percent rate of diabetes in this population—which is 77 percent higher than for whites—and the 40 percent higher mortality rates due to diabetes compared to whites cannot be fully explained by SES or obesity levels; genetic factors may have a stronger role (AOA, 2009; Office of Minority Health, 2007; Otiniano et al., 2003). System-level variables are also salient, with limited prevention initiatives, later diagnoses, and less aggressive treatment of diabetes occurring among older Latinos who lack private health insurance (Angel & Angel, 2006; Roan, 2009). Mexican Americans, Puerto Ricans, and Dominicans, especially those who are female and living alone, suffer considerable chronic and disabling illness earlier in life and experience more limitations in ADLs (Aranda, 2006). For these groups, physiological aging tends to precede chronological aging, with those in their early 50s experiencing health disabilities typical of 65-year-olds and "appearing older" than their chronological age. They are also more likely than the general population to require assistance with personal care and to have greater limitations in carrying out ADLs, although they may resist using in-home services. Lower income, less education, and acculturation are associated with cognitive impairment, as are higher levels of diabetes, cardiovascular disease, and symptoms of depression (Ramirez et al., 2007). Women are more likely than men to experience multiple chronic disorders. Compared with their white counterparts, Latinas have higher mortality rates from cervical cancer and cancer of the uterus (Office of Minority Health, (2007). As with African Americans, this is most likely due to inadequate access to health care and preventive services, resulting in cancer detection occurring too late for successful treatment (Angel & Angel, 2003; Mead et al., 2008; Munet-Vilaro, 2004).

Compared with older adults in general, Latinos are more likely to experience depression than whites or African Americans, which tends to be related to their low SES, chronic economic strains, high rates of diabetes, and short-term financial crises (Angel et al., 2002; Chiriboga et al., 2002). Immigrant or refugee status and living alone also tend to be associated with depressive symptoms (Wilmoth & Chen, 2003). Latinos face an elevated risk not only for experiencing depression but also for its underdiagnosis and undertreatment (Robison et al., 2002). They underutilize specialty mental health care, typically because of system-level barriers, such as lack of bilingual staff and inadequate insurance to cover medication costs and of the stigma they associate with mental health services. Delays in seeking treatment can worsen the depression and result in a sense of fatalism and longer-term health problems (Aranda, 2006; Lopez, 2002; Unutzer et al., 2003).

Early studies suggested that Latino elders were the least likely among all groups to utilize formal health services (Miranda, 1990). As with differences in mortality and morbidity, use of health care services varies within the Latino population. More recent research found that Puerto Ricans and Cuban Americans made more physician visits than whites, but this may be an outcome of better health insurance coverage (Angel & Angel, 2003). Immigrants—especially those who have not attained legal status—lack access to health insurance and thus to adequate health services, particularly preventive care. If they must depend on emergency room care, they typically deal with a new doctor on each visit and do not have the chance to build a rapport and a trusting relationship. In addition, Latinos face communication difficulties that can negatively influence their perceptions of physical and mental health care providers. Language and trust barriers, combined with a greater reliance on home remedies, herbal medicine, and spiritual healing, result in patterns of delayed diagnosis, which can impair their health status (Angel & Angel, 2006; Doty, 2003; Munet-Vilaro, 2004). A study of Mexican American elders found that those with a sense of

personal control over aspects of their health and the health service setting had a greater likelihood of utilizing health services (Angel, Angel & Hill, 2009). Overall, Latino elders are more likely than their white counterparts to lack a usual source of medical care, to experience delays in obtaining health care due to cost, and to feel dissatisfaction with their care (AOA, 2009). Immigrants' ages of arrival influence their degree of acculturation and their access to health care. Across all cohorts, however, Latino immigrants fare worse than Asian immigrants, the other major immigrant group (Kao, 2009). These examples highlight the fact that the wide heterogeneity in immigration experiences and SES profoundly affects how Latinos use health services and perceive their health.

CULTURALLY COMPETENT SERVICES REACH HISTORICALLY UNDESERVED ELDERS

Until 2009, there were only two Latino adult day health centers in Massachusetts, even though the Latino population age 65 and older numbers about 14,000. At the new North Shore Adult Day Health Center, bilingual staff translate for Spanish-speaking elders, lunch is typically Caribbean, English is spoken as a second language, citizenship classes are offered in Spanish, and domino tournaments and bachata and meringue dance competitions are held—all in addition to traditional nursing services. Such centers typically have long waiting lists, especially in March, when many Latin American elders return from their vacations in the Caribbean (Masis, 2009).

Fewer than 3 percent of older Latinos are in nursing homes, rising only to 10 percent among those over age 85. Since families attempt to provide support as long as possible, when older Latinos do enter nursing homes, they tend to be more physically and functionally impaired than their non-Hispanic counterparts. Another reason for this higher level of impairment is that Latinos are less likely to use in-home health services compared to whites (Angel & Angel, 2006).

Social Supports and Living Arrangements

Historically, the extended family has been a major source of emotional support to older Latinos. Living alone is less common among Latino males and females compared to other groups of older adults. Older Latinos are more likely than whites to turn to family than to friends and also to believe that elders should be cared for by family in the community (Williams & Wilson, 2001). They are four times more likely than Anglos between the ages of 65 and 74 and more than twice as likely as those 74 years of age and older to live with their adult children. Widowed women over 75 are generally found in extended-family households. Latino older couples are more likely to head households containing relatives, and older Latino singles tend to live as dependents in someone else's household than are those of other populations of color. Accordingly, their rates of living alone are substantially lower than that of the total older population (AOA, 2009).

Coresidence increases the availability of social supports, including caregivers. Family caregiving among Latinos is influenced by the cultural values and beliefs of:

- *familism* (family unity as central to the life of the individual)
- *marianismo* (veneration of females and the expectation that women are capable of enduring all suffering)
- *machismo* (socially learned and reinforced set of behaviors that guides male behavior)
- *respeto* (respect for people by virtue of age, experience, or service, especially for parents and grandparents)

Accordingly, Latinos value family relations and feel emotionally connected to relatives, believing that the needs of the family as a whole or its individual members should take precedence over one's own (Becker et al., 2003). Although patterns of intergenerational assistance are stronger than among whites, the percentage of Latinos living in multigenerational households has declined. With their urbanization and greater acculturation, some younger Latinos are unable to meet their older parents' expectations to support an extended family in one location. Latino elders who live alone are more likely to live in substandard housing than their white counterparts. Nevertheless, despite cultural, economic, and lifestyle changes, filial piety remains strong and extended family continues to be the most important social institution for Latinos regardless of their country of origin, length of residence, or social class (AOA, 2009; Beyene, Becker, & Mayen, 2002; Kao, McHugh, & Travis, 2007).

Even when Latino families live apart, elders often still perform parental roles; assist with child care, advising, and decision-making; and serve as role models (Martinez, 2003). Although families

---

EL PORTO LATINO ALZHEIMER'S PROJECT: A MODEL FOR CULTURALLY COMPETENT PRACTICE

El Porto Latino Alzheimer's Project in Los Angeles aims to increase the community's capacity to provide culturally and linguistically competent educational, medical, social, and supportive services for Latino elders with dementia, as well as services for their caregivers. These include outreach and education, support groups, day care services, legal services, purchase of services, and case management. The program assumes that public awareness of the diseases and services is limited in the general Latino public. Emphasis is placed on outreach and access, beginning with the project name, meaning "the doorway" or "entrance." Outreach efforts include the use of Spanish and English help lines, bilingual print and electronic media advertising (Spanish-language television and radio stations are the official project sponsors), community fairs, and informal referrals. Access is also enhanced through two agencies serving as points of entry for services; this also ensures a single, fixed point of responsibility for assessing clients' needs. A full-time social work care advocate ("servidora") coordinates case management services, leads support groups, conducts family and community education, and provides informal services and referral (Aranda et al., 2006).

are the most important support for their older members, a division of labor is emerging. This takes place between the family, which offers emotional support and personal care, and public agencies, which provide financial assistance and medical care, along with other institutions such as churches and mutual-aid, fraternal, and self-help groups. These community-based groups provide outreach, advocacy, and information about resources, socialization opportunities, financial credit for services, and folk medicine. The supportive social and cultural context of neighborhood and community is congruent with Latinos' strong sense of cultural identity. Being part of "La Raza" encompasses a shared experience, history, and sense of one's place in the world that can be a powerful base for community and political mobilization.

American Indian elders play a central role in their tribes' cultural activities.

Older American Indians

American Indian, or *First Nations people*, refers to indigenous people of the United States, including Eskimos and Aleuts (i.e., Alaskan Natives).* Their median age is 29.6 years, compared to 36.7 for the general population. Only 7 percent of this population is 65 years of age and older and is projected to remain relatively small in the future. American Indians' life expectancy at birth is now around 74 years compared to 78.1 years for the white population (AOA, 2008; Indian Health Service, 2006; Population Reference Bureau, 2008). There has been some improvement, with life expectancy increasing by 20 years between 1940 and 1980 from 51 to 71.1 years (John, 2004; AOA, 2008). This dramatic improvement is due, in large part, to the efforts of the **Indian Health Service (IHS)** to eliminate infectious diseases and meet acute-care needs earlier in

life. Accordingly, death rates due to tuberculosis, gastrointestinal disease, and maternal and infant mortality have declined the most. Nevertheless, mortality rates for the major killers of older people—heart disease, cancer, and stroke—remain high. For example, cardiovascular disease, while lower among American Indians in the past, is now the leading cause of death beginning at age 45 compared to age 65 in the general U.S. population, thus emerging as a primary health disparity for American Indians (Rhoades et al., 2006). In fact, the rates of chronic and degenerative diseases are rising in this population, creating needs for long-term care that are not addressed by the acute care focus of most Indian health care programs. However, as noted for African Americans, there appears to be a mortality crossover effect. Up to age 75, American Indians have a higher mortality rate than the white population, but this shifts between ages 75 and 85, when their mortality rates are lower than whites (John, 2004).

We know less about the health and well-being of American Indians than other populations. The two federal agencies responsible for collecting data, the **Bureau of Indian Affairs (BIA)** and the U.S. Census Bureau, frequently have different estimates, making it difficult to generalize about

---

*Although the term First Nations is often preferred, American Indians is the category for data-gathering purposes (Weaver, 2005). Both terms are used in our discussion.

First Nation elders. An additional complication in generalizing findings is that there are nearly 562 federally recognized tribes, an estimated 148 unrecognized tribes, and approximately 300 federally recognized reservations. Between 60 to 70 percent live in urban areas rather than on reservations, and therefore their conditions and needs are less visible. A further complication is that approximately 20 percent of American Indian elders who live in federally recognized areas are not enrolled in a tribe and thus would not be seen by providers within the BIA, which is responsible for administration of tribal natural resources, law and justice and economic and agricultural development or the IHS (Baldridge, 2001). Among this highly diverse population, nearly 300 native languages are spoken, and cultural traditions vary widely. Despite the growing urbanization of American Indians, more elders live in rural areas than do other historically underserved older adults, with nearly 25 percent on reservations or in Alaskan Native villages. On the other hand, most urbanized American Indians do not return to their reservations as they age, instead preferring to age in place. Relatively high levels of residential stability characterize the older First Nations population. Over 50 percent are concentrated in southwestern states, with the remainder mostly in states along the Canadian border.

Economic Status

Nearly 30 percent of older American Indians are estimated to be poor, with per capita incomes approximately half that of whites. The median income is barely above the poverty threshold. Although about 50 percent of older urban American Indians live with family members, their families are also more likely to be poor than their white counterparts (AARP, 2000; Barusch, 2006; Redford, 2002). Similar to other historically disadvantaged populations, the poverty of First Nations elders tends to reflect lifelong patterns of unemployment, or employment in jobs not covered by Social Security and poor working conditions. Of all populations, American Indian elders are the most likely to have never been employed. By age 45, incomes have usually peaked among men in this group and decline thereafter. In addition, historical circumstances and federal policies toward tribes have intensified the pattern of economic underdevelopment and impoverishment in "Indian country," which has led to the migration to urban areas mentioned above (Baldridge, 2001).

First Nations women are generally less educated than their male counterparts and seldom earn even half the income of the men, putting them in a severely disadvantaged position. Another factor that negatively affects their socioeconomic and living conditions is that nearly 50 percent of women age 60 and over are widowed. Compared with their male counterparts, older American Indian women are at greater risk of social isolation and economic hardship, resulting in negative health-related consequences as they age (Angel, Jimenez, & Angel, 2007). High unemployment and low income levels often necessitate larger households of intergenerational living arrangements, with the elders often the sole provider of the family through their Social Security or SSI. A surprisingly high percent of American Indian elders do not receive Social Security and Medicare benefits, even though such public supports may be essential to their survival. A substantial percentage also does not receive Medicaid. The reasons for this lack of access to public programs are unclear, but are probably rooted in their negative historical experiences with the federal government.

Health

American Indians may have the poorest health of all Americans, due largely to their high rates of poverty, inadequate housing conditions, and isolation. Older adults have a higher incidence than their white counterparts not only of cardiovascular disease as described above, but also of diabetes, hypertension, arthritis, liver and kidney diseases, gallbladder problems, hearing and visual impairments, strokes, pneumonia, influenza, accidents, tuberculosis, and problems associated with obesity (Office of Minority Health, 2005). The rate of Type II diabetes among First Nations people is nearly three times that of whites and the sixth leading cause of death. In some native communities, approximately 50 percent of adults have Type II diabetes. In fact, the Pima Indian reservation in Arizona has the highest rate of diabetes in the world, and 95 percent of those with diabetes are overweight. Nutritional patterns have shifted from traditional diets to a diet higher in fat and calories, while physical activity has decreased with the use of television and video games for entertainment. For example, Pima Indians in Mexico maintaining traditional diet and physical activity patterns have a lower prevalence of Type II diabetes than Pima Indians living in Arizona. The high rate of diabetes is of concern because it is a major risk factor for cardiovascular disease, a leading cause of death for Americans Indians, as

described earlier (Berry et al., 2009; Denny et al., 2005; Office of Minority Health, 2005; Osier et al., 2005). With diabetes at nearly epidemic proportions, families face heavy demands in managing their elders' diet, exercise, and insulin.

American Indians also have higher rates of smoking and alcoholism. The death rate from alcohol-related diseases, such as chronic liver disease and cirrhosis, is five times higher than the general population (Office of Minority Health, 2005). Alcoholism, however, usually takes its toll before old age. Alcohol-related deaths drop sharply among American Indians who have reached age 55. Automobile accidents also take a disproportionately heavy toll on American Indian men across the life course. In addition, poverty has combined with the historical suppression of indigenous religions and medical practices to place American Indians at higher health risks due to environmental degradation. These risks result from living in poor-quality housing (which may lack electricity and running water), being exposed to local toxins, and lacking safe water supplies and sewage disposal systems. They also are less likely to engage in preventive behaviors, with American Indian women age 40 years and older the least likely of all women to get regular mammograms, colorectal screenings, or immunizations. Therefore, it is not surprising that cancer survival rates are the lowest among all U.S. populations (Mead et al., 2008; Office of Minority Health, 2005). Health promotion efforts focused on American Indians must address community and environmental barriers, as well as personal beliefs and practices—such as their lower likelihood of using Western health services for preventive health measures—and combine native concepts of spirituality and wellness with Western medicine.

For many older First Nations people, medicine is holistic and wellness-oriented. It focuses on behaviors and lifestyles through which harmony can be achieved in the physical, mental, spiritual, and personal aspects of one's role in the family, community, and environment, as well as their connections with ancestors and multiple higher powers (Weaver, 2005). The loss of access to traditional

---

CULTURALLY COMPETENT INTERVENTIONS TO REDUCE DIABETES

Focus groups composed of tribal elders identified the following needs related to prevention and treatment of diabetes in the American Indian population.

- Develop culturally acceptable ways to document family history, given incomplete health histories and the reluctance of tribal members to share personal information
- Locate accessible and knowledgeable diabetes health care providers
- Provide educational programs that take account of historical and cultural factors, including nutrition, time management, how to cook healthy food economically, and stress management
- Design exercise programs on the reservation that are fun and community and family-oriented
- Create a holistic program that encompasses problem-solving skills, improving self-esteem, and building a support system
- Consider the impact of fixed incomes on programs that are offered (Berry et al., 2009)

environments and the suppression of religious and medicine men practices also threaten traditional knowledge derived from the use of plants and herbs. Fortunately, the IHS allows medicine men and other traditional healers to treat patients in some of their clinics. This may help foster and preserve their heritage and enhance IHS professionals' knowledge of non-Western healing practices. Nevertheless, most procedures that focus on treating specific diseases rather than the whole person have typically not incorporated healing elements such as the medicine wheel and sweat lodges. This, then, reduces the effectiveness of such programs with American Indian elders.

American Indian elders have the highest hospitalization rate and the lowest rate of outpatient visits of all historically underserved older adults (John, 2004). As a result of barriers to health care, differences in health practices and their living environments, three times as many American Indians die before reaching the age of 45 than non-Indians (John 2004). American Indians have higher death rates than whites up through age 65. However, between the ages of 65 and 94 the rates are comparable, and after age 85 their death rates are lower than whites (i.e., mortality crossover). But there is no evidence of a "disability crossover." Not surprisingly, their rates of disability, as measured by functional limitations, mobility, and problems with self-care, are higher than their Caucasian counterparts, with fewer years of active life expectancy (i.e., more years of dependent life expectancy, in a state of disability) compared to whites, as a result of their higher incidence of multiple chronic conditions (Goins et al., 2007; Sawchuk et al., 2005). In other words, they experience an *expansion* rather than a compression of morbidity. Over 30 percent of those age 65 to 74 have lost all their natural teeth, the highest proportion of any group in the U.S. Furthermore, the lowest proportion among all groups of color who rate their health as excellent or very good is among First Nation elders (Barusch, 2006; John, 2004). On the other hand, a recent study found that American Indian elders

who rated their health more positively experienced better objective health outcomes during hospitalization (Ruthig & Allery, 2008).

Because of these higher rates, many First Nations people look older than their chronological age, with elders on reservations appearing old by 45 years of age, and in urban areas by age 55 (Barusch, 2006). As a result, American Indians often define an elder in terms of social functioning and decline in physical activities rather than by chronological age. However, this presents barriers to using publicly funded health services, which base eligibility on chronological, not functional, age.

Given the importance of tribal sovereignty, First Nations elders generally believe that health and social services are owed to them as a result of the transfer of their lands and that these services derive from solemn agreements between

---

SHARED CHARACTERISTICS AND EXPERIENCES AMONG HIGHLY DIVERSE FIRST NATIONS ELDERS

Characteristics of American Indians/Alaska Natives that influence their use of health and social services include:

- strong value of tribal autonomy
- nonlinear thought processes, especially related to time
- use of indirect communication and styles
- historical suspicion of government authority
- the rapid and forced change from a cooperative, clan-based society to a capitalistic and nuclear-family-based system as a result of U.S. governmental policies and exploitation of land
- the outlawing by the government of language and spiritual practices
- the past assignment of young members of the tribe to government-runt-funded boarding schools, creating a population of elders whose lives were influenced by such forced removal from their homes
- the high death rates of past generations due to infectious disease or war
- the loss of the ability to use the land walked by their ancestors for thousands of years

sovereign nations. Despite such agreements, the majority of American Indian and Native Alaskan elders rarely see a physician, often because of living in isolated areas, poor transportation, and mistrust of non-Indian health professionals. Accordingly, the prevailing life circumstances for many elders—of poverty, unemployment, alcoholism, and substance abuse—may interfere with their ability to seek preventive health care. Language also remains a barrier. For example, some of the languages of indigenous elders contain no words for *cancer*. Many feel that talking about the disease will bring it on; they may hold fatalistic views or believe that their culture stigmatizes cancer survivors.

To understand American Indian elders' health care patterns, a life-course perspective is necessary that considers their historical trauma and experiences with institutionalized racism, especially the government's efforts to suppress their culture through forced assimilation, boarding schools for youth, religious conversion, and eradication of native languages. The urbanization of the American Indian population during and after World War II created two worlds of aging. For First Nation elders who are dispersed among the general urban population, there is no tribal community or government concerned with their welfare. Nor do they have special government institutions such as the Indian Health Service or the BIA that are responsible for the well-being of American Indians on reservations.

American Indians on reservations have access to the IHS for health care, IHS is severely underfunded and generally focuses on health care for children and young adults, resulting in shortages of personnel, training, and facilities to address elders' needs (Berry et al., 2009; John, 2004). As a result, the majority of American Indian elders receive social and medical services from the BIA and IHS only periodically. As noted earlier, the IHS is effective in controlling infectious diseases and providing acute care earlier in life, thereby extending life expectancy. The IHS generally does not address prevention and management of chronic diseases nor elders'

long-term care needs, however (Barusch, 2006; Berry, 2009; John, 2004; Roubideaux, 2002). For example, the IHS operates less than a dozen nursing homes on reservations, compared to approximately 50 acute-care hospitals. This means that older American Indians who need nursing home care may find themselves in geographically distant facilities that are not oriented to Indian peoples. Such cultural and geographic barriers have resulted in a pattern of repeated short-term stays or revolving-door admissions for chronic conditions. Consequently, among those over age 65, only about 2 percent live in nursing homes (AARP, 2005). Recognizing the need for long-term care services, several tribes have established nursing homes and home health agencies on their reservations, ensuring provision of services

---

SOCIOCULTURAL AND POLITICAL BARRIERS TO ADEQUATE HEALTH CARE AMONG FIRST NATIONS PEOPLE

- Ascribe ill health and disability to the normal aging process and are therefore less likely to seek care for treatable and curable conditions.
- Distrust medical care that is not native.
- Encounter lack of sensitivity to ritual folk healing and cultural definitions of disease among some health professionals.
- Experienced historical trauma, racism, discrimination, and oppression and have been turned away from public clinics where staff insist that IHS is the sole agency responsible for their health care.
- Anticipate adverse contacts and being treated unfairly by non-Indian health professionals.
- Unwilling to sit through long waits at non-native clinics.
- Perceive health care providers as rude because of such behaviors as shaking hands, getting right down to business, addressing strangers in loud, confident voices, and frequent interruptions of the patient.
- Inadequate number of American Indian health care providers.

by American Indian staff who respect cultural values (Barusch, 2006). In urban areas, some intergenerational programs deliver home care as well as facilitate the passing on of cultural traditions and languages.

First Nations elders perceive their mental health to be poorer than do white older adults. Depression is the most common mental health problem, often precipitated by external factors such as chronic unemployment and poverty-level income, but it is difficult to diagnose because of cultural factors and alcohol use. In addition, American Indians tend to somaticize mental health problems and present them as physical health complaints. From their perspective, mind and body are one, so it is reasonable for the body to manifest physical symptoms whenever a person's life is not in balance. Some studies document a higher incidence of suicide, but findings are mixed and suggest that suicide rates may be highest for American Indians age 25 to 34 (John, 2004). Therefore, older American Indians' low utilization of mental health services is not necessarily a reflection of fewer emotional problems, but may represent barriers to treatment and lack of information about services available from their health care providers. It may also reflect the greater respect accorded elders for their wisdom and cultural heritage. To some extent, maintaining a tribal identity may serve to buffer various stresses. With age, American Indians appear to shift to a more passive relationship with their world, accepting age-related changes as a natural part of life and utilizing forbearance to cope. For example, in contrast with all other groups, American Indians are more accepting of dementia, sometimes viewing such elders as communicating with a supernatural "other side" (Henderson & Henderson, 2002).

Mental health problems may be intensified by the degree to which older American Indians' lives are dictated by government bureaucratic policies. Unlike any other historically disadvantaged group, various tribes are sovereign nations that have a distinct relationship with the U.S. government, based largely, but not exclusively, on historical treaties. Congress and the BIA, not the individual states, largely determine daily practices on the reservations. Although the BIA's regulations are intended to ensure basic support, it is criticized for expending most of its budget on maintaining the bureaucracy, with only a small percent actually going to services. It also has undermined some traditional cultural values. As an example, land-grazing privileges were historically extended to all tribal members for as long as they desired. Today, First Nations elders must transfer their grazing rights to their heirs before they qualify for supplemental financial assistance, such as SSI or Medicaid. This deprives the old of their traditional position of power and prestige within the tribal structure. In 2000, the head of the BIA apologized to tribal leaders for the agency's "legacy of racism and inhumanity," including attempts to eliminate Indian languages and cultures, but this apology was not made on behalf of the federal government as a whole (Kelly, 2000). The history of the federal government's mistreatment of American Indian elders must be considered in developing culturally competent social and health services that respect their distinctive values and history.

Social Supports and Living Situations

Historical and cultural factors also strongly influence family and community relationships for American Indians. Family is the central institution; "honoring" and giving respect to elders and sharing family resources are an integral part of their ethos. The term *elder* in Native languages generally means "agent of God." First Nations' deep reverence for nature and a belief in a supreme force, the importance of the clan, and a sense of individual autonomy as a key to noncompetitive group cohesion all underlie their practices toward their elders. Historically, as described in Chapter 2, the old were accorded respect and fulfilled specified useful tribal roles, including that of the "wise elder" who instructs the young and assists with child care, especially for foster children and grand-children. They also maintained responsibility for remembering and passing on tribal philoso-phies, myths, and traditions, and served as reli-gious and political advisors to tribal leaders. These relationships have changed somewhat with the restructuring of American Indian life by the BIA and by the increasing urbanization and assimilation of native populations, fostered by federal policies. Nevertheless, a revival of pride and interest in native cultural history, spir-ituality, and identity have raised the esteem of elders in many tribes.

Not surprisingly, with a gender ratio of ap-proximately 64.5 men to every 100 women age 65 and over, women comprise almost 60 percent of First Nation elders. More than 75 percent of American Indian men, but less than 50 percent of their female counterparts, are married. Approximately 66 percent of all American Indian elders live with family members (e.g., spouse, children, grandchildren, and foster chil-dren), and over 40 percent of these households are headed by older women. Some 25 percent of Indian elders, typically the grandmother, care for at least one grandchild, and over 66 percent live within five miles of relatives (Barusch, 2006). Given cultural values and norms of intergenera-tional assistance, family caregivers may assume elder care to reciprocate for the help they and their children have received from now-aging rel-atives, even though their care responsibilities ad-versely affect the younger generation in terms of financial and interpersonal burden. As noted above, this pattern of helping aging family mem-bers, combined with mistrust of government programs and the lack of long-term care ser-vices, may underlie American Indians' low ser-vice utilization rates. In turn, these factors put undue pressure on families to keep their elders at home, even when they lack sufficient re-sources to do so (Baldridge, 2001). Despite the value of filial responsibilities, unintentional ne-glect may occur because of the caregiver's poverty, inadequate access to resources, uncer-tainty about how to provide health care, or their

own health problems, such as substance use and mental illness. Interventions to prevent abuse that use a community-based participatory ap-proach drawing on the Native community's strengths have been found to be effective (Holkup et al., 2007). Additionally, complemen-tary and alternative medicine therapy (CAM) has been identified to reduce stress, depression, and pain among American Indian family care-givers of individuals with dementia (Korn et al., 2009).

Older Asian/Pacific Islanders*

Asian/Pacific Islander (API) elders encompass at least 30 distinct cultural groups who speak more than 100 different languages:

1. Asians include Burmese, Cambodian, Chinese, East Indian, Filipino, Indonesian, Japanese, Korean, Laotian, Malaysian, Polynesian, Thai, and Vietnamese people.
2. Pacific Islanders encompass Fijian, Guamanian, Hawaiian, Micronesian, Samoan, and Tongan populations.

Some classifications include Native Hawaiians and other Pacific Islanders under Native Americans. Each group represents a culture with its own history, religion, language, values, SES, lifestyle, immigration patterns, and level of accul-turation. They also differ widely in religious affili-ation (e.g., Christian Filipinos and Koreans, Hindu East Indians, Muslim Indonesians and Malay, and Buddhist Cambodians and Laotians). The timing of immigration has resulted in two distinct groupings: (1) Japanese, Chinese, and

*Although *Asian/Pacific Islanders* is the term used to describe Asian Americans *and* Pacific Islanders, most research has been conducted on Asian Americans. The fact that relatively little information is available about Pacific Islander elders is why our discussion largely focuses on Asian American elders' health, economic, and social status. Therefore, we refer primarily to Asian Americans in this chapter.

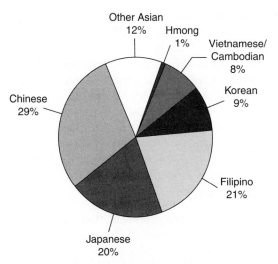

FIGURE 14.3 **Distribution of Asians/Pacific Islanders by Country of Origin**

The grandparent role is highly valued in Asian culture.

Filipino elders who arrived during the late nineteenth and early twentieth century and their U.S.-born children, and (2) older immigrants, primarily from Southeast Asia, who entered the U.S. after the 1970s with their fami- lies. These two waves differ widely in terms of ethnicity and SES. Figure 14.3 illustrates the distribution of API elders by country of origin.

The first wave of immigrants shares the experience of racism and isolation that characterized the early part of the twentieth century. Laws discriminating against Asians were numerous:

- the Chinese Exclusion Act of 1882
- the Japanese Alien Land Law of 1913
- denial of citizenship to first-generation Asians in 1922
- the antimiscegenation statute of 1935
- the Executive Order of 1942 for the internment of 110,000 persons of Japanese ancestry during World War II
- more recently, Public Law 95–507 excluding Asians as a protected minority under the definition of "socially and economically disadvantaged"

Such legislation, combined with a history of racism, contributed to feelings of mistrust, injustice, powerlessness, and fear of government—and thus to a reluctance to utilize services among many API elders who came to the U.S. as young persons in the time period from the 1900s to the 1950s.

In 1965, immigration quotas based on race and nationality were repealed. These changes resulted in a rapid population growth of Southeast Asian immigrants, primarily after 1975, after the conflicts in Cambodia, Laos, and Vietnam. The majority of these more recent refugees were Vietnamese (60 percent), followed by Cambodians and Laotians (20 percent each). However, as described in Chapter 2, education, SES, language, and refugee experiences vary widely among Indochinese refugees, depending on the time of their immigration.

The first wave, shortly after 1975, was largely the highly educated, wealthier Vietnamese who had aided the American military during the Vietnam War. The second, more recent wave of Vietnamese, ethnic Chinese, Lao, Hmong, and Cambodian refugees included illiterate farmers and merchants from lower socioeconomic backgrounds who had experienced the ravages of war and revolution in their homeland. These conditions, combined with the trauma of dislocation and resettlement, adversely affected their health and economic status. For both waves, however, the normal aging process has been complicated by cultural, dietary, and language differences and difficulties with acculturation.

There is even greater diversity within the API population as a result of direct immigration in recent years by Asian American elders, often the parents or grandparents of younger immigrants and primarily from India, China, Korea, and Vietnam. Nearly 80 percent of Asian American elders in the U.S. currently are foreign born and typically linguistically isolated, although their average length of residence is over 20 years (Ruggles et al., 2004). Approximately 60 percent do not speak English, which is higher than the percentage of Latino elders speaking only Spanish (Asian American Justice Center, 2006). Most have deeply rooted Eastern traditional values that differ from the dominant culture, as described in Chapter 2. These differences intensify their difficulties in accessing services, as discussed further below.

The 1996 welfare reform legislation posed new barriers by restricting legal immigrant older adults from receiving government assistance for their first 5 years in the U.S. As described in Chapter 17, although contemporary immigration debates tend to focus on Spanish-speaking illegal immigrants, all immigrants must now provide proof of citizenship in order to receive Medicaid.

Approximately 9.3 percent of the Asian/Pacific Islander population is age 65 and older (AOA, 2008). They are the third largest and the fastest-growing group of color, primarily

because of family reunification laws and high birthrates among many API groups. Between 1990 and 2000, the population of elders among Asian Americans increased 78 percent; APIs are expected to account for almost 8 percent of the older population by 2050. As with other groups, the oldest-old are the most rapidly growing segment. In 2007, 60 percent of API elders lived in just three states: California, Hawaii, and New York (AOA, 2009; Min & Moon, 2006).

Economic Status

A widely held perception is that APIs are a "successful" population of color because, as a whole, they are better educated and better off financially than others. However, this description as the *model minority* tends to trivialize the health problems of Asian Americans, suggesting that they can take care of their elders themselves and do not need public services. It also overlooks the socioeconomic and educational diversity among APIs and the problems faced by the newest refugees. In other words, the success of some masks the severe problems of others. Oldest-old Asians today, who immigrated prior to 1924 (especially Japanese and Chinese), generally differ substantially in their occupational and educational backgrounds from those who came later. As a result of the denial of property rights and discrimination against them for public jobs, most Asian elders who immigrated earlier are less educated and more economically deprived than their white counterparts; however, this pattern has improved dramatically for their adult children and grandchildren. Nevertheless, subgroups living in poverty exist among recent immigrants, especially among Laotians, Hmong, and Cambodians, whose limited English proficiency reduces their ability to access public services and to find and maintain employment.

U.S.-born Chinese American and Japanese American elders tend to be economically better off

Hmong	38%
Cambodian	29%
Laotian	24%
Vietnamese	21%

than other groups. However, over 12 percent of API elders are poor, compared to 9.4 percent for all older adults. As noted above, poverty rates are dramatically higher among recent immigrants. While the median Asian household income is slightly higher than for all older households, the median personal income of older household members is considerably less than for white elders (AOA, 2009; Min & Moon, 2006). Poverty rates may be even higher than reflected in official statistics, because more API adults are self-employed as farmers or in small businesses than other groups, thereby inflating reports of "family" income. Many older Chinese and Filipinos have experienced a lifetime of low-paying jobs, often in self-employment, garment factories, and service or farming work that is not covered by Social Security or other pensions. Filipino men, in particular, were concentrated in live-in domestic, migrant agricultural, or other transient work, often living in homogeneous male camps. This prevented them from gaining an insured work history and from developing close ties with family and neighbors.

For many API elders, their social worlds are limited to ethnic enclaves such as Chinatown and Koreatown, where they have developed small retail and service businesses, mutual-aid or benevolent societies, and recreational clubs, and also have access to traditional health care. Although segregated from the larger society, these ethnic enclaves are nevertheless centers for social support and the delivery of services to elders. These social functions, however, may not exist for future API generations, who will be more geographically and socially mobile and socioeconomically and linguistically diverse. Differences between foreign born and American born, urban residents and suburbanites, old timers and newcomers, Christians and Buddhists, professionals and laborers, and rich and poor frequently override a common ethnic identity, making unity an elusive goal.

As is the case with older Latinos, many API elders who qualify for public financial supports such as SSI, Medicare, and Medicaid do not apply.

In some instances, they may be excluded from Medicare because they do not have the minimal work history and/or the payroll contributions necessary to be eligible or because they are recent immigrants. After years of living under discrimination and fear of deportation, many resist seeking help from a government bureaucracy that they distrust. Their reluctance to seek nonfamilial assistance is also shaped by cultural and linguistic traditions emphasizing hierarchical relationships, personal social status, and self-reliance. When unsure of others' social status, some API elders avoid interacting with them. In the past, they turned to their families and the benevolent societies and clubs in their tightly knit communities. Many are now caught between their cultural traditions of group and familial honor and the values of their Western society that emphaize and self-sufficiency, making them reluctant to seek financial or governmental support

Health

Generalizing about older Asian Americans' health status as a whole is difficult because of the wide variability within population groupings. Immigrants are often healthier than native-born Americans; some studies have defined the API population as a whole as healthier than the general U.S. population, especially in terms of health-promoting behaviors (e.g., healthy vegetarian diets, lower rates of smoking and drinking), and reduced exposure to high risk factors (Min & Moon, 2006). For instance, the incidence of strokes in Chinese Americans and Japanese Americans is actually lower than among their counterparts in China and Japan. The relatively better health status of these two groups may be due to their diet, with lower fat and higher carbohydrate intakes compared with whites, and lower obesity rates compared with other groups. On the other hand, the rates of digestive system cancers, diabetes, and suicide are higher in Japanese Americans than among their counterparts in Japan, in part because Japanese Americans in the U.S. tend to have a higher proportion of fatty

LONG-LIVED ASIAN AMERICAN ELDERS

In Bergen County, New Jersey, researchers discovered a surprising pocket of longevity. Asian American women here live longer than any other group in the United States. Their average lifespan is 91.1 years, compared with 78.1 for the general population, 86.7 for Asian women nationally, and about 80 years for Bergen County as a whole. To researchers, the exact causes of their longevity are unclear, but the women have strong opinions about why they have lived so long. They attribute their longevity to a healthy diet, spirituality, religious participation, close-knit communities, access to quality health care, close families, and structured activities, including exercise through a local Long Life Adult Day Care Center (Murray et al., 2006).

tissue, probably a result of high-fat Western diets (Yee-Melichar, 2004).

Similar to SES, there is a bimodal distribution in health status. Some APIs, such as Japanese and Chinese Americans who immigrated in the 1930s, fare quite well, while others (especially more recent refugees) have very low income and poor health status. As a whole, APIs face higher rates of hypertension, cholesterol, and cancer, especially among low-income groups. Asian American women have the highest incidence of osteoporosis. As examples of within-group heterogeneity of health status, rates of diabetes are higher among Japanese Americans, cardiovascular disease among Korean Americans, hypertension among Chinese and Filipino immigrants than among whites, and mortality rates for heart disease among native Hawaiians compared to other groups. Although Asian Americans are least likely to use health services among all groups of elders, this does not necessarily mean that they are healthier (Braun et al., 2004; Min & Moon, 2006).

More API elders than whites suffer from psychological disorders. The rate of clinically diagnosable depression is slightly greater than that for whites, with the highest rate among Korean Americans, which may be attributed to their more recent arrival in the U.S and difficulties in adjusting to American society (Min, Moon, & Lubben, 2005; Tran, Ngo, & Conway, 2003). As discussed in Chapter 2, the discrepancy between Western culture and their native culture is a risk factor for depression for many immigrant elders, especially for Asian Americans who arrived as refugees (Gorospe, 2006; Mui & Kang, 2006; Nandan, 2005). Data on mental disorders may be underestimates, because cultural factors influence the diagnosis of mental health problems and utilization of services. Furthermore, as noted above for other populations of color, available measures of depression may be culturally biased (Mui et al., 2003). The suicide rate among API elders, especially Chinese women, is higher than for white and African American women. As described in Chapter 6, suicides are often explained by perceived incongruities between the elders' values and past lives and the reality of their relatively isolated lives in an alien culture, the stigma attached to mental health problems, and their reluctance to seek help. Another factor underlying higher rates of depression and suicide is that refugee and immigrant elders from Southeast Asia are likely to have suffered the trauma of war, torture, and loss of loved ones, and thus face mental health problems such as major depression and post-traumatic stress disorders. Yet, as noted in Chapter 2, they are unlikely to seek or use mental health services, and when they do, these services are generally not congruent with their culture and language. Therefore, they often experience poor treatment outcomes (Chow, Jaffee, & Snowden, 2003; Min & Moon, 2006; Yee-Melichar, 2004).

Many API elders with mental health problems do not receive appropriate treatment, partially because mental illness is stigmatized, if not taboo, in the API community. The perception that mental illness is caused by an unexplainable superpower, spiritual forces, or one's predetermined fate and cannot be cured by Western or medical treatment is rooted in traditional Asian cultures. They also attempt to keep mental illness problems within the family. Seeking help for psychological distress is sometimes viewed as a sign of weakness, resulting in loss of face. In addition, they may not trust service providers to keep matters confidential. Some groups somaticize mental distress, in part because of the shame and stigma attached to mental illness and to seeking help from formal services (Yip et al., 2008). APIs' belief in the inseparability of affective and somatic systems and lack of experience in describing and communicating about psychological concerns are also barriers. For example, depression in Chinese culture is expressed by physical symptoms such as fatigue, lower energy, and sleep disturbance, as well as "displaced homemaker syndrome". Korean American women refer to the illness of *Hya-Byung*—prolonged suppression of unbearable pain, suffering, loss, anger, or resentment, which develops into clinical depression, anxiety, and somatic symptoms. Although a commonly accepted expression of one's psychological and physiological status, few Korean Americans seek any kind of professional help for dealing with *Hya-Byung* (Min & Moon, 2006). Such culturally distinctive syndromes are less common in younger generations that have assimilated, suggesting that a clash of divergent cultures contributes to some of these syndromes.

SHARED EXPERIENCES AMONG HIGHLY DIVERSE ASIAN/PACIFIC ISLANDER ELDERS

1. **Health-Seeking Behaviors**
   - lack of knowledge of risk factors and preventive health-promoting behaviors, low participation in formal preventive and health promotion programs
   - lower likelihood than whites or African Americans to get checkups or blood pressure tests
   - lack of knowledge of what blood pressure is and what can be done to prevent heart disease
   - low rates of breast self-exams or screening for breast or cervical cancer
   - limited familiarity with cancer risk factors
   - perceptions that illness always involves symptoms of pain, weakness, dizziness, or nausea; thus failure to seek treatment for diseases without obvious symptoms (e.g., cancer, hypertension, diabetes mellitus)
   - reluctance to accept their diagnoses, particularly if these are from white health care providers or Western treatment regimens
   - holding themselves and their families responsible for their health rather than turning to providers and publicly funded services

2. **Belief Systems**
   - belief in the supernatural powers of ancestral and natural spirits
   - definitions of the use of public services as shameful and an indicator of dependency and inability to care for oneself
   - belief that cancer is inevitably fatal and carries a stigma

   - use of over-the-counter or traditional home remedies rather than going to physicians for prescription medications
   - discomfort with male physicians
   - reverence for authority that may result in not questioning a physician's diagnosis and treatment, and indicating agreement when there is none
   - stigma associated with mental illness and the desire to "keep up appearances" that result in low utilization of treatment for mental health and substance abuse

3. **Structural and Linguistic Barriers**
   - culturally accepted complementary alternative medicine (e.g., acupuncture and herbal medicines) that is usually not covered by insurance
   - noncompliance with Western prescription medications
   - fear of communication problems
   - difficulties in translating English medical/health terminology into Southeast Asian languages and translating Asian health concerns to English (e.g., cancer is not mentioned as a disease in many texts on Chinese medicine)
   - perception of health care providers as "impatient and disrespectful" of their culture
   - fear that seeking medical care will result in deportation if they are residing in this country illegally

Immigrant elders' use of mainstream health services is influenced by their status as a subordinate group and their degree of acculturation. The greater their acculturation, the more likely they are to use services. Overall, however, as noted above, APIs tend to underutilize most social and health services. Cultural values underlie their expectation to rely on family and their reluctance to turn to formal services (Min & Moon, 2006). Filipino American elders, for example, are guided by values of both respect and shame. Respect includes listening to others, self-imposed restraints, loyalty to family, and unquestioning obedience to authority. Shame involves fear of being left exposed, unprotected, and unaccepted. Filipino American older adults are also concerned with good relations or the avoidance of disagreement and conflict. The high value they place on personal relationships may impede their accepting formal assistance, including nursing home care. For first-generation Japanese, or *Issei*, a value that transcends that of family is *group conscience*, characterized by cohesiveness, pride, and identity through devotion to and sense of mutuality among peer-group members. This value has been preserved through the residential and occupational isolation of older Japanese American cohorts from mainstream American culture. Even among the second generation (*Nissei*), the Japanese vision of Buddhism endures in the cherishing of filial devotion and the loving indulgence of the old toward young children. Such interdependence with and respect for elders who have greater life experience, knowledge, and wisdom are widely accepted values. Accordingly, Japanese American older people tend to value intergenerational interactions, hierarchical relationships, interdependency, and empathy—all values that may not characterize formal services. These situations illustrate a lack of person–environment fit between a group's cultural values and the health and long-term care service system's insensitivity to cultural differences. Those who do use home- and community-based services are more likely to be living alone, have lived in the U.S. longer, prefer service providers from their culture, and have higher functional limitations (Kuo & Torres-Gil, 2001; Yip et al., 2008).

The health problems of API elders may thus be exacerbated by this complex and wide set of cultural, familial, linguistic, structural, and financial barriers to care. These result in underutilizing Western health services, as follows:

- lack of knowledge that the services exist, especially those that would support aging in place
- fewer chronic diseases compared with their white peers
- sociocultural, language, and structural barriers to health care
- lack of bilingual staff
- traditional values such as endurance and "looking the other way"
- a fatalistic worldview of the causes of illness and health
- reluctance to use formal Western health services and preference for herbal and acupuncture treatments
- greater likelihood of turning to traditional spiritual healers
- belief in the Yin-Yang equilibrium or balance
- collectivistic values regarding health care decision-making (e.g., shared or deferred decision-making, filial piety, and silent communication), as opposed to the individualistic decision-making styles of Western culture
- perceptions that the Western concept of patient autonomy is burdensome
- the spiritual value of being part of something greater than the individual, harmony with nature, and the importance of family in a quest to achieve a higher state of being (Van Hook, Hugan, and Aguilar, 2001)

Cultural values also provide a source of mutual support and pride. For example, *bayanihan* is the Filipino concept of a community working together, doing heroic deeds, and lending help for community betterment. As younger Filipino immigrants have adopted the individualistic spirit of the U.S., the bayanihan spirit has faded.

The economic value placed on time has hampered volunteerism and devalued unpaid community work and family caregiving in Filipino culture. However, in some communities, advocates seek to resurrect the spirit of Bayanihan to promote the health and well-being of Filipino elders. This spirit is also promoted as a culturally significant health advocacy tool. Similarly, traditional healers provide broader social benefits for native Hawaiian and Korean elders compared to Western medicine. For example, healers typically spend more time with older patients, discuss personal situations thoroughly, are more accessible after hours and on weekends, and have personal contact with family members and friends (Hurdle, 2002).

Social Supports and Living Situations

As discussed in Chapter 2, most Asian cultures are strongly influenced by Confucian teachings of filial piety and respect for older people. In traditional Asian families, age has been a symbol of authority and wisdom, with younger adults expected to obey, respect, and care for their older relatives. With younger generations of immigrants adopting Western values and lifestyles, APIs now face the erosion of filial piety, the status and authority of older family members, and the **law of primogeniture.** This refers to the relationship between aged parents and the oldest son who provides care for them (typically through his wife) and, in turn, inherits their wealth. Today, all adult children, not just the oldest son, are expected to display filial piety and to repay their parents for sacrifices they made. Nevertheless, this value of filial piety is being further eroded due to smaller family size, family mobility, increased employment of daughters and daughters-in-law, and acculturation of younger generations into the larger society. As a result, intergenerational living arrangements have declined, with increasing numbers of elders living by themselves or with a spouse, not with children. In 2007, 84 percent of older Asian men lived with their wives, 6 percent with other relatives, 2 percent with nonrelatives, and 8 percent alone. Among older Asian women, 47 percent lived with their husbands, 30 percent with other relatives, 3 percent with nonrelatives, and 20 percent alone (AOA, 2009).

A strain faced by many families is the duality of cultures and the inevitable clashes when generations have different languages, values, and ethos. Erosion of the traditional family network in some instances has resulted in intergenerational and family conflict. For example, Chinese American elders no longer can offer financial support, land, or other material goods to their children as they would have in their homeland and fear being a burden to their children. They generally live with their children only in cases of extreme poverty or poor health, or when dependent on them for interpreting from English to their native language. In contrast, Korean American elders often accept separation from their upwardly mobile children as a way to promote their children's happiness and success. As noted above, they may prefer to live in urban areas in Asian enclaves rather than the suburban communities favored by younger API familes. Nevertheless, compared with the majority culture, Asian Americans place a higher value on reciprocal exchanges between young and old, and the respect accorded the old. Accordingly, compared to other groups, higher proportions of API elders have extended-family arrangements, and families serve as primary caregivers. Younger Asian Americans are more likely to indicate old age or being old as the main problem of the older family member they care for, rather than a particular illness (National Alliance for Caregiving and AARP, 2004). Similar to Caucasian caregivers, stress has negative health effects on API caregivers. For example, Korean American caregivers were found to experience adverse health effects as indicated by elevated blood pressure and cortisol levels, but their subjective health indicators were not impaired. The fact that physiological effects occurred without self-reported poor health suggests the potential for more serious health problems associated with caregiving stress among this population (Kim & Knight, 2008). Any professional discussion of family living and caregiving arrangements must consider differences in culture, ethnicity, social class, timing of immigration, and generations among APIs and how these variables may influence both the caregiver and care recipient (Hikoyeda & Wallace, 2001; Min &Moon, 2006).

In contrast to other older adults of color and to white older persons, API men somewhat outnumber women until they reach age 75 and older; they also constitute a larger percent of elders living alone. This reflects the continuing influence of disproportionate male immigration in the early part of the twentieth century and past restrictions on female immigration, rather than a higher life expectancy for men. On the other hand, older women in this group are much more likely to be married (42 percent) than their white counterparts (15 percent), with a smaller proportion (21 percent) remaining single in their later years compared to non-Hispanic whites (Angel & Hogan, 2004; Yee-Melichar, 2004).

Although advancing age increases the probability of living alone, nursing home use among older Asian Americans is significantly lower than for their white counterparts. Only about 1.2 percent of API elders age 65 and older are in nursing homes, compared to 4 percent of whites, which partially reflects the continuing importance of filial piety as well as skilled nursing facilities that are culturally congruent (AARP, 2005; NCHS, 2008; Yee-Melichar, 2004).

This chapter highlights only a few characteristics of API elders as a group, since large inter- and intragroup differences exist. Because of population and political pressures in Asian countries, the high rate of immigration is likely to continue, although slowed by the recession, and the diversity among API populations to increase. A major challenge for researchers and service providers is to take account of such diverse history and cultural values when developing culturally competent research and practice models.

Implications for Services

Underutilization of social and health services is a common theme across racial groups. Although some service providers rationalize that elders of color do not use formal services because of their families' assistance, patterns of underutilization cannot be fully explained in this way. Barriers to service utilization can be conceptualized at the level of individual recipients and the delivery system, as illustrated in the box on page 641. Gerontologists increasingly agree that services need to be designed to take account of inter- and intracultural and geographic differences within and across groups. From this perspective, outreach strategies to historically underserved elders are needed to reduce growing social inequities, respond to the range of needs, and increase the participation of various groups. Accordingly, service providers need to be trained to be culturally skilled, and the importance of cross-cultural care or **ethnogeriatrics** is increasingly recognized. Additionally, there has been a shift from cultural sensitivity (awareness of cultural differences) to **cultural competence,** or specific knowledge, attitudes, and skills to work effectively with elders of color and other historically disadvantaged

Shared cultural backgrounds can enhance communication between health care providers and older patients.

BARRIERS TO UTILIZATION OF SOCIAL AND HEALTH SERVICES SHARED BY ELDERS OF COLOR

1. **Cultural and Economic Barriers**
   - cultural isolation, including language differences and inability to speak, read, or understand English
   - perceived stigma of utilizing services, especially mental health, and embarrassment and fear in attempting to describe symptoms
   - confusion, anger at, and fear of health care providers and hospitals, which may be related to present or historical acts of racism by medical providers or institutionalized racism
   - lack of trust and faith in the efficacy of service professionals within a Western biomedical health care system; this distrust may be intensified by cohorts' experiences (i.e., segregated health care and explicit policies—such as the Tuskegee experiment with African Americans, the internment of Japanese Americans in World War II, and the removal of American Indian children to boarding schools)

   - lack of knowledge of services, including how to make appointments, negotiate a clinic visit, and describe symptoms
   - belief in complementary alternative medicine

2. **Structural Barriers Within the Service System**
   - the 1996 Welfare Reform Bill that eliminated some public benefits to legal immigrants
   - lack of services that are oriented toward and operated by members of respective groups of color and ethnicities
   - real or perceived discrimination by service providers and institutionalized racism in agency policies and procedures
   - assessment instruments whose meaning is altered in translation
   - geographic distance of services from neighborhoods where elders of color live
   - lack of low-cost, accessible transportation to services
   - staff with a different racial/ethnic background who are not bilingual and are not culturally competent

groups. In fact, when medical and psychosocial interventions are culturally competent, service utilization by populations of color typically increases. The federal government has established standards for cultural competence in health care to promote respectful care compatible with the patient's cultural health beliefs, practices, and preferred language. Professional associations, such as the National Association of Social Workers, have also developed standards for culturally competent practice (NASW, 2007; Thobaben, 2002; USD-HHS, 2001). Additionally, AARP in 2009 hosted its first national conference on Aging and Diversity that highlighted a theme of inclusion.

Fortunately, a growing number of health providers recognize and respect that elders of color often adhere to traditional paradigms of health and illness, their spiritual orientation, and their associated folk beliefs and behaviors that diverge from mainstream Western scientific medical concepts. Some elders combine these with orthodox or scientific treatments. Accordingly, current health promotion initiatives targeted to older whites may not be appropriate for historically disadvantaged populations. For example, social entities that play a key role in older African Americans' lives, such as the church and religious leaders, are more likely to influence health beliefs and behaviors than are traditional approaches to health promotion through medical settings or senior centers. The involvement of health-promotion experts from the same culture may also help bridge the gap between cultural values and scientific knowledge about the causes and treatment of disease. This is particularly true for American Indian and API cultures, where traditional ways of treating disease are still widely practiced among older cohorts. Health promotion efforts that ignore spirituality and traditional beliefs about harmony between the individual, nature, and the universe are unlikely to be effective in these cultures.

To illustrate, the Chinese believe that health represents a balance between Yin and Yang energy forces, and certain foods are assumed to bring about this balance. Believing that the aging process predisposes people to Yin (or cold forces), Chinese elders avoid eating many cold foods such as leafy green vegetables. Health-promotion facilitators must recognize the basis for such avoidance if they are to encourage healthier diets among older Asians. Accordingly, tools to assess psychological status may not be appropriate for elders of color unless they have been validated with these specific groups. For example, most research on caregiving among populations of color has described lower levels of burden. However, such caregivers may express their burden in different ways than Caucasian caregivers, and available measures of burden may not adequately capture the subjective and objective impact of caregiving on them. In fact, some qualitative studies have found that African American and Puerto Rican caregivers express anger, frustration, loneliness, and resignation similar to their white counterparts, despite their appearance of coping effectively through religion and spirituality (Calderon et al., 2002; Dilworth-Anderson, Williams, & Gibson, 2002).

Service utilization by elders of color is expanded under the following conditions:

- Providers take account of the heterogeneity of populations, including variations by immigration status, time in the country, ethnicity, and gender
- Assessment measures take account of cultural differences and spiritual orientation
- Providers attend to the way that elders describe their spiritual life and its relationship to their illness and health
- Services are located in their local communities, easily accessible, and near complementary supports, such as acupuncture for Asian elders
- Transportation is free or at low cost
- Services adhere to the cultural integrity of the elders' lifestyles; for example, nutrition

programs include favorite ethnic foods, and nursing homes offer culturally appropriate recreation and meals
- The organizational climate is more informal, personalized, open, and less bureaucratic than in mainstream agencies
- Staff include bilingual, bicultural, and/or indigenous workers, or interpreters who are culturally competent, convey respect, and use personalized outreach to establish trust and rapport
- Medical and insurance forms, newsletters, and descriptions of services are bilingual
- Elders from the local community are involved in the planning and delivery of services
- Services are advertised in ways to reach historically underserved elders, such as through ethnic television, radio programs, and newspapers and announced through religious institutions, neighborhood organizations, civic and social clubs, natural support systems, and advocates
- Given major differences in the epidemiology and risk factors of certain diseases (such as diabetes), screening, prevention, and culturally congruent education are essential

Service providers should identify and build upon community strengths to supplement and augment existing services rather than utilize a deficits model in which interventions are designed to ameliorate personal problems. This also suggests the value of utilizing existing organizational structures, such as religious institutions with large memberships of elders of color, to provide services and to link informal and formal sources of help. Assumptions that guide such strategies are that the needs of elders of color are best understood by members of their own communities, that they should have input into decision-making about services in their communities and should be treated as distinct populations, and that research and professional training programs should address issues of cultural competence. It is also important to employ practitioners of color and to implement explicitly

GUIDELINES FOR CULTURALLY COMPETENT PRACTICE

- All staff assessing older adults' cognitive and functional status are trained to deal appropriately with the elder's cultural values and social structure (e.g., decision-making patterns) and how these affect behavior, including reactions to illness and services
- All staff develop ways to monitor their responses for any class, race, gender, cultural, or sexual identity biases that could interfere with the assessment
- Issues of acculturation and language are considered when administering assessment measures and interpreting test results since both the content of the test and the language in which it is administered affects a test's multicultural applicability
- Test instructions are written in simple, concise terminology to enable accurate translations
- "Back translation" is used to obtain an equivalent fair battery for any language: materials produced in one language are translated into another language by a bilingual translator, then translated back into English by a second individual, and then the original and back-translated English versions are compared
- Bilingual staff, when available, are required to conduct assessments in the elder's native language
- Culturally and sociopolitically relevant factors and events (e.g., refugees from war-torn nations) are documented
- Religious and spiritual beliefs and values, including attributions and taboos, are considered because they affect worl views and functioning

SOURCE: Adapted from Bonder, Martin, & Miracle, 2001.

antidiscrimination statutes in federal regulations for aging programs. To advance research on historically underserved populations and thus provide an empirical basis for service interventions, clear and consistent terminology is needed to define and target populations. Issues related to design, data collection, and measurement for and across different groups of color must also be addressed.

Implications for the Future

The recent trend of a faster growth of older populations of color than among whites is expected to continue, although at a slightly slower rate due to the recession and immigration restrictions. Nevertheless, white elders will continue to outnumber their culturally diverse peers. The SES of historically disadvantaged groups is unlikely to improve greatly in the immediate future. This negative forecast is due largely to the growing income inequality in our society, with a worsening of economic conditions for a substantial portion of the population, many of whom are people of color. Accordingly, poor people of all ages face an increased risk of health problems and disabilities. Widening health disparities often parallel growing economic inequities. Since elders of color are overrepresented among lower-income groups, declining health status linked to economic inequities is likely to affect them disproportionately. In addition, increasing length of residence in the U.S. and greater acculturation of Latino and Asian populations will lead to worsening health as they adopt less-healthy Western diets and are exposed to unhealthy environments. The intractability of racism also suggests that racial disparities in health, mortality, and well-being are likely to persist in the foreseeable future. These trends in health status point to increasing demands on caregivers of color, who report worse physical health, and among Asian American and Latino caregivers higher rates of depression than their white counterparts (Pinquart & Sorensen, 2005). Service providers' assumptions of the strengths of families of color may overlook these caregiving strains.

Growing rates of childhood poverty will profoundly affect the well-being of older adults of color in the future. Among all children in the

U.S, about 20 percent are living in poverty; but this rate increases to 40 percent for African American and Latino children. The health status of adults is affected not only by their current SES but also by exposure to economic deprivation and unhealthy living situations over the life course. Early economic and health conditions appear to have long-term adverse consequences for adult health, reflecting cumulative inequality across the life course (Ferraro et al., 2006).

Although the likelihood of chronic illness increases with age, research increasingly shows that the origins of risk for chronic health conditions begin in early childhood or earlier. Furthermore, risk continues to be impacted by factors such as SES and education across the life course. For example, childhood conditions explain a substantial portion of the difference in men's mortality by race, operating indirectly through adult socioeconomic achievement, not lifestyle factors (Warner & Hayward, 2002). This pattern particularly affects African Americans, who have faced the greatest barriers to socioeconomic mobility (Williams, 2004). Increasingly, the importance of improving a group's economic and health status earlier in life is being recognized as critical to well-being in old age. Fundamental changes in social policy that address nutrition, economic security, equitable educational opportunities, quality housing, and comprehensive community-based public health efforts are essential to reduce health disparities across the life course and especially in old age.

New research paradigms are essential to capture the distinctive cultural features of the aging process among elders of color and to implement culturally competent interventions that effectively reduce racial and socioeconomic disparities in health status and health services utilization (Jackson, 2002). Such interventions reflect growing recognition of the dynamic nature of life trajectories and how mobilization of resources can reduce exposure to risk across the life course. Future research also needs to give greater attention to characteristics presumably linked to race, such as SES, acculturation, and discrimination. More recently, social scientists' interest in the concept of accumulation has been supplemented by the work of biologists and behavioral scientists who give greater attention to family lineage as a source of inequality and to genes, gestation, maternal health and childhood as critical to early and enduring inequalities (Ferraro & Shippee, 2009). Regardless of the nature of the research, recruiting and retaining elders of color as research participants presents complex challenges. Empirically tested strategies, participatory action research that builds trust and connection with the community, and involvement of culturally diverse researchers at all levels are vital (Curry & Jackson, 2003). In addition, as noted in the discussion of service implications, social and health providers must improve their level of cultural competence.

Summary

Although age is sometimes called the great equalizer, today's elders are highly diverse. As we have seen throughout this book, differences in income, health, and social supports significantly affect older adults' well-being. An important source of this diversity is racial status. Ethnogerontology is the study of the causes, processes, and consequences of race, national origin, and culture on individual and population aging. An early debate was whether older adults of color experience double jeopardy because of their race or whether age is a leveler of differences in income and life expectancy. Recent studies indicate a narrowing of differences in health status and life expectancy after age 75—or a crossover effect—but health and socioeconomic disparities result in double, and even triple, jeopardy for older women of color in particular.

This chapter reviewed the social, demographic, economic, and health status of African

Americans, Latinos, American Indians, and Asian/Pacific Islander elders. Although we have seen great variability, several common themes also emerge. As a whole, elders of color experience higher rates of mortality from diabetes, heart disease, and cancer, and also higher rates of functional disability, although exceptions to this generalization can always be found. Their resources and status reflect social, economic, and educational discrimination and institutionalized racism experienced earlier in life. In particular, those who immigrated to the U.S. are more likely to experience cultural and language barriers. As a whole, they face shorter life expectancy and increased risks of poverty, poor nutrition, substandard housing, and poor health, although within-group variations exist and life expectancy for Japanese Americans and Chinese Americans is longer than for whites. Nevertheless, many elders of color, especially among the oldest-old, display considerable strengths and resilience. Culturally competent social and health care is of particular concern. Cultural and language difficulties, physical isolation, and lower income, along with structural barriers to service accessibility, contribute to their underutilization of health and social services. Efforts must continue to modify services to be more responsive to the particular needs of older adults of color and to train social and health care providers to be culturally competent.

GLOSSARY

Bureau of Indian Affairs established in 1824, responsible for the administration of law enforcement and justice on tribal lands; agricultural and economic development; tribal governance; and natural resources management

crossover effect the lower death rates among African Americans, APIs, and American Indians after age 75

cultural competence the knowledge and skills to take account of cultural meanings and work effectively with persons from different cultures

double jeopardy hypothesis the hypothesis that aging persons of color are in jeopardy in our society due both to growing old and their racial status

epidemiological paradox refers to the pattern that Latino elders tend to be healthier than Caucasians despite lower SES

ethnogeriatrics cross-cultural geriatric care that recognizes cultural differences in response to health and disease

ethnogerontology study of causes, processes, and consequences of race, national origin, and culture on individual and population aging

health disparities socioeconomic and racial/ethnic inequalities in health, mortality, and other adverse conditions across the life course

health care disparities differences in access, quality, or rate of utilization of health care services, where populations of color have substantially lower utilization rates

Indian Health Service (IHS) federal program that provides health care for Native Americans and Native Alaskans of all ages through hospitals and community clinics

law of primogeniture the exclusive right of the oldest son to inherit his father's estate (traditional among Asian families)

multiple hierarchy stratification the theory that both social class and race status jeopardize older adults of color

RESOURCES

Log on to MySocKit (www.mysockit.com) for information about the following:

- AARP Minority Initiative

- Administration on Aging Minority Initiatives

- National Asian Pacific Center on Aging

- National Association for Hispanic Elderly

- National Caucus and Center on Black Aged

- National Indian Council on Aging

- U.S. Public Health Service

REFERENCES

AARP. (2005). *Racial and ethnic differences among older adults in long term care service use. Fact Sheet Number 119.* Retrieved February 2006, from http://assets.aarp.org/rgcenter/il/fs119_ltc.pdf

AARP. (2008). Public Policy Institute. *From work to retirement: Tracking changes in women's poverty status. Brief.* Retrieved July 2009, from http://www.aarp.org/ppi

Adamson, J. A., Price, G. M., Breeze, E., Bulpitt, C. J., & Fletcher, A. E. (2005). Are old people dying of depression? Findings from the medical research council trial of assessment and management of older people in the community. *Journal of the American Geriatrics Society, 53,* 1128–1132.

Administration on Aging (AOA). (2008). *Profile of Older Americans.* Washington, DC.

Administration on Aging (AOA). (2009). *Facts and figures: Statistics on minority aging in the U.S.* Washington, DC. Retrieved July 2009, from http://www.aoa.gov/AoARoot/Aging_Statistics/minority_aging/2009-plain_format.aspx

Aizenman, N.C. (2009). U.S. Latino population projected to soar: Forecast predicts tripling by 2050. *The Washington Post,* A-Section.

Alwin, D. & Wray, L. (2005). A life-span developmental perspective on social status and health. *Journal of Gerontology: Psychological Sciences, 60B,* PS7–P14.

American Heart Association. (2005). *Heart disease and stroke statistics 2005 Update.* Dallas, TX.

Anderson, R. (2002). Deaths: Leading causes for 2000. *National Vital Statistics Report.* Washington, DC: National Center for Health Statistics.

Angel, J. & Angel, R. (2003). Hispanic diversity and health care coverage. *Journal of Aging and Public Policy, 13,* 8–12.

Angel, R. & Angel, J. (2006). Diversity and aging in the United States. In R. Binstock & L. George (Eds.). *Handbook of aging and the social sciences* (6th ed.). New York: Academic Press.

Angel, J., Angel, R., & Markides, K. S. (2002). Stability and change in health insurance among older Mexican Americans: Longitudinal evidence from the Hispanic Established Populations for Epidemiologic Study of the Elderly. *American Journal of Public Health, 92,* 1264–1271.

Angel, J. & Hogan, D. (2004). Population aging and diversity in a new era. In K. E. Whitfield (Ed.). *Closing the gap: Improving the health of minority elders in the new millennium.* Washington, DC: The Gerontological Society of America.

Angel, J. L., Jiménez, M. A., & Angel, R. J. (2007). The economic consequences of widowhood for older minority women. *The Gerontologist, 47,* 224–34.

Angel, R. J., Angel, J. L., & Hill T. D. (2009). Subjective control and health among Mexican-origin elders in Mexico and the United States: Structural considereations in comparative research. *The Journals of Gerontology Series B: Psychological Sciences and Social Sciences, 64B(3),* 390–401.

Aranda, M. P. (2006). Older Latinos: A mental health perspective. In B. Berkman (Ed.). *Handbook of aging in health and social work*. New York: Oxford University Press.

Asian American Justice Center and Asian Pacific American Legal Center. (2006). *A community of contrasts: Asian and Pacific Islanders in the United States*. Washington, DC.

Baldridge, D. (2001). Indian elders: Family traditions in crisis. In D. Infeld (Ed.). *Disciplinary approaches to aging*. (Vol. 4). *Anthropology of aging*. New York: Routledge.

Barusch, A. (2006). Native American elders: Unique histories and special needs. In B. Berkman (Ed.). *Handbook of aging in health and social work*. New York: Oxford University Press.

Becker, G., Yewoubdar, B., Newsome, E. M., & Rodgers, V. (1998). Knowledge and care of chronic illness in three ethnic minority groups. *Family Medicine, 30*, 173–178.

Beckett, M. (2000). Converging health inequalities in later life—An artifact of mortality selection? *Journal of Health and Social Behavior, 41*, 106–119.

Berry, D., Samos, M., Storti, S., & Grey, M. (2009). Listening to concerns about type 2 diabetes in a Native American community. *Journal of Cultural Diversity, 16*, 56–63.

Beyene, Y., Becker, G., & Mayen, N. (2002). Perception of aging and sense of well-being among Latino elderly. *Journal of Cross-Cultural Gerontology, 17*, 155–172.

Braun, K. L., Yee, B., Browne, C., & Mokuau, N. (2004). Native Hawaiian and Pacific Islander elders. In K. E. Whitfield (Ed.). *Closing the gap: Improving the health of minority elders in the new millennium*. Washington, DC: The Gerontological Society of America.

Calderon, R. V., Morrill, A., Change, B. H., & Tennstedt, S. (2002). Service utilization among disabled Puerto Rican elders and their caregivers: Does acculturation play a role? *Journal of Aging and Health, 1*, 3–23.

Chiriboga, D., Black, S., Aranda, M., & Markides, K. (2002). Stress and depressive symptoms among Mexican American elderly. *Journal of Gerontology: Psychological Sciences, 57B*, P559–P568.

Chow, J., Jaffee, K., & Snowden, L. (2003). Racial/ethnic disparities in the use of mental health services in poverty areas. *American Journal of Public Health, 93*, 792–797.

Cox, C. (2002). Empowering African American custodial grandparents. *Social Work, 47*, 45–54.

Crimmins, E. M. & Sato, Y. (2001). Trends in healthy life expectancy in the United States: Gender, racial and educational differences. *Social Science and Medicine, 52*, 1629–1641.

Curry, L. & Jackson, J. (2003). The science of including older ethnic and racial group participants in health-related research. *The Gerontologist, 43*, 15–17.

Dannefer, D. (2003). Cumulative advantage/disadvantage and the life course: Cross-fertilizing age and social science theory. *Journal of Gerontology: Social Sciences, 58B*, S327–S357.

Das, A. K., Olfson, M., McCurtis, H. L., & Wissman, M. M. (2006). Depression in African Americans: Breaking barriers to detection and treatment. *The Journal of Family Practice, 55*, 30–43.

Denny, C. H., Holtzman, D., & Cobb, N. (2005). Disparities in chronic disease risk factors and health status between Native American/Alaskan Native and White elders: Findings from a telephone survey, 2001 and 2002. *American Journal of Public Health, 95*, 825–827.

Dilworth-Anderson, P., Williams, I. C., & Gibson, R. E. (2002). Issues of race, ethnicity, and culture in caregiving research: A 20-year review. *The Gerontologist, 42,* 237–272.

Doty, M. (2003). *Hispanic patients' double burden: Lack of health insurance and limited English.* New York: The Commonwealth Fund.

Dwight-Johnson, M., Unutzer, J., Sherbourne, C., Tang, L., & Wells, K. (2001). Can quality improvement programs for depression in primary care address patient preferences for treatment? *Medical Care, 39,* 934–944.

Fears, D. (2003). A defining moment for Hispanics. *The Seattle Times,* p. A10.

Federal Interagency Forum on Aging and Related Statistics. (2008). *Older Americans 2008: Key indicators of well-being.* Hyattsville, MD: Federal Interagency Forum on Aging and Related Statistics.

Ferraro, K. F. & Shippee, T. P. (2009). Aging and cumulative inequality: How does inequality get under the skin? *The Gerontologist, 49,* 333–343.

Ferraro, K. F., Shippee, T. P. & Schafer, M. H. (2009). Cumulative inequality theory for research on aging and the life course. In V. L. Bengston, D., Gans, N. M. Putney & M. Silverstein (Eds.). *Handbook of theories of aging* (2nd ed., pp. 413–433). New York: Springer Publishing Company.

Ferraro, K., Thorpe, R., McCabe, G., Kelley-Moore, J., & Jiang, Z. (2006). The color of hospitalization over the adult life course: Cumulative disadvantage in black and white? *Journal of Gerontology: Social Sciences, 61B,* S299–S306.

Flippen, M. (2005). Minority workers and pathways to retirement. In R. Hudson (Ed.). *The new politics of old age policy.* Baltimore: John Hopkins University Press.

Garroutte, E. M., Sarkisian, N., Goldberg, J., Buchwald, D., & Beals, J. (2008). Perceptions of medical interactions between healthcare providers and American Indian older adults. *Social Science & Medicine, 67,* 546–556.

George, L. & Lynch, S. (2003). Race differences in depressive symptoms: A dynamic perspective on stress exposure and vulnerability. *Journal of Health and Social Behavior, 44,* 353–369.

Gibson, P. (2002). Barriers, lessons learned and helpful hints: Grandmother caregivers talk about service utilization. *Journal of Gerontological Social Work, 39,* 55–74.

Goins, R. T., Moss, M., Buchwald, D., & Guralnik, J. M. (2007). Disability among older American Indians and Alaska Natives: An analysis of the 2000 census public use micro data sample. *The Gerontologist, 47,* 690–698.

Gorospe, E. (2006). Elderly immigrants: Emerging challenge for the U.S. healthcare system. *Internet Journal of Healthcare Administration, 4.*

Gullette, M. (2006). Tragic toll of age bias. *The Boston Globe.*

Hayslip, B. & Kaminski, P. L. (2005). Grandparents raising their grandchildren: A review of the literature and suggestions for practice. *The Gerontologist, 45,* 262–269.

Heinz, T., Lewis, J., & Hounsell, C. (2006). *Women and pensions: An overview.* Washington, DC: Women's Institute for a Secure Retirement (WISER).

Henderson, J. & Henderson, L. (2002). Cultural construction of disease: A "supernormal" construct of dementia in an American Indian tribe. *Journal of Cross-Cultural Gerontology, 17,* 197–212.

Hikoyed, N. & Wallace, S. (2001). Do ethnic-specific long-term care facilities improve resident quality of life? Findings from the Japanese American community. *Journal of Gerontological Social Work, 36,* 83–106.

Holden, K. & Hatcher, C. (2006). Economic status of the aged. In R. Binstock and L. K. George, (Eds.). *Handbook of aging and the social sciences* (6th ed.). New York: Academic Press.

Holkup, P. A., Salois, E. M., Tripp-Reimer, T., & Weinert, C. (2007). Drawing on wisdom from the past: An elder abuse prevention program with tribal communities. *The Gerontologist, 47,* 248–58.

House, J., Lantz, P., & Herd, P. (2005). Continuity and change in the social stratification of aging and health over the life course: Evidence from a nationally representative longitudinal study from 1986 to 2001/2002 (America's Changing Lives Study). *Journal of Gerontology: Social Sciences, 60B,* 15–26.

Hurdle, D. E. (2002). Native Hawaiian traditional healing: Cultural based interventions for social work practice. *Social Work, 47,* 183–192.

Indian Health Service. (2006). *Fact Sheet on Indian Health Disparities.* Retrieved February 2007, from http://info.ihs.gov/Files/DisparitiesFacts-Jan2006.pdf.

Jackson, J. S. (2002). Conceptual and methodological linkages in cross-cultural groups and cross-national aging research. *Journal of Social Issues, 58,* 825–835.

Jackson, P. (2005). Health inequalities among minority populations. *Journal of Gerontology: Social Sciences, 60B,* S63–S67.

Jang, Y., Borenstein-Graves, A., Haley, W., Small, B., & Mortimer, J. (2003). Determinants of a sense of mastery in African American and white older adults. *Journal of Gerontology: Social Sciences, 58B,* S221–S224.

John, R. (2004). Health status and health disparities. In K. Whitfield, (Ed.). *Closing the gap: Improving the health of minority elders in the new millennium.* Washington, DC: Gerontological Society of America.

Kao, D. T. (2009). Generational cohorts, age at arrival, and access to health services among Asian and Latino immigrant adults. *Journal of Health Care for the Poor and Underserved, 20,* 395–414.

Kao, H. F., McHugh, M., & Travis, S. (2007). Psychometric tests of expectations of filial piety scale in a Mexican American population. *Journal of Clinical Nursing, 16,* 1460–1467.

Keane, F., Tappen, R. M., Williams, C. L., & Rosselli, M. (2008). Comparison of African American and Afro-Caribbean older adults self-reported health status, functions and substance abuse. *Journal of Black Psychology, 20,* 1–19.

Kelly, M. (2000). BIA head issues apology to Indians. *The Seattle Times,* p. 3A.

Kelley-Moore, J. & Ferraro, K. (2004). The black/white disability gap: Persistent inequality in later life. *Journal of Gerontology: Social Sciences, 59B,* S34–S43.

Kessler, R. C., Berglund, P., Demler, O., Koretz, D., Merikangas, K., et al. (2003). The epidemiology of major depressive disorders: Results from the National Comorbidity Survey Replication. *Journal of the American Medical Association, 289,* 3095–3105.

Kim, J. H. & Knight, B. G. (2008). Effects of caregiver status, coping styles, and social support on the physical health of Korean American caregivers. *The Gerontologist, 48,* 287–99.

King, M. (2006). African American elders helpforge connections. *The Seattle Times,* pp. B1, B4.

Kleinman, A. & Benson, P. (2006). Anthropology in the clinic: The problem of cultural competency and how to fix it. *PLOS Medicine, 3,* 1673–1676.

Korn, L., Logsdon, R. G., Polissar, N. L., Gomez-Beloz, A., Waters, T., & Ryser, R. (2009). A randomized trial of a CAM therapy for stress reduction in American Indian and Alaskan Native family caregivers. *The Gerontologist, 49,* 368–377.

Kuo, T. & Torres-Gil, F. (2001). Factors affecting utilization of health services and home and community-based care programs by older Taiwanese in the United States. *Research on Aging, 23,* 14–37.

LaVeist, T. A. (2003). Pathways to progress in eliminating racial disparities in health. *Public Policy and Aging Report, 13,* 19–22.

LaVeist, T. A., Rolley, N. C., & Diala, C. (2003). Prevalence and patterns of discrimination among U.S. healthcare consumers. *International Journal of Health Services, 33(2),* 331–344.

Lincoln, K. (2000). Social support, negative social interactions and psychological well-being. *Social Service Review, 74,* 231–252.

Lincoln, K. D., Chatters, L. M., & Taylor, R. J. (2005). Social support, traumatic events and depressive symptoms among African Americans. *Journal of Marriage and Family, 67,* 754–766.

Lincoln, K. D., Taylor, R. J., & Chatters, L. M. (2003). Correlates of emotional support and negative interaction among older Black Americans. *Journal of Gerontology: Social Sciences, 58B,* S225–S233.

Lopez, S. (2002). Mental health care for Latinos: A research agenda to improve the accessibility and quality of mental health care for Latinos. *Psychiatric Services, 53,* 1569–1573.

Lum, T. (2003). *Culturally competent practice: A framework for understanding diverse groups and justice issues.* Pacific Grove, CA: Brooks Cole.

Margolis, M. L., Christie, J. D., Silvestri, G. A., Kaiser, L., Santiago, S., et al. (2003). Racial differences pertaining to a belief about lung cancer surgery: Results of a multicenter survey. *Annals of Internal Medicine, 139,* 558–563.

Markides, K. S. & Black, S. A. (1996). Race, ethnicity, and aging. In R. H. Binstock & L. K. George (Eds). *Handbook of aging and the social sciences* (4th ed.) San Diego, CA: Academic Press.

Markides, K. & Eschbach, K. (2005). Aging, migration, and mortality: Current status of research on the Hispanic paradox. *Journal of Gerontology: Social Sciences, 60B,* S68–S75.

Martinez, I. L. (2003). The elder in the Cuban American family: Making sense of the real and ideal. *Journal of Comparative Family Studies, 33,* 359–370.

McDonald, P. & Wykle, M. (2003). Predictors of health-promoting behavior of African American and white caregivers of impaired elders. *Journal of the National Black Nurses Association, 14,* 1–12.

McDonald, P., Wykle, M., Kiley, M., & Burant, C. (2004). Depressive symptoms in persons with Type 2 diabetes: A faith-based clinical trial, *The Gerontologist, 44,* 417.

McGoldrick, M., Giordano, J., & Garcia-Preto, N. (Eds.). (2005). *Ethnicity and family therapy* (3rd ed.). New York: Guilford Press.

Mead, H., Cartwright-Smith, L., Jones, K., Ramos, C., Siegel, B., & Woods, K. (2008). *Racial and ethnic disparities in U.S. healthcare: A chart book*. The Common Wealth Fund.

Min, J. & Moon, A. (2006). Older Asian Americans. In B. Berkman (Ed.). *Handbook of social work in health and aging*. New York: Oxford University Press.

Min, J., Moon, A., & Lubben, J. (2005). Determinants of psychological distress over time among older Korean Americans and non-Hispanic white elders. Evidence from a two-wave panel study. *Aging and Mental Health, 9*, 210–222.

Minkler, M. & Fuller-Thomson, E. (2005). African American grandparents raising grandchildren: A national study using the Census 2000 American Community Survey. *Journal of Gerontology: Social Sciences, 60B*, S82.

Miranda, M. (1990). Hispanic aging: An overview of issues and policy implications. In M. S. Harper (Ed.). *Minority aging*. DHHS Publication #HRS (P-DV-90–4). Washington, DC: U.S. Government Printing Office.

Mui, A. & Kang, S. Y. (2006). Acculturation stress and depression among Asian immigrant elders. *Social Work, 51*, 243–255.

Mui, A., Kang, S. Y., Chen, L. M., & Domanski, M. (2003). Reliability of the geriatric depression scale for use among elderly Asian immigrants in the USA. *International Psychogeriatrics, 15*, 253–271.

Mukamel, D. B., Weimer, D. L., & Mushlin, A. I. (2006). Referrals to high-quality cardiac surgeons: Patients' race and characteristics of their physicians. *Health Services Research, 41*, 1276–1285.

Munet-Vilaro, F. (2004). *Health promotion for older adults: Latino elders*. Seattle: University of

Washington, Northwest Geriatric Education Center.

Murray C., Kulkarni S., Michaud C., Tomijima, N., & Bulzacchelli, M., et al. (2006). Eight Americas: Investigating causes of mortality disparities across races, counties and race-counties. *PLOS Medicine, 3*, 260.

Nandan, M. (2005). Adaptation to American culture: Voices of Asian Indian immigrants. *Journal of Gerontological Social Work, 44*, 175–203.

National Alliance for Caregiving and AARP. (2004). *Caregiving in the U.S.* Bethesda, MD: National Alliance for Caregiving, and Washington, DC: AARP.

National Association of Social Workers (NASW). (2007). *Indicators for the achievement of the NASW standards for cultural competence in social work practice*. Washington, DC: NASW.

National Center for Health Statistics (NCHS). (2008). *National Nursing Home Survey*. Hyattsville, MD: NCHS.

National Center for Health Statistics (NCHS). (2009). *Beyond 20/20 WDS – Chronic conditions U.S. 1999–2007*. National Health Interview Survey. Retrieved May 2009, from http://205.207.175.HDI/Tableviewer.

Office of Minority Health. (2005). *Health status of American Indian and Alaska Native Women*. (2005) Washington, DC: Retrieved July 2009, from http://www.omhrc.gov/templaes/content.aspx?ID=3723.

Office of Minority Health. (2007). *Minority health disparities at a glance*. Washington, DC: Author. Retrieved July, 2009.

Otiniano, M. E., Du, X. L., Ottenbacher, K., & Markides, K. S. (2003). The effect of diabetes combined with stroke on disability, self-rated health and mortality in older Mexican Americans: Results from the Hispanic EPESE. *Archives of Physical Medical Rehabilitation*, *84*, 725–730.

Palloni, A. & Arias, E. (2004). Paradox lost: Explaining the Hispanic adult mortality advantage. *Demography, 41*, 385–415.

Parker, M, et al. (2002). A multidisciplinary model of health promotion incorporating spirituality into a successful aging intervention with African American and White elderly groups. *The Gerontologist, 42*, 406–415.

Phelan, J. & Link, B. (2005). Controlling disease and creating disparities: A fundamental cause perspective. *Journal of Gerontology: Social Sciences, 60B*, S27–S33.

Pinquart, M. & Sorensen, S. (2005). Ethnic differences in stressors, resources, and psychological outcomes of family caregiving: A meta-analysis. *The Gerontologist, 45*, 90–106.

Purcell, P. & Whitman, D. (2006). Income of Americans age 65 and older, 1969 to 2004. *Journal of Deferred Preventive Compensation, 12*, 1–41.

Ramirez, A. G., Suarez, L., Chalela, P., Talavera, G. A., Marti, J., Trapido, E. J., et al. (2004). Cancer risk factors among men of diverse Hispanic or Latino origins. *Preventative Medicine, 39*, 263–269.

Resnick, B., Vogel, A., & Luisi, D. (2006). Motivating minority older adults to exercise. *Cultural Diversity and Ethnic Minority Psychology, 12*, 17–29.

Roan, S. (2009). Doctors target diabetic foot loss. Retrieved July 2009, from topics.latimes.com/health/conditions/diabetes/. . ./2009-03

Robert, S. & Ruel, E. (2006). Racial segregation and health disparities between black and white older adults. *Journal of Gerontology: Social Sciences, 61B*, S203–S211.

Robison, J., Gruman, C., Gaztambide, S., & Blank, K. (2002). Screening for depression in middle-aged and older Puerto Rican primary care patients. *Journal of Gerontology: Medical Sciences, 57A*, M308–M314.

Rooks, R. & Whitfield, K. (2004). Health disparities among older African Americans: Past, present and future perspectives. In K. Whitfield (Ed.). *Closing the gap: Improving the health of minority elders in the new millennium*. Washington, DC: Gerontological Society of America.

Ruggles, S., Sobek, M., Alexander, T., Fitch C., Goeken, R., et al. (2004). *Integrated Public Use Microdata Series: Version 3.0*. Available from the Minnesota Population Center, http://www.ipumis.org

Ruthig, J. C. & Allery, A. (2008). Native American elders' health Congruence: The role of gender and corresponding functional well-being, hospital admissions, and social engagement. *Journal of Health Psychology, 13*, 1072.

Schieman, S., Pearlin, L. I., & Nguyen, K. B. (2005). Status inequality and occupational regrets in late life. *Research on Aging, 27*, 692–724.

Scogin, F., Morthland, M., Kaufman, A., Burgio, L., Chaplin, W., & Kong, G. (2007). Improving quality of life in diverse rural older adults: A randomized trial of a psychological treatment. *Psychology and Aging, 22*, 657–665.

Skarupski, K. et al. (2005). Black-White differences in depressive symptoms among older adults over time. *The Journal of Gerontology: Psychological Sciences, 60B*, P136–P142.

Smedley, B., Stith, A., & Helson, A. (2003). *Unequal treatment: Confronting racial and ethnic disparities in health care*. Washington, DC: National Academy Press.

Tally, T. & Kaplan, J. (1956). The Negro aged. *Newsletter of the Gerontological Society of America, 4*, 111.

Taylor, R. J., Lincoln, K. D., & Chatters, L. M. (2005). Supportive relationships with church members among African Americans. *Family Relations, 54,* 501–511.

Thobaben, M. (2002). Racial and ethnic disparities in health care. *Community-based Health Care Management and Practice, 14,* 479–481.

Tran, T., Ngo, D. & Conway, K. (2003). A cross-cultural measure of depressive symptoms among Vietnamese Americans. *Social Work Research, 27,* 56–65.

Uretsky, M. C. & Matheisen, S. G. (2007). The effects of years lived in the United States on the general health status of California's foreign-born populations. *Journal of Immigrant Minority Health, 9,* 125–36.

U.S. Census Bureau. (2007). *Statistical Abstract of the United States, 2007.* Table 14. Resident Population, by Race, Hispanic Origin, and Age: 2000 to 2005. Retrieved February, 2007, from http://www.census.gov/compendia/statab/tables/07s0014.xls

U.S. Census Bureau. (2009). *Statistical abstract of the United States: 2009.* Retrieved March 2009, from http://www.census.gov/compendia/statab/2009 edition.html

Van Hook, M., Hugen, B., & Aguilar, M. (2001). *Spirituality within religious traditions in social work practice.* Pacific Grove, CA: Brooks/Cole.

Warner, D. F. & Hayward, M. D. (2002). *Race disparities in men's mortality: The role of childhood social conditions in a process of cumulative disadvantage.* Unpublished manuscript. Philadelphia: University of Pennsylvania, 2002.

Weaver, H. (2005). Cultural identity: Theories and implications. In. H. Weaver (Ed.), *Explorations in cultural competence: Journeys to the four directions.* Belmont, CA: Thomson/Brooks/Cole.

Wen, M., Cagney, K. A., & Christakis, N. A. (2005). Effect of community social environment on the mortality of individuals diagnosed with serious illness. *Social Science and Medicine, 61,* 1119–1134.

Whitfield, K. (Ed.). (2004). *Closing the gap: Improving the health of minority elders in the new millennium.* Washington, DC: Gerontological Society of America.

Whitfield, K. E. & Hayward, M. (2003). The landscape of health disparities among older adults. *Public Policy and Aging Report, 13,* 3–7.

Williams, D. R. (2004). Racism and health. In K. E. Whitfield (Ed.). *Closing the gap: Improving the health of minority elders in the new millennium.* Washington, DC: The Gerontological Society.

Williams, D. R. (2005). The health of U.S. racial and ethnic populations. *Journal of Gerontology: Social Sciences, 60B,* S53–S62.

Williams, D. R. & Rucker, T. D. (2000). Understanding and addressing racial and ethnic disparities in health care. *Health Care Financing Review, 21,* 75–90.

Williams, D. R. & Wilson, C. M. (2001). Race, ethnicity and aging. In R. A. Binstock & L. K. George (Eds.). *Handbook of aging and the social sciences* (5th ed.). New York: Academic Press.

Williams, D., Neighbors, H., & Jackson, J. (2003). Racial/ethnic discrimination and health: Findings from community studies. *American Journal of Public Health, 93,* 200–208.

Wilmoth, J. & Chen, P. (2003). Immigrant status, living arrangements and depressive symptoms among middle-aged and older adults. *Journal of Gerontology: Social Sciences, 58B,* S305–S313.

Wingett, Y. & Dempsey, M. (2006). US Hispanics lose Spanish over time, study finds. *Hispanic News.* Retrieved July 2009, from http://www.hispanic7.com/u_s__hispanics_lose_spanish_over_time,_study_finds.htm

Yee-Melichar, D. (2004). Aging Asian Americans and health disparities. In K. Whitfield (Ed.). *Closing the gap: Improving the health of minority elders in the new millennium.* Gerontological Society of America.

Yip, T., Takeuchi, D. T., & Gee, G. C. (2008). Racial discrimination and psychological distress: The impact of ethnic identity and age among immigrants and United States—born Asian adults. *Developmental Psychology, 44,* 787–800.

Yochim, B. P., Kerkar, S. P., & Lichtenberg, P. A. (2006). Cerebrovascular risk factors, activity limitations, and depressed mood in African older adults. *Psychology and Aging, 21,* 186–189.

Zauszniewski, J., Picot, S., Roberts, B., Debanne, S., & Wykle, M. (2005). Predictors of resourcefulness in African American women. *Journal of Aging and Health, 17,* 609–633.

15

The Resilience of Older Women

This chapter covers

This chapter focuses on the experiences of women as they age, and the challenges faced by current cohorts of older women. It reviews some of the content described in earlier chapters (e.g. demographics, health status, home care) from the perspective of older women's lives. More specifically, we will examine:

- The economic conditions faced by older women
- Their health and social status
- Older women's social supports, strengths, and resilience
- A feminist gerontological perspective

Previous chapters have illustrated how women's experiences with aging differ from men's: in patterns of health and life expectancy, relationships, caregiving, social opportunities, employment, and retirement. While referring back to the earlier content, this chapter elaborates on these gender differences, with attention to how personal and environmental factors interact vis-à-vis the challenges facing women in old age. The impact of social factors, especially economic ones, on physiological and psychological well-being is vividly illustrated in terms of women's daily lives of caregiving for others. The concept of resilience, defined in Chapter 6, captures older women's personal, social, and cultural capacities, despite the financial and health adversities they often face. In contrast to earlier chapters, Chapter 15 provides a concise summary of research on older women and examines older women's resilience in the face of multiple economic, health, and social challenges, from a feminist gerontological perspective. It also places more emphasis on documenting structural gender-based barriers, including sexism and ageism faced by women across the life course, particularly in employment and health care.

Rationale for a Focus on Older Women's Needs

A major reason for this separate chapter on older women is that they represent the majority and the fastest-growing segment of the older population, especially among the oldest-old, both in the United States and globally. As noted in Chapter 1, the aging society is primarily a female one. According to Cruikshank (2009), neither women's studies nor gerontology has come to grips with the fact that "old" means "women" (Preface, p. xx). Women represent 58 percent of the population age 65 and older and 68 percent of those over age 85. As illustrated in Chapter 1, women age 65 and older (21.9 million) outnumber men in that age group (16 million) by a ratio of three to two, men age 85 and over by five to two, and centenarians by three to one. Racial variations within the female older population are striking, as described in Chapter 14. Chapter 1 noted that these disproportionate ratios of women to men result from a 5- to 6-year difference in life expectancy at birth for women, which is even greater among African Americans (U.S. Census Bureau, 2008a; Federal Interagency Forum, 2008). This is due to a combination of biological factors, such as the genetic theory that the female's two X chromosomes make her physiologically more robust, and to lifestyle factors, such as women's greater likelihood of preventive health behaviors and their lower rates of smoking, substance abuse, and other high-risk behaviors across the life course. At age 65,

women can expect to live an additional 19.8 years compared to 16.8 more years for their male counterparts. Even at age 85, female life expectancy is 1.2 years longer than that for males (Federal Interagency Forum, 2008). However, men who survive beyond age 85 are likely to have fewer chronic illnesses or disabilities and to have a life expectancy similar to women.

Despite their greater life expectancy, older women face more challenges than men. Therefore, another reason to focus on older women is that gender, intersecting with other forms of oppression, structures opportunities across the life course, making the processes of aging and the quality of life in old age markedly different for men and women. Consistent with the feminist gerontological perspective described in Chapter 8, research on women and aging recognizes that gender and age interact to affect the distribution of power, privilege, economic resources, and well-being for men and women throughout life. In other words, older women do not always become poor with old age, but their circumstances across the life course (e.g., patterns of underemployment, caregiving, limited pensions and private investments, lower wages and Social Security benefits) make them more vulnerable to poverty and chronic illness. As noted by feminist gerontologists, as more women reach old age in Western culture, age compounds a woman's already devalued status and may increase her feelings of powerlessness and sense of becoming "the Other" (Cruikshank, 2009, p. 5). Because gender and age are powerful systems for patterning inequities in roles, relationships, and resources, neither can be understood fully without reference to the other. But feminist gerontologists increasingly recognize the importance of taking account of other intersecting inequalities and theorize about old age itself as social location (Calasanti & Slevin, 2006; King, 2006). As noted by Calasanti (2009), just as gender shapes aging, so too do other hierarchies influence both gender and aging. Older men and women do not exist apart from their racial, ethnic, and sexual identities, functional abilities, and class-based locations.

Because of these inequities, it is not surprising that the problems of aging are increasingly women's problems. As shown in earlier chapters, older women are more likely than older men to be poor; to have inadequate retirement income; to be widowed, divorced, and alone; to live in assisted living or nursing homes; to experience chronic illnesses and disability; and to be caregivers to other relatives. Despite women's overall economic progress as a result of antidiscrimination legislation, they still experience double jeopardy as they age, confronting obstacles both for being old and for being female. Women of color, who are poorer and face more health problems than their Caucasian counterparts, experience triple jeopardy. Women still lag behind men economically; this has implications for their well-being, given the documented association between social class and health. In addition, the emphasis on youth and beauty in our society, which traditionally values women for their physical appearance, sex appeal, and ability to bear children, can mean that older women—particularly low-income women—feel as if they are sexual castoffs. In fact, it is this cultural emphasis on youthful physical appearance as a basis of social acceptance that underlies the growing popularity of anti-aging medicine described in Chapter 4 (e.g., expensive chemical skin peels, laser treatments, cosmetic surgery, and anti-wrinkle creams, available largely to upper-middle-class white women) (Calasanti, 2009).

Given the numerical predominance of older women and their greater probability of problems in old age, it is even more surprising that older women were nearly invisible in social geronto-logical research until the mid-1970s. To illustrate, they were only added to the Baltimore Longitudinal Study (described in Chapter 1) in 1978, because it was previously assumed that women's hormonal cycles would affect the data. The first older women's caucus was not held until 1975 at the annual meetings of the Gerontologi- cal Society of America. And the 1981 White House Conference on Aging was the first to sponsor a special committee on older women's concerns. Research on issues specific to women, such as menopause, breast cancer, hormone replacement therapy, and osteoporosis, was relatively limited until the late 1980s. In 1991, Congress directed the National Institutes of Health to establish an Office of Research on Women's Health to redress the inadequate attention paid to women's health issues in the biomedical and behavioral research communities. One positive result was the Women's Health Initiative; as described in Chapter 4, this was the first randomized controlled study of postmenopausal women and the impact of fat intake and hormone replacement therapy on breast cancer and heart disease. Completed in 2008, its findings, especially related to hormone replacement therapy and to heart disease, have already had an impact on women's health practices and provider behavior. Similarly, the Women's Health and Aging Study, funded since 1994 by the National Institutes of Health, focuses on the causes, prevention, and management of disability among older women as well as rehabilitation. As another indication of greater recognition of older women's issues, most professional associations on aging, such as the Geronto- logical Society of America, now include an older women's caucus or interest group. Perhaps because of the greater attention given to issues distinctive to older women, some feminists and gerontologists now believe that older women's needs have finally received the attention they are due (Cruikshank, 2009).

Research on aging has thus progressed in the following sequence:

1. ignoring gender,
2. merely controlling for gender,
3. describing gender-based contrasts,
4. making efforts to understand the sources of gender-based variations, as well as their implications for both individuals and communities,
5. identifying the intersections of different influences on people's everyday lives (gender and age with race, ethnicity, sexual identity, and disability), and
6. advocating for social change by and on behalf of women (Andersen, 2005).

A feminist gerontological perspective analyzes the intersections of multiple social locations with the long-term goal of gender equity that will benefit both women and men. Feminist theory is grounded in women's lived experience, with feminist inquiry beginning from women's standpoint, which takes subjectivity, oppression, and empowerment into account in its analyses (Allen & Walker, 2006; Calasanti, 2009; Code, 2006). Feminist and postmodern researchers emphasize how women's unpaid and undervalued work as family caregivers, along with their employment mostly in low-status, low-paid jobs, results in economic hardship in old age, with consequent negative effects on their physical and mental well-being and long-term care options. The women's movement has tended to ignore issues specific to older women, although some younger feminists are now aligning themselves with older women around shared concerns, such as those related to caregiving across the life course, health care reform, and economic security. In recent years, older women's resilience and strengths, not only their greater vulnerability to societal inequities, have been made more visible, partly as a result of the education and advocacy of such activist groups as the **Older Women's League (OWL)** and the Women's Institute for a Secure Retirement (WISER). Additionally, organizations representing direct care workers are advocating on behalf of their members to increase wages and other benefits for low-income women, typically immigrants and those of color who are caring for other women.

Older Women's Economic Status

Financial resources—including older women's concerns about their economic situation—are major determinants of their life satisfaction and perceived quality of life. This is not surprising, given that women over age 65 account for 58 percent of the total older population but over 70 percent of the older poor. They form one of the poorest groups in our society, with over 12 percent living in poverty at any one point in time, compared to 7.6 percent of men (AOA, 2008). The **gendered nature of the life course** has created gender differences in employment history, child care, parent care, and other household responsibilities, career interruptions, types of occupations, earnings, and retirement circumstances, all contributing to older women's higher rates of poverty and near-poverty (Gonyea, 2009; Gonyea & Hooyman, 2005; Herd, 2006). Although women among this current cohort of elders have less education and employment experience than both men and younger women, these differences do not completely account for gender-based inequities in income, which persist even among those who have the same educational levels as their male peers.

These income inequities are a result of structural factors, particularly women's marital status and employment history. To some extent, long-lived marriages—irrespective of marital satisfaction—offer economic protection for women in old age. Poverty for women is either created or exacerbated by widowhood or divorce. Being widowed, divorced, or separated renders a woman far more vulnerable to poverty when compared with an older woman who remains married to the same man, who generally receives more retirement income. More specifically, approximately 4.3 percent of older married women face poverty, compared with

18.6 percent of unmarried older women. Widows are over three times more likely to be poor as older married couples (WISER, 2009). Of all widows in poverty, approximately 50 percent become poor only after their husband dies, and divorced older women have even higher poverty rates than their widowed peers (Harrington Meyer & Herd, 2008; Herd, 2006; OWL, 2009a). In addition, the economic gaps between married and widowed women—and between widowed men and women—are increasing, especially among the oldest-old. For lesbians, access to Social Security is not an option, even in states that allow same-sex marriage or same-sex partner benefits, because it is a federal program. Accordingly, older lesbians are denied this basic floor of income security available only to heterosexual married couples (Connidis, 2009; de Vries, 2007; OWL, 2009b).

The difference in women's greater economic vulnerability in old age as compared to men's is a consequence not only of their marital status, but also the domestic division of labor and women's position in the labor market, resulting in lower earnings across the life course and into old age. When all sources of income are taken into account, older women's median annual income is approximately 50 percent of men's, even among employed women (AOA, 2008; Federal Interagency Forum, 2008). This exemplifies the feminization of poverty across the life course. Most women in the current cohort age 80 and older did not consistently work for pay, largely because they were expected to marry, raise children, and depend on their husbands for economic support. Their labor force participation rate was only 9.7 percent in 1950, rose slightly in the 1950s, and then dropped to 7.8 percent in 1983, when many would have been near retirement age. When they were employed, they tended to be concentrated in low-wage clerical, retail, or service positions without adequate pensions and other benefits (OWL, 2009b). Similarly, women are more than twice as likely as men to work part-time—that is, fewer than 25 hours per week, typically in sales, clerical,

and retail jobs (OWL, 2009b). Overall, women age 70 and older generally lacked the opportunities to build up their economic security separate from their husbands' pensions and Social Security earnings for old age. Older women's poverty is due not only to lower lifetime earnings, but also to the fact that they typically have few assets other than a home, which is not a source of cash income (Gorncik, Sierminsk, & Smeeding, 2009).

In addition, 52 percent of women have at least one calendar year without any earnings compared to just 16 percent of men. Women's wages peak on average in their 40s, while men's median earnings continue to climb until their mid-50s. These long-term earnings differentials underscore the fact that women's time spent in performing family care often profoundly limits their economic resources in later life. This is because men typically are employed for the full 35 years required for maximum Social Security benefits, while women spend, on average, about 12 years out of the workforce. These caregiving years are calculated as zero earnings, thereby reducing women's Social Security benefits. For example, women who are caring for older parents are more than twice as likely to live in poverty as noncaregivers (Wakabayashi & Donato, 2004). Finally, women's longer life expectancy means that they may need to stretch more limited financial resources over a greater number of years than men. A growing number of women who never expected to live so long end up outliving their retirement resources (Hartmann & English, 2009; WISER, 2009).

The intersections of age, gender, and race, described above, have a striking impact on economic well-being, with approximately 39 percent of African American and 40 percent of Latina women age 85 and older living below the federal poverty level. A major reason for the higher rates of poverty among women of color is that they earn even less than white women during their working years (approximately 67 cents for African American women and 58 cents for Latinas for each dollar earned by Caucasian men, compared with 77 cents for white women). Overall, poverty rates among African American women are three times that of white women; unmarried black women have four to five times higher poverty rates than married African American women (Federal Interagency Forum, 2008). Because African American and Latino men also earn less, as a whole, than their white counterparts, the gender differences for these two populations narrow compared to the non-Hispanic white population.

Given these inequities structured by race and gender, it is not surprising that poverty rates are highest among women who:

- never married (20 percent)
- are divorced (22 percent)
- are widows (18.6 percent)
- are women of color, with Latina and African American women the poorest
- are age 75 and older (approximately 50 percent among Caucasian women, a rate that increases dramatically among women of color) (OWL, 2009b; SSA, 2006)

These figures may not reveal the full extent of poverty among women, especially widows, who are not counted as poor, despite their low income, if they live in households headed by younger persons whose income is above the poverty line (e.g., with adult children or other relatives) or in long-term care facilities. When these hidden poor are taken into account, as many as 55 percent of older women are estimated to be poor. In addition, older women form 60 percent of the "near poor," falling within 125 to 200 percent of the poverty line (U.S. Census Bureau, 2006). Older women whose income drops below the poverty level may turn to SSI; they comprise about two thirds of older SSI recipients. For women who value economic self-sufficiency, dependency on government support can be stigmatizing. Additionally, the criteria for SSI have not changed since the 1980s, which negatively affects older women's eligibility; increasing the

asset limits for SSI would serve to reduce the number of older women living in poverty (Favreault, 2009).

Income differentials are unlikely to change in the near future, because median earnings of working-age women who work full-time, year-round are approximately $10,000 less than what men earn (WISER, 2009). This wage gap widens throughout women's lives, even for college-educated women; those ages 46 to 64 working full-time earn only 70 percent of what men earn. Over a lifetime, this adds up to more than $440,000 in lost earnings for a woman to save and/or invest in her retirement. The seeming intractability of women's lower earnings raises concerns, especially because it has been over 40 years since the Fair Pay and Equal Pay legislation passed (U.S. Department of Labor, 2008). These patterns suggest the persistence of institutionalized sexism and point to the importance of the White House Council on Women and Girls established by President Obama in 2009 to address inequities (OWL, 2009b, 2009a; American Association of University Women, 2007; WISER, 2009).

Other structural factors underlying women's lower retirement income include:

- interrupted employment histories because of family responsibilities, which reduces Social Security and other pension benefits
- greater likelihood of being divorced, widowed, and unmarried
- lower wages across the life course and resultant lower Social Security and other pension benefits
- greater likelihood of having worked part time, often in temporary positions
- lower likelihood of receiving pensions such as 401(k)s, retirement planning, and investment opportunities to supplement Social Security
- lower probability of having worked in higher-level or professional occupations (Heinz, Lewis, & Hounsell, 2006; Herd, 2006; Lee, 2005; McLaughlin & Jensen, 2000).

OLDER WOMEN WHO CANNOT AFFORD TO RETIRE

For many older women, retirement is not an option. Instead of counting the days until retirement, some count the number of days they have worked in a row. Consider Patsy Secrest, who at age 58 rises at 3 AM. to open up a fast food restaurant at 4 AM, ready to serve the first drive-through customers at 5:30. She has worked in this service job for 28 years, but is paid slightly more than the minimum wage, only $8.50 an hour. She is caught in a vicious circle; employment exacerbates numerous chronic conditions, including high cholesterol and blood pressure, back pain, depression, and insomnia; the resultant rising copayments of her frequent doctor visits ($300 a month) and prescription drugs ($3,600 a year) necessitate that she remain employed to be able to cover her medical expenses. Her job has provided the health care benefits for her husband of 38 years, whose job is threatened by plant layoffs and who last year earned only $11,000. Her life consists of long hours at a physically exhausting job, surrounded by teenagers and young adults. In order to rise early, she needs to be in bed each evening by 6 PM. This leaves her little time for a social life or leisure activities; her one indulgence is $16 for a weekly shampoo and styling. At a time when more affluent couples are anticipating retirement, Mrs. Secrest sees only a future of long, exhausting days, dozens of medications to manage her chronic illnesses, and Social Security as her sole source of retirement income.

SOURCE: Finkel, 2003.

Social Security and Gender Inequities

Social Security is the primary source of income for older women, and they are more likely than men to rely on it as their sole source of income. Women represent 58 percent of all Social Security beneficiaries age 65 and over, and approximately 71 percent of those ages 85 and older. In addition, 47 percent of all older unmarried women compared to 29 percent of men receiving Social Security benefits rely on it for 90 percent or more of their income; 25 percent have no other income. Without Social Security, it is estimated that over 50 percent of all older women would be poor. Yet, as noted above and discussed in Chapter 12, even with Social Security, women are twice as likely to be poor as older men (OWL, 2009a, 2009b; SSA, 2006).

Marital status directly affects Social Security benefits received, just as it affects women's overall financial status. For widows 65 and older, these benefits comprise 58 percent of their total income compared to 41 percent of unmarried older men's income and 33 percent of older couples' (SSA, 2006). Analysis by race further reveals that Social Security provides more than half the retirement income for over 80 percent of non-married older African American and Latina women, compared with 73 percent of older white women. Social Security represents 90 percent or more of the retirement income for more than half of all African American and Latina women, versus 40 percent of white women (Hounsell & Humphlett, 2006; SSA, 2006). Furthermore, their monthly Social Security benefit is often less than for their Caucasian counterparts because, as described above, even among younger persons, African American and Latina women working full-time earn far less than white men and women (Federal Interagency Forum, 2008).

As is true of women's economic status generally, family roles negatively impact their access to Social Security, because benefit levels are tied to earnings and based on the earnings of their best 35 years of employment. Due to family care responsibilities across the life course, women are far more likely than men to have been employed fewer than 35 years, and thus have several years of zero earnings included in the calculations of benefits. A woman in a two-income family who is entitled to both a worker benefit on her earnings and a spousal benefit on her husband's earnings can receive only the greater of the two. Although the percentage of women eligible for benefits from both sources has increased from 5 percent in 1960 to nearly

30 percent today, most women draw a higher Social Security benefit based on their husband's employment record, because he typically received a higher income for more years of employment. As an indicator of women's lower earnings, the dependent spouse's benefit is only 50 percent of the retired spouse's, and women form more than 90 percent of those who collect as dependent spouses. Women thus continue to remain financially dependent on their spouses, receiving the same survivors' benefit they would have gotten if they had never worked outside the home. In fact, Social Security is calculated in such a way that some dual-earner couples receive *less* in Social Security benefits than if they had had the same income, but that income was brought home by one traditional breadwinner (Calasanti, 2009). Although almost all men (95 percent) receive a benefit based fully on their own employment histories, only about 38 percent of women have garnered worker benefits from their own employment (OWL, 2009a). Lower income is also associated with earlier onset of a number of chronic and disabling health conditions that might force earlier retirement decisions, especially among women of color in service and direct care jobs. In general, African Americans, Latinos, and women experience more involuntary job separation in the years immediately prior to retirement, and these periods of forced joblessness often result in permanent labor force withdrawal, as noted in Chapter 12 (Flippen, 2005). The box in the next column highlights some of the reasons why Social Security is so central to the economic well-being of Latinas.

Because women's economic security is so closely tied to their husband's employment history, when they become widowed or divorced and turn to Social Security, their benefits may be less than anticipated. At age 65, a widow can receive full Social Security benefits based on her husband's earnings or her own, whichever is larger. She cannot claim benefits as both a widow and worker. However,

because most women age 60 and over are not employed full time, the majority opt for benefits that are substantially less than what they would have received if their husbands had lived to retire at age 65. On average, widowed women receive nearly 60 percent of their income from Social Security compared to 40 percent of widowed men (SSA, 2006). If a widowed woman becomes disabled more than 7 years after her husband's death, she is not eligible for disability benefits based on his earnings. Instead, she must have been employed at least 10 years to qualify for disability benefits on her own. Widows of color are at highest risk of poverty in late life, because they enter widowhood with lower incomes and fewer assets to begin with (Angel et al., 2007; OWL, 2009a).

Another inequity is that a widow who enters or continues in the workforce past age 65 receives credit for her own retirement benefits for any month after age 65 that she does not draw on Social Security. If her own benefits are greater than her widow's benefits, she will

---

WHY IS SOCIAL SECURITY IMPORTANT TO LATINAS?

- Without Social Security, 51 percent of Latinas over age 65 would be poor.
- Despite their current Social Security benefits, about 21 percent of all older Latinas today live in poverty, increasing to 41 percent among single Latinas.
- Latinas' life expectancy at age 65 is 22.8 years, 3 years longer than non-Hispanic white women and 4.2 years longer than non-Hispanic black women. Therefore, they will receive Social Security benefits for a longer period of time.
- Only about a third of Latinas have savings or asset income.

SOURCE: Federal Interagency Forum, 2008; WISER, 2009.

receive credit toward her own retirement. But if her widow's benefits are the larger amount, she will receive no delayed retirement credits when she retires. The "catch 22" is that her benefits are identical to those she would have received if she had not entered the workforce at all or had retired at an earlier age. To illustrate another inequity, spouses under the age of 62 who are caring for a spouse disabled enough to need regular care cannot receive Social Security benefits. As a result, women under age 62 often rely only on their husband's disability benefits. In contrast, benefits are paid directly to a mother providing care for an adult child who receives disability benefits (OWL, 2009a; WISER, 2009).

Divorced women generally fare worse in terms of Social Security, with 60 times more divorced women than men dependent on their divorced spouse's income (OWL, 2009a). A divorced woman age 62 and older at the time of divorce can receive Social Security based on her former husband's earnings record if:

- she had been married at least 10 years prior to the date of divorce. However, today the average marriage across all ages lasts only 8 years, so many women still lose out on benefits, a pattern that is projected to continue for future cohorts (WISER, 2009).
- she has not remarried, and her former husband is age 62 or older and qualifies for benefits. She can start receiving one-half of his benefits even if she is younger than 62 if she is divorced for two or more years. If her former husband is not yet 62, she must wait until then. For women without other options, this waiting period can be a time of economic deprivation and can have the effect of penalizing women who are divorced. Not surprisingly, women who have been divorced or widowed earlier in their lives tend to have lower retirement incomes than those who have been continuously married (Cruikshank, 2009; OWL, 2009a; WISER, 2009).

Inequities for Women Under Proposals to Privatize Social Security

Although there are no major proposals currently before Congress to privatize Social Security, the concept of privatization is likely to continue to surface under the guise of "individual accounts" in any discussions about the funding crises of entitlement programs. If Social Security were privatized, as will be discussed in Chapter 16, this would negatively affect women, especially women of color, more than men. Under privatization, the progressive benefit formula of Social Security, which replaces a higher percentage of earnings for lower-income workers than higher-income workers, would be lost. Instead, as low-income and part-time employees, many women would have smaller private accounts to invest. This is increasingly the situation with the current recession. With more limited financial resources, women typically avoid higher-risk investments, which means that their accounts generally yield lower-than-average returns. Ultimately, the burden for the management of their investment portfolio falls squarely on individual women's shoulders. And older women who have historically received little training in financial management may be at greater risk for poor investment decisions (Lusardi & Mitchell, 2008).

Given women's longer life expectancy, coupled with their smaller investments, women under a privatized system would face a greater prospect than men of outliving all of their savings and assets. Privatization means that there would no longer be a lifetime guarantee of a benefit, as is true of Social Security currently. Private lifetime annuities, unlike Social Security, are monthly payments based on gender-based life expectancies, resulting in women receiving a lower lifetime benefit even when their investments are equal to men's (Gonyea & Hooyman, 2005). In addition, privatization would eliminate death and disability protection and the cost of living increases available through Social

Security—all changes that would disadvantage women. Women are much more likely than men to be responsible for children and/or themselves after a spouse's disability or death. In a privatized system, the core benefit for divorced individuals might be reduced and division of the private account between husband and wife could fall under the jurisdiction of a divorce court (OWL, 2009a).

Proposals to Reduce Gender Inequities in Social Security

Several other proposals for programmatic reforms to Social Security could eliminate some gender inequities and reduce older women's financial vulnerability. These include raising the minimum benefit, increasing the survivor's benefit for widows, and providing dependent care credits. Raising the minimum Social Security benefit would be particularly valuable to women and persons of color, given their over-representation in low-wage, part-time jobs with few or no benefits. Moreover, many women and persons of color are employed in physically demanding or taxing jobs (e.g., domestic, industrial, and farm labor) that lead to an earlier departure from the paid labor force. Changing the Social Security benefit calculation formula to increase the minimum benefit would be an advantage for women employed as direct care workers in long-term care. It would also help poor working women who either never married or were married less than 10 years and thus receive a benefit based solely on their own employment histories (Gonyea & Hooyman, 2005). In fact, a special minimum Social Security benefit currently exists for low-wage workers with a history of steady employment that provides these retirees with a higher monthly benefit than they would receive under the regular formula. Few individuals, however, are currently eligible for the special minimum benefit due to its restrictive eligibility requirements. As described

---

CARE CREDITS TO IMPROVE SOCIAL SECURITY BENEFITS FOR OLDER WOMEN

Credits for caregiving are available in most Western industrialized countries, but not the U.S. Care credits that reward women's disproportionate caregiving responsibilities would:

- move away from marital status as a criterion for eligibility (e.g., eliminate spousal benefits).
- value women's unpaid care work by moving women into the category of worker benefits, while buffering their low earnings as caregivers.
- improve the progressive nature of benefits
- contrast with earnings-sharing proposals that divide total earnings of married couples between the Social Security accounts of both spouses.

Care credits that drop zero-earnings years from women's benefit calculations have limitations, and only 43 percent of women currently in the workforce would experience advantages

- Women who are most likely to have zero-earnings years are those who can afford not to work outside the home, primarily white upper-income women.

- Women's care labor is only rewarded when they do not participate in the marketplace, but most women combine unpaid care work with paid employment.
- Fewer women in future cohorts are going to have zero earnings years in their benefit calculations.

Care credits that drop low-earnings years (on top of the 5 currently allowed) from the benefit calculation benefit women with high earnings more than those with low earnings. Care credits that place a value on caregiving would:

- reward those who suffer significant cuts in earnings because of caregiving work.
- be a set amount of earnings that would substitute for a certain number of years of earnings that are below this level.
- benefit low-income women and women of color. (Herd, 2002; 2006)

above, women often experience significant declines in income with the death of their husband. For most widows, the loss of Social Security income greatly exceeds the reduction of their living expenses. For these reasons, increasing survivor benefits could benefit widows who did not have long-term employment histories, if that benefit would not be reduced by more than 25 percent of the couple's combined benefit. One possibility would be to shift the widow's benefit from 100 percent of the couple's higher-earner benefit to 75 percent of the couple's combined benefits. This proposal addresses the fact that many older women are not poor until their spouses die. Currently, a widow who works long enough to be eligible for benefits of her own essentially gets no credit for her earnings because the husband's income has typically been higher (WISER, 2009).

Dependent care credits are a way to reward and recognize women's disproportionate responsibilities for raising children, or the "motherhood penalty" (WISER, 2009). In fact, all industrialized countries except the U.S. reward parenthood through their public pension systems (Wisensale, 2009). Some feminists argue that women's economic contributions to households should be recognized, while others advocate for women to move out of the home and into employment. Regardless, dependent care credits would be a more progressive way to distribute benefits than spousal benefits, because women would move onto the worker benefit, and their lower incomes would be buffered by the economic value assigned to their unpaid care work. With dependent care credits, marital status would not be an eligibility criterion. Instead, women would receive benefits based on their contributions to the economy through both their labor force participation and their unpaid work of child and elder care. The most commonly debated proposal is to allow up to 4 to 5 additional drop-out years—when women have been out of the full-time paid workforce because of responsibilities for family members—from women's benefit calculations. Another change is

that such credits could be given for care of family members other than children. A downside of this approach, however, is that it may further exacerbate gender and racial inequities because upper-income white married women, who can afford not to work for pay, are more likely to benefit than low-income married women of color who remain employed out of economic necessity. This means that low-income women are unlikely to have zero-earnings or "drop out" years in their benefit calculations.

Another option is **earnings sharing**, whereby each partner in a marriage is entitled to a separate Social Security account, regardless of which one is employed. Covered earnings would be divided between the two spouses, with one-half credited to each spouse's account. Alternatively, additional low-earnings years (9 years versus 5) could be dropped from the benefit calculations. However, because the rewards for caregiving are directly tied to women's earnings histories, women with high earnings would again fare better than women with low wages.

Placing a value on dependent care is a third way to structure care credits; these would represent a set amount of earnings, which would substitute for a certain number of years of low earnings. To illustrate, if the care credit were $15,000 and a woman within her highest 35 years of earnings had 2 years where she earned only $8,000, she would be credited with an additional $7,000 for those years. This approach would benefit lower-income women and women of color more than those with higher earnings. Generally, low-income women would be hurt most by a system that dropped more zero- or low-earnings years (since they are likely to be employed continuously out of financial necessity), and would benefit most if half of their median wage were substituted into low-earnings years. None of these proposed dependent-care options would benefit all women, but more women would fare better under any of the proposals than they do now under the single breadwinner model (Gonyea & Hooyman, 2005; Herd, 2006). Unlike privatization, there is likely to be more support for these approaches under the Democratic administration. However, none of these proposals to reduce gender inequities inherent in Social Security will be considered in the near future, given the federal deficit and the political pressure to reduce federal spending.

Private Pensions and Gender Inequities

Women are even less likely than men to receive a private pension, either as a retired worker or as a surviving spouse (21 percent of women compared to over 40 percent of men) (OWL, 2009a). Unmarried women are most likely to have no pension. Even when an older woman does have pension income, it is on average less than 50 percent of what their male counterparts receive due to women's relatively lower earnings, for reasons described above (OWL, 2009a; SSA, 2008; WISER, 2009). Women also tend to be concentrated in jobs where pension coverage is not common, and to receive a reduced pension benefit because they retire before the age of full eligibility. Even if women work for a company with pension plans, they are almost twice as likely as male employees to report that their non-participation was due to an insufficient number of hours to qualify for enrollment. The shift to defined contribution plans (e.g., individual investments in IRAs) rather than defined benefits has not benefited women, who typically have less money to invest and have had more years of unpaid family care responsibilities. Also, older women are less likely to have participated in retirement planning and often lack financial literacy (i.e., understanding their financial options) (Lusardi & Mitchell, 2008; Shuey & O'Rand, 2006). These pension and financial planning inequities are exacerbated for women of color, who are significantly less likely to have pension income (Hounsell & Humphlett, 2006; SSA, 2006). Additionally, women are more vulnerable than men to income and savings loss due to marital dissolution.

These findings raise concerns for women's future economic status, given the dramatic expansion of part-time and temporary employment and the declining value of personal investments. Vulnerability to benefit-loss may be an even greater risk for younger cohorts of workers, which are characterized by higher rates of divorce (Shuey & O'Rand, 2006). Not surprisingly, never-married older women who have been employed throughout their lives are far more likely than their divorced or widowed counterparts to derive income from pensions, annuities, interest, and dividends. These figures do not hold true, however, for never-married single mothers who have had child-rearing responsibilities and therefore have not worked regularly outside the home.

A woman whose family role resulted in economic dependence on her husband can benefit from his private pension only if the following conditions exist:

- He does not die before retirement age.
- He stays married to her.
- He is willing to reduce his monthly benefits in order to provide her with a survivor's monthly annuity.

Federal Pension Law requires that an employer-provided defined benefit plan pay a joint benefit and 50 percent annuity unless a spouse gives up such pension benefits and approves the choice of a single life or lump sum payment. Given the economic vicissitudes of aging, some older men choose higher monthly lifetime benefits rather than survivor benefits. That choice, however, can be detrimental to their wives, who typically outlive their husbands, because the lifetime benefit ends when the husband dies. Fortunately, a man is now required by federal law to get his wife's written permission to give up survivor benefits. However, federal laws designed to provide protection to widows of private pension recipients do not apply to state government plans. As a result, over half the states do not have a requirement that the wife of a government employee must agree to her husband's waiving survivor benefits (i.e., **spousal consent requirement**). This means that a wife may discover only after her husband's death that she will no longer be entitled to the government-funded pension benefits that were paid when he was alive. Defined contribution plans provide no such spousal protection, because the account holder for IRAs can name anyone as beneficiary (WISER, 2009).

In summary, women's traditional family roles and limited job options tend to result in discontinuous employment histories with lower lifetime earnings. This pattern, combined with fewer pension opportunities and lower Social Security benefits, produces a double or triple jeopardy for older women's economic status, especially for women of color. These structural barriers and the interaction of gender, age, race, and ethnicity mean that government policies (i.e., Social Security, SSI, and public pensions) are differentially effective in raising older adults out of poverty. Accordingly, women of color remain at the lowest income levels across the life course. Since most changes in Social Security and pension laws have improved women's benefits as dependents rather than as employees, they do not address the growing numbers of divorced, single-parent, and never-married women who are likely to remain poor in the future (Avison & Davies, 2005).

Given these patterns, the economic outlook for future cohorts of older women remains bleak. Poverty and insecurity will continue to be a problem for older women well into the middle of this century, especially because women still earn less than men (Older Women's League, 2009b; WISER, 2006). Even though more middle-aged and older women are employed, they are more likely to hold part-time and poorly paid jobs, increasingly in the service sector. It is predicted that by the year 2020, poverty will remain widespread among older women of color and those living alone because of divorce or widowhood. Social Security and pension systems will have greatly reduced poverty among older men and couples, however. Accordingly, fewer women will receive spousal or survivor benefits due to their increased earnings, declines in marriage rates, and growing rates of divorce and single parenthood (Institute for Women's Policy Research, 2009).

Despite the seeming intractability of these interconnections among gender, age, race, and class, a number of strategies could reduce the poverty rate among older women. These represent additional solutions to those described above to reduce gender inequities in Social Security benefits:

- Increasing survivor benefits would improve the status of widowed women.
- Improving benefits for low earners would help divorced and never-married women.
- Expanding eligibility for the SSI Program would assist the poorest older women.
- Targeting benefits within Social Security, such as an income-tested minimum benefit guarantee of $600 per month for beneficiaries whose net income is less than $400 a month.
- Reducing the number of years of marriage required to qualify for spousal benefits for divorced persons under Social Security.
- Modifying Social Security plans to provide a better return on earnings and improve survivor benefits.

From both a feminist and political-economy perspective, some of these strategies are incremental and fail to address gender inequities across the life course. For example, legislation such as the Family and Medical Leave Act of 1993, which supports women's "taking time off" for caregiving of dependents across the life course, does not promote women's long-term economic security. This is because such legislation fails to provide paid leave, credit toward Social Security, or access to private pensions. As long as women leave the paid workforce to provide unpaid work in the home, they remain dependent on their husband's retirement or Social Security, which is problematic for their future economic security. Feminist and political-economy analyses recognize that women's economic status and retirement are conditioned by gendered employment patterns and by social and economic policies that link women's economic security to that of men's. Solutions that address the interconnections between women's family and employment roles would provide benefits for women's unpaid caregiving in the home (such as care credits), ensure adequate access to pensions in positions typically held by women, and increase women's salaries and wages across all positions. Until such fundamental changes are made, gender and racial economic disparities will persist in old age.

Older Women's Health Status

Women's disadvantaged economic status increases their health risks. Although women in all industrialized countries and nearly all developing countries live longer than men, they have higher rates of chronic diseases, physician visits, and prescription drug use (Moen & Chermack, 2005). As described in Chapter 4, older people who are poor, composed primarily of women and people of color, tend to be less healthy than higher-income older adults. Compared to their wealthier peers, low-income elders as a whole are more likely to live alone, have inadequate diets, have less access to health promotion information, and make fewer dental visits and physician contacts per year. Since women, especially the divorced and widowed, predominate among the older poor, women's health status is more frequently harmed by the adverse conditions associated with poverty than is men's. Older women of color, for example, are more likely to obtain health care from hospital outpatient units, emergency rooms, and neighborhood clinics than from private physicians and specialists. In turn, poor health

combined with inadequate insurance can deplete low-income women's limited resources (Cruikshank, 2009).

Health Insurance and Gender Inequities

As is true of economic security in old age, previous family and employment patterns affect older women's access to adequate health care. For example, the workplace has traditionally determined such access through opportunities to enroll in group insurance plans. Only about 59 percent of American workers today have health insurance through their employers, a percentage that continues to decline with the recession (Kazzi, 2009). Most insurance systems exclude the occupation of homemaker, except as a dependent. As a result, older women are more likely than men to lack private health insurance to supplement Medicare at a time when health care costs are soaring. This is often because women of this current cohort of older adults have never been, or have sporadically been, employed or in part-time service positions that did not provide health benefits. Low-income divorced and/or widowed women, unable to rely on their husbands' insurance, are especially disadvantaged. Divorced women are about twice as likely to lack private supplemental health insurance as married women, and are more likely than widows to be uninsured. Women of color, especially Latinas, also have lower rates of insurance coverage, including Medicaid, than their white counterparts. Some of this differential in publicly funded insurance may be due to immigration status and restrictions regarding proof of citizenship (Christopher, 2006; Xu et al., 2006).

Women in their early 60s are most likely to lack health insurance, even more so than young children who may be able to access health insurance through Medicaid or S-CHIP (State Children's Health Insurance Plan), funded by the federal government (Cruikshank, 2009; Kaiser Family Foundation, 2007). Some uninsured women gamble on staying healthy until qualifying for Medicare coverage at age 65. Because the incidence of chronic disease is higher among older women than among men, many women lose this gamble. For example, if a divorced woman is diagnosed with cancer in her late 50s, she is too young to qualify for Medicare and too sick to obtain private insurance; yet she may fall just above the income limits for Medicaid. As a divorcee, she is unable to turn to her former husband's insurance. Similarly, a woman whose husband retires at age 65 is at risk of becoming uninsured if she is younger than he and has been insured through his job, because he is covered by Medicare but she is not. Fortunately, groups such as OWL have successfully advocated for **conversion laws** Under the Consolidated Omnibus Budget Reconciliation Act or COBRA, insurance companies are required to allow women to remain in their husband's group insurance for up to 3 years after divorce, separation, or widowhood, although 18 months is typically the limit. However, the benefits under conversion health insurance coverage may not be as extensive as when the husband was employed. When their COBRA runs out, uninsured women typically have limited options to find or change jobs in order to get health insurance. And if they have preexisting health conditions, the chances of their buying an individual health insurance plan are reduced even more. After age 65, women comprise the vast majority of Medicare beneficiaries, with women age 85 and over forming 70 percent of beneficiaries. Even with health insurance, older women spend more of their annual income for out-of-pocket health care costs than on food. Since women have more chronic conditions than men, their prescription drug usage is also high. How Medicare Part D (described in Chapter 17) has affected women compared to men is not yet evident, although women are more likely than men to be Medicaid beneficiaries who have been shifted to private drug plans.

Because of their lower SES, older women comprise the vast majority of older Medicaid beneficiaries (Kaiser Family Foundation, 2007). A negative effect of this dependency is that some health care providers, concerned about low reimbursement rates, are unwilling to accept Medicaid patients. This may make it difficult for older women to obtain adequate health and long-term care. Male–female differences in longevity, marital status, and income are central in assessing the impact of recent Medicaid cuts in nearly all states. Women outnumber men two to one among frail elders for whom health and long-term care use and costs are greatest. For example, white women living alone are more likely to use nursing homes and home health services, and for longer periods of time than white males. As more Medicare costs are shifted to the patient through higher copayments and deductibles, more low-income frail women may be unable to afford adequate care. (OWL, 2006).

Higher Incidence of Chronic Health Problems

Limited insurance options and greater dependence on Medicaid are especially problematic, because 85 percent of older women have a chronic disease or disability. A gender and health paradox is that while women are living longer than men, they have higher morbidity rates and, in later years, diminished quality of life. As described in Chapter 4, men experience more life-threatening diseases

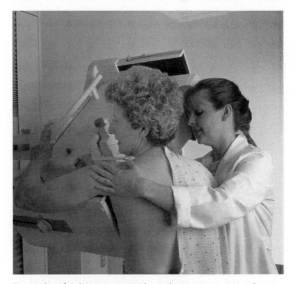

Screening for breast cancer is an important preventive health behavior.

(e.g., heart disease, stroke, and cancer), but are more prone to die from them earlier in life. Women are more likely to face the disabling effects of multiple chronic conditions as they age, particularly hypertension, osteoporosis, gastrointestinal disturbances, autoimmune diseases (e.g., thyroid, systemic lupus), and arthritis. Women also have more acute conditions such as upper respiratory infections. In terms of health trajectories, women face greater odds of functional impairment across time (Cruickshank, 2009; Federal Interagency Forum 2008; Harrington Meyer & Herd, 2008; Liang, 2008; Moen & Chermack, 2005; Rieker & Bird, 2005; Schoenborn, Vickerie, & Powell-Griner, 2006).

Heart disease is the number one killer for both men and women, In fact, older women are more likely to die from heart disease than all kinds of cancer combined. Yet health care providers and women themselves often fail to diagnose the warning signs, especially since symptoms often manifest as back pain for women rather than the chest and arm pain typically experienced by men. Women are less likely than men to be given clot-dissolving drugs during a heart attack and are referred less often for carotid surgery to prevent strokes (Cruikshank, 2009). The primary causes of heart disease are unhealthy diets and sedentary lifestyles, which affect cholesterol levels and blood pressure. The incidence of heart disease increases for women age 65 and over, so that rates are equal for men and women by age 85. This is because, as noted in Chapter 4, women lose the advantage of estrogen's protection against heart disease after menopause (Schoenborn et al., 2006; Wingert & Kantrowitz, 2006).

Women also face health problems specifically associated with their reproductive functions, such as breast, cervical, and uterine cancers, as well as high-risk complications from hysterectomies. Of women with breast cancer, 75 percent are over age 50. In the past 25 years, the chances of a woman developing breast cancer at some point in her life have doubled—from 1 in 16 to 1 in 8 (Horner et al., 2006)—while prevention, diagnosis, and treatment have lagged. One

improvement made by Congress in 1990 was to include **mammography** screening as a biennial Medicare full-coverage benefit. Yet many physicians still do not refer older women for mammography, even though yearly mammograms generally are recommended after age 40. Even when referred, some older women may not get a mammogram, mistakenly believing that they will not get breast cancer because of their age. In reality, the longer a woman lives, the more likely she is to develop breast cancer, although it may be slow growing. At least 50 percent of women diagnosed with breast cancer are age 65 and older. As another illustration of institutionalized ageism, older women are less likely than younger women to receive the more effective two-step procedure of biopsy followed by tumor removal than younger women. They are also less likely to undergo a lymph node dissection essential to treatment, and to be enrolled in clinical drug trials for treating breast cancer (Cruiskhank, 2009; Currey, 2008). A similar pattern is seen where women over age 60, who are most at risk of cancers of the reproductive system, are least likely to have annual pap smears (American Cancer Society, 2007).

Women's chronic health conditions, although not necessarily life-threatening, interfere with daily functioning (ADLs and IADLs), require frequent physician contacts, and can impair quality of life. Some studies find that older women also experience more injuries and more days of restricted activity and bed disability than older men. These measures are generally indicators of chronic disorders, such as high blood pressure and arthritis, although they may reflect women's greater readiness to take curative action and spend more time in bed recuperating when they are ill. Women are less likely than their male peers to engage in leisure-time physical activity, to become more sedentary with age (CDC, 2006). Nevertheless, they often walk and do yard work and household chores as a way to keep active. Women who begin an exercise program even in their 70s and 80s can still improve their fitness and strength (Cruikshank, 2009).

Women also suffer from more depressive disorders than men, as much as 50 to 100 percent greater (Kessler et al., 2003). Women's higher rates of depression reflect real gender-based differences across the life course in health rather than an artifact of variations of help-seeking behavior or willingness to report symptoms. These high rates are of concern because major depression is associated with increased mortality in general and cardiovascular disease in particular. Depression is also associated with immune function and disease severity by magnifying pain and disability. Pain and depression can, in turn, amplify each other. Depressed women are more likely than men to have comorbid anxiety, while men are more prone to comorbid substance abuse. While there are some psychosocial risk factors contributing to women's higher rates of depression, the determinants of these differences remain unclear. What is apparent, however, is that gender differences in mental health contribute in unknown ways to gendered patterns of physical health (Djernes, 2006; Gorman, 2006; Kessler et al., 2003; NIMH, 2009; Rieker & Bird, 2005).

Among people age 85 and over, gender differences in patterns of illness become even more striking, with oldest-old women more than twice as likely as men to enter a nursing home. Women comprise 75 to 80 percent of nursing home residents and 66 percent of home care consumers (Federal Interagency Forum, 2008). Several factors besides health status may account for such differences. As noted in Chapter 1, men who survive to age 75 and older are the healthiest and hardiest of their cohort. As discussed in Chapter 9, older men are more likely to be married, with wives to care for them at home instead of being placed in a long-term care facility. On the other hand, women over age 75, who have higher rates of functional disability than their male peers, have fewer available resources for home-based care and are often unable to afford private home health services.

There is no clear explanation for the **paradox of gender differences in health.** Biological explanations of the health advantages from different hormones and physiological systems that facilitate pregnancy and childbirth have been challenged by recent clinical trials of hormone replacement therapy (see Chapter 4). Evolutionary selection also does not explain differences in men's and women's longevity beyond prime reproductive age. Behavioral theories have focused on lifestyle, including men's higher rates of tobacco and alcohol use and their lower utilization of health services. Sociocultural and environmental theories emphasize social position or class as mediators, and point to environmental factors such as increased occupational hazards for men along with societal expectations for men to engage in more risk-taking behavior.

A growing body of research indicates that the complexity of health differences between men and women extends beyond narrow concepts of the relative disadvantage or advantage of men's and women's biology or how their lives are socially constructed. Several theories attempt to explain these variations. The model of **constrained choice** draws on both biological and social factors, whereby socially structured choices influence biological processes. These, in turn, affect psychological and physiological responses to stress, while gender differences in constraints contribute to health disparities by influencing men's and women's choices and cumulative biological risk (Rieker & Bird, 2005). A process mode of **strategic selection**—whereby the gendered nature of occupational and family-caregiving paths produces patterned disparities in a constellation of health-related resources, relationships, and risks as well as feelings of mastery and control—has also been proposed as a way to explain the paradoxes related to men's and women's health (Moen & Chermack, 2005). Given the range of factors identified in various models, it can be concluded that gender disparities in health are more complicated and nuanced than suggested by biological or medical explanations alone.

Some studies have discovered a "new paradox." Women generally rate their health as better than men, especially among the oldest-old, despite their greater functional impairment (Federal Interagency Forum, 2008). This suggests that associations between gender and health are not necessarily clear-cut and may not be in the direction commonly assumed: e.g., that women experience more health and mental health difficulties as they age. This also highlights the limitations of trying to make "all things equal" in a social order where gender remains such a powerful influence on life chances. Proponents of this gender-based approach also recognize the importance of considering race, class, and sexual orientation along with gender when examining health status (Calasanti & Slevin, 2006). We turn next to some health conditions experienced only or primarily by women.

Osteoporosis

As noted in Chapter 4, women comprise 80 percent of older people with osteoporosis. In fact, 25 percent of women over age 65 and 70 percent of women in their 80s have osteoporosis in their hips or spine. One in two women will have an osteoporosis-related fracture in their lifetime. Caucasian and Asian American women are more likely to develop osteoporosis than African American and Latina women (20 percent, 50 percent, 5 percent, and 10 percent, respectively) (National Osteoporosis Foundation, 2009; NIA, 2008). Over a lifetime, women lose nearly twice as much calcium as men (Cruikshank, 2009). Osteoporosis is called a silent disease because a woman feels no pain as her bones gradually thin to the point where even a slight bump or fit of coughing can cause a fracture. The higher incidence of wrist, spinal, and hip fractures related to postmenopausal osteoporosis is one reason for the greater number of injuries and days of restricted activity among older women. Spinal fractures that are frequent and severe enough to cause kyphosis or dowager's hump (loss of up to 8 inches in height) occur in 5 to 7 percent of women. Over 50 percent of postmenopausal Caucasian women are estimated to have at least one fracture of the spine, wrist, hip, or other bones in their lifetime. Of concern is the fact that the incidence of hip fractures in older women

> **LIFE-COURSE RISK FACTORS FOR OSTEOPOROSIS**
> - being female
> - advanced age
> - family history of osteoporosis
> - smoker; moderate or heavy drinker
> - Caucasian or Asian descent
> - weighing less than 127 pounds; thin, small-boned
> - sedentary lifestyle with little exercise
> - cessation of menstrual periods because of strenuous exercise or dieting
> - low estrogen after premature or surgically induced menopause
> - history of anorexia or bulimia
> - taking steroids, thyroid hormone, or other medicines that can cause osteoporosis
> - a history of fractures, especially from low-impact trauma

doubles every 5 years after the age of 60 (NIA, 2008). The threat of hip fractures can create numerous fears and losses and circumscribe older women's social world—especially because half of those affected lose the ability to walk independently. Indeed, about 24 percent of older patients with hip fractures die within a year from fracture or surgery-related conditions (National Osteoporosis Foundation, 2009).

Since women can lose up to 5 percent of bone mass per year after the menopause, the case for and against hormone replacement therapy (HRT), as discussed in Chapter 4, is not clear-cut. HRT can increase bone mass in the spine and hip by 3 to 5 percent in the first year; this gain is maintained as long as the individual takes hormones. These benefits decline, however, after age 75, when women are most at risk. Because of growing concern about the risk of breast cancer, heart attack, and strokes from HRT, the treatments now recommended to reduce bone loss are diet (increased calcium and vitamin D), calcium supplements, and exercise (NIA, 2008). Fortunately, increasing attention is directed toward both the prevention and treatment of osteoporosis, in large

PREVENTING OSTEOPOROSIS AND RELATED INJURIES

- Be physically active through weight-bearing and strength-training exercises (brisk walking, running, hiking, dancing, climbing stairs, lifting weights, and jumping rope).
- Do not smoke, because smoking weakens bones.
- Get enough calcium (1200–1500 mg) and vitamin D (400–800 mg) through supplements, but do not exceed recommended daily allowances for women.
- Eat yogurt, milk, cheese, sardines, dry roasted soybeans, or leafy green vegetables, which are high in calcium and vitamin D.
- Prevent falls:
  - Avoid high-heeled or loose-fitting shoes, throw rugs, slippery bathtubs, and wet steps.
  - Turn on lights when the room is dark; move things that one could trip on; use nonslip bathmats and bathroom grab bars.
  - Talk to your health care provider about cutting down on drugs that make you more likely to fall and those that lead to bone loss (pain and sleep medications, steroids, epilepsy medicines, and thyroid hormones).

Menopause

The physiological changes associated with menopause were discussed in detail in Chapters 3 and 7. Menopausal symptoms provide another example of the interaction of normal physiological changes with psychological conditions and societal and cultural expectations. For example, many of the discomforts associated with menopause result from Western society's tendency to view it as a disease rather than a normal biological process. Hence, many women assume that depression, loss of sexual desire and sexual attractiveness, and such signs of aging as wrinkled skin and weight gain are inevitable with menopause. Contrary to such expectations, menopause is not an illness or a deficiency, and major mood problems may never

NONMEDICAL APPROACHES TO MENOPAUSE

- Hypnosis, meditation, biofeedback, acupuncture, paced respiration, and muscle relaxation techniques
- Exercise, aerobic and weight-bearing, with paced respiration
- Support groups and use of humor
- Vitamin E to alleviate hot flashes
- Dietary changes to increase intake of vegetables and reduce fats, preservatives, caffeine, alcohol, and spicy foods while increasing fiber, calcium, soy (through tofu, soy milk, tempeh, miso)
- Layered lightweight clothing, portable fans, lightweight blankets for sleeping
- Certain antidepressants and the antiseizure medication gabapentin
- Herbal remedies such as black cohosh roots to reduce hot flashes; kava to minimize mood swings, irritability, and stress; St. John's wort for depression and anxiety. Despite the growing popularity of herbal approaches, most herbs sold in health food stores (as capsules, teas, tinctures, extracts, or infusions) are not regulated by the Food and Drug Administration and have not been tested adequately for effectiveness. Caution also needs to be exercised in terms of possible interactions with prescription medications (Cruikshank, 2009; Manson & Bassuk, 2006; NIA, 2004, 2008).

part because of the escalating health care costs associated with bone fractures. Bone density tests, including x-rays, CT scans, and ultrasound, are now covered by Medicare. The National Osteoporosis Foundation recommends testing all women age 65 and over, as well as younger postmenopausal women who are small-boned, have low estrogen levels, or a family history of the disease. Yet only about 20 percent of eligible Medicare patients have their bone density measured (National Osteoporosis Foundation, 2009). Osteoporosis education is now more widely available, but the extent to which it has increased preventive health behaviors, such as exercise and healthy eating, is unclear More detailed information about osteoporosis can be found in Chapter 4.

occur. With 30 to 50 percent of women having no symptoms as they pass into menopause, many find that it is a positive transition that brings a renewed sense of living and time for oneself, or what anthropologist Margaret Mead termed postmenopausal zest (Gonyea, 1998). For most women, menopause is a critical life juncture, when their choices can shape their physical and emotional lives for years to come.

The culturally prevalent model of menopause as a disease attributes changes to loss of estrogen. When it is thus defined as a "deficiency disease," the implication for treating symptoms has been to replace estrogen. On the other hand, if menopause is viewed as a normative life transition, lower estrogen levels among postmenopausal women can be considered normal. As shown in the box on page 675, women increasingly use nonmedical approaches to minimize uncomfortable symptoms. However, the safety and effectiveness of these alternative therapies have not been fully determined. For example, in a study of 351 women suffering from hot flashes and night sweats, those taking a placebo achieved approximately the same relief as those given the herbal treatment black cohosh (Newton et al., 2006). Menopausal women may find that behavioral changes—dressing in layers of light clothing, sleeping in a cooler room, and avoiding triggers such as hot liquids and alcohol—are an effective way to deal with hot flashes. Larger lifestyle changes—such as intensifying levels of aerobic exercise and weight training, reducing stress, losing weight, pursuing a healthy diet of vegetables, fruit, whole grains, and low-fat dairy products, and stopping smoking—may be the most effective and safest approach to minimizing menopausal symptoms (Manson & Bassuk, 2006).

Although the disease model of menopause suggests that endocrine changes are responsible for depression, this condition in postmenopausal women appears to be more closely associated with psychosocial conditions, particularly changes in women's roles and relationships, than with physiological factors. Those at highest risk are women who have had prior episodes of depression, especially during other periods of hormonal fluctuation (e.g., postpartum depression), those with poor social supports, and those who experience menopause at a younger age. However, menopause itself is *not* a risk factor for depression (NIMH, 2009). Health care providers have often treated the symptoms of depression with drugs or have assumed that postmenopausal women were "too old" to benefit from therapeutic interventions. More recently, efforts have been made to assist women with developing problem-solving skills to exert control over their lives, and to provide cognitive behavioral counseling and social support interventions as a means of combating depression. Support groups can reduce women's feelings of isolation and enhance their self-esteem and self-efficacy (Arthur, 2006; Shearer & Fleury, 2006). Unfortu- nately, women do not always receive user-friendly information for coping with menopause. This is a concern especially for women for whom English is a second language. Some doctors do not talk about alternative methods for mana- ging meno- pausal reactions such as hot flashes or mood swings. In addition, nonmenopausal health conditions may be ignored because they are attributed to the "change of life." Increasingly, middle-aged women are proactive in seeking accurate information, often from the Internet, about what to expect, what therapies work, and their risks and benefits. Regardless of age and marital or socioeconomic status (SES), women can take steps that help active aging.

Older Women's Social Status

Approximately 39 percent of older women (compared to 19 percent of older men) live alone for nearly one-third of their adult lives, primarily because of widowhood or divorce; about 4 percent have never married. With increased longevity, divorced or widowed women are living alone for longer periods of time than ever before. In fact, only about 42 percent of all women age 65 and older live with their spouses, compared to 73 percent of

PLANNING PROACTIVELY FOR ACTIVE AGING

- Promote your health through diet, weight-bearing exercise, stress reduction such as meditation, and screening tests such as mammograms.
- Improve your skills (e.g., computer literacy, health literacy).
- Maximize your workplace benefits.
- Learn as much as you can about your retirement income (i.e., financial literacy).
- Take charge of your finances. This does not mean managing everything on your own, but locating the information and advice needed for making informed decisions.
- Determine if you are eligible for public benefits such as food stamps or Medicaid.
- Research your housing options.
- Learn about resources to assist with caregiving.
- Be prepared for changes in your marital status.
- Continue to build your informal support networks, including with younger members.
- Protect yourself through safety strategies.

men. Only 17 percent live with other family members, generally a daughter. Among women age 75 and over, the proportion living with a spouse drops to less than 30 percent, compared with 70 percent of men; and those living alone increases to approximately 57 percent, a rate almost twice that of older men. Only about 3 percent of older women live with nonrelatives, although a growing number say they would consider asking a friend for assistance and view living with other women as a desirable option (AARP, 2006; AOA, 2008).

Women living alone are four times as likely to be poor as couples. Living alone in itself does not necessarily translate into low SES and loneliness for women; nor does it cause functional health to deteriorate (Harrington Meyer & Herd, 2008). For example, never-married single women in old age have typically developed skills and resources earlier in life, such as autonomy and self-reliance, which prepare them for a lifetime of singlehood. Because the never-married have not experienced marital dissolution and its associated stressors,

they may also feel less strain from living alone as they age than their widowed or divorced peers. Given a higher ratio of women to men, African American women are more likely to never marry compared to whites and less likely to perceive singlehood as a source of strain. Women who were employed throughout their lives may enjoy more stable and secure financial circumstances, higher levels of education, and better health than do widowed, separated, and divorced women. In addition, single women, especially African Americans, often maintain extensive social networks of friends, neighbors, and siblings, as well as levels of social participation in old age that are comparable to those established earlier in life. Such support systems may prevent relocation to a long-term care facility among the young-old, although this social network advantage probably disappears among the oldest-old. The negative consequences of living alone are probably greatest for those who were previously married and unaccustomed to being alone (Pudrovska, Schieman, & Carr, 2006).

Older women of color, especially African American and Latina women who are divorced and widowed, are more likely to live in extended family households with children, grandchildren, other relatives, and fictive kin. As described in Chapters 9 and 14, women of color often extend their households to include children and grandchildren, assuming child care and housekeeping responsibilities into old age. Such grandparenting and caregiving responsibilities can have negative consequences for women's health and finances, although the types of supports and services for grandmothers are increasing.

Widowhood

As discussed in Chapter 13, widowhood is primarily a female experience: 85 percent of all wives outlive their husbands and the average age of widowhood in a first marriage is 59 years. This long-standing pattern results from the fact that women generally marry men older than themselves, live longer than men, and, in their later years, seldom remarry after the death of their husbands. Some 42 percent of women age 65 and older are widowed, in contrast to 13 percent of men in this age-group; this gap increases dramatically with age. Expected years of widowhood are far more than the 7-year difference in life expectancy between women and men at these ages, with some women living up to a third of their lives as widows. Not surprisingly, after age 85, 57 percent of women live alone compared to 30 percent of men (U.S. Census Bureau, 2006). Moreover, this increased time living alone is accompanied by shrinking family size and reduced income, with fewer children available as potential caregivers. The probability of widowhood increases among older women of color; for example, approximately 75 percent of African American women over age 75 are widows (AOA, 2008; Federal Interagency Forum, 2008; Kreider, 2005).

As noted in our discussion of Social Security, the primary negative consequence of widowhood is low SES, with the majority of women becoming poor after they have been widowed. Women who have been widowed longest have the highest poverty rate; within this grouping, women who were widowed in their 50s are among the poorest, often having depleted their assets by the time they reach old age (Cruikshank, 2009; Harrington Meyer & Herd, 2008). Economic status has numerous social implications. Low-income women generally have fewer options for social interactions, affordable and safe living situations, and resources to purchase in-home support services. The worst outcome of widowhood is that their changed economic situation may preclude women from continuing to live autonomously when health problems arise. In fact, widowhood can result in increased health service use and costs and, in some instances, higher rates of hospitalization (Laditka & Laditka, 2003).

Despite these objective disadvantages of widowhood, the "lonely widow" appears to be a stereotype, and widowhood does not necessarily produce the major, enduring negative emotional effects typically assumed. Instead, over the long term, widowhood may represent a positive shift into a new life phase, especially for women who may have felt constrained in their marriages. A growing body of research indicates that, overall, women living alone feel psychologically secure and positive about their lives (AARP, 2006; Carr, 2004a; Cheng, 2006; Cruikshank, 2009).

Limited Opportunities to Remarry

Although remarriage may be viewed as a way to ensure economic security, older widowed and divorced women have fewer remarriage options than do their male peers, as noted in Chapter 9. In addition, they may choose *not* to remarry, either because their marriage was not a positive experience, they now enjoy being on their own, or they do not want to care for an ill or disabled husband. Widowed and divorced men are more likely to remarry than women, especially men with more resources (Pudrovska et al., 2006). The primary obstacles to remarriage for older women are their disproportionate numbers to men and the cultural stigma against women dating and marrying younger men. With a three to one ratio of 80-year-old women to men, their chances for remarriage decline drastically with increasing age. Women who do remarry generally enjoy higher incomes and worry less about finances than those who do not (Moorman, Booth, & Fingerman, 2006).

According to the Changing Lives of Older Couples study, men's interest in dating and remarriage is conditional on the amount of social support received from friends. Six months after spousal loss, only those men with low or average levels of social support from friends report an interest in remarrying someday. Similar patterns emerge for interest in dating 18 months after losing a spouse. Persons who both want and have a romantic relationship report significantly fewer depressive symptoms 18 months after loss, yet this low prevalence is attributable to their greater socioeconomic resources (Carr, 2004b). Such gender and class differences lead to differential needs for support in the face of failing health; most older men are cared for by their wives, whereas most older women rely on their children, usually daughters, for help. Increasingly, adult daughters who assist their widowed mothers are themselves in their 60s or even early 70s and are faced with their own physical limitations. As a result, older women may have to depend more on publicly funded support services available through the Aging Network—described in Chapter 16. As discussed in Chapter 10, women's work as invisible laborers is essential to their relatives' long-term care, but it is not adequately supported by public policies.

In the future, the proportion of older women living alone, including those unmarried throughout their adult lives, will rise more dramatically because of more women living alone across the life course and the growing rates of divorce earlier in life. As noted earlier, the absence of children and a partner also increases the chance of moving into a long-term care facility. This suggests that women may be in such settings for social rather than medical reasons and may be inappropriately placed, when alternative community supports might have permitted more autonomous lifestyles.

Informal Networks and Social Support

In general, older women have fewer economic but more social resources and richer, more intimate informal networks than do older men. Their social

Long-term friendships can provide older women with ongoing strength and support.

networks are larger and more diverse, including more people whom they consider very close. The mutuality and voluntary nature of friendships are highly valued, although the benefits of social support vary with the nature and size of women's networks. Social connectedness is found to buffer some of the adverse effects of widowhood for recently bereaved women, including the risk of hospitalization and health problems (Laditka & Laditka, 2003; Miller, Smerglia, & Bouche, 2004). Some research suggests that women respond to stressful life events by "tending and befriending" rather than men's tendency to "fight and flight" (Taylor et al., 2000). Men's and women's networks result from gender-differentiated experiences within various roles and resulting opportunities for establishing

FORMATION OF COMMUNITY AMONG OLDER WOMEN IN A BEAUTY SHOP

An unintentional community of older women often forms in a beauty shop, based on a shared meaning as mothers, housewives, and caregivers in a society that expects women to be attractive, despite the realities of aging and physical decline. Women in a beauty shop are brought together around a common concern with appearance as a source of self-worth and with taking care of themselves. The face and the body are used to maintain self-respect and community status. Friendships developed in the beauty shop illustrate the diversity of women's connectedness and their varied expressions of mutual support and caring. They talk about illness, aches, and pains, experiencing an outlet for topics they don't feel comfortable discussing with family. Discursive personal stories permit exchange of lived experiences and strengthen social bonds. Shows of physical and verbal affection, humor about the inevitability of wrinkles, sags, and bags, and shared food further strengthen social ties. The beauty shop is a search for a good old age among women disadvantaged by age and gender. In the process of seeking beauty, the women gain a sense of belonging, affirmation, and being cared for. The beauty shop thus also acts as a community of resistance against being old and female in a gendered society.

SOURCE: Adapted from Markson, 1999.

social networks (Ajrouch, Blandon, & Antonucci, 2005). Men tend to have larger non-kin networks, perhaps as a result of employment, but are less resourceful in planning social get-togethers and building networks that substitute for the sociability they typically enjoy in marriage. Even when their friends die, women generally establish new relationships, exchanging affection and material support outside their families, although they may not want to call upon such relationships to care for them (Blieszner, 2006; Shaw et al., 2007). Widowed women in particular and women in retirement communities generally have frequent and intimate contacts with friends. One reason for this is that age-segregated communities provide women with peers at the same stage of life and with similar experiences. A study of female participants in senior center activities who live alone documented their ability to form late-life friendships, which then extended outside the center and had positive effects on their mental and physical well-being (Aday, Kehoe, & Farner, 2006). Simi- larly, support groups for widows and family caregivers build on such reciprocal exchange relations among peers to enhance self-efficacy and personal competence.

In general, social networks and self-efficacy are found to be associated with life satisfaction and improved health outcomes (Antonucci, Birditt, & Akiyama, 2009; Blazer, 2002; Ferreria & Sherman, 2006; Greaves & Farbus, 2006; Stevens, Martina, & Westerhof, 2006). A study of quilting groups among Amish, Appalachian, and Latter Day Saints women identified extensive horizontal and vertical relationships and a sense of collectivity toward others. Specifically, quilting group members exhibited generativity by teaching their skills to others, building bonds with grandchildren through quilting, and leaving legacies through their quilts. Friendships developed with other quilters provided social support to deal with life challenges (Piercy & Cheek, 2004). Some programs specifically seek to enrich friendship and reduce loneliness among women in later life, as a component of active aging (Cattan et al., 2005). One goal-setting intervention found that a combination of developing new friendships and improving existing ones significantly reduced loneliness within a year (Stevens, et al., 2006). Other

> **OLDER WOMEN'S POSITIVE NETWORKS**
>
> I have friends. I have organizational things that I join. I do belong to one senior group, which is very heavily female. You have to build a new network after being widowed. And that's really very important to do. It's helpful because within that network, there's always someone who has been down that road before you (74-year-old respondent to 2006 AARP Survey, p. 19).
>
> I admire a lady down the block from me who's in her 80s. She's ramrod straight. I'm trying to be like her. She lives alone, with grandchildren coming and going. She's an interesting person to talk to. She'll talk about the neighborhood or politics or where she's going next on one of her trips. She drives all over the place. She has a friend out of state she goes and visits. And I thought, that's great. I hope when I'm 80-something, I can do that too (77-year-old respondent to 2006 AARP Survey, p. 18).
>
> [In anticipation of a long life] I keep telling my friends that we all need to buy a big house with a common area downstairs and live together—not like a nursing home, but truly a place where we have communal living....It just doesn't make sense having all these women living alone in these big houses. It would be nice to have some kind of pooled arrangements specifically built for people who want some sense of sharing but do not want to give up their privacy (57-year-old respondent to 2006 AARP Survey, p. 68).

interventions to minimize social isolation among women note greater self-efficacy, resulting in more health-promoting behaviors and better health outcomes (Greaves & Farbus, 2006; Shearer & Fleury, 2006). Increasingly, women across diverse cultural groups also rely on fictive or chosen kin for reciprocal support (Jordon-Marsh & Harden, 2005).

One function of the affirmation of women's competencies by the feminist movement has been to encourage support for each other rather than depending primarily on men. This is evidenced by the growth of shared households, cohousing, older women's support and advocacy groups, groups for caregiving grandmothers, and intergenerational alliances between younger and older women. Increasingly, shared housing has both companionship and financial benefits (AARP,

2006). Many baby boomers want to create new communities for both intellectual stimulation and social support but without the medical connotation of assisted living or retirement homes. Furthermore, as noted in Chapter 9, some women first become comfortable with being open about their lesbianism and their strong emotional bonds with other women in old age. This includes women who earlier in their lives were married, had children, and later accepted their attraction to women, as well as those who lived with women all their lives and had well-established social networks but who hid their identity from coworkers and family. For many in the current cohort, to be "out" publicly was to risk discrimination and marginalization. "When I was in school and I was a teacher—you did not—you were not out. If you were, you were unemployed and not admitted in polite society" (Classen, 2005, p. 238). Coming out for this cohort of older lesbians was typically not about gay pride, but rather an individual process of increasing awareness of who they are, acknowledging their sexual orientation to themselves, and becoming comfortable with it. Despite growing old in a society that criminalized homosexuality, they manage by finding "others of their kind" and display resilience, in part because of the obstacles they faced in the past (Clunis et al., 2005; Heaphy, 2007). Overall, lesbian and heterosexual older women share many of the same concerns about aging because, as we have seen throughout this chapter, all older women's lives are distinctly structured by gender (Cruikshank, 2009; Thompson, 2006).

Consistent with feminist gerontology theory, discussed in Chapter 8, a feminist analysis of older women's social status would articulate their strengths and resilience as well as their vulnerabilities. To be old is defined by our society as being limited in functional ability; but most older women, despite economic and health obstacles, are active, competent, surrounded by other long-living women, and find meaning and spiritual resilience in their lives (Calasanti, 2009). Although cohort, period, and gender-based life circumstances mold older women, they are not passive. By studying gender and age power differentials, feminists seek to deepen our understanding of both women and men, their uniqueness, and their similarities in actively meeting life's challenges (Calasanti & Slevin; 2006).

Feminists are also developing an area of inquiry called **"age studies"** that is less concerned with biological markers than with identifying and critiquing the social meanings ascribed to age (Gullette, 1998; Woodward, 1998). A growing body of feminist research on the aging body or the "rejected body," with its subtext of inactivity, disability, and incompetence, rejects the physical self and focuses on the "actual or inner self." From feminist and social constructionist perspectives, "old" is a label assigned by younger people on the basis of surface appearance and function. It does not accurately describe many women's subjective experience of aging, which often is not centered on the body and how they look (Morell, 2003). Think of women you may know who say, "I don't feel old, until I look in a mirror." A sense of personal power is achieved when a woman refuses to identify primarily with her body. Instead, women who define themselves in terms of an "able self" enjoy new experiences, learning, and relationships. Even women with physical limitations derive meaning from the activities they can continue to do and the adversities that they have overcome.

The concept of an "able self" is also consistent with the theory of gerotranscendence that focuses on inner changes, as described in Chapter 8. While an empowerment approach emphasizes strengths and overcoming limitations, the inevitability of death also must be acknowledged. Some feminists now argue for destigmatizing disability and death, and transforming these into acceptable human experiences shared by all. A dialectical approach to empowerment openly acknowledges the physical changes associated with aging but seeks to integrate power and powerlessness, strength and weakness, life energy and death, and power and vulnerability (Calasanti, 2009). This approach is also congruent with the postmodern perspective discussed in Chapter 8 that views the "aging body" as a social and cultural phenomenon that affects the social construction of the aging identity. Postmodernists maintain that even though physical appearance changes with age, a person's essential identity

Group exercise offers physical and social benefits.

CHANGING CONCEPTS OF BEAUTY AND AGE

Feminist Gloria Steinem, when told that she looked really good for her age, responded, "This is what 60 looks like on me." Model Lauren Hutton, who returned to modeling at age 44, remembers opening the *New York Times Magazine* and seeing a beautiful old face and realizing it was herself. She is now in her 60s and considering returning to modeling. One of her reasons: "It's good to show what beauty is— all ages, all sizes" (Sherill, 2003). Although these women have the financial and social resources to purchase numerous anti-aging products and surgeries, both are conveying a more positive image of older women—celebrating their age rather than focusing on looking younger.

does not (Longino & Powell, 2004; Powell, 2006). As noted on page 678, a survey of midlife and older women provides empirical evidence that many women are thriving, but less so women of color and those with limited retirement income. Even women living alone in this national sample considered their older years as a time to pursue activities that they had always wanted to do (AARP, 2006).

Implications for the Future

Since women's SES compounds problems they face in old age, fundamental changes are needed to remove inequities in the workplace, Social Security, and pension systems. Most such changes, however, will benefit future generations of older women rather than the current cohort over age 75, which was socialized for employment and family roles that no longer prevail. For example, efforts in some states to assure that women and men earn equal pay for jobs of comparable economic worth and to remove other salary inequities may mean that future generations of older women will have retirement benefits based on a lifetime of more adequate earnings and will have more experience in handling finances. Some businesses and government agencies have initiated more flexible work

arrangements with full benefits, which will allow men and women to share employment and family responsibilities more equitably. Recent national and state legislation to increase the minimum wage, including that of direct care workers, will have more economic repercussions for women across the life course than men, because women predominate in low-wage positions.

When such options exist, women may have fewer years of zero earnings to be calculated into their Social Security benefits. Even so, it is predicted that 60 percent of women in the year 2030 will still have 5 or more years of zero earnings averaged into the calculation of their Social Security benefits. This will widen the current gap between older women living alone, married women, and most men (Herd, 2006). This is in large part due to the fact that despite 4 decades of federal legislation, women have not achieved equality in the workforce, still earning less than their male counterparts. Women remain disproportionately in the secondary service sector, marked by low wages, few benefits, part-time employment, and little security. Even the growth of women college graduates and the entrance of more women into previously male-dominated positions has not resulted in a significant restructuring of the distribution of roles within families. In fact, a 2009 report found women particularly stressed by their multiple demands during the 2008–2009 recession (Shriver, 2009).

As noted above, changes in Social Security to benefit women workers have been proposed by federal studies and commissions. The current Social Security system is based on an outmoded model of lifelong marriage, in which one spouse, typically the husband, is the paid worker and the other is the homemaker. As the prior discussion of divorce and changing work patterns suggests, this model no longer accommodates the emerging diversity of employment and family roles. Nor, for that matter, has this model ever represented the diversity of American families. Credits for homemaking and dependent care across the life course, partial benefits for widows under age 62, full benefits for widows after age 65, and the option of collecting benefits as both worker and wife have been proposed by advocacy groups and some policy makers. The likelihood of any such changes being instituted in the future is small, given the record-high federal deficit and the economic crisis of 2008–2009. Instead, more women are losing jobs—as businesses close and downsize—than at any point in recent history.

More corporations and state and local governments in recent years have eliminated pensions for their employees. When pensions do exist, men benefit more than women, although the loss of retirement income through private investments has changed that pattern. In the long run, more fundamental changes are needed in society's view of work throughout the life course, so that men and women may share more equitably in caregiving and employment responsibilities. At the same time, employers must value skills gained through homemaking and volunteer activity as transferable to the marketplace. As discussed in Chapters 9 and 12, the ways in which women contribute to society through their volunteerism, caregiving, housekeeping responsibilities, and informal helping of others need to be recognized under a broader view of productivity rather than only equating productivity with paid work.

Another positive direction is that despite our societal emphasis on physical appearance, more women are comfortable with their aging and accept its visible signs, such as wrinkles and gray hair. They value exercise, nutrition, and meditation as pathways to better health and personal growth, not simply as a way to look younger. Freed from past roles as primarily a wife or mother, they discover strength from learning who they are and sharing their feelings, insights, and fears about aging with each other. Some women collectively identify themselves as "crones" or "sages," rejecting past stereotypes and restoring images of wisdom, honor, and respect to being an older woman. Fortunately, some women who are highly visible—including actresses such as Sally Field and Helen Mirren, who have agreed not to use anti-aging treatments—are also helping to change concepts of old age for women. Another positive trajectory is that older female baby boomers will probably be healthier than current cohorts. Nevertheless, the sheer number of female boomers means that many will still face chronic illness or disability, although perhaps later in life than current cohorts. And the rising rates of obesity among younger and middle-aged women are threatening their future health.

Because of lower rates of marriage, increasing divorce, and growing numbers of single mothers, more women will enter old age accustomed to living alone, even though they may bring fewer economic resources to old age because they are the sole earner. Perhaps because of more years on their own, women of all ages are increasingly supporting one another, as illustrated by the intergenerational advocacy efforts of the Older Women's League, cross-generational support groups, and cohousing for women. Groups of widows and women caregivers encourage members to express their needs and expand women's awareness of available formal support services. This function of educating and politicizing older women also helps many to see the societal or structural causes of the difficulties they have personally experienced. Awareness of external causes of their problems may serve to bring together for common action women of diverse ages, races, social classes, sexual orientations, and functional abilities. Cross-cultural evidence shows that age permits women in a wide range of cultures to experience increased freedom and to become more dominant and powerful, with fewer restrictions on their behavior and mobility, as well as expanded opportunities to engage in roles outside the home. Growing numbers of older women are aiming to resist denigration and invisibility. As women unite to work for social change, they can make further progress in reducing the disadvantages of their economic and social position.

Summary

Older women are the fastest-growing segment of our population, making the aging society primarily female. In addition, the problems of aging are increasingly the problems of women. Threats to Social Security, inadequate health and long-term care, insufficient pensions, and loss of retirement income are issues for women of all ages. Increasingly, older women are not only the recipients of social and health services, but are also cared for by other women who are unpaid daughters and daughters-in-law, or underpaid direct care staff within public social services, hospitals, and long-term care facilities.

Women's family caregiving roles are interconnected with their economic, social, and health status. Women who devoted their lives to attending to the needs of children, spouses, partners, and family members with developmental disabilities or mental illness, or caring for older relatives, often face years of living alone on low or poverty-level incomes, with inadequate health care, in substandard housing, and with little chance for employment to supplement their limited resources. Women face more problems in old age, not only because they live longer than their male peers, but also because, as unpaid or underpaid caregivers with discontinuous employment histories, they have not accrued adequate retirement or health care benefits. If they depended on their husbands for economic security, divorce or widowhood increases their risks of poverty. As one of the poorest groups in our society, women account for the majority of the older poor. The incidence of problems associated with poverty increases dramatically for older women living alone, for women of color, and

for those 75 years and older. Frequently outliving their husbands and sometimes their children, they have no one to care for them and are more likely than their male counterparts to live in long-term care facilities.

On the other hand, many women show remarkable resilience in the face of adversity. With their lifelong experiences of caring for others, for example, women tend to be skilled at forming and sustaining friendships, which provide them with social support and intimacy. Increasing attention is now being given to older women's capacity for change and to their strengths, in part because of the population growth of baby boomers and efforts of national advocacy groups such as the Older Women's League. Current efforts to expand employment and educational opportunities for younger women will eventually mean improved economic, social, and health status for future generations of women, but these changes will occur slowly.

GLOSSARY

age studies an area of study developed by feminists that is less concerned with biological markers than with identifying and critiquing the social meanings ascribed to age

constrained choice model structural factors affect health care choices and biological risk

conversion laws legal requirement for insurance companies to allow widowed, divorced, and separated women to remain on their spouses' group insurance for up to 3 years

dependent care credits proposed change to Social Security where women would receive benefits based on workforce and family care contributions

earnings sharing proposed change in Social Security whereby each partner in a marriage is entitled to a separate Social Security account, regardless of employment status

gendered nature of the life course ways in which gender, which is socially constructed, influences women's caregiving, employment, income and retirement a cross the life course

mammography an X-ray technique for the detection of breast tumors before they can be seen or felt

Older Women's League (OWL) a national educational and advocacy organization on issues affecting older women

paradox of gender differences in health women live longer than men but have higher morbidity rates

spousal consent requirement federal law requiring that a spouse must agree to waiving survivor's benefits from Social Security; not true of state government pension plans

strategic selection a process by which the gendered nature of occupational and family-caregiving paths produce patterned disparities in health-related resources, relationships, risks, and feelings of mastery and control

RESOURCES

Log on to MySocKit (www.mysockit.com) for information about the following:

- AARP Women's Leadership Circle (WLC)
- Institute for Women's Policy Research
- National Black Women's Health Project
- National Program on Women and Aging
- National Women's Health Network
- Older Women's League
- Women's Institute for a Secure Retirement (WISER)

REFERENCES

AARP. (2006). *Looking at Act II of women's lives: Thriving and striving from 45 on.* The AARP Foundation Women's Leadership Circle Study.

Aday, R., Kehoe, G., & Farner, L. (2006). Impact of senior center friendships on aging women who live alone. *Journal of Women and Aging, 18,* 57–73.

Administration on Aging (AOA). (2008). *Profile of older American: 2008s.* Washington, DC: Author.

Ajrouch, K., Blandon, A., & Antonucci, T. (2005). Social networks among men and women: The effects of age and socioeconomic status.

Journal of Gerontology: Social Sciences, 60B, S311–S317.

American Association of University Women. (2007). *Behind the Pay Gap.* Press Release: Women earn less even when working in the same career field, likely due to sex discrimination. Retrieved July, 2009, from http://www.aauw.org/about/newsroom//pressreleases/042307_PayGap.cfm

American Cancer Society. (2007). *Cancer facts and figures.* Atlanta: American Cancer Society.

Arthur, H. (2006). Depression, isolation, social support and cardiovascular disease in older adults. *Journal of Cardiovascular Nursing, 21,* S2–S7.

Avison, W. & Davies, L. (2005). Family structure, gender and health in the context of the life course. *Journal of Gerontology, Special Issue on Health Inequalities across the Life Course, 60B,* 113–116.

Blazer, D. (2002). Self-efficacy and depression in later life: A primary prevention proposal. *Aging & Mental Health, 6,* 315–324.

Calasanti, T. M. (2009). Theorizing, feminist gerontology, sexuality and beyond. (2nd ed). In V. L. Bengtson, D. Gans, N. M. Putney, & M. Silverstein (Eds.). Handbook of theories of aging (2nd ed). New York: Springer.

Calasanti, T. M. & Slevin, K. F. (2006). Age matters: Realigning feminist thinking. New York: Routledge.

Carr, D. (2004a). Gender, pre-loss marital dependence and older adults' adjustment to widowhood. *Journal of Marriage and the Family, 66,* 220–235.

Carr, D. (2004b). The desire to date and remarry among older widows and widowers. *Journal of Marriage and Family, 66,* 1051–1068.

Cattan, M., White, M., Bond, J., & Learmouth, C. (2005). Preventing social isolation among older people: A systematic review of health promotion interventions. *Ageing and Society, 25,* 41–67.

Centers for Disease Control and Prevention (CDC). (2006). *Health characteristics of adults 55 years of age and over: United States, 2000–2003. Advance data from vital and health statistics;* No. 370. Hyattsville, MD: National Center for Health Statistics.

Cheng, C. (2006). Living alone: The choice and health of older women. *Journal of Gerontological Nursing, 32,* 24–25.

Christopher, G. C. (2006). Medicare Part D: A woman's issue. *Joint Center Focus Magazine*, 34(3). Retrieved February, 2007, from http://www. jointcenter.org/publications1/focus/

Clunis, D., Fredriksen-Goldsen, K., Freeman, P., & Nystrom, N. (2005). *Lives of lesbian elders: Looking back, looking forward.* Binghamton, NY: Haworth Press.

Code, L. (2006). Women knowing/knowing women: Critical-creative interventions in the politics of knowledge. In K. Davis, M. Evans & J. Lorber (Eds.). *Handbook of gender and women's studies.* London: Sage.

Connidis, I. A. (2009). *Family ties and aging.* (2nd ed). Thousand Oaks, CA: Sage.

Cruikshank, M. (2009). *Learning to be old: Gender, culture and aging* (2nd ed.). New York: Rowman & Littlefield.

Currey, R. (2008). Ageism in health care: Time for a change. *Aging Well*, 1, 16–21.

Djernes, J. K. (2006). Prevalence and predictors of depression in populations of elderly: A review. *Acta Psychiatrica Scandinavica*, 113, 372–387.

Favreault, M. M. (2009). *Supplementary Security Income benefit payments as stimulus.* Washington, DC: The Urban Institute. Retrieved July 2009, from http://www.urban.org/retirement_policy/recovery.cfm

Favreault, M. M. & Sammartino, F. J. (2002). *Impact of Social Security reform on low-income and older women.* Washington, DC. Public Policy Institute, AARP.

Federal Interagency Forum on Aging. (2008). *Older Americans 2008: Key indicators of well-being.* Hyattsville, MD: Federal Interagency Forum on Aging and Related Statistics.

Finkel, D. (2003, October 7). Stuck behind the counter. Retirement is an elusive dream for women. *The Seattle Times*, p. A3.

Flippen, C. (2005). Minority workers and pathways to retirement. In R. Hudson (Ed.). *The new politics of old age policy.* Baltimore: John Hopkins.

Gonyea, J. & Hooyman, N. (2005). Reducing poverty among older women: The importance of Social Security. *Families in Society*, 86, 338–346.

Gorman, J. M. (2006). Gender differences in depression and response to psychotropic medication. *Gender Medicine*, 3, 93–109.

Greaves, C. & Farbus, L. (2006). Effects of creative and social activity on the health and well-being of socially isolated older people: Outcomes from a multi-method observational study. *Journal of Research on Social Health*, 126, 134–142.

Hartmann, H. & English, A. (2009). Older women's retirement security: A primer. *Journal of Women, Politics & Policy*, 30, 109–140.

Heaphy, B. (2007). Sexualities, gender and ageing: Resources and social change. *Current Sociology*, 55, 193–201.

Heinz, T., Lewis, J., & Hounsell, C. (2006). *Women and pensions: An overview.* Washington, DC: Women's Institute for a Secure Retirement (WISER).

Herd, P. (2002). Care credits: Race, gender, class and Social Security reform. *Public Policy and Aging Report*, 12, 13–18.

Herd, P. (2006). Crediting care or marriage: Reforming Social Security family benefits. *Journal of Gerontology: Social Sciences*, 61B, S24–S34.

Horner, M. J., et al. (Eds.). (2006). *SEER Cancer Statistics Review, 1975–2006*, National Cancer Institute. Bethesda, MD. Retrieved July, 2009, from http://seer.cancer.gov/csr/1975_2006/

Hounsell, C., & Humphlett, P. (2006). *Minority women and retirement income.* Washington, DC: Women's Institute for a Secure Retirement (WISER).

Kazzi, N. (2009). More American workers are losing their health insurance every day. Washington, DC: Center for American Progress. Retrieved July, 2009 from http://www.americanprogress.org/issues/2009/05/insurance_loss.html

Kessler, R., et al. (2003). Screening for serious mental illness in the general population. *Archives of General Psychiatry*, 60, 184–189.

Laditka, J. & Laditka, S. (2003). Increased hospitalization risk for recently widowed older women and protective effects of social contacts. *Journal of Women and Aging*, 15, 7–28.

Lee, S. (2005). *Women and Social Security: Benefit types and eligibility.* Washington, DC: Institute for Women's Policy Research.

Longino, C. F. & Powell, J. L. (2004). Embodiment and the study of aging. In V. Berdayes (Ed.). *The body in human inquiry: Interdisciplinary explorations of embodiment.* New York: Hampton Press.

Lusardi, A. & Mitchell, O. S. (2008). Planning and financial literacy: How do women fare? *American Economic Review*, 98, 413–417.

Manson, J. & Bassuk, S. (2006). *Hot flashes, hormones and your health.* New York: McGraw Hill.

Markson, B. (1999). Communities of resistance: Older women in a gendered world. Review of Frida Furman, Facing the Mirror. *The Gerontologist, 39*, 496–497.

Miller, N., Smerglia, V., & Bouche, N. (2004). Women's adjustment to widowhood: Does social support matter? *Journal of Women and Aging, 16*, 149–167.

Moen, P. & Chermack, K. (2005). Gender disparities in health: Strategic selection, careers and cycles of control. *Journal of Gerontology, Special Issue on Health Inequalities across the Life Course, 60B*, S99–S108.

Moorman, S., Booth, A., & Fingerman, K. (2006). Women's romantic relationships after widowhood. *Journal of Family Issues, 27*, 1281–1304.

Morell, C. (2003). Empowerment and the long-living woman: Return to the rejected body. *Journal of Aging Studies, 17*, 69–85.

National Institute on Aging (NIA). (2004). *Hormones and menopause*. Washington, DC: NIA. Retrieved February 2007, from http://www.niapublications .org/tipsheets/hormones.asp

National Institute on Aging (NIA). (2008). *Age page: Menopause*. Washington, DC: NIA. Retrieved July 2009, from http://www.nia.nih.gov/ HealthInformation/Publications/menopause.htm

National Osteoporosis Foundation. (2009). *Protect patient access to osteoporosis testing*. Retrieved July 2009, from http://www.nof.org/advocacy/Advocacy_Facts.htm

Newton, K., Reed, S., LaCroix, A., Grothaus, L., Ehrlich, K., et al. (2006). Treatment of vasomotor symptoms of menopause with black cohosh, multi botanicals, soy, hormone therapy or placebo. *Annals of Internal Medicine, 145*, 869–879.

Older Women's League (OWL). (2009a). *Gender and the Social Security system*. Washington, DC: Older Women's League.

Older Women's League (OWL). (2009b). *Older women in poverty* Washington, DC: Older Women's League.

Piercy, K. & Cheek, C. (2004). Tending and befriending: The intertwined relationships of quilters. *Journal of Women and Aging, 16*, 17–33.

Powell, J. L. (2006). *Social theory and aging*. Lanham, MD: Rowman and Littlefield.

Pudrovska, T., Schieman, S., & Carr, D. (2006). Strains of singlehood in later life: Do race and gender matter? *Journal of Gerontology: Social Sciences, 61B*, S315–S322.

Rieker, P. & Bird, C. (2005). Rethinking gender differences in health: Why we need to integrate social and biological perspectives. *Journal of Gerontology, Special Issue on Health Inequalities across the Life Course, 60B*, 40–47.

Shriver, M. (2009). A woman's nation changes everything. Washington, D.C. Center for American Progress.

Shearer, N. & Fleury, J. (2006). Social support promoting health in older women. *Journal of Women and Aging, 16*, 3–17.

Sherill, M. (2003). Walk on the wild side. *AARP Magazine*, pp. 10–14.

Social Security Administration (SSA). (2006). *Income of the population 55 or older, 2004*. Washington, DC: Social Security Administration. SSA Publication No. 13–11871. Released May 2006, Retrieved January, 2007, from http://www.ssa.gov/policy/ docs/statcomps/income_pop55/2004/incpop04.pdf

Social Security Administration (SSA). (2008). *Social Security is important to women*. Press Release. Washington, DC: Social Security Administration. Retrieved July 2009, from http://www.ssa.gov/ pressoffice/factsheets/women.htm

Stevens N., Martina C., & Westerhof, G. (2006). Meeting the need to belong: Predicting effects of a friendship enrichment program for older women. *The Gerontologist, 46*, 495–502.

Street, H., O'Connor, M., & Robinson, H. (2007). Depression in older adults: Exploring the relationship between goal setting and physical health. *International Journal of Geriatric Psychiatry, 22*, 1115.

Taylor, S., Klein, L., Lewis, B., Gruenewald, T., Gurung, R., & Updegraff, J. (2000). Behavioral response to stress in females: Tend-and-befriend, not fight or flight. *Psychology Review, 107*, 411–429.

Thompson, E. (2006). Being women, then lesbians, then old: Femininities, sexualities and aging. *The Gerontologist, 46*, 300–305.

U.S. Census Bureau. (2006). *Current Population Survey, 2006 Annual Social and Economic Supplement*. Retrieved January 2007, from http://pubdb3.census .gov/macro/032006/pov/new01_100_01.htm

U.S. Census Bureau. (2008). Population Division, Interim Statistics. Population projections by age, sex and race for 2008. Retrieved March 2009, from http://factfinder.census.gov/servlet/DatasetMainPage Servlet?program=PEP&Submenuid=&lang=en&ts

Wakabayashi, C. & Donato, K. (2004). *The consequences of caregiving for economic well-being in women's later life*. Presented at the annual meeting of the American Sociological Association, San Francisco.

Wingert, P. & Kantrowitz, B. (2006). *Is it hot in here or is it me? The complete guide to menopause.* New York: Workman Publishing.

Women's Institute for a Secure Retirement (WISER). (2006). *Rights of surviving spouses.* Washington, DC: WISER.

Women's Institute for a Secure Retirement (WISER). (2009). *Hispanics and Social Security.* Washington, DC: WISER.

Xu, X., Patel, D. A., Vahratian, A., & Ransom, S. B. (2006). Insurance coverage and health care use among near-elderly women. *Women's Health Issues, 16,* 139–148.

part five

The Societal Context of Aging

The final section of this book examines aging and older people from a broader macro context. The values and beliefs that policy makers and voters hold toward a particular group or issue are often the basis for developing policies and programs. To the extent that these policies also are grounded in empirically-based knowledge, they can enhance the status and resources of that group. On the other hand, policies that are based on misinformation, or on biased or incomplete data may be inadequate and even detrimental.

Throughout this book, the current state of knowledge about the physiological, psychological, and social aspects of aging has been reviewed. We have examined variations among elders of color, men and women, gays and lesbians, and among other segments of the older adult population. The diversity of the aging experience within and across groups has been emphasized. Differences in lifestyle, health behaviors, employment, family caregiving patterns, and social networks in earlier periods of life can significantly impact functioning in old age, often reflecting health and socioeconomic disparities across the life course. This diversity increasingly affects the design, implementation, and effectiveness of social policies and programs. Chapter 16 addresses social and income maintenance policies and programs, while Chapter 17 focuses on health and long-term care policies.

Some age-based programs such as Social Security are directed toward all people who meet age criteria, whereas others such as Supplemental Security Income (SSI) and food stamps are based on financial need. Types of services and their funding and eligibility criteria are often determined by the prevailing social values and by the political party in control of the Presidency and Congress. These values, in turn, reflect beliefs about older people's vulnerabilities and responsibilities to society. For example, attitudes regarding elders' deservingness, whether chronological age should be a basis for services, and whether care of the aging population is a societal or individual responsibility all influence the design and funding of social, health, and long-term care policies. The historical development of aging policy and alterations in existing programs are also reviewed within the context of larger societal changes that influence such values. One societal shift examined in this section is the growing economic well-being of some older adults during the past decade, which is now threatened, and in some cases reversed, by the global economic crisis. Despite the fact that some retirees have seen their investments decline by 50 percent or more (Goldstein, 2009), some policy makers still perceive elders as financially better off than younger age-groups and as concerned about others' well-being. Debates about intergenerational inequity, common in the 1980s, have again surfaced, most often under the guise of declaring (wrongly) that Social Security is in immediate crisis. Health and long-term care policies toward older people have evolved incrementally in response to society's values and expectations of individual responsibility and chronic care needs. Chapter 17 describes these policies; their rising expenditures; the growing need for a system of comprehensive long-term care coordinated with acute care; obstacles to their public funding; current cost-containment initiatives in Medicare and Medicaid, exemplified by the 2003 Prescription Drug Reform; and the expanded emphasis on home-based management of chronic diseases, including innovations in care management and transitions of care. We close with a discussion of national health care reform and its implications for older adults.

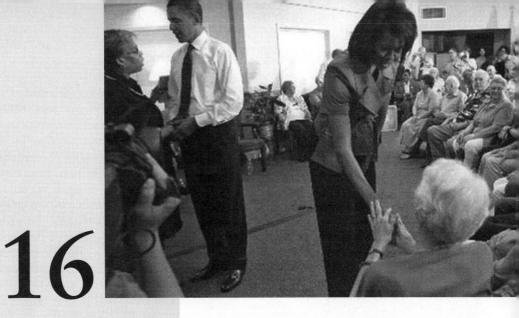

16

Social Policies to Address Social Problems

This chapter focuses on

- Definitions of policy
- Differentiation of types of public policies
- Factors that affect public policy development and that should be considered in policy analyses
- The relatively slow development of aging policies prior to the 1960s, the rapid expansion of programs in the 1960s and 1970s, and the impact of federal budget cuts of the 1980s, 1990s, and today
- Social Security benefits, its fiscal challenges and proposed reforms, including the long-standing debate over privatization
- Other policies that affect economic well-being, such as Supplemental Security Income (SSI), pensions, and tax benefits
- Direct social services funded through the Administration on Aging (AOA) and Title XX of the Social Security Act
- Policy dilemmas and implications for future directions

A wide range of policies, established within the past 8 decades, aim to improve older people's social, physical, and economic environments. Approximately 50 major federal programs are directed specifically toward older persons, with another 200 affecting them indirectly. Prior to the 1960s, however, the U.S. lagged behind most European countries in developing public policy for its older citizens. For example, Social Security benefits were not awarded to American retirees until 1935, publicized by posters such as the one on page 692. In contrast, Social Security systems were instituted in the nineteenth century in Western European countries. The U.S. slowly and cautiously accepted the concept of public responsibility, albeit only partial, for its older citizens. In the 1960s, federal spending for programs for older adults rapidly expanded, resulting in the "graying of the federal budget" and a dramatic change in the composition of expenditures. The growth in federal support for these services

Social Security poster, 1935.

is vividly illustrated through budgetary figures (see Figure 16.1). Currently, expenditures for Social Security and Medicare make up almost 40 percent of the federal budget, compared to 13 percent in 1960. Put another way, federal expenditures for Social Security, Medicare, and Medicaid represent just under 10 percent of the U.S. gross domestic product (GDP); this is expected to increase to 16 percent by 2030 and nearly 20 percent by 2050 (see Figure 16.2 on page 692) (Congressional Budget Office, 2007).

Social Security comprises about 21 percent of federal expenditures, Medicare 16.1 percent, and Medicaid 7 percent. These are **entitlement**

programs that are determined by ongoing eligibility requirements and benefit levels rather than by annual congressional appropriations. Increased federal spending for these entitlements is a result primarily of legislative improvements in income protection, health insurance, and social services enacted in the late 1960s; this spending is projected to continue to rise due to health care costs and the growing number of older adults who will be eligible for them. In fact, by 2030, growth in spending for Social Security, Medicare, and Medicaid will outpace overall economic growth by two to three times (Congressional Budget Office, 2007; Gist, 2007; Steinwald, 2007; Walker, 2007). Concern about the long-term financial viability of these programs and whether older adults are benefiting at the expense of younger groups has intensified among baby boomers. Policy makers are considering different options for managing spending on entitlement programs as part of a larger process of economic sustainability. These are reflected in debates about the need for fundamental changes in Social Security and Medicare, including privatization and individual health accounts, to reduce age-based public expenditures.

It is important to recognize, however, that when Social Security and Medicare are excluded from these federal allocations, less than five percent of the total federal budget is devoted to all other programs that benefit older adults. These growing expenditures also mask the fact that funded aging services are often fragmented, duplicated, and do not reach those with the greatest need, thus perpetuating health and income disparities described in Chapters 14 and 15. Despite growing expenditures for age-based benefits, the U.S. lacks an integrated and comprehensive public policy to ensure older adults' well-being. The complex policy challenges related to entitlement programs for older adults are largely due to past tax cuts, escalating defense spending and health care costs, and the global economic crisis, not the growth of the older population per se. For example, since 2001, funding for defense has jumped at an average annual rate of 8 percent, four times

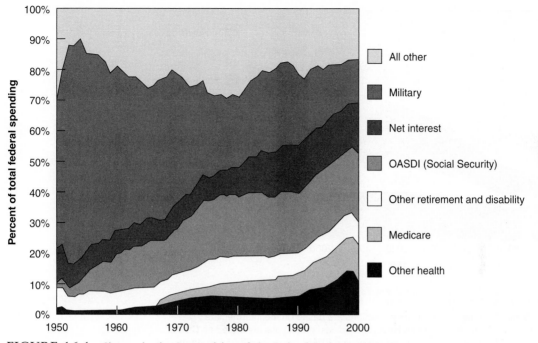

FIGURE 16.1   Change in the Composition of the Federal Budget, 1950–2000

faster than the average growth rate for Social Security, Medicare, and Medicaid (2 percent) and 27 times faster than the average growth rate for domestic discretionary programs (0.3 percent) (Kogan, 2008).

Variations Among Policies and Programs

The purview of **social policy** is not only to identify problems, but also to take action to ameliorate them. Public policy, therefore, must be responsive to changes in systems, practices, beliefs, and behaviors. The procedures that governments develop for making such changes encompass planned interventions, programmatic structures for implementation, and regulations governing the distribution of public funds. Policy for the older population thus reflects society's decisions about what choices to make in meeting their needs and the division of responsibilities between

the public and private sectors. As policies for older adults have developed since 1935, each has served to determine which older persons should receive what benefits, from which sources, and on what basis.

Social programs and regulations are the visible manifestations of public policies. The implementation of the 1965 **Older Americans Act (OAA),** for example, resulted in senior centers, nutrition sites, Meals on Wheels, homemaker and home health services, and adult day care. Some programs are designed specifically for older people, whereas others benefit them indirectly, such as services to support family caregivers. Programs can be differentiated from each other by their **eligibility criteria;** these dimensions are presented in Table 16.1 on page 693 and described next.

1. *Eligibility Criteria for Benefits:* When eligibility for benefits depends on age alone (i.e., a person is entitled to Medicare benefits at

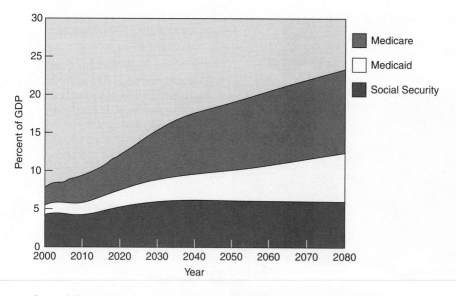

Sources: GAO analysis based on data from the Office of the Chief Actuary, Social Security Administration; Office of the Actuary, Centers for Medicare and Medicaid Services; and the Congressional Budget Office.

Note: Social Security and Medicare projections are based on the intermediate assumptions of the 2006 Trustees' Reports. Medicaid projections are based on CBO's January 2007 short-term Medicaid estimates and CBO's December 2005 long-term Medicaid projections under midrange assumptions.

FIGURE 16.2 **Entitlement Programs Are a Growing Part of the Federal Budget**
SOURCE: Gist, 2007.

age 65), **age-based entitlement programs** are categorical, which means they are specifically for older adults. However, in **need-based programs,** eligibility depends on financial need. These include Medicaid, SSI, food stamps, and public housing. Most programs for older adults are age entitlement programs, with the government automatically paying benefits to anyone who meets the age criteria. In contrast, programs for children and for younger persons with disabilities are typically discretionary and means-based.

2. *Form of Benefits:* Another variation is the form in which benefits are given: either **direct** (cash or commodity) or **indirect,** through a **cash transfer** or **cash substitute.** Thus, Social Security benefits are *direct cash transfers,* and vouchers for the purchase of goods, such as food stamps and rent supplements, are *direct cash substitutes.* Tax policies that

affect selected groups (e.g., personal income tax exemptions for older persons) are *indirect cash transfers* of funds from one segment of the population to another. For example, Medicare benefits paid to health care providers, rather than directly to beneficiaries, are indirect cash substitutes.

3. *Method of Financing:* Programs also vary in how they are financed. Social Security and Medicare are **contributory plans;** entitlement is tied to a person's mandatory contributions to the system as a paid worker across the life course. In contrast, SSI is a **noncontributory program,** available to older adults and persons with disabilities of all ages who meet financial need criteria, regardless of their prior contributions through payroll taxes.

4. *Universal or Selective Benefits:* Programs differ according to whether they benefit populations

TABLE 16.1   **Dimensions Along Which Programs and Policies Vary**

PROGRAM DIMENSIONS	EXAMPLES
Eligibility	
On basis of age	Medicare
On basis of financial need	Supplemental Security Income
	Medicaid
Form of benefits: Direct or indirect	
Cash	
Direct cash transfers	Social Security
Indirect cash transfers	Income tax exemption
Cash substitute	
Direct cash substitutes	Vouchers
Indirect cash substitutes	Medicare payments to service providers
Method of financing	
Contributory (earned rights)	Social Security
Noncontributory	Supplemental Security Income
Universal or selective benefits	
Universal—for all persons who belong to a particular category	Older Americans Act
Selective—determined on an individual basis	Food stamps

on a universal or selective basis. **Universal benefits** are available as a social right to all persons belonging to a designated group; an example is Medicare, which benefits all adults who are age 65 and older. In contrast, **selective benefits** are determined individually. These include Medicaid and food stamps—available on the basis of income, not age. Many public debates have focused on whether aging services should be targeted to low-income elders and subsidized by higher-income older adults. Public consensus on the best approach to service delivery does not exist, as reflected in the following discussion of the factors that influence social policy for older adults.

Factors Affecting the Development of Public Policies

Despite the orderliness of these dimensions, the policy development process is not rational or strategic. Approaches to the financing and delivery of services for older adults evolved in a very different time period, when life expectancy was shorter, chronic disease relatively rare, and federal revenues and deficits of less concern. A major characteristic of the U.S. public policy process is its shortsightedness—its general inability, because of annual budgetary cycles and the frequency of national partisan elections, to deal with long-term economic, demographic, and social trends, or to anticipate future consequences of current policies to meet needs or political imperatives. As the number and diversity of older adults have grown, shortsightedness in public policy development has resulted in a fragmented array of services with separate entitlements and eligibility requirements (Teles, 2005). In fact, this complexity can be so confusing to older people and their families that it has spawned the growth of private case or care managers, websites, and toll-free navigator phone services to locate, access, and coordinate services.

The complexity of the public policy formation process is also magnified by the variety of societal factors influencing it, including:

- individual and societal values and beliefs
- economic, social, and governmental structures

- the configuration of domestic and international problems
- powerful interest groups and their lobbyists

Values Affecting Social Policy

Because public policy reflects what and whom we value as a society, it is fundamentally a matter of values and social justice. Ultimately, it represents our collective definition of a just and caring society that will best promote the common good, including elders' health and income security. Public policy debates also raise issues of older adults' dignity and worth. Although dignity is important at all ages, it is particularly salient in old age because ageism, illness, and other losses threaten elders' identities (Holstein, 2005; Neale, 2005). Two contrasting core values have been played out in American social welfare policies regarding older adults:

1. Individual welfare is essentially the *person's responsibility* within a free-market economy unfettered by government control. This belief in individualism, autonomy, self-determination, and privacy is deeply rooted in our history and culture, is widely embraced by many segments of our society, and underlies many public policies and debates surrounding new policy directions.
2. Individual welfare is a matter of the common stake and thus the responsibility *of both the individual and the community* at large. Government intervention is required to protect its citizens and to compensate for the free market's failure to distribute resources equitably. Nevertheless, because our society values individual productivity and competitiveness, some degree of income disparity is accepted as inevitable.

Our society's emphasis on individual and family responsibility has resulted in placing the government in a *residual* or "back-up" role to informal support systems. Programs are designed to respond *incrementally* to needs, not to prevent problems or to address their underlying causes. This contrasts with the approach of many other countries, where national health and welfare polices represent a consensus that citizens are universally entitled to have basic needs met. Even when our federal government intervenes, it is generally justified because of the failure of the market economy, the family, or the individual to provide for themselves or their relatives. Accordingly, solutions tend to be patterned after private-sector initiatives, as illustrated by many of the changes in Social Security and Medicare proposed by Republican administrations and legislators (Bishop, 2008; Hudson, 2005, 2008).

Since the New Deal of the 1930s, policy has oscillated between these two core values as the public mood and national administrations have shifted. Public perceptions of older people as "deserving" converged to create universal **categorical programs** (e.g., the Administration on Aging, Medicare) available only to older persons, regardless of income. In contrast, policies that use income (e.g., means-testing by Medicaid and SSI) to determine if a person is "deserving" of services reflect our society's bias toward productivity and economic self-sufficiency. Although Social Security was the first federal initiative to address older adults' income needs, it succeeded largely because it was perceived as an insurance plan for "deserving" elders who had contributed through their prior employment and suffered devastating effects from the Great Depression, not as a means-tested income maintenance policy for all vulnerable citizens.

In the past, the American public tended to perceive older people as more deserving of assistance than other groups. Accordingly, Social Security and Medicare have, until recent years, been viewed as inviolate and not to be cut drastically. The passage of such otherwise unpopular programs as national health insurance for older people (i.e., Medicare) and guaranteed income (i.e., SSI) can be partially explained by the fact that older persons in the past aroused public sympathy and support, and therefore a favorable political response. As noted in Chapter 12, such perceptions of deserving elders fueled notable policy enactments and expansions, rather than the heterogeneous older population acting as a unified block to influence legislation (Hudson, 2008). Nevertheless, most politicians do not want to lose older adults' votes, given their high rates of electoral participation (Schulz & Binstock, 2006).

Ongoing debates about the nature and extent of public provisions versus individual responsibility and private philanthropy often have moral overtones. Judgments about the relative worth of vulnerable populations that compete for a share of limited resources (e.g., older persons within the prison system) and about the proper divisions between public and private responsibilities are ultimately based on values regarding individual or group responsibility. A major policy issue, therefore, revolves around the question of whose values shape policy.

Economic Context

Not surprisingly, economic conditions significantly influence policy development. An adverse economy can create a climate conducive to the passage of income-maintenance policies. For instance, Social Security was enacted in part because the Great Depression dislodged the middle class from financial security and from widely held beliefs that older adults who needed financial assistance were undeserving. A strategy to increase the number of persons retiring at age 65 was also congruent with economic pressures to reduce widespread unemployment in the 1930s. With economic constraints, program cost factors were also salient; Social Security as a public pension was assumed to cost less than reliance on local poorhouses, as had been the practice prior to

the 1920s. Thus, a variety of economic and resource factors converged to create the necessary public and legislative support for a system of social insurance. In contrast, periods of economic growth can also be conducive to new social and health care programs. For example, Medicare and the Older Americans Act were passed in the 1960s and early 1970s, respectively. During this period of economic growth and increased social consciousness, government resources expanded under the War on Poverty on behalf of both the younger poor and older people. Similarly, funding for the National Institute on Aging (NIA) increased during the economic boom of the late 1990s.

The influence of both economic resources and cultural values is also evident in the federal government's emphasis, under past Republican administrations, on tax cuts, voluntarism and civic engagement, cost-effectiveness and containment, and targeting services to those most in need. Under the personal responsibility values of the Republican Congresses during the 1990s and until the 2006 takeover by the Democrats, the concept of states' rights and prerogatives was emphasized. Because of federal budget cuts and cost-shifting strategies, states have had to assume a greater role in the development and financing of social programs. This resulted in increased variability of eligibility criteria and benefits for programs such as SSI and Medicaid among the states. Periods of scarcity also tend to produce limited and often punitive legislative responses, as occurred in the 1980s and early 1990s, and have the potential to emerge again under the current economic crisis. Examples include cuts to social and health programs benefiting older adults, such as decreases in Medicaid funds for long-term care options in many states attempting to balance their shrinking budgets. Illustrating the erosion of public support for universal age-based benefits in the 1980s and 1990s, Medicare copayments, deductibles, and Part B premiums increased, Social Security benefits for higher-income older people were taxed, and many legislators proposed cutting Medicare and Medicaid or privatizing Social Security to reduce federal expenditures. Since the 1990s, growing preoccupation with ways to limit public funding placed a priority on the most efficient and least expensive solutions, often by private or faith-based organizations, rather than ensuring equity and the common good by government. Now, with a Democratic President and Congress, the value stance is oriented toward increasing policy and programmatic supports for vulnerable populations, but the recession, the devastating budget reductions by states, and the record high federal deficit are making it increasingly difficult for the Democrats to act on their underlying social justice values.

In sum, American values, fluctuating economic conditions, and the consequent fiscal resources available underlie a *categorical, residual, and incremental* policy approach toward older adults. One of the most vocal critics of this approach, Estes (1979, 1984, 1989, 2000; Estes, Linkins, & Binney, 1996; Kail, Quadagno, & Keene, 2009) maintains that our conceptions of social aging construct the major problems faced by older people and thereby adversely influence age-based policies. These conceptions are described as the political economy perspective in Chapter 8. According to Estes, our society's failure to develop a comprehensive, coordinated policy framework reinforces older persons' marginality and segregates them.

In contrast to Estes, others maintain that the older population benefits at the expense of other age-groups and is "busting the budget." Age-based benefits are viewed as a cause of growing federal expenditures and the allocation of resources away from younger groups who have higher rates of poverty. Spending for entitlement programs is perceived as "mortgaging the future" of succeeding

A FRAMEWORK FOR CRITICALLY ANALYZING PUBLIC POLICIES

- Legislative and historical origins and context of the policy
- Its goal or purpose: Who is the policy intended to benefit?
- The issue or problem that the policy is intended to address, including ways in which the issue or problem is socially constructed:
  - How is the issue or problem defined by both those who support policy and those who do not?
  - Who was involved and who was excluded in defining the issue or problem and its underlying causes?
- Values underlying this policy (e.g., individualism, personal and family responsibility, social justice, common good)
- Competing perspectives on this policy:
  - Who supports the policy? Who opposes it?
  - Whose interests are reflected in the policy and whose are excluded?
  - Who benefits or loses, and in what ways?
- The implementation process and its impact on the intent/outcomes of the policy
- The extent to which the policy promotes social justice and reduces inequities by race, class, gender, functional ability, and sexual orientation
- Changes needed in the policy or in its implementation (e.g., programs and regulations) to promote social justice across the life course

generations. In reality, however, the actual contribution of Social Security and Medicare to the federal deficit has been nearly the same since 1980. In fact, the current reserves in the Social Security Trust Fund help pay for other federal expenditures. Additionally, cuts to programs for older adults do not mean that more resources would necessarily be redistributed into programs that benefit younger generations (Binstock, 2008; Hudson, 2005a). Within this context of the factors affecting policy development, we turn now to the formulation of public policy for older persons. The box on page 698 suggests factors for you to consider whenever you critically analyze public policies, especially in terms of their underlying values and who benefits.

The Development of Public Policies for Older People

1930 to 1950

As noted above, the U.S. had few social programs specifically benefiting older adults prior to the 1930s. Family, community, charity organizations, and local governments (e.g., county work farms)

were expected to be responsible. Factors such as the low percentage of older adults in the population, a strong belief in individual responsibility, and the free-market economy partially explain why our government was slow to respond. Table 16.2 traces these historical policy developments. The Social Security Act of 1935, the first national public benefits program, grew out of the market failure of the Depression and established the federal government as a major player in the social welfare arena (Hudson, 2005a; Schulz & Binstock, 2006). This act legitimated the status of older adults as government's responsibility and is based on an implicit guarantee of social insurance—that the current younger generation will provide for its older members through their Social Security contributions as employees, with the

TABLE 16.2 **Major Historical Developments of Policies That Benefit Older People and Their Families**

1935	Social Security Act
1950	Amendments to assist states with health care costs
1959	Section 202 Direct Loan Program of the Housing Act
1960	Extension of Social Security benefits
1960	Advisory commissions on aging
1961	Senate Special Committee on Aging
1961	First White House Conference on Aging
1965	Medicare and Medicaid, Older Americans Act, establishment of Administration on Aging
1971	Second White House Conference on Aging
1972 & 1977	Social Security amendments
1974	Title XX
1974	House Select Committee on Aging
1974	Change in mandatory retirement age
1974	Establishment of the National Institute on Aging
1980	Federal measures to control health care expenditures
1981	Third White House Conference on Aging
1981	Social Services Block Grant Program
1986	Elimination of mandatory retirement
1987	Nursing Home Reform Act
1989–90	Medicare Catastrophic Health Care Legislation passed, then repealed
1995	Fourth White House Conference on Aging
1996	Family and Medical Leave Act
1999	United Nations: International Year of Older Persons
2000	National Family Caregiver Support Program
2003	Medicare Prescription Drug Bill
2005	Fifth White House Conference on Aging

expectation that future cohorts of workers will do the same for them. The original provisions of the act were intended to be only the beginning of a universal program covering all "major hazards" in life. However, this broader concept, including a nationwide program for preventing illness and ensuring security for children, was never realized.

After the passage of the Social Security Act, national interest in policies to benefit older persons subsided until the 1960s. One exception was President Truman's advocacy to expand Social Security benefits to include farmers, self-employed persons, and some state and local government employees. He also proposed a national health insurance plan, but was opposed by interest groups such as the American Medical Association. However, President Truman succeeded in his push for a 1950 Social Security amendment to assist

---

FACTORS THAT AFFECTED THE DEVELOPMENT OF SOCIAL SECURITY

Demographics

Only 5 percent of the population was age 65 and older in 1935, and dramatic increases in life expectancy were largely unanticipated. As a result, reserves were projected for the system, and early retirees benefited significantly from the "pay as you go" system.

Historical and Economic Context

- The New Deal and federal response to the Great Depression
- Recognition that the private sector could not guarantee economic security for retirees and that the federal government needed to step in
- Compassionate stereotype of older adults as "deserving"
- Incentive for and institutionalization of retirement within the labor market and federal government; the disengagement or exit of older workers from the workforce helped create more opportunities for younger workers
- Influence of Western European countries that had funded social security systems

---

states that chose to pay partial health care costs for needy older persons. This amendment became the basis for establishing Medicare in 1965. Wilbur Cohen, the Secretary of Health, Education, and Welfare (the federal agency that is predecessor to the current Department of Health and Human Services) under President Johnson, noted that major initiatives for older adults come in 30-year cycles (Achenbaum, 2006). The expansion of benefits for elders in the 1960s illustrates this cycle.

Program Expansion in the 1960s and 1970s

Since the 1960s, programs for older people have rapidly evolved, including Medicare, Medicaid, the Older Americans Act (OAA), SSI, the Social Security Amendments of 1972 and 1977, Section 202 Housing, and Title XX social services legislation. The pervasiveness of "compassionate stereotypes"—which assumed that most older adults are deserving poor, frail, ill-housed, unable to keep up with inflation, and therefore in need of government assistance—created a "permissive consensus" for government action on age-based services. A negative consequence of "compassionate ageism," however, was the development of programs that did not take account of economic and racial diversity among the older population. A large constituency—including older adults who are not poor, frail, or inadequately housed—benefited from the policy consensus built on the "compassionate stereotype" of the 1960s and 1970s (Hudson, 2005a). Since old-age constituencies have been viewed as relatively homogeneous (white, English-speaking, and male), many older women, elders of color, the oldest-old, those living alone, and LGBT elders have not always benefited proportionately from program improvements relative to their greater needs.

The first White House Conference on Aging and the establishment of the Senate Special Committee on Aging, both in 1961, addressed age-based needs. Four years later, Medicare and the OAA were passed. Although the OAA established the Administration on Aging (AOA) at the federal level, as well as statewide area agencies and advisory boards on aging services, funding to implement these provisions was low relative to need. Therefore, one of the primary objectives of the 1971 White House Conference on Aging was to strengthen the OAA. In 1972, Social Security benefits were expanded by 20 percent, and the system of *indexing* benefits to take account of inflation **(cost-of-living adjustments or COLA)** was established. Additional funding was provided for the OAA in 1973.

The 1970s, with a prevailing liberal ethos, propelled more developments to improve older people's economic status:

- the creation of SSI
- protection of private pensions through the Employee Retirement Income Security Act (ERISA)
- formation of the House Select Committee on Aging
- increases in Social Security benefit levels and taxes
- the change in mandatory retirement from age 65 to 70 (as noted in Chapter 12, mandatory retirement was abolished for nearly all jobs in 1986)

Public policy on aging, in effect, resulted in more policies, thereby creating its own political constituencies and advocacy. During this period of federal expansion, more than 40 national committees and subcommittees were involved in legislative efforts affecting older adults—most of them created after 1965, the breakthrough year when Medicare, Medicaid, and the OAA were enacted (Hudson, 2009). As a result of the expansion of age-related programs, along with more age-based interest groups, individuals grew to expect that they were automatically entitled to receive benefits based on age rather than income or need. Yet aging advocacy organizations appear to have been more influential in defending existing policy than in affecting the development of new policies (Binstock, 2008; Hudson, 2009). Paradoxically, many older adults assume that they are entitled to continued political support and public benefits, even though their economic needs, along with their political impact, have declined in the past 30 years.

Program Reductions in the 1980s and 1990s

Although compassionate stereotypes and a "permissive consensus" underlay the growth of age entitlement programs in the 1960s and 1970s, fiscal pressures and increasing concern about the well-being of younger age-groups in the 1980s and 1990s raised questions about the size and structure of age-based programs. In those years, a new stereotype of older people as relatively well-off resulted in their being scapegoated and blamed as "greedy geezers." In fact, older people were sometimes seen as responsible for increasing the poverty rates among younger populations (Binstock & Shultz, 2006; Hudson, 2005a; Minkler, 2002).

The impact of tax cuts, reductions in federal programs, the federal deficit, and an overemphasis on economic growth prevented consideration of any large or bold programs for domestic spending on social and health services during the Reagan Administration (1980–1988). Instead, "Reaganomics" implemented policies to reduce or restrain public expenditures for welfare, pensions, and services to older people (Walker, 2007). At the same time, public perceptions of and support for aging programs varied widely. Advocates urged more funding for older adults, particularly for social services, and closely guarded Social Security. Concern over the future of Social Security was fueled by the near-term deficit facing the Social Security Trust Fund in the 1980s. As a result, Social Security was amended in 1983 to address short-term financing problems. As public scrutiny of the costs of Social Security, Medicare, and Medicaid grew, *cost-efficiency* measures were implemented, such as taxing Social Security benefits and providing less generous cost-of-living increases.

During the 1980s, the political reality of the economic, cultural, and social diversity of the aging population—that chronological age is not an accurate marker of financial status or functional ability—became more apparent. The variability in income distribution is reflected among three different groups of older people:

- those who are ineligible for Social Security, including both the lifelong poor and working poor who have discontinuous employment histories, low hourly wages without benefits, and few assets—typically women and elders of color, as described in Chapters 14 and 15
- those who depend heavily on Social Security, with small or no private pensions and few assets except for their homes—typically women and elders of color
- those with generous private pensions and personal savings investments, such as 401(k)s, in addition to Social Security benefits—typically Caucasian males

A number of policies passed in the 1980s recognized older adults' differential capabilities of helping to finance publicly-funded services, so that both age and economic status were considered for eligibility for old-age benefits (Binstock, 2002; Hudson, 2005a). For example, the Social Security Reform Act of 1983 taxed Social Security benefits for higher-income recipients. The Tax Reform Act of 1986 provided tax credits on a sliding scale to low-income older adults and eliminated a second or third exemption on federal income taxes. In addition, OAA programs were gradually targeted toward low-income individuals. These policy changes, combined with public perceptions that older people are better off than younger ones, reflect a transition from the legacy of a modern aging period (1930–1990) of universal benefits to all who qualify because of age to a new period in which old age alone is not sufficient grounds for public benefits to ensure human dignity (Holstein, 2005; Hudson, 2005b).

The Politics of Diversity and Deficit Spending in the 1990s

Efforts to reduce the growing federal deficit profoundly affected public policy development in the 1990s. Two major options were available to shrink the deficit: reductions in spending through program cutbacks or revenue enhancement through higher taxes. National groups that cut across the political spectrum—such as the Bipartisan Commission on Entitlement and Tax Reform and the Concord Coalition—maintained that entitlement programs for older people were growing so fast that they would consume nearly all the federal tax revenues by the year 2012, leaving government with little money for anything else. Increasingly, such groups argued that Social Security, Medicare, and Medicaid must be drastically curtailed to balance the federal budget early in the twenty-first century. Such a perspective is reflected in the Balanced Budget Act of 1997, where Medicare and Medicaid were cut, but not Social Security. In reality, because Social Security is financed by its own dedicated payroll tax, none of the federal deficit has ever been caused by Social Security spending. However, this fact is typically not portrayed by the media nor understood by the general public and even some federal lawmakers (NCPSSM, 2003b).

The broader political arena reflected growing fiscal conservatism, with President Clinton predicting that the federal deficit would be eliminated by 2015. In the 1996 Personal Responsibility Act, President Clinton signed restrictive welfare legislation but vetoed the bill containing changes to alter the nature of entitlements to Medicare and Medicaid. Resistance against dramatically changing these age-based entitlement programs remained strong in the Clinton Administration. However, such entitlements were challenged by Republicans in the White House and Congress during the second Bush administration (2004–2008); they favored privatization of Social Security and other government programs. The fact that such age-based programs have been challenged and that Medicare now uses an income criterion in its prescription drug benefit program (see Chapter 17) reflects a societal shift in attitudes toward the older population. Elders are now less likely to be perceived as a "politically sympathetic" group compared to other segments of the population, particularly children and young families. Yet the U.S. has the second highest poverty rate among older adults when compared to 11 Western European nations (Hudson, 2005b, 2008). At the same time, disparities within the older population are more evident and intensifying, with subgroups of poor, elders of color, women, and persons living alone likely to join political alliances around class, race, gender, or ethnicity that compete with groups of more affluent elders. The "politics of diversity" may thus fragment the political influence of established aging organizations and reduce support for universal programs. In fact, incremental changes in Social Security, the OAA, and Medicare to target benefits toward low-income older people reflect recognition of this diversity and a slight shift away from universality (Hudson, 2008; Torres-Gil & Moga, 2001).

Such diversity among the older population, combined with a focus on reducing federal expenditures, resulted in a greater emphasis on private sector initiatives by the Bush administration that could be utilized by higher-income older adults (e.g., promoting individual retirement accounts—or IRAs—instead of Social Security). Even in the 1990s under a Democratic administration, some members of Congress and the Social Security Advisory Council advocated private savings accounts. With more older adults able to self-finance or privately insure against the social and health costs of later life, the base of support for quality government programs further eroded in the 1990s and the early part of the twenty-first century. To avoid increasing inequality among the older population, a policy challenge in the 1990s was to target resources to those who lacked economic stability, while maintaining public support for quality universal programs. These complex issues set the framework for the 1995 White House Conference on Aging, where delegates voted to maintain Social Security, the basic features of Medicaid and Medicare, and some advocacy functions under the OAA. Reflecting the Democrats' intent to preserve age-based programs, these directions conflicted with the priority of the Republican Congress to reduce the federal deficit by cutting entitlement programs, reducing taxes, and allowing more individual control over Social Security investments. Republican proposals to tax Social Security reflect the shifting base of support compared to earlier time periods when even mentioning such taxes would have been political suicide (Hudson, 2005a; Kail, et al., 2009).

Era of the Market and Personal Responsibility in the Twenty-First Century

Debates about universal entitlements for older adults increasingly reflect political ideology rather than population dynamics. Cost and intergenerational inequity issues that surfaced in the 1980s are still salient, but are secondary to beliefs about the appropriate role of government, private sector, and individual responsibility for elders' economic well-being (Hudson, 2005a, 2008). Instead, the emphasis on private sector competitiveness, tax cuts for upper income adults, and personal responsibility was reflected in a range of proposals under the Bush administration to: (1) privatize Social Security in full or in part, with individuals responsible for making their own investments; (2) encourage enrollment of Medicare beneficiaries in managed care organizations, as exemplified by financial incentives for managed care in the 2003 Prescription Drug Bill or Medicare Part D, described in Chapter 17;

Politicians seek the support of older voters.

(3) provide partial federal tax credits and deductibility for premiums that were paid for private long-term care insurance; and (4) promote individual health savings accounts. The politics of personal responsibility encouraged private sector competition and voluntary enrollment in personal savings plans as a way to "save" Social Security and Medicare. These shifts set the framework for more policy approaches to combine public programs with private mechanisms of incentives for savings (Binstock, 2002; Hudson, 2005a, 2005b, 2008; Kail et al., 2009). They were also reflected in the agenda of the 2005 White House Conference on Aging. Its emphasis on baby boomers and personal responsibility and accountability for

health and well-being was visible in preconference events focused on the Healthy Living Celebration and presentations on civic engagement and community service. It was also the first White House Conference on Aging where the U.S. president did not address the delegates. Despite its focus on individual responsibility, the primary resolution of Conference attendees was to reauthorize the OAA within the first 6 months following the conference. This occurred by the fall of 2006.

We next review specific programs that account for most age-based federal expenditures in the past 65 years:

- Social Security, Old Age and Survivors Disability Insurance (or OASDI), and SSI
- tax provisions and private pensions that provide indirect benefits, primarily to higher income older adults
- social services through Title XX block grants and the Aging Network of the OAA

OASDI, federal employee retirement, and Medicare and Medicaid combined represent the largest and most rapidly growing federal entitlements. However, many younger people also benefit from the intergenerational nature of OASDI and Medicaid, as shown in Figure 16.3.

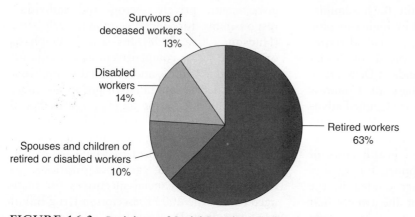

FIGURE 16.3 **Recipients of Social Security Benefits, by Type**
Source: Social Security Administration, 2003. Caldera, 2009.

Income Security Programs: Social Security and Supplemental Security Income

Social Security

As noted earlier, the 1935 Social Security Act aimed to establish a system of income maintenance for older persons to protect against financial disaster. A secondary purpose was to ensure a basic level of protection for the neediest older adults, initially through state plans for OASDI and, since 1974, through the federally funded SSI program. A more recent objective is to provide compensatory income to persons, regardless of age, who experience a sudden loss of income—such as widows, surviving children, and persons with disabilities. The values underlying Social Security were captured in a 1938 radio address by President Franklin D. Roosevelt to mark the third anniversary of the Act. Noting that our individual strengths and wits were no longer enough to guarantee our security, President Roosevelt reminded the nation that each person's safety is bound to that of our friends and neighbors. His comments made clear that Social Security was a *social* insurance program that would give *all* people a basic level of security (Neale, 2005). As such, Social Security aims to protect dignity as a social, not an individual, value and to foster social solidarity and human interdependence. To meet these objectives, Social Security has four separate *trust funds*:

1. Old-Age and Survivors Insurance (OASI)
2. Disability Insurance (DI)
3. Hospital Insurance (HI), which is funded through Medicare
4. revenues for the supplemental insurance portion of Medicare, as described in Chapter 17

Social Security is financed through separate trust funds, with revenues raised equally from the mandatory participation and contributions of

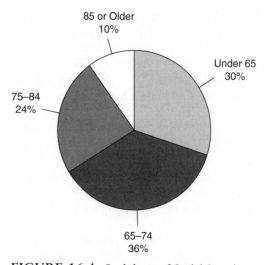

FIGURE 16.4   Recipients of Social Security Benefits, by Age
SOURCE: Social Security Administration, 2008.

employees and employers through payroll taxes, and income based on current tax revenues. This reflects a fundamental concept of Social Security; Individuals pool their resources in order to spread economic risks. Social Security was never intended to be about wealth-building, but rather a shared sense of responsibility for the income security of all older people (Feder & Friedland, 2005; Neale, 2005; Schulz & Binstock, 2006; Williamson & Watts-Ray, 2008). This discussion focuses on the combined OASDI fund, while Medicare is addressed in Chapter 17.

As described in Chapter 12, Social Security is based first on the concept of earned rights as a result of a lifetime of paid work. Benefits can be counted on regardless of inflation and market fluctuations. Initially, only 60 percent of the labor force was eligible to earn future benefits on the basis of the 1935 law. Coverage has since expanded to insure 94 percent of workers (the remainder represent part-time workers whose employers do not pay Social Security payroll taxes and therefore do not qualify), reflecting nearly universal protection across social classes. In addition, wage-price indexing protects recipients against economic changes over which they have no control. Although Social Security creates a pooled mechanism to share the risk, no one is excluded, no matter how "bad" a risk he or she may be. This is a fundamental difference from private insurance or income maintenance programs for children and families (Caldera, 2009; Hudson, 2005; Yee, 2005). Social Security is similar to fire or collision insurance. You may never need to collect on your policy, but that does not mean you do not need to pay the premiums!

Contrary to public perceptions and the attempts of the Bush administration to change it, Social Security is not an investment program or the sole source of retirement income, but rather a minimum floor of protection. Yet, as described in Chapter 12, it is the major source of income for many elders. Twenty-three percent of people age 65 and older live in families that depend on Social Security for 90 percent or more of their income, and another 27 percent receive at least half of their family income from Social Security. Retirees typically need at least 70 percent of their preretirement income to continue living comfortably. But Social Security's average older recipients are paid 41 percent of their preretirement income, a figure that is projected to remain relatively stable through the year 2040 (Caldera, 2009). This average percentage varies with income, however. Social Security accounts for 95 percent of the aggregate income of the lowest-income older households, and only about 26 percent of the income of elders with the highest income (Purcell, 2009). While upper-income workers receive higher benefits in absolute dollars, lower-income workers are assured a greater rate of return for what they have paid into the system (i.e., the *proportion* of preretirement earnings that is replaced after retirement is higher for lower-paid workers). Social Security benefits, therefore, are progressive or most helpful to

those with low and moderate incomes who qualify. In fact, middle-income workers receive benefits roughly equal to their lifetime Social Security taxes (SSA, 2006b). Despite Social Security's progressive benefit formula and its greater relative importance as a source of income for low-income elders, it has not produced a convergence of economic well-being, because the highest income quartile of older Americans still receives substantially higher benefits due to their greater earnings during their working years. This distribution of benefits reflects Social Security's dual goals of social adequacy and individual equity.

- *Social adequacy* refers to a shared societal responsibility and mutual obligation to provide a basic standard of living for all potential beneficiaries, or a "safety net," regardless of the size of their economic contributions.
- *Individual equity* refers to an individual's benefits that reflect that person's actual monetary contributions proportionate to what they have paid into the system, as illustrated above with higher-income elders.

Critics of Social Security often overlook its cross-generational benefits, such as life and disability insurance for workers and their families. It is a myth that Social Security is a funded pension system in which retirees are merely paid back, with interest, the "contributions" made during their working years. Instead, it is a system whereby current workers support retired or disabled workers; thus, it is intergenerational in nature. This "pay-as-you-go" system is like a pipeline: payroll taxes from today's workers flow in, are invested in special U.S. government bonds, and simultaneously flow out to current beneficiaries. Today's retirees generally recoup their Social Security contributions within 7 years. In contrast, today's young workers are unlikely to recoup their contributions for at least

Health care reform mobilized people from culturally diverse backgrounds.

11 years after retirement (NCPSSM, 2003b). In short, Social Security's nearly universal coverage and predictability of income make it the foundation of economic security for most retirees.

Payroll taxes, however, have risen significantly, from a combined 3 percent on employers and employees in 1950 to 12.4 percent today. At the same time, the average return that a worker can anticipate has declined dramatically. A middle-income earner born in 1940 could expect to get back over a lifetime about the same amount that he/she paid into the system ($169,400, adjusted for inflation and interest), while retirees born in 2000 will get back about $249,800 compared to their contribution of $350,900 through payroll taxes. This contrasts with the average retiree born in 1915 who got back about $60,000 more than they paid into the system (SSA, 2006a; Wan et al., 2005). This pay-as-you-go method of financing partially underlies the fiscal crisis in the early 1980s, when the Social Security reserves were inadequate for projected benefits—due largely to the recession during that time period. The box on page 706 summarizes the changing demographic, economic, and political context that now frames debates about the future of Social Security. Figure 16.5 captures the demographic challenges faced by Social Security.

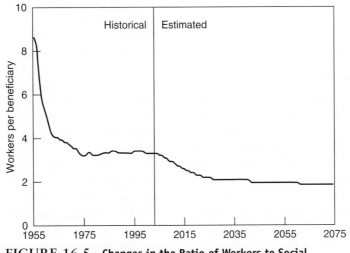

FIGURE 16.5   **Changes in the Ratio of Workers to Social Security Beneficiaries**
SOURCE: 2008 Annual Report of the Board of Trustees of the Federal Old-Age and Survivors Insurance and Disability Insurance Trust Funds, Table IV.B2.

**CURRENT CONTEXT FRAMING SOCIAL
SECURITY DEBATES**

- era of the stock market and personal responsibility
- the longevity revolution (when Social Security was enacted, life expectancy was 61 years, compared with over 78 years today)
- the changing age-dependency ratio from 50 workers to 1 retiree in 1935 to between 4 and 5 currently, only 3 to 1 by 2030 and approximately 2 to 1 by 2050
- a shift from a focus on adequacy of benefits for older adults, persons with disabilities, and survivors to a preoccupation with financing Social Security
- improved economic status of older adults, partly resulting from Social Security and Medicare, although private investments and pensions have shrunk dramatically since 2008 and reduced the income of many older adults
- older adults are healthier, better educated, and can continue to work, although increasing numbers are employed out of economic necessity
- economic pressures on young adults, many of whom are underemployed in the contingent service sector or have lost their jobs because of the recession
- the federal government's focus on the economy, wars in Iraq and Afghanistan, globalization, and health care reform

---

The Future of Social Security

Within this context, many policy makers and the media portray dire predictions about the Social Security crisis. Sometimes described as "merchants of doom," they argue that "apocalyptic demography" will make it difficult for our nation to sustain all age-related benefits through the first half of this century (Schulz & Binstock, 2006). The "graying of the welfare state" is perceived as having catastrophic consequences for the after-tax living standards of most working-age Americans. This view is put forth by groups such as the Third Millennium—which pointed to a 1997 survey

in which more people under age 35 stated that they believed in UFOs than they did in Social Security's future viability, and that they considered Social Security a scam (Schulz & Binstock, 2006). Data such as these, however, are misrepresented as public support for "radical reform." For example, polls show that Americans, even younger adults, overwhelmingly support protecting Social Security, even though they lack confidence in its future and are confused about eligibility criteria (Blendon, et al., 2005; Williamson & Watts-Ray, 2008). In fact, the majority of Americans do not perceive that older people gain at the cost of younger populations or that benefits are too costly. And fewer Americans currently view Social Security in crisis compared to those who did in 1998, although more support incremental reform to ensure that the Trust Fund has enough money for benefits for the next 50 years (Harris Poll, 2007; Wright & Davies, 2007). Any future changes in Social Security must recognize that the vast majority of Americans support protecting this program, believing that the U.S. should do more, not less for older adults, and not privatize it. Such public support may reflect recognition of how Social Security benefits not just retirees but also younger generations (Harrington Meyer & Estes, 2009; Harrington Meyer & Herd, 2007; Williamson & Watts-Ray, 2008), as summarized in the box on page 709. Cross-generational transfer programs may actually receive more public support than typically portrayed by the media and politicians, an issue described below under the intergenerational equity framework.

As noted above, Social Security's short-term danger of bankruptcy was averted through remedial legislation in 1983, which reduced benefits such as a delay in the cost of living adjustment (COLA) and increased the age of full eligibility from 65 years to age 67, beginning in 2003 (to be fully implemented in 2027). The long transition period for this change made it politically viable; in fact, it drew little attention from aging advocates because of its gradual incremental approach (Binstock, 2008; Natali & Rhodes, 2007). These reforms allowed the system to accumulate reserves, even though they currently exceed the benefits paid. As a result, the accumulated surplus is now $2.6 trillion and will rise to $4 trillion by 2023 (Board of Trustees, 2009); It is also essential to recognize that there are great risks of error in making long-range forecasts of 75 years, and dire projections are only speculations about the future, not fact. Nevertheless, current projections are that the Trust Funds will continue to grow only until 2016 or 2017, at which point the benefits payable will exceed the Social Security tax revenues. However, a funding shortfall, due largely to increasing claims by baby boomers, will not occur until at least 2037, although this is 4 years earlier than the date of 2041, estimated in 2008 (Caldera, 2009; Goldstein, 2009; Sahadi, 2009). When a shortfall occurs, where the benefit payouts exceed taxes and interest, the reserves in the Trust Fund would be drawn down. The exhaustion of the Trust Fund, however, would not mean that Social Security benefits would stop; this would happen only if Congress passed legislation ending Social Security payroll taxes. Instead, benefits would have to be reduced by about 24 percent or the payroll tax sharply increased by about 50 percent. This means that Congress would still be able to pay around 76 percent of its obligations promised to future retirees (i.e., 76 cents for every dollar of benefits). On the other hand, the financial security of the Trust Fund would be lost (Goldstein, 2009; Harrington Meyer & Estes, 2009; Social Security and Medicare Boards of Trustees, 2006; Wright & Davies, 2007).

Even if Social Security remains solvent, another concern is that the federal deficit is turning the surplus into paper savings. This could occur because the Treasury Department borrows and then spends the Social Security reserves by investing them in U.S. government securities. The Trust Fund loans its annual surpluses to the general fund of the federal government for use in other programs. In effect, it gives Social Security an IOU

CROSS-GENERATIONAL NATURE OF SOCIAL SECURITY BENEFITS

Contrary to common perceptions, Social Security benefits individuals across the life course, not just older adults. The importance of Social Security to the economic well-being of younger families is well documented:

- It ensures basic protection for the neediest (SSI), regardless of age.
- Every worker contributing to Social Security, regardless of age, has disability insurance worth over $414,000 for workers with major disabilities that prevent them from being employed, and life insurance equivalent to a $433,000 policy for children of deceased workers.
- Social Security ensures compensatory income, regardless of age, to those who experience sudden loss of income (e.g., widows, surviving children, persons with disabilities), as illustrated by the following facts:
  - 33 percent of Social Security beneficiaries are not retirees
  - 17 percent of beneficiaries are younger persons with disabilities
  - 6 percent are children under age 18 who receive Social Security checks as dependents of deceased, disabled, or in a few cases, retired workers
- Social Security lifts 1 million children above the poverty threshold
- Social Security is the largest source of cash benefits for custodial grandparents, who often live on very low incomes. Such survivor or disability support for a grandchild or stepgrandchild is based on the earnings record of a grandparent or stepgrandparent.
- Social Security frees the middle generation from financial support to older relatives, and allows them to direct their resources toward their children (SSA, 2009a).

---

so that the reserves accumulated may be consumed by deficits in later years. Each time the federal government borrows from the Social Security Trust Fund, it issues a legal obligation to pay back the money with interest whenever Social Security

SHOULD A 30-YEAR-OLD WORRY ABOUT FUTURE SOCIAL SECURITY BENEFITS?

If no changes are made to Social Security, when a 30-year-old in 2008 reaches age 64 in the year 2042, benefits for all retirees could be cut by 27 percent and reduced every year thereafter. If this 30-year-old lived to age 100 (which will be more common by then), his or her scheduled benefits could be reduced by 35 percent from today's levels. But this future elder will still receive approximately 65 percent of scheduled benefits (SSA, 2006a).

POINTS TO PONDER

How much will *your* Social Security benefits be when you retire? Since 1988, the Social Security Administration has sent individual statements to every U.S. worker age 25 and older, listing their years of employment, earnings, and Social Security taxes paid each year. Best of all, it lists each person's estimated benefits if they retire at age 62, 67, or 70, based on past contributions to the system, current age, and income. Individual workers can also estimate their benefits by completing the benefits calculator on SSA's website. After you have reviewed this information for yourself, consider the possibility of living with that level of income. Does this seem adequate, especially if you do not anticipate having additional revenue from pensions or continued employment to bolster your income?

needs it to pay benefits. In effect, this is akin to a family borrowing from their college trust fund to pay off their household debts. By 2016, the government will need to begin paying interest and then principles on the securities held by the Trust Fund (Greider, 2009; Ruffing & Van de Water, 2009; SSA, 2009b).

In contrast to the warnings of doom, a more optimistic view is that projected shortfalls can be addressed with relatively minor adjustments. The National Committee to Preserve Social Security and Medicare (NCPSSM) maintains that full solvency can be extended beyond 2037 by expanding the number of workers participating in Social Security (e.g., requiring the approximately 30 percent of local and state government workers who currently do not participate to pay Social Security taxes); raising the cap on taxable income; or allowing the government to invest the funds in equity markets. Such changes are likely to be incremental and represent political compromises between those who favor privatization and those who view Social Security as a "sacred entitlement." But even changes as small as a 0.7 percent reduction in annual cost-of-living adjustments would, over time, result in enormous cost savings. Accordingly, future benefits to older people will not depend solely on the proportion of workers to retirees; it will also rely on whether the economy generates sufficient additional resources to cover Social Security and whether the political will

exists to transfer them to older adults and persons with disabilities. Points of view thus vary widely about the magnitude of the Social Security crisis, along with proposed solutions (Schulz & Binstock, 2006; Williamson & Watts-Ray, 2008). Variations in Social Security reform proposals can be attributed to differing perspectives regarding program goals, whether as:

- *social insurance* (i.e., provide benefits upon disability or death), or
- *income redistribution* (transfer resources from the wealthier to those with fewer resources, both within and between generations).

Some critics of Social Security prefer that it become a savings program that maximizes the "rate of return" to beneficiaries and fosters economic growth by encouraging savings. They argue for privatizing Social Security by greater reliance on individual savings, and predict higher rates of return on individual contributions through stock market investments. This is viewed as the most efficient way to distribute resources across generations, while social insurance is seen as undermining free markets. **Privatization** would divert payroll taxes (or general revenue income tax credits) to new systems of Social Security investment accounts. Because of the persistent theme that "Social Security must be fixed," we briefly review the arguments for fiscal reform, also known as *privatization*. Even if privatization is not pursued under the current Democratic administration, conservatives' ongoing framing of Social Security as a crisis requiring "fiscal and entitlement reform" aim to undermine public confidence in the program as part of a larger effort to reduce government spending (Greider, 2009). Proponents of partial privatization are likely to repackage their arguments to emphasize the ownership and personal economic self-interest aspects of individual accounts, favoring individual responsibility (and risks) (Williamson & Watts-Ray, 2008). Some of these arguments parallel those in health care reform debates about a single-payer system or preserving choice through medical savings accounts. Proponents of partial privatization argue that the fundamental goals of reform should be:

- to promote consumer choice
- to substitute personal savings for tax-financed entitlements
- to take advantage of economies of scale

The most frequently discussed privatization models encompass the following components:

- Workers invest their Social Security retirement funds in the stock market and individual retirement accounts (IRAs).
- Workers contribute to a "first-tier" minimum benefit account through Social Security; above that amount, however, contributions would be deposited in a worker's own personal retirement account.
- Future benefits would be prefunded through direct investments of the trust funds into the stock market (Williamson, 2002).

These privatization models assume a strong economy and stock market, as well as individual

knowledge and skills to make informed investment decisions. Yet these assumptions are undermined by the stock market's poor performance in 2000 and again in 2008–2010, and the fact that most workers are uneducated about the stock market and fail to adequately plan financially for retirement. In fact, the U.S. Securities and Exchange Commission notes that over 50 percent of Americans do not know the difference between a bond and equity (Schulz & Binstock, 2006). Supporters of privatization are primarily Republican lobbyists (e.g., insurance and investment companies that would profit from it) and Washington, D.C. conservative think tanks such as the CATO Institute, the Third Millennium, the Heritage Foundation, the Peter G. Peterson Foundation, and the American Enterprise Institute. They argue that personal investment would lead to higher benefits, and participants would be able to pass wealth to their survivors in the event of a premature death (i.e., before the age of Social Security eligibility). Proponents point to over 20 countries that have established versions of personal accounts and hold Chile up as a model for privatization. Yet even supporters of privatization acknowledge that private accounts would not solve all of Social Security's financing problems, and initial returns would be low because workers would still be committed to paying for the system's past debt (Hudson, 2005).

A wide range of negative outcomes of privatization have been identified by the Social Security Administration (SSA), presidential commissions appointed to study privatization, economists and policy scholars, and even an organization of young adults, the "2030 Center," that aims to strengthen Social Security. These are best captured by the fact that privatization represents a fundamental shift from government to individual responsibility, while not resolving Social Security's long-term financial problems. While proponents argue that privatization is a way to "save universal programs," it would probably destroy Social Security by shifting away from its universal nature and its value of social solidarity. For example, prefunding through individual accounts would actually worsen Social Security's financial problems. The uncertainty of the stock market compared to the guaranteed security of U.S. treasury bonds would mean that investment income may not be sufficient to last until a person dies (Blendon et al., 2005; Caldera, 2009; Herd, 2005; Herd & Kingson, 2005; Holstein, 2005).

Privatization would disproportionately negatively impact low-income workers, especially women and persons of color who depend on Social Security more than other worker groups and have limited resources to invest privately. Low-income workers who lack financial literacy about investment decisions would be disadvantaged, furthering class inequities in retirement income. The primary beneficiaries of a privatized system would be higher-income unmarried workers, largely Caucasian males (Harrington Meyer & Estes, 2009; Herd & Kingson, 2005; Williamson & Watts-Ray, 2008).

Other proposals for future funding of Social Security, separate from privatization, encompass variations on raising payroll taxes, increasing the age of eligibility, using means testing, increasing borrowing, reducing benefits, or relying on economic growth. In addition to the above changes recommended by the NCPSSM, other options frequently discussed are:

1. *Raising the retirement age for full benefits to age 69 or 70, and for partial benefits to age 65.* However, this could negatively impact persons of color, who have lower life expectancies and may be forced to retire for health reasons from low-paying, physically demanding jobs.
2. *Increasing the number of years needed to compute Social Security benefits from 35 to 38 or 40 years.* This would negatively impact women and other low-wage workers who are less likely to have been employed that length of time.
3. *Increasing payroll taxes* These taxes have not changed since the mid-1980s. Raising the employer and employee's share each by 1 percent would keep the system fully solvent for 75 years. However, this would be regressive

SOCIAL SECURITY BENEFITS FOR ELDERS OF COLOR

African American women rely disproportionately more than whites on nonretirement aspects of the Social Security program, given their higher rates of disability and their greater likelihood of surviving their husbands. More than 30 percent of children receiving benefits as survivors and/or dependents of a person with a disability are African American or Latino (Generations United, 2007; Gonyea & Hooyman, 2005; Herd & Kingson, 2005).

in its impact, because the increased tax would represent a greater share of workers' income, especially for women and persons of color. On the other hand, more than 20 countries already have social security taxes that are higher than those of the U.S.

4. *Reducing the cost-of-living adjustments (COLA) to the level equal to actual inflation.* This across-the-board reduction in benefits would create the greatest hardship for the poorest beneficiaries, primarily women and elders of color.
5. *Reducing benefits across the board by 13 percent.* This also is regressive, negatively affecting the lowest-income workers who depend on Social Security for a greater share of their retirement income than do higher-income retirees. In fact, even a 10 percent cut in benefits could lead a 7 percent rise in poverty among older adults.
6. *Raising the cap on the amount of wages and salaries subject to payroll taxes* from the current cap of $106,800 to $140,000 and then index the cap to average wage growth. This would be progressive in its impact, with higher-income workers facing the greater burden of closing the Social Security funding gap.
7. *Increasing the penalty for early retirement* (before the age of full benefits); this would negatively impact elders who must retire due to poor health or unemployment.
8. *Eliminating the "legacy debt"* (i.e., benefits received by early participants well in excess of

their contributions plus interest) by imposing a 3 percent tax on earnings above the maximum earnings base.

9. *Affluence testing by eliminating benefits for higher-income workers above an income threshold ($40,000 in 2003 dollars).* Such proposals alarm even liberal supporters of social insurance, because they are a departure from Social Security's universal age-based nature and would allow higher-income workers to opt out of the system (Diamond, 2004; Diamond & Orszag, 2005; Harrington Meyer & Estes, 2009; Hudson, 2005a; Goldstein, 2009; Greider, 2009; Sahadi, 2009; Schulz & Binstock, 2006; SSA, 2009; Social Security and Medicare Board of Trustees, 2006; Williamson & Watts-Ray, 2008).

Many of these proposals are contrary to the basic philosophy of Social Security as a social insurance plan with universal eligibility. This moral basis of Social Security represents society's willingness to compensate a group of people whose income has been destroyed or lowered by marketplace forces, regardless of their actual contributions. These proposals then challenge the fundamental notion that the federal government should subsidize programs deemed to be in the common good. Many of these options may also undermine Social Security's role in preventing poverty in old age (Herd, 2005; Herd & Kingson, 2005; Holstein, 2005).

Although none of these proposals are currently being debated in Congress, President Obama has committed to build bipartisan consensus on the long-range solvency of Social Security after addressing health care reform (Goldstein, 2009). Concern about the future of Social Security is intensifying, because high rates of unemployment mean that fewer workers are contributing to the Trust Funds. One immediate consequence may be that Social Security recipients will not receive cost-of-living increases in 2010, something that has not happened since automatic adjustments were adopted in 1975 (Crutsinger, 2009). Other modifications

under the guise of fiscal reform are likely to be proposed in the near future in order to bring projected long-term revenues and pension expenditures into balance (Binstock, 2008; Greider, 2009; Natali & Rhodes, 2007; Williams & Watts-Ray, 2008).

Supplemental Security Income (SSI)

As described in Chapter 12, only 27 percent of SSI recipients are age 65 and older. More than 50 percent of these recipients have no sources of income other than SSI. Yet SSI reaches only 40 to 60 percent of eligible low-income persons, often because they lack information about it, have had prior negative experiences with it, or do not want to be stigmatized by receiving "welfare" (SSA, 2008).

SSI is financed fully by federal general revenues (not the Social Security Trust Funds) and administered by the Social Security Administration (SSA). States may supplement federal payments through state revenues, which results in benefit variability. In most states, a person who receives SSI benefits is automatically eligible for Medicaid health benefits. SSI beneficiaries include older adults, adults with disabilities, and those who are visually impaired. Since its inception in 1972, the percentage of older persons receiving SSI benefits has declined, while blind or disabled beneficiaries have increased.

Although SSI was intended to be a protective system or "safety net," it has not eliminated poverty among vulnerable elders. The primary reason is that the federal benefit level equals only about 75 percent of the poverty level for single individuals and 82 percent for couples age 65 and over (SSA, 2009a). When the program was designed, it was assumed that SSI recipients would also receive benefits such as food stamps and that states would contribute revenues to bring their total benefit package up to the poverty threshold. Even with state supplements, however, SSI fails to raise needy older adults out of poverty. In addition, only about 17 percent of all low-income older adults receive food stamps This low percentage is of concern because, in 2007, 11.4 percent of all older aduts faced the threat of hunger, with the rate projected to increase to 33 percent by 2025. The struggle for some older adults to pay for food has intensified during the 2008–2009 economic downturn (Bloom, 2008; Ziliak, Gunderson, & Haist, 2008). One reason for this low participation rate is that older adults who would be eligible think that their income or assets make them ineligible. SSI's eligibility rules related to resource and income limits (i.e., $2,000 for an individual, $3,000 for a couple, and face value of life insurance policy and burial plot) also threaten the dignity of recipients. The monthly benefit is reduced by subtracting *net income,* but in the case of an eligible individual with an eligible spouse, the amount payable is divided equally between husband and wife, further reducing benefits (Choi, 2006; Holstein, 2005; SSA, 2009b). Congress has attempted to facilitate elders' participation in SSI and the food stamp program by enacting provisions to simplify applications and certification of need. Even if outreach is intensified and the application process streamlined and made less intimidating to those with limited education and resources, the means-tested nature of SSI may prevent applications by aging baby boomers (Wu, 2006).

Private Pensions and Income Tax Provisions

Private Pensions

As described in Chapter 12, only 42 percent of the current labor force, primarily middle- and high-income workers, is covered by an employer-sponsored pension plan to supplement Social Security. Overall, the rate of pension growth has slowed due to the changing nature of the workforce and the economic crisis of 2008–2010. Manufacturing jobs that historically provided pensions are slowly disappearing, while service sector and part-time, temporary, contingent, and nonunion jobs have grown. In addition, with the bankruptcy of a growing number of businesses, some pension plans have disappeared, while others have shrunk to levels too low to support retirees.

As noted in Chapter 12, the pension system tends to perpetuate systemic inequities across the life course by income level, race, and gender. Lower-income workers, often women and persons of color, are least likely to work in jobs covered by pensions and to have attained the 5-year vesting requirements. Another inequity is that cash benefits from government-supported private savings plans and favorable tax policies accrue to those who are already relatively well off, intensifying economic disparities over time. Private pension plans that continue to exist thus do not meet the principles of adequacy and shared risk inherent in Social Security. Similar to efforts to privatize Social Security, the growth of voluntary contribution plans such as 401(k)s and 403(b) plans also represents a shift in pension responsibility from the company to the individual.

Income Tax Provisions

Pension plans are not the only "tax expenditures" related to aging. Some older individuals also enjoy extra tax deductions and pay on average a smaller percent of their income in taxes. State and local governments are particularly generous and often provide credits against real estate taxes and partial or full tax exemptions for pensions, veterans' benefits, and Social Security. The federal government does not have many tax provisions that explicitly mention age, but tax law clearly favors Social Security income and saving for retirement. Additionally, older households have lower federal tax rates than households overall, especially households with children (Gist, 2007; Penner, 2008). However, the majority of mortgage interest deductions and state and local tax deductions benefit only the top 20 percent of older households. Higher-income older persons enjoy property tax reductions and preferential treatment when selling their homes (specifically, exemption from capital gains taxation for the sale of a home after age 55). Capital gains realized from the sale of stocks and mutual funds are now taxed at lower rates for those in the highest income brackets. Overall, current tax benefits go to the wealthiest older adults, even more so than to higher income households under age 65. Tax provisions are thus another way that public benefits are inequitably distributed within the older population (Gist, 2007). During the 2008 presidential campaign, both candidates offered additional federal tax benefits to older adults, with Obama proposing to eliminate all federal income taxes on older adults with incomes less than $50,000. Of growing concern, especially during the current economic downturn, is that tax breaks for older adults cost state and federal government billions of dollars a year (Conway & Rork, 2008).

Social Services

Only about one percent of the federal budget allocated to programs for older adults is spent on social service programs. In addition to Medicare and Medicaid, funding for age-based social services derives from **Title XX (**or **Social Services Block Grants)** and the Older Americans Act (OAA) of 1965. Title XX, established in 1975, provides social services to all age-groups. Entitlements are means tested, with most services for older adults targeted to those receiving SSI. In terms of the program classification system discussed earlier, Title XX is a universal program aimed at redressing needs, with income as an eligibility criterion. This means that older people compete for services with families with dependent children and persons who are visually impaired or mentally and/or physically disabled. Title XX encompasses basic life-sustaining, self-care services to compensate for losses in health and functional ability: homemaker and chore services, home-delivered meals, adult protective services, adult day care, foster care, and institutional or residential care services. These have generally ensured a minimum level of support for vulnerable older adults.

Under the federal Omnibus Budget Reconciliation Act (OBRA) of 1981, Title XX was converted to the Social Services Block Grant Program, and federal funds allocated to the states were substantially reduced. The Block

Grant Program was one of the initial decentralization efforts emerging from the new federalism era of President Reagan in the 1980s. Services had to be directed to one of its five goals:

1. Prevent, reduce, or eliminate dependency
2. Achieve or maintain self-sufficiency
3. Prevent neglect, abuse, or exploitation of children and adults
4. Prevent or reduce inappropriate institutional care
5. Secure admission or referral for institutional care when other forms of care are not appropriate (Administration for Children and Families, 2009)

Block grant funding expanded the states' discretion in determining clients' needs and allocating Title XX funds among the diverse eligible groups. But decentralization also decreased revenues for social services under Title XX for older people, despite an increase in demand for services. Competition for funds and variability in services between and within states grew. As a result, states tended to allocate a greater percentage of block grant funds to children than to older adults.

The Older Americans Act (OAA) was funded in 1965 to create a national network for the comprehensive planning, coordination, and delivery of aging services, and is the backbone of services to the aging population. President Lyndon Johnson, signing the law, concluded that the OAA "affirms our nation's sense of responsibility toward the well-being of all of our older citizens" (AOA, 2004). At the federal level, the act charges the AOA, through the Assistant Secretary on Aging, to oversee and support the **Aging Network** (i.e., the system of social services for older adults) and to advocate for them nationally. The establishment of AOA as a discrete unit in the Department of Health and Human Services took more than 27 years, from before the passage of the Act until 1992, and required 13 amendments. At that time, the Administration for Children and Families was also established. This decision to create parallel organizations rather than giving special status to the AOA made a significant statement regarding equity

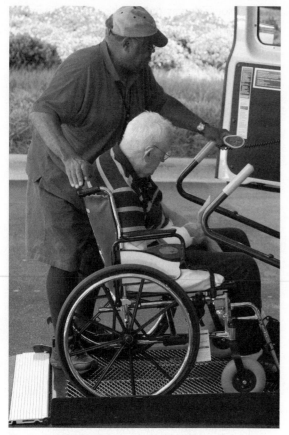

Many agencies funded by AOA provide free or low-cost transportation services.

of responses to the needs of all age-groups. The primary grant programs administered by AOA are:

1. Title III: Grants for State and Community Programs on Aging. Community planning and services to meet older adults' needs
2. Title I: Training, Research and Discretionary Projects and Programs: research and development to promote evidence-based research on program design, including innovative models for service, to individuals with Alzheimer's disease and their families
3. Title V: Community Service Employment for Older Americans. The Senior Community Service Employment Program (SCSEP) offers part-time employment and training

for low-income adults age 55 and older who perform service-type jobs, with the goal of settling them into permanent positions in local agencies and businesses
4. Title VI: Grants for Services to Native Americans provides grants specifically to American Indians and native Hawaiians for supportive and nutrition services
5. Title VII: Vulnerable Elder Rights Protection Activities. Establishes protection systems for the prevention of elder abuse, neglect, and exploitation, including the long-term care ombudsman programs and state legal assistance development

Title III is the single federal social service statute designed specifically for all adults age 60 and over, regardless of income and need. It funds the services typically associated with AOA, such as senior centers, home-delivered and congregate meals, transportation, information and referral, and, more recently, respite and other services for caregivers. In terms of the policy criteria listed in

---

SERVICES PROVIDED UNDER THE OLDER AMERICANS ACT

Access Services: Information and referral; care management.

In-Home Services: homemaker assistance, respite care, emergency response systems, friendly visiting, minor home repairs, and telephone reassurance—and increasingly nonmedical home health care.

Senior Center Programs: social, physical, educational, recreational, and cultural programs, with a growing emphasis on health enhancement and wellness.

Nutrition Programs: meals at senior centers or nutrition sites; in-home meals (Meals on Wheels).

Legal Assistance Advocacy: for individual older adults and on behalf of programs and legislation. The OAA is the only major federal legislation that mandates advocacy on behalf of a constituency.

Additional services are provided based on local community needs and resources.

Table 16.1 entitlement is universal, based on age. The Aging Network encompasses the federal, state, and local area agencies on aging, along with its advisory and advocacy groups. Each of the 56 State Units on Aging (SUAs) has an advisory council to engage in statewide planning and advocacy. The SUAs designate local **Area Agencies on Aging (AAAs)** to develop and administer service plans within regional and local areas. There are nearly 629 AAAs and 246 tribal organizations that fulfill these functions. Each one has an advisory board, which must include older adults in decision-making roles (AOA, 2009).

In addition to government agencies that are responsible for planning and coordination, a fourth tier of the network is composed of about 30,000 direct service providers and 500,000 volunteers in local communities. Many of these OAA services, central to supporting older adults in community settings, overlap with the goals and provisions of the Social Services Block Grants. Within this wide range of programs, the relatively low level of funding means that waiting lists exist for many programs. Additionally, OAA must frequently target services to low-income elders, elders of color, those in rural settings, and frail older adults at risk of nursing home placement, even though it still retains its original goal of universality. Meals on

---

MEALS ON WHEELS: MORE THAN FOOD

When volunteers deliver meals to 90-year-old Ann, they do more than provide meals. They remove rotting food from Ann's refrigerator, check that the gas stove burners are turned off, and make sure that Ann's daughter has dropped by to visit. Harriet, who is age 85 and blind, says that she cannot pay the voluntary stipend because of an $800 pharmacy bill. When a volunteer looks into this, she discovers that the pharmacist forgot to submit the paperwork for Medicare reimbursement. At a battered gray-shingle house, the volunteers leave meals on the front porch because 72-year-old Henry hates anything to do with the government and goes berserk if they enter his home. However, they call on their cell phone and watch from their car when he picks up the meals to make sure he is still alive and functioning.

Wheels programs, for example, are increasingly serving high-risk, vulnerable elders.

Because participation rates in many OAA services are highest among middle-income elders, proposals for cost sharing of services and fee-for-services have been introduced. Some OAA program staff and advocates fear that cost sharing would introduce means testing and stigmatize OAA programs as "welfare," thereby discouraging their use. However, by targeting services to those with the greatest economic need and functional disability, these programs are already implicitly means tested. Another goal is to increase participation by elders of color through targeted outreach and increased recruitment of persons of color as staff and board members for nonprofit agencies receiving OAA funds. Because of projected cuts to OAA funds, cost sharing, targeted services, sliding-fee schedules, private fundraising, and business partnerships are being tested as alternative approaches by increasing numbers of nonprofits to design new or model programs to promote livable communities.

However, each of these alternative revenue strategies challenges the OAA's basic premise of age-based entitlement and raises questions about its effect on the quality and quantity of services for the very poor. For example, senior centers that charge a fee for fitness activities may deter the very elders who would most benefit from these programs—low-income elders and persons of color—even if there is a sliding scale. Alternatively, providing home care services to all who request or require them raises questions of fairness when well-off elders can afford to purchase such care. Advocates of aging services are concerned that the OAA may start to offer a two-tiered system, one for the poor and another for the well-to-do. The fundamental dilemma is whether the Act can meet the increasing demand for services, given significant budget reductions in 2008–2009.

Because of years of flat funding and rising operating costs, current funding levels were unsustainable, even before the economic downturn. Its negative impacts on older adults are illustrated by the fact that 56 percent of AAAs and 59 percent of Title VI tribal programs had to make

A CATCH-22 FOR MEALS ON WHEELS

The Meals on Wheels program, funded by OAA, has delivered food to older adults and persons with disabilities since 1954. Nationwide, approximately 2 million older adults are on waiting lists to receive Meals on Wheels. An important factor underlying the growing waiting lists is a shortage of volunteer drivers, in part due to rising fuel costs and the growing numbers of elders who need to work for pay instead of volunteering. In 2008, more than 70 percent of AAAs found it difficult to recruit and retain volunteers (NCOA, 2009b). This was particularly problematic for the approximately 4,000 Meals on Wheels programs nationwide that depend on volunteers. They typically provide volunteers with a modest payment as well as paying as their mileage to deliver the meals; but with reduced funding for Meals on Wheels, such stipends are not sustainable over time. If you were director of a Meals on Wheels program and had a limited budget, what strategies would you use to recruit and retain volunteers, given the growing demands for this service?

cutbacks in services in 2008, with these numbers projected to rise to 90 and 100 percent respectively in 2009. More than 50 percent of AAAs reported an increase in the number of elders on their waiting lists for services, particularly for transportation, respite care, home-delivered meals, homemaker services, and homecare. In response to these growing needs, the Economic Recovery Act of 2009 substantially increased temporary funding for senior nutrition programs (NCOA 2009a, 2009b). Additionally, NCOA is funding more outreach centers to assist more older adults and younger persons with disabilities to enroll in services for which they are eligible, such as assistance with heating bills, housing, meal programs, and tax relief. This free online service provides enrollment information for more than 1,500 public and private benefit programs nationwide (Bloom, 2008).

Other OAA advocates fear that, in the absence of a national long-term care policy, the AOA has become the nation's de facto provider of many long-term care services targeted to frail homebound elders, but without the benefit of a comprehensive national policy or adequate funding. As an example of this shift to chronic disease management, the OAA increasingly provides home and community-based services (HCBS) for older adults and younger persons with physical disabilities through more than 30 SUAs as the operating agency for Medicaid. As part of President Bush's New Freedom Initiative, Aging and Disability Resource Centers are now jointly funded by the AOA and Centers for Medicare and Medicaid Services (CMS) to access long-term care services. As a result of its successes, some have argued that the Aging Network is best positioned to design an integrated statewide long-term care program (Hudson, 2005; Keigher, 2006; Polivka & Zayac, 2008; Putnam, 2008). The OAA must be reauthorized for funding every 7 years. After years of inaction, Congress in 2006 passed the necessary reauthorization, with a new theme of "Choices for Independence," which emphasized principles of consumer information for long-term care planning, evidence-based prevention programs, and self-directed community-based services to older adults at risk of nursing home placement (AOA, 2009). As has been true for the past 40 years, funding has remained essentially flat, even though needs continue to grow. For example, the 2008 appropriation for the AOA came to about 27 cents for each eligible person (Putnam, 2008). Aging advocates are recommending a 12 percent increase in funding in 2010. The nature of services available through the Aging Network will undoubtedly shift with the aging of baby boomers, with greater emphasis on health and wellness enhancement, elder-friendly communities, and life-long learning opportunities as well as fee-based programs. Service providers will also seek to reach middle-age caregivers willing to pay for assistance with their care tasks. Already, OAA includes several provisions with an intergenerational impact:

- Multigenerational disease prevention, health promotion services, volunteer activities, and civic engagement

- Supportive services and multipurpose senior centers, including services to facilitate regular interaction between school-aged children and older individuals
- The National Family Caregiver Support Act, which applies to caregivers across the life course, including grandparents as caregivers
- Intergenerational Meals Programs
- Community service and employment programs that promote older adults working with younger generations (Generations United, 2007)

The number of cross-generational programs with the potential for other sources of funding is likely to grow in the future, especially because of the modest funding projected for the OAA and the importance of intergenerational partnerships.

Care Coordination

With the growth of various government-funded services under Block Grants and AOA or programs offered by nonprofit agencies, along with structural fragmentation and discontinuity of services, care coordination (or service management) has emerged

---

AN INTERGENERATIONAL PARTNERSHIP WITH LOCAL SCHOOLS

On a designated weekday during the school year, volunteers meet at the senior center and together visit the school, where they talk with their "littles" for an hour about schoolwork or other topics they choose. For many children, this hour brings a welcome opportunity to have a caring adult's undivided attention. Grandparent-aged mentors can be a source of encouragement to the children and, through them, to their families. Their presence in the classroom can also assist teachers. After the mentoring meetings at the school, the volunteers go to a sponsoring restaurant where they receive a $5 certificate for coffee or a snack. During this break, the volunteers have 30 to 45 minutes to discuss their mentoring experiences and build camaraderie. Then they return to the senior center (www.generationb.org).

---

as a critical function in supporting older adults living in the community. It refers to service integration activities to address an elder's lack of resources and accessing of appropriate services. These activities encompass screening, assessment, development and coordination of a care plan, access and linkage to the required resources, and monitoring and regular reassessment of the services being coordinated. These tasks are most frequently performed by social workers and nurses (Naleppa, 2006). Typically, a certified care manager carries out the complete set of functions, but in some instances, multidisciplinary care management teams take over some of the tasks. Linkage and coordination are carried out by one team member. This is the approach used by PACE and On Lok, described in Chapters 11 and 17. Care managers may be employed by nonprofit and governmental agencies or self-employed, often through local Area Agencies on Aging.

Most Frequent Care Management Services

Locating services	Functional assessment
Arranging services	Health status assessment
Family and social support assessment	Development of care plans
Family counseling	Management of care plans (AARP, 2005)

Care managers also play central roles when elders transition from one health care setting to another, as discussed in Chapter 17.

Policy Dilemmas

Age-Based versus Needs-Based Programs

The preceding discussion of Social Security, SSI, and the OAA highlights continuing debates about the need for age-based programs, choices about who should be served, and how to restrict benefits eligibility. Advocates of age-based programs view them as an efficient way to set a minimum floor of protection—less stigmatizing than means-tested services and promoting the values of dignity and autonomy. Similarly, universal programs based on age alone are assumed be more efficient and less administratively intrusive into elders' lives (Holstein, 2005). Neugarten (1982; Neugarten & Neugarten, 1986) was among the first gerontologists to argue strongly against age-based services. She maintained that they reinforce the perception of "the old" as a problem, thereby stigmatizing elders and adding to age segregation. In her view, the OAA implicitly views anyone over age 60 as vulnerable. Yet, as we have seen, some aging network programs benefit growing numbers of young-old who are relatively healthy, have adequate incomes, and do not need traditional support services. Because up to 25 percent of the population qualifies for age-related benefits, a purely age-based approach is politically and economically unfeasible. Rather than age, economic and health needs should be the basis for selectively targeting services. Proposals for income eligibility, such as means-testing for Social Security and Medicare, are congruent with a needs-based approach. Some advocates for targeting services to high-risk older persons favor a combination of categorical and group eligibility mechanisms. For example, a portion of OAA service funds could be allocated only to older SSI and Medicaid recipients, thereby reaching elders with the lowest incomes and presumably the most service needs. Given the increasing economic inequality within the older population, means-testing programs that comprise the "safety net" for the most vulnerable (e.g., SSI and Medicaid) are viewed as priorities for improvement.

The Politics of Productivity versus the Politics of Entitlement

Closely related to the ongoing debate about age-based versus needs-based programs is the "politics of productivity versus entitlement" (Moody, 2002). As implied throughout this chapter, the **politics of entitlement** is characterized as follows:

- In a "failure model of old age," older people are viewed as needy, worthy, and deserving of public support, solely because of their age.

- Issues are defined in terms of needs and rights.
- The emphasis is on what older people deserve to receive as their right rather than what they can give to others.
- Resources are transferred to the older population as a categorical group.
- Other groups must pay for the benefits provided to the older population.

The **politics of productivity** is characterized in contrasting ways:

- The older population is increasingly diverse.
- The implementation of new policies requires an expanding economy toward which older adults can contribute.
- Older people are defined as a resource to help younger populations in an interdependent society.
- "Investing in human resources" and environmental issues across the life course is essential to future economic growth that benefits all ages.

As noted earlier, political conservatives question entitlement programs for all age groups. While they point to the increased socioeconomic diversity of the older population as a rationale for means testing, they do not agree on how much to target resources to benefit those most at risk. In other words, most advocates for changing entitlement programs appear to be motivated by fiscal goals, not by a desire to reduce status inequities within the older population. Similar macro-level patterns are occurring in many Western European countries, where policy makers have rejected the consensus on which social insurance programs were based—that is, older people as deserving poor. Instead, the cost of population aging is questioned and aging is defined as the problem. Even in countries with strong welfare states, pension systems have been reduced or privatized, undermining long-standing public pension and social protection systems for the common good (Walker, 2007).

Intergenerational Inequity Framework

The **intergenerational inequity** argument that measures the relative hard times of one generation (e.g., children) against the relative prosperity of another (elders) is closely related to the entitlement/productivity debate. This inequity debate began in 1984 with Samuel Preston's classic analysis of poverty rates among the young and old, and public expenditures on behalf of older people. The old were perceived to be thriving at the expense of children, as a result of expanded Social Security benefits and inflationary increases in real estate and home equity (Preston, 1984). This generated a rather simplistic picture of generational conflict, expounded in a growing number of newspaper editorials and TV spots on the "crisis" in Social Security. It also resulted in the formation of conservative groups such as Americans for Generational Equity (AGE), which later merged with the American Association of Boomers (AAB) and the National Taxpayers Union. After closing in 1990, AGE has recently become active again, joining with a new group, For Our Grandchildren (FOG), advocating for partial privatization in the name of helping today's children. However, AGE also frames the intergenerational debate around issues of sustainability, efficiency, and waste reduction (Williamson & Watts-Ray, 2008).

Underlying the intergenerational equity arguments is the assumption that significant distribution choices must be made about how to pay for the costs of an aging society, given the demographic bulge of the baby boomers. This political climate surrounded major revisions in the 1980s and 1990s to some of the long-standing features of old-age programs: Social Security benefits at higher-income levels were taxed for the first time; the Tax Reform Act of 1986 eliminated the extra personal exemption for all older adults (although tax credits continue on a sliding scale for very low-income older persons); and the OAA began targeting services to low-income older adults.

Current support for intergenerational equity is fueled primarily by advocates of reducing government size and spending; it resonates with

> **THEMES OF THE INTERGENERATIONAL INEQUITY ARGUMENT**
> - Older citizens, better off financially than the population as a whole, are selfishly concerned only with their retirement benefits and with maintaining their share of the federal budget.
> - Programs for older people are a major cause of current budget deficits, unemployment of younger people, inadequate schools, and increased poverty among mothers and children.
> - Children are the most impoverished and vulnerable age-group.
> - Younger people today will not receive a fair return for their Social Security and Medicare investments in the future.

American values of individualism and self-sufficiency. Mandatory redistribution of resources through Social Security, part of an entitlement ethic, is viewed as infringing on individual freedoms and making people less responsible for their own retirement income. Proponents of this position argue that government programs should be reduced and self-reliance encouraged to ensure an equitable distribution of resources across generations (Williamson & Watts-Ray, 2008).

Critique of the Intergenerational Inequity Framework

Proponents of justice across generations criticize the intergenerational inequity framework as follows:

- It overlooks subgroups of poverty within the older population, which increased with the 2008–09 recession, and the fact that the U.S. has the highest level of old-age inequality among developed nations. The federal government has a responsibility to assure equity between other groups, such as blacks and whites, not only between generations (Ferraro, Shippee, & Schafer, 2009; Kingson, 2007; Meyer, 2005).
- Although the older population's economic status has improved overall, not all older adults have adequate finances, as described in Chapter 12.

Advocates for older adults acknowledge the growing problem of poverty among children and young families, due largely to increasing numbers of single-parent households, unemployment, and declining wages for service jobs. Nevertheless, proponents seek to ensure economic well-being for the oldest members of our society and to prevent elders from being scapegoated for larger societal problems. Advocates for older adults also acknowledge that it is no longer realistic to proceed on the assumption that all age-based benefits are sacrosanct. For example, they now recognize that it is counterproductive to oppose all measures imposed on financially better-off older persons, such as treating part of Social Security as taxable income. Instead, they emphasize the need to focus on other inequities structured by gender, race, and class (Williamson & Watts-Ray, 2008).

• Evidence of significant intergenerational conflict is limited. Younger and older generations generally recognize their interdependence and support benefits for each other across the life course. For example, both the Children's Defense Fund and AARP argue for a collaborative approach and recognize that older people's well-being contributes to the welfare of all other generations.

• The definition of fairness put forth by groups such as Americans for Generational Equity is narrow and misleading. When fairness is equated with numerical equality, this assumes that the relative needs of children and older adults for public funds are identical, and that equal expenditures represent social justice. Even if needs and expenditures for each group were the same, this would not result in equal outcomes or generational justice.

• There is no evidence that cutting Social Security expenditures would result in increased benefits for young families, given other federal priorities. Instead, reducing such benefits would intensify pressures on families to support their aging relatives financially.

• By framing policy issues in terms of competition and conflict between generations, the intergenerational inequity perspective implies that reciprocity between generations does not exist, that programs benefiting one group take resources from another. However, as we have seen in this and earlier chapters, the distribution of benefits extends far beyond the older population, with the majority of families receiving at least one benefit from entitlements such as Social Security or other safety-net programs.

• The intergenerational inequity debate is a convenient mechanism to justify shifting responsibility for all vulnerable groups from the federal level to individuals, the private sector, and local governments.

• It overlooks other ways to expand public resources through efforts to stimulate economic growth, reduce health care costs, or increase tax revenues.

Instead of focusing on entitlement programs, our society must address macro issues of environmental justice across generations, including issues of sustainability, thrift, conservation, and waste reduction (Holstein, 2005; Kail et al., 2009; Kingson, 2007; Minkler, 2002; Williamson & Watts-Ray, 2008; Wisensale, 2003).

The Interdependence of Generations Framework

Consistent with social exchange theory described in Chapter 8, a "contract between generations" exists through sharing of burdens and solidarity across generations. Typically, this is defined as parents to children and adult children to aging parents. The **interdependence of generations framework** recognizes the changing societal and political context: Never before have so many individuals lived so long, and never have there been relatively so few members of the younger generation to support them. Within this larger context, public and private intergenerational transfers are viewed as central to social progress.

Within the broad framework of interdependence, other paradigms are proposed as ways to conceptualize how burdens and opportunities can be fairly shared among generations. Proponents of a broader concept of **generational justice** point to the fact that in all Western societies, older adults are the primary recipients of public income transfer programs while children are, to a large extent, financed privately by their parents. Issues of generational justice are thus primarily economic conflicts—not political or cultural ones—that focus on the distribution of limited resources. The generational justice perspective argues that differential treatment on the basis of age is morally justified because of sequential reciprocity across the life course. That is, as we age, our membership in age-groups changes. The fact that so many Americans are successfully living through all the stages of life makes treating them differently in old age morally acceptable, because so many of us will eventually benefit as well. Intergenerational sharing of burdens and rewards is fair to the extent that each successive generation can expect to receive the same treatment as the preceding and following ones as it moves through each life stage. In such a system, financing older people during one's earning years is fair because one can expect to reap the same benefits in one's retirement, funded by the next generation (Holstein, 2005; Jecker, 2002; Kohli, 2006; Myles, 2005).

Another closely related paradigm is **generational investments,** in which public and private resources tend to flow downwards from older to younger generations. Age-based services and other social programs, such as public education, play an integral part in the system of reciprocal contributions that generations make to one another. Transfers based on public policy (e.g., education, Social Security, and health care programs) also serve intergenerational goals. As noted above, Social Security benefits are distributed widely across all generations and protect against risks to families' economic well-being across the life course, such as when a younger worker becomes disabled or a middle-aged parent dies. As another example of cross-generational benefits, long-term care serves all age-groups—particularly younger adults with developmental disabilities or chronic mental illness. Likewise, it is erroneous to think of education as a one-way flow to children that is resisted by older people. Older adults' support for school levies reflects their recognition that they also benefit from education programs that increase workforce productivity, and that their grandchildren and great-grandchildren learn better in successful schools (Caputo, 2005). Social Security and Medicare are mechanisms through which generations invest in one another and publicly administer returns to older cohorts for the investments made in the human capital of younger groups. As such, old-age benefits represent claims based on merit and social contributions and should not be subject to means testing.

Within the private spheres of families and communities, resources flow downwards from older to younger generations through care for children and dependent adults, financial support, gifts, trust funds, and inheritances. Private intergenerational transfers are essential to meet families' needs across the life course and to transmit legacies of the past (e.g., culture, values, and knowledge). In addition, the growing number of intergenerational programs reflects how both generations gain from these social exchanges (Wisensale, 2003). A broadened welfare consensus can be fostered through an understanding of life-course disparities that lead to problems in old age. This perspective of our common human vulnerability across the life course is not a new one. In fact, President Lyndon B. Johnson's charge to the 1968 Task Force Report on Older Americans was to determine the most important things to be done for the well-being of the majority of older Americans. Because vulnerability in old age is the product of experiences throughout life, the task force concluded that providing social and economic opportunities for young and middle-aged persons is a high priority (Binstock, 1995).

Similar to the "politics of productivity" and the interdependence framework, Torres-Gil and Moga (2001) argue for a **New Aging** paradigm to

---

THE INTERGENERATIONAL COMPACT

- Most intergenerational transfers of resources are from the old to the young.
- More than 3 million children under the age of 18 receive Social Security benefits because their parents are disabled, retired, or deceased.
- Temporary Assistance to Needy Families (TANF) assists children and their caretaker relatives (parents or grandparents).
- More than 3 million children live in households where an adult, often a grandparent, receives Social Security.
- A growing percentage of older adults volunteer to help children, adolescents, and young families.
- Both old and young are increasingly concerned about and working together to solve other societal issues, such as climate change and health care.

---

identify how all generations can contribute to the common good. Our society must alter both our view of older adults as relatively homogeneous to acknowledge their growing diversity and how we respond to differential needs. With such increased heterogeneity, intergenerational conflict cannot be assumed. Although some tensions between young and old will remain, the politics of diversity will become the norm, whereby some older adults have more in common with younger age-groups—perhaps based on race, gender, ethnicity, functional ability, sexual orientation, or immigrant status—than with their chronological age peers. Differences in political opinions among older people and between age cohorts will increase, with more linkages based on political and ideological priorities, not on age per se.

In the politics of the New Aging, advocacy should be rechanneled from special-interest issues toward policies that benefit all future generations. Previously underrepresented groups of older persons—elders of color, women, and rural residents—must establish alliances with younger populations. In fact, this is already occurring through Generations United (described in

Chapter 12), a joint effort by the Child Welfare League of America, the National Council on Aging, and the Children's Defense Fund. This coalition of consumer, labor, children, and senior groups seeks to reframe policy agendas around our common stake in cross-generational approaches. Even AARP is attempting to influence policy in ways that are congruent with generational interdependence. AARP is also forming networks with national organizations based on racial identity, and supports policies to benefit children cared for by grandparents. And the Gray Panthers has intensified its cross-generational advocacy for environmental policies to enhance quality of life for all. Not only should older adults be viewed as a resource that can contribute to the economy, their own income security and the environment, but the young should be educated to assume responsibilities and prepare for their own aging. The real potential of cross-generational advocacy depends on whether the approach pioneered by Generations United is adopted by mainstream age-based social service organizations. However, the increasing emphasis of the OAA on intergenerational programs suggests that this is beginning to occur, although age-based programs will not be entirely eliminated.

For the interdependence framework to address the problems of the underserved, an ideological consensus is required that government should help all people in need, regardless of age. Given that such consensus does not exist, some policy analysts argue that the real issue for the future is not intergenerational interdependence but rather redefining the role of the public sector in caring for its vulnerable citizens and the relationship between the public and private sectors.

Who Is Responsible?

These policy debates ultimately revolve around the role, size, and purpose of the federal government, and the division of responsibility between the public and private sectors. The public-private debate is not new, but long-standing, reflected even in the passage of Social Security. Until recently, Social Security benefits, Medicare, Medicaid, SSI, and OAA services represented society's primary responsibility for older citizens. It was to be a collective responsibility, exercised through the national government, and a protection to which every older citizen was entitled, simply by virtue of age. Since the Reagan era, public officials and policy makers have asserted that the problems of older adults and other historically underserved groups cannot be solved with federal policies and programs alone. Former President Clinton's statement in the 1990s that the "era of big government is over" represents a major shift in society's view of public policy and government intervention (Hudson, 2005a). Individuals were assumed to be responsible for their own well-being, and federal government interventions were considered to be costly and often ineffective. Instead, it was argued that solutions must come from state and local governments, and from private-sector and individual initiatives; such as advocacy, self-help, family care, personal retirement planning and private investments, individual health care accounts, faith-based organizations, and civic engagement and community service. An anti-tax mentality resulted in legislative changes to reduce federal funds and to rely increasingly on the states through block grants. Thus, over the span of 4 decades, the focus of programs for older adults has shifted from ensuring adequacy to managing costs and revenues (Keigher, 2006; Walker, 2009).

The assumption that states can most efficiently and creatively respond to local needs has been used to justify federal cuts to social programs. This decentralized approach, however, is flawed by the fact that states have the fewest resources to provide services, especially during economic downturns, as illustrated by the dramatic cuts they have had to make during the financial crisis of 2008–2009. Historically, decentralization has not assured uniform policy and equity for powerless groups across all states. Stable, uniformly administered federal policies are required to bring the states with the lowest expenditures up to a minimum standard, but are unlikely in the near future. While past changes to Social Security and AOA services may seem modest, the recent emphasis on cost containment, privatization, and federal retrenchment started to dismantle the priority on the common good established in the 1935 Social Security Act (Holstein, 2005; Meyer, 2005).

Reductions in Government Support

Closely related to debates about the extent of federal or state responsibility is the level of public fiscal support. Although public spending for older adults has increased in terms of total dollars, it has declined when measured as a percentage of the gross national product or as government expenditures per capita corrected for inflation. Economically disadvantaged older persons have also been hurt by budget cuts, especially under the Republican "Contract with America," the 1996 "Personal Responsibility and Work Opportunity Legislation," and current reductions in Medicaid and Medicare. Even under a Democratic administration, adequate federal funding for vulnerable citizens of all ages is unlikely in the near future, given the economic crisis and efforts to fund other national priorities (Edwards et al., 2009; Friedman, 2009).

Private and local entities increasingly expected to assume greater responsibility for the care of older adults. Not only are families unable to carry expanded responsibilities on their own, but the private nonprofit service sector, especially faith-based organizations, lacks the resources to fill the gaps created by federal budget constraints. In fact, federal tax laws have reduced tax incentives for corporate giving. In addition, private contributions traditionally have not been targeted to social services and programs for older adults. As a result, increased private giving would not automatically flow into areas most severely cut, nor would this benefit the age-groups most in need. Population aging affects families and communities of all ages; therefore, it must be addressed by adequate government funding and national leadership (Achenbaum, 2006). Strategic public and private funding innovations, including cross-generational policy and funding, are also essential.

Implications for the Future

Our society is faced with complex and difficult policy choices. Even though the current Democratic administration is oriented toward reducing inequities the following macroeconomic, demographic, and social factors will shape its ability to achieve some of its policy goals:

- the demographic bulge of the aging baby boomers
- increasing economic and racial inequities across the life course
- budget cuts, or flat funding, in public programs, along with the escalating federal deficit, currently the largest in U.S. history
- the economic slowdown, nationally and globally, together with fiscal pressures for older adults to be employed longer, thereby gradually raising the average retirement age
- increased competition for limited public dollars, with greater emphasis on cost-effectiveness, fiscal reform, and accountability
- privatization of public policies, such as the 2003 Medicare Modernization Act, and conservatives' advocacy of individual medical savings accounts (described in Chapter 17)
- expectations that the private sector, including faith-based organizations, civic engagement initiatives, and family and other informal caregivers meet the needs of vulnerable populations
- the influential role of AARP in national policy debates, along with the imperative to advocate for cross-generational policies, programs, and funding, as represented by Generations United

- deep partisan divisions at the federal level
- the globalization of aging issues and policies that affect societies and populations as a whole

Given this context of rapid demographic, social, and economic change, an expansion of public policies for older adults is unlikely, unless this growth occurs through privatization. Instead, issues of income security are likely to continue to be addressed in a piecemeal fashion, and deficit-driven budget pressures will collide with the needs of an aging population (Crystal, 2003). As suggested by Ornstein (2002), the challenge of developing a comprehensive policy approach to the problems of an aging society is to adopt a framework larger than the current budget politics and partisan bickering. Compelling proposals for change that can unite legislators from both sides of the aisle are imperative. One such direction is to adopt an intergenerational or multigenerational approach to policy development, as represented by the strong support from both parties for national respite legislation that crosscuts all ages. Such life-course initiatives move away from age-based categorical funding and pool resources across age-groups. They also serve to shift beyond the intergenerational competition and inequity debates that have framed policy discussions since the 1980s. Another way to configure a comprehensive policy approach is to reconceptualize aging policy as family policy and the aging of the baby boomers as a crisis for families, rather than a crisis in Social Security (Binstock, 2002; Hudson, 2005b).

The challenge is even greater when we consider the fact that the older population is not one constituency but several, in which race, gender, class, functional ability, sexual orientation, and rural/urban residence may be greater unifiers than age. A political agenda must be drafted that can unite different older constituencies—low-income, middle-class, and wealthy—as well as diverse populations with common needs that are not based on age. The probability of a comprehensive policy approach that can bring together diverse actors in the near future is extremely low. Yet limited public resources are not the primary barrier to action. For example, the cost of eliminating poverty among both older people and children is well within our societal resources, but our society has lacked the public will, shared social values, and political consensus to ensure a minimum level of economic security and health for all Americans. Progress in eliminating poverty at all ages could occur largely by improving the basic income support of SSI and expanding Medicaid eligibility. Unfortunately, such gains are unlikely to occur without major changes in our political structures and belief systems of democratic pluralism, states' rights, and individual freedom. Historically, social issues have been addressed through partisan, piecemeal, incremental, and short-sighted government intervention. Social Security and Medicare are exceptions to this approach. Another barrier is the fragmentation of political power endemic to and intensifying in our political system. And last remains the challenge of effective implementation that involves both private and public entities. The process of implementation often impedes fulfillment of the intent of policies. Social Security is an exception because it is a relatively self-implementing and therefore successful program (Binstock, 2002). On the other hand, the "crises" entailed by the aging of the baby boomers may force unified action, despite the lack of a forward-looking national policy. Until then, most Americans will continue to be personally generous, but reluctant to support expanding public income-maintenance programs for diverse groups of needy persons or a national long-term care system that would seem to threaten personal choice.

Gerontologists must advocate for programs that benefit individuals across the life course and into old age. Translating gerontological research findings for policy makers and the general public is inherent within effective advocacy. This means that gerontologists need to be visible at the local, state, and federal levels in presenting evidence-based testimony and offering comprehensive, creative, and cost-effective solutions. Given the nature of our political system and the critical

policy and funding challenges created by aging baby boomers, gerontological policy, practice, and research need to be linked in the training and development of professionals who can influence policy making and implementation.

Summary

This chapter reviewed federal programs that assist primarily older persons, although many of these programs have some cross-generational benefits. Since 1960, age-specific spending has increased significantly, mostly through Medicare and Social Security. In the past, such age-entitlement programs were based on public values and beliefs that older people are deserving. However, the rapid expansion of these programs, combined with the improved economic status of the majority of older adults in the 1980s and 1990s, created a growing public and political perception that such age-based entitlement programs must be reduced, perhaps through privatization and means testing to minimize the benefits received by higher-income older adults.

The U.S. developed age-based policies more slowly than did European countries. The Social Security Act of 1935 was the first major policy benefit for older people. Social Security was expanded slightly in 1950 to support partial health care costs through individual states. These changes led to the enactment of Medicare in 1965. Since then, the number of programs aimed at improving older people's lives has grown significantly: the OAA and the Aging Network it created; SSI and the Social Security Amendments of 1972 and 1977; and Title XX social services legislation. National forums such as the 1961 and 1971 House Conferences on Aging strengthened these programs. During the 1980s, however, social service funding declined, despite recommendations from the 1981 White House Conference on Aging to increase funds for aging services. Federal allocations for homemaker, nutrition, chore services, adult day care, low-income energy assistance, respite, and volunteer programs for older adults all diminished during this period. These reductions were based on a national perception that the older population is financially better off than younger age-groups. The fiscal crisis faced by the Social Security system in the early 1980s fueled this stereotype through speculations that the growing numbers of "Greedy Geezers" would drain the system before future generations could benefit. However, numerous structural factors, not the growth of older adults per se, are responsible for many of the problems. Changes that have subsequently been made in this system assure its future viability until approximately 2037.

The debate over age-based versus needs-based programs has also led to the emergence of organizations that argue that older people are benefiting at the expense of younger age-groups. But evidence of such inequities is weak. Numerous other organizations—such as the Children's Defense Fund and Generations United—recognize generational interdependence and the importance of seeking increased public support for all ages through other sources. This framework, known as the interdependence of generations, generational justice, or generational investment, assumes that assistance from young to old and old to young benefits all ages and supports the role of families across the life course.

The policy agenda for older Americans early in the twenty-first century is full and complex. The current emphasis on economic stimulus and fiscal accountability underlies policy debates, frequently divided along partisan lines, about how much the federal government should be expected to provide and for whom. Public perceptions of older people as well off compared to other age-groups, combined with congressional efforts to reduce government expenditures, will undoubtedly affect the types of future programs and policies developed to meet elders' needs. Older adults are less likely to act as a unified bloc in support of age-based programs. Instead, their increased diversity suggests that alliances will be formed between at-risk

elders and other age-groups. Consistent with the frameworks of interdependence and generational investment, such alliances may foster policies that benefit both older people and future generations, including social and environmental justice efforts. Threatening such cross-age efforts, however, is the public's concern about the escalating federal deficit. These pressures suggest that advocates for older adults will need to find new ways to address the complex needs created by elders' increased life expectancy and diversity. A major challenge is the development and funding of long-term care, especially home and community-based care, the topic addressed next, in Chapter 17.

GLOSSARY

age-based entitlement programs programs only available to people of a certain age

Aging Network the system of social services for older adults funded by the Older Americans Act

Area Agencies on Aging (AAA) offices on aging at the regional and local levels that plan and administer services to meet the needs of older adults within that area; established and partially funded through the Older Americans Act

cash substitute a benefit given in a form other than cash, such as a voucher, which may be exchanged for food, rent, medical care, etc.

cash transfer a benefit paid by cash or its equivalent

categorical in this context, a manner of dealing with social issues by addressing the problems of specific groups of persons rather than attempting solutions that are comprehensive to address problems affecting the entire population

contributory plans programs providing benefits that require the beneficiary to contribute something toward the cost of the benefit

cost-of-living adjustments (COLA) changes in benefits designed to maintain steady purchasing power of such benefits

direct benefit a benefit given directly, in the form of either a cash payment or of some commodity such as food or housing

eligibility criteria factors that determine whether people can receive benefits from specific programs

entitlement programs government programs that do not require appropriations from a legislative body; rather, eligibility on the part of applicants triggers receipt of benefits regardless of the program's cost

generational investment investments made by one generation for the benefit of another, such as the payment of Social Security taxes by the working population for the benefit of retirees, the services provided by older persons for child care, and the payment of property taxes to benefit school children

generational justice older adults receiving benefits based on age is morally justifiable because all adults can eventually benefit from age-based programs

indirect benefit a benefit given through tax deductions or exemptions or other indirect means

interdependence of generations framework recognition of intergenerational transfers that occur across the life course

intergenerational inequity the view that one generation or age-group receives benefits that are disproportional to those received by another, or are at the expense of other generations

need-based (or **means-based**) **entitlement programs** social programs delivered to persons who meet defined criteria of eligibility based on economic need or the ability to pay for benefits

New Aging paradigm in which all generations contribute to the common good and advocacy focuses on policies that benefit all future generations

noncontributory programs programs providing benefits that do not require the beneficiary to contribute toward the cost of the benefit

Older Americans Act federal legislation for a network of social services specifically for older people

politics of entitlement political preferences, especially as applied to elders, for the allocation of resources based on the view of older persons as needy, worthy, and deserving of public support

politics of productivity political preferences for the allocation of resources based on the diversity of the aging population: well-off, poor, capable of continued productive work, or ill or disabled

privatization changes in Social Security that would divert payroll taxes to private investment accounts

selective benefits benefits available on an individually determined need or means basis

social policy government policy designed to address a social problem or issue

social programs the visible manifestations of social policies

Title XX (or the **Social Services Block Grant**) funding for social services (e.g., homemaking chores, adult day care) based on need, not age

universal benefits benefits available as a social right to all persons belonging to a designated group

---

RESOURCES

Log on to MySocKit (www.mysockit.com) for information about the following:

- The 2030 Center
- Administration on Aging (AOA)
- Cato Institute
- Generations United
- International Federation on Aging
- National Academy on Aging
- National Association of Area Agencies on Aging (N4A)
- National Center for Policy Analysis
- National Committee to Preserve Social Security and Medicare
- Social Security Administration (SSA)

REFERENCES

Achenbaum, W. A. (2006). Why did old-age policy making lose steam? *Innovations, 1,* 3.

Administration for Children and Families (2009). Social Service Block Grants: Tables of allocations for 2008 and 2009. Retrieved July 2009, from http://www.acf.hhs.gov/programs/ocs/ssbg/

Administration on Aging (AOA). (2004). *Layman's guide to the Older Americans Act.* Retrieved February 2007, from http://www.aod.gov/about/legbudg/oaa/laymans_guide_pf.asp

Administration on Aging (AOA). (2009). *History of evolution of programs for older Americans.* Retrieved July 2009, from http://www.aoa.gov/AOARoot/AoA_Programs/OAA/resources/History.aspx

Binstock, R. H. (1995). A new era in the politics of aging: How will old-age interest groups respond? *Generations, 19,* 68–74.

Binstock, R. H. (2002). The politics of enacting reform. In S. H. Altman & D. I. (Eds.). Schatman, *Policies for an aging society.* Baltimore: Johns Hopkins University Press.

Blendon, R., Brodie, M., Benson, J., Neuman, T., Altman D., et al. (2005). Americans' agenda in aging for the new Congress. *Public Policy and Aging Report, 15,* 20–25.

Bloom, G. (2008). Meals of meds? Benefits CheckUp helps older people struggling with food costs. Retrieved July 2009, from http://www.ncoa.org/contentcfmsectionID=105&detail=2582

Caldera, S. (2009). *Social Security: Ten facts that matter. Fact Sheet 154, April, 2009.* Washington, DC: AARP Public Policy Institute.

Caputo, R. K. (2005). Inheritance and intergenerational transmission of parental care. In R. K. Caputo (Ed.). *Challenges of aging on U.S. families: Policy and practice implications.* New York: Haworth Press.

Choi, N. (2006). Federal income maintenance policies and programs. In B. Berkman (Ed.). *Handbook of Social Work in Health and Aging.* New York: Oxford Press.

Congressional Budget Office (CBO). (2007). *The Budget and Economic Outlook: Fiscal Years 2008 to 2017.* Retrieved January 2007, from http://www.cbo.gov/ftpdocs/77xx/doc7731/01-24-Budget Outlook.pdf

Crutsinger, M. (2009). Social Security, Medicare facing unhealthy future: Benefit programs will be depleted before projections. *The Boston Globe,* News, National, p. 7.

Diamond, P. (2004). *What are the best alternatives for meeting the impending crisis in Social Security financing?* Presented at the Conference on Public Policy and Responsibility across Generations. Newton, MA: Boston College.

Diamond, P. A. & Orszag, P. R. (2005). Saving social security. *Journal of Economic Perspectives, 19(2),* 11–32.

Edwards, B., Gramp, K., Shakin, J., & Woodland, C. (2009). *Monthly budget review, fiscal year 2009: A congressional budget office analysis.* Washington, DC: Congressional Budget Office.

Estes, C. L. (1979). *The aging enterprise.* San Francisco: Jossey-Bass.

Estes, C. L. (1984). Austerity and aging. 1980 and beyond. In M. Minkler & C. L. Estes (Eds.), *Readings in the political economy of aging.* Farmingdale, NY: Baywood.

Estes, C. L. (1989). Aging, health and social policy: Crisis and crossroads. *Journal of Aging and Social Policy, 1,* 17–32.

Estes, C. L. (2000). From gender to the political economy of aging. *European Journal of Social Equality, 2,* 28–45.

Estes, C. L., Linkins, K. W., & Binney, E. A. (1996). The political economy of aging. In R. H. Binstock & L. K. George (Eds.). *Handbook of aging and the social sciences* (4th ed.). San Diego, CA: Academic Press.

Feder, J. & Friedland, R. (2005). The value of Social Security and Medicare to families. *Generations, 29,* 78–85.

Friedman, S. (2009). Gray matters: The federal stimulus package offers measly benefits to seniors. *Newsday,* ACT II, p. B08.

Generations United. (2007). *Intergenerational elements in the Older Americans Act. Fact Sheet.* Washington, DC: Generations United.

Gist, J. R. (2007). Spending and tax entitlements. *Tax Notes, 115(2).* Retrieved November 2009, from http://papers.ssrn.com/sol3/papers.cfm?abstract_id=978884

Goldstein, A. (2009). Alarm sounded on Social Security: Report also warns of Medicare collapse. *The Washington Post,* A-Section, p. A01.

Gonyea, J. & Hooyman, N. (2005). Reducing poverty among older women: The importance of Social Security. *Families in Society, 86,* 338–346.

Greider, W. (2009). Looting Social Security. *The Nation,* February 2009. Retrieved July 2009, from http://www.the nation.com/doc/20090302/greider/print

Harrington Meyer, M. & Estes, C. (2009). A new social security agenda. *Public Policy and Aging Report, 19(2),* 7–11.

Harrington Meyer, M. & Herd, P. (2007). Market friendly or family friendly. The state and gender inequality in old age. New York: Russell Sage.

The Harris Poll #1. (2007). *The American Public strongly supports Social Security reform.* Retrieved

March 2007, from http://www.harrisinteractive .com/harris_poll/index.asp?PID=717

Herd, P. (2005). Universalism without targeting: Privatizing the old-age welfare state. *The Gerontologist, 45,* 292–299.

Herd, P. & Kingson, E. (2005). Reframing Social Security: Cures worse than the disease. In R. H. Hudson (Ed.). *The new politics of old age policy.* Baltimore: Johns Hopkins Press.

Holstein, M. (2005). A normative defense of universal age-based public policy. In R. H. Hudson (Ed.). *The new politics of old age policy.* Baltimore: Johns Hopkins Press.

Hudson, R. H. (2005a). Contemporary challenges to age-based policy. In R. H. Hudson (Ed.). *The new politics of old age policy.* Baltimore: Johns Hopkins Press.

Hudson, R. H. (2005b). The contemporary politics of old age policies. In R. H. Hudson (Ed.). *The new politics of old age policy.* Baltimore: Johns Hopkins Press.

Jecker, N. (2002). Intergenerational justice. In D. Ekerdt (Ed.). *The Encyclopedia of Aging.* New York: McMillan.

Keigher, S. (2006). Policies affecting community-based social services, housing and transportation. In B. Berkman (Ed.). *Handbook of social work in health and aging.* New York: Oxford University Press.

Kingson, E. R. (2007). The greying of the baby boom in the United States: Framing the policy debate. *International Social Security Review, 44*(1/2), 5–26.

Kogan, R. (2008). Federal spending, 2001 through 2008. Washington, D.C: Center on budget and Policy Priorities.

Kohli, M. (2006). Aging and justice. In R. H. Binstock & L. K. George (Eds.). *Handbook of aging and the social sciences* (6th ed.). New York: Academic Press.

Meyer, M. H. (2005). Decreasing welfare; increasing old age inequality: Whose responsibility is it? In R. H. Hudson (Ed.). *The new politics of old age policy.* Baltimore: Johns Hopkins Press.

Moody, H. R. (2002). Should age or need be the basis for entitlement? In H. R. Moody, (Ed.). *Aging: Concepts and controversies* (4th ed.). Thousand Oaks, CA: Sage.

Myles, J. (2005). What justice requires: A normative foundation for U.S. pension reform. In R. Hudson (Ed.). *The new politics of old age policy.* Baltimore: Johns Hopkins Press.

Neale, A. (2005). American values and social justice: Who should pay for elders' income and health-care security? *Generations, 29,* 88–90.

Neugarten, B. (1982). Policy in the 1980s: Age or need entitlement. In B. Neugarten (Ed.). *Age or need: Public policies for older people.* Beverly Hills, CA: Sage.

Neugarten, B. & Neugarten, D. (1986). Changing meanings of age in the aging society. In A. Pifer & L. Bronte (Eds.). *Our aging society: Paradox and promise.* New York: W. W. Norton.

Preston, S. H. (1984). Children and the elderly in the United States. *Scientific American, 251,* 44–49.

Purcell, P. (2009). *Income and poverty among older Americans in 2008.* Washington, DC; Congressional Research Services (www.crs.gov).

Sahadi, J. (2009). *Obama tax panel on treasure hunt.* Retrieved November 2009 from, http://money. cnn.com/2009/03/26/news/economy/obama_tax_ reform_taskforce/

Social Security Administration (SSA). (2006a). *Fiscal Year 2006 Performance and accountability report. Overview of the Social Security Administration.* 2006a. Full report. Retrieved March 2007, from http://www.ssa.gov/finance/ 2006/FY06_PAR.pdf

Social Security Administration (SSA). (2006b). *Updated long-term projections for Social Security.* Retrieved March 2007b from http://www .cbo.gov/ftpdocs/72xx/doc7289/06–14-LongTerm Projections.pdf

Social Security Administration (SSA). (2008). *Supplemental Security Income Annual Statistical Report,* 2008. Retrieved July 2009, from https://www.ssa.gov/policy/docs/statcomps/ssi_asr/

Social Security Administration (SSA). (2009a). *Facts & figures about Social Security,* 2009. Retrieved October 2009, from http://www.ssa.gov/policy/ docs/chartbooks/fast_facts/2009/fast_facts09.pdf

Social Security Administration (SSA). (2009b). *Frequently asked questions about Social Security's future.* Washington, DC: Author.

Social Security and Medicare Boards of Trustees. (2006). *Status of the Social Security and Medicare Programs. A summary of the 2006 annual reports.* Retrieved March 2007, from http://www.ssa.gov/ OACT/TRSUM/trsummary.html

Teles, S. (2005). Social Security and the paradoxes of welfare state conservatism. In R. H. Hudson (Ed.). *The new politics of old age policy.* Baltimore: Johns Hopkins Press.

Walker, D. M. (2007). Fiscal, Social Security, and health care challenges. Government Accountability Office (GAO). Retrieved January 2007, from http://www.gao.gov/cghome/d07345cg.pdf

Walker, A. (2009). Aging and social policy: Theorizing the social. In V. L. Bengtson, D. Gans, N. M. Putney & M. Silverstein (Eds.). *Handbook of theories of aging* (2nd ed). New York: Springer Publishing Company.

Wan, H., Sengupta, M., Velkoff, V., & DeBarros, K. (2005). *65+ in the United States: 2005.* U.S. Census Bureau, Current Population Reports. Washington, DC: U.S. Government Printing Office, P23–P209.

Williamson, J. B. (2002). What's next for social security? partial privatization? *Generations, 26,* 34–39.

Williamson, J. B. & Watts-Ray, D. M. (2008). Aging boomers, generational equity and the framing of the debate over Social Security. In R. B. Hudson (Ed.). *Boomer Bust* (Vol. I). Westport, CT: Praeger Press.

Wisensale, S. K. (2003). Global aging and intergenerational equity. *Journal of Intergenerational Relationships, 1,* 29–46.

Wright, W. & Davies, C. (2007). *Retirement security survey report.* Washington, DC: AARP. Retrieved March 2007, from http://assets.aarp.org/rgcenter/econ/retirement_security.pdf

Wu, K. (2006). *Income and Poverty of Older Americans in 2004.* AARP and Public Policy Institute.

Yee, D. (2005). Insuring health and income needs of future generations. *Generations, 29,*13–20.

Ziliak, J. P. Gundesen, C., & Haist, M. (2008). *The causes, consequences and future of senior hunger in America.* Retrieved July 2009, from http://www.mowaa.org/Page.aspx?pid=183.

chapter

17

Health and Long-Term Care Policy and Programs

This chapter covers

- Definitions, status, and expenditures for acute and long-term care (LTC)
- Medicare, its components and efforts at cost containment
- The increasing burden of health and long-term care costs on elders and their families
- The growing preference and need for community-based home care
- Medicaid as a source of payment for home and community-based services as well as skilled nursing home care
- State innovations under Medicare and Medicaid, including model programs for integrated care and for transitions in care
- Private long-term care insurance, its costs and limitations

Throughout this book, we have examined the interplay of social, physiological, and psychological factors in how older people relate to their environments and how health status affects this interaction. Technological advances oriented toward cure have created the paradox that, while adults now live longer, they also face serious, often debilitating or life-threatening, chronic disabilities that create the need for ongoing care. Although Chapter 4 notes that disability per se in old age does not create dependency, many older adults, especially among the oldest-old, are physically or mentally frail and depend on informal supports as well as medical and social services. This dependence is often intensified by the interaction of age, race, class, gender, poverty, and sexual orientation, as well as changes in family structure described in Chapter 9. And, as we have seen, the oldest-old, persons of color, women, and those who are low-income are most prone to have chronic disabilities that affect their ability to function and increase the likelihood of needing health services.

Health Care Expenditures for Older Adults

Policy makers, service providers, and the general public are all concerned about the "crisis in health care." This crisis refers to the costs, the growing numbers of uninsured individuals of all ages, and the status and future of health care systems. People age 65 and older account for over 30 percent of the nation's annual federal health care expenditures. In fact, the average expenditure for health services for adults age 65 and over is 3.3 times the cost for those under age 65 and increases even more among the oldest-old. This is mostly for long-term care (LTC); in fact, of all LTC expenditures in the United States (e.g., skilled nursing home, home health care), nearly 70 percent are for people age 65 and over, (Bishop, 2008; Moon, 2006; Stone, 2006).

Although cost-containment changes in the private health care marketplace, such as managed care, are intended to slow the rate of acute health care costs, expenses are still rising faster than the cost of living. Spending on Medicare and Medicaid, which consumes approximately 24 percent of the federal budget and accounts for about 5 percent of the gross domestic product, is expanding at several times the economic growth rate (Congressional Budget Office, 2009; Gleckman, 2009). Even though public expenditures for health and long-term care through Medicare, Medicaid, and the Veterans Administration are growing, older individuals and their families continue to pay more out-of-pocket for health care than do younger Americans. Older people now spend a higher proportion (and more in actual dollars) of their incomes on health care services than they did before Medicare and Medicaid were established in 1965. The median older household spends nearly 12 percent of its annual income on health care costs, 50 percent of which pays Medicare and Medigap insurance premiums. Almost one sixth of community-dwelling older adults now spend more than 33 percent of their income on health care. Elders with incomes at or below poverty level spend 29 percent of their income for health care, and these rates continue to rise each year. In addition, LTC costs as part of older adults' overall health expenditures have grown from less than 4 percent in 1960 to over 12 percent (Bishop, 2008; Federal Interagency Forum, 2008; Gleckman, 2009; Neuman, 2009). The sources of personal health care expenditures are illustrated in Figure 17.1. In sum, the financial burdens of health care are expected to expand faster than the older population's capability to pay. At the same time, private health insurance costs are growing more rapidly than Medicare spending, and increases are greatest for home health care and skilled nursing homes.

Factors Underlying Growing Costs

A number of structural factors underlie escalating health care costs.

- The success of modern medical care: At least 50 percent of health expenditures are attributed to technological advances. It is important to recognize that such technology is available to all age-groups thereby increasing per capita health expenditures for everyone, not just older adults (Bishop, 2008).

Visits to doctors for preventive care can help reduce health care costs

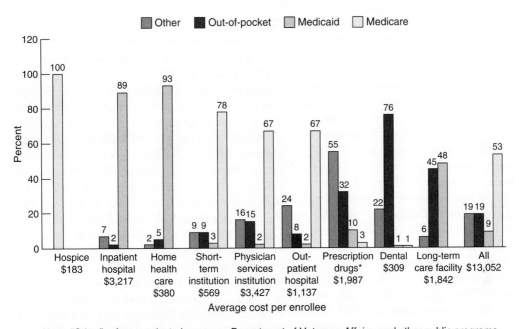

FIGURE 17.1 **Sources of Payment for Health Care Services for Medicare Enrollees Age 65 and Over by Type of Service 2004**

Note: "Other" refers to private insurance, Department of Veterans Affairs, and other public programs.
Reference population: These data refer to Medicare enrollees.
*Figures do not reflect changes with Medicare Part D coverage of prescriptions starting in 2006
Source: Centers for Medicare and Medicaid Services, Medicare Current Beneficiary Survey.

Although advances in medical science produce cost-saving breakthroughs, they also make possible more sophisticated, complex, and expensive medical treatments. These tend to be used in addition to prior services rather than replacements for old technologies or procedures. For example, an older patient now may receive X-rays, CAT scans, and MRIs to diagnose a problem, whereas only radiographs might have been used in the past (Congressional Budget Office, 2009; Gleckman, 2009).

• Related to the success of medical technology in prolonging life is the conflict between the curative goals of medicine and the chronic care needs of older adults. As a result, there is a poor fit between the LTC needs of the older population and the funding mechanisms, regulations, and fragmented services of the health care system that is oriented toward acute care.

• Comprehensive, coordinated health and LTC policy and programs that integrate acute and chronic care are limited.

As seen in Chapter 16, some powerful values and assumptions underlie these systemic factors. They include reluctance to move to government-funded universal health care and a strong belief in the private sector. They combine to produce an approach to LTC and health care that is determined largely by the market, particularly insurance companies. In other words, the shape of health care has been largely influenced by its method of payment. Health services are provided privately, without effective market control or uniform government regulation of expenditures. Patients have been largely free to choose the health care providers they prefer. In turn, physicians have been able to charge patients whatever they choose, with approval by insurance companies. Nevertheless, most health services are financed by a mix of public programs, private insurance, and direct patient payments. Federal and state efforts to limit health care expenditures are now the norm. Described below are modifications to this fee-for-service system in order to control costs, such as Health Maintenance Organizations and managed care, as well as the impetus for health care reform.

A fundamental problem for older people is not costs per se but the fact that acute and long-term care remain two separate, fragmented systems, with relatively distinct providers, treatment settings, financing structures, and goals, although some states have tried to integrate the two. Physicians are the primary care providers in hospitals and outpatient settings, covered mostly by Medicare. When Medicare was passed in 1965, the ability to keep persons with chronic illnesses and disabilities alive, along with the use of medications to do so, was limited. Now chronic care of diseases such as diabetes, dementia, and the interactions of such conditions as osteoporosis, depression, and other illnesses are the primary long-term care needs of older adults, not acute care. Accordingly, more than 80 percent of Medicare beneficiaries have a chronic condition; one-quarter of these beneficiaries who have five or more chronic diseases account for 68 percent of Medicare expenditures (Lawlor, 2008). Older adults who suffer cardiac arrest will have their hospital costs covered by Medicare, but those living with chronic heart disease face barriers to accessing publicly funded in-home care central to quality of life. Nursing staff, direct care workers, and family members are the principal providers of LTC in skilled nursing facilities and private home settings. Medicaid pays for a large percentage of nursing home care and, increasingly, home-based care. In the acute-care setting, the intensity of services that are oriented toward cure determines costs, compared to the duration of services in chronic care settings. Overall, the dissimilar purposes of Medicaid and Medicare are significant barriers to the integration of these two systems.

Medicare

As a social insurance system, **Medicare**, or Title XVIII of the Social Security Act of 1965, is intended to provide financial protection against the cost of hospital and physician care for people age 65 and over. In 1972, the program was expanded to include younger persons with permanent disabilities. Prior to the passage of Medicare, only about 50 percent of older adults had health insurance. A value underlying Medicare is that people are entitled to access *acute medical care* on the basis of age (65 and older), and society has an obligation to cover the costs associated with inpatient hospital care. Medicare's focus on the older population grew out of a compromise with the medical profession, which successfully opposed comprehensive health insurance for the general public. Yet Medicare was also viewed as the "first step" toward increasing access to health care for all age-groups. Today, Medicare funds health care for 45 million people, including 7 million who are younger than age 65 and disabled. The success of this program in covering so many people with so little overhead has made it a model for the health care reform bills in Congress during 2009. Even those opposed to publicly

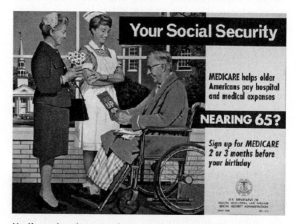

Medicare has been an important part of older adults' health insurance since its inception in 1965.
SOURCE: Social Security Administration History Website http://www.ssa.gov/history/history.html

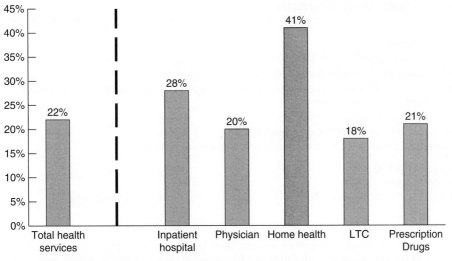

FIGURE 17.2   Medicare's Share of National Personal Health Expenditures: 2007
SOURCE: Federal Interagency Forum on Aging, 2008.

funded health care for the general population have argued that Medicare should be maintained and benefits improved, not reduced in an era of cost-cutting to manage health care costs.

Despite Medicare's goal of financial protection, it covers only 57 percent of health care expenses for older adults, with other funding sources needed for the remaining 43 percent (Congressional Budget Office, 2009). As noted earlier and illustrated in Figures 17.1 and 17.2, the remainder is paid by beneficiaries out-of-pocket through private supplemental insurance or "Medigap" policies (7 percent), by Medicaid (43 percent), and by other public payers such as the Veterans Administration (4 percent). Medicare pays for 22 percent of all health care expenditures in the U.S. and a high proportion of all home health care costs (41 percent), as shown in Figure 17.2.

Contrary to many older adults' assumptions that their acute health care costs will be covered, Medicare pays only 80 percent of the allowable charges, not the actual amount charged by health providers. The patient must pay the difference between "allowable" and "actual" charges, unless the physician accepts "assignment" and agrees to charge only what Medicare pays. Beneficiaries whose doctors do not accept Medicare assignments are responsible for the amount that their doctors charge above the Medicare-approved rate. As illustrated by the vignette about Mr. Fox below. In the current economic downturn, growing numbers of physicians, particularly in rural

---

MEDICARE PAYS ONLY PARTIAL HEALTH CARE COSTS

Mr. Fox went to his physician for a sigmoidoscopy, a procedure to examine the large colon for polyps or cancer. His physician charges $300 for his part of this procedure. Medicare determined that the typical fee for a sigmoidoscopy in Mr. Fox's community is $180, which means that Medicare pays the physician 80 percent of that amount, or $144. If Mr. Fox's physician accepts the assignment, then Mr. Fox owes his doctor the difference between $180 and $144, or $36. Fortunately, Mr. Fox has private Medigap insurance that covers this difference. If Mr. Fox's physician had not accepted the assignment, then Mr. Fox would have been responsible for paying $300 less the amount paid by Medicare, or a total of $156.

TABLE 17.1   Summary of Components of Medicare

Hospital Insurance (Part A)
- Covers 99 percent of the older population
- Financed through the Social Security payroll tax of 2.9 percent
- Available for all older persons who are eligible for Social Security
- Pays up to 90 days of hospital care and for a restricted amount of skilled nursing care, rehabilitation, home health services (if skilled care is needed), and hospice care
- Hospital inpatients pay a $1068 deductible fee
- Beneficiaries are charged copayments for hospital stays exceeding 60 days
- When the 90 days of hospital care are used up, a patient has a "lifetime reserve" of 60 days

Supplemental Medical Insurance (Part B)
- Covers 97 percent of the older population
- Financed through a combination of monthly premiums paid for by the beneficiary and general tax revenues
- Annual $135 deductible
- Since 2007, premiums higher for beneficiaries with annual incomes greater than $80,000

Generally pays 80 percent of physician and hospital outpatient services; home health care limited to certain types of health conditions and specific time periods; diagnostic laboratory and X-ray services, and a variety of miscellaneous services, including 50 percent of the approved amount for outpatient mental health care.

Medicare Advantage (Part C)
- Includes both Medicare Parts A and B services and some additional benefits
- Not a fee-for-service program
- Premiums can range from $50 to $100 per month

---

areas, are unwilling to take more Medicare patients. Medicare beneficiaries must also pay an annual deductible and copayments.

As shown in Table 17.1, Medicare is composed of Part A (Hospital Insurance), Part B (Supplemental Medical Insurance)—although not all older people can afford Part B—and Part C (Medicare Advantage), a more recent option that includes Parts A and B but is not a fee-for-service program like the more traditional components of Medicare. Services covered under Medicare Parts A and B are illustrated in Figure 17.3.

The 1997 Balanced Budget Act created managed care options for older people under **Medicare Plus Choice**, which was renamed in 2003 as **Medicare Advantage** under the Medicare Modernization Act passed that year. **Managed care** refers to a health plan in which Medicare beneficiaries receive care from a network of providers, and all services are coordinated in order to maximize benefits and reduce costs. Plans such as a Medicare Advantage Organization (MAO) could include **Health Maintenance Organizations (HMO)** (health plans that combine coverage of health care costs and delivery of health care for a capitated prepaid premium), a **Preferred Provider Organization (PPO)** (networks of independent physicians, hospitals, and other health care providers who contract with an insurance company to provide care at discounted rates) or a **Private Fee-for-Service plan (PFFS)** (receives a per capita payment from Medicare, rather than from a mix of Medicare reimbursement for services and private supplemental coverage).

To increase the number of beneficiaries, Medicare has expanded federal payments to these MAOs since 2006—on average about 14 percent more than it pays fee-for-service providers (18 percent higher for PPOs and PFFSs,

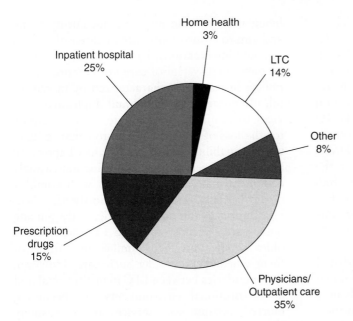

FIGURE 17.3 **Medicare Personal Health Care Spending in 2004**
SOURCE: Federal Interagency Forum on Aging, 2008.

13 percent higher for HMOs) (Kaiser Family Foundation, 2008). Today, almost 25 percent of Medicare beneficiaries, or 10.8 million people, are enrolled in Medicare Advantage, more than double the 5.3 million enrollees in 2003 (Neuman, 2009). MAO plans generally provide more generous benefits than fee-for-service plans. They are able to limit paperwork on claim forms and sometimes offer broader services such as preventive check-ups, vaccines, eyeglasses, hearing aids, and prescription drug coverage in addition to a traditional Medicare benefits package. Most plans initially offer these benefits for no extra premiums and limit co-payments to $5 or $10 per visit. Access to additional services is coordinated by a primary doctor assigned to the Medicare recipient by the MAO. This physician serves as a gatekeeper and must approve the beneficiary's use of any additional services. However, these programs generally recruit elders who are healthier than enrollees in fee-for-service plans. Older adults with multiple chronic illnesses or disabilities typically will not receive such expanded benefits through Medicare fee-for-service and are often not accepted by MAOs.

Overpaying private plans is justified as a way to generate savings for Medicare over time but raises concern about the private sector's ability to offer cost-effective care (Moon, 2006). Because HMOs are a capitated system and thus charge a fixed fee per beneficiary, costs to Medicare are presumed to be more predictable. Yet findings are mixed on whether Medicare expenditures have decreased under Medicare Advantage. After controlling for factors such as health status, some studies find that the costs of HMO enrollment for Medicare are actually about 14 percent higher than through Medicare per se. This is because Medicare only "saves" 5 percent on each HMO participant; the capitated rate is set at 95 percent of the expected expenditure level. In addtion, private insurance companies incur additional administrative and marketing costs to try to make Medicare Advantage more attractive to older adults than traditional Medicare. These "overpayments" were a target of plans to reduce waste in Medicare and eliminate federal subsidies to insurance companies in the 2009 health care reform debates.

Contrary to initial expectations, MAOs do not represent a major savings for Medicare, and managed care does not necessarily deliver promised cost savings nor reduce the regulatory burden on government (Revere, Large, & Langland-Orban, 2004). Although HMO Medicare enrollment is associated with reduced health care utilization (e.g., hospital length of stay), this may result from HMO beneficiaries being healthier than the average older adult, not from less costly service. HMO consumers are generally less satisfied with the quality of care and physicians' skills than those utilizing the fee-for-service system. But they are more satisfied with their lower out-of-pocket expenses (Pourat, Kaqawa-Singer, & Wallace, 2006).

Health care disparities may be exacerbated by some of the managed care models. As noted above, chronically ill elders within HMOs may be denied benefits and access to care. Furthermore, findings are mixed as to whether HMOs and other MAOs have reduced racial disparities in accessing preventive care (Landon et al., 2004; Lin et al., 2005; Trivedi et al., 2005). Class and racial inequities in health care may be exacerbated by **medical savings accounts.** As another alternative to the traditional fee-for-service Medicare model, such accounts are offered as part of Medicare Managed Care and allow beneficiaries to deposit what they would have paid in payroll taxes for Medicare into a tax-exempt account to cover qualified medical expenses.

Long-Term Care Services Under Medicare

As described in Chapter 11, *long-term care (LTC)* refers to a range of supportive services and assistance to persons who, as a result of chronic illness or disability, are unable to function autonomously on a daily basis. The need for LTC does not necessarily correspond to medical conditions, but rather to problems with performing *activities of daily living (ADL)*— bathing, dressing, toileting, eating, and transferring—and *instrumental activities of daily living (IADL)*—shopping, cooking, and cleaning. LTC services are oriented toward managing and

living with chronic illnesses, not curing them, and aim to ensure continuity of care rather than episodic interventions. LTC currently is neither an integrated system of care nor comprehensive policy; instead, it is characterized by incremental, oftentimes fragmented and duplicative, services to minimize, rehabilitate, or compensate for the loss of functioning and to enhance functional capabilities. As described in Chapters 10 and 11, LTC services are becoming increasingly complicated because individuals with complex medical needs are discharged shortly after hospitalization for an acute episode. Since nursing homes are the most common LTC type, many older people and their families first think of them when they consider such care. However, the boundaries between LTC in institutional and non-institutional environments are becoming blurred, because such services are increasingly provided in home- and community-based care settings, such as assisted living, board and care, adult family homes, and adult day centers. Services provided within such *home and residential care settings* encompass personal assistance, assistive devices, and technology, as described in Chapter 11. Those delivered in *community-based settings* include services funded by the Older Americans Act and Title XX Block Grant programs (described in Chapter 16).

Although LTC services also are provided to younger adults with chronic physical and mental illnesses, developmental disabilities, HIV/AIDS, and—increasingly—service-connected disabilities through the Veterans Administration (VA), the focus of this discussion is on the structural, funding, and regulatory aspects of LTC services for older people. Overall, approximately 60 percent of those who report using LTC are age 65 and older. Accordingly, about 66 percent are projected to need some long-term care before they die, with about 20 percent requiring such assistance for 5 years or more (Friedman, 2009; Gleckman, 2009). While only 4 percent of adults age 65 and older are in nursing homes at any one time, more than 12 percent in the community

> ### CHARACTERISTICS OF LONG-TERM CARE
>
> - It is targeted at persons of all ages who have functional disabilities.
> - Disabilities may be physical or mental, transitory, or permanent.
> - It attempts to enhance autonomy in functional abilities and quality of life, including the right to die with dignity.
> - It encompasses a wide range of services, professions, and care settings.
> - Care addresses physical, mental, social, and financial aspects of a person's life.
> - Care is intended to be organized around the distinctive needs of each individual and family.
> - Services change over time as the patient's and family's circumstances alter.
> - It is generally not covered by insurance.
> - Funding sources are a patchwork of federal, state, and local governments; private foundations; and out-of-pocket.

have ADL or IADL restrictions. Among those ages 85 and over, the corresponding rates increase to 21 and 51 percent, respectively. About 47 percent of older women and 33 percent of older men will reside in a skilled nursing facility, if only for a short time period (for over 50 percent of these, less than a year) before they are discharged to community settings. Upon discharge, approximately 75 require some degree of home health care or personal assistance (Schmieding, 2006; Stone, 2006). Although the health care system has traditionally emphasized primary and acute care, the boundaries with LTC are becoming less clear. In fact, our "acute" health care system is increasingly devoted to chronic care by various providers in a range of settings (Gleckman, 2009). Given the high incidence of chronic health needs, it is not surprising that health and LTC costs for persons with chronic illnesses and disabilities are among the most critical policy issues currently facing our nation, as captured by aging advocates' efforts to include LTC in any health care reform legislation.

Medicare's major limitation for persons with chronic illness is its focus on acute care (e.g., inpatient hospital and physicians). Medicare accounts for approximately 18 percent of all national LTC spending, primarily for skilled nursing facilities, home health care, and assisted living (Congressional Budget Office, 2009; Federal Interagency Forum, 2008; Gleckman, 2009). This includes limited coverage for chronic-care expenses (e.g., only 100 days of skilled nursing home care; no dental care or social work services) and minimal coverage for preventive care. The majority of Medicare funding is for hospital care, typically for catastrophic illness and for home care only under restricted conditions. As noted above, nursing home care is limited to 100 days of skilled care or rehabilitation services, with eligibility contingent on acute illness or injury after hospitalization and requiring copayments. This automatically excludes ongoing care for chronic conditions or disabilities. As a result, Medicare covers 53 percent of all health care spending for older people, but a smaller proportion for the oldest-old who require more LTC. In fact, less than 29 percent of the total Medicare budget covers nursing home expenditures. Accordingly, Medicare pays for the LTC expenses of only 5 percent of elders in residential care settings (Federal Interagency Forum, 2008; Neuman, 2009). Many older adults and their families underestimate nursing home care costs and mistakenly believe that Medicare covers LTC expenses. Unfortunately, some older adults become aware of the limited protection offered by Medicare and their supplementary Medigap policies only after they are discharged from a hospital to a home setting or admitted to a nursing home (Berenson & Horvath, 2003; Gleckman, 2009).

Medicare-Funded Home Health Care

Of all health care expenditures covered by Medicare, only about 4 percent is for home health care (Federal Interagency Forum, 2008; Neuman, 2009). A past gap in Medicare funding had been home- and community-based care, but now this is the most rapidly growing Medicare benefit, covering 41 percent of all home health costs, and the fastest-growing component of the overall health care sector (Catlin et al., 2007). With over 20 percent of nursing home placements estimated to be incongruent with older persons' needs, home care is widely advocated as the lower-cost preferred alternative to nursing home placement. Even elders in nursing homes or hospitals may require home care at some point, because 50 percent who stay less than 3 months are able to return to the community, at least temporarily. Not only do most older people require home care after hospitalization or during an acute health episode, but they also tend to recover faster at home, when there is continuity of care. Over time, Medicare has responded to this need, and can now provide unlimited home health care for accredited provider agencies, but only under specific restricted conditions, as noted in the box above. If these criteria are met, Medicare will fund the cost of other services, including home health aides and medical equipment and supplies. In addition, home health care services are available for as long as beneficiaries remain eligible, without any burden of copayments or deductibles. But any personal assistance must be directly related to the medical treatment of an illness or injury, and social work services for nonmedical conditions are not covered. Given elders' preference for home care, it is

not surprising that the number of beneficiaries and the average number of visits per user have grown dramatically.

Whether home care is cost-effective varies with the person's condition and the range and duration of services. In general, home health care is less expensive than hospital care, about 40 percent less than skilled nursing homes, and comparable to adult foster care or adult family homes. However, costs become more comparable if 24-hour care is needed, with private home health aides earning approximately $20 per hour (Gleckman, 2009). It is important to assess each elder's specific health care needs when initiating home care services as an alternative to nursing homes.

A number of factors underlie the extraordinary growth in Medicare-funded *home health care services*:

1. Shorter stays in acute and rehabilitation settings as a result of the 1983 Prospective Payment Systems mean that patients require more technical care at home.
2. A 1989 class action lawsuit created a more flexible interpretation of definitions (homebound), scope of services (both management

and evaluation), regulations (part-time or intermittent care), and skilled nursing assessments, not just skilled nursing care. In addition, some home health care remains a brief recovery "subacute" service, usually after a hospital stay. Medicare-funded home health benefits thus address the short- and some long-term needs of beneficiaries.

3. The number of proprietary, or for-profit, home health agencies reimbursed under Medicare has increased dramatically. For-profit chains grew in response to the 1980 and 1981 Omnibus Budget Reconciliation Acts. These eliminated the requirement for state licensing as a basis for reimbursing proprietary agencies. These regulatory changes stimulated competition for the provision and contracting out of services to new proprietary agencies, including managed care. Such agencies, however, are less likely to concentrate on the ambulatory care of older people after hospital discharge. The 1997 Federal Balanced Budget Amendment reasserted that Medicare home care is only available for patients after an acute episode and cut home care funding. This resulted in a 2-year temporary slowdown of Medicare-funded home care, which was later reversed by expanded funding in 1999–2000.

4. High-tech home therapy, such as intravenous antibiotics, cancer therapy, and pain management, continues to grow. Such care involves expensive pharmaceuticals and equipment that require special staff expertise to use and monitor, and it is costly to the patient or insurer.

As noted in Chapter 11, home health services are delivered by over 11,000 agencies nationwide, a 50 percent increase since 1992. Many are dually certified to serve the needs of both Medicare and Medicaid. The field, however, has shifted from primarily Visiting Nurses Associations and public agencies to hospital-based providers, including the Veterans Administration and private for-profit or nonprofit agencies. Medicare beneficiaries are using home health for longer periods and for less medically intensive services (e.g., more long-term, unskilled personal care by home health aides) after hospital discharge. This has translated into home health aide visits that are lucrative for the agencies, because less skilled and therefore less costly care is still highly compensated by Medicare. On the other hand, incentives for home health agencies to spend as little as possible could place patients who need the most skilled care at greatest risk.

The number of for-profit home health companies that serve primarily private-pay and contract patients has also grown. They fill the demand for home care by patients who, because of age or type of need, do not qualify for Medicare or Medicaid. In general, they offer more services than Medicare-certified agencies. In contrast to the intermittent skilled visits of Medicare home care agencies, noncertified private agencies can provide 24-hour daily care for an indefinite period as well as specialty services. They also offer homemaker/home health aide care services, typically as an on-call service. As with all LTC, recruiting and retaining quality part-time contractual staff is challenging. A dilemma for families, however, is that many private agencies, especially those affiliated with large nationwide chains, require a minimum number of hours of care (typically 8-hour shifts), which can become prohibitively expensive.

Efforts to Reduce Medicare Costs

Medicare currently accounts for 13 percent of federal spending, the fourth largest expenditure following defense, Social Security, and nondefense domestic discretionary spending. Total Medicare spending is projected to double from 3.5 percent of the gross domestic product (GDP) in 2010 to 6.4 percent of GDP by 2030, just to provide the same level of services for a growing Medicare population. The Trustees of the Hospital Insurance Trust Fund continue to warn Congress of the need to restore the balance between income and spending in order to reduce insolvency, which is projected to occur in 2017. At that point, the system would only be taking in enough funds from payroll taxes to pay 81 percent of hospital insurance costs (Crutsinger, 2009; Medicare Board of Trustees, 2008; Montgomery, 2009; Neuman, 2009). The threats to the Medicare Trust Fund are more immediate than those to Social Security, even though most policy makers appear to be more vocal about the solvency of the latter. Medicare's more immediate vulnerability is due largely to the rising cost of health care combined with the decreasing number of workers paying taxes relative to the number of beneficiaries (i.e., the changing age-dependency ratio discussed in Chapters 1 and 16). Within this context of fiscal crises, it is important to remember that Medicare has been highly effective in achieving its initial policy vision of improving access to acute medical care for older adults (Lawlor, 2008).

Several measures over the past 27 years have attempted to reduce Medicare costs:

1. Diagnostic-related groupings (DRGs) were instituted in 1983. Instead of fee-for-service payments that reimbursed providers per service for each patient, Medicare payments were fixed prior to admission, based on the diagnostic category, medical condition, and expected length of stay for each patient. A hospital that keeps patients longer than needed or orders unnecessary tests must absorb the cost difference between the care provided and the amount reimbursed by Medicare. Alternatively, hospitals that provide care at a cost below the established DRG can keep the financial difference. This serves as an incentive for hospitals to discharge patients as soon as possible, putting pressure on families and discharge planners to find a suitable facility or to take the patient home as quickly as possible

Although findings were initially mixed, DRGs appear to have reduced both lengths of

THE COSTS OF EARLY DISCHARGE

Mr. Cohen underwent major surgery—a radical prostatectomy for prostate cancer. Despite the pain that he was still experiencing, he was discharged after 3 days in the hospital and had to return home with a catheter in place that required careful monitoring by a physician or nurse. His wife was in her late 80s and unable to provide the skilled care that a catheter requires. Mr. Cohen was also extremely fatigued. With only his frail wife to care for him, he required the services of a visiting nurse. He continued to experience considerable pain for which his medication was inadequate. If he could have remained in the hospital, his pain could have been relieved by an anesthesiologist. Perhaps the most difficult issue was his uncertainty and anxiety about a variety of symptoms, such as loss of appetite, which could have been resolved with a somewhat longer hospital stay.

stay per hospital admission and number of admissions. Nevertheless, quality of care is sometimes impaired by earlier hospital discharge and restrictions on physician payment levels (Moon, 2006; Stone, 2006), as illustrated by the experience of Mr. Cohen in the box on this page. DRGs have not reduced all the incentives for applying costly high-tech care. In fact, the use of specialists and improved procedures such as knee and cataract surgeries continue to increase, despite other efforts to reduce Medicare costs.

2. Congress passed the Medicare Catastrophic Health Care Act (MCHCA) in 1988 to reduce costs. Expanded benefits were to be financed by a mandatory supplemental premium, which meant that higher-income older adults would pay a surtax for benefits serving primarily low-income elders. This surtax affected approximately 40 percent of older people, many of whom rapidly organized themselves against changes in the basic premise of Medicare, which is its universal nature for all persons age 65 and older (Grogan, 2005). In 1989, Congress voted to repeal the legislation in response

to this public outcry, leaving many legislators wary of making changes in Medicare until the 2003 prescription drug bill.

3. In 1992, reforms were implemented to limit Medicare spending on physician care. This established a physician fee schedule and a system of limiting payment increases when the total cost of physician services billed in a year exceeds estimated levels. It also constrained the amount doctors can charge above the approved Medicare rate.

4. In an effort to maintain the solvency of Medicare, the 1997 Federal Balanced Budget Agreement cut $115 billion in Medicare payments to doctors, hospitals, and HMOs—the largest reduction in the program's history. It also aimed to limit escalating home health care costs and services. The **Centers for Medicare and Medicaid Services (CMS),** the federal agency that approves or denies Medicare claims, froze the licensing of new home health agencies. The **prospective payment system (PPS),** of which DRGs are one component, substantially reduced Medicare's payment for home health care by implementing new payment methods for post-acute (after hospitalization) services. Instead of separate payments for each visit, fixed payments were determined in advance for a general course of treatment. This meant that home care agencies and nursing homes were reimbursed with **capitated payments,** or predetermined amounts per patient per episode of service. This resulted in reducing the number of visits and the average cost per visit. Another iteration of PPS is the **Interim Payment System (IPS),** which sets more stringent caps on costs per home health visit and a cap per beneficiary. The IPS discouraged increases in the number of visits per beneficiary and shortened the duration of services. But they also reduced access for those with high-cost chronic care needs (Spector, Cohen, & Pesis-Katz, 2004; Hans & Remburg, 2005).

As a result of these changes, many home health agencies that had expanded with Medicare funding in the early 1990s closed, and others dropped patients from their client

---

STRATEGIES PROPOSED TO REDUCE MEDICARE COSTS

- Increase the age of eligibility to 67.
- Bill enrollees a modest amount for home health visits.
- Ration services by age.
- Use an income test as a basis for eligibility.
- Boost the combined payroll tax for Medicare and Social Security from 2.9 to 4.11 percent.
- Raise coinsurance and deductibles to shift more financial risk onto the beneficiaries.
- Increase Supplemental Medical Insurance premiums (Part B) for higher-income beneficiaries.
- Reduce the coverage of services and the reimbursement given to providers.

---

rolls. Reductions occurred in the proportion of Medicare beneficiaries who received the service, the number and average length of home health visits per beneficiary, the value of the services, and—as intended—overall Medicare expenditures (McCall & Korb, 2003; Spector et al., 2004).

5. The National Bipartisan Commission on the Future of Medicare was created by Congress in 1997 to study how Medicare can accommodate baby boomers. Some of the commission's recommendations were controversial, including giving beneficiaries a fixed amount of money to purchase private health insurance and to raise the age of Medicare eligibility from 65 to 67. Unable to achieve sufficient unity to forward official recommendations to Congress, the commission was disbanded in 1999. No bipartisan commissions on Medicare have been appointed since then.

6. Because of the 1997 cuts in funding, Medicare expenses declined in 1999. In response, a massive lobbying campaign to restore and expand funding was mounted by national associations of nurses, physicians, nursing home operators, hospitals, managed care organizations, and the home care industry; these providers threatened reduced access

to services if Medicare funding was not restored to address the 1997 cuts. As a result of this intensive lobbying effort, Congress reallocated billions of dollars to various providers in 1999 and 2000.

7. Initiatives to curb home health expenditures and increase fiscal accountability have lowered the number of users, the average number of visits, and lengths of stay. Nevertheless, Medicare-funded home health care costs continue to grow, which suggests that more intensive and expensive services are being provided to high-cost participants (Spector et al., 2004). Ultimately, Medicare's fiscal problems are rooted in the overall increases in health care spending. As noted by AARP (2005), "the problem is not Medicare and Medicaid—the problem is health care."

Not surprisingly, Republicans and Democrats differ on the nature and size of Medicare cuts, although both agree that changes are needed to address Medicare's long-term solvency. Republicans advocate increased application of competitive market principles to health care, privatization (such as individual health care accounts), and private insurance options. Proponents argue that more choices for consumers will lead to increased competition and, in turn, lower costs. But there is no evidence that expanded competition would reduce Medicare costs, in part because more health plans would increase administrative costs and older adults would have to switch plans almost annually, which most are unlikely to do (Herd, 2005). The shift to privatization, however, is reflected in the 2003 Medicare reform prescription drug bill implemented in 2006 and discussed in the next section.

Other strategies to reduce Medicare costs continue to be debated at the national level, most recently as part of the legislation related to health care reform, Contrary to these proposed changes, the majority of Americans agree that the federal government has a basic responsibility to guarantee adequate health care for older people and oppose cost cutting. It is also noteworthy that while Medicare is the current

focus of many budget reduction scenarios and health care reform debates, per capita costs remain below those of private insurers. One major reason for this is that Medicare is administratively far more efficient (3 percent overhead costs vs. 14 percent for private insurance plans), controlling overall health care costs more than the private sector does (Bishop, 2008; Moon, 2006).

Medicare Reform and Prescription Drug Coverage

The most dramatic and controversial change since Medicare's passage is **Medicare Part D**, the **Medicare Modernization, Improvement and Prescription Drug Act,** passed by Congress in November 2003 after the longest roll-call vote in the House chamber's history. What was not disputed was the need for prescription drug coverage for older adults. In fact, Medicare beneficiaries prior to 2006 spent more, on average, out-of-pocket each year on prescription drugs than on physician care, vision services, and medical supplies combined. In addition, the price of the most commonly used drugs had increased by three times the rate of inflation.

The new prescription drug benefit of Medicare was intended to help elders manage rising medication costs.

Of grave concern in 2003 was the 40 percent of Medicare beneficiaries who had no prescription drug coverage at some point each year. Those without drug coverage often restricted their medications because of cost; they skipped filling prescriptions, split drug amounts (e.g., breaking pills in half), eliminated doses, or relied on physician samples. All of these solutions can result in adverse reactions for elders and, over time, increase health care costs, especially for acute exacerbations of chronic diseases (Goulding, 2005; Kaiser Family Foundation, 2006; Safran et al., 2005). The lack of prescription drug coverage under Medicare was a historical accident: When Medicare was enacted in 1965, drugs were not a central part of medical treatment. Now, prescription drugs are often the primary treatment for elders with chronic illness and account for 15 percent of every health care dollar spent (Federal Interagency Forum, 2008).

Because of the lack of restrictions on drug prices, profit margins for drug companies surpass those of nearly every economic sector. Pharmaceutical companies which spend millions lobbying Congress, argue that such costs are necessary to cover research and testing of new, high-risk drugs (Hellander, 2008). Critics of drug companies ask: What good are research and new drugs if no one can afford them? They maintain that too many dollars are spent on marketing drugs, especially the increasing trend of advertising directly to consumers. Such costs and lack of coverage fueled the congressional debate regarding the best way to solve the problem: the government taking more responsibility for controlling prices, better informing consumers, or market competition. Within this context, members of Congress argued whether this entitlement should be age based (i.e., universal) or needs based (i.e., means tested). The central issue being tested under Medicare Part D is whether private health care plans can deliver better care at lower cost than the traditional Medicare program. Part D's administrative reliance on private options reflects an underlying assumption that informed consumers will choose the plan that best fits their needs and that price competition will prevent the government from paying too much for drugs (Stevens, Huskamp & Newhouse, 2008).

In addition to partisan splits over the bill, a controversial and highly visible conflict revolved around AARP's support of it, which did not reflect the will of 65 percent of its members. Critics of the bill accused AARP—which sells insurance and prescription drugs and receives a commission from corporations for these sales—of selling out to pharmaceutical companies, HMOs, and Republican lawmakers. In response, 85 members of Congress canceled their AARP membership and thousands of AARP members burned their membership cards and jammed the association's phone lines protesting AARP's support of the bill. AARP justified its actions by acknowledging that the bill was not perfect, but better than what existed. They also cited polls and focus groups of baby boomers, who are accustomed to employer-sponsored private health care and favored tying private competition to Medicare. Since the bill's passage, AARP has slightly modified its position by lobbying for changes to enable more older adults to qualify for financial assistance and for the government to negotiate lower drug prices directly, as now occurs with the VA. So far neither of these objectives has been met (AARP, 2005; Healthcare Financial Management, 2006).

Medicare beneficiaries may choose to stay in traditional Medicare and obtain drug coverage by paying for a private stand-alone drug insurance policy rather than Part D. But if they decide to join Part D later, they pay an extra percentage in premiums for every month since the deadline for enrollment.

The primary components of the prescription drug legislation implemented in 2006 are:

- The premium for the optional prescription benefit was expected to average $35 a month, although some private plans have cost over $100 monthly.
- The Medicare beneficiary is responsible for the first $250 of drug costs each year.

- After that, Part D covers 75 percent of drug costs up to the first $4,200 in purchases. Although payment of the monthly premium still continues, coverage then stops until the beneficiary has spent $3,600 out-of-pocket, or about $5,451 annually in total prescription expenditures. This difference between $2,400 and $5,451 is known as the **doughnut hole.**
- Above $5,451, catastrophic coverage covers at least 95 percent of the cost until the benefits start again the following year.
- Because of the doughnut hole, the standard plan covers one-third of the average drug bill of $3,051. Of the 24 million beneficiaries enrolled in Medicare Part D in 2007, 3.4 million (or 26 percent) of enrollees reached this "coverage gap."

On January 1, 2006, 3.6 million older adults signed up for Medicare Part D. But its complexity has been a problem for both consumers and providers. In 2006, Medicare was subsidizing almost 3,000 different plans with different premiums, copayments, covered drugs, suppliers, rules for prescribing drugs, and delivery schedules in 34 regions, creating a complex bureaucratic maze for older people to navigate. Older adults and their families often could not determine whether to subscribe to a plan and, if so, which one. Efforts to educate consumers, including phone help lines staffed by 4,500 operators, were often confusing and, in some instances, conveyed inaccurate information. As a result, health and mental health provider organizations and senior advocacy groups devoted considerable resources toward educating their clients. Computer glitches and database errors also added to the confusion and resulted in coverage gaps, especially for low-income elders who were automatically shifted from Medicaid to Part D. In such instances, 20 state governments stepped in to cover drug costs during the transition period. Fortunately, most of these issues were resolved in subsequent years.

Now, several years after its inception, many older adults and their families remain confused by the complexity of Part D. In one survey, up to 66 percent of older people did not know the correct cap level on their drug benefits even if they exceeded the cap, reported difficulty paying for medications, or decreased their medication use because of cost (Tseng et al., 2009).

Who has benefited from prescription drug reform?

- Drug companies are able to maximize profits, because the government agreed not to negotiate lower drug prices. Medicare Part D pays on average 30 percent more for the top 100 drugs than does Medicaid and far more than the VA health care system, resulting in windfall profits for drug manufacturers, as much as $3.7 billion in the first two years of Medicare's Part D program. (Healthcare Financial Management Association, 2008; U.S. House of Representatives, 2008).
- Employers who offer health care plans with prescription coverage to their retirees are subsidized by Medicare to encourage them to continue such coverage. Nevertheless, many employers dropped their prescription drug plans, leaving some retirees to pay substantially more for prescriptions than before, as illustrated in the box on this page.

RISING DRUG COSTS AS A RESULT OF MEDICARE PART D

Under an employer-sponsored drug plan, a couple in their late 70s in Florida paid $40 a month for a powerful cancer medication that was keeping the husband alive. With the passage of Medicare Part D, the husband's former employer canceled their insurance, which had paid a flat $40 fee for any medications through the plan's mail-order program. This flat fee was replaced by a cost-sharing structure that caused the couple's out-of-pocket spending for drugs to skyrocket to $900 a month for the same medicine.

A 68-year old dialysis patient, who worked multiple low-paying jobs all her life, is struggling with Medicare's required copayments for her medications. These drugs were previously covered by her state's Medicaid program but now fall under Medicare Part D. Her income of $660 in Social Security benefits each month does not leave room for even the $3- to-$5 copay she now faces (Shelton, 2006).

• For the first time in Medicare's history, beneficiaries with annual incomes of more than $80,000 must now pay higher premiums for the part of Medicare that covers doctors' care; however, the most affluent elders are able to absorb the additional costs. In this instance, means testing is applied to the wealthy, not to low-income individuals, and reflects a shift from Medicare's universal nature (Antos & Gokhale, 2005).

• Low-income elders who meet eligibility criteria gain by having the premium, deductible, and coverage gap waived. In addition, individuals with incomes below 150 percent of the poverty level and with limited assets (less than $10,000) are also eligible for premium and cost-sharing subsidies, substantially reducing what they spend for drugs. On the downside, however, older Medicaid recipients were often unaware that they had been randomly assigned to a plan and later discovered that some drugs were not covered by the new plan. Still others were uninformed about the low-income subsidies available.

Some of the negative outcomes and limitations of Medicare Part D include:

• Using income levels to determine access to Medicare benefits is counter to the idea that all beneficiaries earn access by virtue of paying payroll taxes throughout their employed years. Privatization of Medicare's prescription drug coverage thus eroded Medicare's universal and entitlement nature. It also represents a shift from a defined benefit to a defined contributions program. With basic Medicare, one's payroll tax assures defined benefits at age 65, but with Medicare Part D, the nature of the benefit varies widely, depending on the insurance chosen (Moffitt, 2006).

• The "doughnut hole" in coverage plus the ongoing deductible and monthly payments make the plan costly for some elders who can easily incur expenses of over $2,400 for drugs in any given year. This gap, which was implemented to save the government money, means that some beneficiaries pay their $35 monthly premium while receiving no help until after they have incurred an additional $3,051 in drug costs. But only about 5 percent of older people require catastrophic care above $5,451 on an annual basis. A 2007 study found that more than 12 million Part D enrollees without low-income subsidies enrolled in plans with limited or no gap coverage (Cubanski & Neuman, 2007; Zhang et al., 2009).

• In addition, older adults who join Part D are no longer able to purchase **Medigap policies** to help cover drug costs created by the doughnut hole. Such costs also increase the risk of medication nonadherence. One study identified that those lacking coverage in the doughnut hole reduced their drug usage by 14 percent (Zhang et al., 2009). Additionally, over 50 percent of older enrollees, even when they were aware of the doughnut hole, did not inform their health care providers that they had reached the cap (Tseng et al., 2009). Fortunately, as noted above, the lowest-income elders are protected since they can apply for subsidies through the Social Security Administration to close the gap (Levin-Epstein, 2006; Song, 2006).

• More than six million low-income elders lost the drug coverage they had under Medicaid, and some had to pay higher copayments to avoid losing access to particular drugs not covered under Medicare. As a result, some low-income older people actually have had less drug coverage than they had through Medicaid. Additionally, some *dually eligible* consumers (i.e., those eligible for both Medicare and Medicaid), because of cost sharing, are paying more than they did under Medicaid.

• The law restricts the importing of less expensive, more readily available generic prescription drugs from Canada and Mexico. Both countries have been important sources for affordable medications.

• The government has been prohibited from using the size of the Medicare program as leverage to negotiate lower drug prices or discounts from drug companies, as it has done effectively through the VA. This may change, however, with the Obama administration's priority to bring down the cost of prescription drugs. Part of the health care reform efforts of 2009 included plans to close the doughnut hole so Medicare beneficiaries do not have to pay as much out-of-pocket.

- The cost of implementation has been higher than initially projected, thereby raising Medicare costs and posing additional threats to its long-term solvency. Additionally, the complexity of Part D and its emphasis on consumer choice are sometimes a poor fit for nursing home residents. It has also added to the administrative burden on nursing home physicians, nurses, and pharmacists, who must balance consumer choice with being able to encourage enrollment in plans that best fit residents' medication needs (Gleckman, 2009; Donohue, Huskamp, & Zuveks, 2009; Health Care Financial Management, 2006; Hellander, 2008; Kaiser Family Foundation, 2006; Shelton, 2006; Washington Post, 2008).

Overall, Part D has met its target of 90 percent coverage, and those enrolled give Part D mixed reviews (Heiss, McFadden, & Winter, 2006). It appears that elders with complex illnesses and those requiring relatively expensive medicines, such as cancer drugs, do not always benefit from this program (Alonso-Zaldivar, 2006; Behavioral Healthcare, 2006; Levin-Epstein, 2006; Slaughter, 2006). In the short-run, 43 percent of enrollees have experienced increases in drug costs. On the other hand, individuals who did not have drug coverage in the past and who are eligible for the low-income subsidy are saving money under Medicare Part D.

The long-range impact of Part D is unclear. Grassroots groups and some members of Congress have mobilized to try to amend Part D to allow Medicare to negotiate directly with drug manufacturers for price discounts and to legalize the purchase of drugs from Canada. The additional savings to taxpayers and beneficiaries would be $156 billion and $86 billion, respectively (U.S. House of Representatives, 2008). As a priority held by the Democratic-controlled Congress, the July 2009 Finance Committee bill for health care reform included an agreement with pharmaceutical companies to provide 50 percent

discounts for brand-name drugs in the doughnut hole (NCOA, 2009).

Mental Health Services Under Medicare

A past limitation of Medicare was its lack of **parity** for mental health services. Prior to 2008, Medicare had a lifetime limit on inpatient psychiatric treatment, while there was no such limit on general hospital care. Of even greater concern, Medicare required a copayment of 50 percent for outpatient mental health services, compared with only 20 percent for all other outpatient services. This disparity persisted from Medicare's inception in 1965, when many believed that mental illnesses resulted from moral defects or character flaws, until 2008. Advocates of mental health parity argued that providing less Medicare coverage for mental health services than for general health services financially discriminated against those seeking treatment for psychological disorders and perpetuated the stigma of mental health care as different from general health care (Sakauye et al., 2005). Now, the copayment for mental health services is the same as it is for other types of services (20 percent rather than 50 percent), to be fully phased in by 2014 (American Association for Geriatric Psychiatry, 2008). The Positive Aging Act of 2007 and 2008 aimed to integrate mental health services for older adults into primary care settings, which would increase the accessibility of such care.

Medicaid

As noted throughout this chapter, there is a disconnect between how the current health care system pays for time-limited, acute services for older adults through Medicare compared to their needs for long-term, continuous, and less costly care (Raphael & Cornwell, 2008). **Medicaid** is a federal and state means-tested welfare program of medical assistance for the

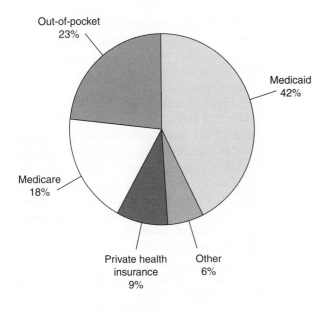

FIGURE 17.4   Spending for Long-Term Care: 2004

SOURCE: "National Health Spending in 2004" in *Health Affairs* by Cynthia Smith, Cathy Cowan, Stephen Hettler, and Aaron Catlin. Copyright 2006 by Project Hope/Health Affairs Journal. Reproduced with permission of Project Hope/Health Affairs Journal in the format Textbook and Other book via Copyright Clearance Center.

poor, regardless of age (e.g., to recipients of Aid to Families with Dependent Children and SSI). Unlike Medicare, it covers LTC but only for the poor or those who become poor by paying for their long-term or medical care, typically by using up their assets. Medicaid also differs from Medicare in that federal funds are administered by each state, which results in considerable variation in the quality and quantity of services provided (see Figure 17.4). Approximately 43 percent of that spending is on nursing home care, largely because of the industry's political clout (Kaiser Commission, 2008). Ironically, when Medicaid was enacted, it was never intended to be a major payer of LTC, especially nursing home care.

Medicaid plays three essential roles related to LTC for qualified older adults:

1. It makes Medicare affordable for low-income beneficiaries by paying Medicare's premiums, deductibles, and other cost-sharing requirements.
2. It pays for medical benefits that Medicare does not cover, such as prescription drugs and LTC.

3. It is the primary public source of financial assistance for LTC in both nursing homes and community-based settings.

Older persons comprise a small percentage (less than 10 percent) of the total Medicaid beneficiaries, yet they account for approximately 40 percent of the total expenditures nationally. The principal cause of this disproportionately high expenditure is that Medicaid accounts for about 42 percent of the nation's $151 billion LTC expenditures, with more than 50 percent of recipients age 65 and older (Federal Interagency Forum, 2008; Kasper et al., 2007; Kaiser Commission, 2009; Kitchener et al., 2006; Smith, et al., 2006). As with Medicare, the growth in Medicaid expenditures is due largely to price increases by health providers and fragmented funding mechanisms, not population growth per se or expansion of care. In fact, participation rates in Medicaid are relatively low because many elders are unaware of potential eligibility or are reluctant to seek help from a "welfare program." Medicaid, like Medicare, provides only 60 to 80 percent of daily care charges. Even though Medicaid is the main funder of nursing home care, over 40 percent of additional expenses associated with such care are still paid by individuals out-of-pocket (Federal Interagency Forum, 2008). Federal regulations require that all state Medicaid programs provide the following comprehensive services: hospital inpatient care, physician services, skilled nursing facility care, laboratory and X-ray services, home health, hospital outpatient care, family planning, rural health clinics, and early and periodic screening. In contrast to Medicare, home health care services are a mandatory area of coverage for Medicaid, while personal-care services and home and community-based services are optional. Although Medicare covers skilled nursing care only for patients with rehabilitative potential, Medicaid can cover skilled care for both rehabilitation and intermediate nursing home care of a long-term custodial nature.

Although Medicaid is the second largest budget item for most states, states vary widely in their eligibility standards; the types, amount, scope, and duration of services; as well as reimbursement rates. For example, states may elect to provide coverage for personal care services but are not required to do so. States differ greatly in the provision of "optional" services such as, intermediate care, prescription drugs outside the hospital, dental services, eyeglasses, and physical therapy. Similar to Medicare, coverage for mental health and social services is limited. Medicaid is a highly visible target for federal and state cost cutting, because it forms a growing proportion of state budgets, while federal Medicaid funds to states have declined in the past decade. Ways that states have sought to reduce expenditures for both nursing home and home care are discussed below.

Older adults qualify for Medicaid in the following ways:

1. Participation in SSI, described in Chapter 16, which encompasses the provision of Medicaid. Although Medicaid is the principal health insurance provided for the poor, only 33 percent of low-income elders meet the stringent categorical eligibility requirements. Those who do qualify for cash assistance under SSI are provided the broadest coverage under state Medicaid programs, including payment of Medicare cost sharing, premiums, and additional services such as prescription drugs, vision care, and dental care.

2. Designated as "medically needy" under state-specific rules (e.g., ineligible for cash assistance but in economic distress after paying medical expenses). Older adults who are "medically needy" can exclude their medical and LTC expenses from income in determining whether they meet specific income limits, and may **spend down** by incurring medical bills that reduce their income and other resources such as assets to the necessary level. These income levels are established by each state and therefore vary.

3. Nursing home residents with income and assets below a state-designated cap of 300 percent of the SSI level. Depletion of almost all personal assets often occurs prior to nursing home admission, and 33 to 40 percent of residents are eligible for Medicaid at admission. Of those who pay out-of-pocket at the time of admission to a nursing home, approximately 66 percent spend down their savings to Medicaid levels. This is due both to the cost of such care and the regulation that nursing home residents must contribute all of their income except a small personal-needs allowance toward the cost of their care. On any given day, up to 60 percent of nursing home residents have Medicaid as their source of payment (Chen, 2006).

4. Dual eligibility, for both Medicare and Medicaid. This applies to those whose income falls 100 percent below the poverty level and with limited financial assets. Dually eligible beneficiaries are the poorest and sickest elders, have significant ADL limitations, and are the highest users of health care services and nursing home care among Medicaid beneficiaries. They obtain help from Medicaid to cover Medicare's copayments and deductibles (e.g., out-of-pocket expenses) and their monthly

premium for physician and outpatient coverage. In other words, even though they have too many financial resources to be eligible for full Medicaid benefits, Medicaid pays for what Medicare does not cover, including nursing home and home care. Not surprisingly, dual eligibles cost the federal government significantly more than what each Medicare-only beneficiary costs. They are also less likely to have a partner or any living children, and more likely to live in a nursing home (Fortinsky, Fenster, & Judge, 2004; Lee, 2006; Stevenson et al., 2008).

Medicaid-Funded Nursing Home Care

As noted above, Medicaid is biased toward institutional care. Medicaid covers almost 46 percent of annual state expenditures on nursing homes and over 33 percent of federal dollars on all types of LTC. Benefits vary widely by state, ranging from nearly $900 to less than $200 (Catlin, et al 2008; Gleckman, 2009).

States have sought a variety of strategies to limit their Medicaid expenditures, especially for LTC. Because states are required to pay for every Medicaid-eligible person residing in a nursing home, one of the earliest approaches was to control the supply of available openings. A majority of states in the late 1970s imposed certificate of need (CON) restrictions on additional Medicaid-certified beds and placed a moratorium on adding new nursing home beds or facilities. These CON restrictions then resulted in high occupancy rates, which inflated charges and bolstered nursing home profits. States have also developed strict preadmission screening procedures and tightened the medical and functional eligibility requirements for nursing home admission, thereby limiting the number of Medicaid recipients entering nursing homes. Other approaches to reduce costs have been:

- to set nursing home reimbursement rates (e.g., managed care models of capitated payments) that result in lower payments for Medicaid nursing home residents

LONG-TERM CARE OMBUDSMAN

The most successful approach to monitoring quality in nursing homes is the long-term care ombudsman. The Older Americans Act requires every state to have an Ombudsman Program, which develops nonregulatory approaches to monitoring care in nursing homes and, in most states, in other LTC facilities as well. Ombudsmen advocate for residents' rights that are guaranteed under the 1987 federal Nursing Home Reform Act. Residents or their families can call on the ombudsman's office in their state to investigate and resolve complaints about resident rights in the LTC facility where they live. In 2007, long-term care ombudsmen received more than 200,000 complaints, such as abuse and neglect and use of physical and chemical constraints (Wells, 2009). The ombudsman's influence is constrained, however, by limited staff funding and reliance on volunteers.

- to restrict eligibility and utilization of benefits covered
- to ration or limit services to those that prove most cost-effective, a concept that is anathema to many Americans who want all possible life-saving technology. This sentiment was expressed by vocal opponents of end-of-life counseling in the 2009 health care reform debates who framed it as rationing care to older adults and persons with disabilities (Maggillis, 2009)

Given such constraints, Medicaid recipients, especially those requiring high levels of care, often have more difficulty finding a nursing home bed—and wait longer to do so—than higher-paying private-pay clients. In fact, some nursing homes do not even accept Medicaid patients and discharge those whose private funding runs out. In addition, the mix of high occupancy rates and the comparatively low payment per bed tends to relegate Medicaid patients to substandard facilities. In fact, a relationship exists between residents' socioeconomic status and the quality of nursing home

Medicaid is the primary source of public funding for nursing home care.

care received. Paradoxically, although many nursing homes need Medicaid residents in order to survive, they have reduced services, especially staffing, to maintain a profit, while offering fewer hours of direct care than nursing homes without Medicaid beds (Chen, 2006; Smith, 2006).

With the growth of the oldest-old, who are most likely to use nursing homes but lack the resources to pay for it, Medicaid is faced with how to provide coverage for low-income and vulnerable populations at a time of intense pressure to limit public spending. Overall, benefit reductions fail to address rising nursing home costs caused by provider price increases. In addition, efforts to control nursing home costs are difficult because of resistance by lobbyists. Another consequence of the nursing home industry's strength is Medicaid's limited funding for alternative LTC, such as assisted living and adult homes, which reduces the options available to low-income older people (Kitchener et al., 2006). On the other hand, as

described both in Chapter 11 and more fully below, every state now offers Medicaid waivers that allow qualified elders to use these less costly options

Medicaid-Funded Home Health Care

As noted earlier, only about 38 percent of Medicaid expenditures go to community-based home health services, even though home-based services are generally more cost-effective and preferred by elders and their families. Given elders' first-choice for home and community-based care, low-income older adults are often on lengthy waiting lists for home care (Catlin, et al., 2008; Gleckman, 2009). Medicaid's bias toward institutional care is slowly shifting, however, and spending on home and community-based services is rising more than for nursing homes (CMS, 2007b). This shift toward alternative models as public policy is driven largely by civil rights, not market interests. Both the Americans with Disabilities Act and the Supreme Courts' 1999 ruling in the landmark Olmstead v. L.C. case require deinstitutionalization by making community-based care choices available to those who prefer it. President Bush's 2001 executive order implementing the New Freedom Initiative mandated immediate compliance with the Olmsted ruling by all federally funded entitlements (Putnam, 2008; Schulz & Binstock, 2006).

Financing of home care services under Medicaid occurs under three different coverage options:

1. Home health care, typically offered by a Medicaid-certified home health agency
2. Personal care, generally semiskilled or unskilled services provided to Medicaid beneficiaries who need assistance with basic activities of daily living in their own home (typically provided by direct care workers) constitute the majority of total spending for home care services under Medicaid
3. Home and community-based waiver services

Eligibility for Medicaid Home Health Care and Waiver Programs

To receive Medicaid-funded home care services, older adults must:

- meet strict income/asset eligibility criteria
- be medically eligible for nursing home placement
- require more services than just home-maker services

In addition, home care must not cost more than nursing home care (i.e., must be budget neutral). Although states are required to cover home *health* services under the Medicaid program, providing personal care at home is optional. Medicaid funds three choices for nonmedical home care coverage: the "personal care services" benefit, the mandatory home health benefit, and the Home and Community-Based Services (HCBS) Waiver program. All states offer at least one of these options, but they vary widely in the extent to which these alternatives are actually available (Gleckman, 2009; Harrington, et al, 2009; Kassner et al., 2008).

If a state provides the optional "personal care services" benefit, it must be made available to all Medicaid beneficiaries who meet the criteria for personal care. There cannot be a waiting list, but states can set coverage limits, regardless of need, and they are not required to pay for all of the personal care services that a Medicaid beneficiary might require.

The Home and Community-based Waiver Program(HCBS) was first authorized under the 1981 Omnibus Budget Reconciliation Act as a way to prevent or delay nursing home placement. This permits the waiver of Medicaid statutory requirements so that states can provide community-based options by targeting benefits to limited geographic areas and to specific groups and numbers of beneficiaries. The **Medicaid waiver program** specifies seven core services that have not been traditionally considered "medical," but which allow people to remain at home—case management, homemaker, home

health aide, personal care, adult day care, rehabilitation, respite care—and other services approved by the federal government as "cost-effective." States must demonstrate that the costs of such services are less than care in institutions and that they can divert at-risk individuals from nursing home placement. Because recipients must be low income and qualify for nursing home care, the number of individuals qualifying for this option is limited (Applebaum & Straker, 2005). In addition, the program's cost-containment goals mean that most states restrict the scope of services and the number of recipients, resulting in waiting lists and continuing levels of unmet needs for low-income elders and adults with disabilities along with widespread inequities across states (Burke, Feder, & Van de Water, 2005; Harrington Meyer et al., 2009). Nevertheless, waiver programs have increased Medicaid spending for community-based LTC, which have overall reduced unmet needs among participants (Galambos, 2006).

Because findings on the cost savings of the waiver programs are mixed, states are focused on increasing the cost efficiency of implementing waivers (Harrington Meyer et al., 2009; Mitchell et al., 2006). In many states, there is a per diem cap on allowable services and long waiting lists. Some states, such as Oregon and Washington, have widely implemented waivers, however. They have deliberately reduced the number of nursing home beds and have supported newer LTC options (described in Chapter 11) such as in-home care, respite services, adult day health care, as well as residential options such as assisted living, adult foster homes, and adult family homes. Several states have demonstration programs that improve the coordination of LTC with the acute care system (Kitchener et al., 2006). Other states use their funds to augment or create their own separate home care programs; a few fund community-based options through lottery revenues or county levies for LTC. How these state innovations are affected by the 2008–2009 recession is as yet unclear. What is clear is that the federal government must address quality as well as cost issues, and must expand Medicaid HCBS funds for states to improve access to home and community-based care (Harrington Meyer et al., 2009).

Aging and Disability Resource Centers are a recent reform initiative that aim to integrate and streamline LTC services into a single coordinated system based on the traditional not-for-profit aging network and funded by AOA and CMS. This integration is assumed to provide easier access to a range of patient-centered, community-based services for older adults and at least one other population with physical or developmental disabilities. These centers have been implemented in 175 sites nationwide (AOA, 2009). In general, states face the challenge of developing not-for-profit integrated LTC systems that can compete with for-profit managed care organizations in a time of greatly reduced public resources (Mitchell et al., 2006).

Consumer-directed care is a Medicaid waiver program, initiated under the 2002 Independence Plus Initiative, that seeks to provide decision-making autonomy to elders and adults with disabilities. This model posits that consumers (in this case, frail adults and their families) have the right and ability to assess their own needs and determine how to meet them. Consumers take on all worker management tasks, including choosing their personal care attendant, with two exceptions: They do not receive a cash allowance to pay the worker directly and they cannot pay their spouse or partner. Within the consumer-directed care approach, **cash and counseling programs** give consumers a cash amount that they can use to hire and supervise their own caregivers; this can include family members who are paid for their services. Recipients of Medicaid personal care or HCBS receive a monthly cash allowance based on a professional assessment of their needs. These allowances are comparable to the value of services that would be given through traditional agencies. Controlling their own budget, consumers become employers, choosing to hire (and fire) family or friends as workers; the states provide bookkeepers to assist with the paperwork. For example, older consumers can decide whether to use funds to make their home more wheelchair accessible, buy a pair of dentures, pay for over-the-counter medications, or hire a grandson to mow their lawn. Counselors or consultants are available to assist them with decision making, but the consumer retains control of the final decision. Cash and counseling projects have been funded and implemented by the Kellogg Foundation in Florida, New Jersey, and Arkansas. Although the three states differ in terms of their goals and political environments, evaluations identify the following outcomes across sites:

- Those who received a cash allowance were able to purchase more services to fit their needs than they could under traditional programs.
- Medicaid costs per recipient per month were slightly higher for both the cash and counseling group than a control group, largely because those in the traditional system did not get the services they were entitled to.
- Being able to hire their own caregivers, even if they were not family members, was associated with greater satisfaction and quality of life for both the care recipient and caregivers (Carlson et al., 2007; Dale & Brown, 2007; Hansen, 2008; Kunkel & Nelson, 2005; Phillips & Schneider, 2007; Schore, Foster, & Phillips, 2007).

With Medicaid waivers and the growth of such alternatives to nursing home care, funding for HCBS has expanded substantially (Chen, 2006; Eiken, Burwell, & Walker, 2005). However, older adults who have too many assets to qualify for Medicaid but cannot afford private home care services typically lack access to these alternatives (Bishop, 2008). Nevertheless, with increasing recognition of the quality of care provided by these newer options and with the aging of baby boomers who are likely to reject

UNDERLYING VALUES AND ASSUMPTIONS OF CONSUMER-DIRECTED CARE

- Adults requiring LTC have a right and ability to make decisions about their care.
- Consumers are experts about their service needs and are capable of managing their own affairs; they have the right to "manage their own risk."
- The dignity of the consumer who needs personal assistance is preserved.
- Choice and control can be introduced into all service delivery systems, including hiring and firing personal care attendants.
- Consumer-directed care should be available to all persons needing LTC, regardless of the payer (public or private).

nursing home care, this pattern of Medicaid and out-of-pocket expenditures may reverse in the future.

Medicaid Spend-Down

Another way to reduce Medicaid costs is to enforce current laws that make it more difficult to qualify. The 1993 Omnibus Budget Reconciliation legislation prohibited the sheltering of assets through trusts during the 5 years prior to an application for Medicaid benefits, and the transfer of assets during the 3 years prior to a Medicaid application. It also mandated estate recovery, forcing states to reclaim Medicaid costs from the estate or property of beneficiaries age 55 and over who lived in nursing homes or received home and community services. States could consider jointly owned property, including homes and bank accounts, as part of the estate recoverable after the death of the recipient or his or her spouse. Most states have not enforced these estate recovery laws, and federal Medicaid officials have been reluctant to impose penalties for noncompliance.

This 1993 legislation, referred to as "Send Grandma to Jail," was extremely controversial and, in 1997, the legal burden was shifted to the Medicaid estate-planning industry. Some lawyers practicing elder law recommend ways for their relatively affluent older clients to shelter up to half of a nursing home resident's financial assets from the spend-down requirement, even within the 3-year time period. Elders with resources are able to establish trusts to preserve family estates without compromising their Medicaid eligibility. Congress also passed measures to protect against spousal impoverishment, raising the amount of income the "community spouse" could keep, and retreated from plans that would enforce adult children's financial responsibility for their parents. About 15 percent of Medicaid beneficiaries are from middle-class backgrounds who have qualified through the Medicaid spend-down process, as well as the conversion and transfer of assets prior to a nursing home stay (Lee, Kim, & Tanenbaum, 2006). The media, politicians, and senior organizations increasingly frame Medicaid for nursing home care as a social entitlement for all older adults. Yet, unlike Medicare and Social Security, Medicaid is not contributory, as defined in Chapter 16. That is, program recipients do not have a legal or moral right to LTC benefits on the basis of tax payments or a lifetime of employment; funding for Medicaid comes from general tax revenues.

This extension of benefits to the middle class within the context of a means-tested program intended for low-income persons has been called "universalism without targeting"; i.e., Medicaid-funded benefits are increasingly available in nursing homes for elders based on age, not income. In fact, the difference between Medicare and Medicaid is often blurred by Medicaid extending its reach to the middle class while the Medicare program often provides extra benefits to low-income dual eligible beneficiaries (Grogan, 2005; Grogan & Patashnik, 2003). As long as the costs of home care, nursing homes, and LTC insurance continue to rise, this tension between Medicaid as an entitlement program for low-income elders and strategies that middle- and upper-income elders use to qualify for Medicaid is likely to continue. Because the cost to Medicaid of assets

POINTS TO PONDER

What is your position on Medicaid "spend down"? Do you think that it unjustly impoverishes older people and their families needing nursing home care? Or do you think that those with assets should hire lawyers to find ways to protect them and still get Medicaid to cover the cost of nursing home care? Reflect on family members or others you know who have used Medicaid spend down strategies to access nursing home care. What were some of their experiences?

transfer is relatively small, it is unlikely that most states will try to "crack down" on this issue, however (Lee et al., 2006; Quinn, 2007).

Private Supplemental and Long-Term Care Insurance

Approximately 45 percent of older adults' LTC care expenditures are paid out of pocket (Federal Interagency Forum, 2008). These elders use a combination of pension income, Social Security benefits, savings, and investments (including reverse mortgages which allow them to tap the equity in their homes) to pay for care. Increasing numbers pay with private supplemental and LTC insurance.

Wide disparities exist among adults in their ability to purchase such private insurance. For those who can afford more extensive coverage than provided by Medicare Parts A and B, private Medigap insurance is available to help with the catastrophic costs of intensive care, numerous tests, or extended hospitalization. As noted earlier, some of these policies have also paid for services not covered by Medicare. These include deductibles and copayments, dental care, eye exams, and hearing aids, but not the critical services of skilled nursing home care and charges exceeding the amount approved by Medicare (in excess of Medicare's "allowable" or "reasonable" charges).

It should be noted that the purchase of such private coverage is not a solution to health costs. Instead, it means that the average spending on health care has increased overall. Since the majority of older people pay fully for this insurance, they still effectively bear the personal burden of health care costs and do not necessarily see a reduction in out-of-pocket expenditures, because they must pay high premiums. Now, with the passage of Medicare Part D, the purchase of Medigap insurance to cover drug costs is no longer an option, although those who had Medigap policies may continue them for other health care costs.

Older adults have purchased some private supplemental health insurance (not private LTC insurance), although less than 6 percent of the expenditures for nursing home or home care are paid by private insurance. Of these, about 30 percent were able to obtain coverage through their former place of employment. Higher-income retirees with employer-sponsored plans have among the lowest out-of-pocket costs, even though they are heavy users of care (Moon, 2006). This translates into unequal access to private health insurance by wealthier elders or those who have access through employment or unions. To avoid scams, elders with financial resources must carefully explore options before purchasing private supplemental health insurance.

Eleven percent of Medicare's recipients have neither assistance from Medicaid (as dual eligibles) nor supplemental coverage to help pay for Medicare's coinsurance, deductibles, and non-covered services. They are less likely to see a doctor in any given year and to have a usual source of care, and more prone to postpone getting care. Not surprisingly, those without supplemental insurance tend to have low incomes and/or to be in poor health. Less than 50 percent of poor or near-poor older persons and less than 18 percent of elders of color, who suffer more from chronic illnesses and disability, have private health insurance, compared to almost 90 percent of their higher-income and healthier peers. Furthermore, older women, who have a greater incidence of chronic illness, are less likely than men to have access to health insurance through employment (Chen, 2006). However, even higher-income retirees may not have access to employer-sponsored plans, because cost-conscious employers are placing more controls on the use of health care, increasing premiums and deductibles, raising the age of eligibility, and changing benefit packages, particularly as a result of the 2008–2009 recession (Gawande, 2009; Gleckman, 2009; Hellander, 2008; Moon, 2006).

Similarly, a growing number of insurance companies are selling private **long-term care insurance** plans. Approximately 7 to 8 million (or 6 percent) of older adults have this type of insurance (Gleckman, 2009). Such plans do not cover all LTC costs, however. Some policies are written to exclude people with preexisting conditions, including psychological disorders such as depression, and contain benefit restrictions that limit access to covered care. The period of coverage is usually only 4 or 5 years, because comprehensive policies for life are very costly. The majority of policies pay a fixed amount for each qualified day in a nursing home. However, home health and adult day-care services are usually reimbursed at lower percentages of the selected nursing home benefit and for a set number of years, although coverage for home health has expanded recently. One's age when a LTC policy is first purchased is important, because the premium paid rises sharply with the age of purchase, although it remains level after that (Ali, 2005). For example, the average annual premium for a couple buying a policy at age 65 for 4 years of coverage is nearly $5,000 a year. However, paying a lower premium at age 50 means paying for perhaps 25 years or more on the 30 percent chance that a person may use the insurance, with no guarantee that the premium will not disappear when the individual most needs it. The high premiums and copayments mean that most LTC insurance policies are beyond the financial reach of

WHAT TO LOOK FOR IN LTC INSURANCE

LTC insurance policies are expensive and complicated. It is therefore important to read about and ask detailed questions about coverage and exclusions when purchasing a plan.

Considerations include:

1. coverage of all types of LTC (nursing home, assisted living, and home health care)
2. coverage of all types of caregivers (some policies state they will cover only "skilled home health workers" such as registered nurses, but insurance should allow for a variety of skilled, intermediate, and custodial home care providers)
3. coverage of a wide range of illnesses and injuries; some exclude the most common reasons why elders seek long-term care
4. protection against inflation, because many policies are purchased 20 or more years before they are needed
5. whether and how much rates can be raised on existing policyholders; this varies across states
6. whether the benefits are for a set period or a lifetime. Given that almost 90 percent of nursing home residents live less than five years after the move, it is more cost-effective to purchase a policy that covers a fixed period
7. whether the benefits are paid daily or monthly. Although most specify a daily benefit, some people prefer the flexibility of monthly benefits to allow for home care as needed
8. the option to pay the entire policy before retiring. This may increase payments initially, but the burden of insurance ends when income decreases
9. flexibility of paying cash benefits so the insured elder can pay a nursing home or home health care provider as needed and is not tied to a particular LTC arrangement
10. the experience level of the insurance agent. The agent may or may not be a specialist in LTC insurance but should sell enough policies each year to understand each buyer's needs.

Americans age 55 to 79 (Friedman, 2009; Gleckman, 2009; Stone, 2006).

The policies are expensive for two reasons: Most are sold individually and therefore carry high administrative costs, and most are bought by older people whose risk of needing LTC is great. Not surprisingly, women are less likely than men to be able to afford LTC insurance, and they spend a higher proportion of their income when they do, reflecting both gaps in coverage and their lower median income. It can also be financially prohibitive for older couples, where each partner must purchase individual coverage. The cost of purchasing some LTC services and insurance can be deducted from federal income taxes, but this benefits only those with higher-income levels who can take deductions (Chen, 2006; Stone, 2006). Not surprisingly, people who are most likely to purchase and benefit from LTC insurance are those:

- in relatively good health—that is, without serious preexisting chronic conditions
- in their 60s
- with higher income and more assets
- with more education
- with a partner to protect
- without children living nearby (although informal networks have little overall effect on whether one purchases LTC insurance)
- state employees in states that offer private LTC insurance to their workers
- federal employees, who along with their parents, have access to such insurance (Stone, 2006)

In addition to cost, the complexity of options and limited awareness about them are barriers to purchasing LTC insurance. Non-purchasers are also skeptical about the viability and integrity of private insurance companies and often feel overwhelmed by the process. In educating consumers about the value of LTC insurance, it is important to attend to behavioral and psychosocial factors as well as financial issues (Cramer & Jensen, 2006; Curry, et al,

2009; Friedman, 2009). The number of beneficiaries may grow in the future with workplace education to encourage planning for LTC among employees, tax incentives to purchase such insurance, increasing benefits for state employees, and younger policyholders who want to guarantee their lifestyle in old age by protecting their retirement assets. Nevertheless, private LTC insurance is likely to remain a relatively small market, and boomers who had once anticipated buying such insurance may be less likely to do so because of the global economic crisis, now that they are focused on paying for more immediate expenses (Cramer & Jensen, 2006).

Resultant Disparities

Because public funding is biased toward nursing home and acute care, and private insurance policies are beyond the financial reach of low-income elders, a *two-tier system of health and long-term care delivery* has emerged: one for those with private health insurance or the means to pay for expensive medical treatment, and another for those forced to rely on Medicaid or Veterans' Assistance—often entailing long waits for services—or making do without health care insurance altogether.

Disparities exist even among Medicare recipients. Older people who have Medicare only, many of whom may be near-poor, tend to have fewer doctor visits and hospital stays and buy fewer prescription medications than those who can afford cost-sharing provisions and supplementary insurance. In fact, low-income Medicare beneficiaries are nearly twice as likely to delay seeking health care as those with private insurance or Medicaid to supplement Medicare. Not surprisingly, the proportion of income spent on health care increases as income decreases (Lee, 2006). Out-of-pocket expenditures are highest for those in poor health, without Medicaid or supplemental insurance, and for near-poor women who are not eligible for Medicaid. This pattern means that many moderate-income older adults who are admitted to nursing homes incur catastrophic financial expenses prior to admission.

Medicaid also perpetuates class inequities. In fact, less than 50 percent of all low-income Medicare beneficiaries benefit from Medicaid, even though they are dually eligible. Dispari- ties are intensified for elders of color who generally underutilize services that could enhance their health. Even in programs designed for the poor, such as Medicaid, older adults of color are represented far less than their reported objective needs indicate. Such low participation levels are attributed to lack of awareness and understanding of Medicaid, complex enrollment processes, limited government outreach, and reluctance to apply for help from a welfare-linked program. A 2006 ruling that Medicaid applicants must be able to prove citizenship by means other than signing a declaration presents another barrier to immigrant and low-income populations, many of whom do not have a passport, certificate of naturalization, or birth certificate. While federal officials sought to reduce costs with this reform, most states contend that noncitizens are not a significant drain on the Medicaid program and that this law will result in more uninsured elders using hospital emergency rooms and clinics. Fortunately, more providers are recognizing the need for targeted outreach to historically underserved populations.

Physicians who refuse to take Medicaid patients, especially those with a high level of need, or limit them to a small proportion of their patient load are another obstacle. This occurs because Medicaid reimbursement rates are generally far below prevailing fees—even lower than Medicare rates. As noted above, Medicaid patients must also wait longer for nursing home placement than do private-pay patients. These burdens fall disproportionately on older women and elders of color. Another disparity is experienced by approximately 40 percent of the older population with incomes that are too high to be eligible for Medicaid but insufficient to pay out-of-pocket for LTC. These middle- and lower-income individuals often receive inadequate care or must depend on their families to help pay for LTC (Gardner & Zodikoff, 2003).

Innovations in Care Transitions

Medicare regulations promote systems of separate and distinct providers delivering and monitoring acute care services and little attempt to link with LTC services once discharged from an acute care setting Additionally, Medicare does not reimburse for chronic disease management programs or initiatives to prevent further illnesses in an effort to reduce expensive emergency, hospital or nursing home care. To address such gaps in care, models of transitional care are being designed and evaluated, primarily through demonstration grant funding. Transitional care includes a broad range of services and settings to promote the effective movement of patients between levels of care and across care settings. Such care is critical for older adults with multiple chronic illnesses, often involving many health providers and settings. If the transitions are not managed well, high rehospitalization rates and increasing costs can result. When older people must be moved between the acute care of hospital settings to LTC settings—and perhaps back again—they often experience discontinuities of care (e.g., conflicting medical advice, medication errors, and inadequate follow-up care) and a lack of coordination that increases their vulnerability and results in higher costs to Medicare.

Transitional care is the relatively brief time interval that begins with preparing a patient to leave one setting and concludes when the patient is received in the next. Transitions are often unplanned, result from unanticipated medical problems, occur on nights or weekends, involve clinicians who may not have an ongoing relationship with the older patient, and happen so quickly that formal and informal support systems cannot adequately respond (Coleman, 2004a, 2004b).

Barrier to effective transitions include poor communication, cultural differences, health literacy issues, inadequate education of elders

---

A COACHING MODEL OF TRANSITIONAL CARE

A Colorado medical center developed the Care Transitions Intervention where patients receive specific skills and tools that are reinforced by a "transition coach" who follows them across settings for the first 30 days after leaving the hospital. This "patient-centered care" encompasses four areas: medication self-management, creation of a personal health record maintained by the patient, timely follow-up care, and designing a plan to best seek care if particular symptoms arise. Patients who participated in this intervention were less likely to require rehospitalization in the first 30 days, significantly cutting their health care costs, especially hospital costs. Positive effects continued up to 6 months later. Given its favorable impact on both costs and quality of care, this intervention has been implemented in 12 health care organizations nationwide, with funding from the John A. Hartford Foundation (Coleman & Berenson, 2004).

---

and their family caregivers, and the lack of a single point person to ensure continuity of care (Naylor, 2003; Naylor et al., 2004; Naylor & Keating, 2008).

Three critical transitions are identified:

- Increasing older adults' access to evidence-based transitional care services
- Improving transitions within acute hospital settings
- Improving patient discharges to and from acute care hospitals.

Several effective models of care transitions organized by community-based care, transitions within settings, and transitions from to and from acute care hospitals, are:

COMMUNITY-BASED CARE:

Hospital at home model. Chronically ill elders who otherwise would be hospitalized are identified in the emergency room and then discharged to home and provided with nursing, physician and other services according to a prescribed template. In addition to clinical outcomes similar to those attained in traditional settings, lengths of stay and overall costs are reduced (Leff et al., 2005, 2006)

Day hospital model. The Collaborative Assessment and Rehabilitation for Elders (CARE) program at the University of Pennsylvania provides high risk elders with a range of health, palliative and rehabilitation services for a few days a week up to nine weeks. Improved function and decreased hospital use are outcomes (Naylor and Keating, 2008).

TRANSITIONS WITHIN SETTINGS:

Acute Care for Elders (ACE). At the University Hospitals in Cleveland, this model improves discharge readiness by adapting the physical environment, holding daily interdisciplinary team meetings, using nurse-initiated guidelines for preventive and restorative care, and starting discharge planning immediately at admission to include family caregivers (Naylor and Keating, 2008; Panno et al., 2000).

Professional-patient partnership. This Baltimore-based model engages the patient and caregiver in the discharge planning process by having them complete a questionnaire to assess their needs upon discharge, watch a video on post-discharge care management, and receive information on accessing community services. Satisfaction after discharge is generally high.

TRANSITIONS TO AND FROM ACUTE CARE HOSPITALS:

Care Transition coaching at the University of Colorado, detailed in the box on this page (Coleman & Berenson, 2004).

In the **Transitional Care model** at the University of Pennsylvania, Transitional Care Nurses design and implement the plan for follow-up care, including traditional visiting nurse services, home visits and being available 7 days a week by phone. Outcomes include high satisfaction among older adults, reduced hospitalizations and lower health care costs (Naylor, 2004).

Both of the above models have been introduced as bills to Congress in 2009, which reflects growing recognition that care coordination should become the standard of care.

All of these transition models point to the centrality of clear communication among patients, caregivers and health care providers (Zimmerman & Dabelko, 2007). An area for further development is the transition to and from skilled nursing facilities (Nishita et al., 2008; Naylor & Keating, 2008).

Service Integration Innovations

Models of service integration attempt to bring the acute-care and LTC sectors together into a single system The **On Lok** model of social care is a service integration approach tested in a wide range of communities and first implemented in San Francisco's China Town. Meaning "peaceful happy abode" in Cantonese, On Lok aims to integrate a full continuum of acute and chronic care into one agency, thereby preventing nursing home placement of frail elders certified as needing a nursing home level of care. As a capitated system, On Lok is paid a flat amount for each person served. A comprehensive day health program is integrated with home care, including nursing, social work, meals, transportation, personal care, homemaker, and respite care. The On Lok model is found to be effective at serving low-income elders and elders of color in their communi-ties and is replicated to varying degrees nationwide, often through the **Program of All-inclusive Care for the Elderly (PACE),** described in Chapter 11.

Similar to On Lok, PACE focuses on reducing costs by coordinating primary and LTC within an adult day health model for frail adults age 55 and older who are eligible for nursing home placement (Hansen, 2008). In addition to "one-door access" to a comprehensive care package of preventive, acute, and LTC services, adults may keep their own doctor. PACE must provide basic Medicare and Medicaid services but programs are given the flexibility to use less typical interventions, including activities such as fishing trips and drama groups as preventive services. It also tries to address root causes of health care problems. For example, a

Medicare beneficiary may show up at the emergency room on a monthly basis to be treated for skin infections due to flea bites. Rather than just treat the bites, the PACE team may decide to fumigate her home and provide a flea dip for her dog. Interdisciplinary teams of physicians, nurses, social workers, aides, therapists, and even van drivers are central to coordinating care management at predetermined reimbursement rates. Evaluations of both On Lok and PACE have found reduced home visits by nurses and decreased inpatient hospital admissions and hospital and nursing home days. Overall, enrollees demonstrated enhanced quality of life, satisfaction with care, improved functional status, and ability to live longer in the community (Grobowski, 2006; Hansen, 2008). Despite its success, PACE has reached only a small proportion of Medicare beneficiaries, partially because of low referral rates and high start-up costs for the provider organization (Fortinsky et al., 2004; Kane et al., 2006; Naylor, 2006).

States and for-profit providers are also attempting to integrate acute and LTC, especially for the population that is dually eligible for Medicare and Medicaid. Some are experimenting with innovative financing and service delivery of acute and LTC for older people on Medicaid and younger people with disabilities.

Many older adults are advocating for health care reform for all ages.

A LIFETIME OF SAVINGS DISAPPEARS WITH LONG-TERM CARE

LTC is a health care need for which virtually every American is unprepared. Helen thought she did everything right. She worked hard for 40 years as a secretary for churches and libraries. She and her husband lived modestly and saved. After her husband died, Helen felt secure because she had savings of well over a half million dollars. In her early 80s, she suffered a series of small strokes as well as an unusual brain disease that caused temporary amnesia. Although she rarely needed a doctor's care and would live with her chronic illnesses for many more years, she could not take care of herself. She needed assistance with getting in and out of bed, dressing, and fixing her meals. After paying for such personal care, it is not surprising that Helen ran out of money and had to go on Medicaid. She spent her last months in a nursing home, impoverished and sharing a small room with a stranger.

Plans pay for community-based care, case management for high-risk patients, up to 180 days of nursing home costs, and financial incentives to minimize nursing home use and encourage early nursing home discharge. However, gaps in care are unlikely to be filled by limited Medicaid allocations to states, and by programs funded entirely by states, (Stone, 2006). In addition, some for-profit providers have created integrated service systems, in part for altruistic reasons and in part for market incentives. Hospitals have integrated vertically—buying nursing homes, rehabilitation centers, and home health agencies—in an effort to become all-purpose providers in the community. Skilled nursing facilities, and to some extent home health agencies, have integrated horizontally, building alliances with hospitals, physicians groups, assisted-living developers, and other community-based providers. To what extent these innovations have continued during the 2008–2009 recession is as yet unclear.

Some states have developed a consumer-friendly single entry point approach to LTC.

Accessible information and assistance is at the core of this model to assure service coordination, efficient assessment and screening, consumer choice, support for informal caregivers, and a strong social infrastructure of nonmedical services such as accessible, affordable housing, transportation, and other home- and community-based services. A designated "gatekeeper" or advocate is responsible for providing information, application assistance, and help navigating the maze of programs and services. Every region of the state must conduct a "service readiness assessment" to determine service gaps and to implement innovative programs such as telemedicine, telehealth, and telehomecare to reduce barriers. While these and a range of other programs attempt to integrate care and reduce costs, only a relatively small proportion of older persons currently participate in such options (Applebaum & Straker, 2005; Healthcare Association of New York State, 2005; McGeehan, 2005).

Debates about health care reform are not new. Since 1912, several attempts were made to create a program of access to health care for all Americans. Yet the U.S remains the only industrialized nation that does not provide some form of universal health coverage regardless of the ability to pay, has the highest health care costs in the world, and has lower quality of care compared to many other industrialized countries. For example, among 19 industrialized countries, the U.S. had the highest rate of deaths from conditions that could have been prevented or treated successfully (Robert Wood Johnson, 2009b). Without health care reform, the cost of health care for businesses could double in ten years and the number of uninsured Americans, currently around 47 million, could reach 65.7 million (Robert Wood Johnson Foundation, 2009a). Under the Clinton Administration (1993–2001), health care reform moved from academic debates to the legislative process but ended in gridlock. What ultimately killed national health care reform in the 1990s was the disproportionate influence of powerful special-interest lobbies, particularly insurance and drug companies, and small businesses that sought to protect their financial interests. Despite escalating costs,

HISTORY AND STATUS OF NATIONAL LONG-TERM CARE LEGISLATION

- **1988:** The first comprehensive LTC legislation was introduced by the late Florida Representative Claude Pepper, who linked an initiative to fund LTC in the home to the ill-fated catastrophic health care legislation.
- **1990:** The Pepper Commission recommended public funding of home, community, and nursing home care for Americans with serious disabilities.
- **1992:** The Democratic leadership in the House and the Senate introduced bills for LTC, known as the Long Term Care Family Security Act.
- **1992:** Bill Clinton was the first presidential candidate to call for expanded public funding for home care services provided on a non-means-tested basis.
- **1990–1994:** The National Committee to Preserve Social Security and Medicare and the Leadership Council of Aging Organizations proposed universal and comprehensive LTC plans for all people with disabilities; this encompassed institutional, home- and community-based care, and personal assistance.
- **1993:** President Clinton's National Health Security Act offered new LTC benefits and set forth the principles of universal access, comprehensive health care benefits, and high-quality care, but was not passed.
- **2000:** The Long-Term Care Security Act enables federal employees to purchase LTC insurance at group rates.
- **2007:** Americans who purchase LTC insurance can deduct their payment premiums from their federal income taxes

growing numbers of uninsured citizens, and discriminatory and restrictive insurance policies, attempts to change the health care system have been blocked by the philosophy of individual choice and responsibility versus guaranteeing access to all, not to mention fear mongering by groups opposed to health care reform for their own political and financial gain.

Partially as a result of such inaction on reform, the number of uninsured and underinsuranced Americans continues to grow. Of these, 7 million are age 65 and older who have Medicare but are still faced with rising health care costs. At age 50 nearly one in six people applying for individual health insurance are rejected because of pre-existing conditions and by age 60, this increases to one in four. For those who are fortunate to have health insurance, their premiums grew nearly 80 percent between 2002 and 2007 and are, on average, three times higher than premiums paid through employer coverage (Barry, 2009; Hellander, 2008; Kaiser Commission, 2007; Older Women's League, 2008). Although older adults have Medicare, health care reform cannot be viewed as separate from health and long-term care of older adults. Consistent with the life course perspective, inadequate health care earlier in life has implications for the health status, costs and quality of life for future older adults and their family caregivers. As concluded by analyses by the Tax Policy Center, the Urban Institute and Brookings Institution, "it is difficult to imagine a well-designed health reform that fails to address these issues" (Gleckman, 2009).

Advocates for older adults and persons with disabilities initially pushed for the LTC to be included as part of health care reform legislation in 2009. In fact, the first nursing home reforms since the 1987 Omnibus Budget Reconciliation Act were included in early versions of health care reform (Well, 2009). Advocacy organizations, such as the National Council of Aging, promoted expansion of HCBS and nursing home diversion programs, care coordination, chronic disease management, and single point of entry information and referral, and improving Medicare low-income assistance programs to reduce out-of-pocket expenses—all directions away from a primarily medical model of care toward one based on functional ability that we have discussed as needed in this chapters (Kirchheimer, 2008; NCOA, 2009). But attention to LTC issues was less visible in the heated debates about a public option for health insurance, end-of-life counseling, and concerns about how to pay for reform (Kazzi, 2009; Pear & Herszenhorn, 2009). A significant proportion of older adults mobilized against health reform because of misperceptions of health care rationing and the concepts of voluntary end-of-life counseling and proposed reductions to Medicare, even though such cuts were primarily to eliminate the federal subsidy to insurance companies through Medicare Advantage.

Implications for the Future

Long-term care is characterized by the lack of a comprehensive policy, resulting in fragmentation, segmentation, and often bitter debates among advocates for various services. Past changes have focused on short-term fixes and responding to fiscal and regulatory concerns, particularly those of providers. Without dramatic changes in how LTC is delivered, costs will continue to escalate for the individual and for society as a whole.

Although concerns about LTC costs are widespread, there are many unresolved issues regarding potential solutions. As noted in Chapter 16, the economy and political factors profoundly shape public policy. The sluggish economy early in this century followed by the global economic crisis of 2008–2009, the federal and state emphasis on cost containment, and the growing federal deficit suggest that cost-cutting of programs, especially Medicaid, and subsidies for private market solutions to address LTC may dominate the national agenda. The implementation of Medicare Part D represents a shift toward privatization and means testing of what had been a universal program based on age. However, under the current Democratic administration, the pattern of reduced governmental responsibility and increasing reliance on private sector solutions is changing in the face of intense conservative opposition. Although the future of LTC is difficult to predict, the following factors will continue to shape the need for LTC:

- the growing numbers of older adults who rely on informal caregivers for the majority of care
- the preference of elders for home- and community-based care

- baby boomers' desires for choice and having more say about health care for themselves and their older relatives
- the increasing number of veterans with serious disabilities who fought in Iraq and Afghanistan
- the human tendency to avoid planning for potential disability or frailty, thus denying the need for LTC and the purchase of LTC insurance
- the importance of culturally competent LTC models that reduce disparities by race, gender, class, and sexual orientation across the life course
- the need for publicly funded, comprehensive, coordinated, and accessible in-home and community-based supportive services
- nursing homes taking on more rehabilitation and short-term skilled nursing responsibilities after hospitalization because they are no longer the primary provider of LTC
- the emphasis on ambulatory care rather than hospitalization for acute conditions, and the growth of managed care
- the use of technology, including electronic medical records, to coordinate care, provide information to consumers, and extend medical care to underserved areas
- the shortage of health care professionals trained in geriatrics
- the shortage of direct care staff, such as certified nursing assistants and home care aides

Some agreement is emerging about the major components of an ideal LTC system, but, as noted above, the national political will to achieve this does not currently exist. These components include:

- integrated administration and financing, such as flexible funding streams with incentives to combine dollars and minimize cost-shifting
- adoption of mechanisms that can effectively integrate care, including care transitions (e.g., care planning protocols, easy access to a single point of entry, uniform client needs

assessment, interdisciplinary care teams, and integrated information systems)

- broad and flexible benefits, including supports for informal caregivers
- far-reaching delivery systems that encompass home- and community-based care, care management, social services, supportive housing and transportation, and overarching quality control systems with a single point of accountability (NCOA, 2009; Stone, 2006)

As noted in Chapter 4, the growing number of older adults surviving with multiple chronic conditions requires health care providers trained in gerontology and clinical geriatrics. These specialists need the knowledge and skills to understand and manage the health needs of elders who live in LTC facilities, along with those who receive community-based LTC services. Geriatricians, nurses and nurse practitioners, pharmacists, social workers, dentists, physical therapists, and occupational therapists who can work with elders requiring LTC will be in even greater demand as baby boomers reach their 80s. The shortage of geriatric specialists in these health professions, estimated to be only 25 percent the number needed in 2030, will place significant demands on available providers. This projected shortage of geriatric specialists, especially those with LTC experience, may also put frail elders at greatest risk if their chronic conditions are not effectively managed in the community and hospitalization is required. Fortunately, the national Eldercare Workforce Alliance, encompassing approximately 30 national professional organizations, aims to address these workforce needs, including direct care workers, through federal legislation. In the 2009 congressional session, there was widespread support for a federal bill known as the "Retooling the Healthcare Workforce for an Aging America Act" which would fund geriatric training, education, and loan forgiveness.

Given these contextual factors, the need for public/private partnerships for LTC insurance, service delivery, and accountability is critical. However, partisan debates about the role of government versus the marketplace and private sector, the modes of service delivery, and societal responsibility toward vulnerable low-income elders will determine whether LTC reform is considered as well as older adults' support for such reform.

Summary

The growing acute care and LTC expenditures by both federal and state governments and by older people and their families are a source of concern for most Americans. Escalating hospital and physician costs have placed enormous pressures on Medicare—the primary financing mechanism for older Americans' acute care. The government's primary response to these Medicare costs has been cost containment, particularly moving away from fee-for-service delivery models to managed care, financial incentives for shortening hospital stays of Medicare patients, requiring higher deductibles and copayments, and cuts in Medicare funding. Efforts have also been made to offer more choices for Medicare beneficiaries, as represented by Medicare Advantage. On the other hand, for most older adults, Medicare fails to provide adequate protection against the costs of home- and community-based care. In fact, changes in Medicare funding have affected the availability of nonprofit home care agencies. They have also meant that many elders and their families have had to pay privately for home care or do without. As a rapidly growing portion of the federal budget, Medicare is under intense scrutiny. The prescription drug bill that was fully implemented in January 2006 attempts to address the problem of rising prescription drug costs, but costs to both consumers and the federal government have actually risen under Medicare Part D.

Medicare is the major payer for hospital and physician care for older adults, but it is almost absent from nursing home financing. The reverse applies to Medicaid, however. The largest portion of the Medicaid dollar goes to services needed by older persons but not covered by Medicare—nursing home, home, and personal care. However, as Medicaid has been increasingly subject to cost-cutting measures at the state level, benefits have been reduced. For example, copayments for health care services have increased as a way to reduce Medicaid spending, but this cost is borne disproportionately by low-income elders. Another disadvantage for Medicaid recipients is that most nursing homes and doctors limit the number of Medicaid recipients they will accept. Although Medicaid waivers have allowed state funding of some innovative community-based alternatives, Medicaid remains biased toward nursing home care. As described in Chapter 16, Title XX and Older Americans Act home care programs continue to have relatively flat funding levels and limited impact. Given the gaps in public funding for LTC, private insurers are offering LTC insurance options, but these are beyond the financial reach of most elders and not widely understood. These health and LTC needs will be a major issue debated by the U.S. Congress in the coming years.

GLOSSARY

Aging and Disability Resource Centers reform initiative that aims to integrate and streamline long-term care services into a single coordinated system

capitated payments payments for services based on a predetermined amount per person per day rather than fees for services

cash and counseling programs funded by the Robert Wood Johnson Foundation, older adults in three states receive a cash payment to purchase services and products they need to remain at home

Centers for Medicare and Medicaid Services (CMS) the federal agency that administers the Medicare and Medicaid programs; prior to 2001, known as the *Health Care Financing Administration (HCFA)*

consumer-directed care under the Medicaid waiver system, older adults can hire personal care attendants, including family members (except for spouses)

diagnostic-related groupings (DRGs) Medicare payments are fixed prior to admission to hospital or home care, based on diagnostic category, medical condition, and expected length of stay

doughnut hole Prescription costs that a Medicare enrollee must pay 100% out of pocket each year between $2400 and $5451. Amounts below and above this gap are covered partially by Medicare Part D

Health Maintenance Organizations (HMOs) health plans often associated with Medicare Advantage that combine coverage of health care costs and delivery of health care for a capitated prepaid premium low-income older adults eligible for both Medicare and Medicaid)

Interim Payment System (IPS) sets stringent caps on cost per home health visit and per beneficiary

long-term care insurance private insurance designed to cover the costs of institutional and sometimes home-based service for people with chronic illnesses and disabilities

managed care policies under which patients are provided health care services under the supervision of a single professional, usually a physician

Medicaid a federal and state means-tested program of medical assistance for the categorically needy, regardless of age

Medicaid waiver program allows states to provide home care services to elders at risk of nursing home placement "outside" of Medicaid regulations; must be budget neutral

medical savings accounts proposed Medicare program that will allow beneficiaries to carry private "catastrophic" insurance for serious illness and pay routine costs from a special account

Medicare the social insurance program, part of the Social Security Act of 1965, intended to provide financial protection against the cost of hospital and physician care for people age 65 and over

Medicare Advantage (formerly known as Medicare Plus Choice) beneficiaries can choose between traditional Medicare and a Choice Plan that includes HMOs

Medicare Part D (Medicare Modernization, Improvement and Prescription Drug Act) prescription drug reform legislation; older adults pay for a private insurance plan to cover medications; also known as the Medicare Modernization Act

Medigap policies private supplemental insurance to help with the catastrophic costs of intensive care, numerous tests, or extended hospitalization

On Lok a comprehensive program of health and social services provided to very frail older adults, first started in San Francisco, with the goal of preventing or delaying nursing home placement

parity mental health services covered by Medicare at the same rate (20 percent) as health care services for physical disorders

Preferred Provider Organizations (PPOs) networks of independent physicians, hospitals, and other health care providers who contract with an insurance entity to provide care at discounted rates

Private Fee-for-Service plan (PFFS): health care providers receive a per capita payment from Medicare

Program of All-inclusive Care for the Elderly (PACE) federal demonstration program that replicated On Lok's integrated services to attempt to prevent nursing home placement

prospective payment system (PPS) a system of reimbursing hospitals and physicians based on the diagnostic category of the patient rather than fees for each service provided, as applied to inpatient services; includes DRGs

spend down to use up assets for personal needs, especially health care, in order to become qualified for Medicaid

transitional care care during the interval between preparing a patient to leave one setting and receiving the patient in the next setting

RESOURCES

Log on to MySocKit (www.mysockit.com) for information about the following:

- American Association for Home Care
- American Health Care Association
- American Medical Directors Association
- Centers for Disease Control and Prevention
- Centers for Medicare and Medicaid Services (CMS) (formerly HCFA)
- Committee to Preserve Social Security and Medicare
- Families USA
- Henry J. Kaiser Family Foundation
- MetLife Foundation
- MetLife Mature Market Institute
- National Association of Directors of Nursing in Long Term Care
- National Association of Local Long-term Care Ombudsman Program
- National Association of Professional Geriatric Care Managers
- National Citizen's Coalition for Nursing Home Reform
- National Council on the Aging

REFERENCES

AARP. (2005). *Reimagining America: AARP's blueprint for the future.* Washington, DC: Author.

Administration on Aging. *Aging and Disability Resource Centers.* (2009). Retrieved July 2009, from http://www.aoa.gov/AoARoot/AoA_Programs/HCLTC/ADRC/index.aspx

Ali, N. S. (2005). Long-term care insurance: Buy it or not! *Geriatric Nursing, 26,* 237–240.

Alonso-Zaldivar, R. (2006). Medicare drug plan is scoring. *The Seattle Times,* p. 1.

Antos, J. & Gokhale, J. (2005). Medicare prescription drugs: Medical necessity meets fiscal insanity. *Cato Institute Briefing Papers,* 91.

Applebaum, R. & Straker, J. (2005). Long-term care challenges for an aging America. *Public Policy and Aging Report, 15,* 3.

Barry, P. (2009). New health care reform proposals aim to help older Americans too young for Medicare: Without employer health coverage millions of people ages 50 to 64 can't afford-able insurance. *AARP Bulletin Today.*

Berenson, R. A. & Horvath, J. (2003). Confronting the barriers to chronic care management in Medicare. *Health Affairs, 22,* W337–W353.

Burke, S., Feder, J., & Van de Water, P. N. (Eds.). (2005). *Developing a better long-term care policy: A vision and strategy for America's future.* Washington, DC: National Academy of Social Insurance.

Catlin, A., Cowan, C., Hartman, M., & Heffler, S. (2008). National health spending in 2006: A year of change for prescription drugs. *Health Affairs, 27*(1), 14–29.

Catlin, A., Cowan, C., Heffler, S., & Washington, B. (2007). National health spending in 2005: The slowdown continues, *Health Affairs, 26,* 142–153.

Carlson, B. L., Foster, L., Dale, S. B., & Brown, R. (2007). Effects of cash and counseling on personal care and well-being. *Health Services Research, 42,* 467–487.

Centers for Medicaid and Medicare Services (CMS). (2006). *Medicare Program Rate Stats, 2006.* Retrieved January 18 2007, from http://www.cms .hhs.gov/MedicareProgramRatesStats/downloads/ MedicareMedicaid Sumamries2006.pdf

Chen, L. M. (2006). Policies affecting long-term care and long-term care institutions. In B. Berkman (Ed.). *Handbook of social work in health and aging.* New York: Oxford University Press.

Coleman, E. A. & Berenson, R. (2004). Lost in transition: Challenges and opportunities for improving the quality of transitional care. *Annals of Internal Medicine, 141,* 533–536.

Congressional Budget Office. (2009). *Health care reform and the federal budget.* Washington, DC: Author.

Cramer, A. & Jensen, G. (2006). Why don't people buy long-term care insurance? *Journals of Gerontology: Social Sciences, 61B,* S185–S193.

Crutsinger, M. (2009). Social Security, Medicare facing unhealthy future: Benefit programs will be depleted before projections. *The Boston Globe,* NEWS, National, p. 7.

Cubanski, J. & Neuman, P. (2007). Status report on Medicare part D enrollment in 2006: Analysis of plan-specific market share and coverage. *Health Affairs, 26,* w1–w12.

Curry, L. A., Robison, J. Shugrue, N., Keenan, P., & Kapp, M. B. (2009). Individual decision-making in the non-purchase of long-term care insurance. *The Gerontologist, 49,* 560–569.

Dale, S. B. & Brown, R. S. (2007). How does cash and counseling affect costs? *Health Services Research, 42,* 488–509.

Donohue, J. M., Huskamp, H. A., & Zuvekas, S. H. (2009). Dual eligibles with mental disorders and Medicare part D: How are they faring? *Health Affairs, 28,* 746–759.

Eiken, S., Burwell, B., & Walker, E. (2005). *Medicaid HCBS waiver expenditures FY 1999 through FY 2004.* Cambridge, MA: Thomson Medstat.

Federal Interagency Forum on Aging and Related Statistics. (2008). *Older Americans 2008: Key indicators of well-being.* Hyattsville, MD: Author.

Fortinsky, R., Fenster, J., & Judge, J. (2004). Medicare and Medicaid home health and Medicaid waiver services for dually eligible older adults: Risk factors for use and correlates of expenditures. *The Gerontologist, 44,* 739–749.

Friedman, S. (2009). Add long-term care for the aged to the national priority list. *Newsday (New York),* Gray Matters, ACT II, p. B06.

Galambos, C. (2006). Policies affecting health, mental health and caregiving: Medicaid. In B. Berkman, (Ed.). *Handbook of social work in health and aging.* New York: Oxford University Press, 2006.

Gardner, D. & Zodikoff, B. (2003). Meeting the challenges of social work practice in health care and aging in the 21st century. In B. Berkman & L. Harootyan (Eds.). *Social work and health care in an aging society.* New York: Springer.

Gleckman, H. (2009). What about long-term care?: Forgotten in today's health care reform debate: The frail elderly and the disabled, who need a little help, not just high-tech medicine. *USA Today*, News, p. 11A.

Goulding, M. (2005). Trends in prescribed medicine use and spending by older Americans. U.S. Department of Health and Human Services, Centers for Disease Control and Prevention, *Trends in Health and Aging*, 5, 1–20.

Grogan, C. M. (2005). The politics of aging within Medicaid. In R. Hudson, *The new politics of old age policy*. Baltimore: Johns Hopkins Press.

Grogan, C. M. & Patashnik, E. M. (2003). Universalism within targeting: Nursing home care, the middle class and the politics of the Medicaid program. *Social Service Review*, 77, 51–71.

Hansen, J. C. (2008). Community and in-home models. *Journal of Social Work Education*, 44, 83–88.

Harrington, C., Ng, T., Kaye, H. S., & Newcomer, R. J., (2009). Medicaid home and community-based services: Proposed policies to improve access, costs and quality. *Public Policy and Aging Report*, 19, 13–18.

Healthcare Association of New York State. (2005). Point of entry. *Long-Term Care Reform Series* [Issues Brief #1].

Healthcare Financial Management Association (2006). To address Medicare Part D confusion, states take matters into their own hands. *News Watch*, p. 16–17.

Healthcare Financial Management Association. (2008). Medicare pays more for medications under part D: Report. *Healthcare Financial Management*, Retrieved September 2009 from http://www.hfma.org/hfm/2008archives/month09

Heiss, F., McFadden, D., & Winter, J. (2006). Who failed to enroll in Medicare part D, and why? Early results. *Health Affairs*, 25, w344–w354.

Hellander, I. (2008). The deepening crisis in U.S. health care: A review of Data. *International Journal of Health Services*, 38, 607–623.

Herd, P. (2005). Universalism without the targeting: Privatizing the old-age welfare state. *The Gerontologist*, 45, 292–298.

Kaiser Family Foundation. (2006). *Medicare: Tracking prescription drug coverage under Medicare: Five ways to look at the new enrollment numbers.* Retrieved February 2006, from http://kff.org/medicare/upload/7466.pdf

Kaiser Family Foundation. (2008). *Medicare: Medicare spending and financing.* Retrieved September 2008, from http://www.kff.org/medicare/upload/7305_03.pdf

Kane, R. L., et al.(2006) Variations on a theme called PACE. *Journal of Gerontology: Biological Sciences*, 61B, 689–693.

Kazzi, N. (2009). More Americans losing health insurance every day: Analysis of health coverage losses during the recession. *Center for American Progress*. Retrieved July 2009, from http://www.americanprogress.org/issues/2009/05/insurance_loss.html/ print.html

Kirchheimer, B. (2008). A gray tsunami cometh: Long-term care is challenged by the onslaught of the baby boomers, but concern is muted by a lack of immediacy [Healthcare opinion leaders' survey]. *Modern Health Care*, 22.

Kitchener, M., Hernandez, M. Ng, T., & Harrington, C. (2006). Residential care provisions in Medicaid home and community-based waivers: A national study of program trends. *The Gerontologist*, 46, 165–172.

Kunkel, S. & Nelson, I. (2005). Consumer direction: Changing the landscape of long-term care. *Public Policy and Aging Report*, 15, 13–16.

Landon, B., Zaslavsky, M., Bernard, S., Coffey, E., & Cleary, P. (2004). Comparison of performance of traditional Medicare vs. Medicare managed care. *Journal of the American Medical Association*, 291, 1744–1752.

Lee, J. (2006). Policies affecting health, mental health and caregiving: Medicare. In B. Berkman (Ed.). *Handbook of social work in health and aging*. New York: Oxford University Press.

Lee, J., Kim, H., & Tanenbaum, S. (2006). Medicaid and family wealth transfer. *The Gerontologist*, 46, 6–13.

Levin-Epstein, M. (2006). A troubled beginning for Part D. *Behavioral Healthcare*, 26, 4.

Lin, C., Musa, D., Silverman, M., & Degenholtz, H. (2005). Do managed care plans reduce racial disparities in preventive care? *Journal of Health Care for the Poor and Underserved, 16,* 139–151.

McGeehan, S. (2005). *The role of case management in integrated models of care.* Oxford, Ohio: Miami University. Unpublished master's thesis.

Mitchell, G., Salmon, J., Polivka, L., & Soberon-Ferrer, H. (2006). The relative benefits and cost of Medicaid home- and community-based services in Florida. *The Gerontologist, 46,* 483–494.

Moffitt, R. E. (2006). *The President's modest Medicare budget proposal.* Retrieved February 2006, from http://www.heritage.org/Research/HealthCare

Montgomery, J. (2009). CBO paints dire portrait of long-term revenue, spending. *The Washington Post,* Financial, p. A18.

Moon, M. (2006). Organization and financing of health care. In R. Binstock & L. George (Eds.). *Handbook of aging and the social sciences* (6th ed.). New York: Academic Press.

National Council on Aging (NCOA). (2009). President Obama signs economic stimulus plan. *NCOA's Public Policy Update,* 3.

Naylor, M. D. (2003). Nursing intervention research and quality of care. Influencing the future of healthcare. *Nursing Research, 52,* 380–385.

Naylor, M. D. (2006).Transitional care: A critical dimension of home healthcare quality agenda. *Journal for Healthcare Quality, 28,* 48–54.

Naylor, M. & Keating, S. A. (2008). Transitional care. *Journal of Social Work Education* [Supplement], *44,* 65–74.

Neuman, T. (2009). *Medicare 101: The basics.* Kaiser Family Foundation Medicare Policy Project. Retrieved August 2009, from www.kff.org/medicare/index.cfm

Pear, R. & Herszenhorn, D. M. (2009). Health care vote illustrates partisan divide. *The New York Times.*

Phillips, B. & Schneider, B. (2007). Commonalities and variations in the cash and counseling programs across the three demonstration states. *Health Services Research, 42,* 397–413.

Pourat, N., Kaqawa-Singer, M., & Wallace, S. (2006). Are managed care Medicare beneficiaries with chronic conditions satisfied with their care? *Journal of Aging and Health, 18,* 70–90.

Quinn, J. B. (2007). How to pay for old-age care. *Newsweek.*

Revere, L., Large, J., & Langland-Orban, B. (2004). A comparison of inpatient severity, average length of stay and cost for traditional fee-for-service Medicare and Medicare HMOs in Florida. *Health Care Management Review, 29,* 320–329.

Safran, D. G., Neuman, P., Schoen, C., Kitchman, M. S., Wilson, I. B., Cooper, B., Li, A., Chang, H., & Rogers, W. H. (2005). Prescription drug coverage and seniors: Findings from A 2003 national survey. *Health Affairs: The Policy Journal of the Health Sphere, Web Exclusive,* November 16, 2009.

Sakauye, K., Blank, K., Cohen, C., Cohen, G., Kennedy, G., et al. (2005). Medicare managed mental health care: A looming crisis. *Psychiatric Services, 56,* 795–797.

Schmieding, L. (2006). *Caregiving in America.* New York: International Longevity Center and Schmieding Center for Senior Health and Education of Northwest Arkansas.

Schore, J., Foster, L., & Philips, B. (2007). Consumer enrollment and experiences in the cash and counseling program. *Health Services Research, 42,* 446–466.

Shelton, R. (2006). Medicare drug plan benefits some; others fall through cracks. *Seattle Times,* p. A3.

Slaughter, L. (2006). Medicare Part D: The product of a broken process. *New England Journal of Medicine, 354,* 2314–2315.

Smith, G. (2006). *In search of quality care: Low-income seniors left behind.* Seattle, WA: Northwest Federation of Community Organizations.

Smith, G., Cowan, C., Heffler, S., & Catlin, A. (2006). National health spending in 2004. *Health Affairs, 25,* 186–196.

Song, K. M. (2006). Drug-plan gap trips up many older Americans. *Seattle Times,* p. 1.

Spector, W. Cohen, J., & Pesis-Katzh, I. (2004). Home care before and after the balanced budget act of 1997: Shifts in financing and services. *The Gerontologist, 44*, 39–47.

Stone, R. (2006). Emerging issues in long-term care. In R. Binstock & L. George (Eds.). *Handbook of aging and the social sciences* (6th ed.), New York: Academic Press.

Trivedi, A., Zaslavsky, A., Schneider, E., & Ayanian, J. (2005). Trends in the quality of care and racial disparities in Medicare managed care. *New England Journal of Medicine, 353*, 692–700.

U.S. House of Representatives. (2008). *Medicare Part D: Drug pricing and manufacturer windfalls.* Washington, DC: U. S. House of Representatives.

Zhang, Y., Donohue, M., Newhouse, J. P., & Lave, J. R. (2009). The effects of the coverage gap on drug spending: A closer look at Medicare part D. *Health Affairs, 28*, W317–W325.

INDEX

Note: *Italic* page numbers indicated where items are defined.

Group conscience, 638
Group counseling, for caregivers, 416
Group housing, 466, 469
Group therapy, 258
Growth hormones, 76
Guardians, elder abuse and, 428
Guardianship, *581*
Guildford's structural model of
  intelligence, 204
Guilford-Zimmerman Temperament Survey
  (GZTS), 221

Hair, 81–82
Hall, G. Stanley, 31
Hastened death, *570–582*
HDL (high-density lipoprotein), 86, 138,
  157, 158
Health, 117–119
  of African Americans, 614–617
  of American Indians, 627–631
  of Asian/Pacific Islanders, 635–639
  disparities in, 325
  of homeless elders, 480
  of Latinos, 121, 622–624
  quality of life in, 119–121
  religious activity and, 520
  retirement and, 500
  self-rating of, 120
  volunteering and, 530
Health and Retirement Study, 242
Health behaviors, quality of life and, 119–121
Health care
  for African Americans, 616, 617
  Alzheimer's costs and, 251
  for American Indians, 630–631
  barriers to utilization, 643
  durable power of attorney for, 580
  expenditures for, 120
  GDP for, 49–50
  goals of, 155–156
  innovation programs for, 760–762
  intergenerational fight, 705
  for Latinos, 622–624
  Medicare coverage of, 735, 743
  need for reform, 761–762
  payment for Medicare services, 733
  policy and programs, 731–765
  reasons for growth of costs, 732–734
  services and, 164–165
  spending on, 152
  two-tier system of, 760
Health care disparities, 9, 610–611
Health care providers, 14–15, 164–165, 483
  for African Americans, 619
  assessment by, 432–433
  grieving process and, 585
  questions about sexuality, 300–302
Health care reform, 734, 744–748
Health disparities, 9, 610
Health insurance, reimbursement by, 108
Health literacy, 476

Health Maintenance Organization (HMO), *736*
Health outcomes, from caregiver's stress, 397
Health practices, outcomes and, 157–158
Health promotion, 120, *155–164*
Health services
  health care system and, 164–165
  uses of, 152–155
Health status, *118*
  of women, 668–674
Health technology, 52–53
Healthy aging, 164–165
Healthy Families Act (HFA, 2009), 411
Healthy life span, *78*
Healthy People 2000, 162 *2010,* 135,
  141, 156, 157, 162, 164
Hearing, 100–105
Hearing aids, 104
Heart disease, 123, 125, 127–129, 672
Heart rate, 86, 87
Heat stroke, 81
Height, reduction in aging, 82
Hemicentin-1, 99
Heminanopsia, 130
Hemiplegia, 130
Hemlock Society, *582*
Hiatus hernia, *144*
High blood pressure. *See* Hypertension
High-frequency hearing loss, 102, 104
Hip fractures, 135, 139
Hispanic paradox, 622–623
Hispanics. *See also* Elders of color; Latinos
  use of term, 606n
Historically underserved groups, 5, 8, 25, 36,
  607, 612, 616, 620, 627, 629, 640, 643
HIV, 58–59, 145–148, 285, 302
HMO. *See* Health Maintenance
  Organization
Hoarding, 422–423
Home. *See also* Cohousing
  adapting to P-E incongruence in, 452
  nursing home as, 465
  services needed by elders in, 471
Home and community-based services
  (HCBS), 466–467, 469, 753–754
Home-based care, Medicaid payments
  for, 736
Home equity conversion mortgages
  (HECM), 458–459
Home Fall Hazard Assessment Tool, 152
Home health care
  Medicaid-funded, 752, 753–755
  Medicare and, 738, 739–741
  services for, 471–472, 743
Homelessness, 479–480, 481, 484–485
Homosexuality. *See also* Lesbian, gay,
  bisexual, and transgender (LGBT)
  partners
  formerly classified as mental illness, 352
  women's support networks and, 678
Hormone replacement therapy (HRT), 287,
  659

alternatives to, 288
  for osteoporosis prevention, 135–138,
    672–674
Hormones, 90
  growth, 76
  sexuality and, 286–287
Hospice, 562, *564–570*
Hospital insurance (Medicare Part A), *736*
Hospital Insurance Trust Fund, 741–742
Hospitalization, 154, 631
Hospitals
  depressed older adults in, 236–237
  palliative care in, 562, 564
  utilization of, 122, 152–153
Hot flashes, *286, 287–288*
Households, family structures in, 344
Housing
  affordable, 480
  characteristics of older homeowners, 458
  cohousing and, 454
  government programs and, 477–479
  homelessness and, 479–480
  independent, 457–460
  long-term care and, 461–470
  patterns of, 457–461
  planned, 460
Housing and Urban Development,
  Department of (HUD), 469
HRT. *See* Hormone replacement therapy
Human agency, in life-course perspective, 325
Huntington's disease, 243
Hya-Byung, 639
Hypertension, 123, 124, 128–129
Hyperthermia, *81*
Hypoglycemia, 139
Hypokinesia, *158*
Hypotension, 129
Hypothermia, *81*
Hysterectomy, 286, 294

IADLs. *See* Instrumental Activities of
  Daily Living
Iconic memory, *186*
Identity
  accommodation of, 223
  assimilation of, 223
  grandparent, 361
  retirement and, 500
  of widows, 587–588
Illness. *See* Diseases; specific conditions
Immigrants and immigration
  Asian and Latin American, 608–609
  cultures of, 605–606
  as direct care workers, 429, 430
  finances of, 62–63
  in Japan, 51
  Latino health profile and, 623
  older, 59–61
  as oldest-old, 19
  resistance to, 51
  Southeast Asian, 623–634

Photo Credits